P9-CIU-824

115385601153856011538

Current Biography Yearbook 1978

CURRENT BIOGRAPHY YEARBOOK

1978

EDITOR
Charles Moritz

ASSOCIATE EDITORS
Evelyn Lohr
Henry Sloan
Kieran Dugan
Judith Graham

THE H. W. WILSON COMPANY
NEW YORK

PHOTO CREDITS

Russ Adams, United States Tennis Association, Guillermo Vilas; © *1977 Bandana Mdse., Inc.,* Peter Frampton; *Jerry Bauer,* Richard Adams; *Belgian Institute of Information and Documentation,* Leo Tindemans; *BMI Archives,* Neil Sedaka; *British Information Services,* David Steel; *Photo Division, CBS Television Network,* Lucille Ball; © *1977 Columbia Picture Industries, Inc.,* Steven Spielberg; *Columbia Records,* Bruce Springsteen; *Nancy Crampton,* Susan Brownmiller; *Dean Drury,* Andrei Serban; *John Engstead,* Lillian Gish; *Mary Lloyd Estrin,* Joan Didion; © *Henry Grossman,* Thea Musgrave; *Lee Gurst,* Barry Manilow; *Ronald Hoeben,* Paul Theroux; *Hook Bros., Memphis, Tenn.,* Benjamin L. Hooks; *ICM Artists,* Pinchas Zukerman; *Julie Jensen,* Maggie Kuhn; *Martha Kaplan,* John Gardner; *Jorge Lewinski, London,* Henry Moore; *Neil Libbert—N Y Times,* Edward Bond; *Adam Lubroth, Madrid, Spain,* Vicente Alexiandre; *Marion Morehouse,* Robert Graves; *MCA Records,* Olivia Newton-John; *Metropolitan Museum of Art, Reprinted with the permission of New York News,* Diana Vreeland; *Minnesota Twins,* Rod Carew; *Museum of Modern Art/Film Stills Archive,* Elizabeth Ashley, Catherine Deneuve; © *Arnold Newman,* Richard Anuszkiewicz; *New York Knicks,* Earl Monroe; *Courtesy of New Yorker Films,* Werner Herzog; © *Nordisk Pressefoto, Copenhagen, Denmark,* Anker Jorgensen; *Novosti Press Agency,* Anatoly Karpov; *Planco, William Morris Agency,* Sissy Spacek; *Lynn Saville,* Chryssa; *Scavullo,* Margaux Hemingway; *Layle Silbert,* José Donoso; *Nancy Sirkis,* Louis Auchincloss; *R. D. Smith, Yale University,* A. Bartlett Giamatti; © *Svenskt Pressfoto,* Thorbjörn Fälldin; *Tadder/Baltimore,* Lloyd McBride; *Jim Theologos,* Irving Howe; *United Press International,* Muhammad Ali, Bibi Andersson, Emperor Bokassa I, Leonid I. Brezhnev, Vladimir Bukovsky, Robert C. Byrd, Lillian Carter, Frank Church, Mairead Corrigan, Bruce Dern, Morarji Desai, Michael S. Dukakis, Uri Geller, Pope John Paul I, Diane Keaton, Archbishop Marcel Lefebvre, Nancy Lopez, George Lucas, Michael J. Mansfield, Russell Means, John D. Rockefeller 4th, Felix G. Rohatyn, Linda Ronstadt, Anastasio Somoza, Ben Vereen, Jorge Rafaél Videla, Gene Wilder; © *Thomas Victor,* Eleanor Clark, Kenneth Koch; *Warner/Reprise,* Steve Martin; *The White House,* Margaret Costanza, Walter Mondale; *Wide World,* Rosalynn Carter, Sammy Davis Jr., Farrah Fawcett-Majors, Mark Fidrych, Henry Geldzahler, H. R. Haldeman, David Mamet, Craig Morton, Qabus bin Said, Daniel Schorr; *Yeshiva University,* Norman Lamm.

THIRTY-NINTH ANNUAL CUMULATION—1978

PRINTED IN THE UNITED STATES OF AMERICA

International Standard Serial No. (0084-9499)

Library of Congress Catalog Card No. (40-27432)

PREFACE

The aim of CURRENT BIOGRAPHY YEARBOOK 1978, like that of the preceding volumes in this series of annual dictionaries of contemporary biography, now in its fourth decade of publication, is to provide the reference librarian, the student, or any researcher with brief, objective, accurate, and and well-documented biographical articles about living leaders in all fields of human accomplishment the world over.

CURRENT BIOGRAPHY YEARBOOK 1978 carries on the policy of including new and updated biographical sketches that supersede earlier, outdated articles. Sketches have been made as accurate and objective as possible through careful researching by CURRENT BIOGRAPHY writers in newspapers, magazines, authoritative reference books, and news releases of both government and private agencies. Immediately after they are published in the eleven monthly issues, articles are submitted to biographees to give them an opportunity to suggest corrections in time for CURRENT BIOGRAPHY YEARBOOK. To take account of major changes in the careers of biographees, sketches have also been revised before they are included in the yearbook. With the exception of occasional interviews, the questionnaire filled out by the biographee remains the main source of direct information.

In the back of the volume under *Organizations* can be found the names of men and women who head organizations. Persons who are not professional authors but who have written books are included under *Literature* in addition to their vocational fields. The pages immediately following contain: *Explanations; Key to Reference Abbreviations; Key to Pronunciation;* and *Key to Abbreviations.* The indexes at the end of the volume are *Biographical References; Periodicals and Newspapers Consulted; Classification by Profession;* and *Cumulated Index—1971-1978.* The 1940-1950 index can be found in the 1950 yearbook; the 1951-1960 index, in the 1960 yearbook, and the 1961-1970 index in the 1970 yearbook. The three decennial indexes are cumulated in CURRENT BIOGRAPHY CUMULATED INDEX 1940-1970.

For their assistance in preparing CURRENT BIOGRAPHY YEARBOOK 1978, I should like to thank the associate editors and Dorothy McEntee, editorial assistant.

Charles Moritz

Explanations

Authorities for biographees' full names, with some exceptions, are the bibliographical publications of The Wilson Company. When a biographee prefers a certain name form, that is indicated in the heading of the article: for example, Niemöller, (Friedrich Gustav Emil) Martin means that he is usually referred to as Martin Niemöller. When a professional name is used in the heading, as, for example, Anne Bancroft, the real name (in this case Annemarie Italiano) appears in the article itself.

The heading of each article includes the pronunciation of the name if it is unusual, date of birth (if obtainable), and occupation. The article is supplemented by a list of references to sources of biographical information, in two alphabets: (1) newspapers and periodicals and (2) books. (See the section *Biographical References,* found in the rear of this volume.)

Key to Reference Abbreviations

References to some newspapers and periodicals are listed in abbreviated form; for example, "Sat Eve Post 217:14 S 30 '44 por" means *Saturday Evening Post,* volume 217, page 14, September 30, 1944, with portrait. (For full names, see the section *Periodicals and Newspapers Consulted,* found in the rear of this volume.)

January—Ja
February—F
March—Mr
April—Ap
May—My
June—Je

July—Jl
August—Ag
September—S
October—O
November—N
December—D

Journal—J
Magazine—Mag
Monthly—Mo
Portrait—por
Weekly—W
Review—R

Key To Pronunciation

ā āle
â câre
a add
ä ärm

ē ēve
e end

g go

ī īce
i ill

K German ch as in *ich* (iK)

N Not pronounced, but indicates the nasal tone of the preceding vowel, as in the French *bon* (bôN).

ō ōld
ô ôrb
o odd
oi oil
o͞o o͞oze
o͝o fo͝ot
ou out

th *then*
th thin

ū cūbe
û ûrn; French eu, as in *jeu* (zhû), German ö, oe, as in *schön* (shûn), *Goethe* (gû'te)
u tub

ü Pronounced approximately as ē, with rounded lips: French u, as in *menu* (mə-nü); German ü, as in grün

ə the schwa, an unstressed vowel representing the sound that is spelled
a as in sofa
e as in fitted
i as in edible
o as in melon
u as in circus

zh azure

' = main accent

" = secondary accent

Key To Abbreviations

AAAA	Amateur Athletic Association of America
A.A.U.	Amateur Athletic Union
ABA	American Bar Association
ABC	American Broadcasting Company
ACA	Americans for Constitutional Action
A.C.L.U.	American Civil Liberties Union
ADA	Americans for Democratic Action
AEC	Atomic Energy Commission
AEF	American Expeditionary Force
AFL	American Federation of Labor
AFL-CIO	American Federation of Labor and Congress of Industrial Organizations
ALA	American Library Association
AMA	American Medical Association
A.P.	Associated Press
ASCAP	American Society of Composers, Authors and Publishers
ASNE	American Society of Newspaper Editors
B.A.	Bachelor of Arts
BBC	British Broadcasting Corporation
B.D.	Bachelor of Divinity
B.L.S.	Bachelor of Library Science
B.S.	Bachelor of Science
CAA	Civil Aeronautics Administration
CAB	Civil Aeronautics Board
C.B.	Companion of the Bath
C.B.E.	Commander of (the Order of) the British Empire
CBS	Columbia Broadcasting System
C.E.	Civil Engineer
CEA	Council of Economic Advisers
C.E.D.	Committee for Economic Development
CENTO	Central Treaty Organization
CIA	Central Intelligence Agency
CIO	Congress of Industrial Organizations
C.M.G.	Companion of (the Order of) St. Michael and St. George
Com.	Commodore
CORE	Congress of Racial Equality
D.A.R.	Daughters of the American Revolution
D.C.L.	Doctor of Civil Law
D.D.	Doctor of Divinity
D.Eng.	Doctor of Engineering
DEW	Distant Early Warning Line
D.F.C.	Distinguished Flying Cross
D.J.	Doctor of Jurisprudence
D.Litt.	Doctor of Literature
D.Mus.	Doctor of Music
DP	Displaced Person
D.Pol.Sc.	Doctor of Political Science
D.Sc.	Doctor of Science
D.S.C.	Distinguished Service Cross
D.S.M.	Distinguished Service Medal
D.S.O.	Distinguished Service Order
ECA	Economic Cooperation Administration
ECOSOC	Economic and Social Council
EDC	Economic Defense Community
EEC	European Economic Community
ERA	Equal Rights Amendment
ERP	European Recovery Program
ESA	Economic Stabilization Administration
FAO	Food and Agriculture Organization
FBI	Federal Bureau of Investigation
FCC	Federal Communications Commission
FEPC	Fair Employment Practice Committee
FHA	Federal Housing Administration
FOA	Foreign Operations Administration
FPC	Federal Power Commission
FSA	Federal Security Agency
FTC	Federal Trade Commission
GATT	General Agreement on Tariffs and Trade
G.B.E.	Knight or Dame, Grand Cross Order of the British Empire
G.C.B.	Knight Grand Cross of the Bath
G.O.P.	Grand Old Party
H.M.	His Majesty; Her Majesty
HUD	Housing and Urban Development
IBM	International Business Machine Corporation
ICBM	Intercontinental Ballistic Missile
ICC	Interstate Commerce Commission
I.C.F.T.U.	International Confederation of Free Trade Unions
IGY	International Geophysical Year
I.L.A.	International Longshoremen's Association
I.L.G.W.U.	International Ladies' Garment Workers' Union
I.L.O.	International Labor Organization
INS	International News Service
IRO	International Refugee Organization
J.D.	Doctor of Jurisprudence
K.B.E.	Knight of (the Order of) the British Empire
K.C.	King's Counsel
K.C.B.	Knight Commander of the Bath
L.H.D.	Doctor of Humanities
Litt.D.	Doctor of Letters
LL.B.	Bachelor of Laws
LL.D.	Doctor of Laws
M.A.	Master of Arts
M.B.A.	Master of Business Administration
MBS	Mutual Broadcasting System

M.C.E.	Master of Civil Engineering
M.D.	Doctor of Medicine
M.E.	Master of Engineering
METO	Middle East Treaty Organization
MGM	Metro-Goldwyn-Mayer
M.Lit.	Master of Literature
M.P.	Member of Parliament
M.P.P.D.A.	Motion Picture Producers and Distributors of America
MRP	Mouvement Républicain Populaire
MSA	Mutual Security Agency
M.Sc.	Master of Science
Msgr.	Monsignor, Monseigneur
NAACP	National Association for the Advancement of Colored People
NAB	National Association of Broadcasters
NAM	National Association of Manufacturers
NASA	National Aeronautics and Space Administration
NATO	North Atlantic Treaty Organization
NBC	National Broadcasting Company
NEA	National Education Association
NLRB	National Labor Relations Board
N.M.U.	National Maritime Union
NOW	National Organization for Women
NRA	National Recovery Administration
NRPB	National Resources Planning Board
NYA	National Youth Administration
O.A.S.	Organization of American States
O.B.E.	Officer of (the Order of) the British Empire
OCD	Office of Civilian Defense
OEEC	Organization for European Economic Cooperation
OMB	Office of Management and Budget
OPA	Office of Price Administration
OPEC	Organization of Petroleum Exporting Countries
OPM	Office of Production Management
OWI	Office of War Information
PBS	Public Broadcasting Service
P.E.N.	Poets, Playwrights, Editors, Essayist and Novelists (International Association)
Ph.B.	Bachelor of Philosophy
Ph.D.	Doctor of Philosophy
PWA	Public Works Administration
Q.C.	Queen's Counsel
RAF	Royal Air Force
RCA	Radio Corporation of America
REA	Rural Electrification Administration
RFC	Reconstruction Finance Corporation
RKO	Radio-Keith-Orpheum
ROTC	Reserve Officers' Training Corps
SAC	Strategic Air Command
SALT	Strategic Arms Limitation Talks
S.J.	Society of Jesus
SCAP	Supreme Command for the Allied Powers
SEATO	Southeast Asia Treaty Organization
SEC	Securities and Exchange Commission
SHAEF	Supreme Headquarters, Allied Expeditionary Force
SHAPE	Supreme Headquarters, Allied Powers Europe
S.J.D.	Doctor of Juridical Science
SLA	Special Libraries Association
S.T.B.	Bachelor of Sacred Theology
S.T.D.	Doctor of Sacred Theology
TVA	Tennessee Valley Authority
T.W.U.A.	Textile Workers Union of America
UAR	United Arab Repubic
U.A.W.	United Automobile, Aircraft, and Agricultural Implement Workers of America
UMT	Universal Military Training
U.M.W.A.	United Mine Workers of America
U.N.	United Nations
UNESCO	United Nations Educational, Scientific, and Cultural Organization
UNICEF	United Nations Children's Fund
UNRRA	United Nations Relief and Rehabilitation Administration
U.P.I.	United Press and International News Service
USO	United Service Organizations
U.S.S.R.	Union of Soviet Socialist Republics
U.S.W.A.	United Steel Workers of America
VA	Veterans Administration
V.F.W.	Veterans of Foreign Wars
W.F.T.U.	World Federation of Trade Unions
WHO	World Health Organization
WMC	War Manpower Commission
WPA	Work Projects Administration
WPB	War Production Board
YMCA	Young Men's Christian Association
YMHA	Young Men's Hebrew Association
YWCA	Young Women's Christian Association

Current Biography Yearbook 1978

Adams, Richard (George)

May 10, 1920- Writer. Address: "Knocksharry House," Lhergy-Dhoo, near Peel, Isle of Man

Animal fantasy fiction, a genre extending back to Aesop's *Fables*, has a new master in Richard Adams, a former British civil servant who was a late starter, already in his fifties when he published his first book, the "instant classic" *Watership Down* (1972), a rabbit odyssey set in Berkshire and concerned with survival and leadership. That best-selling novel, popular with both adults and older children, won the *Guardian* and Carnegie awards for distinguished fiction and drew from critics comparisons with Lewis Carroll, Kenneth Grahame, and J. R. R. Tolkien. With his usual descriptive and imaginative brilliance, Adams evoked an ancient kingdom of his own invention as the setting for *Shardik* (1975), a terror-filled religious epic involving a bear-god. He returned to the English landscape for *The Plague Dogs* (1977), an antivivisectionist story about two garrulous canine fugitives from an experimental laboratory. That third novel, heavy-handed in its satirical treatment of human villains, is, like its predecessors, distinguished by richness of naturalistic detail and a sustained narrative skill.

Richard George Adams was born on May 10, 1920 in Newbury, England, where his parents owned a spacious house with three acres of garden amidst the rolling Berkshire countryside that would become the locale of *Watership Down*. His mother was Rosa (Button) Adams; his father, Evelyn George Beadon Adams, a surgeon who read Hugh Lofting's Dr. Doolittle stories to his children. "I was the youngest child," Adams told Al Burt of the Miami (Florida) *Herald* (April 20, 1975). "My sister and brother were nine and seven years older. So I had time to myself. . . . I had the run of the fields. . . . I fantasized. I made up games." In another interview, for *Newsweek* (April 28, 1975), he described himself as "a solitary little boy with an enormous fantasy life" who imagined himself to be "a king of an imaginary country [with] quite a lot of comrades."

From boarding school—where he was a classmate of Christopher Milne, the son of A. A. Milne and the real-life counterpart of Christopher Robin in Milne's *Winnie the Pooh*—Adams went to Bradfield College, a prep school in Berkshire, and from there to Oxford University in 1938. At some point in his formative years he underwent Jungian psychoanalysis. After World War II service with the British Airborne Forces, he returned to Worcester College at Oxford, where he received an M.A. degree in modern history in 1948. From Oxford, Adams went directly into the British home civil service, where he worked up through the ranks of the Ministry of Housing and Local Government to become, after twenty years in various positions, assistant secretary in charge of the clean air section of the ministry's Department of the Environment.

In the interview with Al Burt for the Miami *Herald*, Adams recounted the genesis of *Watership Down:* "My own children [Juliet and Rosamond] came late in our lives. There was some difficulty. When they did come, I made up my mind to be the best father possible. The stories started out of that. I also had the idea of interesting them in Shakespeare and Mozart [and] it was while we were driving to Stratford once, and they were begging for stories, that *Watership*

Down began. All the principal ingredients were extemporized off the top of my head. It was about a fortnight before I finished telling it to them the first time."

The story Adams told began with a psychic young rabbit named Fiver having a vague but terrible vision of imminent destruction. He is correct—the home warren is to be razed and its inhabitants gassed to make way for a suburban housing development—but only a few of the other rabbits, including Fiver's older brother Hazel, take him seriously. Under Hazel's leadership, the small band flees the warren to look for a new home. Their expedition is a long and adventurous one, through woods and across a stream, into contact with an effete warren whose lotus-eating inhabitants lack the self-defensive instincts necessary for survival, and finally to Watership Down, where they decide to settle. Just as they are doing so, a neighboring warren, a totalitarian state ruled by a rogue rabbit named General Woundwort, makes war on them, and it is only after they win a bloody, climactic battle that they can turn their attention to building a democratic society on Watership Down.

At the urging of his daughters, Adams set about putting his rabbit story down on paper. For solid scientific background, he consulted R. M. Lockley's *The Private Life of the Rabbit*, and, as he explained in the interview included in Justin Wintle and Emma Fisher's *The Pied Pipers* (1974), he adopted Rudyard Kipling's formula for anthropomorphic animal fantasy: "You attribute to your animals motives and incentives and ideals that real animals wouldn't have. On the other hand they are very animal to this extent: they never do anything of which real animals would be physically incapable—they don't wear clothes or smoke cigars or walk about on their hind legs or anything like that. They're allowed to keep their animalian dignity."

Adams stretched out his basic plot to a story of epic length consisting of fifty chapters, each introduced with a pithy literary quotation from such writers as Shakespeare, Clausewitz, Malory, Milton, and Auden and each ending with a cliff-hanging device. In and around the scrupulously authentic details regarding rabbit biology and physiology he fashioned a complete rabbit civilization, with folklore (including a creation myth), politics, and even, in addition to English, a special lapine language consisting of words described by Adams as having "a wuffy, fluffy sound, the sort of noises a rabbit might make." The scientific undergirding and imaginative superstructure were created to enhance, with plausibility, the author's essential project: the narration of the perilous adventures of a band of rabbits whose "only motives from start to finish" are "food, survival, and mating."

Writing evenings, Adams spent two years putting *Watership Down* on paper. After rejections by four publishers and three literary agents, the manuscript was accepted by Rex Collings Ltd. in 1970. Collings came out with the first edition of *Watership Down* in 1972, and the following year Penguin issued the novel in its children's series, Puffin Books.

British critics greeted *Watership Down* with raves, ranking it beside George Orwell's *Animal Farm* and the fantasy fiction of C. S. Lewis, J. R. R. Tolkien, Jonathan Swift, Kenneth Grahame, and A. A. Milne. When the book received the children's fiction award of the *Guardian* (March 29, 1973), Edward Blishen, writing in that newspaper, called it "a true original," setting "the rabbit free from all previous literary overtones, including sentimental and whimsical ones." Blishen wrote: "Mr. Adams has provided the creature with perfectly convincing and precisely imagined physical and mental characteristics of its own —together with a language so persuasive that one seems always to have known it. All this is totally absorbed into a story of epic weight and excitement."

Like many other reviewers, Blishen saw "hidden meanings" in *Watership Down:* "A double comment seems constantly to be made on the world of human affairs. The plight of the rabbits in a countryside trembling under the impact of human enterprise is one such comment; the other is offered by the experiences of the rabbits among themselves, their struggle for peace, the constant threat of enslavement, corruption, war. Altogether, it's a book that, through the originality of its creatures and theme, refreshes a reader's feeling for the world of men."

In the United States, Macmillan, having first intended *Watership Down* for its juvenile list, published it as an adult title in 1974. As in England, it was an instant success. Within two weeks it was the number one best seller, and it remained on the New York *Times* best-seller list for thirty-three weeks. In addition, it was a Book-of-the-Month Club selection, and Avon paid $800,000 for the paperback rights. By April 1975, when the first Avon edition was issued, hard-cover sales totalled 700,000.

Writing in *New York* magazine (March 4, 1974), Eliot Fremont-Smith said that what makes *Watership Down* "a very grand book" is "Adams's wonderfully rich imagination, together with an extraordinary and totally disarming respect for his material. Tone is all important in a tale like this, and Adams's is straight, confidently controlled, never maudlin, never cute." He summed up *Watership Down* as "a marvel, a wise and sunny book, a suspenseful epic that readers twelve and up are going to enjoy for a long time to come.'" Reviewing the book in the Los Angeles *Times* (March 26, 1974), Robert Kirsch wrote that "one reads on in these pages" because "the prose, the drama, the imaginative meld of the factual and the experiential will not allow us to stop."

There were dissenters from the praise heaped on *Watership Down*. Among the many who thought that the novel was too long and "laboriously drawn out," was Geoffrey Wolff, who reviewed it for *Newsday* (April 14, 1974). But, Wolfe wrote, "*Watership Down*, for all its faults and forfeits, works and lives," as a "reduced world, where clarity of vision seems to resemble breadth and length of vision, where shamans and heroes can still save the tribe. . . . Such reduction and reconstruction, for visionary rather than moral ends, has from the beginning been imaginative fiction's function and life."

Adams's own favorite among his books is the second one published, *Shardik* (Rex Collings, 1974; Simon and Schuster, 1975), described by the author as "a Rider Haggard story," a "spiritual and religious novel," and "an attempt to write a major, large-scale tragic novel for children." The book, which begins with an epigraph from Carl Jung ("Superstition and accident manifest the will of God"), has as its title character a mammoth bear who is alternately worshipped as a divine avatar and victimized by the barbarian inhabitants of an ancient empire in Asia Minor, a complex fictional world invented by Richard Adams with his usual imaginative power.

Unlike *Watership Down*, *Shardik* teems with human characters, who illustrate both the cruelty and destruction, on the one hand, and the nobility, on the other, that can ensue from religious belief. At one pole is Genshed, the slave dealer who finds pleasure in torturing and murdering young children; at the other is Kelderek, a morally regenerate leader whose utopian vision contributes to the frightening story's happy ending.

Typical of the mixed notices *Shardik* received was that in the *Listener* (January 2, 1975), where reviewer Kenneth Graham observed that while "there is no real grasp of the inward reaches of character, only of the grand simplicities of archetype . . . there is enough creative endeavor, careful planning, integrity, and sheer multifarious detail in *Shardik* to make a dozen ordinary novels." Comparing *Shardik* to *Moby Dick*, Graham wrote: "As in the case of Melville's extraordinary amalgam of prosaic whaling treatise and poetic meditation, *Shardik* is an attempt to create an entire world that is memorably real and, at the same time, incandescent with immemorial meaning. And for a time—at the beginning and again near the ending—it almost works as intended. There can be few books on which more loving, energetic inventiveness have been expended."

In *Time* (April 28, 1975) John Skow wrote of *Shardik*: "The author spins out his romance entertainingly, but without dealing seriously with the questions he raised: of belief and its perversion, of authority and its corruption. Good as he is at nature walks, Adams does not venture far into the forests of the mind." Peter Wolfe, writing in the *New Republic* (May 3, 1975), called attention to the book's "majestic language, heroic theme, and sustained power," and in the *Saturday Review* (May 31, 1975) Bruce Allen wrote: "Among this book's greatest strengths is its rejection of the modern novel's emphasis on subjective uncertainty. It urges that truth is knowable."

Adams provided some of the prose for *Nature Through the Seasons* (Felix Gluck Press; Simon and Schuster, 1975) and *Nature Day and Night* (Viking, 1978), both containing nature drawings by David A. Goddard and scientific notes by Max Hooper, and he wrote *The Tyger Voyage* (Knopf, 1976), a simple tale of two tigers living in Victorian England inspired by a picture by Nicola Bayley. He also wrote the verse for *The Ship's Cat* (Knopf, 1977), an account of the adventures and brave deeds of a feline swashbuckler on the Spanish Main, illustrated by Alan Aldridge with Harry Willock.

Having resigned his government post after writing *Shardik*, Adams was a visiting professor of poetry appreciation at the University of Florida in 1974-75, and the following academic year he became a writer-in-residence at Hollins College in Virginia, where he continued working on his third novel, *The Plague Dogs*. That book, published in England by Allen Lane in 1977 and in the United States by Knopf in 1978, is the story of two dogs who escape from an animal experimentation laboratory in the English Lake District. One is Rowf, a large black mongrel who, having been repeatedly immersed and nearly drowned, is deathly afraid of water. The other is Snitter, a small fox terrier who, having undergone brain surgery designed to "confuse the subjective and the objective," wavers between lucidity and hallucination. Befriended by a fox, the dogs make their way across the countryside in an adventure that turns into a nightmare when newspapers report that the dogs may carry bubonic plague as a result of experiments at the laboratory from which they escaped. Army, police, and citizenry join in hunting them down.

"*The Plague Dogs* is not just an attack on animal experimentation," Adams told Jan Rodger of the Toronto *Globe and Mail* (November 16, 1977). "It is about the way in which, in modern life, almost all of us have a motive for what we do which is other than a simple, direct, honest motive, straightforward hunger or love. The animal experimenters are one thing. . . . Then the journalist, he wants his story. . . . Then there is the man who feeds the animals. He knows very well he is participating in this inhuman research but he needs his wages. If you are put off by tracts, you are probably not going to like *The Plague Dogs*. But I do feel very indignant about animal experimentation and perhaps my indignation got the better of me."

There were those in the scientific and medical communities who agreed that Adams's indignation *had* "got the better" of him, and some critics outside of those communities accused Adams of "sentimentality," of bias in treating the human characters strictly in terms of satire or melodrama, and of indirect moralizing. But even John Leonard, who panned *The Plague Dogs* mercilessly in his review in the New York *Times* (March 7, 1978), acknowledged that Adams "is uncanny at making us believe that animals think and feel precisely the way he says they do." In the Washington *Post* (February 26, 1978) Joseph McLellan wrote: "By his repeatedly felt presence behind the scenes, manipulating the action and commenting on it, Adams underlines a fact that is already apparent: like them or not, his novels differ from all others being written today. He clearly aspires to the literary big leagues. . . . As the book weathers into a classic (if it does, and it well may) the idiosyncrasies that are a distraction on its first appearance will become part of its charm. And the prospect for the foreseeable future is that its central image—that of two creatures victimized by society, unable to live by its rules but also unable to work out and live by their own outlaw code—is one in which many people will see reflected some part of themselves."

Richard Adams is a blue-eyed, ruddy-faced man with graying blond hair, an erect posture, a restless temperament, and a well-tailored wardrobe. In conversation he can be warm or pugnacious, as the situation demands. Holding political and social views that are as old-fashioned as his manner and appearance would suggest, he is obsessed with the permissiveness and lack of leadership in contemporary society, and he dislikes cities, where "God's earth has been covered with concrete." An Anglican who takes his religion seriously, he has pointed out that one of the ideas in *Shardik* is "that we ought to rethink from scratch the basic corpus of religion." Independent of spirit and fancy-free, he can lose himself in the interest of the moment, becoming oblivious of traffic, for example, when reciting a classic from memory in the street. Once, in Los Angeles to appear on *The Tonight Show Starring Johnny Carson*, he never reached the television station because he was too engrossed in conversation with the late Groucho Marx, one of his screen favorites.

Adams and Barbara Elizabeth Acland, a writer and lecturer on chinaware, were married in 1949. They now live on the Isle of Man in the Irish Sea, where Adams likes to walk up and down the glens and to swim. The author, who is vice-president of the Royal Society for the Prevention of Cruelty to Animals, has two pets, a dog and a cat. Adams writes in longhand, with pen or pencil, never a typewriter, and he writes slowly, revising constantly and producing a maximum of 1,000 words a day. Before beginning each writing session he usually reads aloud from Milton's *Paradise Lost*, Spenser's *The Faerie Queene*, or C. K. Scott-Moncrieff's translation of Proust, whom he acknowledges as his master. His other favorite authors range from Beatrix Potter to William Butler Yeats. Adams does not care for modern novels that are "dominated by the problems of their heroes or heroines, who are constantly questioning their values," he told Jenny Rees of the London *Times* (November 8, 1974). "As an orthodox Christian I feel there really isn't a lot of agonizing to be done. I couldn't write a story about right and wrong." In an interview with Dick Adler for the Los Angeles *Times* (July 20, 1975) he confessed: "It would be quite beyond me to write a true novel—a story of contemporary people in a contemporary setting, by implication examining contemporary morality. . . . I need, if you will, the anthropomorphic distance of using animals."

References: Biog N 2:475+ My/Je '75 por; Guardian p13 Mr 29 '73 por; London Times C p12 N 8 '74; N Y Post p35 Mr 30 '74 por; N Y Times Bk R p38 Ap 9 '78 por; Newsday A p13 Ap 16 '74 pors; Pub W 205: 6+ Ap 15 '74 por; Washington Post B p1+ My 27 '75; Contemporary Authors, vols 49-52 (1975); Who's Who, 1978; Wintle, Justin and Fisher, Emma. Pied Pipers (1975)

Aleixandre (Y Merlo), Vicente

Apr. 26, 1898- Spanish poet. Address: h. Wellingtonia 3, Madrid 3, Spain

When the members of the Swedish Academy awarded the 1977 Nobel Prize for Literature to the Spanish poet Vicente Aleixandre, they cited Spain's remarkable "Poetic Group of 1927," in which he had figured so notably during the past half-century. They also expressed admiration for Aleixandre's "strength to survive" that had enabled him to transcend such formidable obstacles as frail health, a bitter Civil War, and the enforced separation from many of his friends and colleagues, who left him behind in his sickbed after the Franco victory drove them into exile. The wording of the award made it clear, however, that the distinction was mainly

Vicente Aleixandre

based on Aleixandre's long lifetime of poetic output, rooted both in the Spanish lyric tradition and in his modernism, which "illuminates man's condition in the cosmos and in present-day society."

Vicente Aleixandre came belatedly to the literary profession after having prepared himself for a career in law and commerce. His cadenced free verse, evolving at times into prose poems, has love, death, and eternity as its abiding themes. Although absent on doctor's orders from the Stockholm award ceremony in December 1977, Aleixandre declared by proxy from Madrid his "spiritual presence" in a toast that accepted the Nobel Prize honor as "above all a symbol of human solidarity." Although not widely known outside the Spanish-speaking world, Aleixandre is highly admired in Latin America, and in his native land, where he has exerted a major influence upon younger poets. He has defined his poetry as "a longing for the light" and views the poet as a man who speaks for the earth, whose primal forces he can feel even through the soles of his feet.

Vicente Pio Marcelino Cirilo Aleixandre y Merlo was born in Seville, Spain on April 26, 1898 to Cirilo Aleixandre Ballester, a native of Valencia, and Elvira Merlo García de Pruneda, whose family belonged to the Andalusian upper middle-class. Cirilo Aleixandre came from a family of prosperous artisans in the Levante region of Spain. The birthplace of Vicente Aleixandre, the Palacio de Yanduri, was occupied by General Francisco Franco years later at the outset of the Spanish Civil War.

The Aleixandres' first child, a girl, died at an early age, and Vicente's birth in 1898—the year that witnessed the end of Spanish colonialism and the genesis of the "Generation of 1898" literary movement—was followed in 1899 by that of his sister Concepción (Conchita). As the biographer and poet Leopoldo de Luis has pointed out, the Aleixandre-Merlo family formed an affectionate and close-knit unit (until the mother's death in 1934 and that of the father six years later) that helped to shield Vicente from outside adversity at the same time that it allowed him freedom of movement.

In 1902 the family moved from Seville, where the father had worked as a civil engineer for the Andalusian Railways, to Málaga on the Mediterranean coast. Its sunny skies, luxuriant flora, and picturesque seascape left an indelible impression on Vicente Aleixandre's memory. He has mentioned that his earliest childhood recollection of those tranquil and happy years is of sitting on the floor at his grandmother's feet, playing with some marble figurines while watching in fascination the Columbine and Harlequin revolving on top of her antique music box. Aleixandre also has fond memories of his primary schoolmaster, Buenaventura Barranco Bosch, and of a fellow primary school student in Málaga, Emilio Prados, who later published Aleixandre's first poetry.

Vicente Aleixandre's grandfather Merlo was another important figure in his early life. He not only fired the boy's imagination with tales about his military adventures in Cuba, but influenced his precocious reading habits and helped establish his literary loyalties. To him Aleixandre owes his early fondness for novels, especially those of Benito Pérez Galdós, which he found in his grandfather's library, and his nonreligious, though not anticlerical, education. He went on to read the Spanish historian Modesto Lafuente, the nineteenth-century realists, the dramatists of Spain's Golden Age, and the prose writers of the Generation of 1898. His foreign favorites included Fyodor Dostoyevsky and Friedrich Schiller.

When the family moved to Madrid in 1909 and set up housekeeping in the aristocratic quarter of the Barrio de Salamanca, Vicente Aleixandre attended a secular school to prepare for the secondary-level exam for his *bachillerato* degree, which he obtained in 1913. The following year he entered the law school of the University of Madrid. While spending a summer vacation at Las Navas del Marqués in the province of Ávila in 1917, Aleixandre met a student his own age named Dámaso Alonso, who became a deciding factor in his choice of a career. Now the president of the Royal Spanish Academy, a distinguished philologist, and still a close friend, Alonso was amazed to learn that Aleixandre had read virtually no poetry, for all of his wide reading, and gave him a volume by the Modernist Nicaraguan poet Rubén Darío that afforded him a new perspective on literature.

In addition to foraging through the works of Gustavo Adolfo Bécquer (who had been a friend of his grandfather Merlo) and the Catalan poet Juan Maragall, Aleixandre began reading contemporary Spanish and French poets. But he has attributed his genuine poetic formation to his exposure to Antonio Machado, Juan Ramón Jiménez, Paul Valéry and the Symbolists; they, along with Arthur Rimbaud (his prose more than his verse) and James Joyce, are responsible for his being a poet. Later influences were the German and French romantics, the English poets, the surrealists, and the German mystical poet Novalis. His facility with foreign languages and his travels abroad, made possible by his private means, cosmopolitanized him as a poet.

In 1919 Vicente Aleixandre took both his law degree and a diploma in business administration. In October of that year he became an associate professor at the Central School of Commerce in Madrid, where he taught courses in commercial law. Two years later he accepted a position in the Madrid offices of Ferrocarriles Andaluces, the railway for which his father had worked as a civil engineer, and he began writing for a business weekly called *La Semana Financiera* (Financial Week). He first broke into print as the author of an article on railway problems. During the summer course for foreigners at the famous Residencia de Estudiantes, where Luis Buñuel and Federico García Lorca lived during the 1920's, Aleixandre taught a course in business terminology in 1921.

At an art exhibit held in Madrid's Ateneo in 1922 Vicente Aleixandre first met Rafael Alberti, then an artist and later a surrealist poet and fellow member of the Poetic Group of 1927. In that year Aleixandre fell victim to an attack of infectious arthritis that proved to be the first in a lifelong series of illnesses and physical pain. The tuberculosis of the kidney that afflicted him in 1925 forced him to give up his professional activity, and his father took a house in the countryside near Madrid to accelerate his son's convalescence. In 1931 Aleixandre suffered a relapse that led to an operation in the following year for removal of one kidney, and in 1937 he experienced a recurrence of the same malady.

Nevertheless, Vicente Aleixandre managed to intersperse his debilitating bouts of illness with extraordinarily fecund periods of poetic creativity. He also succeeded in traveling, lecturing, and sustaining many productive friendships over the years. Although he had begun to write poetry at eighteen, he kept that a virtual secret until he was twenty-seven. In 1924 he began work on the poems that would be included in his first book, and on returning to Madrid after recuperating in the country he brought with him the completed manuscript of the volume eventually entitled *Ámbito* (Ambit). The discovery by some friends of poetry that he had been writing in the privacy of his room led in 1926 to the first publication of his work in the intellectual review *Revista de Occidente*, which was founded by Ortega y Gasset.

The year 1927 marked a milestone not only in Vicente Aleixandre's life but also in modern Spanish literature. In May of that year the Aleixandre family moved into the small villa on the northern outskirts of Madrid, near the university campus on a short street named Velintonia (after a tall conifer) but mistakenly listed in municipal directories as Wellingtonia. That house with its garden facing the Guadarrama mountains became the poet's haven and creative habitat for the next half-century. The year 1927 was a turning point for Spanish letters because it witnessed a joint homage by young writers to Luis de Góngora on the tercentenary of the death of that last great poet of Spain's Golden Age.

In turn, that collaboration of Aleixandre with Jorge Guillén, Dámaso Alonso, Luis Cernuda, Rafael Alberti, Gerardo Diego, Pedro Salinas, Federico García Lorca, and others produced a flowering of poetic production that poet and essayist Lewis Hyde, who has translated Aleixandre into English, has called "the most fruitful current in modern poetry." The American poet Robert Bly, who has also translated Aleixandre, wrote in the New York *Times* (October 30, 1977) of Vicente Aleixandre and his contemporaries: "His generation was the astounding one, a concentration of genius unheard of in Spain for centuries, amazing in any country." They came to be known as the Poetic Group of 1927 after the Góngora anniversary celebration that had served them as catalyst. Although its members never really constituted a movement, as Bly put it, they "welcomed Neruda when he came to Spain in the 30's, jumped feet first into surrealism, which they felt not as a clique but as an ocean, [and] encouraged each other."

Vicente Aleixandre's first book of poetry, *Ámbito*, was published in 1928 by the Litoral press in Málaga, which was operated by Aleixandre's childhood friend Emilio Prados and Manuel Altolaguirre. That same year Aleixandre began reading Freud, a major influence in his subsequent evolution. The latter years of the 1920's brought the deepening of his friendships with García Lorca and Cernuda, and in 1929 Aleixandre was invited to Málaga by Prados and Altolaguirre, a trip that helped him to recover his Andalusian roots.

Aleixandre's presence and participation in the Poetic Group of 1927 coincided with its third phase, a surrealism not altogether loyal to the orthodoxy of André Breton's manifesto and before long known in Spanish as "superrealismo." The key books of poetry by Aleixandre during that period are *Pasión de la tierra* (Passion of Earth), written between 1928 and 1929 but not published until 1935, in Mexico; *Espadas como labios* (Swords Like Lips), written during 1930-31 and published in 1932; and *La Destrucción o el amor* (Destruction, or Love) begun in 1932 and completed in 1933, when it won the poet that year's National Literary Prize in Spain. *La Destrucción o el amor,* published in 1935, has been singled out by Leopoldo de Luis as the most outstanding of those works, one of the best books of surrealist poetry anywhere and, indeed, of any love poems of all time. The last of the series, *Mundo a solas* (The World Alone), was begun in 1936 shortly before the outbreak of Spain's Civil War.

Again Aleixandre was confined to his sickbed as the armed conflict and the eventual Franco triumph drove his friends abroad one by one; his house on Wellingtonia Street was on the edge of the Madrid front during the war, and by 1939 had been bombed out. Towards the end of hostilities, the poet and his sister had lived not far away; with their father dead in March of 1940, they determined to rebuild the villa and have lived there ever since. During the first autumn of uneasy peace, Vicente Aleixandre began writing poems for his *Sombra del paraíso* (Shadow of Paradise), which the rigid censorship kept from publication until 1944. The second editions of *La Destrucción o el amor* and *Pasión de la tierra* (the latter, in a first edition for Spain) appeared in 1945 and 1946 respectively, and in 1948 Aleixandre published in a Zaragoza review his "Elegy" dedicated to the memory of the poet Miguel Hernández.

On June 30, 1949 the Spanish Royal Academy elected Vicente Aleixandre a member, the fifteenth man of letters to occupy its so-called "O" seat since the Academy was founded in 1714. His acceptance address, entitled "The Poet's Life: Love and Poetry," was delivered at the Academy in January 1950. That same year brought other honors: a de luxe edition of *Mundo a solas* appeared; Aleixandre lectured at Oxford and the University of London; and Carlos Bousoño published his important critical exegesis titled *La Poesía de Vicente Aleixandre: imagen, estilo, mundo poético* (The Poetry of Vicente Aleixandre: Image, Style, Poetic World). In 1953, the year he visited Morocco for lectures in Tangier and Tetuán, Aleixandre published *Nacimiento Último* (Final Birth), and the following year a major work called *Historia del Corazón* (The Story of the Heart) appeared. The latter marked a turning point in his evolution that led Lewis Hyde to consider Vicente Aleixandre as one of the few pessimistic poets of the twentieth century capable of emerging from the darkness to find something higher. Death and loss still shadow those later poems, Hyde notes, but they give way to human fellowship. "Man rises to the foreground," according to the article on Aleixandre in *World Authors,* and for the first time the poet recognizes that, although he remains separated from the eternal, "man must still live and love in the brief reality allowed to him."

"Where before he had been attentive to nature and longed to join it," Hyde wrote in his New York *Times* article, "now nature is just the background for the lives of human beings." One of the best of his few prose works, *Los Encuentros* (Encounters, 1958), contained affectionate glimpses of his fellow writers. In 1960 Aleixandre's complete poems were published; two years later appeared his *En un vasto dominio* (In a Vast Dominion), which critics described as so accessible that it was even prosaic. Anthologies of his work were translated into Italian and German in 1961 and 1963. After *Relatos con nombre* (Stories with a Name, 1965) appeared *Poemas de la consumación* (Poems of the Final Consummation, 1968), which a London *Times Literary Supplement* reviewer called "of almost aphoristic brevity" for the most part, and some of his bleakest poems. "Their treatment of old age and the passing of love is uncompromisingly honest and devoid of any kind of easy consolation," the critic wrote. "If the poet himself sees his whole work as a constant clarification of means and material . . . these new poems at last break through to the kind of difficult simplicities which are occasionally the reward for a lifetime's major work."

Aleixandre won the Spanish Critics' Prize in 1969, the year another edition of his complete works appeared, and in 1970 he began work on *Diálogos del Conocimiento,* which was published in 1974. Homage was paid to him in one form or another throughout the 1970's, and in 1974 scholars in Spain and abroad suggested his name for the Nobel Prize. He had been proposed several times, once in conjunction with Jorge Luis Borges of Argentina and again with Léopold Senghor of Sénégal, but political considerations related to the 1975 execution of Spanish terrorists and Borges' enthusiasm for the Videla regime in Argentina ruled out Aleixandre's selection.

Vicente Aleixandre expressed great surprise when the Swedish Academy's Nobel Committee chose him as recipient of the Prize for Literature in the autumn of 1977. Unable to attend the award presentation because of his chronic ill health complicated by a heart disorder and failing eyesight, Aleixandre delegated Justo Jorge Padrón, a young Spanish poet living in Stockholm and his official translator into Swedish, to receive his prize. A few days later he was visited by King Juan Carlos I of Spain, who decorated him with the Grand Cross of the Order of Carlos III in an informal ceremony attended by several of his contemporaries from the Spanish Royal Academy. Aleixandre belongs to the Hispanic Society of New York, the Académie du Monde Latin of Paris, and the Academia Hispanoamericana of Bogotá. He continues to live quietly with his sister Conchita, a dog, and some goldfish in the same house that he moved into in 1927 and that he seldom leaves. He is gratified that the Nobel distinction will further familiarity with his work, since he has often said that poetry is either "potentially multitudinous" or else can advance no claim to be poetry at all.

References: N Y Times A p1+ O 7 '77 por; A p12 O 7 '77; N Y Times Bk R p3+ O 30 '77 por; International Who's Who in Poetry, 1974-75; Quién es Quién en las Letras Españolas, 1969; Who's Who in Spain, 1963; World Authors 1950-1970, 1975

Ali, Muhammad

Jan. 18, 1942- Boxer. Address: b. Deer Lake, Pa. 17972

NOTE: This biography supersedes the article that appeared in *Current Biography* in 1963, under the name of Cassius Clay.

The most recognized face in the world is probably that of Muhammad Ali—self-described as "the Greatest"—the first prizefighter ever to win the world heavyweight championship three times. Ali began his professional career in 1960, when he was Cassius Clay, a brash eighteen-year-old Olympic medal winner from Louisville, Kentucky who soon became as well known for the boastful doggerel with which he predicted the rounds of his victories as for his skill, power, speed, and dazzling dancing style in the ring. His international reputation soared when, after taking the heavyweight title from Sonny Liston in 1964, he announced his membership in the Nation of Islam (now the World Community of Islam) and his refusal to fight in Vietnam, but at home he paid dearly for his principled defiance of the establishment: heavyweight boxing authorities lost little time in stripping him of his title and his boxing license, forcing him into three and a half years of professional exile, from 1967 to 1970. Ali regained the championship by defeating George Foreman in October 1974, lost it to Leon Spinks in February 1978, and took it back from Spinks in September 1978, when his professional career totals stood at fifty-eight wins, three losses, and thirty-seven knockouts. His claim to the title is recognized by the World Boxing Association but not by the World Boxing Council, which recognizes that of Larry Holmes. The W.B.C.'s stand is based on Leon Spinks's backing out of an agreement to face Holmes after the first bout with Ali.

Muhammad Ali was born Cassius Marcellus Clay Jr. in the General Hospital in Louisville, Kentucky on January 18, 1942, the elder of two sons of Cassius Marcellus Clay Sr. and Odessa (Grady) Clay. According to some genealogical accounts, Ali's maternal grandfather was a white Irish-American and his paternal great-great-grandfather was a freed slave who took the name of his former master, Cassius Marcellus Clay, the diplomat, pioneer abolitionist and relative of Henry Clay. But Arnold Hano in *Muhammad Ali, The Champion* (1977) cites May Clay Turner, an aunt of the prizefighter, as insisting that the Clay name, and the "white blood," came down from Henry Clay himself, a direct ancestor. In his autobiography, *The Greatest: My Own Story* (Random House, 1975), written with Richard Durham, Ali dismisses the latter assertion with scorn: "The fact is that in my part of the family there was very little knowledge, if any, of 'white blood' from any source. . . . If slave owner Clay's blood came into our veins along with the name, it came by rape and defilement."

Cassius Marcellus Clay Sr. provided for his family by painting signs and, when he could find the extra work, murals for churches and taverns. According to Ali, he was also, avocationally, a "natural actor," singer, impressionist, and "the fanciest dancer in Louisville." The father's attraction to show business was reflected in the name he gave his younger son—Rudolph Valentino Clay (now Rahaman Ali). Cassius and Rudy, as they were then known, grew up in what the prizefighter describes as "semi-poverty." To help make ends meet, especially when mortgage payments on their four-room frame house came due, Odessa Clay worked as a domestic for four dollars a day, and when he was old enough, Cassius did part-time custodial work at Nazareth College, a Catholic school near his home that has since become Spalding College.

Clay's boxing career dates from the time his bicycle was stolen, when he was twelve years old and attending a bazaar at the Columbia Auditorium, a community recreation center across the street from Nazareth College. Someone told him to report the theft to Joe Elsby Martin, a white policeman who was supervising boxing in the basement gym of the auditorium. After making note of the theft, Martin invited him to join the boxing sessions, and he began to do so, regularly. According to Martin, Cassius Clay was a "little smart aleck—I mean he's always been sassy," but "he had more determination than most boys, and he had the speed to get him someplace." Soon Martin was booking Clay on *Tomorrow's Champions*, a local weekly television boxing show.

To his two hours of daily training under Joe Martin, Cassius Clay added four under Fred Stoner, a black trainer at the Grace Community Center, a gym in the all-black section of Louisville, and he credits Stoner with molding his style, his stamina, and his system. Watching Floyd Patterson, Archie Moore, and other top professional heavyweights on television, he knew that one day he would "be able to whip these men very easily, because they are not moving, not circling, not moving backwards at the right time." Every day he practised how to hit without being hit, to jab and then lean back. "Soon I develop a built-in radar. I know how far I can go back, when it's time to duck or time to tie my man up. I learn there is a science to making your opponent wear down. I learn to put my head within hitting range, force my opponent to throw blows, then lean back and away, keeping eyes wide open so I can see everything, then sidestep, move to the right, or to the left, jab him again, then again, put my head back in hitting range. It takes a lot out of a fighter to throw punches that land in thin air. When his best combinations hit nothing but space, it saps him. Throughout my amateur days, old boxers think I'm easy to hit, but I'm not. I concentrate on defense. I concentrate on timing and motions and pulling back. When I throw a jab, I know my opponent will throw a punch, and I pull back."

As a boy, Clay worshipped at the church attended by his parents, Mount Zion Baptist Church, and he attended DuValle Junior High School and Central High School in Louisville. He confesses that his "mind was so wrapped up in boxing" he "didn't work too hard in school," with the result that in high school he ranked near the bottom of his class academically, and he remains a poor reader to this day. On the positive side, he escaped the dangers of delinquency because he "ate, drank, and slept boxing" and "didn't have time for nothin' else."

As Cassius Clay the amateur, Ali won 100 of 108 fights and captured six Kentucky Golden Gloves championships, two national Golden Gloves championships, and two national Amateur Athletic Union championships. The veteran sportswriter Lester Bromberg, who saw the young pugilist at the Olympic trials in Madison Square Garden in New York City early in 1960, recalled in the New York *Post* (February 10, 1978) that "the instant impression was of his easy and ready garrulous manner." Bromberg remembered him boasting that he was "the best-looking, the fastest, the cleverest." Ali says that he picked up the art of ring chatter during the Olympic trials, from Allen Hudson, who talked to him during the whole bout and made fun of his mistakes, rattling him. Despite the rattling, Clay defeated Hudson, and the following summer he went on to the Olympic Games in Rome, Italy, where he took the light heavyweight title. In Rome, his indefatigable affability made him the most conspicuous resident of Olympic Village, and a fellow member of the Olympic team remembers him behaving as if "he were running for office."

Back home in Louisville, the Olympic gold medalist's hero's welcome had a bitter anticlimax, described in detail in his autobiography. What happened, in brief, was that an incident in which he was refused service in a restaurant escalated into a fight with a white motorcycle gang leader from which he emerged alive and without serious injury—and with his Olympic gold medal, which the cycle punk had demanded as a "souvenir"—thanks only to quick reflex action. "Then and there," Ali says, "occurred one of the two split-second moves in my life without which my career would have been forever altered." (The second happened during his first championship fight with Sonny Liston.) Following the incident in Louisville, Ali, in sudden disgust, threw his cherished gold medal into the Ohio River.

Cassius Clay turned professional in the autumn of 1960 under the sponsorship of eleven wealthy Louisville citizens. The Louisville Sponsoring Group, as it was called, brought in ex-champ Archie Moore to train

Clay, briefly, before turning to Angelo Dundee, who has been with Clay/Ali ever since. Right away, Dundee knew he had a winner. "Of all the fighters I've ever known, only he could make the heavy bag sing when he hit it. . . ," he told James Wilde in an interview for a cover story in *Time* (February 27, 1978). "He ran eleven miles to the gym from the hotel and back every day along the causeway. He was always the first in and the last out of the gym. He is the most unspoiled kid I've ever had."

In his first professional match, arranged before the Louisville sponsoring group went into operation, Clay won a six-round decision over Tunney Hunsaker in Louisville on October 29, 1960. In Miami Beach in January and February 1961 he knocked out, in succession, Tony Esperti, Jim Robinson, and Donnie Fleeman, and back in Louisville in April he KO'd Lamar Clark. Ten-round decisions over Duke Sabedong and Alonzo Johnson in the summer of 1961 were followed by knockouts of Alex Miteff and Willi Besmanoff in the fall.

Angelo Dundee "knew for sure" that he "had a winner" when Clay fought Sonny Banks in Madison Square Garden on February 10, 1962. In the *Time* interview he recalled: "Banks hit Ali with the finest left hook I've ever seen. It would have floored King Kong. Ali's eyes glazed like he was out of it, and his keester hit the canvas. Then he sprang back up, bright-eyed and bushy-tailed and stopped the guy cold." Ali dispatched Banks with a knockout in the fourth round, and he racked up an identical victory over Don Warner in Miami Beach eighteen days later. During the following five months he had three more KO's, over George Logan and Alejandro Lavorante in Los Angeles and Billy Daniels in New York.

Meanwhile, Clay was developing his showman's strategy—based partly on the example of Gorgeous George the flamboyant wrestler —of attracting public attention abrasively, through loud-mouthed braggadocio, as he relates in his autobiography: "I was predicting the round my opponent would fall in each fight with an accuracy the papers found unbelievable. I created a poem for every opponent: 'They'll all fall in the round I call!' I shouted. And each time the boos for me were getting stronger and stronger. But I won and I kept the world heavyweight title in focus. The louder the boos, the surer I was that some promoter would see that there was more money to be made with me fighting a title match than any so-called contender above me."

Before his match with Archie Moore, his first opponent capable of drawing worldwide attention, Clay predicted, "When you come to the fight,/Don't block the halls,/And don't block the door,/For y'all may go home/ After round four." After disposing of Moore in the predicted time on November 15, 1962, Clay found an unexpectedly tough opponent in Doug Jones, whom he defeated by decision in ten rounds in New York City. In London on June 18, 1963 the British heavyweight champion Henry Cooper knocked down and stunned Clay badly just before the bell ended the third round. The extra minute between rounds that was required to fix a broken seam in one of Clay's gloves gave him the chance to clear his head, and he went on to score a technical KO over Cooper in the fifth round, just as he had predicted he would.

Finally, Clay was given the chance to face the opponent he had been stalking all along, the late heavyweight champion Sonny Liston, a hulking stone-faced "monster," as Clay called him, who was a preeminent representative of the old school of brutal slugging. At the weigh-in before the fight in Miami Beach, Florida on February 25, 1964, Clay shocked reporters and officials with a carefully rehearsed display of hysteria, in which he screamed "chump," "ugly old bear," and other epithets at Liston and, seemingly, had to be restrained from lunging at the older fighter. In the fight itself, Clay, dancing, circling, and heckling Liston, goaded him into clumsy rushes and then peppered him with hard punches. Although nearly blinded by a caustic wound ointment—transmitted accidentally from Liston by glove—Clay persevered, and he jarred his opponent with such potent combinations that Liston failed to answer the bell for the seventh round. The slogan, "Float like a butterfly, sting like a bee," suggested to him by his second, Drew (Bundini) Brown, dates from that first bout with Liston.

In a return match with Liston in Lewiston, Maine on May 25, 1965, Ali retained his world heavyweight title, flooring Liston with a short, lightning-quick right punch in the first round. He successfully defended the title against Floyd Patterson (whom he baited and mocked mercilessly, in the view of Patterson sympathizers) by a twelfth-round KO in Las Vegas in November 1965. The following year, probably the finest of his career, he repulsed five challengers: George Chuvallo by a decision and Henry Cooper, Brian London, Karl Mildenberger, and Cleveland Williams by knockouts. In February 1967 he won an overwhelming fifteen-round decision over Ernie Terrell, and the following month he knocked out Zora Folley in the seventh round.

Meanwhile, the controversy over Clay/Ali had made a quantum leap to a new dimension. Originally the controversy was simply over his loquacious self-adulation and whether one found it amusing or not. But behind the scenes the clowning prizefighter was undergoing a serious spiritual and intellectual transformation. As soon as he won the championship, in 1964, he announced that, like his brother before him, he had joined the black nationalist Nation of Islam, popularly known as the Black Muslims, at that time widely but mistakenly viewed by Middle America as a subversive "race hate" sect. When, two years later, his Selective Service board took away his deferred status of 1-Y (he had failed the intelligence test, probably because of his slow reading), and reclassified him 1-A, he responded by appealing for conscientious objector status on religious grounds. "I ain't got no quarrel with those Vietcong, anyway," he added. "They never called me nigger."

Denied exemption, and refusing, according to reports, to make a face-saving deal with the Selective Service, Muhammad Ali, as he was by then known, was called up by the Army on April 18, 1967. When he formally refused induction, the World Boxing Association stripped him of his title as well as his license and announced that it would hold an elimination tournament to determine his successor. The action of the W.B.A., effective in forty states, was followed up by a similar decision by the New York State Athletic Commission. On June 20, 1967 a federal court in Houston, Texas found Ali guilty of violation of the Selective Service Act and imposed a $10,000 fine and a five-year sentence. He remained out of jail pending appeal.

Ostensibly in disgrace, the disbarred Ali gained an immense constituency he never would have had simply as a prizefighter. Throughout the Third World, the peace movement, the counterculture, and the masses of poor, alienated, or rebellious American blacks, he became a folk hero, a spokesman of resistance to injustice and oppression and for social change. As Harry Edwards wrote in *The Revolt of the Black Athlete* (1969), "To us he was, is, a god . . . the saint of this revolution in sports . . . enhanc[ing] the most crucial factor in the minds of black people everywhere—black dignity."

Deprived of his pugilistic livelihood, Ali lectured on college campuses, addressed peace rallies and Muslim meetings, and, in December 1969, starred in the short-lived Broadway musical *Buck White*, written by Oscar Brown Jr. The United States Supreme Court reversed Ali's conviction on June 20, 1970, and four months later a federal court ruled that the revocation of his boxing license had been "arbitrary and unreasonable."

Returning to the ring, Ali scored a third-round knockout of Jerry Quarry in Atlanta in October 1970 and a fifteenth-round KO of Oscar Bonavena in New York City on December 7, 1970. In Madison Square Garden in March 1971 he challenged Joe Frazier, the champion then recognized by the W.B.A., and lost by decision. Later in 1971 Ali won by knockouts over Jimmy Ellis and Jurgen Blin and by decision over Buster Mathis. The following year he defeated Mac Foster and George Chuvalo by decision and Jerry Quarry, Al Lewis, Floyd Patterson, and Bob Foster by knockouts, and in February 1973 he scored a twelve-round decision over Joe Bugner.

On March 31, 1973 Ali, suffering a broken jaw, lost by a split decision to Ken Norton. In a return twelve-rounder with Norton six months later he was victorious by decision, and he tallied a similar victory over Rudi Lubbers in October 1973. On January 28, 1974 Ali again faced Frazier, who had meanwhile lost the title to George Foreman. Ali avenged his earlier loss by a close decision, thus clearing the way for a crack at Foreman.

The "rumble in the jungle," as Ali called his bout with Foreman in Kinshasa, Zaire, Africa on October 30, 1974, was a classic instance of the cunning of the latter-day Ali. Beforehand, he psyched Foreman with verbal intimidation, and in the fight itself he would attack and then retreat into his "rope-a-dope," letting Foreman punch away, usually harmlessly, as he, Ali, protected his face with his gloves and his midsection with his forearms. By the eighth round Foreman had run out of power, and Ali, with a barrage of punches, knocked him out.

During the following three years Ali successfully defended his championship against Chuck Wepner in Cleveland (KO), Ron Lyle in Las Vegas (KO), Joe Bugner in Kuala Lumpur, Joe Frazier in Manila (KO), Jean-Pierre Coopman in San Juan (KO), and Ken Norton in New York. But his physician, Dr. Ferdie Pacheco, "grieved for the continuous erosion of . . . health and longevity" that was going on within the "beautiful fighting machine." "There was mounting damage that only a doctor could see," Pacheco said. "I saw what was happening to him. That terrible fight with Jimmy Young, which many felt he lost. The travesty with Alfredo Evangelista. Then Earnie Shavers almost knocked him out."

After pleading in vain with Ali to quit the ring, Dr. Pacheco deserted his camp just before the first fight with young Leon Spinks. In that bout, in Las Vegas on February 15, 1978, Ali loafed through the first six rounds, expecting his young opponent to tire, but Spinks remained fresh to the end and won the fifteen-rounder by a split decision. Still deploring Ali's stubbornness, Pacheco told a reporter before the rematch with Spinks: "I think he has a chance. I never underestimate Ali when his mind is made up—resourceful, powerful, determined."

It was indeed a resourceful and determined —and superbly conditioned—Ali who faced Spinks in New Orleans on September 15, 1978. In a lackluster but workmanlike display of boxing tactics and tricks, Ali eschewed rope-a-dope and was in command almost from the start, exploiting his height, weight, and backpedaling advantages, countering Spinks's right uppercut with a left jab, scoring enough points to win each round, and then tying Spinks up in clinches. Spinks never ran out of energy, and he was never hit badly, but his relentless flailing and lunging became almost desperate and were, in the end, to no avail. As if for old time's sake, Ali even danced his famous "Ali shuffle" in the last round. The unanimous decision went to Ali, and Spinks was the first to raise his opponent's arm. "He was always my idol," Spinks said. "He still is." Somber before and during the fight, Ali laughed afterward, saying: "That wasn't me dancing, was it? A thirty-six-year-old man? If I did that, I must be the greatest."

Ali grossed an estimated $3,000,000 from the second bout with Spinks. Before that fight his career income was estimated at $48,951,117. A third of the money made since 1966 went to Herbert Muhammad, who replaced the Louisville group as Ali's financial manager in 1966. At least half of the remainder was taken by the Internal Revenue Service, sizeable hunks were eaten up by professional expenses and by divorce settlements, and other sums went into gifts for his parents, needy friends, and various charities and causes, from UNICEF to a Jewish home for the elderly in New York. Ali was left with a net worth estimated variously between $2,000,000 and $6,000,000 in cash and holdings. The holdings include a training camp at Deer Lake, Pennsylvania, a farm in Berrien Springs, Michigan, a vacant department store building in Cleveland, a Rolls-Royce, and two custom-made buses.

Although old by ring standards, Ali is, of course, young enough to go into any of a number of other careers. One possibility is business, and Ali Enterprises, based in Chicago, is already handling business and merchandising spinoffs of his prizefighting career. Another is acting, where Ali has credits going back to 1962, when he played a small part in *Requiem for a Heavyweight* (Columbia). As the star of *The Greatest* (Columbia, 1977), the film version of his autobiography, he was generally praised by critics as a "natural performer" with "presence" and "charm." "Ali's unique charisma dominates the screen," William Wolf wrote in *Cue* (June 11-24, 1977), "and he even handles the difficult dramatic moments surprisingly well." Because of his love for children and his ease in communicating with them, the champion especially enjoyed lending his name and his voice to the children's cartoon series *Muhammad Ali,* which began syndication on television during the 1977-78 season. "We're enormously impressed by his sense of responsibility and his purpose in making the series something of value," Fred Calvert, the executive producer of the show has said.

But Ali's chief ambition is to serve his global constituency. In his world travels he has conferred with heads of state in the Soviet Union, Africa, and elsewhere, and recently he said he was founding an organization called the World Organization for Rights, Liberty, and Dignity (WORLD). "It's going to have sixty countries represented," he said, as quoted by Michael Katz in the New York *Times* (August 4, 1978). "Brezhnev gave me a spot in the Kremlin to have an office. . . . The President of Bangladesh gave me an office in his government building. I'm going to be my own United Nations. We're going to build boys camps in this country, give people relief when they're hit by floods and other disasters, build hospitals wherever they're needed around the world, and work for better relationships between countries."

Muhammad Ali is six feet three inches tall and weighs, when he is in condition, 220 pounds. His face, is, as he boasts, "pretty," free of the pulpy defects accrued by most prizefighters. A sparring partner testifies that Ali is "real vain about his body—you tell him his legs don't look as good as they used to and he'll go out and run ten miles." Ali neither smokes nor drinks, and he is generally puritanical in his attitudes. In conversation he tends to be a monologist. The champion lives with his third wife, the former Veronica Porche, and their two children in a mansion he owns in Chicago. His two previous marriages, to Sonji Roi and Belinda Kalilah Boyd, ended in divorce. By the second, he has four children. Fears that used to haunt him, such as that of flying, he now takes in stride, because, he says, he knows that "it's all up to Allah."

References: Ebony 27:145+ S '72 pors; 33:112+ S '78 pors; N Y Post p23 Mr 1 '71 por; p35 Mr 5 '71 por; Time 111:72+ F 27 '78 pors; Sports Illus 49:20+ S 11 '78 pors; Ali, Muhammad, with Durham, Richard. The Greatest (1975); Lipsyte, Robert. Free to be Muhammad Ali (1978)

Andersson, Bibi

Nov. 11, 1935- Swedish actress. Address: h. Tykö Vägen 28, Lidingo, Sweden

When grappling with the complexities of human relationships and the enigmas of life, death, and art, the Swedish film maker Ingmar Bergman often chooses images that allow different personal meanings for different viewers. But for about a decade in such films as *The Seventh Seal* (1956) and *Wild Strawberries* (1957), there was never any ambiguity as to

Bibi Andersson

what his blond, blue-eyed protégée Bibi Andersson usually symbolized—freshness, simplicity, and docility. Partly because of her own creative interpretation of the role of Nurse Alma, she broke from that stereotype with harrowing intensity in *Persona* (1966). Of her 1970 movie for Bergman, David Thomson wrote in *A Biographical Directory of Film*, "*The Touch* shows that she is the warmest, most free-spirited of Bergman's women, more broadly compassionate than [Ingrid] Thulin or [Liv] Ullman. Being more robust, her distress is more moving, and her doggedness more encouraging." In productions of both the Swedish and American stage and television, as well as film, she is admired as an actress of subtlety and sensitivity and of an integrity that the New York *Times* critic Clive Barnes, in reviewing the play *Full Circle* (1973), described as an "absolutely unforced naturalness."

Bibi Andersson was born in Stockholm, Sweden on November 11, 1935, the younger of two daughters of Josef and Karin (Mänsson) Andersson. Her sister, Gerd (Mrs. Viet Bethke), is a ballerina with the Swedish Royal Opera. During the girls' early childhood their father, the head of a Stockholm express firm, and their mother, a social worker, were divorced. When Bibi was about seven, her mother had a nervous breakdown. "I never regarded her as sick," Sylviane Gold quoted Miss Andersson in the New York *Post* (July 9, 1977) as saying. "She collapsed because her circumstances were too tough. . . . She is, for all the problems—today I can see it objectively—admirably healthy and strong."

Her mother was, moreover, responsive to Bibi's early ambitions to become an actress, assuring her that she had talent and that someday she would find the courage to develop it. After attending public schools, she studied at the Terserus Drama School and then, from 1954 to 1956, at the Royal Dramatic Theatre School in Stockholm, which counts Greta Garbo and Ingrid Bergman among its alumnae. Since the age of fourteen she had been acquiring practical experience by working as an extra on movie sets. There she was discovered by Ingmar Bergman, who at a time of economic distress in the Swedish film industry was making a series of television advertisements for Bris soap. For one of them he hired the seventeen-year-old Bibi Andersson to play a princess who offers a swineherd a hundred kisses if he will give her a bar of Bris soap.

One of Bibi Andersson's movie idols was Maj-Britt Nilsson, a regular of Bergman's Svensk Filmindustri productions and an actress noted for the naturalness and spontaneity of her projection. Sincerity, too, as Peter Cowie wrote in *Film in Sweden* (1977), "is the abiding gift that Bibi bestows on a film audience. . . . But Bibi's early directors mistook that sincerity for naivety." She appeared, for example, as a scrubbed-clean innocent in such non-Bergman movies as *Stupid Bom* (1953) and *A Night at Glimminge Castle* (1954).

In her first film for Bergman, the playful *Smiles of a Summer Night* (Svensk Filmindustri, 1955), Miss Andersson spoke a few lines as a young actress in the little-play scene. From that bit part she advanced immediately to one of the leads in Bergman's *The Seventh Seal* (1956), a film that grew out of a training play he had written for his students at the school of the municipal theatre in Malmö, to which Miss Andersson at his suggestion had transferred from the Stockholm theatre. The role he wrote for her in his eschatological fable was that of Mia, an innocent young woman devoted to her husband. Cowie summed it up in *Film in Sweden*, "The long blonde hair, the milk-white skin, the ample mouth, the demure gaze: at one blow—in a single shot—the character of Bibi Andersson is caught by Bergman and registered by the spectator so that her Mia is forever a symbol of goodness and fidelity."

Cast in a dual role in Bergman's allegorical *Wild Strawberries* (1957), Miss Andersson portrayed the boyhood sweetheart of Professor Isak Borg, played by Victor Sjöström, for whom she is many years later reincarnated as a hitchhiker representative of modern youth. As an unwed prospective mother in *Brink of Life* (1957), she was an appealing teenager whose elfin charm and brashness hide a fragile interior of uncertainty and insecurity. For her performance in that study of physical and psychological ordeal in a Swedish maternity ward, she shared the best-acting award of the Cannes Film Festival. She had a minor role in Bergman's *The Face*, or *The Magician* (1958); in his light-hearted variation on the Don Juan legend, *The Devil's Eye* (1960), she played the chaste maiden whom the devil tries to seduce; and in *The Pleasure Garden* (1961) she again symbolized wholesomeness.

From time to time, but not often, Bibi Andersson also appeared in non-Bergman films, including a 1961 Yugoslavian movie. With Bergman serving as production supervisor, his disciple Vilgot Sjöman directed her in *The Mistress* (1962) in a role requiring unaccustomed duplicity as a young woman who has to conceal from her fiancé her infatuation for an older, married man. Sjöman was also the director of the disquieting period piece *My Sister, My Love* (Sandrew-Ateljeerna, 1966), a tale of incest in eighteenth-century Sweden. "The exquisite blonde, Bibi Andersson, turns in a commanding performance as the proud, spoiled, impetuous and doomed heroine who loves her brother as a husband," Joan Fox commented in the Toronto *Globe and Mail* (July 14, 1967). Other critics felt that Miss Andersson projected a tenderness that effectively contrasted the purity of her forbidden love with the debauchery of a hypocritical society.

The women that Bibi Andersson created for her two Sjöman films were markedly different from the ingénues that Bergman chose for her, including Bumble Bee of *Now About These Women* (1964). Referring to that typecasting, she said, as Richard Eder quoted her in the New York *Times* (February 24, 1977), "It bothered me—until *Persona* he put me in uncomplicated roles, symbolizing simple, girlish things. I used to be called 'a professional innocent.' " Bergman's generative idea for *Persona* (1966), one of his finest films, came to him when he saw a photograph of Miss Andersson and the Norwegian actress Liv Ullmann, who were appearing together in a film version of Knut Hamsun's *Pan* (Sandrew, 1965). Their resemblance to one another persisted in his mind. "I thought it would be wonderful to write something about two people who lose their identities in each other," he recalled in *Bergman on Bergman* (1970).

Bergman cast Liv Ullmann in *Persona* as a strong-willed actress, Elisabeth Vogler, who has a nervous breakdown and retreats into silence. Bibi Andersson plays her nurse, Alma, a talkative and apparently secure younger woman whose blurted out confidences to her patient, however, include erotic experiences of troubling consequence. In exploring the possibility of a transfer or merging of the personalities of Elisabeth and Alma, Bergman encourages multiple interpretations. Several critics pointed out that the various meanings and implications of the film unfold only with repeated viewings. *Persona* was voted the best movie in 1967 by the National Society of Film Critics in the United States, which also voted Bibi Andersson best actress. The director himself said of her performance in *Bergman on Bergman*, "Bibi becomes something so infinitely better than her role."

From the Baltic island of Färo, where Bergman found the isolated atmosphere for *Persona*, Bibi Andersson went to southern Utah for the filming of Ralph Nelson's ethnically mixed western of torture and carnage, *Duel at Diablo* (United Artists, 1966), in which she was the captured, out-of-wedlock mother of the son of an Apache chief. Under the direction of Jacques Doniol-Valcroze she played another captive woman, Marianne Séverin, in the Swedish-French production *Le Viol* (*The Rape*, 1965). Her other international ventures include *The Black Palm Trees* (1968), a Lars Magnus Lingren picture filmed in Brazil, and *Story of a Woman* (1969), Leonardo Bercovici's Italian-Swedish indulgence in sentimentality. The role of an actress touring Sweden in Aristophanes' *Lysistrata*, who is also a wife in search of emancipation, enabled her in *The Girls* (1968), as Cowie reported, "to articulate her views (and those of the director, Mai Zetterling) on the position of women in modern society and she [did] so with forthright intensity."

Returning to Färo, Miss Andersson rejoined Bergman and Liv Ullman for *A Passion*, or *The Passion of Anna* (1969), portraying Eva, a well-to-do architect's wife who is plagued by a feeling of uselessness. In her next Bergman film, *The Touch* (Cinematograph/ABC Pictures, 1970), she spoke both Swedish and English to create the seemingly placid wife of a Swedish doctor (played by Max von Sydow) who risks her comfortable marriage for an affair with a neurotic American archaeologist (played by Elliott Gould). Her stirring characterization endeared her to almost all critics. Derek Malcolm of the *Guardian* (October 7, 1971) thought her performance "superb even by her exalted standards," and Stanley Kauffmann, who lambasted the movie in the *New Republic* (August 21-28, 1971), conceded, "Bibi Andersson could not give less than truth and appeal to anything she does, and she gives them here even in this dull role."

A more recent Bergman production in which Miss Andersson performed was a six-part series for television, made in 1972 and later compressed into a 168-minute film and released under the title *Scenes from a Marriage*. Bergman wrote the series as a vehicle for Miss Ullmann, and Bibi Andersson appears in only one episode, but memorably, as the embittered wife in a failed marriage who during a dinner party fights an excoriating and, to others, embarrassing verbal battle with her husband.

Meanwhile, the American director John Huston had chosen Bibi Andersson to head the star-studded cast of his melodrama about the skulduggery of international spying, *The Kremlin Letter* (Twentieth Century-Fox, 1970).

In that critically disappointing film she portrayed Erika, a world-weary prostitute married to the sadistic head of Soviet intelligence. The role of a compassionate psychiatrist, Dr. Fried, who guides a teen-age girl out of schizophrenia in *I Never Promised You a Rose Garden* (New World Pictures, 1977) offered a fascinating challenge to Miss Andersson. In her interview with Sylviane Gold she said that the role went "against everything acting is about. Acting is to reveal yourself. As a psychiatrist you conceal yourself." Reviewers in general credited her with a performance praiseworthy for its freedom from platitudes in interpretation of character. In the 1978 film adaptation of Henrik Ibsen's *An Enemy of the People* (Warner Brothers) Miss Andersson portrayed the wife of a village doctor embroiled in an environmental dispute with the officials of his community. A critic for *Variety* (August 30, 1978) considered Miss Andersson's performance "highly effective" in what was otherwise a preachy and miscast film.

Swedish theatregoers in Stockholm, Malmö, and Uppsala had long enjoyed Bibi Andersson's luminous acting in such classics as Molière's *Tartuffe* and *L'École des femmes*, Chekhov's *The Three Sisters* and *Uncle Vanya*, Ibsen's *A Doll's House*, and *As You Like It* and *Twelfth Night*. In the latter Shakespearean comedy she was directed as Viola by Ingmar Bergman in 1975 at Stockholm's Royal Dramatic Theatre. Her roles in modern plays included Honey in 1963 in Edward Albee's *Who's Afraid of Virginia Woolf?* and Maggie (the Marilyn Monroe character) in 1964-65 in Arthur Miller's *After the Fall*.

Bibi Andersson made her American stage debut in an adaptation of Erich Maria Remarque's drama about Berliners in the closing days of World War II, *Full Circle*, which was produced and directed by Otto Preminger. After opening in Washington, D.C. in October 1973, the play moved to Broadway's ANTA Theatre, where it ran for only about three weeks. The star herself, however, won excellent personal notices for her portrayal of a German widow who shelters an escaped prisoner from a Nazi concentration camp. In his comments for the New York *Times* (November 8, 1973) Clive Barnes called her "a superlative actress" and went on to say, "As in the Bergman movies, one is impressed by the total reality of her playing."

Another politically concerned play, Arthur Miller's *The Archbishop's Ceiling*, set in an Eastern European country, featured Miss Andersson as, to use the phrase of one reviewer, "the communal strumpet" of a group of writers. Although intended for Broadway, the play had only a shortened run of a week in Washington in the spring of 1977. Per Olvo Enquist's *The Night of the Tribades*, which uses a play within a play to dramatize August Strindberg's tempestuous relationships with women, opened in New York in the fall of 1977 in a production starring Bibi Andersson, Max von Sydow, and Eileen Atkins. Miss Andersson played the wife of Strindberg, who suspects her of being a tribade, the Greek word for lesbian. As a New York *Times* reporter put it, the play was a "noble failure" on Broadway, closing after twelve performances. American audiences also saw the Swedish actress in a television presentation of *After the Fall* (NBC, December 1974), in which her role this time was not Maggie, but Holga, a German woman to whom the tormented protagonist, Quentin, turns for amorous comfort.

Along with the awards she won for *Brink of Life* and *Persona*, Bibi Andersson's tributes include the Swedish Silver Bear as best actress in 1963 for *The Mistress*, the French Film Academy's 1967 Étoile de Cristal as best actress for *My Sister, My Love*, and the British Film Academy's 1971 best foreign actress award for *The Touch*. She also won a prize in Sofia for her performance on Swedish television in the title role of Strindberg's *Miss Julie*.

In 1960 Bibi Andersson married the film director Kjell Grede; they were divorced thirteen years later. Grede more recently directed her in a series for Swedish television based on a work of Strindberg. After encountering tax problems similar to those that drove Bergman into temporary exile, she moved to New York City in 1976 with her then five-year-old daughter, Jennifer Matilda, for an indefinite stay. One of Miss Andersson's closest friends is Liv Ullmann, who recalled in her autobiography, *Changing* (1977), their first meeting, on a Norwegian island for the filming of *Pan*. "I admired her for her generosity and her honesty," Miss Ullmann wrote. "The ties between us became stronger than those I had had with any other woman friend, and through the years the friendship has endured." When he interviewed her for his New York *Times* article, Richard Eder was impressed by her buoyancy and directness and, like other interviewers, by her reflective and analytical attitude toward her life and work: "She does not guard herself. She talks on whatever subject is proposed, and after she answers questions, she goes on to answer their implications." Although at first she had misgivings about working in the United States, she realized that receptivity to change was important to her career. "Part of an actress is aliveness, alertness," she once said, as quoted in the Washington *Post*, "and it comes from not letting yourself stiffen."

References: N Y Post p15 N 3 '73, p42 Jl 9 '77 por, p38 O 8 '77 por; N Y Times C p17 F 23 '77 por; Washington Post E p1+ Ap 29 '77 pors; Cowie, Peter. Film in Sweden: Stars and Players (1977); International Who's Who, 1977-78; Thomson, David. A Biographical Directory of Film (1976); Vem är Det, 1973

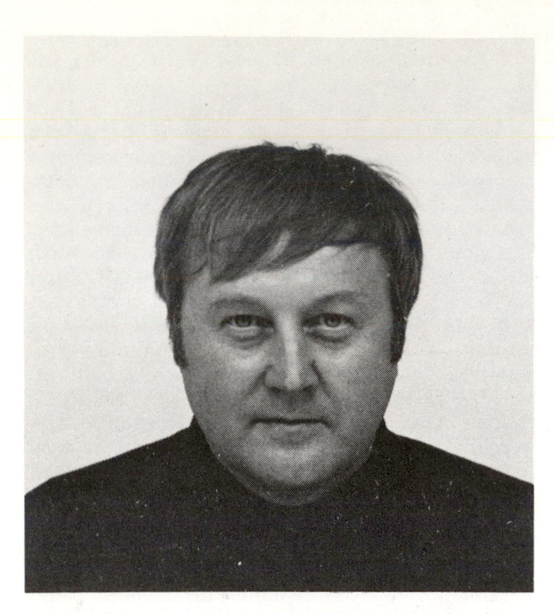

© *Arnold Newman*

Anuszkiewicz, Richard (Joseph) (an-ə skā′vitch)

May 23, 1930- Artist. Address: b. c/o Andrew Crispo Gallery, 47 E. 57th St., New York City, N.Y. 10022; h. 76 Chestnut St., Englewood, N.J. 07631

Having begun in 1960 to "dazzle," as the critics said, New York gallerygoers with his paintings of geometric shapes in compositions scientifically determined by the interaction of complementary colors, Richard Anuszkiewicz was in line a few years later to be dubbed an old master of Op art. Practitioners of that newly recognized art movement happened to share certain stylistic characteristics inspired largely by the optical illusions achieved in the paintings of Josef Albers in the United States and the French artist Victor Vasarely. But as he continued to make his individualistic discoveries about the play of color off color and the effect of light on color, Anuszkiewicz' retinal kineticism became not the eye-shattering, dizzying tricks often associated with Op art (although he has proved himself capable of that magic), but rather a vibrating image that has been likened to musical cadence or a luminous, shimmering flow of advancing and retreating colors. What he told Grace Glueck in a 1965 interview for the New York *Times* applies also to his work of nearly a decade later, such as his delightful *Sunrise Chroma* (1974), "I really love color. I try to manipulate it in schemes that give the viewer a particular feeling of excitement. If you want to call it emotion, that's fine."

Richard Joseph Anuszkiewicz was born in Erie, Pennsylvania on May 23, 1930 to Adam Jacob and Victoria Ann (Jankowski) Anuszkiewicz, natives of Poland who grew up there in villages not far apart, but did not meet until after both had settled in Pennsylvania. His father was employed in an Erie paper mill. By an earlier marriage of his mother, Richard Anuszkiewicz has a half sister and four half brothers. The youngest of those children was about eleven years old when Richard was born.

"I wanted to be an artist from the first," Anuszkiewicz told the art scholar and critic Gene Baro in a conversation that was printed in the catalog of the painter's 1975 exhibition at the Andrew Crispo Gallery. His formal training began at a vocational high school in Erie, where his teacher, Joseph Plavcan, introduced him to the impressionist and other orthodox theories of color. Largely under the influence of his teacher, who was interested in American provincial art, he captured in realistic pictures, mainly watercolors, atmospheric details and moods reminiscent of the paintings of the Ashcan School and the WPA representational artists. Among the townscape canvases of his high school years were *From My Kitchen Window* (1945) and *Bonfire* (1946).

The talent that Anuszkiewicz showed in those and other pictures won him a scholarship in his last year of high school to the Cleveland Institute of Art. During his five years there he continued to develop as "a sort of Midwest regional painter," as he described himself when he recalled his student output in an interview with Grace Glueck of the New York *Times* (February 21, 1965). Echoes of Charles Burchfield and Edward Hopper, for example, appear in *Negro Wedding* (1949), *The Bridge* (1950), and other paintings of his Cleveland years. Referring to his work in realistic genre subjects, still lifes, and landscapes, he explained to Grace Glueck, "In a sense, though, it was related to what I'm doing now. I painted that way because I was interested in the shapes, not the subjects." As Karl Lunde pointed out in his comprehensive study *Anuszkiewicz* (1977), two paintings of 1951, *Six Altar Boys at Sanctus* and *Eight Windows,* clearly indicate a tendency toward abstraction in arrangement of forms.

In 1953 Anuszkiewicz was awarded both his Bachelor of Fine Arts degree from the Cleveland Institute of Art and a Pulitzer Traveling Fellowship by the National Academy of Design. He used the Pulitzer stipend of $1,500 to enroll in the Yale University School of Art and Architecture to study with Josef Albers, a painter whose explorations of optical phenomena in geometric color configurations made him a progenitor of the movement eventually known as Op art. Anuszkiewicz' investigation at Yale of the findings of several psychologists who were experimenting with perception—the laws by which the eye structures whatever is presented to it—led him to write a master's thesis entitled "Study in the Creation of Space with Line Drawing."

When Anuszkiewicz left Yale with his M.F.A. degree in 1955, he enrolled in Kent State University to work for a B.S. degree in education, which he received in 1956. While at Kent he had his first one-man show, at the Butler Institute of American Art in Youngstown, Ohio in 1955. One reason for his decision to spend a year on courses in education was that he would have the advantage of academic qualification if he were to follow Albers' example and combine teaching with painting. Another reason was that he needed time to accept the change that his study at Yale was making in the direction of his art, as he went, almost reluctantly, through a transitional stage from realism to abstraction. "I struggled to preserve what I already had," he admitted to Grace Glueck. He moved to New York City in 1957, worked for a time at the Metropolitan Museum of Art on repairs to architectural models, and during 1958 traveled abroad studying the art treasures of Europe and North Africa.

Besides learning from Albers how to work methodically and how to look at a painting abstractly, Anuszkiewicz through his teacher had become more aware of color relativity, of how colors relate to one another and change startlingly with changes in position, shape, scale, and light. Aesthetic exploitation of the interaction of color had long been obvious in the paintings of impressionists, neoimpressionists, Fauves, and others—more specifically, for example, of Georges Seurat, Paul Klee, and Robert and Sonia Delaunay. Soon after his graduation from Yale, Anuszkiewicz began experimenting with the impact on each other of saturated complementary colors, such as blue on red and green on red. As he recalled in his discussion with Baro, "I had discovered an area of color unexplored previously, the use of complementary colors of full intensity and the dynamic effect to be found in the use of this particular mode." He maintained that the territory into which he was moving was uncharted inasmuch as the use of complementary colors in the work of other artists had been only partial.

Anuszkiewicz' early optical paintings were two-color or, less often, three-color experiments with figure-ground relationships. Irregular forms roam at random over the entire canvas in *On Blue* (1957), *Green on Red* (1957), *Dissolving the Edge of Green* (1959), *Emerald Tablet* (1959), and other paintings of the late 1950's. His pictures of that type, he has said, were influenced by abstract expressionism. Most of his work, however, like Op art itself, is a reaction against abstract expressionism, a repudiation of the drip and splatter school of action painting. His hallmark became calculated, rather than haphazard or impulsive, painting of hard-edged color shapes, preferably squares, that disclose the beauty of color and have no personal or associative content.

Turning from his tentative attraction to the abstract expressionist manner, during the early 1960's Anuszkiewicz painted several color mix pictures in which many shapes—sometimes regular and sometimes irregular, but always more fully controlled—tend to congregate toward the center of a square canvas, as in *Plus Reversed* (1960) and *The Vaulted World* (1961). He used a pattern of squares and rectangles to produce an illusion of depth in *Knowledge and Disappearance* (1961) and a pattern of concentric circular lines in *Water from the Rock* (1961-62), which is becoming a classic example of the illusion of advancing and receding forms. The circles, or dots, of his yellow, green, and silver *Fluorescent Complement* (1960); blue, red, and green *Triangular Prism* (1962); blue, red, and green *Injured by Green* (1963); and the multicolored diamonds of *All Things Do Live in the Three* (1963) had such direct public appeal that by the mid-1960's he was applying polka dots in commercial designs of fur coats and stockings.

Even though enthusiasm for abstract expressionism had begun to cool by the time Anuszkiewicz arrived on the New York art scene, acceptance of his work came only slowly. He had his first one-man New York show in 1960 at the Contemporaries gallery, of which Karl Lunde was the director. On that occasion an art critic of the New York *Times* (March 5, 1964) noted the violent collision of his colors and went on to say, "These pictures are fascinating chromatic experiments. Whether they would be bearable on the wall is another matter. For they sorely try the optic nerve."

The following year, when Anuszkiewicz had his second show at the Contemporaries, his work received somewhat grudging attention in the New York *Herald Tribune* (April 8, 1961): "Few of his designs, which are fascinating superficially, are more than tasteful semicommercial applications, such as excellent designs for tiles or floorcoverings." Remarking on the effect of Anuszkiewicz' paintings on normal vision, Stuart Preston wrote in the New York *Times* (April 2, 1961), "After lengthy looking at them, one cannot positively identify either shape or color. This could be a tedious optical trick, were it not for this artist's composing patterns of appealing liveliness and variety." Inclusion of his work in the Museum of Modern Art's group shows "Americans, 1963" and "The Responsive Eye" (1965) brought him prestigious notice. He was saluted in *Life* magazine (December 11, 1964) as "one of the new wizards of Op."

Op as an art movement proved less influential and less durable than some of its admirers had predicted. But Anuszkiewicz' aesthetic independence, agility, and resourcefulness assured his continuing development. He enriched his work, for instance, through an experimental series of black and white paintings, beginning with *Unit* in 1966, that used a grid pattern to create spatial illusion. Translating his ideas into optical constructions, he produced three-dimensional cubes of enamel on plywood, some of which he set on a mirrored base: *Convex & Concave. 1: Dimensional (1967) and Sectional (1967).*

In his color canvases, meanwhile, Anuszkiewicz had progressed so far in his effects of vibration that his exhibitions at the Sidney Janis Gallery in 1967 and 1969 were praised with exceptional warmth in the New York *Times*. Explaining what he called his "evolution of image," he told Gene Baro, "Initially, I was interested in movement; later in the interplay of formal arrangements whose dynamics were essentially interaction of chroma. My introduction of more color led me to the greater use of line. Always color determines the form." His expanded palette in the use of warm and cool colors and the increased subtlety of his color modifications are evident, for instance, in the glowing acrylic square modulars of the series that includes *Moonbow* (1968), *Orange Delight* (1969), and *Sun Game* (1970).

While not entirely abandoning his pattern of "quiltlike squares," as one critic termed them, in the early 1970's Anuszkiewicz painted many canvases of nested rectangles, also made up of lines or stripes of varying width and color. *Trinity* (1970), *Winter-Summer Reds* (1973), *Spring-Warm* (1973), and *Spring-Cool* (1973) belong to that group. He used triangles in a similar way on a square canvas in *Rosafication* (1970) and *Triangular* (1970). Later in the decade the lines and color variations of Anuszkiewicz' paintings tended to become peripheral, although in some, like *Bisected Gray* (1974), the composition is central. Commenting on the thirty new acrylics in the Andrew Crispo Gallery show in 1975, Louis Chapin wrote in *Art News* (May 1975), "Anuszkiewicz now embroiders solid colors with strips that change hue fractionally and look like gradations from a slide rule. The effect is to return the eye to the color field and to so deepen and invigorate this field that it seems to be producing light rather than reflecting it."

Apart from his canvases, Anuszkiewicz has produced many prints and lithographs and also some screen prints that have been used as posters for art exhibitions. In the 1960's he applied certain techniques of Op art in fashion enterprises, designing stockings with dots or diverging and converging lines, along with matching packages, and painting coats, wall hangings, and rugs for the New York furrier Georges Kaplan. He also designed ceramic tile coasters commissioned by the periodical *Art in America* and a multiple of one hundred porcelain enamel tiles, *Centum* (1970), for Abrams Original Editions. Also on commission, in the early 1970's he designed exterior murals for a YWCA building in New York City and an office building in Jersey City.

The execution of Anuszkiewicz' designs for *Centum* and the exterior murals required the skills of craftsmen whose work the artist directed closely, as he does the assistants who help him on his canvases. His painting has been said to be architectural in structure, and he himself has described it as architectural in technique, because each picture develops from a carefully prepared plan that at any stage in its realization may call for new decisions, even spontaneous change, but does not accommodate chance or accident. To assure consistency of color he mixes the paint for the entire canvas before he begins painting; he achieves sharpness of edge by using architectural charting tapes to protect one layer of paint from another.

Since the early 1960's art critics seem to have been shaking their heads in wonder at the scientific precision of Anuszkiewicz, who carries out his visual ideas through use of color mathematically planned and exactly calibrated. Lunde pointed out in *Arts* (March 1975) that a basic concept of Anuszkiewicz' work "is the energy of color that is produced when two lines of different colors approach each other in certain relationships. Anuszkiewicz experiments with this color energy like a laboratory technician." John Canaday reasoned in the New York *Times* (April 5, 1969) that since Anuszkiewicz' paintings are "works of art created entirely by calculation" and also "executed with mechanical precision," they contradict his (Canaday's) premise that "no painting of real interest can be produced entirely by rule." While having to admit himself baffled in regard to Anuszkiewicz' aesthetic sensibilities, Canaday found the paintings of the 1969 show to be "really beautiful."

One of Anuszkiewicz' recent one-man shows was a United States Information Service exhibition that circulated to American embassies in foreign countries from 1974 to 1976. His work has been seen in scores of group shows throughout the United States and abroad, and he is represented in many private collections and in collections of leading museums. He taught at Cooper Union Art School from 1963 to 1965 and was artist in residence at Dartmouth College in 1967 and visiting artist at the University of Wisconsin, Cornell University, and Kent State University in 1968.

On November 26, 1960 Richard Anuszkiewicz married Elizabeth (Sally) Feeney, a schoolteacher. Their children are Adam, Stephanie, and Christine. Anuszkiewicz is a blond, husky man whom Lunde described as "socially comfortable, relaxed, and direct." Lunde said further, "But his conversation is highly abstract, and his restlessness and search for variety drive him to pace the floor when he is alone or to jump into his car impulsively and drive for hours. Not only has he a need for variety, but he enjoys all kinds of art and music, people, and experience." Among his hobbies is cooking, especially preparing salads. "Food should be visually appealing," he was quoted as saying in *Museum of Modern Art Artists' Cookbook* (1977). "We do unorthodox things with Easter eggs and Christmas cookies." Far more spontaneous when cooking than painting, he said of making cookies, "I never know what I'm going to do until I get there."

References: N Y Times II p19 F 21 '65; Contemporary Artists (1978); Hirshhorn Museum and Sculpture Garden (1974); Lunde, Karl. Anuszkiewicz (1977); Who's Who in America, 1976-77; Who's Who in American Art (1976)

Ashley, Elizabeth

Aug. 30, 1939- Actress. Address: b. c/o APA, 9000 Sunset Blvd., Los Angeles, Calif. 90069

The first clear sign that Elizabeth Ashley's career would someday become what the New York *Times* critic Mel Gussow has called "a one-woman conquest of the American theatre" flashed in her 1961 Tony-winning creation of the college freshman of *Take Her, She's Mine*. Then, although her inability to cope with early success, among other pressures, resulted in her temporary retirement later in the 1960's, she gradually progressed from captivating ingenue portrayals to such *tour de force* characterizations as that of her electrifying Maggie the Cat of the 1974 revival of Tennessee Williams' *Cat on a Hot Tin Roof*. She has also performed in scores of television dramas and in some ten movies, including *The Carpetbaggers* (1964), *Rancho Deluxe* (1975) and *Ninety-two in the Shade* (1975).

Elizabeth Ashley was born Elizabeth Ann Cole on August 30, 1939 in Ocala, Florida, the daughter of Arthur Kingman and Lucille (Ayer) Cole. Descendants of Civil War heroes, her family had belonged to the Southern gentry, but the devaluation of land and their lack of professional training left them particularly vulnerable to the Depression. When Elizabeth was five, her parents were divorced and she went with her mother to Baton Rouge, Louisiana, where they shared a two-bedroom house with her grandmother, her invalid grandfather, an aunt, and a cousin. To support them all, Mrs. Cole took a job as a secretary and eventually worked her way up to administrative assistant to the state commissioner of agriculture. In girlhood Elizabeth Ashley devoted much of her time to the movies, especially to films starring Jane Powell, and occasionally she accompanied her mother to performances of plays put on at Louisiana State University. At the age of twelve or thirteen she saw Tennessee Williams' *Summer and Smoke*, which made her aware that the theatre could be concerned with people like those she knew. She herself never seriously considered becoming an actress.

Mrs. Cole tried hard to mold her daughter into a "proper young woman," but without much success. "To her the rules of the game were truth, integrity, and character," Elizabeth Ashley explained to Shaun Considine in an interview for *After Dark* (February 1974). "And as a kid I never measured up to her standards. She wanted me to go to college, get an education, be true to myself. I didn't want any of that. I hated school. I wanted to be a cheerleader, to stay out and drink beer with the boys. I was Miss Looney Tunes in my head. My main ambition was to get pinned." She did, however, study ballet with Tatiana Semenova in Baton Rouge, and after graduating from University High School, she entered Louisiana State University. At the end of her freshman year she left Baton Rouge for New

York City in pursuit of glamour and adventure.

With only about $135 in her pocket, Miss Ashley was soon compelled to consult the Manhattan telephone book for leads to employment and almost immediately found a job as a model for the Seventh Avenue firm of Jonathan Logan. Five weeks later she quit, having heard that it was possible to make up to $100 a day doing TV commercials. She became the "Chiffon-Light Jello Pudding and Pie Filling Girl" on *The Price is Right* and later toured New York State as Miss Genny for Genessee Beer.

When Miss Ashley realized that her Southern accent was costing her the plum assignments in television commercials, she enrolled in acting classes, in 1958, at the Neighborhood Playhouse School of the Theatre, in the hope of receiving speech training. There, as she portrayed Esmeralda in a student production of *Camino Real* and Abigail in *The Crucible*, her ambitions began to center on acting as a career. To finance her drama study, she worked as a waitress and a guitar-playing folksinger in a Greenwich Village coffeehouse and economized by sharing a cold-water flat with three other girls.

During the summer of 1959 the name Elizabeth Cole appeared in the cast of two professionally produced plays—Sartre's *Dirty Hands*, an Off-Broadway presentation at the Actors Playhouse, in which she played Jessica, and *Marcus in the High Grass*, a stock company offering at the Westport Country Playhouse in Connecticut. She made her Broadway debut on November 4, 1959 at the Longacre Theatre in the minor role of Jane Ashe in *The Highest Tree*, Dore Schary's talky and static protest play against nuclear bomb testing, but the show closed after twenty-one performances. In her continuing apprenticeship she understudied Inga Stevens in the role of Elizabeth Brown in *Roman Candle* on Broadway in 1960 and Barbara Bel Geddes in the title role of *Mary, Mary* on Broadway in 1961. She performed in stock during the summer of 1960 at the Green Mansions Theatre in Warrensburg, New York and appeared on television in "Heaven Can Wait" on the *Dupont Show of the Month* in November 1960 and "The Big Splash" on the *U.S. Steel Hour* in February 1961, both on CBS. To avoid confusion with another actress named Elizabeth Cole, she changed her name to Elizabeth Ashley.

In keeping with his reputation for recognizing the potentialities of novices in the theatre, the Broadway producer and director George Abbott opened the way to stardom for Elizabeth Ashley by casting her in *Take Her, She's Mine* as the bouncing, nubile daughter of a bewildered and overprotective father, played by Art Carney. The exceptionally warm notices that greeted the comedy after its opening at the Biltmore Theatre on December 21, 1961 hailed Miss Ashley as one of the stage's most promising newcomers. For her portrayal of Mollie Michaelson, she won the Tony award for best supporting actress, a Theatre World award, and the Southern Woman's Achievement Award for 1962.

After *Take Her, She's Mine* ended its run of nearly a year, Elizabeth Ashley went to Hollywood to make her movie debut in *The Carpetbaggers* (Paramount, 1964) as Monica, the rejected wife of a ruthless, egocentric industrialist, played by George Peppard. Many reviewers panned the movie as a tawdry and salacious extravagance, but as its producer, Joseph E. Levine, predicted, its slick combination of action, sex, and violence made it a box-office smash. Their appearance together in *The Carpetbaggers* marked the beginning of a much-publicized romance between Peppard and Elizabeth Ashley, both of whom were married and were negotiating for divorce, Miss Ashley from the actor James Farentino, her husband since September 1962.

It was reportedly with Elizabeth Ashley in mind that the playwright Neil Simon tailored the role of the somewhat featherbrained young wife, Corie, in his hit play *Barefoot in the Park*, in which Miss Ashley returned to Broadway in October 1963 to costar with Robert Redford. In his review of the Mike Nichols-directed comedy about the ordeal of newlyweds coping with life in a fifth-floor Manhattan walk-up, Richard Watts Jr. wrote in the New York *Post* (October 24, 1963), "Miss Ashley is nothing short of adorable as the spirited bride, playing with wonderfully humorous charm and expert skill"—an appraisal with which most critics agreed.

Taking a leave of absence in June 1964 from *Barefoot in the Park*, Miss Ashley went back to Hollywood to work on her second film, Stanley Kramer's *Ship of Fools* (Columbia, 1965), based on the novel by Katherine Anne Porter. Its sterling cast created a score or more of fairly well realized characters, including—some reviewers thought—Miss Ashley's fun-loving, but unhappy Jenny. In the opinion, however, of Richard Roud of the *Guardian*, (October 22, 1965), "Elizabeth Ashley has the worst role in the film—smart girl tied up to a social-protest painter—but she does as much as can be done with it."

Instead of returning to *Barefoot in the Park* when the film was completed, Miss Ashley bought up the remainder of her contract for $35,000, a sum that she delights in telling interviewers is $10,000 more than Richard Burton had to pay to leave *Camelot*. Free of obligation, she flew to England to be near George Peppard, who was making a film there. The resulting publicity prompted Warner Brothers to cast the two as husband and wife in the thriller *The Third Day* (1965). Both stars received good personal notices but the film's torpid and old-fashioned story line about an amnesia victim guaranteed audience boredom.

Years later Miss Ashley revealed that she had undergone a severe emotional crisis during that period of her life and had been briefly hospitalized because of a nervous breakdown. "I had a feeling of terrible pressure," she confided to Joan Barthel of the New York *Times* (September 22, 1974). "What happened, as nearly as I can assess it, is that a kind of animal rage took over and I became really monstrous." Shaun Considine quoted her as saying, "I was one of those girls who had become successful too fast." Shortly after finishing *The Third Day*, Elizabeth Ashley married Peppard, in 1966, and startled the entertainment world by announcing her retirement. "I'd looked at myself; I seemed to be sad and crazy," she said in the New York *Times* interview, "and I thought maybe what I ought to do was live life as a woman, to live a real life. So what did I do? I married an actor, I moved to Beverly Hills, and my career became shopping, traveling and lunch. It did not make me happy." In 1969 she announced her return to acting and the following year filed for a divorce from Peppard.

At first Miss Ashley found it difficult to land a guest shot even on the more routine television series. But after performing on the *Hallmark Hall of Fame's* "The File on Devlin" on NBC in November 1969, she reaffirmed her comeback during 1970 with appearances on *Love American Style* (ABC), *Men from Shiloh* (NBC), and *Medical Center* (CBS). Since then she has played in many made-for-television movies on various networks, including *Harpy* (1971), *When Michael Calls* (1972), *One of My Wives is Missing* (1976), and *The War Between the Tates* (1977). In 1975 she portrayed Kate Chase Sprague in the second program in NBC's *Sandburg's Lincoln* series.

Meanwhile adding to her screen credits, Elizabeth Ashley was the nasty, meddling sister in *The Marriage of a Young Stockbroker* (Twentieth Century-Fox, 1971); the scheming American charmer in *Golden Needles* (American International, 1974); the loyal, long-suffering barmaid in the Canadian-produced *Paperback Hero* (Rumson, 1976); and the foul-mouthed, kidnapped wife of a railroad tycoon in *Great Scout and Cathouse Thursday* (American International, 1976). Although none of her films created much of a stir at the box office, critics singled out two as rather interesting failures: the funny, surrealist western with a present-day Montana setting, *Rancho Deluxe* (United Artists, 1975), in which she had the role of the sexually deprived rancher's wife, and *Ninety-two in the Shade* (United Artists, 1975), which featured her as the baton-twirling wife of a Key West guide service operator.

Miss Ashley's return to Broadway began rather inauspiciously with the starring role of Maggie Train in *Ring Round the Bathtub*, a nostalgia piece about an Irish-American family surviving the Depression. It opened—and closed—on April 29, 1972. In the fall of that year she assumed the title role in the Los Angeles production *Mary C Brown and the Hollywood Sign*, a musical written by her close friend Dory Previn, who closed the play for revision after a total of ten performances. At the John F. Kennedy Center in Washington, D.C. Elizabeth Ashley began recapturing the unstinted applause of theatregoers when she opened in Jean Giraudoux's fantasy *The Enchanted* in March 1973. As the French schoolmistress who falls in love with a ghost, she conveyed "an ideal mixture of softness, independence of spirit and romantic susceptibility," Alan M. Kriegsman reported in the Washington *Post* (March 8, 1973).

Any possible doubt about Miss Ashley's reputation as one of the most gifted stage actresses in America disappeared in 1974 when she electrified audiences in Stratford, Connecticut, New York, and Washington with her interpretation of Maggie, the Southern beauty married to an alcoholic, in the American Shakespeare Theatre revival of *Cat on a Hot Tin Roof*. John Simon, theatre critic for *New York* magazine, echoed the reaction of most of his colleagues when he wrote of Miss Ashley in his review of August 12, 1974, "She absorbed me into herself and made me see Maggie more from inside than from without. . . . She is, if anything, too beautiful for the part, but performs with such astonishing, such uncanny precision that not even her heady loveliness distracts us from her acting. Miss this performance at your soul's peril." Other adjectives that critics used to describe her performance included "brilliant," "superb" and "incomparable." She was nominated for a Tony award as best actress, but perhaps the greatest compliment came from the playwright himself, Tennessee Williams, who was overheard to remark that she might possibly be "the definitive Maggie."

The following year audiences at the Kennedy Center and on Broadway delighted in the gift for broad comedy that Miss Ashley showed as Lily Sabina, the indestructible maid in José Quintero's revival of Thornton Wilder's *The Skin of Our Teeth*. "There is one good reason for seeing it—Elizabeth Ashley's saucily irreverent performance as Sabina," Mel Gussow declared in the New York *Times* (September 10, 1975). *Legend*, an original spoof of the wild West by Samuel Taylor, was Miss Ashley's vehicle for 1976, but it proved to be a disappointing one, closing in New York after only five performances. One of the critics who had nothing but praise for its star, Brendan Gill observed in the *New Yorker* (May 24, 1976), "Miss Ashley has intelligence, beauty and energy, and all are on display in *Legend*."

Miss Ashley's string of personal successes hit a temporary snag early in 1977 when she costarred with Rex Harrison in an ambitious but lifeless revival of Shaw's *Caesar and Cleopatra*. Critics called her performance "unbelievable," "uneven" and "clichéd," and the show limped to a close within a month. Regarding that failure, Miss Ashley was quoted in *Time* (May 2, 1977) as saying, "It just breaks your heart, but you do the same thing you do when a man breaks your heart—you go out and get another one." As soon as *Caesar and Cleopatra* closed, Miss Ashley went to Chicago to rehearse for Jack Heifner's three-character comedy, *Vanities*. She was cast as a sexually precocious cheerleader who yearns for liberation and ends up running a pornographic art gallery. The play was scheduled to run through the summer of 1977, but Miss Ashley left the cast early to make another film, *Coma* (United Artists, 1978).

Because of her earthy, sometimes unprintable vocabulary, combined with her candor and unorthodox views, the articulate Miss Ashley has long been a favorite subject of interviewers. She is a fragile-looking beauty, five feet six inches in height, with brown hair, dark eyes, and a remarkably flexible voice. A militant supporter of the women's movement, she believes, as she told Tom Donnelly of the Washington *Post* (February 28, 1973), "The roles for males and females that have been passed down by the various cultures are mutilations of the human soul." By her marriage to George Peppard, she has a son, Christian Moore Peppard, who before reaching school age often traveled with her to the various cities of her film, TV, and stage engagements.

Elizabeth Ashley thinks of herself as something of a gypsy, or vagrant, has "tribes" of friends in several parts of the United States and in Europe, and likes to spend her free time "hanging out" with rock musicians. Intensely serious in her devotion to the theatre, she once explained to Bess Winaker of the Chicago *Sun-Times* (March 30, 1977), "When I'm on stage, I guess it's like the way it is for a lot of people when they take a drug It's another place. It's a privilege to get on a stage." Miss Ashley was a member of the board of directors of the American Film Institute and served on the first National Council on the Arts, during the Lyndon B. Johnson Administration.

References: After Dark 6:65+ F '74 por; Esquire 83:104+ Mr '75 por; N Y Sunday News III p1+ Ag 18 '74 por; III pl My 16 '76 por; Newsday A p4+ O 31 '74 por; Washington Post F p1+ F 9 '75 pors; Ashley, Elizabeth, with Firestone, Ross. Actress: Postcards from the Road (1978); Notable Names in American Theatre (1976); Who's Who in America, 1974-75; Who's Who in the Theatre (1977)

Asner, Edward

Nov. 15, 1929- Actor. Address: c/o Jack Fields and Associates, 9255 Sunset Blvd., Los Angeles, Calif. 90069

In his persona of twice-born Lou Grant, Edward Asner has become one of the genuine folk heroes of television—an unglamorous, middle-aged man who nevertheless projects charm and lovability, a figure with whom millions of viewers can readily identify. Lou Grant was introduced to the American public in 1970 on *The Mary Tyler Moore Show*, where he played the boss of the television newsroom in Minneapolis where Mary worked. After that program finally ended its long run in March 1977, Grant reemerged that autumn as the editor of the city desk of a large metropolitan newspaper called the "Tribune" in *Lou Grant*, an unusually intelligent dramatic show about the grittier realities of newspaper reporting and publishing. In fact, Lou Grant is only the best-known of Asner's creations, for the veteran character actor has been playing thugs, cops, and businessmen in films and on television since the early 1960's. During the lengthy tenure of *The Mary Tyler Moore Show*, Asner varied his work on that situation comedy with acclaimed dramatic roles that included the part of the embittered German immigrant father in the TV mini-series *Rich Man, Poor Man*, Huey Long in the TV film *The Life and Assassination of the Kingfish*, and the sea captain in the mini-series *Roots*.

Edward Asner was born on November 15, 1929 in Kansas City, Missouri, the youngest of the five children of Morris David and Lizzie (Seliger) Asner. "My father was a scrap iron dealer. That's one of several euphemisms my brothers taught me when we moved to a middle-class WASP neighborhood," Asner, who grew up in the rigorous pieties of an Orthodox Jewish home, recalled to Ellen Cohn of the New York *Times* (September 23, 1973). "Sometimes he was called a junk man." Elsewhere the actor has described his late father as "a patriarch, very controlling." Asner has two sisters and two brothers one of whom, Ben, owns a record store in Kansas City.

At Wyandotte High School in Kansas City, Asner worked on the school newspaper and was an all-city tackle on the football team. His first exposure to acting occurred in a high school radio class that broadcasted a fifteen-minute weekly program over a local station. After graduation, he went to the University of Chicago, although, he confided to Ellen Cohn, "I really wanted to be an adventurer, to lay pipelines in South America or be a cabin boy on an Alaskan cruiser, but I didn't have the guts."

In college Asner was active in dramatics, making his stage debut as Thomas à Becket in a production of T. S. Eliot's *Murder in the Cathedral*. After two years, however, he dropped out of the university and returned home, where, he has recalled, almost too graphically, he "lay around like a slug." In Kansas City, Asner worked at a variety of jobs, including driving a cab and selling advertising space, shoes, and encyclopedias. Returning to the Chicago area, he found employment in a steel mill in Gary, Indiana, and on an auto assembly line.

In 1951 Asner was drafted into the Signal Corps of the United States Army and sent to France. There he managed a basketball team that became the second highest-rated Army team in Europe. Shortly before he was discharged, he received a letter from Paul Sills, who had seen him act at the University of Chicago, inviting Asner to join his new Playwrights Theater Club in Chicago. At that repertory theatre Asner appeared in twenty-six plays over the next two years, working with Mike Nichols, Zohra Lampert, Tom O'Horgan, and Barbara Harris. When the group began to get involved in improvisation, however, Asner left. "My conservative Middle West upbringing had taught me that you have to work for what you get," the actor told a reporter for *TV Guide* (May 22, 1971), "and improvisation sounded like too much fun."

In 1955 Asner left Chicago for New York. In February 1956 he joined the cast of the long-running Off-Broadway production of Bertolt Brecht's and Kurt Weill's *The Three-Penny Opera* as Mr. Peachum, a part he kept for two years and nine months, for the remuneration of $65 a week, an income that he fattened with work on local television. In October 1959 he appeared in an Off-Broadway production of Jean Anouilh's *Legend of Lovers* as Dulac, but the play closed after less than a month. That was followed by another short stint as Prospero in Shakespeare's *The Tempest*, which ran Off Broadway from December 27, 1959 until January 10, 1960. Asner's Broadway debut was equally short-lived. He had a small part in *Face of a Hero*, starring Jack Lemmon, which opened at the Eugene O'Neill Theatre on October 20, 1960 and closed on November 19. Meanwhile, Asner was accumulating a number of credits in summer festival productions of Shakespeare. During the summer of 1959 he appeared at Stratford, Connecticut, for example, as Sampson in *Romeo and Juliet* and as Bardolph in *The Merry Wives of Windsor*. The following summer he played the Duke of Exeter in the New York Shakespeare Festival's Central Park Production of *King Henry V*.

During the spring of 1961 Asner flew to Los Angeles to appear in a segment of the television series *Naked City* (ABC). Having decided to move to California, he arrived in Los Angeles as a permanent resident on May 30, 1961. In Southern California he fared better financially than he had in New York, obtaining a steady supply of character parts in episodes of television series. In the fall of 1964 he costarred, as Frank Radcliffe, in his first series, *Slattery's People*, with Richard Crenna, who played Slattery, a crusading lawyer. The series ran through November 1965 on the Columbia Broadcasting System.

Asner made his film debut in 1965 as the villain's hired henchman in *The Satan Bug* (United Artists), a disappointingly bland science-fiction melodrama. In *The Slender Thread* (Paramount, 1965), a drama starring Sidney Poitier and Anne Bancroft, Asner played a police detective helping Poitier, a suicide center volunteer, to rescue Miss Bancroft, who has taken an overdose of barbituates. Asner again played a cop in the Elvis Presley film *Change of Habit* (Universal, 1969).

Despite his occasional Hollywood film appearances, however, Asner remained primarily a television actor. Among the series that he appeared in during the 1960's and early 1970's were *Medical Center* (CBS), *Name of the Game* (NBC), *Mod Squad* (ABC), *Ironside* (NBC), *Felony Squad*, and *Peter Gunn* (NBC; ABC). Various reporters have recalled his outstanding performances as an ex-convict turned kidnapper on an episode of *The FBI*, as an aging policeman terrified of his impending retirement on a segment of *Police Story*, and as the boss of the special robbery squad on the pilot of *Police Story*.

In 1969 Asner's portrayal of an ill-tempered police chief in a television movie called *Doug Selby, D.A.* was seen by Grant Tinker, Mary Tyler Moore's husband. Although Asner's experience in comedy up to that time had been limited to two assignments, Tinker, a television producer, sensed that the actor might be ideally suited for the role of Lou Grant in the upcoming *Mary Tyler Moore Show*. By auditioning Asner obtained the part as the irascible but lovable Grant, who is Mary's boss in the fictitious newsroom of WJM-TV in

Minneapolis. After the CBS show had its premiere on Saturday, September 19, 1970 at 9:30 P.M., it became a hit both with viewers and with critics, who praised its ensemble acting. Asner, who received more than his share of critical approval, was awarded Emmys in 1970-71, 1971-72, and 1974-75 for his work on the *Mary Tyler Moore Show*.

While appearing on *The Mary Tyler Moore Show*, Asner continued his concurrent dramatic career. In the summer of 1973 he toured the American Midwest in a stock production of Garson Kanin's *Born Yesterday*. The following year he starred in a low-budget film called *The Wrestler* (Entertainment Ventures, 1974), in which he played an honest wrestling match promoter who is struggling to keep the business from being taken over by criminals. His next starring role was as a Chicano bush pilot in *Hey, I'm Alive*, a television movie that was aired on the ABC network on November 7, 1975. Based on a true incident, the film tells the story of how the pilot, through his strength and faith in God, managed to keep himself and his young female passenger (Sally Struthers) alive for forty-nine days after their crash-landing in a Yukon forest in the dead of winter. "Asner as the Mexican pilot, peering through ice-covered spectacles, is splendid," wrote Cecil Smith of the Los Angeles *Times* (November 7, 1975).

In 1976 Asner played the volatile owner of a ludicrously inept football team in the Walt Disney comedy film, *Gus*. In a change of pace, he contributed a much-admired performance as the patriarch of the Jordache sons to the ABC-TV mini-series *Rich Man, Poor Man*, based on the best-selling novel by Irwin Shaw. After watching the first episode the reviewer for *Variety* (February 4, 1976) commented, "Strongest presence in Part I was Edward Asner, who plays the boys' father, a German immigrant, in superb style. His power and emotional shadings made the other performances seem shallow and mechanical." For his portrayal Asner was granted his fourth Emmy in May 1976.

In 1977 Asner added considerably to his already impressive collection of television credits. In the now famous ABC-TV mini-series *Roots*, telecast in January, he played Davies, the captain of the slave ship that brought Kunta Kinte and other oppressed Africans to the United States. On March 21 he starred in *The Life and Assassination of the Kingfish*, CBS's made-for-television film biography of Huey Long, the controversial Louisiana politician who was murdered in 1935. "He's a bit florid at times," Harriet Van Horne conceded in *New York* magazine (March 28, 1977), "and that bayou accent does slip a vowel or two under stress. But oh, what a performance! Asner grows into the part, builds it, varies it with bravura touches and sudden stabbing insights." Then, in December, Asner costarred with Maureen Stapleton as a ruthless businessman who is reunited with his estranged wife and children a short time before his death in *The Gathering*, a TV film on ABC. In 1977 Asner became the only actor ever to win, in a single year, both the award for best supporting actor in a drama (*Roots*) and in a comedy (*The Mary Tyler Moore Show*) from the Television Critics Circle.

The Mary Tyler Moore Show finally reached its end with an episode telecast on March 19, 1977, in which Lou Grant was sacked from his longtime job as newsroom chief of WJM. All was not lost, however, for Asner had already signed a contract with MTM Enterprises to star in a spinoff from the show, which follows the fortunes of Grant after he left Minneapolis and moved to Los Angeles to start a new career as the city editor of a large newspaper. Unlike *The Mary Tyler Moore Show*, a half-hour situation comedy, the new *Lou Grant* is an ambitious and serious-minded one-hour dramatic show. "Edward Asner," wrote Frank Rich in *Time* (September 19, 1977) ". . . has been developing the character [of Lou Grant] for seven seasons. On *Mary Tyler Moore* he first played his role as another gruff but lovable TV sitcom boss. . . . By the time that series concluded last season, Asner had given Lou three dimensions: he was still a comic figure, but he was also a lonely, somewhat self-destructive man. Now [in the new series] Asner takes the character still further. . . . To Lou Grant, the disheveled loner, Asner now adds Lou Grant, the self-assured, two-fisted journalist."

When *Lou Grant* premiered on CBS-TV on Tuesday, September 20, 1977 at 10:00 P.M., it was soon commended by critics for its uncompromising realism, mature scripting, and its star. "It is Asner who dominates the show," wrote Rich in the *Time* article. "Whether Lou Grant is sitting disconsolately alone in his sterile L.A. hotel room or counseling reporters in a rundown newspaper bar, he comes across as a man who has been knocked around by the real world, rather than by writers at a Hollywood story conference." Although the show suffered from low ratings during its first months, by late January 1978 it had climbed to eleventh place. Since January 30, 1978 *Lou Grant* has been broadcast at 10:00 P.M. on Mondays. Somewhat tardily, the television critic of the *Saturday Review*, Karl E. Meyer, joined in the chorus of praise in its June 24, 1978 issue: "Ed Asner, who portrays Grant, has a face right out of the *Gnomes* book and a hard-soft manner that anyone who has been a cub reporter will instantly recognize. He seems more at home as city editor of *The Tribune* than in his old job as the producer of a television news program in Minneapolis. It now seems clear that Grant is at heart a print journalist and was only a temporary exile in the land of tubes."

While a struggling young actor in New York, Edward Asner met Nancy Lou Sykes, a literary agent. They soon fell in love but delayed marriage for over two years because they worried about their parents' reactions to the difference in their religious backgrounds. (Nancy was raised as an Episcopalian.) Finally they married on March 23, 1959 in a civil ceremony. Their children, Matthew and Liza, who are twins, and Kathryn, have been brought up in the Jewish faith. The Asners live in an unostentatious home in Los Angeles' wealthy Bel Air section, where their household includes several dogs, cats, birds, and fish. Phyllis Battelle of the *Ladies Home Journal* (March 1978) described them as "a close and caring family. Their values are traditional and their way of life modest." Asner contributes both time and money to liberal and ecological causes, and is a member of the American Civil Liberties Union, Americans for Democratic Action, National Committee for an Effective Congress, Common Cause, and SANE. Although Asner told Miss Battelle that through psychotherapy he has "recently discovered I am not the ideal person to live with," the actor, like his alter ego Lou Grant, is invariably described as "lovable." Asner is five feet nine inches tall, balding, and perennially overweight, although he recently lost thirty-five pounds with the aid of a liquid protein diet. He has tried unsuccessfully to stop smoking.

References: Ladies Home J 95:138+ Mr '78 por; N Y Times II p19+ S 23 '73 por; TV Guide 19:33+ My 22 '71, 25:26+ O 15 '77 por; Who's Who in America, 1978-79

Auchincloss, Louis (Stanton)

Sept. 27, 1917- Writer. Address: b. Hawkins, Delafield & Wood, 67 Wall St., New York City, N.Y. 10005; h. 1111 Park Ave., New York City, N.Y. 10028

NOTE: This biography supersedes the article that appeared in *Current Biography* in 1954.

Except for one brief interval, for thirty years Louis Auchincloss has successfully pursued a twin career as a Wall Street lawyer and as a writer of novels, short stories, biographies, and criticism. *The Rector of Justin, Portrait in Brownstone, Powers of Attorney, The Embezzler, Tales of Manhattan*—among the best known of his many books of fiction—reflect his abiding interest in the psychological and moral dramas played out along New York City's corridors of money, power, and social position, and on the narrow stages occupied by affluent lawyers, bankers, corporation heads, brokers, and their wives, daughters, and mistresses. His firsthand explorations of the *haut monde* have made him, as one critic put it, "the last of our genuine novelists of manners" in the line of William Dean Howells, Henry James, Edith Wharton, and J. P. Marquand. That solitary position also makes him something of an anachronism—a self-confessed (Henry James) Jacobite whose traditional moral vision and techniques run counter to most modern trends. Hence, his work is little discussed by the academic establishment, and he is sometimes criticized for the supposed irrelevance of his material, repetitiveness, and lack of stylistic flair. Yet his civilized novels of manners are sometimes best sellers, esteemed for their assured narrative skills, solid craftsmanship, accurate observations of character and background, and honest feeling. "Not since Dreiser has an American writer had so much to tell us about the role of money in our lives," novelist Gore Vidal, a staunch Auchincloss supporter, has written. "What I've been trying to do," Auchincloss has said of his circumscribed goals, "is to see the New York I know in depth. . . . That's the heart of my work, its essential purpose."

Louis Stanton Auchincloss was born in Lawrence, Long Island on September 27, 1917, the third of four children of Priscilla (Stanton) and Joseph Howland Auchincloss, a Wall Street corporation lawyer. Like his parents, grandparents, and great-grandparents before him, he lived in New York City, as part of an aristocratic clan of Dixons, Howlands, Stantons, and Auchinclosses whose high social status was assumed and whose antecedents uniformly made their fortunes in the professions and in the higher echelons of corporations. He has a sister who married an architect, one brother who is a lawyer and diplomat, and another who is a doctor. His boyhood was happy, crowded with an interesting variety of relatives and characterized by private clubs, summer homes in Long Island and Bar Harbor, attendant servants, and, when he reached his teens, by debutante parties and foreign travel. During the 1920's he attended the Bovee School for Boys on Fifth Avenue, and in 1929, following a class tradition, he entered Groton. A hopeless athlete and unmotivated student, Auchincloss was at first unpopular at Groton, but by the time he reached the sixth form he had achieved superior status as scholar, editor of the literary magazine, and president of the drama society. His first "passionate literary experience" was a class he attended in Victorian fiction, and his first short stories appeared in the *Grotonian*.

In *A Writer's Capital* (Univ. of Minnesota, 1974), a candid autobiographical study of his background, Auchincloss reveals his painful youthful struggle to define himself as man and writer. When he was still a boy, his father unwittingly gave him the "gloomiest anticipations" of a man's professional life during a grim visit to Wall Street. Horrified by "those dark narrow streets and those tall sooty towers," Auchincloss gravitated towards the carefree women of his class, "a privileged happy lot" exemplified by the literary personality of his mother. Those two worlds remained unreconciled in 1935 when he entered Yale, where, a Phi Beta Kappa, he avoided campus activities except for small Dramatic Society roles and writing stories for the *Yale Literary Magazine*. When Scribners rejected his first novel, a highly derivative "Madame Bovary" about a woman of his caste, he melodramatically concluded "that a man born to the responsibilities of a brownstone bourgeois world could only be an artist or writer if he were a genius." Renouncing writing to pursue a "serious" career, he skipped his senior year at Yale and entered the University of Virginia law school in 1938.

To his surprise, Auchincloss liked the study of law. "There seemed no reason any more to suppose that even a lawyer's life might not be an enjoyable one," he recalled in *A Writer's Capital*. Further assurance came with his election to the editorship of the *Law Review* and the discovery of his keen interest in estates law while serving as "summer boarder" in 1940 with the Wall Street firm of Sullivan & Cromwell. He kept writing, however, and completed a novel about a snobbish dilettante, Beverly Stregelinus, who was largely a self-caricature. Disappointed with its bathos, he disposed of the manuscript in a trash pail, only to find when he changed his mind an hour later that the garbage truck had made its collection. After his admission to the bar in 1941, Auchincloss joined Sullivan & Cromwell as a regular associate, but he soon enlisted in Naval Intelligence. During World War II he spent over a year of "torpid shore duty" in the Panama Canal Zone, then went to sea as commander of an LST in England during the buzz-bombing of London; he later experienced the Normandy invasion and the final Pacific amphibious campaigns.

Still drawn to fiction when he returned to Sullivan & Cromwell at the war's end, Auchincloss finished a novel he had begun on shipboard entitled *The Indifferent Children*. It was published in 1947 by Prentice-Hall, Inc., under the pseudonyn "Andrew Lee." Once again he followed the ironic adventures of his patrician hero, Beverly Stregelinus, this time through love and war in the high society of New York, Panama, and London. Although he and his parents had anticipated damaging effects of the novel upon his law career (hence the pseudonyn), predominantly favorable reviews bolstered his confidence in his avocation. Working nights and weekends, he began writing short stories, which were published under his own name in the *Atlantic, New Yorker, Esquire,* and other magazines. In 1950 eight of them were brought together in *The Injustice Collectors* by Houghton Mifflin Company, the publisher of all his fiction thereafter.

A capsule review in the *New Yorker* announced that *The Injustice Collectors* is about "people who have beautiful manners, plenty of money, and a perfectly ghastly time all around." That summary might be applied as well to Auchincloss' later fiction. In fact, points raised in the earliest reviews set an ambivalent pattern of judgment for Auchincloss criticism thereafter. Some praise has been fulsome. William McFee, for example, in the New York *Sun* (May 27, 1947) called *The Indifferent Children* "a remarkable novel about the war," and, fixing Auchincloss in the tradition of Henry James like many reviewers since, saw him "alive to our times . . . [with] the psychological alertness and mastery of English the master would have enjoyed." From the start, Auchincloss was recognized as a knowing, astute observer of his special world. Like many later reviewers, Leslie Bell in the New York *Herald Tribune* (June 29, 1947) applauded his sense of irony in *The Indifferent Children*, a blend of satire tempered with understanding and forgiveness. However, forecasting charges of irrelevance and blandness that were to be repeated over the years, Merle Miller in the *Saturday Review* (June 14, 1947) saw in it a novel dealing with "a rather unimportant minority in American life," and Virgilia Peterson in the New York *Herald Tribune* (October 1, 1950) regarded *The Injustice Collectors* "as anachronistic as the society it depicts . . . lacking in passion and power to move."

In 1951 Auchincloss resigned his law post to write full time, and, as he says in *A Writer's Capital*, "to find out, once and for all, what I am." He began undergoing psychoanalysis. In 1954 he returned to law, joining Hawkins, Delafield & Wood at 67 Wall Street, where he has remained ever since as an associate and, since 1958, as partner. "I ceased to think of myself as a 'lawyer' or a 'writer,'" he wrote. "I was simply doing what I was doing when I did it." Meanwhile, during his three-year respite he published two novels, *Sybil* (1952) and *A Law for the Lion* (1954). Both were about a society woman divorced under scandalous circumstances, and both were lukewarmly received. More successful was *The Romantic Egoists* (1954), eight short stories originally published separately, but unified by a single narrator, and by development of one topical theme of the 1950's: an individual's need to stand up against crowd conformity. In the New York *Times* (May 16, 1954) James Stern wrote: "This volume reveals Louis Auchincloss as a writer of unusual brilliance . . . with an economy of style, an alertness of eye, an artful, disarming modesty."

Governed by an upper-class code of conduct in which any deviation from honor and integrity demands its retributive punishment, characters in Auchincloss' fiction often seek relief from guilt through self-destructive actions. The theme of how culpability shapes human lives is dealt with in his next three novels: *The Great World of Timothy Colt* (1956); *Venus in Sparta* (1958); and *Pursuit of the Prodigal* (1959). In Auchincloss' first full-scale assay of the legal world, his Timothy Colt destroys his marriage and idealistic law career after being lured into malpractice by the blandishments of the larger world. Michael Parrish, the emotionally ill-equipped hero of *Venus in Sparta,* is a bank executive whose success in business and love is soured by self-motivated crises that lead to his ruin. The Long Island high society rebel, Reese Parmalee, in *Pursuit of a Prodigal* discovers that breaking out of the confines of one's class and family simply engenders more painful dilemmas. More tightly and organically structured than Auchincloss' previous work, all three novels were looked upon by reviewers as promises of more important things to come.

In the 1960's, with his first ventures into historical fiction, Auchincloss fulfilled those promises. He has always disagreed with those who maintain that the rich are essentially different from other people, and that environment inevitably determines personality. "Irked by the insistence of critics and friends that the most important thing in the shaping of my characters had to be their money, I decided . . . to write the novel everyone thought I had been writing," he says in his autobiography. Since American wealth often involves inherited fortunes, he was led to their origins in the nineteenth century. The result was *The House of Five Talents* (1960), followed by *Portrait in Brownstone* (1962), extensive family chronicles tracing the effects of wealth through several generations up to our day. Narrated principally by two elderly matriarchs, the novels are social histories that "offer a bittersweet portrait of 'the image of lost elegance and virtue,'" according to James W. Tuttleton, an authority on the novel of manners in America.

Critics generally agree that Auchincloss' next two novels rank among his finest accomplishments. In *The Rector of Justin* (1964) his hero is Frank Prescott, the charismatic headmaster of a Protestant New England boys school, now deceased, who is refracted through six glaringly different viewpoints by people who once knew him. When the novel appeared, Prescott was often identified as Endicott Peabody, founder of Groton, but Auchincloss later disclosed a very different model, Judge Learned Hand. Despite his failings, Prescott was intended to emerge as a man "of giant intellect, of passionate idealism, of searing doubts, of mordant humor." Not all reviewers concurred with that judgment—one labeled Prescott "a petrified old windbag"—but the majority regarded the portrait as did Virgilia Peterson in the New York *Times* (July 12, 1964): "not only a passionately interesting, but a spiritually important study of the American character." In *The Embezzler* (1966) Auchincloss returned to his preoccupation with scions of the old New York establishment with Guy Prime, self-exiled in Panama City after his imprisonment for financial misappropriations during the Depression. Again employing multiple viewpoints, he created a tantalizingly ambiguous portrait of his protagonist.

As Auchincloss continued to mine the limited field of New York upper-class society, some critics tended to regard each successive novel as simply a "representative product," one more piece of testimony to his undoubted talents, but now weakened by predictability and overly neat manipulation of material. Three recent novels were indifferently received, even though he introduced fresh elements of interest. *A World of Profit* (1968), for example, is about an "outsider," Jay Livingstone, an attractive but opportunistic Jewish land developer whose rise hastens the fall of an old New York family, as well as his own. Auchincloss first entered the world of politics in *I Came as a Thief* (1972), which, while echoing earlier themes of crime, guilt, and atonement, tells a story of a Security and Exchange Commission member who betrays his public trust. *Dark Lady,* published in 1977, is one of Louis Auchincloss' most literary, freighted with references to Euripides, Shakespeare, and Tolstoy, as it traces a twice-married, failing actress through her marriage to a wealthy Jewish investment banker, her Phaedra-like affair with his son, and on to her membership in the United States Congress after her husband's death. In *Newsweek* (August 7, 1978) James Atlas described the cast of *The Country Cousin,* Auchincloss' most recent novel, as being "familiar to readers of his 20 previous works of fiction: the calculating but sympathetic adventuress from a deprived background; an older sponsor scornful of the conventions of New York Society; taciturn, philandering businessmen with ruddy faces; and their thwarted wives, thirsting for uninhibited affairs."

In addition to extolling Auchincloss' novelistic treatment of America's ruling class in a long review in the *New York Review of Books* (July 18, 1974), Gore Vidal called him "a superb short-story writer." Auchincloss regularly publishes his short fiction in prestigious magazines. In his collections, however, he deliberately blurs the area separating "short stories" and "novel" by dealing with a unifying theme or topic. Thus, *Powers of Attorney* (1963), one of his most successful books, is a loosely structured group of episodes about the fictional law firm of Tower, Tilney & Webb, with steady attention paid to its senior partner, Clitus Tilney, a principled man of the old school. In the fifteen stories of *Partners* (1974), clashes between traditional values and questionable modern business practices surface in another law firm. *The Winthrop Covenant* (1976) presents variations upon the Puritan ethic in nine nearly self-sufficient stories spanning the period stretching from 1630 to our day, each of them dealing with a Winthrop family descendant. Although divided into three sections, *Tales of Manhattan* (1967) achieves the same collective effect by clustering together thematically related stories about art, the law, and society matrons. Deftly plotted, expert in limning character with minimal strokes, illuminated with intelligent observations, the best of Auchincloss' short fiction reveals, as one critic noted, "a shrewd understanding of the small battles that fill so much of our lives."

While Auchincloss has said that his fiction does not imitate Henry James, in *Reflections of a Jacobite* (1961), his first collection of his literary essays, he acknowledges James as a "starting point" and as a "kindly guide" for his lifetime's reading. The essays express his admiration for novelists of manners ranging from William Makepeace Thackeray, George Eliot, and George Meredith in the nineteenth century, through Henry James and Edith Wharton, and on up to J. P. Marquand and John O'Hara. To him, the peaks in the genre were scaled by Henry James and Marcel Proust. In the *Saturday Review* (June 3, 1961) James Gray typified the general reception of Auchincloss' criticism when he described the essays as "spontaneous, personal, and, despite the air of casual modesty with which they are presented, surcharged with awareness and conviction." Auchincloss expanded upon his earlier essays in his *Edith Wharton* (Viking, 1971), a biography, and *Reading Henry James* (Univ. of Minnesota, 1975), a critical survey of James's work. *Pioneers and Caretakers* (Univ. of Minnesota, 1965) is a collection of levelheaded essays on nine American women novelists from Sarah Orne Jewett to Mary McCarthy, and *Motiveless Malignity* (Houghton, 1969) deals with Shakespeare's "sense of the perverse and irrational." He has also written a biography, *Richelieu* (Viking, 1973); *The Club Bedroom*, a play shown over public television; and four other, as yet unproduced, plays.

"If a human being is described completely," Auchincloss once wrote, "his class makes little difference. He becomes a human being on the printed page, and other humans, of whatever class, can recognize themselves in his portrait." Nevertheless, depending upon which critic one reads, Auchincloss' fixation upon New York's upper crust remains either his most distinctive asset or his most serious flaw. The socially conscious Granville Hicks, Gore Vidal's principal target of attack in his Auchincloss article, wrote in the New York *Times* (September 3, 1972): "My recurrent quarrel . . . is that the little world of his novels usually seems to me to be detached from the real world." Critics more virulent than Hicks are impatient with Auchincloss' seeming captivation by the mannered rich, and with his serious attention to "trivial people with clockwork insides," as one put it. But many others, more willing to accept his remoteness from current literary fashions and from America's topical concerns, concur with Bill Perkins in the *National Observer* (March 30, 1974): "His range may be limited, but within it his pitch is perfect." Lucid, intelligent, knowledgeable, a moralist of subtle sophistication, a confident storyteller, judiciously distanced from his material, Auchincloss is not a major American writer, most critics agree, but he is a "literary artist," and, as Christopher Lehmann-Haupt has said, a reader "can always count on him for highly polished entertainment."

Louis Auchincloss lives on Park Avenue with his wife, the former Adele Lawrence, and their three sons, John, Blake, and Andrew. They summer at their country place in Bedford, New York. Auchincloss is a well-knit six-footer with something of a military bearing. He was described by interviewer Fern Marja Eckman in the New York *Post* (March 25, 1973) as fast-moving and fast-talking, a man of "wit, intellectual perspicacity, and graciousness." Besides law and writing, his chief interests are the theatre and bookcollecting. "I love being tied up and busy all day with things going on all around," he has said, "and I don't like the solitude of writing." (He now writes at home only on weekends, never at night). To add to his busyness, he is board chairman of the Museum of the City of New York; trustee of the New York Society Library, the Josiah Macy Jr. Foundation, and St. Barnard's School; counsel for the National Institute of Arts and Letters; and a member of the administrative committees of the Dumbarton Oaks Research Library and the New York Bar Association. He lists his club as the Century Association.

References: Life p53+ Ap 16 '66; Nat Observer p21 My 15 '76 por; N Y Post p33 Mr 25 '73 por; Saturday R p24 Jl 14 62; Auchincloss, Louis. A Writer's Capital (1974); Contemporary Authors 1st rev vol 1-4 (1967); Whos Who in America, 1978-79; World Authors: 1950-1970 (1975)

Backe, John D(avid) (bok'ē)

July 5, 1932- Broadcasting executive. Address: b. CBS, Inc., 51 West 52d St., New York City, N.Y. 10019

John D. Backe capped an unusually rapid rise through the ranks of corporate executives when, on May 11, 1977, at the age of forty-four, he succeeded William S. Paley as chief executive officer of CBS, Inc., the giant multi-media conglomerate. It numbers among its properties CBS-TV and CBS Radio, Columbia Records, several major publishing houses, a score of magazines, Creative Playthings, musical instruments, and the Needle Arts Society. Just seven months earlier, Backe had been named president of the corporation. He took over the reins of the $2 billion empire shortly after CBS-TV, the largest network in the country, lost its longtime hold on first place in the network rankings, and in an effort to regain its supremacy, reorganized the network's operations, funneled money into program development, and initiated in-house management training programs. CBS's other divisions received similar attention. "I want this to be a quality corporation," Backe said in a recent interview. "We haven't scratched the surface on what we can do in this corporation to maximize our resources."

Of German and Austrian descent, John David Backe was born in Akron, Ohio on July 5, 1932 to John A. Backe, an employee of the B. F. Goodrich Rubber Company, and Ella A. (Enyedy) Backe. He has one sister, Patricia (Backe) Ohendorf. Backe attended Miami University in Oxford, Ohio, where he majored in business administration and marketing. After receiving his B.S. degree in 1954, he enlisted in the United States Air Force and spent the next four years as a B-57 bomber pilot in the Strategic Air Command. Backe's years in the military matured him. "I went through some hairy experiences, so I guess maybe very early in life I learned a lot about myself," he told Rance Crain in an interview for *Advertising Age* (March 28, 1977). "I had some very close calls. Some men go through life and they're never really challenged, or they step away from some real challenges, and they never understand what it's all about. . . . If you're about to have your tail busted flying an airplane and you survive that, you mean to tell me that things that happen in a business environment are more serious?"

After his discharge from the Air Force in 1957, Backe returned to Ohio to take an entry-level position with General Electric in Cincinnati. Over the next nine years he held a variety of jobs with the company in marketing, engineering, and finance. To improve his chances for job advancement, he enrolled in the evening graduate program in business administration at Xavier University and earned his M.B.A. degree in 1961.

In 1966 Backe left General Electric to become vice-president and director of marketing for Silver Burdett Company, the textbook publishing sector of General Learning Corporation, a joint venture of General Electric and Time Inc., for developing new teaching techniques. Quickly climbing the corporate ladder, he became president of Silver Burdett in 1968, executive vice-president of General Learning in 1969 and, later the same year, its president and chief executive officer. He remembers that assignment as "the most fun job" of his career. "It was small enough to sit in on all the editorial meetings, marketing meetings, everything was under [my] control and [I] could truly influence the whole thing."

Backe remained at General Learning until March 1973, when Arthur R. Taylor, the new president of CBS, persuaded him to join the huge conglomerate as president of its publishing group and corporate vice-president. Four months later, Backe was named a director of CBS. Hired specifically to rescue the floundering publishing division, Backe set about to generate increased income, which in 1972 had fallen to a pre-tax low of about $100,000. With that end in view, he completely reorganized the various components of the publishing group: Holt, Rinehart and Winston, a trade and textbook publishing house; Popular Library, the paperback publisher; W. B. Saunders, a firm that specializes in the publication of scientific and medical books; and a consumer publishing division that publishes twenty-five special interest magazines, among them, *Field and Stream, World Tennis,* and

Road and Track. By 1975 Backe had boosted the publishing group's sales from a low of $149,000,000 in 1972 to $207,000,000 and its pre-tax income from its pitiful $100,000 to a respectable $18,000,000. Moreover, he engineered the potentially lucrative acquisition of Fawcett Publications, Inc., a paperback publishing house, and its subsidiaries, *Woman's Day* magazine and a book distribution division.

William S. Paley, the chief executive officer of CBS, Inc., watched Backe's spectacular career with more than average interest. Since the mid-1960's Paley, who founded the Columbia Broadcasting System in 1928, had been searching for his successor. He had a change of heart about his first heir apparent, Dr. Frank Stanton, a pioneer in broadcast journalism who, during his years as president of CBS, Inc., was a widely respected spokesman for the broadcasting industry. Charles T. Ireland, Stanton's successor, was Paley's second choice, but he died after only eight months in office. To replace Ireland, Paley handpicked Arthur R. Taylor, an aggressive young executive and financial wizard of the International Paper Company, leading industry insiders to assume that Taylor was being groomed to take over the corporation on Paley's retirement. As expected, Taylor steadily increased corporate profits, but his "business school mentality" irritated some of the more creative program executives. To make matters worse, in January 1976 CBS-TV lost the top spot in the prime time ratings for the first time in twenty years to ABC.

Media observers attributed some of CBS's problems to the networks' acceptance of the 8:00-to-9:00 P.M. "family viewing hour," a concept developed largely by Taylor to stave off anticipated FCC programming regulations. That voluntary restriction on adult programming forced CBS to shift its entrenched satirical comedies, such as *All in the Family* and *Maude*, to a later viewing period. Taking advantage of the situation, ABC unveiled a group of youth-oriented situation comedies, most notably *Happy Days* and *Laverne and Shirley*, that propelled the network into first place in the standings. To attract the adult audience, CBS began televising violent action series and such controversial made-for-television movies as *Helter Skelter*, a chillingly graphic depiction of the mass murders committed by Charles Manson and his followers, prompting renewed criticism from outraged consumer groups and congressmen.

Disappointed by Taylor's performance, Paley demanded his resignation and named Backe as his successor. "I was shocked," Backe said later, as quoted in *Fortune* (May 1977). "It took a full week of thinking before I could decide." The broadcasting industry was equally stunned when Paley made his decision public at an annual stockholders' meeting on October 13, 1976. At the same time, he announced his intention to step down as the corporation's chief executive officer in six months.

Backe approached his new post with his characteristic energy and enthusiasm. His first priority, he assured Albin Krebs, who interviewed him for a New York *Times* (October 14, 1976) profile, was "learning." "I've been so entirely immersed in the company's publishing activities that its others, like radio and television for which CBS is best known, are mostly new ground to me," he explained. "There are four disparate operating groups, and I must quickly grasp the workings of the whole complex organization, see what makes it tick." Backe immediately embarked on a self-prescribed crash course in programming, under Paley's tutelage. By his own estimation, he devoted more than 50 percent of his time to the broadcasting medium, attending all program meetings and previewing all the pilots of projected series. "My imagination was never captured by hardware, though I was known as a hardware man," he said, as quoted in *Variety* (March 30, 1977). "But it was different with publishing, and now with television. The creative process is fascinating."

In his first year in office, Backe appropriated $32,000,000 for the development of new television programs. Convinced that the regular series is still the underlying foundation of the networks, he and his programming executives methodically rebuilt the CBS program roster, concentrating on urbane thirty-minute situation comedies and hour-long dramas. "Four times in my career, I've come into turnaround situations where I walk in and the cupboard's bare," Backe explained to Larry Michie of *Variety* (July 14, 1977). "I came into this job and asked what our inventory was and they said, *'Ball Four.'* That's not going to happen again. . . . We're going to have shows and made-for-television movies on the shelf this fall if quick changes are necessary."

Although he sees the family viewing hour as a dead issue, Backe is still intent on lowering the sex and violence quotient of CBS programs. "It's an easy thing in a situation comedy to get into sex or salacious material as being funny," he told one reporter. "It's a hell of a lot less easy and more creative to get funny material and not take that route." Unlike his counterparts at the other networks, Backe adamantly refuses to schedule programs that flout accepted standards of morality, such as ABC's controversial *Soap*. Because the networks automatically "ratify anything [they] put on the air, right or wrong," they have an obligation to upgrade program content, he believes. The phenomenal success of the ABC mini-series *Roots*, which he praised as "one of the best damned things that's happened to TV in a long time," proved beyond question that "the American public can be led to something better." Following that example, Backe enthusiastically supported the production of a number of limited series of high quality.

More "inward-looking" than his immediate predecessors, Backe chose not to become an industry spokesman and preferred to focus his attention on the concerns of CBS. To facilitate internal corporate development and promote managerial effectiveness, he set up a training course for CBS middle managers, the first of its kind in the broadcast industry. "We want them to learn how to set up management objectives and how to measure people," he said, as quoted in *Fortune* (May 1977) magazine. "In our industry, you run into a lot of people who are very glib and attractive and bright. They are not always effective. I want to find the people who make things happen."

Although Backe's style of management is formal and, in his words, "pretty much according to the book" from the standpoint of business procedure, he is informal with corporate subordinates. "I get very involved in operations [and] I run formal business reviews on a regular basis," he admitted to Rance Crain, "but the other side of it is that I'm a very informal guy. I'm not hung up by the trappings of the office. I try to have personal relationships with people and humanize the organization as much as I can, because this office has enough of a horror about it that you do everything possible to knock down the built-in majesty, to get people to communicate with you."

At the annual stockholders' meeting in Los Angeles on April 20, 1977, Paley announced that Backe would take over the running of CBS's day-to-day operations as the company's chief executive officer on May 11. Paley retained his position as chairman of the board. Despite Paley's assurances that Backe had a free hand in the management of CBS's corporate operations, some business analysts speculated that the former chief executive's huge stock holdings and control of the board of directors guaranteed him continued power. "Paley has given up every position except emperor," one unidentified CBS official remarked, as quoted in *Time* (May 2, 1977) magazine. Backe was well aware of his delicate situation. "The toughest thing," he told the reporter for *Fortune*, "will be to impart my style of management to people who are obviously still wondering if Paley is really stepping down."

Intent on making CBS "as competitive as possible in every aspect," Backe was determined to be more of an activist than Paley, who concentrated on broadcasting. Among other things, Backe planned to expand CBS's publishing group by acquiring selective newspapers, such as shoppers' guides and business publications, and data collection and dissemination systems. Furthermore, he expected to make huge capital investments in CBS Records, with a view to the future, and he is committed to making further diversifications as long as they make sense.

As rumors of a massive talent hunt for a successor to Backe circulated through "Broadcasting Row" in October 1977, he made his most important move to date as chief executive officer. In an effort to reverse CBS's falling prime time ratings, Backe ordered a sweeping reorganization of the network's broadcast operations, patterned after those made earlier by ABC, the prime time leader in ratings. He replaced the presidents of both the broadcast group and the television network and created two new divisions, CBS Sports and CBS Entertainment, previously under the aegis of the network president. Despite repeated CBS denials, some media columnists, among them, Kay Gardella of the New York *Daily News*, conjectured that Paley, not Backe, was the driving force behind the structural changes.

John D. Backe stands about six feet tall and weighs about 175 pounds. He has brown eyes and black hair, graying at the temples. In his rare off-hours he plays an occasional game of tennis or reads historical novels, but his favorite pastime is flying his twin-engine, seven-passenger Cessna 411. He and his wife, the former Katherine A. Elliott, whom he married on October 22, 1955, and children, Kimberly and John, live in Basking Ridge, New Jersey. Backe was recently awarded an honorary Doctor of Laws degree from his undergraduate alma mater. He is a director of the Association of American Publishers and a Trustee of the Morris County (New Jersey) United Fund.

References: Advertising Age 48:53+ Mr 28 '77 pors; Fortune 94:33 N '76 por; N Y Times p74 O 14 '76 por, D p1 Ap 21 '77 por; Time 108:52 O 25 '76 por; Who's Who in America, 1976-77

Ball, Lucille

Aug. 6, 1911- Actress; producer. Address: b. Lucille Ball Productions, Inc., 780 N. Gower St., Hollywood, Calif. 90038; h. 1000 N. Roxbury Dr., Beverly Hills, Calif. 90213

NOTE: This biography supersedes the article that appeared in *Current Biography* in 1952.

Speaking "a universal language of wacky humor and warmth," the irrepressible redheaded actress Lucille Ball has gone on from

Lucille Ball

her instant success in *I Love Lucy* in 1951 to brighten TV screens with her inspired slapstick for over a quarter of a century. By the time of her announced retirement in 1974, after 179 episodes of her original situation comedy, 156 of *The Lucy Show*, 144 of *Here's Lucy*, plus many specials, her face had been seen "by more people, more often, than the face of any human being who ever lived," according to Terrence O'Flaherty's estimate in *TV Guide*. Variously called a "national treasure," a monument, an institution, a legend, and a daily habit, Lucille Ball is also an international personality whose shows have been dubbed in several different languages and aired in seventy-seven foreign countries over the years. In *Lucy* reruns and repeats of her films (nearly eighty in all) devoted Lucy-watchers can enjoy her comic expertise indefinitely. She is both a lovable clown and a shrewd business executive who successfully managed the mammoth film factory Desilu Productions from 1962 to 1967 and, beginning in 1968, Lucille Ball Productions. To further the cause of film as pure entertainment that provides, in her words, "hope, faith and fun" as an antidote to the "violence, sex, muck and mire on the screen" prevalent today, in 1974 Lucille Ball essayed the most demanding cinema role of her career: the heroine of *Mame*, an elaborately gowned, matronly woman rather than a madcap.

Of mixed Irish, Scottish, English, and French ancestry, Lucille Désirée Ball was born on August 6, 1911 in Celoron, a suburb of Jamestown, near Lake Chautauqua in western New York. Her parents were Henry Dunnell Ball, a telephone lineman who died before she was four, and Désirée (Hunt) Ball; they had one other child, a younger son, Fred. From her grandfather, Fred C. Hunt, a woodturner in a Jamestown furniture factory and an ardent Socialist, Lucille Ball derived her instinct for family loyalty and for survival by hard work.

In childhood Lucille Ball loved going to vaudeville shows and movies in Jamestown with her grandfather and then acting out two-reel comedies and serials like *The Perils of Pauline*. Encouraging her interest in home theatricals and school plays, her mother was in the habit of "making the costumes and storin' up the makeup and sending to Samuel French for plays," as the actress told James Gregory, who wrote *The Lucille Ball Story* (1974). Eventually, "DeDe" Ball became a faithful member of Lucy's studio audience, and before her death in 1977 her laugh could be heard on nearly every sound track. Telling about a high school performance of *Charley's Aunt*, Lucille Ball once remarked, as quoted in *Time* (May 26, 1952), "I played the lead, directed it, cast it, sold tickets, printed the posters, and hauled furniture to the school for scenery and props." She also appeared in a community theatre production of Bayard Veiller's melodrama *Within the Law*.

Nonetheless, Lucille Ball was a washout at the John Murray Anderson-Robert Milton Dramatic School in New York City, where she enrolled at the age of fifteen. Spellbound by the school's star pupil, Bette Davis, she felt, as she recalls, "terrified and useless." After six weeks she returned home to high school, but periodically renewed her courage to try again on Broadway. Although several sources report that Lucille Ball became a successful showgirl, she has said that her Broadway experience was limited to "some rehearsals and some calls." With her new theatrical-sounding name, Diane Belmont, she was hired for Earl Carroll's *Vanities* and the Shuberts' *Stepping Stones* and promptly fired. She then rehearsed for the third road company of Ziegfeld's *Rio Rita* and later for *Step Lively*, but was not called.

After a stint as a soda jerk in a Rexall drugstore on Broadway, Miss Ball turned to modeling as another means of paying the rent. She worked at Hattie Carnegie's elegant dress salon and in the evenings freelanced for commercial photographers and for the magazine illustrators McClelland Barclay and John Lagata, until a bout with rheumatoid arthritis disabled her for two years. Later, her nationwide exposure as the Chesterfield Cigarette Girl led to her selection in the summer of 1933 as a last-minute replacement for one of twelve Goldwyn Girls in Eddie Cantor's film *Roman Scandals* (United Artists, 1933). Moviegoers had earlier glimpsed Miss Ball as a walk-on in a beach scene in the New York-filmed *Broadway Thru a Keyhole* (United Artists, 1933).

During her first eighteen months in Hollywood, Lucille Ball merely decorated a total of ten films with unbilled parts under her $150-a-week contract with Goldwyn-United Artists. Sensing that her forte was comedy, she secured a contract with Columbia's stock company, for which she appeared in two-reel comedies with Leon Errol and the Three Stooges and had bit parts in five full-length films. As a nurse in *Carnival* (1935), the last of these, she won her first screen credit. She then spent seven years on the RKO lot, where she became "Queen of the B's" and enjoyed a gradual raise in salary from $50 a week to $3,500. After playing an anonymous mannequin in the fashion-show sequence of *Roberta* (1935) and making another unbilled appearance in *The Three Musketeers* (1935), she insisted, "I am *not* going to work as a show girl in a background anymore." Consequently, Lucille Ball was cast in a brief speaking role, with an individual identity for the first time on screen, in *I Dream Too Much* (1935). Between assignments she had been studying her craft at RKO's Little Theater. In the sixth of her 1936 releases, the musical *That Girl From Paris,* she stepped up to second lead, giving a performance that landed her a leading role in a Broadway-bound musical, *Hey Diddle Diddle,* which closed prematurely in early 1937 because of the death of its star, Conway Tearle.

The standouts among Lucille Ball's largely unrewarding roles in her twenty-two pictures over the next six years were a plucky, wisecracking, aspiring actress in *Stage Door* (1937); the temperamental, fading movie star of *The Affairs of Annabel* and *Annabel Takes a Tour* (both 1938), in which she teamed with Jack Oakie as her overenthusiastic press agent; the hardhearted woman on the rebound in *Five Came Back* (1939); the gold-digging burlesque queen of *Dance, Girl, Dance* (1940); and the top-billed spoiled heiress of *Too Many Girls* (1940), an adaptation of the Richard Rodgers-Lorenz Hart Broadway musical hit, in which, as before, her singing was dubbed. One of the four football-hero bodyguards of the last-named film was Desi Arnaz, a Cuban bandleader and bongo player whom Miss Ball married on November 30, 1940.

In RKO's *The Big Street* (1942), as Her Highness, an embittered, crippled nightclub singer, Miss Ball elicited James Agee's encomium, much quoted from *Time* (September 7, 1942): "Pretty Lucille Ball, who was born for the parts Ginger Rogers sweats over, tackles her 'emotional' role as if it were sirloin and she didn't care who was looking." Impressed by her dynamic trouping in that Damon Runyon story, MGM officials created her new look as a "strawberry-pink" redhead and signed her to star in the Cole Porter musical *DuBarry Was a Lady* (1943), opposite Red Skelton. While she was learning the use of props from the silent comedian Buster Keaton, she graced such routine programmers for MGM as *Best Foot Forward* and *As Thousands Cheer* (1943), *Meet the People* (1944), and the lavish *Ziegfeld Follies* (1946). She found more satisfying screen moments in lively comic scenes with Keenan Wynn, as a flip realtor in *Without Love* (1945) and as a tempestuous, scatterbrained show girl in the farcical *Easy to Wed* (1946).

Partly because of her disenchantment with such mediocre cinema fare as United Artists' *Lured* (1947) and Columbia's *Her Husband's Affairs* (1947), Lucille Ball accepted a role in the CBS radio show *My Favorite Husband* in July 1947 as Liz, the featherbrained wife of a Midwestern banker, played first by Lee Bowman and then by Richard Denning. The comedy series ran to March 1951. Miss Ball had earlier appeared on radio in 1938 as featured comedienne on Phil Baker's show and on Jack Haley's *Wonder Bread Show* and later had been heard on such programs as *Lux Radio Theatre, Suspense,* and *Screen Guild Playhouse.* She also turned to the legitimate stage, touring during late 1947 and early 1948 for twenty-two weeks in Elmer Rice's *Dream Girl.* In the challenging role of bemused Georgina Allerton, she demonstrated "her efficiency as a comedienne" and was able to "tinge a scene delicately with pathos," as Edwin Schallert attested in the Los Angeles *Times.*

At Bob Hope's request Miss Ball went to Paramount to portray another nightclub singer for *Sorrowful Jones* (1949) and rejoined him for the slapstick and sight gags of *Fancy Pants* (1950). But her talents had been "shockingly wasted," her admirers complained, as secretaries in *Easy Living* (RKO, 1949) and *Miss Grant Takes Richmond* (Columbia, 1949). Her amusing *The Fuller Brush Girl* (Columbia, 1950) had only limited success, and she lost the prize lead in the film version of *Born Yesterday* to Judy Holliday. Soon afterward, however, in *I Love Lucy* she found the showcase for her comedic gifts.

Before the premiere of *I Love Lucy* on October 15, 1951, Lucille Ball and Desi Arnaz went on a nationwide vaudeville tour to persuade CBS executives that the public would accept the comedy team of an American redhead and a Cuban bandleader with a marked accent. Their twenty-minute act, which included a trick-cello bit, a seal routine, and a "Cuban-Pete"—"Sally Sweet" medley, as they played themselves, was transmuted into a half-hour situation comedy about a young couple, Ricky and Lucy Ricardo, and their best friends, Fred and Ethel Mertz, who are also their landlords. The innovative production method, with each episode performed in sequence, like a play, before an audience and filmed with a revolutionary three-camera technique, had a direct influence on the general shift from live television to film. *I Love Lucy* rated as the number-one show within six months; accumulated over 200 awards, including five Emmys (it was nominated twenty-three times); and became, along with Milton Berle's Texaco show, *The Beverly Hillbillies,* and *All in the Family,* one of TV's four "all-time hits." It is indicative of the series' extraordinary emotional hold that on the occasion of Little Ricky's birth more people watched *I Love Lucy* than the inauguration of President Dwight D. Eisenhower. Through advanced filming, the birth of the fictional son coincided with that of Lucille Ball's second child, Desiderio Alberto Arnaz y de Acha IV, on January 19, 1953. Her daughter, Lucie Désirée Arnaz, had been born on July 17, 1951.

The production of the show, with complete plot summaries of each episode, has been generously documented in *Lucy and Ricky and Fred and Ethel: The Story of "I Love Lucy"* by Bart Andrews (1976). Earlier, Jack Gould of the New York *Times* (March 1, 1953) had analyzed the distinctive appeal of its treatment of the husband-versus-wife theme: "[It is] the extraordinary discipline and intuitive understanding of farce that gives *I Love Lucy* its engaging lilt and lift. . . . Only after a firm foundation of credibility has been established is the element of absurdity introduced. It is in the smooth transition from sense to nonsense that *I Love Lucy* imparts both a warmth and a reality to the slapstick romp which comes as the climax." While Lucille Ball has always credited her then-husband with the concept and execution of the undertaking, in his autobiography, *A Book* (1976), Desi Arnaz accords her "ninety percent of the credits," among all those involved, for its success. In an assortment of such mirth-provoking guises as a ballerina, matador, Indian, Martian, grape stomper, statue, and toothless hillbilly, Lucille Ball exhibited unflagging physical stamina and comic flawlessness. Her superb sense of timing made her, according to Jack Gould, "the distaff equivalent of Jack Benny."

During the six-season run of *I Love Lucy*, which ended on May 6, 1957, moviegoers saw an amiable variation on the "yelp-mates" of TV in *The Long, Long Trailer* (MGM 1954), which one critic called "a comedy with gorgeous moments." Another Desi-Lucy film, however, *Forever, Darling* (MGM, 1956), in which a guardian angel saves a troubled marriage, was judged a weak meld of comedy and fantasy. With the sale of the rerun rights of *I Love Lucy* to CBS, the producing company Desilu, formed in 1950, was able to acquire its own studio, the former RKO lot, where many landmark TV shows had been made. From November 1957 through April 1960 the *I Love Lucy* format persisted through thirteen hour-long specials, each a lavishly budgeted *Lucille Ball-Desi Arnaz Show* focussing on the familiar quartet's world-hopping antics with many top guest stars. But increasing business stresses together with personal differences led to the divorce of the seemingly ideal TV couple on May 4, 1960.

As she began to follow a separate career, Lucille Ball at last realized her dream of Broadway success, opening in the musical comedy *Wildcat* on December 16, 1960. To prepare for the limited but arduous role of Wildy Jackson, a lithe, tomboyish oil driller, she had months of vocal exercises with Carlo Menotti as her coach. "Hey, Look Me Over," which she sang in her husky voice, became a smash hit, but some New York critics were unenthusiastic about an otherwise rather awkward and unamusing libretto. "I kept fixing and changing *Wildcat* up to the night I closed," she told Rex Reed in an interview for the New York *Times* (October 8, 1967). The show ended its standing-room-only run of 171 performances on June 3, 1961 because of the star's illness.

To the delight of the many fans of her zany Lucy character, Lucille Ball portrayed widowed Lucy Carmichael of *The Lucy Show* during the five and a half years from October 1962 to the spring of 1968. In that series she shared a house with her two children and the divorcée Vivian Bagley, played by Vivian Vance, and worked for the banker Theodore Mooney, played by Gale Gordon. About the time of the premiere of *The Lucy Show* she had bought out the shares of her former husband in Desilu. The personal touch that she brought to her presidency helped to build the company into one of the country's largest producers of filmed television shows before the vast complex was sold to Gulf & Western Industries in early 1967 for $17,000,000. In March 1968 she formed Lucille Ball Productions, whose first major undertaking was *Here's Lucy*. Lucille Ball starred as another widow, Lucy Carter, who supported herself and her son and daughter (played by her own offspring) by toiling for her irascible brother-in-law (another role filled by Gale Gordon) in a predictably wacky employment office. The series was seen on CBS-TV from the fall of 1968 through the spring of 1974.

On two of her periodic returns to motion pictures Miss Ball costarred again with Bob Hope—in *The Facts of Life* (United Artists, 1960), a spoof of extramarital flirtation, and *Critic's Choice* (Warner, 1963), a farce about a drama critic whose wife writes a play. After taking a cameo role in *A Guide for the Married Man* (Twentieth Century, 1967), she appeared opposite Henry Fonda in *Yours, Mine and Ours* (United Artists, 1968), an innocuous but warmly received family film in which the widow she portrayed resembled a matured, somewhat subdued Lucy.

There were traces of Lucy also in *Mame* (Warner, 1974), a synthesis of Lucille Ball's acting, singing, and dancing talents. The role is a favorite of the actress because she feels in tune with high-spirited, sophisticated Mame's attitude toward life in the song "Open a New Window." Despite the thorough drubbing that many anti-*Mame* critics gave the expensive, old-fashioned production, Miss Ball, who promoted the movie on a lengthy personal appearance tour, won such accolades as Judith

Crist's validation in *New York* (March 18, 1974) of her "penetrating warmth and inner humor." Conceding that Miss Ball "has some great moments," Vincent Canby of the New York *Times* (March 8, 1974) anticipated the popular reaction: "I have great reservations about *Mame*, but I suspect a lot of people couldn't care less."

Miss Ball's more recent TV performances included her portrayal of the dowdy, overweight, sharp-tongued Norma Michaels of *Happy Anniversary and Goodbye* (November 19, 1974), in which she played opposite Art Carney, who rejoined her in *What Now, Catherine Curtis?* (March 30, 1976), a modest script about a woman confronting life alone after twenty-three years of marriage. She headlined the *Lucille Ball Special Starring Lucille Ball and Dean Martin* (March 1, 1975) and the *Lucille Ball Special Starring Lucille Ball and Jackie Gleason* (December 3, 1975) and impersonated the late Sophie Tucker on NBC-TV in Bob Hope's *All-Star Tribute to Vaudeville* (March 25, 1977). In another of her specials, aired over CBS-TV in November 1977, the President's mother, Lillian Carter, made a special appearance. Also featured in the show were Vivian Vance, Gale Gordon, Ed McMahon, and Steve Allen, among others.

Among Lucille Ball's countless honors were the "Lucy Day" at the New York World's Fair on August 31, 1964 and the "Comedienne of the Century" designation at a benefit show, *To Lucy with Love*, at the Los Angeles Music Center on May 23, 1971. Testimonials and vintage film clips in the two-hour *CBS Salutes Lucy—The First 25 Years*, aired on November 28, 1976, capped her tributes.

Blue-eyed Lucille Ball, who has been described as "sleek, serene, and stunning," stands five feet six inches tall and weighs about 120 pounds. She is a Scrabble enthusiast, a dog lover, an admirer of the painters Norman Rockwell and Andrew Wyeth, and a disciple of Norman Vincent Peale's doctrine of positive thinking. Although politically conservative, back in 1936 in an effort to please her beloved, elderly grandfather she registered to vote for the Communist party. During the 1950's, however, the House Un-American Activities Committee cleared her of any charges of Communism. Uninterested in the women's movement, she once declared, as quoted in the *Christian Science Monitor* (April 14, 1975), "I'm so liberated that I'm just delighted to have a husband who does things for me." Her husband, Gary Morton, whom she married on November 19, 1961, was formerly a stand-up comedian and is now her executive producer. They have homes in Beverly Hills and Palm Springs and a hideaway at Snowmass, Colorado, where Lucille Ball suffered a multiple leg fracture in a skiing accident in 1972. Indefatigable as ever, she turned up on the *Mame* set a year later to begin rehearsing the dances.

References: Films in R 22:321+ Je '71 pors; Good H 166:50+ Je '68 pors, 183:118+ N '76 pors; Look 35:54+ S 7 '71 pors; McCalls 100:72+ Je '73 pors; N Y Times II p19 O 8 '67; Sat Eve Post 244:60+ Winter '73 pors; TV Guide 22:15+ Jl 6 '74 por; Andrews, Bart. Lucy and Ricky and Fred and Ethel (1967); Foremost Women in Communications (1970); Gregory, James. The Lucille Ball Story (1974); Parish, James Robert. The RKO Gals (1974)

Beene, Geoffrey

Aug. 30, 1927- Fashion designer. Address: b. Geoffrey Beene, Inc., 550 7th Ave., New York City, N.Y. 10018; h. 333 E. 69th St., New York City, N.Y. 10021

Quality, originality, and surpassing elegance in ready-to-wear fashions are the hallmarks of Geoffrey Beene, the internationally popular designer who became, in 1976, the first American in his field to open a manufacturing branch in Europe. That same year Geoffrey Beene, Inc., which he founded on a shoestring in 1963, grossed $47 million at wholesale. The creative and unorthodox Beene first attracted attention in the late 1960's for his sophisticated, figure-flattering, simple styles that were, at once, classic and contemporary. "I no longer look at a sketch and say 'Is it beautiful?'" Beene remarked recently. "If it's logical, it's beautiful. It's more conceptual design than fashion design." The winner of three Coty American Fashion Critics' Awards, Beene was elevated to the Fashion Hall of Fame in 1974.

Geoffrey Beene was born in Haynesville, a small town in northwestern Louisiana, on August 30, 1927, the son of Albert Beene, an automobile salesman, and Lorene (Waller) Beene, the daughter of a prosperous cotton planter. After graduating from Haynesville High School at age sixteen, Beene enrolled in the premed program at Tulane University in New Orleans. "In the South, if you're not a doctor, lawyer, merchant or thief, everything else is a hobby," he explained to Jerry Bowles in an interview for *Vogue* (January 1977) magazine. "So my family thought I ought to be a doctor. The first two years weren't bad, because it was classroom work, but the third year we got into vivisection, cadavers, and all that horrendous stuff. And every disease we studied I got."

During lectures, Beene amused himself by sketching the elaborate gowns Adrian had designed for the 1943 film version of the costume musical *DuBarry Was a Lady*. He eventually realized that he lacked, in his words, "the proper dedication or constitution to be a good doctor," and dropped out of college without taking his degree. His disappointed parents sent him to California for what he has since called "a rest cure" and completion of his studies at the University of Southern California. But before classes began, Beene took a job as an assistant in the display department of the downtown Los Angeles branch of I. Magnin, the fashionable clothing store chain. Recognizing Beene's flair for design, a Magnin executive advised the young man to pursue a career in fashion.

In the mid-1940's Beene moved to New York City, where he studied at the Traphagen School of Fashion. He then went on to Paris for intensive training in sketching, designing, and sewing, a terrifying experience for a man who by his own admission had "never been good at little things with [his] hands." Beene learned the art of cutting fabric from Molyneux, a retired tailor and a master of the figure-flattering bias cut. On his return to New York in 1949, he worked briefly for Samuel Winston, a custom salon, before accepting a job as assistant to the chief designer of Harmay, a new ready-to-wear house in the garment district. He was fired eight years later, because, as he explained to Jerry Bowles, "I began to get into very modern clothes and was affected by chemises and very loose things. . . . They didn't believe in that sort of thing. I still like that sort of thing and they're out of business; that's a commentary on that."

Teal Traina, another promising young designer, immediately asked Beene to join his fledgling firm. His first collection for Teal Traina, in 1958, was widely acclaimed for its originality. His unconventional designs for Traina's 1961 summer line were no less than "sensational," according to the fashion reporter of the New York *Herald Tribune*, who singled out a low-waisted, flapper-style raspberry linen dress with a flaring, knee-baring skirt as "one of the major hits" of the New York summer fashion season. His fall collection featured a sexy 1930's look with face-framing hats, fur pieces, and hip-length pullovers worn over pleated or flared "cloche" skirts. One delighted fashion reporter, who lavishly praised the entire line, commended Beene for his uncommon ability to "combine the kookie and the commercial."

In June 1963 Geoffrey Beene set up shop under his own name in a champagne-colored showroom on Seventh Avenue, the center of the fashion industry in the United States. His partner in the new enterprise was Leo Orlandi, the former production director for Teal Traina. Unveiled in the spring of 1963, Beene's first collection had the looser fit, eased waistlines, bloused tops, and flared skirts that characterized his designs throughout the 1960's. The clothes, priced from $90 to $375, were snapped up by enthusiastic dress buyers from such prestigious Fifth Avenue stores as Henri Bendel, Lord & Taylor, Bergdorf Goodman, Saks Fifth Avenue, and Bonwit Teller. In its first year of operation Geoffrey Beene, Inc., sold $500,000 worth of clothes. Within two years, the figure jumped to $4 million.

Always aiming for a simple, comfortable, contemporary look, Beene stressed in his 1964 spring collection unadorned, sleeveless linen shifts; his fall designs included subtly shaped wool coats and dresses and slinky, close-to-the-body evening dresses. "Each season I try to achieve a greater simplicity," he told Bernadine Morris in an interview for the New York *Times* (May 13, 1964). "The more you learn about clothes, the more you realize what has to be left off. Cut and line become increasingly important. Simplification becomes a very complicated procedure."

To emphasize the simplicity of his designs, Beene paid special attention to intricate dressmaking details, such as tiny wrist buttons, white collars and cuffs, narrow belts, and tucked bodices, as well as to fabric. He regularly made the rounds of European textile houses in search of unusual fabrics and in 1965 built a large part of his spring collection around the dramatic prints of Tzaims Luksus. Following the lead of the more trendy British designers, he lifted the skirt length of his spring suits to just above the knee. Beene argued that the short skirts were in better proportion to the long, narrow jackets, but many buyers, as yet unused to the mini, specified regular length when ordering the suits.

In one twelve-month period in the mid-1960's Beene won the Coty American Fashion Critics' Award, the most prestigious of the fashion awards, the Ethel Traphagen Award, the Neiman-Marcus Award, and the first of two awards from the National Cotton Council of America for his trend-setting use of the native American fiber. Regarding Beene as the quintessential American designer, the Fashion Group chose him to represent the United States at the first International Fashion Week in Mexico in 1966. That same year, he was asked to contribute a dress to a new costume and fashion museum in Cincinnati. He selected as a representative design a chiffon evening gown that effectively combined a 1930's-style bias cutskirt, a very contemporary high turtleneck collar, and batwing sleeves.

With his reputation firmly established, Beene presented the most varied, imaginative, and, in the eyes of many buyers, the best collection of his career in 1967. His huge spring line included high-waisted "little girl" dresses, short "rice paddy" pants, rather conservative flannel jumpers, sexy silk print harem pajamas, short but full evening dresses trimmed with dyed-to-match ostrich feathers, and a long black dress tailored like a cassock and worn with the traditional padre's hat. For fall, he turned out ten-shaped, long-sleeved "pseudo-coatdresses" in well-mannered fabrics like gray flannel, tailored suits, pantdresses, and many minidresses. His evening creations were even more striking: a white poet's blouse over a pale pink satin bell skirt belted in acid green; a long, slim gray flannel column buttoned with rhinestones; tweed evening pants paired with jeweled or lamé jackets; short, sequined dresses in abstract or argyll patterns; and long, sequined gowns cut like oversized football jerseys, complete with numerals. His most publicized creation of the year, however, was the "rather regal and a little austere" pure white silk faille bridal gown he designed for the White House wedding of Lynda Bird Johnson, the older daughter of President Lyndon B. Johnson.

Over the next few years Geoffrey Beene continued to mingle contemporary designs with fanciful creations evoking bygone eras. His 1968 collection, for example, included long-sleeved, full-skirted evening gowns with see-through bodices as well as severely tailored, 1930's-style gangster suits, one of them whimsically named "Alice Capone." Other popular designs from that period were a long, clinging, backless black velvet dress sprinkled with silver spangles inspired by an Art Nouveau poster; high-necked Victorian gentlewoman dresses with small, tight-fitting bodices and full skirts; Sicilian peasant costumes; and restaurant-length dresses with narrow skirts reminiscent of the hobble skirts of the early 1920's. To keep his shows from becoming boring, Beene always included at least one tongue-in-cheek creation. His outrageous designs include a coat entirely constructed of black, wooden buttons, a short evening dress cut like a tutu, with a sequined bodice and feather skirt; and a pink lamé coat with an eight-foot boa of ostrich feathers and aluminum foil.

His phenomenal success afforded Beene an opportunity to venture into other sectors of the fashion industry. In the late 1960's Dan Grossman introduced a collection of Beene-designed fur jackets, boleros, dinner skirts, and street-length coats, and Roxanne presented his unorthodox "covered-up look" swimwear line, which featured a long-sleeved, gray "sweatshirt suit." To avoid the designer's nightmare of trying to find the perfect accessory to complement each outfit, Beene began creating his own abstract print silk scarves and shiny, industrial-looking bracelets and necklaces, which were manufactured and marketed at modest prices by Kramer, a costume jewelry company. He even tried his hand at designing for the Broadway stage, when he acted as fashion consultant, in 1968, for *Avanti!*, a short-lived comedy by Samuel Taylor about an American businessman and an English girl who meet in Rome and fall in love.

Branching out into menswear, Beene designed a twenty-five-piece wardrobe for Eagle Clothes, Inc., in 1969. Markedly influenced by American films of the 1930's and 1940's, the line included wool blazers and jersey slacks, aviator jackets in both jersey and leather, and business suits with wide lapels, fitted jackets, and straight, full, cuffed trousers. The unquestioned hit of the collection was a maxicoat of taffy-colored ciré cut like a duster and worn with a ten-foot-long white silk muffler. He showed no evening clothes because he wanted to liberate men from tuxedos, starched shirts, and funereal black ties.

In the wake of the midi debacle and the slump in the fashion industry in the early 1970's, Geoffrey Beene began experimenting with softness, fullness, and movement in practical, comfortable clothes. His new direction, first evident in the easy, unfitted styles of his 1973 summer collection, was an immediate success. Buyers were particularly enchanted by his handsome crepe de chine evening shirts, worn unbuttoned almost to the waist and tucked into long, full pajama pants in such sensuous fabrics as silk, lamé, and chiffon. Those timeless creations earned him, in 1974, his third Coty award and a place in the Coty Fashion Hall of Fame.

The unmistakable stamp of quality that distinguished Beene's opulent couture designs was equally obvious in his relatively inexpensive, almost disposable Beene Bag sportswear. Priced from $12 to $150, Beene Bag's clean-cut, casually elegant cotton separates, all with such custom-made touches as Madeira embroidery edgings, particularly appealed to younger women. The soft, sensuous smocks and chemises with just a hint of the figure underneath that highlighted his spirited and contemporary 1975 spring and summer collections for both the couture line and Beene Bag won him a standing ovation from buyers at the opening in November 1974.

Admittedly excited by the possibilities of fabric, Beene mixes seemingly incompatible "poor and rich" materials to achieve his contemporary look. He haunts street markets in New York City and in Europe looking for scarves, ropes, belts, bags, and other common objects he can turn into something new and personal. Unlike his more staid counterparts at the European high fashion houses, Beene does not hesitate to use plastic sandals and a dishtowel hat to serve as accessories for a dress with a $1,000 price tag. Similarly, he often uses unexpected fabric combinations, such as wool and satin, handkerchief linen and raw silk, quilted ticking and chiffon, and jersey and taffeta. Although he favors neutrals to bright colors, he has, on occasion, created eye-catching outfits in chrome yellow or red.

Anxious to see if his clothes could succeed internationally, Beene eagerly accepted when he was invited to show his collection in Milan, Italy in 1975. Encouraged by his success there, he decided to manufacture and distribute his clothes on the continent, thus avoiding the prohibitive taxes and duties on imported American fashions. Cofil S. P. A., founded in Italy by Beene in 1976, produces and markets a somewhat edited collection of the couture and Beene Bag line for sale in Europe and the Far East. (His New York base still supplies North America and Australia.) Beene's pioneering effort brought him a special citation from the Coty Awards jury for his leadership in promoting respect for American fashion abroad. Moreover, the sales of his couture line increased by almost 100 percent after just one year of European operation.

Previewed in Milan, Beene's 1977 and 1978 collections centered around the unstructured, supple shapes that have become his trademark. Among his most applauded designs were ankle- or mid-calf-length full skirts, sensuous wrap tops, soft Italian cotton fishnet T-shirts, suits with easy skirts and unfitted, quilted cotton jackets, and minimally designed strapless evening dresses.

Shy and reticent, Beene rarely accompanies his models and staff on the traveling "trunk shows" showcasing his clothes. "It's like a zoo," he has reportedly protested. "People come to see how much I weigh, how nearsighted I am, how short I am. Then they throw me a peanut and leave."

In recent years, Beene has made dozens of profitable franchising arrangements. Under those agreements, he designs, among other things, resort jewelry for Bergère Originals, shoes and handbags for Andrew Geller, scarves for Jewel Case, eyeglass frames for Victory Optical, panty hose for Bonnie Doon, loungewear for Swirl, and linens for Fieldcrest. He also introduced a men's cologne, Grey Flannel, and two fragrances for women: the woodsy, slightly fruity signature scent, Geoffrey Beene, and the ultra-sophisticated Red. Despite dozens of tempting corporate offers, Beene has refused to sell his company. "I'd never sell the firm," he told Bowles. "I do exactly what I want now and I have a clear idea of what I want from my work. I don't care if I ever get any bigger."

Geoffrey Beene is a "round, teddy-bearish" man, standing about five feet five inches tall, with dark brown hair and dark eyes shielded by owlish spectacles. A genial host, the designer often caps a rigorous work week with relaxed Sunday night dinner parties in his elegant New York duplex apartment. Among his hobbies he lists collecting regional cookbooks, paintings, antiques, and stamps. At his Fire Island beach cooperative Beene finds gardening "the most rewarding" of all his pastimes.

Beene once described his typical customer as an "outgoing," "terribly knowledgeable" woman with an "intelligent approach to fashion." "She will no longer take the word of any one designer," he said. "I simply want to present a certain feeling, and then let her select for herself whatever suits her character and sense of humor." Numbered among his legions of fans are Jacqueline Onassis, Gloria Vanderbilt Cooper, and former First Lady Patricia Nixon. One fashionable admirer explained Beene's almost universal appeal to Jerry Bowles: "Geoffrey's dresses may be a little square compared to what some others are doing, but they're beautiful and they're exquisitely made. When you see a woman wearing a Halston dress, you say, 'That's a Halston dress.' When you see someone wearing one of Geoffrey's things, you will probably recognize them as his, but you'll say, 'My God, what a well-dressed woman.' That's why we love him."

References: N Y Post p53 D 1 '67; N Y Times III p 1+ N 20 '77 por; N Y Times Mag p48+ Ja 9 '77; Vogue 167:126+ Ja '77 pors; Who's Who in America, 1976-77

Bokassa I, Emperor

Feb. 22, 1921- Sovereign of the Central African Empire. Address: Imperial Court, Beringo, Central African Empire

On December 4, 1977 Bokassa I of the Central African Empire, who calls himself "the world's first socialist emperor," formally crowned himself, in imitation of Napoleon I, who placed the imperial crown of France on his own head on December 2, 1804. The extravagant coronation ceremony, estimated to have cost as much as $30,000,000, lent a comic opera atmosphere to the otherwise grim re-

Emperor Bokassa I

ality of poverty and oppression prevailing in the landlocked former French colony of some 1,800,000 people.

A career soldier with over two decades of service in the French army, Jean-Bedel Bokassa took control of what was then the Central African Republic in a military coup in 1966, was named President for life in 1972, and became constitutional monarch in December 1976 when a new constitution turned the republic into an empire. Although some observers, including United States Embassy officials, maintain that Bokassa has brought some progress to his people, others agree with Los Angeles *Times* correspondent David Lamb's assessment of Bokassa as "one of Africa's most forgettable presidents, a tragi-comic figure who was never able to come to grips with the problems facing his impoverished country."

Jean-Bedel Bokassa, one of the twelve children of Mindogon Mgboundoulou and his wife, Marie Yokowo, was born on February 22, 1921 in the village of Boubangui, Lobaye Province, in the colony of Oubangui-Chari, in what was then French Equatorial Africa. His father, like his grandfather before him, was a land-owning village chief of the Mbaka ethnic group, which provided administrative aides to the French authorities as well as leaders of the resistance to colonial rule. The late Barthélémy Boganda, who launched Oubangui-Chari on the road to independence before his death in an airplane crash in 1959, was Bokassa's uncle, and David Dacko, who became the first President of the Central African Republic in 1960, is his cousin. When Bokassa was six, his father was assassinated at a local prefect's office in a tribal conflict (or, according to one source, died as a result of official mistreatment), and his grief-stricken mother committed suicide.

Educated at the Ecole Sainte Jeanne d'Arc in M'Baiki and at Roman Catholic missionary schools in Bangui and Brazzaville, Bokassa originally planned to study for the priesthood. He decided, however, after the outbreak of World War II in 1939, to join the French army as a private, and after the fall of France became a member of an African unit of General Charles de Gaulle's Free French forces. In August 1940 he took part in the campaign at Brazzaville that led to the capture of General Husson, the Vichy regime's acting governor-general of French Equatorial Africa, and the establishment of a Free French government there. Promoted to company sergeant in 1950, Bokassa compiled a distinguished combat record in Indochina and survived the defeat of French forces in 1954 at Dien Bien Phu. In 1956 he was commissioned a second lieutenant. He returned to Bangui, now the capital of the new Central African Republic, in 1960 and retired from the French army the following year with the rank of captain. His dozen decorations included the Croix de Guerre and membership in the Légion d'Honneur.

Asked by President David Dacko to build up the new nation's armed forces, Bokassa began in 1960 to organize an efficient, French-trained 400-man Central African army. In 1963, then a major, he was designated army commander in chief, and, in 1964, chief of the general staff. He represented his country at international meetings, including the defense councils of the Afro-Malagasy Union, a grouping of French-speaking African states, and in February 1965 he was elected president of the defense committee of the Organization of African Unity.

Despite President Dacko's efforts at economic reform, his government was unable to cope with growing budget deficits and a stagnant economy, brought on by corruption and inefficiency. Although Dacko eliminated the political opposition in late 1960 and made the Mouvement pour l'Evolution Sociale de l'Afrique Noire (MESAN) the country's only political party, discontent was widespread. His move in 1964 to establish diplomatic relations with the People's Republic of China dismayed military circles and French commercial interests in the Central African Republic. To cope with disastrous financial conditions, Dacko introduced such unpopular austerity measures in 1965 as a 10 percent reduction in civil service salaries. His demand for a substantial cut in the 1966 military budget angered Bokassa, now a colonel, who had taken control of the Ministry of War.

On December 31, 1965 Bokassa seized control of the Central African Republic in a relatively bloodless military coup d'etat. Acting on information about a Chinese-inspired plot to take over the government, he put the police chief and several government ministers in custody, surrounded the Presidential palace with loyal paratroopers, and placed Dacko under house arrest. In the early hours of January 1, 1966, after obtaining a signed statement from Dacko turning over power to him, Bokassa declared over Radio Bangui: "The hour of justice has sounded. The bourgeoisie is no more, and a new era of equality between all citizens is beginning." Some sources indicate that Bokassa acted with French support, to prevent the rich uranium deposits recently discovered in the Central African Republic from falling into the hands of hostile powers.

Immediately after his takeover, Bokassa suspended relations with Communist China, expelled some fifty Chinese advisers, and seized large stores of Chinese weapons. During the next few days he dissolved the National Assembly, established a governing Revolutionary Council composed of military officers, former Cabinet ministers, and civil servants, proclaimed himself President, Prime Minister, commander in chief of the armed forces, and leader of MESAN. Although Bokassa freed most political prisoners, he dealt harshly with such alleged conspirators as former security chief Jean-Baptiste Mounoumbaye, who was eventually executed. Disavowing long-range political ambitions, he declared that he was "a soldier, not a politician," and promised that he would hold elections as soon as order was restored and the economy placed on a firm footing.

In the beginning Bokassa tried to restore a sound economy and alleviate the inequalities of the Dacko regime. He instituted an agricultural modernization plan called "Operation Bokassa" and expanded exports of cotton, coffee, groundnuts, timber, and livestock. In June 1966 his government established a national diamond bureau and permitted the formation of an international consortium of American, French, Dutch, and Israeli companies for the marketing of diamonds. In 1968 a $11,600,000 textile complex, the country's largest economic enterprise, was established with French aid, and in 1969 a French-built uranium processing plant began operations at Bakouma. Cotton production increased by 25 percent during 1967-68, and diamond exports doubled between 1965 and 1968. After 1970, however, the economy stagnated, partly because of climactic and geographic factors, but perhaps more importantly, because of mismanagement and political instability.

A major factor was undoubtedly Bokassa's erratic behavior and megalomania, for notwithstanding his initial assertion that his regime was to be only temporary, he became obsessed with maintaining himself in power. Portraits of Bokassa appeared everywhere, streets and public buildings were named after him, and the mere mention of democracy and elections was forbidden. As provided for by treaty, the French government dutifully dispatched a company of paratroopers to the Central African Republic at his request in November 1967 to forestall a real or imagined plot against him. In April 1969 Bokassa ordered the execution of the Health Minister and paratroop commander, Lieutenant Colonel Alexandre Banza, once one of his closest assistants, for allegedly plotting to assassinate him.

After becoming lieutenant general in December 1970 Bokassa outlawed strikes and demonstrations, imposed strict censorship on foreign news, and barred civilians from military installations. To celebrate Mothers Day in 1971, he freed all women prisoners and ordered the execution of men convicted of serious crimes against women. A year later, incensed by a crime wave that included a burglary of the presidential palace, Bokassa supervised the beating, by soldiers using clubs and rifle butts, of forty-six prisoners convicted of theft. Three died as a result, while the rest were displayed in Bangui's public square.

At odds with his own government team, Bokassa reshuffled his Cabinet as often as six times in a single year and took over a large number of ministerial posts. In addition to being President, Prime Minister, and head of the armed forces, he served as Defense Minister from 1966 to 1976 and as Minister of Justice from 1966 to 1970. He held the portfolios of Information and of Agriculture and Stockbreeding from 1970 to 1974, and those of Civil and Military Aviation, of Land, River, and Air Transport, of Civil Service, and of Mines from 1973 to 1976. From 1971 to 1976 he headed the Ministry of Public Health and Population, in 1973-74 and again in 1976 he held the portfolio of Trade and Industry, and in 1976 he was Minister of Posts and Telecommunications. In March 1972, Bokassa—who in the previous year had assumed the rank of full general—convened a national congress of MESAN, which unanimously proclaimed him President for Life. In 1974 Bokassa added to his many titles by becoming Marshal of the Central African Republic.

Bokassa's unpredictable nature was reflected in his foreign policy. Although the Central African Republic, as a member of the French Community, depended on France for economic and defense aid, relations were frequently strained. When in February 1968 Bokassa's government broke ties with the moderate, French-oriented Union Douanière et Economique de l'Afrique Centrale (UDEAC) and joined with Chad and Zaire (then known as Congo-Kinshasa) in forming the Union des Etats de l'Afrique Centrale (UEAC), the move was interpreted as a blow to France. But UEAC succumbed to internal tensions within less than a year, and Bokassa became reconciled with France after bringing his government back into UDEAC. Relations tensed again when Bokassa, who had established diplomatic relations with several Eastern European countries and led a delegation to the Soviet Union, declared in October 1970 that he was turning toward the socialist nations. But when the expected economic aid from the Communist bloc failed to materialize, Bokassa returned to the Western camp, and at de Gaulle's funeral in November 1970 he was led away from the graveside sobbing "Papa, Papa!"

With de Gaulle's successors, Presidents Georges Pompidou and Valery Giscard d'Estaing, Bokassa observed his familiar routine of occasional skirmishes, followed by reconciliations. In 1971 conflicts arose over Bokassa's abortive plan to transfer the Banque Centrale des Etats de l'Afrique Equatoriale from Paris to Bangui, and his insistence on establishing an independent airline, separate from the French-controlled Air Afrique. Other controversies arose over Bokassa's nationalization schemes, introduced in 1974, which affected French businesses, and his periodic harassment of the French press. With the United States, Bokassa has maintained cordial relations, despite a formal American protest against the arrest and mistreatment of two Western newsmen in Bangui in the summer of 1977 and a more recent announcement by the State Department that it was phasing out its aid program to his country because of Bokassa's human rights violations. On the whole, Bokassa has managed to establish working relationships with most of the world's rival power blocs. He is now friendly with both China—which he visited in 1976—and the Soviet Union, and he receives aid from the major Western nations and the U.N. Through an Israeli intermediary he deals with South Africa, and he also has a Lebanese adviser to help him maintain relations with Arab countries.

Although in January 1975 Bokassa relinquished the Prime Ministership to MESAN vice-president Elizabeth Domitien—the first woman to become formal head of an African government—he remained the undisputed ruler of the Central African Republic. In March 1975 his international prestige was enhanced when he acted as host to French President Giscard d'Estaing and leaders of thirteen French-speaking African countries at a summit conference in Bangui to stress the overwhelming need for a new world economic order.

Bokassa reorganized his government once more in September 1976, when he established a thirty-one-member Council of the Central African Revolution with himself as President and David Dacko as his closest personal adviser. When, in October, President Muammar el-Qaddafi of oil-rich Libya paid a visit to him, Bokassa converted to Islam and adopted the Moslem name Salah Eddine Ahmed (Defender of the Faith). But after the Libyan ruler's promises of financial aid proved to be empty ones, he dropped the name and returned to the Christian fold.

On December 4, 1976, after a new constitution was approved by a special congress of MESAN, the Central African Republic became the Central African Empire, and Jean-Bedel Bokassa was proclaimed Emperor Bokassa I. The constitution provided for a parliamentary monarchy, with a National Assembly, a Supreme Court, and a government headed by a Prime Minister chosen by the Emperor. According to imperial protocol, anyone approaching the Emperor must observe an elaborate ceremonial etiquette. The Emperor was to move his imperial court from Bangui to Beringo, his "ancestral place of origin," and would appear in public only under exceptional circumstances, while the Prime Minister would preside over most public functions. Although Bokassa received congratulatory messages from French President Giscard d'Estaing and from President Idi Amin of Uganda, who saluted him as a "true brother," many observers failed to take his new status seriously. According to *Le Nouvel Observateur* of Paris, "Bokassa's eleven years of power . . . caricature the worst aspects of the colonial heritage," while the *Standard* of Kenya observed: "His mania for titles, decorations, and other trappings of power is bound to ridicule him in the eyes of the world and his fellow African leaders."

For months committees toiled under Bokassa's personal supervision in preparation for his coronation, which took place amid an atmosphere of "Napoleonic pageantry mixed with the strains of Mozart and tribal drums," on December 4, 1977. Some 240 tons of food and drink, including vast quantities of French champagne and wine, and Chivas Regal scotch, were imported for the ceremony, along with 450 pounds of rose petals, 25,000 fresh cut flowers, a ton and a half of fireworks, sixty Mercedes-Benz limousines, and eight pale gray horses brought in from Normandy to draw the Napoleonic style green and gold carriage. Bangui bristled with wooden triumphal arches and plaster pillars, and a huge gilded throne in the shape of an eagle was constructed in France. Two imperial portraits were commissioned for Bokassa from a West German artist, his robes were prepared by the Paris firm of Guiselin, which once embroidered Napoleon's uniforms, and his diamond-studded gold crown, valued at as much as $5,000,000, was crafted by a noted Paris jeweler. Brought in for the occasion were a French navy band, a contingent from the Pygmy Women's Association, and a song-and-dance group of former bar girls from Saigon.

Arriving at the coronation ceremony at Bangui's Yugoslav-built sports stadium ninety minutes behind schedule, Bokassa crowned himself Emperor and swore "before my people and before history" to uphold the constitution. He then led the royal procession along a route decked with the country's red, white, blue, green, and yellow flags, to the cathedral of Notre Dame de Bangui, where the coronation was sanctified by a High Mass. Although some 3,500 guests from about forty countries attended, the only head of government present was the Prime Minister of Mauritius, and royalty was unrepresented. The French government sent its Minister of Cooperation and the United States was represented only by its Ambassador. Pope Paul VI sent an archbishop as his delegate and prepared a message calling on Bokassa to promote social and religious progress for his people. In his original plans for the coronation, Bokassa had envisioned the Pope as attending the ceremonies and serving as the bearer of the crown, just as Pope Pius VII had done for Napoleon. Pope Paul declined the invitation, however, explaining that present Vatican policy prohibited his active participation in the crowning of emperors.

Emperor Bokassa I is said to have three wives, thirty children, and several mistresses. Ranking first among his wives is the former Catherine Dengueade, a native of Central Africa some thirty years his junior, who was crowned Empress Catherine. His second-ranking wife is a Romanian woman named Gabrielle. In November 1977 he designated two-year-old Prince Jean-Bedel Georges as his successor. His other children include Prince Georges Bokassa, the oldest, who is chief of the imperial armed forces, St. Jean de Bokassa, the youngest, born in March 1977, and Martine, his daughter by a Vietnamese woman whom he met during his service in Indochina. Another young woman from Vietnam, who first claimed to be Martine, was invited to remain a member of the household after she was exposed as an impostor.

A short, bull-necked, bearded man, Bokassa has been described as moody and arbitrary, but also as fearless and hard-working. To display his many medals he had to have a special coat tailored for him. Although he has amassed one of the largest personal fortunes in Africa, he still draws a pension as a retired French army officer. Bokassa regards Ivory Coast President Felix Houphouet-Boigny as his "spiritual father" and President Mobutu Sese Seko of Zaire as his "younger brother."

References: Africa p14+ N '77 pors; Africa Research Bulletin p4251+ D '76; International Who's Who, 1977-78; Kalck, Pierre. Central African Republic (1971); Reuters News Agency, The New Africans (1967); Who's Who in Africa (1973)

Bond, Edward

July 18, 1934- English playwright.
Address: c/o Margaret Ramsay, 14a Goodwin's Court, St. Martin's Lane, London WC2N 4LL, England

At forty-four, Edward Bond is no longer the *enfant terrible* of the British theatre, but he remains one of its most controversial playwrights. Bond first attracted attention in 1965 when his play *Saved* was banned by the Lord Chamberlain, the once-powerful British censor, for a scene that depicted the stoning to death of a baby by a gang of street toughs. The angry debate over *Saved* and over Bond's next play, *Early Morning*, is often credited with leading to the abolition of the Lord Chamberlain's censorship powers. Ten years later Bond treaded on even more sacrosanct ground with a play called *Bingo*, which presented Shakespeare, in his retirement at Stratford, as grasping, self-loathing, and suicidal. In other plays he has portrayed Queen Victoria as a murderous lesbian, concluded that the venerated Japanese poet Matsuo Basho had "the attitude of a criminal," and dared to rework *King Lear*. For Bond, and for the many who see value in his work, his plays are neither slanderous nor gratuitously violent, as their critics have charged time and again. They are, instead, a carefully structured and deeply felt examination of the relation between violence and oppression and, in the later plays, between oppression and art itself.

Edward Bond, the son of Gaston Cyril and Florence Kate (Baker) Bond, was born on

July 18, 1934 in north London, England. Among his early memories is the evacuation of his family, which included a brother and two sisters, from the city during the Blitz of World War II. He spent part of his boyhood in Cornwall and also lived for a time with his grandparents in East Anglia, a residence that is reflected in the dialect and setting of *The Pope's Wedding* and *The Sea*. Gaston Bond was a laborer, and his son has said that he himself would probably be a laborer if he had not had the ability to make a living as a playwright. At fifteen he left school, the last of several state schools, Crouch End Secondary Modern in Hornsey, London. Although he prizes knowledge, he is, if anything, proud of his lack of schooling, which he believes spared him the indoctrination that is standardly inflicted on those who follow a regular course of study. "I think universal education is one of the worst disasters that has hit Western society since the Black Death," he told Jack Hall of the *Guardian* (September 29, 1971).

From Bond's school years one cherished experience remains in memory: in 1949 at the old Bedford Theatre in Camden Town, London, he saw Donald Wolfit in *Macbeth*. Recalling the event to Ronald Bryden of the London *Observer* (February 9, 1969), he said, "It was the first thing that made sense of my life for me; the first time I'd found something beautiful and exciting and alive. Naturally, when I wrote I wrote for the theater." Unable, however, to write professionally for many years, he was thirty-two before he earned enough as a writer to support himself.

For ten years Bond worked in factories and offices, using his spare time to compose fifteen unproduced plays, none of which he has published. He followed two years of national service in the army with two years of intensive theatregoing in London, literally attending every professional production presented in the city, including those of the music halls. For his stagecraft he is indebted at least in part to the Writers Group at London's Royal Court Theatre, which he joined in the early 1960's. That workshop, whose members included Keith Johnstone, Ann Jellicoe, John Arden, and Arnold Wesker, had been initiated by William Gaskill, then the associate director of the English Stage Society at the Royal Court. The company of the Royal Court was instrumental in bringing Bond's work before the public, with Gaskill directing the first productions of some of his early plays.

In 1962 the Royal Court gave Bond's play *The Pope's Wedding* a single Sunday performance for members of the theatre's private drama club. Based loosely on Raleigh Trevelyan's book *A Hermit Disclosed*, his play traces its young protagonist's growing fascination with a misanthropic recluse. The protagonist is pictured as comfortably belonging to a group of local layabouts in a country town, but his interest in the hermit causes his alienation from his friends and his East Anglian environment. In the climactic scene he kills the hermit, apparently believing that by that means he can take his place. The critical reception to the play, which was performed without props or scenery, was meager and generally mixed. In the London *Times* the street gang scenes were found to be "unsatisfactory and unrelated," and the London *Observer* reviewer called the play "too long, too portentous and too elliptical," although he praised Bond as a "born mood evoker."

The English Stage Company showed its satisfaction with *The Pope's Wedding*, however, by commissioning another play from its author. Bond worked for two years on *Saved*, the play that was to make him both famous and notorious. Written in dense street dialect, *Saved* is about lower-class life in south London. Its central character, Len, has a casual love affair with Pam and moves in with her and her parents. Pam soon wearies of Len and takes up with the leader of a gang of toughs who, at the end of the first act, kill her child by stoning it to death in its carriage in a public park. The world of *Saved* is so emotionally stunted and numbed that the murder of the child causes barely a ripple, and Bond meant the scene as an explosive demonstration of the suppressed aggressions that throughout the drama motivate characters dehumanized and exploited by society. Len stays on in the flat despite his estrangement from Pam, exhibiting a plodding innocence and a genuine desire to communicate with others that emerge as the saving virtues of the play's title.

When William Gaskill was named the artistic director at the Royal Court in 1965, he selected *Saved* as one of a three-play repertory program to be presented at the theatre during the 1965-66 season. Like *The Pope's Wedding*, *Saved* was shown only to a private theatre-club audience because Bond had refused to make cuts in the text required by the Lord Chamberlain, the British censor. The London critics were even less approving than the censor, J. C. Trewin of the *Illustrated London News* (November 31, 1965) calling the play the "nastiest" thing he had seen on any stage and Irving Wardle of the London *Times* (November 4, 1965) referring to its "systematic degradation of the human animal." *Saved* had run only three months when the Lord Chamberlain's office, deciding that it was not suited even for private audiences, began a prosecution that resulted in the banning of further performances of the play in England.

Bond's protest in an open letter to newspapers was not without support. Kenneth Tynan, Penelope Gilliatt, and Mary McCarthy all saw merit in the play, and Laurence Olivier testified on its behalf in court and wrote eloquently in its defense. "*Saved* is not for children," he conceded, "but it is for grownups, and the grownups of this country should have the courage to look at it." In the next five years the play was produced in Germany,

Czechoslovakia, the United States, and Canada, winning critical approval and respect. Edith Oliver of the *New Yorker* (November 7, 1970), thought *Saved* "one of the strongest and most unsettling plays to come along in years." In his critical study *The Plays of Edward Bond* (1976) Richard Scharine wrote, "*Saved* clearly is one of the most important English plays of the 1960's, just as John Osborne's *Look Back in Anger* was probably the most pivotal English play of the 1950's. Osborne unintentionally revolutionized the English theater. Bond intentionally aims to revolutionize English society."

The realistic London dialogue in *Saved* attracted the attention of the Italian motion picture director Michelangelo Antonioni, who hired Bond to collaborate on the screenplay of his internationally produced *Blow-Up* (1966). Since then, to supplement his income he has worked on scripts for several films, including *Laughter in the Dark* (1969), based on the novel by Vladimir Nabokov, and *Walkabout* (1971), adapted from James Vance Marshall's novel about survival in the Australian outback. He also supplied some of the dialogue, especially for Laurence Olivier's scene, of Sam Spiegel's *Nicholas and Alexandria* (1971). Screenplay writing, however, has proved to be an unsatisfactory outlet for his talents; as he told Charles Marowitz, who quoted him in the New York *Times Magazine* (January 2, 1972): "Money controls filmmaking, and there's no pretending it can be otherwise."

Early Morning, the third of Bond's produced plays, is a hectically plotted historical farce that pits Queen Victoria and her lesbian lover, Florence Nightingale, against Prince Albert and Benjamin Disraeli in plot and counterplot. Also involved are George and Arthur—the Siamese-twin children of Victoria and Albert—William Gladstone, and several Cockneys named for these in *Saved*. At a frantic pace the characters do each other in by hideous means until Arthur, who seems to be the hero of *Early Morning*, devises a method to destroy utterly all sides in the conflict. The last scenes are set in heaven, where the same characters, now immortal, cannibalize each other's miraculously regenerative flesh. Like *Saved*, *Early Morning* had its share of puzzled and outraged critics. Kenneth Tynan, an early defender of *Saved*, considered the new play not so much shocking as incompetent. "If only it had been better done," he wrote in the London *Observer* (April 7, 1968) of its first performance, "we would have realized how bad a play it was."

In what was to be its last gasp, the Lord Chamberlain's office banned *Early Morning* after that one performance in April 1968. Parliament relieved the Lord Chamberlain of his censorship powers in November of the same year. Now that not only *Early Morning* but also *Saved* could be performed in Britain, William Gaskill set about planning a three-play Bond retrospective to be performed at the Royal Court in the spring of 1969. The third play in the repertory was *Narrow Road to the Deep North*, which Bond had written in two and a half days on commission for the international conference on people and cities at Coventry Cathedral. "I disliked being told over and over that I couldn't construct a play," Bond disclosed to Marowitz, "so I decided that I would just sit down and write one off."

The result was a short Japanese epic that condemns both the imperialist adventurism of the West and the withdrawn quietism of the East. Based on an experience recorded by the seventeenth-century Japanese poet, Matsuo Basho, the play depicts Basho refusing to aid an abandoned child whom he sees along the way as he is journeying to the North to seek wisdom. The child survives and grows to be a tyrannical shogun who wars with a couple of Victorian English colonialists in meaningless conflicts reminiscent of the struggles in *Early Morning*. When he returns from the North without having found enlightenment, Basho seeks to stand apart from the battle but is drawn in on the side of the English and eventually becomes their apologist and a symbol of the corrupt poet. Compared both favorably and unfavorably with Brecht's work, *Narrow Road* was as controversial as any of Bond's plays. Ronald Bryden judged it Bond's "most accomplished work so far" in his comments for the London *Observer* (June 30, 1968), and Clive Barnes, reviewing its American premiere in Boston, declared it "a remarkable play" in the New York *Times* (December 2, 1969). The 1972 production at Lincoln Center in New York was a critical disaster, however, with Walter Kerr panning it in the New York *Times* (January 16, 1972) as "a thin, confused, extremely tardy venture into schoolboy symbolism."

Lear, first produced in 1971 at the Royal Court, was perhaps Bond's most audacious venture. Asserting that he was rewriting Shakespeare's masterpiece to make it "more relevant," Bond turned *King Lear* into a modern political parable. The tyrant king, who is using slave labor to build a wall protecting his kingdom, is overthrown by his daughters and blinded by a mechanical device that, with a blunt irony characteristic of Bond's writing, preserves his eyes so that they can be put to "good use." Cordelia is not Lear's daughter but a revolutionary leader who conquers the king's tormentors only to establish a repressive regime of her own. Lear renounces power politics and is killed trying to destroy the wall whose construction he initiated and Cordelia is continuing. For Helen Dawson of the London *Observer* (October 3, 1971), *Lear* was "unmistakably the work of a visionary craftsman," and others who liked the play saw it as a gigantic and important drama. Its critics were inclined to use words like "boring" and "heavy-handed." Walter Kerr, who watched much of the audience walk out of the Yale Repertory Theatre production of *Lear* in 1973, insisted that the theatregoers were not disgusted by the violence in the play but rather unpersuaded by it.

Violence is not an essential element of *The Sea*, a play that Bond based on an image of a drowned man remembered from childhood. His comedy of manners, enlivened with absurdist and surreal elements, is set in a small town on the British coast in 1907. The action centers around the drowning of a young man and the indifference of the townspeople to his death. *The Sea* seems to have struck many critics as a strange, sometimes funny, yet largely unrealized work. The American drama critic Robert Brustein, who saw one of the first performances of the play at the Royal Court, wrote in the London *Observer* of May 27, 1973, that it was "permeated by a dour and morose temperament, rather as if Thomas Hardy were trying to write a farce," but he called *The Sea* "intriguing" and Bond "a writer whose voice and vision are unique."

In *Bingo*, Bond returned to the theme of the corrupt poet that he had treated in *Narrow Road to the Deep North*. This time the poet is the Bard himself, William Shakespeare, who in his retirement years is involved with the Stratford aristocracy in a land enclosure scheme that will assure his income but pauperize the common people. He is abused by a termagant wife and visited by a drunken and profane Ben Jonson, who tries to persuade him to return to playwriting. Throughout the play Shakespeare remains a sullen presence, a guilty artist imprisoned in the life of a prosperous burgher. His solution to those contradictions is suicide, and his last words, as Bond writes them, are "Was anything done?" *Bingo*, with John Gielgud playing Shakespeare, was both a critical and a commercial success in London in 1974. There were dissenters, but most agreed with Michael Billington's assessment in the *Guardian* (August 24, 1974) that the play was a "deeply moving study of the artist's impotence." In America, without Gielgud, *Bingo* did not fare so well among reviewers, although some admired the conception of the play. Walter Kerr, who had disliked Bond's other work, accused *Bingo* in his comments for the New York *Times* (February 15, 1976) of being "a cheat because it uses Shakespeare as a lure."

The London premiere of *The Fool* in 1975 left Bond's uncertain critical status unresolved. It deals with the life of John Clare, the nineteenth-century poet-peasant who was driven to madness by poverty and neglect. The background of the play is the resistance of the common people to the fencing in of common land by the enclosure act. Siding with the commoners, Clare is a poet who has made the opposite choice to Shakespeare in *Bingo*, but his actions are just as ineffectual. In the London *Observer*, Robert Cushman described the Clare character as undeveloped and incapable of uniting a play of more than forty roles.

Bond's most recent play, *The Bundle*, is a variation on the theme he explored in his earlier work, *Narrow Road to the Deep North*. It received mixed reviews when it opened at the Royal Shakespeare Company's London studio theatre, The Warehouse, in January 1978. Eight months later, his reworking of Homeric myth entitled *The Woman* was seen by Michael Billington of the *Guardian* (August 27, 1978) as a sign that Bond was "moving away from stark pessimism to unsentimental hope."

Although Bond is quite often compared with Brecht, the playwright he most admires is Chekhov, whose *The Three Sisters* he adapted for a Gaskill production in 1967. Bond is the author of the libretto of the opera *We Come to the River* (1976), for which Hans Werner Henze wrote the music. Since 1971 he has been advisory editor of the *Theatre Quarterly*. For *Early Morning* he won the 1968 George Divine Award of the English Stage Society and for *Narrow Road to the North* the John Whiting Playwrights Award of the Arts Council.

Edward Bond has blue eyes and brown hair and is a "shortish, frazzle-bearded man," as described by Charles Marowitz, who went on to say, "He is inconspicuous until he begins to speak and then he transmits energy like some hyperactive mission control." Since 1971 he has been married to Elisabeth Pablé, an Austrian theatre critic. Their home is in Cambridge. Bond votes socialist in British elections, was once an avowed anarchist, and is an atheist. A rather sanguine man, despite the enveloping gloom of his plays, he wrote in the Author's Note to the published *Saved*, "Like most people, I am a pessimist by experience, but an optimist by nature. . . . Experience is depressing, and it would be a mistake to be willing to learn from it."

References: Contemporary Authors 1st rev ed vols 25-28 (1977); Contemporary Dramatists (1973); Hinchliffe, Arnold P. The British Theatre, 1950-70 (1974); Scharine, Richard. The Plays of Edward Bond (1976); Taylor, John Russell. The Second Wave: British Drama for the Seventies (1971); Who's Who, 1977-78

Brezhnev, Leonid I(lyich) (brezh'nəf)

Dec. 19, 1906- General Secretary of the Central Committee of the Communist party and Chairman of the Presidium of the Supreme Soviet of the U.S.S.R. Address: b. Central Committee of the Communist party, 4 Staraya Ploshchad, Moscow, U.S.S.R.

NOTE: This biography supersedes the article that appeared in *Current Biography* in 1963.

When Leonid I. Brezhnev succeeded Nikita S. Khrushchev in October 1964 as head of the

Leonid I. Brezhnev

Soviet Communist party—sharing the top leadership of the U.S.S.R. with Chairman of the Council of Ministers Aleksei N. Kosygin —many observers predicted that his tenure would only be temporary. But in the years that followed, Brezhnev demonstrated his talent for survival and his shrewd grasp of power politics, so that by the early 1970's he had fallen heir to the mantle of Lenin, Stalin, and Khrushchev as the supreme leader of the Soviet Union and nominal head of the international Communist movement. An orthodox Marxist, he is the author of the "Brezhnev doctrine," which sought to justify the 1968 invasion of Czechoslovakia, and at home he suppresses dissent. Yet, as one of the principal architects of détente, he has presided over a more relaxed atmosphere in relation to the West and an easing of cold war tensions.

Leonid Ilyich Brezhnev—who refers to himself as a "fifth-generation steelman"—was born on December 19, 1906 in a working-class slum district of the Ukrainian industrial town of Kamenskoye (known since 1936 as Dneprodzerzhinsk) to Ilya Yakovlevich Brezhnev and his wife, Natalya Denisovna. He has a sister and a younger brother, Yakov, who is a metallurgist. His father, a native of the Kursk Gubernia in southern Russia, worked at the local steel plant, the Kamenskoye Zavod, which was under French and Belgian ownership. Brezhnev remembers his father's accounts of the abortive 1905 revolution and of steelworker strikes. "The way of life at the plant, the thoughts and hopes of working people and their approach to life—all this had a decisive influence in forming my world outlook," Brezhnev later recalled.

In 1915 Brezhnev entered the Klassicheskaya Gymnaziya, a school subsidized by the steel plant. During his six years at the school, where he was an average student, he experienced the hardships imposed by World War I, Revolution, foreign intervention, and a lingering civil war between Red and White forces. In the revolutionary struggles, the Brezhnevs, like most steelworker families, cast their lot with the Bolsheviks.

Following his graduation in 1921, Brezhnev reportedly obtained his first job, as a manual laborer, and studied for a time at a metallurgical vocational school in the abandoned buildings of the Kamenskoye steel plant. By the summer of 1923 he was a student at the Technicum for Land Organization and Reclamation in Kursk and that same year joined Komsomol, the Communist youth organization. After graduating from the Kursk Technicum in 1927 he worked briefly as a surveyor in Byelorussia and in the Kursk Gubernia. He then went for three years to the Urals as a land use specialist, eventually becoming head of the district land department, deputy chairman of the Bisert district soviet executive committee, and deputy chief of the Urals regional land administration. Much of his work involved the distribution of land taken over from kulaks under Stalin's agricultural collectivization program. After attending the Timiryazeff Academy, an elite agricultural institute in Moscow, in 1930-31, Brezhnev decided to leave agriculture and work once more in metallurgy.

Returning to his hometown, Brezhnev studied at its metallurgical institute from 1931 to 1935. At the same time he worked at its steel plant—now known as the F. E. Dzerzhinsky metallurgical factory—as a stoker, oiler, and fitter. Meanwhile, Brezhnev became a full-fledged member of the Communist party in 1931. He served as chairman of the trade union committee in his factory, as secretary of the party organization at the institute, and, from 1933 to 1935, as director of the steel plant's metallurgical workers' faculty.

On obtaining his degree in metallurgical engineering at the institute, Brezhnev spent a year, beginning in November 1935, in the Red Army, serving in the Trans-Baikal military district. Returning to his hometown, he was for several months, in 1936-37, the director of the Dneprodzerzhinsk Metallurgical Technical College, and in 1937 he was elected deputy chairman of the executive committee of the Dneprodzerzhinsk town soviet of working people's deputies.

In May 1938 Brezhnev joined the Dnepropetrovsk regional Communist party committee as a department head. He became the committee's propaganda secretary in February 1939 and its agriculture secretary in the fall of 1940. As the regional party committee's secretary for the defense industry on the eve of war between the Soviet Union and Nazi Germany, Brezhnev was responsible for the conversion of factories from civilian to military production. Although he reportedly worked in cooperation with Nikita S. Khrushchev, then the Communist party chief in the Ukraine, there is no evidence that he took part in the massive Stalinist purges carried out by Khrushchev during that period.

During the war, Brezhnev was among party officials sent to the armed forces by the Central Committee as high-level political officers. Serving successively as deputy chief of the political directorate of the southern front, chief of the political department of the eighteenth Ukrainian army, and chief of the political administration of the fourth Ukrainian front, he was promoted in 1944 from colonel to major general. He took part in combat operations, including the successful amphibious action near Novorossisk on the Black Sea, and toward the end of the war he was involved in preparations for the liberation of Czechoslovakia. After the defeat of Germany he was named chief of the Carpathian military district with headquarters in Czernowitz.

In the fall of 1946 Brezhnev became first secretary of the Communist party organization in the Ukrainian industrial region of Zaporozhe. Returning to his home territory in November 1947 as first secretary of the Dnepropetrovsk party regional committee, Brezhnev helped to promote postwar recovery there. In July 1950, after working for a few months with the Central Committee apparatus in Moscow, he was named first secretary in the former Romanian province of Moldavia, which had become one of the sixteen Soviet republics after the war, and that year he was for the first time elected a deputy to the Supreme Soviet of the U.S.S.R. His tasks in Moldavia included consolidation of the newly established collective farm system and extension of Communist party control in the countryside.

At the nineteenth congress of the Soviet Communist party in October 1952, Brezhnev moved into the central leadership of the party, becoming a full member of its Central Committee, a candidate member of its Presidium, and one of its ten secretaries. In the power struggles that followed Stalin's death in March 1953, he was temporarily dropped from the Presidium and secretariat. Until February 1954 he served in the rank of lieutenant general as first deputy chief of central political administration in the Defense Ministry, responsible for political supervision of the navy.

Named second secretary of the Communist party in the Central Asian republic of Kazakhstan in February 1954, Brezhnev then served as its first secretary from August 1955 to February 1956. There he played a key role in administering Khrushchev's "virgin lands program" which was aimed at increasing the Soviet Union's agricultural output by placing vast areas of land under cultivation in Central Asia and Siberia. The scheme was at least temporarily successful and contributed to a record wheat harvest in 1956.

Over the next few years Brezhnev emerged as one of an inner circle of party functionaries loyal to Khrushchev, whom they supported in 1957 in his successful struggle with an "anti-party" faction. Meanwhile, at the twentieth party congress in February 1956, Brezhnev's positions as a candidate member of the Presidium and as a secretary of the Central Committee were restored; in July 1957 he became a full member of the Presidium; and in 1958 he was elected deputy chairman of the Central Committee's bureau for the Russian Federation. In his role as a party secretary he took on responsible domestic and foreign assignments and presided over periodic shakeups in party ranks.

When Marshal Kliment Y. Voroshilov retired on May 7, 1960 as Chairman of the Presidium of the Supreme Soviet of the U.S.S.R., Brezhnev became his successor. Two months later, Brezhnev relinquished his position as a secretary in the party's Central Committee to devote himself fully to his new post which, although largely ceremonial, enjoyed great prestige. During his four years as titular chief of state he traveled in Europe, Asia, and Africa, and acted as spokesman for the Khrushchev regime's foreign policies. He also devoted much effort to promoting the Soviet space program. Reelected Chairman of the Presidium in April 1962, Brezhnev was also reappointed in June 1963 to the Central Committee's secretariat, as a replacement for Frol Kozlov who, until illness forced him to resign, reportedly was being groomed as Khrushchev's successor. On July 15, 1964 Brezhnev relinquished the Chairmanship of the Presidium to Anastas I. Mikoyan to devote himself more fully to party matters. As unofficial second secretary he was, during the next few months, responsible for much of the day-to-day supervision of party affairs.

On October 14, 1964 Khrushchev was suddenly relieved of his two top-level posts. In his place, the Central Committee chose Brezhnev as the party's First Secretary, while Khrushchev's position as Chairman of the U.S.S.R. Council of Ministers, or Prime Minister, was filled by Aleksei N. Kosygin. Although Khrushchev ostensibly stepped down for reasons of advanced age and declining health, later reports indicated widespread dissatisfaction among top Soviet officials with his policies, especially with his personality cult and failure to rely on collective leadership. Whether Brezhnev had any hand in his former mentor's downfall is not known. Several sources suggest that he was placed into the forefront by his party colleagues as a competent and colorless bureaucrat and technician unlikely to evoke a personality cult of his own. The historian Bertram Wolfe in 1965 described him as "an insignificant transition figure in a new interregnum."

Although the difference between the ebullient Khrushchev and the low-keyed Brezhnev-Kosygin team was more one of style than of substance, the two officials instituted some significant changes soon after taking power, especially in economic policy. They relaxed restrictions on private farming, raised farm income, and ended the division of the party into agrarian and industrial branches. Wages increased, welfare measures improved, and consumer goods became more readily available. In cultural matters, the new regime proved as restrictive as its predecessor. The nonconformist writers Andrei Sinyavsky and Yuri Daniel were imprisoned in 1966, and similar action was taken against other dissenters. In what seemed, in terminology at least, a reversion to Stalinism, the twenty-third party congress in March 1966 changed Brezhnev's title from First Secretary to Secretary General and renamed the party's Presidium the Politburo.

In foreign policy, Brezhnev and Kosygin generally tried to enhance the Soviet Union's influence while avoiding major confrontations with other powers. The new leaders at first attempted to modify Khrushchev's anti-Chinese policies, but in 1969 relations deteriorated to the point that fighting broke out on the Sino-Soviet frontier. By 1970 diplomatic contacts had brought some measure of stabilization, even though the ideological conflict continued. When in late 1965 the United States escalated its military involvement in Vietnam, the Soviet Union condemned the American actions and furnished massive military aid to North Vietnam but shunned any direct involvement. Similarly, after the Israelis decisively defeated Egyptian, Syrian, and Jordanian forces in the six-day war of June 1967, the Soviet leaders, fearing that direct intervention might bring war with the United States, did not go beyond giving some material aid to their Arab allies and breaking off relations with Israel.

A cardinal principle of the Brezhnev-Kosygin regime has been its insistence on maintaining the solidarity of the Communist world under the guidance of the Soviet Union. When in the spring of 1968 the Czechoslovakian Communist party leader Alexander Dubcek departed from standard Marxist policies to institute "Communism with a human face," orthodox Communist leaders feared disintegration of Soviet hegemony. Having failed to persuade Dubcek to return to the fold, on the night of August 20, 1968 the Soviet Union and its Warsaw Pact allies invaded Czechoslovakia and deposed him. Expounding what became known in the West as the "Brezhnev doctrine," the Soviet Communist party leader later explained that a threat to the cause of socialism in one Communist country was the concern of all Communist countries.

Meanwhile, Brezhnev, who at first had been overshadowed by Kosygin, consolidated his power as Communist party chief by quietly placing his supporters from the provinces in key positions and by dropping potential rivals. By 1970 he was the Soviet Union's leading spokesman in negotiations with foreign heads of state, and at the twenty-fourth Communist party congress at Moscow in the spring of 1971 he emerged as "first among equals." In the ninth five-year plan, for 1971-75, announced by Brezhnev that year, the main emphasis was placed for the first time on consumer goods and a higher standard of living rather than on defense production and heavy industry.

Despite occasional setbacks, the relaxation of tensions, known as détente, between the Soviet Union and Western nations, has been the dominant feature of the Brezhnev regime. In November 1969 United States-Soviet Strategic Arms Limitation Talks (SALT) began in Helsinki. In August 1970 West German Chancellor Willy Brandt concluded a goodwill treaty with the Soviet Union, and the following year a four-power agreement was signed providing for unhindered traffic between West Berlin and West Germany.

In line with United States policy, engineered by Secretary of State Henry Kissinger, to seek accommodation with both the U.S.S.R. and China, in May 1972 President Richard Nixon visited Brezhnev in Moscow, where the initial phase of the SALT talks concluded with the signing of interim agreements limiting antiballistic missile systems and strategic offensive weapons. The Paris cease-fire agreement of January 1973, ending hostilities in Vietnam, further improved relations between the two superpowers, even though the Soviet Union was not a party to it. As a result of the relaxation of tensions, the Soviet Union, following its 1972 crop failure negotiated major purchases of wheat from the United States, and during 1973 Soviet trade with Western countries increased by over 40 percent.

In June 1973 Brezhnev made an eight-day visit to the United States, during which he and Nixon signed eleven treaties dealing with arms limitation and other matters. He reached further agreements on armaments with Nixon in Moscow in July 1974, and with President Gerald R. Ford in Vladivostok that November. At the Helsinki Conference on Security and Cooperation in Europe, which Brezhnev attended in the summer of 1975 as one of thirty-five government representatives, the Soviet Union scored a triumph, for by recognizing the territorial status quo the Helsinki accord seemed to legitimize the gains made since World War II by the Soviet Union and other Communist countries. But the conference also committed its participants to certain human rights practices, such as the easing of restrictions on travel and exchange of information.

Although the Brezhnev regime's methods of dealing with dissidents are a far cry from the blood purges of the Stalin era, such actions as the enforced exile of Nobel Prize-winning author Aleksandr Solzhenitsyn in 1974, harassment of scholars like Andrei D. Sakharov, and prosecution of lesser-known dissenters, especially those of Jewish background who have applied for immigration to Israel, have caused a stir in the West. Dismissing President Jimmy Carter's criticisms of Soviet human rights violations, Brezhnev told a trade union meeting in March 1977: "Washington's claims to teach others how to live cannot be accepted by any sovereign state." The controversy over human rights was one of the reasons why the SALT talks remained stalled as of the fall of 1978.

On the international scene, where earlier cold war initiatives have given way to a more cautious approach by the Soviet Union, the Brezhnev regime suffered setbacks in the 1970's. Its goal of "proletarian internationalism," already impaired by the continuing conflict with China and the independent positions taken by the Yugoslav and Romanian Communist governments, was further weakened by the emergence of "Eurocommunism" among the Communist parties of France, Italy, and Spain, which have asserted their independence of Moscow in internal affairs. In the Middle East, following the defeat of its Arab allies by Israel in the Yom Kippur war of 1973, the Brezhnev regime has favored an all-embracing settlement, including the creation of an independent Palestinian state, while rejecting Egyptian President Anwar Sadat's 1977 and 1978 peace initiatives toward Israel.

In Latin America, the Soviet Union under Brezhnev has continued to give material aid to the Cuban government of Fidel Castro but has withheld support from Cuba's efforts to export the revolution to other Western Hemisphere countries. While backing Cuban military initiatives in Africa, notably in Angola, and providing aid for the Marxist government of Ethiopia and for black guerrilla groups in Rhodesia and South Africa, the Soviet Union has avoided direct military involvement on the African continent.

As the Soviet Union celebrated the sixtieth anniversary of the Bolshevik Revolution in November 1977, Brezhnev basked in the height of his power and prestige. Earlier, on June 16, 1977, he had once more been elected Chairman of the Presidium of the U.S.S.R., following the unceremonious dismissal of Nikolai Podgorny—his chief rival during the Khrushchev era—who had occupied the post since 1965. A new Soviet constitution, adopted in October 1977, was said to have been largely the work of Brezhnev, who had chaired the constitutional commission since 1964. Although the document contains no major changes in power relationships from those provided in the 1936 Stalin constitution, it enhances the authority of the Presidium Chairman. Geared to the stage of "developed socialism," the constitution for the first time spells out the role of the Communist party as "the leading and guiding force" in the Soviet Union and implicitly justifies intervention in other countries in the name of "socialist internationalism."

Several volumes of Brezhnev's speeches and essays have been translated into English, including *On the Policy of the Soviet Union and the International Situation* (Doubleday, 1973). Among his many honors are five Orders of Lenin, two Orders of the Red Banner, the Lenin Peace Prize, the Order of Victory, and designation as a Hero of the Soviet Union. In May 1976 Brezhnev was promoted to marshal of the Soviet Union, the nation's highest military rank, and a bronze bust of him was dedicated in his hometown. Recent sources list Brezhnev as supreme commander of the Soviet armed forces and as chief of the defense council.

Leonid I. Brezhnev's wife, Viktoria Petrovna, whom he married about 1932, is said to be of middle-class Jewish background. According to one source, she was a fellow metallurgy student, while another maintains that she is a gynecologist. Their daughter, Galina, has been an employee of the Novosti Press Agency; their son Yuri was named Deputy Minister of Foreign Trade in 1976; another son, Mikhail, is said to be a journalist. The Brezhnevs have several grandchildren and at least one great grandchild. They make their home in a five-room apartment on Moscow's Kutuzovski Prospect and have a country dacha in the village of Kolchuga, near the capital. Brezhnev is about five feet ten inches tall, weighs over 200 pounds, has blue eyes, graying brown hair, and bushy eyebrows, and dresses meticulously.

Although he has reportedly suffered at least two heart attacks in recent years, Brezhnev often puts in a sixteen-hour workday and persists in chain-smoking American filter cigarettes. He has a fleet of foreign automobiles and a yacht. A philistine, he is said to prefer cowboy movies to the Bolshoi Ballet. Once adept at ice-skating, cross-country skiing, swimming, and long-distance cycling, he still enjoys hunting and rooting for his favorite soccer team.

In *Current History* (October 1977) Robert G. Wesson wrote: "Brezhnev . . . can be proud of the order and stability over which he has presided. . . . But in terms of fulfilling Lenin's dreams, his reign has hardly been a success. . . . The Soviet Union, which under Khrushchev still spoke in messianic tones, . . . has acquired the image of a staid bureaucracy, whose chief bureaucrat is Leonid Brezhnev."

References: Academy of Sciences of the U.S.S.R. Leonid I. Brezhnev: Pages From His Life (1978); Dornberg, John. Brezhnev: The Masks of Power (1974); Institute of Marxism-Leninism. Brezhnev: A Short Biography (1978); Robinson, Donald. 100 Most Important People in the World Today (1970); Simmonds, George W., ed. Soviet Leaders (1967); Swearingen, Rodger, ed. Leaders of the Communist World (1971)

Brownmiller, Susan

Feb. 15, 1935- Writer; feminist leader. Address: h. 61 Jane St., New York City, N.Y. 10014

When, in the fall of 1975, Susan Brownmiller's best-selling *Against Our Will: Men, Women and Rape* made its opportune appearance, rape had become the fastest growing violent crime in the United States, with an increase of 62 percent in five years. The most comprehensive study of rape ever made, her book is probably also the most controversial analysis of the subject, because it propounds rape as a weapon to subjugate women in the male-female power relationship. Susan Brownmiller therefore brought the grave social problem of rape even closer to the concerns of the women's liberation movement, from which she had drawn inspiration and support in her undertaking. As a free-lance journalist, she has written articles on a wide range of issues—in addition to film, TV, and book reviews—for *Vogue, Esquire,* the New York *Times Magazine,* and other nationally circulated periodicals.

Susan Brownmiller was born in Brooklyn, New York on the anniversary of the birth of the nineteenth-century feminist leader Susan B. Anthony, February 15, 1935, a coincidence of some importance to her. She grew up in a Jewish middle-class family in the Flatbush section of Brooklyn, the only child of a New York City clothing salesman and his wife, a hard-working secretary who imparted to her daughter a sense of self-dependence. In an interview with Sally Quinn of the Washington *Post* (November 2, 1975), Susan Brownmiller spoke of her regret that neither of her parents had lived long enough to share her satisfaction in the publication of *Against Our Will.* "I'm really sorry Mother died before I finished this book," she said. "She would have understood every word of it."

With the intention of preparing for a career in law, Susan Brownmiller enrolled in Cornell University in 1952, the year of the Presidential election in which Dwight D. Eisenhower defeated Adlai E. Stevenson. Although college students of the 1950's were later known as the Silent Generation because of their general compliance, she became radicalized in her freshman year and joined a small campus group called Students for Peace. Peace organizations were suspect in that period of flourishing McCarthyism, and, as she recalled in an article, "Up from Silence," which she wrote for *Esquire* magazine (March 1969), her worried parents made a trip to Ithaca, New York to ask the Dean of Women to talk her out of belonging to the group. She was also a member of the Cornell chapter of the National Association for the Advancement of Colored People.

Leaving Cornell in 1955, a year before she would have graduated, Susan Brownmiller went to Manhattan to study acting. It was about that time, at the age of twenty, that she decided to change her long, distinctly ethnic surname. She would have preferred "Winemiller," because one of her favorite roles was Alma Winemiller of Tennessee Williams' *Summer and Smoke,* but as she explained to Sally Quinn, if she were ever to portray that heroine on the stage, it would seem strange for her to have the same name. She therefore adopted "Brownmiller." After playing in two off-Broadway productions and suffering through years of tryouts and rejections, she concluded that she was not suited to the theatre, although she believes that many bright, serious-minded women found the stage of the 1950's highly congenial.

In search of a radical cause with which she could fully identify, Susan Brownmiller tried a variety of directions during the 1950's and 1960's, enrolling, for example, in a course at New York's Marxist-oriented Jefferson School of Social Science with the American Communist historian Herbert Aptheker. To Aptheker, as she acknowledged in her book, she is indebted for her knowledge of the tools of dialectic logic, as well as insights that influenced her thinking about the nature of rape. During the mid-1960's she spent two summers in Mississippi as a civil rights worker. After she had relinquished her ambition to become an actress, she turned to writing at the suggestion of her analyst and took a succession of jobs in journalism, editing and writing for *Coronet* magazine and researching for *Newsweek*. She was employed as a reporter for NBC-TV in Philadelphia in 1965 and as a network newswriter for ABC-TV in New York from 1965 to 1967. Disappointed in her hopes of getting on camera, she quit the latter job to become a staff writer for the *Village Voice*.

Free-lancing over the next few years, Miss Brownmiller wrote a string of first-rate articles for magazines on such diverse personalities as the New York fashion designer Jacques Tiffeau (New York *Times Magazine*, January 15, 1967), the redoubtable urbanologist Jane Jacobs (*Vogue*, May 1969), Democratic Senator Eugene McCarthy (New York *Times Magazine*, July 20, 1969), and Consolidated Edison's chief executive officer, Charles Luce (New York *Times Magazine*, April 12, 1970). Some of her articles dealt with subjects relating to activist causes in which she was personally interested, like, for instance, "As the First Black Woman Congressman Herself Puts It, This Is Fighting Shirley Chisholm" (New York *Times Magazine*, April 13, 1969). From that article on one of Brooklyn's Democratic Representatives she developed a biography for young readers, *Shirley Chisholm*, which was published by Doubleday & Company in 1970 and was issued as an Archway paperback in 1972.

Another of her articles, "Sisterhood Is Powerful" (New York *Times Magazine*, March 15, 1970), concerned the women's liberation movement, an effort that she early recognized as her own. "I've always been a gut feminist, no doubt about it," she told Sally Quinn in the Washington *Post* interview. "I've tried to trace it back, the feeling I've always had, the gut reality that women were as good as men." A pioneering feminist meeting that she attended in the late 1960's turned out to have a stronger appeal for her than the usual group activity in which she participated, including anti-Vietnam War demonstrations. "All of a sudden I knew I was home. I knew I was where I belonged," she has said, as quoted in *Time* (October 13, 1975). In 1968 she helped to found the New York Radical Feminists.

One of the immediate targets of New York Radical Feminists was the annual Miss America Pageant in Atlantic City, New Jersey, which the group picketed in 1968. In collaboration with members of other women's liberation groups, Susan Brownmiller helped to organize more than 100 militant feminists whom she led in a sit-in at the offices of the *Ladies Home Journal* in March 1970. The protesters chose that magazine, she explained, partly because they found it to be "one of the most demeaning magazines toward women." Their demands included putting out a liberated issue of the magazine and ending exploitative advertising. The speak-out on rape and conference on rape that she organized in 1971 constituted other milestones in militant feminism. What she learned from discussions with women who attended the meeting caused her to question her views on rape, made her aware of the need for research on the subject, and provided the impetus for her book. Referring to that source of encouragement, she affirmed, as was reported in *Time*, "I'm grateful to the Movement for giving me a channel, a constructive way to use my rage."

As Mary Ellen Gale pointed out in the New York *Times Book Review* (October 12, 1975), "*Against Our Will* is in part a moving and persuasive record of Brownmiller's personal odyssey." Before the 1970's Susan Brownmiller, who herself has never been raped, had regarded rape as a sex crime committed by a madman. During one of Aptheker's lectures on slavery in the South, she had for the first time heard rape spoken of as a political act, a means used by the white man to further humiliate and oppress the black woman. But black women raped by black men and white women raped by black men or by white men were not recognized in Aptheker's dogma as victims of a political crime. Like others of middle-class liberal background, Miss Brownmiller tended to suspect that a black man accused of raping a white woman was the prey of racial prejudice. Her "knee-jerk reactions," as she later called them, were reflected in her article "Rashomon in Maryland" (*Esquire*, May 1968), an account of the Giles-Johnson rape case, in which three black men were accused and convicted of raping a white girl. Distrustful of judicial fairness in an interracial case, she did not even think it would be worthwhile for her to interview the alleged victim. Many years later, however, although rape charges had been dismissed, she said during a TV discussion of the case that she had eventually become convinced that the girl had been raped, had "submitted herself to an act of sex . . . believing that her life was threatened."

Most of the change in Susan Brownmiller's perspective on rape resulted from research that she at first thought would take six months. She planned to spend another six months writing up her findings. Her book required, in fact, a total of four years of work. Aside from obtaining information through interviews, she carried out research at several libraries, mainly the New York Public Library, where she also wrote most of the book. When her savings and an advance from her publisher, Simon and Schuster, ran out, she applied for and received grants from the Alicia Patterson Foundation and the Louis M. Rabinowitz Foundation, which supported her for two years.

Upon its publication in October 1975 *Against Our Will: Men, Women and Rape* gained immediate recognition as a major and much-needed contribution to the urgent discussion of the changing relationship between the sexes. It became a selection of the Book-of-the-Month Club and an alternate selection of *Women Today, Saturday Review,* and *Psychology Today* book clubs. Besides winning a spot on the best-selling list, it earned its author a reported $250,000 in the sale of paperback rights alone. The editors of the New York *Times Book Review* listed it among the outstanding books of the year in the issue of December 28, 1975 and described it as "a feminist tract that seems destined to take its place beside De Beauvoir's *The Second Sex,* Friedan's *The Feminine Mystique,* and Kate Millett's *Sexual Politics.* Susan Brownmiller, moreover, was one of *Time's* twelve Women of the Year, whose photographs appeared on the cover of the January 5, 1976 issue. Her book, it was suggested, "may significantly change the terms of the dialogue between and about men and women."

Against Our Will offers an analysis of history in which men have always dominated women through physical force and have used rape as a weapon to maintain their power. Susan Brownmiller's thesis is that rape "is nothing more or less than a conscious process of intimidation by which *all men* keep *all women* in a state of fear." Not all men are rapists, but men as a group tolerate rape and perpetuate myths about rape that keep women subjugated. Miss Brownmiller theorizes that women originally agreed to monogamous marriage with men to protect themselves from rape by other men. Since a woman was traditionally regarded as a man's property, "a crime against her body became a crime against the male estate."

Some reviewers thought Susan Brownmiller's generalizations were too sweeping, her conclusions too grim, and her tone too truculent, and some questioned the accuracy of certain interpretations. But most were impressed by her extensive documentation and the scope of her presentation of historical, literary, legal, psychological, and sociopolitical perspectives on the wartime rapist, the police blotter rapist, and the homosexual rapist in prison, among others. Her recommendations on how to contend with the incidence of rape through reform of the law and of police and court procedures and through the strengthening of women's physical defense were approved in some reviews as thoughtful and constructive.

Critical commentary on *Against Our Will* tended to be somewhat polarized. M. J. Sobran, for example, wrote mockingly in the *National Review* (March 5, 1976), "What she is engaged in, really, is not scholarship but henpecking—that conscious process of intimidation by which all women keep all men in terror," and Michael Novak in *Commentary* (February 1976) rejected the book as "a tract in celebration of lesbianism and/or masturbation." In her appraisal for the New York *Times Book Review,* on the other hand, Mary Ellen Gale commended it as "a chilling and monumental study [that] deserves a place on the shelf next to those rare books about social problems which force us to make connections we have long evaded, and change the way we feel about what we know." Diane Johnson wrote in the *New York Review of Books* (December 11, 1975) that Brownmiller's study "is not a model of surpassing tact and delicacy, [but] may in fact succeed where reticence has failed to legitimate the fundamental grievance of women against men."

Practising what she preaches about learning techniques of self-defense, in early 1973 Susan Brownmiller enrolled in a training program in jujitsu and karate. She wrote about the course in "Women Fight Back," the concluding chapter of her book, and in "Street Fighting Woman," an article for the New York *Times* (April 18, 1973), and discussed its value in an interview about antirape techniques for *Harper's Bazaar* (March 1976). In her personal battle against rape she has also vigorously denounced pornographic magazines like *Penthouse* and *Hustler* and films like *Snuff,* convinced, as she insisted in *Against Our Will,* that "the case against pornography and the case against the toleration of prostitution are central to the fight against rape." She was a leader of a recently formed antismut feminist group that met in July 1977 to plan strategy in an educational campaign against new forms of pornography specializing in the dehumanization and brutalization of women.

Among those whom Susan Brownmiller thanked in the Acknowledgements of *Against Our Will* was the Reuters correspondent Kevin Cooney: "It was the lot of Kevin Cooney to live with the book as he lived with me." She and Cooney no longer share an apartment. By preference she is unmarried and expects to remain so. "I'd be a poor wife and an anxiety-ridden mother," Sally Quinn quoted her as saying. Miss Brownmiller stands five feet six inches tall and weighs 122 pounds and is a small-boned, graceful, and attractive woman who once wrote that "femininity" is central to her image of herself. Her royalties from her book have enabled her to indulge an interest that she could not earlier afford, travel: she has ridden horseback in Montana, climbed mountains in Peru, visited Hawaii, and gone on an African safari.

References: Guardian p16 D12 '75 por; Mlle 82:122+ Je '76 pors; N Y Daily News p38 S 28 '76 pors; Time 106:48+ O 13 '75 por; 107:20 Ja 5 '76; Washington Post C p1+ N 2 '75 por; Writers Digest 56:14+ Ap '76 por; Foremost Women in Communications (1970)

Bukovsky, Vladimir

Dec. 30, 1942- Soviet dissident. Address: c/o Amnesty International USA, 2112 Broadway, New York City, N.Y. 10023

The Soviet exile Vladimir Bukovsky is one of the more celebrated of the Eastern European dissidents who have helped to make the question of human rights a central international issue. Between 1963, when he was twenty, and 1976, when he was thirty-three, Bukovsky was incarcerated for a total of eleven years in Russian prisons, labor camps, and hospitals for political offenses that included the international dissemination of the first documents exposing the Soviet practice of using psychiatry and psychiatric hospitalization in repressing political nonconformity. His release to the West in December 1976 in an exchange for imprisoned Chilean Communist leader Luis Corvalán Lepe was the first acknowledgment by the Kremlin, however implicit, that there are political prisoners in the Soviet Union.

Vladimir K. Bukovsky was born on December 30, 1942 into a Moscow home that was broken by divorce. His late father, an orthodox, hard-line Communist, was a member of the Soviet writers union. His mother, Nina (Ivanovna) Bukovsky, who once wrote children's programs for Radio Moscow, went into exile with her son, as did Vladimir's sister, Olga, and Olga's son, Mikhail. Mrs. Bukovsky, Olga, and Mikhail now live in Switzerland.

According to Ludmilla Thorne—a Russian-speaking American member of Amnesty International who first contacted Bukovsky's mother by telephone in 1972 and came to know her well—Nina Ivanovna has "an abiding wonderment over having reared such a heroic rebel." Anxious to protect the "natural flow of his life," she at first tried to discourage her son's nonconformity, and it was only gradually that she accepted the fact that she is, in her words, "a hen that has given birth to an eagle."

Bukovsky's rebellion began early, and relatively innocently. As a high school student in Moscow he was suspended for publishing a typescript satirical magazine, and one semester after he matriculated at Moscow University with the intention of majoring in biophysics he was expelled for behavior that did "not correspond to the character of a Soviet student." That behavior consisted of involvement with a heterodox literary group that championed abstract art, issued a typescript review called "The Phoenix," held poetry readings in Mayakovsky Square, and was generally guilty of "Western decadence."

After his expulsion, Bukovsky worked on the staff of a geological expedition and at a computer center while engaging in the distribution of clandestine newsletters and literature. Arrested in 1963 for possession of two photocopies of Milovan Djilas' book *The New Class*, a criticism of the Yugoslavian Communist party elite, he was placed in solitary confinement in Lubyanka Prison, Moscow, and interrogated repeatedly by General Svetlichny, who was then in charge of the Moscow branch of the K.G.B., the Soviet security police. Svetlichny offered to release him if he would recant and reveal who gave him the book and who helped him make the photocopies. When he refused, he was given a psychiatric examination, declared mentally ill, and sent to a special prison mental hospital in Leningrad. Unlike the regular mental hospitals, which come under the Ministry of Health, the special *psikhushki* are institutions for the criminally insane run by the M.V.D., the Ministry of Internal Affairs. According to Bukovsky, there are now at least eleven special hospitals—nine more than there were thirty years ago—and a tenth of the inmates are mentally healthy political dissenters.

As a psychiatric inmate in 1963, Bukovsky was witnessing what he has called "the breaking point in . . . people's [viewing] such institutions as havens of 'salvation.'" In the Stalinist era, when millions of political prisoners were condemned to slave away their lives in the dreaded "Gulag archipelago," the immense, inhumane system of labor camps exposed by Aleksandr Solzhenitsyn, a diagnosis of insanity and consignment to a psychiatric hospital was a blessing, a form of escape, and forensic psychiatry was considered an agency of mercy. After the death of Josef Stalin the political situation changed rapidly, so that in 1959 Premier Nikita Khrushchev was compelled to declare that there were no longer any political prisoners in the Soviet Union. (Actually there were still a few thousand prisoners in the slave labor system, according to Bukovsky.)

Coping with dissenters remained a problem, however, and psychiatric hospitalization became the easy solution, acceptable without qualm to anyone conditioned to accept the assumption that, in Soviet society, dissent is by definition a symptom of mental illness. Thus, in contrast with its earlier, beneficient role, psychiatry became a common instrument of repression. Fortunately, at the time of Bukovsky's first incarceration, the Moscow-oriented Snezhnevsky school of psychiatry, which fostered the aforesaid assumption, was still being challenged by the Leningrad school headed by Professor Sluchevsky. Any diagnosis of "sluggish schizophrenia" in Moscow was almost automatically rejected in Leningrad. Bukovsky attributes his early release, in February 1965, not to any humane leniency he found in the Leningrad institution—life there was "hell"—but to "the fact that the Leningrad school was still trying to carry on its dispute with the Moscow school and to refute [Moscow's] diagnoses."

The intrepid Bukovsky was a principal organizer of a student demonstration—the first such since 1927—in Pushkin Square in Moscow on December 5, 1965 in protest against the arrests of Andrei D. Sinyavsky and Yuli Daniel, presumably on charges of smuggling their anti-Soviet writings out of the Soviet Union. Brandishing the slogan "Respect your Constitution," the demonstrators demanded that the two writers be given a public trial in keeping with Soviet constitutional law. Article 190-3 was soon afterward promulgated specifically to deal with such demonstrations, but at the time the Soviet criminal code had no provision for legally punishing the participants. The K.G.B. released the arrested student leaders after a brief detention, but, hoping for a confirmation of his previous psychiatric diagnosis, they sent Bukovsky to two Moscow hospitals, at each of which doctors refused to declare him mentally ill. After two months, he was transferred to the Serbsky Institute in Moscow for observation, and he might have remained there indefinitely had not Amnesty International, an organization devoted to the rescue of political prisoners throughout the world, threatened to take his case before the Bertrand Russell tribunal, another nongovernmental, international agency of justice. In August 1966, after spending six months in the Serbsky Institute, Bukovsky was released.

In January 1967 Bukovsky was arrested a third time, for organizing a demonstration in Pushkin Square in protest against the imprisonment of four fellow dissidents. Defending himself at his trial, he said, "We demonstrate, for instance, in defense of Greek political prisoners. Are we to remain indifferent to the fate of our own?" His sentence was three years, which he served in the "ordinary regime" labor camp at Bor, near Voronezh, working as a carpenter. After his release he earned his living as secretary to the writer Vladimir Maksimov (now also exiled).

The Washington *Post* for May 17, 1970 carried an interview with Associated Press correspondent Holger Jensen in which Bukovsky recounted his experiences and observations in the Leningrad special psychiatric hospital from 1963 to 1965 and in the Bor labor camp from 1967 to 1970. His most serious indictment was of practices in the Leningrad hospital, where, he said, healthy nonconformists were "turned into vegetables" with punitive injections of aminazin (Thorazine), triftazin, and sulphazin. (He himself was not given those drugs.) On June 9, 1970 he was interrogated by Assistant Moscow City Prosecutor Vankovich regarding the "libels on the Soviet system" contained in the interview. Bukovsky's description of the interrogation was published in summary form in the underground typescript Moscow journal "A Chronicle of Current Events" and in longer, translated form in the *New York Review of Books* of March 9, 1972.

Meanwhile Bukovsky had been using his periods of freedom to compile eight case histories, including his own, exemplifying the abuse of psychiatry in the punishment of political dissenters. Smuggled out of the Soviet Union, the document was released to the outside world in Paris on March 10, 1971. Arrested nineteen days later, Bukovsky was subjected to psychiatric examination for months, found sane, and given a one-day trial on January 5, 1972. Found guilty of "anti-Soviet agitation and propaganda . . . aimed at undermining and weakening Soviet power," he was sentenced to a total of twelve years: two in prison, five in a "strict regime" labor camp, and five in exile. "Our society is still sick," he said at his trial. "It is sick with the fear that we inherited from the time of Stalin's terror. But the process of society's spiritual regeneration has already begun and there is no stopping it."

At Vladimir prison, 110 kilometers north of Moscow, Bukovsky went on hunger strikes to protest the treatment of other prisoners and was kept much of the time in punitive conditions in an isolation cell, to the detriment of his health, which was already threatened by a rheumatic heart. After two years he was transferred to the Perm labor camp, about 700 miles northeast of Moscow, where he met Semyon Gluzman, a young psychiatrist incarcerated for writing a dissenting diagnosis of dissident former Soviet Army General Pyitr Grigorent Grigorenko. With

Gluzman, he put together "A Dissident's Guide to Psychiatry," a hand-written manual telling the offender what to expect and how to behave when confronted "by a qualified psychiatrist who has received his orders to hold him unaccountable." A copy of the manual was smuggled out of the Soviet Union, and the text was published in Great Britain in the winter-spring 1975 issue of the periodical *Survey*.

Chiefly through Bukovsky's mother, Nina Ivanovna, who often communicated by telephone with Ludmilla Thorne and Amnesty International, news about Bukovsky and his plight regularly filtered out of the Soviet Union, and prominent Westerners, including labor leader George Meany, actress Geraldine Fitzgerald, and writers Arthur Miller, Vladimir Nabokov, Norman Mailer, Jerzy Kosinski, and Clive Barnes (whose wife collected many of the signatures) lent the weight of their names to petitions sent to Soviet leaders in Bukovsky's hehalf.

The idea of exchanging the freedom of Bukovsky for that of Luis Corvalán Lepe, the jailed leader of the Chilean Communist party, was reportedly suggested by Andrei Sakharov, the dissident Soviet atomic physicist and Nobel Peace Prize winner who is the leader of the Soviet human rights movement. After six weeks of negotiation, in which the United States, on the suggestion of President-elect Jimmy Carter, acted as intermediary, the exchange took place on December 18, 1976 at Kloten Airport in Zurich, Switzerland, where the Aeroflot plane carrying Bukovsky and his family from the Soviet Union and the Lufthansa airliner bearing Corvalán and his wife landed within five minutes of each other.

While his mother, sister, and nephew settled into an apartment in a village eighteen kilometers outside of Zurich, Bukovsky embarked on a round of speeches, interviews, and other engagements. In England, he spoke before Parliament and was interviewed by Peter Williams on Thames Television's *This Week* program. In France, in an interview for *Le Nouvel Observateur*, he noted that the 1975 Helsinki declaration, for all its provisions on human rights and political prisoners, was followed by increased harassment and ill treatment of dissidents in Eastern Europe. "There will be no changes," he said, "unless . . . firmness is maintained with perseverance." He expressed his support for Senator Henry Jackson's proposed amendment to the United States-Soviet trade bill, an amendment calling for an increase in exit visas for Jews desiring to emigrate from the Soviet Union, and he warned that American-made goods, such as the handcuffs the K.G.B. put on his wrists in the plane that took him to Zurich, can be used repressively in the Soviet Union. "I am not calling for a blockade," he said, "but I ask that you not sell us handcuffs, in both the literal and the figurative sense."

On March 1, 1977 Bukovsky met with President Jimmy Carter and Vice-President Walter Mondale in the White House. In an address before the American Psychiatric Association in Toronto, Canada on May 3, 1977 he observed that psychiatric repression in the Soviet Union had been lessened "because both the K.G.B. and Soviet forensic psychiatry are now forced to work under publicity—they must pay heed to Western public opinion and, in part, to Western psychiatrists." He ended by saying: "Soviet psychiatry is not monolithic: The conflict between honest scientists and the authorities' accomplices has never ceased. Consequently, it is not a question of instituting a total boycott against all Soviet psychiatrists. . . . It is possible and necessary . . . to strive for contacts with honest Soviet psychiatrists and give them your support."

Vladimir K. Bukovsky, who is sometimes addressed as Volodya (the diminutive for Vladimir), is a dark-haired man with intense eyes and a sharp wit. His English is excellent but a little stilted because, as he has explained, he was taught it from "old and very formal texts." Unlike most other dissidents, who have strong political or religious beliefs, Bukovsky is ideologically free. "Whose camp do I fall in?" he once responded to a reporter. "The concentration camp." Asked what he thinks of the "socialism with a human face" that European Communist parties profess to aim for, he replied: "All that interests me is the human face." Unlike Solzhenitsyn and other permanent Soviet exiles, Bukovsky has a five-year passport. His plans include writing a book and studying biophysics at Cambridge University in England.

References: American Teacher 61:16+ Mr '77 pors; Christian Sci Mon p1+ F 22 '77 por, p18+ Mr 29 '77 pors; N Y Post p7 D 29 '72, p4 O 5 '73; N Y Review of Books p3+ Mr 9 '72, p16+ F 17 '77; N Y Times A p5 Mr 2 '77, p41 My 3 '77; N Y Times Mag p38+ F 26 '77 pors; p26+ Je 12 '77 pors; Bukovsky, Vladimir. To Build a Castle: My Life as a Dissenter (1978)

Bunker, Ellsworth

May 11, 1894- Diplomat. Address: b. Department of State, 2201 C St., Washington, D.C. 20520; h. 4341 Forrest Lane, Washington, D.C. 20007; Putney, Vt. 05346

NOTE: This biography supersedes the article that appeared in *Current Biography* in 1954.

Ellsworth Bunker's reputation as a patient, tough-minded negotiator and a skilled diplo-

Ellsworth Bunker

matic troubleshooter is rivaled only by that of W. Averell Harriman. Turning to diplomacy in the early 1950's after serving for more than thirty-five years as a top executive in the sugar industry, Bunker served as a special envoy and mediator during crises in the Middle East and Latin America and as ambassador to Argentina, Italy, and India. As the ambassador to Vietnam for six contentious years, from 1967 to 1973, he almost became a symbol of American involvement in the Indochinese war, and on completing that tour of duty, he was named ambassador-at-large. Recently, at eighty-three, he completed the most difficult assignment of his career: the negotiation of a new Panama Canal treaty that will, in his words, "not only protect but strengthen our national security interests."

A descendant of Nantucket whalers and New York Dutch Reformed ministers, Ellsworth Bunker was born on May 11, 1894 in Yonkers, New York to George R. Bunker, a founder of the National Sugar Refining Company, and Jean Polhemus (Cobb) Bunker. After graduating from the Mackenzie School, a private institution in Dobbs Ferry, New York, Bunker matriculated at Yale University, where he majored in history and economics. After taking his A.B. degree in 1916, he joined his father's firm.

Eager to learn the sugar business from top to bottom, Bunker began his career by hand-trucking raw sugar on a Yonkers dock. Over the next decade, he worked his way up through all the refinery operations to become manager of the Warner Sugar Refining Company of New Jersey, a subsidiary of National Sugar. Bunker was named a director of the parent company in 1927, secretary in 1931, and vice-president and treasurer in 1934. He served as president of National Sugar from 1940 to 1948, sat as chairman of the board from 1948 to 1951, and remained a member of the board of directors until 1966.

A recognized leader in the sugar industry, Bunker was chairman of the newly formed United States Cane Sugar Refiners Association, helped to set up the Sugar Research Foundation and, during World War II, headed the Cane Sugar Refiners War Committee, a governmental advisory agency. In the early 1940's he extended his industrial interests by serving as president of the Portrero Sugar Company of Mexico and as a director of the Guantánamo Sugar Company of Cuba and of Central Aguirre Associates of Puerto Rico. At various times he was also a trustee or director of a steamship company, a bank, two insurance companies, a publishing house, and a manufacturing concern.

At mid-century Secretary of State Dean Acheson, who as a sophomore had coached Bunker on the freshman rowing team at Yale, remembered his old friend when President Harry S. Truman began looking for a successor to Stanton Griffis, the American ambassador to Argentina. Because of his extensive business experience in Latin America, Bunker seemed an ideal choice for the sensitive assignment. Nominated by Truman on February 5, 1951, Bunker presented his credentials to Argentine President Juan Perón three months later. By following a policy of "masterly inaction," which he developed to frustrate the Peronists' repeated attempts to provoke American representatives in Buenos Aires, Bunker patiently mended the rift between Argentina and the United States. In a diplomatic shuffle early in 1952 he was transferred to Italy, where he performed admirably, winning widespread approval in the American press for his skillful handling of potentially explosive issues in the politically and economically unstable nation.

In 1953 Bunker returned home after the newly elected President, Dwight D. Eisenhower, appointed a Republican, Clare Booth Luce, as his replacement in Italy. On January 1, 1954 the former ambassador became the first salaried president of the American National Red Cross. But it was not long before he returned to government service. President Eisenhower appointed him a United States delegate to the Eleventh General Assembly of the United Nations in 1956 and then named him ambassador to India, a post he held until 1961. For several years in the late 1950's, he served at the same time as ambassador to neighboring Nepal. Bunker's forthright explanations of American policy won him the respect of Indian Prime Minister Jawaharlal Nehru, and of such influential publications as the *Indian Express,* which commended him in an editorial for having "prepared the ground for the closer relationship to which both countries are looking forward."

Through a series of special assignments in the early 1960's, Bunker earned a reputation as an accomplished troubleshooter and, in the words of one *Time* magazine correspondent, "an inspired contriver of compromises." At the request of the United Nations he mediated a 1962 dispute between the Netherlands and Indonesia over Irian Barat, a Dutch dependency on the western half of the island of New Guinea. After several months of negotiation, Bunker persuaded the Dutch to surrender the territory to Indonesia, pending a U.N.-supervised plebiscite. Engaged as a consultant to Secretary of State Dean Rusk in 1963, he convinced Prince Faisal, the Prime Minister of Saudi Arabia, and President Gamal Abdel Nasser of the United Arab Republic, who were interfering on opposite sides in the Yemeni civil war, to withdraw their troops from the conflict. (The disengagement agreement and a subsequent tacit truce collapsed within days.)

In January 1964, just one week after Ellsworth Bunker was appointed United States Representative to the Organization of American States, a clash between Panamanian and American students in the Canal Zone precipitated bloody riots that took the lives of a score of Panamanian civilians and several American soldiers. After two months of talks, Bunker and his Panamanian counterpart drafted a joint declaration announcing the resumption of normal relations between their countries and the beginning of negotiations to eliminate the causes of conflict, including a possible revision of the sixty-year-old canal treaty. The following April, Bunker addressed himself to resolving the problems between the United States and Indonesia, but his efforts to minimize their differences failed.

In November 1964 Bunker, who speaks both Spanish and Portuguese, was elected chairman of the Council of the O.A.S., the first American to hold that post in thirteen years. He found himself in a difficult position when President Lyndon B. Johnson, in violation of O.A.S. principles of hemispheric cooperation, ordered American troops into the Dominican Republic after supporters of the exiled former president, Juan Bosch, toppled the military-supported government of J. Donald Reid Cabral in April 1965. Contending that the United States had acted "purely and solely for humanitarian purposes," Bunker convinced two-thirds of the member nations to sponsor an O.A.S. peace-keeping force, composed mainly of American troops, in the Dominican Republic. Appointed to a three-man, *ad hoc* peace committee, Bunker arrived in Santo Domingo in June. He eventually persuaded the constitutionalist rebels, led by Colonel Francisco Caamaño Deñó, and the junta government forces of Brigadier General Antonio Imbert Barreras to accept the installation of a provisional government under the direction of Héctor García-Godoy, the moderate ex-foreign minister, until new national elections could be held in May 1966.

In recognition of his immeasurable value to the diplomatic corps, President Johnson named Bunker ambassador-at-large on October 6, 1966. Just five months later, the President asked him to take on his most difficult assignment to date: the ambassadorship to South Vietnam. At the time of his appointment, American troop strength in Southeast Asia was steadily growing, and the shaky Saigon regime, then under the leadership of Premier Nguyen Cao Ky, controlled little of the countryside. In testimony before the Senate Foreign Relations Committee, Bunker identified as his objectives in Vietnam the establishment of a durable peace, the development of a viable economy, and the protection of the right of self-determination.

Hastily confirmed by the Senate, Ambassador Bunker landed in Saigon on April 25, 1967. On his arrival Bunker told reporters that "military power—important as it is—cannot alone provide any lasting answer to the real problems in Vietnam." "The larger tasks will take longer and will depend ultimately on the Vietnamese people themselves," he added. One of those larger tasks was the so-called pacification program, which was intended to restore South Vietnamese government control to hundreds of rural hamlets that had become havens for Viet Cong guerrillas. Dismayed by the snail-paced progress of the program, Bunker transferred it from civilian to military control, arguing that "the indispensable first step of pacification is providing continuous local security."

By mid-summer 1967 Bunker could report encouraging progress in South Vietnam, particularly in political reform. To avoid charges of campaign abuses in the upcoming national elections supervised by the United States, Bunker prevailed on Premier Ky, who had been accused of illegal campaign practices, to withdraw from the presidential race in favor of the second-place spot on a ticket headed by Nguyen Van Thieu. His wholehearted support of Thieu in that 1967 contest and in subsequent elections—most notably in 1971, when Thieu was unopposed for reelection—sparked charges of election rigging from other Vietnamese candidates. Criticized by Congressional doves for his behind-the-scenes maneuvering in an election that was, in the words of Senator Robert F. Kennedy, "a fraud and a farce," Ambassador Bunker defended his cooperation with Thieu as part of his obligation to deal with the government to which he was accredited. Bunker maintained a close working relationship with Thieu and, over the course of his tenure in Saigon, talked the increasingly dictatorial South Vietnamese leader into instituting a few minor socio-economic reforms. But despite repeated efforts he was unable to end Thieu's boycott of the Paris peace talks, which began in November 1968.

A staunch supporter of President Richard M. Nixon's policy of a phased American troop withdrawal from Vietnam, Bunker insisted that his government's objective was a negotiated settlement that would permit the South Vietnamese to determine their own future. As early as 1970 he fully expected the Vietnamese to reach "a purely Vietnamese solution, one we may not even understand." "We must make a judgment about what is most effective, especially in the Asian context," he explained to Robert G. Kaiser in an interview for the Washington *Post* (January 18, 1970). "The object of diplomacy, here as elsewhere, is not to win arguments but to achieve goals. . . . The yardstick of our success is not what we do, but what the Vietnamese do for themselves." Bunker had always intended to leave Saigon after a negotiated peace settlement was reached, and he therefore resigned on March 30, 1973. On the day of his departure, he told reporters that "the tunnel was longer and the light was dimmer and farther away than any of us realized at the time," but that the situation in Vietnam, imperfect as it was, was "far better than it [had been] before the Paris agreement was signed."

After being reappointed ambassador-at-large by President Nixon in September 1973, Bunker took on two major assignments. He headed the American delegation to the first Geneva peace conference on the Middle East between the Arabs and the Israelis and, perhaps more importantly, he took charge of the deadlocked Panama Canal treaty negotiations. Bunker began talks with deputies of Panama's strongman, Brigadier General Omar Torrijos Herrera, on November 27, 1973. From the beginning he recognized the need for the United States to make concessions in renegotiating the sixty-year-old Hay-Bunau-Varilla treaty, which allowed the United States to build the canal and operate it "in perpetuity." Recognizing how important the talks were to Panamanian national prestige, Bunker immediately moved the site of the negotiations to Panama. "It was psychologically useful for both countries not to appear to be always summoning the Panamanians to Washington," he explained later. Meeting in isolation on a resort island off the Panamanian coast with Foreign Minister Juan Antonio Tack and Nicolas González Revilla, the Panamanian ambassador to Washington, Bunker hammered out a working agreement on eight broad principles of the new treaty, among them, the end of American sovereignty in perpetuity over the canal, the right of the United States to operate and defend the canal, and higher canal fees for Panama.

For the next three and one-half years, Bunker was enmeshed in the most delicate and complex negotiations of his career. Meeting regularly with Panamanian representatives, he dealt with successive obstacles to the completion of a treaty satisfactory to both sides. The Panamanians were especially concerned about the duration of the treaty and the amount of annual rent to charge the United States (Torrijos reportedly wanted to increase the fee from $2,000,000 to $300,000,000 per year); the Americans worried about the canal's vulnerability to attack without a continued United States military presence. By mid-1975, Bunker had convinced the Panamanians to consider the operation and defense of the canal separately. Two years later, the major hurdle was finally overcome when the Torrijos government agreed on a limited role for the United States in the canal's defense even after operational control of the waterway had been relinquished to Panama.

The remaining legal problems were settled during a three-hour conference call that involved Bunker and his colleague, Ambassador Sol M. Linowitz, Torrijos, and the presidents of Mexico, Venezuela, Colombia, and Costa Rica. The Americans then returned to Panama and on August 10, 1977 concluded an accord, comprising two treaties and a separate economic agreement. One treaty grants Panama immediate civil jurisdiction over the Zone and full operational and administrative control of the canal by January 1, 2000. In the meantime the United States will pay Panama between $40,000,000 and $70,000,000 per year to operate the waterway under a new Panama Canal Commission that it will dominate. The United States also agreed to grant Panama $345,000,000 in loans and credits for defense and development. The second treaty authorizes the United States to retain five military bases in Panama through 1999. After that date, primary responsibility for the canal's security will shift to Panama, although the United States retains the right to intervene if the neutrality of the canal were threatened.

The new treaty was signed by the two chiefs of state—President Jimmy Carter and General Torrijos—in a formal ceremony in Washington, D.C. on September 7, 1977. A few days later, it was overwhelmingly confirmed by the Panamanian people in a special plebiscite, but Bunker foresaw a problem with its ratification by the United States Senate. "The canal has a constituency," he explained to one reporter. "The new treaty has no constituency. One has to be created for it. Voting for the canal is like voting for motherhood."

To counter widespread opposition to the treaty, led by such ultraconservatives as Ronald Reagan, who made retention of the canal a key element in his bid for the 1976 Republican Presidential nomination, Ambassador Bunker traveled across the country, making speeches supporting the pact. In virtually every one, he stressed the fact that the United States, contrary to popular opinion, bought not territory, but rights, in 1903. Failure to ratify the treaty, he argued, might well cost the United States its basic objective: an open, safe, efficient, and neutral canal. Pointing out that disgruntled Panamanians could easily disrupt the canal's operations, he warned that "the most likely avenue to the canal's closure and loss would be to maintain the status quo," thus creating permanent tension in Panama. "Eventually, without a treaty," Bunker warned, "we'll face a confrontation with the Panamanians and find ourselves engaged in hostilities with an otherwise friendly nation."

The long-awaited settlement, coming after thirteen years of sporadic negotiations, was a testament to Bunker's diplomatic finesse. "You have to inspire confidence in the people with whom you're negotiating," he told Connecticut Walker in an interview for *Parade* magazine, a Sunday supplement to the Washington *Post* (August 31, 1975). "You have to inspire trust that you are dealing with them fairly and openly. It requires perception, a sensitivity to the other side's problems," he continued. "Obviously, it requires patience, perseverance, and a sense of humor. . . . But it also requires a sense of humility—an awareness that you don't know all the answers and that you have to keep on trying to find them." Although his fellow diplomats attest to Bunker's humanity, they are quick to point out that the ambassador drives a hard bargain. Commenting on Bunker's tactics in an interview for *Newsweek* (August 22, 1977), Torrijos told Ron Moreau, "I have never in my life dealt with people as hard as Linowitz and Bunker. They fought for 1,440 square kilometers of the Zone like the Russians at Leningrad." "He's the most considerate man I ever met," a longtime associate said recently, "but you've heard of the velvet glove and the iron fist. Well, with him the steel is only just a little bit below the velvet."

An austere, dignified man with an aristocratic bearing, Ellsworth Bunker stands six feet two inches tall and has white hair and blue eyes. He wears rimless eyeglasses to correct a vision deficiency resulting from a childhood attack of typhoid. According to one interviewer, Bunker's self-control gives him "an air of having bathed every day of his life in cold spring water." Although outwardly reserved, Bunker is a warm and witty man who frequently regales his colleagues with personal anecdotes, jokes, and limericks. His favorite leisure activity is reading, but he also enjoys golf, sailing, and an occasional game of tennis. Bunker's first marriage, to Harriet Allen Butler, ended with her death in 1964. On January 3, 1967 he married Carol Clendening Laise, then the American ambassador to Nepal. Mrs. Bunker is currently the director general of the foreign service. By his first marriage, he has two sons, John Birbeck and Samuel Emmett, and a daughter, Ellen Bunker Gentil. The Bunkers have a home in Washington, D.C. and a 600-acre farm in Vermont.

References: N Y Post p28 Mr 18 '67 por; N Y Times p9 Mr 16 '67 por; N Y Times Mag p23+ Mr 26 '67 pors, p22+ Ap 28 '68 pors; Newsweek 90:28+ Ag 22 '77 pors; International Who's Who, 1976-77; Who's Who in America, 1976-77

Byrd, Robert C(arlyle)

Nov. 20, 1917- United States Senator from West Virginia. Address: b. 133 Russell Senate Office Building, Washington, D.C. 20510

NOTE: This biography supersedes the article that appeared in *Current Biography* in 1960.

On January 4, 1977 Robert C. Byrd, a self-made scrambler from the hills and hollows of West Virginia's desolate coal-mining region succeeded Senator Mike Mansfield as Majority Leader of the United States Senate. First elected to the Senate in 1958 on the strength of his three-term record in the House of Representatives, Byrd was for many years the prototypical Southern conservative, but after his election as Majority Whip in 1971, he moved closer to the moderate mainstream. A shrewd parliamentary tactician with an inborn talent for political hardball, Byrd is, in the eyes of some seasoned Washington analysts, the most effective Majority Leader in years. "I want to be a part of making the Senate the institution it was meant to be," he said in a recent interview. "The Senate has an independent role. This doesn't mean that it can't cooperate, or won't cooperate with the executive, but the role of the Senate is not to be a rubber stamp for any President."

Robert Carlyle Byrd was born Cornelius Calvin Sale Jr. on November 20, 1917 in North Wilkesboro, North Carolina. (He learned his real name at the age of sixteen and his true birthday from an elder brother in 1971. Until that time, he believed his date of birth to be January 15, 1918.) When his mother died in the influenza epidemic of 1918-19, his father sent him to live with his aunt and uncle, Vlurma (Sale) and Titus Dalton Byrd, in Stotesbury, a coal-mining town in the mountains of West Virginia. As his foster father, a miner, drifted from job to job, Robert Byrd spent a rather bleak childhood in a succession of company towns. He remembers suppers with only "lettuce and a little butter . . . and sugar" on the table and Christmases without "a present in the house, not even a stick of candy." His only toy, he told Martin Tolchin in an interview for the New York *Times* (March 27, 1977), was "a little automobile [he] could pedal." "I kept that automobile until I was an adult," he added.

Byrd was the valedictorian of the 1934 graduating class of Mark Twain High School in Stotesbury, but because of the Depression he could not afford to go to college. He worked briefly as a gas station attendant, then took a job as a produce boy at a local market. Eager to improve himself, he studied a meat cutter's manual in his spare time and, by the end of the 1930's, he was earning $85 a month as the head butcher at a grocery store in nearby Crab Orchard. He moved to Baltimore, Maryland in the early 1940's to work as a welder in the wartime shipyards, but returned to West Virginia after the war ended and opened his own grocery store in Sophia.

Byrd, a born-again Baptist, taught an adult Bible class in Sophia that soon outgrew its quarters as scores of people flocked to the church to hear his spellbinding fundamentalist lectures. When the local radio station in nearby Beckley began to broadcast his weekly sermons to a wider audience, Byrd became so well-known that it seemed inevitable that he would run for public office. He set his sights on the West Virginia House of Delegates. Campaigning alone, he called on every voter in the district. At each stop, he outlined his political program, then took out his fiddle and regaled his listeners with performances of such country classics as "Cripple Creek" and "Rye Whiskey." In 1946 he won election to the state house by an overwhelming majority, and two years later he captured a state senate seat by a similar margin. In his spare time Byrd took night courses at several local colleges, including Morris Harvey College in Charleston and Marshall University in Huntington. He earned straight "A's," but never found the time to complete his undergraduate degree.

Early in 1952 Byrd announced his candidacy for the United States House of Representatives from West Virginia's Sixth Congressional District. During the Democratic primary campaign, H. D. Ragland, his principal opponent, revealed that Byrd had been a kleagle, or organizer, for the Ku Klux Klan in 1942 and 1943. Taking the offensive, Byrd bought radio and television time to acknowledge his brief membership in the Klan as a "mistake of youth." Impressed by his candor, the voters rewarded Byrd with a primary victory, but shortly before the general election, the Klan issue was resurrected by the Republican candidate, who made public a letter that Byrd had written to the Imperial Wizard of the Ku Klux Klan in 1946—three years after he had allegedly left the organization. In that letter Byrd wrote, "The Klan is needed today as never before and I am anxious to see its rebirth here in West Virginia" and "in every state in the Union." The incriminating letter cost Byrd the support of the governor and of most of the state's newspapers. Relying on small donations from hundreds of voters to continue his campaign, Byrd countered that exhuming his former membership in the Klan was nothing more than a diversionary tactic to distract voters from the real issues: crime, moral corruption, and Communism. He took 57.4 percent of the vote to win election to Congress by a respectable majority; he was reelected by even greater margins in 1954 and 1956.

A liberal on most domestic economic issues but generally conservative in other areas, Byrd was outspoken on legislation directly affecting his constituents, most of whom depended on the coal mines for their livelihood. For example, he supported repeal of the Taft-Hartley Act, voted for most prolabor measures, and warned against increased reliance on imported natural gas as a principal energy source. Meanwhile, he attended night classes at the law schools of George Washington University and American University, taking his J.D. degree, *cum laude*, from American University in 1963.

With both West Virginia Senate seats up for election in 1958, Byrd decided to make his move to the upper house. After winning the primary contest by a huge majority, he moved confidently into the campaign against the Republican incumbent, Chapman Revercomb. Taking advantage of the usual off-year antipathy toward the White House, Byrd chastised President Dwight D. Eisenhower for his "lack of strong leadership" in foreign policy, his weak response to the growing Soviet scientific threat, and his failure to turn the recessionary economy around. West Virginia voters responded at the ballot box, giving Byrd 381,745 votes to Revercomb's 263,172 votes. He was reelected by substantial majorities—he routinely garners 80 percent of the vote—in 1964 and 1970 and was unopposed in 1976. Although he has never faced a serious challenge, Byrd does not take his Senate seat for granted. He often telephones local officials for their opinions on key bills and makes regular flying visits to the state to "let the folks know [he didn't] forget them."

As a freshman Senator, Byrd was guided and counseled by Texas Senator Lyndon B. Johnson and, after Johnson's election to the Vice-Presidency in 1960, by Senator Richard B. Russell of Georgia. Although he had supported past civil rights measures, he joined Russell and other Southern Democrats in a filibuster against the bill that became the Civil Rights Act of 1964. "Men are not created equal today, and they were not created equal in 1776, when the Declaration of Independence was written," he argued during one all-night session. "Men and races of men differ in appearance, ways, physical power, mental capacity, creativity, and vision." He disapproved of the voting rights bill of 1965 for similar reasons and often spoke out against such antipoverty legislation as rent supplements. "We can take the people out of the slums, but we cannot take the slums out of the people," he said. "Wherever some people go the slums will follow. People first have to clean up inside themselves."

As chairman, from 1961 to 1969, of the Senate Appropriations subcommittee on the predominantly black District of Columbia, Byrd cracked down on welfare "cheaters," drastically trimmed the assistance rolls, and funneled "the monies that were saved in welfare" into health services, education, recreational facilities, and public safety. When spontaneous riots erupted in Washington following the murder of Martin Luther King Jr. in 1968, Byrd, a longtime law-and-order advocate, recommended that federal troops be called up to "put the troublemakers in their places." Although initially opposed to home rule for the District of Columbia, he eventually changed his mind and came out in favor of self-government because it would "place the responsibility right where it ought to be and there would be no further passing of the buck to Congress."

During his first decade in the Senate, Byrd generally voted with the other members of his party in support of the New Frontier and Great Society programs of Presidents John F. Kennedy and Lyndon B. Johnson. Domestically, he was particularly concerned about the quality of education in the United States. A firm believer in continuing education, Byrd supported additional funding for vocational training, career counseling, adult education, community colleges, and cooperative education programs. He was also a leader in the fight for realistic social security benefits and sponsored legislation strengthening the administration and financing of the plan. In foreign affairs, he wholeheartedly supported the escalation of the war in Southeast Asia and condemned antiwar demonstrators as "hypocritical, self-centered, selfish, long-haired, know-it-all students and pseudo-intellectuals" who wanted to "encourage Hanoi and help kill American boys."

By the end of the 1960's Byrd's views were conservative enough for him to rate a place on President Richard M. Nixon's list of possible Supreme Court nominees. During the Ninety-second Congress, he took Nixon's position on 59 percent of the issues before the legislature, voting against him on only 34 percent. His agreement with the majority of Congressional Democrats dropped from a high of 83 percent during the Eighty-sixth Congress to just 65 percent, while his agreement with the conservative coalition rose from 42 percent to 56 percent. He supported preventive detention, no-knock entry and anti-riot legislation, approved additional appropriations for the supersonic transport plane and the antiballistic missile system, and voted against the Hatfield-McGovern and Cooper-Church end-the-war amendments. To combat the "activist" nature of the Supreme Court under Chief Justice Warren E. Burger, he backed the nominations of G. Harrold Carswell and Clement F. Haynesworth Jr., the conservative Nixon appointees, to the Court, and when the Senate refused to confirm the nominations, he complained that the two men were victims of a lynching bee at the hands of the liberal establishment.

Over the years, the diligent Byrd earned the admiration of his colleagues for his detailed knowledge of bills under consideration and for his grasp of parliamentary procedures. In 1967 he was elected secretary of the Democratic Conference, a housekeeping position of relatively little importance until Byrd assumed that post. Always available, he helped his fellow Democrats draft legislation, scheduled bills for debate, counted noses on important issues, and occasionally delayed votes until the Democratic contingent assembled. He remembered birthdays and anniversaries, attended family funerals, and kept a careful account of favors given and received. Because he cheerfully took on tedious and seemingly insignificant tasks, Byrd became known among his detractors as "the Senate's garbage man."

But within three years Byrd was virtually running the day-to-day operations of the

Senate and in 1971 challenged Edward M. Kennedy, the incumbent, for the position of Democratic Whip. "I've been doing the work all along," he told reporters. "The only difference is I would like the title." On the strength of votes from Southern and border-state Democrats and a deathbed proxy from Senator Russell, Byrd unseated Kennedy by a vote of thirty-one to twenty-four. Most observers credited his stunning victory to his attention to legislative details and to his willingness to look out for the interests of absent Senators.

At the time he became Majority Whip, Byrd was the third most conservative Senator outside the South, but within weeks of taking office his voting record moderated. He continued to vote with the liberals on such bread-and-butter issues as housing, unemployment benefits, Social Security, and public works projects. He also approved most civil rights bills, including the Equal Rights Amendment, but he steadfastly opposed busing to achieve racial integration in the schools as a "monstrous and costly madness." In contrast to previous positions, he supported "certain selective" cuts in defense spending and in October 1973 joined his colleagues to override Nixon's veto of a bill limiting the President's war-making powers. Byrd criticized a proposed arms sale to South Vietnam, recommended that SEATO be abolished, and supported the resumption of diplomatic relations with Cuba and with the People's Republic of China. He readily acknowledged that the shift to a more liberal viewpoint was deliberate. "A leadership role is different," he explained to newsmen, "and one does represent a broader constituency."

A member of the Senate Judiciary Committee since 1969, Byrd led the opposition to the confirmation of L. Patrick Gray 3d as the director of the Federal Bureau of Investigation. Under the Senator's relentless cross-examination, Gray admitted that John W. Dean 3d, counsel to President Nixon, had probably lied to the FBI during the early months of the Watergate investigation. Gray's testimony virtually forced Dean to cooperate with the special prosecutor. Well-versed in earlier impeachment trials, Byrd opposed Presidential resignation as an alternative to impeachment because "the question of guilt or innocence would never be fully resolved" and "confidence in government would remain unrestored."

A superlative legislative technician and expert political maneuverer, Byrd was one of the most productive whips in the history of the Senate, so that by the time Senator Mike Mansfield, the Senate Majority Leader for fifteen years, resigned in January 1977, he was ready to take on the administrative leadership of the Senate. After his only serious challenger, Hubert H. Humphrey, withdrew from contention, Byrd was chosen Majority Leader by acclamation. He immediately pledged his full cooperation to Jimmy Carter, but reminded the newly elected Democratic President that his "first responsibility will be to represent the United States Senate."

As Carter's point man in the Senate, Byrd smoothed the way for Administration programs. He was not, however, a Carter cheerleader and on more than one occasion publicly chastised the President for failing to consult the Senate leadership on key appointments and legislative policies. Refusing to waste time on bills that had little chance for passage, among them, the welfare reform package, Byrd concentrated on such vital issues as energy conservation. When the Carter energy package, which had passed the House virtually intact, met with determined opposition in the Senate in September 1977, Byrd resorted to what some observers called "steamroller tactics" to end a fourteen-day filibuster over deregulation of natural gas prices. To stall passage of a deregulation bill, Senators James Abourezk and Howard M. Metzenbaum offered some 500 amendments. Acting on a prearranged plan, Vice-President Walter F. Mondale, as presiding officer of the Senate, summarily ruled about three dozen of the amendments out of order as Byrd brought them up, one after another, for a ruling. That parliamentary maneuver broke the filibuster, and the Senate voted, 50 to 46, to exempt natural gas from price controls. Responding to protests from outraged liberals, Byrd maintained that he had "not abused [his] leadership." "I am trying to keep Senators from abusing the Senate," he said. "I am trying to put a stop to this filibuster. . . . The Vice-President is here to get the ox out of the ditch."

Byrd often employed his tactical skill to save Carter foreign policy proposals from almost certain defeat. For example, to broaden support for the proposed withdrawal of American troops from South Korea, he introduced a compromise amendment insuring Congressional participation in the final plan. Because the controversial new Panama Canal treaties were, in his words, of "such far-reaching importance" that "they ought not to be rushed," he postponed a ratification vote for several months to give Senators the chance to study the facts. "The judgment should be based on merits, not on jingoism or knee-jerk reactions," he explained. Byrd himself led a Senate delegation to Panama to get "a better understanding of the problem."

Recently described by one reporter as "a short, slightly paunchy figure with a pinched expression and canny gaze," Robert C. Byrd is five feet nine inches tall with slicked-back gray hair and blue eyes. He spends virtually all his time on the job, foregoes annual vacations, and, in his few hours away from the Hill, is likely to be involved in some self-improvement project. Several years ago, for instance, he read a dictionary from cover to cover. In infrequent fits of energy, he jogs in place. He shuns the cliquish Washington cocktail party circuit because he hates to stand around and squander his time. A rather reserved, private man, he prefers the company of his family to that of his political colleagues. He and his wife, Erma Ora (James) Byrd, whom he married on May 29, 1936, have two daughters, Mona Carol and Marjorie Ellen, and six grandchildren. "One of these days, I'll be over in a hospital somewhere with four walls around me and the only people who'll be with me will be my family," he told Martin Tolchin. "The rest will be pretty busy with their responsibilities. It's pretty easy to be fast forgotten."

References: Atlan 236:29+ S '75 por; N Y Times A p14 Ja 5 '77 por, p1+ Mr 27 '77 por; N Y Times Mag p9+ F 28 '71 pors; U S News 83:29 O 17 '77; Douth, George. Leaders in Profile: The United States Senate (1975); Who's Who in America, 1976-77

Carew, Rod(ney Cline)

Oct. 1, 1945- Baseball player. Address: b. Minnesota Twins, Metropolitan Stadium, 8001 Cedar Ave. S., Bloomington, Minn. 55420

The professional baseball player now active who is most likely to duplicate Ted Williams' feat of a .400-plus average is Panamanian-born Rod Carew of the Minnesota Twins, who has just won his sixth American League batting title, with an average of .388. The Minnesota first baseman, who throws right and bats left, aims for hits, not homers, and with his quick, easy stroke he connects to all fields with assured regularity. Although ranking with the all-time hitting greats, the low-keyed Carew received little publicity until recently because, in an era when commercial hustling and insatiable aggrandizement are too often the rule among players as well as teams and leagues, he has preferred the peace and quiet—and relatively low pay—of his niche in the Midwest's "north country." "There's nobody quite like him," Gene Mauch, the Twins's manager says. "He's got everything—intelligence, strength, confidence, speed afoot, and hand-eye coordination. Many ballplayers are pleasant to manage, but managing Rodney is a privilege." On November 16, 1977 the Baseball Writer's Association of America, by vote of its members, named Carew the American League's Most Valuable Player.

"All this publicity has been great for me," Carew told Dave Anderson when Anderson was preparing an article on him for *Sport* (October 1977), "but . . . it's not going to make me different. . . . I'll always look back to what I had as a kid. I know where I came from." Rodney Cline Carew was born to Panamanian parents on October 1, 1945 on a train taking his mother, Olga Carew, from her home in Gatun, a town near the Caribbean Sea end of the Panama Canal Zone, to a clinic in Gamboa, in the middle of the Canal Zone. He was named after Dr. Rodney Cline, a physician who happened to be on the train and who delivered him. Assisting at the delivery was another passenger, a nurse, Margaret Allen, who became his godmother.

Growing up in Gatun, Carew was, according to his mother, "quiet and alone . . . always walking around with a bat and ball in his hand." Dave Anderson in his *Sport* article quoted Carew: "At school I could never be in plays or recite poetry. It seemed like I was never really comfortable except when I was playing ball." In *An Interview with Rod Carew* (1977), a Children's Press Creative Education Book, Larry Batson quoted the Minnesota first baseman: "We were poor, really poor. I almost never had shoes or clothes good enough to go to church and Sunday school like the other kids. That was one of the reasons I was so shy, I guess. But no matter what, my mother always saw that I had baseball shoes and a glove. She knew how much the game meant to me."

When he was eleven, Carew was hospitalized for six months with rheumatic fever. It was during or shortly after his period of recuperation from the disease that he first saw a major leaguer swing a bat—in old newsreels incorporated into the motion picture *The Babe Ruth Story*. After his recovery, he played

Little League baseball, under the tutelage of an uncle, Joseph French, to whom he was much closer than he was to his father, a Canal tugboat worker. "They thought I had to be older than twelve because I was getting five, six hits a game," he recalls. "I had to show them my birth certificate. . . . The next year I was only thirteen but I was playing in a senior league with kids who were seventeen and I still hit. That's when I realized I must be a good hitter."

In 1962 Margaret Allen, Carew's godmother, wrote his mother from New York City, suggesting that life there might be easier than in Panama. Carew's father told his wife to go on ahead with the children, and that he would follow when he could. (Apparently he never did.) Olga Carew flew to New York with Rod, her older son Eric, and her daughters and settled with them in the Washington Heights section of Manhattan, near where the Polo Grounds, home of the baseball Giants, still stood, across the Harlem River from Yankee Stadium.

Carew, whose native language is Spanish, remembers the years he spent at George Washington High School in Washington Heights as a "terrible" time. "I didn't speak a whole lot of English then [and] the classes were in English. . . . I'd walk around the streets and wish I were home. Panama was so different. In Panama there was room to run and room to play and room to breathe. This was like a whole new world. It took some getting used to." There were some "nice people," he recalls, but there were also "hoods and dope-pushers and junkies and killers." "I never really left the neighborhood. I stayed by myself. I learned I could keep out of trouble by being alone, thinking, studying, playing ball. My whole world was that area." (Several years after he graduated from high school, Carew went back to visit the school and was saddened by what he found, as he told Larry Batson: "I couldn't believe it. The kids were blank. Just blanks. Dope.")

Afternoons, Carew had a part-time job in a grocery store. On weekends he played sandlot ball with a team called the Cavaliers in Macombs Dam Park, adjacent to Yankee Stadium, or in Babe Ruth Park, across the street from the stadium. Eventually he caught the eye of a teammate's father, Herb Stein, a New York City Transit Authority detective who was a "bird dog," or unofficial, unpaid lookout for the Minnesota Twins. Alerted by Stein, the Twins sent a regular scout, followed by the director of their farm system, to look Carew over, and the next time the Twins came to Yankee Stadium to play the Yankees they gave the eighteen-year old a tryout in the stadium. (It was his second time in a major-league ball park; the first had been to see Willie Mays play in a game in the Polo Grounds.)

A month after the tryout, Carew signed with the Twins for a bonus of $5,000. He spent three years in the minor leagues, with Minnesota farm teams in Melbourne and Orlando in Florida and Wilson in North Carolina, batting .325, .303, .292 respectively. As the first black player with the Orlando team, Carew was under severe tension, with the result that when he arrived in Wilson he was "moody," according to Vern Morgan, the Wilson manager. "Part of the moodiness was . . . he was homesick. Part of what made him homesick was his experience at Orlando." Under Morgan's encouraging guidance, he came out of his funk and worked hard at his weak points. "Morgan made sense," Carew recounts. "He kept reminding me that if you don't play in the big leagues, then you've wasted your time and you're nowhere. I was a terrible fielder. We started there."

The following year, 1967, Carew was in Minnesota, playing second base, a position he held until 1976, when he was shifted to first base. In his first major league season he hit .292 and was voted the American League's Rookie of the Year. The next year his average slipped to .273, but in 1969 he won the first of his American League batting titles, with an average of .332. Also in 1969, he stole home seven times, tying the major league record. His manager at the time, Billy Martin, later commented: "I taught him how to steal home. That's all I ever taught him. As for hitting, he knew how to do that all by himself. And he could bunt .330 if he tried."

In 1970 Carew batted .366, but he was not in contention for the batting title that year because, sidelined by an injury, he was at bat only 191 times in fifty-one games. The injury, a torn cartilage that required surgery, was incurred when a base runner crashed into him while he was pivoting at second base on a double play. For some time thereafter Carew tended to be over-cautious in pivoting, and his effort to conquer his fear was not helped by public gibes by Bill Rigney, who had replaced Billy Martin as manager of the Twins. The effects still linger, in reverse: Carew's determination not to capitulate to physical pain or fear of the same is such that Gene Mauch, the present Minnesota manager, calls him "a man and a half" for remaining in games despite injuries.

In 1971 Carew had an average of .307, and beginning in 1972 he won four consecutive batting titles, with averages of .318, .350, .364, and .359. The only other American Leaguer ever to lead the league in batting four or more years in succession was Ty Cobb, who did it nine times in a row; in the National League, Rogers Hornsby had six in succession and Honus Wagner had four.

In 1976, when he lost the American League's Silver Bat to George Brett (.333) of the Kansas City Royals with a .331 average, Carew drove in ninety runs. Going into the 1977 season his career major-league totals were 1,328 games played, 5,055 times at bat, 737 runs, 1,658 hits, 241 doubles, sixty-four triples, fifty-five home runs, 563 runs-batted-in, 466 bases on balls, and an average of .328. In the All-Star balloting by fans in mid-season 1977, when his average was again above .400—as it had been in mid-season 1974—he received the most votes for the second time in three years—a record 4,292,740. He finished the 1977 season in first place in the league in batting (.388) as well as hits (239), runs (128), and triples (sixteen) and tied for third place in doubles (thirty-eight). His average was the best in either league since 1957, when Ted Williams hit .388, and the second-best since 1941, when Williams hit .406. Among National League players, the last to have a higher average was Bill Terry, with .401 in 1930. In addition to the American League's Most Valuable Player Award, Carew received the *Sporting News*'s 1977 American League and Major League Player of the Year awards, by poll of the players. As for the Twins—who had not won a pennant since 1965, although they came close in 1967, and finished first in the Western Division in 1969 and 1970—their fourth-place divisional finish was true to recent form.

The trim but muscular Carew, who throws right but bats left, adapts to different pitchers and their variety of throws with twelve batting stances, which are, as he points out, actually four with variations. "The main reason[s] for changing stances [are] to get comfortable [and] unstring . . . the pitcher." He stands as deep in the batter's box as possible, he says, the better to let his extraordinary eye size up the pitch. "They [most batters] guess at what is coming. I don't guess. I wait to see what the pitch is going to be, then I swing at it." The swing is a quick outward slash, seldom a "pull" (unless the pitch is inside), and almost never the "glory homer" pull for the shortest distance to the nearest fence—a trap for so many potentially high-average hitters.

Pitcher Jim "Catfish" Hunter of the New York Yankees says of Carew: "He has no weaknesses as a hitter. Pitch him inside, outside, high, low, fast stuff, breaking balls—anything you throw he can handle. He swings with the pitch; that's why he's so great. Trying to sneak a pitch past him is like trying to sneak the sunrise past a rooster." Nolan Ryan, the California Angels' strikeout ace, as quoted by Melvin Durslag in *TV Guide* (September 3, 1977), expresses similar sentiments: "When he [Carew] finds himself troubled with a certain kind of pitch, he will make quick adjustments. For a while, he had trouble with inside stuff, but he developed a wrist movement allowing him to slap the ball to left field. When he had trouble with off-speed stuff, he changed his stance and hit the hell out of us. I don't try to outfox him any more. I just throw hard stuff, as close to the outside corner as possible." Minnesota manager Mauch says, "Carew has fantastic hand-eye coordination. Just unbelieveable. And so is his bat control. The great similarity between him and [Ted] Williams is this: they hit the ball hard, often." But Carew differs from Williams in hitting to all fields, so that a "Williams shift" defense cannot be used against him by the opposing team.

Fleet of foot, Carew picks up many "leg hits," reaching first safely on slow ground infield balls, and he steals about forty bases a year. Since 1969 he has stolen home sixteen times. His speed makes possible one of his favorite ploys, the bunt, to which he resorts to break a slump. To maintain and refine his control at the plate, especially in such specific situations as hitting to the opposite field and hitting behind a runner, Carew takes extra batting practice about three days a week, and he finds it hard to understand players with low batting averages who can't be coaxed out to the field early for practice. Like all great hitters, he picks his bats fastidiously and cares for them scrupulously, bathing them with alcohol and storing them in a locked closet reserved for them by the Twins, next to the clubhouse sauna.

Rod Carew is six feet tall, weighs 182 pounds and has the wrists and forearms of a heavyweight boxer, the result of a regular routine of weight lifting. Carew, an Episcopalian, and Marilynn Levy, a white, Jewish native of North Minneapolis, were married in 1970. As of October 1977 they had two children, Charryse and Stephanie, and a third was on the way. The Carews live in a split-level home with a two-car garage in Golden Valley, an upper-middle-class suburb of Minneapolis, where the Minnesota first baseman can be seen working in the garden, shoveling snow, cleaning out the rain gutters, and puttering around like any average suburban home owner.

Among the trophies displayed in the Carew residence are the six Silver Bats he has won as best American League hitter, the American League's Joe Cronin Award, presented to him when he won his fourth consecutive Silver Bat, and the Roberto Clemente Award, for community service. (Carew has devoted much time to fund-raising for various causes, and less conspicuously, he often visits patients at the Mayo Clinic in Rochester, Minnesota.) The award of which he is proudest is Panama's Medal of Honor. Considered a national hero in his native land, especially by young people, Carew has felt that it is his duty to retain his Panamanian citizenship.

Although not as moody, intense or socially awkward as he once was, Carew is still essentially a loner. "I still like to be alone, in my hotel room on road trips, for instance," he told Larry Batson. "I think things through. I think of what's important to me and how to work things out." He feels that his strength and peace of mind as a player are nourished by his happy family life and his location away from the distractions of metropolises like New York and Los Angeles. He could have become a free agent in 1976 but instead accepted a three-year contract at a salary (reportedly below $200,000 annually) that would elsewhere be considered ludicrously low for a superstar. "Some of the free agents who get big money aren't in my calibre, but that's not my business," he says. "Dollars only buy so much. I'd prefer to finish my career here." When that career is finished, he wants "to be remembered as a complete ball player, because I can hit, I can run, I can throw, and I can field."

References: Sport 44:61+ N '67 pors, 57:62+ Je '74 pors, 48:73+ O '69 pors, 64:35+ O '77 pors; Sports Illus 48:57+ Je 19 '78 por; Time 110:52+ Jl 18 '77 pors; TV Guide 25:24+ S 3 '77 por; Batson, Larry. An Interview with Rod Carew (1977)

Carter, (Bessie) Lillian

Aug. 15, 1898- Mother of Jimmy Carter; nurse; social service worker. Address: h. Plains, Ga. 31780

Lillian Carter, the feisty and outspoken matriarch of the Carter clan, has been described by her son, President Jimmy Carter, as "the most liberal woman in Georgia," and by one enchanted reporter as "a Rose Kennedy without the hair dye." The grande dame of Plains, Georgia prefers to be known as Miss Lillian. "Don't call me Mrs. Carter," she chided newsmen covering her son's Presidential campaign. "That's Jimmy's wife." At seventy-eight Miss Lillian became the darling of the media—the most candid, refreshing, and unpredictable personality of the election year. Always independent during her long lifetime, she defied her family to become a registered nurse, withstood the slights of her neighbors when she nursed poor blacks, and, when most of her contemporaries had quietly retired, served two years in India as a Peace Corps volunteer. When, in September 1977, the Synagogue Council of America presented Miss Lillian with the Covenant of Peace Award for "outstanding contributions to the cause of peace," she became the first woman to be so honored.

Lillian Carter was born Bessie Lillian Gordy in the southwest Georgia town of Richland on August 15, 1898, the fourth of the nine children of James Jackson ("Jim Jack") Gordy, the local postmaster, and Mary Ida (Nicholson) Gordy. The family also included two adopted children and a grandmother. Lillian Gordy "adored" her father, whom she described as "the best, biggest politician in this part of the world." Although he never ran for public office himself, Jim Jack Gordy managed Tom Watson's successful district Congressional campaign and later developed the idea of Rural Free Delivery, which Representative Watson pushed through Congress.

The Gordy family moved in 1921 to nearby Plains, where Miss Lillian, ignoring her parents' objections, began nurses' training at Wise Hospital. "I always wanted to be a nurse," she explained in an interview for the *Ladies' Home Journal* (August 1977). "I guess if I had my life to live over, I would realize that what I really wanted to be was a doctor." While working at the hospital, she became engaged to James Earl Carter, who managed the local farm supply store. With his encouragement, Miss Lillian went to Atlanta to complete her nurses' training before the two were married on September 25, 1923. On October 1, 1924 their first child, James Earl (Jimmy) Carter Jr. was born; a daughter, Gloria (now Mrs. Walter Spann, a farmer's wife and author), was born two years later, on October 22, 1926. During the early years of their marriage the Carters lived in a succession of apartments in Plains, but in 1927 Earl Carter bought a 700-acre farm in Archery, about three miles outside of Plains. He eventually purchased the neighboring 3,300 acres of farmland and added a fertilizer bagging and selling plant, a peanut warehouse, and a general store for his black farmhands to his growing line of flourishing businesses.

Lillian Carter laughingly discounts her son Jimmy's "log-cabinizing" accounts of his early years. "We weren't poor," she told James Neyland in an interview for his book, *The Carter Family Scrapbook* (Grosset & Dunlap, 1977). "We just didn't have the modern conveniences. . . . But we lived just as well as anybody else who lived in the country before rural electrification." About two years after the Carters moved into the sprawling, frame farmhouse in Archery, Ruth Carter (now Mrs. Robert Stapleton, a lay Baptist minister and faith healer) was born on August 7, 1929. The Carters' fourth and youngest child, William Alton (Billy) Carter, who now manages the Carter peanut warehouse, was born on March 29, 1937.

Throughout the 1920's and 1930's Lillian Carter continued to work as a nurse. But despite her heavy work schedule, Miss Lillian, assisted by a cook and a nanny, efficiently managed the Carter household and attended to her growing children. "I do believe in working women and I feel so strongly that a child is better off not to have the mother every minute of the time," she said years later, as quoted in *Ms.* magazine (October 1976). "Children who cling to their mothers . . . grow up being babies." The Carter children acquired their habit of reading at the dinner table from their mother, who often went through four or five books a week, most of them purchased from a bookstore in Columbus, Georgia or from a mail-order book club.

To the astonishment of her white neighbors and the silent disapproval of her conservative husband, Miss Lillian regularly nursed the Carters' black farmhands and occasionally received black visitors in her parlor. "I've always had a feeling for the underdog, right or wrong," she told Kandy Stroud, who interviewed her for *How Jimmy Won* (Morrow, 1977). "And I guess it's the fact that I'm just different. I'm not in the same mold as some of the people I know. I'm just different." She excuses her husband's segregationist beliefs as those common to a man "of his time."

In the late 1940's the Carters moved back into Plains, where both were active in church and community affairs and in politics.. Earl Carter was elected to the state legislature, but during his first term in office, he died of cancer on July 23, 1953. Too shocked by her husband's death to accept the customary offer to complete his term in office, Miss Lillian was, in her words, at first "bitter . . . because everyone had a husband and I didn't," then "bored." At the suggestion of her sister, a college housemother for many years, she signed on as the housemother of Kappa Alpha fraternity at Auburn University in Alabama. Around 1961 she resigned because she was "getting nervous over things" and returned to Plains. A few months later, however, she was back at work, this time managing a nursing and convalescent home in Blakely, Georgia. Complaining that most of the patients were younger than she was, Miss Lillian left that post two years later.

Although she had never taken part in the mass demonstrations and marches of the civil rights movement in the early 1960's, Miss Lillian often spoke out in favor of equal treatment for blacks and other minorities. She attended the Democratic National Convention in 1964 and cochaired the Sumter County campaign for the election of President Lyndon B. Johnson, a task that demanded a certain amount of courage. "People hated Johnson down here because of his stand on civil rights, and it got very ugly," she told Claire Safran in an interview for *Redbook* magazine (October 1976), "[but] I [was] never . . . afraid, not even when they threw things at my car and yelled 'nigger-lover, nigger-lover' at me." With other members of her family, she was among the few to vote against a 1965 resolution banning "Negroes and other civil rights agitators" from membership in the Plains Baptist Church. Although she despairs of her church being fully integrated in her lifetime, Miss Lillian believes that the racial situation in the South is "a thousand times better than it used to be."

In 1966, while Jimmy Carter was making his first run for the governorship of Georgia, his sixty-seven-year-old mother, intrigued by a televised public service message that "age [was] no barrier" to membership in the Peace Corps, volunteered for the Corps and requested assignment to India. To her surprise and delight, she was accepted and sent to Chicago for several months of orientation and intensive study in languages and family planning. From her psychological counselor, she learned the subconscious motive for her decision. "I was frustrated in the South," she explained to Jonathan Steele, who interviewed her for the *Guardian* (October 23, 1976). "I wanted to go and work with people who were underdogs, and I realized why I had asked for India. I wanted a dark country with a warm climate."

Admittedly "a little scared," Lillian Carter left for India in December 1966 to begin work in the family planning clinic of Godrej Industries, a complex of factories and mills in Vikhroli, about thirty miles from Bombay. There she shared a small flat with another elderly Peace Corps volunteer, Mabel Yewell. Although the two women were, in Miss Lillian's words, "as far apart emotionally as [Lester] Maddox and [Robert F.] Kennedy are politically," they learned to tolerate and even to like one another—once Miss Lillian had overcome her desire to "push her [roommate] down the steps." At the family planning clinic Miss Lillian taught various methods of contraception to unreceptive male factory workers and assisted with vasectomies. She was convinced that "[her] God doesn't want babies hatched like fish" but grew to resent "having to talk the men into it, for . . . the poor Indian man has only his feeling of manhood to keep him going."

Dissatisfied and frustrated with her family planning work and depressed by the "poverty, starvation, and the dreadful disease," Miss Lillian became more and more despondent. She was especially depressed by her inability to help a woman with terminal infectious leprosy, who had been left to die at the side of a road by the officials of the local leprosarium. Looking back on those dark days, she told Helen Dewar of the Washington *Post:* "India was killing me. I just couldn't bear it. I couldn't touch the dirt, the blood, the lice, the leprosy. I hadn't the strength to bear the horrible cruelty and indifference." One day, she went up on a hillside, away from the filth of the city, to pray. "And Christ let something come into me and I knew I could do anything. I could wipe up blood—and blood had always appalled me—and I could touch leprosy without running to scrub my hands. . . . I could stay in India."

Transferred to the factory complex's treatment clinic, Miss Lillian suppressed her immediate dislike of the "hateful" surgeon and set about to correct the deplorable unsanitary conditions. As many as 300 people, many of them seriously ill, trooped through the clinic each day. Miss Lillian gave injections, administered intravenous feedings, cared for lepers, and even performed minor surgery. Forbidden to treat anyone not employed at the complex, she surreptitiously pocketed bandages and drugs to give to the poor. In desperation, she appealed to the factory owners, who finally consented to distribute medical supplies at her expense. She coaxed contributions from her friends and relatives back home and, by pretending she knew the presidents of their companies, persuaded representatives from Parke-Davis and other pharmaceutical houses to donate drug samples. Within a year, she had created a well-stocked, American-style free clinic.

Buoyed by letters and packages from home and by her indomitable faith, Miss Lillian survived occasional homesickness and recurrent bouts of cabin fever. The most welcome packages contained favorite foods, books (including Mickey Spillane thrillers, which she devoured "like a hungry man eating a grape"), and small gifts for her Indian friends. When she was feeling especially downcast, she attended the lectures of Swami Chinmayananda, whose religious beliefs she found very similar to her own. When her two-year tour of duty ended late in 1968, Lillian Carter, so weakened by her hard work and by her virtually vegetarian diet that she had lost nearly twenty pounds, almost reluctantly returned home. "[My stay in India] meant more to me than any other one thing in my life," she said in a recent interview. "It strengthened my faith in God, and my relationship with minorities. Whether I did anything for the Indian people, they did so much for me." Her lively, occasionally humorous, and always candid letters home, collected and edited by Gloria Carter Spann, were published in 1977 by Simon & Schuster as *Away From Home.*

After she regained her strength, Lillian Carter stumped the state to drum up support for what turned out to be Jimmy Carter's successful 1970 gubernatorial candidacy. A few years later, she took to the campaign trail again, making, by her own count, 600 speeches for the Carter for President campaign. During the all-important primaries she remained behind in Plains to babysit with her granddaughter, Amy Carter, the chief joy of her life. Nearly every day she stopped in at Carter campaign headquarters in Plains to give interviews to newsmen seeking background information on the relatively unknown candidate, sign autographs for tourists, and buttonhole potential Carter voters. Although she never counseled her son on matters of policy, Miss Lillian advised him, in her words, "to quit that stuff about never telling a lie and being a Christian and how he loves his wife more than the day he met her" and to select a "good-looking" running mate.

Much to the delight of television interviewers, Miss Lillian attended the Democratic National Convention in New York City in July 1976. She appeared on television talk shows, gave many interviews, met with the black women's caucus and the Gray Panthers, an activist organization for the elderly, and watched with pride as her son accepted his party's nomination as President of the United States. "I had such a feeling of awe that I wanted to weep," she told Jonathan Steele. "I believe it was the first time I realized what Jimmy was doing, and that if he were elected, he would be the most powerful man in the world. . . . I said, 'Oh Lord, this is the truth. That is my son.' It was almost like being in a cathedral."

Since Jimmy Carter's inauguration as President in January 1977 Miss Lillian has, for the most part, remained at home in Plains. But in February 1977 she returned to India as the official American representative to the funeral of Indian President Fukhruddin Ali Ahmed. Following the ceremony and a brief social meeting with Prime Minister Indira Gandhi, Miss Lillian visited Vikhroli, where she was met by the governor of Maharashtra and 7,000 cheering Indians. "I never knew you thought so much of me," she told the crowd. "The first time I came here, I walked so much it seemed like a thousand miles. But I give you my word, I was happier here then than I am now in the President's plane." In 1978 she also embarked on tours to Italy and West Africa.

A small but solid-looking woman, Lillian Carter has a grandmotherly face etched with fine lines, thick, wavy, white hair, "startlingly clear Carter Caribbean blue" eyes, and "the original of the famous Carter smile, toothy and face-splitting." Although she is convinced that God "planned [her] way of life," she does not consider herself to be deeply religious. "I am a Christian but that doesn't mean I'm a long-faced square," she told Claire Safran. "I do the things I want to do." She smokes an occasional cigarette, takes "a toddy now and then," and plays bridge for money. Casual about clothes, she favors pantsuits and wears dresses only to go to church on Sunday.

Still a voracious reader, she is especially fond of *Anna Karenina*, Kahlil Gibran's *The Prophet*, the novels of Jane Austen, contemporary political analyses, and mysteries. Because she is an admitted soap opera addict, she sets aside time each day to follow the tangled tale of *All My Children*. Miss Lillian enjoys football, baseball, hockey, and basketball, and wrestling matches. She has been a fan of the Dodgers, now based in Los Angeles, ever since Jackie Robinson, the first black major leaguer, joined the then Brooklyn Dodgers in the late 1940's. Realizing a lifelong dream, she threw out the first ball at the fourth game of the 1977 World Series in Dodger Stadium.

Once described by a journalist as "a lovable interview junkie," Miss Lillian recently cut down on the number of interviews she grants because they had become burdensome. She distrusts aggressive women reporters and, despite her reputation for candor, has been known to tell "white lies." "I lie all the time," she told one correspondent, adding, "I have to—to balance the family ticket." Miss Lillian divides her time between her red-brick, ranch-style home in Plains and the angular, airy "Pond House," a gift from her children upon her return from India, on the outskirts of town. There, she fishes for bass with her daughter, Gloria, takes long walks with her Secret Service agent, and entertains her fourteen grandchildren and her great-grandson.

"When Earl died, my life lost its meaning and direction," Miss Lillian wrote from India on her seventieth birthday. "For the first time, I lost my will to live. Since that time, I've tried to make my life have some significance. I felt useful when I was at Auburn, serving as housemother for my bad, sweet KA's. And I'm glad I worked at the nursing home, but God forbid that I ever have to live in one! I didn't dream that in this remote corner of the world, so far away from the people and material things that I had always considered so necessary, I would discover what life is really all about. Sharing yourself with others, and accepting their love for you, is the most precious gift of all."

References: Guardian p9 O 23 '76 por; Ladies Home J 93:73+ Ag '76 por, 94:73+ Ag '77 por; Modern Maturity 20:11+ Ag-S '77 pors; Ms 5:51+ O '76 pors; Neyland, James. The Carter Family Scrapbook (1977); Schram, Martin. Running For President 1976 (1977); Stroud, Kandy. How Jimmy Won (1977)

Carter, Rosalynn (Smith) (rōz′ə-lən)

Aug. 18, 1927- Wife of the President of the United States
Address: The White House, 1600 Pennsylvania Ave., NW, Washington, D.C. 20500

"An almost equal extension of myself"—that is how President Jimmy Carter describes his wife, Rosalynn Carter, with whom he shares a political partnership unequaled in the White House since the days of Franklin and Eleanor Roosevelt. Partnership is nothing new in the thirty-year Carter marriage, for Mrs. Carter took an active role in the family business in Plains, Georgia, campaigned vigorously for her husband's election as Governor of Georgia, and chalked up a record of independent accomplishment while living in the Georgia Governor's mansion. During Carter's race for the American Presidency Rosalynn Carter campaigned alone across the country for nearly two years. Acknowledged as one of President Carter's most influential advisers, the First

Lady often sits in on Cabinet meetings and diligently pursues her special interests, including mental health programs, the needs of the elderly, and passage of the Equal Rights Amendment. Because of her activism, Rosalynn Carter has often been compared to Eleanor Roosevelt, but the current First Lady seems determined to develop her own style. Unlike Mrs. Roosevelt who eventually evolved an identity separate from that of her husband, Mrs. Carter is still, as one reporter put it, "a woman who has a clear sense of mission but whose husband comes first."

Rosalynn Smith was born on August 18, 1927 at 6 A.M. on her mother's family farm a few miles outside Plains, Georgia. She was the first child of Allethea ("Miss Allie") Murray Smith, whose Scotch-Irish ancestors had come to the United States from the Isle of Skye, and Wilburn Edgar Smith, an indirect descendant of Captain John Smith. The Smith family eventually included another daughter, Allethea Smith Wall, who is now an Ellenwood, Georgia housewife, and two sons, William Jerald Smith, an industrial engineer who lives in Illinois, and Murray Lee Smith, who is employed as a teacher in the high school in Plains.

Remembered by one longtime Plains resident as "neat, pretty, clean, smart, reserved and not a blab-mouth or high roller," Rosalynn led a normal and carefree life as a young child. All that changed in the summer of her thirteenth birthday, when her father, who worked as a mechanic and the school bus driver, died a lingering death from leukemia. Left with only a small life insurance policy and a meager pension, Rosalynn's mother scrambled to make ends meet by taking in sewing, working part-time in a grocery store, and finally obtaining a position as Plains postmistress. Meanwhile, her eldest daughter took over many of the household chores and the responsibility of looking after the younger children. Rosalynn also helped with the sewing and earned a few dollars by shampooing hair in the local beauty parlor.

Despite her heavy responsibilities at home, Rosalynn Smith kept up her grades at school, played basketball on the girls' team, and went dancing with local beaux. At school she was looked upon as the best-dressed girl in her class because of the smart clothes that she and her mother made, and one year she was elected May Queen, an honor that took into account both beauty and brains. On his deathbed, Rosalynn's father had urged his children to get an education, and his widow made sure that funds were put aside so that they could attend college. Therefore, after graduating as valedictorian of her high school class, Rosalynn commuted to Georgia Southwestern College, a two-year college in nearby Americus, where she took a secretarial course and was active in the Tumbling Club and the Young Democrats.

As a college girl Rosalynn had a number of admirers, but she developed her most serious crush on the older brother of her best friend, Ruth Carter. At that time Jimmy Carter, three years her senior, was a cadet at the United States Naval Academy in Annapolis and was regarded as the town's most eligible bachelor. He took little notice of his younger sister's friend until late in the summer of 1945, just before he was to return to the academy. After having one date with her, so the story goes, he announced to his mother that Rosalynn was the girl he intended to marry. There followed a whirlwind courtship that consisted of frequent letters, a few dates at Christmas, and a couple of weekends at Annapolis. On July 7, 1946 Rosalynn married him in Plains after she graduated from Georgia Southwestern and he from the United States Naval Academy. "He planned to make the navy a career, so I just thought it would be exciting to get married and travel around," the First Lady recalled to Gail Sheehy (*New York*, November 22, 1976) of her youthful decision to marry. "At that age, I hadn't seen the world, and I thought there was more to it than Plains, Georgia."

For the next seven years Rosalynn Carter got to see at least part of the world, living first in Norfolk, Virginia and then a succession of cities reflected by the birthplaces of her sons. John William (Jack) was born in Portsmouth, Virginia in 1947, James Earl III (Chip) in Honolulu, Hawaii in 1950, and Donnel Jeffrey (Jeff) in New London, Connecticut, in 1952. Since her husband was often away at sea, the young mother was able to gain a large measure of confidence and independence by managing the children and her successive households singlehandedly much of the time.

When his father died of cancer in 1953, Jimmy Carter decided to give up his navy career to return to the family peanut warehouse in Plains. According to the Carters, that decision led to their only serious disagreement. Violently opposed to Jimmy's decision, Rosalynn argued that he was giving up a promising career and that their lives would be restricted by living in such a small town in the midst of their relatives. But Jimmy was adamant, and eventually his wife capitulated. In 1954 the Carters returned to Plains.

Back in Plains, the Carters were faced with a failing business that cleared under $200 the first year. But with characteristic vigor, they plunged into their new work, with Rosalynn keeping the books and Jimmy doing the labor. When the business began to prosper and expand, Mrs. Carter studied accountancy so that she could handle the complicated accounts, and she has recalled that she would probably have taken the CPA exam if her husband's political career had not interfered with her plans.

When Jimmy Carter ran for the Georgia state senate in 1962, his wife took charge of all his campaign correspondence, and after he was elected, she managed the family business alone during the three months each year that he was away in Atlanta. She again took part in Carter's campaign when he ran for governor in 1966 and shared in the disappointment of his defeat by Lester Maddox. A year later, however, she was able to raise his spirits by satisfying his longtime desire for a daughter with Amy Lyn, who was born in October 1967, a few months after Rosalynn turned forty.

During her husband's early political campaigns Mrs. Carter stayed out of the limelight, but when he made his second gubernatorial try in 1970, she gamely took to the stump despite a shyness that made public speaking an agony for her. With her new role as Governor's wife after Carter won, however, Rosalynn gradually gained confidence, learning that she could handle her tasks as the state's official hostess and even master the art of public speaking with a minimum of discomfiture. In addition to performing the ritual round of ceremonial duties, she took an interest in the mentally retarded by serving as a member of the Governor's Commission to Improve Service for the Mentally and Emotionally Handicapped, by also serving as honorary chairman of the Georgia Special Olympics for Retarded Children, and by helping to establish 134 day-care centers for the mentally retarded in Georgia. To gain first-hand experience with the problems of those afflicted with mental illness, she served as a volunteer at the Georgia Regional Hospital in Atlanta.

In 1973, when Carter decided to run for the Presidency, Mrs. Carter not only helped him make that decision, but persuaded him to run in every primary. She then went on to crisscross the country on her own, campaigning for her "Jimmy," as she always called him, in thirty-four primary states. After Carter's nomination at the Democratic National Convention in July 1976, Rosalynn Carter redoubled her efforts by putting in eighteen-hour days campaigning, via her own chartered Learjet, in ninety-six cities and thirty-six states. Impressed with her self-discipline, determination, and soft-voiced Southern charm, reporters nicknamed her the "Steel Magnolia," and many observers felt that she outshone her husband as a public speaker.

In the months following President Carter's January 1977 inauguration, Mrs. Carter concentrated on organizing her eighteen-member staff and settling into a White House workday that included making telephone calls, answering correspondence, attending meetings, and, once a week, holding a working luncheon with her husband. She also instituted the simpler, more relaxed mode of entertaining that has characterized the Carter White House.

When she entered the White House, Mrs. Carter pledged that mental health programs and the needs of the elderly would be among her primary concerns. She therefore persuaded her husband to appoint a twenty-member President's Commission on Mental Health, of which she became honorary chairman, since as the President's wife, she could not legally serve as the official chairman. Tireless in her work for the commission, she chaired public hearings on mental health problems in cities across the United States during the spring of 1977. And in May she held the first of a projected series of round-table discussions at the White House on the problems of the aging.

Another high priority of Rosalynn Carter's has been working for the passage of the Equal Rights Amendment, which she has done mainly through telephone calls and letters to legislators in states where the amendment has come under consideration. She has also spoken out unequivocally in favor of extending the period for ratification of the E.R.A. In the future, Mrs. Carter plans to devote much of her time to building what she calls "a more caring society," which she hopes to encourage by establishing programs that will get "people working together in communities."

During the election campaign, Carter promised that his wife would serve as a sort of roving ambassador during his tenure. Her first major junket took place in late May and early June 1977, when she made a seven-nation tour of the Caribbean and Latin America, calling on heads of state in Jamaica, Costa Rica, Ecuador, Peru, Brazil, Colombia, and Venezuela. The White House made it plain that the trip was to be of a more substantive nature than the traditional goodwill tours on which First Ladies have sometimes embarked. It was emphasized that she would explain the President's views and elicit feedback in wide-ranging talks with leaders of Latin American countries.

To prepare herself for the tour, Mrs. Carter spent several months studying Spanish and receiving briefings from the State Department. Nonetheless, news of the trip was received coolly by most of the macho-minded countries she was to visit, largely because it was considered unseemly for a woman to handle such an important mission. When she actually arrived, however, Mrs. Carter managed, according to most observers, to dispel such male chauvinistic sentiments because of the competent and businesslike way in which she conducted herself.

In addition to making her Latin American trip, Mrs. Carter has served as official representative of the President at the inauguration of President José López Portillo of Mexico and at ceremonial occasions in United States cities. Late in December of 1977 she left with her husband on a seven-nation tour of Europe, India, and the Middle East. At each stop she had her own itinerary that included meetings with health officials and briefings on the status of women.

Mrs. Carter's honors have included election to the board of directors of the National Association of Mental Health, the award of merit of the National Organization for Women for her support of E.R.A., and the volunteer of the year award from the Southwestern Association of Volunteer Services. A Harris poll in the summer of 1977 revealed that Mrs. Carter was one of the most popular First Ladies in recent years.

Although reared as a Methodist, Rosalynn Carter switched her church affiliation to the Baptist denomination of her husband when they married. Like him, she considers herself a "born-again" Christian, and has said that the turning point of her life occurred when she was first lady of Georgia. "I had all those new responsibilities, new things to learn, things I had never done before," she told Dennis Farney of the *Wall St. Journal* (October 26, 1977). "I came to a point where I felt I just couldn't do it myself. And then all of a sudden I realized that I didn't have to, that God was there and He would help me."

The First Lady is a pretty, youthful-appearing woman with naturally curly brown hair and intelligent, wide-set eyes that are variously described as brown, hazel, or blue-green. She is five feet five and a half inches tall, weighs a trim 118 pounds, and is a perfect size 6 or 8, depending on the designer. For clothing, Mrs. Carter prefers conservatively cut, ready-made fashions and shows little patience with reporters who are preoccupied with what she wears.

Rosalynn Carter has been described as a complex and ambitious woman with a relentless drive toward self-improvement. In the New York *Times Magazine* (March 20, 1977) Kandy Stroud called her "a self-contained, basically happy woman with a very stable personality." Despite her considerable warmth and social ease, the First Lady has only a few close women friends. She looks instead to her husband for intimate friendship and enjoys her other close family ties. For a time the White House held the most extended family since the FDR administration, with, besides the President, Rosalynn, and Amy in residence, son Chip and his wife Caron, their baby, James Earl IV, son Jeff, and his wife Annette. Chip and Caron have since moved back to Plains, where he is employed in the family business. The Carters have a second grandson, Jason, the son of Jack and his wife Judy. Amy Lyn Carter is a student at the Thaddeus Stevens School, a progressive public school located not far from the White House. The Carters jealously guard their privacy together, enjoying trips back to Plains or weekends at Camp David, the Presidential retreat in Maryland. Rosalynn Carter has taken music and literature appreciation courses with her husband, and they recently took a brush-up class in speed-reading. Her recreations include playing tennis, which she took up at her husband's urging, and sewing. The First Lady, who reinstituted the pre-Kennedy White House custom of serving only wine, rarely takes anything stronger than an occasional glass of wine herself, and she never smokes.

References: Family Circle 89:4+ O '76 pors; Good Housekeeping 185:102+ Ag '77 pors; N Y Times p45 S 15 '76, p20 F 14 '78 por; N Y Times Mag p19+ Mr 20 '77 por; New York 9:50+ N 22 '76 pors; People 6:22+ N 15 '76 pors; Wall St J p1+ O 26 '77 por; Norton Howard. Rosalynn: A Portrait, 1977

Chryssa (Vardea)

Dec. 31, 1933- Artist. Address: 15 E. 88th St., New York City, N.Y. 10028

The most dramatic and most beautiful sculptures of the Greek-born artist Chryssa are probably her "luminates," as she has called them, constructions in which slender, flowing lighted colors of neon tubing appear either alone or in combination with other materials, as in her masterwork *The Gates to Times Square* (1964-66). Light, however, is only one aspect of the sculpture, whose aesthetic worth remains when neon is exhausted. Chryssa works in a great variety of media —scrap metal, aluminum, bronze, plaster, plexiglass, wood, asbestos, canvas, newsprint, oil, and acrylic—whatever best captures and transmits her image, which sometimes carries considerable emotional force. More essential to Chryssa's art than a particular medium is her preference for using means of communication characteristic of our times, including newspapers and advertising signs, and elements of language, such as alphabetical letters and other written symbols, in explorations that release them from their function, turn them into abstract shapes, and reveal their structural potentialities.

Chryssa Vardea, whose Greek given name translates as "golden one," was born in Athens, Greece on December 31, 1933, the youngest of three daughters in a family originally from Mani in the southern Peloponnesus. As a child during World War II she endured the frightening ordeals of the German and Italian occupations of Athens, where members of the Greek underground would venture into the darkened streets after curfew to write messages on the walls of buildings informing their compatriots about wartime developments. The Fascists hastened to erase the words before they could be read. John Gruen, to whom Chryssa recalled those events in an interview for the New York *Herald Tribune* (March 27, 1968), suggested, "This may have been the beginning of Chryssa's obsession with letters and words—and, indeed, with neon lights, going on and off like those underground messages."

Another of Chryssa's memories of childhood is of the contributions she herself made to the abundant chalk graffiti of the city's streets as she walked to and from school. Prefiguring also the particular forms of expression that she eventually gave to her aesthetic concepts were the wire and plaster constructions that she fashioned at an early age and the largely abstract painting that she executed while studying with Anghelos Prokopion. Before deciding, however, to commit her life to art, Chryssa attempted a career in social work. As a representative of the national welfare ministry, she served at the age of nineteen in the Dodecanese Islands, and she later worked on the Ionian island of Zante to help the homeless victims of a disastrous earthquake.

According to Pierre Restany, in his in-depth study *Chryssa* (1977), it was Chryssa's disillusionment with social justice as she observed the administration of welfare programs that led her to intensify her training in art. In 1953 she left Athens for Paris, where she attended the Académie de la Grande Chaumière and met the surrealist poet André Breton and the surrealist artist Max Ernst, among other luminaries of the postwar Parisian cultural scene. The following year she moved on to San Francisco to study at the California School of Fine Arts and to experiment during her rather brief stay in theatrical design.

Not until after Chryssa had reached New York City in late 1954 did she achieve what Sam Hunter in *Art News* (January 1973) considered to be "her first distinctly personal work": the *Cycladic Books* of 1954-55. The simple, barely distinct vertical and horizontal markings, resembling the letter T, on those plaster or baked-clay raised tablets vaguely suggest the geometric features of the masks or faces of prehistoric Cycladic sculpture. As the title indicates, the reliefs reflect both Chryssa's Hellenic links and her concern with means of communication.

Her fascination, in fact, with symbols of communication, especially mass communication, is what attracted Chryssa to Manhattan, which she has called "the new Byzantium," and specifically to Times Square, "the kingdom of light." For her, the flashing, garish signs of the city were invested with poetic meanings. "I was naturally drawn to Times Square," Hunter quoted her in *Art News* as saying. "Times Square I knew had this great wisdom—it was Homeric—even if the sign makers did not realize that." One of her first reactions to Times Square was to analyze the elements or fragments of its signs in bronze or aluminum tablets composed of letters of the alphabet. She usually either aligned various letters, as in *Bronze Tablet, No. 2* (1956) and *Bronze Tablet: Homage to the Seagram Building* (1957), or scattered them, as in *Study of Light* (1958), a cast aluminum plaque painted white. Some of her configurations of multiple letters have themes expressive of her love of music, such as *Bach* (1956), *Composition for Requiem (Mozart)* (1959), and *Guitar* (1960).

In other structural studies of letters Chryssa juxtaposed modular elements to form individual letters. One of her most effective sculptures of that type is the painted cast aluminum *Letter T* (1958), of which the modular element is itself a T. Rows of rectangular modulars make up another sign, the arrow, in *Arrow: Homage to Times Square* (1958), one of a series devoted to the arrow. The modular elements of the letters and arrows compositions, like those of the earlier *Flight of Birds* (1956), are projected from a background panel against which each casts a dark shadow. That shadow play produces what Chryssa terms "static light." As Restany pointed out in *Chryssa,* the shadow "doubles the real structure of the form while dematerializing its contours. The form plus its shadow create a kind of symbiotic ensemble, a 'formless form.' . . . The repetition of the element or fragment, while altering the integrity of form, carries it beyond its single, simple meaning into an extradimensional continuity of life: communication becomes identified with the very flow of energy."

When Chryssa's work was first seen in solo shows in New York City in 1961, at the Betty Parsons Gallery in January and at the

Guggenheim Museum in November and December, the nature of her art was not so fully perceived. Stuart Preston found some of her sculpture constructions "impressive" in his comments for the New York *Times* (January 13, 1961), in which he also mentioned the artist's "clear, classical, daylight sense of order" and concluded, "Chryssa is a good letterer, one whose talents could be used to advantage in the designing of architectural inscriptions or of text to be put on medals." Predicting in the New York *Herald Tribune* (November 26, 1961) that the show at the Guggenheim would be "confounding" to most visitors, Emily Genauer approved of Chryssa's original approach and concluded: "If the artist possesses or can release any emotional or spiritual depth, her future work may turn out to be very good indeed."

Some of the compositions included in those shows had been inspired by the *Times* and *Herald Tribune* themselves. With *Newspaper* (1958-59), an oil painting on canvas and newsprint, Chryssa had begun a series in which she experimented formally with the structure of the newspaper page. She reworked the typographical spacing of the front page and of pages devoted to advertisements, stocks, real estate listings, classified ads, weather maps, and crossword puzzles. In addition to large newspaper paintings and many preparatory studies, she produced a series of twenty-two lithographs for her *Newspaper Book* (1962), and several newspaper sculptures, including *Folded Newspaper* (1963). An exhibition of lithographs and drawings that Chryssa made during the years from 1959 to 1962 using elements from the medium of the newspaper was presented by the Whitney Museum of American Art in New York in 1972.

Chryssa's preoccupation with the newspaper image tied her, though tentatively, to the pop artists, who chose to work with the forms of everyday, often commercial, things in developing their own idiom. Some of the pop artists, Jasper Johns and Robert Indiana, for instance, shared her involvement with alphabetical letters. Another link with pop art was her utilization of ready-made, or found, objects—discarded metal newspaper plates and later junk metal advertising signs, which she introduced into her constructions in 1959. Typically, she used fragmented or fractured signs and letters. Fragmentation is central in Chryssa's impression of the character of contemporary culture and is also a technique of her work. "I have always felt that when things are spelled out they mean less, and when fragmented, they mean more," she explained in the interview with Gruen. In a landmark sculpture of 1962, *Times Square Sky*, she topped a stack of metal letter fragments with the word "air" in blue neon cursive letters, an inspiration that proved to be a significant step beyond her earlier use of neon lighting, to frame her newspaper painting *Times Square Puzzle* (1961-62).

The problem of light had absorbed Chryssa ever since her first view of Times Square, whose brilliant nighttime sky, she has said, reminded her of the gold of Byzantine icons: "It comes and goes in the foreground instead of remaining in the background." She has also compared Times Square to "a garden of light" that she experienced visually and emotionally in a way that she could not convey through painting. Chryssa came to recognize that neon was the appropriate medium for her image.

To transmit her ultimate understanding of Times Square, Chryssa had to overcome the intricate technical difficulties of working creatively with neon lights. She did so in part through a series of highly original constructions that are aesthetically an end in themselves as well as a means to an end. Again combining metal letter fragments with neon tubing, she produced *Americanoom* (1963), *Positive/Negative* (1965), and *Delicatessen* (1965). Beginning in 1962 she also gained mastery over her new material by creating pieces using neon alone, housed in plexiglass boxes. Among her most satisfying sculptures of that group are *Analysis of Letter B* (1962) and *Five Variations on the Ampersand* (1966).

Renting a studio in Brooklyn large enough to accommodate a sculpture of architectural scale, Chryssa began work in 1964 on the execution of *The Gates to Times Square*, which required a concentrated effort of two years. Her ten-foot-square walk-through complex—an amalgam of welded stainless steel, cast aluminum parts, fragments of commercial signs, neon, plexiglass, and rolled plans (or working drawings) of the forms—is structured on a three-dimensional triangle analyzing the letter A. Restany praised her achievement as a "magnum opus [in which] she embodied the anthropological fact of Times Square in a superlative phenomenon of language." *The Gates* was first exhibited at a major solo show of Chryssa's work in March-April 1966 at the Pace Gallery in New York. During 1968 it was included in the City Sculpture Exhibit in Grand Central Terminal, and a few years later it was acquired by the Albright-Knox Gallery in Buffalo, New York as a gift of Mr. and Mrs. Albert List, who thus gratified the feeling of art critics and art lovers that the work should be made available to the public.

The Gates generated fifteen sculptures called *Studies for the Gates*, on some of which Chryssa continued to work after the completion of her masterpiece. Most of them encase tubular neon shapes in plexiglass boxes and incorporate programming devices such as timers in the total design. Two exceptions are the unencumbered, or wholly exposed, black glass, neon tubing constructions *Clytemnestra: Study for the Gates No. 14* (1967), subtitled *First Scream from 'Iphigenia in Aulis' by Euripides,* and *Study for the Gates No. 15* (1967), subtitled *Flock of Morning Birds from 'Iphigenia in Aulis' by Euripides.* Discussing the latter in a statement quoted in *Hirshhorn Museum and Sculpture Garden* (1974), Chryssa explained that she used a particular form from *The Gates* that resembled a bird shape and that the five sections of the sculpture light up progressively, suggesting a birdlike movement. "This motion," she pointed out, "is also related to the way the chorus moves on the stage in Euripides' play," which opens with a reference to morning birds. *Flock* was described in the New York *Times* (February 24, 1968) as "a pure lyrical form [that] transcends 'neon-ness' to become a sculpture of light devoid of pop or Broadway associations."

Variations on the bird theme occurred among a later group of poetically splendid light boxes that included *Automat* (1972), which Hunter has singled out as an example of "Chryssa's mysterious, effective ability to achieve sensuous beauty." He went on to say, "It is the light intensity of the work veiled by the dark plexiglass, which has the potential of ecstasy as the controlling rheostat is adjusted to its highest pitch of brilliance." In some of her fairly recent work Chryssa has combined neon with painted letters, such as *Today's Special,* part of her calligraphic triptych of 1970-73; *White Plaster with Yellow Ns* (1975-76); and *Rhythm* (1975-76). Several of her compositions of painted plaster or wood letters are without neon.

Restany has attributed the greater diversity of materials in Chryssa's output of the 1970's and her increased involvement with calligraphic fragmentation to her work on the decoration of the reception rooms of Count Metternich's castle in Adelebsen, near Kassel, Germany—a painting commission that she accepted in 1968. That undertaking, though it exacted careful planning and large-scale effort, spared her the enormous expense of the materials, special fabrication, and technological assistance that she needs for much of her sculpture. Some of her aesthetically successful pieces have been financial disasters, and she no doubt welcomed the stipend as well as the honor of the Guggenheim foundation fellowship awarded her in 1973. Chryssa is herself a superb technician whose "fastidious craftsmanship," in the words of James R. Mellow, art critic of the New York *Times,* "has been a hallmark of her work." Her insistence upon nothing less than perfection from the artisans she employs has contributed to her reputation for temperament.

The Museum of Modern Art, Whitney Museum, Guggenheim Museum, Hirshhorn Museum, Walker Art Center, and Tate Gallery are among the world-renowned art institutions that include Chryssa's work in their permanent collections. She has been represented in many group shows in the United States and abroad, especially in Europe, to which she retained her close ties after becoming a naturalized American citizen.

Chryssa is an intense, enthusiastic brown-haired and brown-eyed woman who stands five feet seven inches tall and has what one press interviewer described as the "compact robustness" needed to wield the designs of her larger sculptures. "For the creative person," she once reflected in a conversation with Hunter, "life is like a play —you continue until you reach your destiny." At times she becomes so deeply immersed in her work that she loses awareness of the transition from days to nights. Her recreational interest of music is also part of her art. Asserting that she learned everything about sculpture from Bach, she asked Gruen rhetorically, "Who, with the exception of Mozart has ever made technical structure synonymous with big and powerful emotions?" She has a collection of bouzouki records that may have inspired her, soon after she settled in the United States, to make a sculpture in which she fitted the strings of a bouzouki in the hollowed-out center of a bronze Ionic capital.

References: Art N 72:63+ Ja '73 por; Christian Sci Mon p12 My 31 '68 por; N Y Herald Tribune p6 N 26 '61, p12 Ja 29 '62, mag p36 Mr 27 '68 por; N Y Times p26 F 24 '68, p23 Ap 21 '73; Contemporary Artists (1975); Hirshhorn Museum and Sculpture Garden (1974); Hunter, Sam. Chryssa (1974); Restany, Pierre. Chryssa (1977); Who's Who in America, 1976-77; Who's Who in American Art (1976)

Church, Frank (Forrester)

July 25, 1924- United States Senator from Idaho. Address: b. Room 245, Russell Senate Office Building, Washington, D.C. 20510; 304 Federal Office Building, Boise, Idaho 83702

NOTE: This biography supersedes the article that appeared in *Current Biography* in 1958.

The United States' involvement in the Vietnam war and recent government scandals troubling many Americans have weighed heavily in determining the priorities of Democratic Senator Frank Church of Idaho, a liberal leader who is next in line for the chairmanship of the Senate Foreign Relations Committee. One of the first prominent critics of direct United States military intervention in Southeast Asia, he feels that America must avoid overextending itself abroad and concentrate on its internal problems. The na-

Frank Church

tion's major domestic goal, Church contended during his unsuccessful 1976 race for the Democratic Presidential nomination, should be restoration of the people's confidence in their government. His belief was fostered by his role as head of a 1975-76 Senate probe that revealed extensive violations of individual liberties by the FBI, CIA, and other intelligence agencies. Among the legislative measures that Church has sponsored since his election to the Senate in 1956 are those dealing with the water needs of Idaho, conservation, and social welfare, particularly the problems of the aging.

The grandson of a pioneer who settled in Idaho shortly after the Civil War, Frank Forrester Church was born in Boise on July 25, 1924 to Frank Forrester Church 2d and Laura (Bilderback) Church. He has an older brother, Richard B. Church. His father owned a sporting goods store. Like most residents of southern Idaho, the older Church was a conservative Republican who generally denounced the domestic policies of Franklin D. Roosevelt. To stimulate family debate his son would take the other side of political questions, and after doing his own research on the President's programs at the public library, he became a New Deal supporter. Idaho's Republican Senator William E. Borah remained his political hero, however.

As a high school junior, Church won a first prize college scholarship in the American Legion's 1941 national oratory contest and afterward toured Idaho to demonstrate his public speaking talent. In 1942 he entered Stanford University, but during his first term he enlisted in the United States Army as a private for service in World War II. After taking officer training at Fort Benning, Georgia in 1944, he was commissioned a second lieutenant of infantry and later assigned to serve as a military intelligence officer in Asia.

When the war ended, Church resumed study at Stanford, where he won honors in debate, was elected to Phi Beta Kappa, and in 1947 received his B.A. degree. He enrolled in Harvard Law School in the fall of 1947, but after a New England winter he returned to Stanford hoping that a milder climate would ease his back pains. In 1948 the cause of the pains was diagnosed as cancer, and he was given six months to live. But X-ray treatment and surgery restored his health. Years later Church was quoted in the Philadelphia *Inquirer* (September 21, 1975) as recalling, "When I found out I wasn't going to die, I thought I'd take all the chances that came my way. As a result, I was much more inclined to gamble."

Having earned his LL.B. degree from Stanford and gained admittance to the Idaho bar, in 1950, Church entered the Boise law firm of Langroise, Clark & Sullivan, one of the most prestigious in Idaho. While practising law during the next six years, he taught public speaking at Boise Junior College. Although he lost a 1952 bid for a seat in the state legislature, he was elected to serve as chairman of the Young Democrats of Idaho. He also acquired some recognition in public life as state chairman of the Crusade for Freedom in 1954-55.

Still relatively unknown in the predominantly Republican state of Idaho, Church ventured into the Democratic primary for the United States Senate in 1956. He edged out Glen Taylor, a former United States Senator and the 1948 Progressive party vice-presidential candidate by 170 votes. In the campaign for the general election, when Church faced incumbent Senator Herman Welker, an avid supporter of Senator Joseph R. McCarthy, he emphasized the need for economic development in Idaho and alleged that Welker had done nothing to reverse a decline in population and per capita income in the state. Although Idaho had a long isolationist tradition, Church ran on an internationalist platform and pledged to back the nation's bipartisan Cold War foreign policy. In a campaign speech quoted in the *Reporter* (November 1, 1956), he commented, "We can no longer afford the luxury of isolation. Should we resort to the 'Fortress America' concept, it could mean enemy bombers over Blackfoot or Pocatello some morning." President Dwight D. Eisenhower carried the state by a 61,000-vote margin, but Church defeated Welker by some 46,000 ballots. At the age of thirty-two he became the youngest member of the Senate.

During his first year in Washington, Senator Church, showing that he could be flexible in his liberal stand, won the favor of Majority Leader Lyndon B. Johnson by cosponsoring a compromise jury trial amendment that facilitated passage of the Eisenhower Administration's civil rights bill without a Southern filibuster. In gratitude Johnson removed Church from the minor Post Office and Civil Service Committee in 1958 and placed him on John L. McClellan's rackets committee, investigating improprieties in labor and management. When a seat on the Foreign Relations Committee became available in 1959, the Majority Leader gave it to Church.

A supporter of social welfare programs, the freshman Senator backed efforts to override Eisenhower vetoes of two housing bills and an area redevelopment bill and favored a Social Security health insurance plan opposed by the President. In his keynote speech at the 1960 Democratic National Convention, he accused the White House of fostering a mentality of conspicuous consumption while ignoring social problems such as the need for additional classrooms, medical care for the aged, and expanded public transportation. He asserted, moreover, that under Republican leadership the United States had lost its military superiority over the Soviet Union. Much more favorable toward the programs of President John F. Kennedy, he voted in 1961-62, the first two years of the new Democratic Administration, for school aid, minimum wage, housing, area redevelopment, and medicare legislation.

Among the disadvantages that Church faced in seeking reelection in 1962 was his support of conservation legislation opposed by Idaho mining and lumber interests, such as the National Wilderness System bill, of which he had been Senate floor manager in 1961. Because of his membership on the Interior Committee, however, he also had the political asset of being able to attend to the water needs of his state. In 1957 he backed federal construction of a dam at Hell's Canyon near the Idaho-Oregon border. Two years later he cosponsored a bill for erecting a reregulating reservoir in the upper Snake River Valley. A month before the 1962 election, by threatening to filibuster a water projects bill, he succeeded in retaining appropriations for the long-delayed Bruces Eddy dam project on the Clearwater River in the final bill signed into law by President Kennedy. Church had also won the favor of Idaho voters by returning regularly to his state and meeting with his constituents. On election day his victory by 25,000 votes made him the first Democrat ever to be returned to the United States Senate from Idaho.

The Vietnam war became Church's primary concern in the mid-1960's. As early as 1963 he urged an end to American aid to South Vietnam if its government continued repressing political opposition. Two years later, after President Johnson had directly deployed United States combat forces in the war, Church argued in the New York *Times Magazine* (November 28, 1965) that since the Communist world no longer presented a monolithic front, the United States should be less obsessed with the threat of Communism. Furthermore, he continued, America would be playing a "self-defeating role" in the underdeveloped nations if it backed unpopular dictatorships simply because they were anti-Communist. He concluded, "The lesson to be learned from Vietnam is that when the outcome of a guerrilla war does not threaten the vital interests of this country, we had better deal with it at arm's length." In 1966 he was among fifteen Democratic Senators who signed a letter to President Johnson urging him to continue his suspension of air strikes against North Vietnam. But in a 1967 warning to Hanoi he gave notice that although favoring a negotiated settlement to the war, he opposed unilateral American withdrawal from Vietnam.

As a member of the Senate Foreign Relations Committee, Church came to be regarded as one of the prominent "doves" on Vietnam. That distinction had repercussions in Idaho, where in 1967 prowar rightwingers launched an effort to collect signatures for the Senator's recall. The attempt, however, was ruled illegal. Challenging Church's bid for a third term in 1968, Republican Representative George V. Hansen stressed the Vietnam issue, calling for military victory over North Vietnam. He also criticized the incumbent's support of President Johnson's civil rights and antipoverty legislation. Church campaigned on his representation of the state's interests, citing his consistent opposition to gun control and his successful effort on the Interior Committee earlier in the year to block a measure to divert Colorado River water from Idaho to the Southwest. He won easily by 59,000 votes.

After the incursion into Cambodia ordered by President Richard M. Nixon in April 1970, Church began a series of efforts to end American participation in the Indochinese conflict and reassert Congressional powers on questions of war that he believed had been abdicated. With Senator John S. Cooper he introduced an amendment to the 1970 foreign aid bill that, as passed by Congress in a limited version, prohibited funds for American combat troops or advisers in Cambodia. A 1971 Cooper-Church amendment sought to bar expenditures for United States forces in Indochina except to protect withdrawing American troops, but the Senate rejected it. The next year Church joined Senator Clifford Case in an unsuccessful bid to pass a similar proposal. While the Senate debated the amendment, Church took the floor to denounce the mining of Haiphong harbor by President Nixon without consulting Congress, stating that the decision "continues a conscious policy of disregard for Capitol Hill which has been in effect throughout this senseless war, a Presidential war."

Church was also involved in broader efforts to limit American overseas commitments because he believed, he declared in a foreign policy address at Washington University in 1970, "the first mission of the federal government . . . [is] to attend to the genuine needs of the American people." In 1971 he advocated a 50,000-man cut in the 310,000 United States force in Europe by the end of the year. Opposed to the 1971 foreign aid authorization bill, he argued on the Senate floor that "reactionary regimes . . . value aid from the United States as a means of maintaining, not of abolishing, inequalities of wealth and power." In 1972 the Senator urged scrapping the SEATO alliance so that it would not draw the country into new entanglements or interfere with President Nixon's recent rapprochement with mainland China.

Chairman of the Foreign Relations Committee's subcommittee on multinational corporations, Church headed several well-publicized investigations in the mid-1970's, including a 1973 probe that revealed that International Telephone and Telegraph (ITT) had offered to finance the CIA in an effort to prevent the election in 1970 of Marxist Salvador Allende as President of Chile. Church recommended legislation barring private contributions to the CIA. Spurred by the Arab oil embargo, in 1974 Church's subcommittee investigated the relationship between United States oil companies and Middle East oil-producing nations. His findings led him in 1975 to urge an antitrust investigation by the Justice Department and to suggest the creation of a government corporation to buy oil directly from foreign suppliers. During the same year his subcommittee revealed the full extent of the Arab blacklist of Jewish and allegedly pro-Israeli businesses. After the panel heard testimony in 1975-76 on the bribery of foreign officials by American companies doing business abroad, Church proposed legislation for monitoring major corporations to prevent that practice.

Because of reports of improper or illegal use of the CIA and FBI under the Nixon Administration, the Senate in January 1975 appointed Church chairman of a Select Committee to Study Government Operations With Respect to Intelligence Activities, popularly known as the Senate Intelligence Committee. A formal, almost scholarly public figure, Church sought a fair, responsible probe free of sensationalism and received considerable national attention and praise from both parties for his work. The security measures imposed by Church and ranking panel Republican John Tower made the committee "leakproof."

Early in the Intelligence Committee investigation Church explained in a meeting with newsmen, as quoted in the *Christian Science Monitor* (March 21, 1975), that the major reason for the inquiry was "to determine where a threat to the freedom [of American citizens] is involved." The committee's probe revealed that, among other abuses the CIA, FBI, and National Security Agency had intercepted telephone calls, cables, and letters; the FBI had staged burglaries and disruptive activities to harass dissidents; and the Internal Revenue Service had initiated audits for political reasons. In February 1976 Church urged the appointment of a special prosecutor to investigate criminal activity by the CIA and FBI. The following May he fought successfully on the Senate floor for the establishment of a permanent Select Committee on Intelligence with exclusive legislative and budgetary authority over the CIA.

On March 18, 1976, shortly after the Intelligence Committee had completed its hearings, Church declared himself a candidate for the Democratic Presidential nomination. A late entry into the race, he founded his strategy on the belief that no strong front-runner would emerge from the primaries. In an interview for *Time* (June 7, 1976) he stated that the campaign's overriding issue was "to reestablish the legitimacy of the Government in the eyes of the people." Church backed the Humphrey-Hawkins jobs bill, which called for government help in reducing unemployment, but stressed the need for reviving the private economy. He advocated an end to government policies that encouraged investments abroad, costing Americans their jobs. Appealing to another group of voters, he could point to solid achievement as the chairman of the Special Committee on Aging. In his first primary contest Church defeated former Georgia Governor Jimmy Carter in Nebraska on May 11. The Senator then won the Idaho and Oregon primaries on May 25 and the Montana race on June 1. But on June 14, after Carter had virtually clinched the nomination, Church withdrew his candidacy and endorsed the Georgian, who later named Church among those being considered for his running mate.

While serving as chairman of the energy research and development subcommittee of the Energy and Natural Resources Committee (formerly the Interior Committee), Church disagreed in 1977 with President Carter's opposition to the development of plutonium as a power reactor fuel. He stated in May that the policy of the President, who favored halting construction of the Clinch River nuclear reactor demonstration plant at Oak Ridge, Tennessee, would diminish the influence of the United States in the formulation of worldwide nuclear policy. The ranking member of the Foreign Relations Committee and a supporter of President Carter on that panel, Church visited Cuba the following August on an Administration-encouraged trip aimed at improving relations with that Caribbean nation. His three days of talks with President Fidel Castro culminated in an announcement by the Cuban leader that he would permit eighty-four American citizens to leave the island with their Cuban wives and children. Senator Church was scheduled to become chairman of the Foreign Relations Committee in January 1979 on the retirement of Senator John J. Sparkman of Alabama.

On June 21, 1947 Frank Church married Jean Bethine Clark, the daughter of a prominent Democrat, Chase A. Clark, who had been Governor of Idaho in 1941-42. According to Linda Charlton of the New York *Times* (March 19, 1976), Mrs. Church is one of her husband's major political advisers and has been referred to as Idaho's "third Senator." The couple has two sons, Forrest and Chase. The still-boyish looking Church is six feet tall with slightly graying dark hair and brown eyes. He loves to talk, both as a public speaker and as a father at the dinner table, and his family used to joke about his habit of talking to himself while shaving. Louise Sweeney of the *Christian Science Monitor* (July 1, 1975) wrote that on television Church seems to have "a certain heaviness of manner" that is deceptive because in person he is a man of warmth and ebullience. She also described him as an "unaccomplished pianist." Another of his recreations is trout fishing. In 1965 the National Wildlife Federation named him winner of the Conservationist of the Year award.

References: Biog N p956+ S/O '75 por; Christian Sci Mon p22 Jl 1 '75 por; N Y Times p1 Mr 19 '76 por; Newsweek 87:20 Mr 29 '76 por; Time 107:15+ My 3 '76 por; U S News 78:15 Je 30 '75 por; Douth, George. Leaders in Profile: The United States Senate (1975); Ralph Nader Congress Project, 1972; Who's Who in America, 1976-77

Clark, Eleanor

July 6, 1913- Writer. Address: b. c/o Pantheon Books, 201 E. 50th St., New York City, N.Y. 10022; h. 2495 Redding Rd., Fairfield, Conn. 06430

So far in her career of over forty years Eleanor Clark's nonfiction, particularly the enduring *Rome and a Villa, Oysters of Locmariaquer,* and book reviews in *Partisan Review* and other periodicals, has accounted more than her fiction, including her major novel, *Baldur's Gate,* for her luster as a writer. But whatever her literary form, "an integral element in her art," as the novelist Peter Sourian once pointed out, is her "cultivation." Her short stories and her novella, *Dr. Heart,* as well as her recent memoir, *Eyes, Etc.,* are also rich in literary echoes and references that signify a lifelong love of reading. Whatever her theme, moreover, she unfolds it with an often ironic juxtaposition of values, with adroit, illuminating turns of phrase and thought, sometimes with a Yankee's social consciousness, and almost always with a keen perception of place and what Sourian called a "sense of past-present as a constantly deliquescing oneness."

Although Los Angeles, California is Eleanor Clark's birthplace, she spent only the first few weeks of her life in that city and is a New Englander by heritage, rearing, and preference. She was born on July 6, 1913, the younger of two daughters of Frederick Huntington Clark, a mining engineer, and Eleanor (Phelps) Clark. On both sides of her family her ancestors were among the early settlers of Massachusetts, Rhode Island, and Vermont. She grew up in what she has called "a highly literate ambiance." Her paternal grandfather, John Bates Clark, wrote books on economics, and her Grandmother Clark, an early graduate of Vassar College, was dedicated to the values of education. Her maternal grandfather, Charles Henry Phelps, practised law, wrote poetry, and enjoyed the friendship of Longfellow and Melville.

The first home that Eleanor Clark remembers is Roxbury, Connecticut, of which she considers herself a native. An outdoorsman, her father often took her and her sister, Eunice, on camping trips. She also spent part of her childhood in Manhattan, where as a first-grade pupil she attended the first of many schools in a series of changes that in some part may perhaps be attributed to the breakup of her parents' marriage. For two years she went to a one-room country schoolhouse in Roxbury, later to convent schools in France and Italy, and for four years of college preparation to Rosemary Hall in Greenwich, Connecticut. Writing, editing, and acting ranked high among her extracurricular interests. In an autobiographical sketch for *Twentieth Century Authors; First Supplement* (1955), she wrote, "Also inclined, always, to waste a lot of time on various sports and hope not to outlive the possibility of doing so."

Music, moreover, particularly the piano, had become so important to her that she devoted a year of study to that art in Rome before enrolling in Vassar College in 1930. There she majored in English. "In my college years I was mainly writing poetry and I wrote a great deal," Eleanor Clark told R. W. B. Lewis in an interview for the New York *Times Book Review* (October 16, 1977). "I consider this in retrospect an important exercise. Any art has got to have a strong element of cryptology . . . something that holds further meanings on further scrutiny. And poetry is an essential teacher in this." At Vassar she joined two of her classmates, Elizabeth Bishop and Muriel Rukeyser, who, unlike her, did go on to become poets, in forming a literary magazine to protest some policies of the *Vassar Review*. Another member of that rebel group was Mary McCarthy, like Eleanor Clark, a sharp ironist and stern, individualistic moralist. All four young writers shared a gift for verbal subtlety.

On leaving Vassar with her B.A. degree in 1934, Miss Clark worked at an assortment of free-lance jobs, contributing short stories and essays to magazines and ghostwriting and editing for German refugee scholars and others. From 1936 to 1939 she was employed in editorial work by W. W. Norton and Company, the publisher of *New Letters in America* (1937), a collection of short stories, essays, and poetry mainly by new American writers, which she edited with Horace Gregory. Later she translated from the Spanish Ramon José Sender's *Dark Wedding* (Doubleday, 1943).

Along with many others who reached maturity during the Depression-stricken 1930's, Eleanor Clark was exposed to compelling forces for change in social and political attitudes. She has described herself as having been "a Trotskyite sympathizer," as quoted in the New York *Times* (October 15, 1977). "But I was never a political person," she went on to make clear. ". . . I figure my function is to be a writer." Her interest in the political agitation of the 1930's is evident in some of her early fiction, such as her short story "Call Me Comrade" and her first novel, *The Bitter Box* (Doubleday, 1946). An ironic study of an innocuous, unsuspecting bank teller who becomes involved, to his ruin, in a radical political party, *The Bitter Box* delighted Diana Trilling, who praised it in the *Nation* (April 27, 1946) as "a serious, funny, and truthful picture of Communist doings in this country, and therefore a work of courage."

Between the writing of much of the novel and its publication after World War II, Miss Clark served for two years, from 1943 to 1945, in Washington, D.C. in the Office of Strategic Services, which put to use in its foreign nationalities branch her knowledge of French and Italian. The war's ending, together with an award in creative writing from the National Institute of Arts and Letters and a Guggenheim fellowship, enabled her to make several prolonged visits to Italy, especially to Rome and its surroundings. From time to time she returned to her inexpensive, cold-water apartment in New York City, whose occupants and comings and goings she wrote about nostalgically in a section of *Eyes, Etc.*

While in Italy, Eleanor Clark lived in a ruined sixteenth-century fortress north of Rome. Her intention was to work on fiction, but she became so often diverted by the seductions of the city that she began writing the sketches and essays that evolved into *Rome and a Villa* (Doubleday, 1952). To her impressions of Rome—the grandeur of its past and the present, its buildings, fountains, statues, streets, people, and cats—she brought the distinctive qualities of her fiction, such as "an almost polished beauty, a poetic absorption with the inner meaning of the outward symbol," which Rose Feld had admired in *The Bitter Box* (New York *Herald Tribune Book Review*, April 14, 1946).

Katherine Anne Porter remarked in the New York *Times* (April 13, 1952) on Miss Clark's "faculty of discrimination" and on her "immensely bold use of language" in *Rome and a Villa*, and she went on to point out, "The whole book is the distillation of a deep personal experience; it is autobiographical in the truest sense." Discussing *Rome and a Villa* in "The Art of Seeing" (*The New Leader*, 1975), Pearl K. Bell wrote, "Rarely has the love affair between a modern sensibility and an ancient locale—consummated in every glance, with every step —been more exuberantly recorded."

By the time that an expanded edition of *Rome and a Villa* was issued by Pantheon Books in 1975, in honor of the new Holy Year, Eleanor Clark's work had become acknowledged as a classic. "Perhaps the finest book ever to be written about a city," Anatole Broyard asserted in the New York *Times* (March 25, 1975), "*Rome and a Villa* is an implicit comparison between 'the farthest flaunting of the human spirit' and the way we live now." To bring the new edition up to date with a chapter about the changes that had taken place during the intervening years, Miss Clark revisited Rome. Her magnificent description of Hadrian's Villa at Tivoli, which epitomizes much of Rome, is a central chapter of her book, but she has said that if she were seeing that country palace for the first time as it is now, bustling with tourists and buses, she perhaps would have lacked the enthusiasm to write about it.

Like *Rome and a Villa* and some of her other writing, *The Oysters of Locmariaquer* (Pantheon, 1964) testifies to Eleanor Clark's remarkable sense of place and of the aliveness of the past in the present. Also like the earlier book, it is *sui generis*, originating desultorily with notes for a few prospective articles and evolving its own singular form. From a childhood summer vacation in Brittany, she has said, "the images of this book flow (in the subterranean fashion of such things)." When, years later, she vacationed with her husband and children in Brittany, she became fascinated by the people of the village of Locmariaquer on the Gulf of Morbihan and by their occupation of oyster cultivation.

The winner of the 1965 National Book Award in arts and letters, Eleanor Clark received a citation that read, "Humor, history, local color, landscape, romance, melodrama, are all summoned out of oystering." That tribute does not render full justice to the scope of *Oysters*, the delightfulness of the author's literary allusions, and the wit and charm of her depiction of the village postmistress and other Bretons. Although the novelist and poet John Wain, in his review for the *New Republic* (August 8, 1964), was not equally enthusiastic about all aspects of the book, he admired its overall construction and recognized that it "could not have been written by anyone who wasn't, potentially or actually, a fine novelist, with the novelist's instinct for the 'flavor of life itself.' "

"If you turn it inside out," Miss Clark once said of *Oysters*, as quoted in *Newsday* (March 25, 1965), "it's about America and a nostalgia I feel for something gone from this country. What we lack in this country is an exciting sense of the past and an attachment to one's work." She attempted another and more explicit treatment of that theme in her ambitious novel of several themes, *Baldur's Gate* (Pantheon, 1970). Here the place is one long-familiar to her, the New England countryside—a semirural Connecticut village named Jordan in the middle of the twentieth century. The central character, Eva Buckingham, an unhappy young wife and mother, narrates the events that trouble and change her world as she eventually reaches a new view of life's values.

Baldur's Gate became a Book-of-the-Month Club selection for July 1970, with the endorsement of Gilbert Highet, then a member of that organization's board of judges, who enjoyed "its delicate evocations of country scenery" and admired its "inner coherence" and careful organization. In her critique for the *Saturday Review* (July 4, 1970) Glendy Culligan acknowledged, "Panoramic as it is in scope, the novel is equally rich in narrative modes. Social comedy coexists with personal tragedy, realism with symbolism, depth psychology with fairy tales. Half a dozen time levels, a dozen themes, and a score of characters merge in the intricate structure." But to her it seemed to be "somehow hollow at the core" and to lack convincing characterization. Phillip Corwin of the *National Observer* (July 6, 1970) and the poet and fiction writer F. D. Reeve, reviewing for the Washington *Post* (June 23, 1970), turned in more favorable verdicts on its overall achievement.

Another work that grew out of Miss Clark's personal involvement with place, *Dr. Heart* was inspired by a year-long stay in Grenoble, the birthplace and early home of the French novelist Stendhal. Her story of an American graduate student, Tom Bestwick, who goes to an unfriendly French city, X., to research his doctoral dissertation on the Great Writer S., was published in *Dr. Heart: A Novella & Other Stories* (Pantheon, 1974). The dozen short stories in the book had been written over a period of four decades and had earlier appeared in the *Partisan Review*, *Kenyon Review*, *New Yorker*, and other periodicals and in collections.

Pier-Maria Pasinetti's comment on *Rome and a Villa* in the *Yale Review* (Autumn 1952) applies also to *Dr. Heart*: "The book presupposes information and some of its keenest remarks are hints given to a knowing and conditioned reader." As Peter Sourian, accordingly, observed in the New York *Times Book Review* (January 12, 1975), "Much of the reader's pleasure in [*Dr. Heart*] derives from the intricate and rather subtle interplay between the themes in Stendhal's work and the themes of Bestwick's life." Although Sourian commended what he considered to be an "excellent new novella," reviewers generally seemed disconcerted by its intellectual content and by Miss Clark's stinging wit in, for instance, having her Stendhalian hero at one point become infatuated with the *nouveau roman* and assume an air of boredom and indifference to hide his outgoing nature and help him win friends.

While working on *Dr. Heart*, Eleanor Clark suffered a retinal hemorrhage that impaired the vision in one of her eyes. About three years later, in the winter of 1975-76, a recurrence in the other eye of the condition, known as macular degeneration, resulted in a distortion of vision that made it very difficult for her to read and impossible for her to use a typewriter. Out of her need for self-preservation and at the suggestion of her daughter, she tried a new method of writing, using Magic Markers on large gray drawing pads. In Vermont in the summer of 1976 she began *Eyes, Etc.: A Memoir* (Pantheon, 1977), with an opening sentence that read: "Try first to write a page a day this way. Get used to it." About three and a half months later, in a form determined to some extent by her new writing technique, she completed her recording of memories and of reflections on everyday events of the summer and early fall of 1976, including the family's reading aloud of Homer.

Neither self-pitying nor Pollyannic, *Eyes, Etc.* grapples unyieldingly with affliction; it is the protest of an outraged writer who cannot be reconciled to not being able to read. In press interviews at the time of its publication, Eleanor Clark said, in effect, that she did not want reviewers to present her book as a message about something like "How bravely we bear our burden." One of the many reviewers who respected her intention, Doris Grumbach wrote in the *Saturday Review* (October 29, 1977), "Her book is not a comforter to the afflicted or a palliative for the suffering. . . . In reading it, we learn a great deal about the old-fashioned quality, character, or what the Victorians might have called Eleanor Clark's 'quality.' "

Even though *Eyes, Etc.* appears to be, and sometimes is, an intensely personal book, it is hardly a key that unlocks Eleanor Clark's heart. During an interview for the New York *Times* (October 15, 1977) she characterized herself as "a very quiet, secretive person." But if much is withheld in *Eyes, Etc.*, many of Miss Clark's strong opinions and likes and dislikes are clearly exposed. As readers of *Dr. Heart* already knew, she loves skiing and skiing terrain. She plays tennis and enjoys cooking, entertaining friends, and gardening, and cares greatly about music, but not as a substitute for reading. Also interested in the theatre, she has written two plays that were performed by different troupes at Yale University. She deplores, on the other hand, speed reading, the generalizations of sociology, and the debasement of the English language. Her organizational ties are with the National Institute of Arts and Letters and the Corporation of Yaddo, the arts foundation in Saratoga Springs, New York.

Eleanor Clark is five feet seven inches tall, weighs 135 pounds, and has brown eyes, blond hair, and a gracefulness that athletically inclined women often possess. On December 7, 1952 she married Robert Penn Warren, one of America's most highly honored men of letters. They have two children, Gabriel Penn and Rosanna, who are referred to as Prodge and Ennie in *Eyes, Etc.*, to the bewilderment of quite a number of readers. The Warrens' Connecticut home is a reconditioned barn, part of which dates from the Revolutionary period, where husband and wife each has a studio for writing. In the summer Eleanor Clark sometimes writes in a cabin across the road from their house in Vermont, where in the winter she goes for skiing. Although she herself has appeared on television in interviews and accepts neighbors' invitations to watch essential telecasts, she does not have a TV set in her home, quite likely resisting its intrusion on the preoccupation of a writer, whether or not at the desk.

References: Book-of-the-Month Club p4+ Je '70 por, p6 Je '75 por; N Y Post p43 Ap 18 '65 por, p33 Mr 1 '75 por; N Y Times p24 O 15 '77 por; N Y Times Bk R A p11+ O 16 '77 por; Pub W 212:6 O 24 '77 por; Contemporary Authors 1st rev vols 11-12 (1974); Contemporary Novelists (1976); Twentieth Century Authors; First Supplement (1955); Who's Who in America, 1976-77

Clark, Roy

Apr. 15, 1933- Singer; musician; comedian.
Address: b. c/o Jih Halsey Co. Inc., 5800 E. Skelly Dr., Tulsa, Okla. 74135

As much an international ambassador for country music as Louis Armstrong was for jazz, Roy Clark is a performer of multiple talents: a virtuoso on the banjo, guitar, and fiddle; a vocalist, whose light tenor has produced many recorded hits; and a comedian, whose hayseed routines have been a mainstay of the television show *Hee Haw*, which he has hosted with Buck Owens since 1969. Clark's rise to stardom paralleled the spread of the popularity of country music beyond its traditional confines in the rural South. Among other distinctions, he was named Entertainer of the Year by the Country Music Association in 1973, and his celebrity extends as far as the Soviet Union, where he toured in 1976. "It took a long time for him to be discovered," *Hee Haw* producer Frank Peppiatt has said of Clark, "but he deserves his success because he is one of the best musicians alive."

Roy Clark

One of seven children of a family of tobacco farmers, Roy Linwood Clark was born on April 15, 1933 in Meherrin, Virginia, some sixty miles southwest of Richmond. He spent part of his childhood in Staten Island, New York, and while still in grade school he moved with his family to Washington, D.C., where his father, Hester Clark, now retired, obtained a job with the federal government. "We didn't have a whole lot," Clark told Jerry Parker in an interview for *Newsday* (February 16, 1975), "but we were never poor, especially after Dad went to work for the government." Clark remembers teachers at Kramer Junior High School and Chamberlain Vocational High School in Washington, D.C. warning him that he would never amount to much in the world when he grew up because he refused to take anything seriously.

Although Roy Clark at one time weighed the possibilities of a career in baseball, his main interest from childhood was in music, —which he never studied formally or learned to read. His father and uncles were part-time musicians who played the guitar, banjo, and fiddle at local barndances and Moose and Elks socials. His passion for aviation also dates from his boyhood, and he once constructed a glider of oak planks and bedsheets that was, however, grounded by his father. By his early teens, Clark had mastered the banjo, guitar, and fiddle with his father's tutelage, and he soon joined the members of the family band in their weekend engagements. In the late 1940's he competed in the national country music championships at Warrenton, Virginia, where he won the banjo competition two years in a row. His first victory led to his television debut on a local Washington station, on the program *Hayloft Conservatory of Musical Interpretation*, and his second earned him a bid to appear on the legendary *Grand Ole Opry* at Nashville, Tennessee.

In 1951, when he was eighteen, Clark's prowess as a baseball player came to the attention of scouts for the old St. Louis Browns, who invited him to take part in spring training, but he turned down the offer because he could not afford the fare to Florida. Also trying out as a light heavyweight boxer in the arenas of Washington, D.C., he won his first fifteen fights but ended his boxing career after losing the sixteenth. "I guess [I quit] because I found another guy more serious about it than I was," he told Jerry Parker of *Newsday* (February 16, 1975).

Concentrating instead on his career as an entertainer, Clark became adept with piano, trumpet, trombone, and drums, and as a vocalist, in addition to acquiring virtuosity on the banjo, guitar, and fiddle. At twenty-one he was appearing regularly with his own band on local television and in such Washington clubs as the Famous, the Shamrock, the Dixie Pig, the Harmony, the Covered Wagon, and Strick's. Eventually he gained a reputation as "a sort of down-home Bob Hope," doing comedy routines during band intermissions. "I would do anything within reason to make people laugh," he told Lawrence Laurent of the Washington *Post* (May 19, 1974).

For a time in the mid-1950's Clark played lead guitar with Jimmy Dean's Texas Wildcats, on whose televised Washington programs *Town and Country Time* and *Town and Country Jamboree* he was featured until he was reportedly fired for his incorrigible tardiness. Later, as a member of Marvin Rainwater's ensemble, he was dropped, according to one account, because he got more applause than the star himself. By that time he had won a substantial following among country music fans as a top instrumentalist. After appearing as a guest on the Arthur Godfrey show in 1956, Clark attained wider popularity, and in the late 1950's he gained further exposure on cross-country tours and radio and television shows. In 1960 Clark was featured in Wanda Jackson's show at the Golden Nugget in Las Vegas as bandleader and comedian, after which he provided background music for several of her recordings. After appearing with the Hank Thompson show in Reno and Las Vegas in 1961, Clark went on tour with Thompson.

While appearing at a small nightclub in Arizona in the summer of 1962, Clark received a call from his old friend Jimmy Dean, who served as one of the guest hosts on NBC-TV's *Tonight* show in the interregnum between Jack Paar and Johnny Carson. Accepting Dean's invitation to appear on America's longest-running gabfest, he turned in a performance that led to offers from the networks. His rustic buffoonery helped him to land roles as the musical Cousin Roy and his mother, Big Mama Halsey, in CBS-TV's top-rated comedy series *The Beverly Hillbillies*. In 1963 he was featured on George Hamilton IV's summer replacement show on ABC-TV, and during 1964 and 1965 he toured the state fair circuit with Andy Williams. In the mid-1960's Clark also appeared on Williams' television show, the Jimmy Dean show, *Grand Ole Opry,* and the *Tonight Show Starring Johnny Carson*. For six months in 1966 he performed on the NBC-TV daily daytime show *Swingin' Country* and that year he stood out, amidst formidable competition, in the Andy Griffith spectacular in Las Vegas. His nightclub and supper club engagements included the Playboy Club in Chicago and the new Century Plaza Hotel in Los Angeles.

Meanwhile, Roy Clark had begun to make an impression as a recording artist. His early recordings, for Four Star—as Roy Clark and the Wranglers—and then for the Debbie and Coral labels, lacked impact, and it was not until he signed with Capitol, following his association with Wanda Jackson, that he began to establish a reputation as a recording star. His first hit LP, the instrumental album *Lightning Fingers of Roy Clark,* released by Capitol in 1962, made the country music charts, but although highly praised, it sold only moderately well. The following year Clark reached the top ten of the country music charts with his vocal recording of Bill Anderson's sentimental ballad "Tips of My Fingers," and he scored equally well with his album of the same title. By 1977 he had recorded some thirty-five albums on the Capitol, Dot, ABC, and other labels, as well as scores of hit singles, such as "I Never Picked Cotton" (1970), "Thank God and Greyhound" (1970), "A Simple Thing Called Love" (1971), "The Lawrence Welk Counter Revolution Polka" (1972), "Come Live With Me" (1973), "Honeymoon Feeling" (1974), "Somewhere Between Love and Tomorrow" (1974), and "If I Had to Do It All Over Again" (1976). Clark's single of Charles Aznavour's "Yesterday, When I Was Young" was a pop best seller in 1969, and his album *Superpicker* reached both the pop and country music charts.

Clark's hit albums include *The Best of Roy Clark, Do You Believe This?, Everlovin' Soul, Happy to Be Unhappy, Family Album, Classic Clark, Family and Friends, Heart to Heart, So Much to Remember, Roy Clark Sings Gospel,* and *The Magnificent Sanctuary Band*. He collaborated with Buck Trent on albums of banjo tunes entitled *A Pair of Fives* and *Banjo Bandits*. His other instrumental albums include the guitar pieces on *Urban, Suburban,* and *Hookin' It* (ABC, 1977), of which the title tune is Clark's own composition. His albums sell briskly in the United States, Canada, Great Britain, Germany, the Scandinavian countries, Australia, and Japan.

In addition to current country and western hits, Clark includes in his albums and concert performances such country classics as "Ghost Riders in the Sky," "The Last Letter," "The Great Pretender," "Roomful of Roses," and "High Noon"; Broadway musical standards like Kurt Weill's "September Song"; such traditional folk ballads as "Jesse James" and "John Hardy"; and works of contemporary folk-country composers, like Glen Campbell's "Back in the Race," Kris Kristofferson's "Me and Bobby McGee," and Johnny Cash's "Folsom Prison." His instrumental repertoire ranges from the country favorites "Orange Blossom Special," "Sweet Georgia Brown," and "Steel Guitar Rag" to newer standards like "Lara's Theme" from *Dr. Zhivago* and "Never on Sunday," as well as older ones like "St. Louis Blues," "Twelfth Street Rag," Hoagy Carmichael's "Lazy River" and "Georgia on My Mind," and Irving Berlin's "Alexander's Ragtime Band." But the pièce de résistance of many of Clark's concerts is his masterly rendition of the Spanish guitar classic "Malagueña."

In the spring of 1969, while appearing on the *Jonathan Winters Show,* Clark was invited by producers Frank Peppiatt and John Aylesworth to become cohost with Buck Owens of a new country and western comedy program to be called *Hee Haw*. Originally intended as a summer replacement for the *Smothers Brothers Comedy Hour, Hee Haw* had its premiere on CBS-TV in May 1969 and obtained its own spot on the regular schedule later that year. A sort of "country cousin" of NBC-TV's much more sophisticated *Rowan and Martin's Laugh-In, Hee Haw* is a kaleidoscopic collection of musical numbers, comedy sketches, and one-liners, featuring pretty girls, animated barnyard beasts, and leading country musicians and comedians. In addition to its regular cast of about ninety, including Grandpa Jones, Cousin Minnie Pearl, Junior Samples, the Hager Brothers, Archie Campbell, Lulu Roman, Lisa Todd, Honi Stoneman, and George Lindsey, *Hee Haw* regularly features such guest performers as Loretta Lynn, Charlie Pride, Waylon Jennings, George Jones, and Roy Rogers. Although critics condemned its corniness as "an insult to the intelligence of a nursery school dropout" and as "possibly the worst . . . ever seen," *Hee Haw* soon won a devoted following, not only in the boondocks but in big cities and on campuses. Explaining its appeal, Roy Clark observed, as quoted in *TV Guide* (October 8, 1977): "It has no messages. It's not topical. It's so fast-paced that if a joke really fails, it doesn't hurt much because there's another coming right behind it."

To slough off its rural image, CBS divested itself of *Hee Haw* in 1971, along with *The Beverly Hillbillies, Green Acres,* and *Petticoat Junction*. Managing to raise enough money to continue production, its producers offered *Hee Haw* for syndication on a station-to-station basis, and in the years that followed it continued to prosper. By the fall of 1977 it was seen weekly by an estimated 35,000,000 viewers over 220 markets from coast to coast, and commanded the highest rating on the Nielsen scale among non-network programs. Clark's antics on *Hee Haw*, which is taped on an "assembly-line" basis at Nashville, are usually completed during two three-week sessions each year. In *TV Guide* (August 24, 1973) Neil Hickey observed that *Hee Haw* was the vehicle that brought Clark "from the penumbral half-light of minor celebrity to the blinding glare of full public favor."

Making about 200 concert appearances a year throughout the United States and Canada, Clark reportedly receives as much as $35,000 for a single night, with an entourage that includes music director Bill Hartman, Buck Trent, and a team of back-up singers. He is a fixture at the Hughes Hotels in Las Vegas and at Harrah's in Reno and Lake Tahoe. When, in February 1975, Clark headed a show in the "Country in New York" series at Manhattan's Felt Forum, a critic for *Variety* (February 5, 1975) conceded: "It may be too hokey for some, but it draws the *Hee Haw* crowd . . . and it works." Under a cultural exchange program, Clark went on a two-week tour of the Soviet Union in January 1976, visiting Moscow, Leningrad, and Riga, where his concert performances were so enthusiastically received that he has been invited to return. In September 1977 he hosted the third annual Roy Clark Celebrity Golf Classic in Tulsa, which raised funds for a children's medical center.

Much in demand for television talk and variety shows, Clark regularly substitutes for Johnny Carson, has served as cohost with Mike Douglas, and has made frequent guest appearances with Flip Wilson, Dinah Shore, and Merv Griffin. Other programs on which he has been a guest include *The Odd Couple*, *The Captain and Tennille*, the *Country Music Hit Parade*, and John Wayne's 1971 NBC-TV special, *Swing Out Sweet Land*. On Labor Day 1973 he was one of the cohosts of Jerry Lewis' nationally televised muscular dystrophy telethon. In 1975 he helped brighten the Grand Ole Opry's fiftieth anniversary program on ABC-TV and Mac Davis' Christmas special on NBC-TV, and he sang the theme song, "Mississippi," by Earl Robinson, in the ABC-TV film *Huckleberry Finn*. In 1976 Clark appeared on the Bell System Family Theatre's NBC-TV comedy-variety special *Jubilee* and on Joe Garagiola's NBC sports special *It's Anybody's Ball Game*. On the large screen, he portrayed "Wild Bill Wildman" in the comedy *Matilda* (American International, 1978), starring Elliott Gould.

In 1970 the Country Music Association designated Clark Comedian of the Year. In 1973 he was named Entertainer of the Year by both the Country Music Association and the Academy of Country Music, and Country Music Star of the Year by the American Guild of Variety Artists, and in March 1974 he became the first artist to win honors as Entertainer of the Year from the Academy for the second time in a row. In early 1975 Clark was nominated best male country vocalist both at the American Music Awards, where he served as cohost with Helen Reddy and Sly Stone, and at the Grammy awards ceremony. He was chosen Best Guitarist by *Guitar Player Magazine* in 1975, 1976, and 1977 and Country Guitarist of the Year in *Playboy* magazine's annual readers' poll in 1976 and 1977. At the fourth annual Truck Drivers Country Music Award show, held in Kansas City in the summer of 1978, Clark was named the year's best country instrumental recording artist.

Roy Clark and his wife, Barbara Joyce, were married in 1957. She has two children from a previous marriage. Clark also has two children from his first wife, whom he married at seventeen and divorced five years later. Somewhat contradicting the simple country image, the Clarks, who lived for a number of years in Davidsonville, Maryland, moved in 1976 to Tulsa, Oklahoma, where they have a thirty-seven room, three-story, brick Colonial-style house with space for seven cars, including the *de rigeur* Rolls Royce. They also have two motorcycles, a boat, and twelve race horses. A licensed pilot since 1956, Clark flies for relaxation and owns three airplanes: a Stearman PT 17 biplane of 1941 vintage, a single-engine Tri-Pacer, and a seven-passenger Mitsubishi turboprop that he pilots on his concert tours. Clark holds financial interests in the advertising, broadcasting, music publishing, and recording industries. He is part-owner of the Tulsa Drillers baseball team in the Texas League.

A brawny man, Clark is six feet tall and weighs 212 pounds. A woman acquaintance, quoted in *Newsday* (February 16, 1975), has said of Clark: "He's not a sex symbol, that's for sure. He's just a fellow you feel right at home with." And Jimmy Dean has said of his old friend: "Everybody loves him. When he walks out on stage with his bungling attitude as though he didn't know what was going to happen next, the audience is immediately on his side. It's like cheering for the underdog or the hometown boy."

References: Biog N p628 Je '74 por; Newsday II p4+ F 16 '75 pors; People 8:28 S 26 '77 pors; TV Guide 21:14+ Ag 24 '73 por; Washington Post TV Channels p5 My 14 '72; p7 My 19 '74 pors; Ewen, David. All the Years of American Popular Music (1977); Illustrated Encyclopedia of Country Music (1977); Shestack, Melvin. Country Music Encyclopedia (1974); Stambler, I. and Landon G. Encyclopedia of Folk, Country, and Western Music (1969); Who's Who in America, 1976-77

Cleland, (Joseph) Max(well) (clē-lənd)

Aug. 24, 1942- United States government official. Address: b. Veterans Administration, 810 Vermont Ave., Washington, D.C. 20420; h. 2440 Virginia Ave., NW, Washington, D.C. 20037

Few Americans have overcome such grave physical disabilities to attain prominence in public life as has Max Cleland, who was appointed Administrator of Veterans Affairs by a fellow Georgian, Jimmy Carter, and was sworn in by President Carter on March 2, 1977, succeeding Richard L. Roudebush. An "authentic American hero," in the words of Senator Sam Nunn of Georgia, Cleland earned Bronze and Silver Stars and the Soldier's Medal for his service in the Vietnam war. Undeterred by the loss of both legs and a right forearm in a grenade accident, Cleland was elected to two terms in the Georgia state senate, then served on the staff of the Senate Committee on Veterans' Affairs before taking over the V.A. He is the youngest man and the only Vietnam veteran to head the huge agency.

Joseph Maxwell Cleland was born in Atlanta, Georgia on August 24, 1942, the only child of Joseph Hugh Cleland, an automobile supplies salesman, and Juanita (Kesler) Cleland, a secretary. Max Cleland, as he prefers to be known, grew up in nearby Lithonia, a small, close-knit community with, in his words, a population of "2,400 happy people and two grouches." An early achiever, Cleland was determined "to be Number One" by his teens. At Lithonia High School, he got excellent grades, played in the band, headed several student organizations, and earned letters in basketball, baseball, and tennis. In 1960 he was awarded the Atlanta *Journal* trophy as the school's outstanding senior.

At Stetson University in De Land, Florida, Cleland, who majored in history, overcame early academic difficulties to become one of the outstanding students in his class. He spent a semester of his senior year at American University in Washington, D.C. under Stetson's "government in action" program. "I came away from Washington feeling a deep sense of the importance of the decisions made there, a feeling that nobody had all the answers, and a knowledge that even one person's interest and enthusiasm can go a long way," he told Charlotte Hale Smith in an interview for the Atlanta *Journal* (August 18, 1968). "I felt I had discovered the basic truth of our government—the direction of which is determined by those who involve themselves—that when our government does not act it is because we Americans do not act, and when we act, the government acts."

After receiving his B.A. degree in 1964, Cleland took a year of graduate courses in history and political science at Emory University in Atlanta and then returned to Washington to work for a few months as a Congressional intern. By virtue of the ROTC commission he had earned at Stetson, Cleland entered the United States Army in October 1965 with the rank of second lieutenant and was assigned duty as a communications officer in the Signal Corps. A qualified paratrooper, he volunteered for a tour in Vietnam but drew instead assignment to Fort Monmouth, New Jersey as aide-de-camp to Brigadier General Thomas M. Rienzi. Feeling increasingly guilty "shaking hands and serving sherry" while other young men, less trained than he, were being drafted to fight, Cleland ignored the advice of his parents, his friends, and his commanding general and once again volunteered for Vietnam. This time he succeeded. Reassigned to the First Air Cavalry Division, he rushed his master's thesis to the typist just thirty minutes before boarding a plane for Southeast Asia. He received his M.A. degree, *in absentia*, from Emory University in 1968.

Stationed at An Khe in the Central Highlands, Cleland was, in his words, "apprehensive" but "eager" for action. "I felt ready to prove myself to myself," he told Charlotte Smith. "It was a pretty good life for the first seven months . . . just characteristic boredom and routine. Then came the Tet offensive and all hell broke loose." On leave during the Tet battles, Cleland, who had been recently promoted to captain, rejoined his unit north of Hue. He was seconded to an infantry battalion as a signal officer at his own request and spent most of March waiting. "It was like sitting on a tack and trying to keep calm," he recalled for one reporter. Then, on April 1, 1968, the First Air

Cavalry moved to relieve the beleaguered Marines at Khe Sanh. During one intense fire fight, some of Cleland's men left their refuge in a bomb crater and, ignoring a heavy enemy rocket barrage, rendered first aid to several fallen comrades. Cleland, as commanding officer of his unit, received the Silver Star.

On April 8, 1968, just five weeks before he was scheduled to end his Vietnam tour, Cleland was helping his men set up a radio site a few miles east of Khe Sanh when he spotted a live grenade lying on the ground. Instinctively, he attempted to dispose of it, but before he could pick it up, it went off. "The explosion deafened me and blew me backwards," he recalled to Charlotte Smith. "I opened my eyes and saw my right hand was gone, the bone sticking out. My right leg was gone and my left foot." Doctors at a military hospital in Quang Tri amputated both his legs above the knee and his right forearm before flying him to Walter Reed General Hospital in Washington for intensive rehabilitation. "I had my rough moments," he admitted to Jack Fuller in an interview for the Chicago *Tribune* (March 6, 1977). "You experience a total exhaustion of your will. Then there is a reaching out in the darkness for help or guidance or forgiveness or understanding. Then the help comes. . . . In the hospital bed I had the strongest, most primitive urge. I think it was God. It said, 'Live on.' "

Cleland was determined to learn to walk on artificial legs, but because he was a triple amputee, doctors estimated the odds against a successful rehabilitation at four to one. Giving him "more discouragement than encouragement," they urged him to reconcile himself to life in a wheelchair. Cleland was adamant, however, and his doctors finally agreed to fit him with "stubbies"—short, unjoined artificial legs. With the stubbies, Cleland, who once stood a strapping six feet two inches tall, was only slightly over four feet in height. After months of pleading, he was finally fitted with laminated plastic artificial legs at a V.A. clinic in New York.

When he was finally released after eighteen months of agonizing rehabilitation in a succession of hospitals, Cleland was deeply angry at the Veterans Administration for treating him like a "claim number." Members of the hospital staffs were particularly insensitive to his efforts to adjust psychologically to his handicaps. With the exception of some sympathetic V.A. personnel, who presented him with "the possibilities rather than the difficulties," Cleland found the V.A. too indifferent, bureaucratic, and impersonal. He testified to that effect before the United States Senate's Committee on Veterans' Affairs.

Having accepted his physical handicap, in 1970 Max Cleland decided to run for the Georgia state senate from the fifty-fifth district. In the course of that campaign, he met Jimmy Carter, who was making his second bid for the governorship. The two candidates became friends and, after election to their respective offices, they collaborated on legislation benefiting the handicapped. Among other things, Cleland was largely responsible for the passage of a bill making public buildings more accessible to handicapped citizens. The only Vietnam veteran in the Senate, he fought for state educational aid to supplement the G. I. bill and, in 1972, headed a special commission created to study the problems of returning veterans. During his successful reelection campaign in 1972, he exchanged his painful artificial legs for a wheelchair—a sign that he had, in his words, "healed up . . . psychologically."

Cleland suffered his first political defeat in mid-1974 when he finished third in a field of ten in the Democratic primary for lieutenant governor. In March of the following year he joined the professional staff of the Senate Committee on Veterans Affairs. Responsible for monitoring veterans' medical care, he paid regular visits to major V.A. hospitals. To eliminate the "bureaucratic rigor mortis" that plagued most V.A. installations, he recommended revitalizing government service so that the individual did not get lost in the shuffle. Cleland was especially concerned about the inadequate counseling offered returning Vietnam veterans, many of whom suffered from profound and persistent malaise. Contributing to the problem was the mass media's false image of the veteran as a "drug-oriented, crazed, psychologically maladjusted, walking time bomb." Cleland believed that all veterans—the physically whole as well as the physically and mentally disabled—should be treated with the same compassionate and understanding attitude. "It's important to end up on your feet—even if you don't have any feet," he said, as quoted in the Washington *Post* (July 31, 1977). "It's great to conclude peace on the battlefield, but the most important thing for each veteran is to conclude peace within his own mind."

Nominated to the post of Administrator of Veterans Affairs by President Carter on February 18, 1977, Cleland was confirmed by acclamation in the Senate one week later. When he took charge of the V.A., it had an annual budget of more than $19 billion, the largest of any non-Cabinet department of the federal government, and over 220,000 employees, a total exceeded only by the Department of Defense and the Postal Service. More than 180,000 of those employees worked in the V.A.'s medical system, which, with its 171 hospitals and an average daily patient census of 75,000, is by far the largest health care operation in the country. The V.A. also manages a $35 billion life insurance program, a compensation and pension program covering some 5,500,000 veterans and their survivors, and the largest adult education program in the world under the G. I. bill.

In recent years the V.A. has been widely criticized for its allegedly inadequate patient care, inefficient management, and indifference to human problems. Some of that criticism came from Cleland himself, who shortly after taking office acknowledged that the V.A.'s situation was "every bit as bad" as he had thought it would be and "maybe a little worse." He immediately embarked on an intensive six-week study to identify the specific problems and develop possible solutions. From the outset Cleland had to stave off concerted efforts to dismantle the cumbersome agency and shift its functions to other existing governmental departments. Contending that the V.A. was uniquely suited to serve the veterans of the United States, he attacked the National Academy of Sciences' proposed integration of veterans' medical services and private health care plans into a nationalized system under federal health insurance. Such a reorganization was not only unfounded and unrealistic, Cleland argued, but also substantially more expensive than his revitalization program.

In addition to preserving the V.A.'s structural integrity and improving its general health care system, Cleland's priorities include expanding treatment facilities for alcoholics; computerizing records and benefit payments; preparing for the huge number of World War II veterans who will reach retirement age in the 1980's and 1990's and thus become automatically eligible for V.A. pensions and medical care; and making the huge V.A. bureaucracy more compassionate and sensitive. He also drew up plans for a research center to develop new treatments for amputees and patients with spinal cord injuries.

Since taking office, Cleland has sought media exposure to call attention to his mission, which is to serve as a symbol of all veterans, especially the disabled. "By sitting in my wheelchair and through my speeches, appearances and general leadership I see myself as public reminder of the price that's been paid," he explained, as quoted in the Washington *Post* (July 31, 1977). Cleland's critics, some of whom contend that he is using his position as a springboard to higher elective office, have argued that he lacks the managerial ability to correct the V.A.'s shortcomings. Thorne Marlow, a spokesman for the Veterans of Foreign Wars, told one reporter that two terms as a Georgia state senator did not prepare Cleland for the administration of a $20 billion program. Nevertheless, the V.F.W. has not blamed Cleland for the inadequacies of Carter's veterans' program, contending that, as "a tool of the Office of Management and Budget," he lacks the power to effect revolutionary changes in the bureaucracy.

Max Cleland is a big, powerfully built man with dark blond hair and sparkling blue eyes. Energetic and unfailingly cheerful, he propels his wheelchair up and down office corridors at top speed and, according to one reporter, "thrusts doors open with his shoulders as ferociously as a linebacker hits opponents." To maintain his strength, he does 125 push-ups each morning, swims, plays wheelchair basketball, and works out at a local V.A. hospital at least once a week.

Cleland, who is unmarried, lives alone in a one-bedroom apartment in Washington, where he does some of his own cooking and housecleaning. Instead of using a government-chauffeured limousine, he drives a specially equipped 1977 Oldsmobile. He spends his leisure hours listening to soft rock music and reading. A Methodist, he bases his optimistic philosophy of life on the "Serenity Prayer": "God grant me the serenity to accept the things I cannot change . . . courage to change the things that I can, and the wisdom to know the difference." "If you can do that and live one day at a time," Cleland said in a recent interview, "then you're in good shape, whether you're handicapped or not." Cleland is the recipient of the New York Department of Disabled Veterans' Outstanding Veteran Award and the Jefferson Award.

References: Atlanta Constitution A p22 S 9 '77 por; N Y Times p9 F 26 '77 por; People 7:12+ Mr 26 '77 pors; Washington Post B p6 Ap 18 '77, B p1 Ag 28 '77; Who's Who in American Politics, 1973-74

Corrigan, Mairead (mä-rād')

Jan. 27, 1944- Peace activist. Address: b. Peace House, 224 Lisburn Rd., Belfast 9, Northern Ireland

Because they followed their convictions that each individual can contribute significantly to peace, the 1976 Nobel Peace Prize was awarded, belatedly in October 1977, to a secretary, Mairead Corrigan, and a wife and mother, Betty Williams, for having mobilized a grassroots "Peace People" movement in violence-ravaged Northern Ireland. Begun in August 1976, their effort was so new—coming a half year after the deadline for nominations—that the Nobel Prize committee could not consider them for the award that year. Although neither Miss Corrigan nor her associate had ever before engaged in public activities other than those relating to church, school, and home, within a few months they stirred the imagination and captured the support of peoples throughout the world for their attempt to bridge religious and national divisions in

Mairead Corrigan

Ireland and break a tradition of hatred. Both women are natives of Belfast, the capital of Ulster, or Northern Ireland, the only part of the island of Ireland that remains under British rule. The Catholic population of Ulster numbers about 500,000, roughly one-third the total population of the Protestant-controlled country. Neighborhoods of religious homogeneity dividing the city of Belfast reflect centuries-old conflicts exacerbated by the bitterness of many Catholics who want reunion with Ireland.

Mairead Corrigan was born on January 27, 1944 in the Falls, a Catholic section of west Belfast, the second of seven children (five girls and two boys) of a working-class family. Her father is a window cleaner. Mairead attended Catholic schools, which differed from the state schools not only in religious instruction, but in political interpretations of Irish history, the state schools reflecting Protestant and British influence. She grew up, she has said, both fearing the Irish Republican Army and hating the British soldiers whom she saw beat up children, damage homes, and so thoroughly antagonize young men that they joined the IRA.

Even as a child, however, Mairead Corrigan was not revolutionary and felt indifferent to her father's reminiscences of the great 1916 Easter Rebellion. Today, Miss Corrigan denies having any strong feeling about Irish reunification. Her identity, she says, is Irish, but Northern Irish, and she finds more in common with Belfast Protestants than with Catholic Dubliners. But although she personally has never experienced job or housing discrimination, she thinks many Catholics have good reason to feel that they are second-class citizens.

When she was fourteen, Mairead Corrigan left school because her father did not have the funds for her high school tuition. While learning skills for a livelihood at business school, she worked as a babysitter. At sixteen she got a job as assistant bookkeeper in a textile factory and at twenty-one she became a secretary in the Guinness brewery. There she rose to be private secretary to a director of the firm and was holding that position when she began organizing the Community of Peace People.

The Legion of Mary has exerted a strong influence on Mairead Corrigan ever since she joined it at the age of fourteen. Like other members of that lay Catholic welfare organization, she was required to devote to it one or more evenings a week, mainly in helping others. When her parents moved to Andersonstown, another Catholic section of Belfast, Miss Corrigan, at eighteen, took charge of a new group of children and teen-agers that increased from about six to 150. She helped to set up the first nursery school and organize recreational activities in an area of bleak residential housing devoid of stores and facilities for amusement. During 1972 she and a Protestant pastor from the Shankill Road in the Protestant section of Belfast attended the meeting of the World Council of Churches in Thailand. Her later description of herself at the time was quoted by Richard Deutsch in *Mairead Corrigan/Betty Williams* (1977): "I was pretty much the typical young Catholic from the Catholic ghetto." The following year she visited the USSR to make a film for the Legion of Mary on how people of religious belief live in the Soviet Union.

In 1968-69, spurred by student civil rights activity, leaders of the Catholic minority in Northern Ireland launched a campaign against alleged discrimination. Its program included electoral reform that would give Catholics an increased share of political power, better housing, and more job opportunities. Reporters drew a somber picture of the escalation of conflict from that phase of protest—which involved rallies, marches, and other forms of peaceful demonstration—to serious disorder and, eventually, to violence. Protestant backlash against the demonstrations led to the collapse of the government of Prime Minister Terence O'Neill, who was succeeded by James D. Chichester-Clark, an exponent of moderate reform. New religious riots precipitated the intervention of the British, who introduced direct rule and in mid-August 1969 sent military units into Northern Ireland to keep peace between the Catholic and Protestant communities.

Although the British insisted that they were maintaining civil law, their intervention failed to alleviate Catholic-Protestant tensions. In the early 1970's members of the Irish Republican Army regrouped. Organized as the Provisionals ("Provies"), they planned to protect Catholic neighborhoods against Protestants and began a campaign of violence that they threatened to continue until the withdrawal of the British. Opposing the IRA was its Protestant, pro-British counterpart, the Ulster Defense League. The two organizations established a form of paramilitary rule, policing their respective Catholic and Protestant areas and reducing the effectiveness of the British army, the Protestant police, and British and Northern Ireland politicians. They also established taxi service, co-ops, gas stations, hotels, advice centers, and informal procedures for punishing such crimes as stealing and drug use.

Opposed to the fighting from the outset, Miss Corrigan watched with horror the first burning of Catholic houses, the retaliatory arson, the heightening atmosphere of mutual fear. Her activities with the Legion of Mary brought her to the core of the conflict as she worked with the organization to keep children safe during the 1969 outbreak. After the British opened camps for revolutionaries in August 1971, she visited prisoners as a member of the Legion of Mary. She understood the dilemma of the young men, she has said, of the sons who joined the defensive group after seeing their parents molested, feeling it was the only route open to them. Yet she insisted that violence was not the way of Christ and felt that part of her mission was to persuade the paramilitary to adopt pacificist views.

On August 10, 1976 in Belfast an event that was just another episode in eight years of terrorism touched Miss Corrigan's life directly and tragically. An IRA getaway car, its driver killed by a British police bullet, crashed into an iron railing, fatally crushing a daughter and two sons of Mrs. Anne Maguire, who herself was seriously injured. Anne Maguire is Mairead Corrigan's sister. One onlooker of the accident was Mrs. Betty Williams.

At first independently, the two women began an immediate assault on terrorism whatever its source. In a public move unprecedented for a Roman Catholic, Miss Corrigan condemned the IRA on television, as did her brother-in-law, Jackie Maguire. (The Maguires later immigrated to New Zealand with their remaining child.) Mrs. Williams went from door to door asking people to sign a petition for peace and had obtained 6,000 signatures by the time she read the petition over television two nights after the episode. Miss Corrigan invited Betty Williams to join the family at the children's funeral as soon as she heard of her activities, and the two combined forces to form what was first called Women for Peace and then became the Community for Peace People. By the end of August they had organized three marches, gaining 30,000 followers. On the third march Catholic women from the Falls crossed the army's dividing line and proceeded into the Loyalist Protestant Shankill Road to be welcomed by Protestant women.

In their campaign for broader financial support and membership backing and in other efforts, Miss Corrigan and Mrs. Williams relied greatly on the journalist Ciaran McKeown, who gave up his job on the *Irish Press* to work as the ideological leader of the movement. His account of an early meeting with the two women after the accident appears in Deutsch's book: "We talked, and we formed a kind of agreement to trust each other—three people who didn't know each other and who were going to work together. Just by looking at them, I knew I could count on them. And they felt the same way about me, implicitly, just as they did about one another. We had to establish that bond for the movement to be able to exist."

Within a few months they had organized rallies in the provinces and marches in cities outside Belfast, drawing large but quiet crowds, and had established 120 small groups. They took "peace walks" in confrontation zones, opened two offices, issued pamphlets, and launched a magazine called *Peace by Peace*. They arranged escapes for Protestants and Catholics on terrorists' blacklists. In December 1976 Miss Corrigan left her position with the Guinness brewery to work full time for the movement. She and Mrs. Williams began drawing salaries and expense allowances in 1977.

Media interest in the seemingly tireless activities of Miss Corrigan and Mrs. Williams both in Northern Ireland and on visits to other countries helped to carry their message on a tide of international sympathy and admiration. The American folk singer Joan Baez, in one of her endorsements of the peace movement, joined them at a rally in London. Trips abroad won them moral support and financial aid from New Zealand, Australia, Canada, Mexico, and Ireland, and from Germany and elsewhere on the continent of Europe. In October 1976 they traveled to the United States to exhort the Irish-American community not to contribute funds to organizations involved in the conflict, since their support would go, directly or inadvertently, to bolster terrorist activity in Ulster. (In 1977 President Jimmy Carter, along with a number of other politicians, issued a similar appeal against donating money to the terrorists.)

By the fall of 1976 the accomplishments of the Peace People had prompted recommendations that the leaders be considered for the Nobel Peace Prize, but the February 1 deadline for nominations prevented their eligibility. Reviewing a list of fifty candidates, however, the Nobel Peace Prize committee decided that none warranted the award for

1976. Before the end of the year a group of Norwegian newspapers and civic organizations cooperated in the creation of a Norwegian People's Peace Prize for Miss Corrigan and Mrs. Williams, who went to Oslo to accept combined donations of $340,000, which they earmarked for expansion of the Peace People program. The Nobel Peace Prize, according to some sources, was meanwhile held open for them for a year, although conflicting rumors in fall 1977 indicated that the outcome was not certain. The belated award, carrying $140,000, of which the two women were designated as winners in October 1977, was given concurrently with the 1977 award, which went to Amnesty International. No woman had received the Peace Prize since 1944; moreover, both "grass-roots" choices reversed a trend toward choosing statesmen. After splitting part of the money they received from the Nobel Peace Prize committee, the two activists removed themselves from the peace movement's payroll and became full-time volunteers.

Once they had launched their campaign, Miss Corrigan, Mrs. Williams, and Ciaran McKnown drew criticism from many quarters. Paramilitary groups on both sides called them traitors because they had urged informing on the IRA and other terrorists—especially after May 1977, when they began a "demilitarization" campaign and asked all such groups to turn in their weapons by September. Mrs. Williams, a Catholic married to a Protestant, was doubly suspect. Death threats were not uncommon. At one meeting—held, ironically, to protest an incident of British army brutality—the two leaders were beaten and forced to take sanctuary in a church while their cars were smashed. Working-class pro-IRA Catholics, objecting to their "peace at any price" philosophy, called them British collaborators, and Protestant loyalists accused them of fence-sitting. The Northern Ireland civil rights activist Bernadette Devlin, although opposed to the new IRA, which replaced the abortive civil rights movement, expressed the opinion that the Peace People leaders were being manipulated. Other criticism was focused on globe-trotting trips that allegedly neglected operations at home; the lack of a concrete program or political impact; and the emphasis on ethnic interaction—youth clubs, peace houses, and sports activities.

Miss Corrigan and Mrs. Williams, nevertheless, affirmed both the direction and the effectiveness of the movement, which had turned from demonstrations to community work and had shaken the macho hero image and cult of violence. Despite continuing explosions, aggregate violence declined 54 percent, Mrs. Williams maintained on the day of the announcement of the Nobel award. Another source compared the fewer than two killings a week in 1977 with more than 4.5 a week in 1969, a decline that may have been due less to a desire for peace than a reduction in arms from the Irish-American community, which the Peace People leaders called for on their visits to the United States. The money, moreover, from the Nobel Peace Prize, as from the Norwegian People's Peace Prize, assured fulfillment of some of the projects of a nonsectarian, apolitical movement whose earliest efforts were directed toward the building of community centers and the restoration of damaged factories and schools.

Much to the surprise of many of their supporters, Mairead Corrigan, Mrs. Williams, and Ciaran McKeown announced their resignations from the leadership of the Community for Peace People on April 15, 1978. McKeown, who planned to return to journalism, cited as the main reason their interest in fostering the democratization of the movement. He added, however, that the three former leaders intended to remain at "the disposal of the Peace People."

Among the tributes paid to Miss Corrigan and Mrs. Williams were the Carl von Ossietzky Prize of the Federal Republic of Germany, awarded in December 1976; honorary doctorates from Yale University, conferred in June 1977; and an invitation to an interview with Queen Elizabeth II during the summer of 1977. In *Mairead Corrigan/Betty Williams*, Deutsch described Miss Corrigan as "small, dark, green-eyed, straightforward, always smiling, and always ready with a retort." Some saw her as a foil to her fellow leader—slighter, more emotional, softspoken, and religious. "They call us the saint and the sinner," Betty Williams once quipped. Regarding her purpose in the peace movement as similar to that of her work in the Legion of Mary, Mairead Corrigan has a "spiritual and magnetic quality" that tends, according to Deutsch, to "'electrify' the crowds she is addressing."

References: Family Circle 91:38+ Mr 27 '78 por; Ms. 5:62+ D '76; N Y Daily News p2+ O 11 '77 por; N Y Times p1+ p14 O 11 '77 por; N Y Times Mag p29 D 19 '76 pors; Newsday p4 O 11 '77 por; Newsweek 90:61 O 24 '77 por; Deutsch, Richard. Mairead Corrigan/Betty Williams (1977)

Costanza, Margaret

Nov. 28, 1932- Former assistant to the President of the United States. Address: b. c/o The White House Office, 1600 Pennsylvania Ave., NW, Washington, D.C. 20500

When newly elected President Jimmy Carter announced the appointment of Margaret

Margaret Costanza

("Midge") Costanza as special assistant to act as his liaison with organized special interest groups, she was referred to in some quarters as the administration's "token woman." While that factor no doubt entered into Carter's choice, it was clear that Miss Costanza possessed a number of impressive qualifications: she was the only one of the President's special assistants who represented in her own person Northerners, Roman Catholics, ethnics, and liberal activists—and, more importantly, she was experienced in dealing with business, labor, and political interest groups.

The job that Miss Costanza held existed in the two administrations that preceded Carter's, but she was the first incumbent to bring to it a concept of its function and conduct that recognizes the importance of public input into the President's store of working information. Thus she had been readily accessible, an impartial listener regardless of her own convictions on any subject brought to her attention, and a hard worker. She was, as well, volatile, outspoken, and a magnet for controversy.

Born in LeRoy, New York on November 28, 1932, Margaret ("Midge") Costanza is one of the four children of Philip Joseph and Concetta (Granata) Costanza, immigrants from Palermo, Sicily, who settled in upper New York State and founded a sausage-making business that they called "The House of Costanza." The Costanzas never became wealthy, but, their daughter says, there has never been a time when they did not have enough. The business is still being run by the Costanzas' other daughter; the elder Costanzas, now retired except for running a small grocery store, maintain a lively interest in "Midge's" political career.

Midge Costanza (she prefers the nickname) grew up in Rochester, where she attended East High School and ended her formal education with graduation. Intelligent rather than intellectual or scholarly, she has never felt that her lack of a formal education handicapped her successful business career; recently she has speculated in interviews whether a college background would have given her opinions more weight with "professional administrator types". Always a willing and energetic worker, she entered the business world via the usual jobs open to a girl just out of high school—file clerk, switchboard operator, and secretary. Eventually she became administrative assistant to John Petrossi, head of a cement construction business in Rochester and real estate developer. In her twenty-five years with Petrossi she engaged in business-related community activities: she served as a member of the advisory committee of the Community Savings Bank of Rochester, of the American Cancer Society, the Woman's Council of the Rochester Chamber of Commerce, the committee of the Rotary Horse Show, and the Hudson Avenue Businessmen's Association. She was also a member of the board of directors of the Rochester Community Chest, the Italian Civil Rights League, the Sons of Italy, and the Italian Woman's Civic Club.

Activities such as those served as a springboard into local politics, an interest that Miss Costanza had had since her high school days, when she ran for president of the student body and was defeated. One of her political colleagues has recalled that when Midge Costanza decided to take an active part in politics she inquired about the best way to start, and was told to take the odd jobs route at the grassroots level. She did accordingly, licking envelopes, scrubbing floors and walls, and canvassing door-to-door. Her first political involvement was with the W. Averell Harriman gubernatorial campaign in 1954. Thereafter she served as executive Democratic committeewoman for the 22d ward in Rochester, 1959-1964; executive director for the Robert F. Kennedy senatorial campaign in Monroe County, 1964; vice-chairman of the Monroe County Democratic Committee, 1966-1970; chairman, New York State Democratic Women's Conference, New York State Democratic Committee, 1968; member of the advisory committee of the Small Business Administration, 1968; alternate delegate (1972) and delegate (1976) to the Democratic National Convention; and member of the Democratic National Committee, 1972-1977. She has also been active in the National Women's Political Caucus, an organization dedicated to the greater involvement of women in politics.

Ready by 1974 to try for office, Midge Costanza became the Democratic candidate for Congress from the Thirty-fifth District, running against the veteran Republican incumbent, Barber Conable. She was defeated, but that campaign brought her to the notice of Jimmy

Carter, then a political unknown with a long view, who volunteered his help in her campaign. In the same year Miss Costanza was elected a member-at-large of the Rochester city council. Inasmuch as she polled the largest number of votes, she should, by custom, have been named mayor, but her fellow council members chose not to abide by the unwritten rule and named her vice-mayor, a largely ceremonial post. In spite of a lack of encouragement from her fellow Democratic councilmen, she chose to take an active part in council deliberations, and came to function most effectively as a gadfly. Oddly enough, her greatest support came from the lone Republican council member.

As the Carter bid for the Presidential nomination began to materialize, Costanza, a staunch admirer since their meeting on the occasion of her 1974 Congressional campaign, became one of the first New York politicians of any stature to endorse him. She was subsequently named cochairman with William Vanden Heuvel of Carter's New York campaign and shared honors with Representatives Peter W. Rodino Jr. and Andrew Young in making seconding speeches for the Carter nomination. With the election over, Miss Costanza prepared to resume her duties on the Rochester city council, but was overjoyed to receive the President-elect's Christmas Day call offering her a place in his circle of special assistants

The White House office assigned to the woman who was to be called "the President's window to the nation" was small, low-ceilinged, mail-cluttered, and much less pretentious than those in the Executive Office Building allotted to her staff of ten. Yet it was considered a choice one, since it was next door to the Oval Office. From there Miss Costanza directed her staff as they coped with thousands of pieces of mail, up to 350 phone calls, and an average of 150 meetings a week. The agenda in her first year of office included consultations with groups concerned with everything from big business to endangered wildlife—business women, Indians, gays, minorities, senior citizens, consumers, vegetarians, women attempting to save the porpoise, disabled citizens, groups for and against abortion, the Equal Rights Amendment, and amnesty—to list a representative sampling. All were given a hearing, but no promises were made. Ordinarily Midge Costanza personally talked with those whose concerns were relevant to legislation that the President was preparing for Congress at the moment. Resulting memos from her to the President tended to be astute and to the point, and had been known to carry weight with him.

Although Midge Costanza had much that was constructive in her record, it was her most controversial activities that were emphasized in news reports. She attracted headlines at the outset by supporting an amnesty coalition for Vietnam deserters and draft evaders and talking to picketing groups. The first real furor arose during the height of the Anita Bryant controversy over her much publicized meeting with representatives of the National Gay Task Force, who had hitherto been barred from the White House. She also sponsored a meatless buffet on Vegetarian Food Day at the White House, which brought down the wrath of cattlemen incensed at low market prices. She next supported a campaign by a women's coalition to pressure Carter to change his stand on denying federal aid to indigent women seeking abortions. When she became persuaded that a march planned by the coalition would not be a good idea, she called instead for individual letters from top-level women in the administration, thereby provoking Carter's tight-lipped public statement that her action was "inappropriate." General reaction to the effect that one does not openly oppose one's leader apparently had little impact on her, since she soon risked Presidential wrath again by openly calling for the resignation of beleaguered Bert Lance as Director of the Office of Management and Budget when the news of his financial involvements became public.

Her stand on the Bert Lance matter intensified reactions to reports a short time later of a fund-raising party Midge Costanza gave two months after coming to work in the White House. Her unsuccessful 1974 campaign for a House seat ended with a deficit of $17,615, all but $570 of it advanced by Costanza herself. In reply to questions raised by critics, she said that she could have raised the funds in Rochester at any time, but did not explain why she waited until going to work in the White House. Having conceived the idea of a fund-raising party, she consulted White House legal counsels and was advised that there was nothing illegal in the proposal. The party took place in New York City, the charge was $500 a ticket, and the featured attraction was Vice-President Walter F. Mondale. The successful affair brought in $21,035, much of it from such groups as the Brooklyn Longshoremen, United Auto Workers, and communications workers, and some from individuals who did not know Midge Costanza but wished to oblige her sponsors; few contributions came from Rochester sources. After all obligations were met there was a surplus of $3,400, which brought up the knotty question of how best to dispose of it. By law a report was due the Federal Elections Commission, and Costanza duly notified the Commission that she would be unable to meet their deadline until complete figures were available and the surplus question resolved. The report continued to be unavailable, the Commission made its complaint public, and there were the inevitable calls for her resignation. When Republican Representative Samuel Devine of Ohio called for her resignation on the House floor on the grounds that she "failed to meet President Carter's test of being above suspicion," Democratic Representative John Burton of

California called his remarks "the most sexist statement" he had ever heard. Midge Costanza herself saw nothing improper in the situation.

Although she maintained that she neither sought nor feared controversy, Midge Costanza continued to attract it. She was, for example, scheduled to be keynote speaker at the 1978 Jefferson-Jackson Day Dinner of the Virginia Democratic Party, but when word reached officials of her caustic comments concerning certain Virginia Democrats who had voted against the Equal Rights Amendment, their retort was "She's going to be uninvited." And while helping Democratic Representatives to campaign for reelection in Denver, she produced some unflattering comments on persons in the news whose views on ERA and abortion were at variance with her own.

On April 12, 1978 Miss Costanza announced that although she would probably keep her title of special assistant to the President for public liaison, she would in the future narrow her concerns to issues such as women's rights and to domestic human rights in general. Squelching speculation that the shrinkage of her areas of responsibilities implied a demotion, she made clear that the change was being effected merely so that she could be free to concentrate on those matters closest to her heart. Despite her protestations to the contrary, Miss Costanza's influence in President Carter's inner circle was greatly reduced when Anne Wexler, a former deputy Under Secretary of Commerce, was assigned the major duties of the public liaison office formerly under Miss Costanza. In what many observers viewed as an addition of insult to injury, Midge Costanza was then asked to vacate her office just down the hall from President Carter's own and to move into cramped quarters in the White House basement.

All in all, it is clear that one reacts either positively or negatively to Midge Costanza; few comments are neutral. Some people who have dealt with her appreciate her vigor and efficiency, like the man who commented that it used to be that if you succeeded in getting an appointment you were presented with a portrait of the President in addition to a recital of the administration's accomplishments, whereas under Miss Costanza the responsibility for acting as liaison between the American public and the President was interpreted literally and resulted in action. Such partisans, who praise her forthrightness, breeziness, deft handling of all sorts of people, and the broad humor she brings to discussions and public speeches, saw evidence that her opinions were highly valued by the President. That admiration seemed to be mutual, since Midge Costanza had been quoted in *U.S. News and World Report* (April 24, 1978) as saying: "There are very few things he and I are not compatible about. Perhaps my commitment is a little stronger and deeper for gay rights. My sensitivity toward women must be stronger because I am a woman,"

Although she continued to insist that she respected and loved the President and that she would support him if he ran for reelection, Midge Costanza resigned as his assistant on August 1, 1978. Her appearance six weeks later at the celebration for New York Governor Hugh L. Carey's victory in the primary seemed to indicate that she would play a major role in his campaign and would probably be in line for a position in his administration if he were reelected.

Midge Costanza is five feet one inch tall ("I used to be eight feet tall before I got involved in politics," she has said), weighs around 110 pounds, and has close-cropped black hair, and expressive brown eyes. She favors pantsuits, and, for work, blue jeans. She has never married because, as she puts it, she has never met a man who was more interesting than what she was doing. Her close friends include such independent-minded celebrities as Bella Abzug and Shirley MacLaine, but she sees little of them, since she has scant time for recreation.

Her much-quoted self-characterization as "a loud-mouthed, pushy little broad" sums up a complex and supercharged personality described accordingly to the speaker's particular bias. They vary from the antagonistic Rochester council member's "all personality and not much substance" to such more or less admiring comments as "feisty," "a complex mixture of toughness, explosive temper, and insecurities," "a hell of a woman," "smart," and 'a regular guy with lots of moxie." Midge Costanza is said to be a disorganized worker who knows where everything is, a political maverick, a paradoxical combination of aggressiveness and shyness, and a tireless worker who thrives on cigarettes, coffee, and long hours. She uses humor as a weapon, but it often boomerangs by alienating the target.

References: Who's Who in American Politics, 1977-1978; Who's Who of American Women, 1975-76

Davis, Sammy Jr.

Dec. 8, 1925- Entertainer. Address: c/o Warner Bros. Records, Inc., 44 E. 50th St., New York City, N.Y. 10022

NOTE: This biography supersedes the article that appeared in *Current Biography* in 1956.

The liveliest human vestige of old-time vaudeville still working the boards—not to mention today's big and small screens and recording studios—is that self-described "little

Sammy Davis Jr.

one-eyed colored guy" with the broken nose, defiant jaw, and big, crooked smile, Sammy Davis Jr. The versatile, restlessly energetic Davis, who entered show business half a century ago as a toddler mugging in his father's arms, is the complete variety performer—one of those individuals who, all alone on a stage, with nothing but a mike in his hand, can keep an audience entertained for hours, with dancing, comic patter, impressions, and acting. Davis, who learned his nonstop "flash" dancing as the featured member of the Will Mastin Trio, went on to accumulate credits on Broadway, in Hollywood, and on the pop music charts. Working out of Las Vegas, where he owns 8 percent of the Tropicana Hotel, he regularly takes his act to top nightclubs, supper clubs, and concert halls throughout the United States and, occasionally, abroad. As a recording artist, Davis, who was previously with Capitol, Decca, and Reprise, is now heard on the Warner Brothers label.

Sammy Davis Jr. was born in Harlem, New York City, New York on December 8, 1925. His father was a lead dancer in adopted uncle Will Mastin's "Holiday in Dixieland," a vaudeville troupe in which his mother, Elvera (Sanchez) Davis, was the lead chorus girl. When he was two, his parents had a daughter, Ramona, who was raised by maternal relatives while they, the father and mother, stayed on the road. The paternal grandmother, Rosa B. ("Mama") Davis, brought up Sammy Jr. in Harlem—specifically, at 140th Street and Eighth Avenue—until, when he was two and a half, his parents broke up professionally as well as maritally and Sam Sr. took custody of his son.

Sammy Jr.—who was called, facetiously, "Poppa" by his father and, inexplicably, (even to him), "Mose Gastin" by his uncle—traveled and performed with the Mastin troupe first as a cute, silent human prop and, gradually, as a full-fledged entertainer. To appease truant officers, Mastin and Sam Sr., whenever they could, found someone around whatever theatre they were working to tutor the boy in the three R's. In a respite from the vaudeville circuit, Davis made his first motion picture, *Rufus Jones for President* (Vitaphone-Warner, 1933), a two-reeler filmed at the old Warner studios in Brooklyn. In that comedy he played the title role, a little boy who falls asleep in the lap of his mother (Ethel Waters) and dreams that he is elected President of the United States. Immediately afterward, he was cast in another Vitaphone-Warner talkie, *Season's Greetings,* starring Lita Grey.

As the popularity of vaudeville waned with the rise of motion pictures, the Mastin troupe was progressively reduced from a twelve-member organization to a trio, and it underwent several name changes, including "Will Mastin's Gang, Featuring Little Sammy" and, finally, "The Will Mastin Trio, Featuring Sammy Davis Jr." Touring with his father and uncle in the late 1930's and early 1940's, Davis met, among other entertainers, Bill ("Bojangles") Robinson, the legendary tap dancer, and Frank Sinatra, who was then singing with Tommy Dorsey's band. (One of the standard songs in Davis' act today is his "cover" of "Mr. Bojangles," earlier popularized by Jerry Jeff Walker and the Nitty Gritty Dirt Band.)

Drafted into the wartime United States Army when he turned eighteen, Davis was assigned to the infantry's basic training center at Fort Francis E. Warren in Cheyenne, Wyoming. There he had the good fortune to come under the guidance of a bookish black sergeant who gave him remedial reading lessons and lent him books from his own small library. (Davis had read only comic books up to that time.) On the negative side, he encountered blatant racial prejudice for the first time, and he responded to the cruel bigotry of some of the white enlisted men in his barracks with his fists. "I had scabs on my knuckles for the first three months in the Army," he recounts in *Yes I Can* (Farrar, Straus, 1965), the autobiography he put together from tape recordings with the help of writers Jane and Burt Boyar.

Transferred to Special Services, Davis did shows in camps across the country, "gorging" himself, as he says in his autobiography, "on the joy of being liked," combing every audience for "haters" and, when he spotted them, giving his performance "an extra burst of strength and energy" because he "had to get to those guys," to "neutralize them and make them acknowledge" him. Alan Ebert, an NBC publicity man who later worked with Davis, has written that he is "sure" that "in Sammy's mind he still thinks of himself as the kid in the Army, the one who got stomped on, spat upon, and beaten" and that "Sam knocks himself out in a vain attempt to make the whole world love him and to erase from his mind those early years."

After the war, with theatrical vaudeville virtually dead, the Will Mastin Trio put in several lean years breaking into nightclubs in Las Vegas—which was just beginning to become a show town—and in Los Angeles, New York, and other places across the country, including the boondocks. Davis was constantly adding to or perfecting his contributions to the act: impressions of popular screen stars and singers, dance steps, and the playing of trumpet and drums. (Later, he learned to play piano and vibes.) While the three men always did some flash dancing together, the trio more and more became a showcase for Sammy, with father and uncle providing tap and soft-shoe background.

In his ample spare time, Davis hung out in the popular show-business watering spots open to him in that segregated era, places like Bill Berg's club in Los Angeles and the old Ritz Hotel on Chicago's South Side, figuring to "make a connection that could do us some good." He became a friend of singer Mel Torme and an acquaintance of singer Billy Eckstine, and through Jesse Price, a drummer, he made a "connection" at Capitol Records for fifty dollars a side. One of the songs he recorded for Capitol, "The Way You Look Tonight," was chosen Record of the Year by *Metronome,* and that magazine named him "Most Outstanding New Personality" of 1946.

For six months in 1947 and 1948 the Will Mastin Trio toured with a show starring Mickey Rooney. A three-week engagement on a bill headed by Frank Sinatra at Manhattan's Capitol Theatre (the last of the big-time vaudeville bastions) was followed by an opening gig at Slapsie Maxie's in Los Angeles and a featured spot in Bob Hope's police benefit show in the same city. Through Jack Benny, the trio won a coveted booking at Ciro's in Hollywood, and an appearance on Eddie Cantor's *Colgate Comedy Hour* on NBC-TV led to a contract for the trio as the summer replacement for that network show. Following a smash engagement at New York's Copacabana, Decca Records signed Sammy Davis Jr. to a contract. Released in mid-1954, his first Decca album, *Starring Sammy Davis Jr.,* contained impersonations of Dean Martin and Jerry Lewis, Jimmy Durante, Johnny Ray, and Bing Crosby, among others. Another Decca LP, *Just for Lovers,* was done in his own persona, and songs from both were given wide play by disk jockeys.

The automobile accident in which Davis lost his left eye occurred on November 19, 1954, as he was driving from an engagement in Las Vegas to Hollywood. During his confinement at Community Hospital in San Bernadino he began, as he recounts, "thinking about [his] faults" and "started to change," especially religiously. His father was Baptist and his mother was Roman Catholic, but he had not until then taken religion very seriously. However, he had been wearing a mezuzah given him by Eddie Cantor—although, as he was careful to note, he was not wearing it on the night of the accident—and his conversion to Judaism was accelerated, partly through the instrumentality of a rabbi visiting the hospital who admonished him, "In the Talmud . . . it is written, 'Whom the Lord loveth, He correcteth.' Therefore, 'Should a man see suffering come upon him, let him scrutinize his actions.' " Davis' conversion was completed in the months following his recuperation, when he studied Judaism deeply and found "an affinity" between Jews and blacks as oppressed peoples and "joy" in the emphasis on trying to make a Godly kingdom on earth.

Publicity from the accident had been such that when Davis left the hospital clubs all over the country were clamoring for him and the trio, with offers averaging $15,000 a week. With battered face and eye-patch (later replaced by a "glass"—actually plastic—eye), Sammy Davis Jr. made his return to the nightclub stage, with Mastin and Sam Sr., before a celebrity-packed audience at Ciro's that gave him a ten-minute standing ovation. Triumphal appearances followed at such night spots as Copa City in Miami, the Chez Paree in Chicago, and the Latin Casino in Philadelphia.

Davis, with enthusiasm, and his father and uncle, with some reluctance, made their Broadway debut in *Mr. Wonderful,* a musical comedy created specifically for Davis. The show, the story of a young black nightclub entertainer succeeding against racial odds by dint of talent and will, was produced by Jule Styne and George Gilbert and written by Joseph Stein and Will Glickman. It opened at the Broadway Theatre on March 22, 1956 to mixed reviews—mixed in the sense that the critics panned the production while acknowledging Davis' "dynamism," his "amiably urgent personality," and his "unusual versatility." Sustained at the box office chiefly on the strength of Davis' personal following, *Mr. Wonderful* ran for 383 performances, closing on February 23, 1957.

After the closing of *Mr. Wonderful,* the Will Mastin Trio began to disintegrate, but even after it broke up completely, around the end of the decade, Davis continued for some time to divide his income three ways. His first solo television appearance was on Ed Sullivan's popular CBS variety show, and in the late 1950's and early 1960's he acted in episodes of the *General Electric Theatre* and the *Dick Powell Theatre,* among other dramatic series. On the *Patty Duke Show* on ABC on March 3, 1965 he played himself in "Will the Real Sammy Davis Please Stand Up?" and his appearance on the musical show *Hullabaloo* in the spring of 1965 boosted that program to the top of the weekly ratings.

Meanwhile, as a recording artist, Davis had made dozens of albums and a number of top-selling singles. (His all-time best seller remains "Candy Man," trailed by "Hey There," "Birth of the Blues," "The Lady is a Tramp," "Gonna Build a Mountain," and "Who Can I Turn To?") In Hollywood he played Fletcher Henderson in *The Benny Goodman Story* (Universal, 1956); costarred as the jive-talking sailor Danny Johnson opposite Eartha Kitt in *Anna Lucasta* (United Artists, 1958); and stood out in the screen version of George Gershwin's folk opera *Porgy and Bess* (Columbia, 1959) as the mischievous Sportin' Life. Davis appeared as himself in a cameo role in the picaresque comedy *Pepe* (Columbia, 1960); was one of the title-role prisoners in *Convicts Four* (Allied Artists, 1960); sang the title song for the soundtrack of *Of Love and Desire* (Twentieth Century-Fox, 1963); was the Street Singer in the Kurt Urlich production of *Three Penny Opera* (1963); and had a supporting role in *Nightmare in the Sun* (Zodiac, 1965).

As a member of the "Rat Pack," a bon-vivant group of Hollywood actors led by Frank Sinatra and including Dean Martin, Tony Curtis, Peter Lawford, Joey Bishop, and Henry Silva, Davis lived at a faster pace than ever. He and various members of the pack made several movies together: *Ocean's Eleven* (Warner, 1960), *Sergeants Three* (United Artists, 1962), *Johnny Cool* (United Artists, 1963), *Robin and the Seven Hoods* (Warner, 1964), *Salt and Pepper* (United Artists, 1968), and *One More Time* (United Artists, 1970).

In the mid-1960's Davis returned to the legitimate stage at the instigation of producer Hillard Elkins, who conceived the idea of turning Clifford Odets' play *Golden Boy* into a musical about a young Negro trying to break out of the ghetto through boxing. Despite repeated "doctoring," pre-Broadway reviewers in Philadelphia, Detroit, and Boston, each in their turn, found the new book unconvincing. Revisions continued all the way to New York, and on Friday, October 16, 1964, four days before the opening at the Majestic Theatre, Davis, voice-weary and harried, learned from Arthur Penn, the director, that more changes were to be made. He failed to appear for a preview performance on Saturday, October 17, but rallied in time for the opening curtain on October 20. Expecting the worst, he was elated when Howard Taubman of the New York *Times* gave him a rave notice and Walter Kerr of the *Herald Tribune* was at least sympathetic, and when *Cue* magazine named him Entertainer of the Year. *Golden Boy* ran for 568 performances, until March 5, 1966.

During the run of *Golden Boy*, Davis' most serious cinematic effort up to that time was filmed by his own company, Trace-Mark Productions, in a Harlem nightclub and other locations in New York City. That picture, *A Man Called Adam* (Embassy, 1966), the story of the decline and fall from greatness of an embittered, guilt-ridden black jazz musician, was generally faulted by critics for its "poor script" and praised for the "pluck" exhibited by Davis. Later, Davis sang and danced as the hip revivalist Big Daddy in *Sweet Charity* (Universal, 1969) and performed in *Save the Children* (Paramount, 1973), an all-star music documentary filmed at a 1972 benefit show for the Reverend Jesse Jackson's Operation Push in Chicago.

Following the success of the variety special *The Swinging World of Sammy Davis Jr.* on WABC-TV in New York City on February 18, 1965, Davis did an ABC network special, *Sammy and His Friends*, and a short-lived NBC network series, the *Sammy Davis Jr. Show*, both in the 1965-66 season. Davis blamed the failure of the series partly on himself, partly on problems caused by a contractual conflict between ABC and NBC, but mostly on the fact that he was a spontaneous, free-wheeling entertainer locked into a strict cue-card situation.

In the late 1960's Davis' network television credits included roles in episodes of *The Beverly Hillbillies* and *Mod Squad*, among other shows. He hosted the *Tonight Show* several times in place of Johnny Carson, and he revived Pigmeat Markham's old "Here Come De Judge" vaudeville routine in appearances on the NBC kaleidoscopic comedy series, *Rowan and Martin's Laugh-In*. In 1970 he was in segments of *Here's Lucy* (CBS) and *Make Room for Granddaddy* (ABC), and when he made an appearance as the first celebrity guest actor on CBS's *All in the Family* on February 19, 1972, that show set a new Nielsen record.

Maligned in previous years in much of the black press for "living white," Davis drew liberal as well as black community fire when he, a registered Democrat, allowed himself to be photographed with President Richard Nixon in Miami Beach during the August 1972 Republican Convention there. His public endorsement of Nixon was reinforced when he did a special performance in honor of American Vietnam war prisoners at the White House the following year. He had previously been known for his support of liberals in politics, and the black community causes to which he had contributed generously of time, talent, and money ranged from the NAACP through the civil rights movement of the 1960's to the defense of Angela Davis, the jailed militant Marxist.

His political image, as reported in the press, was not reflected in Davis' professional engagements, where his mastery of the art of establishing immediate, joyful rapport with audiences was undiminished. On May 28, 1973 Davis hosted a twenty-hour nationally syndicated telethon that brought in $1,107,653 in pledged contributions for the Highway Safety Foundation. The following November *Sammy*, a one-man network tour de force in which Davis recounted his half-century in show business, was immensely successful, but his second attempt at a regular variety hour, *NBC Follies*, was cancelled in midseason 1973-74. Meanwhile, the fast living, heavy smoking, and hard drinking to which he had become habituated as an alumnus of the Rat Pack were taking their physical toll. He developed liver and kidney trouble, and in February 1974 he was hospitalized with chest pains.

By April 1974 Davis, modifying his vices, was well enough to do a revue in New York City's Uris Theatre, *Sammy on Broadway*, with his old effervescence. He paced himself more carefully, emphasizing his casual strut and capitalizing on his naturally relaxed manner as a seasoned trouper, but he could, at the right moments, as he said, "rev it up." In his club appearances he tried to restrain what he called the "monster" of perpetual motion in which he had trapped himself, but the energy seemed the same, as Louie Robinson of *Ebony* (February 1976) reported from Caesar's Palace in Las Vegas: "The coat and tie having come off . . . and the face grown moist with perspiration . . . he reaches for a tambourine, slaps it against his hip. [Later, having] donned a straw hat given him by the late Maurice Chevalier, . . . he goes into an excellent impression of its donor, singing 'Me and My Shadow' to the accompaniment of a delicate tap dance. Then he is off on a string of mimicry: Bogart, Cagney, Stewart, Brando, Dean Martin." Some perfectionist critics quibble about the "untrained," sometimes "overblown" quality of Davis' singing, failing to note that he professes to be, not a complete singer, but a complete entertainer, and that he certainly succeeds in entertaining audiences with his upbeat style, his flexible voice, and his resonant projection, especially when the song is a "belter." At the New York State Theater in Lincoln Center in August 1978, Davis starred in *Stop the World, I Want to Get Off*, an adaptation of the Leslie Bricusse-Anthony Newley musical.

Sammy Davis Jr. and Altovise Gore, a black dancer whom he married in 1970, live in Davis' luxurious home in Beverly Hills. Davis was married twice before, to Loray White, also a black dancer, for a few months in 1959 and 1960, and to May Britt, the Swedish actress, from 1960 to 1968. By Miss Britt he has a daughter, Tracey, and with her adopted Mark and Jeff (named for Davis' late friend Jeff Chandler). Both marriages ended in divorce. Davis' favorite recreations are photography, playing golf, and driving automobiles, of which he has several, including a Rolls-Royce. His carefully chosen, well-tailored, stylishly hip wardrobe, ranging from tight-fitting jeans to sharp evening clothes, is huge; he tends to dress more flamboyantly on stage than off, and to wear a plethora of jewelry. He has reported his income to be somewhere between $2,500,000 and $3,000,000 a year.

Davis is a wiry man, five feet six inches tall and weighing about 129 pounds, with a "childlike" body that has been described as "incongruous" with his "fierce" head. In explaining why he refuses to be bitter about past hurts, including the threats on his life he received when he was dating white actresses in the days of rampant segregation and the daily hate mail he and May Britt used to receive, he once said that "bitterness makes for ugliness" and he "can't afford ugliness because . . . if he [the man he sees in the mirror] isn't pretty, the awards, the applause, the money, they don't mean a thing." Those who know him well say that Davis is a warm, vulnerable man, and after interviewing him for *Newsday*'s *Long Island Magazine* (June 16, 1974), Al Cohn reported that he "discussed his politics, his problems, and his goals the way he seems to handle everything—with emotion, obvious sincerity, and relentless vigor."

References: Coronet 5:181+ Ap '67 pors; N Y Sunday News III p1 Jl 8 '73 pors; N Y Times Mag p32+ O 15 '72 pors; Sat Eve Post 238:89+ F 13 '65 pors; Biographical Encyclopedia & Who's Who of the American Theatre (1966); Davis, Sammy Jr., and Boyar, Jane and Burt. Yes I Can (1965); Who's Who in the Theatre (1977)

Deneuve, Catherine (de-nûv')

Oct. 22, 1943- Actress. Address: b. c/o Artmedia, 10 Avenue George-V, 75008 Paris, France

Although admired as one of the most beautiful women to decorate the contemporary motion picture screen, Catherine Deneuve has also, perhaps less flatteringly, been called the "ice maiden" because of the aloof and enigmatic personality she has glacially projected in such classic art films as Polanski's *Repulsion*, Buñuel's *Belle de Jour* and *Tristana*, and Truffaut's *The Mississippi Mermaid*. Miss Deneuve, who is often compared with Grace Kelly because of her patrician beauty, has won critical acclaim in the United States, commands a devoted following in Europe, and in her native France enjoys the status of a superstar.

Catherine Deneuve

Catherine Deneuve was born on October 22, 1943 in Paris, France, the third of the four daughters of Maurice Dorléac and the former Renée Deneuve, who were both fairly successful actors. As a child, Catherine was in frail health and showed signs of reserve —a quality that has remained with her. Her closest companion was her older sister Françoise Dorléac, who died in an automobile accident in 1967, at the height of a successful acting career. "My parents were what one might call bourgeois—though without mean, small minds," Miss Deneuve told Edward R. F. Sheehan for an interview in *Holiday* (August 1969). "We lived on the first floor of a little house in the sixteenth [arrondissement]. I knew everybody in the neighborhood. It was very provincial, but I was very happy when I was young. I was always together with my parents and sisters." She also remembers weekend outings in the country, where the Dorléacs owned a house. Miss Deneuve attended the École Lamazou, a private Roman Catholic girls' school, until the age of eleven, when she entered the exclusive Lycée La Fontaine. "The nuns were very old-fashioned, but the lycée was very snob," she told Sheehan. "I was really more comfortable with the nuns in spite of their strictness."

In keeping with the French bourgeois tradition, Catherine Deneuve was shielded from the theatre by her parents during her childhood, and she only saw her father perform on stage on rare occasions. Although more interested in interior design than in acting, she did appear in small roles, while still a schoolgirl, in the films *Les Collégiens* (1956) and *Les Petits Chats* (1959). In 1960 she was featured with her sister Françoise in the low-budget *Les Portes Claquent*. Although her early film experiences failed to inspire her with any real commitment to acting, she gradually established herself as an actress, with the encouragement of her sister. Together they appeared in Michel Deville's light comedy *Ce Soir ou Jamais* (1960), and on her own, Miss Deneuve acted in small roles in *L'Homme a Femmes* (1960) and in Marc Allegret's *Les Parisiennes* (1962).

At seventeen Catherine Deneuve met director Roger Vadim, who saw in her just the right combination of sex appeal and innocence to cast her as the virtuous Justine in his World War II film *Le Vice et la Vertu* (1962; *Vice and Virtue,* MGM, 1965). Vadim has said of her, as quoted in *Newsweek* (August 26, 1968): "She never had that drive to be in films. But, living with me, she wanted to get involved in that part of my life." In 1962 she gave birth to Vadim's son Christian, but despite social pressure she refused to marry the director. Meanwhile, she appeared in Vadim's *Et Satan Conduit le Bal* (1962), an exposé of life among the sons and daughters of the rich, and in Pierre Kast's *Vacances Portugaises* (1963), about fashionable couples on holiday, but neither film did much to advance her still halfhearted career.

After becoming a close friend of Jacques Demy and his wife, Agnes Varda, both directors, Catherine Deneuve was cast as the heroine of Demy's successful musical *Les Parapluies de Cherbourg* (1963; *The Umbrellas of Cherbourg,* Allied Artists-Landau, 1964), a dream-like film set against the prosaic everyday life of the French provincial town. Although Miss Deneuve received only $5,000 for her performance, she fondly remembers the congenial ambiance in which *The Umbrellas of Cherbourg* was made. Her interpretation of Geneviève, the umbrella dealer's daughter who is maneuvered into an unhappy marriage with a jewelry merchant after her lover leaves for the army, brought her superlatives from the critics and the *palme d'or* —the best actress award—of the 1964 Cannes film festival. Miss Deneuve credits Jacques Demy with her success. "Before *Umbrellas of Cherbourg,* I did not take acting seriously," she told Tom Burke of the New York *Times* (August 18, 1968). "Jacques made me feel that I am beautiful. He sees, too, that I am sensitive. He made me learn to act, to love acting for the first time, to *believe* what I act."

Catherine Deneuve next appeared in Claude Chabrol's episode "L'Homme qui Vendit la Tour Eiffel" in the omnibus film *Les Plus Belles Escroqueries du Monde* (1963); in Philippe de Broca's farce *Un Monsieur de Compagnie* (1964; *Male Companion,* International Classics, 1966); in the comedy *La Chasse à l'Homme* (1964), again with her sister; and in the Italian production *La Costanza della Ragione* (1964). She scored her second triumph when she played a schizophrenic young woman whose sexual hangups lead to emotional withdrawal and murder in Roman Polanski's harrowing *Repulsion* (Royal Films International, 1965). According to Polanski, he cast her in the role because he needed "an angelic girl who could kill a man with a razor." Writing in *Cue* (October 9, 1965), William Wolf found that Catherine Deneuve played the disturbed girl "with haunting detachment," and Bosley Crowther, reviewing *Repulsion* in the Toronto *Globe and Mail* (October 6, 1965), judged her as "simply splendid in the central role—secretive in nursing her obsession and starkly sad in her insanity." Describing the experience of playing a character who, in her words, "was one of those dirty jokes of nature, without reason or point," Catherine Deneuve told Tom Burke that she was "able to discard the emotion completely" the moment a take was finished. "You must never become so involved that you bring the role away from work with you," she said.

On August 18, 1965 Catherine Deneuve married the British fashion photographer David Bailey in an unconventional ceremony in London, with Mick Jagger as best man. Meanwhile, she was seen in Marcel Camus' *Le Chant du Monde* (1965), a film about a vendetta in the south of France, and then in Jean-Paul Rappeneau's *La Vie de Chateau* (1966; Royal Films International, 1967), a romantic comedy set in occupied France at the end of World War II. In the latter she received glowing notices for her performance as a restless wife whose affections are fought for by a member of the French Resistance, a German officer, and her own husband, a dull Norman orchard owner who emerges as the hero. Less successful was the Austrian sex comedy *Liebeskarusell* (1965), in which she appeared in an episode with Gert Fröbe, and the science-fiction allegory *Les Créatures* (1965), a French-Swedish production written and directed by Agnes Varda, in which she played a writer's wife who is shocked into speechlessness by an automobile accident.

Catherine Deneuve and Françoise Dorléac appeared together for the last time in Jacques Demy's *Les Demoiselles de Rochefort* 1966; *(The Young Girls of Rochefort,* Warner Brothers-Seven Arts, 1968), a good-natured spoof of Hollywood musicals inspired by the success of *Umbrellas of Cherbourg*. Although some reviewers praised the sisters for their singing and dancing talents, critical opinion was by no means unanimous. Wendy Michener, writing in the Toronto *Globe and Mail* (June 24, 1968), felt that "as a team, Deneuve and Dorléac" were "a disappointment" and that the "two beauties" cancelled "each other out." The death of Françoise Dorléac in 1967, only a few months after the film was completed, left Catherine Deneuve emotionally scarred. Her childless marriage to David Bailey broke up in the following year and ended in divorce in 1970.

In spite of the emotional wounds she sustained in private life, Miss Deneuve achieved another triumph in Luis Buñuel's "surrealist fairytale" *Belle de Jour* (1967; Allied Artists, 1968). She appeared as Séverine, who although apparently happily married to a physician, is aware that she can reach sexual fulfillment only by suffering humiliation, and embarks on a part-time career as a prostitute in a high-class brothel. The film alternates between her real and fantasy worlds so deftly that it is virtually impossible to distinguish one from the other. Although she had had misgivings about appearing in some of its nude scenes, Miss Deneuve felt that her performance in *Belle de Jour* was the best of her career up to that time—an opinion seconded by critics. She told Edward R. F. Sheehan during the *Holiday* interview: "Buñuel called me an Anglo-Saxon, someone with a static visage, a constant deadpan. We kept it that way. . . . It corresponds to my own nature. . . . My theory of acting . . . is to communicate through nuances—by keeping things very natural, simple, hidden, dissimulated." *Belle de Jour* received the Golden Lion award at the 1967 Venice film festival.

Miss Deneuve was next seen in Michel Deville's "libertine farce" *Benjamin* (1967; Paramount, 1968) as Anne, an eighteenth-century coquette, and then in Jean Aurel's *Manon '70* (1967). She was featured as the Baroness Marie Vetsera in Terence Young's big-budget French-British production of the nineteenth-century historical tragedy *Mayerling* (1968; MGM, 1969), filmed in Austria with Omar Sharif as Crown Prince Rudolf. In the view of most critics she was grossly miscast and failed to convey the deep passion that characterized the ill-fated love affair between the young baroness and the crown prince. Judith Crist reported in *New York* magazine (February 24, 1969) that "Miss Deneuve successfully lays to rest any delusions . . . about her being able to act beyond simulating a lovely blank-eyed marble statue."

For her American debut, in *The April Fools* (National General, 1969), director Stuart Rosenberg—who called her "one of the most professional people I've ever worked with" —cast Miss Deneuve as the neglected wife of a wealthy New Yorker who runs off to Paris with a less successful man, played by Jack Lemmon. But despite her generally favorable reviews, *The April Fools* did not as yet bring her any wide recognition in the United States.

Alan Cavalier's *La Chamade* (1968; Lopert, 1969), based on a novel by Françoise Sagan, featured Catherine Deneuve as a "super-chic flower child" torn between two lovers—a wealthy Parisian businessman and a poor young painter—opting, in the end, for comfort and luxury. Next she played the mysterious mail-order bride of a tobacco planter (Jean-Paul Belmondo) in *La Sirène de Mississippi* (1969; *The Mississippi Mermaid*, United Artists, 1970), Francois Truffaut's romantic melodrama about loneliness and love, filmed on the island of Réunion. While on location she confessed in an interview with Nadine Liber in *Life* (January 24, 1969): "It's a very tough part for me. The girl is so different from me, so strong, so sure of herself, so aggressive." The critic for *Time* (April 27, 1970) felt that Miss Deneuve exhibited in the role "all the frosty, mysterious elegance" of the Hitchcock heroines Ingrid Bergman and Grace Kelly, and Louise Sweeney observed in the *Christian Science Monitor* (April 25, 1970) that she gave "a disarming and complex performance as the woman who manages to 'look like the innocent flower but be the serpent under it.' "

Catherine Deneuve again distinguished herself in the title role of Luis Buñuel's Spanish-Italian-French production of *Tristana* (Maron Films, 1970), loosely based on a novel by Benito Pérez Galdós about a young orphan corrupted by her cultivated but libertine guardian—played by Fernando Rey. In her interview with Joseph Gelmis in *Newsday* she explained that she approached the role with the idea that "intentions are more important than 'acting,' " and that she tried to "play the situation, not the scene." The overwhelmingly favorable reviews called Miss Deneuve's performance "perfect," "splendid," "impeccable," and "magnificently controlled." In the New York *Times* (September 21, 1970), Vincent Canby wrote: "Never before has her beauty seemed more precise and enigmatic, so that while, at the beginning, there is just the slightest hint of the erotic woman inside the schoolgirl, there is, at the end, an awareness of the saint that once lived within the majestically deformed woman."

In Jacques Demy's version of Charles De Perrault's fairy tale *Peau d'Ane* (1970) Miss Deneuve appeared in a dual role as a mother and daughter. She gave what was described as a "very adept" performance as a mother faced with the death of a child in Nadine Marquand Tritignant's *Ça n'arrive qu'aux autres (It Only Happens to Others*, GSF Productions, 1971), costarring Marcello Mastroianni, with whom she also appeared in *Lisa* (1972). Among her other recent films are the gangster movie *Un Flic* (1972) with Alain Delon and Richard Crenna; *L'Evènement le Plus Important depuis que l'Homme a Marché sur la Lune* (1973); and *La Femme aux Bottes Rouges* (1975). She was seen as a Place Pigalle entertainer and part-time hooker in Lazzlo Szabo's comedy *Zig-Zig* (1975), and as a high-class Hollywood call girl in her second American film, Robert Aldrich's hard-boiled crime melodrama *Hustle* (Paramount, 1975), with Burt Reynolds.

Her passive portrayal of Giancarlo Giannini's afflicted sister in Mauro Bolognini's French-Italian production *La Grande Bourgoise* (1975; Atlantic Releasing Corporation, 1977), about the downfall of a prominent family of Italian socialists, evoked mixed reviews. To most critics she seemed inordinately out of place as the elegantly groomed daughter of a murdered archaeologist in a Moroccan desert outpost in Dick Richard's Foreign Legion epic *March or Die* (Columbia, 1977).

In recent years Catherine Deneuve has displayed her photogenic charms on television commercials for Mercury cars and Chanel perfumes. Since 1971 she has been president and director-general of Films de la Citrouille. Among her latest films is *Lovers Like Us*, in which she stars with Yves Montand.

Catherine Deneuve's romance with Italian film star Marcello Mastroianni ended about three years after she gave birth to his daughter, Chiara-Charlotte, in 1972. She now lives with her two children in an apartment in the St. Germain-des-Prés district of Paris. A former brunette who is five feet four inches tall, Miss Deneuve was described by Christina Kirk in the New York *Daily News* (May 5, 1968) as "a fragile French blonde with wide, amber eyes and an air of startled innocence" who blends "sex," "sweetness," and "sophistication." In his *Memoirs of the Devil* (Harcourt, 1977) Roger Vadim refers to her development from "the shy and discreetly perverse adolescent figure of a Colette heroine" to "the elegant romantic of the French cinema" who, "when she brings her cold, faultless features to a Buñuel role, . . . comes close to perfection." Miss Deneuve characterizes herself as a "pessimist" and a "spendthrift," and she dislikes being referred to as a "sex symbol"—a label she regards as strictly American. She guards her privacy fiercely, maintaining a certain formality and distance even with those closest to her. Diane de Dubovay, who interviewed her for *Viva* (December 1977), quoted her as saying: "Love is the most important experience a woman can have. Otherwise life would not be worth living."

References: Holiday 46:48+ Ag '69 por; McCalls 105:177+ O '77; Viva 5:44+ D '77 por; Celebrity Register, 1973; International Motion Picture Almanac, 1977; International Who's Who, 1977; Shipman, David. The Great Movie Stars (1973); Thomson, David. A Biographical Dictionary of Film (1975); Who's Who in France, 1977-78

Dern, Bruce

June 4, 1936- Actor. Address: c/o Creative Artists Agency, Inc., 1888 Century Park E., Suite 1400, Los Angeles, Calif. 90067

One of Hollywood's most admired character actors, Bruce Dern has portrayed a dazzling variety of psychotic killers, tough guys, hillbillies, drug freaks, and business promoters. A veteran of over 100 television and thirty-five film roles, Dern has paid his dues by appearing in many television and film Westerns—he became the first actor ever to kill folk hero John Wayne onscreen—and in exploitation pictures like *Bloody Mama, Cycle Savages*, and *The Incredible Two-Headed Transplant*. On the college-town revival house circuit, Dern is a favorite for his starring roles in such cult films as Bob Rafaelson's *The King of Marvin Gardens* and the ecology-science fiction picture, *Silent Running*. In recent years Dern has won critical praise for major roles in *The Great Gatsby* (1974), *Family Plot* (1976), *Black Sunday* (1977), and *Coming Home* (1978). Trained at the Actors' Studio in New York, Dern began his career on the New York stage, and was scheduled to return there in the fall of 1978 as the costar of a Broadway play about the marriage of Sinclair Lewis and Dorothy Thompson.

A member of one of the Midwest's most distinguished families, Bruce MacLeish Dern was born in Chicago, Illinois on June 4, 1936 and raised in the Chicago suburb of Winnetka. His father, John Dern, was Adlai Stevenson's law partner. His grandfather, George H. Dern, served as governor of Utah and as Secretary of War under President Franklin D. Roosevelt. Bruce Dern's mother, Jean (MacLeish) Dern, was the daughter of the chairman of Carson, Pirie, Scott, and Company, one of Chicago's leading department stores. Dern's great-uncle is Archibald MacLeish, the poet. Dern has an older brother, Jack, who is an executive of Carson, Pirie, Scott, and a sister, Jean.

"I was a rebel in my family," Dern told Joan Levine of *Viva* (April 1976). "When I was six, I started telling lies and I had a terrible temper. They had to send me to a doctor for it." When he was fourteen, his family packed him off to the exclusive prep school, Choate, in Connecticut, but he was miserable there. After his sophomore year, he transferred to New Trier High in Winnetka, where he became a star on the track team. Track was also his major interest at the University of Pennsylvania, where he majored in journalism. In 1956 he tried out for the Olympics, but did not qualify for the United States team.

In 1957 Dern saw James Dean in *Rebel Without a Cause* and was profoundly affected. Shortly afterward the track coach kicked him off the team for refusing to shave the sideburns that he had grown for a school play. Despite the protests of his family, who were determined that he become a lawyer, Dern dropped out of college and began to study acting. At first he studied in Philadelphia under Gordon Phillips at the American Foundation of Dramatic Art; later he transferred to the Actors' Studio in New York, where he was coached by Lee Strasberg.

Dern made his Broadway debut on November 20, 1958 as Maguire in an Actors' Studio production of Sean O'Casey's *The Shadow of a Gunman*. The following year Elia Kazan cast him as the bartender in Tennessee Williams' *Sweet Bird of Youth*, which opened on Broadway on March 10, 1959. Later Dern toured as Tom Junior, the part Rip Torn created on Broadway. In 1960 he took over the leading role of Val Xavier in Williams' *Orpheus Descending* in an Off-Broadway production. Around the same time Elia Kazan gave him his first film role, a bit part in *Wild River* (Twentieth Century-Fox, 1960), as a small-town Southern bigot.

After *Orpheus Descending* closed in April 1960, Dern's promising theatre career stalled, and for a year he supported himself as a taxi driver. Gradually, however, he began to get bit parts in TV episodes, and in 1962 he decided to move to Los Angeles. Soon after his arrival, he landed a job as Jack Lord's sidekick in *Stoney Burke*, an ABC-TV series about rodeo riders that ran for a year starting in the fall of 1962. Meanwhile, he continued to perform walk-ons in episodes until 1964, when he was cast as the villain in an episode of *The Alfred Hitchcock Theatre* (NBC). As he recalled to Rex Reed of the New York *Sunday News* (April 16, 1972), he portrayed "a hillbilly psychotic peach-picker who terrorized Teresa Wright and made her eat a dead squirrel."

Dern's performance for Hitchcock convinced casting directors that he could play a chilling villain, and the young actor was in frequent demand after that to do cowboy or hillbilly outlaws and killers. In 1965 and 1966 his television credits included over twenty-five episodes of such shows as *Wagon Train* (ABC), *Rawhide* (CBS), *The Virginian* (NBC), *Gunsmoke* (CBS), *Shenandoah* (ABC), *12 O'Clock High* (ABC), *The Fugitive* (ABC), *The Big Valley* (ABC), *Run for Your Life* (NBC), and *Laredo* (NBC).

In films Dern had a short run as a corpse —he was bludgeoned to death with a poker in Hitchcock's *Marnie* (Universal, 1964) and decapitated in *Hush . . . Hush, Sweet Charlotte* (Twentieth Century-Fox, 1965)—before he began getting villain and psycho parts in B pictures. His first was *The Wild Angels* (American International Pictures, 1966), directed and produced by Roger ("King-of-the-B's") Corman, in which he played a Hells Angel type killed by the police while trying to steal one of their motorcycles. Thereafter he delighted second-string reviewers obliged to sit through such films as *The Trip* (AIP, 1967), a Corman picture in which Dern played Peter Fonda's guide on an LSD trip; *The War Wagon* (Universal, 1967), a routine Western in which he portrayed one of the villain's scurrilous henchmen; *Will Penny* (Paramount, 1968), another Western, in which he menaced Charlton Heston; and *Psych-Out* (AIP, 1968), in which Dern portrayed an LSD user "flipped out" in the Haight-Ashbury district of San Francisco. In *Support Your Local Sheriff* (United Artists, 1969), a good-natured Western spoof with James Garner, Dern played the town's most ornery outlaw. For once he appeared on the side of the law in another comic Western, *Waterhole No. 3* (Paramount, 1967), in which he was an inept deputy sheriff.

In 1968 Dern temporarily broke away from B films with a small part in *Castle Keep* (Columbia, 1969), directed by Sidney Pollack, but that antiwar movie scored neither at the box office nor in the reviewers' columns. In 1969 he appeared in another film that went nowhere, *Number One* (United Artists), a football film in which he portrayed a businessman. Dern then returned to the B's, appearing as a sadistic bisexual in Corman's *Bloody Mama* (AIP, 1970); as a psychotic motorcycle gang leader in *Cycle Savages* (AIP, 1970); as another heavy in *Thumb Tripping* (Avco Embassy, 1972); and as an evil scientist who creates a monster in *The Incredible Two-Headed Transplant* (AIP, 1971). In the latter film he was called upon to take a bite out of a baby's arm.

Meanwhile, Dern was getting a few respectable assignments. In Sidney Pollack's much acclaimed depiction of Depression dance marathons, *They Shoot Horses, Don't They?* (Cinerama Releasing Corporation, 1970), Dern had a supporting role as an Okie who enters the contest with his pregnant wife. He appeared in his first "necktie role" as the authoritarian, relentlessly clean-living basketball coach in *Drive, He Said* (Columbia, 1971), a film about student activism and restlessness in the 1960's that was written and directed by Jack Nicholson. Booed and hissed at the Cannes Film Festival and rejected at the American box office, *Drive, He Said* nonetheless won some admiring notices for Dern and the National Society of Film Critics Best Supporting Actor award.

If his role in *Drive, He Said* did much to persuade directors that Dern was capable of portraying ordinary human beings that impression was once more nearly dispelled when the actor appeared in *The Cowboys* (Warner Brothers-Kinney, 1972). Dern not only played another of his crazed killer roles, but had the temerity to murder John Wayne on camera, thus desecrating an American institution as sacred as apple pie or Mother. "Dern," the big Duke told him before they filmed the scene, "you're gonna be hated everywhere in the world for this one."

Luckily Dern's career survived the cinematic showdown with Wayne, and he went on to star as the offbeat hero of *Silent Running* (Universal, 1972), a science fiction film directed by one of Stanley Kubrick's technical assistants on *2001, a Space Odyssey*. The story of an astronaut-ecologist who escapes into space to save the world's only remaining greenery from destruction by a plastic-obsessed society, the film was dismissed as simplistic and sentimental by many critics, but others were enthusiastic. Among the latter was Richard Schickel, who wrote in *Life* (March 24, 1972), "[The film] provides a great, near-solo role for Bruce Dern, known heretofore as one of Hollywood's best young character actors. . . . As a gentle, practical humanist among the hardware, Dern gives a quiet, resourceful performance in which strength and determination, nuttiness and squareness are combined."

With Jack Nicholson, Dern costarred in *The King of Marvin Gardens* (Columbia, 1972), Bob Rafelson's enigmatic portrait of two brothers destroyed by their fantasies. Most critics commended the two star performances, but they almost universally labeled the film a pretentious failure. Although both *Silent Running* and *The King of Marvin Gardens* have enjoyed some status over the years as cult films, neither fared well at the box office. Dern was next seen on the screen in 1974, when he portrayed detective Walter Matthau's sidekick in the San Francisco-based crime melodrama, *The Laughing Policeman* (Twentieth Century-Fox). That year he also appeared as Tom Buchanan, Daisy's caddish, polo-playing husband in *The Great Gatsby* (Paramount). Jack Clayton's expensively mounted production of the F. Scott Fitzgerald novel was panned, but Dern was one of the few actors who came away from that misguided project with critical approval. For his performance he was nominated as Best Supporting Actor of 1974 by the Hollywood Foreign Press Association.

In 1975 Dern starred in two admired, but commercially unsuccessful films. Written and directed by Kirk Douglas, *Posse* (Paramount) gave him the opportunity to costar with Douglas as a hunted outlaw. In *Smile* (United Artists), a satire on beauty contests that delighted audiences at the 1975 New York Film Festival, Dern portrayed Big Bob Friedlander, the beauty pageant's energetic promoter, a man who sells automobiles and still subscribes to the American dream.

In *Family Plot* (Universal, 1976) Dern again displayed his comic talents as the con-man hero, but few critics found the Hitchcock film more than a minor effort of the suspense master. The critical verdict was even less generous for *Won Ton Ton, the Dog Who Saved Hollywood* (Paramount, 1976), a comedy about the silent film era in which Dern starred as a would-be producer who promotes the talents of a Rin Tin Tin-type performing dog. That same year Dern also starred in *The Twist*, an English-language picture filmed in Paris by French director Claude Chabrol, as a best-selling author married to Stéphane Audran and having an affair with Ann-Margret. The film has never been released in the United States.

In *Black Sunday* (Paramount, 1977), John Frankenheimer's thriller about a Goodyear blimp menacing a superbowl crowd with thousands of death-dealing darts, Dern played the blimp's deranged Vietnam war-veteran pilot, seduced into terrorism by sultry Black Septembrist Marthe Heller. "Happily, there are some fine performances in potentially cartoonish roles—and Dern's work in particular borders on the extraordinary," wrote Frank Rich of the New York *Post* (April 1, 1977). "I've always admired this actor's ability to convey both all-American stolidity and out-and-out insanity—and in *Black Sunday* his uniquely schizophrenic screen personality is exploited better than it ever has been before."

Bruce Dern portrayed another soldier emotionally destroyed by his experiences in Vietnam in *Coming Home* (United Artists, 1978), the antiwar film in which he costarred with Jane Fonda and Jon Voight, under the direction of Hal Ashby. Although most critics felt that the script was stacked against the Dern character—a gung ho Marine captain who goes off to Vietnam with visions of glory—they were divided in their estimation of the actor's ability to transcend the limitations of the script. "With Bruce Dern in the role, Captain Hyde—who is supposed to be driven mad by the war—looks buggyeyed and crazily distracted even before he goes to Vietnam," complained Pauline Kael in the *New Yorker* (February 20, 1976); "when the war deranges him, who can tell the difference? It's a fatally wrong piece of casting." Judith Crist, on the other hand, was more admiring. "Dern's performance is equally subtle within the rigid confines of the role. . . ," she wrote in the New York *Post* (February 16, 1978). "His transition from the secure Marine 'lifer' to the displaced individual is signified by the pace of speech, the tightening of jaw, the jerky movement."

For years baffled movie critics have wondered why Bruce Dern has failed to achieve the level of stardom attained by such of his contemporaries as Jack Nicholson and Robert Redford. "I was sold wrong," he explained to Bob Lardine of the New York *Sunday News* (May 23, 1976). "I would have been much further along if I had gotten a better agent earlier. Everyone in this business is sold, and I was sold as a cuckoo, a bad guy, a psychotic." But things are looking up for Dern now that he is represented by Fred Spector of the Creative Artists Agency, even if his most recent film, *The Driver*, did open at the end of July 1978 to mostly negative reviews.

"When he is not talking about his career, his monologue is a shower of throwaway lines, spoken softly and quickly and underscored by a sly smile whenever he says something particularly outrageous," Tom Topor wrote after interviewing Bruce Dern for the New York *Post* (March 26, 1977). Dern lives in Malibu in a beachfront house built by Frank Capra, and fraternizes with Robert Redford and Jack Nicholson. He shuns Hollywood social life, however, preferring to go off when he can to his mountain retreat at Lake Tahoe. Still a dedicated runner who logs up to ten miles a day and competes in amateur track meets, the slim and muscular Dern is six feet two inches tall and weighs 170 pounds; he has blue eyes and light brown hair. In keeping with his athleticism, he neither drinks nor smokes. Dern has told interviewers that he does not read, but likes to listen to music, especially that of Brahms, Erik Satie, and Aaron Copland. Professing to have no interest in politics, he claims to have voted only once, for Barry Goldwater in 1964. On October 20, 1969 Dern married his third wife, Andrea Beckett, whom he met when she was a student and he a teacher at the Actors and Directors Lab in Los Angeles. By his second wife, the actress Diane Ladd, he has a daughter, Laura Elizabeth. Their other daughter accidentally drowned in a swimming pool as an infant.

References: *Los Angeles Herald Examiner* F p1+ Ap 23 '78 pors; *N Y Post* p40 Ap 24 '76 por, p34 Mr 26 '77 pors; *N Y Sunday News* II pS9 Ap 16 '72 pors, III p13 Ja 27 '74 por, III p9 My 23 '76 por; *Time* 106:48 Ag 15 '75 pors; *Viva* 3:55+ Ap '76 por; *Washington Post* B p1+ My 4 '78 por; *White Plains Reporter Dispatch* p27 Ap 11 '72 por; *Who's Who in America*, 1976-77

Desai, Morarji (Ranchhodji) (de-sī′ mō-rär′ jē)

Feb. 29, 1896- Prime Minister of India. Address: b. Office of the Prime Minister, New Delhi, India; h. 5 Dupleix Rd., New Delhi, India 110011

NOTE: This biography supersedes the article that appeared in *Current Biography* in 1958.

Crowning a career that has spanned nearly six decades, Morarji Desai, India's oldest active politician, succeeded Indira Gandhi as his country's Prime Minister on March 24, 1977. Paradoxically, Desai, who has been described as the most autocratic political figure in India, was chosen to restore democracy following twenty-one months of emergency rule. A disciple of Mohandas K. Gandhi, Desai spent several years in prison for his part in India's independence movement. Later he made his mark as an effective but puritanical administrator in the state government of Bombay and skillfully handled the portfolios of Commerce and Finance in the Cabinet of Prime Minister Jawaharlal Nehru. In 1969, after his dismissal as Finance Minister by Indira Gandhi, Desai resigned as Deputy Prime Minister and became leader of the opposition to the ruling Congress party. Although the 1977 election victory of his newly organized Janata party was greeted with collective euphoria, India, under Prime Minister Desai, continues to face immense difficulties, including its perennial problems of hunger, disease, and overpopulation.

A native of Bhadeli, a village near the city of Bulsar, in what is now the state of Gujarat, Morarji Ranchhodji Desai was born on February 29, 1896, the oldest of the six children of Ranchhodji Desai, a teacher, and Vajiaben (or Maniben) Desai. He is a member of the Anavil ("without blemish") Brahmin caste, which consists mainly of farmers and civil servants. Desai obtained his primary education in Bhadeli and in the village of Kundla, where his father was for a time headmaster of an English middle school, and he graduated from the Bai Avabai High School in Bulsar.

At fifteen Desai married Gajraben, the eleven-year-old daughter of a local revenue official. Since his father had died, an apparent suicide, three days before the wedding, Desai now headed a household consisting of his wife, mother, grandmother, two sisters, and three brothers. In 1913 he entered Wilson College in Bombay under a scholarship sponsored by the Maharajah of Bhavnagar. "I was very timid . . . till I was sixteen," Desai has recalled. "It was after I went to the college that I developed courage and strength of character."

At Wilson College, Desai studied science and mathematics, served as secretary of the debating society, and attended meetings of the Home Rule movement and the Indian National Congress. In 1915 he heard Mohandas K. Gandhi for the first time and was profoundly impressed by his personality. After graduating in 1917 with a B.S. Desai remained at the college for an additional year as a Dakshina Fellow and was a Viceroy's commissioned officer in the University Training Corps.

In 1918 Desai joined the Bombay state civil service and during the next twelve years served in various parts of the state as a deputy collector—a post that under the British Raj included the duties of local executive officer or district magistrate. According to Welles Hangen, in *After Nehru, Who?* (Harcourt, 1963), "His reputation for efficiency and incorruptibility was proverbial, although he often clashed with arrogant British superiors." Dismayed by the patronizing attitude of British officials toward Indians, Desai left the civil service in May 1930 to devote himself to the national cause. "After resigning from government service . . . , I had decided that I would not . . . undertake any task just for the sake of an income," he has recalled. "I had . . . an awareness that I had ill-served my country by serving a foreign government for twelve years."

Joining Gandhi's civil disobedience movement, Desai took part in the "no tax" campaign aimed at persuading peasants to withhold revenues from the British authorities. He was arrested for the first time in October 1930, after the Congress movement was declared illegal, and served two additional prison terms between 1932 and 1934. In accordance with Gandhi's Satyagraha principles, he improved himself physically and mentally during his imprisonment by practising strict self-discipline.

In 1931 Desai joined the All-India Congress Committee and was elected secretary of the Guajarat Pradesh Congress Committee, serving until 1937, and again from 1939 to 1946. When the British granted provincial autonomy to India in 1937, he was elected to the legislative assembly of Bombay province and named Minister for Revenue, Cooperation, Forests, and Agriculture in the provincial government. In 1939 he and other Congress party members resigned from the government in protest against Great Britain's commitment of India as a belligerent in World War II without prior notice.

During 1940-41 Desai was imprisoned for a fourth time, for civil disobedience. After Gandhi launched the "Quit India" movement—calling for passive resistance in the event of a Japanese invasion, while insisting on unconditional independence from Great Britain as the price of India's participation in the Allied war effort—Desai had misgivings about anti-British strikes and sabotage campaigns favored by its more radical adherents. Nevertheless, he became active in the movement and was again imprisoned, from 1942 to 1945, along with Gandhi and other Congress leaders.

Desai became Minister for Home and Revenue in the newly reconstituted Congress party government in Bombay, headed by Chief Minister B. B. G. Kher, in April 1946, and he continued to serve after India became independent in August 1947. During his six years in that office he put his puritanical views into effect by trying unsuccessfully to close Bombay's brothels and campaigning against polygamy, cosmetics, popular music, and public dancing by unmarried couples. His efforts to impose total prohibition on Bombay state gave rise to a flourishing bootlegging industry and contributed to his unpopularity.

On the whole, however, Desai was credited with running an efficient administration. Among his reforms were safeguards for tenant farmers against arbitrary eviction and exorbitant rents; organization of a citizens' volunteer police force; nationalization of bus transportation; and removal of some restrictions against members of the Harijan (or "Untouchable") caste. From 1950 to 1958 he served as treasurer of the All-India Congress Committee.

In 1952 Desai was designated by retiring Chief Minister Kher as his successor and was chosen Congress party leader in the legislative assembly. As Chief Minister of Bombay state, he introduced far-reaching administrative reforms, including the separation of the judiciary from the executive. His most serious problem was the turbulent campaign for division of Bombay state along linguistic lines, between the economically backward Marathi-speaking people and his own more prosperous Gujarati minority.

To suppress the riots, reportedly stirred up by Communists, that erupted over the language issue in several cities in Bombay state, Desai ordered police to fire on the demonstrators, and an estimated 100 persons were killed. When violence broke out in Ahmedabad in August 1956, Desai tried to use Gandhian tactics in dealing with it, vowing to "fast unto death" to restore peace, but he ended his fast after eight days and reverted to police action when the riots failed to subside.

In November 1956 Desai accepted an invitation from Prime Minister Nehru to join the national Cabinet as Minister for Commerce and Industry. In 1957 he was elected to the first of five terms as representative of the Surat district of Bombay in the Lok Sabha—the lower house of India's parliament. After India's Minister of Finance, T. T. Krishnamachari, was ousted as a result of a financial scandal in March 1958, Nehru appointed Desai to succeed him. As Finance Minister, Desai acquired a reputation for husbanding India's meager resources and for pursuing an even-handed policy in dealing with business and organized labor. Among his most controversial measures were the Gold Control Order, forbidding the production of gold artifacts of greater purity than fourteen karats, to make gold smuggling and hoarding less lucrative, and the Compulsory Deposit Scheme, compelling Indians of certain income levels to deposit a percentage of their earnings.

Desai made his first trip abroad in the fall of 1958 to attend a Commonwealth finance ministers' conference at Montreal, Canada. He also visited the United States and Great Britain, after those countries exempted him from the requirement of undergoing vaccination, a practice to which he objected for religious reasons. In 1960 he visited the Soviet Union and Eastern Europe, and in 1961 he had a friendly meeting with President John F. Kennedy in Vienna. In his dealings with foreign statesmen Desai made clear that his government welcomed economic aid and investments from abroad but was determined to remain independent of all outside control.

Although Desai had been a leading contender for the Prime Ministership, by the early 1960's his claim seemed less secure. In his book *Nehru's Mantle* (Praeger, 1966), Michael

Brecher wrote: "Throughout the fifties . . . Nehru showed respect, even affection for Morarji. . . . However, . . . with years of close contact came disenchantment. Nehru never lost his respect for his administrative talents but . . . he became increasingly concerned that Morarji's brittleness could cause grave damage to the unity of India." A major issue of controversy between Nehru and Desai was the latter's insistence on the designation of Hindi as India's official language. In 1961 Nehru reduced the importance of the post of deputy leader of the parliamentary Congress party majority, a move regarded as an effort to forestall Desai's bid for what had traditionally been the second-ranking position in the party.

Desai and other senior Cabinet members resigned in August 1963 in accordance with the Kamaraj Plan, designed by Congress party leader Kumaraswami Kamaraj Nadar in the wake of recent electoral setbacks suffered by the party. Under its provisions, key officials on the national and state levels were to step down and devote themselves to a grass-roots revitalization of the party. After Nehru's death in May 1964, Desai made a bid for the Prime Ministership, but the party caucus, headed by Kamaraj, decided on the lesser-known Lal Bahadur Shastri. Although Shastri offered to take Desai into his Cabinet, he refused, because the new Prime Minister would not guarantee him the post of Home Minister, the second-ranking position. During 1966-67 Desai was chairman of the Administrative Reforms Commission.

Meanwhile, after Shastri's death in January 1966, he made another bid for the Prime Ministership as the sole challenger of Nehru's daughter, Mrs. Indira Gandhi, whom he dismissed as a mere "schoolgirl." Sponsored by Kamaraj, Mrs. Gandhi won election as parliamentary Congress party leader with 355 votes against 169 received by Desai. When Mrs. Gandhi took office as Prime Minister later that month, Desai declined her invitation to join her Cabinet. A year later, in February, the Congress party suffered a setback in national elections, making the establishment of a new government necessary. Desai withdrew his opposition to Mrs. Gandhi under a compromise agreement that brought him into the Cabinet as Deputy Prime Minister and Minister of Finance after her reelection in March 1967. Thanks to his adroit maneuvers in Parliament and party councils and his ability to conciliate both his own conservative wing of the Congress party and Indira Gandhi's socialist faction, Desai soon became a dominant personality in the government.

When, in 1969, members of the Congress party's conservative old guard, known as the Syndicate, challenged Mrs. Gandhi's socialist program, especially her plans to nationalize the country's leading banks, Desai adopted a compromise stance, advocating "social control" of the banks rather than outright nationalization. But at the Bangalore convention in early July, Mrs. Gandhi obtained passage of a resolution endorsing her nationalization scheme. Another conflict arose over the question of choosing a successor to Indian President Zakir Husain, who died in May. While the Syndicate leaders and Desai favored Neelam Sanjiva Reddy, a conservative, Mrs. Gandhi threw her support to V. V. Giri, who was elected.

On July 16, 1969 Prime Minister Gandhi relieved Desai of his post as Finance Minister, taking over that portfolio herself. Three days later she ordered the nationalization of India's fourteen largest commercial banks. Dismayed at his abrupt dismissal, Desai rejected Mrs. Gandhi's offer to retain him as Deputy Prime Minister and to give him another Cabinet post and resigned from the government. After reconciliation efforts by party officials and Cabinet members failed, Desai more openly identified himself with the Syndicate.

The Congress party formally split in November 1969 into the Indian National Congress—Ruling (INC-R) under the continued leadership of Indira Gandhi, and the Indian National Congress—Opposition (INC-O), or Old Congress, which under Desai's parliamentary leadership claimed the support of sixty-five of the 281 Congress party members then in the Lok Sabha. Over the next few years Desai devoted much of his effort to opposing what he regarded as the increasingly dictatorial and highhanded methods of Prime Minister Gandhi. In 1970 he proposed a grand alliance of opposition parties, but his plan was rejected in favor of a more informal working arrangement for the 1971 elections. Four years later, he launched a massive anticorruption campaign in his home state of Gujarat aimed against the ruling Congress party, and on April 7, 1975 he embarked once more on a "fast unto death" to force Mrs. Gandhi to permit early state elections in Gujarat, which had been placed under direct rule of the national government. He ended his fast six days later, when the Prime Minister acceded to his demands.

Because of mounting opposition to her rule, Prime Minister Gandhi proclaimed a state of national emergency on June 26, 1975, suspending civil liberties. Desai was immediately arrested, along with other opposition leaders, and spent the next nineteen months in confinement. He was released on January 18, 1977, a few hours before Mrs. Gandhi announced the relaxation of authoritarian rule and promised national elections in two months.

Preparing for the elections, Desai and other opposition leaders organized the Janata (People's) party—a coalition of such disparate elements as the Congress opposition, the Hindu nationalist Jana Sangh, the right-wing

Indian People's party, and the moderately leftist Socialist party—which waged a vigorous campaign under the slogan "Democracy over Dictatorship." Although the country's relative prosperity under her rule made her confident of victory, Mrs. Gandhi's position was weakened by the unpopularity of her drastic emergency measures, opposition to the growing influence of her son, Sanjay Gandhi, the overzealousness of her birth control campaign, and the defection of Jagjivan Ram, the leader of India's untouchables, from her Cabinet.

In the elections to the Lok Sabha, held from March 16 to 20, 1977, the Congress party was removed from power for the first time in thirty years of Indian independence. Emerging as the strongest political force, the Janata party won 271 seats in the 542-member lower house, while the Congress party's representation dwindled to 153. In the interest of party unity, the choice of the new Prime Minister and Janata party leader was left to the elder statesmen Jaya Prakash Narayan and J. B. Kripalani, who after discussion with party members chose Morarji Desai. His only rival, Jagjivan Ram, who headed the new Congress for Democracy, agreed a few days later to join Desai's Cabinet as Defense Minister. After being sworn in as India's fourth Prime Minister by acting President B. D. Jatti on March 24, 1977, Desai told the cheering crowds: "You need not fear this government as you had feared all these months. We are your servants and not your masters."

In the months that followed his inauguration, Desai substantially restored democratic institutions, took steps to institute a less coercive birth control program, and announced plans for a reversal of large-scale industrialization and a greater emphasis on cottage industries. His government was strengthened when Defense Minister Jagjivan Ram formally merged his Congress for Democracy with the Janata party in May 1977 and again when Janata won substantial victories in state elections. On the other hand, the government drew considerable criticism for its short-lived arrest of the still popular Indira Gandhi on ill-prepared corruption charges in October 1977. Desai also found that with the removal of the coercive apparatus crime and unrest increased, while the problems of poverty remained.

In foreign relations, Desai tried to replace Mrs. Gandhi's Moscow-oriented policy with genuine nonalignment. He inaugurated a friendly correspondence with President Jimmy Carter, made overtures for improved relations with China and Pakistan, and declared his intention to examine Arab-Israeli problems with greater impartiality. "We have cordial relations with all countries and no relation with any country at the cost of any other country," Desai declared when he returned from a visit to the Soviet Union in October 1977.

Morarji Desai and his wife, Gajraben, have a house in a fashionable district of New Delhi. Their two surviving children are a married daughter, Viru, and a son, Kantilal, a former businessman who has recently served as his father's aide. Two sons died in infancy, and a daughter, Indu, committed suicide in 1953. Welles Hangen described Desai in 1963 as a clean-shaven man of "medium height and spare build" who "moves with youthful agility" and has the "appearance and manner . . . of a fastidious professor." Two volumes of Desai's projected three-volume autobiography, *The Story of My Life,* were published by Macmillan India in 1974. His opinions are found in the volumes *Selected Speeches of Shri Morarji Desai* (1956) and *In My View* (1966).

A devout Hindu, who once committed the entire Bhagavad-Gita to memory, Desai devotes three to four hours each day to prayer, meditation, and yoga exercises, and works daily on the *charkha*—the Indian-style spinning wheel—in the tradition of Mahatma Gandhi. He takes pride in having practised celibacy since the late 1920's. A vegetarian, but not an ascetic, Desai indulges in choice fruits and nuts, carrot juice, milk, honey, cheese, raw garlic, and Swiss chocolate and rejects modern medicine in favor of nature cures. He considers himself an "instrument of God" and believes that "one should form no habits except the one of telling the truth."

References: Asian Recorder 23:13705+ Ap 23-29 '77; India News 15:1+ Mr 28 '77 por; New Yorker 53:119+ O 17 '77; Desai, Morarji. The Story of My Life 2 vols (1974); International Who's Who, 1977-78; Times of India Directory and Yearbook, 1976

Didion, Joan

Dec. 5, 1934- Novelist; journalist; screenwriter. Address: c/o William Morris Agency, Inc., 1350 Ave. of the Americas, New York City, N.Y. 10019

The technical virtuosity of Joan Didion's intensely personal journalism pieces and of her understated, elliptical novels has led a number of critics to second the opinion of James Dickey, who has called her "the finest woman prose stylist writing in English today." In all of her work Miss Didion communicates her apocalyptic view of postwar America, especially of her native California, with fierce eloquence. She views the United States as a world in disintegration, a place where, as she quotes from William Butler Yeats: "Things fall apart; the center cannot hold." The quotation comes from the preface

Joan Didion

to her brilliant collection of magazine essays, *Slouching Toward Bethlehem* (1968), but it could just as well serve as an introduction to her two best-selling novels, *Play It As It Lays* (1970) and *A Book of Common Prayer* (1977). In both novels Miss Didion explores the problems of the individual living in a world where nothing seems to hold. Although Maria Wyeth, the heroine of *Play It As It Lays* comes to view the terrifying emptiness of her life in Los Angeles and Las Vegas with nightmarish clarity, Charlotte Douglas, mother of a political terrorist in *A Book of Common Prayer*, clings tenaciously to her delusions. Joan Didion's first novel, *Run River* (1963), was about a family living in her birthplace, Sacramento. With her husband, the author John Gregory Dunne, she has written several screenplays, including the film version of *Play It As It Lays*. Her articles have appeared in many magazines, and she has been a columnist for the *Saturday Evening Post, Life*, and *Esquire*.

Joan Didion was born into a family that had lived for five generations in the Sacramento Valley which, she has written in *Slouching Toward Bethlehem*, is the *real* California, "a place in which a boom mentality and a sense of Chekhovian loss meet in uneasy suspension." She was born on December 5, 1934, the daughter of Frank Reese and Eduene (Jerrett) Didion. Her father's family originally came from Alsace-Lorraine. Her mother is descended from English settlers who came to America during the War of Independence and kept pushing westward along the frontier. Miss Didion has one younger brother, Jimmy, who is an executive with the large Western real estate firm, Coldwell Banker, and her father is also in the real estate business.

During World War II Joan Didion left Sacramento with her family to follow her father, an Army Air Corps finance officer, from base to base. After the end of the war she returned to Sacramento, where during the week she attended public schools and on Sundays, religious classes at the Trinity Episcopal Cathedral. Although she has insisted that her childhood was happy, Miss Didion has admitted to being "one of those children who always thought the bridge would fall in if you walked across it." "I was just one of those fearful children," she confessed to Sally Quinn of the Washington *Post* (April 4, 1977), "always working out how the funicular at Royal Gorge would crash. Yes, I did have a happy childhood . . . except for these terrible fears. I thought about the atomic bomb a lot . . . after there was one."

By the age of thirteen Joan Didion was typing pages from the fiction of Hemingway and Conrad just to see "how sentences worked." After graduating from high school, she attended the University of California at Berkeley, where she majored in English literature and edited the school paper. Shortly before her graduation in 1956, she submitted a long article she had written on William Wilson Wurster, the father of the San Francisco style of architecture, to *Vogue* magazine's *Prix de Paris* contest for young writers and won first prize.

Entitled either to a free trip to Paris or a cash award and a job at *Vogue*, Miss Didion prudently chose the job and arrived in New York City in the summer of 1956. At *Vogue* she worked her way up from writing merchandising and promotional copy to a position as associate feature editor. By the early 1960's she was also free-lancing for *Mademoiselle* and the *National Review*. In 1963 she began writing *Vogue*'s movie reviews and went on leave from her staff position to finish her first novel.

Set in the Sacramento Valley that Joan Didion knows so well, *Run River* (Obolensky, 1963) centers on the gradual self-destruction of an old Sacramento family during the years after World War II. "I started . . . *Run River* in New York because I was homesick," the author explained to Elizabeth Fishel of *Newsday* (October 2, 1971). "That's why there's too much landscape in it, too much social detail." Although it lacked the spare, sinewy quality of her later fiction, the novel encountered an admiring critical reception. "She is, above all, cool, and an impressively skilled writer," wrote Robert Maurer in the New York *Herald Tribune Books* magazine (May 12, 1963). "Even in this first novel there seems to be nothing technically that she cannot do."

A few months after the publication of *Run River,* on January 30, 1964, Joan Didion married John Gregory Dunne, who was then working on the staff of *Time.* In April they both took temporary leave from their jobs to visit Southern California and have been living there as free-lance writers ever since. Over the next few years Miss Didion continued contributing film reviews to *Vogue* and wrote for the *Saturday Evening Post, Holiday,* the New York *Times Magazine,* and *The American Scholar.* She became a contributing editor to the *National Review,* and in 1967 she and her husband began alternately writing a column for the *Saturday Evening Post* called "Points West," which continued until the *Post* stopped publication in February 1969.

A selection of Miss Didion's brooding essays from the *Saturday Evening Post* and other journals were included in *Slouching Toward Bethlehem* (Farrar, Straus, 1968). Those articles, including her celebrated title piece on the hippies of San Francisco's Haight-Ashbury district during the summer of 1967, deal mainly with contemporary life in California and her reactions to it. "A substantial element of spiritual biography is present in these pieces of wary skepticism," wrote Melvin Maddocks in the *Christian Science Monitor* (May 16, 1968). "Though she has a journalist's weakness for converting her themes into 'myths,' 'dreams,' and 'folk' symbols—she is an original observer and even better. an original thinker."

In 1970 Miss Didion completed her second novel, *Play It As It Lays* (Farrar, Straus), which she has characterized as "a book in which anything that happened would happen off the page, a 'white' book to which the reader would have to bring his or her own bad dreams." Written in tough, jagged prose, the novel consists of eighty-four terse chapters, some only a few lines long. Chapter fifty-two, for example, reads: "Maria made a list of things she would never do. She would never: *walk through the Sands or Caesar's alone after midnight.* She would never: *ball at a party, do S-M unless she wanted to, borrow furs from Abe Lipsey, deal.* She would never: *carry a Yorkshire in Beverly Hills."* Its deliberately disjointed narrative relates the story of Maria Wyeth, a second-rate Hollywood actress who aimlessly drives the freeways of Southern California and keeps a precarious grasp on life despite adultery, divorce, abortion, the institutionalization of her brain-damaged daughter, and the suicide of her best friend.

"Miss Didion is shocking in the way that Jane Austen is shocking," wrote Robert Nye in the *Guardian* (March 17, 1971) in an admiring review typical of the others: "She calculates her effects with imperturbable iciness. like a soul on the make. . . . *Play It As It Lays* deserves the attention of anyone still interested in the possibilities of narrative prose." A commercial as well as a critical success, the book became a best-seller, earned the author a six-figure income, and was nominated for a National Book Award.

In December 1969 Miss Didion began a biweekly column for *Life* magazine, introducing herself to her readers with characteristically dramatic directness as a woman sitting in a hotel room in Honolulu "in lieu of filing for a divorce." The column lasted for only a few months, but her marriage to Dunne endured, and the husband and wife team went on to write several screenplays together during the 1970's. The first was *Panic in Needle Park* (1971), a modestly budgeted Cannes Film Festival prize-winner about youthful heroin addicts on the Upper West Side of New York. The pair then adapted *Play It As It Lays* into a 1972 screen version that was directed by Frank Perry and starred Tuesday Weld and Anthony Perkins. Having come up with the idea of updating the perennial *A Star Is Born* as a rock musical, they wrote three screenplays for the film that after many tribulations eventually became the Barbra Streisand-Kris Kristofferson vehicle of 1976. Although they later withdrew from the film and had nothing to do with the final screenplay, they had the consolation of receiving a percentage of its considerable profits. Miss Didion has told interviewers that she finds screenwriting a lucrative and welcome break from writing fiction. "It's not like writing," she explained to Evelyn Renold of *Newsday* magazine (April 24, 1977). "You're really making notes for a director. . . . It's like working a puzzle; there's no real involvement in it."

In 1977 Miss Didion's third novel, *A Book of Common Prayer,* was published by Simon and Schuster. Like Maria Wyeth, its heroine is a wanderer; Charlotte Douglas drifts through the American South and the countries of Central America refusing to come to terms with her eighteen-year-old daughter's career as an airplane hijacker and political terrorist. Charlotte's final stop is a steamy, decadent banana republic called Boca Grande, where she is killed during one of the country's periodic "colorful" revolutions. As in *Play It As It Lays,* Miss Didion tempers the melodrama of *Common Prayer* with a spare, ironic narrative, in this case using the technically difficult device of a first-person narrator. Although a few critics found her narrative pyrotechnics obtrusive, the reviewer for *Library Journal* (February 15, 1977) praised the book as "an almost Faulknerian reconstruction in which the drama of the action is matched by a second drama of narration." Equally admiring was Peter S. Prescott of *Newsweek* (March 21, 1977) who wrote, "Her laconic prose, compressed into short chapters and staccato paragraphs, allows for occasional repetitions that lend a liturgical echo to her tale. Her exposition of situations and details adroitly conceals their significance—until much later their meaning flares before our eyes. This is a remarkably good novel."

In an interview with Chris Chase of the Chicago *Tribune* (April 3, 1977), Miss Didion admitted that she hated doing magazine columns. "I do it to force myself to go out and report," she said. "It's a way of forcing yourself into other people's worlds. . . . An awful lot of stuff in my novels came out of stuff I encountered reporting." Her latest stint as a columnist was in 1976 and 1977 when she and her husband alternated in writing a column called "Points West" for *Esquire*.

In 1976 Joan Didion was a visiting regents lecturer in English literature at the University of California in Berkeley. Miss Didion's future projects include a nonfiction book about California called "Fairytales," a novel set in Hawaii to be called "Angel Visits," and, with Dunne, a screenplay entitled "Water," about a family in California's Owens Valley.

In an article entitled "Why I Write" for the New York *Times Book Review* (December 5, 1976), Miss Didion once described herself as "a person whose most absorbed and passionate hours are spent arranging words on pieces of paper." A slow and painstaking writer, she works daily in a small office in her home from eleven in the morning until four or five in the afternoon. When it is time to finish a novel, however, she has always returned to her parents' home in Sacramento, where she works in the bedroom she slept in as a child.

Joan Didion lives with her husband and adopted daughter Quintana Roo—who is named for a territory in the Yucatan—in a white-painted brick house fronting on the ocean in Trancas, just north of Malibu, California. Socially the Dunnes see many members of the Hollywood film and television colony, including Warren Beatty, Jack Nicholson, Jane Fonda, Robert Towne, Norman Lear, and assorted screenwriters, studio heads, and record company executives. Soft-voiced and fragile-looking, Miss Didion chainsmokes Pall Mall cigarettes and drinks large quantities of coffee. When asked to draw a portrait of herself for *Ms.* magazine, the writer submitted a thumb print accompanied by the following word sketch: "This is Joan Didion Dunne, five feet two inches, ninety-five pounds, hair red, eyes hazel. Must wear corrective lenses. Too thin. Astigmatic. Has no visual sense of herself." When she is not working, Miss Didion enjoys reading, cooking, and taking an occasional vacation in Hawaii.

Intensely individualistic, Joan Didion shuns psychoanalysis and women's groups, and takes little interest in politics or the women's movement. In 1972 she wrote an article critical of modern feminism for the New York *Times Magazine* and has in turn been attacked by feminists for creating what they regard as passive losers for heroines. Although she listed herself as a Republican for her entry in *Contemporary Authors*, Miss Didion told Sara Davidson in the New York *Times Book Review* that she seldom votes. "The politics I personally want are anarchic," she said. "Throw out the laws. Tear it down. Start all over." Admittedly shy and reticent, the author has often said she never feels articulate unless she is in front of her typewriter. "In many ways writing is the act of saying *I*, of imposing oneself upon other people, of saying *listen to me, see it my way, change your mind*," she wrote in her essay, "Why I Write." "It's an aggressive, even a hostile act. You can disguise its aggressiveness all you want with veils of subordinate clauses and qualifiers and tentative subjunctives, with ellipses and evasions—with the whole manner of intimating rather than claiming, of alluding rather than stating—but there's no getting around the fact that setting words on paper is the tactic of a secret bully, an invasion, an imposition of the writer's sensibility on the reader's most private space."

References: Chicago Tribune Ap 3 '77 pors; Harper's 243:112+ D '71 por; Ms. 5:65+ F '77 por; N Y Post p17 Jl 25 '70 por; N Y Times Bk R p1+ Ap 3 '77; People 6:50+ Jl 26 '76 pors; Wash Post D p1+ Ap 4 '77 por; Contemporary Authors 1st rev ed vols 5-8 (1969); Contemporary Novelists, 1976; Didion, Joan. Slouching Toward Bethlehem (1968)

Donoso, José (do-nō'sō)

Oct. 5, 1924- Chilean novelist. Address: Calaceite, Province of Teruel, Spain; c/o Carmen Balcells, Urgel 241, Barcelona 11, Spain

In *The Boom in Spanish American Literature*, his "personal history" of the outstanding Latin American writers who erupted upon the literary scene of the 1960's, the novelist José Donoso traced his own career from obscurity in his Chilean homeland to the international renown that today links his name with those of Carlos Fuentes, Jorge Luis Borges, Gabriel García Márquez, Julio Cortázar, and Mario Vargas Llosa. Although early recognized for his brilliant talents and agile imagination, Donoso was first labeled a *criollista*, a writer in the limited slice-of-life tradition of Chilean regional realism. Abounding with details of his nation's customs, language, and class conflicts, his first short stories and novels appeared unified by the recurrence of one central theme: the death and decay of Chile's rigidly structured society.

José Donoso

Only with the 1970 publication of *El obsceno pájaro de la noche (The Obscene Bird of Night)*, a monumental novel hailed in Europe and on both American continents as his fantasy masterpiece, was Donoso regarded as transcending Chilean boundaries and joining his Latin American counterparts in experiments with legends and myths, discontinuous plotting, multiple identities, shiftings of time and points of view, and grotesque fantasy. In *The Boom*, which he wrote while living in Spain, he attributed his later stylistic techniques to the overall internationalization of Latin American writers and to his belated realization that "the irrational could have intellectual significance." He has dissociated himself from any coherent metaphysical system or sociopolitical purpose, summing up himself for one interviewer: "I have no social vision. Mine is an interior exercise."

José Donoso was born on October 5, 1924 in the sparsely populated suburb of Providencia in Santiago, Chile, the first of three sons of José and Alicia Donoso. His brothers are Gonzalo and Pablo Donoso. In his self-revealing "Chronology" in *Review 73* (Fall, 1973), he told of an early life surrounded by ne'er-do-well, slightly Bohemian *nouveau riche* relatives, in an atmosphere of class privilege and eccentricity often echoed in his fiction. His father, he wrote, was "a young physician more addicted to horse racing and to playing cards than to his profession"; and his mother, "a pretty and amusing woman, who somehow coped," was related to the owners of the newspaper *La Nación*, on which her husband had been given work. In 1929 the family moved into a house in the old part of Santiago with three of his father's wealthy great-aunts. Surrounded by "courts" of relatives and servants, in a microcosm of Chile's antiquated class structures, his father served as "royal" physician and his mother, as glorified "lady-in-waiting." For Donoso and his brothers it was a heady world of limousines and classical music, English tutors, boxing lessons, costumed childhood mimicry of operas, and youthful sexual dalliance with compliant maids.

For almost a decade, beginning in 1932, Donoso attended The Grange, an English day school in Santiago, and it was there, in reaction against the stiff-lipped regimen of British education, that he developed his "lifelong incapacity to belong to groups of any kind—political, social, or recreational." He fled to the romance and haphazardness, sometimes bordering upon madness, of his family life and to wide, indiscriminate reading. "I caught the bug," Donoso wrote in his "Chronology," "together with a fateful feeling of guilt related to reading literature. . . . As father predicted, literature was my undoing." At thirteen he wrote and illustrated a costume play imitating Victor Hugo's *Hernani*, and soon he was writing poetry. Depressed by The Grange and compulsory sports, he feigned stomach trouble to avoid duties, the first sign of physical and mental illnesses, real and imaginary, that were to plague him all his life.

As a teenager, Donoso played the role of the lost poetic soul—a school truant, announced atheist, frequenter of Santiago's most disreputable quarters, and reader of forbidden books. Dropping out from school in 1943 before completing his *bachillerato*, he took a brief fling at acting like a social dandy modeled after Proust's Marcel, while working at short-term jobs. Wanderlust led him to book third-class passage on a steamer south through the Straits of Magellan to Punta Arenas, to take a job on the pampa as a shepherd for nearly a year, and then to wander through Patagonia to Buenos Aires, where he worked in the port and hobnobbed with sailors and stevedores. He returned to Santiago in 1947 to complete high school at the Pedagogical Institute and entered the university to study English and literature.

An intimation that literature was not "the source of guilt and destitution," but "involved much delight" became a certainty at Princeton University, where Donoso went in 1949 as a Doherty Foundation scholar. Despite his poor academic performance, he remembers Princeton fondly, particularly some of his professors, among them the noted critic Richard P. Blackmur, under whom he wrote in English his first short stories. After receiving his A.B. degree in 1951, he roamed for six months through the United States, Mexico, and Central America before he returned to

Chile. Suffering from one of his recurrent bouts with gastritis and from writer's block in what he recalls as the most chaotic period of his life, he began his first sessions of psychoanalysis. Analysis helped, and in 1954 he became a professor of conversational English at the Catholic University of Chile. Later he taught techniques of expression in the Journalism School of the University of Chile. "China," his first story in Spanish, won inclusion in 1954 in a well-known anthology after Donoso had entered it in a Santiago story contest.

With the private publication in 1955 of *Veraneo y otros Cuentos* (Summertime and Other Stories) Donoso first encountered the limits that confined any aspiring Chilean writer. Rejected by three Santiago publishers who anticipated low sales, the volume appeared only after he had sold 100 subscriptions to pay the first installment on 1,000 copies. "I stood on street corners to offer *[Veraneo]* to passing acquaintances while my friends did the same in other sections of the city," he recalls, describing actions that he was to repeat with his first novel. Although the stories eventually won high critical praise and the Municipal Short Story Prize for 1956, they were not reprinted until ten years later. *El Charleston (The Charleston)*, his second collection, followed in 1960, and selected stories, all but one taken from the earlier books, were published as *Cuentos* by Barcelona's Seix Barral in 1971 and as *Charleston & Other Stories* by David R. Godine in Boston in 1977.

Although the early short stories made few departures from the realistic techniques that dominated Chilean *criollismo* in the 1950's, they contain "glimpses of the direction Donoso would eventually pursue," according to Larry Rohter in a Washington *Post* (August 14, 1977) review of the *Charleston* collection. Predictably for a young writer, the stories often deal with children and adolescents as they first encounter the hypocrisy, indifference, and evils of adults. However, their scope spread widely, sometime touching upon the class conflicts developed later by Donoso, more often focusing upon isolated, obsessed characters perched dangerously between damnation and salvation, reason and madness, loneliness and love—an isolated boy who controls others with magical powers of his whistling; a man who spends his life sleeping, in the hope that one day in his dreams he will find "something real and magical"; a collector of feline pictures driven insane from recurrent nightmares of ferocious animals. At their best, Robert Maurer commented in the *Saturday Review* (July 9, 1977), Donoso's "dark, terrifying account of human existence . . . moves step by step from our real world towards a realm of dream, magic, fantasy, and mystery."

The work that publicized Donoso's name outside Chile was the novel *Coronación* (*Coronation*, Knopf, 1965), completed near Santiago in Isla Negra during 1957 after he had given up his jobs. Published that year by Nascimento, the book brought its author compensation only of 700 copies, which he again peddled wherever he could. "A mixture of poetry and brutality," according to K. Schwartz in *A New History of Spanish American Fiction*, the novel "offers us a multiple viewpoint of Chilean society as seen by *los de arriba* (the ups) and *los de abajo* (the downs.)" Set in the tomb-like manor of a wealthy ninety-four-year-old widow and her middle-aged bachelor grandson, Donoso's story depicts the debilitation of those two oligarchs when a young peasant girl, brought in to nurse the widow, introduces instead the disturbing vibrancy of sexual attraction and the violence of Santiago's criminal element. Fragmented and separate, the lives of the characters are all somehow crippled by social station, inhibitions, or tenuous grasps upon reality. The novel closes with a grotesque mock coronation of the widow by her two mad cap servants that climaxes in her death and in her grandson's insanity. While Chilean critics praised the substantiality of Donoso's grim social portrait, recognition of Donoso's more universal concerns came later only as the novel was passed hand to hand among the growing underground of Latin American writers with international literary interests. In 1962 *Coronación* was awarded the William Faulkner Foundation Prize, set up by Faulkner's will to encourage translations of outstanding Spanish American fiction.

"Asphyxiated in my Chilean surroundings," Donoso wrote in *The Boom*, "dissatisfied with the limitations placed upon me, six months after *Coronación* appeared and without a nickel in my pocket, I decided to begin a tour of America with the purpose of learning what was happening outside my country." During two years in Buenos Aires his horizons expanded with copious reading of other Latin American writers, some of whom—Borges and Miguel Angel Asturias among them—became his friends. In 1959 he returned to work for Santiago's *Revista Ercilla* as a journalist, for five years covering "everything from earthquakes to new books, from fashion shows to revolutions." He won the Chile-Italia Prize for Journalism in 1960. Two Writers' Congress meetings, one in Concepción in 1962 and the other at Chichén Itzá, Mexico, in 1964, confirmed for Donoso the widespread isolation of Latin American writers, but also gave him signs that "The Boom," as it soon was called, had begun. His close friendship with the Mexican novelist Carlos Fuentes dates from the Congresses. From 1964 to 1966 Donoso lived in Mexico City, doing literary criticism for *Siempre* magazine while completing his next two novels, both published in 1966: *Este domingo* (*This Sunday*, Knopf, 1968) and *El lugar sin límites* (*Hell Has No Limits*, Dutton, 1973).

Este domingo, Donoso's second novel about familial and social disintegration, repeats many of *Coronación*'s conflicts between rich and poor, masters and servants, old and young, impotency and sexual power; but critics generally found it more skillfully composed and profound. Beginning with a prologue by a boy who describes the ritualized Sundays spent with his middle-class grandparents, the slightly absurd Alvaro Vives and his frivolous wife Chepa, the novel moves to analyses of the couple's futile attempts to find significance in their empty lives, Alvaro through a past affair with their servant Violeta, Chepa through do-gooder social work that leads her to a dominating mother-love for Maya, a criminal. As in *Coronación*, a dark, ominous sense of violence lies just beneath the veneer of civilized forms, whose breakdown triggers the murder of Violeta by Maya and a vicious attack on Chepa by slum children she is dedicated to helping. "Donoso's cool and biting intelligence demonstrates once again that he is one of the major novelists now writing in Latin America," Alexander Coleman said of the novel in the New York *Times* (November 26, 1967).

Together with novels by Fuentes and Cuba's Severo Sarduy, *El lugar sin límites* appeared in English in the collection *Triple Cross*. It marked a distinct break from realism and toward such stylistic devices as symbols, multiple viewpoints, and character transformations. Covering the events of one day in a brothel of a decaying village, the novel centers on the ambiguous relationships among four characters: La Manuela, a transvestite brother owner; his daughter Japonesita, the madam; Don Pancho, a brutish customer; and Don Alejo, the patriarchal village *jefe*. "The material sounds sensational, but to Donoso's credit, he does not allow it to get out of hand and become merely perverse and stupidly shocking," Ronald de Feo concluded in a *Nation* review (June 11, 1973). Along with other critics, de Feo applauded Donoso's striking techniques, as well as his portrayal of desperate people lacking clear identity, hoping for a change of skin. According to Kirsten F. Nigro's essay on the novel, "From *Criollismo* to the Grotesque," the book lies in "a clear line of progression in chaos," along which Donoso increasingly moved toward innovative structures while exposing a universal false myth "that man possesses an internal symmetry."

His reputation now established abroad, Donoso was invited to teach writing and modern Spanish American literature at the University of Iowa's Writers' Workshop during 1965-1967 and briefly in Fort Collins, Colorado in 1969. He found teaching and writing incompatible, and he went to Spain to complete *El obsceno pájaro de la noche*, which reached forty drafts over eight years of composition before its completion in Barcelona in 1970. Convalescing from surgery for a hemorraging ulcer he had undergone in Colorado, unable to take pain-killing drugs, Donoso in Spain had fits of hallucinations, paranoia, and suicidal urges. "My experience of madness," he said in his "Chronology," had perhaps given "the material [of my novel] an organization." It was published in 1970 in Latin America and Spain to immediate acclaim. Many translations followed, including one in English by Hardie St. Martin and Leonard Mades in 1973 under the Knopf imprint.

"*The Obscene Bird of Night*," Robert Coover wrote in a New York *Times* review (June 17, 1973), "is a dense and energetic book, full of terrible risk-taking, populated with legendary saints and witches, mad old crones and a whole estate-full of freaks and monsters, and narrated by a deaf-mute, many times disguised." Like most critics, Coover found its plot indescribable. However, the narration of the deaf-mute, Mudito, is once again about the fall of a powerful dynasty, this time of Don Jerónimo and Ines de Azcoitía. Settings alternate between their mansion, La Rinconado, and The House of the Incarnation of La Chimba, once a convent and later a labyrinthine residence for old women attended by nuns. Central images are those of the legendary Ines, a witch-saint, and of Boy, the only Azcoitía offspring, a deformed monster. Like all the characters, the two images are abstractions, not real, lacking firm identity, containing opposites, constantly changing, reflecting a world, as one critic put it, "where ambiguity is an all-encompassing principle."

A few critics found *El obsceno pájaro de la noche* an overpraised, sometimes tedious, or incomprehensible work, but most regarded it as a masterwork about Chile to rival Gabriel García Márquez's *One Hundred Years of Solitude* about Colombia. Critical interpretations are multiple and varied. Michael Wood in the *New York Review of Books* perceived it as suggesting "that reality can be seen as presenting such a dearth of life that our frightened, starved minds will take refuge in nightmare," while Coover discovered "a book about an author being driven mad by the book he is trying to write." Donoso himself has denied "any intention of a precise meaning." The novel, he told one interviewer, reflects his "obsession with the non-unity of the human personality," his terror of non-existence, and is a "parody . . . of my whole previous narrative work." Walter Clemons in a *Newsweek* article (June 4, 1973) concluded: "With this book Donoso becomes a world novelist."

Donoso has published only one other work of fiction since 1970, *Tres novelitas burguesas*, three novellas issued first by Barcelona's

Seix Barral in 1973 and translated as *Sacred Families* by Knopf in 1977. Two of the novellas, all three of which are set amidst today's glittering Spanish jet set, display Donoso's humorous fantasy put to satirical purposes; the third, "Gaspard de la Nuit," harkens back to his earlier stories in its murky vision of experience. The volume, according to Larry Rohter's review, exhibits "the mind of a fully formed writer, confident in his manipulation of narrative and more cosmopolitan in outlook than his younger self."

Also originally published in Barcelona, by Editorial Anigrama in 1972, was Donoso's *Historia personal del "Boom"*, which appeared in English translation in 1977 under the title *The Boom in Spanish American Literature: A Personal History* (Columbia Univ. Press). It is less an analysis of a movement that brought Latin American writers into the mainstream of world literature than it is a chatty, rambling account of Donoso's firsthand experiences with other writers and of his own development. Among those writers who influenced him most he discusses Borges, Fuentes, Alejo Carpentier, and Mario Vargas Llosa.

Although José Donoso can be strikingly open about himself in his own writing and in interviews, little is known about his day-to-day personal life, perhaps because he stresses so strongly his inner self. Photographs show him as a handsome, broad-faced, virile-looking man with full dark hair, heavy gray mustache and beard, and large-rimmed glasses. Like his characters so often, Donoso is a multiple personality, fearing nonidentity above all else. He once told Emir Rodriquez Monegal in an interview, "I don't believe that a psychological unity exists in the human being. I have taken too many pills; I've smoked grass; too many psychological accidents have happened to me to believe that I am a single person. I am thirty persons and I'm nobody." After a hectic courtship described in his "Chronology," in 1961 he married María Pilar Serrano, and the couple has a daughter born in Madrid in 1967. They now live in the charming Spanish village of Calaceite, Teruel province, in a seventeenth-century stone house.

References: Review 73 (Center for Inter-American Relations) p11+ Fall '73 por; Sat R 4:30+ Jl 9 '77; Donoso, José. The Boom in Spanish American Literature (1977); International Who's Who, 1977-78; Who's Who in the World, 1974-75

Dukakis, Michael S(tanley) (dōō-kä'kis)

Nov. 3, 1933- Governor of Massachusetts.
Address: b. State House, Boston, Mass. 02133

When Michael S. Dukakis, a reform Democrat with strong liberal credentials, took office as Governor of Massachusetts in January 1975, he was faced with a staggering budget deficit that allowed him no course but to reduce expenses drastically. In ambivalent collaboration with a conservative, although predominantly Democratic, state legislature, Dukakis proceeded to remove "employable" persons from the general relief rolls, to end medical assistance to welfare recipients and the working poor, and to whittle down cost-of-living increases for welfare families with dependent children. Fellow liberals accused him of betraying their cause by trying to balance the state budget "on the backs of the poor," and other observers categorized him, along with Edmund G. Brown Jr., of California, as the exemplar of a "new breed"of liberal governor, a pragmatist who had become a "fiscal conservative" under the pressure of hard times. Dukakis rejected such categorization as "nonsense—we just don't have the money," and he vindicated himself when, as the fiscal crisis abated somewhat under his frugal management, he cautiously began to restore some of the human services that had been cut.

Dukakis established his reputation as the most conscientious, uncompromising of Massachusetts Democratic reformers during eight years in the State House of Representatives, where his best-known achievement was the passage of the nation's first no-fault auto insurance law. Nationally he is highly visible as the photogenic, articulate moderator of *The Advocates*, a weekly series of debates on public issues televised in Boston by station WGBH-TV and nationwide by the Public Broadcasting Service. What many liberal critics of Governor Dukakis do not understand is his view of the proper or expedient division of responsibility in the governmental hierarchy: he believes that the federal government, through job and health programs, should relieve the states of the burdens of welfare, Medicaid, and unemployment compensation and thus leave them free to devote more resources to crime-fighting, education, mass transit, mental health, consumer protection, and environmental control.

An only child, Michael Stanley Dukakis was born on September 3, 1933 in the upper-class Boston suburb of Brookline, Massachusetts—where he still lives—to Panos S. and Euterpe Dukakis, both of whom had emigrated from Greece. The father is a Boston obstetrician who worked his way through Harvard Medical School as a laborer in a textile mill. Dr. Dukakis' most oft-repeated and emphatic admonition to his son when he was growing up was, reportedly, "Michael, economize."

After graduating from Brookline High School, in 1951, Dukakis entered Swarthmore College, where he majored in political science. According to William A. Henry 3d, writing in the *New Republic* (January 15, 1977), "As a schoolboy athlete Dukakis found his five foot seven height a disadvantage but doggedly switched from sport to sport until he became a competition class runner." Dukakis himself lists his college sports as cross country running, basketball, and tennis. He notes that he was a member of the student council, that he worked in the college library and on summer construction jobs; that he "cut hair for sixty-five regular customers during [a] boycott of Swarthmore barbers who refused to cut black's hair"; and that he was chairman of Students for Democratic Action on campus and active in Philadelphia Democratic campaigns. He says he was strengthened in his interest in public policy and politics by his "concern about the direction the United States [had taken] during the [Joe] McCarthy years" and by the example of President John F. Kennedy.

In 1955 Dukakis received his B.A. degree, with Phi Beta Kappa key, and from 1956 to 1958 he served with the United States Army in Korea. After his discharge from the Army, in the rank of specialist third class, he entered Harvard Law School, where he took his J.D. degree with honors in 1960. Upon his admission to the Massachusetts bar, he joined the Boston law firm of Hill and Barlow, where he specialized in housing law, usually condominium cases.

In Brookline, Dukakis became a member of the town meeting in 1959 and served as chairman of the town committee in 1960 and 1961. In the wake of the scandal-ridden administration of Democratic Governor Foster Furcolo, he helped to organize a reform movement within the Democratic party, and he was elected to the State House of Representatives as a candidate of that movement from Brookline in 1962 and again in 1966. As the most energetic and intrepid of the reformists, he set himself apart from the State House establishment from the beginning of his career.

During his eight years as a legislator, Dukakis sponsored many consumer protection, housing, and environmental protection measures, and he was a pioneer in the drive to divert funds from highway construction to mass transit in Boston. His outstanding achievement was the nation's first no-fault auto insurance law, introduced by him and pushed by him, with typical obstinacy and endurance, against bitter opposition for four years. The no-fault system, finally authorized by the legislature in 1970 and put into effect the following year, has saved Massachusetts drivers millions of dollars in reduced bodily injury rates and has served as a model for similar no-fault systems in a number of other states.

In 1970 Dukakis lost a bid for lieutenant governor on a ticket headed by Boston Mayor Kevin White. Out of office, he devoted himself to public-interest law, organizing a Nader-type organization to monitor state agencies. He also began building the statewide power bases for his anticipated assault on the governorship, a work of construction abetted by the high profile he assumed as moderator of the public television debate forum *The Advocates*.

With a campaign staff and volunteers drawn largely from the ranks of veterans of the 1972 McGovern Presidential campaign and the anti-Vietnam war movement, Dukakis began his overt gubernatorial campaign in October 1973. Running against another liberal, Republican incumbent Francis W. Sargent, Dukakis stressed not the social issues on which both sides presumably agreed but rather his long-held belief that "good government," freed of waste, inefficiency, and political patronage, could solve its financial problems and deliver more services without increasing taxes.

As William A. Henry 3d observed in his *New Republic* article, "Dukakis was an early admirer—for style and substance—of another come-from-behind populist tactician, Jimmy Carter." Henry, an editorial writer and columnist for the Boston *Globe*, was not the only observer who saw, beneath differences in personality, a similarity to Jimmy Carter in Dukakis the campaigner. In what reporters described as an "intensely earnest," "business-like," "serious," and even "righteous" or "self-righteous" manner, Dukakis stressed the need for better "management" of state affairs and programs. "The first thing" he was going to do as governor, he said, was "to begin to introduce the idea of productivity and efficiency goals into state government." He promised to cut the governor's staff and generally institute a "no-hire no-fire" policy of attrition where possible, to balance the state budget without recourse to new taxes, and to improve the cost efficiency of government by 5 percent.

When he did address himself to issues during the campaign, Dukakis' stands tended to reflect his belief that the time of knee-jerk liberalism is past and that the Democratic politics of the future cannot ignore the alienation of working and lower-middle-class voters and the legitimate bread-and-butter grievances of the so-called "ethnics." On the explosive issue of artificially achieved racial balance in the public schools, he avoided discussion of busing and went on the record for "community control."

At the polls on November 5, 1974, Dukakis and his running mate, Thomas P. O'Neill 3d, son of the Democratic leader in the United States House of Representatives, defeated Governor Sargent and Lieutenant Governor Donald Dwight, taking 56 percent of the vote. On January 2, 1975 Dukakis was sworn in as the sixty-fifth Governor of Massachusetts.

Before the gubernatorial election of 1974, the Sargent administration claimed a budget surplus for the fiscal year 1974. After the election, state officials had told Dukakis to be prepared to deal with a serious budget deficit in 1975, but he did not know just how serious the deficit was until he took office. "What we found was appalling," he said later. "The state was in worse financial shape than any other state in the Union. If we had not taken immediate and drastic steps, we would rapidly have become the New York City of state governments."

Faced with a $450,000,000 deficit in 1975 and headed for a total deficit of more than $1.2 billion within two years, Dukakis looked into every corner of the state bureaucracy for ways to save money, beginning with his own office. The state police detail that traditionally guarded the executive suite was sent out to patrol the highways; the governor's staff was cut in half; limousines and other state vehicles were sold off, and the Governor began commuting between his home and his office by public transit trolley-subway; and instead of ordering new stationery, he continued using that bearing the name of Francis W. Sargent. In other economy moves, he cut the staff of the state fraudulent auto claims investigating board from fifty-six to four and that of an antiquated civil defense unit from ninety-eight to forty-three.

But such economies proved to be mere gestures in the face of the problem at hand. Trying to keep his campaign promise of no new taxes, he went into the bond market to raise between $450,000,000 and $500,000,000, but the financing—and eventually the refinancing—of the bond issue would be impossible, he saw, without realistic budget-tax packages. Reluctantly, when he took the bond issue to the legislature in the spring of 1975 he asked for a $110,000,000 tax program to back it up as a means of coping with the 1975 budget deficit. The following November he asked for a $3.3 billion 1976 budget—$300,000,000 below the amount requested by state agencies—and another $690,000,000 tax increase. Even after the drastic trimming of human services, $1.8 billion of the requested budget money was for that purpose, and all but $400,000,000 of the human services allocation was for welfare.

The legislature approved Dukakis' 1975 requests with relative speed but balked at his proposals for 1976 until the Governor publicly apologized in a television address for his tardiness in recognizing the need for tax increases and took upon himself the onus of the budget cuts in human services. The cuts included staff reductions at state hospitals, reductions in medical assistance, and the termination of general relief payments to "employable" persons.

Slashing away at human services even deeper than Dukakis had requested, the legislature passed a budget-tax package calling for $3 billion in expenditures in fiscal 1976 and for $445,000,000 in new taxes. Some of the services cut—which included termination of medical assistance to the working poor—were restored in the Governor's 1977 budget of $3.74 billion, but the "pork barrel" riders forced on the Governor by the legislature led him to describe the budget bill as enacted "one of the worst pieces of junk" he had ever seen.

The Governor's handling of the fiscal crisis lost him many of his closest supporters among the liberal political leaders of Massachusetts, including State Representative Barney Frank of Back Bay and State Senator Jack Backman of Brookline, both of whom broke with him on the issue of his "workfare" program, which they feared would take jobs away from the working poor and give them to hard-core unemployed fathers whose families were on welfare. (In the workfare program, unemployed fathers must work three days a week in state or nonprofit agency jobs or forfeit financial assistance.) In the Boston *Herald American* for October 10, 1977, Frank was quoted as saying flatly that he would not vote for Dukakis in 1978. Backman was quoted as saying: "I'm with Dukakis when I think he's right. I don't like what he's doing to the poor people. I don't like his cutbacks on medical assistance to them. Just before the 1974 election, I introduced Dukakis to about 1,000 senior citizens. His exact words to them were, 'I will never turn my back on the elderly of Massachusetts.' Then, in his first address to the legislature, he said he was going to eliminate the cost of living for Social Security recipients receiving supplementary aid from state funds. This has epitomized his actions."

Whatever the political side effects, the fiscal crisis seemed to abate under Dukakis' stern management. In June 1977, when the state legislature was about to include in the 1978 budget increased payments to 80,000 recipients of general relief—payments not reimbursed by the federal government—the Dukakis administration protested that it did not know if the money would be available, and the legislators worded the legislation accordingly, so that it would be effective only on the condition of sufficient funds in the state treasury. Later the Dukakis administration announced that it had realized a surplus of $72,000,000 from fiscal 1977, that it had increased its estimates of tax revenue by approximately $31,000,000, and that it was the beneficiary of unspent budget funds and a $74,000,000 settlement from the United States Department of Health, Education, and Welfare. In view of the combined financial windfall, David S. Liederman, chief secretary to Dukakis, announced on November 25, 1977 that not only was there enough money in the general relief account, but that the administration was considering asking the legislature for a special deficiency appropriation of $14,000,000 to fund 3 percent increases in benefits to approximately 385,000 recipients of Aid to Families with Dependent Children. Half of the amount of such benefits is refunded by the federal government.

At the same time the Dukakis administration announced that it would propose legislation raising state aid to municipalities from $1 billion to approximately $1.15 billion. To that aid it intended to attach controls on local spending and property taxation. Because the property tax, the most regressive of all sources of revenue, has a higher rate per capita in Massachusetts than in any other state, relieving the property tax burden was one of the three top priorities Dukakis had set forth in his "state of the state" message on January 12, 1977. The others were court reform and the Coastal Zone Management environmental control plan, which were saved from defeat or mutilation in the state legislature through the strenuous efforts of Kevin Harrington, the president of the State Senate.

"Dukakis' major political asset [is] his reputation for stern integrity," William A. Henry observed in his *New Republic* article. "Most of his remaining supporters see him as a fighter, battling entrenched interests, notably a corrupt legislature dominated by his own party. . . . His reputation for financial probity is unchallenged. . . . He has an abiding faith in himself and a conviction that virtue will be rewarded."

When the Democratic primary election was held on September 19, 1978, however, Dukakis' political assets were not enough to assure his victory over his opponent, Edward J. King, executive director of Massport, the state transportation authority. King, who won by a margin of over 70,000 votes, cited his victory as proof that the voters of Massachusetts wanted a Proposition 13. Referring to King's campaign call for big cuts in state taxes and his opposition to Dukakis' stands against the death penalty and mandatory jail sentences for drug pushers, Angelo Berlandi. King's campaign aide, commented after the election, "We put all the hate groups in one pot and let it boil."

Brown-haired, brown-eyed Michael S. Dukakis is a neatly groomed man with sharp, handsome features, a polished manner of speaking, a businesslike demeanor, and an intelligence that is at ease with statistics. He is five feet eight and a half inches tall and weighs about 160 pounds. The Governor does not smoke and he drinks sparingly. Seemingly indifferent to food as well as frugal, he eats dollar lunches; in similar manner, he wears off-the-rack clothes, probably bought in Filene's bargain basement, as one Boston journalist has observed. For recreation and exercise, he plays tennis and jogs, and he used to compete in the Boston marathon. He is a member of the Greek Orthodox Church. According to Albin Krebs in the New York *Times* (August 16, 1977), the Governor's signature on routine notes and documents is in many instances actually written by a stand-in, Sergeant Arthur Beaulieu, a plainclothes Boston policeman assigned to him who has an uncanny talent for duplicating handwriting.

Michael S. Dukakis and the former Katherine Dickson, who teaches modern dance at Lesley College, were married on June 20, 1963. With their three children, John, Andrea, and Kara, they live in a Victorian row house in Brookline that has a living-room library stocked with books on the social sciences and a front-yard vegetable garden tended by the Governor. Even at his busiest, Dukakis tries to walk his children to public school and to eat with his family at least once daily.

Governor Dukakis' compassion for children is reportedly in inverse ratio to his impatience with adult fools, incompetents, and wastrels. "You could put him in charge of an alcoholic rehabilitation program and it would be the most efficient one you ever saw," Boston Mayor Kevin White, no longer friendly to him, has observed. "But he wouldn't pick up a drunk in the street." A pragmatist, Dukakis rejects the pigeonholing that political pundits inflict on him and Governor Jerry Brown of California. He does "sense certain similarities" with Governor Brown, as he explains: "I think we're both part of a new generation of politicians who share an abhorrence of waste and government inefficiency and abhorrence of the fancy trappings of office. [But] trying to put tags like liberal or conservative on guys like Brown and me is of utterly no value."

References: Boston Globe A p5 N 27 '77 por; Nations Bsns 13:22+ O '75 por; N Y Times p3 N 6 '74 por; New Republic 176:20+ Je 15 '77; Newsweek 84:28 N 18 '74 por; Time 104:16 N 18 '74 por; Washington Post C p3 Je 27 '76 pors; International Who's Who, 1977-78; Who's Who in American Politics, 1977-78; Who's Who in the East, 1977-78

Elliott, Osborn

Oct. 25, 1924- Former Deputy Mayor of the City of New York; journalist. Address: h. 10 Gracie Sq., New York City, N.Y. 10028

After thirty years in journalism, twenty-one of them at *Newsweek*, which he transformed into a force for *Time* to contend with in the weekly newsmagazine field, Osborn Elliott joined the administration of Mayor Abraham Beame in financially distressed New York City as deputy mayor for economic development on October 20, 1976. Between 1969 and 1976 firm after firm left New York, taking with them 650,000 jobs and $1 billion in annual tax revenues, an amount sufficient to have prevented the city's near-bankruptcy. Elliott acknowledged that the task of reversing the business and industry drain is "enormous," but he addressed himself to it with the calm confidence that "we can make an important beginning" in reinvigorating New York City's economic base. After the election of Edward I. Koch as Mayor of New York in November 1977, Elliott resigned his city post in order to give Koch "total freedom" in selecting his appointees.

The scion of an old, socially prominent, New York "WASP" family, Osborn Elliott was born in Manhattan on October 25, 1924 to John Elliott, a Wall Street stockbroker and investment counselor, now retired, and Audrey N. (Osborn) Elliott, a former suffragette who was vice-president of the real estate firm of Douglas Gibbons-Hollyday & Ives Inc. until shortly before her death in 1976. His maternal grandmother, Josefa Neilson Osborn, was a noted designer and importer of women's clothing and the personal costumer of actress Ethel Barrymore. John Elliott, better known as Jock, chairman of the board of the Ogilvy & Mather advertising agency, is his older brother.

Raised in Manhattan, where his family owned a town house on East 67th Street, Elliott grew up in a social circle in which the Mellons, Walter Lippmann, John Gunther, and Robert Moses were familiar figures. He received his elementary education at the Browning School in Manhattan and his prep schooling at St. Paul's School in Concord, New Hampshire, where, according to Merle Miller in *Esquire* (June 1973), "he played a fair game of hockey, and he was a gentleman scholar, meaning he never did anything at all memorable scholastically."

After his graduation from St. Paul's, in 1942, Elliott entered the accelerated wartime Navy ROTC program at Harvard College. Commissioned an ensign in 1944 (he did not receive his B.A. degree until 1946), he saw action in the Pacific as junior damage control officer on the heavy cruiser USS *Boston*. Following his discharge, in the rank of lieutenant junior grade, in 1946, he decided against a career in advertising or finance and joined the staff of the New York *Journal of Commerce*.

At the *Journal of Commerce* Elliott was successively reporter, nonferrous metals editor, and tax-exempt bonds columnist. "He liked it," Merle Miller recounted in his *Esquire* article. "Not so much the writing. . . . But business itself fascinated him." Miller quoted Elliott's old friend, Richard Clurman: "Until he happened onto journalism Oz never took anything seriously. Journalism changed his whole life; it has become the ruling passion of his life. But if that had not happened, it would have been quite possible for Oz to have worked downtown [on Wall Street] and succeeded. There is something in his genes that suggests he would never have been a dull fellow, a failure."

On the recommendation of his first wife, the former Deirdre Marie Spencer, who was working in the personnel department at *Time*,

Elliott was interviewed for a job with that weekly newsmagazine. He joined the staff of the magazine in January 1949 as a contributing editor specializing in business, and three years later he was advanced to associate editor. In 1955 he was offered a job as a senior business editor at *Newsweek*, a magazine at which, as he later said, he had "hardly looked" up to that time. Founded in 1937 through the merger of *Today*, a magazine backed by Vincent Astor and W. Averell Harriman, and *News-Week*, started in 1933 by Thomas J. C. Martyn, *Newsweek* was *Time's* weak competitor, and to a great extent its imitator, in the weekly newsmagazine field.

Accepting the offer, Elliott moved from *Time* to *Newsweek*, which, like *Time*, is headquartered in New York City. In 1959, his fourth year at *Newsweek*, Elliott made the United States Junior Chamber of Commerce's list of the ten outstanding young men in the United States. That same year, drawing on interviews with more than 100 leaders in business and industry, he published *Men at the Top* (Harper), in which he examined, in a lively, popular style, the backgrounds, characters, and attitudes of the denizens of America's executive suites. The book was well received. "No profound analysis here," read the notice in the *Library Journal* (October 15, 1959), "but good reporting," and in the New York *Times Book Review* (November 8, 1959) Eliot Janeway credited Elliott with providing "an authentic sense of life as it is lived in the corporate stratosphere."

When Philip L. Graham, the liberal publisher of the Washington *Post*, bought the controlling interest in *Newsweek* in 1961 he made Elliott the weekly's executive editor. Elliott recalled in an interview with Anthony Mancini of the New York *Post* (October 9, 1976): "*Newsweek* needed somebody to open the windows and doors and let a gust of fresh air blow through. Phil Graham made it possible by the tone he set and the budget he gave me. We attracted top people who attracted others and rebuilt the whole editorial department."

The productive publisher-editor relationship at *Newsweek* continued under Katharine Graham, Philip's widow, after her husband's death in 1963. "The style of the magazine was no longer grey; at times it was as lively as that of *Time*, and it was not burdened with the backward-running, mind-reeling sentences that still burdened *Time's* pages," Merle Miller observed in his unabashedly biased *Esquire* article. "Nor was it burdened by the reactionary political stance imposed on *Time* by Henry Robinson Luce. . . . In the years that followed, *Newsweek* not only became the magazine to read [for] those who detested *Time*, . . . it became the place to work."

One advantage *Newsweek* had over *Time* as a place to work was the pride of craft and sense of responsibility that came with signed articles and reportage published in the words of the correspondents themselves. Departing from the anonymous group journalism tradition of *Time*, Elliott began bylining, first, selected analytical stories on major national and international issues, then, all art, music, and book reviews, and, ultimately, news stories in general, including team efforts requiring multiple bylines.

Under Elliott, *Newsweek* began doing depth polling on such national issues as civil rights, and one such project was spun off into the book *The Negro Revolution in America* (Simon & Schuster, 1964), edited by Elliott and containing field work done by William Brink and Louis Harris. In its issue of November 20, 1967 the magazine ventured into advocacy journalism for the first time with a twenty-three-page symposium titled "The Negro in America: What Must Be Done"—a reaction to recent racial ferment and especially the black urban riots of the summer before. In the editorial he wrote to accompany the symposium Elliott asserted: "To deal with the racial crisis effectively, there must be a mobilization of the nation's moral, spiritual, and physical resources, and a commitment on the part of all segments of U.S. society." (In a talk to newspapermen that week he said, "Our conclusion is that the United States has the ability to cope with the problem, but we have a question as to whether it has the will.") For the symposium, *Newsweek* won the Columbia University School of Journalism's Magazine of the Year Award.

Newsweek's new vigor was reflected in its circulation, which rose from 1,493,000 in 1961 to 2,150,000 in 1967 and 2,716,148 in 1976. *Time* continued to lead in circulation, however, with a 3,700,000 domestic figure in 1967 and 4,341,978 in 1976. (The international edition of *Time* in 1976 had a circulation of 1,427,626 compared to *Newsweek's* 367,057.) Regarded by ad agencies as "the hot book," and having lower advertising rates, in keeping with its circulation, *Newsweek* was running neck-and-neck with *Time* in advertising linage in 1967, selling 1,124 pages of ads to *Time's* 1,184. It jumped ahead in 1968, amassed 2,918 pages in 1970, and has held the lead ever since. Such changes at *Time* in recent years as the liberalizing of its political tone and the trend to bylines or reporter-researcher-writer credits were influenced at least in part by innovations earlier made by Elliott at *Newsweek*.

"The 60's and early 70's were enormously challenging for journalists of every stripe," Elliott wrote in an autobiographical article in the New York *Times Magazine* (August 28, 1977), "and from the moment I became editor of *Newsweek* . . . I had a front row seat for that wonderful, awful period—for the space age, the Kennedy years, the assassinations, civil rights, the war in Vietnam, the campus revolt, the sexual revolution, the women's movement. But while the job was fun, it was also gruelling, and in the mid-60's, being something of a space nut, I secretly resolved to extricate myself as editor as soon as man had landed on the moon. I figured that eight or ten years of editing were enough for any man—and more than enough for any magazine. And so, in late 1969, my bosses, Kay Graham and Fritz Beebe (then chairman of the company) allowed me to step into the nonexistent job of editor-in-chief." He later accrued the additional titles of president, chief executive officer, and board chairman as well.

"[In 1972] I was back at the old editing grind, and two or three years after *that* I was once again ready to move on," Elliott went on. "But what to do next? I was just turning fifty-two. How about writing a book? Or teaching? Or running a college? Or acting? . . . The Walter Mitty juices really flowed at times." [Meanwhile] I had come to know a good deal about New York in a year as chairman of the Citizens Committee for New York City, a group that stimulates self-help activities throughout the five boroughs. . . . I had . . . come to realize my love for this place that has been hometown to my family for close to 150 years."

Alfred Eisenpreis resigned as New York City's economic development administrator in June 1976. The following autumn, as the city continued to teeter on the brink of bankruptcy, Mayor Abraham Beame asked Elliott to take over and restructure the city's economic development agency. After the Mayor agreed to establish a new deputy mayorship, and thus vest the agency with the prestige and clout of his own office, Elliott agreed to leave his $133,000 job at *Newsweek* to take the city post. A generous separation settlement with *Newsweek* made is possible for him to waive his $47,093 city salary and to work *pro bono*, for one dollar a year, in order to put distance between himself and the political process and enhance his credibility in City Hall and in the business community. ("I hasten to announce, however," he said in 1977, "that, should anyone feel the urge to ask me to stay on beyond this year, I'd gladly accept the pay. In fact, I'd have to.")

Elliott's predecessor, Eisenpreis, concentrating on the corporations, had become convinced that efforts to sell New York as a business or industrial location were doomed to failure. Elliott, however, noting that 98 percent of the 190,000 businesses and industries in the city were not large companies but small enterprises, insisted that much could be done. He established a research division to locate potential growth areas in the city's private economy; set up the Business Action Center as a kind of "ombudsman" agency to help businesses cut through red tape in dealing with the city's bureaucracy; and initiated a major marketing-and-promotion campaign, stressing tax incentives and other advantages, to retain existing businesses and attract new ones. "The path ahead is uphill," Elliott said. "It can be eased . . . by Federal actions. . . . But in the long run, any real progress that New York City makes will depend on the commitment, hard work, and common sense of New Yorkers themselves."

On November 21, 1977 Elliott resigned his city post, effective at year's end. In accepting his resignation, Mayor Beame thanked him for his "energetic efforts" benefiting the city and the business community. In departing, Elliott said that his office had completed or made significant progress in seventy-four of the crucial tasks it had undertaken, and offered Mayor-elect Koch four items of advice: cut city taxes on business and increase incentives for private investment; continue to encourage the private sector to participate in the solution of the city's economic ills; create a new industrial and commercial development corporation; remember that the real key to New York City's economic revitalization is helping small enterprises—of less than 100 employees—to prosper.

"Subjectivity in Journalism," a lecture delivered by Elliott in the M. L. Seidman Memorial Town Hall series, was published along with lectures by Howard K. Smith and Merriman Smith in *The News Media—A Service and a Force* (Memphis State University, 1970), edited by Festus Justin Viser. Elliott is a trustee of the New York Public Library, the Asia Society, and the Museum of Natural History, a fellow of the American Academy of Arts and Sciences, and a member of the Century Association, the Council on Foreign Relations, the Harvard Club, and the Coffee House. His honors include the Van Anda Award of the Ohio University School of Journalism (1969) and an honorary doctorate from the University of Michigan (1970).

Osborn Elliott, better know as "Oz," is five feet eleven inches tall and has blue eyes, a ruddy complexion, aquiline features, a head of graying and thinning blond hair, and a manner often described as "patrician" and "elegant." By his twenty-four-year marriage to Deirdre Marie Spencer, which ended in divorce in December 1972, Elliott has three grown daughters, Diana, Cynthia, and Dorinda. On October 20, 1973 he married Inger Abrahamsen McCabe, a photographer and designer who is founder and president of China Seas Inc., an importer and merchandiser of fine oriental fabrics, wallpapers, and carpets. With Mrs. Elliott's three children by a previous marriage and her adopted son, the Elliotts live in a spacious Gracie Square apartment and, for part of each year, in their country house in Stonington, Connecticut. Elliott's conservative wardrobe is enlivened by the colorful ties designed for him by his wife. In his leisure time Elliott sails, reads magazines avidly, plays the piano, and, as the writer of his New York *Times* "Man in the News" profile (October 7, 1976) observed, "welcomes frequent interruptions from the children."

References: Esquire 76:169+ Je '73 por; N Y Post p26 O 9 '76 por; N Y Times p42 O 7 '76 por; Contemporary Authors vols 1-4 (1962-67); Who's Who in America, 1976-77

Fälldin, Thorbjörn (Nils Olof) (fel-dēn')

Apr. 24, 1926- Former Prime Minister of Sweden; political leader. Address: Ås 870 16 Ramvik, Sweden

In Sweden's 1976 election, Thorbjörn Fälldin, a man-of-the-people sheep farmer, and his non-Socialist three-party coalition ousted Western Europe's longest ruling Socialist party by a narrow margin. Conservatives abroad hailed the Socialist defeat as a turn to the right, but Swedish voters seemed more interested in Fälldin's promises to ban nuclear power, cut taxes, and decentralize the economy. Instead, he continued nuclear development, raised taxes, and nationalized more industries, angering his supporters, tarnishing his credibility, and leading the defeated Olof Palme to accuse him of betrayal. Sweden's first non-Socialist Prime Minister in recent history also tried to preserve the Socialist cradle-to-coffin welfare legacy in the face of worsening economic conditions. On October 5, 1978 Fälldin resigned "on a point of principle" over the support among politicians for even greater nuclear energy development.

Thorbjörn (Nils Olof) Fälldin, son of Nils Johan and Hulda (Olsson) Fälldin, was born on April 24, 1926 on a farm in Västby in north central Sweden. He grew up with politics, since both of his parents were active members of the Agrarian (now Center) party. His father was the Agrarian party representative in the nearby Högsjö municipal council, and his mother helped to found the party's first woman's branch in the Fälldin home.

Largely self-educated, Fälldin managed to complete elementary school but had to postpone secondary school to help with the farm work after his father suffered a gastric hemorrhage. He rounded off his "formal" education with correspondence courses and biweekly classes at a nearby village. The university remained beyond his reach, and Fälldin is the only Swedish political party leader without the benefits of a university education. "Many years of working at all levels of life in the community has taught me more than I could learn in fifteen years at a university," Fälldin maintains.

Fälldin's political activities began early. At fourteen he attended his first Agrarian party Youth League meeting to watch a poetry dramatization. He soon joined the local chapter and was almost immediately elected to its executive committee. Two years later he became its chairman and a member of the Youth League district committee. After time out for compulsory military service as a reserve army officer, he became, at twenty-two, the Ångermanland district committee general secretary and served as its president from 1950-55.

In 1951 Fälldin won his first local election, when he succeeded his father as a municipal council member of the Agrarian party. He also served on the local building committee and was joint industrial committee chairman and municipal council vice-chairman. But in 1956 the Agrarian party suffered its worst electoral setback—garnering only 9.4 percent of the national vote—and Fälldin resigned as Youth League district chairman. Renamed the Center party, it fared better in 1958, the year in which Fälldin was elected to the Lower Chamber of the Riksdag (Parliament). It was then that he began the commuting between politics and weekend farmwork, somewhat like a latter-day Cincinnatus, that later became his trademark.

Fälldin's political career was not without its setbacks, however. He lost his Riksdag seat by eleven votes in 1964, but he continued working as a member of the National Environment Protection Board (1963-71) and of the Labor Market Board (1965-71). He was elected to the Center party's National Executive in 1967, was reelected to the Riksdag as an Upper Chamber member that same year and became the first vice-chairman of the Center party in 1969. While serving as a Riksdag member, Fälldin was a deputy member of the standing committees on finance, foreign affairs, and the Nordic council and a member of the advisory council on foreign affairs. During those years he took part in governmental studies of unemployment insurance, recreational facilities, nature conservation, and aid to developing countries.

Although a member of an opposition party, Fälldin kept his views of the political process well within the traditional Swedish framework of rule by consensus. "I see politics as teamwork where all members of the team work out the basic principles of a decision or stand we take," he has said. "This gives a sense of security that I think is very important." He once told reporters that although political differences became more acute during campaigns, they did not preclude ultimate consensus. "Together we have built our Sweden—not just the Social Democrats. And we live in a good country," Fälldin said.

In 1971 Fälldin succeeded Gunnar Hedlund as chairman of the Center party and began consolidating its position as Sweden's only substantially growing party through the next two general elections. The Center party had always mustered considerable support from farmers and small tradesmen, but it now sparked an appeal to the urban middle class by focusing on the Swedish people's widespread dissatisfaction with the centralized, bureaucratized, industrialized, and highly taxed society that had developed under four decades of Social Democratic rule. The Center party symbol—a green clover—represented its "green dream"—the Swedish yearning for a simple, clean, unfettered life.

In the 1973 election Fälldin, as leader of the largest opposition party, made his first attempt to oust Social Democratic Prime Minister Olof Palme. Under Fälldin, the Center party enhanced its "green dream" appeal by proposing tax cuts and measures to stimulate rural area industry, and by taking a strong stand against environmental pollution. The Center party also took an aggressive stance against rising unemployment, a problem laden with political dynamite for a government committed to full employment. Fälldin promised to create 100,000 jobs, largely by giving financial incentives to the small entrepreneurs and family-owned firms who make up much of the Center party constituency.

In the heat of battle Fälldin proved to be a capable campaigner, both calm and confident. Although Palme remained as Prime Minister when the votes were counted, the Center party had increased its share from less than 14 percent of the 1966 vote to 25 percent. Because its coalition with the two other opposition parties—the Liberals and Conservatives—controlled half the Riksdag seats, the Social Democrats and their unofficial Communist party partners were left with little parliamentary leverage.

The nuclear power issue on which Fälldin was later to stake his career played no part in the 1973 election, although the Center party officially opposed it. Fälldin's opposition to Palme's ambitious nuclear power program had begun after the Swedish Nobel laureate in physics, Hannes Alfven, told him of the unresolved American debate over the storing of radioactive wastes, nuclear proliferation, and the risks of terrorism. Fälldin reacted angrily, since he had served on the environmental protection board responsible for approving nuclear plant sites, and the experts who testified had said nothing about radioactive wastes or nuclear blackmail. In his words, he felt that the "city slickers had put something over on the country boy."

It was not until the oil embargo raised prices and lowered temperatures that Sweden's rapid nuclear development became a public issue. All parties studied it, and the members of the Center party continued its opposition. But the Social Democrats announced a policy of "cautious increase" in reliance on nuclear energy, even though Sweden already produced more atomic power per capita than any other nation, more than double the amount produced by the United States. Voters seemed to agree with the Social Democratic leaders who worried about jobs and the need for energy, since opinion polls revealed that less than half of those persons questioned opposed nuclear development. Polls taken early in 1976 showed that Center party strength dropped 20 percent below its 1973 share. On that issue, the Center party stood alone, for the Liberal and Conservative parties also disagreed with the Centrists' anti-nuclear stance.

But on other issues, the members of the three opposition parties forged a moderate coalition. They spent the year leading up to the election of September 19, 1976 in an attempt to exploit the voters' growing anger with high taxes and their uneasiness over the nation's pervasive bureaucracy and the long rule of the Social Democrats. The opposition charged that the government put security and welfare ahead of initiative, free choice, and opportunity, citing as a prominent example film director Ingmar Bergman's self-exile from Sweden because of tax harassment.

Although the government's accusation of tax evasion directed at Bergman was the only such affair that received substantial foreign publicity, the Social Democrats were plagued by four others during the campaign. One union whose members were Social Democrats conducted a well-publicized tourist boycott against Spain, but its beer-bellied and bare-chested chief was photographed in Spain's sun-drenched Canary Islands. The Finance Minister, who imposed the world's highest taxes upon Swedes, paid almost nothing himself. A beloved children's author claimed she had to pay 102 percent of her income in taxes. At first not everyone took those "affairs" seriously, but following Ingmar Bergman's exile, polls showed that Social Democratic support had dropped to a record 38.5 percent low.

Fälldin characteristically refused to exploit the woes of the Social Democrats. But just as the Social Democrats began to recover, the Meidner Fund controversy began. The national labor organization's chief economist, Rudolf Meidner, proposed to have all companies with 50 or more employees change 20 percent of their before-tax profits into company shares and put them into union-controlled funds each year. Palme could not disavow the plan, which would have given workers majority control of all companies in a couple of decades, without angering union members, all of them Social Democrats. The opposition, however, attacked his evasiveness, arguing that the Meidner plan would drastically cut back investments and industrial growth.

Despite the Meidner Fund controversy, polls showed that the Social Democrats were slowly recovering their earlier strength, until Fälldin reaffirmed the anti-nuclear position of the Center party at his first major radio press conference. He insisted that nuclear plants in the planning stage never leave the drawing board and that the five under construction be stopped or completed but never used, and that the ones in use be phased out. According to Fälldin, none of those demands was negotiable. "No minister's post in the world is so attractive that I am prepared to compromise with my conscience," he told reporters. Because Swedish politicians rarely make such strong statements, Fälldin's remarks had a great impact on public opinion. The ensuing emotional debate cut across all party lines and electoral alliances. In a two-man televised debate with Palme, Fälldin challenged him again and again in his North Swedish dialect. "Olof Palme, can you stand here tonight on this rostrum and assure us that you are giving this generation and coming generations a better society when you give them a nuclear power society?" he asked. Palme did not reply, and the solid, sincere sheep farmer came out ahead. While the urbane, multilingual, and sharp-tongued Palme often seemed overbearingly arrogant and turned many Swedes off, the baggy-suited, pipe-smoking Fälldin seemed to exude common sense and honesty. "He's like your next door neighbor," a Social Democratic politician said at the time. "He's what people think of as typically Swedish, a plodder . . . a clever, honest man." But another Social Democrat characterized him as lacking in experience, imagination, or intelligence. "He knows nothing of foreign affairs. He can't speak English. A disaster!" he complained, according to the New York *Times* (September 21, 1976).

During the last two weeks of the campaign Fälldin concentrated on the nuclear issue, and it arrested the Center party's decline. On September 19, 1976 nearly six million Swedes voted in one of their country's closest elections and narrowly ousted Palme, the longest ruling leader in Western Europe. The non-Socialist bloc, consisting of the Center, Liberal, and Conservative parties, got 50.8 percent of the vote and 180 of the Riksdag's 349 seats, five more than a majority, while the informal ruling alliance of Social Democrats and Communists got 47.6 percent of the vote and 169 seats in the Riksdag. Thorbjörn Fälldin became the new Prime Minister of Sweden. "This non-Socialist victory will revitalize the whole political system in Sweden," he predicted.

When the three parties had organized their coalition government, Fälldin delivered his first policy speech to the Riksdag on October 8, 1976. He pledged to preserve the social welfare system but eliminate waste, to maintain a strong defense, and to continue Sweden's nonaligned foreign policy. He also promised an equal rights law for women, stressed the need to decentralize decision-making, to reform the tax system, and to ease the burden on small business owners. But Fälldin also pledged that his government would implement social reforms like those carried out by Social Democrats in the past. "The new Swedish government will improve things rather than change them," Fälldin promised.

What drew most attention, however, was Fälldin's eventual retreat from his nuclear power position, before the year was out. His Liberal and Conservative party partners, who had never endorsed his views, argued that it was irresponsible to threaten jobs and future energy supplies, and with his coalition at odds, Fälldin gave in. His action sent shock waves through Sweden. Palme called Fälldin's backdown "the greatest fraud in Swedish political history," and Bernt Carlsson, international secretary of the Social Democratic party, said, "The Center party has sold out, not only on their program but on their principles. What happened is that the realities of Swedish industrial society have waked them up. They have to face reality, and the new government is following precisely along the plans of the old." Anti-nuclear forces marched in protest against what they viewed as Fälldin's betrayal. Stung by criticism from his own party as well as from the Social Democrats, Fälldin placed what he called "tough" conditions on new reactor start-ups. Meanwhile he tried to buy time by naming a special commission to prepare a draft energy program for the Riksdag in 1978 and to study the possibility of a referendum on the issue, a rare phenomenon in Sweden.

As the economic situation deteriorated, Fälldin's government was forced to take other unpopular moves. Inflation ran at about 12 percent in 1977 and huge wage hikes boosted the prices of Swedish goods, making them less competitive in world markets. Although continued government subsidies amounting to nearly 10 percent of total government spending prevented layoffs and kept unemployment at a record 1.5 percent low, a $3 billion foreign trade deficit forced the government to borrow money abroad for the first time in memory. Fälldin finally introduced an austerity program aimed at increasing Swedish exports by making them more competitive, thereby reducing the trade gap and creating more jobs at home. Despite his glowing promises to expand the welfare system while cutting taxes and letting market forces operate more freely, he was forced to cut spending, boost taxes, nationalize the bankrupt shipbuilding industry, and pump money into the ailing steel sector. In addition, Fälldin froze prices for two months and devalued the krona by 10 percent, a move deplored by Swedish socialists and other Scandinavian government officials, who complained that they were forced to go and do likewise against their will. Not surprisingly, Sweden's economic woes and Fälldin's stringent measures cut into the new government's initial popularity. In mid-1977 Fälldin's coalition was trailing far behind the Social Democrats in public opinion polls.

Despite its economic troubles in 1977 Sweden responded to persistent Third World demands by cancelling more than $200 million in debts owed by governments in eight developing countries, nearly 85 percent of Sweden's overall foreign aid credits. Third World diplomats immediately hailed the move as a generous one, and an example that other countries should follow. In the future, Sweden plans to discontinue development loans and provide outright grants, something for which developing nations have also campaigned.

While Prime Minister, Fälldin returned to his farm each weekend to help his wife raise barley, oats, and potatoes. He has sixty-two acres of field and 645 acres of forest. "I think best when I am sitting on a tractor," he has said. He was thirty when he married twenty-one-year-old Solveig Oberg in 1956. Soon after their marriage, which produced two daughters and a son, they bought their farm in Ås, a tiny village in the hilly central district where Fälldin was born. Fälldin's blue jeans and work-gnarled hands are almost as much a part of his popular image as his pipe and his addiction to coffee. He has been a cross-country runner and a center forward on his home football team for years. He preferred swimming, skiing, fishing, and saunas to his official duties, which he did "not enjoy" but had "gradually learned to live with."

References: Current World Leaders 20:87 Fall 1977; New Yorker 52:104+ N 1 '76; International Who's Who, 1977-78

Fawcett-Majors, Farrah

Feb. 2, 1947- Actress; model. Address: b. William Morris Agency Inc., 151 E. Camino Dr., Beverly Hills, Calif. 90212

Farrah Fawcett-Majors, the "poster girl" of 1977, came to fame through the cops-and-robbers show with sex appeal called *Charlie's Angels*, the top-ranking network television show of the 1976-77 season. That weekly showcase for the actress with the cascading hair and dazzling smile boosted sales of the poster showing her in a wet, skin-tight swimsuit to a record-breaking figure estimated at over 7,000,000 by October 1977, while the Farrah look in hair was copied by women everywhere. Before the success of *Charlie's Angels* Farrah's face was well known more from her modeling assignments than from her acting, which was limited for the most part to secondary roles in made-for-television movies. Now that she is more than an anonymous "pretty face," she has dropped out of the cast of *Charlie's Angels* to concentrate on a motion picture career for herself, to form a film production company with her husband, actor Lee Majors, and to fulfill a contract with Fabergé Inc., which has created a "Farrah Fawcett" line of hair products and beauty preparations.

Farrah Fawcett-Majors, who is of mixed French, English, and one-eighth Choctaw Indian descent, says that her mother, Pauline

(Evans) Fawcett, "just made ['Farrah'] up" as a name to "go nicely with Fawcett." The actress and model was born Farrah Fawcett on February 2, 1947—some sources say 1948—in Corpus Christi, Texas, where her father, James William Fawcett, was working as a pipefitter for an oil refinery. Fawcett later founded a pipeline construction company, and he now runs a custodial service in Houston. Farrah has an older sister, Diane Fawcett Wells, who is Fabergé's liaison for the southeast United States.

Born with a tumor obstructing her digestive tract, Farrah underwent a delicate operation to correct the condition when she was twenty-eight days old. "I was never rebellious as a child," she informed Helen Dorsey, a Hollywood-based journalist who wrote a series of three articles on the star for the New York *Post* in March 1977. "I listened to my parents, helped my mother with the dishes, and studied hard in school." With the other members of her family, she was a communicant of St. Patrick's (Roman Catholic) Church in Corpus Christi, and she received her early education in the parish school. "Farrah was a little ray of sunshine in the classroom," Sister Aloysius Young recalls. "She was a very cooperative student . . . an honor student. She was outgoing and friendly—but never a show-off."

After completing the sixth grade of St. Patrick's, Farrah transferred to public school. Joseph Alexander Cain, her art teacher at W. B. Ray High School, recalls: "She was sort of a contradiction. She was quiet and reserved in class, but her eyes sparkled with ideas." Not all of her memories of public school are happy, as she told Connie Berman, author of *Farrah & Lee* (1977): "Many [teachers] thought I believed all I had to do was just sit and look pretty to make good grades. In the long run I didn't get the grades I deserved because of their attitudes." She dated less than other girls in high school, and most of her dates were family affairs. "I was always protected by my family," she says. "I liked being protected. It kept me from getting too wise too soon."

Farrah entered the University of Texas in Austin as a microbiology major but switched to art in her sophomore year. "I'm ashamed to remember the way I used to make fun of Farrah," a former classmate has confessed, as quoted by Claire Susans in *Farrah's World* (1977). "She stood out like a painted pony, with her beauty and those clothes. . . . She looked like she just stepped out of a bandbox, and the rest of us were hanging around in beat-up jeans and sweatshirts. We were marching for peace, and Farrah was sitting there, smiling and looking pretty. . . . To us, Farrah looked like a leftover from the fifties. We were experimenting with sexual freedom, and a little bit of dope. And Farrah, of course, would have none of that."

As a college student, Farrah did professional modeling for an Austin clothing store advertising in the campus newspaper, and she was also a favorite amateur model, especially of one of her teachers, sculptor Charles Umlauf, who has a bronze bust of her in his sculpture garden. After seeing a photograph of her, the Hollywood publicist David Mirisch repeatedly urged her to drop out of school and come to the film capital. She was easier to persuade than her parents, particularly her father, who wanted her to finish college before beginning a career.

Finally, at the end of her junior year, Farrah's parents gave their permission for her to try her luck in Hollywood. Mirisch wasted no time in bringing her to public notice in such promotions as Queen of the Los Angeles Boat Show and Miss Pro Tennis, while in her spare time Farrah worked under a voice coach to improve her diction. She also tried a general acting class, but the "Method" repelled her.

Her acting prospects improved when Farrah met Lee Majors—an already established television actor who arranged to be introduced to her after publicity agent Dave Gershenson showed him her picture—and signed a contract with Screen Gems as a recruit in that company's new talent program. Still, for many years her most lucrative work was in commercials and modeling. Eventually she was making $100,000 a year for her appearances in television commercials for Ultra-Brite toothpaste, Noxema shaving cream (with Joe Namath and others), Wella Balsam shampoo, and Mercury Cougar cars and for her modeling chores for *Vogue, Cosmopolitan,* and other fashion magazines.

Farrah's first engagements as an actress were on television during the 1968-69 season in segments of NBC's situation comedy *I Dream of Jeannie,* where her most memorable exchange was "I have to change," with a male actor responding, "Don't change too much." Her first motion picture roles were bit parts in *Myra Breckinridge* (Twentieth Century-Fox, 1970) and *Un Homme Qui Me Plait (Love Is a Funny Thing,* United Artists, 1970), and later she had a two-scene part as a twenty-third-century maiden in the science-fiction fantasy *Logan's Run* (MGM-United Artists, 1976).

On televison in the early 1970's Farrah was seen in episodes of ABC's *Owen Marshall, Counselor at Law,* and shortly after Lee Majors' hit series *The Six Million Dollar Man* premiered on ABC in 1974 she joined her husband in some of the episodes of that show. In 1974 she had a brief role in the series *Apple's Way* on CBS, and during the 1974-75 television season she was seen occasionally on ABC's *Harry O* with David Janssen.

In made-for-TV movies, Farrah played minor roles in *The Feminist and the Fuzz* (ABC, 1971), starring Barbara Eden and David Hartman, and *The Girl Who Came Gift Wrapped* (ABC, 1974), starring Karen Valentine and Richard Long. She was cast as a waitress who enters a beauty contest in *The Great American Beauty Contest* (ABC, 1973), and as a stewardess in *Murder on Flight 502* (ABC, 1975). Her comic role in *The Great American Beauty Contest* was her first real "opportunity to shine," as Kevin Thomas observed in his review of the movie in the Los Angeles *Times* (February 13, 1973). As a "toothy, breezy blond waitress from Texas," Thomas wrote, she was "reminiscent of Dorothy Malone in looks and flair."

The made-for-TV movies in which Farrah played were produced by Leonard Goldberg, who had been head of production at Screen Gems, and Aaron Spelling. In 1976 Spelling and Goldberg came up with a series idea about three beautiful young women working as agents for an off-screen private detective who gives his orders to them by telephone. After selling the idea to Fred Silverman at ABC, they cast Farrah Fawcett-Majors, Jaclyn Smith, and Kate Jackson in the female roles and John Forsythe as the unseen detective agency head. *Charlie's Angels* produced at Universal Studios, premiered in September 1975 with Farrah Fawcett-Majors in the role of the gaminesque, athletic Jill Munroe, a poker-playing private eye with an ebullient sense of humor, Kate Jackson as the intellectual Sabrina Duncan, Jaclyn Smith as the street-wise Kelly Garrett.

"The *Charlie's Angels* phenomenon . . . was as startling to us as the Farrah phenomenon that grew out of it," Leonard Goldberg told Bill Davidson when Davidson interviewed him for an article in *TV Guide* (May 21, 1977). "We thought it was a nice little show, nothing more, and we were totally unprepared for what happened. It was a hit from the start." *Charlie's Angels* became the only entry among the 1976-77 television season's new series to place consistently among the top ten in the weekly A. C. Nielsen ratings, and the Farrah phenomenon grew apace, as indicated by the adulatory mail from people of all sexes and ages that poured into ABC, from the rate of sales of the famous poster of Farrah, and from the ubiquity of her face on the covers of publications ranging from *Time* and *People* to women's magazines and scandal tabloids.

Many of those trying to explain the success of *Charlie's Angels* saw the program as the original prime-time girlie show disguised as an action-adventure series, full of changes of sexy wardrobe, décolletage, plots requiring less than ingenuous bondage scenes, situations in which the Angels are decoy prostitutes or go-go dancers, and other such devices. In the Los Angeles *Times* (September 22, 1976), Lee Margulies wrote that *Charlie's Angels* "drips with sexuality" consisting of "good-natured but quite intentional teasing" and walks "a fine line between sexism and sexiness." At the same time the show appealed to women, Margulies noted, perhaps because in the story line itself, apart from the visual "sexploitation," boss Charlie's only interest is in the professional talents of employees who are "independent, intelligent, resourceful and brave, adept at race-car driving and poker, effective with their hands and guns." The reviewer for *Time* (November 26, 1976) described the series as "family-style porn, a mild erotic fantasy" that appeals to women as well as men because the heroines "remain pleasant and feminine while performing roles until now reserved for men." "The plots are merely convenient pegs on which to hang . . . soft-core fantasies," John J. O'Connor wrote in the New York *Times* (November 21, 1976). "[But] the pornographic presence is more a matter of tone or atmosphere than of specific incident."

"Certainly it is the illuminated evanescence of Farrah Fawcett-Majors that is largely responsible for the success of *Charlie's Angels,*" Tom Shales wrote in the Washington *Post* (January 2, 1977). "People must be tuning in just to watch Farrah bounce around." Farrah herself said: "I think people want to see some glamour, some clothes, some hair styles, you know—they want to see girls." Yet there were times when she refused to don a bikini because she felt "they had reached a quiet point in the script and needed my body to liven things up," and she protested when lines or scripts made her seem "too silly" or "too giggly." With all the attention that was being paid to the sexiness of the show, perhaps its most important aspect was almost ignored—it was, as David Doyle, who plays Charlie's male assistant, pointed out, "a crime-suspense show without the usual violence."

Farrah posed for her best-selling poster, produced by Pro-Arts Inc., of Medina, Ohio, before *Charlie's Angels* first went on the air. The poster is a blown-up color photograph of her in a revealing one-piece maillot, sitting leanly at poolside, "smiling like thirty-six Rockettes," as one observer noted, and tugging at a curl on her blondish tawny, tousled hair. By March 1977 it had already sold 5.000,000 copies at between two and three dollars apiece, leaving far behind the marks reached by Marilyn Monroe, Henry ("The Fonz") Winkler, and the shark from the movie *Jaws*. Later estimates of sales went as high as 8,000,000. Two additional posters of Farrah went on sale: "Farrah Flower," in which she is shown wearing blue jeans and white top and holding a red flower in her hand, and "Farrah Collage," a combination of five poses. Also available for purchase by her fans were Farrah T-shirts, transfers, pins, pillows, dolls, and wigs.

When Farrah announced that she would not be returning to *Charlie's Angels* in 1977-78, the producers began contract litigation, and one studio executive was reported to have quipped: "Farrah's replacement, must of course, be another well-stacked blonde with good bod and great looking legs, who can wear a T-shirt well and read four lines of dialogue off an idiot card." The replacement found by Universal and Spelling-Goldberg was Cheryl Ladd.

By the fall of 1977 Farrah Fawcett and Lee Majors' new company, Fawcett-Majors Productions, had completed its first TV movie, *Just a Little Inconvenience*, which was aired on NBC, and under an independent producer, Martin Poll, Farrah was in New York City for the shooting on location of the motion picture *Somebody Killed Her Husband*. When it was released in October 1978, Frank Rich, the reviewer for *Time* (October 9, 1978), summed up the general critical reaction with the protest: "To buy this film's plot, it isn't enough to suspend disbelief; you have to submit to a lobotomy."

Earlier in her career, Farrah had signed a contract with Fabergé calling for her participation in the creation and promotion of a line of Farrah Fawcett products—shampoo, hair spray, creme rinse and conditioner, which began appearing on the market in 1978, with combs, brushes, suntan lotion, and beauty preparations perhaps to follow. According to Richard Barrie, the president of Fabergé, Farrah's percentage of the profits will probably be "several million dollars."

Farrah Fawcett-Majors is five feet six inches tall, weighs 112 pounds, and has wide-set aquamarine eyes and a figure that has been described as "scrawny" and "flat." "I don't know how I got to be a sex symbol," she told Judy Kessler when Miss Kessler was writing an article on her for *People* (October 24, 1977). "My body isn't that great. I don't think I'm too much of a threat." Contributing to her acceptance among female as well as male fans are her healthy good looks—maintained by daily calisthenics and regular swimming, scuba diving, and playing tennis (competition calibre)—and the wholesomeness she projects in general. "There's more to it than *looking* your best," she points out. "You have to *be* at your best, too—bopping along all the time, happy, upbeat, friendly." When she has time, Farrah also likes to read historical novels and to make cornbread and a number of other Southern specialties in the kitchen.

Farrah Fawcett and Lee Majors were married on July 28, 1973. With Lee Jr., Majors' son by a previous marriage, they live in a spacious Bel Air, California home decorated in French provincial style. The actress and model, who categorizes herself as "a contemporary girl with old-fashioned standards," is kept from feeling either guilt or hubris over her success by her philosophy of compensation. "God balances things out," she told Judy Kessler in the *People* interview. "My theory is that God gives you either straight white teeth with lots of cavities or crooked stained teeth with no cavities. I have lots of cavities. In the same way, if someone were not as attractive, then she might be much more intelligent."

References: Good H 185:128+ Ag '77 pors; Esquire 88:97+ S '77 pors; Ladies Home J 94:34+ Je '77 pors; N Y Post p51 Mr 21 '77 por, p49 Mr 22 '77 por, p43 Mr 23 '77 por; People 8:28+ O 24 '77 pors; Sat Eve Post 249:54+ S '77 pors; Time 108:67+ N 22 '76 pors; TV Guide 25:24+ My 21 '77 por; Washington Post B p1+ Ja 2 '77 pors; Berman, Connie, Farrah & Lee (1977); Burstein, Patricia. Farrah (1977); Susans, Claire. Farrah's World (1977)

Fidrych, Mark (fid'rich)

Aug. 14, 1954- Baseball player. Address: b. Detroit Tigers, Tiger Stadium, Detroit, Mich. 48216

The most refreshing "flake" to come along in baseball in a long time—probably since Dizzy Dean, nearly half a century ago—is Mark Fidrych, the Detroit fast-ball pitcher who was voted the American League Rookie of the Year by the Baseball Writers Association of America in 1976, when he led major-league starting hurlers with his earned-run average of 2.34 per game. Aside from his ability to throw hard, low strikes, the uninhibited Fidrych electrified the crass world of professional baseball and caught the imagination of fans with his boyish enthusiasm, relative indifference to money, buoyant good nature, and eccentricities of personality and style. The twitchy, gangly, loose-limbed right-hander, nicknamed "the Bird" because of his avian body kinetics, "psychs" himself by talking to the ball, pats the mound smooth on his hands and knees between innings, and stomps around the infield after a strikeout or putout, with arms flapping and mouth emitting squawks of joy or words of congratulation for his teammates. Sidelined with a knee injury and a sore shoulder during most of the 1977 season, Fidrych worked himself back into shape by pitching in the Florida Instructional League in the winter of 1977-78. On April 17, 1978, however, he was ordered to rest for three weeks because of a recurrence of tendonitis, and in August he was sidelined for the rest of the season.

Mark Fidrych was born in Worcester, Massachusetts on August 14, 1954 to Paul Fidrych, a public schoolteacher of Polish descent, and Virginia Fidrych, whose ancestry is Danish. With his older sister, Paula, and his younger sisters, Carol Ann and Lorie Jean, he grew up in Northboro, Massachusetts, where the Fidryches live in a modest one-family house. "He's always been hyperactive, Markie, just like me . . . ," Mrs. Fidrych told Ron Fimrite in an interview for *Sports Illustrated* (April 11, 1977). "He's so honest and gullible, it's pathetic. Just like me. Markie's been talking to things as far back as I can remember —bikes, wagons, cars, you name them. He never had to read instructions on how to put things together. He could just do it automatically. He's a genius that way."

A fidgety student, Fidrych was held back in the first and second grades of public elementary school in Northboro. "I couldn't read," he told Tom Clark in one of the interviews making up *No Big Deal* (Lippincott, 1977). "I could do all the other work [but I] used to have to go to summer school . . . when I was a little kid. . . . School just wasn't my bag."

Growing up, Fidrych was more interested in hunting, fishing, and tinkering with cars —he owned several in succession in his late teens—than in baseball, but his father, a rabid fan, saw his son's potential on the diamond, and especially the mound, and cultivated it. The elder Fidrych, who did some schoolboy coaching, instilled in his son the practice of landscaping the mound between innings. "I don't want to get in another guy's groove," Fidrych explains. "So I smooth the dirt and find my own."

As a boy, Fidrych pitched Little League and American Legion as well as high school ball, and when not on the mound played shortstop and outfield, except on the American Legion team, where he was in the lineup solely as a pitcher. At Algonquin High School in Northboro he was also on the basketball and football teams. When his age disqualified him from playing in his senior year at Algonquin, his father enrolled him in Worcester Academy, a prep school within commuting distance of home. Although he did not become a star at Worcester—he had a losing season—he earned a reputation as a good, hard "thrower" against high-calibre competition, including the freshman teams of Harvard and other nearby colleges and universities. During vacations and on weekends Fidrych worked at a gas station in Northboro.

Fidrych received no offers of athletic scholarships, but New Mexico Highlands University in Las Vegas, New Mexico accepted him in its two-year engineering program. When the Detroit Tigers, alerted by their New England scout, Joe Cusick, picked him in the tenth round of the 1974 player draft, he changed his plans and signed with the Tigers instead of going on to college.

With Bristol, Tennessee in the Appalachian League in 1974 Fidrych pitched thirty-four innings as a reliefer and ended the season with a 3-0 record. Jeff Hogan, the Bristol coach, bestowed the nickname "Bird" on him because, as Hogan explained to him at the time, "Fidrych is too hard to say [and] you look like that goofy bird on *Sesame Street* [the children's educational television program]." In 1975 Fidrych was, successively, starting pitcher with Lakeland in the Florida State League, relief pitcher with Montgomery, Alabama in the Southern League, and starting pitcher with Evansville, Indiana in the American Association. His total tallies were eleven wins and ten losses.

Called up by last-place Detroit for the beginning of the 1976 season, Fidrych in his first start for the Tigers pitched a two-hit 2-1 victory over the Cleveland Indians on May 5. After a 0-2 loss to Boston in his second start, he racked up a string of eight straight victories. As Fidrych became a local hero, attendance in Tiger Stadium more than doubled, averaging 33,649 a game, or 19,756 more than usual. When the Tigers, with Fidrych on the mound, faced the championship-bound Yankees on July 28, 1976, a sell-out crowd filled the stadium. In addition, a national television audience had its first glimpse of Fidrych as he pitched a 5-1 win over the powerful New York team. After the game, thousands of cheering fans refused to leave the stadium until Fidrych came back out of the locker room in his stocking feet to take a bow, thus initiating a fad. "Fidrych popularized the curtain call in baseball," Bowie

Kuhn, the Commissioner of Baseball, has observed. "Now it's become a baseball tradition."

After the Yankee game, teammate Rusty Staub explained Fidrych's popularity to correspondent Steve Serby of the New York *Post* (June 29, 1976): "It's because you love him. He's real. He has the most enthusiasm of any person I've seen in my life. There's not one thing in this world that is contrived that he's doing. I think we're more protective of him than anybody. I've never seen anybody who has been able to make such an impact on a city as he has. . . . When he goes out to pitch, it's like nothing I've ever seen. It's everything about him. He brings everything out in people. All the frustrations people have in their lives, everything. He must touch every heart in a different way."

The Yankee game made Fidrych a national celebrity. In his next three starts in Detroit he drew crowds of 51,032, 51,041, and 45,905, and on the road the average attendance at his games was 26,869. By mid-season he had finished twelve of his thirteen starts and had a league-leading earned-run average of 1.97. His designation as the American League's starting pitcher in the mid-season All-Star game marked the first occasion in fifty years, and the second in history, that a rookie was so honored. In the game the National League beat the American, 7-1.

Fidrych finished the 1976 season with nineteen wins and nine losses, the best record by a rookie Tiger pitcher in sixty-eight years. His earned-run average of 2.34 was the lowest in the majors, and his twenty-four complete games and his fielding average of 1.000 in seventy-eight chances were the best in the American League. Attendance at the games that he pitched at home and away totaled 901,239. Detroit remained probably the worst defensive team in the American League, but he helped it to escape last place and to finish fifth among the six teams in the league's East Division and eleventh out of the twelve teams in the league as a whole. Besides American League Rookie of the Year, he was named Major League Man of the Year, by the Association of Professional Baseball Leagues. The Tigers awarded him a $20,000 bonus, and his father helped him negotiate a new contract, reportedly for $230,000 over three years. His first-year contract had been for the minimum of $16,500, an unusually low salary for a superstar in a game where lesser talents were demanding seven figures. Some of his outraged fans sent donations of money for him to the Detroit front office (which returned the money) during the 1976 season, but Fidrych himself tended to think in terms of the pay he had been getting back at the gas station in Northboro. He was in no hurry to ask for more, he explained, because he was happy in Detroit and grateful to the Tigers for bringing him there, and anyway, too much money too soon might give him a "big head."

During the winter of 1976-77 Fidrych traveled the banquet circuit. Shagging flies in the Detroit training camp in Lakeland, Florida on March 22, 1977, he suffered an injury to his left knee that was at first thought to be minor, but when he attempted to return to action seven days later the knee popped in and out of joint repeatedly. On March 31 surgeons at Henry Ford Hospital in Detroit removed torn cartilage from the knee. After recuperating, Fidrych finally entered the Tigers' 1977 lineup and won six out of ten games—as of July 12, when he took himself out of a game complaining of pain in his right shoulder. The condition, diagnosed at Henry Ford Hospital as tendonitis, became so bad he could hardly raise his arm, and on August 28 he was sent home to Northboro, Massachusetts to give the shoulder a rest.

In October 1977 Fidrych traveled to St. Petersburg, Florida to ease his way back into action by pitching in the Florida Instructional League. After throwing in batting practice a couple of times a week, he returned to competition on November 5, pitching for the Tigers' instructional team against Philadelphia Phillies' rookies. In two innings he threw twenty pitches, fifteen of which were fast balls and only one of which was hit safely, for a scratch single. He struck out one and walked none. "He talked to the ball, gyrated on the mound, exhorted the pitches with his hand, patted the dirt, and congratulated his unknown rookie infielders," Jerry Green reported in the *Sporting News* (November 26, 1977). Green quoted Jim Campbell, Detroit's general manager, as saying, "He looked great," and Fidrych himself as saying that his arm felt "good."

On November 10 Fidrych again took to the mound, throwing forty-five pitches and allowing but two infield singles by the Baltimore instructional team in three scoreless innings. "I hope to have a better third year than any year I've ever had," he told Jerry Green. "What's going to happen will happen." Asked if he thought the crowds, which had declined in his absence, would return to Tiger Stadium in 1978, he replied: "If I win, they'll come out. If I lose, they won't. Correct me if I'm wrong."

Despite his antics, once an inning begins, Fidrych pitches quickly, keeping the game moving at a fast pace. His basic pitch is the knee-high fast ball, which, even if hit, is more likely to be an infield out than a home run. His catcher Bruce Kimm says, "His greatest asset is that he doesn't make mistakes. When he misses, he misses low." While not as fast as, say, Nolan Ryan's, his fast ball is lively, clocking in at ninety-three miles an hour. In addition to the fast ball, he has a slider, and he has been developing a change-up. He cannot throw a curve because, as he explains, he "can't twist [his] wrist right."

Mark Fidrych is six feet three inches tall, weighs about 173 pounds, and has a luxurious head of curly blond hair, eyes that have been described as "manic," and the "hip-sprung" gait of a plowboy. His idiosyncratic mannerisms contribute to his concentration, which is, according to Stubby Overmire, who coached him at Lakeland, "incredible—he doesn't seem to know anyone else is in the park." "He's liable to say anything that comes into his mind," Overmire adds, and many an embarrassed radio and television interviewer can vouch for the spontaneity of Fidrych's language. His actions are also often startlingly unpredictable. Typical was the instance when he was playing in Florida and, on his way to the bullpen, remembered that he was not wearing his protective groin cup. Unabashed, in full view of the stands, he took the cup from his pocket, dropped his pants, and inserted the cup in his jockstrap. But according to Ralph Houk, manager of the Tigers, he is "far from being whacky." "What he has is enthusiasm," Houk says. "Everybody in the park throws every pitch with the kid." And Fidrych's mother describes her son as "a down-to-earth child."

Fidrych is unusually considerate of fans. He worries, for example, about slighting a single person in an autograph-seeking crowd, and few if any other players could have borne with the same equanimity the gross invasions of privacy he suffered during his rookie year. He found the solitary traveling life and the speaking chores of the winter of 1976-77 harder to bear.

Outside of his actual playing experience, Fidrych is surprisingly ignorant of major-league history, and current facts and statistics because, as he confesses, he does not "follow baseball." He is more interested in rock 'n' roll music—he was "thrilled" to meet Elton John and the Beach Boys—and in his cars. (Tiger General Manager Tim Campbell has made him get rid of his motorcycles.) His other recreations include golf (low 100's), pinball, pool, drinking beer with his buddies, and dancing. He avoids steady dating, hoping that a hometown girlfriend whom he "lost" in 1974 will come back to him. His business transactions outside of baseball, such as his endorsements of Aqua Velva shaving products, are handled by Steve Pinkus of the William Morris Agency. Fidrych's chief plan for the future is, he told Ron Fimrite in the *Sport* interview, to go to an automobile technical training school even though he "won't have to go to work right away" when he gets his baseball pension—"say when [he is] thirty."

Raised in Roman Catholicism, his father's faith, Fidrych is a "religious" person, as he told Dave Marsh, who interviewed him for *Rolling Stone* (May 5, 1977): "I don't go to church much, but . . . I can talk to God right here in this room." He wears a Lady of Mount Carmel medal given to him by his mother, a Protestant who has taken on Catholic ways. She says, as quoted by Earl McRae in *Sport* (July 1977): "Markie is a very religious boy, you know. He doesn't show it, but he is. I once thought he'd become a priest, but, well, I'm proud of him anyway. It's not always the ball he's talking to out there."

References: N Y Times Mag p12+ Ag 22 '76 pors; Rolling Stone p43+ My 5 '77 pors; Sport 65:23+ Jl '77 pors; Sporting News p53 N 26 '77 por, p51 Ja 7 '78 por; Sports Ill 46:44+ Ap 11 '77 por; Fidrych, Mark and Clark, Tom. No Big Deal (1977); Official Baseball Register (1977)

Flood, Daniel J(ohn)

Nov. 26, 1904- United States Representative from Pennsylvania. Address: b. Rm. 108, Cannon House Office Bldg., Washington, D.C. 20515; Rm. 1015, United Penn Bank Bldg., Wilkes-Barre, Pa. 18701

"Dapper Dan" Flood, the fifteen-term septuagenarian Democratic United States Representative from Pennsylvania's Eleventh Congressional District, is far and away the most colorful legislator on Capitol Hill. With his brilliantined hair, waxed, winged mustache, spiffy but eccentric wardrobe, and flamboyant mannerisms and orotund rhetoric carried over from his youthful career as an actor, Flood has been amusing his colleagues and constituents for three decades. Behind his stylized buffoonery, Flood has been a shrewd, methodical manipulator of the reins of power available to him, notably Defense, Labor, and Health, Education, and Welfare appropriations subcommittee senior memberships that identify him with more than three-fourths of the federal budget. Generally a liberal on social welfare, he is hawkish on foreign policy.

Flood denies recent allegations that he has on occasion sold his influence for personal gain, but he openly boasts of his preeminent success in the practice of pork-barrel politics. As a master of the *quid pro quo,* he has been instrumental in obtaining for the Eleventh District—which almost died economically with the decline of anthracite coal mining—millions of Health, Education, and Welfare dollars and untold millions more in defense contracts. Largely because of him, the district has attracted new businesses and diversified its industrial base, so that the unemployment rate has dropped from 19 percent in the 1950's to a figure on a par with the national average. Regarded as a savior by his constituents, he is not likely to be turned out of office by them, whatever the outcome of Federal investigations into his affairs. He may lose some of his power on Capitol Hill, but advancing age is probably the only real threat to his tenure in Washington.

Of Irish Catholic descent, Daniel John Flood was born on November 26, 1904 in Hazleton, Pennsylvania to Patrick and Sarah (McCarthy) Flood. At Syracuse University, where he was on the boxing team, he received a B.A. degree in 1924. After his graduation from Syracuse he did a few months postgraduate study at Harvard University and toured the country with a theatrical troupe for several years, playing in some fifty productions, including Shakespearean plays. His Simon Legree-style mustache was originally grown for one of his stage roles.

Leaving the stage to pursue a career in law, Flood earned an LL.B. degree at Dickinson College in Carlisle, Pennsylvania in 1929. Admitted to the Pennsylvania bar the following year, he set up a law office in Wilkes-Barre, where the most important of his early legal clients was the Home Owners Loan Association. In 1936 Flood was appointed Deputy Attorney General of Pennsylvania and counsel for the Pennsylvania Liquor Control Board. From 1941 to 1944 he was director of the Bureau of Public Assistance of the Pennsylvania Treasury Department and executive assistant to the State Treasurer.

In 1944 Flood was elected to the United States House of Representatives from Pennsylvania's Eleventh Congressional District, which encompasses the city of Wilkes-Barre and five counties in the northeastern part of the state. He has been reelected biennially since then, except in 1946 and 1952, when the Republicans swept Congressional elections nationwide. During his first term in Congress he also served briefly as special United States Ambassador to Peru.

Having the only major known deposits of anthracite coal in the United States, northeastern Pennsylvania was a booming mining region through the early decades of the twentieth century, attracting large numbers of immigrant workers from eastern Europe. By the end of World War II the demand for anthracite had all but disappeared, chiefly because of the competition from bituminous coal, which is cheaper, easier to mine, and more abundant, and from gas and oil. The depressed economy of his district and the ethnic background of his constituents were important factors in the formation of Flood's two fundamental Congressional stands: endorsement of social welfare programs and vigilance against the "menace" of Communism.

Typical of Flood's actions on the Communist-watching front in Congress in the 1950's were a resolution requesting the Truman Administration to "explore" ways of aiding resistance movements behind the Iron Curtain; an amendment to the National Science Foundation Act making an F.B.I. security screening a prerequisite for the foundation's employment of any foreign national "in any capacity whatever"; and constant, vociferous opposition to the Eisenhower Administration's efforts to make military economies in the interest of a balanced budget, which he viewed as "a sham" because "you know the budget won't be balanced."

On the economic home front, Flood futilely fought the St. Lawrence Seaway because it would expedite the importing of coal from Europe, and he proposed plans for the federal purchase of enough hard coal to maintain operations in the dwindling anthracite fields and for the attraction of new industries to northeastern Pennsylvania. He missed no opportunity to attach to legislative vehicles of wider regional or national priority riders of benefit to his district, which had no full-scale hospital or airport until he brought one of each home from Washington. Nor did it have a modern highway, until he, sitting on a transportation subcommittee, balked at voting for Interstate 83, linking Montreal and New Orleans, unless that highway was rerouted through Wilkes-Barre. It was so rerouted. And the Pentagon was persuaded by him to turn the Tobyhanna Army Base from a shooting range into the principal East Coast base for overhauling military communications equipment.

Aside from Department of Defense contracts, the chief instrument by which Flood effected an infusion of new jobs in northeastern Pennsylvania was a series of federal area redevelopment programs, begun exactingly under a reluctant President Eisenhower, reaching significant proportions in the Area Redevelopment Act signed by President John

F. Kennedy in 1961, and culminating in the establishment of the Economic Development Administration under President Lyndon B. Johnson in 1965. Flood has recounted, as quoted by George Crile in *Harper's* magazine (January 1975): "The first big thing was the so-called Flood-Douglas bill, which provided federal funds [including long-term, low-interest loans for businesses] for depressed areas. You can imagine what kind of funds my district got. The bill was too parochial, though, and we couldn't get enough votes to keep it going, so we expanded it into the Appalachian bill. I got Robert Kennedy in on that one, and lo and behold, thirteen counties on the New York-Pennsylvania border turned up in Appalachia. That must have surprised them. But we had to get more votes, so we gave birth to the Economic Development Act, and everybody got included in that."

Through Flood's efforts, Wilkes-Barre became the EDA's regional headquarters for the eastern United States, the Virgin Islands, and Puerto Rico. The Model Cities program was to have been limited to the inner-city ghettos, but the original bill ran into trouble in the House. Flood cosponsored a modified bill, which passed, and Wilkes-Barre became the first city accepted for help in the Model Cities program. When the Office of Economic Opportunity tried to cut back its programs in the Eleventh District, in keeping with national reductions, Flood would not hear of it. The OEO capitulated, adjusting the funding for the entire state of Pennsylvania in order to keep the programs in the Eleventh District intact.

In 1960 Flood pressured the United States Army into converting its 8,000 coke-burning barracks furnaces in West Germany to anthracite use. When the Army later attempted to back out of the anthracite deal, in order to save $20,000,000 a year by reconversion to oil, the appeal for reconversion funds died annually in the Defense Appropriations Subcommittee on which Flood sits. "I stopped it," Flood boasted to George Crile. "I did it by twisting arms and hammering heads. I'd break a few arms if I had to."

In 1962 Flood underwent surgery for advanced cancer of the stomach and esophagus. Previously portly and round-faced, he came out of the operation stick-thin, as he remains to this day. Colleagues assumed he was moribund, and for some time it was true that only his great fortitude and will power enabled him to carry on as usual, despite pain and weakness. His recovery was widely viewed as a near-miracle.

Flood supported most of President Johnson's Great Society programs and was a hawk on Vietnam. In 1968 he was rated 58 by Americans for Democratic Action, the liberal lobby, 100 by the National Farmers Union, and 16 by the conservative Americans for Constitutional Action, and his scores with the same groups in the following two years were 47, 100, and 12 and 36, 100, and 29.

One of Flood's most spectacular coups was the passage in 1969 of the Coal Mine Health and Safety Act (Public Law 91-173), including a provision for compensation to victims of "black lung" disease. House Majority Leader Thomas P. ("Tip") O'Neill later recalled the impassioned speech Flood gave on the day of the vote in the House: "Most of us hadn't even heard of black lung before that day. It [the speech] completely killed the opposition. He got a standing ovation." Under the black lung measure, 25,000 incapacitated miners in Carbon County, south of Wilkes-Barre, began receiving approximately $165 a month each in compensation.

After he became chairman of the Labor-HEW subcommittee, in 1967, Flood's power was significantly enhanced, and the IOU's he accumulated throughout the Washington power structure multiplied. Collection of those IOU's contributed to some of his extraordinary performances, the grandest of which took place in June 1972, when Hurricane Agnes devastated Pennsylvania's Wyoming Valley, flooding Wilkes-Barre and other cities along the Susquehanna River, leaving 200,000 people homeless, and causing $4 billion in damage. As soon as he heard that the Susquehanna was rising, Flood flew to Wilkes-Barre in the commandeered heliocopter of Melvin Laird, an old Congressional friend who was then Secretary of Defense. In Wilkes-Barre he personally took charge of the rescue and relief missions, demanding and getting troops and equipment from the Pentagon and food, medicine, and personnel from the General Services Administration. Two days later, standing on a hill overlooking Wilkes-Barre, dressed in fatigues, he told a television audience: "This is Dan Flood. Today I have ordered the Army Corps of Engineers not to allow the Susquehanna to rise one more inch." Because of Flood's lobbying, the amount of federal assistance to victims of the disaster was twice as much as what might otherwise have been expected.

The Eleventh District's share of federal military-industrial and other outlays in 1972 was $378,030,209. Among the recipients were Kennedy Van Saun Inc., manufacturers of projectiles, Philco Ford and Medico Industries, manufacturers of telecommunications equipment, United States Steel-Berwick (unspecified products), and the Benton Air Force Station. Among the new industries contributing to healthy diversification were finance, insurance, and real estate companies, manufacturers of apparel and other textile products and electrical equipment and supplies, and processors of food and kindred products.

In key votes in the early 1970's Flood was for prayers in public schools, public television funding, the no-knock crime law, consumer protection, family assistance, a clean-water appropriations bill, jets for Taiwan, and the Safeguard antiballistic missile system; and he was against breaking up the highway trust, ending the House Internal Security Committee, and accepting the Cooper-Church amendment to limit Presidential authority to conduct Cambodian military operations. His ADA, or liberal, ratings in 1971, 1972, 1973, and 1974 were 35, 44, 56, and 35, and his ACA, or conservative, scores for the same years were 41, 29, 15, and 20. Flood's yea votes in 1975 included those for funds for the B-1 bomber, nerve gas, and public transportation.

As the leading champion on Capitol Hill for American retention of the Panama Canal, Flood frustrated the efforts of four successive Presidents to amend the Canal treaty. Consistently, he opposed the two new treaties negotiated by President Jimmy Carter in 1977, under the terms of which the canal is to be turned over to Panama in the year 2000. After the Senate approved the treaties, Flood joined four other legislators in a Supreme Court suit challenging the right of the President to dispose of the Canal Zone without the consent of the House of Representatives in addition to that of the Senate.

Also in 1977, Flood opposed as insufficiently stringent a Senate amendment to the Labor-HEW appropriations bill denying Medicaid funds for abortions except when "medically necessary." The House rejected his own proposal to bar aid for abortions except when the mother's life is in danger. In the House-Senate conference on the matter, he helped tighten the Senate provision so that rape, incest, or danger to the mother's life or physical health are the only instances in which the prohibition can be lifted.

In July 1977 the United States Attorney's office in Philadelphia began investigating possible improprieties in the implementation of a $14.5 million federal grant for a new wing for Philadelphia's Hahnemann Hospital that Flood had helped push through Congress. The construction contract was handled by the law firm of Joshua Eilberg, another Pennsylvania Representative, and monitored by an engineering firm recommended by Flood. The probe widened when Stephen Elko, Flood's administrative aide from 1970 to 1976, began cooperating with federal authorities following his conviction in October 1977 for taking a bribe from a California trade school chain. Elko asserted that Flood had received $100,000 in cash and bank stock from the trade school chain and other institutions that had obtained federal financing with the Congressman's help, and he also charged that an attempt had been made to buy his, Elko's, silence. By March 1978 the Department of Justice and the House Committee on Standards of Official Conduct were also looking into allegations that Flood profited behind the scenes from influencing legislative and administrative decisions involving foreign aid to Haiti, an Agency for International Development project in the Bahamas, and antipoverty funds received by Rabbi Leib Pinter's Brooklyn-based B'nai Torah Institute.

Reactions to the charges against Flood among those close to him varied. Some younger members of the House of Representatives observed that the seniority system of power politics of which Flood is an exemplar is a natural breeding ground of corruption and should be changed. Older members who viewed Flood as a "Congressman's Congressman," an "old boy" who understands "the way we operate around here," were more sympathetic. In his home district, where a school, a park, and other institutions are named for him, most people seemed more protective of him than ever, viewing the trouble he was in as "persecution" by "liberals." On March 16, 1978, when Dan Flood Day was celebrated in Wilkes-Barre, Bill Cherkes, chairman of the event, told a reporter: "We don't care what outsiders say. They're just trying to hurt a member of the family." One of his constituents called Flood "the next closest thing to God." Notwithstanding his proximity to the Divinity, in late 1978 Flood was indicted twice by federal grand juries for perjury, bribery, and conspiracy. But on November 7, 1978 the voters of his district returned him to the House of Representatives for yet another term.

Daniel J. Flood married Catherine Swank, a former actress, on September 24, 1949, not long after the two met at a church social. Since his bout with cancer, the plucky Representative's health has not been robust, and privately, on occasion, he has been seen taking the arm of a companion for support. But he refuses to betray any weakness in public, and his energetic performances in the House of Representatives continue to be fulsome demonstrations of the ham actor's art, full of bombast and oratorical flourishes.

Aside from his white Cadillac and his extravagant, foppishly surreal wardrobe, which includes such items as ice cream-colored Tom Brown suits, silk top-hats, cerise-lined capes, ruffled shirts, red-white-and-blue sneakers, and canes, Flood is said to be frugal to the point of stinginess. His home in Wilkes-Barre is a modest white frame house, and in Washington he and his wife live in a one-bedroom apartment in the old Congress Hotel, where they were allowed to remain after the building was turned into a House Office Building annex. As the beleaguered Representative leaves for work every day, his wife reminds him, "Every night's a first night," and Mrs. Flood recently assured a reporter that her pugnacious husband, old trouper that he is, would not be daunted by the troubles currently besetting him, because "he always gives his best performance."

References: Harper's p60+ Ja '75; N Y Times p12 Ja 31 '78 por; Washington Post B p1+ Mr 17 '78 pors; Biographical Directory of the American Congress, 1774-1961 (1962); Who's Who in America, 1978-79; Who's Who in American Politics, 1977-78

Ford, Henry, II

Sept. 4, 1917- Industrialist. Address: b. Ford Motor Company, The American Rd., Dearborn, Mich. 48121; h. Grosse Pointe Farms, Mich. 48236

NOTE: This biography supersedes the article that appeared in *Current Biography* in 1946.

When he was called upon some thirty-five years ago to reverse the downward trend of his family's automobile enterprise, Henry Ford II proved his managerial skills to be as great as were the mechanical skills of his grandfather, the Henry Ford who founded the Ford Motor Company in 1903. With operations in thirty countries and sales of nearly $29 billion in 1976, the company ranks among the world's largest industrial complexes. Spurred by his sense of corporate responsibility and feeling of family pride, Ford has been the leader in both fact and title of the Ford Motor Company, holding the office of president from 1945 to 1960, when he became chairman of the board, serving on all its committees, and making the final decision on all major matters. In April 1977 he announced that henceforth the company would be run by a three-man office of the chief executive, consisting of himself, Philip Caldwell, and Lee A. Iacocca; if the three should not agree, he, Ford, would have the tie-breaking vote. In June 1978 he gave Caldwell the additional title of deputy chief executive and made his brother, William Clay Ford, chairman of the executive committee. On July 14 Iacocca resigned from the company.

Henry Ford II, the oldest son of Edsel Bryant and Eleanor (Clay) Ford, was born on September 4, 1917 in Detroit, Michigan, where he spent a childhood carefully guarded from publicity and kidnappers, along with his brothers and sister, Benson, William Clay, and Josephine. Benson was a vice-president of the Ford Motor Company at the time of his death on July 27. 1978 and was also the owner of the Detroit Lions football team. William has held various positions within the family organization. Josephine, sometimes called "the Ford Ford," is married to Walter Buell Ford, a designer related to the Henry Ford family only by his marriage.

An indifferent student both at Detroit University School and at Hotchkiss School in Lakeville, Connecticut, Ford preferred the athletic fields to the classrooms. After he enrolled in Yale University in 1936, he gave more of his attention to such extracurricular activities as Zeta Psi fraternity, the Book and Snake Club, and management of the Yale crew than to his studies. He began in college with engineering as his major subject in preparation for his expected role in the Ford company, but after a year he changed to sociology. He left Yale in June 1940 without graduating because his senior thesis was discovered to have been ghostwritten and he had passed up the chance to write another.

In 1938 Ford had become a director in his family's company, and on his departure from Yale, he went to work at Ford's River Rouge plant in Michigan to learn the automobile business from the bottom up. He had, however, little mechanical inclination and no sense of urgency about his training. When, in 1941, his being drafted for World War II service seemed imminent, he enlisted in the Navy, where he spent the next two years on shore duty and rose from ensign to lieutenant. In 1943, just after he had requested transfer to sea duty, his father died, at the age of fifty.

Edsel Ford had been the unassertive president of the Ford company since 1919, while his father had kept tight control over the organization. As he grew older, Henry Ford had become increasingly dependent upon Harry Bennett, a former prizefighter who presided over a secret police force that he had set up within the company to spy on the business and personal activities of everyone from high-echelon executives to workers on the assembly line. With his small army, which included ex-policemen and ex-convicts, Bennett promoted obedience and loyalty to the Ford Motor Company and fostered his own career. His Rasputin-like influence over Henry Ford increased after the old man suffered strokes in 1938 and 1941.

On the death of his son, the eighty-year-old founder, indecisive, unpredictable, and forgetful, resumed the presidency of the company and, according to rumor, made plans to turn it over after his death to Bennett and a group of men under his control. In 1943, however, the wartime priorities of the United States government, which had contracted with Ford for thousands of airplanes to be manufactured at Willow Run, led Secretary of the Navy Frank Knox to decide that Henry Ford II should serve his country by working at the Ford company instead of staying in the Navy. Accordingly, he was released on August 1, 1943. When he returned to the Ford company, this time to learn the industry from the top down, he found the family business a dying giant. Between 1930 and 1941 its output had dropped from 40 percent of all American cars to less than 20 percent, and profits had plummeted from $80,000,000 in 1929 to $6,000,000 in 1941. Besides lacking leadership, having lost several top executives, the company had no accounting system, property books, or adequate research and design departments. During its forty-year history there had never been an audit.

On December 15, 1943 Henry Ford saw his grandson elected vice-president in charge of sales and promotion, and four months later, with his advancement to executive vice-president, Henry II became second in command to the founder himself. In his claim to the top spot, he had the support of other executives and of the senior Mrs. Henry Ford and Mrs. Edsel Ford, his grandmother and mother, who were major stockholders in the family-owned business. Mrs. Edsel Ford is reported to have told her father-in-law that unless her son were made president, she would sell her sizable block of shares. On September 20, 1945 Henry Ford bowed to her ultimatum, and the following day Henry II was made president and chief executive officer. He immediately fired Harry Bennett.

Despite the fact that the Ford Motor Company was losing some $10,000,000 a month when he took office, Ford felt confident that he could restore its prosperity. He took on the task, moreover, when all American industry was starting to make the transition from wartime to peacetime production. Among his other problems was the United Automobile Workers' demand for a 30 percent wage increase, which posed the threat of strikes throughout the automobile industry. Ford took the trouble to establish good personal relations with Walter Reuther, a leader of the automobile union, and with the resumption of limited automobile production in October 1945, after a brief work stoppage, he invited union officials to a get-acquainted meeting with him. He thus paved the way to a continuation of collective bargaining on November 20, just one day before employees at General Motors walked off their jobs. Negotiations at Ford ended on January 26, 1946 with the union's gaining a 15 percent wage increase in return for guaranteeing the company against illegal strikes and worker inefficiency. A proponent of the concept of company security against costly production interruptions, Ford had said in a speech before the Society of Automotive Engineers earlier in January, "If we can solve the problem of human relations in industry, I believe we can make as much progress toward lower costs during the next ten years as we made during the past quarter century through the development of the machinery of mass production."

In addition to securing a labor settlement, Ford gave prompt attention to finding managerial talent. One of his first moves was to persuade Ernest R. Breech, president of Bendix Aviation Corporation, to join the Ford Motor Company in 1946. Breech had the experience and expertise to implement Ford's desire for a decentralized organization patterned on General Motors, where Breech had held various executive posts since the 1920's. In 1946, also, Ford recruited the so-called "Whiz Kids," a group of ex-Air Force officers who wanted to continue working together in civilian life, applying military management techniques to a business organization. Included in the group were Robert S. McNamara, Arjay Miller, and Charles B. Thornton.

To regain the company's leadership among car manufacturers, Ford also began divesting the Ford empire of many sidelines instituted by his grandfather, including all but five of a fleet of lake- and ocean-going vessels, a rubber plantation in South America, soybean and antibiotic research projects, experimental farms, and parts of vast forest holdings. At the same time, while shunning diversification, as he continued to do, except for Philco, he began investing in an expansion program that totaled $1 billion by 1953 and that included thirteen new manufacturing plants throughout the United States, sixteen parts depots, and four engineering buildings.

Company prospects quickly brightened. Although the first half of 1946 showed a loss of about $50,000,000, at year's end there was a profit of $2,000. Three years later new Ford, Lincoln, and Mercury models helped bring the company its best year since 1929, with sales of over a million automobiles and a profit of $177,000,000. Net profit for 1950 reached $265,000,000, and by 1953 the Ford Motor Company had moved past the Chrysler Corporation into second place in the automobile industry. It has held that position ever since, averaging a 21 to 25 percent share of total annual automobile sales in the United States each year.

The momentum of the company's progress slowed down in 1957, when it introduced a new car, the Edsel. Clinching the decision in 1955 to produce that model, Henry Ford II had pushed the project despite the misgivings of some of his executives. The expected sales figure of 200,000 for the first year never materialized, a total of only 110,247 Edsels being sold by 1959, when the car was discontinued. That major attempt of the Ford company to penetrate the medium-priced automobile market represented a $250,000,000 loss, and Ford himself shouldered the blame for the Edsel's failure.

With subsequent new cars, Ford had far greater success. The Falcon in 1959 was the first compact that any of the "Big Three" automobile manufacturers put on the market; it set a first-year record of 417,107 sales. The sporty Mustang, aimed specifically at the youth market, was introduced at the New York World's Fair in 1964 and sold 417,811 during its first year, a record that still stands. Largely the creation of Lee A. Iacocca, a Ford vice-president not yet forty years old, the Mustang contributed much to his rise in the company. Ford's low-priced Maverick compact in 1969 and the even smaller Pinto in 1970, both of them attempts to meet the growing competition from small foreign cars, such as the Volkswagen, were also Iacocca models. However, the final approval to go ahead with any of those automobiles had to come from Henry Ford II, just as it had with the Edsel, and he also made the decision to put $250,000,000 into his company's Lincoln-Mercury Division between 1967 and 1969, part of an effort to grab a piece of General Motors' Buick, Oldsmobile, and Pontiac market.

Outside the industry Ford himself was becoming widely known as a highly visible and articulate multimillionaire executive who often, and sometimes bluntly, expressed his views on social, industrial, and governmental problems. He spoke in 1969 at Vanderbilt, Yale, and Harvard universities on the relationship between business and government and the social challenges and responsibilities faced by both, voicing doubt as to whether business can do all that society expects of it. He suggested that the profit motive might bolster business efforts for new social service through meeting new demands and, if that should not be possible, he regarded government intervention as advisable. Ford's lectures appeared in book form in 1970 under the title *The Human Environment and Business* (Weybright & Talley).

Automobile safety had emerged as a major issue affecting business, government, and society, so that by 1966 Ford was concerned that the controversy over safety would push Congress into enacting legislation that, by hamstringing the automobile industry, would harm the American economy. Ford has long felt that better driver training and highway laws would make significant contributions to reducing accidents. With the later emergence of air pollution and demands for higher gasoline mileage as issues, Ford's worries over governmental intervention have grown. He deplores the additional problems with which the automobile industry must cope because of "uncertainties over governmental regulation."

Action that Ford himself has taken on air pollution includes a commitment by his company to reduce polluting emissions from manufacturing plants as well as from automobiles, and in 1970 he demanded that oil companies increase the production of unleaded gas. The gasoline economy problem has involved Ford, as well as other automobile makers, in making smaller cars, such as the twenty-six-miles-per-gallon Fairmont that Ford introduced in the fall of 1977. Ford's executives also expect the Fairmont to beat the first-year sales record still held by the Mustang and to recover for the Ford company a 25 percent share of the automobile market.

Both business and government leaders, Ford has argued, must be apprehensive of the social dangers posed by poverty. After the riots in Watts, California and elsewhere in the United States, he warned in a speech in Detroit in May 1966, "The greatest danger to a civilized nation is the man who has no stake in it and nothing to lose by rejecting all that civilization stands for." The riots of the next year in Detroit seemed to Ford "the most serious domestic crisis since the Civil War." He asked 10,000 Ford supervisors to support his company's attempts to give "people who have been held back by prejudice and poverty a chance to earn a decent life." The company began hiring illiterate blacks from the ghetto, some with police records, and putting them into entry-level jobs. On November 17, 1967, speaking before the National Urban League, Ford said that genuine equal opportunity "is, in fact, the most urgent task our nation faces." He viewed urban unrest as a "social cancer that threatens the vitality and peace of communities where we do business."

In 1968 President Lyndon B. Johnson named Ford chairman of the National Alliance of Businessmen, to direct a program involving cooperation between industry and government to find employment in private enterprise for the hard-core unemployed. During that year the alliance found jobs for 125,000 previously unemployed people. When the Nixon Administration took office, Ford resigned his post, but later served under Nixon as chairman from 1970 to 1972 of the National Center for Voluntary Action, a clearinghouse organization that set up centers throughout the country to bring together people who wanted to volunteer their social service skills and institutions most in need of help.

According to *Time* (July 20, 1970), moreover, as a trustee of the Ford Foundation, Henry Ford II had "supported most of its widely debated actions, including aid to community-organizing projects among the poor." Ford had inherited his seat on the board of trustees on the death of his father in 1943. His resignation on January 11, 1977 left no family member on the board of the foundation that his grandfather had established in 1936 and that had become the largest philanthropic institution in the country. In a statement that he made at the time of his resignation, he criticized the foundation for trying to do too many things in too many areas and for failing to promote an appreciation of the capitalistic economic system.

It was to diversify the Ford Foundation's holdings that the Ford Motor Company's stock was sold publicly for the first time, in 1956, when the foundation disposed of 15 percent of its company stock, then worth about $650,000,000, in the largest transaction of its kind thus far in history. Although his grandfather would have objected to sharing the Ford company with a lot of other stock owners, Henry II saw advantages in the move and, according to Booton Herndon in his book *Ford* (1969), "seems to enjoy his role as head of a large public corporation," presiding patiently but firmly over stockholders' meetings.

Ford is one of America's richest men and also one of its most highly paid executives, with salary and bonuses in 1976 amounting to $970,000; in addition, he receives several millions of dollars annually in dividends from the Ford Motor Company, nearly 40 percent of whose voting stock he and his family control. A hard worker, he often puts in ten-hour days in shirtsleeves at a desk that he likes to keep uncluttered. He seldom arrives at work much before nine in the morning, but takes papers home for study in the evening and on occasion stays overnight at his office, where he has a bed.

On July 13, 1940 Henry Ford II married Anne McDonnell, daughter of a financier and utility executive. The marriage, for which he converted from Methodism to Roman Catholicism, ended in divorce in February 1964. On February 19, 1965 he married thirty-five-year-old Maria Cristina Vettore Austin, the divorced wife of a British naval officer. The separation of Ford and his second wife was confirmed in January 1976. By his first marriage Ford had three children. His daughter, Charlotte, married the Greek shipping magnate Stavros Niarchos in 1965 and divorced him in 1967; she later married J. Anthony Forstmann. Ford's daughter, Anne, married and later divorced Giancarlo Uzielli, an investment banker. Ford's third child, Edsel Bryant Ford II, who married Cynthia Layne Neskow in 1974, is one of five great-grandsons of the first Henry Ford and has been active in the family business in product planning and sales.

Because of his international travels, for both business and pleasure, his enthusiasm at parties, and his love for dancing, Ford acquired something of a jet-set image, especially after his second marriage. He is six feet tall and sartorially impeccable. He enjoys hunting, usually at his lodge in Ontario, and spending a holiday shooting in England, but aside from that and an occasional game of golf, he gives little attention to sports. Although he is said not to be seriously devoted to art, he spent heavily, particularly during the 1950's, on his art collection, which contains work by such artists as Van Gogh, Degas, Matisse, Cézanne, and Renoir.

One of Ford's absorbing personal interests in recent years has been Detroit Renaissance, for which in 1971 he revealed a gigantic urban renewal plan involving shopping centers, hotels, and office buildings, all to be built by a consortium of fifty-one companies at a cost of some $337,000,000 in downtown Detroit. In April 1977 he helped to dedicate Renaissance Center. For his efforts on behalf of minority employment and training, he was awarded an honorary Doctor of Laws degree from Yale in 1972. Another tribute paid to him is the Presidential Medal of Freedom, awarded in 1969 by President Johnson.

References: Biog N p994+ S/O '75 por; Fortune 87:188+ My '73 pors; London Sunday Times Mag N 16 '75 pors; N Y Times III p1+ O 23 '77 pors; N Y Times Mag p25+ O 19 '69 pors; p12+ Mr 5 '78 pors; p22+ Mr 12 '78 pors; Time 96:66+ Jl 20 '70 pors; Herndon, Booton. Ford (1969); International Who's Who, 1977-78; Who's Who in America, 1976-77

Fox, Carol

June 15, 1926- Opera producer; manager. Address: b. Lyric Opera, 20 N. Wacker Dr., Chicago, Ill. 60606

Chicago's pre-Depression operatic glory has been restored largely through the vision and hard work of one person—Carol Fox, cofounder and general manager of the Lyric Opera of Chicago, sometimes called "the Met of the Midwest" but more appropriately known as "La Scala West" because of the international dimensions of its casts, crews, repertoire, and reputation. In its twenty-two seasons of existence, the Windy City's resident opera company has presented approximately 100 different operas in some 900 performances, and it has been the site of the American operatic debuts of the late Maria Callas and numerous other international stars. In addition, the Lyric Opera now trains a select group of young singers in the New Opera School of Chicago.

An only child in a wealthy family, Carol Fox was born in Chicago, Illinois on June 15, 1926 to Edward Fox, an office supply company executive, and Virginia (Scott) Fox. According to Miss Fox, she was encouraged to pursue the theatrical arts by her mother, a "persuasive" woman who had been "thwarted" from doing so in her own youth by her family. Growing up, Carol Fox had lessons in singing, piano, ballet, elocution, dramatics, and opera, in addition to languages (French, German, Italian) and the other subjects considered *de rigueur* in the education of a lady. At Girls Latin School in Chicago she played leads in dramatic productions, and in her leisure hours she often sailed on Lake Michigan.

At her father's insistence, Miss Fox took and passed the entrance exams for Vassar, but Mr. Fox respected her wishes and did not force her to go to college. Instead, she studied acting at the Pasadena (California) Playhouse and took voice lessons under Edith Mason and Vittorio Trevisan in Chicago and Virgilio Lazarri and Giovanni Martinelli in New York, where she was also coached in operatic repertory by Fausto Cleva. After Martinelli returned to Italy she continued her voice studies with him there. She lived in Italy for two years, staying with Martinelli's family in Rome and at Villa Ca'Rossa near Lake Como. During her sojourn in Italy she completed her mastery of Italian and took advantage of the opportunity to sing some minor roles in amateur opera productions.

Miss Fox returned to the United States determined to found an opera company, and no major city cried out for one more than Chicago. Samuel Insull's Chicago Civic Opera Company had died simultaneously with Insull's utilities empire at the beginning of the Depression, in 1932, and later attempts at a resident company—the last by the Music Foundation, between 1945 and 1947—had been abortive. With seed money from her father and in collaboration with business promoter Lawrence Kelly and conductor Nicola Rescigno, Miss Fox founded her company, first called the Lyric Theatre of Chicago, in 1952. She and her collaborators made arrangements to take over the then empty Civic Opera House built by Insull—which remains the company's home to this day—as well as its nearby gigantic warehouse, full of scenery, costumes, and props, and they recruited a group of thirty young people, called the Lyric Guild, to spearhead fund-raising and promotion campaigns.

In February 1954 Miss Fox's fledgling company presented a two-performance "calling card" performance of *Don Giovanni* with a cast including Nicola Rossi-Lemini, Eleanor Steber, Leopold Simoneau, and Bidu Sayao. In the audience was Claudia Cassidy of the Chicago *Tribune,* who two decades later recalled, "I could not believe that stage. The Lyric did not exist, except in faith, hope and a vast amount of charity. Yet on that . . . stage was true, luminous Mozart. Chicago accepted the calling card and said, 'Come again.' "

In preparation for her company's first full season, Miss Fox went to Europe and, aided by the enthusiasm of Rossi-Lemini, signed Maria Callas and other leading singers in Italian opera houses who had never performed in opera houses in the United States. Mme. Callas' American debut in the title role of *Norma* at the Civic Opera House on November 1, 1954 was a spectacular success, with worldwide reverberations. On a later occasion in the Lyric's first three-week season Mme. Callas drew a twelve-minute standing ovation with her interpretation of the mad scene in *Lucia di Lammermoor.* The season's eight productions included *Il Barbiere di Siviglia* (Rossini), *La Bohème, La Traviata, Carmen,* and *Tosca,* and the first fully staged and costumed production of *The Taming of the Shrew,* with an all-American cast. The international stars in the Italian opera productions included Tito Gobbi, Giulietta Simionato, and Giuseppe di Stefano. In its first season the Chicago company played to 84-percent capacity in the 3,500-plus-seat Civic Opera House. In subsequent years it never played to less than 90-percent capacity, and in recent years the attendance has averaged about 99 percent. In a typical season the audiences total more than 60,000.

Callas, Rossi-Lemeni, di Stefano, and Ettore Bastianini opened the second season in Chicago on October 31, 1955 in Bellini's *I Puritani.* Among the other productions presented in the five-week 1955 season were de Banfield's *Lord Byron's Love Letter,* Mascagni's *Cavalleria Rusticana,* and the ballet *Revanche,* on a triple bill. The 1956 season in Chicago opened on October 10 with Puccini's *The Girl of the Golden West* under Dimitri Mitropoulos. Later in the season Georg Solti conducted the Lyric Opera's first excursions into German opera, productions of Strauss's *Salome* and Wagner's *Die Walküre.* Among the twelve 1956 productions was a gala concert recorded by London Records. In 1956 Carol Fox's colleagues Kelly and Rescigno left Chicago, ultimately to found the Dallas Civic Opera, and the Lyric Theatre was reorganized as the Lyric Opera of Chicago, with Miss Fox as general manager.

During the late 1950's and early 1960's the financial condition of the Lyric Opera improved. In 1957, when twenty-nine performances were sung to a succession of full houses, contributions totalled $252,000; in 1958 there was a grant-in-aid from the Italian government; and beginning in 1959, twenty-five productions were—or have been—underwritten by rich friends of the Lyric Opera or by such agencies as the Ford Foundation. But with every rise of the curtain, even in the best of times, the company lost upwards of $11,000, and Miss Fox faced other problems, including the aesthetic conservatism of her public and the financial caution of the Lyric Opera's board. (The board was seen as a "problem" by outside observers, not by Miss Fox, who regards it as "the most cooperative board in the world.") Not the least of the problems were the reorganization pains the company continued to suffer, as Peter Jacobi noted in the New York *Times* (December 8, 1963): "Staging too often has been negligible; directors unable to cope with the rapid and limited rehearsal schedule have been brought from Europe only to allow matters to fall apart. Young American artists have had scant opportunity to present their credentials. And the repertory has receded to conservatism, sprinkled with lapses of good sense."

Peter Jacobi gave the tenth anniversary season, ending November 29, 1963, as an example of "repertory planning gone awry"—"five old Italian works, two old German operas, and the most staple of French staples [Gounod's *Faust*]." Looking back, he complained that in ten seasons the Lyric Opera had presented thirty-nine Italian works out of a total repertory of fifty-six, or 70 percent, and that only four of the fifty-six works had been written within the previous forty years. The four were *Turandot, Lord Byron's Love Letter, The Taming of the Shrew,* and *The Harvest.* The last mentioned, commissioned under a Ford Foundation grant and produced in 1961, had failed with public and critics and there were "apparently no plans to try again."

In the mid-1960's the Lyric Opera's season was progressively expanded from nine to ten to eleven weeks. Carol Fox's willingness to balance the familiar with the unfamiliar, and to share musical planning with two capable new artistic codirectors, Pino Donati and Bruno Bartoletti, was reflected in such presentations as the Chicago premieres of Berg's *Wozzeck* and Ravel's *L'Heure Espagnole* in 1965 and of Prokofiev's *Angel of Fire* in 1966, in the double billing of Stravinsky's *Oedipus Rex* and *Le Rossignol* in 1968, and in the first professionally staged production of Britten's *Billy Budd* in the United States in 1970. In an *Opera News* interview (November 1972) with Speight Jenkins, Miss Fox pointed out that since the advent of Bartoletti as principal conductor the company had been trying to build an audience for newer works, but within limits, for several reasons. One was that "with our Strauss and our growing *Ring* we're doing the things that a company our age should have in its repertory." Another was that the Lyric Opera was less equipped for the visual than for the aural, and "the Henzes and the Dallapiccolas and the other more modern sounds are very expensive to realize visually." A third reason she gave for moderation in tackling newer works was that "our audiences might take a lot of hearings to comprehend and enjoy them" and she didn't "know that it's our job to do all these things." The most important job, she said, "is to content the public, to get them to come, and bit by bit to indoctrinate them to the new. It takes some time to make someone enjoy an unknown piece, even a new boom-boom-boom piece."

In the interview with Jenkins, Miss Fox took pains to stress that "this is *not* an Italian house." She explained: "We started this company with the fanaticism of doing what we did well, and the chorus master is very adept in Italian opera. If you put on French, German, English, modern, Italian grand opera, and baroque all at once, it takes enormous resources. You should be well rounded, but you can't do everything at one time."

In February 1973 the Lyric Opera inaugurated its apprentice artist program, taking into residence, at a $9,000 salary each, a first batch of ten young American singers for eleven months of training and chorus experience. The small stage of the Chicago Civic Theatre, next door to the giant Lyric Opera house, became a showcase for apprentice productions. Chicago radio station WFMT-FM began broadcasting the Lyric Opera's opening night performances in the autumn of 1973, and those broadcasts are now heard beyond the greater Chicago area via national radio syndication. In September 1974 the Lyric Opera hosted the Fourth International Verdi Congress, climaxed by an all-new production of *Simon Boccanegra.* The 1974 season also saw the Chicago premieres of *Peter Grimes* and *Don Quichotte* and the first production in nearly half a century of *Götterdämmerung.* The 1974 season, the company's twentieth anniversary season, was underwritten by the Gramma Fisher Foundation. In 1975, when artistic codirector Pino Donati died and chorus master Michael Lepore retired, the repertoire was cut to seven productions but the number of performances remained at the customary fifty-two.

During its 1976 season the Lyric Opera scored brilliant successes with company premieres of Offenbach's *Les Contes d' Hoffmann* and Prokofiev's *The Love of Three Oranges.* The other operas included *La Cenerentola, Un Ballo in Maschera, Rigoletto, Khovanshchina,* and *Tosca.* Among the singers were tenors Placido Domingo, Alfred Kraus, José Carreras, and Luciano Pavarotti. In celebration of the American Bicentennial, Krzysztof Penderecki composed his *Paradise Lost,* commissioned by the Lyric Opera and underwritten by James C. Hemphill. The premiere of *Paradise Lost* was scheduled for 1978.

At the Lyric Opera Miss Fox leaves no doubt, as one of her assistants has observed, that "she is the boss," involved in every aspect of the company's operations, from the mailroom to the choosing and casting of operas, an activity that is the work of a triumvirate consisting of herself and her two artistic codirectors. The codirectors as well as the chorus master, the artistic assistant manager, and three business assistant managers report directly to her. To her permanent staff of thirty and her full season company of approximately 500, she is an omnipresent, demanding matriarch, forever walking the hallways, the wings, and the rehearsal rooms, cajoling, encouraging, inviting all to buttonhole her with problems or grievances. She knows everyone by name, down to the lowliest stagehand.

The personalized nature of relations and the spirit of common endeavor at the Lyric Opera extends to huge Thanksgiving dinners at Miss Fox's apartment and company parties where, as she says, "nobody is secondary." New guest artists, from assistant conductors up through star singers, are informed before their arrival in detail, in a variety of languages, about such matters as their hotel accommodations, and they are met at the airport by Miss Fox or her surrogates and given advance money on the spot.

To meet the Lyric Opera's annual budget of approximately $5,000,000 Miss Fox applies all the charm, guile, and drive at her disposal to fundraising. She is tightfisted in using the money raised, and to cut costs she has entered into arrangements for the interchange of costumes, sets, and production plans with other opera houses. Still, she has energy left for civic and other causes, such as the Junior League and advisory boards at the University of Chicago and Loyola University. Her many honors include the Steinway Award, the Chicago Medal of Merit, and decorations from Italian and American organizations for promoting ties between the two countries.

Carol Fox is a big, brown-eyed woman with a deep, booming, musical voice. In the New York *Times* (November 25, 1973) Stephen E. Rubin described her as "formidable," exuding "enough authority and confidence to give the word *chutzpah* a new meaning," but "strangely, for an enormously aggressive woman, she is not interested in personal publicity." When Bess Winakor interviewed her for *Chicago Today* in September 1974 she found her to be "a gracious, charming hostess who almost seemed vulnerable." She told Winakor that she is sometimes a "diplomat," but when diplomacy doesn't work she can raise her voice and take a "firm hand." In an earlier interview for *Chicago Today* (July 5, 1973), society editor Margaret Carroll noted that she has a "strong" personality and that her eyes can "smile warmly or flash anger." But Miss Fox said that she is "not a women's libber at all" and that she despises the term "Ms." and won't allow it to be used on the Lyric Opera's mail partly because she thinks "it's a smokescreen for insecurity" and partly because she likes old-world formality. Italian, which she speaks as if it were her native language, is used as much as English by Carol Fox in her work and at home. That home is an apartment on Lake Shore Drive, although her real home, her assistants say, is the Lyric Opera of Chicago.

References: Chicago Today p27+ Jl 5 '73 por; Christian Sci Mon p4 Je 14 '61 por; N Y Times II p15+ N 25 '73 pors; Opera News 35:13+ O 3 '70 pors, 37:14+ N '72; Who's Who in America, 1976-77

Frampton, Peter

Apr. 20, 1950- British musician; recording artist. Address. b. c/o A & M Records, 595 Madison Ave., New York City, N.Y. 10022

Peter Frampton, the British rock musician whose *Frampton Comes Alive* (1976) broke all records to become the best-selling double live album in the history of the recording industry, is one of the few performers who has achieved enormous popularity without the benefit of critical acclaim. An exceptionally talented guitarist and gifted songwriter, Frampton served an apprenticeship with such groups as the Herd and Humble Pie before striking out on his own in 1971. His five years of almost unbroken touring finally paid off in 1976, when he generated over $67 million in revenue through the sale of records, concert tickets, and posters and other paraphernalia. That same year he was named Rock Personality of the Year by *Billboard* magazine, voted "Number One" by *Rolling Stone*'s readers, and selected Artist of the Year by his peers at the annual Rock Music Awards. Like Elton John, Stevie Wonder, and Paul McCartney, the performers he most nearly resembles in onstage dynamism, Frampton has the ability to mesmerize audiences, who respond to his energetic performances with unrestrained delight. "I do what Jolson, Sinatra, Tony Bennett, and the Beatles did," he explained recently. "I communicate."

Peter Kenneth Frampton was born on April 20, 1950 in Beckenham, Kent, a middle-class bedroom suburb of London, England, the older of the two sons of Owen Frampton, a high school art teacher and amateur musician, and his wife Peggy. Even as a child, Peter Frampton showed an unusual interest in music, and encouraging that interest, Owen Frampton taught his son the basic chords on the banjulele, a four-string cross between the banjo and the ukelele and, one Christmas, gave him a guitar. Enthralled, the boy practised for hours, often in the family bathroom—the "original echo chamber," in Frampton's words—and used his two tape recorders, recording melody on one and rhythm on the other, to simulate two guitars. "I never wanted to be a train driver," he told Steve Clarke in an interview for Clarke's book, *Peter Frampton: The Man Who Came Alive* (Bunch Books, 1977). "I wanted to be the best guitar player in the world."

When he was nine years old, Frampton made his debut as a performer at a Boy Scout show at nearby West Wickham. A year later he was playing lead guitar in his own group, the Trubeats. The quartet played their first gig in a local pub, where, Frampton remembers, "everybody giggled at us," then began making the rounds of the local church halls and fetes. Gradually, the Trubeats added to their repertory of songs recorded by the Ventures, the Shadows, and Johnny and the Hurricanes tunes by Chuck Berry and the Beatles. In an effort to cash in on the growing popularity of the Liverpool groups, they began billing themselves as "the Wickham boys with the Mersey sound."

When Frampton was about twelve years old, the press began to take notice of the Trubeats. Despite enticing offers from music agents, he acceded to his parents' wish that he concentrate on his studies until his sixteenth birthday and left the group. Having no one to jam with and taking little interest in the classical guitar lessons he had been having for the past two years, Frampton began playing along with the albums of such jazz guitarists as Django Reinhardt, Wes Montgomery, and Kenny Burrell.

After passing the eleven-plus scholarship exam, Frampton enrolled at Bromley Technical High School, where he became friendly with two older students, George Underwood and David Jones, the latter of whom later became famous as David Bowie. The three invariably spent their lunch hours in a school stairwell, playing Buddy Holly and Everly Brothers songs on acoustic guitars. The following year Frampton transferred to Bromley Grammar School, where he spent much of his time in empty classrooms, practising his guitar for weekend gigs with such local rhythm and blues groups as Denny Mitchell and the Soundsations and the Konrads.

In April 1965 Frampton joined the Preachers, an aggregation of some of the best blues musicians in southwest England. In addition to being the group's lead guitarist, he was the featured vocalist on such numbers as Mose Allison's "If You Live," Bobby Bland's "You're the One," and "Wild Thing," the raucous, raunchy, and chart-topping Troggs' hit. The pressure of school work forced Frampton to leave the group as a full-time player in August, but before his departure he contributed a sizzling guitar riff to the Preachers' only single recording, "Hole in My Soul." Late in the year the Preachers joined forces with the Other Two to form the Train. With Frampton once again on board, the group performed as a supporting act at London's most important rock clubs and, in the spring of 1966, recorded "Deed I Do," an undistinguished, soul-oriented number. After passing his "O" level exams in June 1966, Frampton left the stalling Train.

At about the same time the Herd, another popular local band, lost one of its guitarists. The group's manager, Billy Gaff, who had often heard Frampton play with the Preachers and the Train, sounded him out about signing on with the group as lead guitarist. He was eager to join, but his parents, who still wanted their son to enter a more conventional career, had yet to be convinced. Gaff eventually won their consent, and by late fall Frampton and the Herd were playing to sell-out crowds at London's Marquee Club, the mecca of British rock groups in the mid-1960's. Their kinky, flamboyant act, which pop critic Chris Welch analyzed as "a mixture of cool camp and smart musicianship," increased their following in the South of England, but they still lacked a hit record to make them a national success.

To that end, the Herd signed with Ken Howard and Alan Blaikley, the hip young manager-songwriters who had composed a number of top twenty hits. The Herd's first Howard and Blaikley single, "I Can Fly," received little air play and failed to score commercially. Recognizing Frampton's potential as a pop idol, the Herd's new managers pushed the reluctant guitarist to the forefront of the group and relentlessly promoted him as a teenybopper sex symbol. The next three Herd singles—"From the Underworld," "Paradise Lost," and "I Don't Want Our Loving to Die"—all made the top ten on the pop record charts. Capitalizing on the latest trend, the rock music press promptly dubbed Frampton "the face of 1968." "We were on TV every week, *Top of the Pops*," Frampton recalled, as quoted in *Newsweek* (April 19, 1976). "I was lip-synching to the records, being screamed at, having my clothes ripped and people cutting bits of my hair. It was like a dream." Despite their success, the group's members, Frampton in particular, resented the pop packaging, which included, according to Frampton, glycerine drops to make his eyes sparkle. "We were puppets," he told one interviewer. Disenchanted, he left the Herd in February 1969, shortly before it disbanded.

Almost immediately Frampton, his friend Steve Marriott, the leader of the Small Faces, one of the most successful groups of the mid-1960's, and two other musicians formed Humble Pie. After rehearsing throughout the spring and summer in a small village in Essex, the group signed with the Immediate label, recorded their first single, "Natural Born Boogie," a low-key rock 'n' roll number written by Marriott, and an album, *As Safe As Yesterday*, and went on the road. After triumphant engagements in Britain and on the Continent, Humble Pie traveled to the United States for appearances at New York City's Fillmore East and a tour with the Moody Blues. Because they continued to rely on acoustic instruments, they were not well received by American audiences, who preferred the hyperamplified, electronic sound of acid rock. Shortly after their return to England, Immediate Records went bankrupt, leaving the group bereft of funding and management. Within weeks, however, Frampton and Marriott had negotiated a five-year contract with A & M Records, calling for two albums a year.

Early in 1970 Humble Pie hired as their new manager Dee Anthony, an American rock promoter who had helped Ten Years After, Jethro Tull, Traffic, and other British groups achieve superstar status in the United States. When their second and third albums, *Town and Country* and *Humble Pie*, failed to score in Britain, the band returned to the grueling but potentially profitable American circuit. At Anthony's suggestion, they discarded their earlier material and concentrated on the hard rock that American audiences seemed to prefer. Anthony's strategy of one-nighters and national tours with established acts, such as Grand Funk Railroad, a popular heavy metal group, eventually paid off when *Rock On*, Humble Pie's fourth album, hit the charts in the spring of 1971. Their next LP, *Rockin' the Fillmore*, notable for Frampton's dazzling guitar vamps, made a million dollars within a matter of weeks. But Frampton felt frustrated musically and in September 1971 he decided to try his luck as a solo musician.

For the next seven months Frampton filled in as a session man on such studio LP's as George Harrison's *All Things Must Pass* and Harry Nilsson's *Son of Schmilsson* and worked diligently on his *Wind of Change*. Released by A & M Records in April 1972, that album represented an experiment in various musical styles that Frampton has since described as "almost . . . schizophrenic," although it won praise from British rock critics for its creative arrangements, well-crafted tunes, and excellent musicianship. But *Wind of Change* proved more of a success with the critics then with the public, and in September 1972 Frampton once again hit the road in the United States.

Frampton's Camel, as his group was known, played everything from tiny backstreet rock clubs to outdoor stadiums. "I was on call all the time, not to tour but to work constantly," he told Steve Clarke. "I needed a lot of work to bolster my confidence and learn to be a front-man, which I'd never been before." Nevertheless, with expenses running up to $1,500 a performance, the band failed to make money, and at one point, Frampton was reportedly $250,000 in debt. Although his 1973 album, *Frampton's Camel*, did little to reduce the group's staggering deficit, it did confirm Frampton's reputation as one of rock music's most accomplished lead guitarists. Two of its numbers—"Lines on My Face," a lament for a deteriorating relationship, and "Do You Feel Like We Do," a group composition—have since become standards in Frampton's concert repertory, as have "Something's Happening" and "Doobie Wah," a pair of solid rockers from *Something's Happening*, which was released in April 1974.

In November 1974 a discouraged and depressed Peter Frampton returned to England to record *Frampton*. On the strength of the heavy air play given "Money," "Show Me the Way," and "Baby, I Love Your Way" by American disc jockeys, the album sold more than 300,000 copies in 1975 and nearly made the top twenty category. "If that album hadn't made it, it would've been the end," Frampton told one interviewer. "There would have been no way to keep going. We'd hit rock bottom." Riding the crest of his popularity, Frampton returned to the United States for a national tour. Backed by drummer John Siomos, bassist Stanley Sheldon, and guitarist Bob Mayo, all first-class professionals, he galvanized audiences with his combination of hard-driving rock and laid-back ballads. Reviewing his explosive performance at the Schaefer Music Festival in New York City's Central

Park for the New York *Times* (June 29, 1975), Ian Dove applauded the "stimulating and articulate" Frampton's "spare, lean, and unfrilled" melodies, "direct and unfussy" lyrics, and rhythmic guitar lines. "The whole performance seemed to take us back to when rock 'n' roll had a sure sense of direction, before it became fudged and fuzzed with too much art form," Dove wrote. "Yet in no sense is Mr. Frampton's work to be termed nostalgia; he just belongs to the mainstream of rock that will always be around."

Throughout his customary three-hour performance Frampton jumps, leaps, and prances around the stage like "a sort of benign Mick Jagger," as John Rockwell, the New York *Times*'s rock critic once observed. Tutored in audience control by Dee Anthony, he plays upon his listeners as skillfully as he plays his guitar, manipulating their responses to fever pitch with hand signals. "It's all very natural," he insisted to Cameron Crowe in an interview for a *Rolling Stone* (February 10, 1977) profile. "We have a good time onstage 'cause we realize it gets through to the audience. Gone is the age of doing a seventy-two-bar guitar solo with your back to the audience, wearing a ripped pair of Levis. They want to be entertained. And when I'm applauded for doing that, all it makes me want to do is entertain more."

The rapport that Frampton enjoys with his audience is nowhere more apparent than on *Frampton Comes Alive*. Released by A & M on January 30, 1976, the album sold 1,000,000 copies in one week and shot to the top of the chart. It hovered in the top five until June, when it regained first place, remaining there, unchallenged, for seventeen consecutive weeks. Despite the fact that every song was already available on earlier Frampton recordings, *Frampton Comes Alive* sold more than 13,000,000 copies and spawned three hit singles. Critics were stunned by its phenomenal sales, and Frampton himself was equally mystified. "If it had just gone gold, and that was it, I'd say it was because I'd been touring for so long, and 'meeting the people,' and playing with every group I could," he told John Rockwell in an interview for the New York *Times* (October 3, 1976). "But . . . I don't really know. And I don't really want to analyze it."

The ambiguously titled *I'm In You*, the long-awaited followup to *Frampton Comes Alive*, sold a million copies within one week after its release in June 1977. His first studio LP in two years, *I'm In You* is an eclectic collection of personal love ballads and classic rock, including cover versions of two driving Motown oldies, "Signed, Sealed, Delivered" and "Road Runner." Mick Jagger is featured on background vocals and Stevie Wonder on harmonica. When it was released as a single, the title track, which Frampton describes as "a song about the audience" (he insists he was unaware of its sexual implications), followed the album to the top of the charts.

Almost to a man, critics denounced what they considered *I'm In You*'s "sugary romanticism" and its "preposterously lame" and "ultracompetent but ultimately uninspired" melodies. Even Larry Rohter, who had extolled *Frampton Comes Alive*, complained that much of the album sounded bland and timid, "like a watered-down version of someone else." "The main weakness," he wrote in a review of *I'm In You* for the Washington *Post* (June 9, 1977), "is Frampton's reluctance to rely on what is probably his greatest gift —a sense of melody that is exceeded only by [Stevie] Wonder's and perhaps Elton John's and Paul McCartney's."

Although he had expected some adverse reaction to *I'm In You*, Frampton was deeply hurt by what he saw as "almost personally vicious" criticism. It was therefore with some trepidation that he returned to the concert stage in June 1977 after an absence of seven months. After his first performance before 91,000 cheering fans at John F. Kennedy Stadium in Philadelphia, he remarked with relief, "I feel like I've just come from the dentist. I feel alleviated of a ton of pressure. It's nice to know they're still there." Later on in the sold-out three-month tour of forty-four cities Frampton, a "gadget freak" since his childhood, delighted audiences by using a talkbox —a device that electronically distorts his voice through his guitar—to converse with a replica of R2-D2, the stubby robot in *Star Wars*. Frampton then went to Hollywood to portray Billy Shears in Robert Stigwood's production of *Sgt. Pepper's Lonely Hearts Club Band*, a motion picture fantasy based on the classic 1967 Beatles album. When the film was released in July 1978 it was greeted with mostly negative reviews.

Often described as the archetypal androgynous rock star, Peter Frampton is a slight, boyishly handsome man with shoulder-length, curly blond hair, large, hypnotic hazel eyes, and a sensuous mouth that easily breaks into a "cover-boy grin." He is five feet seven inches tall and weighs 115 pounds. Affable and unaffected, he remains indifferent to the synthetic glitter of rock stardom. Frampton rarely goes out, preferring to read, watch television, play guitar, or go walking with his dogs on his fifty-three-acre country estate in Westchester County, New York. Although he occasionally spends a few days at his house in the Bahamas, he seldom takes vacations because he likes to keep in practice.

Frampton is a vegetarian who drinks sparingly, usually beer or brandy, and is frightened of drugs. "I've always had the capability to sit alone in a room and flake out, not say anything, just completely turn off, whether I'm happy or sad," he told one interviewer. "I guess that's *some* kind of release." Frampton and his British wife, the former Mary Lovett, whom he married on August 24, 1972, were divorced in 1976. In the past two years, his most frequent companion has been Penny McCall, an American for whom he composed "Penny For Your Thoughts," an intricate, haunting melody for acoustic guitar.

References: N Y Daily News Mag p13+ Ag 21 '77 pors; N Y Post p33 Je 25 '77 por; Newsweek 87:64 Ap 19 '76 por; People 7:25+ Je 22 '77 pors; Rolling Stone p11+ F 10 '77 por; Clarke, Steve. Peter Frampton (1977); Daly, Marsha. Peter Frampton (1978)

Gardner, John (Champlin, Jr.)

Jul. 21, 1933- Writer. Address: b. c/o Bosdydell Artists Ltd., 72 Monument Ave., Bennington, Vt., 05201

Eight inventive and innovative books of fiction since 1966 account chiefly for John Gardner's reputation as one of the most original of contemporary American writers. Yet, in his latest book, *On Moral Fiction* (1978), Gardner takes his stand as a conservator of traditional values and forms, a voice of affirmation in a literary world resonant with despair and alienation. In his prodigious output of novels, short stories, poetry, translations, biography, criticism, and children's books, Gardner has searched for meaning and stability in an alien and indifferent universe. Trained as a medievalist and classicist, Gardner was until recently a university professor who translated Old and Middle English texts, and when his fiction began appearing, he was identified as a philosophical writer who drew upon his learning for characters, structures, and themes. However, his successive books, including the highly acclaimed *Grendel* (1971), *The Sunlight Dialogues* (1972), and *October Light* (1976), displayed an extraordinary range of settings, language, themes, and tones. What has remained constant is Gardner's goal as a shaper of conduct. "I agree with Tolstoy," he writes in *On Moral Fiction*, "that the highest purpose of art is to make people good by choice."

John Champlin Gardner Jr. was born on July 21, 1933 in Batavia, a small town near Rochester, New York that provides the setting for two of his novels. To his father, a farmer, and his mother, Priscilla (Jones) Gardner, an English teacher, he attributes the greatest influence upon his early literary training. In a conversation with Don Edwards and Carol Polsgrove in the *Atlantic* (May 1977) he told how his father "does sermons, goes around to these little churches and preaches. He knows the Bible backwards and forwards, as well as Shakespeare and poetry. He reads that stuff and he loves language. . . . It's in the family." Gardner's attraction to "the metaphoric and indirect," he says, came from his parents' admiration for such "nonrealists" as Shakespeare, Scott, and Dickens. Gardner grew up in a culture of church singers, poets, and storytellers. Other childhood influences were opera, Disney animated films, and Melville. "When I was a little kid," Gardner recalls, "I was writing poetry and, in fact, novels."

Gardner continued to write in the fifteen years before his first novel appeared in 1966, but meanwhile he "just sort of slid" into an academic career. He studied at DePauw University from 1951 to 1955 and in 1955 received his A.B. degree from Washington University, St. Louis. He then went to the State University of Iowa with a Woodrow Wilson Fellowship, earning his M.A. degree in 1956 and his Ph.D. in 1958 in classical and medieval literature. At Iowa he entered the creative writing program, but became discouraged by the low quality of student writing and the publishing world that sometimes printed it. In contrast, Gardner recalls that when he discovered Chaucer, he could not "believe there was such great literature."

After he received his doctorate, Gardner began teaching in 1958 at Oberlin College. In 1959 he moved to Chico State College, California, and in 1962 to San Francisco State. In 1965 he settled down at Southern Illinois University, in Carbondale, where he remained until 1976. He has been a visiting professor in English and writing at the University of Detroit, Northwestern University, Williams College, Skidmore, Bennington, and George Mason University, and he took part in writing workshops at Breadloaf in Vermont and other literary centers.

Throughout those years, he told C. E. Frazer Clark in *Conversations with Writers* (1977), scholarship and imaginative writing were for him closely related, as parts of a common endeavor to enlarge human understanding.

Gardner's scholarly writing is aimed less at academic specialists than at students and generalists, for whom he serves as a knowledgeable and enthusiastic guide. He has put into modern English or done interpretative introductions for *The Complete Works of the Gawain-Poet* (Univ. of Chicago, 1965) and *The Alliterative Morte Arthure, The Owl and the Nightingale, and Five Other Middle English Poems* (Univ. of Southern Illinois, 1971). He is editor, with Lennis Dunlap, of *The Forms of Fiction* (Random House, 1961), a critical anthology; and, with Nicholas Joost, of *Papers on the Art and Age of Geoffrey Chaucer* (Univ. of Southern Illinois, 1967). Other critical works include *The Construction of the Wakefield Cycle* (Univ. of Southern Illinois, 1974), which views the medieval mystery and miracle plays as a coherent single work; *The Construction of Christian Poetry in Old English* (Univ. of Southern Illinois, 1975), a study of Christian and classical rhetorical methods in old English texts; *The Poetry of Chaucer* (Univ. of Southern Illinois, 1977); and *The Life and Times of Chaucer* (Knopf, 1977.) While some reviewers of his recent books on Chaucer have faulted Gardner's critical methods, such as his free use of the novelist's prerogative to invent portions of Chaucer's life where gaps exist, and his failure at times to credit his scholarly sources, most have agreed with Charles Muscatine in the New York *Times* (April 24, 1977) that "'Gardner's good taste and good sense are in the ascendant, and his instinctive love for Chaucer's poetry is everywhere."

Themes that Gardner explored in his scholarly writing are reflected in his fiction, starting with his first novel, *The Resurrection* (New American Library, 1966.) According to Bruce Allen in *Sewanee Review* (Summer 1977), "The medieval poet's assertion of man's imperfect nature is the clear precursor of medievalist Gardner's fiction patterns. All of his stories concern themselves with initiatory journeys towards knowledge." *The Resurrection* traces the journey of James Chandler, a young philosophy professor dying of leukemia, who returns to his native Batavia with his family during his last few weeks of life. Conventionally structured, accurate in its presentation of characters and small-town life, and surcharged with philosophical concepts, the novel, as Gardner describes it, "is the story of modern man's 'absurd' search for the answer to what he knows beforehand is a meaningless question: 'What is the meaning of life?' " Helped by people in Batavia, says Gardner, Chandler finds an "unreasonable affirmation, an aesthetic theory." "It was not the beauty of the world we must affirm," Chandler concludes, "but *the world,* the buzzing blooming confusion itself. . . . *One must make life art.*"

The Resurrection was quietly received, and it was not until 1970 that Harper published Gardner's second novel, *The Wreckage of Agathon.* "For a long period of time, my writing was not liked," Gardner told J. D. Bellamy. "Finally people began to publish my things. Actually, *The Wreckage of Agathon* broke it." A metaphysical satire set in ancient Sparta during the slaves' revolt against Lycurgus the Lawgiver, the novel was described by one reviewer as "an inventive if rather baroque meditation on the status of imaginative freedom within an oppressive political order." It takes the form of alternate monologues by Agathon, an irreverent Athenian sage, and Peeker, his young apprentice, both of whom have been imprisoned for advocating humane tolerance of learning, and even of anarchy. Their black-humored talk provides many energetic and provocative moments, although Gardner's philosophizing occasionally seems forced and bloated.

On the other hand, Gardner's third novel, *Grendel,* (Knopf, 1971), is a model of compressed speculation in action. Once again he deals with the conflict between social order and a rebellious alien, in retelling the Anglo-Saxon *Beowulf* from the viewpoint of the monster Grendel, whom he transforms into a tortured, complex being—at once a nihilistic man-eating brute destined to be killed by Beowulf, and a comic, but pathetic figure doomed by his longing for human beings, the "patternmakers" of poetry and beauty. Unable to subscribe either to order or chaos, Grendel becomes the evil force that makes affirmation possible for men in song and heroic action. Complicated in structure, sometimes farcical, *Grendel* is written in prose whose eloquence often approaches poetry. It was described by Richard Locke in the New York *Times* (September 4, 1971) as "very funny, original, and deft, altogether lovable, poignant, rich with thought and feeling," a work that made Gardner "a major contemporary writer." It was named as one of 1971's best works of fiction by both *Time* and *Newsweek* magazines.

One critic has said that *The Wreckage of Agathon* and *Grendel* are like "small jewels, scholarly tours de force almost, and flawed to a degree by [their] remoteness." In contrast, Gardner's next novel, *The Sunlight Dialogues* (Knopf, 1972), represents an ambitious attempt to locate no less than a total myth for contemporary America in the midst of the quotidian realities of life in Batavia during the 1960's. A sprawling saga that drew comparisons with Melville, James, and Faulkner, *The Sunlight Dialogues* soon made the best-seller lists. Mixing philosophy and reportage, it ranges through subjects as varied as law, justice, religion, politics, myth, magic, time, and good and evil. Although its multileveled, many-stranded plot involves dozens of characters, it is essentially the story of Batavia's aging police chief, Fred Clumly, and of an escaped prisoner from Clumly's jail, the Sunlight Man, who, in a Cain-like fall from grace as a member of one of the town's leading families, has become a daemonic, anarchistic magician, the embodiment, as one reviewer said, "of all that is newly restless, newly rebellious in the American spirit." The two men struggle in the dialogues of the title, Clumly in an inflexible defense of the social order, his antagonist in a perverse mockery of ethical conventions. Ultimately Clumly learns, as Susan Strehle put it in an essay in *Critique* (1976), "that justice is obscure and that compassion is the only adequate response to the gloomy confusion of human motives. Clumly's growth localizes and justifies the tentative affirmation, the hope for blessing, that the novel offers."

In *Jason and Medeia* (Knopf, 1973), a "Homeric" epic poem of twenty-four books that retells in freely syllabic hexameter lines one of the major Greek legend cycles, Gardner returned to ancient material in a display of what critics agreed was "his amazing virtuoso dexterity." Drawing upon Euripides, Pindar, Apollonius, and other sources, Gardner spins a dark, sometimes satirical tale of defeated faith and ideals in Jason's quest for the Golden Fleece and Medeia's revenge when he abandons her in Corinth. Jason relates his own past adventures in flashbacks, with intermittent intrusions by "a poet from the world's last age," who is John Gardner himself. For that distortion of an imitative form, as well as for other faults, D. S. Carne-Ross scored *Jason and Medeia* as "a full-scale literary disaster" in the *New York Review of Books* (October 4, 1973), but other critics praised its imaginative daring, rhetorical brilliance, and sharply drawn actions, reminiscent of Robert Graves or Robinson Jeffers.

In another abrupt turnabout, Gardner returned to the simplicity and directness of his first novel in *Nickel Mountain* (Knopf, 1973). Since it was his fifth book in three years, it led critics to speculate upon both his fecundity and the sequence in which his works were written. Their questions were answered in Gardner's interview with J. D. Bellamy, in which he described himself as a slow, methodical writer. "But when you've been writing for fifteen years and nobody liking you," he said, "you do build up a backlog. I've been publishing an early work, a late work, an early work." He then identified *Grendel* and *Jason and Medeia* as recent, *The Sunlight Dialogues* as early, and *Nickel Mountain* as very early.

Paradoxically, the originality of *Nickel Mountain* lies in its submission to the ancient literary form named in its subtitle, "A Pastoral Novel." Set in the Catskills of New York during the 1950's, the novel makes a case for the ordinariness of plainspoken country people such as its main character, Henry Soames, the middle-aged and fat proprietor of a truck diner, the meeting place for some of the area's most garish and destructive types. Told unpretentiously and concretely, without Gardner's usual overt philosophical interludes, *Nickel Mountain* is the story of Soames's marriage out of kindness to a pregnant teenager deserted by her lover, and of his growth in perceptivity with the long passage of time. Soames survives his vicissitudes through innocence and decency, becoming in the process one of Gardner's most sympathetic characters.

A collection of eight short stories and a novella (the title piece), *The King's Indian* (Knopf, 1974) contains such a wealth of technical variety and literary derivations that one reviewer described Gardner as "the Lon Chaney of contemporary literature . . . a writer of enormous range and inventiveness." Labeled by Gardner "a celebration of all literature and life," the book echoes writers from Homer to Kafka, sometimes with arch playfulness. To some reviewers, Gardner's gallery of fairy tales, Poe-like horror stories, allegories, sea yarns, romances, and realistic slices of life seemed self-indulgent, and show-offish, traits of a writer perhaps "too cunning for his own good." But others found his self-consciousness made tolerable by immaculate craftsmanship and thematic intensity. Two pieces won repeated acclaim: "The King's Indian," a long sea-detective story about a ghostly whaling ship reminiscent of Melville's *Pequod;* and "Pastoral care," a moving encounter between an up-to-date Presbyterian minister and a student "into revolution" who "bombs things."

October Light (Knopf, 1976), a novel appropriately published in America's bicentennial year, takes place on a granitic farm near Bennington, Vermont, where Gardner had moved after leaving Illinois. It chronicles the struggle between two aged, muleheaded Vermonters—James Page, who views America's past as uplifting and its present as rubbish; and his octogenarian sister, Sally, who celebrates the liberating present she sees on her television set, including woman's lib and the sexual revolution. Driven to her bedroom after her brother destroys the set, Sally sulkily plots revenge and reads a trashy modern novel, *The Smuggler of Lost Soul's Rock,* which Gardner unravels as a novel within a novel, one of the many devices that add dimension and complexity to his brooding pastoral comedy. *October Light* won a National Book Critics' award for fiction.

In *On Moral Fiction* (Basic Books, 1978), Gardner presents his manifesto on the destitute state of contemporary writing and on the life-affirming relationships that should exist among art, criticism, and values. An essay of separate pronouncements rather than a tightly reasoned argument, *On Moral Fiction* stands upon familiar and time-tested views of the artist as moral agent. Art is good, Gardner declares, "only when it has a clear positive moral effect, presenting valid models for imitation, eternal verities worth keeping in mind, and a benevolent vision of the possible which can incite human beings towards virtue." Some reviews found Gardner's strictures upon his contemporaries (Bellow, Heller, Updike, Mailer, Vonnegut, and others) "harsh but invariably shrewd and worthy of attention," but many saw his overall argument as deficient, less a convincing explanation of the current situation in art than an extended apologia for his kind of writing.

Even before the appearance of *On Moral Fiction,* critics had discovered beneath Gardner's remarkable variety of experiments in form a basically conservative writer, a man dedicated to those "eternal verities" he finds in his literary sources—whether he draws upon them forthrightly as in *Grendel* and *Jason and Medeia,* or indirectly for allusions and thematic referents in his contemporary settings. As Paul Gray pointed out in *Time* (December 30, 1974), his strategy frequently "sets conflicting metaphysics whirling, then records the patterns thrown out by their lines of force." Gardner sometimes remains neutral in presenting those conflicts; more often he sides with traditional literary values such as truth, love, faith, innocence, beauty, repudiating both a nihilistic world view and the angst-ridden society that view produces. The main targets of adverse criticism, therefore, have been Gardner's bookishness and philosophical bent, which give his work, said one reviewer, "an element of the arbitrary, of the willed, that too often interrupts the natural momentum of his material." Nevertheless, Gardner has repeatedly been identified as a major writer with multiple talents: verbal eloquence, imaginative invention, extraordinary powers of execution, a humane intelligence, and a well-stocked mind. He takes a place beside such figures as Cheever and Updike, said one critic, "as one of the presiding portrayers of life in late 20th-century America."

John Gardner is of medium height, with a "tidy barrel of a body," shoulder-length silver hair, a youthful Buster Brown face, and very light eyes. He wears country clothes and work boots, smokes a churchwarden pipe, and is quick in his movements, soft and rapid in his speech. On June 6, 1958 he married Joan Louise Patterson, a pianist, composer, and music teacher, who has collaborated so closely with him in his writing that, as he told J. D. Bellamy, "Perhaps I should have used 'John and Joan Gardner' on the titles all along." They have two children, Joel and Lucy, who along with their mother, contributed to and illustrated *A Child's Bestiary* (1977). Gardner's other stories and poems for children include *Dragon, Dragon* (1975), *Gudekin the Thistle Girl* (1976), and *In the Suicide Mountains* (1977).

Gardner rides a motorcycle and plays French horn—two sides of him that escape resolution. "I am on the one hand a kind of New York State Republican, conservative," he says. "On the other hand, I am a kind of bohemian type." Gardner has written librettos for two operas by Joseph Baber, *Frankenstein* and *Rumpelstiltskin* and although he candidly admits to being one of the best of today's writers, when once asked by an interviewer how he wants to be remembered, he replied, "As the greatest librettist of the twentieth century."

References: Atlantic 239:43+ My '77 pors; Washington Post p25 Ja 24 '77, p23 N 6 '77 pors; J. D. Bellamy, The New Fiction (1974); Contemporary Authors vols 65-68 (1977); Conversations with Writers (1977)

Geldzahler, Henry

July 9, 1935- New York City government official; art historian. Address: b. Department of Cultural Affairs, City of New York, 830 Fifth Ave., New York City, N.Y. 10021

In December 1977 Henry Geldzahler ended his colorful and at times controversial seventeen-year association with the Metropolitan Museum of Art to join New York City Mayor-elect Edward I. Koch's administration as cultural affairs commissioner. An art historian, Geldzahler rose from curatorial assistant in contemporary art to curator of the museum's newly created department of twentieth-century art in only seven years. Because of his personal involvement in the Pop Art movement of the 1960's, he was often at odds with some of the museum's mossbacked trustees. Nevertheless, he managed to generate an interest in collecting and exhibiting contemporary art, and his mammoth exhibition of mid-twentieth-century American painting and sculpture was the *succès de scandale* of the Metropolitan's centennial celebration in 1970. Since assuming his new post in January 1978, Geldzahler has devoted most of his time to fundraising.

Descended from Polish-Jewish immigrants who had settled in the Low Countries in the nineteenth century, Henry Geldzahler was born in Antwerp, Belgium on July 9, 1935. He is the younger of the two sons of Joseph Geldzahler, a prosperous diamond broker, and

Henry Geldzahler

Charlotte (Gutwirth) Geldzahler. Because Mrs. Geldzahler had spent part of her youth in the United States and was a naturalized American citizen, it was relatively easy for the family to arrange immigration to the United States when World War II broke out. Just a few weeks before the German invasion in 1940, the Geldzahlers fled Belgium and took up residence in New York City, where Joseph Geldzahler soon established a thriving business.

Henry Geldzahler attended the local public elementary schools in his Upper West Side neighborhood, then went on to the prestigious Horace Mann School for his college preparatory work. There he finally overcame the speech impediment that had been the underlying cause of his poor scholastic performance up to that time and rose to the top of his class. It was while he was a high school student that Geldzahler decided on his future career. "I'd been hanging around museums since I was fourteen," he explained to Francesco Scavullo in an interview for *Scavullo on Men* (Random House, 1977). "I went to see [an Arshile] Gorky show at the Whitney Museum in 1950, when I was fifteen. And I came home and threw up, then slept for eighteen hours. I was completely knocked out, and that's when I first realized that art could be that moving or upsetting. I went back two days later and the same thing happened. When I was seventeen, I came home and said I wanted to be a curator."

After graduating from Horace Mann, Geldzahler enrolled at Yale University, where he majored in art history. He spent virtually every weekend visiting New York museums and galleries and, during the summer of his sophomore year, worked as a volunteer in the Metropolitan Museum's department of European paintings. He spent his junior year in Paris, studying at the Ecole du Louvre and at the Sorbonne's Institut d'Art et d'Archéologie, then returned to Yale for his senior year and graduated, *magna cum laude,* with a B.A. degree in 1957.

Immediately Geldzahler went on to Harvard University to work on a Ph.D. degree. In addition to taking a full load of graduate units, he taught undergraduate courses in the fine arts. Remembered by his students as a knowledgeable and conscientious but rather dull lecturer, Geldzahler was in his off-hours an amusing conversationalist. His seemingly inexhaustible supply of information about a vast range of subjects made him a popular figure at campus coffeehouses despite his reputation for having what one former classmate has since described as a "low threshold of boredom."

Shortly after he completed his course work and passed his preliminary doctoral examinations, Geldzahler was asked by James J. Rorimer, then the director of the Metropolitan Museum of Art, to join its staff. Because of his interest in twentieth-century art, Geldzahler bluntly told Rorimer that he would prefer to work for the Whitney Museum of American Art. A few weeks later, Rorimer again offered him a job, this time as curatorial assistant in contemporary art in the Metropolitan's department of American painting and sculpture. Geldzahler immediately accepted and left Harvard in mid-1960 without completing his doctoral dissertation on the sculpture of Henri Matisse.

With the encouragement of Robert Beverly Hale, the head of the department of American art, Geldzahler spent most of the next two years out of the museum, visiting artists' studios and scouring out-of-the-way galleries for examples of current trends in contemporary American art. "I didn't have fixed ideas about art being this or that," he explained to Scavullo. "Instead, I had a strong background in art history and could relate whatever I was seeing to traditional art. . . . I was associated with the avant-garde, but my training was so classical that nothing really freaked me out." Geldzahler once traced the lineage of Lichtenstein's cartoon-like paintings back through Stuart Davis and Fernand Léger to Jacques-Louis David and Nicolas Poussin. He often fell back on his ability to "legitimatize . . . things that freaked a lot of people out" to defend his proposed purchases to more conservative Metropolitan authorities.

Contending that "the artist . . . decides what is art," Geldzahler was an early promoter of Pop Art and helped to establish the reputations of such then unknown artists as Jules Olitski, Helen Frankenthaler, Kenneth Noland, Robert Rauschenberg, James Rosenquist, Roy Lichtenstein, Frank Stella, Claes Oldenburg, and Jasper Johns. Much to the dismay of some staid Metropolitan trustees, Geldzahler was often more of an active participant in than an objective observer of the contemporary art scene. He was painted by Larry Rivers, Marcia Marcus, Alice Neel, David Hockney, and Frank Stella, sculpted in wood by Marisol, and cast in plaster by George Segal; he took part in several notorious "happenings" staged by Claes Oldenburg; and he appeared in Andy Warhol's monumentally boring experimental film, *Henry Geldzahler*, in which he smoked a cigar for ninety minutes.

As interest in Pop Art waned, Geldzahler devoted more time to expanding the Metropolitan's small collection of contemporary American art. In the spring of 1966 he took a leave of absence from the Metropolitan to serve as program director of visual arts for the National Council on the Arts, a government organization created to encourage and enrich the cultural resources of the United States. To "make it easier for the artist of quality to get on with his work," as he put it, Geldzahler made grants of $5,000 each to 119 artists of his own choosing; to make that work "more available" to the American public, he persuaded the Council to give to fifteen museums across the country matching grants of $10,000 to purchase art works by contemporary Americans. Furthermore, he was instrumental in the awarding of federal grants for the commission of original drawings for reproduction, the production of a comprehensive art history slide set for schools and libraries, and the formulation of a federal housing assistance program geared to the special needs of artists.

Asked by the director of the National Collection of Fine Arts to choose the artists who would represent the United States in the thirteenth Venice International Biennale exhibition, Geldzahler settled on Helen Frankenthaler and Jules Olitski, both color-field painters, Ellsworth Kelly, an abstractionist painter, and Roy Lichtenstein. When a number of influential but conservative American art critics, including the editor of *Arts* magazine, denounced the selection of such "second-rate artists," Geldzahler defended his choice as "serious, weighty, and worthy of international exposure." Knowing his fondness for Pop Art, some critics speculated that Geldzahler personally favored Lichtenstein and the New York *Times*'s Hilton Kramer even went so far as to suggest that he was behind a "steamroller movement" to win first prize for that pop artist. Annoyed by the implication that he was part of the widespread backstage maneuvering, Geldzahler deplored "the mechanics and politics of prizes" in a public statement issued on June 14, 1966. "No committee or jury, no matter how constituted, can proclaim aesthetic quality," he said. According to some observers, his outburst may have prevented the Americans from taking the top international prize that year, but just two years later, the system of prizes and awards was abolished.

Returning to the Metropolitan in 1967, Geldzahler was promoted a few months later to curator of the museum's new department of contemporary arts, later the department of twentieth-century art, by Thomas P. F. Hoving, who had succeeded Rorimer as director. In its first eighteen months of existence, the new department staged only three small exhibitions, two of which were arranged by Hoving without Geldzahler's approval. Irritated, Geldzahler tendered his resignation, but Hoving persuaded him to stay on.

With Hoving's renewed support, Geldzahler expanded his department and made several major purchases. "The burden of what I'm trying to do is to catch up on what we missed during the last heroic period of painting," he explained to Calvin Tomkins in an interview for a *New Yorker* (November 6, 1971) profile. "I don't subscribe to Alfred Barr's idea that if one out of ten things you buy works out well, then you're doing a good job. That's all right for a museum that's devoted strictly to contemporary art, but I'm in the fortunate position of taking the long view, since I work for a museum that takes in the whole history of art."

For the Metropolitan's centennial celebration in 1970, Geldzahler put together a monumental exhibition of twentieth-century art that represented, in his words, "the culmination" of his ten years at the museum. Convinced that the New York School was "the historical successor to the School of Paris," he selected 400 representative pieces by forty-three artists whose work had, as he put it in the exhibition catalog, "commanded critical attention or significantly deflected the course of recent art." He further limited his choices to those artists whose "distinctive styles emerged and were viewed before 1965 in galleries, group shows, and museums." Among those artists not meeting Geldzahler's criteria were such luminaries as Larry Rivers, Robert Indiana, Louise Nevelson, Marisol, Jim Dine, and Richard Pousette-Dart.

Admittedly a personal "sorting out of major themes and figures," the exhibit included examples of abstract expressionism, "cool" realism, "soft" sculpture, and conceptual, minimalist, and op art. Explaining the absence of works by some pop artists whom he had enthusiastically supported in the 1960's, Geldzahler observed that while Pop Art had been an "interesting episode," it was "not a major movement which continues to spawn new artists."

After selecting each piece, choosing "familiar masterpieces" as well as "surprises" and "lesser-known works" by such artists as Barnett Newman, Robert Motherwell, Edward Hopper, Arshile Gorky, Willem de Kooning, Frank Stella, Helen Frankenthaler, Robert Rauschenberg, Mark Rothko, Mark di Suvero, and Alexander Calder, Geldzahler supervised the installation of the collection in the thirty-five galleries set aside for the show. Not interested in "fairness," but in "quality," he devoted entire rooms to the works of Jasper Johns, Jackson Pollock, Hans Hofmann, and Josef Albers. "I don't want anything to be uniform about this show," he told a reporter for *Newsweek* (October 20, 1969), "so some of the rooms show a miniature retrospective of an artist's work, others show examples from only one period of an artist's work, and others show the early work of a group of artists. . . . No period, not even the Renaissance, has ever had forty-three major artists."

When "New York Painting and Sculpture: 1940-1970" opened on October 18, 1969, some influential art critics immediately condemned it. The New York *Times*'s John Canaday called it "a boo-boo on the grand scale"; Hilton Kramer dismissed it as "modish, arbitrary, and confused"; Emily Genauer of *Newsday* belittled "Geldzahler's playground" as "another predictable assemblage" of works backed by the curator and "his coterie of taste-and-value makers"; and Harold Rosenberg, writing in the *New Yorker*, complained that the show was "merely the latest and largest in a series of survey exhibitions in which works of art are employed to serve the career strategies of the curator who assembled them or to call attention to their mental fixations." *New York* magazine's Barbara Goldsmith put it more succinctly: "The show is simply Geldzahler's choice. He could have called it 'Painters I Like.'" Other critics, citing the "insight," "evident love," and "extraordinary care" with which Geldzahler selected and installed the "stimulating" and "refreshing" exhibition, defended "Henry's show," as it came to be known in art circles. The controversy continued for a long time after the show closed.

Throughout the early 1970's Geldzahler acquired for the Metropolitan important pieces of contemporary art, concentrating on the areas in which its sister institutions, the Museum of Modern Art, the Whitney Museum of American Art, and the Guggenheim Museum, were weakest. His criteria for selection were "memorability" and a "visceral physical reaction." Although he and Everett Fahy, the curator of West European paintings, resisted the sale of some pieces, Geldzahler readily approved sales of paintings that were, as he put it, "not hangable in [his] galleries." In June 1972 he played a key role in the controversial secret trade of six paintings—a Modigliani, a Bonnard, two Juan Grises, a Picasso, and a Renoir—for two works by the contemporary artists David Smith and Richard Diebenkorn. His position at the museum was reportedly further weakened when he refused to organize the Andrew Wyeth exhibition that later proved to be extraordinarily popular with the public when mounted by other staff members. Because of the publicity accorded those controversies, it became increasingly clear that although Geldzahler was, as New York *Times* critic John Russell observed, "a gifted and knowledgeable curator of twentieth-century art," the Metropolitan had "neither a coherent collection nor a long-term policy" for the collection and preservation of contemporary art. Moreover, as Russell reported in the *Times* of December 14, 1977, Geldzahler's department increasingly found itself in "an isolated position in the Met's councils."

That untenable situation, coupled with Thomas Hoving's intention to retire as director of the museum at the end of 1977, apparently predisposed Henry Geldzahler to accept Mayor-elect Edward I. Koch's offer of the post of cultural affairs commissioner for New York City. Geldzahler was in Moscow to supervise the installation of an exchange exhibition of American paintings at the Pushkin Museum when the announcement was made public on December 13, 1977. In discussing the appointment with American correspondents, he compared the post to "that of commissioner of wheat in Kansas and spices in India." "Culture is our best crop," he said. "It nourishes and excites." Countering criticisms that, because of his background in the visual arts, he might slight the performing arts in the allocation of funds, Geldzahler told a reporter for the New York *Times* (December 13, 1977), "Whoever came to this would come to it from a field. I'm not a monoculture person. I have a great interest in ballet, theatre, and opera as well as the visual arts, and I'll try to be fair to all."

Because his new job included recommendations for city funding to the Metropolitan, Geldzahler resigned from the museum's staff to avoid conflict-of-interest charges, but he delayed his resignation long enough to present a number of prospective purchases to the Metropolitan's acquisitions committee. After taking his oath of office on January 10, 1978, Geldzahler immediately set out to provide "definition and visibility" to city programs in support of the arts that would, as he put it, "foster the new while preserving the best." Since most of the $24 million allotted to the department of cultural affairs is earmarked for the city's major cultural institutions, there is little money to support experimentation in the arts. To make up the deficit, Geldzahler immediately began soliciting funds from foundations and corporations to pay for specific projects and set up a special liaison office in Washington, D.C. to lobby for federal money.

A short, stocky man with blue eyes and a neatly trimmed beard, Henry Geldzahler, as more than one reporter has noted, bears a striking resemblance to Charles Laughton, the British actor. Belying the man-about-town image he cultivated in the 1960's, he rarely goes out, and when he does, he restricts himself to what he calls "fulcrum events." He prefers to spend his evenings in his townhouse near Washington Square, where he listens to classical music or reads Trollope, and his weekends at his rented home in Southampton, New York. Still fascinated by artists "for whom the world isn't quite ready," he collects works by Edward Avedesian, Michael Hurson, Richard Hennessey, Christopher Wilmarth, Stephen Buckley, and others.

References: Life 60:41+ F 18 '66 pors; N Y Herald Tribune Mag p14+ N 21 '65 pors; N Y Times C p19 D 14 '77 por; New Yorker 47:58+ N 6 '71; Washington Post F p1 Ja 15 '67 por; Scavullo, Francesco. Scavullo on Men (1977); Who's Who in America, 1978-79; Who's Who in American Art, 1976

Geller, Uri

Dec. 20, 1946- Psychic. Address: b. Kadima Productions, Inc., P.O. Box 5175, F.D.R. Station, New York City, N.Y. 10002

Parapsychology's current sensation is the controversial Uri Geller, an Israeli with seemingly paranormal powers who moved to the United States six years ago. Geller rejects the title "psychic," thinking of himself rather as the instrument of "some great, intelligent interspatial energy." The powers that allegedly come to or through him—seldom on cue, it might be noted—are in the areas of clairvoyance and telepathy to some degree, but his celebrity rests on his purported feats of psychokinesis, the power of mind over matter. Aside from his mightier claims (which include levitation and translocation of objects, projecting his image to film through a closed camera lens, and halting cable cars and escalators), Geller professes routinely to bend or break metal objects such as keys, cutlery, and nails and to start watches virtually by mental force alone, with perhaps a touch of the hand. In his contribution to *The Amazing Uri Geller* (1975), edited by Martin Ebon, Robert Brier reported witnessing, close-up, a demonstration by Geller, and in doing so he pinpointed the essence of the controversy over him: "What he does seems very much like a magician's act, but no magician can duplicate it under the same conditions. That is, it fails to meet scientific standards, but is not a clear case of fraud."

Uri Geller was born in Tel Aviv, Israel on December 20, 1946, the only child of Itzhaak Geller, a professional soldier who had emigrated from Hungary, and Berlin-born Margarete (Freud) Geller, a seamstress and hotel-keeper who is, according to her son, a distant relative of Sigmund Freud, the founder of psychoanalysis. In his autobiography, *Uri Geller: My Story* (Praeger, 1975), Geller recalls a mystical experience he had at the age of three or four that he "connects" with his "ability." He was playing alone in a garden near his home in Tel Aviv when suddenly there was a high-pitched ringing in his ears; all other sounds ceased, and the trees stopped moving in the wind, "as if time stood still." Looking up at the sky, he saw "a silvery mass of light" coming toward him. "This was not the sun, and I knew it. The light was too close to me *[and]* the color was brilliant. I felt as if I had been knocked over backward. There was a sharp pain in my forehead. Then I was knocked out. I lost consciousness completely. I don't know how long I lay there, but when I woke I rushed home and told my mother. She was angry and worried. Deep down, I knew something important happened."

From about the time of the strange happening, Geller's mother recalls, Uri could often read her mind, anticipating what she was going to say to him and telling her how much she had won or lost at cards.

In school, where he was bored and unhappy, the hands of his wristwatch would race ahead, as if in sympathetic response to his wishes. He called the attention of classmates and teachers to the phenomenon, until he realized it made them laugh at him. At the age of eight or nine he began having trouble with silverware: spoons would bend or break in his hand, spilling soup in his lap, or flatware on the table would curl up without his even touching it. If friends or outsiders were present, as in restaurants, his mother would become embarrassed at what others considered his "clumsiness" or "mischievousness." "My mother gradually began to accept it, but only up to a point," Geller remembers. "When I told her of the things that would happen at school, she finally said she didn't want to hear anything more. . . . When my father was home they *[talked]* about taking me to a psychiatrist. They were hoping I would outgrow this strange thing." Geller himself learned to conceal his "difference."

After his parents separated, Geller lived in a kibbutz until his mother remarried and took him with her to live with his stepfather, Ladislas Gero, on the island of Cyprus, where Gero ran a small hotel in Nicosia. On Cyprus, Geller, who already spoke Hebrew, Hungarian, and some German, learned to speak English and some Greek. He attended a Roman Catholic secondary school, Terra Sancta College, situated on a hill overlooking Nicosia, where a lay English teacher, Mrs. Julie Agrotis, noticed and encouraged the "strange energy powers" that he had been trying to hide. "I still remembered all the teasing I used to take back in Tel Aviv, and I didn't want that to start up again," Geller recounts. "But I had some problems. I was not a bad student, but I certainly wasn't a good one. During some examinations, when I was stuck for an answer, I would *[select]* the brightest kid in the subject, concentrate on the back of his head, and come up with the answers." Other teachers accused him of copying, but Mrs. Agrotis was "sure this wasn't something ordinary happening," especially when, as Geller recalls, he "began picking up her thoughts, in words, on this crazy screen in my mind." Put at ease by the sympathetic teacher, Geller showed her how he could bend keys and spoons and start broken watches, and he engaged in experiments in telepathy with her.

Following the death of Ladislas Gero, Geller and his mother moved back to Israel, where Uri became an army paratrooper. Wounded in the Six-Day War of 1967, he was first sent to a rehabilitation center and then given a three-month vacation leave. During the leave he worked as a counselor at a summer camp, where one of his charges was a twelve-year-old boy named Shipi Strang, with whom he became fast friends and discovered an extraordinary extrasensory rapport, as he recounted in an interview with the editors of *Psychic* (June 1973): "I would demonstrate things to them [Shipi and his sister, Hannah] and discovered that when *[Shipi]* was around I could do unbelievable things, like reading his mind and passing thoughts to him. One day he came to me and asked if I'd perform at his school, which would pay me ten dollars for my time. I agreed and appeared for nearly four hours; the students wouldn't let me stop and the teachers were really impressed. That was the beginning. Word got around and I was invited to perform at other schools. Then an article about me appeared in the paper, and the whole thing just grew, very rapidly and large. Agents began contacting me."

Released from military service at the end of 1968, Geller worked as a photographer's model and handled the export correspondence of a Tel Aviv textile company until March 1970, when he signed with a talent manager and became a full-time professional entertainer. Beginning with an engagement at the Kolno'ah, a theatre in Bat Yam, he had bookings before standing-room-only audiences at theatres and clubs throughout Israel, and within months his name was a household word in the country—a word eventually tainted by rumors of fraud. The rumors were partly correct, as Geller admits in his autobiography: "I would do telepathy while members of the audience wrote or drew things on a blackboard; pass thoughts directly into people's minds; describe what people were wearing without looking at them; start up watches that hadn't run for some time; bend keys and other objects they brought in; and then have a question-and-answer period. All the experiments would work about 70 or 80 percent of the time [but] the manager came and told me . . . there ought to be more to the act."

The "more" was a stage trick: "He [the manager] would watch people get out of their cars and write down their license plate numbers. Then he would have them ushered to selected seats as they came into the theatre. He'd give me the numbers before I started the demonstrations, and I would point to these people and tell them their license plate numbers. I [being] young and inexperienced [did not] know that this power, this force, this unknown energy was going to be taken so seriously by the scientific world [but] I hated myself every time I did it [the license plate trick]."

Andrija Puharich, an American physician and neurophysiologist who has made important contributions to psychic research and to medical electronics, went to Israel to look first-hand into the "Geller effect" in August 1971. Puharich impressed Geller as a "hippie Einstein"; Geller, Puharich became convinced, was "the ambassador of an advanced civilization," the "intermediary between [extraterrestrial] messengers and earth people." Together, as they reported in their respective books, they experienced UFO sightings and heard "voices," among other purported encounters with higher intelligences.

With the assistance of Captain Edgar D. Mitchell, the astronaut who walked on the moon during the Apollo 14 mission and who since had been devoting himself to "theoretical and applied consciousness research," Puharich brought Geller to the United States in 1972 to be tested at the Stanford Research Institute (which has no connection with Stanford University) in Menlo Park, California. In the tests, conducted under the scientists Harold E. Puthoff and Russell Targ, Geller correctly read the roll of dice in a closed metal box in eight out of eight guesses (two additional times, he passed, venturing no reading), overcoming odds of a million to one; against odds of a trillion to one, he twelve times divined which of ten identical film cans contained ball bearings or other objects and which were empty; he caused a laboratory balance under a bell jar to respond as if a force were applied to its pan; without touching the measuring head of the instrument, he caused a deflection of the chart recorder monitoring the magnetometer output of a Bell gaussmeter; and in a shielded room he reproduced, with a reasonable degree of correspondence, random drawings done by researchers outside the room. The S.R.I. experiments with Geller were documented in a twenty-five-minute S.R.I. film, *Experiments with Uri Geller*, and reported by Puthoff and Targ in a paper published in the prestigious British journal *Nature* (October 18, 1974) under the title "Information Transmission Under Conditions of Sensory Shielding."

Simultaneously with the publication of Puthoff and Targ's report in *Nature*, the British physicist Joseph Hanlon published an article in the *New Scientist* (October 17, 1974) challenging the worth of the S.R.I. tests. "A dry scientific paper can never capture the feelings of an experiment," Hanlon wrote. "In this case the Targ-Puthoff paper totally fails to communicate the circus atmosphere that surrounded all of the tests with Geller. As Targ commented to me: 'Deliberately or accidentally, Geller manipulates the experiments to a degree of chaos where he feels comfortable and we feel uncomfortable. Then he bends something.' "

Actually, Puthoff and Targ made no claims for Geller's alleged ability to affect metal by force of his mind, but in later tests, including those at the University of London and the laboratory of the Foch hospital in Suresnes, France, Geller reportedly bent metal without touching it. After European television appearances by him, especially in England, Germany, and Scandinavia, stations were flooded with calls from viewers who claimed that forks, spoons, and other metal objects in their homes had bent while Geller was demonstrating on TV.

Geller made his first major public appearance in New York City at Town Hall on September 25, 1973. Typically, that performance (or demonstration, as he prefers to call it)—approximately the one-thousandth of his career—began with a half-dozen telepathy readings in which he asked the audience to concentrate on a word written on a blackboard that he could not see. The readings, some of which failed, were followed by a question-and-answer period in which Geller established a strong rapport with the audience. "The audience loved it. . . ." Jay Levin reported in the New York *Post* (September 26, 1973). "He asked for broken watches, had several women hold them in their hands, held his hands over theirs and concentrated. None of the watches started ticking. 'Okay, no, I did my best,' he said with a shrug. Then he asked for heavy rings to bend. [Again] no success. Finally, when it seemed he was about to quit in disgust for the night, Geller shrugged and offered to try just one more. When the woman opened her hands, Geller gasped faintly and raised the ring aloft, holding it seemingly lightly by the bottom. The heavy metal slowly spread apart [until] the ring was fully spread out and twisted."

When Dotson Rader interviewed Geller for *Esquire* (March 1976), he experienced a "nightmarish" series of poltergeist phenomena, including a wooden sculpture flying across the living room of Geller's apartment. Rader, "too scared to move," was reassured by Geller: "It is nothing. It happens all the time." Rader was not reassured: "His attitude was so dissimilar to my own, more . . . like a mother with an unmanageable, if unseen child making mischief in the house [that he] seemed suddenly foreign to me, unlike me in some essential way."

Abraham Weinberg, a doctor and a self-described meditherapist and psychosomaticist who was asked by the editors of *Esquire* to comment on Rader's article, said that Rader "could have been hypnotized, either by self-inducement or by someone else. . . . Most of what occurred, however, described but not explained, must remain a mystery." Those more skeptical of Geller's "powers" have offered various explanations other than hypnosis for the effects he achieves. James Zwinge, a professional magician whose stage name is The Amazing Randi, the fiercest of Geller's critics, says flatly that he is a fraud, a sleight-of-hand artist posing as a Messiah. "Geller brings disgrace to the craft I practice . . . ," Randi wrote in *The Magic of Uri Geller* (1976). "I am angered at Geller and his ilk, who have wasted the valuable time and talents of these men [the scientists who have tested him]—not to mention huge amounts of money—by leading them to believe in supposed miracles."

Others find significance in the fact that Andrija Puharich is the inventor of a microelectronic device for the deaf, a receiver small enough to be implanted in the teeth. No knowledgeable observers doubt the integrity of Puharich, but there are those who suspect that in his demonstrations of clairvoyance or telepathy Geller might somehow be in electronic communication with, say, Shipi Strang, who usually (although not always) tours with him. As for psychokinesis, when a spoon bent and broken "paranormally" by Geller was examined by the Federal Institute for Material Testing in Berlin, Germany at the request of the editors of the German news magazine *Der Spiegel*, researchers at the institute suggested that the break might have been caused by the application of silver nitrate.

But, as Paul Langdon observed in the article he contributed to *The Amazing Uri Geller*, "a layman is inclined to doubt such chemical conjuring as too elaborate a trick for Geller's seemingly free-and-easy performances, and for the frequency with which he does this sort of thing." Langdon points out that even the stage magicians who view Geller as "nothing but another magician, but with a good gimmick," tend to agree that he is "much too impatient and jumpy, has too short a span of attention" for "elaborate mechanisms." "The magicians say that his personality [or] the way he projects it is [his] greatest asset. He comes on with a mixture of bafflement about his own ability and a childlike delight whenever something goes right. [Geller's] patter has a pattern: he is very tired but will try his best; he apologizes for being on the run but is gracious and disarming, eager to please, downhearted when things don't come out all right. The audience is on his side, eager, in fact, to please him by going along, possibly by seeing and testifying to something of which it is not fully convinced."

Many magicians have called Geller a master of "distraction" and "misdirection," and Robert Brier in his article in *The Amazing Uri Geller* corroborates that description: "Just as in a magic show, Geller pretty well calls the shots. He tells people what to hold, when to hold it, and so on. Also, as in a magician's show, Geller seems to carefully manipulate the audience's attention: while we were watching Geller attempt something else, the key [with which he had earlier failed] bent. Geller then pointed out the amazing fact to us." In his summation at the end of the book, Martin Ebon wrote: "I do believe that Uri Geller may have psychic abilities—but also that he helps them along, in psychological and physical ways, to gain maximum dramatic effect, admiration, fame and money. The argument about his psychic power will certainly never end."

In addition to his demonstrations on the lecture and TV talk show circuit, Geller has been writing poetry and, reportedly, science fiction. "Poems come to me in strange ways," he has said. "I don't think I write them myself." Some of his poems, set to music by his friend Byron Janis the pianist (whom he believes to be a reincarnation of Chopin), may be heard on an album released by CBS Records. On the LP, Geller himself does the reading, backed up by vocalist Maxine Nightingale and a choir.

A handsome man of commanding presence, Uri Geller is six feet two inches tall, tries to keep his weight down to 170 pounds, and has piercing dark eyes, thick black hair, a manner that has been described as "nervous" but "ingratiating" and "charming," and a casual but sleek wardrobe. "The impression he makes," Dotson Rader wrote in his article in *Esquire*, "is that of a highly successful fashion model, which he was in Israel, or a movie star, something he badly wants to be." Andrija Puharich has described him as "a nice Jewish kid interested in cars and girls" who can be "like a temperamental rock star." Others have referred to Geller's "narcissism" and "vanity," and Geller himself confesses to having "a very healthy ego." In an interview with Martin Ebon for *The Amazing Uri Geller*, Captain Edgar D. Mitchell said: "Uri is a very warm, personable, human sort of young fellow, energetic, eager, and bouncy. But as he has received more attention . . . his ego has asserted itself and he [has] become more demanding, irascible, and difficult to work with."

Geller now resides permanently in Manhattan, in a luxury apartment on the Upper East Side, and English is now, he says, the language that he thinks in. "I like to live a full, well-rounded life," Geller says. "I like television and films and sports. I like to date girls, to travel, and to meet people everywhere." One thing he does not like to do, and does not do, he has said on several occasions, is read books, because he does "not want to change [his] theories." In her article in *The Amazing Uri Geller*, Mary Bringle writes: "He makes no claims to intellectualism and operates only as an instinctual and highly developed instrument for powers outside himself. [But] the triviality of Uri's miracles has prompted more than one expression of impatience."

References: Esquire 85:116+ Mr '76 por; Viva 2:20 S '75 por; Ebon, Martin, ed. The Amazing Uri Geller (1975); Geller, Uri. My Story (1975); Panati, Charles, ed. The Geller Papers (1976); Puharich, Andrija. Uri: A Journal of the Mystery of Uri Geller (1974); Randi. The Magic of Uri Geller (1976)

Giamatti, A(ngelo) Bartlett

April 4, 1938- President of Yale University. Address: b. Office of the President, Yale University, New Haven, Conn. 06520; h. Hillhouse Avenue, New Haven, Conn.

As the new president of Yale University, America's third-oldest institution of higher learning, A. Bartlett Giamatti is faced with some difficult decisions. Since 1970 the university has been operating at a deficit, and with the value of its endowment dropping because of inflation, it can no longer sustain the extensive programs it began during an era of greater prosperity. Giamatti, a respected scholar of medieval and Renaissance literature, and one of Yale's most popular professors of English and comparative literature, must find ways of saving money without endangering Yale's educational excellence. Because he is known to be a man who values the traditional educational verities, Yale's teachers and students are confident that he will manage that difficult achievement, and in addition bring new vitality and color to the university community.

Angelo Bartlett Giamatti was born on April 4, 1938 in Boston, Massachusetts. His father, Valentine Giamatti, a 1932 Yale graduate, taught Italian at Mount Holyoke College, where he is now a professor emeritus. His mother, Mary (Claybaugh Walton) Giamatti, graduated from Smith College in 1935.

"Bart" Giamatti grew up in South Hadley, Massachusetts, which is near Springfield. Although not himself an athlete, he developed a lifelong interest in sports, especially baseball. From an early age he displayed an aptitude for languages and literature, which his parents encouraged. He learned Italian from his father while still a child, and often took part in dinner-table conversations on such topics as Dante's *Divine Comedy*. After attending South Hadley High School for a time, Giamatti spent a year at the International School of Rome while his father was in Italy on a sabbatical leave. He completed his secondary education at Phillips Academy in Andover, Massachusetts and then entered Yale, where he majored in English and was elected to the exclusive Scroll and Key Society.

In 1960 Giamatti obtained his B.A. degree *magna cum laude* from Yale College. He then went on to the Yale Graduate School as an honorary Woodrow Wilson Fellow. Sustained by a Woodrow Wilson Fellowship and guided by the supervision of Professor Lowry Nelson Jr., he received his Ph.D. degree in comparative literature in 1964, after submitting a doctoral dissertation on "The Earthly Paradise in the Renaissance Epic." As a graduate student, Giamatti had taught Italian at the Yale Summer Language Institute in 1961 and 1962. Entering upon his full-time teaching career, in the autumn of 1964 he became an instructor in Italian and comparative literature at Princeton University. Giamatti was promoted to assistant professor in 1965, and in the autumn of 1966, after teaching a summer course at New York University as a visiting professor of comparative literature, he joined the Yale faculty as an assistant professor of English.

Giamatti advanced rapidly through the academic ranks at Yale, becoming an associate professor of English in 1968, an associate professor of English and comparative literature in 1970, and a full professor in 1971. Outside the classroom he served as Master of Ezra Stiles College, one of Yale's twelve undergraduate residential colleges, from 1970 to 1972 and as director of the university's Visiting Faculty Program from 1974 to 1976. During three summer sessions, 1972, 1973, and 1974, he taught at the Bread Loaf School of English, at Ripton, Vermont. In 1976 Giamatti became Frederick Clifford Ford Professor of English and Comparative Literature and director of the Division of the Humanities in Yale's Faculty of Arts and Sciences, but he relinquished the Ford chair in 1977 to assume the newly founded John Hay Whitney Professorship of English and Comparative Literature. In the spring semester of 1977 he also served as associate director of the National Humanities Institute at Yale.

During those years Giamatti came to be known as both a teacher and a scholar, two fields of endeavor that too many university professors seem to regard as mutually exclusive. Teaching was in some respects his first love, something that he did so well and so enjoyed doing that he gave up the Ezra

Stiles post in 1972 because its administrative responsibilities kept him out of the classroom. Unlike many of his colleagues, Giamatti was as much at home in basic freshman courses as in advanced electives and graduate seminars. Always interested in undergraduates, he devoted much of his time to planning Yale's freshman English program.

A traditionalist in his views on education, Giamatti favored a more structured curriculum with fewer optional courses, and he often spoke out against the vogue for unmarked or pass-fail courses, explaining that "students are owed a sense that the faculty knows what is important, which means setting reasonable demands and holding to them." He also favored an intensive freshman writing program, because, as Giamatti explained in a New York *Times* interview (December 25, 1977), "the question of writing is crucial. It is the fundamental pedagogical problem in American education at all levels: How do you get people to write clearly and in an organized fashion? That means nothing other than how do you get them to think clearly."

His educational conservatism notwithstanding, Yale's student body responded to Giamatti with great enthusiasm, packing his classes in such subjects as epic poetry and Renaissance literature to overflowing, although because of his reputation as a tough marker, many preferred to sit in as auditors rather than take the courses for credit. One of his students, as quoted in the New York *Times* (December 21, 1977), has said of Giamatti: "He's the best English teacher I've ever had. He makes you excited about the subject even if you're not."

Giamatti's scholarly reputation is largely based on the revised version of his doctoral dissertation, *The Earthly Paradise and the Renaissance Epic,* which was published in 1966 by Princeton University Press. In that analysis of the works of classical and medieval authors and of such Renaissance poets as Petrarch, Ariosto, Camoëns, Spenser, and Milton, he examined "the desire for a state of repose and life eternal [that] has always haunted mankind." That idea of a "blessed place," or earthly garden, he demonstrated, recurred in the Western literary tradition from ancient times through the end of the Renaissance. It then disappeared as a significant literary theme, not because man no longer sought "the lost state of bliss and innocence" that the garden represented, but because he had lost that Renaissance sense of tolerance, spaciousness, and inclusiveness; that faith in man, in ourselves, which the earthly paradises . . . always implied."

By and large, the response to *The Earthly Paradise* was highly favorable. John L. Lievsay, in *Comparative Literature Studies* (1967), commended Giamatti for his "ingenious and painstaking detective work," while a reviewer for *Choice* (February 1967) praised the book as "a well written and significant study." Even Bernard F. Huppé, who in *Speculum* (July 1967) carped that Giamatti had not sustained his thesis, regarded the work as an important contribution. The general critical opinion was perhaps best summed up by Frances Yates in the *New York Review of Books* (February 28, 1967), who called Giamatti "a subtle psychologist, extremely sensitive to poetry," and added: "This is comparative literature as it ought to be done, not the superficial tracing of 'sources,' but the organic study of a theme at a deep level."

Giamatti has also written *The Play of Double Senses: Spenser's "Faerie Queene"* (Prentice-Hall, 1975), an introductory guide to the great English epic poem for undergraduates, which was appraised in *Choice* (July-August 1976) as "a balanced, coherent reading that is both enlightening and full of delight." He coedited *The Songs of Bernart de Ventadorn* (University of North Carolina Press, 1965), *A Variorum Commentary on the Poems of John Milton* (Columbia University Press, 1970), and, with Stewart A. Baker, an edition of the *Orlando Furioso* of Ariosto (Bobbs-Merrill, 1966), for which he prepared the introduction and bibliography. In addition, Giamatti served on the editorial board of the "Princeton Studies in English and Comparative Literature" from 1968 to 1971, and was the general editor of the three-volume anthology, *Western Literature* (Harcourt, 1971). His lifelong passion for sports is reflected in his articles on pitcher Tom Seaver and boxer Muhammad Ali that appeared in *Harper's*.

While Giamatti was teaching at Yale, that university was entering one of the most precarious periods in its almost 300-year history. Ironically, the crisis followed an era of optimism and expansion. In the 1960's, when the economic situation had been favorable, and funds had been forthcoming from foundations, wealthy alumni, and the government, Yale had experienced considerable growth, adding new programs and facilities, broadening its admissions policies to include more members of minority groups, and raising the quality of its student body and faculty.

As economic conditions deteriorated in the 1970's, however, Yale began to encounter grave financial problems. Its spending and investment policies, formulated in the affluence of the previous decade, proved eminently unsuitable in a time of plummeting stockmarket prices and double-digit inflation. The buying power of its $563 million endowment declined by 40 percent, and contributions began to fall off as well. As a result, by 1970-71 Yale was running a deficit of $2.6 million. The deficit continued to grow despite a freeze on nonacademic hiring and a 10 percent cut in the faculty, amounting to an accumulated total of $16 million by 1977, with increases predicted. To make matters worse, a few band-aid managerial reforms failed to have much of an effect on the outmoded administrative structure with which the university was saddled. A major fund-raising drive, however, begun in 1974 and scheduled to run through 1979, raised more than $250,000,000 of its $370,000,000 goal by mid-1978, despite the straitened economic climate and a certain restiveness among the alumni. Although largely loyal to Yale, they were unhappy about its lackluster athletic record and the liberal and activist image projected by President Kingman Brewster and University Chaplain William Sloane Coffin Jr.

When, in May 1976 Brewster resigned the Yale presidency to become ambassador to Great Britain, Hanna Holborn Gray, the provost, became the acting head, and the Yale Corporation named William P. Bundy, editor of *Foreign Affairs* and former CIA official, to chair a seven-member search committee charged with finding a new president. In the interim, Hanna Gray brought in an outside consultant to make a detailed study of Yale's grave financial plight. A special faculty committee was also appointed to come up with ways of reducing the deficit, and Giamatti became one of its members.

The eight-month effort to find a new president proved more arduous than had been anticipated, since word had gotten around that the person selected would have to bear the onus of making the radical cuts and operational changes demanded by Yale's budgetary crisis. The search committee worked in absolute secrecy, reportedly burning all leftover papers at the end of each session as if conducting a military intelligence operation, but news about its proceedings was continually leaked to reporters. Quite a number of prospects were considered, among them Richard Lyman and David Saxon, the presidents of Stanford and the University of California respectively, but most bowed out and others proved unsuitable.

The search finally narrowed down to two men, A. Bartlett Giamatti and Henry Rosovsky, the dean of Harvard's Faculty of Arts and Sciences. Early in December 1977 a formal offer was made to Rosovsky, but he turned it down, to the great embarrassment of members of the committee, who had been certain that he would accept. In the ensuing confusion, it sometimes looked, according to *Newsweek* (December 26, 1977) as if "the Yale presidency was the tag-end remnant of a garage sale." A few days later Giamatti was offered the post. He accepted, and on December 20 it was announced that he had been elected Yale's nineteenth president, effective July 1, 1978. Until that date Hanna Holborn Gray, who in the meantime had accepted the presidency of the University of Chicago, would continue to serve as acting president.

The choice of Giamatti, who would be Yale's youngest president in more than 200 years, and the first of at least partly non-WASP ancestry, delighted both students and faculty. Many felt it would be easier to endure the forthcoming budget retrenchment now that it would be coming from one of their own, a humanist committed to learning, rather than a managerial type. "It's good to have someone who really cares about students," said Yale's Roman Catholic chaplain, and a history professor speculated: "A human being as president of a university—my God, what will that be like?" The consensus was that Giamatti would bring a special panache to the office of president, and that the eloquence, drama, and rigorous thinking of his public speaking should stand him in good stead as a fund-raiser.

After jestingly telling newsmen that his only ambition in life was to be president of the American League, not of Yale, Giamatti admitted that it had been hard to accept the job. "It is a giving up of what one thinks one is," he said. "I'm a teacher; I'm a private type. I like to go to the library." He added: "I'm going to hate some of the things I'll have to do, and people are going to hate me. One of the advantages of having a young president is that he can remember a time when he was a non-tenured faculty member."

In an interview that appeared in the New York *Times* on December 25, 1977, Giamatti restated his belief that the university's curriculum should be revised, with more emphasis on the fundamental areas of the liberal arts, and possibly with the reintroduction of required courses in science, the social sciences, and foreign languages. While admitting that the budget crisis might make it necessary to cut whole programs or departments, he indicated that he was concerned about the deleterious effect that might have on morale and on educational excellence. So far as his role as president was concerned, he said: "If there's anything I've learned from watching the academic world, it is that the president persuades—or tries to persuade—the faculty. He doesn't command or issue fiats."

A. Bartlett Giamatti is a member of the Mediaeval Society of America. He served on the new study commission of the Modern Language Association from 1969 to 1973 and on the council of the Renaissance Society of America, was vice-president of the Dante Society of America from 1973 to 1975, and from 1968 to 1971 was treasurer of the American Comparative Literature Association. A member of the board of the Foote School and of the Arts Council of Greater New Haven, he was a trustee of Phillips Academy from 1971 to 1974, and from 1971 to 1975 was vice-president of the Connecticut Ballet, Inc. In 1969-70 Giamatti was a Guggenheim fellow.

In 1960 A. Bartlett Giamatti married Toni Smith, a graduate of Columbia University and the Yale School of Drama who now teaches English at Hopkins Grammar-Day Prospect Hill School. The couple has three children: Marcus Bartlett (born 1961), Elena Walton (born 1964), and Paul Edward Valentine (born 1967). Formerly the occupants of a modest gray frame house, the Giamattis now live in Yale's imposing presidential residence on Hillhouse Avenue in New Haven. Noted for his irreverent wit and for his conviviality, Giamatti sports what a writer for *Newsweek* (January 2, 1978) called "a slightly satanic beard," and he usually dresses in rumpled slacks and sports jackets, often with construction boots as his footgear. In December 1977 he made his ballet "debut" in the nondancing role of Herr Drosselmeyer in a production of Tchaikovsky's *The Nutcracker* by the Connecticut Ballet Company.

References: Newsweek 91:45 Ja 2 '78 por; N Y Times B p18 D 21 '77 por; Time 111:68 Ja 2 '78 por; Directory of American Scholars, 1974

Gish, Lillian

Oct. 14, 1896(?)- Actress. Address: h. 430 E. 57th St., New York City, N.Y. 10022

NOTE: This biography supersedes the article that appeared in *Current Biography* in 1944.

From naïve road company melodramas at the turn of the century through the era of the silent movies to the more sophisticated theatre, screen, and television productions of today's entertainment industry, Lillian Gish has always pursued her vocation of acting with the disciplined professionalism of what the drama critic Brooks Atkinson has admiringly called "a trouper." Atkinson also has pointed out, "Although Miss Lillian is the least pretentious and the least self-conscious of women, she is an American institution. Her life story is part of the American mythology." With the pioneering director D. W. Griffith showing the way, Lillian Gish helped to shape the art form of the motion picture, which she contends is "the only new art form of the twentieth century" and "the only art form America can lay claim to."

In its early decades Lillian Gish's career was inextricably tied to that of her sister, Dorothy Gish, with whom she appeared in *Orphans of the Storm*, *Romola*, and other silent film classics. Although less closely associated professionally in later years, they performed together on a summer theatre tour in *The Chalk Garden* in 1956. Her sister, as well as Griffith and herself, made major contributions to the development of the motion picture industry, whose early history Lillian Gish presented in over a hundred film lectures that she began giving in 1969.

The older of the sisters, Lillian Diana Gish was born in Springfield, Ohio on October 14, 1896 or thereabouts. Reference books differ on the year, and in her autobiography she does not disclose her exact age. The ancestors of her parents, James Lee and Mary Robinson (McConnell) Gish, were early German and English settlers of the American colonies, whose descendants, on her mother's side, included President Zachary Taylor. When her father, an unsuccessful candy merchant, deserted the family in New York City, her mother found work as an actress and took in lodgers who were also actresses. They persuaded her to let her daughters go on the stage with touring companies. Remarking that in childhood she learned security from her mother and insecurity from her father, Lillian Gish has said that she values both and that insecurity at an early age is important to the development of character.

At the age of five or six Lillian Gish began to earn her own living, making her debut in Rising Sun, Ohio in the melodrama *In Convict's Stripes*, which starred Walter Huston. Soon afterward Dorothy Gish, only four years old, toured in the role of Little Willie in *East Lynne*. On a few joyful occasions in later years, the mother and daughters all had roles with the same traveling company. One of the performances of her early career still memorable for Lillian was dancing in a Sarah Bernhardt production in New York City in 1910.

Except for brief attendance at several schools, notably Ursuline Academy, a convent in East St. Louis, Lillian Gish is wholly self-educated, having learned to read and write in the dressing rooms of theatres across the United States. At one time she used to feel inferior to her cousins who had gone to college. But in *The Movies, Mr. Griffith, and Me* (Prentice-Hall, 1969), she wrote, "Now I realize that, although I never went much to school or received a diploma, I have kept right on learning. I never wanted to own anything but books."

While barnstorming in a dozen melodramas, the Gish girls struck up a friendship with another juvenile actress, Gladys Smith, whose name soon became Mary Pickford. Lured by the higher earnings to be had from working in the so-called "flickers," Mary Pickford regularly made movies between stage plays. In 1912 at the American Mutoscope and Biograph Company in New York City, she introduced Lillian and Dorothy Gish to D. W. Griffith, who immediately hired them to take part in an audience scene he was about to direct. Recalling that meeting in his autobiography, Griffith wrote, "Lillian had an exquisite ethereal beauty." But when he rehearsed the sisters for their first film, *An Unseen Enemy* (1912), he gave Lillian a blue hair ribbon and Dorothy a red one so that he could tell them apart.

First on tour and then in New York, Lillian Gish played the fairy Morganie in David Belasco's *A Good Little Devil* (1913), in which Mary Pickford had the leading role. That was the last stage production in which Miss Gish appeared for seventeen years. She devoted herself instead to the movies, working both in Los Angeles and New York in close association with Griffith, who helped her to develop her talents through dancing lessons and voice lessons and instructions of his own, such as advice that she study the movements of animals as well as people. Along with Dorothy, Miss Lillian, as Griffith called her, learned much about the techniques of acting in films by appearing in a score or more of one and two reelers, including *The Musketeers of Pig Alley* (1912) and *The Mothering Heart* (1913), before playing in the more ambitious Biograph productions like *Judith of Bethulia* (1914).

When Griffith left Biograph after the filming of *Judith*, Lillian Gish went with him to the Mutual Film Corporation, the releasing agency for the Reliance-Majestic productions. Among the many that featured the Gishes were *Home, Sweet Home* (1914) and *The Sisters* (1914). As Elsie Stoneman, the virtuous daughter of a Northern family, Lillian Gish helped to make *The Birth of a Nation* (Epoch, 1915), Griffith's masterpiece. That Civil War epic, which became an immediate box-office success, is a landmark in the development of modern films. But its sympathetic presentation of the Southern cause aroused much criticism. In answer to what he considered bigotry, Griffith produced the spectacular but commercially unrewarding *Intolerance* (Wark, 1916). Between each of its four historical episodes Lillian Gish rocked the cradle of humanity.

In *Diane of the Follies* (Triangle-Fine Arts, 1916), which was not directed by Griffith, Miss Gish portrayed a vamp, a welcome change for her from the "gaga-baby," or sweet girl, roles that she was assigned to play by the dozens and that she has maintained are far more difficult to handle effectively than the wicked characters. Of one of her saccharine roles, that of Susie in *True Heart Susie* (Paramount-Artcraft, 1919), David Thomson wrote in *A Biographical Dictionary of Film* (1976), "Only great discretion and integrity prevented her from seeming coy or sententious."

True Heart Susie followed a string of rather grim Gish-Griffith World War I movies, such as *Hearts of the World* (Comstock-World, 1918), and belongs to a group of films that Thomson has called "the finest flowering of Griffith's view of a virginal, self-sacrificing heroine." Her roles in that genre included a twelve-year-old Limehouse waif beaten to death by a drunken father in *Broken Blossoms* (Griffith-United Artists, 1919); an unwed mother driven out by her father into a blizzard in *Way Down East* (Griffith-United Artists, 1920), and an orphan separated from her blind sister during the French Revolution in *Orphans of the Storm* (United Artists, 1922).

Soon after the completion of *Orphans of the Storm*, Lillian Gish parted from Griffith, who as an independent producer could not afford to pay her what her popularity had come to deserve and who advised her to capitalize on her celebrity. In working with Griffith she had often helped to write the story and the subtitles and had discussed ideas for promotion and other matters with him. She had, moreover, proved her understanding of film making by directing Dorothy in *Remodeling Her Husband* (Paramount-Artcraft, 1920). After she joined Inspiration Films in 1922, she continued in some measure to guide her own career, and as her first picture for that new company she suggested *The White Sister* (1923), in which she played a young woman who becomes a nun. Also for Inspiration she portrayed the title character of *Romola* (1924), based on the George Eliot historical novel set in fifteenth-century Florence at the time of Savonarola.

Both pictures, costarring Ronald Colman and filmed in Italy, fared well commercially and critically. But as a result of actions on the part of Charles Duell, president of Inspiration, that almost involved Miss Gish in a scandal, she signed an $800,000 contract with MGM, for which she made five movies in two years. As her first MGM role she herself chose Mimi in *La Bohème* (1926). When that film was recently shown in New York's Town Hall, Harold C. Schonberg reported in the New York *Times* (March 30, 1978) that the audience was genuinely moved, and he commented that "Miss Gish, with that aura of femininity, that lightness which allows her to walk without apparently touching the ground, that incredible beauty—Miss Gish was able to rise far above period and give us a touching portrait of the little French seamstress." Her Hester Prynne of *The Scarlet Letter* (1926), made at her suggestion, is one of her most affecting characterizations and the picture itself is a classic. Among her other MGM movies is *The Wind* (1928), a drama of the Texas prairie that Thomson regards as "her greatest film."

By the time Miss Gish's first "talkie," *One Romantic Night* (United Artists, 1930), was filmed, New York City had become her home. There she enjoyed close friendships with George Jean Nathan, H. L. Mencken, F. Scott and Zelda Fitzgerald, and other literary figures. She may also have preferred living in New York because it served as a center for the theatre, to which she returned in 1930 as Helena in Jed Harris' production of Chekhov's *Uncle Vanya*. As before, her stage engagements required much travel, and in 1932 she went to Colorado to star in a gala production of *Camille* at the Central City Opera House. Although Brooks Atkinson, in his introduction to her autobiography, thought that she was miscast as Marguerite Gautier, he praised her "shining, touching performance."

The acting skills that Lillian Gish had acquired in the movies sustained her on Broadway as Effie Holden in *Nine Pine Street* (1933), based on the Lizzie Borden story; as the saucy Young Whore, a striking departure from typecasting, in Sean O'Casey's *Within the Gates* (1934); and as Ophelia in Guthrie McClintic's production of *Hamlet* (1936), among other roles during the 1930's. In Great Britain she played Charlotte Lovell in *The Old Maid* in 1936 and performed in Chicago during 1940-41 for a record run of sixty-six weeks as Vinnie in *Life with Father*.

In her many later stage plays in New York and on tour or in other out-of-town presentations, Lillian Gish continued to delight audiences with generally well-rounded characterizations that sometimes shattered and other times strengthened her stereotyped image: as the pretentious and preposterous Katrina Ivanna in a dramatization of Dostoyevsky's *Crime and Punishment* (1947); the half-daft title character of John Patrick's *The Curious Savage* (1950); the gentle, weary widow longing for her early home in Horton Foote's *The Trip to Bountiful* (1953); one of the aunts, Agatha, in T. S. Eliot's verse play *The Family Reunion* (1958); the mother of the grief-stricken widow in Tad Mosel's *All the Way Home* (1960); the dominating mother, one of her rare comic roles, in Shaw's *Too True to Be Good* (1963); a fussy, fluttery Nurse in the Stratford, Connecticut American Shakespeare Festival of *Romeo and Juliet* (1965); the Dowager Empress of Russia in *Anya* (1965), a musical version of *Anastasia;* the old nurse, Marina, in Mike Nichols' production of *Uncle Vanya* (1973); and others.

Lillian Gish has remained disdainful of the changes that the advent of sound made in an art form in which the universal language of pantomime had been essential, but after an absence of a decade from Hollywood, she readily alternated motion picture and stage roles. She added to her screen credits with, among others, *The Commandos Strike at Dawn* (Columbia, 1943), in which she played a Norwegian wife during the Nazi occupation; *Miss Susie Slagle's* (Paramount, 1946), in the title role of a proprietor of a boarding house for medical students; *Duel in the Sun* (Selznick International, 1947), portraying a wife driven to drink by her brutal husband, a Texas cattle baron played by Lionel Barrymore, who had been a fellow performer of her earliest Hollywood days; and *Night of the Hunter* (United Artists, 1955), directed by Charles Laughton in the part of a kindly eccentric who shelters two children being pursued by a murderous evangelist. Her later films include *Warning Shot* (Paramount, 1967) and Graham Greene's *The Comedians* (MGM, 1967). In the spring of 1978 she appeared as a moribund matriarch in her hundredth motion-picture, *A Wedding* (Twentieth Century-Fox), which was produced and directed by Robert Altman.

Television performances have enlarged Miss Gish's audience since 1948, when she appeared in *The Late Christopher Bean,* which Fred Coe produced on NBC's *Philco Playhouse*. She was also seen on TV in Coe's productions of *The Trip to Bountiful* (NBC, 1953), which then became her Broadway vehicle, and *The Sound and the Fury* (NBC, 1955). Two highlights of her work in television were her portrayal of the American primitive artist Grandma Moses on *Schlitz Playhouse of Stars* (CBS, 1952) and her costarring performance with Helen Hayes in *Arsenic and Old Lace* (ABC, 1969). Her many other TV dramas include *The Day Lincoln Was Shot* (NBC, 1956) and *The Spiral Staircase* (NBC, 1961). She was also the hostess in 1975 of *The Silent Years*, a series of early movies shown on public television.

Classic silent films in which she had performed were, moreover, the subject of "Lillian Gish and the Movies: The Art of Film, 1900-1928," a film lecture on the evolution of the movies to the talkies. Her program covered in another form much of the information of the early chapters of her autobiography, *The Movies, Mr. Griffith, and Me,* written with the help of Ann Pinchot. Miss Gish gave her program its premiere at the McMillan Theatre of Columbia University in April 1969, about the time of the publication of her book, and then went on tour for two or three years, taking her show to cities in Europe, the United States, and Canada and winning enthusiastic attention at film festivals and from school and college audiences. "My hope for 'The Art of Film' program," she explained in *Dorothy and Lillian Gish* (Scribner, 1973), "is to reach the young in colleges, universities and schools who will make our future pictures and to impress upon them the power they leave on the world and [their] responsibility of where they direct this power." Just as her autobiography celebrates the work of Griffith, *Dorothy and Lillian Gish*, which has over 800 photographs and other illustrations, is largely a tribute to her sister, whose gift for comedy she greatly admired. Dorothy Gish had died in 1968.

Asserting that "only Chaplin, and later on Garbo, ever matched Lillian's eminence as a serious film artist," Irving Drutman called Lillian Gish "the loveliest of perennials" in an article for the New York *Herald Tribune* (June 13, 1965). He also reflected, "What probably has kept her image fresh is a sense of protectiveness she evokes in an audience, combined with a stage personality whose precise quality has baffled many a critic." After directing her in *The Comedians*, which was filmed under trying conditions in Dahomey, Peter Glenville attested, "As a professional she is impeccable." In David Thomson's appraisal, "She has a secure place among the great actresses of the cinema, even if her emotional range was uncommonly narrow."

Lillian Gish's honors include an A.F.D. degree from Rollins College and an H.H.D. degree from Mt. Holyoke College. In 1971 the Academy of Motión Pictures Arts and Sciences awarded her an honorary Oscar, and in 1973 Mayor John V. Lindsay presented her with the Handel Medallion for achievement in the arts, a medal inscribed "To Dorothy and Lillian Gish, for the joy they have given to generations of Americans." The French film critic, actor, and producer François Truffaut dedicated his *Day for Night* (1973) to Lillian and Dorothy Gish because, he said, "they were the first real actresses of the American cinema." At a luncheon in New York's Plaza Hotel on May 11, 1978 she was presented with a diamond and rubies brooch by the United Service Organization in recognition of her being honored as its Woman of the Year.

Fragile in appearance, Lillian Gish has ash-blond hair, blue eyes, and a graceful, slender figure. Her height is five feet six inches. But she is far more energetic than frail, and believing that it is part of an actress' job to maintain good health, she follows a set of dietary rules and practises yoga. Although courted by many suitors, she has preferred to remain single because she feels that her dedication to her career would not mix with marriage. She is said to be low on vanity and free of malice and envy. Her formula for happiness is to hold to a "balance of living equally in the mind, body, and spirit." Peter Glenville wrote in an introductory tribute in her autobiography, "Lillian would be equally at home with the Beatles and with the Archbishop of Canterbury. And they would equally appreciate her."

References: After Dark 11:16+ Je '69 pors; N Y Post p47 Ap 17 '69 por; N Y Times p26 D 27 '60, p21 Je 11 '66 por; Newsday II p1+ Ja 6 '74 pors, A p3+ Je 24 '75 pors; Gish, Lillian. The Movies, Mr. Griffith, and Me (1969), Dorothy and Lillian Gish (1973); Notable Names in the American Theatre (1976); Thomson, David. A Biographical Dictionary of Film (1976); Who's Who in the Theatre (1977)

Giulini, Carlo Maria (jōō-lē'nē)

May 9, 1914- Conductor. Address: b. c/o Hurok Attractions Inc., 730 5th Ave., New York City, N.Y. 10019; h. Via Jacopo da Ponte 49, Rome, Italy

The newly named music director of the Los Angeles Philharmonic Orchestra is meticulous, unassumingly aristocratic Carlo Maria Giulini, who is known for the combination of self-effacement and elegance he brings to the podium. The Italian-born, internationally celebrated Giulini was primarily a conductor of opera until, a decade ago, he decided to concentrate on symphonic work. For three years he was music director of the Vienna Symphony, and since 1969 he has been the Chicago Symphony Orchestra's principal guest conductor. His tenure with the Los Angeles Philharmonic begins with the 1978-79 season.

Carlo Maria Giulini was born on May 9, 1914 in Barletta, in the province of Bari, Italy. The first musical experience he remembers was hearing an itinerant violinist at his parents' farm near Verona when he was three or four. A year or two later, after the family had moved to Bolzano, he asked for and received a three-quarter-sized violin from his father and learned to play the instrument with the help of the nun who taught his kindergarten class. Later he studied at the local music school until he was sixteen, when he went to Rome to study with Remy Principe, at whose suggestion he took up the viola. In Rome he also studied composition with Alessandro Bustini at the Accadèmia di Santa Cecilia, and in 1934 he won a national competition to fill a vacancy in the viola section of the orchestra of Rome's Teatro Augusteo.

As a member of the Augusteo orchestra, Giulini had the opportunity, while still a student, to play under many great guest conductors, including Bruno Walter, Wilhelm Furtwängler, Erich Kleiber, Otto Klemperer, and Willem Mengelberg. Among the soloists who performed with the orchestra were Vladimir Horowitz and Bronislaw Huberman. In his spare time, away from the Augusteo orchestra and from his classes, he formed an amateur string quartet with three fellow students of Principe, and the four young men worked on chamber music together for three years.

Asked by Alan Blyth of *Gramophone* (July 1971) how he switched from string playing to conducting, Giulini replied that he didn't "know quite how and when it was" but that he "gradually felt this absolute necessity to produce a sound through a gesture." In another interview, with Maurice Fleuret for *Le Nouvel Observateur*, reprinted in translation in *Music and Musicians* (November 1972), he explained: "The conductor is the only musician without the right to work on his instrument. When he arrives in front of the orchestra he must already know everything. . . . He is forbidden to use the orchestra for his own practice. Further, of all musicians the conductor is the only one to produce sound without any physical contact . . . [with] a gesture in the air. . . . To tell the truth, gesture is an interior fact, never an exterior one. Nothing is in the arm, everything is in the head."

In his final semesters at the Accademìa di Santa Cecilia, Giulini was a prize-winning student of interpretation. During World War II he served as an officer in the Italian army until the Germans occupied Rome and he went into hiding. When Rome was liberated by the Allies in June 1944, he made his public debut as a conductor, directing a concert in celebration of the occasion in the Teatro Adriana. Giulini was with Radio Italiana, as the second conductor of the orchestra of the radio station in Rome from 1944 to 1950 and as the founding conductor of the Milan radio orchestra beginning in 1950. A Milan broadcast of Haydn's *Il Mondo della Luna* in 1951 was heard by the venerable conductor Arturo Toscanini, who arranged to meet Giulini. The younger conductor remained a close friend and disciple of Toscanini for six years, until the older man's death in 1957.

Giulini's first opportunity to conduct a staged opera was at the 1951 Bergamo Festival, where he led performances of Verdi's *La Traviata*, with Renata Tebaldi and Maria Callas successively singing the title role. After conducting Manuel de Falla's *La Vida Breve* at La Scala, he became assistant to Victor de Sabata, and in 1953 he succeeded Sabata as principal conductor at the hallowed Milan opera house.

Some of Giulini's most successful productions during his tenure at La Scala, and after, were collaborations with the designer and director Franco Zeffirelli, the late director Luchino Visconti, and the late Miss Callas. In preparing a production of Verdi's *La Traviata*, Visconti, Miss Callas, and Giulini, perfectionists all, spent three weeks working on the character of Violetta alone. Giulini recalls one instance of disagreement with his friend Zeffirelli: "We were doing *Falstaff* and in the scene where Falstaff has emerged from the waters of the Thames, Zeffirelli introduced a group of ragamuffins making fun of him. He did this despite the fact that Verdi specifies that Falstaff is alone, gloomily meditating on this *mondo ladro*—this thieving world. I had to say to Zeffirelli: 'The boys go or I go.' "

In 1955 Giulini left La Scala to become principal conductor of the Teatro dell'Opera in Rome. In the same year he made his debut in Great Britain, conducting *Falstaff* at the Edinburgh Festival. In 1958 Giulini and Visconti staged Verdi's *Don Carlo* at Covent Garden, and they presented the same composer's *Il Trovatore* at the same London house in 1963. Their most successful collaboration, Giulini feels, was their 1964 production of *The Marriage of Figaro*, the production that became the highlight of the Rome opera company's visit to the Metropolitan Opera House in New York City in 1968

Before his 1968 visit, American opera audiences knew Giulini only through his Angel recordings, which included *Don Carlo* and *The Marriage of Figaro*. (Outside of opera, he had already recorded on the Angel label the four Brahms symphonies, and he had begun recording the symphonies of Beethoven.) Because of his insistence on the right cast and sufficient rehearsal time for operas, he had limited his engagements in the United States to orchestral performances, beginning with an engagement with the Chicago Symphony in 1955. In 1960 he led the Israel Philharmonic in a seven-week tour of American, Canadian, and Mexican cities. The opening 1960 concert, at the Metropolitan Opera House, consisted of Carl Maria von Weber's Overture to *Der Freischütz*, Brahms's Symphony No. 1, Naom Sheriff's Two Symphonic Movements from *Psalm*, and Stravinsky's Suite from *The Firebird*. Reviewing that concert in the New York *Times* (October 17, 1960), Harold C. Schonberg judged Giulini to be "a superior technician and a first-class interpreter," especially in his reading of the Stravinsky piece: "Mr. Giulini conducted a performance that was almost startling in its clarity. . . . The idea is to avoid a Rimsky-Korsakoffian type of color, and instead to make the timbres as lean and clear as possible. Stravinsky . . . has bewailed the excessive 'interpretation' given to the score. He would have had little about which to complain last night."

After recuperating from a near-fatal bout of peritonitis in the mid-1960's, Giulini gradually phased himself out of opera, not because his demands regarding casts and rehearsal time could not be met—several opera houses had expressed willingness to meet them—but because of two other factors, as he explained to Alan Blyth in the *Gramophone* interview: "There must be rapport between music and action in any operatic performance, and today I feel just that productions go too far; they have become the dominating part of the opera. The second factor is a personal one and follows on from the first. At a concert I'm 100 percent in charge and I'm not distracted by what's going on elsewhere. I may make a thousand mistakes but at least they are my own."

When Giulini made his debut as conductor of the New York Philharmonic Orchestra with Arturo Benedetti Michelangeli as his soloist in the D-minor Piano Concerto of Mozart, Irving Kolodin wrote in the *Saturday Review* (December 28, 1968): "Giulini is no 'type' of today's conducting cadre, but a gifted, deeply involved man of music whose means of expression happen to be conducting an orchestra. . . . He does little, if anything, for the audience. All his energies are directed toward evoking the kind of musical expression he craves from the men around him. It goes so far indeed as to invade his most characteristic kind of hand signal—an outstretched left arm dipping deep into the space between conductor and players, the fist clenching spasmodically now and then as if to draw physically, from the bows and the breath of his associates, that indispensable vibrance."

At the London Festival in 1968 Giulini conducted Beethoven's *Missa Solemnis* and Verdi's *Requiem*, and the following year he became principal guest conductor of the Chicago Symphony Orchestra. Georg Solti, the music director of the Chicago orchestra, wanted him to be his permanent codirector, but Giulini demurred, explaining: "It's not right that two persons should make such decisions. Besides, I have no talent or patience for organization." In 1971 Giulini led the Chicago Symphony in eleven of the twenty-five concerts the orchestra gave on its first European tour, and he took responsibility for eight weeks of performances by the orchestra in each of his nine seasons as its principal guest conductor. For three years beginning in the fall of 1973 Giulini was the principal conductor of the Vienna Symphony Orchestra, which he took on a world tour in 1975.

At the conclusion of a ninety-minute performance of Gustave Mahler's Ninth Symphony, led from memory by Giulini in New York's Philharmonic Hall in 1972, the members of the Philadelphia Orchestra, in a rare act of homage to an associate, rose and applauded him. Similarly, the members of the Chicago Symphony gave him an ovation at Carnegie Hall in December 1975 after he conducted them in Anton Bruckner's Eighth Symphony from memory. Musicians respect Giulini not only because he can conduct long works without a score but also because he marks his own orchestra parts, including bowing instructions and phrasings—a fundamental task in conducting but one that most conductors today delegate to others.

After attending the December 1975 Carnegie Hall concert, Andrew Porter, writing in the *New Yorker* (January 5, 1976), contrasted Giulini's conducting of the Chicago Symphony with Solti's: "For Giulini, the Chicago Orchestra is a less high-tension and insistently virtuoso body. . . . Its tone . . . becomes broader and somewhat more tender. . . . The playing of the Chicago Symphony at this concert was just about as good as orchestral playing can be—string tone firm and singing at every level; woodwinds cohesive, perfectly balanced, exactly tuned; brass big and round but not aggressive." In *New York* magazine (December 12, 1977), Alan Rich reported on a Mozart program performed by the Chicago Symphony under Giulini in Chicago's Orchestra Hall: "This was a deeply moving experience: two works, the *Linz* Symphony and the [Verdi] *Requiem*, played with such elegance, such regard for the power of the melodic line, as to leave this tourist virtually speechless."

On April 17, 1977 Thornton F. Bradshaw, the board president of the Los Angeles Philharmonic Orchestra, announced that Giulini had been named music director of the orchestra, to succeed Zubin Mehta, who was moving to the New York Philharmonic. Giulini's three-year contract, which became effective in October 1978, requires him to give the orchestra ten weeks each year in Los Angeles and another four to six weeks touring and recording.

Giulini insisted on a relatively light schedule because, ever since his brush with death from peritonitis he has felt the need for "a little time for life, for simple things, to sit down with a friend, talk, have a glass of wine . . . time to do nothing, to think about life, about what should be the most important part of our lives—the spiritual part." Also, he needs time between concerts "to recover, to recharge," because, as he told Maurice Fleuret, he becomes so emotionally involved in music that it causes him "suffering in both body and spirit."

Carlo Maria Giulini and his wife, Marcella, have three sons. The well-tailored Giulini, who looks younger than his years, is a tall, slim man with a high-bridged, aristocratic nose, blue eyes, slender, tapered hands, and a reserved, gentle manner. What Eugene Rizzo wrote of him in *Opera News* (June 15, 1968) a decade ago still essentially applies: that several of his "well-known attributes as conductor—vitality, elegance, passion for detail—are uncannily borne out by his appearance. . . . Looking closely, one thinks of the cleanness of Mozart and the vigor of Verdi—his two favorite composers for the stage." Writing in the Washington *Post* (June 16, 1973), Alan M. Kriegsman observed that Giulini's "look of the romantic Italian film star" is deceptive: "He is a romantic by nature, but there's nothing of the film star's preening or self-absorption about him. He has a kind of quiet grace, and a charm all the more impressive for being unconscious." Sailing is the favorite recreation of this conductor who knows that "there isn't only music," that "there are many other fascinating things to see and do before leaving everything forever."

References: Gramophone 49:166+ Jl '71 por; Hi Fi 25:MA38 Ap '75; Music and Musicians 21:34+ N '72 por; Opera News 32:14+ Je 15 '68; Washington Post B p1+ Je 16 '73 pors; International Who's Who, 1976-77; International Who's Who in Music, 1975; Jacobson, Robert. Reverberation (1974); Who's Who, 1977-78; Who's Who in America, 1976-77; Who's Who in Opera, 1976

Goldwater, Barry M(orris)

Jan. 1, 1909- United States Senator from Arizona. Address: b. 427 Russell Senate Office Building, Washington, D.C. 20510. h. P.O. Box 1601, Scottsdale, Ariz. 85252

NOTE: This biography supersedes the article that appeared in *Current Biography* in 1955.

Now in his fourth term, Senator Barry M. Goldwater, Republican of Arizona, is best known as the man who made conservative political ideology an important factor in contemporary American politics. When he ran for President in 1964, Goldwater, who stressed opposition to big government and militancy in foreign policy, was buried under an avalanche of votes for the Democratic incumbent, President Lyndon B. Johnson, but he polled enough votes in the South to establish the Republicans for the first time as a truly national political party.

Although Ronald Reagan, the former governor of California, recently replaced him as titular head of right-wing Republicans, the conservative movement that Goldwater developed has steadily gained momentum. Goldwater's own views, however, have moderated to such an extent that many of his former followers have accused him of apostasy. As more than one political analyst has discovered, he has learned to compromise, to "talk first and fight later." "Politics has never been the making or breaking point of my life," he said in one recent interview. "I worked hard to make Arizona a better state and my country a better country. If I failed, I've taken the criticism."

Barry Morris Goldwater was born on January 1, 1909, the first child of Baron and Josephine (Williams) Goldwater, prominent and prosperous residents of Phoenix, Arizona. His paternal grandfather, Michael Goldwasser (the surname was Americanized to Goldwater), an immigrant Polish Jew, had parlayed a territorial trading post into a flourishing mercantile establishment with branch stores in several neighboring towns. Baron Goldwater managed the Phoenix branch. A high-spirited boy who enjoyed sports, especially boxing and football, practical jokes, and tinkering with electrical and mechanical gadgets, Barry Goldwater showed little interest in academic subjects. After he failed two courses in his freshman year at Phoenix Union High School, his parents sent him to Staunton Military Academy in Lexington, Virginia. Although never an outstanding student, he fared somewhat better at Staunton and, at the graduation ceremonies in 1928, he received the Kable Legion of Honor, the academy's highest award, as the best "all-around" cadet. That autumn Goldwater enrolled at the University of Arizona at Tucson, intending to study liberal arts and business. Bored by his studies, he dropped out of school a year later, an action he has come to regret as "the worst mistake [he] ever made," to enter the family business.

Starting as a junior clerk in piece goods, Goldwater worked his way up to general manager in 1936 and to president in 1937. At that time Goldwaters, Inc., was Phoenix's prestigious department store and Goldwater, a shrewd businessman with a flair for merchandising, further added to the luster of the store's reputation as the town's leading specialty shop. Concerned with his employees' welfare, he initiated a five-day work week and set up hospitalization and life insurance plans and a generous profit-sharing arrangement. Goldwater remained president until 1953, when he was elevated to chairman of the board, a post he continues to hold, even though the Goldwater family no longer owns the department store chain.

A licensed pilot, Goldwater volunteered for active duty with the Army Air Force several months before the Japanese attacked Pearl Harbor. At that time, he was rejected because of his age, astigmatism, and basketball injuries to both knees. But he persisted and, through the intercession of both Arizona Senators, he was finally accepted into the infantry. At first assigned to duty as a gunnery instructor, he eventually proved himself as an aviator and spent the next few years ferrying fighter planes and supplies to Europe and Asia. After being mustered out of the service in 1945 with the rank of lieutenant colonel, he helped organize the Arizona Air National Guard and served as its chief of staff until 1952.

Despite his family's long involvement in the Democratic party (his father and his uncle, Morris Goldwater, founded the state's Democratic organization), Barry Goldwater, always the maverick, remained aloof from politics after registering as a Republican in 1930 to protest the power of the Democratic machine. In 1949, however, his friends talked him into running for the Phoenix city council on a nonpartisan businessmen's reform slate. He was easily elected and, with characteristic energy, devoted the next year to adapting the local government to a more efficient city-manager system.

Having learned the techniques of statewide electioneering as manager of Republican Howard Pyle's successful 1950 gubernatorial campaign, Goldwater decided to try for the United States Senate in 1952. His opponent was Senate Majority Leader Ernest W. McFarland, a favorite in the traditionally Democratic state. Campaigning as a conservative, Goldwater described himself as being "not a me-too Republican," but "a Republican opposed to the superstate and to gigantic, bureaucratic, centralized authority." He rode into office on the coattails of the party's enormously popular Presidential candidate, Dwight D. Eisenhower, who carried the state by more than 40,000 votes. Goldwater edged out McFarland, the two-term incumbent, by fewer than 7,000 votes, polling 51.3 percent of the votes cast to McFarland's 48.7 percent.

In his first speech to the Senate, addressed to "all sincere men and women who are concerned with retaining the social gains which have been made in the last twenty years," the new junior Senator from Arizona sounded more like a resurrected New Dealer than a conservative Republican. He listed Social Security, old-age assistance, aid to dependent children and to the disabled, and unemployment insurance as "things [that] have been of great benefit to the people." "[No] responsible Republican, and especially not this Republican, has any . . . desire to abolish any of them," he promised. But in later floor speeches and in Senate votes, Goldwater consistently opposed federal spending for such domestic programs as aid to economically depressed areas, training for the unemployed, public housing, urban renewal, and mass transit. At one point he argued that Social Security be made voluntary, but he later revised his position and voted for measures to strengthen the program. Goldwater continued to oppose using Social Security funds to finance medical care for the elderly, contending that such a plan would not only bankrupt the system, but lead inevitably to socialized medicine.

Goldwater's quarrel was not so much with social programs themselves as with the federal government's increasing assumption of responsibilities better left to the states, churches, charitable organizations, and the individual citizen. In his view, federally funded welfare and relief programs not only demeaned the individual but served to institutionalize poverty. "I do not undertake to promote welfare, for I propose to extend freedom," he proclaimed in his book *The Conscience of a Conservative* (Victor, 1960), in which he set forth his political creed. "My aim is not to pass laws, but to repeal them. It is not to inaugurate new programs, but to cancel old ones that do violence to the Constitution . . . and if I should be attacked for neglecting my constituents' 'interests,' I shall reply that I was informed their main interest is liberty and that in that cause I am doing the very best that I can."

Distrustful of the growing power of organized labor, Goldwater went so far as to suggest that antitrust laws be applied to the unions, although he later discarded that solution as impractical. Believing that state right-to-work laws are a matter of "individual freedom" based on "constitutional and moral grounds," he sponsored legislation requiring a union to have the support of 95 percent of the employees in a plant before claiming exclusive bargaining rights. Appalled by the McClellan Committee's disclosures of union corruption in the late 1950's, Goldwater was instrumental in the passage of the comprehensive Landrum-Griffin labor reform bill, which guaranteed union members the right to a democratically run union.

Although personally opposed to racial discrimination in any form, Goldwater was one of twenty-seven Senators to vote against the landmark 1964 Civil Rights Bill, insisting that its public accommodations and fair employment provisions violated states' rights. Moreover, he was convinced that the racial problem was "essentially moral" and that it was "impossible to legislate moral conduct." "You cannot pass a law that will make me like you or you like me," he said. "This is something that can happen only in our hearts."

In 1954 Goldwater joined twenty-two of his colleagues to vote against the censure of Senator Joseph R. McCarthy, calling the militant, redbaiting Wisconsin Republican a leader in the fight against communism. A hardliner on communism, Goldwater favored a policy of "peace through strength" as the best way to combat what he saw as the worldwide communist threat. He consistently supported a strong but flexible defense establishment and repeatedly indicated his willingness to consider the use of "appropriate nuclear weapons" in certain situations. Moreover, he denounced arms control negotiations, urged a resumption of nuclear testing in the atmosphere, and defended his opposition to the 1963 nuclear test ban treaty as a vote for "the strength to prevent [war]."

In *Why Not Victory? A Fresh Look at American Foreign Policy* (McGraw-Hill, 1962), Goldwater accused the United States of vacillation and timidity in its dealings with foreign governments, particularly those of communist countries. Because he considered such programs as generally "ill-conceived, ill-administered, [and] characterized by waste and extravagance," he habitually opposed foreign economic and military aid except where it could be "used as a 'rifle' aimed at specific areas where we can gain advantage over the Russians." Goldwater so distrusted the Soviet Union that he recommended an end to Russian-American cultural exchanges and called for a break in diplomatic relations.

Goldwater's views brought him increasing popularity in his home state. In 1958 he handily defeated McFarland for a second time, winning reelection by 35,563 votes. Since conservative Republicans fared badly almost everywhere that year, Goldwater's stunning victory thrust him into the national spotlight as potential Presidential material. Among party professionals he had already made a name for himself as one of the most skilled and dedicated campaigners in behalf of the Republican cause to come along in years. Elected to the first of three consecutive two-year terms as chairman of the Republican Senatorial Campaign Committee in 1955, he literally stumped the entire nation for Republican candidates and, by 1960, he was the party's leading fundraiser, making him a strong contender for a spot on the 1960 Republican national ticket. His name was placed in nomination for the Presidency, but he withdrew and threw his considerable support to Richard M. Nixon. In a plea for party unity, he told his disappointed supporters, "Let's grow up, conservatives. If we want to take this party back, and I think we can some day, let's go to work."

Over the next few years, Goldwater repeatedly denied reports that he was considering a run for the Presidency in 1964, even though a number of "Goldwater-for-President" clubs sprouted around the country. Without the Senator's encouragement, a National Draft Goldwater Committee was formed early in 1963 to appeal to Goldwater's natural constituency of rightwing extremists, disaffected Southerners, who shared his opposition to forced desegregation, states' rights advocates and, most importantly, to the small-town conservatives who made up the bulk of the Republican National Convention delegates. Much of Goldwater's strength came from the relative weakness of the other Republican hopefuls, among them Richard M. Nixon and Nelson A. Rockefeller. Although he was openly disdained by the so-called Eastern Establishment, that bloc of liberal and moderate leaders who had been choosing Republican Presidential candidates for nearly three decades. Goldwater moved past Rockefeller into first place in a Gallup poll of Republicans in mid-1963.

On January 3, 1964 Goldwater announced his candidacy for the Republican Presidential nomination. Uncomfortable in what he has described as the "baby-kissing, hand-shaking, blintz-eating" atmosphere of the primaries, Goldwater concentrated on the state conventions, where he captured an overwhelming majority of delegates. Moreover, he modified some of his more controversial stands to such a degree that he took most of the primary contests he entered and, to reach even more voters, publicized those concessions in *Where I Stand* (McGraw-Hill, 1964), a collection of his campaign speeches. By the time the Republicans met in San Francisco for their national convention in July 1964, Goldwater seemed virtually unbeatable.

Turning back a last-minute bid by William W. Scranton, the moderate governor of Pennsylvania, Goldwater won the nomination on the first ballot. His Vice-Presidential running-mate was William E. Miller, a little-known New York Congressman. In his acceptance speech, Goldwater chastised the Kennedy-Johnson Administration for its failure to maintain America's security and for its weakness in the face of the threat of world communism. He pledged that his administration would regain respect abroad and reestablish reason in government at home. "Extremism in defense of liberty is no vice," he reminded his listeners, and "moderation in pursuit of justice is no virtue."

Goldwater's failure to reconcile the differences between the conservative and moderate factions of the party left Republicans bitterly divided. Many Republican candidates disassociated themselves from the national ticket, and scores of Republican newspapers came out in favor of President Lyndon B. Johnson. His stump speeches, stressing military preparedness and "brinksmanship" in foreign policy did little to contradict his popular image as a trigger-happy warmonger. "The whole campaign was run on fear of me," Goldwater said later. "In fact, if I hadn't known Goldwater, I'd have voted against the s.o.b. myself." On November 3, 1964 Goldwater lost to Johnson by a landslide of nearly 16,000,000 votes, polling only 38.7 percent to Johnson's 61.3 percent.

After his staggering defeat, Goldwater returned to Arizona where, as he put it, he was "shunned like a bird of ill omen" by Republicans until 1968, when he easily won election to the United States Senate, besting Roy Elson, his Democratic opponent, by more than 70,000 votes. Back on Capitol Hill, he staunchly supported President Nixon's Indochina war policies and during one heated floor debate on the escalated air war over North Vietnam in April 1972 he denounced those who opposed the increased bombing as "weak-kneed and jelly-backed." "I would rather blow the living daylights out of Haiphong than lose one more American life," he argued. To the surprise of his fellow conservatives, he applauded the President's diplomatic overtures toward the People's Republic of China. But the Senator was troubled by the loss of seniority occasioned by the break in his Senate service and by his infrequent invitations to the White House. Consequently, his voting participation record of 45 percent was the worst in the Ninety-first Congress. "I feel a little out of it," he admitted in August 1972, and he talked privately of retiring.

The Watergate scandals restored Goldwater to his former national prominence. Shortly after Nixon's record reelection victory in 1972, he began publicly prodding the President to make a full disclosure, to "get rid of the smell," and for the next eighteen months he relentlessly criticized Nixon's handling of the affair. Suddenly Goldwater was once more a political hero, and, according to a Gallup poll, one of the world's ten most admired men. On August 7, 1974, after Nixon admitted withholding Watergate evidence, Goldwater accompanied the Republican leaders of the House and Senate to the White House and, acting as their spokesman, warned the President that he would have a maximum of fifteen supporting votes in a Senate impeachment trial and that he, Goldwater, would probably vote for Nixon's conviction for abuse of power. On the following night Nixon announced his resignation.

Riding the crest of his popularity, Goldwater rolled up his biggest margin ever in November 1974, beating Democrat Jonathan Marshall by almost 91,000 votes. During his current term Goldwater has continued his strong support for the military, voting "yes" on such controversial issues as the B-1 bomber and the neutron bomb. Scoring the "unseemly haste" and "feverish eagerness" of President Jimmy Carter's foreign policy, he voted against the Administration's renegotiated Panama Canal treaty. As one of the most enthusiastic defenders of the space program, he approved appropriations for the development of the space shuttle and for space exploration.

Goldwater has continued to work for an end to federal paternalism, a balanced national budget, and a healthy, free economy without runaway inflation. In his most recent book, *The Coming Breakpoint* (Macmillan, 1976), he predicted that the American people, "fed up" with taxes and federal supervision, would one day revolt. "All the great civilizations fell when people lost their initiative because government moved in to do things for them," he explained to Clare Crawford in an interview for *People* (March 22, 1976). "When you don't have any morals left, and you don't have people with ambition, the inevitable result is anarchy."

A tanned and trim six-footer, Barry Goldwater has blue eyes and wavy silver hair. In his spare time he explores the mountains and deserts of his native state, and his photographs of Arizona's spectacular scenery and its Indian tribes have been collected in his *The Face of Arizona* (F. P. Middleton, 1964) and *People and Places* (Random, 1967). Long interested in Amerindian culture, he has a large collection of Hopi Kachina dolls and has for many years belonged to the Smokis, an organization devoted to the preservation of Arizona's Indian tradition. Still fascinated by gadgetry, he recently constructed a garbage compacter, a digital timer, an electric organ, and three television sets. His ultramodern, hilltop house outside Phoenix and his cooperative apartment in Washington, D.C. are crammed with ham radio equipment. Senator Goldwater and his wife, the former Margaret Johnson, an heiress to the Borg-Warner automotive fortune, were married on September 22, 1934. They have four children: Joanne, Barry, Jr., a Republican Congressman from California, Michael, and Margaret, and several grandchildren. Goldwater is a member of the Royal Photographic Society, the American Association of Indian Affairs, the American Legion, and the Veterans of Foreign Wars. His religious affiliation is Episcopal.

References: Life 57.93+ S 18 '64 pors; 57:88+ O 23 '64 pors; N Y Times p9 Ja 4 '64; p23 Ag 17 '76 por; Time 83:31+ Je 12 '64 pors; Washington Post E p1+ Ag 18 '76 pors; Almanac of American Politics, 1978; White, Theodore. The Making of the President 1964 (1965); Who's Who in America, 1976-77

González (Márquez), Felipe

Mar. 5, 1942- Spanish political leader; lawyer. Address: c/o Partido Socialista Obrero Español, Joaquín García Morato 165, Madrid 3, Spain

A major political force in post-Franco Spain is Felipe González, secretary general of the Partido Socialista Obrero Español (PSOE), or Spanish Socialist Workers' party, which, after years of clandestine activity, emerged from the general elections of mid-June 1977 as the country's strongest single party. Virtually unknown to most Spaniards as recently as the early 1970's, González has become a familiar figure not only in his native Andalusia but throughout Spain, and he has acquired increasing prestige among the Social Democrats of Europe and Latin America. González, who insists that Socialism never died out in Spain, even during the long night of Franco's dictatorship, defines true democracy as a system under which "human beings are not only allowed freedom of expression, but social equality and equality of economic opportunity."

Felipe González Márquez, who was born in Seville into a farming family on March 5, 1942, is the second of the five children of Felipe and Juana (Márquez) González. His father, then a livestock handler employed by the García Carranza family that belonged to the local oligarchy, admired the Spanish Republican statesman Manuel Azaña and remained aloof from the Franco regime. During the Second Republic, the elder González had been president of the Casa del Pueblo in the Seville suburb of Pueblo del Rio. Although neither his brothers nor his sisters were able to attend college, Felipe González enrolled at the University of Seville law school after completing his secondary studies with the Claretian Fathers. During his second year of law school he helped to organize a lecture series on labor problems through such groups as Juventudes Obreras Católicas (JOC), or Young Catholic Workers, and Hermandades Obreras de Acción Católica (HOAC), or Catholic Action Brotherhood of Workers. At that time all those organizations were tolerated by the Franco government. His wife, Carmen Romero de González, recalled in an *International Herald Tribune* interview (August 16, 1977) that González was not involved in student politics as much as she was during their university years together but that he was mainly concerned with the workers' cause. She also remembered that he "came to class many mornings smelling of the cows that he had had to deliver to the slaughterhouse for his father before school."

According to González, his family status was not a decisive factor in his choice of a political career. A more likely influence was the sociological conditioning of having lived for twenty years in the typical Seville quarter known as Bellavista, which was located near a penal colony for political prisoners on the lower Guadalquivir River canal. On their release, many of them chose to settle nearby rather than return to their hometowns to face their families and neighbors. That proximity to the "prisoners' canal" inclined him towards Socialism during his university days. Another influence was that of the late Professor Manuel Giménez Fernández, whose Christian Democratic organization maintained a critical posture toward the Franco regime along with a commitment to freedom. In 1962 González joined the Juventúdes Socialistas, then being clandestinely reorganized in Andalusia, and two years later he became a member of the Partido Socialista Obrero Español, because the latter seemed to offer an alternative to dictatorship and capitalism within a framework of internal democracy.

On obtaining his law degree from the University of Seville in 1966, González decided to specialize in labor law, and, with several other young lawyers, opened the first labor counsel office in Seville, furnishing legal advice to thousands of workers throughout the province. It served as a model for others that were later established throughout Spain. As a labor relations lawyer, González was also involved in some celebrated labor-management disputes outside of Seville, including those at the FASA-Renault plant in Valladolid, at La Felguera in Asturias, at the Firestone plant in Bilbao, and at the Astilleros shipyard in Cádiz. At the same time he was lecturing on labor law at the University of Seville.

González' involvement in labor relations diminished as he became more and more active in politics. From 1965 to 1970 he was a member of the PSOE provincial committee for Seville, and also of its national committee. His rise to prominence as a rival of the veteran Socialist leader Professor Enrique Tierno Galván coincided with a growing discord among Socialists of different factions, and he became increasingly aware of the urgent need for the renewal and broadening of the bases of Spanish Socialism. As a result of his activities in behalf of the illegal PSOE, González was arrested several times by the Franco regime.

At the eleventh PSOE congress, held at Toulouse, France in August 1970, González was elected to the party's executive committee. There he defended the right of Socialists inside Spain—rather than those in exile—to make political decisions for the party, and it was at that congress that the "interior" faction managed to gain majority control of the executive committee. Meanwhile, the Juventudes Socialistas and the Union General de Trabajadores (UGT)—the PSOE's autonomous trade union organization—had likewise recognized the changing realities of modern Spain and resolved to undertake a reappraisal program to keep abreast of them.

In 1972, at the twelfth PSOE congress, also held at Toulouse, the conflict between the "interior" and "exterior" factions came to a head when Tierno Galván established an independent Partido Socialista del Interior, which later became the Partido Socialista Popular (PSP). The congress gave rise to a further split in the PSOE, between the so-called "renovated" and "historical" sectors, with the latter group, headed by Rodolfo Llopis, refusing to recognize the authority of the twelfth congress. Eventually, it was the "renovated" sector, in which González worked as an increasingly respected militant, that won recognition from the Socialist International as the sole voice of Spanish Socialism.

The last phase in the process of consolidating the "renovated" sector's dominant position in the Spanish Socialist movement occurred at the thirteenth PSOE congress in Suresnes, France, a Paris suburb, in October 1974, when González, then operating under the code name Isidoro, was elected secretary general—just a decade after he had joined the party ranks. Since his name was then still largely unknown to the average Spaniard, his election surprised some observers in political circles, including the PSOE itself. According to González, his election as secretary general resulted from a "team effort," in the aftermath of the turbulent 1972 congress, to find "a person who in some way might symbolize the party" and thereby forge unity among the various sectors of the PSOE. As a result of his election, González was called in for questioning by the Spanish police later in 1974 and charged with belonging to what was then still an illegal organization. He received an eight-year sentence which was, however, never carried out.

After the congress in Suresnes, France the PSOE leadership engaged in negotiations with Christian Democrats and others to formulate a common policy for the restoration of democracy in Spain. The result was the Programa Democrática (PD), agreed upon in June 1975. Earlier, in July 1974, another opposition group, encompassing such diverse elements as the Communist party of Spain (PCE), liberal monarchists, and Tierno Galván's PSP, had been organized under the name Junta Democrática (JD). In March 1976—after reaching a consensus on such goals as a general amnesty, freedom of political and trade union organization, and the eventual drafting of a new constitution based on popular sovereignty—the PD and the JD merged into the Coordinación Democrática (CD), a temporary alliance under the joint leadership of Felipe González, Communist party leader Santiago Carrillo, and Christian Democrat José María Gil Robles. González ruled out, however, the prospect of a coalition government with the Communists, maintaining that they were not "believable as democrats." Although González kept in touch with world Communist leaders—including Cuban Premier Fidel Castro, whom he visited in Havana in June 1976—he chose to identify himself with the German Social Democrats and other moderate European Socialist parties.

In keeping with the PSOE's radical Marxist legacy, González' early public pronouncements, still geared to the Franco era, were generally militant and uncompromising. At public rallies he was noted for his fiery oratory and clenched-fist salute. After the death of Franco in November 1975, the PSOE leaders at first resisted the accession of Juan Carlos to the throne, regarding him as little more than "Franco's heir," but they gradually decided to give the new King an opportunity to fulfill his reform promises. The performance of Adolfo Suárez González, whom Juan Carlos appointed to succeed Carlos Arias Navarro as Spain's Prime Minister in July 1976, led Felipe González and other opposition leaders to hope that the Spanish government was willing to accelerate the nation's progress toward democracy. Among other actions, Suárez declared a general amnesty; approved a far-reaching political reform law; authorized the legalization of the parties of the opposition, including the PSOE and the Communists, effective in April 1977; and scheduled national elections for June of that year.

Even before formal legalization, the PSOE received government permission to hold its first congress on Spanish soil in forty-four years. That historic congress, which took place at Madrid in December 1976, was attended by such prominent foreign Socialists as Willy Brandt, Olof Palme, Pietro Nenni, Michael Foot, and François Mitterrand, and was considered a milestone on the road to normalization of Spanish political life. In his opening address to the enthusiastic gathering, González spelled out the pragmatic line he had been striving to follow, charting a careful course between the "negativism" of the extreme left and the "abandonment of Socialist principles." According to Joe Gandelman of the *Christian Science Monitor* (December 10, 1976), the results of the 1976 congress seemed to indicate that González had tamed the militant activists within PSOE ranks and had led his party out of "the leftist ghetto." Earlier that year he had enhanced his international stature by attending Socialist conferences in Denmark, Portugal, and Venezuela.

For González and his Socialists, as for the rest of Spain, 1977 was a year of supercharged political significance because of nationwide general elections held on June 15 and municipal and trade union elections announced for the final quarter of the year. To prepare for the midyear voting that marked Spain's first free election in more than four decades, González embarked on "American-style campaigning" that included trips around the country by chartered jet for two or three meetings a day. According to James M. Markham of the New York *Times* (June 20, 1977), González and the PSOE conducted "by far the smoothest and most professional campaign" during the official three-week period preceding the election.

When the ballots were counted, the PSOE was found to have polled 28.5 percent of the popular vote—as compared with about 34 percent received by Suárez' Union of the Democratic Center (UCD), a coalition of centrist and moderately rightist parties. González himself was elected to the lower house of the new Chamber of Deputies from Madrid, becoming one of the 118 PSOE representatives in that 350-member body. Several political analysts have observed that González and the PSOE leadership apparently did not want to win that first election because of the party's lack of experience in dealing with the vast problems facing the country and because of the risk of a major confrontation with right-wing officers within the military. Joe Gandelman noted in the *Christian Science Monitor* (June 17, 1977) that the PSOE, widely regarded as "possibly the most stable political force in Spain in the long term," apparently would be reluctant to take part in any ruling coalition required to take unpopular economic measures likely to limit its options and thus make the Communists the favorite left-wing opposition alternative.

Despite his charge during the campaign that Suárez' UCD coalition was merely "renovated Francoism," González met after the election with Suárez and King Juan Carlos in his capacity as parliamentary spokesman for the largest single political party in Spain. Meanwhile, González had become increasingly critical of the Communists. In an interview in the French magazine *Le Point* in August 1977 he noted that the PCE—despite its adherence to "Eurocommunism," which made it more independent of Moscow—retained its totalitarian character, and he warned of the danger of yielding to the temptation of a new "Popular Front."

In August 1977 González flew to Colombia, Chile, and Venezuela. In Bogotá, where he met with President Alfonso López Michelsen and addressed both houses of the Congress, he pointed out the uselessness of dictatorship as an historical experience and commented favorably on the accomplishments of Spain's monarchy. In Chile he was received by Cardinal Primate Silva Henríquez and interceded with the Justice Minister in behalf of two imprisoned Chilean leftists. During his stay in Caracas, where he was the guest of President Carlos Andrés Pérez, the PSOE leader again commented on the political situation in Spain, declaring himself opposed to any coalition with the UCD and in favor of new legislative elections within two years, once a new constitution had been approved, and he called for a Spanish foreign policy independent of the world's major power blocs. His Caracas agenda also included a meeting with the son of Hubert Matos—a political prisoner in Fidel Castro's Cuba. On his return from Latin America in early September, González held a two-hour meeting with Suárez, at which the two leaders assessed the results of the trip and reportedly agreed on a legislative course of action.

On October 8 and 9, 1977 Suárez held negotiations at Moncloa Palace in Madrid with the leaders of the major opposition parties, including both González and Carrillo, to formulate a program of economic revitalization and political reform. The subsequent agreement, which was signed by all parties involved on October 25, 1977, contained provisions setting limits on future price and wage increases and on the amount of new money placed in circulation during 1978. Also instituted as part of the economic package were tax reform measures designed to shift the burden of payment to the wealthier sectors of society. To insure the support of the government's economic austerity measures by both the PSOE and the Communist party, Suárez agreed to make changes in the penal code that would guarantee police reorganization, greater freedom to hold meetings and demonstrations, and reform of the articles banning contraceptives and requiring punishment for adulterers.

In 1968 Felipe González married Carmen Romero, the daughter of an army doctor, over her conservative family's objections. A member of the UGT trade union movement and of the Frente de Liberación de la Mujer (Women's Liberation Front), Carmen Romero de González teaches English in Carabanchel, a working-class district of Madrid. The PSOE leader and his wife make their home in a comfortable middle-class Madrid neighborhood with their two sons, Pablo (named for Pablo Iglesias, who founded the PSOE in 1879) and David. González has been described as "tall, dark-haired, and intense" and as a "dynamic" and "charismatic leader" whose "easy charm and insistent appeal" has been largely responsible for his party's success. He favors casual jackets, blue jeans, and open-necked shirts, but generally wears ties and business suits for official meetings. Although fond of soccer, he has little time for leisure activities other than reading, and during the mid-1977 election campaign he made a point of re-reading Cervantes' *Don Quixote*. González is a member of the Madrid bar association. In his booklet *¿Qué es el Socialismo?* (1976) he observed: "The fullness of democracy is not going to be achieved except in a Socialist society. . . . Socialism and democracy are indissolubly united concepts."

References: Christian Sci Mon p6 D 10 '76 por, p16 My 9 '77 por; Los Líderes (Madrid) I:1+ '76 pors; International Who's Who, 1978-79

Goodson, Mark

Jan. 24, 1915- Television producer. Address: b. 375 Park Ave., New York City, N.Y. 10022; 6430 Sunset Blvd., Los Angeles, Calif. 90028; h. 1 Beekman Pl., New York City, N.Y. 10022

Daytime and nighttime, the perennial standby of television has been the game show, offering home viewers a chance to match wits with studio contestants who hope for cash, prizes, or perhaps just a moment of glory. The impresario who has probably dreamed up more successful programs of that type than any of his rivals is Mark Goodson, whose senior status in television production has led him to call himself, in jest, "the John Foster Dulles of television." Trained in radio during the 1940's, Goodson launched his video career in 1950 with *What's My Line?*, one of the best-known and longest-lived programs in the history of American television. Since then, he has created many other popular shows, including *I've Got a Secret, To Tell the Truth, The Price is Right, Password,* and *Match Game.* Throughout his television career Mark Goodson has worked in tandem with Bill Todman, and their company, Goodson-Todman Productions, has been the leading packager of television game shows since the mid-1950's.

Mark Goodson was born in Sacramento, California on January 24, 1915, the son of Abraham Ellis and Fannie (Gross) Goodson, who immigrated to the United States from Russia in the early years of the century. Abraham Goodson worked as a masseur, ran a chicken farm in Hayward, California for a few years until it failed during the Great Depression, and eventually opened a health-food store in Berkeley. "We were very poor,"

Goodson recalled of his childhood to Gilbert Robin of *Sports Illustrated* (June 24, 1963). ". . . My memory was always of where to eat, who would pay the rent, five-day-old bread, second-hand clothes. . . . There was a whole feeling of catastrophe right around the corner."

Goodson became involved in the entertainment world as a child, acting in amateur little theatre productions in Sacramento and occasionally earning money for professional appearances with the Plaza Theatre Stock Company of Sacramento. Not surprisingly, after graduating form high school in Hayward in 1932, Goodson was interested in an acting career, but his parents were determined that he become a lawyer, a profession they regarded as more financially stable. Therefore, after entering the University of California at Berkeley, Goodson majored in economics and political science to prepare himself for law school, but he retained his interest in theatre and became a regular member of the Berkeley acting troupe and a director of several campus plays. An enthusiastic debater, he won the Robert Gordon Sproul Gold Medal for extemporaneous debate.

To finance his college education, Goodson won a series of scholarships and worked in the Lincoln Fish Market in Berkeley. There his tasks included dipping into the herring barrel each Friday night to retrieve the last herring, a duty which, he has recalled ruefully, left him with a hopelessly ineradicable fishy odor for the weekend. After dropping out of school for a year because of illness, Goodson was graduated *cum laude* from Berkeley in 1937 with a B.A. degree and a Phi Beta Kappa key.

Instead of going directly on to his professional studies, Goodson decided to work for a while, and in the course of time forgot all about law school. His first job was that of a part-time disc jockey at radio station KJBS in San Francisco, which paid him $35 a week. Soon he was working full time, and in 1939 he was hired by the Mutual Broadcasting System station KFRC in San Francisco as an announcer, newscaster, and station director. At KFRC he originated his first game show, called *Pop the Question*, it consisted of contestants throwing darts at multicolored balloons to determine the stakes for the questions.

In 1941 Goodson moved to New York City, where he continued his radio career as a freelance announcer. Among his assignments were those of acting as master of ceremonies of the game show *The Jack Dempsey Sports Quiz* in 1942; playing *The Answer Man* in 1942, announcing such soap operas as *Just Plain Bill* and *Front Page Farrell;* and doing Nazi and Japanese voices on the *We the People* program. In 1943 Goodson created his first network show, a dramatic series presented daily on ABC entitled *Appointment with Life* that was based on the files of a marriage counselor. Subsequently he wrote and directed the dramatic episodes on the *Kate Smith Variety Hour*, directed the United States Treasury Department's bond-selling show, *The Treasury Salute (1944-45)*, and produced the daytime soap opera *Portia Faces Life.*

Soon after moving to New York City, Goodson met Bill Todman, a young radio writer and director, while both were working on a quiz program for WABC called *Battle of the Boroughs*—Goodson as the master of ceremonies and Todman as the writer. The two men became friends, and after a time Todman started peddling an idea for a quiz show that Goodson had originated called *Winner Take All.* With its sale to CBS radio in 1946, the Goodson-Todman partnership began. Over the next four years the partners prospered as packagers of radio shows, and Goodson created a series of audience participation radio shows, including *Stop the Music,* a telephone quiz show that spawned a host of imitators, and *Hit the Jackpot.*

In 1950 Goodson and Todman ventured into the emerging world of network television with a lively panel show created by Goodson. First shown on Wednesday, February 1, 1950, *What's My Line?* proved so popular that it was soon moved to the 10:30 p.m. slot on Sunday night, where it remained on CBS-TV for seventeen years, with John Daly as its host. Dorothy Kilgallen, the newspaper columnist for the now defunct New York *Journal-American,* was one of the original panel members, and she remained until her death in 1965. Long-time panelists Arlene Francis, the actress, and Bennett Cerf, the publisher, joined the show not long after it began. The fourth place on the panel was occupied by a guest celebrity. The task of the panelists was to guess the unusual occupations of the people who were guests on the show. Over the years the panel was stumped by such unusual jobs as pea picking, sword swallowing, cow washing, and sausage stuffing. Each week the program would also be visited by a famous guest. While trying to guess the identity of those mystery guests, the panelists wore blindfolds, and the visitors tried to disguise their voices. Prominent mystery guests included Frank Sinatra, Eleanor Roosevelt, Carl Sandburg, Sister Kenny, Barbra Streisand, Gerald A. Ford, Jimmy Carter, and Elizabeth Taylor. Although long one of the most popular shows on the CBS roster, *What's My Line?* finally began to slip in the ratings during the 1960's. By the time it was dropped in the fall of 1967, it was the second longest-running show on television, right behind *The Ed Sullivan Show,* which had premiered only a few months before it.

During the early 1950's Goodson also developed such quiz shows as *I've Got a Secret* (CBS), hosted by Garry Moore, *It's News to Me, The Name's the Same, Two for the Money* (CBS), and *Judge for Yourself,* which was presided over by Steve Allen. By 1956 the Goodson-Todman team had become the largest packager of game shows in the United States.

Extending their empire into the field of drama, they opened a California division that produced such dramatic series as *The Rebel* (ABC), starring Nick Adams, *Jefferson Drum, Branded,* and *The Richard Boone Repertory Theater.*

In 1956 Goodson developed one of his most successful shows, *To Tell the Truth,* which was telecast for many years on CBS with Bud Collyer as its host. Its format, which Goodson has called the best game concept he ever devised, was a variant on *What's My Line?* and consisted of a panel of quick-witted celebrities cross-examining three persons who claimed the same identity. After each panelist hazarded a guess as to which of the three contestants was authentic, Collyer would make the now famous request, "Will the real [so-and-so] please stand up."

In 1961 Goodson created another long-running hit, *Password* (CBS), with Allen Ludden as its host. Probably the most cerebral and ingenious of any of his formats, the "password" game represented a variation on the time-honored parlor game of charades. It required contestants to communicate a word to an associate by using one-word clues. *Password* was broadcast until 1975, when it expired after a decline in its ratings.

Two longtime favorites by Goodson that are still being telecast are *The Price is Right* (1956), a takeoff on an auction in which contestants estimate the prices of merchandise, and *Match Game* (1962), which trafficks in double entendres without trespassing into bad taste. Both are broadcast daily on CBS-TV, as is a third Goodson game show, *Tattletales.* All three programs also appear once a week in nighttime versions, which are widely syndicated. Goodson also created *Family Feud,* which is seen during the day on ABC and syndicated for nighttime viewing weekly. It is now the top-rated game show. A fifth Goodson creation, *Concentration,* is currently produced solely for syndication.

In the Goodson-Todman partnership, Goodson serves as the fountainhead of creativity, while the semiretired Todman attends to the complex business dealings. Over the years, Goodson has introduced many features now standard on game shows, including the ubiquitous bells and buzzers. It was Goodson who innovated the stratagem of having contestants compete against each other, and it was he who first thought of the champion contestant who keeps appearing on the show until he meets defeat at the hands of a challenger. Goodson never developed any shows that awarded huge cash prizes, like *Twenty-One* or *The $64,000 Question,* and the Goodson-Todman company was never implicated in the quiz show hanky-panky that scandalized the nation in the late 1950's. In the early days of television the shows were recorded live but in recent years the producers have taped them a few weeks before showing, without too much loss of spontaneity.

To improve his current game shows and to develop new ones, Goodson meets in California regularly with his creative group of producers and directors, although his brightest ideas still occur to him in private. As he explained to Stephen Steiner in an interview for *TV Guide* (January 7, 1978): "We subject an idea to internal battering. I don't want to suddenly wake up and say, 'Oh, I forgot that.' I never get angry at people in our company who poke and poke and say that something's not going to work. Most people in the game-show business settle too early. They get a concept and dash forward with that idea, and every once in a while it works. With us, by the time we are ready with something, it may not be great, but it's been through the kind of white-hot heat that makes it better."

Game shows have made Goodson a multimillionaire, complete with Rolls-Royce, art collection, and chauffeured limousine. Although the most lucrative kind of television programming today, the game show is inexpensive to produce and, unlike a risky dramatic series, makes money from the very first day it hits the home screen. According to a 1975 report in the business magazine *Forbes* (April 1), the average daily game show costs no more than $35,000 to produce weekly and can be sold by the packager to the network for around $50,000 a week, while syndication can yield even higher profits for the producer.

Since 1958 Mark Goodson has been a principal stockholder and vice-president of the Ingersoll Newspaper group, which publishes newspapers in Connecticut, Massachusetts, Rhode Island, New York, and Pennsylvania. He also has holdings in real estate and in publishing companies. Goodson has received the national television award of Great Britain (1951), three Emmy awards (1951; 1952; 1977) and a Sylvania award. He is a member of the Academy of Television Arts and Sciences and a former president (1957-58) of the New York chapter, a director of the New York City Center of Music and Drama, and a member of the American Film Institute.

A compulsive workaholic, worrier, exacting boss, and self-proclaimed perfectionist, Mark Goodson confessed to Gilbert Rogin of *Sports Illustrated* in 1963, "I'm really quite helpless at a cocktail party, a real *schlepper.* I feel most comfortable of all in an office or the studio. I feel I belong there; I truly come to life." The pipe-smoking television producer is tastefully dressed, distinguished-looking, white-haired man of average height, who sometimes puts on a few extra pounds. Although he maintains a home in New York City, he spends much of his time on the West Coast. Goodson has been married three times. By his first wife, Bluma Neveleff, whom he married in 1941, he has a daughter Jill and a son Jonathan. His daughter Marjorie was born during his second marriage, to Virginia McDavid. Since August 17, 1972 he has been married to the former Suzanne Russell Waddell of Greeneville, Tennessee.

In defending himself against the slings and arrows of caustic television critics, Goodson has said: "There's a vast, pluralistic society out there and the dial is its weapon. There are millions of people out there who love to watch game shows." Nevertheless, he is the first to admit that there are some rotten ones. "One of the prices I pay," Goodson complained to Stephen Steiner, "is that the game-show business is essentially without status. I regret it and I resent it. There aren't many people at the Yale Drama School studying game shows. The first thing people ask is, 'Why is somebody as literate and articulate as you in games?' It's like they're saying, 'Why is an engineer picking up garbage?' "

References: N Y Sunday News II p13+ Ap 15 '62 por; N Y Sunday News Mag p6 D 29 '57 por; Sports Illus 18:52+ Je 24 '63 por; Who's Who in America, 1976-77

Gould, Laurence M(cKinley)

Aug. 22, 1896- Educator; explorer.
Address: b. Department of Geoscience, University of Arizona, Tucson, Ariz. 85721; h. 9451 E. Rosewood, Tucson, Ariz. 85710

Dr. Laurence M. Gould, an expert in polar geology who has been studying Antarctica for fifty years, served as second-in-command of Commander Richard E. Byrd's expedition to the South Pole in the late 1920's and, three decades later, guided the American team's efforts in the Antarctic during the International Geophysical Year. In the interim, he taught geology at the University of Michigan and at Carleton College and, later, as Carleton's president, masterminded its development into one of the finest small liberal arts institutions in the United States. Gould has received some two dozen honorary degrees and a number of prestigious decorations, including the Explorer's Club medal, the Norwegian Cross of St. Olaf, and the United States Navy's Distinguished Service Award. The Norwegian-born American explorer, Finn Ronne, named Gould Bay, an inlet of Antarctica's Weddell Sea, after him.

Laurence McKinley Gould was born in Lacota, Michigan on August 22, 1896, the son of Herbert and Anna (Updike) Gould. At seventeen he left the farm on which he had grown up and moved to Boca Raton, Florida, where he taught kindergarten through eighth grade in a "little red schoolhouse" for two years. Returning to his home state, he enrolled at the University of Michigan in Ann Arbor. He had intended to study law, but he switched his major to geology, a subject in which he became interested while rooming in the house of the chairman of the geology department.

But Gould's promising academic career was temporarily interrupted by military service in World War I. As a member of the United States Army ambulance service from 1917 to 1919, he took part in the Meuse-Argonne offensive and, later, in the occupation of Germany. After his return to civilian life he continued his studies at the University of Michigan, where he earned his B.S. degree *magna cum laude* in 1921, his M.A. degree in 1923, and his D.Sc. degree in 1925. His doctoral dissertation dealt with the geology of the La Sal Mountains in Utah. Originally hired by his alma mater as a geology instructor in 1921, he was advanced to assistant professor in 1926 and promoted to associate professor in 1930. Meanwhile, he had embarked on what was to be a lifelong career in polar geology. During the summer of 1926 he served as geologist on an Arctic expedition sponsored by the University of Michigan, and the following summer he was the geographer and topographer for the Putnam expedition to Baffin Island in the Canadian Arctic.

In March 1928 Commander Richard E. Byrd, the celebrated aviator and polar explorer, chose Gould as one of eighty men to accompany him on a privately sponsored expedition to the Antarctic. The first American explorers to investigate that continent in ninety years, the members of the Byrd party were suitably outfitted to "winter over" in Antarctica. They set sail from Newport, Virginia in September 1928, and three months later, on December 28, reached the Bay of Whales, an inlet on the Pacific side of Antarctica where Roald Amundsen, the Norwegian discoverer of the South Pole, had established his base in 1911. A few miles inland, on the outer edge of the Ross Ice Shelf, Byrd set up camp and put Gould in charge of constructing the barracks and workrooms and readying them for the long Antarctic winter. The sprawling camp eventually included more than a dozen buildings, among them a small gymnasium, a fairly well-stocked library, a "maternity ward" for the sled dogs, and a machine shop and storehouse made out of airplane crates.

Commander Byrd was so impressed by Gould's technical know-how and by his affability that he named him his second-in-command. "If any man was liked by all, it was he," Byrd wrote in *Little America* (Putnam, 1930), his personal account of the expedition. "Larry was a blend of coolness and warmth. His friendly ways and his fairness endeared him to the Winter Party at Little America. Larry mingled, and yet was always respected. He was not above the telling of an occasional anecdote, distinguished for its dry and incisive wit. But most of all he was the oracle," Byrd continued. "When arguments waxed and flamed and drew to no conclusion, Larry was resorted to as the seat of judgment. His mind seemed to have held every fact that came into it."

While making his first aerial exploration of the interior in late January, Byrd discovered a great mountain range in Marie Byrd Land, and a few weeks later, Gould headed a small party on a geological expedition to that area. He collected his samples, but before the group could return to base, a blizzard destroyed their Fokker aircraft. The men were marooned until a search plane rescued them three days later. Gould spent the next six months preparing for the first extensive geological and glaciological survey of the Queen Maud Mountains, which he has described as "a veritable paradise for a geologist." In October he set off with five companions on the 1,500-mile sledge trek to Mt. Nansen and, several weeks later, established a base camp a few miles from the awesome 15,000-foot peak.

Under Gould's direction, the party mapped and charted large areas of the surrounding mountains and collected samples of low-grade lignite, indicating that Antarctica had once been densely forested, along with pre-Cambrian gneisses, schists, and granites. In snow-free areas they found patches of crusty lichen—the only indigenous life to be found in the region—clinging to the rocks. To confirm his suspicion that Mt. Nansen was part of a great uplifted fault system that stretched across the continent for more than 1,000 miles, Gould led his team up the mountain's steep southern slope. "We roped to climb and 'herringboned' and 'sidebilled' our way up on our skis," he wrote in his journal on December 7, 1929. "Had to climb even steeper slopes beyond these first crevasses to reach the coveted rocks—a bit hazardous this, for we were climbing along a steep side hill, and some 200 feet below us, paralleling our course, was a great yawning chasm. The snow was crusted over, and it was hard to make our skis stick, but we finally reached our rocks, the very rocks I wanted most to find in the Antarctic."

The rock formations on the peak—a series of sandstones with impure coaly material in the top seams—proved that Gould's supposition was correct. "No work of art of which I have stood in awe, no symphony I have ever heard, ever gave me the thrill that came when I picked up a piece of rock and found it was the sandstone I had come all the way to Antarctica to find," Gould wrote later. As the group began the slow, difficult descent, it began to snow. "We slipped and fell time after time, knowing the big open crevass was a few feet below us, got up, swallowed our hearts, and skidded on again." Gould finally "sat down on [his] skis and disgracefully slid to the bottom." He described his experiences in *Cold: the Record of an Antarctic Sledge Journey* (Brewer, Warren & Putnam, 1931). For his pathbreaking work, he was awarded an honorary Sc.D. degree by the Polytechnic Institute of Brooklyn, the David Livingston Centenary Medal of the American Geographical Society, and a Congressional Gold Medal.

In February 1930 Gould left the Antarctic and returned to his teaching post at the University of Michigan. Two years later, he accepted an appointment as professor of geology at Carleton College, a small coeducational college in Northfield, Minnesota. There he taught introductory and advanced courses in geology and continued his research in polar geology and in the geological history of the upper Mississippi Valley. During World War II he doubled as chief of the Arctic section of the United States Air Force's Arctic, Desert and Tropic Information Center. In 1945 Dr. Gould "reluctantly" gave up teaching to become Carleton's president. His inaugural address, delivered on October 16 of that year, stressed his concern for the future of "science and the other humanities" and typified his interdisciplinary approach to education.

Over the next few years Gould transformed Carleton from a relatively obscure coeducational college into a topflight private liberal arts institution. Working closely with its admissions director, he recruited the best students from the nation's high schools and instilled in them a commitment to intellectual excellence that brought the college scores of academic awards. Because he believed that scholarship requires "constant renewal through some kind of research activity," he attracted faculty members who were dedicated researchers as well as teachers. Moreover, he toughened the requirements for graduation and revised the curriculum to emphasize the humanities. "There is no excuse for a small private college any more unless it specializes in excellence and sets standards," he explained to a reporter for *Look* magazine (June 7, 1960). "Free of political control, it can experiment with curriculum and ideas and be a bearer of values. If America's academic life accepts the mores of the marketplace, we are really sunk."

In 1955—nearly thirty years after his first exploration of the polar regions—Gould headed the United States delegation to a multination planning conference on Antarctic research programs to be carried out during the 1957-58 International Geophysical Year (IGY). Appointed director of the United States IGY Antarctic program the following year, he took a sabbatical from Carleton, and on December 27, 1956, once again sailed for the Antarctic. Working out of the main American base on Ross Island in McMurdo Sound, Dr. Gould supervised scientific operations at five other United States stations.

In contrast to earlier expeditions, which concentrated on exploring and mapping uncharted areas, IGY teams from twelve countries conducted sophisticated experiments in oceanography, geomagnetism, cosmology, seismology, ionospheric physics, and glaciology. Although the scientific knowledge gained from the IGY research programs was enormous, Dr. Gould believed that the "human and social results" would prove more important in the long run. "This vast global effort was carried out in a period of almost unprecedented worldwide turmoil and unrest," he wrote more than a decade later in the *Bulletin of the Atomic Scientists* (December, 1970). "It was the IGY cooperative efforts in Antarctica, coldest of all the continents, that witnessed the first thawing of the Cold War. . . . It demonstrated, as never before, that the international community of science is the most hopeful of all examples of world cooperation and organization." As chairman of the Committee on Polar Research of the National Academy of Sciences, he testified before the Senate Foreign Relations Committee in favor of a treaty dedicating Antarctica as a peaceful scientific preserve. Calling the agreement "indispensable to the world of science which knows no national or other political boundaries," he urged its ratification as the first step toward "some kind of permanent cooperation" between governments.

Refreshed from his months in Antarctica, Dr. Gould returned to Carleton and immediately set about raising $10,000,000 to finance an extensive campus construction project. To prod corporations and well-heeled alumni into donating funds, he occasionally resorted to Cold War rhetoric. "We are like penguins wrapped in blubber," he told one group of potential contributors, as quoted in *Time* magazine (December 29, 1958). "We have wrapped ourselves in such a layer of luxury we are virtually impervious to what goes on in the world around us. We may be unable to wake up in time to meet the crisis that Sputnik graphically posed for us." Within three years he raised more than $12,000,000 for the redevelopment program. After retiring from the Carleton presidency in 1962, he joined the faculty of the University of Arizona in Tucson as professor of geosciences, a post he still holds.

Throughout his career Dr. Gould has been active in professional and academic organizations. Elected to the senate of Phi Beta Kappa in 1946, he served, in the late 1950's, successive terms as vice-president, then president of its United Chapters. He was a member of the board of the National Science Foundation from 1952 to 1962 and a trustee of the Ford Foundation and the Carnegie Foundation for the Advancement of Teaching from 1958 to 1962. As a Ford Foundation trustee, he made a two-month trip around the world in 1961 to review Ford-supported programs. He also served as president of the Scientific Committee on Antarctic Research and of the American Association for the Advancement of Science.

Through the years Dr. Gould has followed the exploits of his fellow polar scientists and has twice returned to the continent himself, most recently in January 1977. In articles for professional journals and in speeches to learned societies, he has stressed the immeasurable importance of Antarctica as a scientific laboratory, as a "dated record" of the earth's history, and as a potential source of protein-rich food. The discovery in 1969 of a fossilized skull of a lystrosaurus, a medium-sized reptile somewhat resembling the modern-day salamander that thrived during the Triassic period, proved "beyond a doubt," in Gould's words, that Antarctica had at one time been the keystone of Gondwanaland, the gigantic, hypothetical, pre-Mesozoic continent composed of India and all other southern hemispheric land masses. One of the truly great fossil finds of all time, it made probable the long-discredited theory of continental drift.

Although he concedes that a dangerous gap has developed between science and the humanities, Gould dismisses C. P. Snow's theory of "two cultures" as "greatly overstated." Like Jacob Bronowski, he believes that the concept of values in the humanities and the sciences is similar. "Both the scientist and the poet seek to explore and to understand," he wrote in an article for the February 1968 issue of the UNESCO *Courier*. "It is only the form of exploration which is different." Gould argued that "many supposed conflicts rise from a gross misunderstanding of what science is all about." "There is a fallacious idea that science is objective while the humanistic studies are subjective," he continued. "This is complete nonsense. Science is always the record of someone's personal experience." To "bring the disciplines of our academic world into order," to "recover the Renaissance," he recommended using "history, broadly conceived," as a "cultural bridge." "Science, viewed historically, is the great untapped reservoir of humanism which can help fill the void caused by the decay of classical humanism," he concluded. "We must have humanists who comprehend and include scientific and technological knowledge in their dreams of the world, else we shall have no world at all."

On August 2, 1930 Laurence Gould married Margaret Rice. Burly and still vigorous, he has the creased, weathered face of a man who has spent most of his life outdoors. During his years at Carleton, cartoonists for the college newspaper affectionately caricatured him as a jovial penguin. Gould is easy-going and imperturbable and friends claim that he can "swear better than any other man without using a single cuss word." Most comfortable in casual attire, he has a penchant for red ties that dates back to his undergraduate days. "Larry Gould simply cannot be adequately described by words alone," a longtime colleague has said. "One has to know him and work with him. . . . I know of no one who has worked with Larry who has not in some way been affected by the association."

References: Look 24:7+ Je 7 '60 pors; Newsweek 59:84 Je 25 '62 por; Science 139:612-14 F 15 '63 por; Time 72:30 D 29 '58 por; Who's Who in America, 1976-77

Graves, Robert (Ranke)

July 24, 1895- Writer. Address: "Canelluñ," Deyá, Majorca, Spain

For sheer scope, versatility, and sustained brilliance of achievement there is probably no man of letters currently writing in English to equal the octogenarian Robert Graves, the stoic sage of Majorca. During a sixty-year career spiced with frequent controversy over his highly idiosyncratic viewpoint, Graves has published 140 books and 800 short pieces, establishing a reputation as a remarkable, multifaceted talent: poet, novelist, short-story writer, biographer, critic, essayist, translator, and mythographer. He is perhaps best known for his early, classic autobiography, *Good-bye to All That* (1929), a valedictory to Georgian England especially notable for its recounting of his experiences in World War I; for his two best-selling historical novels about ancient Rome, *I, Claudius* (1934) and *Claudius the God* (1934); and for his studies in myth, especially the monumental *The White Goddess* (1947), his exploration into the folk origins of the idealized woman identified with the poetic Muse. But he is first and last a poet, whose prose is written to support the verse that he writes in service to his Goddess.

During the long hegemony of what he calls "Franco-American modernism," the experimental movement in poetry typified by Ezra Pound and T. S. Eliot, among others, Graves was a spiritual exile, dismissed as a "minor poet" because of his adherence to traditional metrical forms and a subjective romanticism unacceptable to the "mechanarchy," the name he gave to the world he left behind when he moved from England to Majorca in 1929. Beginning with Edwin Muir in the 1950's, critics increasingly upgraded his rank as a poet, and today he is widely regarded as perhaps the best contemporary English lyric poet, the master of hard-edged, vigorous love poetry, precise and clear in its diction, sensuous in its imagery, and ironic in its wit. "The main theme of poetry," Graves believes, "is, properly, the relations of man and woman rather than those of man and man, as the Apollonian classicists would have it," and his chief emphasis, paradoxically is on "the practical impossibility, transcended only by belief in miracle, of absolute love continuing between man and woman." In his prose as in his verse, he is a technically impeccable craftsman, in total control of syntax, and even those who consider some of his excursions into myth, history, and biography "perverse" acknowledge the dazzling range of his maverick erudition.

Robert Ranke Graves was born on July 24, 1895 in Wimbledon, England, the third of five children of Amalie (von Ranke) Graves, the daughter of a professor of medicine at the University of Munich, and Alfred Perceval Graves, a Scotch-Irish London school inspector and man of letters who had five additional children by a previous marriage (terminated by his first wife's death). The father, the son of a Protestant bishop of Limerick, was a poet, songwriter, and translator who contributed to the Irish literary renascence through such books as *Irish Songs and Ballads* (1879). Graves credits his paternal heritage with saving him "from any false reverence of poets" and giving him sufficient "coldness" to check "the goodness of heart from which my mother's family suffers." On the maternal side he acknowledges a debt to his grandfather Heinrich von Ranke for his "clumsy largeness, endurance, energy, seriousness, and thick hair" and to his great-uncle Leopold von Ranke, the historian, for his historical method, his passion for finding out "how the things actually occurred."

Randall Jarrell in his essay "Graves and the White Goddess," reprinted posthumously in his *The Third Book of Criticism* (1969), quoted Graves as saying that, as a poet, he owes more to the von Rankes than to the Graveses, that the Graveses have good minds "for examinations . . . and solving puzzles," are "inclined to petulance" and subject to "most disconcerting spells of complete amnesia," and "rely on their intuition and bluff to get them through." Jarrell commented that "this is a fine partial summary of one side of Robert von Ranke Graves," the side including his "professional, matter-of-fact-to-the-point-of-insolence, complacent, prosaic competence."

According to legend, Graves received a literary baptism of sorts when, as a babe in his pram on Wimbledon Common, he was patted on the head by Algernon Charles Swinburne, one of the many literati who frequented the Graves family circle. In *Good-bye to All That* Graves describes a pleasant upper-class childhood in Wimbledon, London, and, during vacations, Germany and Wales. At Charterhouse, the famous old public school in Godalming, Surrey, he pursued sports (boxing, rugby, and mountain climbing) and his studies with equal vigor. The teacher who most influenced him in both lines of endeavor was George Mallory, who would later die in an attempt to climb Mount Everest. Mallory showed Graves's poetry to Edward Marsh, then secretary to Winston Churchill, who encouraged him, with the caveat that he modernize his diction and rid his verse of the saccharine tendencies inherited from his father. "Since the age of fifteen," Graves later wrote, "poetry has been my ruling passion and I have never intentionally undertaken any task or formed any relationship that seemed inconsistent with poetic principles."

From Charterhouse, Graves went directly into action in World War I as a captain in the Royal Welch Fusiliers, where one of his fellow officers was another "war poet," Siegfried Sassoon. In July 1916, after two traumatic years in the trenches of northern France, he was grievously wounded in the chest by an exploding shell on the Somme front and mistakenly reported dead. Reading the announcement of his death in the London *Times* gave him a sense of posthumous reprieve, but the relish for living that came with that feeling was overshadowed for more than ten years not only by the problems of bronchitis and neurasthenia but by a deep psychological funk. Until 1928, Graves says, he was afflicted by recurring visions of horror, flashbacks to the bloody, stinking trenches that persisted "like an alternate life."

Graves's first book was the slim collection of Georgian verse *Over the Brazier* (Poetry Workshop, 1916). A second small volume, *Goliath and David* (Chiswick Press, 1916), was followed by *Fairies and Fusiliers* (Heinemann, 1917; Knopf, 1918), a collection of war poems that reveal a young man shocked out of complacent gentility but whose bitterness, absorbed in part from his association with Siegfried Sassoon, who published his *Collected War Poems* in 1919, was relieved by irony and even, at times, by flippancy.

In January 1918 Graves married Nancy Nicholson, daughter of the painter William Nicholson and a staunch feminist. With his wife, he settled near Oxford University, where he studied fitfully for a degree, wrote steadily, and numbered among his friends T. E. Lawrence ("of Arabia") and the poets John Masefield, Edmund Blunden, and Robert Bridges. Lawrence introduced him to Ezra Pound, saying, presciently, "Graves . . . Pound. Pound . . . Graves. You'll dislike each other."

When Peter Quennell visited Graves in his cottage near Oxford in 1923 or 1924, Graves had not yet emerged from his "puritanical phase . . . nor had he yet been able to cast off the neurotic legacy of his war adventures," Quennell recounted in *Horizon* (January 1962). "But he was already engaged, slowly and patiently, in accomplishing his own self-salvation; and he had evolved an odd and original theory about the nature and purpose of the poet's work: every poem was the solution of a problem that could not otherwise be formulated and resolved."

Graves himself informs us, in *Good-Bye to All That,* that he regarded poetry as "first, a cathartic for the poet suffering from some inner conflict, and then as a cathartic for readers in similar conflict" and that he made a "tentative connection" between poetry and dream in the light of the dream psychology in which he was then interested as a means of self-therapy. That Freudian, psychoanalytical approach was the one he took in *On English Poetry: Being an Irregular Approach to the Psychology of This Art, from Evidence Mainly Subjective* (Heinemann, 1922; Knopf, 1922), *The Meaning of Dreams* (Cecil Palmer, 1924; Greenberg, 1925), and *Poetic Unreason and Other Studies* (Palmer, 1925).

The romantic poems and ballads of *Country Sentiment* (Secker, 1920; Knopf, 1920) were in large measure escapist verse, sometimes marred, Graves later felt, by "falsities for public delectation." In *The Pier-Glass* (Secker, 1921; Knopf, 1921) he took a brave step forward, to hunt down the phantasms haunting his mind to their source. He did not, however, wish to exorcise "these mysterious ghostly influences" completely, for fear that the power of writing poetry would disappear and he would "become merely a dull easy writer."

In 1926 Graves took his B.Litt. degree at Oxford. By that time he and Nancy Nicholson had four children, two girls, Jenny and Catherine, who were given the last name Nicholson, and two boys David and Samuel, who were surnamed Graves. (David was killed in action in Burma in World War II.) Under financial pressure, Graves took the only salaried job of his career, as professor of English literature at the University of Cairo in Cairo, Egypt, a position secured for him partly through the instrumentality of his friends Arnold Bennett and T. E. Lawrence. After one year, the academic year 1926-27, he left the teaching post and returned to England with the determination never to tie himself down to a job again. To free himself, he began to turn out books of prose calculated to sell. The first was the authorized biography *Lawrence and the Arabs* (J. Cape, 1927), published in the United States as *Lawrence and the Arabian Adventure* (Doubleday, 1928). With the huge success of *Good-bye to All That* (J. Cape, 1929; Cape and H. Smith, 1930) he was able to pay off his debts and move to the Balearic island of Majorca, 140 miles east of Spain's Mediterranean coast, a retreat suggested to him by Gertrude Stein as a "paradise—if you can stand it."

In *Good-bye to All That* Graves bade farewell to his whole past, including not only the England of his schooling, the British literary establishment, and the World War I era, but also to his first marriage. Having separated from Nancy Nicholson, he set up a ménage as well as a literary partnership with Laura Riding, the American "Fugitive" poet and critic. Teaching themselves hand printing, Graves and Miss Riding established the Seizin Press in London and continued to operate the press after they moved to Majorca. Together they edited the semiannual critical journal *Epilogue,* translated Georg Schwarz's *Almost Forgotten Germany* (Random, 1937), and wrote several books, including the satirical *No Decency Left* (J. Cape, 1935). Under the influence of Miss Riding, who preached a rigorous literary gospel of "truth in words," Graves purified his poetic diction, arriving at a greater economy, clarity, and precision in his use of language.

Forced to leave Majorca when the Spanish Civil War broke out in 1936, Graves and Miss Riding moved to Switzerland, to England, to Brittany, and finally to the United States, to a farm near New Hope, Pennsylvania, where they broke up in 1939. The books published by Graves during his decade-long association with Miss Riding included *Collected Poems* (Random, 1938); *The Future of Swearing and Improper Language* (K. Paul, Trench, and Trubner, 1936); the collection of short fiction *But It Still Goes On* (J. Cape, 1930); *The Real David Copperfield* (Barker, 1933), a condensation of Dickens' novel; and the novels *Antigua, Penny, Puce* (Seizin Press and Constable, 1936) and *Count Belisarius* (Random, 1938), which won the Femina-Vie Heureuse and Stock prizes.

Graves established himself in the front rank of historical novelists with the best-selling *I, Claudius* (Smith and Haas, 1934), winner of the Hawthornden and James Tait Black Memorial prizes. Along with its sequel, *Claudius the God* (Barker, 1934; Smith and Haas, 1935), *I, Claudius* is a masterful reconstruction of Roman life, seen through the eyes of the Emperor Claudius I. Maligned by history as a half-mad despot, Claudius is rehabilitated by Graves into a seemingly slow-witted, gentle man who surprises the soldiery who put him on the throne by becoming a wise, forceful administrator in a society full of violence and intrigue. A film based on the Claudius novels was begun by Alexander Korda in 1937 but never completed. A stage version by John Mortimer was produced in London in 1972, and a thirteen-part BBC version was shown in the United States by the Public Broadcasting Service during the 1977-78 television season.

In 1939 Graves returned to England, where he married his present wife, Beryl Pritchard. With Alan Hodge he wrote *The Long Week-End* (Faber, 1940; Macmillan, 1941), a lively social history of England in the years between 1918 to 1939, and *The Reader Over Your Shoulder* (Macmillan, 1943), a handbook for writers of English prose. During the World War II years he also wrote two novels based on the diary of a British soldier in the American Revolutionary War, *Sergeant Lamb of the Ninth* (Methuen, 1940) and *Proceed, Sergeant Lamb*, (Random, 1941); an unsympathetic novel about John Milton narrated by the poet's wife, *Wife to Mr. Milton* (Creative Age Press, 1944); *Hercules, My Shipmate* (Creative Age Press, 1944), a re-creation of the Jason legend in which the Golden Fleece is transformed from mere treasure sought by the Argonauts into a symbol of matriarchal worship predating the male-dominated religion of the Olympian gods.

After World War II Graves returned to Majorca with his second family. In 1946 Creative Age press published his daring fictionalization of the life of Jesus, *King Jesus*, a book that shocked believers with what they considered its blasphemous distortions. Two years later the same publisher issued Graves's monumental "historical grammar of poetic myth," *The White Goddess*, in which he explored pagan, Mediterranean and Celtic mythology and found in it the central monomyth of a Goddess whose worship ended when patriarchal civilization began. Source of the seasons and moon phases, that Goddess is both the Muse that inspires true poetry and the instrument of human creativity, fulfillment, and destruction. Graves's mixture in *The White Goddess* of scholarship and intuitive discovery, a mixture that he calls "analeptic thought," is dismissed as unsound by many scholars, but in his study *Robert Graves* (1956) Martin Seymour-Smith places the book "beside *The Anatomy of Melancholy* as an eccentric classic of English literature." As a personal statement of poetic faith the book remains central to Graves's thought. Graves related other myths to the monomyth in his later studies *The Greek Myths* (Penguin Books, 1955), *The Hebrew Myths* (Doubleday, 1964), written with Raphael Patai, and *Mammon and the Black Goddess* (Doubleday, 1965).

In retrospect, Graves realized that the White Goddess is a personal Muse who has been with him so long that he "cannot recall her first entry" into his heart and who comes to him periodically incarnate in the women he loves. "There are two distinct but complementary orders of women, both of them honored by poets," he explains. "First, the ideal woman of patriarchal civilization . . . heroine of all old-fashioned songs and stories . . . the guardian of the sacred hearth. . . . Then the other woman, the multitudinously named White Goddess, a relic of matriarchal civilization or (who knows?) the harbinger of its return. She scorns any claim on her person, or curb on her desires; rejects male tutelage, hates marriage, and demands utter trust and faithfulness from her lovers. . . . The love bestowed on a poet, however briefly, by a Muse-possessed woman heightens his creative powers to an unparalleled degree."

After the publication of *The White Goddess* Graves's critical writings tended to be either defenses of his view of true poetry as the invocation of the Muse or attacks on poets he considered remiss in paying her tribute, among whom were Ezra Pound, T. S. Eliot, and W. H. Auden. Ranked high by Graves were Robert Frost and Ben Jonson, and he paid special homage to John Skelton, whose strong influence on his own poetry he acknowledged. Among the volumes containing his literary criticism are *The Common Asphodel: Collected Essays on Poetry*, (H. Hamilton, 1949); *The Crowning Privilege* (Cassell, 1955; Doubleday, 1956), comprising the Clark lectures that Graves delivered at Cambridge University in 1954-55; and *Poetic Craft and Principle* (Cassell, 1967).

As a translator, Graves produced English versions of *The Golden Ass* of Apuleius, entitled *Metamorphoses* (Penguin, 1950; Farrar, Straus, 1951), Pedro Antonio de Alarcón's *Infant with the Globe* (Faber, 1955), George Sand's *Winter in Majorca* (Cassell, 1956), and Seutonius' *Lives of the Twelve Caesars* (Cassell, 1957), among other works. When "analeptic thought" pushed him into interpretative areas, his translations stirred controversy. Such was also the case with his and Joshua Podro's revision of the New Testament, *The Nazarene Gospel Restored* (Cassell, 1953; Doubleday, 1954), a reconstruction of and commentary on the Gospels, considered by the author to be one of his most important books. His *The Anger of Achilles* (Doubleday, 1959) was a rendering of the *Iliad* as an entertaining satire written not by a single poet but by a guild of Ionian bards. Perhaps the most controversial of his translations was his blank-verse rendition of *The Rubaiyyat of Omar Khayaam* (Cassell, 1967), done in collaboration with Omar Ali-Shah, which repudiated the melodic style and romantic hedonism of Edward Fitzgerald's translation, replacing them with the plain declarations of a Sufi religious devotee.

Meanwhile, with the passing of the years, Graves was becoming ever more productive as a poet, honing and culling for each successive collection. As Randall Jarrell observed, "Mr. Graves is one of the few poets alive who can write a first-rate poem, and one of the very few who are getting better as they get older." In Jarrell's opinion, "Graves's richest, most moving, and most consistently beautiful poems—poems that almost deserve the literal [appellation] magical—are his mythical-archaic pieces, all those the reader thinks of as 'White Goddess poems': 'To Juan at the Winter Solstice,' 'Theseus and Ariadne,' 'Lament for Pasiphaë,' 'The Sirens' Welcome to Cronos,' 'A Love Story,' 'The Return of the Goddess,' 'Darien,' and eight or ten others. The best of these are different from anything else in English. . . . 'The Sirens' Welcome to Cronos,' for instance, has a color or taste that is new because it had been lost for thousands of years."

In 1957 Graves made the first of many lecture and reading tours of the United States, under the sponsorship of the Institute of Contemporary Arts. In his introduction to Graves's *New Collected Poems* (Doubleday, 1977), James McKinley recalled that occasion: "The United States embraced Robert Graves. . . . We found his rebellious nature refreshing, his matriarchal notions fetching. His explorations with hallucinatory drugs, magic mushrooms served with ancient history, were *à la mode.* We wondered at a man who could construct an operative code for living out of the belief that man's role is to be alternately inspired and dejected by his love for women."

As Graves himself observes, he became recognized in England by "repercussion from America." That recognition was officially confirmed by his election to the Oxford University Chair of Poetry, a position in which he gave three lectures a year between 1961 and 1966. Among the books Graves published during those years were two children's books, *The Big Green Book* (Crowell, 1962), illustrated by Maurice Sendak, and *Two Wise Children* (Harlin Quist, 1966). Beginning in 1966, the British rare book dealer Bertram Rota Ltd., brought out limited, signed editions of new small books of poetry by Graves from which the poet would select verse at two or three year intervals for inclusion in the successive editions of his collected poems. Reviewing *Poems 1970-72* (Doubleday, 1973) in the *New York Times* (March 11, 1973), Stephen Spender wrote: "Of all poets of this time, Robert Graves is the one who, without solemnity but with total dedication, has kept the idea of poetry sacred and the idea of the poet true. . . . His work is the nearest thing we have to Latin poetry."

The independence that Graves displays in his poetry extends to academic and political affiliations. "The fact is," he told an interviewer, "that I really hate all organizations. I've refused several D. Litts because I don't want to commit myself. I refused the C.B.E., too. . . . The only things I believe in, really, are love and honor." He accepted a Gold Medal from the National Poetry Society of America in 1960, and the Queen's Gold Medal for Poetry in 1968. He is also the recipient of two unusual Olympic Games medals: a Bronze Medal for Poetry, Paris, 1924; and a Gold Medal for Poetry, Cultural Olympics, Mexico, 1968. The Lockwood Memorial Library of the State University of New York at Buffalo maintains an archive of Graves's poetry, and Southern Methodist University in Texas owns his prose manuscripts.

Robert Graves and his present wife, Beryl, have four children, Lucia, William, Juan, and Tomás, and Graves has grandchildren from both his marriages. The writer is a burly man, six feet two inches tall, with an athletic build that belies his years, blue eyes, a grizzled head of white hair, a stubborn set to his face, a hooked nose, broken in schoolboy rugby, and an imposing presence, suggesting hauteur. He writes compulsively, he says, with a steel-nibbed pen, beginning a poem in "a fit of possession" or "induced trance" and going through as many as thirty-five drafts before he is satisfied. His prose works he puts together with the aid of a secretary, in about six drafts.

Occasionally Graves will take time out to walk, swim, or entertain visitors to his stone-walled, tile-roofed home, surrounded by citrus orchards on a mountain that rises above the village of Deyá in Majorca. The village has a population of some 300 Spanish natives and scores of expatriate artists and writers, many from the United States, attracted by Graves's presence in Deyá. He rolls his own cigarettes and has never learned to drive a car or typewrite. "I seem," he says, "to be the last of the old-fashioned men of letters."

References: Esquire 74:144+ S '70; N Y Times p43 N 20 '64 por; N Y Times Mag p36+ O 30 '66; Pub W p50+ Ag 11 '75; Show 2:78+ D '62 pors; Washington Post E p5 N 21 '65 pors; Contemporary Authors 1st rev vols 5-8 (1969); Matthews, T. S. Jacks or Better (1978); Twentieth Century Authors (1942; First Supplement, 1955)

Guthrie, Janet

Mar. 7, 1938- Race driver. Address: c/o United States Auto Club, 4910 W. 16th St., Speedway, Ind. 46224

The sex barrier in championship auto racing in the United States has been broken by Janet Guthrie, the first woman to qualify for the Indianapolis 500, the major American event of its kind and one at which women were not even allowed in the repair and refueling pits until 1972, when the ban was lifted by lawsuit. Miss Guthrie began her driving career in sports car competition, road racing that is supervised by the Sports Car Club of America. The high-powered USAC type of motor car racing on an oval track epitomized by the lucrative, sensational 500-mile event at the Indianapolis Motor Speedway every Memorial Day is under the jurisdiction of the United States Auto Club. Miss Guthrie first qualified at Indianapolis in 1977, in her second attempt, and she finished ninth there in 1978. In addition to her achievements on the USAC circuit, she has acquitted herself well in many Grand National events on the NASCAR (National Association for Stock Car Auto Racing) circuit, where she is also the female pioneer.

Janet Guthrie

The eldest of five children, Janet Guthrie was born in Iowa City, Iowa on March 7, 1938. Her father, William Lain Guthrie, a pilot, operated an airport on the outskirts of Iowa City until he took a job with Eastern Airlines and moved with his family to Miami, Florida. In Florida, Miss Guthrie attended Miss Harris' Florida School, a prep school for girls, then in Miami, now in Stuart.

As the daughter of an airlines captain, Miss Guthrie early displayed a taste for daring adventure. "I've always enjoyed challenges," she told L. H. Whittemore in an interview for the Sunday supplement *Parade* (August 1, 1976). "I used to ask myself, 'Why am I involved in these men's activities? What's wrong with me?' Then I realized that they're intrinsically exciting."

Quickly learning to handle the controls of a Piper Cub, Miss Guthrie flew at thirteen, soloed at sixteen, and earned a private pilot's license at seventeen; later she also earned an instructor's license. By the age of twenty-one she had logged more than 400 hours in the air, was able to handle at least twenty different types of aircraft, and had some experience as a parachutist.

In the meantime, from prep school Miss Guthrie had gone to the University of Michigan, where she took a B.S. degree in physics in 1960. For seven years following her graduation from college she worked as an aerospace research and development engineer at the Republic Aviation Corporation in Farmingdale, Long Island. While working at Republic Aviation she was one of four women who passed the National Aeronautics and Space Administration's first tests for the scientist-astronaut program, but she was later eliminated, presumably because she did not have a Ph.D. degree.

With money saved from her earnings at Republic Aviation, Miss Guthrie in 1961 bought a used Jaguar XK 120, a sports car she had coveted since adolescence. Her original intention was to use the XK 120 only as a street vehicle, but, unable to resist venturing beyond simple road testing in the sleek coupé, she joined local sports car clubs and entered their gymkhana competitions, low-speed events stressing precision driving, such as contests on zigzag courses marked with pylons. In 1962 she was named the women's gymkhana champion of Long Island.

When Miss Guthrie attended a driving school at the sports car track in Lime Rock, Connecticut, veteran driver Gordon McKenzie, impressed with her combination of daring and carefulness, asked her if she had ever considered becoming a sports car racing driver. His encouragement was all she needed: she enrolled in race driving classes and bought a used Jaguar XK 140, built expressly for racing, taught herself the mechanics of its assembly, and rebuilt its engine.

During 1964 Miss Janet Guthrie finished thirteen races in her Jaguar XK 140, including several endurance runs. After placing sixth overall in the Watkins Glenn (New York) 500, she won two SCCA meets, placed second in three, and finished third in Three more.

In 1967 Miss Guthrie quit her job at the Republic Aviation Corporation, and later she became a technical editor for the Sperry-Rand Corporation, a job allowing her more time for racing. For five years, until 1971, she was one of the Macmillan Ring-Free Motor Maids, a team sponsored by the Macmillan Ring-Free Oil Company. In a variety of cars, she and her codrivers finished thirty-first in the Daytona (Florida) twenty-four-hour endurance race in 1966, took the KLG-Nisonger Trophy in the same race the following year, and won the trophy a second time at Sebring in 1969. By 1971 Miss Guthrie had a record of nine straight finishes in the country's top endurance events. (Only approximately half of the drivers who start in those events finish.)

Among the events in which she finished was the Watkins Glen six-hour race. In the Sebring twelve-hour race she was second in class in 1967 and she won the under-two-liter prototype class at Sebring in 1970. She was a member of a women's team that beat out an international male team at Sebring in 1970, and she was first overall and first in class at a Bridgehampton, Long Island meet in 1972.

Sponsored by the Goodyear Tire and Rubber Company in addition to the Macmillan Ring-Free Oil Company, Miss Guthrie and codriver Kent Fellows finished first overall in a Camaro at Bridgehampton, Long Island in August 1971. Under new sponsorship, that of the A-1 Toyota Co. of East Haven, Connecticut, Janet Guthrie, driving a Toyota Celica, won the North American Road Racing "B Sedan" championship in 1973. At Bridgehampton in 1975 she won both the Vanderbilt Cup race and the Bridgehampton 400. By that time she had well over 100 races behind her.

In October 1975 Janet Guthrie began working for Toyota as a "consumer information specialist," demonstrating safe-driving techniques around the United States—and incidentally promoting Toyota automobiles. Four months later she was surprised to receive a telephone call from Rolla-Vollstedt, asking her to become the first woman driver in the Indianapolis 500. Vollstedt, an Oregon lumber executive and championship car builder who had been entering cars at Indianapolis since 1962, said that he was planning on entering two cars at Indy that year: one was to be driven by veteran Dick Simon; would Miss Guthrie agree to drive the second?

Accepting Vollstedt's offer, Janet Guthrie underwent secret trials at the Ontario Motor Speedway near Los Angeles in February 1976, hitting an average speed of 172.58 miles per hour and a top speed of 196 miles per hour. After the Bryant Heating and Air Conditioning Company assured her of its sponsorship, she announced her Indianapolis bid in March 1976. To establish her status in the United States Auto Club by proving her ability to handle USAC-level cars in competition, she first entered the Trenton (New Jersey) 200 on May 2, 1976 in the *Bryant Special*.

At Trenton, Miss Guthrie placed fifteenth in a field of twenty-two after a gearbox break forced her out. At Indianapolis later in the month she passed the rookie test with a top speed of 171.42, but she was unable to push the *Bryant Special* up to 181 miles per hour, the qualifying speed. (She did achieve that speed in another car in practice.) Making up for her disappointment in Indianapolis was the opportunity to become the first woman ever to qualify for a Grand National Speedway event sponsored by the National Association for Stock Car Racing. Some admirers of hers in Charlotte, North Carolina, saw to it that she could race in the Charlotte World 600 on May 30, 1976, at the same time that the Indy 500 was under way. In a 1975 Chevrolet Laguna provided by Lynda Ferrari, a bank executive, and tuned up by veteran mechanic Ralph Moody, she came from the twenty-seventh pole position to finish fifteenth at Charlotte. Moving on to five other NASCAR events in 1976, she finished fifteenth twice and earned $8,179 in prize money. Early in the 1977 season she raced in two NASCAR Grand National events, the Daytona 500 and the Richmond 400, and finished twelfth—and top rookie—in both. She ran nineteen Grand National stock car races in 1977 and finished third in that year's fierce Rookie-of-the-Year contest.

At Indianapolis in 1977 Vollstedt provided Miss Guthrie with a new, faster car, the *Lightning*. On a practice run at the Speedway on May 10 she crashed into a wall seconds after she was clocked at 191 mph. She recuperated and her car was repaired in time for the qualifications, which she passed with a four-lap average of 188.403 miles per hour. On May 29, 1977 Tony Hulman, the late president of the Indianapolis Motor Speedway, in his last call to the drivers beginning the 500, made the historic statement: "In company with the first lady ever to qualify at Indianapolis—gentlemen, start your engines." Engine trouble forced Miss Guthrie to make eight pit stops for repairs, and she retired from the race after completing only twenty-seven laps, to finish in twenty-ninth place. Sponsored by the Texaco Company, Miss Guthrie raced at Indianapolis on May 28, 1978 in the Texaco *Star*, a "Wildcat" built by George Bignotti, in which she finished ninth.

"There has been a big change in the reaction to me," Miss Guthrie told Bill Lyon in an interview for *Sporting News* (July 1, 1978). "The hostility has cooled down quite a bit. I think the worst is over. The initial reaction to me was one of a lack of respect. What you really need is endurance. And some tests show that women have more endurance than men. But that's not the point. I'm not trying to establish the superiority of one sex over another. I'm a good driver, but I'm no superwoman. What I'm trying to emphasize is that a driver is primarily a person, not a man or a woman, and that a great deal of driving is mental. You cannot afford to get angry behind the wheel. A good driver needs emotional detachment, concentration, good judgment, and desire."

Janet Guthrie is a slender woman, five feet nine inches tall and weighing 135 pounds, with light brown hair and hazel eyes. Even on the racetrack she is as well groomed and manicured as conditions will permit, and in private life she is a fashionable dresser. She impresses most interviewers as serene and composed, and she herself says that she is an introvert by nature. When he interviewed her for the *Sporting News*, Bill Lyon found her to be "articulate" and giving the impression that "she would prefer an afternoon in the library [or] a box at the ballet [to] shrieking engines, coaxing two tons of steel and rubber to go faster, faster, faster." As a matter of fact, going to the ballet in Manhattan (where she maintains an apartment) is one of her recreations. The others include raising plants, listening to Bach, Berlioz, and the like on her stereo, reading, cooking for guests, and picnicking on Long Island.

Regarding marriage, she told L. H. Whittemore in the *Parade* interview: "Well, I've had long-standing relationships with a couple of guys, one of whom was a driver. But it would be difficult to be married and continue racing, especially with kids. Racing is notorious for breaking up marriages. It takes so much time and travel. But believe me, living alone is hell." But whatever the sacrifice it requires in her social life, racing is worth it for her, as she stated in another interview, with Margaret Roach for the New York *Times* (March 4, 1978): "Racing is a passion, . . . at this level, a source of immense gratification. So the rest is no problem."

In response to the common assertion that race drivers have a "death wish," Miss Guthrie quotes scientific authority to the effect that drivers are "less suicidal" than most people because they have "an outlet for their aggressions." "There is," she pointed out in the *Sporting News* interview, "very little in civilized life that demands everything you've got intellectually, physically, and emotionally. Auto racing demands all of this, and more. Driving is living. It's aggressive instead of passive living."

References: N Y Post p19 Mr 20 '76 por; N Y Times C p10 Mr 4 '78 por; Newsday p3 Ja 30 '77 pors, p10+ Mr 6 '77 pors; Parade p9 Ag 1 '76 pors; Sporting News 185:26 Jl 1 '78 por; Time 107:62 My 31 '76 por; Olney, Ross R. Janet Guthrie (1978)

Haldeman, H(arry) R(obbins)

Oct. 27, 1926- Former government official. Address: b. c/o Times Books, 3 Park Ave., New York City, N.Y. 10016

Among the events precipitated by the Watergate scandal, the resignations in 1973 of President Richard Nixon's two top aides, H. R. ("Bob") Haldeman and John Ehrlichman, had an impact exceeded only by the resignation of the President himself the following year. Haldeman, then an advertising executive, joined the Nixon team in 1956, managed the successful Presidential campaign of 1968, and became Presidential chief of staff when Nixon took office in 1969. The core of "Watergate" was the involvement of high Nixon campaign organization and Administration officials in the political conspiracy that came to light after an espionage break-in at the Democratic National Committee headquarters in Washington in 1972. The cover-up, or attempted cover-up, of that involvement led to the worst Constitutional crisis in American history. For his part in the cover-up, Haldeman, after losing appeals, served eighteen months in jail.

Harry Robbins Haldeman was born on October 27, 1926 in Los Angeles, California, the son of Harry Francis and Katherine (Robbins) Haldeman. The grandparents on both sides of the family had migrated to California from Indiana, bringing with them staunchly conservative political, social, and economic attitudes. Harry Marston Haldeman, the paternal grandfather, the owner of what was at one time the largest independent plumbing supply firm in Los Angeles and a philanthropist interested in advancing the cultural life of the city, was a cofounder of the Better American Federation of California, one of the first anti-Communist organizations in the United States. When the family business began to falter, during the Depression, Haldeman's father revitalized it by turning from plumbing to heating and air conditioning.

Bob Haldeman was raised in comfortable homes in Beverly Hills and the San Fernando Valley, and, when he did not achieve up to his capacity in public school, he was sent to private schools. In the Boy Scouts he attained the rank of Eagle. In his first two years in college he was enrolled in the United States Navy's wartime V-12 officer training program, at the University of Redlands in 1944-45 and at the University of Southern

California the following academic year. He completed his college work at the University of California at Los Angeles, where he began his long association with John Ehrlichman. Both were members of the UCLA graduating class of 1948, and they served together on the university's interfraternity council. Frank Mankiewicz, the journalist and prominent Democrat, a member of the UCLA class of 1947, remembers Haldeman as a militant anti-Communist on campus, but Haldeman challenges that recollection. In *The Ends of Power* (Times Books, 1978), written with Joseph Di-Mona, Haldeman recalls: "In school I was not only apolitical, but had gone completely the other route. I was a rah-rah college type, a Homecoming Chairman, no less, and a campus leader."

After taking his B.S. degree in business administration at UCLA and working briefly as a market researcher with the advertising firm of Foote, Cone & Belding, Haldeman joined the J. Walter Thompson Company in 1949. As an account executive in New York, San Francisco, and Los Angeles, until 1959, and, thereafter, as a vice-president and manager of the J. Walter Thompson office in Los Angeles, he handled or supervised such accounts as Disneyland, 7-Up, Aerowax, Aeroshave, Diaper Sweet, Sani-Flush, and Black Flag insecticide.

The creative aspects of advertising interested Haldeman less than promotional strategy and building a good staff. Among the young men he hired at J. Walter Thompson were several who would later go with him to the White House, where they became known as the "beaver patrol" because of their eagerness. They included Ronald Ziegler, President Nixon's press secretary, Dwight Chapin, the President's appointments secretary, and Lawrence Higby, Haldeman's closest aide throughout the years. According to Higby, Haldeman was an easygoing advertising executive, and it was only the intensity with which he did his job in the White House, and the pressure of Watergate, that made him seem "a robot type." While managing the J. Walter Thompson office in Los Angeles, Haldeman served as a regent of the University of California.

What first attracted Haldeman to Nixon was the "fighting" spirit exhibited by the future President when he was a member of the House Unamerican Activities Committee investigating the alleged Communist affiliation of Alger Hiss, a former State Department official, in 1948 and 1949. That attraction was reinforced by the so-called "Checkers" speech, the emotionally charged radio-television appeal to the people by which Nixon saved his Vice-Presidential candidacy in 1952 when his place on the Eisenhower ticket was threatened by the disclosure that seventy-six Californians, including Haldeman's father, had contributed $18,235 to a private political expense fund for him.

Haldeman's offer to work for Nixon was ignored in 1952 but accepted in 1956. In *The Ends of Power* Haldeman recalls his "dismay" when he first saw Nixon "close up," late one night in a San Francisco hotel room during the 1956 Republican Convention. Not knowing that Nixon's late-night "almost incoherent," rambling monologues were caused by "the utter fatigue of long days of campaigning," he thought the Vice-President "had been drinking." "I was embarrassed when I first saw him, but the next day I heard him speak, looking fit and contained, and I signed on as [an] advance man for the reelection campaign."

Haldeman's work in the 1956 campaign and in the Republican Congressional campaign of 1958 so impressed Robert Finch that when Finch became manager of Nixon's 1960 campaign for the Presidency he persuaded Haldeman to take a leave of absence from the J. Walter Thompson Company to serve as the chief advance man in that campaign, which Nixon lost to John F. Kennedy. "From that point on," Haldeman recounts, "I was very close to Nixon during the political campaigns. . . . Nixon rarely spared the rod or the knife in his speeches and, to put it mildly, he wasn't averse to using all possible means to try to defeat his opponents. I believed in tough campaigning too, but even from my hard-line standpoint, Nixon went too far at times. But political strategy wasn't my province, only the mechanics. For political advice Nixon consulted experts such as John Mitchell, Robert Finch, Len Hall, Bill Rogers, or Murray Chotiner."

Haldeman tried to persuade Nixon not to run for Governor of California in 1962, but when he failed he agreed to manage the campaign against the Democratic incumbent, Edmund G. ("Pat") Brown. During the campaign a public relations firm hired by Haldeman with Nixon's approval conducted a spurious $70,000 mail poll calculated to discredit Brown within his own party. On the letterhead of a "Committee for the Preservation of the Democratic Party," 900,000 Democrats were asked if they agreed that Brown was a left-wing extremist and, if so, to send contributions to help move their party back to a more moderate position. Judge Byron Arnold of the San Francisco Superior Court found that the poll constituted a violation of the state election laws, but by the time the judgment was rendered the gubernatorial campaign had ended, in Brown's favor.

On November 7, 1962 a crushed, bitter Nixon conceded defeat to Brown in what he described as his "last press conference," which took even Haldeman by surprise. Lashing out at the press, he told reporters, "You won't have Nixon to kick around any more," and in a telegram sent to several newspapers ten days later he reaffirmed that his unsuccessful California gubernatorial bid was his "last campaign for public office." However, the struggle between Goldwater and Rockefeller forces in 1964 badly divided the Republican party, and in his stumping for Republican candidates in the mid-term elections of 1966 Nixon became aware that he still had much support. As anti-Vietnam war sentiment eroded Democratic President Lyndon B. Johnson's popularity, Nixon decided that American voters might accept him as a leader who could bring the country together, and he set his sights on the Presidential election to be held in 1968.

As campaign manager in 1968, Haldeman worked out a strategy for the packaging and merchandising of the "new" Nixon with two interlocking factors uppermost in mind. One was Nixon's tendency when extremely fatigued "to start losing his faculties and appear foolish." The other was the fact that astute use of the media in this electronic age made exhausting tours of the hustings unnecessary. With the help of John Ehrlichman, who left his law practice in Seattle to join the campaign, and a team of media experts, Haldeman plotted a restrained campaign, in which a studiously relaxed Nixon made a few carefully selected public appearances calculated to reach maximum audiences with a minimum danger of challenge or heckling. Ever at Nixon's side, yellow legal note pad in hand, Haldeman exercised tight staff control in acting as the liaison between the protected candidate and the campaign apparatus. Haldeman's campaign strategy, which gave Nixon the edge he needed for victory over Hubert H. Humphrey in 1968, was adapted by the Committee to Reelect the President under John N. Mitchell and Clark MacGregor four years later. Enjoying the benefit of incumbency over a weak Democratic opponent, Senator George McGovern in 1972, Nixon conducted an outwardly easy, statesmanlike campaign and was returned to office by a landslide vote.

Haldeman says that he performed "with gusto" his demanding job as Presidential chief of staff—Nixon's "S.O.B.," the gatekeeper of the Oval office, the "zero-defects" boss of the White House staff, and "the focal point for the whole range of problems that concerned the staff and the President." He forsook any independent schedule of his own in order to plan the President's schedule and keep himself "totally at the President's beck and call." "I based my plans for each day completely on the President's. I traveled with him on all trips, including holiday and vacation weekends. I was rarely more than a few feet away from him during the working day, and never out of immediate touch at any hour of the day or night. In order to assure adequate staff work and avoid duplication, I reviewed all paperwork before it went to the President and most of what came from him for action."

In the press Haldeman was depicted as an "arrogant" man, an "Iron Chancellor" who "says No for the President" with "a singleness of purpose and an authority that are respected—and feared—throughout official Washington." "My image bothered reporters, no doubt about it," Haldeman writes. "Bad enough that Nixon was President; did he have to have a 'Nazi' as his Chief of Staff? That German name. Those eyes that would freeze Medusa! . . . Of course I realize that what fostered the 'Nazi' image wasn't merely a German name and a crew cut. It was both my personality and my approach to my job. I am naturally reclusive [and] I had to be tough. I was tough. Add to that a reputation for 'puritanism.' "

Haldeman built "a wall" around Nixon not only because the President had to be protected from "the unending flow of public officials who 'just had to see the President' " but also because "*this* President had to be protected from himself." According to Haldeman, the wall was effective "until this other character," special counsel Charles Colson, the "Chief of Dirty Tricks," entered the White House and "encouraged the dark impulses in Nixon's mind, and acted on those impulses instead of ignoring them or letting them die." Colson, Haldeman writes in *The Ends of Power*, became the President's "personal hit man," his "impresario of 'hard ball' politics." "Nixon was behind him all the way, on projects ranging from his long-dreamed-of hope of catching Senator Teddy Kennedy in bed with a woman not his wife to more serious struggles, such as the ITT antitrust 'scandal.' "

In *The Ends of Power* Haldeman describes the "dark side" of Nixon as "petty vindictive," "insecure," "personally awkward with people," "trying to shield strong emotions with an iron self-discipline," seeing "enemies (most of them real) everywhere," and, in "despair at his lack of natural charisma," trying "to attack and destroy the enemy" as if "the end justifies the means." The enemy included political opponents, the liberal press, and those persons, known and unknown, in the State Department and elsewhere, who were making government secrets public. He was furious over the public disclosure of the secret bombing of Cambodia, and even over the leaking of the "Pentagon Papers" by Daniel Ellsberg. (The Pentagon documents covered only the Kennedy and Johnson phases of the Vietnam war, and not the Nixon phase, but Henry Kissinger, as quoted by Haldeman, persuaded Nixon that the release of the papers was dangerous because "it shows you're a weakling, Mr. President.") Also, Nixon was fearful of the possible revelation of a secret Administration deal in the settlement of the International Telephone and Telegraph antitrust case.

Haldeman recounts that Nixon, having "given up on the FBI and CIA for any real help in trying to track down and plug up the leaks from the White House and the rest of the Administration," ordered John Ehrlichman, his domestic affairs adviser, to set up "a little group right here in the White House." The group, the Special Investigations Unit, was nicknamed the Plumbers because of its assignment to fix leaks.

On September 4, 1971 two of the Plumbers, Howard Hunt, an ex-CIA agent who had been brought into the White House by Colson, and G. Gordon Liddy, burglarized the office of Daniel Ellsberg's psychiatrist, allegedly to look for evidence of "Ellsberg's weird habits" that could be used against him in court. Federal investigators did not learn of the burglary until a year and a half later. In the meantime, after the disbanding of the Plumbers, Hunt and Liddy joined the Committee to Reelect the President (familiarly known as CRP, or CREEP). It was, reportedly, "laundered" money from CREEP that, at least in part, financed the break-ins at the Democratic National Committee headquarters in the Watergate complex of buildings in Washington, where documents were photographed and electronic surveillance equipment was installed.

"The Watergate break-in itself came about as a result of President Nixon telling Charles Colson to get some information regarding Larry O'Brien [then chairman of the DNC]," Haldeman reveals in his book; "of Colson assigning the job to Howard Hunt, of Hunt using Gordon Liddy and the CRP capability and resources to repeat the pattern of their earlier Ellsberg break-in."

Actually, there were at least two DNC break-ins, the first, apparently, in late May 1972. The break-in that made headlines occurred on June 17, 1972, when Hunt and Liddy, with five accomplices, returned to the scene of the crime and were apprehended with cameras and wiretapping equipment in their possession.

During the 1972 election campaign the Democrats charged that the Watergate break-in was part of a larger conspiracy to undermine Nixon's political opposition, and intrepid investigative work by reporters for the Washington *Post* established, as early as October 1972, that the break-in was not the "third-rate burglary" that CREEP and the Administration tried to make it out to be. But the "containment" of Watergate succeed-according to Haldeman, Nixon's sweeping plan ed through the election and into 1973. Although, for the reorganization of the executive branch of government was not the program for a "coup" but a legitimate attempt at greater efficiency, liberals, libertarians, and other suspicious parties, especially in the legislative branch, became alarmed, and therefore more watchful, when implementation of the plan began early in 1973. That was the setting when, in March 1973, one of the convicted Watergate burglars, James W. McCord Jr., broke the silence he had been maintaining out of fear of "retaliatory measures" and revealed that at least two Administrative officials, John W. Dean 3d, and Jeb Stuart Magruder, had prior knowledge of the conspiracy. Dean and Magruder in their turn talked to federal prosecutors, implicating CREEP and White House officials, all the way up to President Nixon, in the cover-up. Under mounting pressure, Haldeman and Ehrlichman resigned on April 30, 1973, and other resignations followed. Under threat of impeachment, Nixon himself left office on August 9, 1974, turning over the Presidency to Vice-President Gerald R. Ford.

Pardoned by Ford, Nixon was named a conspirator but not indicted by the Watergate grand jury. Indicted along with other Administration and CREEP officials, Haldeman was found guilty of perjury, conspiracy, and obstruction of justice and sentenced to two-and-a-half to eight years in jail, later reduced to one to four years. After the Supreme Court refused to review his conviction, he began serving his sentence at the federal minimum security facility at Lompoc, California on June 21, 1977. A federal parole board in Washington, D.C. announced on June 14, 1978 that he would be freed on December 20, 1978.

A chastened Haldeman sees his culpability in Watergate chiefly as that of a perfectionist taskmaster ("natural for me") who forced the men under him to become "'little generals', which was out of character for them." "I put on too much pressure, and in the process laid the groundwork for the mental attitude that 'the job must be done,' which badly served the cause when Watergate struck. By then, our whole crew was so strongly indoctrinated in the principle that there were to be results, not alibis, that they simply once again swung into action—doing what they felt was expected of them."

H. R. Haldeman is a lean man with piercing blue eyes, a self-described "passion for precision and punctuality," and, according to his wife, an ability to organize and "get things done" with "no confusion and no doubt." A devout Christian Scientist, he neither smokes nor drinks, and his social life is largely confined to his family. His recreations include gardening, body surfing, following baseball, playing tennis and chess, taking home movies, and listening to religious-oriented rock and country music. Testifying to his sense of humor, are the framed originals of two less-than-flattering "Doonesbury" comic strips by Garry Trudeau depicting him as a member of the "Watergate Alumni Club" which hang in the den of Haldeman's home in Los Angeles.

Haldeman and Joanne Horton, who were married on February 19, 1949, have four children: Susan, Peter, Hank, and Ann. In his book Haldeman reveals that his job in the

White House "hurt" his marriage: "Or at least it temporarily cost me the understanding of my wife, Jo. It wasn't until years later, after I resigned and was back in California, that Jo revealed what was bothering her. 'I thought you were blind about Nixon, that you couldn't see his faults. I'd hear you on the telephone, coddling and flattering him. It just wasn't like you.' I told her I saw his weaknesses better than anyone—but I viewed it as my job, purely professionally, to emphasize his strengths. I believed he was a great President, and I didn't want those flaws to impede him." According to his ghostwriter, Joseph DiMona, the ultra-loyal Haldeman might never have come around to discussing those flaws publicly had he not seen the televised David Frost interviews of May 1977, in which the ex-President admitted some guilt in Watergate: he had been too soft-hearted, not "a good butcher," he said, in holding on so long to old employees Haldeman and Ehrlichman.

References: N Y Times p12 F 8 '72 por; N Y Times Mag p59+ Ag 3 '69, p38+ My 6 '73 por; Newsweek 72:30+ D 16 '68 por; Washington Post B p1+ F 15 '78 por; Haldeman, H. R., with DiMona, Joseph. The Ends of Power (1978); Rather, Dan, and Gates, Gary Paul. The Palace Guard (1974); Who's Who in America, 1977-78

Hayden, Sterling

Mar. 26, 1916- Actor; writer. Address: b. c/o G.P. Putnam's Sons, 200 Madison Ave., New York City, N.Y. 10016

An eagerness to keep moving on has been a driving force in the life of Sterling Hayden, who quit school at sixteen to go to sea. At twenty-four he exchanged the sea for Hollywood, which immediately celebrated him as a handsome, blond "male starlet." Within fewer than twenty years he had made some thirty-five movies, of which he once said, with characteristic belittlement of his achievements as an actor, that he could recall only about five titles. One of the films was John Huston's impressive *The Asphalt Jungle*. Abruptly repudiating his own readiness to sell out to Hollywood, in 1959 Hayden made a spectacular voyage to Tahiti with his children in violation of a court order. He then fulfilled a childhood ambition to write a book, *Wanderer*, an autobiography that proved him to be a colorful writer of unaffected literary power. Since then, while enjoying writing as his preferred occupation and completing a novel, *Voyage*, he has also steadily gained stature as an actor for his performances in *Dr. Strangelove*, *The Long Goodbye*, and *1900*, among other films.

Sterling Hayden was born Sterling Relyea Walter on March 26, 1916 in Montclair, New Jersey, the only child of well-to-do parents, George and Frances Walter. His father sold advertising for a newspaper, the New York *World*; his godfather, whom he called Uncle Mont Sterling and after whom he was named, was a New York City business executive. "I could tell from the start that the main thing in life was to make a success of yourself," he wrote in his autobiography. "Success meant money." The family had a comfortable home and spent summer vacations in the Catskill Mountains.

When Sterling was nine years old, his father died. While his grandmother took care of the house in Montclair, his mother worked for *Good Housekeeping* magazine in Manhattan. Recalling an early experience of fear and loneliness, he told Neal Ashby, who interviewed him for *Newsday* (May 1, 1977), "Night after night I would kneel on the chair in our dining room, looking out the window . . . , watching for the lights of my mother's car, terrified that she wouldn't come home." About four years after the death of her husband, his mother married James Watson Hayden, to whom Sterling owes his surname. From that time on, the family led a nomadic life, moving from town to town along the East Coast, sometimes visiting relatives, as the stepfather whiled away his time, and whatever money he could borrow, on one unsuccessful business deal after another. Sterling acquired a somewhat sporadic education in public and private schools, including a few months at Wassookeag School, a boarding school in Dexter, Maine.

One of the Haydens' many temporary homes was on an island in Boothbay Harbor, Maine, where they spent the year 1931-32. In *Wanderer*, Sterling Hayden recalled his first sight of the harbor in his early teens: "The glow inside me turned to a dancing flame." Because of the fascination he felt for the sea and ships, he sat for days in public libraries reading about sailing vessels and ocean voyages, an absorption that led in time to a wider interest in reading. He discovered that the sea and books "both were distilled of silence and solitude." Dropping out of school at sixteen, he ran away to sea as an ordinary seaman aboard the schooner *Puritan*, bound from New London, Connecticut to San Pedro, California. During the next few years he found other berths on fishing vessels and sailing ships out of New England ports. At twenty he sailed from Gloucester, Massachusetts as first mate of the schooner *Yankee* on a voyage around the world, and at twenty-two he took his first command, sailing from Gloucester to Tahiti as skipper of an eighty-nine-foot brigantine.

In one of the Boston newspapers' reports of his feats aboard ship, Sterling Hayden, who stood six feet five inches tall and weighed 200 pounds, was compared to a movie idol in "masculine pulchritude." The idea of a Hollywood career grew on him, and after a ship of which he was part owner sustained irreparable damage in a storm, he became persuaded that acting in films would be a quick and easy way to make money to buy another ship. He took a screen test in New York in March 1940, signed a seven-year contract with Paramount Pictures, and arrived in Hollywood in May. After his screen debut in a B-movie, *Virginia* (1941), which starred the English actress Madeleine Carroll and Fred MacMurray, he was hailed as a "Viking god over whom the females swooned."

"I learned one thing very quickly," Hayden said in the *Newsday* interview of his early days as an actor. "And that was that I was simply not professional. . . . Now, the way Hollywood used to be structured, if you were brought into a 'stable,' they just went to work on you. . . . It was a lot like a sawmill. They took you in as a tree, and if they wanted a two by two, you came out a two by two, and if they wanted a two by six, you came out that way." Hayden's acting in his second film, *Bahama Passage* (Paramount, 1941), probably reflected his attitude toward Hollywood. Bosley Crowther of the New York *Times* (February 19, 1942) described his performance as "unenthusiastic" and went on to say, "He just stands straight as a mainmast and speaks his lines in truculent monotone."

Again in *Bahama Passage* Hayden's leading lady was Madeleine Carroll, whose skepticism about Hollywood matched his own. The love story of the movie had a counterpart in their own lives, and in 1942, after Miss Carroll had fulfilled her film commitments, they were married in New England. America's involvement in World War II provided Hayden with a quick way to cut his own ties with Hollywood. After completing boot training at Parris Island, South Carolina, he was commissioned a lieutenant in the Marine Corps, from which he soon obtained a transfer to the Office of Strategic Services, the United States wartime intelligence agency. At that time he had his name legally changed to John Hamilton, which has often been given erroneously in news stories as his original name.

Among the assignments in which Hayden won the Silver Star was running supplies and ammunition to Tito's partisan guerrillas in Yugoslavia, a mission that brought him a citation from Tito's government. He also served as an OSS operative in Italy, Germany, and other European countries before being discharged at the end of the war in the rank of captain. During much of the war Madeleine Carroll was serving in Europe with the Red Cross, but Hayden saw his wife only infrequently. He wrote in *Wanderer* of their last, brief meeting in Paris in September 1945: "We knew, without knowing why, without much discussion, that the marriage had dissolved." Their divorce was granted in 1946.

Like several other former servicemen who had been fledgling stars before the war, Hayden received a warm welcome back from Hollywood and from some of the film critics when he resumed his screen career, in *Blaze of Noon* (Paramount, 1947), an adventure movie about the pioneering days of commercial flying in which he played a pilot. Roles in *Manhandled* (Paramount, 1949), *El Paso* (Paramount, 1949), and other pictures had made him a fairly familiar figure in crime melodramas and westerns by the time that John Huston chose him for the lead in the gangster classic *The Asphalt Jungle* (MGM, 1950). Most critics thought him excellent as Dix Handley, the reluctant, but vicious hoodlum who wants to go home and raise horses.

Less successful, but not without merit, were Hayden's portrayals of a former minister and skid-row bum saved by a mission girl in *Journey into Light* (Twentieth Century-Fox, 1951); of Pervus DeJong, the poor, stolid Midwestern farmer in a remake of *So Big* (Warner Brothers, 1953), adapted from Edna Ferber's novel; and of a conscience-stricken cavalry deserter who leads a wagon train to safety and thus redeems himself in *Arrow in the Dust* (Allied Artists, 1954). He had Bette Davis as his leading lady in *The Star* (Twentieth Century-Fox, 1953) and Joan Crawford in *Johnny Guitar* (Republic, 1954), in which he gave a quiet, thoughtful performance in the title role. As Sir Gawain in the star-studded cast of *Prince Valiant* (Twentieth Century-Fox, 1954), he played, in what one reviewer criticized as a bootscuffing, self-conscious manner, the burly knight who teaches jousting and dueling to the comic strip hero.

In the string of crime movies that followed, Hayden played a bullying cop in *Crime Wave* (Warner Brothers, 1954); an independent-minded chief of detectives in *Naked Alibi* (Universal-International, 1954); a small-town sheriff in *Suddenly* (United Artists, 1954); a laconic fisherman victimized in a blackmail scheme in *The Come On* (Allied Artists, 1956); a gangster in Stanley Kubrick's *The Killing* (United Artists, 1956); and a policeman forced to arrest his own wife in *Crime of Passion* (United Artists, 1957). His performances were variously described as "strongly felt," full of "gruff power," and "restrained but hard and efficient."

Shallow characterization and trite dialogue in sometimes hastily thrown together scripts of sex and violence accounted largely for the dissatisfaction that led Sterling Hayden in early 1959 to stop making movies and to take his children on a voyage to Tahiti in search of a new lifestyle. "I spent a lifetime selling out," he explained years later to Harry J. Stathos, who quoted him in the New York *World-Telegram and Sun* (April 13, 1963). "I always hated acting but I kept on acting . . . a commuter on a tinsel train." Hayden embarked on his ten-month cruise to the South Pacific amid a whirlwind of headlined publicity because he was acting in defiance of a court order. He had gained legal custody of his four children—Gretchen, Matthew, Christian, and Thor—after a prolonged court battle with his second wife, Betty Ann (De Noon) Hayden, to whom he had been married from 1947 to 1955. But Superior Court Judge Emil Gumpert, who had awarded Hayden custody, in January 1959 ruled against the projected voyage on the grounds that the ninety-eight-food schooner *Wanderer* was unseaworthy and its crew inexperienced.

Almost as soon as Hayden returned to California in late 1959, he had to face contempt of court charges. In January 1960 he received a suspended sentence from Judge Gumpert, who pronounced the actor's action a "regrettable and foolish violation of the court's order," but added, "The court is not blind to forces which control human behavior under emotionally charged circumstances." Public sympathy, moreover, favored Hayden for his daring and determination, and he emerged from the experience with a renewed sense of purpose and self-respect. The voyage itself became the point of departure for his autobiography, *Wanderer*, which was published by Alfred A. Knopf in 1963 and reissued, with a new introduction, by W. W. Norton & Company in 1977.

Discussing *Wanderer* in the interview with Stathos, Hayden said, "The book's about the struggle of a tortured individual to be himself in a society which is hostile to breakaways from the herd." But his attitude is one of self-searching and self-questioning, rather than self-justification. He is especially candid in relating the circumstances of his brief membership during 1946 in the Communist party, U.S.A., which he joined partly because of his respect for the Yugoslav partisans, who he believed had fought for "the interests of the people" over "the interests of the privileged few." When called to testify before the House Committee on Un-American Activities in April 1951, he cooperated by informing on others associated with the party. "I was a real daddy longlegs of a worm when it came to crawling," he wrote in *Wanderer*. Acknowledging the boost to his career from what he called his "one-shot stoolie show," he reflected, "Not often does a man find himself eulogized for having behaved in a manner that he himself despises."

The exhilaration that Hayden has said he feels in writing conveyed itself particularly in passages about the sea. "Here he is writing of people and places and ships he understands and loves; he writes beautifully and with compassion," Joe Hyams concluded in *Book Week* (December 22, 1963). Joseph Wershba of the New York *Post* (December 15, 1963) raved, "This is a superb piece of writing. It ranks with the best of modern self-examination. It illuminates a generation's heroism, foolishness and juvenile retardation. It is literate and literary, in and out, rebellious and beatnik—and thoroughly American Gothic. Everything is here, with echoes from Poe and Melville to Steinbeck and Mailer. But it's all of one piece, a work of fascination on every level."

During the 1960's Sterling Hayden began to appear in films that for the most part were of more substance and of an otherwise higher quality than those of his earlier career. In Stanley Kubrick's "nightmare comedy," *Dr. Strangelove: Or How I Learned To Stop Worrying And Love The Bomb* (Columbia, 1964), satirizing the Cold War, the American military, and the political right, he earned lavish praise as the paranoid General Jack D. Ripper, whose fear of a Communist plot to fluoridate the water and pollute the vital juices of his body leads to nuclear destruction. In the opinion of Judith Crist, then reviewing for the New York *Herald Tribune* (January 30, 1964), Hayden was "perfection." Mike McGrady of *Newsday* (January 30, 1964) considered him to be "at his deadpan best," and Frank Morriss of the Toronto *Globe and Mail* (January 30, 1964) felt that he performed with "gritty realism" and kept the film on a "sharp satirical edge." Further escaping his old typecasting, Hayden played a successful self-made businessman in *Loving* (Columbia, 1970), a Cheeveresque film about the dark side of suburban life. Gary Arnold, critic for the Washington *Post* (March 28, 1970), thought

Hayden revealed "surprising and touching facets" in his characterization of "a businessman who seems sanctimonious until he flashes a hidden bit of guile." In *The Godfather* (Paramount, 1972), Francis Ford Coppola's blockbuster about the Mafia, he turned in a convincing portrayal of the crooked police captain, McCluskey.

One of Hayden's favorite roles was Roger Wade, the bearded, alcoholic novelist with a strong resemblance to Hemingway in *The Long Goodbye* (United Artists, 1973), Robert Altman's adaptation of the detective novel by Raymond Chandler. Even less enthusiastic reviewers of the movie, such as Stanley Kauffmann of the *New Republic* (November 10, 1973), singled out Hayden's performance for special comment. David Sterritt, critic for the *Christian Science Monitor* (April 16, 1973), felt that he acted his part with his "usual strength and insight." More recently Hayden has appeared in Bernardo Bertolucci's romantic epic of class conflict in turn-of-the-century Italy, *1900* (Paramount, 1977), playing a patriarchal peasant, an "old oak" with a "noble, weather-beaten presence," in the words of one critic. Vincent Canby, commenting in the New York *Times* (October 8, 1977), was impressed by his "severe passion."

A bright aspect of Hayden's career as an actor has been his work in television, especially during the late 1950's and early 1960's, when he appeared on CBS in several *Playhouse 90* productions and a *Du Pont Show of the Month* play. TV critics wrote of the power, control, emotional effectiveness, and unusual merit of his performances as an intellectual rebel in a totalitarian society of the future in Robert Alan Aurthur's *A Sound of Different Drummers* (1957); an avenger in Aaron Spelling's western *The Last Man* (1958); a resigned convict in an adaptation of William Faulkner's *Old Man* (1958); and Ethan Frome in a 1960 drama based on the Edith Wharton novel. Hayden also appeared in a 1964 program on ABC-TV to champion the values and goals of the United Nations, *Carol of Another Christmas*, in which he played Grudge, a Scroogelike character who refuses to become involved in the fate of Mankind.

Having in recent years spent his happiest hours in writing, in 1976 Hayden published a 700-page epic novel of the sea, *Voyage* (Putnam), a meticulously researched book in which the conflicts aboard a ship sailing from New York to San Francisco via Cape Horn serve as a microcosm for the class struggle in American society during the time of the 1896 presidential election. According to one reviewer, John Skow of *Time* (January 24, 1977), "The novel's heft and subject suggests a routine costume epic. But stripped of its ornaments, *Voyage* is in fact a somber study of the human condition." Judson Hand, books editor of the New York *Daily News* (December 26, 1976), discovered narrative crudities in spots, but felt the book was "never boring or false." *Voyage* was chosen as a main selection by the Book-of-the-Month Club.

Sterling Hayden lives half the year in Wilton, Connecticut with his third wife, Catherine Denise (McConnell) Hayden, whom he married in 1960, and their two teen-aged sons. The other half of the year he lives alone on a Dutch canal barge in France. He seemed to Judson Hand to resemble Poseidon, god of the sea: "His curly hair pointed in several directions at once. His long beard hung like seaweed from his chin. He seemed to exude superhuman energy from his enormous frame." Disparaging his public image as a "free spirit," Hayden told *Newsweek*'s critic Walter Clemons in an interview of December 27, 1976 that he became a free man only very late in life: "When I was younger, I tried to be tough. Now I find myself seeing more, feeling more, hurting more, crying more. I've grown up late. . . . I feel sometimes as though I've never grown up, and I like that. There are still possibilities."

References: Book-of-the-Month Club N p3+ Ja '77 por; N Y Post p29 S 13 '64 por; Newsday LI p21+ My 1 '77 pors; Newsweek 88:58+ D 27 '76 por; Celebrity Register (1963); Hayden, Sterling. Wanderer (1977); International Motion Picture Almanac, 1977; Thomson, David. Biographical Dictionary of Films (1976)

Hemingway, Margaux

Feb. 1955- Model; actress. Address: b. c/o Fabergé, Inc., 1345 Avenue of the Americas, New York City, N.Y. 10019

In 1975, within less than a year after embarking on her modeling career, Margaux Hemingway, the granddaughter of Ernest Hemingway, was earning one hundred dollars an hour and appearing on the covers of *Vogue* and *Time*. One of her host of admirers, the New York fashion artist Joe Eula called her the "photographer's ideal," with "the face of a generation, as recognizable and memorable as Lisa Fonssagrives and Jean Shrimpton." In that same year Margaux Hemingway went on to capture what the *New Yorker* (June 2, 1975) called "the largest single advertising contract ever involving a female personality," when she became Fabergé, Inc.'s "Fabulous Babe," the symbol of their new and much touted perfume. A movie contract with Dino De Laurentiis quickly followed and led to her starring role in Paramount Pictures' 1976 release *Lipstick*. Fully aware that her famous name is partly responsible for her instant celebrity, Miss Hemingway attributes much of her tenacity and drive to her family background. "I'm proud of my

Margaux Hemingway

heritage," she has said, "because my grandfather was completely in love with life, always moving, always churning. His spirit is in my marrow."

The second of the three daughters of John Hadley ("Jack") Hemingway, and Byra (Whitlock) ("Puck") Hemingway, Margaux Hemingway was born in Portland, Oregon in February 1955. Her younger sister is Mariel; her older sister, Joan, is a coauthor and translator of the French suspense novel *Rosebud,* which Otto Preminger made into a movie in 1975. Her father and mother spent several years with their children on Ernest Hemingway's farm in Cuba. They then moved to San Francisco, where Jack Hemingway, a former resistance fighter in the French underground, worked as a stockbroker. In 1967 the Hemingways again moved with their daughters, this time to Ketchum, Idaho (the town in which Ernest Hemingway had committed suicide six years earlier), located in the Sawtooth Mountains, near the affluent ski resort community of Sun Valley.

There Jack Hemingway became a member of the state fish and game commission and instilled in his daughters his own love of outdoor activities and sports. Margaux (who reportedly changed the spelling of her name from Margot when she learned that she was conceived by her parents during the euphoria they experienced after consuming a bottle of Château Margaux) grew up skiing, hiking, playing soccer and tennis, fly-fishing, horseback riding, and hunting ducks and doves. Her precocious physical dexterity moved a reporter for the local newspaper, the *Valley Sun,* to write: "Margaux is the only child we know who has mastered the art of riding a sting-ray bike with her feet over the handle bars, eating an ice-cream cone with one hand and waving with the other."

Margaux Hemingway, who refers to her father as her "closest buddy," feels that she takes after his side of the family. "They're the free ones, and that made me independent," she has said. Her independence and self-determination left her feeling so restricted in the local Ketchum schools that she left her hometown at fourteen for a boarding school in Portland, Oregon. Much to her family's embarrassment, she dropped out of school two years later. She drifted around, often in her 1951 pickup Chevrolet, frequented local bars, and, as her father has admitted, became expert at getting herself out of trouble.

After taking art classes for several days at the University of Oregon in Portland, Margaux Hemingway once again left school. She has explained: "I have so much energy. I constantly thought of a million other things to do—like hitchhiking downtown to Ketchum to see my friends at the bar. Or have a shot of tequila. Or hike up some mountain." After traveling in Europe and North Africa, she returned to the United States and worked in Hollywood as guardian and chauffeur for actor George C. Scott's daughter, Devon, who was appearing in a network television series. She did publicity for Evel Knievel's motorcycle jump over the Snake River Canyon in Twin Falls, Idaho on September 8, 1974 and spent much of her time hot dogging (stunt skiing) on slopes in Idaho.

During a three-day stay in New York City in mid-September 1974, where she was to promote a women's free-style skiing event on CBS-TV, Margaux Hemingway met and fell in love with Errol Wetson, the wealthy former owner and cofounder of the Wetson hamburger chain of fast-food restaurants. After spending a brief period back home in Ketchum she decided to return to New York City to live with Wetson. At first she contemplated opening a flower shop or trying her hand at television commercials; instead, at Wetson's urging, she registered for singing, acting, and dancing lessons in preparation for a modeling career. She reduced her weight from 180 to 140 pounds at that time, partly because she got rid of the temptation-laden refrigerator in her East Side apartment.

Confounding the warnings of some magazine editors and of the executives of her first modeling agency, Wilhelmina Models, Inc., that she would never succeed until she lost another twenty pounds and tweezed her bushy eyebrows, Margaux Hemingway soon appeared on the covers of many of the nation's most prestigious publications. Her career took off from the launching pad with a front-page interview, arranged by Errol Wetson, in the November 6, 1974 edition of *Women's Wear Daily*. It was followed by cover photos in *Vogue* and *Town and Country*, and feature articles in *People* magazine and *Sports Illustrated*. In May 1975 Margaux Hemingway switched to the Eileen Ford Agency and one month later, on June 16, she appeared on the cover of *Time* magazine.

In less than a year Miss Hemingway had become the pet of the New York fashion industry. No less an authority than Halston assured a writer for the *Time* cover story that she had "all the components to become a modern young superstar—openness, infectiousness, beauty and the ambition to follow through." Fashion photographer Francesco Scavullo, a personal friend of Miss Hemingway and an early adviser, characterized her in the *Time* article as being not the least bit temperamental. "I once made her sit down in a black swamp in San Diego full of tule weeds and bugs, completely topless, in a bikini bottom, and she roared with delight," he recalled. Many of her other new acquaintances in New York were charmed by her addiction to such expressions as "Scoobie doo," "Yippie skippie," and "hoyah." According to a close family friend back in Ketchum, however, she deliberately spoke that way to make her friends laugh, not because she lacked sophistication. Despite her success, she frankly admitted to Joan Zyda in an interview for the Chicago *Tribune* (May 29, 1977) that she finds modeling dull unless she is working with such photographers as Francesco Scavullo and Richard Avedon. "Modeling is basically a gig," she told Miss Zyda. "It gives us money to live the way we want."

Margaux Hemingway's freedom to live the way she wants was considerably amplified in July 1975, when she signed a one-million dollar, four-year contract with Fabergé, Inc., to promote their new perfume, Babe. The deal was initiated by Errol Wetson and Peggy Nestor of Gemeaux Ltd., who brought photos of Margaux Hemingway to the attention of Fabergé's chief operating officer and executive vice-president, Richard Barrie. Miss Hemingway, who used to make her own perfume back home by crushing sagebrush and wildflowers, helped determine the scent, packaging, and promotion of the perfume. By the end of 1976 sales for Babe exceeded twelve million dollars, and in the spring of 1977 its trademark was expanded to include cosmetics and skin care products, which Miss Hemingway promoted through national and international tours and television and magazine advertising.

Less than a month after she signed the Fabergé contract, Margaux Hemingway conferred in Hollywood with Dino De Laurentiis, movie producer Freddie Fields, and director Lamont Johnson. That encounter led to the signing of a $75,000 movie contract three weeks later, a deal that included an unusual percentage-of-profits clause for a fledgeling like Miss Hemingway. "I'm going to make you a star," De Laurentiis promised Miss Hemingway at the time. "A star like Sophia Loren. I'm going to make you the greatest star in this country since Marilyn Monroe." Lacey Fosburgh of *Redbook* (May 1976) reported that in response to the effusive Italian's braggadocio the amused and down-to-earth starlet poked a little fun at De Laurentiis by asking, "Do people still say that?"

Lipstick, the film for which Miss Hemingway was chosen, is about a young model who is raped and later again humiliated during a trial in which the sex offender is acquitted by a jury convinced that she had enticed him. The rapist later attacks the model's younger sister, played by Margaux's real-life sister, Mariel, and gets his just deserts when a revengeful Miss Hemingway blasts him in the genitals with a rifle. Margaux Hemingway told Bert Green for an interview in *Viva* (January 1977) that she "was never interested in movies because they never seemed important." "I did *Lipstick* because it *was* important. Because the subject had to be brought out from under the rug. This is something that's been going on since the beginning of time: women getting screwed over. . . ." Five million dollars were spent to publicize *Lipstick* and to groom Miss Hemingway for her performance with speech lessons, acting classes, and physical therapy. Its director, Lamont Johnson, explained to Lacey Fosburgh: "I worked with her like she was a race horse. Every day we started with hours of yoga and breathing exercises to loosen her up. Then we got into improvisations and theatrical games. I wanted to break through to her insides and get her to use her own feelings."

Despite all the time and money squandered on *Lipstick*, most reviews were damning. Frank Rich in the New York *Post* (April 3, 1976) condemned it as a "movie whose real intent is to revel, as much as possible, in lurid sexist fantasies," and described one of the two rape scenes as "hideously graphic and blatantly designed to titillate." In his *Newsday* (April 5, 1976) review Joseph Gelmis blasted the film as "vile" and "an index of the soul-rot corruption of Hollywood and its agent-flesh peddlers like Freddie Fields who now are packagers-producers." Richard Schickel in *Time* (April 19, 1976) also took a swipe at the film makers when he vituperated them as "moral morons."

Margaux Hemingway also came under fire from the critics, who evaluated her performance as "bland," "klutzy," and "dreadful." One critic made a special mention of her voice, which he described as a "muffled sneeze." Some praise for the movie was forthcoming, however, from a few feminist organizations and the redoubtable Pauline Kael of the *New Yorker*, who called it a "major film that asks important questions." Miss Hemingway, who felt somewhat wistfully that the critics might have been kinder, was gratified when the California legislature passed the Margaux Hemingway Resolution Number 109, which prohibits the mention of a rape victim's sexual history during a trial, and when the California bar association presented her with a citizenship award for her role in *Lipstick*.

In her *Redbook* profile Lacey Fosburgh wrote: "There has always been a willful self-determination about Margaux, which is why so many of her old friends find it hard to understand her current status—that of being manipulated by a handful of powerful Hollywood men. She has, in effect, turned over the reins of her life and said, 'Here—you drive for a while.' And her old friends think that one day she will realize this—and rebel." The prediction of those who knew her best later proved right, for she broke her contract to do more pictures after the release of *Lipstick*.

On April 28, 1977 Miss Hemingway made her singing debut on the *Mike Douglas Show* on CBS-TV. A writer for *People* magazine (April 18, 1977) quoted Miss Hemingway as saying that, for her, "singing is a real upper. It makes me feel dizzy and energetic." She prefers blues, jazz, and country music and has said that she would enjoy performing in a musical comedy someday. Among the songs that she has composed is " 'Goin' Fishing with Daddy and the Boys."

Margaux Hemingway and Errol Wetson were wed in Paris in June 1975. They held their reception at the Ritz Hotel, from which a furious Ernest Hemingway reportedly once fired at enemy aircraft with a machine gun during World War II, in an attempt to save it for his friends Cesar and Charles Ritz. The couple was divorced in 1978.

The striking physical appearance of the six-foot tall Miss Hemingway prompted a writer for the *Time* cover story to glorify her as the "American Dream incarnate, a prairie Valkyrie," but according to the more matter-of-fact Margaux Hemingway, she achieves that image only at the cost of a constant diet. Recently she added karate and gliding to her many athletic activities. Of her jet-set lifestyle she has said: "It may be pretentious, the way I want to live, but maybe I wouldn't [have made] the movie or [done] some of the other things I've done if I didn't respect the importance of money. I want to live a lot and be at the center of things. I need money. Money is freedom." Jack Hemingway, her father, is convinced that if Ernest Hemingway had had a daughter, Margaux is what he would have wanted. "She's very womanly. She has a true capacity for suffering and for enjoying and for loving." Of the few works in the Hemingway canon that she has read, she is most fond of *A Moveable Feast*.

References: Glamour p94+ Ap '77 por; Newsweek 85:69 Mr 17 '75 por; Redbook 147:10+ My '76 pors; Washington Post B p1+ Mr 26 '76 pors

---

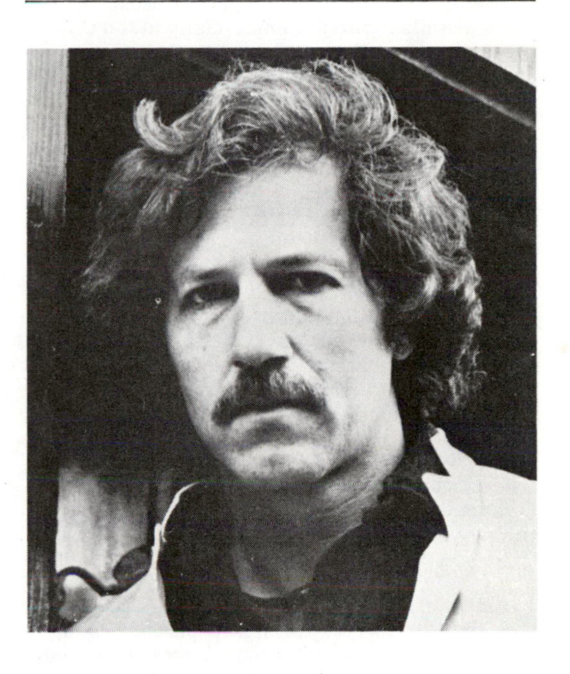

Herzog, Werner (her′tsōk)

1942- German filmmaker. Address: c/o New Yorker Films, 43 W. 61st St., New York City, N.Y. 10023

Often considered the leading figure in West Germany's critically acclaimed new wave of cinema, Werner Herzog is a visionary who explores the essence of humanity through depicting it at its most precarious extremes, in films peopled with madmen, dwarfs, social outcasts, and the physically handicapped. For the locales of his visually stunning films he has sought out some of the most exotic and remote areas of the world. Uncompromisingly personal in his filmmaking and a loner by temperament, Herzog writes, directs, and produces his films on a low budget, using a small film crew and many of the same actors. His two best-known works are both based on bizarre historical incidents. Set in the sixteenth century, *Aguirre, der Zorn Gottes* (*Aguirre, the Wrath of God*) is about Pizarro's mutinous, power-mad lieutenant who led a small band of followers to destruction in the Amazon jungles on a futile quest for El Dorado. *Jeder für Sich und Gott gegen Alle* (*The Mystery of Kasper Hauser*), a parable of innocence destroyed, is based on the story of the nineteenth-century young man of Nuremberg who became a public oddity after apparently spending his entire youth locked in a cellar.

Especially admired by French and English critics, Herzog has become a favorite on the European film festival circuit. In the United States, where he has been showcased at the New York Film Festival, he has his widest following on college campuses. Most of his films are distributed commercially in the United States by New Yorker Films.

Werner Herzog was born Werner H. Stipetic in Munich, Germany in 1942, under the zodiac sign of Virgo (August 22-September 22). In order to escape the Allied bombing of Munich, his mother took him a few months later to the small village of Sacrang, about ninety kilometers away in the Bavarian mountains. Herzog's parents were divorced when he was young, and he grew up with his mother and two brothers. "Of his father," wrote Gideon Bachmann in *Film Quarterly* (Fall 1977), "he speaks with respect as a mixture of scientist and clochard, a man who never got anything off the ground throughout his life except a series of marriages and relationships with women, off whom he lived, fathering small tribes of children in various places." Herzog has more admiration for his grandfather, an archaeologist who conducted excavations on the Greek island of Kos.

"I was very much alone in my early childhood," Herzog recalled to Alan Greenberg in *Heart of Glass* (1976). "I was quite silent, and wouldn't speak for days. My parents thought I was insane, or retarded. I was very dangerous, my character was peculiar; it was almost as if I had rabies." When Herzog was twelve, his family moved back to Munich, where they lived in abject poverty, the four of them sharing a single room. He attended an academic high school, but his heart was not in his studies. "When he was in school, Werner never learned anything there," his mother, Elizabeth Herzog, told Greenberg. "He never read the books he was supposed to read, he never studied, he never knew what he was supposed to know, it seemed. But in reality, Werner always knew *everything*. His senses were remarkable. If he heard the slightest sound, ten years later he would remember it precisely, he would talk about it, and maybe use it some way."

At about fourteen Herzog left home for the first time, hitchhiking to Greece with some friends. From there he tried to enter Albania, which, he told Jonathan Cott of *Rolling Stone* (November 18, 1976) was for him "*the* mysterious country in Europe." Unable to get across the border, he walked along the Albanian frontier in Yugoslavia. Not long afterward, Herzog decided to convert to Roman Catholicism, precipitating a battle with his militantly atheistic father. "I had a very profound religious feeling at the time, a strong religious need. I took it very, very seriously," the filmmaker assured Alan Greenberg. He chose Catholicism over Protestantism because of its rituals and unbroken tradition, even though he recognized that its hierarchy and dogma were unattractive to him. "All of this didn't last very long," Herzog told Greenberg. "It was over in a couple of years. The result of all of this is obvious to me. Since I had become so deeply involved in religion, I have become much more violently against it."

It was also around the age of fourteen or fifteen that Herzog decided to become a filmmaker. He began developing projects and writing screenplays, but they were rejected by the producers to whom he submitted them. Meanwhile, he continued his periodic travels. In 1960 he was in the Sudan while riots were taking place in the nearby Congo. At another point he worked on the docks in Manchester, England. After graduating from school in 1961 he went to the United States, where he lived in Pittsburgh and supported himself by working in a factory, parking cars, and riding in a rodeo. Around that time he also experimented with writing, submitting poems to competitions and little magazines in Germany and the United States.

Since it became apparent to Herzog in his late teens that he would have to raise the money to produce his own films, he got a job working the night shift in a steel factory. That job financed his first three film shorts: *Herakles* (1962); *Spiel im Sand* (*Game in the Sand*, 1964), in which the principal character is a rooster; and *Die Beispiellose Verteidigung der Festung Deutschkreuz* (*The Unprecedented Defense of Fortress Deutschkreuz*, 1966), a fierce satire about war. Herzog's fourth film, a short entitled *Letzte Worte* (*Last Words*, 1967) won him his first film prize, at the Oberhausen (West Germany) Film Festival.

In 1967 Herzog made his first feature-length film, *Lebenszeichen* (*Signs of Life*). Filmed in Crete, it concerns three German soldiers stationed there during World War II. Slowly the men are overcome by the landscape until one of them completely loses his sanity at the sight of a valley full of windmills. *Signs of Life* introduced Herzog to the United States with a well-received showing at the 1968 New York Film Festival.

Herzog braved the Sahara in summer to film his second feature-length film, *Fata Morgana* (1970), an idiosyncratic documentary that uses the desert as a metaphor for man's destruction of his environment. Accompanied by ecclesiastical music and a narration in German of a Guatemalan myth of creation, the film centers on the landscape of the desert, and, as A. M. Kriegsman wrote in the Washington *Post* (May 4, 1972), "The optical panorama is a great deal more vivid than one could guess from literal description. With mesmerizing fluidity, the camera roves across dappled dunes, braids of fire and smoke from the stacks of refineries, the blinding white of adobe settlements, bleached bones, startling oases of greenery and falling waters, heaps of oil drums like huge bullets on the barren sand." Herzog recognized *Fata Morgana* as a highly personal, inaccessible film, and has said that he never planned to let it be shown. Nonetheless, the film was released in West Germany in 1970 and was exhibited at the 1971 New York Film Festival.

At the same time that he filmed *Fata Morgana* Herzog shot a short documentary called *Die Fliegenden Ärtzte von Ostafrika (The Flying Doctors of East Africa,* 1969). His next project was also a short film, *Massnahmen gegen Fanatiker* (*Precautions Against Fanatics,* 1969). In 1969 he again launched an ambitious project with the filming, in the Canary Islands, of *Auch Zwerge haben klein Angefangen (Even Dwarfs Started Small, 1970).* With a cast made up totally of midgets and dwarfs, the film depicts the way in which the inmates of a desolate island prison run amok when they revolt against their captors. During the course of the film, accompanied by a soundtrack of demented, cackling laughter, the dwarfs cut down trees, set fire to flowerpots, tie a monkey to a cross, butcher a nursing sow, start two cockfights, and humiliate the weaker members of their band. The film is, as Gideon Bachmann commented in *Film Quarterly* (Fall 1977), Herzog's "most pessimistic statement on the *condition humaine,*" and it drew outraged reactions from most of the critics who saw it at the 1970 New York Film Festival and even from dwarfs, who picketed it on several occasions.

Having used dwarfs to comment on the human condition in *Even Dwarfs Started Small,* Herzog employed the physically handicapped in his next two feature-length documentaries, *Behinderte Zukunft* (*Handicapped Future,* 1970), and *Land des Schweigens und der Dunkelheit* (*Land of Silence and Darkness,* 1971). The better known of the two and one of his most admired films, *Land of Silence and Darkness* chronicles the life of a fifty-six-year-old woman, who has been deaf and blind since childhood. After watching the film at the 1972 Cannes Film Festival, Richard Roud observed in the *Guardian* (May 10, 1972), "Herzog is fascinated by marginal situations. . . . this [film] . . . deals with deaf, dumb, and blind people. A scary subject, but the effect of his film is to make us feel how something in man survives even when deprived of what we think of as the essentials."

Based on the doomed expedition of a group of Spanish conquistadores through the Amazon jungle in 1560, Herzog's next film, *Aguirre, the Wrath of God* (1972), was shot on location in the Peruvian Amazon. Perhaps the most visually arresting of Herzog's films, *Aguirre* opens with an acclaimed scene in which clumsily armored soldiers and their Indian slaves snake slowly down the steep slope of a jungle mountain, accompanied by such cumbersome trappings of civilization as a horse, a cannon, and two litters bearing the wife of one leader and the daughter of another. Equally admired is the film's closing scene in which Aguirre, the power-mad megalomaniac who has seized control of the expedition and driven it to self-destruction, stands alone, amid the rotting corpses of his comrades, on a raft afloat in a wild jungle river. As his rantings echo through the indifferent jungle, the camera moves 360 degrees around the death-filled raft, which has been overrun by hundreds of romping, chattering monkeys.

Although some critics found the film pretentious and slow, most praised it as highly as David Sterritt of the *Christian Science Monitor* (April 4, 1977) who wrote that *Aguirre* "ingeniously combines Herzog's gift for deep irony, his strong social awareness, and his worthy ambition to fashion a whole new visual perspective on the world around us via mystical, evocative, yet oddly direct imagery. It is a brilliant cinematic achievement." Among Herzog enthusiasts *Aguirre* is generally considered his most successful film, and in Paris it broke previous attendance records set by *Last Tango in Paris* by running for eighteen months. In the United States, however, the film was not released commercially until 1977, four years after its American premiere at the 1973 New York Film Festival. Meanwhile, Herzog had gained recognition in the United States for his next film, *Every Man for Himself and God Against All* (1974), which won the 1975 Cannes Film Festival Jury Prize and proved to be the hit of the 1975 New York Film Festival. It was commercially released later that year in the United States under the title *The Mystery of Kasper Hauser.*

"An innocent is thrown into the world, unprepared, encounters despair and destruction, fights with the means at his disposal, suffers, rebels, and loses, leaving behind an emptier, more desperate landscape," wrote Bachmann in *Film Quarterly.* "This, in a nutshell, has been the story line of each film Herzog has made." That description is especially apt for *Kasper Hauser,* which the filmmaker based on the true story of a young man who was apparently brought up in solitary confinement in a cellar until the day, in 1828, that he was found standing in the town square of Nuremberg, bearing an anonymous note. Hauser was taught to speak and walk, was widely exhibited as a curiosity, and then was mysteriously murdered. To play the role of Kasper Hauser, Herzog chose Bruno S., a compelling but emotionally damaged man who had been featured in a West German television documentary entitled *Bruno the Nigger.* Bruno had been placed in an asylum for mentally retarded children by his prostitute mother when he was three years old, although he was in no way retarded. He stayed there for ten years, and then spent the next twenty years in and out of hospitals, reformatories, and prisons. Although he had never acted, "it didn't take too long for me to convince him to take the part," Herzog told

Sheila Benson and Mal Karman of *Mother Jones* magazine (November 1976), "because he understood right away that it was about him, too." Most critics not only admired the film but also the performance that Herzog had obtained from his extraordinary star. Even Pauline Kael, no ardent fan of Werner Herzog, conceded in the *New Yorker* (October 20, 1975) that "Bruno S. is never ordinary; as an actor he's as awkward, hallucinatory and stylized as Herzog is as a filmmaker, and he begins to take hold of the part."

Herzog's next project was a short documentary entitled *Die grosse Extase des Bildschnitzers Steiner* (*The Great Ecstasy of the Sculptor Steiner,* 1975), which deals with the life of a woodcarver named Walter Steiner who is also, according to Herzog, the world's greatest ski jumper. The following year Herzog made another documentary short, *La Soufrière,* about a volcano in Guadaloupe. He and his film crew arrived at the island just before Soufrière was expected to erupt, and they filmed the smoldering volcano, the abandoned city at its base, and the few old men who had refused to be evacuated. Although the volcano failed to erupt as expected, Janet Maslin of the New York *Times* (October 1, 1977) called the film "a serene, strangely clearheaded documentary about the end of the world" when she saw it at the 1977 New York Film Festival.

Less successful was Herzog's next feature-length film, *Herz aus Glas (Heart of Glass,* 1976), which was also shown at the 1977 New York Film Festival. For that parable about a nineteenth-century Bavarian town that goes mad when its main industry—a ruby-colored glass factory—fails, Herzog hypnotized the entire cast in order to emphasize the trance-like state of the town's inhabitants. Although visually beautiful like all his works, *Heart of Glass* was generally considered, rather paradoxically, to be one of his more opaque efforts.

Herzog again used Bruno S. to star in *Stroszek* (1977), a film about a trio of born losers who leave West Germany with vain hopes for a better life in the United States. Although most critics felt that the film had flaws, the majority of them found much to admire. "Even a minor Herzog film is filled with images that startle and disturb—such as the sight of a premature baby instinctively clutching a doctor's hands," wrote the reviewer for *Newsweek* (August 15, 1977). "Like Bruno, he's hanging on for dear life."

In order to produce his own films, Herzog relies on foreign sales of his pictures, television sales, and cash awards and loans from the West German government. He employs no secretaries or permanent staff and handles his operations out of his Volkswagen bus and his house in a suburb of Munich. Late in 1977 he was working on a remake of Friedrich W. Murnau's film about Dracula, *Nosferatu,* which he hoped to have ready for release by December 1978.

Herzog and his wife of some twelve years, Martje, are the parents of one son, Rudolph Amos Achmed, who is nicknamed "Burro." "I am not a bad father, but my family life is not always the most normal," the filmmaker told Bachmann. "For the first two or two and a half years after marriage, I didn't live with my wife. And my son—I've told him to call me Herzog—I don't think I've accepted him yet as my son." Herzog is a tall, broad-shouldered man with thick brown hair and moustache, hazel eyes, and a gentle manner. He speaks fluent English. "People don't often recite statistics about him," observed Alan Greenberg in *American Film,* "or reel off abstract accounts of his honors and glories. Rather, they tell tales." Many stories make up the legend of Werner Herzog: how he stole a camera to make his first film; how he got in the way of a *coup d'etat* in the Cameroons while filming *Fata Morgana* and was tortured and imprisoned for several weeks; how he jumped in a large clump of cactuses to humor the diminutive cast of *Even Dwarfs Started Small*; how he once walked 600 miles during winter from Munich to Paris as a tribute to the German film historian Lotte Eisner; or how he risked death to film *La Soufrière.* Herzog has sometimes been described as a nineteenth-century romantic, but he insists that he is closest in spirit and aesthetics to the late Middle Ages.

References: Film Quarterly p2+ Fall '77 por; Horizon 20:88+ S '77; Mother Jones 1:40+ N '76 pors; N Y Times II p19+ S 11 '77 por; Rolling Stone p48+ N 18 '76 pors; Greenberg, Alan. Heart of Glass (1976).

Hooks, Benjamin L(awson)

Jan. 31, 1925- Organization official. Address: National Association for the Advancement of Colored People, 1790 Broadway, New York, City, N.Y. 10019

Benjamin L. Hooks, a lawyer and Baptist minister from Tennessee, resigned his position as the first black member of the Federal Communications Commission in order to succeed Roy Wilkins as executive director of the National Association for the Advancement of Colored People upon Wilkins' retirement in 1977. The moderate NAACP, founded in 1909, is the oldest and largest organization of its kind in the United States. The major pioneer in the establishment of civil-rights beachheads through litigation and lobbying in earlier decades, it tended to be eclipsed by more radical and vociferous groups in the tumultuous 1960's, when its membership and contributions began to decline.

Benjamin Hooks

In addressing himself to the revitalization of the NAACP, Hooks explains that "after the heady days of the so-called 'civil rights revolution' [in which] black and white folks felt they had to attack [such] elementary wrongs" as disenfranchisement and segregated public accommodations, a period of "reconsolidation and regrouping" was "normal." Now that the stress of blacks is on the same problems of employment and economic development that beset poorer Americans in general —although not in equal measure—the "battle is much more sophisticated." We are dealing, he says, "with the fact that in order [for blacks] to get jobs some white persons may feel that they have to lose theirs" and with the danger that "affirmative action" may be misinterpreted by former liberal allies as "reverse discrimination" or "preferential treatment." The membership of the NAACP, which declined by 100,000, to 427,000, between 1963 and 1977, has increased by 25,000 under Hooks, whose goal is a membership of 1,000,000 by 1980 and 2,000,000 by 1985.

Benjamin Lawson Hooks was born in Memphis, Tennessee on January 31, 1925, the fifth of seven children of Robert B. Hooks Sr. and Bessie (White) Hooks. His father, who ran a photography studio that is now operated by Hooks's brother Charles, was a stern taskmaster, according to Hooks, and mother and father both tried to instill perfectionist attitudes in their children. "So many today have a harum-scarum life," Hooks told Myra MacPherson of the Washington *Post* (November 8, 1976), "but because of that training I have a fairly disciplined life. That's why I get a lot done." He said that his grandmother, a piano teacher who was partly white and "very Indian looking," was the second black woman in the United States to graduate from college —Berea College in Kentucky. The whole family was imbued with a sense of service, he told Miss Macpherson, citing as an example his older sister, who was a secretary of the Memphis branch of the NAACP "in the days when you took your life in your hands even to join."

The Hookses were among the elite in Memphis' black community, but their affluence was only relative, especially during the Depression. "I had three older brothers and I wore hand-me-downs, never anything else," Hooks recalled in the Washington *Post* interview. "But mother could make things stretch. We were better off than many; we always had something to eat."

The Reverend G. A. Long, a local minister, was a boyhood hero of Hooks. When Long invited the famed black labor leader A. Philip Randolph to speak at his church in defiance of Mayor Ed ("Boss") Crump's prohibition, Hooks was in attendance as fire marshals made a show of trying to close the church. Eventually the Memphis segregationists tired of trying to cope with the troublesome Long and left "the crazy nigger" alone. "That's what they did with people they couldn't handle. . . , dismissed you as crazy, to restore their manhood."

Hooks attended Porter Elementary School and Booker T. Washington High School in Memphis. Drawn to the ministry but influenced by his father, who was antipathetic to organized religion, Hooks, when he graduated from high school in 1941, went into prelaw studies at LeMoyne College in Memphis. As a student, he recalls, he suffered so acutely from shyness that he sometimes asked himself why he was preparing for the profession of law when he could "not even speak."

After two years at LeMoyne College, Hooks was drafted for World War II service in the United States Army, where he found himself in the ironic position of guarding Italian prisoners of war who were allowed to eat in "for whites only" restaurants in Georgia that were off limits to him. At the end of the war he was discharged from the Army in the rank of staff sergeant. Because no law school in Tennessee would admit blacks at that time, he matriculated at De Paul University in Chicago, where he took his J.D. degree in 1948. Although opportunities were brighter in Chicago, he chose to go back to Tennessee, vowing to help "break down that segregation, to end those days."

Recalling his experience practising law in segregated courts in Memphis, beginning in 1949, Hooks told Robert A. Deleon in an interview for *Jet* (December 21, 1972): "At that time you were insulted by law clerks, excluded from white bar associations and when I was in court, I was lucky to be called 'Ben.' Usually it was just 'boy.' [But] the judges were always fair. The discrimination of those days has changed and, today, the South is ahead of the North in many respects in civil-rights progress." Hooks was among the pioneers of that progress, participating in the NAACP's restaurant sit-ins of the late 1950's and early 1960's. "I was always served —sometimes sullenly, but I was served," he recalls. He was also on the board of directors of Martin Luther King's Southern Christian Leadership Conference.

In 1961 Hooks became assistant public defender of Shelby County, the Memphis jurisdiction; as a black man he had no chance of becoming chief public defender. In elective politics, he made unsuccessful bids for the Tennessee state legislature, in 1954, and juvenile court judge, in 1959 and 1963. One positive factor in his 1963 defeat was the endorsement of the Memphis daily *Commercial Appeal*, an indication of his acceptability to a significant segment of the white power structure. In 1965 Governor Frank G. Clement appointed him to fill out a vacancy in the Shelby County criminal court, thus making him the first black criminal court judge in Tennessee history, and the following year Hooks won election to a full term in the judgeship.

Hooks says that it was in the pulpit that he first overcame his shyness in speaking, as a guest preacher in Chicago about the time that he received his law degree. Ordained a Baptist minister, he was called to the pastorate of the Middle Baptist Church in Memphis in 1956, and in 1964 he took on, in addition, the pastorate of the Greater New Mount Moriah Baptist Church in Detroit, where he flew to conduct services twice a month. On December 31, 1968 he resigned his seat on the criminal court bench in order to devote more attention to his ministries and to assume the presidency of Mahalia Jackson Chicken Systems Inc., a fast-food chain that went out of business after two years.

During his 1968 election campaign, President Richard Nixon promised to appoint a black person, the first ever, to the Federal Communications Commission, which licenses radio and television stations and regulates those stations as well as telephone, telegraph, and satellite communication. Under pressure from black media coalitions and the Congressional Black Caucus, which charged that the FCC ignored the needs of black Americans in license renewal cases, Nixon kept his word, announcing on April 12, 1972 his nomination of Hooks to succeed Robert T. Bartley, who was retiring from the seven-member commission. Among his qualifications for the post, aside from his background in law, was his experience in local television in Memphis, where he produced and hosted the television show *Conversations in Black and White*, co-produced *The 40 Percent Speak* (a program deriving its title from the fact that 40 percent of the population of Memphis is black), and served as a panelist on *What Is Your Faith?*

After confirmation by the Senate, Hooks was sworn in on July 6, 1972. As an FCC commissioner he tended to be activist, liberal, and a consumer advocate. On one occasion he defended the right of a racist politician to express his views on the air. On another, he dissented from the FCC ruling limiting the amount of prime-time network programming—a limitation that was aimed at encouraging more local community service programs but which resulted in the buying of more syndicated "junk" by the local stations.

As the first black member of the FCC, Hooks was especially concerned with the influence of minorities in radio and television, because, as he observed, "until we become part of the image-making process we are foredoomed to failure." Blacks own only twenty of the 7,000 radio stations in the United States and not a single television station; the minority employment figure in broadcasting rose from 3 percent in 1968 to a little more than 15 percent today.

On November 6, 1976 the board of directors of the National Association for the Advancement of Colored People elected Hooks executive director of that civil rights organization, effective with the retirement of Roy Wilkins nine months later. "One of the first things I'm going to do," Hooks said, "is look at the hiring policies of all our government agencies and at discrimination in the print media—which is far behind broadcast journalism in its hiring of minorities. There was a time when the young blacks called us [the NAACP] backward. But now the Black Panthers aren't doing much. There is a more neutral attitude toward our cause and I intend to change that."

In his public statements between the time of his election as executive director of the NAACP and his assumption of office on August 1, 1977, Hooks stressed the plight of blacks and other minorities in American society, describing "affirmative action" (which takes past inequities as well as present ability into account in such matters as hiring and education) as the "only workable, humane means" of redressing "handicaps growing out of centuries of black exclusion" and warning that "white folks had better understand that we're going to enjoy it [the American dream] too, or, like the flies, we're going to make sure nobody enjoys it." On the other, he acknowledged that, the degree of opportunity aside, "the problem transcends race—it is employment, education, and a decent welfare system." In an interview with Keith Moore of the

New York *Daily News* (July 31, 1977) he said: "I think you will find us dealing with issues that are not always perceived as concerns of the NAACP. We will take stands on the Humphrey-Hawkins full employment bill . . . on the environment, ecology, and energy . . . the problems of the cities [and] national health insurance, welfare, [and] the criminal justice system."

On NBC's *Meet the Press* on November 14, 1976 Hooks asserted that "racism in all of its sensitive implications is still a part of American life, and we plan to fight that," particularly as it results in under-representation of blacks in corporate entities. . . . We are not necessarily saying that those who head the corporate entities now are directly responsible, but it is the product of years of discrimination."

In a rousing speech at the NAACP's sixty-eighth national convention, in St. Louis in July 1977, Hooks announced that he intended to reorganize the NAACP without changing the organization's basic method of affecting local and national policy through litigation, legislation, voting, direct action, and negotiation. The list of priorities he announced included the search for new alliances, with, for example, corporations, businesses, and foundations, in addition to or outside of government, labor, Jewish groups, liberal organizations, and other past sources of financial and moral support; encouraging United States businesses to withdraw totally from South Africa and the United States government to play a larger role in promoting self-determination there; the creation of two new departments within the NAACP—one for church work, to make the association more grass-roots oriented, and the other for communications, to improve the NAACP's image in the media.

Addressing a conference of 400 local NAACP chapter heads in New York City in January 1978, Hooks assured his audience that, while turning to the problems of employment and economic development, the organization would maintain its concern for "quality education" and wage legal battles in communities where school integration had been resisted. Noting the high unemployment rate among blacks—about 14 percent, or double the national average—he accused President Jimmy Carter (who would not have been elected without the margin contributed by a solid black vote) of having "failed to move forward adequately," particularly with a public works program, and he announced that the NAACP planned to submit economic proposals of its own calling for the federal government to become "employer not of last resort but of first resort."

At a news conference on January 9, 1978 Hooks said that his criticism of President Carter's "preoccupation with the budget" to the detriment of "human needs" did not imply he had changed his view of the President as "compassionate and decent." He also announced that the Rockefeller Foundation was contributing $500,000 to the NAACP for employment and education litigation. The donation brought to almost $2,000,000 the total given to the NAACP's Special Contribution Fund by the Rockefeller Foundation since 1969.

At the same conference Margaret Bush Wilson, the chairman of the board of directors of the NAACP, announced that for the first time in fifteen years the organization's budget was in "black ink and not red ink." The flow of money, she said, was mostly in the form of contributions to help finance a large bond that had to be posted after the NAACP lost a law suit over an economic boycott of merchants in Port Gibson, Mississippi. The Mississippi court decision is being appealed.

According to a Los Angeles *Times* dispatch by Grayson Mitchell appearing in *Newsday* for January 29, 1978, Hooks was considering resigning as executive director of the NAACP because of a "feud" with the board of directors over recent policy decisions "that Hooks felt undercut his authority and limited his ability to administer." The decisions reportedly included reluctance or refusal to approve expenditures for hiring a chief aide selected by Hooks and for raising the wages of key staff members. Also cited was the NAACP's support of deregulation of oil and natural gas prices as "a symptom of the problems between Hooks and the board." Hooks was reported as saying that he was not involved in the NAACP deliberations that produced the policy paper, which went against the Carter Administration's energy program on the ground that the program's strict standards would lead to "massive" layoffs in the industry and contribute to an inflationary pressure falling "harder on minorities than on any other group in the country."

Hooks is vice-president and treasurer of the Mutual Federal Savings and Loan Association of Memphis, which he cofounded. He is a thirty-third degree Mason and a member of the Elks, the Knights of Pythias, and the American Legion. He ran for office in Tennessee as a Republican chiefly because of the local Democratic party's traditional association with segregation, but he describes himself basically as an "independent" with "Democratic leanings." "The Democrats take black people for granted," he observes, "and the Republicans don't do anything for you anyway."

Benjamin L. Hooks is five feet seven inches tall and keeps his weight down to approximately 165 pounds by dieting. He has short salt-and-pepper hair, long sideburns, a ready smile, a quick, jaunty gait, and a modishly conservative wardrobe. He wears glasses in private but is seldom seen in them in public. "There is something in him of the Southern don and more than a trace of the dandy," Les Payne observed in *Newsday* (July 11, 1977). Hook's favorite recreation is reading, and he is given to quoting from the works of Shakespeare, Churchill, Thoreau, Longfellow, and W. E. B. Dubois. His other recreations include spectator sports and walking, the form of exercise he prefers as therapy for a weak back.

Hooks and Frances Dancy, a teacher, were married on March 21, 1951 and have an adopted daughter, Patricia, and two grandchildren. Mrs. Hooks, an NAACP volunteer, spends much of her time working and traveling with her husband. As executive director of the NAACP, Hooks makes $50,000 a year. If and when he leaves his present post he will probably go back to his ministries, and he often takes advantage of invitations to serve as a guest preacher. "The Church is my first love and I'll always go back to preaching," he says. "The Church has kept black folks together and I believe it will encourage another civil rights movement, which we need right now."

Soft-spoken in private, Hooks is a fiery orator who delivers his speeches and sermons in a vibrant, ringing tenor voice. According to Les Payne in the *Newsday* article, Hooks modeled his oratorical style on that of Martin Luther King and other Baptist preachers he has admired, adapting it to his own delivery. "Some intellectuals feel ashamed of the Southern Baptist tradition . . . ," Hooks told Payne. "To me that is insincere. Blacks have a rich tradition in speaking and singing." Hooks says that he is an emotional man who has "no hangups" about shedding tears. "A good song could do it. A good prayer. A good sermon—but never my own. I cry from happiness or sorrow, but mostly from happiness."

References: Biog N p654 Je '74 por; Broadcasting 82:22+ Ap 17 '72 por; Ebony 30:54+ Je '75 pors; Jet p20+ D 21 '72 pors; N Y Post p20 Ag 5 '72 por, p23 N 13 '76 por; N Y Times p15 Ap 15 '72 por, p26 N 7 '76 por; Newsday A p3 Jl 11 '77 por; Time 108:22 N 22 '76 por; TV Guide 20:16+ D 2 '72 por; Washington Post A p16+ N 8 '76 por; Ebony Success Library vol 1 (1973); Who's Who in America, 1978-1979

Howe, Irving

June 11, 1920- Writer; critic; historian; university professor. Address: b. Graduate Center, City University of New York, 33 W. 42d St., New York City, N.Y. 10036

Social history and literature, the two main concerns of Irving Howe's work during the three decades that he has been a luminary on the American literary scene, coalesce in *World of Our Fathers* (1976), the masterpiece of a writer who grew up speaking Yiddish as his first language and learned English only later on the streets and at school. One of America's foremost critics, Howe is a member of the New York literary intelligentsia, a long-standing leader of the anti-Communist left, and a prolific author and essayist. The humanity and breadth of his interests make him, in the words of R. Z. Sheppard in *Time*, "one of those writers for whom the designation 'gentleman and scholar' was minted." Since 1970 Howe has been Distinguished Professor of English at the Graduate Center of the City University of New York and at Hunter College.

Born on June 11, 1920 in New York City, Irving Howe is the only child of Ukrainian-born parents who immigrated to the United States in 1912. By a curious coincidence they made the transatlantic voyage together on the same ship, but they did not know each other at the time, and it was only later that they met and married. After living for a while in Manhattan's teeming Lower East Side, they moved to the Bronx, where they opened a small grocery store.

Business was good until the onset of the Depression, when, in 1930, his father went bankrupt and lost his store. He then became a "customer peddler," selling sheets and linens door to door. He was able to earn very little, however, and during the years that followed the family led a cruelly impoverished existence. To save money they moved in with relatives—five adults and a child crammed into a three-room apartment.

In an interview with John F. Baker of *Publishers Weekly* (January 26, 1976), Howe reminisced about how he had shared a small bedroom with his grandmother and an unmarried aunt. "For many years," he said, "my greatest wish in life—and, I suspect, that of countless urban Jews, was to have a room of my own." Elsewhere, in "A Memoir of the Thirties" *(Steady Work)*, he wrote in the same vein: "The thought of bringing my friends home was inconceivable. . . . Where would people sit in those cramped apartments? . . . So we walked the streets, never needing to tell one another why we chose this neutral setting for our escape at evening. . . . I remember those night walks as carefree and relaxed, away from the pressures of family and politics, though always with some secret anxiety that I would get home too late—for my parents, in their sweet blind innocence, were more distressed by my irregular hours than my irregular opinions."

Growing up poor in the Depression was a decisive formative experience of Howe's life, one about which he wrote eloquently in later years. In "A Memoir of the Thirties," for instance, he recalled, "To be poor is something that happens; to experience poverty is to gain an idea as to what is happening. . . . Only after I had begun to go to high school did the idea of poverty start creeping into my consciousness, and I learned to regard it with the familiar blend of outrage, shame, and ambition. When I was thirteen or fourteen I began to buy a magazine that was printing Sherwood Anderson's reports about hunger in the North Carolina textile towns, and I would read these articles with tears of indignation, barely aware of the extent to which I was perhaps feeling sorry for myself."

Troubled always by their parents' money worries and by the fear that they would be unable to find jobs on completing school, Howe and his boyhood friends were isolated, both by their poverty and by Bronx provincialism, from many aspects of New York's cultural richness. Nonetheless, they attended free concerts at the Metropolitan Museum of Art and went often to the cheap movie houses on Forty-second Street, "where amid clouds of steam and stench [their] political virtue was compromised by sophisticated European art films." In addition, they benefited from "public schools that really were schools and devoted teachers whose faces lived in memory longer than their names." They also gained much from the ambiance of the immigrant ghetto in which they lived, for "while the East Bronx was a place of poverty, it kept an inner discipline: Jews felt obligated to look after each other, they fought desperately to avoid going on relief, they would treat with the outer world only under extreme duress."

At the age of fourteen, while attending De Witt Clinton High School. Howe began to develop an intensely leftist political consciousness, acquired in part from his grandmother, who had been a teen-age activist in Europe. He joined a socialist youth organization. "From then on," he has recalled, "all through my teens and twenties, the Movement was my home." Looking back in "A Memoir of the Thirties," he explained that it was not simply ideology which attracted him to Marxism, but the sense it gave young people "that they had gained, not merely a 'purpose' in life but, far more important, a coherent perspective upon everything that was happening to us." Perhaps more fundamental yet, he continued, it offered "a profoundly *dramatic* view of human experience . . . [a] pattern of drama which made each moment of our participation seem so rich with historical meaning."

Howe's political militancy came into full flower around 1936, when he graduated from Clinton and entered CCNY (College of the City of New York, now City College of the City University of New York), a hotbed of radicalism throughout the Depression era. As was typical of many CCNY students in those days, he devoted himself more to politics than to academic activities, often cutting classes for the sake of participating in discussions and demonstrations and giving far more effort to mastering ideological minutiae than to conventional subjects. Irving Kristol, a former classmate, writing about CCNY in the New York *Times Magazine* (January 23, 1977), remembered Howe as "a pillar of ideological rectitude. Thin, gangling, intense, always a little distant, his fingers incessantly and nervously twisting a cowlick as he enunciated sharp and authoritative opinions." Known as the chief leader and theoretician of CCNY's anti-Stalinist Trotskyist faction, Howe intellectually dominated Alcove No. 1 of the college's lunchroom, "the place where you went if you wanted to be a radical and have a theory as to the proper kind of radical you should be."

After receiving his B.S. degree from CCNY in 1940, Howe completed a semester of graduate work at Brooklyn College. In 1942 he entered the United States Army, which stationed him for eighteen months of his military service in Alaska. There, as he told Harvey Breit of the New York *Times Book Review*

(July 20, 1952), he used his free time to read more than 400 books on a wide range of subjects—the kind of reading, he said, that he would never have a chance to do again unless he were to suffer a heart attack. On his discharge from the army in 1945 or 1946, Howe turned to writing, making frequent contributions to political and literary journals —a combination of interests that has typified his output ever since. His first major work was a new English version, based on a 1936 British translation from the German original, of Leo Baeck's *The Essence of Judaism* (Schocken, 1948).

With B. J. Widick, a chief steward at the Chrysler plant, Howe collaborated on a sympathetic and highly informative study of the automobile union, the world's largest trade union, *The UAW and Walter Reuther* (Random House, 1949). Two extremely well-received literary studies followed: *Sherwood Anderson: A Critical Biography* (Sloane, 1951), a book that Howe called "an act of love," and *William Faulkner: A Critical Study* (Random House, 1952). Later in the decade Howe wrote *Politics and the Novel* (Horizon, 1957), which Melvin Maddocks in the *Christian Science Monitor* (April 25, 1957) praised as "a full-blooded and three-dimensional approach to literature, and, incidentally, a brilliant compensation for the textual analyses conducted in a kind of literary vacuum that have surfeited the critical scene in recent years." Politics in America's recent past rather than in fiction concerned Howe in his collaboration with Lewis Coser on the widely reviewed *The American Communist Party: A Critical History* (Beacon, 1958).

The abiding interest in politics that Howe showed in many of his books is reflected also in his work since 1953 as editor of *Dissent*, a periodical noted for its literate and nonauthoritarian expression of themes relating to the political trend known as social democracy, or democratic socialism. Moreover, although he had never acquired the usually mandatory Ph.D. degree for a university career, he began teaching as a guest lecturer at the University of Vermont and the University of Washington. In 1953 he held a Christian Gauss Seminar Chair at Princeton University. That same year he joined the faculty of Brandeis University as an associate professor of English, subsequently rising to the rank of full professor. In 1961 he left Brandeis to become a professor of English at Stanford University, where he remained until 1963. He then joined the faculty of Hunter College of the City University of New York as a professor of English, a post he still holds.

After he had become occupied in university education, Howe's literary output remained as profuse and varied as it had been earlier. For *Modern Literary Criticism; An Anthology* (Beacon, 1959), which he edited, he wrote an introduction that one reviewer described as "temperate, generous, and broad minded" and another, as "admirably lucid and judicious." He himself was a regular book critic for *Harper's Magazine* from 1968 to 1971 and has contributed an abundance of essays, some of them literary, to the *New Republic*, *New York Review of Books*, New York *Times Book Review*, *Commentary*, *Partisan Review*, *Dissent*, and other periodicals.

Some of Howe's best literary and political writings were assembled in *A World More Attractive: A View of Modern Literature and Politics* (Horizon, 1963); *Steady Work: Essays in the Politics of Democratic Radicalism, 1953-1966* (Harcourt, 1967); *Decline of the New* (Harcourt, 1969); and *The Critical Point: On Literature and Culture* (Horizon, 1973). His *Thomas Hardy* (Macmillan, 1967) is, moreover, largely a critique on Hardy's novels and poetry, and he has prepared critical editions of works by George Gissing, George Orwell, Isaac Bashevis Singer, and William O'Neill.

Other anthologies and collections that Howe has edited include *Edith Wharton: A Collection of Critical Essays* (Prentice-Hall, 1962); *The Basic Writings of Leon Trotsky* (Random House, 1963); *The Radical Imagination* (New American Library, 1967), a collection of essays from *Dissent; The Idea of the Modern in Literature and the Arts* (Horizon, 1968); *Poverty: Views from the Left* (with Jeremy Larner, Morrow, 1968); *A Dissenter's Guide to Foreign Policy* (Praeger, 1968); *Beyond the New Left: A Confrontation and Critique* (McCall, 1970); *The Seventies: Problems and Proposals* (with Michael Harrington, Harper, 1972); and *The New Conservatives: A Critique from the Left* (with Lewis Coser, Quadrangle, 1974). His most recent book, *Leon Trotsky* (Viking, 1978), was praised by Jack Beatty in the *New Republic* (October 28, 1978) as "a work full of the rarest sort of political wisdom."

Within his broad range of tastes, values, and concerns as a literary and social critic, Howe has long had a particularly appreciative regard for Jewish culture. He collaborated with Eliezer Greenberg on the compiling and editing of *An Anthology of Yiddish Stories* (Viking, 1954), for which he prepared several of the translations; *A Treasury of Yiddish Poetry* (Holt, 1970); *Voices from the Yiddish: Essays, Memories and Diaries* (Univ. of Michigan Press, 1972); and *Ashes Out of Hope: Fiction by Soviet-Yiddish Writers* (Schocken, 1977). He also anthologized *Yiddish Stories Old and New* (Holiday, 1974) and *Jewish-American Stories* (New American Library, 1977).

Yiddish literature and other aspects of the culture of *Yiddishkeit* is central to Howe's major work, the book that more than any of his others won him the attention and acclaim of the general reading public: *World of Our Fathers* (Harcourt, 1976). Howe's compelling social and cultural history of the East European Jewish experience in America begins with the mass immigrations of the late nineteenth century, covers the full gamut of immigrant life in the new country in the twentieth century, and concludes with an overview of the present-day children and grandchildren of the immigrant generations.

A comprehensive and well-illustrated study of 714 pages, *World of Our Fathers* is the fruit of more than a decade of thought and scholarship by Howe, aided by a staff of research assistants, the chief of whom, Kenneth Libo, received the unusual distinction of being mentioned on the title page. Heralded as an important publishing event, the book almost immediately fascinated both critics and readers, climbing to the top of the best-seller lists almost overnight. By early 1978 it had exceeded the 120,000 mark in sales.

Because of the book's broad scope, it was perhaps unavoidable that some critics should have detected omissions or oversights in its coverage of the subject matter. In addition, some felt that Howe had overemphasized certain themes, such as Yiddish secular culture, socialism, and the Jewish labor movement, while slighting others, in particular the influence of religion in the immigrant community and the contribution of Jewish immigrants to American business and the communications industry. Those criticisms notwithstanding, *World of Our Fathers* was almost universally hailed as a masterwork. Walter Clemons in *Newsweek* (February 2, 1976), for instance, described it as "a model of distillation and clarity," while Theodore Solotaroff in the New York *Times Book Review* (February 6, 1976), termed it "a great book." Enumerating its various merits in the *National Observer* (March 6, 1976), Clifford A. Ridley found it "richly rewarding in its abundant evidence that the simple English sentence remains an instrument of unsurpassed communication."

In the *New Republic* (April 24, 1976) Nathan Glazer offered an especially thoughtful appraisal: "*World of Our Fathers* is a remarkable book. One approaches big books with suspicion, and particularly big books by intellectuals. . . . And after all, Irving Howe, with all his accomplishment . . . is neither a historian nor a sociologist. . . . But Howe succeeds, better than the sociologists and the historians have. He is not engaged in simply retelling us what they have already told us in different languages: his own sharp and deep insight into the life and problems of East European Jews in America is everywhere evident, illuminating some aspect of their experience better than the specialists have. . . . Howe does more than retell the story; he justifies in this book the marriage of historical and sociological materials with that high seriousness, that grasping for brilliance, that is the special mark of the New York Jewish intellectual tradition."

In April 1977 *World of Our Fathers* received the National Book Award in the history category. It was also cited by the American Jewish Public Relations Society, which chose Howe winner of its 1978 Magid Award for his contributions to Jewish communications. A projected documentary film, in a series of six-to-eight hour-long segments, being made for educational television (Channel 13 in New York City) is expected to bring *World of Our Fathers* before a vast new audience.

Among the many distinctions that Irving Howe enjoys is his increasing recognition as an elder statesman of the democratic left in America. Often in conflict with the New Left during the tumultuous 1960's, because of what he sees as its lack of humanistic values, its authoritarianism and fawning to leftist dictatorial regimes, and its kneejerk anti-Americanism, Howe regards socialism not simply as a matter of public ownership, and indeed not simply as an economic matter, but as the ultimate fruition of true democracy. As a leading exponent of democratic socialism, he is grimly aware that when viewed from his standpoint, every attempt to implement socialism in the twentieth century has been a disaster. Nonetheless, he continues to believe in the cause. "To remain a socialist," he wrote in *Commentary* (August 1976), "is to be convinced that the values and procedures of democracy must be spread through areas of our social life to which they have barely penetrated." And in the *Partisan Review* (Spring 1967) he asserted, "The society in which we live urgently needs the most scathing, fundamental and serious social criticism. But only that criticism merits our support which emerges unambiguously from a devotion to political liberty."

Irving Howe was a Guggenheim fellow in 1964-65 and 1971, a Bollingen fellow in 1959-60, and a fellow of the School of Letters of Indiana University. He has served as a National Book Awards judge and has received awards from the National Institute of Arts and Letters, the Longview Foundation, and the Kenyon Review Foundation. He lives in Manhattan. He has two children: Nicholas, a medievalist, and Nina, a clinical psychologist. Always looking forward to new projects, Howe includes among his current plans a memoir of his early experiences in the American Socialist party, a study of Rudyard Kipling, and a picture book on the Lower East Side.

References: Contemporary Authors 1st rev vols 9-10 (1974); Directory of American Scholars (1974); Encyclopaedia Britannica (1974); Encyclopaedia Judaica (1972); Twentieth Century Authors, First Supplement (1955); Who's Who in America, 1976-77

Jay, Peter

Feb. 7, 1937- British Ambassador to the United States. Address: British Embassy, 3100 Massachusetts Ave., NW, Washington, D.C. 20008

When Peter Jay was named by Foreign Secretary David Owen in April 1977 to succeed Sir Peter Ramsbotham as Great Britain's Ambassador to the United States, the appointment touched off a flurry of criticism among his countrymen, who cited his relative youth, his lack of diplomatic experience, and the fact that he is the son-in-law of Prime Minister James Callaghan. But Jay's reputation as a skilled journalist, television reporter, economic analyst, and something of an authority on the United States, eventually outweighed the misgivings voiced by some of his compatriots. A member of the Labor party's right wing, Jay has at times been an outspoken critic of government policy, but since assuming his ambassadorial post in Washington, D.C. in July 1977 he has devoted much of his time to explaining to Americans how the British Labor government has managed to put the country back on the road to economic recovery.

Peter Jay was born on February 7, 1937 to Douglas and Margaret Christian (Garnett) Jay. He has a brother, Martin, and two sisters, Catherine (Mrs. Stewart Boyd) and Helen (Mrs. David Kennard). His father, a Labor Member of Parliament since 1946, began his career as a journalist with the *Times* of London and the *Economist* and later was city editor of the *Daily Herald*. During World War II and the postwar years he served with the Ministry of Supply and the Treasury, and from 1964 to 1967 he was in the Cabinet of Prime Minister Harold Wilson as President of the Board of Trade.

Peter Jay attended Winchester College, one of England's most famous public schools, in Winchester, Hampshire, where he was head boy and an outstanding athlete. He made his first foray into politics standing as a Labor party candidate in a 1955 student mock election in which he made use of old campaign posters of his father's that said "Vote for Jay." After spending two years in the Royal Naval Volunteer Reserve, where he attained the rank of sublieutenant, he went to Oxford University. There he concentrated on philosophy and also studied politics and economics, at Christ Church College. While at Oxford, Jay belonged to the Labor Club, wrote a weekly column for a student newspaper, and was president of the Oxford Union, the university debating society. Working at his studies as much as twelve hours a day —even though one of the dons told him that eight hours were enough—Jay constructed a device for his record player that enabled him to time himself by automatically replaying a half-hour recording of one of Bach's Brandenburg Concertos twenty-four times. After obtaining his M.A. degree with first-class honors in 1960, Jay continued at Oxford with a term of postgraduate work in economics at Nuffield College.

In 1961 Peter Jay married Margaret Ann Callaghan, a fellow student at Oxford, whose father, James Callaghan, a Laborite Member of Parliament, was at the time "shadow" Chancellor of the Exchequer, or chief parliamentary spokesman for the opposition on economic matters. In the year of his marriage, Jay went to work at Her Majesty's Treasury, where he served as assistant principal from 1961 until 1964, when he was promoted to principal and became private secretary to the Joint Permanent Secretary of the Treasury, Sir William Armstrong. But when his father-in-law became Chancellor of the Exchequer in the Cabinet of Prime Minister Harold Wilson in October 1964, Jay was talked into leaving the Treasury, even though he did not feel that his relationship to Callaghan made resignation necessary. Taking another civil service post, in the Department of Education, he worked from 1964 to 1967 on education budgets. At the end of three years, however, he was still at a level where, in accordance with the traditions and practices of the British civil service, advancement to more challenging responsibility would take another twenty years. In 1967 he therefore resigned from the civil service and accepted an offer from William Rees-Mogg, the editor of the *Times* of London, to become economics editor of that newspaper, a post he continued to hold until 1977.

In 1969 Jay was in addition appointed associate editor of the *Times*'s new business news supplement, and that same year he served as a correspondent for that paper in Washington, D.C., where he made friends with World Bank president Robert S. McNamara and other noted Americans. On his return to London later that year he approached Labor party leaders, hoping to become a candidate for a House of Commons seat representing London's East End, but he was turned down, apparently because he had never been an enthusiastic campaigner for his party.

Although Jay pursued his career as journalist with energy and enthusiasm, some of his associates felt at times that his critical and pessimistic articles about Great Britain's economic crisis were too erudite. Once, when a colleague told him that his column could not be understood by anyone except a few individuals high up in the Treasury, he replied: "Those are the people I am writing for." From his ideological position on the right wing of the Labor party, Jay made recommendations for the British economy that were described by Peter Pringle in the New York *Times Magazine* (July 2, 1978), as "a mixture of hard-headed monetarism" and "soft-headed socialism." Jay expressed the view that government investment in leading industries should go hand in hand with marketplace competition, since the latter encourages individual freedom of choice. He also suggested that workers be helped to understand the responsibilities of management by becoming owners of shares of stock in the companies in which they work and by more direct involvement in decisions concerning production.

In 1972 Jay began to present a weekly Sunday morning current affairs program, *Weekend World,* on Great Britain's Independent Television network (ITV), where he indulged in congenial conversation, posing questions to his guests that were often longer than the answers he received. The program soon became one of the more important weekly broadcasts dealing with current affairs. Following up on that success, in 1975 Jay inaugurated a television series of his own, *The Jay Interview.* In 1973 he was named political broadcaster of the year and Harold Wincott financial and economic journalist of the year, and in 1974 he received the Royal Television Society's Pye Award as the male personality of the year and the Society of Film and Television Arts' Shell International Television Award. That year he also was one of six Britons on a *Time* magazine list of 150 future leaders of the world. In 1975 he was Wincott Memorial Lecturer and was elected a fellow of the Royal Society of Arts, and in 1976 he was the subject of a *Sunday Times* profile titled "The Cleverest Young Man in England?" Jay's writings include a study of the British budget, published in 1972, and a number of articles in American and British periodicals.

Jay's appointment as British Ambassador to the United States followed a visit to Washington, D.C., in April 1977 by his long-time friend, Foreign Secretary David Owen, who decided that the youthfulness prevailing in President Jimmy Carter's White House staff would be more congenial to a younger man than to the incumbent Ambassador, Sir Peter Ramsbotham. According to some reports, Owen considered Ramsbotham an elitist who lacked rapport with the Carter Administration and the informality and permissiveness prevailing in the United States of the 1970's. When he officially made the appointment on May 11, 1977, Owen who himself was under forty, described Jay as "one of the most able people of my generation" and expressed confidence that he would be able to "establish an easy and informal relationship with many of the people of his own generation who have prominent positions in the new American Administration." Jay's familiarity with the United States was also considered an asset. He had first visited the country in 1966 on a Ford Foundation grant and after joining the *Times* made several trips there each year. Finding America stimulating, he said during one of his early visits that he liked its people because of their "unquenchable source of faith that problems can always be solved if one only tries hard and long enough."

Owen's announcement that he was naming Jay ambassador aroused a storm in Parliament. Some critics felt that Jay was too young, while others favored assigning a career diplomat to so important a post. But the negative reaction centered in particular on Jay's relationship by marriage to James Callaghan, who had succeeded Harold Wilson as Prime Minister in April 1976. Criticized from both the left and the right, the appointment was labeled "blatant, naked nepotism," "indefensible favoritism," and "total disgrace." According to the *Guardian,* the idea of naming Jay an ambassador was "an eccentric notion"; the Toronto *Globe and Mail* (May 14, 1977) suggested that the choice was "a daring one for a minority government to make"; the *Daily Express* headlined its story "The Son-in-Law Also Rises"; and one Labor party spokesman called the appointment "reminiscent of the practices of seventeenth-century monarchs."

In the House of Commons, Prime Minister Callaghan defended the appointment and became so disturbed by the attacks that he threatened at one point to step down as leader of the government. But the criticism subsided almost as quickly as it had arisen, and some important political figures spoke out in behalf of Jay. One prominent Laborite, Jack Ashley, observed that the Jay appointment "recognizes brains and ability rather than orthodoxy and dullness," and Lord Boothby, a former member of Conservative Cabinets, praised Callaghan as "the first Prime Minister in my experience who has really given a chance to the young."

During his years as a journalist, Jay had been known as a critic of government economic policies, but after becoming Ambassador to the United States he began promoting those policies. According to Peter Pringle, Jay saw no inconsistency in his analyses of the past and the present. He conceded, for example, that the government's ceiling on wages, about which he previously had misgivings, had dealt successfully with the crisis of inflation. A supporter of Great Britain's National Health Service, Jay told American government officials who were considering a federal medical insurance program that "developing a national health plan is like sex—people get in a tiz about starting it, but once they have, they never go back." Jay's only setback during his first few months in office was the rejection by a British Cabinet committee of his recommendation for a 50 percent staff cut in the British Information Services office in New York City.

In a speech at the National Press Club in Washington, D.C. on September 7, 1977 Jay noted with satisfaction that his country was "back in business" because of government success in gaining control over the budget deficit, halting the collapse of the British stock market, and producing a balance of payments surplus, partly as a result of recent North Sea oil discoveries. He said that as long as unemployment and inflation exist together in the economies of the democracies there must be a "fundamental rethinking" of traditional concepts about the relationship between capital and labor and suggested that such rethinking has been going on in Britain, which had "touched bottom first" and was now on its way to recovery. Referring to the "new realism" of the present British leadership, Jay asserted that his government was giving up the "illusory role of world power," and while willing to help the developing nations of the Third World, it would do so "without any lingering pretensions beyond [its] means."

Margaret Ann (Callaghan) Jay, who was designated "co-ambassador" at her husband's request, was born in Surrey in 1939. Since her marriage she has combined a successful career as a British Broadcasting Corporation producer with being a wife and mother. The Callaghans have two daughters, Thomasina (called Tamsin) and Alice, and a son, Patrick. Margaret Jay first came to the United States in 1966 on a Ford Foundation scholarship to study educational television and in 1969 she was a political assistant to Senator John V. Tunney of California. Later, as a reporter on American politics for the BBC she covered the 1972 and 1976 political conventions and helped to prepare documentaries on the American bicentennial. Her chief function as "co-ambassador," aside from being hostess at the British Embassy in Washington, is to make speeches during the one week a month that she spends traveling around the United States with her husband.

Tall and athletic in build, Peter Jay was described by Sally Quinn in the Washington *Post* (July 19, 1977) as "very good-looking in a sort of scruffy English Oxford journalistic way." His hobby is sailing, and in 1976 he navigated his forty-seven-foot sloop, *Norvantes*, across the Atlantic Ocean from England to Maine in a month. He also plays tennis, and one of his regular opponents is Zbigniew Brzezinski, President Carter's national security adviser. Although Jay makes himself more accessible to newsmen than his predecessors, he is considered arrogant by some, a characterization that he rejects. "There are times when, deliberately or unconsciously, I appear not to take other people's ideas or propositions seriously," he explained to Pringle. "It isn't that I'm not listening to them, but that I know very quickly what they're saying." He told a correspondent for *Newsweek* (May 15, 1978) that he considers his ambassadorial duties "the most enjoyable and fulfilling work" he has ever done. Now a confirmed optimist about his country's future, he wrote in an Op-Ed article in the New York *Times* (September 5, 1977): "History may yet say that the nation which lost its empire in the 1940's had by the late 1970's found a new role—as the proving ground of Western societies."

References: Guardian (Manchester) Weekly p3 My 3 '77 por; N Y Times A p3 My 12 '77; N Y Times Mag p10+ Jl 2 '78 pors; Newsweek 91:18 My 15 '78 por; People 7:31 My 30 '77 por; Who's Who, 1978-79

John Paul I, Pope

Oct. 17, 1912- Supreme Pontiff of the Roman Catholic Church. Address: Vatican City

BULLETIN: Pope John Paul I died of a heart attack on the evening of September 28, 1978, bringing to an end the briefest Papal reign in 373 years. *Obituary:* Newsday p1+ S 29 '78

The crisis in faith and discipline that agonized Pope Paul VI in his reign as the 262nd Supreme Pontiff of the Roman Catholic Church did not end with Pope Paul's death in Au-

Pope John Paul I

gust 1978. Indeed, Paul's excruciating, inflexible efforts to hold the church steady in the turbulence following Vatican Council II served only to leave traditionalists and progressives more divided than ever over such issues as birth control, divorce, the reformed and de-Latinized liturgy, priestly celibacy, and the ordination of women. The Cardinals of the church, in quickly choosing Albino Cardinal Luciani of Venice as Paul's successor, laid the current heavy burden of the Papacy on a moderate conservative, a hardline traditionalist in politics and doctrine who is apparently flexible in many areas of discipline. How Pope John Paul I—as he chose to be called, to indicate continuity with both the openness of John XXIII and the caution of Paul VI—will handle the problems of the church is a question held in abeyance for the moment by a world stunned and reassured by the fatherly presence of the new Pope, who, with his infectious smile and self-effacing manner, clearly suggests a pastor rather than a prince.

Pope John Paul, who characterizes himself as "only a poor man, accustomed to small things and silence," is the first Roman Pontiff to come from the working class. The elder son of a peasant scullery maid and an itinerant stonemason, metalsmith, and glassworker, he was born Albino Luciani in the impoverished rural mountain hamlet of Canale d'Agordo—then called Forno di Canale—in the Dolomite Alps of northeastern Italy on October 17, 1912. His health was precarious from birth, when his chances of survival seemed so slim his mother had him baptized immediately instead of waiting for a formal church ceremony. Later he spent a year in a tuberculosis sanitorium, and a not very successful tonsilectomy left him with periodic laryngitis.

The Pope's mother, Bertola Luciani, was, as he describes her, "strong and devout," but his father, Giovanni Luciani, was an anticlerical Socialist. "It's a scandal, the election of this Pope," an eighty-year-old resident of Canale d'Agordo was quoted as saying in *Time* (September 11, 1978). "He's a very good man, but his father burned crucifixes in his stove." The Pope's younger brother, Edoardo, a retired schoolteacher and the father of nine, said, according to the same source, that he and Albino grew up "torn between the devil and holy water."

The holy water prevailed, partly because the father was home only periodically, between stints of work in Switzerland, France, and Germany. After the death of Bertola Luciani, in 1948, Giovanni married again, worked in Argentina for two years, and finally settled down as a glassworker on the Venetian lagoon island of Murano. By his second marriage Giovanni Luciani, who died in 1952, had one child, a daughter, Antonia, who is married to a bricklayer in Santa Giulian di Levico, near Trent.

Recalling his and his brother's childhood, Edoardo Luciani told reporters who converged on Canale d'Agordo at the time of Albino's election as Pope: "You just cannot imagine what it was like in those days. From May to October we went without shoes. The rest of the year we had to have them because the place was covered with snow." He said that his brother "used to love working in the fields," cutting hay, and that he, Edoardo, always looked up to Albino as an example of gentleness and kindness. "I can honestly say that I never remember my brother losing his control. His self-discipline is really quite unbelievable. But he was not a goody-goody. At school he was very lively and once when his teacher failed to give him back a book he called her a thief to her face."

Influenced by an old country priest, Albino aspired to the priesthood from an early age. A schoolmate has recalled that when their fourth-grade teacher asked the children what they wanted to be, "Albino spoke right up and said he was going to be a priest. 'What!' said the teacher, 'A naughty boy like you? What kind of priest could you be?' " Don Giulio Gaio, a ninety-two-year-old priest who taught Albino fifty years ago remembers him as "very intelligent and gifted with an exceptional memory" but "so modest it seemed he had no idea of his capabilities."

When he was ten, Albino wrote to his father, who was then working in France, for permission to study for the priesthood. Despite his anticlericalism, the elder Luciani sent an affirmative answer, and, according to his brother, the Pope still carries the letter from his father around in his pocket. At eleven, Albino entered the minor seminary in Feltre, and he went on to graduate in philosophy and theology from the major seminary in Belluno. During summers and other holiday periods he returned home to work in the fields.

Following his ordination, on July 7, 1935, Father Luciani was assigned to parish work in his native village and in nearby Agordo, where he also taught religion in a mining school. For ten years, beginning in 1937, he was on the faculty of the seminary in Belluno, ultimately as deputy director. In the meantime he earned a degree in dogmatics from the Pontifical Gregorian University in Rome, with a thesis on the controversial theology of Antonio Rosmini, a nineteenth-century priest.

In 1948 Father Luciani became deputy to the Bishop of Belluno, in charge of catechetics, or religious education. The simple catechism lessons he devised, full of breezy metaphors, were brought together in the book *Catechesi in Briciole* (Catechism Crumbs, 1949), which is now in its seventh edition. After four years in Belluno, he became vicar general of the provincial diocese.

During Luciani's early years in Belluno, the most controversial issue in the Roman Catholic Church was the priest-worker movement, then flourishing in France and threatening to widen. Luciani was among those who rejoiced when Pope Pius XII squelched the movement with an official condemnation. Then as now, he believed that "Marxism is incompatible with Christianity" and that the priestly vocation is incompatible with engagement in the class struggle.

Pope John XXIII's first episcopal appointment was the naming of Luciani as Bishop of Vittorio Veneto in northern Italy in 1958. The initial major problem Bishop Luciani faced was a scandal involving two priests of the diocese who had purloined, under cover of a series of bad checks, tens of thousands of dollars in contributions from the faithful. His handling of that situation initiated the reputation he has throughout Italy as a prelate of down-to-earth honesty. Calling together the 400 priests of the diocese, he delivered a stern lecture on the necessity of the church to identify with the poor and of churchmen to carry out their stewardship accordingly. Refusing to invoke ecclesiastical immunity under Italian law, he announced that restitution would be made with revenues earned from diocesan holdings. He went on to establish during his tenure in Vittorio Veneto the simple style that would mark his entire episcopal career, refusing, for example, to wear the bejeweled ring symbolizing his office and making the rounds of his diocese on bicycle.

Bishop Luciani kept a low profile during Vatican Council II, commenced in 1962 by Pope John for the reformation, or, as it was more delicately put officially, "renewal," of the Roman Catholic Church. He was among those prelates who had difficulty in adjusting to some of the liberalizing steps taken by the council, such as the lessening of Papal authority in favor of the "collegiality" of the world's bishops. "The thesis I found hardest to live with was the one on religious freedom," he said later. "For years I had taught the public law theses of Cardinal [Alfredo] Ottaviani, according to which only the truth [as held by the Roman Catholic Church] had rights. In the end, I convinced myself we had been wrong."

Like other conservatives at the council, Luciani disagreed with the liberal faction when, in the conservative view, it seemed to be calling for an interpretation of the church's mission that would reduce it to a mere worldly agency of social action. Like them also, he was repelled by the efforts of some progressives from Germany and Holland to challenge such traditions as clerical celibacy and an exclusively male priesthood. But unlike most of the others, he tried to keep lines of communication open and participated in many meetings with the widely shunned progressives.

Bishop Luciani was a consultant to the sixty-member international commission formed by Pope Paul VI in 1963 to make recommendations for dealing with the problem of birth control. Luciani personally concluded that some accommodation for artificial birth control could be made within the teachings of the church, and he wrote to the Pope to that effect. The majority view in the report submitted by the commission in 1965 was that a modification of the traditional ban on contraception was possible and that, at the very least, no blanket prohibition should be made. Against the majority's recommendation, Pope Paul in 1968 issued the encyclical *Humanae Vitae,* which firmly restated the papal opposition to birth control in all its forms, including the "pill." Although saddened by the drift of middle-class Catholics from the church that was accelerated by the encyclical, Bishop Luciani, loyal to his Pope, suppressed any negative thoughts he might have entertained about *Humanae Vitae.*

In 1969 Pope Paul appointed Luciani to the archdiocese of Venice, the only episcopal seat in Europe outside of Lisbon where the archbishop is honored with the title of patriarch, deriving from the Venetian churches' dependence on the Byzantine Empire during the barbarian invasions. Two twentieth-century Popes, Pius X and John XXIII, had been among Luciani's predecessors in the Venice see, which has a population of 3,600,000 Catholics. It came as no surprise when, four years after Luciani's installation there, Pope Paul named him a Cardinal.

As Patriarch of Venice, Luciani continued to travel by bicycle—when feasible, in the mainland parishes—visiting factories, canal ferries, hospitals, and other institutions in simple clerical garb. He sold his patriarchal ring and other precious ornaments and gifts, including valuable works of art, donating the proceeds to charity, and urged the priests throughout his see to do likewise. "The church's real treasures are the poor, the little ones, who should not be helped by mere occasional alms," he wrote on one occasion, "but in such a way as to insure the bettering of their condition."

A priest who served under Cardinal Luciani at St. Mark's Basilica has said: "He wanted to be close to people, to live with them and through them, especially the children. But he is a strong defender of the faith. Over men he may yield and make exceptions, but he will never compromise over ideas or beliefs." Luciani's self-abnegation and charity were matched by his repugnance at the libertarian and sometimes "immoral" life-style of Venice, typified in his view in some of the offerings of the annual film festival and the biennial art show. He threatened those of his priests who were taking part in proabortion rallies with suspension of their right to say Mass; opposed a new concordat between the Vatican and the Italian government because it called for the removal of compulsory religion classes from the public schools; and disbanded the United Italian Federation of Christians, a Catholic youth group, charging it with a "false sense of pluralism," when, without consulting him, it sent a letter to Italy's bishops asking them to support the 1974 referendum to repeal the country's tough divorce law.

In a sermon in 1976 Cardinal Luciani condemned the French physician-priest Marc Oraison for asserting that homosexual love could be Christian. "If a priest preaches as he does, everything is ruined," he said. "Now even nuns are starting to dress like young ladies. And what about certain theologians? They have forgotten that a theologian is not just someone who speaks of God but also someone who speaks to God." In the national elections that year, Luciani was a leader among the Italian bishops urging a strong Christian Democratic vote to counter the growing strength of the Communists in the Italian government. When terrorists kidnapped Christian Democratic leader Aldo Moro in the summer of 1978, Luciani commented: "Tell children that sin is only a fairy tale [and] print school textbooks that ignore God and deride authority? Then don't become amazed at what is happening."

Following the death of Pope Paul VI, on August 6, 1978, 111 Cardinals from forty-nine nations gathered in secret conclave in the Vatican, on August 26, and elected Luciani with surprising speed, in the fourth round of the first day's voting, eight hours and fifty-four minutes after they began. The election of Pope Pius XII in 1939 had been quicker, done in a record seven and a half hours, but that was an exception. Modern conclaves have normally lasted at least several days, and in past centuries they often went on for weeks or months. The celerity in this instance was credited in several reports to the deftness with which Giovanni Cardinal Benelli, Archbishop of Florence and former chief of staff to Pope Paul VI, persuaded his colleagues to settle on the Patriarch of Venice—an Italian, but not a Curia bureaucrat, a conservative who was not frightening to the Third World Cardinals and the liberals. When Luciani began to see the "danger" of his election, he later said, he was consoled by the two Cardinals sitting on either side of him. One said, "Courage. If the Lord gives a burden, he also gives the strength to carry it," and the other, "The whole world prays for the new Pope." When the election was completed, Luciani's response was: "What you have done to me—may God forgive you."

Despite his reluctance to ascend the Papal throne, and his confessed feeling of being "so ignorant" of the mechanisms of the Vatican, Pope John Paul has, in his public appearances since his election, given the impression that he is a joyful man, at ease in his station and at peace with himself. His warm smile and his simple ways have won him, instantly, the hearts of his audiences in the Vatican and, by television, around the world.

The Holy Father's intelligence, wit, cultural flexibility, writing skill, and love of literature combined with love of God are manifest in articles he contributed to the Italian press over the years. Among them were a series of imaginary letters to famous figures of the past, including Sir Walter Scott, Mark Twain, Carlo Goldoni, St. Bernard of Clairvaux, and G. K. Chesterton. The letters were published under the title *Illustrissimi* (Il Messaggero di Sant' Antonio, 1976). In one of them, addressed to Charles Dickens, he thanked the English novelist for "disgracing" the "oppressors" of the poor with a "pen dipped in anger and irony," adding: "The whole world is a poorhouse, and has such need of God."

Pope John Paul I is a frail, bespectacled man with close-cropped hair, demonstrative hands, and a weak voice that often cracks. He suffers from rheumatism, among other ills, and he has been operated on for gallstones twice, for a condition in his left eye once, and for a broken nose after a fall once.

He eats little, perhaps a few nuts for lunch and minuscule portions for dinner, along with a glass of wine. The Pope speaks fair French, some German and Slavic, and very bad English. He smokes cigarettes and cigars, enjoys the music of Vivaldi, and regularly reads such devotional works as Thomas à Kempis's *The Imitation of Christ.* This Supreme Pontiff with the common touch is a compulsive hugger with a genuine love of people, but as the spiritual leader of the world's 732,000,000 Catholics he is reported to suffer heavy anxiety beneath his genial, beaming exterior.

References: Boston Globe p1+ Ag 28 '78; N Y Catholic News p1+ Ag 31 '78 pors; Newsweek 92:66+ S 11 '78 pors; Time 112:78+ S 11 '78 pors; Washington Post p1+ Ag 28 '78 pors

---

Johnson, Frank M(inis), Jr.

Oct. 30, 1918- United States District Judge. Address: b. P.O. Box 35, Montgomery, Ala. 36101

For more than twenty years, the most influential, innovative, and controversial trial judge in the United States has almost certainly been Frank M. Johnson Jr., a self-described "conservative hillbilly" lawyer who has been issuing precedent-shattering decisions almost since the day he took office as a judge of the Federal District Court for the Middle District of Alabama in November 1955. During the late 1950's and 1960's Johnson's uncompromising defense of civil liberties was the basis for most of the advances in civil rights in the South. More recently, his sweeping decisions overhauling the administration of mental hospitals and prisons turned his courtroom into a major battleground in the conflict between the states and the federal bench over the rights and responsibilities of governments. In August 1977 Johnson was nominated for the directorship of the FBI by President Jimmy Carter, but three months later he asked that his name be withdrawn from consideration because he needed to undergo a prolonged period of recuperation from heart surgery.

Frank Minis Johnson Jr. was born in the tiny community of Haleyville, Alabama, on October 30, 1918, the oldest of the seven children of Frank and Alabama (Long) Johnson. His father, a farmer and high school teacher, served as a postmaster and a probate judge and, during the early 1940's, was the only Republican member of the state legislature; his mother was a teacher. Johnson's attitudes were shaped by the rigors of farm life, his mother's discipline, and the independent traditions of his home county in the backwoods of northern Alabama. (A longtime Republican stronghold, Winston County had attempted to secede from the state after Alabama withdrew from the Union in 1861 and had tried to remain neutral throughout the Civil War. Johnson's forebears fought on both sides of the conflict.)

Johnson attended grade school and two years of high school in Haleyville, then, at his parents' insistence, enrolled at the Gulf Coast Military Academy at Gulfport, Mississippi. Following his graduation from the academy in 1936, he worked for about a year as a highway surveyor before entering Birmingham Southern College on a football scholarship. After his freshman year, he transferred to Massey Business College in Birmingham, where he studied bookkeeping and accounting, then enrolled as a junior in the prelaw program at the University of Alabama. He went on to the university's law school and, in 1943, graduated at the top of his class with an LL.B. degree. He gained admission to the state bar later the same year.

Having joined the United States Army as a private late in 1943, Johnson was commissioned an officer in the infantry and rose to the rank of captain. Wounded during the Normandy invasion, he completed his tour of duty as a legal officer stationed in England. Returning to Alabama after his discharge, he settled in Jasper, where he cofounded the law firm of Curtis, Maddox & Johnson. Although most of the firm's clients were businessmen, Johnson practised some criminal law and quickly earned a reputation as an excellent defense lawyer. In 1952 he headed Alabama Veterans for Dwight D. Eisenhower and was one of the state campaign managers for Eisenhower's Presidential bid. Johnson's reward for his devotion to the Republican party came in August 1953, when the victorious Eisenhower appointed him United States Attorney for Alabama's northern district. Two years later, on November 7, 1955, the President named him to a lifetime job on the federal bench. He was, at thirty-seven, the country's youngest federal judge.

Johnson's first big case came three months later when Rosa Parks, the black seamstress who had refused to relinquish her seat to a white rider, as required by Montgomery's bus segregation laws, challenged the constitutionality of those laws in a class action suit in federal court. On June 5, 1956 Johnson and Judge Richard T. Rives, a majority of the three-judge panel, citing the Supreme Court's historic 1954 school desegregation decision, ruled that the bus segregation ordinances violated the "due process and equal protection" clauses of the Fourteenth Amendment. It was the first time a court had applied the 1954 school integration decision to a non-school case and it cleared the way for the eventual desegregation of all public facilities in the South. Over the next two decades, Johnson, alone or as a member of a three-judge panel, desegregated Montgomery's parks, libraries, museums, YMCA, bus depot and airport. Some of those rulings were the first of their kind in the country.

Johnson was opposed on many of those landmark decisions by Alabama Governor George C. Wallace, a staunch segregationist. The first clash between the two former law school classmates came in January 1959 when Wallace, then a state judge, impounded voting records sought by the federal Civil Rights Commission, in an attempt to impede black voter registration. The commission appealed Wallace's decision in federal court and Johnson threatened his old friend with contempt unless he released the records. Although Wallace remained publicly defiant, Johnson ruled that, by giving the records to a local grand jury which, in turn, passed them on to the commission, he had complied with the court order, "even though it was accomplished by means of subterfuge." But when Wallace ran for governor three years later, he berated Johnson as a "carpetbagging, scalawagging, integrating, baldfaced liar" for suggesting that he had in any way cooperated with federal integration orders.

By the mid-1960's Johnson had gained a national reputation as a champion of civil rights. The judge, however, repeatedly insisted to the press that he was not a crusader but simply a judge upholding "the supremacy of the law." In fact, several of Johnson's rulings dismayed civil rights advocates who had come to look upon him as their special friend in court. In 1958, for example, he ruled that he had no power to reverse the state legislature's gerrymandering of Tuskegee, which left only four black families of the overwhelmingly Negro city eligible to vote in municipal elections. Strictly following the letter of the law, Johnson based his opinion on an earlier Supreme Court decision that "modification of a municipality is the prerogative . . . of the state alone." When the high court reversed his ruling, thereby altering its own stand, Johnson promptly restored Tuskegee's original boundaries.

Even in *U.S. v. Alabama*, the 1959 Macon County voter registration case that led to a national revision of black voting rights, Johnson threw out the Justice Department's first effort to enfranchise more black voters, contending that the Civil Rights Act of 1957 did not give the federal government the right to sue county registrars who had resigned to avoid prosecution for interfering with black voting rights. As a direct result of his ruling, a provision allowing the federal government to cite states and their agencies as defendants was written into the Civil Rights Act of 1960. The following year Johnson ordered the Macon board of registrars to stop making "puny excuses" and to register any Negro whose voting qualifications equalled those of the "least qualified white." That standard, known as the "freeze doctrine," was later incorporated verbatim into the 1965 Voting Rights Act. In an effort to remove the remaining barriers to black participation in local and national elections, Johnson outlawed the poll tax and, in 1962, as a member of a three-judge panel, voided Alabama's scheme to base apportionment of the state legislature on geography rather than on population. The panel issued the first court order for legislative reapportionment in American history, anticipating the Supreme Court's one-man, one-vote ruling.

Many legal analysts maintain that Johnson's decision permitting Dr. Martin Luther King Jr. and thousands of his supporters to march the fifty miles from Selma to Montgomery to petition Governor Wallace for their voting rights was vital to the passage of national voting rights legislation. Contending that the massive demonstration was dangerous to public safety, Wallace prohibited the march, but after three days of hearings, Judge Johnson threw out the governor's ban. "The right to assemble, demonstrate, and march peaceably along the highways and streets in an orderly manner should be commensurate with the enormity of the wrongs that are being protested against," Johnson said. "In this case, the wrongs are enormous."

Following the march, Viola Liuzzo, a white civil rights worker from Detroit, Michigan, was shot to death while riding in her car with a black youth. In one of the most widely publicized trials of the decade, an all-white jury acquitted three Ku Klux Klansmen of the murder in state court, even though an FBI informant testified that he saw one of the men kill her. When the three were later tried in Johnson's court for violating the dead woman's civil rights, the jurors declared themselves "hopelessly deadlocked" after several hours of deliberation. Johnson coolly ordered them back to the jury room, saying, "You haven't commenced to deliberate long enough to reach the conclusion that you're hopelessly deadlocked." Then, employing a rarely used legal device to prevent a mistrial, he reminded the jurors that "the case cannot again be tried better or more exhaustively on either side." A few hours later, the jury found the Klansmen guilty—"the only verdict [they] could possibly have reached," in the judge's opinion—and sentenced the defendants to the maximum ten years in prison.

Throughout the turbulent years of the early 1960's, Johnson worked to implement the Supreme Court's 1954 directive, in *Brown v. Board of Education,* that racial segregation in the public schools was unconstitutional. His 1963 order to desegregate the schools in Alabama precipitated yet another clash with Governor Wallace, who stood "in the schoolhouse door" to block the enrollment of two black students at the University of Alabama. After four years of legal wrangling, a four-judge court, presided over by Frank Johnson, handed down an order that desegregated every public school, trade school, and state college in Alabama. In applying the order, Johnson preserved "free choice" wherever possible, protected the neighborhood school concept, and restricted busing to such an extent that he upset civil rights activists.

Some other important rulings handed down by Judge Johnson or by panels on which he sat include decisions that struck down the state law barring blacks and women from juries; outlawed the practice of paying justices of the peace from the fines they collected; broadened the Supreme Court's Gideon rule on the right of defendants to counsel by requiring that court-appointed lawyers be paid; stopped state university officials from barring a speaker invited to the campus by the students; ordered a complete revision of Alabama's property tax system; desegregated the state trooper force; and forbade discrimination against women by employers in salaries and promotions.

In an unprecedented decision of a 1971 class action suit filed on behalf of all patients involuntarily committed to Bryce Hospital, the largest of Alabama's mental hospitals, Johnson ruled that the patients had a constitutional right to "adequate treatment." Appalled by the deplorable conditions at Bryce and other state mental institutions, Johnson held that there was no legal (or moral) justification for the state's failure to provide medical care. He therefore ordered a complete reorganization of every mental hospital in the state.

In another equally unprecedented and even more sweeping and controversial ruling in 1976, Johnson declared that Alabama's prisons were unfit for human habitation and threatened to close them unless they were cleaned up and made safe for the prisoners. In his opinion, the prevailing conditions were blatant violations of the Eighth Amendment's stricture against "cruel and unusual punishment." He set up a Human Rights Committee to see that his guidelines for prison administration were followed. Wallace, who had attacked Johnson's mental hospitals ruling as a usurpation of state legislative powers, was even more bitter about the prison decision and frequently accused the judge of creating a hotel or resort atmosphere in the state's jails. The judge countered, "The elimination of conditions that will permit maggots in a patient's wounds for over a month before his death does not constitute the creation of a hotel atmosphere."

In 1977 the United States Court of Appeals significantly weakened Johnson's prison ruling and, in its majority opinion, warned the courts not to become too intrusive in state governmental affairs, thus joining the debate between activist unelected federal judges like Johnson and elected state officials. With Johnson, sometimes called the state's "real governor," overseeing the operations of Alabama's schools, prisons, mental hospitals, and political elections, one observer remarked that Wallace had not "much to run but the highways and the liquor stores." Johnson himself objects to what he calls "improper" judicial intervention in state government, but he also believes that "a blind and unyielding deference to legislative and executive action is judicial abdication and is equally to be condemned." He has repeatedly insisted that he has taken action only when state officials have plainly ignored their duty.

Because of his superlative record on the bench, Johnson has often been considered for higher federal offices. In 1969, for example, he was then-Attorney General John N. Mitchell's choice to succeed Justice Abe Fortas on the United States Supreme Court, but his nomination was blocked by angry Alabama Republicans who disapproved of his civil rights stands. His reputation as a hardline law-and-order judge who regularly handed out stiff sentences in criminal cases is one of a number of factors that led President-elect Jimmy Carter to offer him the directorship of the FBI in December 1976. At that time, Johnson declined, but eight months later, when Carter was still without an acceptable candidate, he agreed to head the bureau.

When the President officially nominated Johnson to the post on August 17, 1977, calling him "a tough, fair-minded protector of justice and the law," the appointment was universally acclaimed. Even Wallace and other diehard segregationists praised their old enemy, and he seemed headed for easy Senate confirmation. But the day after his nomination, Johnson's physician found an aortic aneurysm. The judge underwent surgery to correct the defect and his surgeon, Dr. Michael De Bakey, the heart specialist, predicted complete recovery in six weeks. Several months later, however, Johnson suffered a relapse and, when his doctor estimated that it might be several more months before he could take on his new job, the judge asked the President to withdraw his nomination. After regaining his health, he returned to the bench, where he continued to break new legal ground. In May 1978, for instance, he ordered Alabama State University, the state's oldest and largest traditionally black college, to stop "its practice of discrimination against whites" in hiring faculty and staff. It was the first time a federal court had found that a black institution discriminated against whites.

Judge Johnson is a stern and forbidding figure in the courtroom and his authority there is unquestioned, although he never raises his voice. Until he was ordered to do so by a higher court, he never wore a robe or used a gavel, explaining that a judge who needs such trappings "hasn't established control." Although one Montgomery lawyer once described him as being as "hard-boiled as a ten-minute egg," virtually every attorney who has brought a case before him attests to his fairness.

Frank M. Johnson Jr. stands six feet one inch tall and weighs 175 pounds. He has brown hair, now graying at the sides, brown eyes, and craggy facial features. His gravelly drawl was compared by one reporter to a "banjo twang." Johnson, whose hobbies are golf, fishing, and woodworking, stopped hunting several years ago because he "just didn't like to kill things." Although intense and remote on the job, among his small circle of close friends he is known as an engaging storyteller and practical joker.

Johnson and his wife, the former Ruth Jenkins, have been married since January 16, 1938. Their adopted son, James Curtis Johnson, is no longer living. Johnson's desegregation rulings have provoked cross burnings on the lawn of his home in an integrated section of Montgomery, the fire bombing of his mother's house, frequent death threats, and bags of hate mail. For years he was guarded around the clock and he is still ostracized by many prominent Montgomery residents. Nevertheless, Johnson insists that the animosities aroused by his controversial rulings have failed to impair his social life.

References: Economist 264:25+ Ag 20 '77 por; New Times 9:31+ D 9 '77 por; New York 9:37+ Ap 26 '76 por; N Y Times A p1+ Ag 18 '77 por; Newsweek 90:26 Ag 29 '77 por; Time 89:72+ My 12 '67 por, 110:11 Ag 29 '77; U S News 83:20+ Ag 29 '77; Wall St J p1+ Ap 15 '76 por; Washington Post A p17 Mr 21 '65 por; Kennedy, Robert F. Jr. Judge Frank M. Johnson, Jr. (1978); Political Profiles: the Eisenhower Years (1977); Who's Who in America, 1978-79

Jorgensen, Anker (Henrik)

July 13, 1922- Prime Minister of Denmark. Address: b. Statsministeriet, Christiansberg, 1218 Copenhagen, Denmark; h. Borgbjergvej 1, 2450 S.V. Copenhagen, Denmark

Although Denmark has long been considered a showcase welfare state, its growing economic woes—notably unemployment, inflation, high taxes, industrial strife, and a perennial balance of payments deficit—have posed serious difficulties for its Prime Minister, Anker Jorgensen, whose minority Social Democratic government depends for its stability on support from among the country's ten other political parties. A former blue-collar worker and trade-union leader and a member of Denmark's parliament, the Folketing, since 1964, Jorgensen had no previous Cabinet experience when he succeeded Prime Minister Jens Otto Krag in October 1972. After leading the parliamentary opposition during the Liberal government of Poul Hartling, from December 1973 to January 1975, Jorgensen returned to the Prime Ministership, and his position was substantially strengthened as a result of the general elections of February 1977. Although he stands to the left of center of his Social Democratic party, Jorgensen—who believes that "socialism is democracy conclusively carried out"—supports the European Common Market, NATO, and cooperation with the United States.

Anker Henrik Jorgensen was born in a working-class district of Copenhagen on July

13, 1922. His father, Johannes Jorgensen, was a driver of a horse-drawn streetcar. Orphaned at the age of four, Anker went to live with his father's sister, a worker in a tobacco factory, and her husband, a van driver. While staying with his aunt and uncle, whom he called mother and father, he lived in modest circumstances but never experienced any real hardship. (When his aunt, who is now in her eighties, was informed in 1972 that her nephew had become Prime Minister, she reportedly remarked: "What could be more sensible?") Jorgensen received his formal education in the strict religious atmosphere of the Copenhagen School for Orphans, which he attended until 1936. He enjoyed sports as a boy, especially football, and at one time he held a Zealand swimming championship.

After leaving school at fourteen, Jorgensen went to work as a general helper in a lock factory. There he took part in his first industrial dispute, which resulted in a 20 percent wage increase for the workers. Later he worked as a messenger with the Federation of Danish Cooperative Societies (FDB), but at eighteen, when he moved into a higher wage bracket, he was dismissed. For a time he also worked as an unskilled shipyard and factory laborer. During one extended period of unemployment Jorgensen devoted himself to self-education. Spending many hours in the public library, he read voraciously—but without any particular plan—in poetry, philosophy, geography, and history and became familiar with the works of Marx and Lenin. Eventually he again found employment with the FDB, this time as a warehouse worker.

During World War II Jorgensen served with the Royal Danish Hussars at Naestved until German occupation troops disarmed the remnants of the Danish armed forces in August 1943 and seized control of the government. Then he joined the Resistance as a member of a group that specialized in sabotage of transport facilities. On one occasion he took part in a raiding party that invaded the offices of the Ministry of Trade and appropriated files valuable to the Resistance forces. During the later war years, Jorgensen continued his schooling by taking evening classes in Copenhagen, and in 1945 he qualified for a general certificate of education.

Jorgensen began his trade union career in 1947, when his coworkers at the FDB warehouse elected him shop steward. In 1950 he left the warehouse job to work full-time as the salaried vice-president of the 5,000-member Warehouse Workers Union in Copenhagen, and from 1956 to 1962 he served as its president. To gain more background in his chosen field, in 1957 Jorgensen completed a course in trade union activities at the Roskilde Workers' Folk High School, and two years later he attended a three-month course in economics and labor market problems at Harvard University.

From 1962 to 1968 Jorgensen was union manager (or group secretary) of the transport section of Denmark's largest union, the Dansk Arbejtmans og Specialarbejder Forbund (DASF), or Danish General and Semiskilled Workers' Union, and he also served from 1964 to 1968 as editor of the official DASF journal. A DASF congress in 1968 elected him union president by a large majority. The 250,000-member DASF—known since 1974 as Specialarbejderforbundet i Danmark (SID), or Union of Semiskilled Workers in Denmark —represents workers in such areas as construction, manufacturing, transportation, agriculture, and horticulture.

During his four years as DASF president, Jorgensen devoted much of his effort to improving conditions for lower-paid workers. He conducted a vigorous campaign to create jobs in areas of Denmark where unemployment was high and took steps to streamline the union's organizational structure. Under his leadership the DASF sponsored a number of initiatives that were channeled through the official programs of the Social Democratic party. On the cultural level, the union under Jorgensen supported small theatrical groups that toured factories, schools, and construction sites, and it published books, magazines, and pamphlets. Jorgensen also promoted international cooperation among labor movements. He was an early protester against United States military action in Vietnam and a consistent advocate of diplomatic recognition of East Germany.

Along with his trade union activities, Jorgensen was active in Social Democratic politics. From 1961 to 1964 he was a member of the Copenhagen city council, and since 1964 he has represented a Copenhagen working-class district in the national Folketing. As a member of parliament, Jorgensen promoted programs beneficial to labor, including an elaborate plan for the gradual transfer of ownership and control of Danish industry from the capitalists and managers to the trade unions. "We want to be represented on the boards," Jorgensen said in an interview in mid-1972 that was published in *Forbes* magazine (November 12, 1972). "We will try to realize a system where the workers will get more than just wages for their work." Since the Social Democrats remained in the minority, however, there was little likelihood that such a program would be put into effect in the near future.

Of more immediate concern was the question of Danish membership in the European Economic Community, or Common Market. Jens Otto Krag, the Social Democratic Prime Minister, signed an agreement at Brussels in January 1972 providing for Denmark's admission to the EEC along with Great Britain, Ireland, and Norway, but the country was sharply divided on that issue. So were the labor movement and the Social Democratic party. In April 1972 a majority of his own union, the DASF, voted against the Common Market. Nevertheless, Jorgensen, who had long championed international cooperation, both on the Scandinavian level and in the broader European context, vigorously supported EEC membership. He was, he explained, motivated by political rather than economic considerations. "The left wing of the trade union movement and the Social Democratic party is wrong in believing that rejecting the EEC represents a leftist attitude," he told fellow party members. "I maintain that the only practical possibility available to us for putting our leftist mark on developments in Europe comes through membership."

On October 3, 1972, a day after a national referendum was held in which 63.5 percent of those who voted favored EEC membership, Prime Minister Krag announced his intention to retire now that the government had won a resounding victory on the Common Market issue. The Social Democratic party immediately named as his successor Jorgensen, who had gained much popularity within the party and the trade union movement, despite his lack of government experience. In proposing him as his successor, Krag was motivated not only by Jorgensen's support of the EEC but also by the fact that his left-wing reputation would appeal to party dissidents and to members of the more radical Socialist People's party, on whom the Social Democrats depended for support.

The national executive of the Social Democratic party unanimously approved Jorgensen's appointment on October 4, 1972, and he was formally invested as Prime Minister by Queen Margrethe II on the following day. Commanding only seventy seats in the 179-member Folketing, his Social Democratic government had to rely on the seventeen votes of the Socialist People's party and two votes of Greenland representatives to survive. Although Jorgensen had kept his predecessor's government intact, in September 1973 he reshuffled the Cabinet in a leftward direction. That same month a Social Democratic congress in Copenhagen unanimously elected him party chairman. Meanwhile he met with little success in coping with the country's economic problems, including an increasingly unstable currency, a balance of payments deficit that had more than doubled within a year, and a crippling three-week strike by some 280,000 workers. Because of his expressed sympathy for Israel, Denmark was adversely affected by the Arab oil boycott, and in late 1973 Jorgensen had to institute austerity measures to conserve fuel.

On November 6, 1973 Jorgensen's government was defeated by an eighty-six to eighty-six tie vote on an income tax bill because one of the Social Democratic party's right-wing members, Erhard Jacobsen, had defected from its ranks to form a new party. Two days later the Jorgensen government resigned. In the new national elections on December 4, in which the Social Democrats, while still the strongest party, found their representation reduced to forty-six, the traditional parties all lost ground. Dismayed by high taxes and a burgeoning bureaucracy, many voters cast their votes for two new parties—Mogens Glistrup's Progress party and Erhard Jacobsen's Democratic Center. On December 19, 1973 a new government was formed by Poul Hartling, who, although his Liberal party controlled only twenty-two seats, obtained support from other moderate factions in the Folketing. But Hartling's economic measures, including a temporary freeze on wages and profits, reductions in income taxes, and cutbacks in the budget, proved insufficient, and in December 1974 he called for new elections with the hope of gaining support for his more far-reaching plans.

In the elections of January 9, 1975 the Social Democrats received fifty-three seats, and the Liberals nearly doubled their representation, to forty-two, but at the expense of the other moderate parties. On January 28 Hartling lost a vote of confidence and resigned as Prime Minister, and on February 13, after the failure of two weeks of negotiations among the leaders of the ten parties for the formation of a viable coalition, Anker Jorgensen took office once more as the head of a minority Social Democratic government. Because he could no longer command a majority with the Socialist People's party and now depended for support upon the parties of the moderate right, he had to move more cautiously. His compromise program for limited wage raises and cost of living adjustments, adopted in March 1975, is credited with having averted a wave of strikes. "I think we do need a slowing down of social welfare programs," Jorgensen said in an interview, as quoted in the New York *Times* (February 12, 1976). "My party doesn't have a majority in Parliament, so we have to move more slowly. And the economic situation dictates that we move slowly, too."

In June 1975 Jorgensen suffered a minor setback when a court found him guilty of having slandered the right-wing newspaper *Minuit* at a 1974 rally, but no penalties were imposed on him. At the time he reportedly asserted that the paper represented the "darkest fascism imaginable" and accused it of receiving support from international oil companies.

In August 1976 the Jorgensen government provoked wildcat strikes by imposing a new austerity program aimed at reducing the foreign trade deficit, and in December a price, wage, and rent freeze was enacted. Unable to come to terms with the moderate parties with regard to housing policy and other issues, Jorgensen dissolved the Folketing on January 22, 1977 and called for new elections.

In that campaign the Social Democrats represented themselves as the party of responsible government, ready to make unpopular decisions if necessary to restore equilibrium to the economy. The elections of February 15, 1977 resulted in an increase to sixty-five seats for the Social Democrats, who continued to work with the moderate parties of the right—the Center Democrats, Christian People's Party, Radical Liberals, and Conservatives—while the antiwelfare state Progress party now displaced the Liberals as the leading opposition party. In September 1977, after protracted negotiations between the Social Democrats and their allies on the right, a new anti-inflationary program for higher consumer taxes, called the "Midway Compromise," was enacted. In the local elections of March 1978, the Social Democrats, with 38 percent of the vote (as compared with 32 percent in 1974) scored substantial gains.

On the international level, Jorgensen made an official visit to the Soviet Union in the fall of 1973 and hosted an EEC summit meeting in Copenhagen later that year. In 1975 he attended the European Security Conference at Helsinki, visited Venezuela and Mexico, and met with President Gerald R. Ford in Washington, D.C. In 1976 he was host to a summit meeting of European Social Democratic leaders at Elsinore, and in 1978 he served as president of the EEC council of ministers. Jorgensen played an active role in the effort to strengthen democratic socialist forces in Portugal and Spain following the emergence of those countries from right-wing dictatorship.

Since 1956 Jorgensen has been a teacher at the Social Democratic Workers' School. From 1956 to 1962 he was chairman of the board of the Ellebjerg School, where he has continued to serve as a board member. He belonged to the General Workers' joint council from 1957 to 1962 and became a member of the Social Democratic Union in 1966. Since 1969 he has served on the board of directors of the Workers' Bank of Denmark. When asked by an interviewer for the liberal Danish newspaper *Jyllands-Posten* which half of his party's name was more important to him, he said: "The Democratic. There is no doubt in my mind. Democracy means free elections, free speech, a free press, everything that means anything. . . . Democracy is the cornerstone, and it is up to us to preserve it."

Prime Minister Anker Jorgensen and his wife, Ingrid, a former children's nurse, whom he met at a Social Democratic function and married in 1948, have four children. The youngest son, Lars, still lives with his parents in their five-room apartment in a cooperative housing project near Copenhagen's south harbor, in the working-class district that Jorgensen represents in the Folketing. A small, corpulent man with thinning black hair, a mustache, and a goatee, the Danish Prime Minister is five feet seven inches tall, weighs about 170 pounds, and keeps fit by taking brisk evening walks. His leisure activities include reading, painting, and writing poetry for family celebrations. The Jorgensens spend weekends and vacations in their small holiday cottage near the North Zealand coast. A hard worker who is meticulous in his habits, Jorgensen is relaxed, unpretentious, and informal. He belongs to the Church of Denmark but considers himself a rationalist. His trade union experience has taught him, he has said, that one has to be "a little bit of an idealist and a little bit of a cynic."

References: Current World Leaders 16:13+ N '73; N Y Times p5 O 6 '72 por; Dictionary of Scandinavian Biography (1976); International Who's Who, 1977-78; Kraks Bla Bog, 1977

Karpov, Anatoly

May 23, 1951- Grand master of chess. Address: b. c/o State Committee for Sports and Physical Culture of the U.S.S.R. Council of Ministers, Moscow, U.S.S.R.

On April 3, 1975 the world chess championship went by default to Anatoly Karpov, a young economics student at Leningrad University, after the American grand master

Bobby Fischer forfeited it in a dispute with the Fédération Internationale des Échecs (FIDE), the world governing body of chess. At the time, Karpov had been the leading contender for the title, a position that he had struggled long and hard to attain. A child prodigy, he won the world junior championship in 1969 and became the world's youngest international grand master in 1970, and he has since been a fairly consistent winner in tournament play. A strategist rather than a tactician, Karpov is rated "the best chess player in the world in our time" by his mentor Mikhail Botvinnik, who lists as his strong points "his ability for self-programming, a keen sense of danger, calculation of variants, and skillful buildup of domination on the board." In the summer and fall of 1978, at Baguio City in the Philippines, Karpov defended his title against challenger Viktor Korchnoi. The longest title match in chess history ended on October 18, after more than thirteen weeks, with a score of six games to five in favor of Karpov, who remained world champion.

Anatoly Evgenyevich Karpov, one of the two children, and the only son, of Evgeny Stepanovich Karpov and Nina Karpova, was born on May 23, 1951 in the old Russian city of Zlatoust, in the Chelyabinsk district, in the southern Urals mountains. His father, a steelworker in a metallurgical plant at Zlatoust, later moved with his family to the city of Tula, where he became chief engineer of a factory after qualifying for an engineering diploma at the Bauman Higher Technical School in Moscow. Tolya—as Anatoly Karpov is known to his friends—learned the rules of chess from his father when he was only four. "I recall being tremendously upset when I lost a game," Karpov told Ivetta Knyazeva of *Soviet Life* (July 1975). "But Father used to say that without defeats there would be no victories, and that if I let myself get so upset, he wouldn't play with me."

Later, Karpov played the game with neighborhood boys and took part in chess matches at his school, at the metallurgists' sports palace in Zlatoust, and at the local clubhouse of the Pioneers—the leading Soviet children's organization. At seven he won a third-category chess rating and the following year he achieved second-category rating and won the scholastic championship of the Chelyabinsk region. When he was eleven—two years after he had qualified for the first-category rating—he tied for second place with two others for the Chelyabinsk region men's championship and became the youngest candidate master of chess in the Soviet Union.

Among Karpov's boyhood chess heroes were Mikhail Tal of the Soviet Union, who had won the world title in 1960, and the late Cuban grand master José Raúl Capablanca, who had been noted for the clarity and unpretentiousness of his positional play. In the beginning Karpov shunned chess literature, preferring to rely on his instincts, but when he was around thirteen he used his school lunch money to buy a series of Capablanca's published games and studied them in detail. In 1964 he enrolled in a chess correspondence school organized by the Trud Sports Society and headed by the three-time world champion Mikhail Botvinnik, and he remained under Botvinnik's tutelage for four years. At fifteen he became the Soviet Union's youngest chess master.

Karpov's international career began in early 1967, when the Soviet Chess Federation mistakenly sent him to Trinec, Czechoslovakia to take part in a tournament intended exclusively for adults. Nevertheless, the fifteen-year-old Karpov was permitted to compete and won first place without a single loss. At the International Youth Tournament—considered the *de facto* European junior championship competition—held in Groningen, the Netherlands, in the winter of 1967-68, he won the European cup for juniors. Later in 1966 he won the Moscow University championships and helped the Armed Forces team win the Soviet team championships at Riga. It was at the latter tournment that Karpov first came to the attention of grand master Semyon Furman, who became his trainer.

In a three-player tournament in March and April 1969 Karpov defeated his two opponents to qualify as the Soviet representative in the World Junior Championships, and during the next few months, under Furman's tutelage, he devoted himself to perfecting his game and improving his physical condition through exercise, in preparation for the world junior event. Although he was off to a slow start in the tournament, held at Stockholm in August 1969, he won the junior title with a final score of ten points, and was designated an international master.

By winning the Russian Federation (RSFSR) championship in the spring of 1970, Karpov became qualified to compete for the U.S.S.R. championship. At the international tournament in Caracas, Venezuela in the summer of 1970 he finished in a fourth-place tie with two others, but his performance was dazzling enough to earn him designation as an international grand master of chess. On his return to the Soviet Union he finished in a three-way tie for fifth place in the U.S.S.R. championships at Riga.

In addition to distinguishing himself at chess, Karpov performed brilliantly in school. When he graduated from high school he was awarded a gold medal, and his name was included on the list of honor students in the school's annals. Although, according to his parents, his boyhood ambition had been to become a pilot, he decided, when he enrolled at Leningrad University in the early 1970's, to combine a career as an economist with chess as a pastime. "Economics requires logical thinking, the ability to analyze," Karpov observed in the *Soviet Life* interview. "Chess helps develop that ability."

In the summer of 1971 Karpov attained a nearly perfect score in the Student Olympiad held at Mayagüez, Puerto Rico and made good showings with the Armed Forces team in the Soviet team championships and the Leningrad team in the army team championships, and that fall he finished fourth in the U.S.S.R. championships. In November and December 1971, at the Alekhine Memorial Tournament in Moscow—considered the most competitive in over thirty years—Karpov was up against four former world champions and fourteen other grand masters. His first place tie with Leonid Stein for a score of eleven points in eighteen rounds was the most notable achievement of his career up to that time.

Karpov next went to England for the sixteen-round Hastings International Congress. Recalling his impressions of Karpov at Hastings, the British chess master P. R. Markland wrote: "He may look frail . . . but he is able to inject tremendous mental energy into every tournament in which he plays. . . . Observing all the customary courtesies, he becomes a player of phenomenal calculating powers. . . . It is as though he possesses the ability to win at will." Of his own encounter with Karpov, in the final round, Markland wrote: "He squeezed, pushed, and eventually demolished my position with his customary ease." With a final score of eleven points, Karpov finished the Hastings tournament in January 1972 in a first-place tie with Viktor Korchnoi.

On his return to the Soviet Union, Karpov helped his team win second place in the Soviet team championships, and in the Student Olympiad, at Graz, Austria in July 1972, he contributed to the Soviet team's victory. At the twentieth World Chess Olympiad at Skopje, Yugoslavia that fall, Karpov won the prize for the best performance on the fifth board. In November and December 1972 Karpov was in San Antonio, Texas to compete in an international tournament sponsored by the indisputably capitalistic Church's Fried Chicken drive-in chain. Playing with what one American chess expert, quoted in *Newsweek* (December 11, 1972), called "a leisurely boa-constrictor style," Karpov obtained 10.5 points in sixteen rounds and finished in a three-way tie for first place. From San Antonio, Karpov went with Tigran Petrosian and Paul Keres to Chicago for a series of exhibition games.

By the end of 1972 Karpov was regarded as a potential world champion, and Petrosian called him the Soviet Union's "great hope" to regain the title, lost for the first time in twenty-four years when Bobby Fischer defeated Boris Spassky at Reykjavik in September 1972. In his *Grandmasters of Chess* (Lippincott, 1973), Harold C. Schonberg called Karpov the "new Russian threat," who "played a solid, old-man's game and was being talked about as the one young player who could give Fischer some real competition." In March 1973, at the Budapest International Tournament, Karpov came in second to Yefim Geller, and in a "double-round, triangular match" between three Soviet teams in Moscow in April he scored victories against Boris Spassky and Mark Taimanov.

In the Leningrad Interzonal Tournament in June 1973—the first of the qualifying events for the world championship—Karpov, with 13.5 points in eighteen rounds, finished in a first-place tie with Korchnoi. The tournament narrowed the field of Fischer's potential challengers down to eight. The following month Karpov helped the Soviet team to achieve victory in the European team championships at Bath, England, and in October 1973, in the fortieth U.S.S.R. championships in Moscow, he finished in a five-way tie for second place, behind Boris Spassky. He completed the year with another triumph, in the eighth Madrid international tournament. In January 1974 Karpov for the first time received the gold "Oscar," presented annually by the International Association of Chess Journalists for the best overall score in match and tournament play in the previous year.

Pitted against Soviet grand master Lev Polugayevsky in the quarter-final candidates' match at Moscow in January and February 1974, Karpov defeated him in eight games with a score of three to nothing. Then, in the semi-final, at Leningrad in April and May, Karpov, after losing the first game to Boris Spassky, went on to score a four-to-one victory over him in eleven games. At the twenty-first World Chess Olympiad, played in Nice in June 1974 to commemorate the fiftieth anniversary of FIDE, Karpov achieved the best score in the history of the event, with twelve points out of a possible fourteen.

On September 15, 1974, before a capacity audience of 1,800 at Moscow's Trade Union Hall, the frail, austere Karpov and the burly, genial four-time Soviet titleholder, Korchnoi, nearly twice his opponent's age, confronted each other in the first round of the final candidates' match that was to determine who would qualify to challenge Fischer for the title in 1975. Meanwhile, in June 1974, the temperamental Fischer had resigned the championship because of a dispute with FIDE officials over rules. But the world body refused to accept Fischer's resignation, and the American continued to be recognized as the world titleholder. Under FIDE rules, the Karpov-Korchnoi match consisted of a maximum of twenty-four games, with the victory going to the player who won five games or scored 12.5 points. In the often tense ten-week contest—described in *Newsweek* (December 9, 1974) as "a classic confrontation between the young man's coldly mathematical chess and the veteran's complex attempts at innovative counterpunching"—Karpov took an early lead, and Korchnoi failed to overtake him. The final result, after the twenty-fourth game, on November 22, 1974, was three wins for Karpov, two for Korchnoi, and nineteen draws. With 12.5 points to Korchnoi's 11.5, Karpov emerged as Fischer's challenger for the world title.

FIDE officials announced in January 1975 that a world championship match between Karpov and Fischer was tentatively scheduled to take place in Manila later in the year and that a $5,000,000 purse—the highest in chess history—had been posted for the event. Meanwhile, however, Fischer continued to insist that he would not play unless the rules for the match were amended to suit him. Atfer some debate, federation officials reluctantly agreed to some of Fischer's conditions, designed to accommodate the champion's aggressive playing rather than Karpov's more reserved style. They included the demand that the world title match be of unlimited duration rather than being limited to thirty-six games, and that the title should go to the first player to win ten games. The officials balked, however, at Fischer's demand that he retain the title in the event of a nine-to-nine tie, maintaining that it would give the champion an unfair advantage.

After Fischer failed to meet the deadline set by FIDE for formal acceptance of federation rules, he was stripped of his title on April 3, 1975, and Karpov was proclaimed world chess champion. Lamenting the fact that he had been denied the "moral satisfaction" of victory, Karpov later said that he hoped to meet Fischer in a private match under mutually acceptable conditions at some future date. Although Karpov was referred to in some quarters as a "paper champion" and the official mood in the Soviet Union on his accession to the title lacked the usual euphoria, he continued to prove himself a winner in international tournament play.

Among Karpov's most notable victories after he became world champion were those in Portoroz and Ljubljana, Yugoslavia and Milan, Italy in 1975; in Amsterdam, Holland, Skopje, Yugoslavia, and Montilla, Spain in 1976; and in Bad Lauterberg, West Germany, Las Palmas in the Canary Islands, and Tilburg, Holland in 1977. That year, playing board one in the 1977 European team championships in Moscow, Karpov obtained a perfect score in his five games. In the grand master's tournament at Bugojno, Yugoslavia in March 1978 he finished in a ten-point tie for first place with Boris Spassky. Between the time he assumed the championship and July 1978, Karpov lost only six out of 188 games.

Meanwhile, Korchnoi, in disfavor with Soviet authorities ever since his 1974 defeat by Karpov, defected from the U.S.S.R. in July 1976 and asked for asylum in Holland. Stripped of his Soviet titles and honors, Korchnoi continued to compete in exile, contending that the Soviet Chess Federation had discriminated against him and that the world title should have rightfully been his rather than Karpov's. In January 1978 Korchnoi defeated Boris Spassky in the candidates' final at Belgrade and emerged as Karpov's challenger for the world title.

The Karpov-Korchnoi world championship match—billed as a "grudge match"—opened on July 18, 1978 in Baguio City, a mountain resort in the Philippines. At stake, in addition to the title, was a prize fund of $553,900 —the highest ever awarded in chess—of which five-eighths was allocated to the winner. Under revised FIDE rules, the victor is the first to win six games, with draws not counting in the scoring.

During the match—which was off to a slow start—Karpov virtually secluded himself in his leisure time, while Korchnoi made headlines by charging that he was being subjected to hypnotism and radiation bombardment by the Soviet team, by adding members of a Hindu mystical sect to his entourage, and by asserting that he would defeat Karpov and "prove once and for all that the Soviet system produces only robots." Contrasting the styles of the two contenders, J. D. Reed wrote in *Sports Illustrated* (July 31, 1978): "Korchnoi . . . plays chess as if it were street theatre. He is the Stravinsky of chess. . . . Karpov is the game's Bach, passionless at the board, an enigma of classic perfection. . . . His game is pure counterpoint." Although Korchnoi rallied within a two-week period from a two-to-five deficit to a five-to-five tie, his resignation from the thirty-second game, on October 18, 1978, enabled Karpov to claim his sixth victory of the match and retain the championship.

On February 10, 1978 Karpov presented his diploma thesis—dealing with the uses of leisure time under socialism—to the economics faculty of Leningrad University. That same day he was informed that the chess "Oscar" had been awarded to him for the fifth consecutive year. He belongs to the central council of FIDE, and under that organization's official ELO rating system he had a score of 2,716—higher than that of any other player in the world—as of early 1978. Karpov is a member of the central committee of Komsomol, the Young Communist League. He travels throughout the U.S.S.R. giving lectures and consultations and taking part in exhibition games, and he occasionally writes for chess publications. The book *Karpov Vs. Korchnoi: World Chess Championship 1978* was published by David McKay three days after the end of the match. Karpov's autobiography is not yet available in English.

Anatoly Karpov makes his home in Leningrad, maintains another apartment in Moscow, and rides around in a chauffeured Mercedes-Benz. A slightly-built man, five feet seven inches tall and weighing 120 pounds, he has gray eyes and a neatly brushed shock of brown hair. He keeps fit with running, swimming, skiing, rowing, calisthenics, and tennis. Despite his reputation for being self-contained and taciturn, he leads a crowded social life and has a lively sense of humor. Among his favorite recreations are reading, attending the theatre and movies, listening to popular and classical music, collecting stamps, watching sports, especially hockey and football, and playing bridge. His favorite author is the nineteenth-century Russian poet and novelist Mikhail Lermontov.

References: Chess Life & Review 32:647 D '77; Christian Sci Mon p13 Jl 10 '78 por; N Y Post p43 Ap 18 '75 por; N Y Times Mag p12+ Jl 9 '78 pors; Newsday p10 Ap 7 '77; Sports Illus 41:78+ S 30 '74 por; 49:22+ Jl 31 '78 por; Brace, Edward R. An Illustrated Encyclopedia of Chess (1977); Markland, P. R. The Best of Karpov (1975); Sunnucks, Anne. Encyclopaedia of Chess (1976)

Keaton, Diane

Jan. 5, 1946- Actress. Address: c/o Paramount Pictures Corp., 9440 Santa Monica Blvd., Beverly Hills, Calif. 90210

In 1977 Diane Keaton emerged as one of America's most accomplished film actresses with her portrayal of the vulnerable title character in Woody Allen's multiple Oscar-winning *Annie Hall,* a young woman who beguiled audiences with her flustered murmurings, outlandish costumes, and waif-like smiles. Although she danced and sang her way through the original production of *Hair* on Broadway and played Al Pacino's wife in the blockbuster *Godfather* films, Miss Keaton had until recently been best known as Woody Allen's daffy sidekick in his *Play It Again, Sam, Sleeper,* and *Love and Death.* Again teamed with Allen in *Annie Hall,* his somewhat autobiographical account of their love affair, she took full advantage of the opportunity to exhibit her wide-ranging abilities as a comedienne and actress. Late in 1977 she went on to make a spectacular debut as a dramatic actress with her interpretation of the sex-obsessed cruiser of singles bars who is savagely murdered by one of her pickups in Richard Brooks's *Looking for Mr. Goodbar.* Although a Hollywood outsider, like Woody Allen, on April 3, 1978 Diane Keaton won an Oscar as best actress from the Academy of Motion Picture Arts and Sciences for her performance in *Annie Hall.*

Like her film alter ego, Diane Keaton was born with the surname Hall, but she later adopted her mother's maiden name in order to avoid confusion with another actress named Diane Hall. Miss Keaton was born in Los Angeles, California on January 5, 1946, the first child of Jack and Dorothy (Keaton) Hall. Jack Hall is a civil engineer who now heads his own consulting firm. Diane Keaton assured Ben Fong-Torres of *Rolling Stone* (June 30, 1977) that her mother is "a crafty person. She did rock collages, and she became a photographer, too. She's a very emotional, sensitive woman, a journal keeper, a letter writer." Miss Keaton has a younger brother, Randy, who writes poetry and works as a draftsman in his father's business, and two sisters, Robin, a nurse, and Dorrie, a recent college graduate with a degree in art.

From an early age Diane clowned and performed for her family, a warm and loving group. She sang in the choir of the Methodist church, and by the time she was in junior high school in Santa Ana, California, where the Halls had moved when she was ten, she was trying out for school talent shows. When she was at first turned down, she organized and starred in her own show, which was performed by the children in her neighborhood. At Santa Ana High, a school with about 2,500 students, she won a "Miss Personality" contest and sang in the Debutantes, a girls' choir. She also appeared in school musical productions and began acting in the local little theatre. Despite her exaggerated makeup and clothing—she favored white lipstick, black net stockings, and grotesquely ratted hair—she was still considered strictly "a nice girl" in high school. "But I wanted to be more than a nice girl," the actress told Ben Fong-Torres. "I felt I wasn't really interesting enough. I was a California girl—I mean, *beach*. I think that's one of the reasons I went into acting."

After high school Diane Keaton briefly attended Santa Ana College and Orange Coast College, and then, at nineteen, went to New York City on a scholarship to study acting with Sanford Meisner at the Neighborhood Playhouse School of the Theater. While in school she sang and danced with an obscure rock 'n' roll band called the Roadrunners, which played $10 gigs in out-of-town nightclubs.

After finishing acting school in 1967, Miss Keaton performed in the Woodstock, New York, summer theatre and then returned to New York City for four discouraging months of unsuccessful auditions. Early in 1968 she attended tryouts for the Broadway production of Jerome Ragni and James Rado's paean to 1960's counterculture, *Hair,* "the American Tribal Love-Rock Musical." Hired for a minor part as a member of the Tribe and as understudy to Lynn Kellogg, the female lead, Miss Keaton made her Broadway debut with the show when it opened on April 29, 1968 at the Biltmore. When Miss Kellogg left the show a few months later, Diane Keaton took over her role as Sheila, singing "Easy to be Hard" and "Good Morning Starshine." Diane Keaton is also remembered as the one cast member of *Hair* who refused to shed her clothes for the final number.

Although Miss Keaton was technically the female lead in *Hair,* "that play wasn't much for individual performances," as the actress observed to a reporter for *Time* (September 26, 1977). She therefore decided to attend the tryouts for *Play It Again, Sam,* which had been written by a young standup comedian named Woody Allen. In it Allen portrayed one of the sexually insecure characters that were to become his stock in trade—in this instance a film critic who imagines that his pitiful love life is directed by Humphrey Bogart. Miss Keaton obtained the role of his best friend's wife, a lovable neurotic who proves to him that he can make it on his own romantically by falling in love with him. Although *Play It Again, Sam* was primarily a vehicle for Allen, Miss Keaton came in for her share of critical praise after it opened on February 12, 1969 at the Broadhurst. "Diane Keaton played . . . [the wife] with confidence and charm," wrote Martin Gottfried in *Women's Wear Daily* (February 13, 1969), "which made up for the role's absence of character (other than being a good girl)."

After *Play It Again, Sam* closed on March 14, 1970, Diane Keaton obtained a small role, as a young wife who wants to divorce her husband, in the offbeat New York-made film *Lovers and Other Strangers* (ABC Pictures, 1970), a marital comedy based on a Broadway play. Over the next couple of years Miss Keaton paid the rent by making three television commercials for Hour After Hour deodorant that required her to jog around a kitchen wearing a track suit, holding a can of deodorant and yelling, "This stuff is great." She also began appearing on talk shows, especially on *The Tonight Show,* where she would sing and chat with a bemused Johnny Carson. Of her routine on *The Tonight Show* Fong-Torres wrote, "She would scrunch up on the couch, or sit spread-legged, like some spaced-out love child, and Johnny, concerned and paternal, would ask about her love life, and she would invariably say she didn't have one, to his invariable disbelief. And he would tell her how talented she was, and she would shake her head and giddy-yap: 'Oh, no-o-o. No. I mean, no.' "

Aside from a couple of guest shots on the *FBI* and *Night Gallery* television shows, Diane Keaton did not have another acting assignment after *Lovers and Other Strangers* until she was chosen to play Kay, the WASP wife of Mafia heir Michael Corleone (Al Pacino), in Francis Ford Coppola's *The Godfather* (Paramount, 1972). She repeated her role in Coppola's sequel, *The Godfather, Part II* (Paramount, 1974). Although the critics who took note of her in those films agreed that she performed competently, Miss Keaton was, as she herself has put it, merely "background music" to the performances of Al Pacino, Robert De Niro, Marlon Brando, and the other male stars.

Miss Keaton had more of an opportunity to display her abilities when she again teamed with Woody Allen in the film version of *Play It Again, Sam* (Paramount, 1972) and, the following year, in *Sleeper* (United Artists, 1973). In the latter film the actress portrayed Luna Schlosser, an overcivilized poetess of the twenty-second century who scribbles atrocious verse modeled after that written by her literary hero, Rod McKuen. Miss Keaton again joined Allen in *Love and Death* (United Artists, 1975), the comic's takeoff on Tolstoy's *War and Peace,* in which she played Sonja, the dizzy cousin and eventual wife of Boris (Allen). In true Woody Allen style, the capricious Sonja's reply to Boris' advances in their nuptial bed is, "Don't. Not here."

Although Miss Keaton earned admiring notices for her roles in the Allen films, she was still, as Pauline Kael observed in the *New Yorker* (December 31, 1973), "really just there to be Woody's girl." Recognizing the imperative of launching her film career as a comic actress independent of Allen, Miss Keaton next costarred with Elliott Gould in *I Will, I Will . . . For Now* (Twentieth Century-Fox, 1976). Although the film was dismissed as an embarrassingly tame sex comedy, Diane Keaton's performance as a rich, neurotic New

Yorker trying to achieve a reconciliation with her husband won some rapturous reviews. "Much laughter, many cheers and at least one low wolf whistle for Diane Keaton, who looks like the brightest light comedienne in movies," wrote Jay Cocks of *Time* (March 15, 1976). "She brings nicely scrambled wit and bushwhacked sex appeal to even the lowliest undertakings." Less successful was her appearance in *Harry and Walter Go to New York* (Columbia, 1976), a banal comedy that squandered the considerable talents of James Caan and Michael Caine as well as those of Miss Keaton and Elliott Gould.

Returning to the New York stage, Diane Keaton starred in an Off-Broadway production of Israel Horovitz's comedy, *The Primary English Class,* which opened at the downtown Circle in the Square on February 7, 1976. "Her hound dog-sad eyes baying desperate messages of hysterical panic, Diane Keaton plays a neurotic instructor trying to teach basic English to a class of foreigners who don't speak a word of the stuff," wrote Marilyn Stasio in *Cue* (February 28, 1976), adding that the actress gave the teacher "a nice touch of vulnerability." Although Miss Keaton received appreciative reviews, the play itself failed to generate much interest, and the show folded three months later, on May 16, 1976. Meanwhile, Diane Keaton was pursuing a singing career between her acting assignments. In 1974 she played an engagement at the New York cabaret Reno Sweeney and has since sung at the club downstairs at the American Place Theatre, also in New York, and, in California, at the Ice House in Pasadena.

Miss Keaton renewed her collaboration with Woody Allen in his bittersweet romantic comedy *Annie Hall* (United Artists, 1977). The film tells the story of a love affair between Annie, a flaky Midwestern WASP who has come to New York in pursuit of success as a singer and actress, and Alvy Singer, a gloomy New York Jewish comic. Although details are fictionalized, the screen personalities of Annie and Alvy are comic exaggerations of the real Diane and Woody, and the plot roughly parallels the course of their relationship. Miss Keaton and Allen became lovers while appearing on Broadway together in *Play It Again, Sam* and lived together for about a year in 1971. Like the characters they play onscreen, Miss Keaton and Woody Allen then broke up, but unlike Annie and Alvy Singer, they have remained close friends and professional colleagues.

The critical verdict for *Annie Hall* and Diane Keaton was almost unanimously favorable. Among the very few dissenters was the acerbic John Simon of *New York* (May 2, 1977), who dismissed the film as "everything we never wanted to know about Woody's sex life and were afraid he'd tell us anyway." "And then there is Diane Keaton's scandalous performance," Simon grumbled. "Her work . . . always consists chiefly of a dithering, blithering, neurotic coming apart at the seams—an acting style that is really a nervous breakdown in slow motion—but it has never before been allowed such latitude to deliquesce in." A more typical response to the Keaton acting style was expressed by the writer of her *Time* cover story (September 26, 1977): "Audiences begin cheering *Annie Hall* with the first scene, when Annie and Alvy meet after a tennis game (she wearing men's brown pants, an unpressed white shirt, a black vest, and a ridiculously long polka-dot tie, an outfit Diane might have found on the floor of her own closet). She starts to compliment him on his tennis, gets lost in one of her enchanted word-forests, then subsides into pretty embarrassment: 'Oh, God, Annie . . . Well, oh, well . . .' And then the murmur of defeat: 'La-de-dah, la-de-dah.' Heartbreaking."

In a complete change of pace, Diane Keaton switched from the kookiness of *Annie Hall* to the fiendishly demanding role of Theresa Dunn in *Looking for Mr. Goodbar* (Paramount, 1977), Richard Brooks's nightmarish film version of the best-selling novel by Judith Rossner. As Terry Dunn, a dedicated teacher by day who picks up sadistic lovers at singles bars at night until one of them kills her, Diane Keaton gave what many critics considered the best performance of her career. "As delightful and skillful as Keaton has been in Woody Allen's comedies," wrote William Wolf in *Cue* (October 29-November 11, 1977), "one is unprepared for the range of her dazzling, many-leveled dramatic performance. Whether teaching deaf children, wriggling loose from the constraints of her family, asserting her sexual freedom, fencing with the strangers she encounters, or facing brutal death, Keaton makes Theresa Dunn turbulently alive."

For her performance in *Annie Hall* Diane Keaton received the 1977 Golden Globe award of the Hollywood Foreign Press Association as best actress in a comedy, the National Society of Film Critics best actress award, the New York Film Critics Circle award, and an Oscar as best actress of 1977. Her performance in *Looking for Mr. Goodbar* brought her a Golden Globe nomination as best actress in a drama, and third place in the New York Film Critics Circle polling.

By the end of January 1978 Diane Keaton had finished working in Woody Allen's Bergmanesque *Interiors,* his first excursion into serious drama, in which she was cast as Renata, a death-obsessed poet. Miss Keaton continues to sing—one of the delights of *Annie Hall* was her stylized renditions of "Seems like Old Times" and "It Had to Be You"—and she was scheduled to cut her first record album in 1978. She was one of only two women—the other was Barbra Streisand—to appear on the 1977 moviehouse owners' annual list of top ten box-office draws.

Diane Keaton lives with Buster, her Abyssinian cat, in a two-bedroom apartment on East 68th Street in New York City, just a few blocks away from Woody Allen. Photography is the actress' favorite hobby, and she has converted one bedroom in her sparsely furnished apartment into a darkroom. A slim and leggy five feet seven inches tall, Diane Keaton has light brown hair and blue-hazel eyes. Since 1973 she has been seeing an analyst from three to five times a week, and in the *Rolling Stone* interview Fong-Torres reported that "she knows all about her self-deprecatory act." "Sure," Miss Keaton told him, "and that's manipulative on my part, to get that response, that you're okay. 'It's all right, nice Di.' Absolutely . . . in my past I've done an awful lot of apologizing. I always liked to say I'm sorry before anything happened, but I don't do that as much anymore."

References: N Y Sun News III p17 Mr 24 '74 por; N Y Times II p9+ My 28 '72 por, II p1+ Ap 17 '77 pors; People 8:34+ D 26 '78 pors; Rolling Stone p72+ Je 30 '77 pors; Time 110:68+ S 26 '77 pors

---

Kennedy, Edward M(oore)

Feb. 22, 1932- United States Senator from Massachusetts. Address: b. 431 Russell Office Building, Washington, D.C. 20510; h. 636 Chain Bridge Rd., McLean, Va. 22101

NOTE: This biography supersedes the article that appeared in *Current Biography* in 1963.

First elected to the United States Senate in 1962 on the strength of his family name, Edward M. Kennedy, the political heir apparent to the Kennedy Camelot, has matured into an influential legislator of national stature and, in the eyes of many Democratic stalwarts, Presidential caliber. Kennedy is a pragmatic liberal with a special interest in social welfare legislation; he is also an excellent floor strategist and a masterful political maneuverer whose commitment to public life was only deepened by the deaths of his two older brothers, President John F. Kennedy and Senator Robert F. Kennedy, who influenced and inspired him.

Edward Moore ("Ted") Kennedy was born in Brookline, Massachusetts on February 22, 1932, the ninth and last child of Joseph P. and Rose (Fitzgerald) Kennedy, third-generation Americans from prominent Irish-Catholic families with a foothold in state Democratic politics. His maternal grandfather, John F. ("Honey Fitz") Fitzgerald, was a former mayor of Boston and his paternal grandfather, Patrick J. Kennedy, served in both houses of the Massachusetts legislature. His father, a multimillionaire businessman, went to Washington in 1933 to serve in President Franklin D. Roosevelt's Administration as chairman of the Securities and Exchange Commission, then as head of the Maritime Commission. Edward remained with his mother in New York City, where the Kennedys had moved in 1926, but the family was reunited in London in 1938 when Joseph Kennedy was named United States Ambassador to the Court of St. James's. Ted Kennedy's three older brothers are no longer living: Joseph P. Kennedy, Jr. was killed in World War II, John was assassinated in 1963, and Robert was shot and killed during his quest for the Presidency in 1968. One sister, Kathleen, died in a plane crash in 1948. His surviving sisters are Rosemary, Eunice, Patricia, and Jean.

As the Kennedys moved between London, Boston, New York, and Palm Beach, Edward Kennedy studied at one private boarding school after another before enrolling at Milton Academy, a coeducational institution near Boston, in 1946. Kennedy was an undistinguished student, but he was popular with his classmates, an excellent debater, and a fine athlete. From Milton, Kennedy went to Harvard University where, in his freshman year, he asked a friend to take his examination in Spanish, one of his weaker subjects. Both students were expelled. To redeem himself, a repentant Kennedy enlisted in the United States Army and served a two-year hitch in France and Germany. After his discharge as a private first class in 1953, he returned to Harvard, graduating three years later with a

B.A. degree in history and government. In 1956 he studied at the International Law Institute at The Hague and spent some time in North Africa as a reporter for the International News Service. Kennedy completed his education with an LL.B. degree from the University of Virginia Law School in 1959 and was admitted to the Massachusetts bar later that same year.

Like his older brothers, Edward Kennedy gravitated naturally toward public life. He got his first taste of politics in 1958, when he managed John F. Kennedy's successful campaign for reelection to the United States Senate. Two years later, his skillful coordination of John's Presidential primary campaign in thirteen Western states helped secure the Democratic nomination for his brother. Following John F. Kennedy's election to the Presidency in November 1960, Ted Kennedy took a job as an assistant to the District Attorney of Suffolk County, Massachusetts, as a dollar-a-year man. He also began laying the groundwork for his own political career. Traveling at his own expense, he accompanied members of the Senate Foreign Relations Committee on a fact-finding tour of Africa in December 1960 and, in the months that followed, he visited Latin America, Israel, the European Common Market countries, and several East European nations.

Before taking office in January 1961, President-elect Kennedy prevailed upon Massachusetts Governor Foster Furcolo to appoint Benjamin Smith 2d, a family friend untried in politics, to his vacated Senate seat until the special election scheduled for November 1962, prompting speculations that Smith was merely holding the spot until Ted Kennedy reached thirty, the minimum age for a United States Senator. As expected, when the youngest Kennedy announced his candidacy for the Democratic nomination on March 14, 1962, Smith stepped aside. Kennedy's chief rival for the nomination was Edward J. McCormack Jr., the state attorney general and the nephew of John W. McCormack, the Speaker of the United States House of Representatives. Although Kennedy avoided a potentially damaging issue by revealing the story of his expulsion from Harvard before his opponents could expose it, the primary campaign was unusually bitter. McCormack repeatedly reminded the voters that his opponent, who had "never held elective office," lacked the "qualifications" and the "maturity of judgment" to be a Senator and, in the first of two televised "Teddie-Eddie debates," lashed out: "If your name was simply Edward Moore instead of Edward Moore Kennedy, your candidacy would be a joke." Such attacks generated an enormous sympathy backlash for Kennedy and, in the September primary, he beat McCormack by a margin of more than 300,000 votes. He went on to defeat the Republican aspirant, George Cabot Lodge, in the November general election, amassing 1,143,021 votes to Lodge's 863,460. He was sworn into office at the opening of the Eighty-eighth Congress in January 1963.

Kennedy was presiding over the Senate on November 22, 1963 when a press officer brought him the news of his brother John's assassination. Seven months later, on June 19, 1964, he had his own brush with death when the light plane carrying him, Senator Birch Bayh of Indiana, and several other persons crashed in an apple orchard near Southampton, Massachusetts. Pulled from the wreckage by Senator Bayh, Kennedy suffered serious spinal injuries. He spent the next six months in hospitals, totally immobilized in a rotating Stryker frame. The long incapacitation, however, did not affect his chances for election to his first full Senate term. With the well-oiled Kennedy organization running smoothly and his wife campaigning in his place, the Senator easily defeated a weak Republican candidate, Howard Whitmore Jr., taking an unprecedented 74.4 percent of the ballots.

Ted Kennedy, as the youngest man ever elected to the Upper House, was at first considered something of an upstart by his older colleagues, but he soon won respect and admiration as a hard-working legislator who played by the book. He received his first major leadership assignment in 1965 when he guided the Lyndon B. Johnson Administration's Immigration and Nationality Act, which ended the national origins quota system, through the Senate. Although he usually supported President Johnson, Kennedy occasionally acted independently of the White House. For instance, acting against the President's wishes, he attached to the Administration's voting rights bill of 1965 a rider outlawing state and local poll taxes. That the rider was defeated by only four votes, despite high-pressured lobbying by the White House, is evidence of Kennedy's legislative skill. Like most of his legislation, the rider was well-researched, clear, and limited in scope.

Because he inherited the "Cold War legacy" of his brother John, Kennedy initially expressed "no reservations" about the American military commitment in Southeast Asia, although he foresaw a "long and enduring struggle." But as American involvement escalated toward the end of the decade, Ted Kennedy, like Robert Kennedy, then the junior Senator from New York, came to believe that the war was "a monstrous outrage" and that "continued optimism" about its outcome was unjustified. While Robert Kennedy, an announced antiwar candidate for the 1968 Democratic Presidential nomination, excoriated the Johnson Administration's hard-line Vietnam policies, Ted Kennedy labored to reform the "unfair" and "inequitable" draft laws and to aid hundreds of thousands of refugees.

After Robert Kennedy's assassination on June 5, 1968, Edward Kennedy temporarily withdrew from public life. He managed to deliver the eulogy, in a cracked, tremulous voice, at his brother's funeral in New York City's St. Patrick's Cathedral, but "the events of June," as he came to call them, took a heavy toll. He spent ten weeks brooding and sailing, often alone, off Cape Cod. Finally, on August 21, in a speech before the Worcester, Massachusetts Chamber of Commerce, he resumed his "public responsibilities." "Like my brothers before me, I pick up a fallen standard," he said. "Sustained by the memory of our priceless years together, I shall try to carry forward that special commitment—to justice, excellence and to courage—that distinguished their lives."

His first priority was ending the war in Vietnam. To that end, he offered a four-point plan calling for, among other things, an unconditional bombing halt in North Vietnam and unilateral reduction of American forces. Over the next few years his opposition intensified. In scores of antiwar speeches in the Senate and across the country, he condemned President Richard Nixon's Vietnamization program as "a policy of violence" that "means war and more war." On the Hill, he supported all end-the-war resolutions and, in hearings before his Subcommittee on Refugees and Escapees, focused attention on the plight of the refugees up to and after the fall of the Saigon government in 1975.

In the bleak period immediately following Robert Kennedy's death, Ted Kennedy's popularity was such that many political observers believed the 1968 Democratic Presidential nomination was his for the asking. Kennedy, however, declined to put his name in contention. Instead, Kennedy set his sights on wresting the post of Senate majority whip from Russell B. Long of Louisiana. As the chairman of the powerful Finance Committee, Long was a formidable opponent, but susceptible to an overthrow by the liberals. On January 3, 1969, after four days of backroom politicking, Kennedy was elected whip by a margin of five votes. At thirty-six, he was the youngest majority whip in the history of the Senate.

The year 1969, begun so auspiciously for Kennedy, turned sour on July 18 when he was involved in a fatal automobile accident following a small get-together for former Kennedy campaign workers on Chappaquiddick Island, off Martha's Vineyard, Massachusetts. The car the Senator was driving ran off a narrow, rickety wooden bridge and plunged into a tidal pool. His only passenger, Mary Jo Kopechne, one of the "boiler room girls" in Robert Kennedy's 1968 campaign, drowned. Kennedy, who failed to report the accident to police for about nine hours, pleaded guilty to a misdemeanor charge of leaving the scene of an accident, received a two-month suspended sentence, and lost his driver's license for a year.

In a television appeal to the voters of Massachusetts a week after the accident, Kennedy conceded that his conduct on that night had been "indefensible," but he denied rumors of intoxication and of a "private relationship" with Miss Kopechne. He asked the viewers to tell him whether his standing among them had been "so impaired" that he should resign his Senate seat. Apparently touched by his candid admission of culpability, the people responded heavily in his favor, and on July 30 Kennedy announced that he would remain in office. Nevertheless, lingering doubts about the "Chappaquiddick incident" produced a spate of articles and books, ranging from Robert Sherrill's meticulously researched *The Last Kennedy* to *Teddy Bare; The Last of the Kennedy Clan,* a potboiler by Zad Rust. Over the years, Kennedy has "come to terms" with the Chappaquiddick gossip and feels he can face it in a campaign if he has to.

Kennedy won reelection in 1970, stressing in his stump speeches the continuation of his brothers' legacy. The 63 percent of the vote that he gathered against Josiah A. Spaulding, his attractive but comparatively unknown Republican opponent, was substantial but some 500,000 votes short of his stunning 1964 achievement. Meanwhile, his position on the Hill had declined in importance as Senator Robert C. Byrd, the ambitious secretary of the Democratic Conference, gradually assumed many of the whip's duties and generally ran the day-to-day operations of the Senate. On January 21, 1971 Byrd, who had put together an unbeatable coalition of Southern and border-state Democrats, unseated the frequently absent Kennedy as party whip. "It hurts like hell to lose," Kennedy remarked later, "but now I can get around the country more, and it frees me to spend more time on issues I'm interested in." Always frank, he spoke out more boldly than ever before on matters of national and international interest. He warned England not to create another Vietnam in Northern Ireland, condemned Pakistan for genocide in Bangladesh, and accused President Nixon of using American prisoners of war as political pawns.

As the ordeal of Chappaquiddick faded, Kennedy regained his status as a major figure in American politics, once again prompting talk of a Kennedy Presidency. A midsummer 1978 Gallup poll showed that rank-and-file Democrats preferred Kennedy over incumbent President Jimmy Carter by a margin of 54 to 32 percent. Although he attracts voters from all levels of society, Kennedy's appeal is perhaps strongest among blue-collar and ethnic voters.

Over the past decade journalists and politicians have regularly reported that Kennedy was running for President. Lending credence to those reports, he often acted like a candidate by accepting countless speaking engagements, making frequent cross-country fence-mending trips, openly courting such old foes as George C. Wallace, and, in 1974, by visiting the Soviet Union for a private meeting with Leonid I. Brezhnev. But he continually denied all rumors of his candidacy. On the August 6, 1978 edition of ABC-TV's *Issues and Answers* Kennedy dismissed suggestions that he planned to challenge Carter in the 1980 primaries, saying that "for any foreseeable future," his work would be in the Senate. "I would like to be President," he admitted to Robert Ajemian in an interview for *Time* magazine (August 21, 1978). "I feel I can do the job. But this isn't the time."

Senator Kennedy ascribes his reluctance to run to family considerations. "I feel certain responsibilities to my family, my mother, my wife, my children, Bobby's children," he explained to one interviewer. "I have to think about running in terms of other people." Because of the dozens of death threats he receives annually, the possibility of an assassination attempt is never far from his mind, but he has learned to live with that danger.

Reelected to a third term in 1976 with 70 percent of the vote, Kennedy, who ranks seventeenth in seniority among the Democratic majority, has become one of the most powerful Senators. He chairs important subcommittees and will succeed James O. Eastland as chairman of the Judiciary Committee upon Eastland's retirement in January 1979. As chairman of the Senate's health subcommittee, Kennedy has concentrated on one of his primary concerns: health care. The author of *In Critical Condition: The Crisis in America's Health Care* (Simon & Schuster, 1972), he believes that decent health care is a basic right. The health security program he envisions provides for comprehensive national health insurance to bring high quality medical services to every citizen and, at the same time, improve the organization and delivery of that health care. Fearing that national health insurance will be "dead for at least the next ten years'" unless Congress acts soon, Kennedy tried for several months to work out a compromise with the White House, then split publicly with President Carter over his "conditional" and "piecemeal" approach to the problem.

Throughout his Congressional career Kennedy has served as an advocate for the "people left out of the system." He has supported measures to aid the elderly, the unemployed, the young, immigrants, women, and ethnic minorities, and he has long defended busing to achieve racial desegregation in the schools. To the astonishment of his more conservative followers, Kennedy approved federal payment of abortions. An early advocate of consumer protection legislation, he led the fight for airline deregulation, no-fault insurance, and more consumer-oriented antitrust laws. Seeking relief for low-and middle-income taxpayers, he urged Carter to be bold in developing a tax reform package and submitted a forty-one-page list of suggestions for eliminating loopholes and corporate tax shelters.

Appalled by Watergate and its attendant political scandals, Kennedy was a leading force behind the passage of the Federal Election Campaign Acts Amendments of 1974, which provides for some public financing of Presidential campaigns, and has sought similar legislation for Congressional contests. For more than a decade he has been the Senate's chief spokesman for stringent gun control legislation and tougher law enforcement. Calling criminal sentencing a "national scandal," Kennedy, as cosponsor of the far-reaching Criminal Code Reform Bill that passed the Senate in January 1978, successfully pushed for mandatory sentences for street crimes, less judicial discretion in sentencing, and severe parole restrictions. He outlined a number of his legislative proposals in *Decisions for a Decade; Policies and Programs for the 1970's* (Doubleday, 1968).

In foreign affairs Kennedy has continued to work for an end to the escalating arms race and has repeatedly voted down increased appropriations for defense. He sees hunger as perhaps the most important international problem, but does not believe that food should ever become a weapon in politics. In recent months Kennedy recommended ending the thirteen-year American trade embargo with Cuba, voted for the new Panama Canal treaties, and called for a "normalization'" of relations with the People's Republic of China. Still concerned about the fate of Indochinese refugees, he persuaded the government of the Socialist Republic of Vietnam to allow some thirty Vietnamese to join their relatives in the United States.

Edward M. Kennedy stands six feet two inches tall and carries a lean 210 pounds on his large-boned frame. He has a wide, square, "Irish-potato" face, "whitewater-pale green" eyes, and moderately long, thick, reddish-brown hair tinged with gray. Despite occasional bouts of back pain, he still enjoys tennis, skiing, and sailing. Ted Kennedy and Virginia Joan Bennett were married on November 29, 1958. They have a daughter, Kara Anne, and two sons, Edward M., Jr., who lost a leg to bone cancer in 1973, and Patrick Joseph. The surrogate father to his brother Robert's brood, he is especially close to Robert's oldest son, Joseph. Joan Kennedy, who has freely discussed with the press her several hospitalizations for the treatment of alcoholism and emotional distress, recently moved from their large house overlooking the Potomac River in McLean, Virginia to their Boston apartment, explaining that she wanted to explore "options other than being a housewife and mother."

References: Esquire 70:97+ S '68 pors; Look 33:38+ Mr 4 '69 pors, 35:43+ Ag 10 '71 pors; N Y Times Mag p25+ F 23 '69 pors, p25+ My 24 '70 pors, p27+ N 28 '71 pors; Newsweek 73:13+ Ja 13 '69 pors, 85: 19+ Je 2 '75 pors; Time 93:12+ Ja 10 '69 pors, 98:16+ N 29 '71 pors; Burns, James M. Edward Kennedy and the Camelot Legend (1976); Douth, George. Leaders in Profile (1975); Lippman, Theo, Jr. Senator Edward Kennedy (1976)

Klein, Calvin (Richard)

Nov. 19, 1942- Fashion designer. Address: b. Calvin Klein Inc., 205 W. 39th St., New York City, N.Y. 10018

American fashion has come into its own, on a par with Paris internationally, partly through the influence of three-time Coty award winner Calvin Klein, a New York designer who, by his talent and sense of timing, has helped to pioneer casual chic, or the unstructured style in couture. Klein made his first hit with an attractive trench coat a decade ago, a time when the fashion industry was entering a slump brought on by the predilection of young people for wearing informal clothes in defiance of the dictates of high fashion. In 1972 he began creating flexible collections of interchangeable separates, at once sporty and elegant, trim and fluid, that offer women—and, to a lesser extent, men—a wide range of choices for round-the-clock wear.

Using the best natural fabrics, generally in earth tones or neutral colors, Klein designs, sweaters, jackets, shirts, blouses, pants, skirts, bikinis, capes, coats, and other pieces that fit his definition of classicism: "clothes that work over and over," in varying ensembles, from day to night and from season to season. A Klein resort or winter collection gives the woman of expensive taste the range of clothes she might design for herself had she the talent and time, but the woman accustomed to wearing jeans is equally at home in a Klein wardrobe, which, with its simplicity and flexibility, leaves the degree of formality up to the individual wearer. After winning a record-breaking third Coty "Winnie", he told a reporter: "I never try to overpower the woman who wears my clothes. True, my customer is a spender, but her home, travel, living get a big part. It is ridiculous to spend everything on wearing apparel. Therefore I design for the new look but with an everlasting feeling." In addition to clothes, Klein markets a line of characteristically subtle cosmetics, among other products.

Calvin Richard Klein was born in the Bronx, New York on November 19, 1942 to Leo and Flore (Stern) Klein. "I have always wanted my own business," Klein has recounted. "When we were only five, my best friend, Barry Schwartz [now his business partner] and I wanted to open a pet shop. I was going to find the fauna and Barry was going to keep us from going broke. We grew up in different directions professionally; while I was at FIT [the Fashion Institute of Technology, in Manhattan], Barry attended NYU [New York University]. I apprenticed in the fashion industry while Barry worked in his family's food business."

As an adolescent, while his peers were playing sandlot sports, Klein was sewing, sketching clothes, and going regularly to Loehmann's, a high-fashion discount store in the Bronx, to look at the Norman Norell samples and other couture. After graduating from the Fashion Institute of Technology in 1962, he went to work in the garment district, as a $75-a-week apprentice designer for Dan Millstein, in the very quarters now occupied by Calvin Klein Inc. In 1968, with $2,000 of his own and $10,000 from Schwartz, who had taken over his family's supermarket in Harlem, Klein founded his own company, originally called Calvin Klein Ltd. The company operated out of a small suite at the York Hotel on Seventh Avenue for five years, until Klein bought out Millstein and moved Calvin Klein Inc. to its present site, at 205 West Thirty-Ninth Street.

The early years of Calvin Klein Inc. marked a low period in the fashion industry. Dressing "down," hippie style, was the fad, and where designer clothes were in at all they were typified by the miniskirt and plastic boots. Biding his time, Klein succeeded with a snappy trench coat, a genre always in style. His first big order was from Bonwit Teller for $50,000 worth of coats. Mildred Custin, Bonwit's president, recalled in an interview with a reporter for *Newsweek* (November 3, 1975) the day that Klein personally wheeled his samples the twenty or so blocks up Seventh Avenue and over to her office: "What impressed me most was the purity of his line and the simplicity of his designs. 'Young man,' I said to him, 'you better raise your prices by ten dollars or you'll never make any money.' "

In his first year of operation, Klein shipped orders totaling $1,000,000 and gross sales rose $1,000,000 or more annually in succeeding years—years in which he helped to pioneer the transition from the mini to longer lengths in skirts and coats. He knew the time had come for a change, as he told Isadore Barmash of the New York *Times* (June 1, 1970), when he realized that many of the young women absenting themselves from the fashion market were "going into their attics to look at the old clothes, or going into antique shops."

Klein designed mostly two-piece suits as well as coats until 1972, when he came out with a coatless collection and began concentrating on sportswear, an aspect of his line that was drawing less attention than he felt it deserved. The step to sporty separates, such as sweaters, skirts, dresses, shirts, and pants—which could be intermixed for a complete day-and-evening wardrobe—virtually dictated itself. "I felt that the American lifestyle had changed and that there was certainly a need for clothing to express and relate to that change," he later explained. "Women could no longer be dictated to. For the most part, women today spend their time and energy working, participating in all aspects of home, community, and business. Their lives have changed and there is little time for wardrobe planning."

In 1973 Klein was among the first American designers to translate Paris' full-skirt style into proportions right for American women, who worked at keeping a slim figure and did not want that figure disguised. In presenting his seventy-four-piece fall line in a show in May 1973, he emphasized the perfect coordination of the pieces by having models exchange coats and jackets as they passed on the runway. On that occasion he told Ruth Preston of the New York *Post* (May 24, 1973): "It's all in understanding who your customer is, her lifestyle and needs and filling those needs, not fantasizing. I believe in classic clothes—not the faddishness that looks right this season and is dead the next."

Klein also said that he was emphasizing the sweater "for the sportswear feeling in important suits and coats" and that his own favorite among the luxury touches he had added to some of his pieces was fur. Ruth Preston summed up the few items of men's clothing he introduced that year as "a breeze," because "he does it with the same comfortable, softly tailored feeling, snappy young shapes, and classic fabrics as he uses for the women." She noted also that Klein had, as usual, produced the "niftiest rainwear" of the season, including a cotton gabardine pants outfit with a matching pile-lined coat and a checked wool coat with a color-coordinated skirt, pants, and turtleneck.

In a nationwide poll of 400 fashion reporters, Klein and Stephen Burrows were selected winners of the 1973 Coty American Fashion Critics Awards, announced on June 21, 1973. The citation with Klein's award, presented the following October, commended "his superlative and consistent taste, his innate but nonconformist sense of classic line, never banal but always strong and feminine, and his unique understanding of today's blend of casualness, luxury, and moderate price." The fashion show staged by Klein on the occasion of the awards presentation at Lincoln Center included almost identical men's and women's styles in pea jackets, fur-collared melton overcoats, wool turtlenecks, and slacks. Klein, who noted that many of the best-tailored classics for women had been borrowed from the men to begin with, said that his men's clothes were based on the same philosophy as his women's apparel, so as "to make a person feel comfortable without taking over his personality."

Klein's earlier clothes were priced for a relatively inexpensive market and his Trevira overblouses and polyester print dresses were available to about 1,000 stores. In 1973 he became more exclusive, cutting back his distribution to 250 stores. Also, as his success mounted his prices rose, partly because he stopped using economical man-made fabrics. "Polyester feels slimy," he told one reporter. "It represents everything I hate. It's synthetic, it's fake, it's cheap." In addition, he generally stopped using bright colors when his 1974 resort collection, stressing shocking shades of pink, red, and green, sold poorly in the stores. He said later that he "got bored" with color, which, if excessive, tends to be "tacky."

In addition to his own collections, Klein in 1974 did a fur collection for Alixandre, his first venture into licensing. Later, he licensed the manufacture of Klein-designed umbrellas, belts, dress patterns, scarves, and bags. In 1974 and 1975 he won his second and third Coty "Winnies," and on June 25, 1975 he was elected to the American Hall of Fame of Fashion. Klein's 1975 resort collection contained 350 pieces from T-shirts and bikinis to evening casuals in natural-fiber fabrics, mostly cottons, and in colors "influenced by flowers." His 1976 resort collection included an ivory silk jumpsuit with a neckline that plunged, characteristically, to a drawstring waist and hooded terry cloth ponchos that doubled as hostess dresses or bikini cover-ups.

The collection that Klein took to the sport shop at the Neiman-Marcus department store in Houston, Texas in January 1976 was a typical, brilliant interlocking, with perfect color-keying, of silk crepe de chine and striped or panne velvet daytime separates with evening clothes, designed to take the prospective buyer from a morning on the golf course or beach to a night at a discotheque. After working with brushed flannel plaids in the fall of 1976, Klein turned to more "feminine" clothes, such as printed silk jacquards for evening and light-weight combinations of silk and cashmere. In a short bylined fashion forecast in the New York *Times* (December 8, 1976), he predicted that sportswear would continue to flourish, but that it would be "less tailored" and "more romantic." He wrote: "When I think about romantic clothes, I don't think of frilly clothes. I don't think of a blouse with a lot of ruffles. I think of a blouse with perhaps a new cut and a refined kind of softness. . . . The more fabrics lend themselves to unconstructed clothes, the better. We've been talking about unconstructed clothes for years. Now they're beginning to take over. . . . I think that movement will continue for the next few years. The standard outfit for most of the 1970's has been the shirt and pants. Now I think this will change over to the blouse and skirt. The skirt will be full, it will move. For me, fashion is not moving in an ethnic direction. It has to be what I consider clean. I think quality means more than price. Luxury fabrics, even cotton, are expensive. I don't see any way of changing that. But if women enjoy their clothes, then they're worth the price."

In 1977, when designers generally went for the ethnic "big look," Klein's clothes remained relatively slim and close to the body, soft but racy. As for his designer jeans, early in 1977 they were selling for from $40 to $70; later in the year he embarked on a licensing arrangement with the Puritan Fashion Corporation for the mass marketing of jeans similar in style and quality to sell at approximately half the price.

Reviewing the spring fashion collections shown in November 1977, Beverly Stephen wrote in the New York *Daily News* (November 20, 1977): "Thank God there are designers like Calvin Klein, John Anthony, and Kasper, who understand how to interpret the current fashion trend of bigger, looser clothes in sophisticated, subdued ways. You can never go wrong wearing one of Calvin Klein's unconstructed linen blazers, linen pants [or] shawl collar charmeuse shirts. The clothes are young and sophisticated, but not bizarre." In a similar vein, Nina S. Hyde, writing in the Washington *Post* (November 8, 1977), noted the prevalence of sexy, see-through clothes done with restraint: "Unlike the Paris designers, the Americans pull back. . . . The styles here are softer and more feminine." Among the Klein pieces she singled out were a crepe de chine wrap dress and a big-pocket pants suit, both with plunging necklines.

When Klein presented his first full collection of menswear in January 1978, Ron Alexander of the New York *Times* (January 28, 1978) characterized the clothes as "soft and easy," not just because of the flannel, camel's hair, and similar fabrics used or the clay, dark olive, and other muted colors employed, but also because of the "relaxed manner" in which Klein employs the fabrics and colors and the "almost offhanded" way he accessorizes them. In March 1978 Klein introduced his beauty line, encompassing fragrances, cosmetics, and skin care products. His concept of makeup deals with the whole face, or five basic "faces"—mauve, rose, honey, coral, and rouge—each designed as a range within which a woman has a choice of tones of eye, cheek, lip and nail colors created to complement each other perfectly.

In April 1978 Klein showed a fall and winter line of sixty-eight outfits with two, three, or four pieces, such as a silk skirt and V-neck cashmere sweater or satin blouse and crepe de chine pants topped by a short alpaca pile overcoat, each of which could be carried over into a variety of other combinations. The look was at once loose, in keeping with the prevailing "Annie Hall" vogue, and typically Klein—"simple and unfussy," as Bernadine Morris observed in her review in the New York *Times* (April 29, 1978)—with coats hanging straight from broadened shoulders, jackets either falling in a straight line or sashed at the waist, and slightly narrowed skirts. "It was one of those smash successes," Miss Morris wrote. "No clinkers. . . . No memorable music or even drop-dead outfits at Calvin Klein. He simply continues doing for next fall and winter what has made him a leading fashion figure for the last decade: He makes clothes women like to wear."

Months before each collection, Klein goes to Europe, chiefly France, to look at fabrics. After his return to the United States he works with domestic mills, sampling approximately fifty yards of each fabric in order to see how each feels, drapes, and cuts. Then, after he sketches his designs, his team of cutters, pattern makers, drapers, button and trim buyers, and others, goes into action. About 800 pieces of clothing are made up and photographed with a Polaroid camera and the photographs are grouped and edited. Only those pieces that can function alone, as well as coordinate with other designs in the Klein line, are selected for the new collection.

Shipping and delivery schedules are planned in accordance with fabric arrivals from Europe, so that Bloomingdale's and Saks Fifth Avenue in New York City, Britton's in South Carolina, Isetan's in Tokyo, and the other stores with Klein boutiques will get new styles on time every month. The business side of the operation is computerized and Klein and Schwartz delegate as many as possible of the details of designing, manufacturing, and merchandising to others. The chemists and others involved in the preparation of Klein's perfume and makeup work under the direction of Stanley Kohlenberg. Klein is planning soon to design sunglasses and home furnishings, to expand his cosmetics line to include hair products and suntan oils, and to add a line of belts and other small leather goods to his franchises for shoes, scarves, and bedding.

Calvin Klein is a tall, slim man with sandy hair who spends time regularly with dermatologists and in health spas partly because, as he says, he has "this thing about health and the body" and wants to maintain his youthful vigor and appearance and partly because his hard-working habits have taken a heavy toll on his nervous and digestive systems. His boyish charm, gregariousness, and straightforward manner are definite assets in his relationships with department store executives, buyers, and the others with whom he deals in the course of his work.

Klein and Jayne Centre were married in 1964 and divorced ten years later. Klein unwinds with an occasional drink of vodka, and, on his rare days off, he entertains friends, does acrylic painting, plays tennis, goes bicycling or horseback riding, or takes his daughter, Marci, to the theatre, ballet, or concerts. On February 3, 1978 Marci was kidnapped by a former babysitter, ransomed by her father, and released unharmed, all within a ten-hour period.

In addition to his spacious, starkly decorated apartment overlooking the East River in Manhattan, Klein has homes in Connecticut and on Fire Island. That brown is Klein's signature color is evident in the decor of his residences, in much of his wardrobe, and in his Mercedes. Klein is a member of the Council of Fashion Designers of America and a consultant at the Parsons School of Design, and he holds advisory positions at the Museum of Modern Art, the Metropolitan Museum of Art, the Whitney Museum, and the Guggenheim Museum.

References: Houston Post p1+ Ja 19 '76 por; N Y Post p42 O 11 '73; Newsweek 91:80+ My 8 '78 pors; Who's Who in America, 1976-77; Who's Who in Fashion (1975)

Koch, Edward I(rving) (käch)

Dec. 12, 1924- Mayor of the City of New York. Address: b. City Hall, New York City, N.Y. 10007; h. Gracie Mansion, New York City, N.Y. 10028

Edward I. Koch, who on January 1, 1978 succeeded Abraham D. Beame as mayor of the City of New York, has been charged with the responsibility of governing what some consider an "ungovernable city." Relatively unencumbered by machine connections and political debts, Koch has for a number of years been a leader of New York City's liberal-oriented Democratic reform movement, although some of his political views also appeal to conservatives. Known for his capacity for hard work, his quiet competence, and his low-keyed personal style, Koch is widely acknowledged to have a sincere concern for the well-being of his constituents. Before becoming mayor, he served with distinction for four terms as a United States Congressman, and before that he was a member of the New York City Council.

The second of three children, Edward Irving Koch was born to Polish Jewish immigrants Louis and Joyce (Silpe) Koch on December 12, 1924 in New York City. His father, who remarried after his wife's death, now lives in retirement in Fort Lauderdale, Florida. Koch's older brother, Harold, is part-owner of a carpet firm in Orange, New Jersey, and his sister, Pat (Mrs. Alvin Thaler), lives in Pomona, New York. Louis Koch, a furrier by trade, was a partner in a small fur shop until 1931, when the business became a casualty of the depression. The family then moved from the Crotona Park section of the Bronx to Newark, New Jersey, where Louis Koch's brother ran a catering hall. There they shared a two-bedroom apartment with the brother's family of four. In the years that followed, Louis Koch worked parttime in the fur industry, and at night he and the family operated the hatcheck concession in his brother's catering establishment.

Ed Koch began working in the checkroom at the age of nine. He later worked as a delicatessen clerk in a grocery store while attending Newark's Southside High School, where he was an honor student. One year, while his family summered in the Catskills, he organized a teenage babysitting cooperative in the resort area. From 1941, when the family moved to Ocean Parkway in Brooklyn, until 1943, when he entered the United States Army, Koch attended the College of the City of New York and worked at the same time as a shoe salesman in a Brooklyn department store. Serving in the European Theatre of Operations as a combat infantryman, he earned two battle stars, and after V-E Day he was a denazification specialist in occupied Bavaria.

Following his discharge with the rank of sergeant in 1946, Koch entered New York University law school, where he obtained his LL.B. degree in 1948. From 1949, when he was admitted to the bar, until 1969, when he entered Congress, he was a practising attorney, and in 1963 he helped to found the Wall Street law firm of Koch, Lankenau, Schwartz & Kovener, in which he became the senior partner. Meanwhile, in 1952 Koch had begun his political career as a streetcorner speaker in Adlai E. Stevenson's Presidential campaign. In 1956, after moving to his own modest, rent-controlled apartment in Manhattan's Greenwich Village, Koch became a charter member of the Village Independent Democrats, a newly founded reformist group. He briefly left the VID to join the Tamawa Club, the Village's regular Democratic organization headed by Carmine De Sapio, but soon returned to the VID because he was coldshouldered by the Tammany regulars. Koch also did volunteer work for local causes and served as an unpaid counsel for tenant committees.

Determined to wrest control of the Democratic party organization in the Village from Tammany Hall, and unable to find a better-known candidate, the VID in 1962 ran Koch against incumbent William F. Passannante for state assemblyman, but although he had the backing of Mrs. Eleanor Roosevelt he received only 32 percent of the vote. In September 1963, after waging a hard-fought campaign backed by Mayor Robert F. Wagner, Koch defeated Carmine De Sapio for the post of Democratic district leader by 4,656 to 4,615 votes. Because of the closeness of the contest the state Court of Appeals ordered a new election for June 1964, which Koch won by 164 votes. He defeated De Sapio a third time, in 1965, thus ending the political career of the long-time party boss.

Now solidly entrenched as the standard-bearer of New York City's burgeoning reform movement, in 1966 Koch, nominated by both the Democratic and Liberal parties, became the first Democrat in thirty-eight years to be elected to the City Council from Manhattan's prosperous second councilmanic district. As a City Council member, he became an outspoken advocate of extension of the city's controversial rent-control law among other liberal causes. Known for his dedication, he often visited subway stations and bus stops in his district to meet his constituents informally and ask their opinions on issues.

Winning a three-way Democratic primary fight in June 1968 in which his opposition to United States involvement in Vietnam and his support of Senator Eugene J. McCarthy for the Presidential nomination were major issues, Koch became the Congressional candidate of the Democratic and Liberal parties for the seat in the United States House of Representatives for Manhattan's Seventeenth Congressional District, which was more or less coextensive with his councilmanic district. Extending from Greenwich Village to Spanish Harlem, and taking in the fashionable Upper East Side, it was known as the silk-stocking district because of its high proportion of well-to-do residents. The Seventeenth District—renumbered the Eighteenth in 1972—had previously been represented by John V. Lindsay, who became mayor in 1966. Defeating progressive Republican blueblood Whitney North Seymour Jr. to become the district's first Democratic Representative since 1934, Koch received 84,627 out of 163,743 votes, or 52 percent of the total, in a race that Michael Alonge of the New York *Daily News* (October 6, 1968) termed "an almost classical American contest . . . pitting the son of immigrant parents against the offspring of a family with roots deep in American history."

Reelected four times by substantial majorities, Koch won 62 percent of his district's ballots in 1970, 70 percent in 1972, 77 percent in 1974, and 75 percent in 1976. He was a member of the space sciences and applications subcommittee of the House Science and Astronautics Committee in 1969-70; the urban mass transportation, consumer affairs, small business, and international trade subcommittees of the Banking and Currency Committee from 1970 to 1974; the printing and electronic equipment subcommittee of the Committee on House Administration in 1973-74; and the District of Columbia, transportation, and foreign operations subcommittees of the Appropriations Committee in 1975-76. Koch also served as secretary of New York's faction-ridden bipartisan thirty-nine-member Congressional delegation; as one of the two House members of the Federal Privacy Study Commission; and as one of four Congressional observers on the Emergency Financial Control Board set up to cope with New York City's fiscal crisis.

Avoiding, in the words of the *Almanac of American Politics*, "the contentiousness that characterizes some New York reform veterans," and aware "that there is a world beyond Manhattan, one that has legitimate claims on government," Koch displayed a broad understanding of the public interest on a national scale. Known as one of the hardest-working members of the House, he usually returned to New York on Thursday nights to spend three-day weekends meeting with his constituents at bus and subway stops and in a "traveling office" that held sessions in churches, synagogues, storefronts, and other locales.

From the outset, Koch lined up with the opponents of United States involvement in Indochina. On the domestic scene he supported public transportation, public housing, social security and tax reform, and measures to alleviate tax and legal discrimination against the unmarried. He introduced a bill to provide home health care for the elderly; promoted aid to Israel and legislation to permit Jews from the Soviet Union and Asians from Uganda to immigrate to the United States; helped bring about federal subsidies to urban mass transit systems; and introduced the bill that set up the President's Commission to Study the Effects of Marijuana. In a 1970 debate about a proposed increase in the space budget, Koch declared: "I cannot justify approving monies to find out whether or not there is some microbe on Mars, when in fact I know there are rats in Harlem apartments."

A random sampling of Koch's positions on key issues indicated that he supported repeal of the Hatch Act, amnesty for draft resisters, solar energy research funds, aid to daycare centers, federal funds for abortion, public funding of Congressional elections, reductions in military aid to South Korea, suspension of arms aid to Turkey, and establishment of a federal consumer protection agency. He opposed loan guarantees for Lockheed Aircraft Corporation, deregulation of natural gas, ending the ban on importation of Rhodesian chrome, arms sales to the Chilean junta and production of the B-1 bomber. Criticizing government plans in 1975 for involvement in Angola, Koch called for "sensible criteria" rather than "random intervention" in dealing with foreign disputes.

Demonstrating an independence that won him the respect of such conservatives as William F. Buckley Jr. and Representative Barry Goldwater Jr. of California—with whom he shared sponsorship of the bill that became the landmark Federal Privacy Act of 1974—Koch at the same time maintained his unimpeachable credentials as a liberal. His voting record won him a 100 percent rating from Americans for Democratic action in 1976, and he also received consistently high ratings from such groups as the Committee on Political Education of the AFL-CIO (COPE), the League of Women Voters, and the Consumer Federation of America. His colleagues rated him as the most effective member of New York's Congressional delegation.

As early as 1966, Koch's friends and political associates considered him a likely candidate for mayor of New York City. He finally cast his hat into the mayoral ring on February 12, 1973 in a race for the Democratic nomination that at one point included seven hopefuls. Abandoned by many liberals, however, partly because of his insistence that street crime was the most important issue, Koch had trouble raising funds and failed to secure the support of the influential New Democratic Coalition. At the end of March 1973 he withdrew from the race, and for some time thereafter he refused to discuss the possibility of running for mayor.

In November 1976, while New York City was still reeling from the financial crisis that had brought it to the brink of bankruptcy, and there was widespread dissatisfaction with the mayoral administration of Abraham D. Beame, Koch again declared himself candidate for mayor. Known in the beginning to barely 6 percent of the city's voters, he faced a long uphill battle to win the Democratic nomination. He did, however, have a small following of intensely loyal supporters and a well-defined strategy. Proclaiming himself a "liberal with sanity," he stressed management reform, continued to take a tough line on crime, even advocating capital punishment in some instances, and he emerged as incumbent Mayor Beame's most vocal critic.

Throughout the winter of 1976-77 Koch steadily won more and more backers, and cash contributions began pouring in. Retaining David Garth, a top political consultant, he became the beneficiary of a brilliant public-relations effort, including thousands of television and radio announcements that parlayed his reputation for hard-working, honest, but dull efficiency into the image of "Mr. Competence," just what the city needed after John V. Lindsay's "charisma" and Abe Beame's clubhouse politics.

The Democratic ballot in the primary election on September 8, 1977 offered New Yorkers seven candidates for mayor. Among them were incumbent Beame and former Congresswoman Bella Abzug, both of whom had led in the polls through the end of August. Also in the running were Mario M. Cuomo, Secretary of State of New York State, who had the backing of Governor Hugh L. Carey; Manhattan Borough President Percy E. Sutton, a black; Congressman Herman Badillo, a Puerto Rican; and Joel Harnett, a businessman.

In the primary, on September 8, 1977, some 910,000 New York Democrats went to the polls—a substantial 48 percent of registered party members as compared to 32 percent who voted in 1973. With such a broad field of contenders, none was able to win a majority, but Koch, with 20 percent of the vote, came in first, followed closely by Cuomo, Beame, and Abzug, who had 19, 18, and 17 percent, respectively. In the primary runoff, on September 19, Koch won an easy victory, receiving 431,849 votes to Cuomo's 354,222.

Since the Democrats were New York City's majority party, Koch's winning of the nomination was considered tantamount to a victory in November. Nevertheless, he refused to relax, campaigning hard against the three adversaries he would face on election day: State Senator Roy M. Goodman, the Republican standard-bearer; Conservative Barry Farber; and Cuomo, who had won the Liberal party nomination.

During the campaign Koch continued to take a hard line on crime and spoke out against excessive municipal labor union demands, welfare waste, and inefficiency in the police department and other city agencies. He indicated that he would oppose construction of low-income public housing in middle-class neighborhoods and came out in favor of gambling casinos in the city, mayoral control of the board of education, legislation requiring municipal employees to live in the city, and increased federal and state financial aid. To offset the impression that he was Manhattan-oriented, Koch made frequent expeditions to the "outer boroughs." He joined with Cuomo in refusing to exploit the possibilities of polarizing the campaign on ethnic lines and ridiculed the rumor that he was an Episcopalian. Reportedly to counter a whispering campaign that he was homosexual, Koch appeared often with former Miss America winner Bess Myerson, a close friend and astute political adviser, and he did not squelch speculation that they intended to be married.

Although Koch's victory on November 8, 1977 was generally predicted, some observers felt that he should have made a better showing against Cuomo, who, with 42 percent, trailed him by only 125,000 votes. Overall, Koch received slightly more than 50 percent of the total vote cast in the four-way race, winning pluralities in four of the city's five boroughs. Settling down after the election to plan his new administration, Koch attended a seminar for new mayors at Harvard University later in November.

Inaugurated on January 1, 1978 as New York City's 105th mayor, Edward I. Koch succeeded Abe Beame to a post regarded as second only to the Presidency of the United States for political and administrative headaches. Heading a governmental unit encompassing the nation's largest and most diverse city, with more than 200,000 employees, Koch was immediately confronted by problems similar to those that had plagued his predecessors: a budget deficit officially set at $249,000,000 but estimated to be as much as $400,000,000; far-reaching demands from labor unions; and a municipal bond market in which New York City securities, considered unreliable, could not readily be sold, thus depriving the city of long-term major financing. In addition, the city's physical plant, because of delays in maintenance and repair, was rapidly deteriorating. Many major businesses were moving out of the city, as were members of the middle class, with concomitant losses in jobs and tax revenues. Public schools remained woefully inadequate, while crime, racial tensions, and unemployment continued unabated.

On January 20, 1978 Koch, at the request of the United States Treasury Department, presented a fiscal recovery plan for the city that envisioned a balanced budget by the beginning of fiscal year 1983 by means of a complex program involving the state and federal governments, the municipal unions, and the city banks. His scaled-down $13.5 billion budget for 1978-79, presented to the City Council and Board of Estimate in April, included a plan for elimination of some 20,000 city jobs by attrition over a four-year period. Although Koch's hard bargaining position during two months of negotiations earned him the enmity of some city labor leaders, he reached a manageable contract settlement with the unions, giving the city's employees increases totaling $757,000,000 over two years. His financial program seemed to satisfy Congress, which in June, through intercession of President Jimmy Carter, approved legislation granting New York City loan guarantees up to $2 billion, thereby helping the city to resume its place in the municipal bond market in the foreseeable future.

Among Koch's other actions during the early months of his administration were the issuance of an executive order forbidding discrimination on the basis of "sexual orientation or affectional preference" in city jobs; creation of a committee on intergroup relations under Deputy Mayor Herman Badillo, to ease racial, religious, and ethnic tensions; and appointment of inspectors to root out corruption in city agencies. He drew some fire from environmentalists and community leaders for shifting from opposition to support of Westway, an elaborate, federally financed project for an interstate highway along Manhattan's West Side, after receiving guarantees from Governor Carey that adequate funds for mass transit would be made available to the city.

Mayor Edward I. Koch, who has remained a bachelor, is six feet one inch tall, weighs

195 pounds, and has a fringe of graying brown hair. To some he seems "arrogant and acerbic"; to others, "open and frank." Ed Koch lives frugally, has virtually no leisure time, and does not own a car. Although the mayor's official residence is Gracie Mansion, Koch has retained his apartment on Washington Place in Greenwich Village. In a report filed in April 1978, he indicated that his net worth was slightly over $100,000. The mayor swims to keep fit, enjoys reading books on politics and history, and collects inexpensive modern paintings. In an interview with Dennis Duggan of *Newsday* (January 1, 1978), Koch revealed that New York City's Mayor Fiorello H. LaGuardia and President Harry S. Truman were the two men he admired most in American political life.

References: N Y Times Mag p15+ O 30 '77 pors; Almanac of American Politics, 1978; New York Red Book, 1977; Who's Who in America, 1978-79

Koch, Kenneth (Jay) (kōk)

Feb. 27, 1925- Poet; playwright; educator. Address: b. Dept. of English, Columbia University, Broadway and 115th St., New York City, N.Y. 10027; c/o Commission for Educational and Cultural Exchange between Italy and the United States, Via Boncompagni, 16, 00187 Rome, Italy

The reputation of Kenneth Koch rests as firmly on his innovative experiments in teaching the writing of verse as it does on his own witty, ebullient poetry, which, like his teaching techniques, presses for the free play of feeling and imagination. A principal alumnus of the so-called New York School of poetry and a member of the faculty of Columbia University, Koch has described the methods and results of his unusual creative writing workshops outside the university in three books: *Wishes, Lies, and Dreams: Teaching Children to Write Poetry* (1970), *Rose, Where Did You Get That Red?: Teaching Great Poetry to Children* (1973), and *I Never Told Anybody; Teaching Poetry Writing in a Nursing Home* (1977). His own verse thus far fills eight volumes, the most important of which are the collections *Permanently* (1961), *Thank You and Other Poems* (1962), *The Pleasures of Peace* (1969), and *The Art of Love* (1975) and the antic epics *Ko* (1960) and *The Duplications* (1977), zany, free-wheeling, multiplotted narratives exuding, like all of his work, the joy of creation. Dramatic works by Koch, mostly short dada-like burlesques of academic or patriotic pageantry, are collected in the volumes *Bertha and Other Plays* (Grove, 1966) and *A Change of Hearts* (Random House, 1973).

The New York School, consisting essentially of the triumvirate of Koch, John Ashbery, and the late Frank O'Hara, flourished in the 1950's in close conjunction with the abstract expressionist movement then in the ascendancy in painting and especially with the work of the restive, rebellious abstract expressionist Larry Rivers. In varying degrees and ways the three poets applied the principles of abstract expressionism to verbal constructs, using words abstractly and evocatively. Much of the writing that Koch did during his New York School "apprenticeship" was "very far out" and at times, "incomprehensible, even to himself," as Hayden Carruth observes in his entry on the poet in *Contemporary Poets* (1975), edited by James Vinson. "The freedom of his earlier verbal technique has given him a felicity which occasionally still descends to surrealistic glibness but which at its best is remarkably inventive and accurate," Carruth writes. "At the same time, substantially fixed in his poems is a depth of metaphysical concern that gives them the drive and intensity of genuinely serious experiments."

Kenneth Jay Koch was born on February 27, 1925 in Cincinnati, Ohio, the son of Stuart J. and Lillian Amy (Loth) Koch. Koch says that he began writing when he was five but produced nothing "very good" until he read Dos Passos and started writing stream of consciousness when he was seventeen. "It's natural to like writing," he told Bill Zavatsky, "just as it's natural to like drawing or singing, unless, of course, someone interferes with the process." When he showed some of his "obscene and angry" literary outbursts to Katherine Lappa, his third-year high school English teacher, her response was, "That's exactly the way you should be feeling when you're seventeen years old." Koch observes, "This was an . . . instance of the benevolent influence that Freud has had on my life. I was able to enjoy the benefit of a teacher who in Cincinnati in 1942 had undergone psychoanalysis."

After graduating from high school, Koch saw action in World War II with the United States Army in the Pacific. When the war was over he enrolled at Harvard University, where he studied writing under Delmore Schwartz and began his lifelong friendship with John Ashbery, a fellow student. Inspired by the writings of William Butler Yeats and Wallace Stevens, to which Schwartz introduced him, he wrote his first playlet, *Little Red Riding Hood*.

In 1948 Koch received his B.A. degree and moved to New York City, where he began graduate work at Columbia University and became a friend of Jane Freilicher, the painter responsible for persuading Larry Rivers to turn from jazz musicianship to art. Mrs. Freilicher introduced Koch to Rivers, and soon he, Ashbery, and O'Hara were ensconced in the avant-garde circle of artists exhibiting at the Tibor de Nagy Gallery, musicians playing at the Five Spot Cafe, and poets publishing in the journal *Locus Solus* (on the editorial board of which Koch served for two years). The vortex of the circle was the intense Larry Rivers and what O'Hara described as Rivers' "Bohemian household . . . of staggering complexity." Rivers and Koch collaborated on the painting-poems "New York, 1950-1960," and "Post Cards," and Rivers and O'Hara wrote a play to which they gave the title "Kenneth Koch: A Tragedy," a work so riddled with art world gossip that it was unpublishable.

When Bill Zavatsky in his New York *Times* interview asked Koch to generalize about the New York School style, the poet responded cautiously, lest he put words in the mouths of the school's other principals. "As I look back on it now, we were anti-traditional. . . ," he said. "I was attracted to the allusiveness in Pound and Eliot but not especially to what they alluded to. I liked the way they jumped from one thing to another. I think we may have been more conscious than many poets of the surface of the poem . . . and how we were using words. I don't think we saw any reason to resist humor." In France on a Fulbright grant during the academic year 1950-51, Koch was influenced by the psychological particularism he found in the poetry then being published there.

During the 1950's and the early 1960's Koch wrote a score of short plays, dadaistic and surrealistic farces and burlesques, many of which were produced Off and Off Off Broadway. Among the best known of them were *Bertha*, a pastiche of blackout sketches produced in 1959, and *George Washington Crossing the Delaware*, produced at the Maidman Playhouse in Manhattan in March 1962.

George Washington Crossing the Delaware was inspired by a painting of the same name by Larry Rivers, a spoof, done in a mixture of historical styles, of Emanuel Leutze's academic, cliché-ridden *Washington Crossing the Delaware*. Richard Gilman, in a review reprinted in his *Common and Uncommon Masks* (1971), called *George Washington Crossing the Delaware* "the funniest play" he had seen in 1962, a "set of interlocking parodies [with] the purest kind of fantastic innocence [and] a childlike vision of American origins." Of Koch's plays in general, Robert Brustein has written: "[Koch] has discovered an inexhaustible vein of dramatic material: the corpus of Western myth, historical anecdote, and fairy tale, all of which he mocks gently in the anachronistic accents of romantic verse drama." Ruby Cohn, in a chapter on Koch in her book *Dialogue in American Drama* (1971), wrote: "His wit is of cabaret quality, depending on brevity and expert timing. . . . As in his equally witty and more imaginative volumes of poetry, Koch runs the danger of repeating his own facility."

In 1953 Koch took his M.A. degree at Columbia University. In the years following, while working for his doctorate at Columbia, he taught at Rutgers University (1953-54, 1955-56, and 1957-58) and Brooklyn College (1957-59) and directed a poetry workshop at the New School for Social Research, beginning in 1958. In 1959 he took his Ph.D. degree at Columbia after submitting a dissertation titled "The Reception and Influence of American Poetry in France, 1918-1950."

Also in 1959 Grove Press published Koch's comic epic *Ko; or A Season on Earth*, a 115-page poem with myriad interrelated plots set simultaneously in many locations, including Cincinnati, Tucson, Paris, and Tahiti, and involving a cast of characters ranging from a Japanese baseball star to a neurotic financier seeking exclusive control of the world's canine population. Writing in *Library Journal* (April 1, 1960), Ray Smith dismissed the satire as an "exercise in odd-rhyme virtuosity," but the critic for *Time* (March 14, 1960), using a mountain-climbing metaphor, called the poem "a kind of lesser Catskill among epics —not very strenuous . . . but good comedy."

Of *Thank You and Other Poems*, Stanley Kunitz wrote in *Harper's* (October 1962): "In an age of dialectical poets . . . Koch is that genuinely rare bird, an accumulative poet, one who delights in composing loose incremental structures, associational houses-that-Jack-built, word-capped towers." Burton A. Robie in his comments for the *Library Journal* (November 15, 1962) called attention to Koch's "love of living" and the "vitality" of his poems.

Three small volumes of verse—*Poems from 1952 and 1953* (Black Sparrow Press, 1968), *When the Sun Tries to Go On* (Black Sparrow, 1969), which had illustrations by Larry Rivers, and *Sleeping With Women* (Black Sparrow, 1969)—were followed by another major collection, *The Pleasures of Peace and Other Poems* (Grove, 1969). Most reviewers of the last-mentioned work agreed that it marked Koch's arrival at a new stage of maturity. In his review in *Poetry* (November 1971), Paul Carroll observed that Koch's most successful poems dealt with the art of poetry itself and were variations on the theme of "the celebration of the power and the glory and the comedy of the poetic imagination." Koch himself has said of the title poem: "When I wrote 'The Pleasures of Peace,' I was very unhappy about the Vietnam war and about everything that was happening there and about my students who had to go fight in it or else go to jail or leave the country. And I tried to put into that poem a lot of feelings about suffering and anguish . . . and they didn't make good poetry for me. Starting with poems like 'The Circus' in my last collection, *The Art of Love,* I think I've been able to include some experiences like that."

The erotically boisterous *The Art of Love* (Random House, 1975) contained seven reflective, didactic, and mock-didactic poems about which Victor Howes wrote in the *Christian Science Monitor* (July 31, 1975): "Koch manages to weave in and out of the instructive mode like a mad bicyclist in a downtown traffic jam. . . . [He] is a breath of fresh air among academics." Sandra M. Gilbert in *Poetry* (August 1976) noted the "kind, flexible, winsome, soulful irony" used by Koch "to enable both poet and reader to distance feelings, ideas, experiences, so as to perceive them strangely, freshly, as if they were rare or even alien curiosities." Gilbert quoted the poet as wanting to leave the reader "distressed and illuminated, ready to believe/It is curious to be alive."

At Columbia University, Koch became an associate professor in 1966 and a full professor of English and comparative literature five years later. He began teaching elementary school children to write poetry in 1968, at Public School 61 on New York's Lower East Side, and he reported on the experiment in *Wishes, Lies and Dreams* (first published by Chelsea House in 1970 and reissued by Random House in 1973), a combination "how-to" guide for teachers and an anthology of poems by students.

Koch's motivation was partly his awareness of the breakthrough in teaching art to schoolchildren and the need for a similar breakthrough to make possible in children's verse the "happy creative energy of children's art." His approach was to give the students simple "poetry ideas," like asking them to express deeply felt wishes or recalled dreams. In his relaxed classroom, spelling, grammar, and neatness—matters which could be taken care of later—were ignored; the use of rhyme was eschewed because it might restrict imagination and feeling, and devices such as repetition of key words, phrases, or clauses were used instead; and collaboration was encouraged. Herbert Kohl, writing in the *Saturday Review* (March 20, 1971), testified that he had tried Koch's ideas in his writing classes and that "they work."

In the next stage of the experiment, Koch shifted to teaching great poetry to the children. His method was to read selections aloud and encourage the students to emulate the core feelings or ideas. Thus, after reading William Blake's "The Tyger," he asked them to "write a poem in which you are talking to a beautiful and mysterious creature and [asking] it anything you want." One fourth-grader responded with, "Rose, where did you get that red?," which became the title of Koch's next book. Reviewing *Rose, Where Did You Get That Red?* in the New York *Times* (December 23, 1973), John Gardner wrote, "Koch . . . has clearly proved . . . that writing poetry can be as exciting as anything in a child's experience," and the reviewer for the *New Yorker* (November 19, 1973) called the children's verse "an outburst of genuine creativity."

In the spring and summer of 1976 Koch carried his experiment into the American Nursing Home, also on the Lower East Side. There were numerous problems inherent in such an undertaking, including disabling infirmities and failing memories, but Koch knew that those elderly and sick people had, like the young and robust, fantasy lives that might be tapped through poetry. Gradually responding to Koch's techniques, including the use of music and other aids, the twenty-five nursing home residents made the transition from collective to individual composition. By the final sessions, many had gone beyond the general themes suggested by their teacher and were writing on a very individual level, about personal feelings, dreams, and memories. Out of that experience came *I Never Told Anybody; Teaching Writing In A Nursing Home* (Random House, 1977), a collection of the patients' poems and Koch's account of how he elicited them. In his review in the Washington *Post* (April 4, 1977), Alex Comfort called Koch a "considerable pioneer" in helping the patients "overcome nearly as many stereotypes about 'poetry' as we have to overcome about age" and "a rare teacher" in "giving them models which did not require metrical virtuosity and [in] letting the structure of the ideas provide the skeleton of the poem." Koch spent ten months in France in 1976 and 1977 and during part of that time he taught poetry writing to French schoolchildren.

A perception running through Koch's own work is the illusoriness of tranquility or stasis and the prevalence of flux and diversity, "continual activity or excitement," in nature and life. He told Bill Zavatsky in the New York *Times* interview: "You find out, as soon as you study a little biological science or physics, that everything is jumping all over the place and . . . everything is always changing . . . and as we're sitting here talking, monkeys are jumping around in the trees and waves are going across the Hudson and new poets are being born and . . . people are picking flowers in Tuscany. . . . That has a lot to do with what my novel, *The Red Robins,* is about, and *The Duplications* also."

The Red Robins (Random House Vintage Books, 1976), a pop-cult entertainment showing the influence of rock singers such as the Beatles and Cat Stevens, comic strips, and writers like Kurt Vonnegut Jr., J.R.R. Tolkien, and Ken Kesey, is a fantasy about a squadron of young aviators led by Santa Claus who give international chase to a group of villains that includes evil Dr. Pep and Dracula. In the 450 Byronic *ottava rima* stanzas of *The Duplications* Koch took up again the kind of project he had attempted years before in *Ko*—a contemporary epic poem in which he makes nonsense of a world of which he cannot make sense. The narrative in *The Duplications* is essentially a tour de force in which, as Robert Coles pointed out in the New York *Times* (April 10, 1977), the poet gives free rein to his "delicious sense of ironic detachment," his "lyric, if not ecstatic, celebrations of the flesh," and his "naturalist's pantheistic, humorous advocacy." Koch's verse has been anthologized in *The Poets of the New York School* (1970), edited by J. R. Myers.

Kenneth Koch is a bespectacled man who looks younger than his years, whose smile is quick and broad, and whose voice has been described as "low," "pleasant," and "slow." Koch and the former Mary Janice Elwood, who were married on June 12, 1952, have a daughter, Katherine. They live in Manhattan, where Koch continues to teach English and comparative literature at Columbia University. He has accepted an appointment with the Commission for Educational and Cultural Exchange to teach Italian schoolchildren. Koch considers poetry a useful art capable of connecting us with Blake's "immense work world of delight," which, as he observed to Bill Zavatsky, "may exist in things without our knowing it."

References: N Y Times Bk R p27+ Ap 10 '77; Time 109:52 Ap 4 '77 por; Contemporary Poets (1975); International Who's Who in Poetry (1974-75); Who's Who in America, 1976-77; World Authors: 1950-1970 (1975)

Kuhn, Maggie (kōōn)

Aug. 3, 1905- Social activist. Address: b. Gray Panthers, 3700 Chestnut St., Philadelphia, Pa. 19104; h. 6342 Greene St., Philadelphia, Pa. 19144

"We are on a pilgrimage but also a lark," Maggie Kuhn said in October 1977 at the close of the second biennial convention of the Gray Panthers, a coalition of older, middle-aged, and younger activists and advocates pulling together for social change. A founder in 1960 and the national convener of the Gray Panthers, Miss Kuhn views the work of her organization as part of the present-day struggle for human liberation—freedom from the oppressive practice of agism, which is related to, and just as demeaning as, sexism and racism. She is an ebullient, resolute radical who minces neither words nor convictions, who scoffs at substituting "senior citizens" for "old people," and who regards retirement communities as "big playpens for wrinkled babies."

Margaret E. Kuhn was born in Buffalo, New York on August 3, 1905 to Samuel Frederick and Minnie Louise (Kooman) Kuhn. Social consciousness appears to have been a strong force in her life from its beginning: her mother journeyed from Memphis to Buffalo so that the baby would not be born in the South, whose practices, at that time, of social segregation she deplored. Maggie's father had begun his career in business as an office boy for Bradstreet, which developed into Dun & Bradstreet, the financial rating firm, and over the years he advanced to the position of credit manager of his company's offices in various cities. There was one son in the family, Samuel Kooman Kuhn, who became a credit investigator.

"Father was of German extraction and he ruled the household. 'Head of the house' was his motto. He never could understand where I got my strange ideas," Maggie Kuhn told Helen Dudar during an interview for the New York *Post* (May 27, 1972). The household was moved from Buffalo to Memphis to Cleveland, as the Bradstreet home office transferred Kuhn from one city to another. Maggie Kuhn completed high school in Cleveland, West High School, in 1922 and remained in that city to attend Flora Stone Mather College of Case-Western Reserve University. While majoring in English and sociology, she spent much of her time outside the classroom writing for the college magazine and helping to organize a college chapter of the League of Women Voters.

Since teaching was one of the few professions open to women in the mid-1920's, Maggie Kuhn began training as a practice teacher at the Fairmount Junior High School in Cleveland. But when a relay race that she devised to sweeten a grammar lesson turned into an eraser-throwing contest unexpectedly witnessed by the regular teacher, her prospects for a career in education ended. "I never did like the structured classroom system," she observed wryly to Helen Dudar. Not yet sure how to make the best use of the B.A. degree she had received in 1926, she kept busy as a volunteer for the Cleveland Young Women's Christian Association, which hired her within a year as a full-time staff member.

For eleven years Miss Kuhn worked at a variety of organizing assignments among young, employed women for the YWCA in Cleveland and in Philadelphia, Pennsylvania. She soon became what was later known as a "women's libber." As she explained to Bill Mandel, who interviewed her for the Philadelphia *Inquirer* (April 27, 1975), "So many of our members at the YWCA were women working for rotten-paying clerical or commercial jobs. They were working six days a week for $10. In the Depression, of course, it got worse. My work with these women as they started to organize and unionize cemented my radicalism. . . . Yes, I've been a radical for a long time."

In the last of several positions with the YWCA, Maggie Kuhn was employed as publications' editor on the national staff in New York City, a post from which she resigned in the late 1930's. After working for a time with the General Alliance of Unitarian Women in Boston, she began a twenty-five-year professional association with the United Presbyterian Church in New York City, where she served as associate secretary in the office of church and society and as coordinator of programming in the division of church and race. She helped to edit and wrote for the church magazine *Social Progress* (later the *Journal of Church and Society*), which was published in Philadelphia, and was alternate observer at the United Nations for the Presbyterians.

As a church bureaucrat, Miss Kuhn proved to be well ahead of prevailing attitudes on such pivotal social issues as race relations, women's rights, medical care, housing, and problems of the aged. Her own firsthand observation of the church's ministry made possible her books *Get Out There and Do Something About Injustice* (Friendship Press, 1972), a resource guide for adult groups in churches, and *Maggie Kuhn on Aging* (Westminster Press, 1977). The latter is a dialogue between her and a group of students, mostly ministers, enrolled during the mid-1970's in a week-long course of the advanced pastoral studies program of the San Francisco Theological Seminary. Defining *agism* as "the arbitrary discrimination against people on the basis of their chronological age," she told the students, "I propose to attempt to challenge the present mind-set of the church that is largely accommodative to the existing wasteful system." And she urged that the church "launch a massive attack on agism in all its oppressive and constraining forms."

At the time that Maggie Kuhn was teaching that course on what the church and older Christians need to do for one another, she was no longer working for the United Presbyterian Church, having been forced into mandatory retirement in 1970 at the age of sixty-five. To prepare for her years in pasture, in June 1970 she met for lunch at the Interfaith Center in New York City with five friends whose employment in various national organizations had involved them in social causes that they did not want to forsake and who had been or were about to be retired. They shared a sense of freedom, no longer bound by the constrictions of their bureaucratic roles, to act upon their beliefs in regard to such controversial questions as American policy on the war in Indochina, which they all opposed.

Almost from the beginning, in fact, objection to United States participation in the Vietnam War served as a bridge between young and old. Within a year after the June meeting, the group had grown to about a hundred retired men and women who came together to discuss programs for social action. Their status as retired persons, with nothing to lose, emboldened them to a militancy matching that of the college students whose protests against the war and the draft they were eager to support. Concern for other matters of social justice, as well as the recognition of the necessity for mutual help in meeting economic and social needs of young and old, encouraged the formation of an organization that was first known as Consultation of Older and Younger Adults for Social Change. Some years later, discussing the affinity between the two age groups in their early association, Maggie Kuhn said in the Philadelphia *Inquirer* interview, "We realized that the young and the old in this society are equally discriminated against. Both groups have identity crises. Both groups can't get credit from banks. Both groups are in the drug scene, although there are different drugs and different pushers."

Both younger and older adults, moreover, had been ignored in what Maggie Kuhn calls "the decision-making process." To begin to counter that failure to listen to the aged, she and some other members of her fledgling organization joined with older adults of black and Puerto Rican groups to make their voices heard at the 1971 White House Conference on Aging. Again they targeted the government's expenditure of vast funds on the fighting in Vietnam, arguing that the money should be shifted to paying for human services.

The Gray Panthers owe their name to a television newsman on New York's WPIX who apparently saw in the activism of the Consultation of Older and Younger Adults a similarity to the radicalism of the Black Panthers. What made the name stick was its wide circulation by reporters of the AP and of the New York *Times* and other major newspapers who covered Maggie Kuhn's press conference in May 1972 in Denver during the 181st general assembly of the United Presbyterian Church. In later interviews she has acknowledged that the term "Gray Panthers" turned off quite a number of persons, but, she reasoned, they were the very ones who would not be ready anyway to work toward the group's goal of social change. "Gray," furthermore, is appropriate to an organization made up mainly of gray-haired members, but eager to include people of all ages as well as all colors. "Gray is a symbolic color," Miss Kuhn explained, as quoted in *MS.* (June 1975), "—everyone gets old, and if you put all the colors of the rainbow together, you get gray."

College students were among the volunteers who set up the Gray Panthers' first office, in a church basement in Philadelphia, the city that became the headquarters of the organization, which has tried to shun traditional bureaucracy in structuring a national network of leadership. Its regional organizers and enablers interpret and expound Gray Panther objectives in local meetings, addresses before many types of professional groups, college lectures, and radio and television appearances.

Since 1971, in its pursuit of such goals as ending age discrimination and training older persons to use their skills in various kinds of public-interest work, the Gray Panthers had been cooperating with the Retired Professional Action Group, one of Ralph Nader's Public Citizen Groups. Maggie Kuhn's organization merged with Nader's on December 1, 1973. Two of the projects that the Gray Panthers took over from the RPAG concerned the promotion of legislation affecting the hearing aid industry and nursing homes. The Gray Panthers also organized a number of citizen-action groups into the National Coalition for Nursing Home Reform and in 1973 began a three-year study of the nursing home industry that resulted in the publication of *Nursing Homes: A Citizens' Action Guide* (Beacon Press, 1977) by Linda Horn and Elma Griesel.

Nursing home reform is just one aspect of the overall problem of medical care on which the Gray Panthers has concentrated much effort. With typical straightforwardness Maggie Kuhn asserted in the New York *Post* interview, "The American Medical Association spent millions lobbying against a national health program and now the same doctors who tried to defeat Medicare are getting rich out of the maladies of the aged. Doctors prey on the infirmities of the old, and you can quote me." In a later interview, for *Retirement Living* (December 1975), she explained that the Gray Panthers want to eliminate the profit motive from health care, to adopt a system somewhat like the British health service program. When the interviewer pointed out that "socialized medicine" is an inflammatory term in the United States, she replied, "If it's so great for the armed forces, *and* Congress, *and* the President and his family, we would like to have it for everybody."

The Gray Panthers have staged demonstrations at meetings of the AMA, to which they have also presented positions papers. In July 1973 Miss Kuhn testified on behalf of her organization before members of the subcommittee on health of the Senate Special Committee on Aging. Health care, furthermore, was one of two kinds of services on which she testified in April 1977 before the House Select Committee on Aging in a public hearing on fragmentation of services. On that occasion she told the legislators, "Old people constitute America's largest untapped and undervalued human energy source, yet I have observed only token effort to give us a chance to be self-determining and substantively involved in planning and developing the programs that are designed to help us." In another appearance on Capitol Hill she commented in the fall of 1977 for the Gray Panthers on the Carter Administration welfare reform bill, which she called "a great disappointment." She went on to say, "Public welfare in this country does not need re-forming; it needs radicalization. To merely rearrange the out-dated, unworkable concepts of the Elizabethan Poor Laws is not the solution."

Much of the public-interest work for which the Gray Panthers want to train, or recycle, older people concerns monitoring the operations of the courts, of banks and insurance companies, and of municipal agencies such as planning commissions and zoning boards. Another area of watchdogging involves the way older people are depicted on radio and television and in advertising. Through a Gray Panthers' group called the Media Watch they target programs that use insipid dialogue and erratic behavior to make older people look useless and helpless. Objecting particularly, for example, to the portrayal of an elderly woman on *The Carol Burnett Show*, they protested to CBS executives and to the National Association of Broadcasters Code Board. In a hearing on the television industry of the House Select Committee on Aging in September 1977, Maggie Kuhn criticized the negative stereotyping of the elderly on TV and the failure of the media to use the opportunity to correct the age bias that she contended contributes to the alienation of the young and the old.

Delegates from over thirty states and the District of Columbia attended the first general convention of the Gray Panthers in October 1975, attesting to the national scope of the organization. When Maggie Kuhn convened the second biennial convention in Chevy Chase, Maryland in October 1977, some 350 delegates represented 8,000 affiliate members of about seventy network groups across the country. In resolutions covering a score or more of national issues the Gray Panthers called for legislation to provide for a tax-supported program to make health care available to everyone without charge or discrimination, the adoption of "publicly owned and democratically controlled" utilities services, and the establishment of an Office of Consumer Representation. They also went on record as opposing mandatory retirement "in any form, at any age."

Another Gray Panther resolution affirmed "the right to sexuality at all ages and the right to celebrate and express it." A discussion on the sexuality of the elderly in *Maggie Kuhn on Aging* noted that the churches have given scant attention "to the sexual needs and the human sexuality of people who are in their late years. It's assumed that sex is a no-no—that sexual competence, interest, and the ability to attract members of the opposite sex are lost when one gets old. Such mythology must be eliminated from the thinking of people and from the practice of society."

Maggie Kuhn is a member of the national advisory board for Hospice, Inc., and for the *Over Easy* public TV series. She helped to organize the task force on older women for the National Organization of Women (NOW) and serves on the Federal Judicial Nominating Committee of Pennsylvania and the Committee for a Responsive Philanthropy. Maintaining what she calls a "horrendous" travel schedule, she covers thousands of miles a year to give hundreds of speeches. In many television appearances, such as a recent one on the PBS *Black Perspective on the News*, telecast in New York in March 1978, she persistently reiterates the need for fundamental social change if services, not just novocaine, are to be provided for the elderly.

Some of Maggie Kuhn's trips from home are taken to collect tributes: the first annual Award for Justice and Human Development of the Witherspoon Society (1974), Distinguished Service Award in Consumer Advocacy of the American Speech and Hearing Association (1975), Freedom Award of the Women's Scholarship Association of Roosevelt University (1976), Annual Award of the Philadelphia Society of Clinical Psychologists (1976), Peaceseeker Award of the United Presbyterian Peace Fellowship (1977), Humanist of the Year Award of the American Humanist Association (1978), and honorary Doctor of Humane Letters degree from Swarthmore College (1978).

The birdlike fragility of Maggie Kuhn's appearance contrasts with her firmness of manner, moral fiber, and intellectual toughness. She stands five feet three inches tall, weighs 105 pounds, and has brown eyes and bright gray hair. Her home is a spacious old stone house in the Germantown section of Philadelphia that she bought in the late 1950's. There in rare hours of leisure she enjoys cooking, gardening, listening to music, birdwatching, and watercolor painting.

References: Biog N 1:556 My '74 pors, 2: 576+ My/Je '75 por; Ms. 3:91 Je '75 por; N Y Post p23 My 27 '72 por; Kanin, Garson. It Takes A Long Time to Become Young (1978)

Kuhn, Margaret E. See Kuhn, Maggie

Laker, Sir Frederick A(lfred)

Aug. 6, 1922- British airline executive. Address: c/o Laker Airways, Gatwick Airport, Horley, Surrey, England

The patron saint of budget-minded tourists has long been Frederick ("Freddie") A. Laker, the

Sir Frederick A. Laker

maverick British entrepreneur who owns Laker Airways. During the 1960's Laker pioneered low-cost holiday package deals and the so-called "affinity charters," which provided cut-rate group flights for members of organizations. He later championed the travel arrangement called Advance Booking Charters, or ABC's, a less restrictive charter plan that was finally approved by the United States Civil Aeronautics Board (CAB) in October 1976. Laker's major boon to the nonaffluent traveler is Skytrain, a dirt-cheap, no-reservation air shuttle service between London and New York and London and Los Angeles. Skytrain, which was vigorously opposed by the major scheduled Atlantic carriers, was only approved by the British and United States governments after several years of legal wrangling. Since it began the London-to-New York run in September 1977, Skytrain has ushered in an era of unprecedented transAtlantic flight bargains, with other airlines competing to match its low fares.

Frederick Alfred Laker was born in Canterbury, England on August 6, 1922, the son of a merchant seaman and his wife, Hannah. The father, a sadistic man who devised cruel punishments for his young son, deserted the family while Freddie was still a young child. When the boy was about eight, his mother remarried a man whom Laker has described as "wonderful" and "loving." Both Laker's father and stepfather are no longer living. His mother, a lively septuagenarian, lives in a pleasant three-room apartment that he bought for her in a seaside English town.

Although Laker's mother eventually achieved some prosperity as a scrap dealer during World War II and then as the owner of a general store, the family was bitterly poor when Freddie was a boy during the Depression. For a time the Lakers were forced to live in primitive quarters that lacked an indoor toilet. As a student at the Simon Langston School in Canterbury, Freddie was impatient and rebellious. "I hated school," the British multimillionaire told Gitta Sereny during an interview for the New York *Times Magazine* (September 4, 1977). "And I was terrible, academically and otherwise. I can still remember the roars of laughter, from boys and master alike when, in answer to the question what I wanted to be, I replied, 'A millionaire.' " Freddie did excel, however, in more practical pursuits: he built a radio at the age of ten, reconstructed a car at twelve, and ran his school's candy store at a profit, at fourteen.

Laker first became fascinated by aircraft at fourteen, when he saw the ill-fated *Hindenburg* airship and a Handley Page biplane crossing the sky over Canterbury at the same time. Two years later he quit school and persuaded Shorts Brothers in Rochester, manufacturers of flying boats, to hire him as a sweeper and tea boy. As an apprentice at Shorts he learned the fundamentals of aviation engineering and at night school he studied mathematics and economics.

Not long after the Shorts factory was bombed in 1940, Laker joined the British Air Transport Auxiliary, for whom he worked as an engineer and pilot, ferrying airplanes between squadrons. After the war, he worked briefly for British European Airways, but soon realized that he needed to strike out on his own. In the next couple of years he parlayed his mother's and his own modest savings into a tidy sum by buying and selling government surplus trucks, a cherry orchard, and some aircraft-radio and electrical spare parts. In 1948 he received his first big break when a friend to whom he had given some good advice on aircraft sales lent him 38,000 pounds. Laker took that money and his own 4,500 pounds in savings and purchased twelve Halton aircraft with spare parts and engines from BOAC. A few months later the Berlin airlift began, and all the planes were chartered. For the next year and fourteen days, until the airlift was halted in 1949, Laker kept his Haltons flying in and out of Berlin around the clock.

After the Berlin airlift Laker remained in the charter business, ferrying passengers and cargo wherever he could turn a profit. He also continued to amass government surplus planes and spare parts until, as the story goes, he found himself with 100 aircraft and 6,000 engines. He smelted them down and sold the scrap to a manufacturer of saucepans. During the 1950's Laker began to design and produce his own aircraft. His most successful project during that period was his modification of the Douglas DC-4 into a craft capable of carrying five cars and twenty-two passengers. That plane, which he named the Carvair, is still in use.

In 1958 Laker sold his charter business to an outfit that acquired several other companies and in 1960 became British United Airways. Laker stayed on with British United Airways as managing director, increasing its sales until the company became Britain's most profitable independent airline. While with the company Laker continued to design, having the BAC-111 built to his specifications and modifying the VC-10 to carry cargo. He also launched the world's first Hovercraft service.

Laker left British United Airways in 1965, and the following year he established Laker Airways. Soon he was pioneering the cheap package tours and charter flights that made holiday traveling possible for thousands of moderate-income Europeans, and around 1969 he entered the trans-Atlantic "affinity charter" business. Operated under rigorous British and American rules, those low-cost flights were legally available only to persons who had belonged for six months to bona-fide groups not organized just for the purpose of travel. The rules were so widely flouted, however, that it has been estimated that 50 to 90 percent of affinity charter passengers traveled illegally. During a 1972 crackdown on nonscheduled carriers who were alleged to have infringed the strict affinity charter regulations, Laker was charged by the CAB with having operated sixty-three unauthorized charter flights in 1970-71 and 1972.

Eventually, Laker settled his case with the CAB out of court by paying a $101,000 settlement. Although he has always protested his innocence of the charges, Laker has freely admitted that many people did defy the regulations. The fact that "decent people were committing perjury [by pretending to be members of sometimes nonexistent clubs] to get back and forth across the Atlantic at dirt-cheap fares," indicated to him, he told Dennis Duggan of *Newsday* (August 3, 1973) that "there was this vast market for cheap air travel."

Skytrain was Laker's proposal to provide that cheap travel, which he envisioned as an alternative for budget-minded travelers who could not plan ahead far enough to take advantage of charter flights. He saw it, for example, as a way that persons of moderate means could visit seriously ill relatives and attend funerals across the Atlantic. Laker first applied for permission from the British government to operate the Atlantic shuttle service in mid-1971. Certain that the American CAB would never approve a plan providing guaranteed reservations for passengers (since it would take business away from the conventional airlines), he proposed that Skytrain tickets be sold on a first-come, first-served basis a few hours before the flight. For $90 one-way at the peak of the tourist season, Laker said he could transport passengers between New York and London. If they wanted food, movies, stereo, or drinks—all the "frills" the conventional airlines provide—they could buy them for an extra fee.

The British Civil Aviation Authority did not approve Laker's application for Skytrain until late in 1972. But Laker was confident that American approval would follow soon after, since under the terms of the aviation agreement then in effect between the two nations, the CAB was more or less obligated to rubber-stamp Britain's approval. He was, in fact, so confident that he put up $70,000,000, much of it borrowed, in order to buy three McDonnell Douglas DC-10's that he painted with the Skytrain insignia. But the Americans did not approve the project. Besieged by furious anti-Skytrain lobbying from the major scheduled American airlines and already on the outs with Laker over alleged charter violations, the CAB kept putting off approval.

For years it appeared that Skytrain was permanently grounded, until February 9, 1976, when British Secretary of State for Trade Peter Shore revoked Laker's ten-year license to operate the shuttle, ostensibly to protect the interests of the government-owned British Airways, which plied the same route at regular prices. In a rare move, the feisty Laker sued his government for reinstatement of the license, and won. The British government subsequently lost an appeal to overturn that decision, and in February 1977 the British Civil Aviation Authority announced that it would request United States approval of Laker's Skytrain. The CAB complied in June 1977, and a few days later President Jimmy Carter formally approved the venture for a one-year trial period.

The years of delays and legal battles cost Laker more than $1,000,000 in American legal fees and expenses alone, but meanwhile his business flourished. By the time that Skytrain won approval for landing in the United States, Laker Airways had become the world's second-largest charter operator across the Atlantic, second only to Pan American. With net assets of over $14,000,000, Laker owned a fleet that included two Boeing 707's, five BAC-111's, and four DC-10's. During the period that he was being frustrated in his efforts to get Skytrain off the ground, Laker was able to lobby for the adoption of the Advance Booking Charter plan, which allowed Laker and other airways to offer low-cost charters with fewer restrictions than earlier plans.

By the time that Skytrain was authorized, Laker had had to raise his original budget fare of $180 roundtrip to approximately $236 ($135 eastbound and 59 pounds or about $101 on the London-New York run). Although they had protested vociferously for years that Laker's low fares would prove economically disastrous, the scheduled airlines immediately countered with an assortment of transportation plans of their own, at prices almost as low as his.

Under the terms of Laker's license, he was allowed one daily roundtrip of Skytrain, starting on September 26, 1977. During the peak of the summer tourist season, he could run eleven Skytrain flights each week. Originally the London flights were scheduled to land and take off from Stansted Airport, well outside London, but Laker was later able to obtain permission to operate out of the more conveniently located Gatwick Airport.

The first flight of Skytrain on September 26, 1977 was a gala event, with hordes of journalists in attendance, free-flowing champagne, and the ebullient Laker himself on board. The Gatwick-Kennedy flight took off on Monday evening with only 270 passengers, or 85 percent capacity in the wide-bodied DC-10, which seats ten across, but on the late-night Kennedy-Gatwick return flight, the plane was filled to its 345-seat capacity by passengers who had begun lining up for the trip as early as the previous Friday evening. Blair Sabol of *New York* magazine (October 10, 1977), one of the 150 or so reporters present, described the Skytrain waiting room scene as "the typical student/charter-flight sight. The kind so reminiscent of cheapie 'vomit comit' Icelandic Airlines trips to Europe."

By the end of November 1977 Laker could report that his Skytrains had averaged around 80 percent of capacity, and that his trans-Atlantic shuttle service had already netted a profit of almost $700,000. Shortly after the shuttle began Laker purchased two more DC-10's to add to the Skytrain fleet. In December 1977 he announced that he had applied for a license to operate a daily air shuttle between Los Angeles and London. Those flights began on September 26, 1978 at a round trip price of $382. Crediting his tightfistedness for much of his business success, Laker keeps the headquarters for his Airways in a collection of small offices crowded into the Laker hangar at Gatwick Airport. In addition to his airline, the only one on the North Atlantic run named after an individual, he owns two tour companies and four travel agencies.

Although Laker keeps his business headquarters modest, there is nothing spartan about his lifestyle. He makes his home in a twenty-two-room farmhouse in Surrey that is furnished with fine antiques. Also in Surrey he maintains a 1,000-acre sheep and cattle ranch, a stud farm where he indulges his passion for raising racehorses, and a turkey farm that supplies his employees with birds at Christmas. Laker, who for years purchased a new Rolls-Royce annually, keeps a fleet of seven cars for his personal use. But his most prized possession is his 70-foot yacht, the *Tutinella*, which he keeps moored in Majorca. It was in Majorca in 1974 that he met his present wife, the former Patricia Bowden Gates, a widow from Tulsa, Oklahoma. They were married in 1975 and Laker adopted her teen-aged daughter, Tina. Their newborn son, Freddie, died hours after his birth in November 1976. Laker married his first wife, Joan, in 1942. They had two children, Elaine, now a housewife, and Kevin, who was killed in a car accident in 1965 at the age of seventeen. Joan, who was divorced from Laker during the 1960's, remains on the board of directors of Laker Airways. Laker was subsequently married for a second time, but that union was dissolved in 1974.

"A faint whiff of cannon smoke clings to the persona of Freddie Laker," wrote Tim Murari (*Guardian*, August 24, 1974). ". . . He relishes any kind of battle and after a few hours with him the grapeshot is flying so thick and fast that occasionally it gets impossible to see the target for all the smoke." Gitta Sereny in her New York *Times Magazine* article described the brash and colorful airline executive as "a friendly, but not a gentle, person . . . [with] an engagingly open face that can close up within seconds." Laker is six feet one inch tall and heavy-set. His clubs are the Eccentric and the Little Ship. In recognition of his achievements, he was knighted by Queen Elizabeth II on June 2, 1978.

References: Bsns W p60+ Mr 3 '73 por; Guardian p11 Ag 24 '74 por; N Y Times Mag p14+ S 4 '77 pors; People 8:34+ S 19 '77 pors; Who's Who, 1977

Lamm, Norman

Dec. 12, 1927- President of Yeshiva University; rabbi. Address: b. Yeshiva University, 500 W. 185th St., New York City, N.Y. 10033; h. 101 Central Park West, New York City, N.Y. 10023

As the president of Yeshiva University since August 1976, Rabbi Norman Lamm stands at the helm of America's oldest and largest university under Jewish auspices, a school whose commitment to two often opposed spheres of learning is reflected in its motto, *Torah u-mada* ("Torah and worldly knowledge"). A creative and independent thinker whose academic training, appropriately, encompassed both rabbinic studies and organic chemistry, Lamm is especially well known for his interest in the problems of religious doubt engendered in modern society. Before becoming Yeshiva's third president (and its first to be American-born), he taught philosophy and was the spiritual leader of one of New York City's most important Orthodox Jewish congregations.

Norman Lamm, the son of Samuel Lamm, a civil servant, and Pearl (Baumol) Lamm, was born on December 12, 1927 in Brooklyn, New York. He has two married sisters, Sondra Sittner and Miriam Auslander, the former of whom lives in Israel and the latter in Suffern, New York. His younger brother

Norman Lamm

Maurice, who is also a rabbi, lives in Los Angeles and is the author of *The Jewish Way in Death and Mourning*. Raised in the Williamsburg section of Brooklyn, a neighborhood then heavily populated by traditionally observant Jews, Lamm attended the Yeshiva Torah Vodaath, an Orthodox parochial institution, for his primary schooling, and then went on to the Mesivta Torah Vodaath, where he was the editor of his class yearbook, for his secondary education. In 1945 he matriculated at Yeshiva College, majoring in chemistry but also taking a required course of studies in traditional religious subjects.

While still a student at Yeshiva during the Israeli War of Independence in 1947-48, Lamm was recruited by Dr. Ernest D. Bergmann, who later became the head of Israel's Atomic Energy Commission, to work on a secret munitions project at a laboratory sequestered in upstate New York. The lab's activities were illegal, and on one occasion it was raided by the FBI. Lamm and his associates, however, managed to persuade the naïve agents that they were really trying to develop a new fertilizer.

In 1949, after compiling a brilliant academic record that won him prizes in both Talmud and general scholarship as well as the honor of being chosen class valedictorian, Lamm received his B.A. degree *summa cum laude*. While continuing his Jewish studies at Yeshiva under two of the most outstanding Orthodox scholars of the period, Dr. Samuel Belkin (who since 1943 had been Yeshiva's president) and Dr. Joseph B. Soloveitchik, Norman Lamm also did graduate work in organic chemistry at the Brooklyn Polytechnic Institute.

At that juncture Lamm won a four-year medical school scholarship, and he was forced to make a long-deferred decision—whether to enter the rabbinate or pursue a secular career. After consulting with Belkin, his *rebbe* (spiritual mentor), he began the course of rabbinic studies at the Rabbi Isaac Elchanan Theological Seminary, a branch of Yeshiva University. Ordained in 1950, Lamm became the assistant rabbi of Congregation Kehilath Jeshurun in New York City in 1951, and in 1954 he became the rabbi of Congregation Kodimoh in Springfield, Massachusetts. He also served for a time as an associate editor of *Hadarom*, a journal of Jewish law, and in 1957 he founded, and for some years edited, *Tradition*, a quarterly that soon came to be recognized as the foremost English-language journal of Orthodox Jewish thought. In 1958 The Jewish Center on West 86th Street in Manhattan, one of New York City's most prestigious Orthodox synagogues, called Lamm to its pulpit, a post he retained until September 1976.

Meanwhile, in 1959 Lamm had joined the faculty of Yeshiva University as an instructor in philosophy. Rising through the academic ranks while working on his doctorate in Jewish philosophy at Yeshiva's Bernard Revel Graduate School, Lamm became the Erna and Jakob Michael Professor of Jewish Philosophy in June 1966, the same year he received his Ph.D. degree. In 1970 he spent a half-year sabbatical teaching in Israel, and in 1974-75 he was visiting professor of Judaic studies at Brooklyn College.

Over the years Lamm's writings, particularly those in which he sought to present and interpret traditional Jewish law in the light of contemporary scientific, technological, philosophical, and social developments, won him wide recognition. A striking example of the esteem in which his work was held occurred in 1966, when Chief Justice Earl Warren, rendering the Supreme Court's majority opinion in the *Miranda* case, made reference to Lamm's essay "The Fifth Amendment and Its Equivalent in the Halakhah" (*Judaism*, 1956). The same article was later quoted by Justice William O. Douglas in a 1967 decision concerning self-incrimination. That year, too, Lamm appeared before a Senate subcommittee to explain the Jewish view of the right of privacy, a subject he also covered in "The Fourth Amendment and Its Equivalent in the Halakhah" (*Judaism*, 1967; reprinted in the *Congressional Record*).

Lamm's most important scholarly work, *Torah Lishmah* (Torah for Its Own Sake; Mosad Harav Kook, 1972), dealt with the theology of the Mitnaggedim, opponents of the pietistic Hasidic movement in eighteenth and nineteenth century Europe. He turned to the subject of Hasidism in his work in progress.

tentatively entitled "A Reader in Hasidism." It will comprise annotated translations, with extensive introductions, of the primary theological writings of the early Hasidic masters.

Lamm's interests have ranged far beyond Hasidism, however. In *A Hedge of Roses*, published in 1966 (Feldheim) and subsequently translated into Hebrew, Portuguese, French, and Spanish, he treated the Jewish laws on sex and the marital relationship. He also wrote a number of articles for the *Encyclopedia Judaica* (Jerusalem: Keter, 1972), including a major essay on "Judaism and the Modern Attitude to Homosexuality" which appeared in *Encyclopedia Judaica Yearbook*, 1974, and he has written on strictly scientific subjects, such as the article on caffeine withdrawal on which he collaborated with Dr. Morris A. Shorofsky for the *New York State Journal of Medicine* (February 1977). He edited the anthology *The Good Society; Jewish Ethics in Action* (Viking, 1974).

Most notably, however, Lamm has been a prolific contributor to both popular and scholarly Jewish periodicals, including *Judaism*, *Jewish Heritage*, *Jewish Quarterly Review*, *Jewish Education*, *Jewish Life*, and the *National Jewish Monthly*, to name but a few, as well as *Hadoar*, a Hebrew-language periodical, and *Tradition*. A number of his essays, dealing with such diverse themes as faith, ecology, the new morality, the religious implications of life on other planets, and the Jewish ethic of leisure, were gathered in the volume *Faith and Doubt: Studies in Traditional Jewish Thought* (Ktav, 1971), while some of his best sermons, on similar themes, were collected in *The Royal Reach: Discourses on Jewish Tradition and the World Today* (Feldheim, 1970). Lamm has also co-edited two anthologies, the *Leo Jung Jubilee Volume* (1962), a *festschrift* in honor of his predecessor in the pulpit of The Jewish Center, and *A Treasury of Tradition* (Hebrew Publishing Co., 1967). Since 1974 he has been the editor of Ktav's "Library of Jewish Law and Ethics," and he was also a contributing ditor of *Sh'ma*, a Jewish monthly.

Along with his congregational and university responsibilities, and his writing and research, Lamm kept up a busy schedule of speaking engagements throughout the United States for The Jewish Center Lecture Bureau and on behalf of Yeshiva University service units. He also lectured in many foreign countries, visiting the Jewish communities of India and Pakistan in 1961, South Africa in 1964, and Australia and New Zealand in 1973. In 1975 he attended an international colloquium in Italy on world hunger and poverty.

Lamm has also been much involved in the organizational life of American Jewry, especially of its Orthodox branch. A forthright and articulate spokesman for Orthodoxy, he has also insisted on the necessity of Orthodox Jews to cooperate with Reform and Conservative Jews in confronting problems that concern the American Jewish community as a whole, a viewpoint unpopular in certain extremist Orthodox circles. In 1974 he was largely responsible for preventing the withdrawal of the Union of Orthodox Jewish Congregations from the interdenominational Synagogue Council of America.

In 1970 Lamm displayed his unusual combination of an insistence on traditional observances with a sympathetic understanding for the nonobservant, when he submitted his unique "Rosh Hodesh Plan" to the Israeli Knesset. He was concerned about the widespread public desecration of the Sabbath in the Jewish state, yet aware that Israel's six-day work week made the situation unavoidable, since the nonobservant had no other opportunity to engage in secular leisure activities. Therefore Lamm proposed that Rosh Hodesh, the first day of each month in the Jewish religious calendar, be declared a legal holiday expressly for leisure purposes. Although tabled indefinitely for further study, the plan aroused widespread favorable comment both in Israel and abroad.

When Samuel Belkin died in the spring of 1976, Yeshiva University began a search for a new president. Such searches are often difficult, but in Yeshiva's case the difficulty was compounded. Facing the same problems that confronted most American institutions of higher learning in that period, Yeshiva needed a president who, like the head of any other school, would possess administrative, fund-raising, and educational expertise —in itself often a hard bill to fill. In addition, however, Yeshiva's unique attempt to effect a synthesis of two intellectual worlds—the religious and the secular—caused it to require a very special kind of leadership. Its new president would have to be at home in both, and would have to be spiritually and intellectually acceptable to all of Yeshiva's diverse constituencies and contributors, which include Orthodox Jews of many different persuasions and outlooks, not to mention non-Orthodox Jews who support the university's Jewish ambiance but are more concerned with its achievement in other spheres.

In due course the search focused on Lamm. In past years, because he preferred to remain at his alma mater, he had turned down presidential offers from two other American schools and from Bar-Ilan University in Israel, as well as invitations to accept the post of chief rabbi of Great Britain and of the Israeli city of Haifa. This time, however, he accepted. In August 1976 the university's trustees elected him to the presidency, and on November 7, 1976 he was formally invested in a ceremony at Yeshiva's main campus in the Washington Heights section of Manhattan.

The institution that Lamm took over traces its origins back to the tiny Yeshiva Eitz Chaim, founded in 1886 on New York's Lower East Side. Now occupying facilities at several locations in Manhattan and the Bronx, it consists of five undergraduate colleges, a seminary and a cantorial institute, a major library of Hebraica-Judaica, graduate schools in the sciences, the social sciences, the humanities, and social work, a law school, a medical school and affiliated hospital, and many other branches and divisions. Its student body numbered about 7,000, and its annual budget amounted to $100 million.

Convinced, as he told Eric Fettmann of the New York *Post* (August 23, 1976), "that the future of American Jewry depends on a vital Yeshiva University," and aware that Yeshiva cannot survive if its academic standards are anything less than excellent, Lamm began his presidency with a massive reappraisal of the school's current state and goals. Eight distinguished educators from outside the university were appointed to a presidential planning commission that was charged with reviewing and evaluating all aspects of Yeshiva's operations. Task forces and committees representing various disciplines within the university were assigned to help the commission. Lamm himself, in an ongoing effort to sound out Yeshiva's faculty, staff, and student body, met frequently with teachers and student leaders, and he traveled to many parts of the country to consult Yeshiva's alumni and supporters. On June 8, 1977, while that evaluation was still in progress, Lamm presided at his first commencement, a moving experience for one who had received his own baccalaureate degree in the same place nearly thirty years before.

Dr. Norman Lamm is a director of the Union of Orthodox Jewish Congregations of America, a charter member of the board of governors of the Association of Orthodox Jewish Scientists, a member of the board of overseers of Bar-Ilan University, a trustee of the American Zionist Youth Federation, and a member of the advisory council of the World Jewish Congress. His other memberships include the honorary advisory board of the Greater New York Conference on Soviet Jewry, the publication committee of the Jewish Publication Society of America, the advisory board of the Jewish Association of College Youth, the Halakhah Commission of the Rabbinical Council of America, and the Brith Milah Board. In 1972 he received Israel's Abramowitz-Zeitlin Award for Religious Literature and was designated Outstanding Educator of the Year in the United States. In 1977 he was awarded the honorary degree of Doctor of Hebrew Letters by Hebrew Theological College in Skokie, Illinois.

On February 23, 1954 Norman Lamm married Mindella Mehler, a teacher. He and his wife live with three of their four children —Joshua, Shalom, and Sara—on Manhattan's Central Park West. Their oldest daughter, Chaye, who is an occupational therapist, is married to David Warburg, an attorney. Lamm, who stands five feet eight inches tall and weighs around 165 pounds, has been described by a colleague as moving with the speed and vitality of a sprinter. Other associates have mentioned his ready wit and sense of humor.

The religious views of Norman Lamm were summarized for the lay public by Tina Levitan in a series of articles that ran in the *Jewish Press*, a Brooklyn weekly, in January and February 1976. In her words: "He believes that the main source of the present-day conflict between the spheres of science and religion lies in the concept of a personal God. . . . Dr. Lamm states that Judaism's unique contribution to modern man may well lie in its insistence that God is very much alive, that He is not absent from society, even secular society, for those who invite Him in. The best way to achieve this goal is . . . through a sanctification of all life, meaning, and purpose."

References: Jewish Press p15 Ja 16 '76; N Y Post p23 Ag 23 '76 por; N Y Times p24 Ag 9 '76 por; Contemporary Authors vol 49-52; Encyclopedia Judaica, 1972; Who's Who in Israel, 1976; Who's Who in the East, 1975-76; Who's Who in World Jewry, 1972

Lefebvre, Marcel (François) (le-fe'vr)

Nov. 29, 1905- French prelate. Address: Fraternité Sacerdotale Internationale Saint Pie X, Séminaire Internationale Saint Pie X, "Ecône," 1908 Riddes, Valais, Switzerland

A threat of schism in the Roman Catholic Church is posed by Archbishop Marcel Lefebvre, a French prelate who is opposed to the liberalizing changes in the Church that were set in motion by Vatican Council II. In 1969 Lefebvre founded the International Society of Priests of St. Pius X—named for the Pope (1903-1914) who formally condemned the "heresy" of "modernism"—and the following year he established the St. Pius X Seminary in the villa "Ecône" near Riddes, Switzerland, where he trains and ordains his priests in the "old" rite. The center of that rite is the Tridentine Latin Mass, approved by the Council of Trent (1545-63) in the midst of the Counterreformation. What distinguishes Lefebvre from other "traditionalist" leaders, as one Vatican spokesman has explained, is, aside from the degree of his rebellion, the fact that he is "a captain in

Marcel Lefebvre

Egypt": as a bishop, he is able not only to ordain priests but also to consecrate bishops and thus set up a line of succession for a breakaway church. (He has reportedly already consecrated at least one bishop.) Earlier in his ecclesiastical career, Lefebvre was Archbishop of Dakar in Senegal and Superior General of the Holy Ghost Fathers, a French Roman Catholic missionary congregation working chiefly in Africa.

Marcel François Lefebvre was born to René Lefebvre, a textile manufacturer, and Gabrielle (Watine) Lefebvre in Tourcoing, Nord, France, near the Belgian border, on November 29, 1905. "I am a man of Nord, a region where Flemish blood runs in most people's veins," the Archbishop remarked in one of the interviews with José Hanu that comprise *Non* (Stock, 1977), a book that is subtitled *Mais Oui a l'Église Catholique et Romaine*. In a typical display of his sense of humor, he added: "The Flemish, you know, have a reputation for frank speech. The same cannot be said of the Italians, and that perhaps is one of the reasons for the friction between the Vatican and me."

Religious devotion and patriotic activism were Lefebvre family traditions. Daily prayers were said in Latin, and Marcel's vocation along with those of four of his siblings brought the number of priestly and religious callings on his mother's side of the family alone to sixty in four generations. A sister of the Archbishop is the founder of a traditionalist convent near Castel Gandolfo, Italy, the Pope's summer residence.

Archbishop Lefebvre remembers his father as a rigorous disciplinarian who held monarchist views in politics. During World War I the elder Lefebvre, who spoke several languages, including English and German, served as a spy, under the name Lefort, and he died as a German prisoner during the next Occupation, in 1941. Madame Lefebvre, who managed the family factory during her husband's absence in the 1914-1918 war, was jailed briefly by the Germans for refusal to cooperate with them. Both parents were conspicuously involved in works of charity, especially the care of war casualties.

Lefebvre traces his efficiency in practical manual tasks and his love of "tinkering" to the apprenticeships he served in the family factory during his vacations from school and seminary. After graduating from the Collège du Sacré-Coeur in Tourcoing, Lefebvre entered the French Seminary in Rome, where his superior was Père Le Floch, a follower of monarchist Charles Maurras whose influence in the Vatican, strong under Pope Pius X, was waning in the pontificate of Pius XI. On December 20, 1926 Pius XI issued a condemnation of Maurras and Action Française, the ultra-rightist, allegedly anti-Semitic Catholic political movement headed by Maurras.

On September 21, 1929 Lefebvre was ordained by Archbishop (later Cardinal) Achilles Lienart of Lille, France. After his ordination he was assigned to Lomme, a working-class suburb of Lille—where he is remembered by older parishioners as "a young priest of shining faith," according to José Hanu—and three years later he followed an older brother into the Holy Ghost Fathers (Les Pères du Saint Esprit). Assigned to the Holy Ghost seminary in Gabon, French Equatorial Africa, as a professor, he ultimately served as superior of the seminary, until 1947, when he was named Vicar Apostolic of Senegal, French West Africa, and consecrated a bishop by Cardinal Lienart.

In 1948 Lefebvre became Archbishop of Dakar, Senegal, and Apostolic Delegate for all of French West Africa, positions he held for eleven years—a time of great expansion for the missions under his jurisdiction. To the charge that he is *"déphasé,"* or "out of touch" with the times, that he is "still in Africa, in 1950," the Archbishop says that he must, in a sense, plead guilty, as he explained to José Hanu. His "African experience," he told Hanu, showed him "the dangers of false ecumenism" and "the misinterpretation of spiritual liberty" that causes the "sectarian fragmentation" of which "Protestants themselves complain." "For Africa, in any case, the dissolution of Catholic unity and the initiation of 'dialogue' with the Muslims and Protestants has proved disastrous," Lefebvre said. "The Church in Africa before [Vatican Council II] was respected because it dared proclaim that it was the Truth. But once the impression is given that one cult is as good as another . . . there is general dissolution of morals . . . especially concerning marriage [and] the law of priestly celibacy." He observed that while Islam expands because it has "absolute confidence in its principles," Catholics, and especially priests, "are forever questioning their faith." "That is what is happening right now, in 1977. If a Catholic bishop who deplores that situation is *déphasé,* well then, yes, I am *déphasé,*" Lefebvre said.

After his return to Europe, Lefebvre served as a member of the preparatory commission for Vatican Council II, from 1960 to 1962; as Bishop of Tulle, France, in 1962; and as Superior General of the Holy Ghost Fathers, from 1962 to 1968. In keeping with Roman Catholic custom as it applies to bishops lacking a bishopric, for purposes of rank and precedence in protocol he was named titular Archbishop of the defunct see of Synnada in Phrygia in 1962.

As a participant in Vatican Council II, Lefebvre became ever more apprehensive over the "progressive" drift of the conclave, the "dangerous course" it was taking in "confusing spiritual values and human values," in "paying too much attention to the world and too little to the heavenly city for which we are destined." He warned against liturgical reform that would open a Pandora's box of "continual change" in the texts and translations of missals, breviaries and rituals; against a "collegiality" of bishops that would weaken the primacy of the Pope; and against a new latitude in such matters as priestly and religious dress. Not only does external form affect internal attitude, he admonished, but permissiveness or deference to worldly fashion in externals can blur the distinction that Jesus demanded of his followers when he said, "You do not belong to the world. . . . I have chosen you out of the world."

Lefebvre especially objected to the council's constitution on "The Church in the Modern World," for what he saw as its failure to describe the Christian calling as special, distinct from a vague goal toward which all of humanity is moving. Shortly before the conclave ended, Lefebvre rose to declare before the full assembly of council fathers: "This constitution is not pastoral . . . evangelical . . . [or] apostolic. . . . The clothing is that of a sheep; the voice is [more] that of a wolf." He later pointed out that what he was saying was that, in his view, "the Holy Spirit had not inspired the Council, but, more likely, the Devil had."

What Lefebvre feared in the changes he saw sweeping the Church was dramatized for him when, visiting Paris during the "new left" riots that nearly toppled the government of President Charles de Gaulle in 1968, he saw long-haired young priests joining their students in the disturbances. He became convinced that a "new Ark" was needed, a seminary that would stand above the "modernist" flood. His conviction was reinforced by the young men of similar mind who came to him for guidance, aspirants to the priesthood who felt they could not receive proper sacerdotal training in the existing seminaries, "reformed" as they were becoming in accordance with the decrees and the spirit of Vatican Council II.

In 1969 Lefebvre founded the International Society of Priests of St. Pius X in Fribourg, Switzerland under the aegis of Bishop Charrière of the Diocese of Lausanne-Geneva-Fribourg. The following year he set up the society's seminary near Riddes in the canton of Valais, Switzerland, in "Ecône," a villa formerly owned by the Canons of St. Bernard. To the villa—purchased for him by local Catholics—he added other buildings gradually, as the necessary donations of money came to him, as he says, through "Providence, by the intercession of Saint Joseph."

In November 1974 two envoys from the Vatican paid a visit of inspection to Ecône, as Lefebvre later recounted: "In the course of questioning the seminarians on the subjects of married priests, the notion of Truth, and the resurrection of Our Lord Jesus Christ, they expressed [the] scandalous propositions . . . that the ordination of married people is inevitable, that the Church is not a unique guardian of [revealed] Truth, and that the resurrection of Our Lord is not a certainty!" He went on to explain, "Deeply incensed to think that it was Rome itself bringing us these errors . . . I wrote, on November 21, the now well-known 'declaration' that . . . ignited the powder keg."

The declaration of November 21, 1974, written in the heat of Lefebvre's indignation, read in part: "We adhere with all our heart, with all our soul, to Catholic Rome, guardian of the Catholic faith and the traditions necessary for maintaining that faith. . . . On the contrary, we refuse . . . to follow Rome in the neo-modernist and neo-Protestant tendency clearly manifest in Vatican Council II and the "reforms" that have issued from it. Those reforms have contributed and continue to contribute to the destruction of the Church, . . . the priesthood, . . . the Sacrifice [of the Mass] and the sacraments, [and] religious life and to naturalistic and Teilhardian teaching in the universities, the seminaries, and the catechism. . . . You cannot drastically modify the *lex orandi* [ritual, or practice] without modifying the *lex credendi* [faith, or dogma]. There is a connection between the new Mass and the new catechism, the new priesthood, the new seminaries, the new universities, the charismatic Church, the pentecostal Church—all departures from orthodoxy."

Archbishop Lefebvre concluded his historic declaration with a positive statement of his position: "Without rebellion, bitterness, or resentment, we go on with our work of training priests . . . , persuaded that we could not render a greater service to the holy Catholic Church, to the Sovereign Pontiff, and to future generations [while waiting for] the light of tradition to pierce the darkness that obscures the sky of eternal Rome."

The Vatican withdrew its canonical endorsement of the International Society of Priests of St. Pius X in May 1975. After Lefebvre ordained thirteen priests at Ecône, on June 29, 1976, the Sacred Congregation of Bishops at the request of Pope Paul VI on July 24 suspended him, forbidding him to exercise his sacerdotal or episcopal functions, including preaching, in public. The suspension affected only the legality of Lefebvre's functions, not their validity, because sacerdotal power—as well as episcopal consecration—is, according to Roman Catholic teaching, irrevocable, however illegally it may be exercised. Even such an unhappy turn of events failed to dampen the Archbishop's sense of humor. "We have," he said, twisting the facts a bit, "been forbidden to say the 'new' Mass, administer 'new' sacraments [or] teach the 'new' catechism—none of which we would want to do anyway."

In defiance of the papal proscription, Lefebvre celebrated a Latin rite Mass before 6,000 people in a sports arena in Lille, France on August 29, 1976—an event that had been scheduled before the interdict. Regarding the "political polemic" that critics detected in his sermon on that occasion, especially in his praise of the state church in Argentina, he later said: "I had just been told that the situation in that country [Argentina] had much improved and that the leaders responsible were Catholics. Very simply, I wanted to give an example of a country that had returned to Christian [social] principles. . . . I should have realized that to speak of Argentina in particular or South America in general in any but the most derogatory terms is unfashionable. Have we reached the point where anarchy and disorder are the norm, the ideal to be sought by modern states? If I had cited Solzhenitsyn, that Christian who has said nothing different, after all, than I have said, would there have been the same hue and cry about my being a 'right-wing' bishop?"

In a second act of defiance, Lefebvre celebrated a Tridentine Mass before a congregation of 2,000 people in a sports stadium in Besançon, France on September 5, 1976. Six days later he had an audience with Pope Paul VI in which, he later reported, the Pope spoke to him "like a father to a son" but out of which came nothing in the way of reconciliation. Subsequently he celebrated public Masses in Friedrichshafen, West Germany, in Paris, and in Geneva. He ordained a Benedictine monk at a monastery in Flavigny-sur-Ozerain, France on June 26, 1977 and fourteen priests and sixteen subdeacons at Ecône three days later. Writing in the New York *Post* of July 1, 1977, Malachi Martin, a former Jesuit priest, revealed that Archbishop Lefebvre had consecrated at least one bishop, "presumably as his own successor —unmistakable evidence that he intends his movement, or his church, to continue after him."

In July 1977 Lefebvre flew to the United States to consecrate a church in Dickinson, Texas that now serves as a regional headquarters of the International Society of Priests of St. Pius X. Denied permission to enter Mexico, he flew on to Bogotá, Colombia and thence to Buenos Aires, Argentina, where he celebrated Masses in private homes when police barricades prevented him from doing so in public places. Later in 1977 he returned to the United States to dedicate a headquarters of the Society in Oyster Bay Cove, Long Island.

The followers of Archbishop Lefebvre claim to number upwards of 10,000 in the United States and 50,000 in Europe. Many in the traditionalist movement as a whole cannot be counted among his followers or sympathizers because, like Father Gommar A. De Pauw, they are devoted to the Tridentine Mass but deplore Lefebvre's disobedience to the Pope. Worldwide, the International Society of Priests of St. Pius X has some twenty-five centers, including several in England and Australia. The typical facility is makeshift, such as the society's seminary in a former farmhouse in Armada, Michigan. A second American seminary is in the planning stage.

Archbishop Lefebvre is the author of *J'Accuse le concile* (I Accuse the Council, Éditions Saint-Gabriel, 1976), and his sermons, other speeches, and short writings delivered or written between 1963 and 1974 were published under the title *Un Évêque parle* (A Bishop Speaks, Morin, 1974). The periodical *Ecône: portes ouvertes* (Ecône: Open Doors) is published by the Society of St. Pius X.

Marcel Lefebvre is a frail, white-haired man of erect posture who delivers his sermons in a soft voice that sometimes cracks with emotion—when it is not edged with acid wit. He is an even-tempered man with a serene disposition and a mild manner. Also a practical man, good with his hands, fond of tinkering and efficient at housekeeping, he personally made the rounds of stores choosing the drapes, furniture, and other appointments for the Ecône seminary when it was being set up. The seminary, which now houses about 100 students (some from the United States) and a score of professors, is situated above the village of Riddes in the valley of the Rhône. The Archbishop's charisma and the loyalty it inspires are such that a corps of local men with automobiles have formed themselves into the so-called "Chauffeurs de Monseigneur," ready at a moment's notice to transport him wherever his duty calls, across Europe if necessary.

The Archbishop points out that he has "never lent [his] name to any political party whatever," that his "only cause, that of Our Lord Jesus Christ, permeates [his] every thought." Regarding his disobedience of the Pope—paradoxical in a prelate who stresses the primacy of the Pontiff over the collegiality of bishops—he says: "When the Pope is in error, he ceases to be Pope. . . . It is not us but Rome which is moving toward schism. They are the ones moving toward heresy. I am with twenty centuries of the Church and all the saints in heaven."

References: N Y Daily News p31 Jl 1 '77 por, p72 Jl 3 '77 por; N Y Post p14 Jl 2 '77 por; N Y Times p39+ N 9 '76 por; National Review 28:951 S 3 '76; Newsweek 88:90+ S 13 '76 por; Hanu, José. Vatican Encounter (1978); International Who's Who, 1977-78; Lefebvre, Marcel, with José Hanu. Non (1977); Who's Who in France, 1971-72

Lightfoot, Gordon

Nov. 17, 1938- Canadian singer; composer. Address: b. c/o Early Morning Productions Ltd., 350 Davenport Rd., Toronto, Ont., Canada

Transcending international frontiers and the tenuous boundaries between folk, country, and pop music, the Canadian singer and songwriter Gordon Lightfoot is one of the few survivors of the bardic tradition. In the more than 400 songs, including several all-time hits, that he has written since the early 1960's, Lightfoot evokes the grandeur of Canada's mountains, lakes, and rivers, the turbulence of its cities, the loneliness of the wanderers who take to its open roads, and the pangs of unrequited love. They have been recorded by such stars as Peter, Paul, and Mary, Bob Dylan, Marty Robbins, Johnny Cash, Glen Campbell, and Barbra Streisand, among others.

Lightfoot sings in an unpretentious style, in a hearty baritone, and with impeccable guitar technique. "His personality on stage is strong, virile, and yet curiously understated and modest throughout," Milton Okun wrote in a sketch about Lightfoot in his book *Something to Sing About* (Macmillan, 1968). "He seems to offer the sort of restrained self-composure so often seen in highly talented performers. He has no need to shout, because he feels he has something of musical and poetic validity to say." One of his countrymen, Jack Batten, writing in the Toronto *Globe and Mail* (May 4, 1970), ascribed a variety of roles to Lightfoot, including those of "journalist, poet, historian, humorist, short-story teller, and folksy recollector of bygone days."

Gordon Lightfoot was born on November 17, 1938 in the rural community of Orillia, Ontario, on Lake Simcoe, some sixty miles north of Toronto. Recognizing his vocal ability, his mother encouraged him to sing at Kiwanis festivals and before women's clubs even as a small boy, and at the age of nine, as a member of a junior choir, he received further encouragement from his choirmaster. While attending high school in Orillia, Lightfoot performed in plays and operettas, took part in barbershop quartets, sang and played drums in a dance band, and taught himself the rudiments of folk guitar. He also made his mark as an athlete, establishing school records in shot putting and pole vaulting.

In 1958, after graduating from high school, Lightfoot attended the Westlake College of Music in Los Angeles, where he became interested in the jazz idiom and studied composition and orchestration. For a time he made a living as a singer on demonstration records and as a writer, arranger, and producer of commercial jingles. About 1960 he became involved in folk music by listening to Pete Seeger and Bob Gibson and to his fellow Canadians Ian and Sylvia Tyson, who became his close friends. After hearing a recording of a Carnegie Hall concert by the Weavers he bought his first "decent guitar," and within a year played well enough to perform professionally, although his repertoire at that time consisted largely of songs written by others.

Back in Canada, Lightfoot worked at a variety of musical assignments, mainly in Toronto. He was a drummer in a revue, a member of a folk duo called the Two Tones and of an ensemble known as the Gino Silvi Singers, and finally a studio singer and dancer on the Canadian Broadcasting Corporation's television show *Country Hoedown,* where he earned about $100 a week. "I'm not particularly proud of my alumniship on *Country Hoedown,* but it sure taught me a lot of things," Lightfoot told an interviewer for *Canadian Composer* (September 1970). "I don't envy the kids who make it overnight—and I'll tell you why: There's no security in this business, but experience and training sure helps."

During the summer of 1963 Lightfoot was in England as host of a series of eight one-hour shows on the BBC-TV program *Country and Western.* It was during that period that he began to apply himself to writing songs, largely in the country and western vein. Returning to Canada later that year, he toured bars and coffeehouses, made solo appearances on such Canadian television programs as *Nightcap, Take Thirty,* and *A la Carte,* was featured on Oscar Brand's series *Let's Sing Out,* and had some of his material recorded by Ian and Sylvia, who helped him to gain recognition. A major influence during that period was Bob Dylan, who had drawn his main inspiration from Woody Guthrie, the balladeer of an earlier generation, and who himself was then near the beginning of his career as a folksinger and composer. "Dylan changed my whole viewpoint about songwriting," Lightfoot told Kristin Baggelaar and Donald Milton, as quoted in *Folk Music: More Than a Song* (Crowell, 1976). "After getting turned on to Bob Dylan, I started getting some identity into my own songwriting. It's not that Dylan's acceptance . . . made it easier. . . . It just changed my outlook. I'd already written about seventy-five songs by the time I first heard him on record but most of them didn't really mean anything."

During 1965 Lightfoot lived for a time in Detroit, staying at Joni and Chuck Mitchell's third-floor walkup apartment near Wayne State University, and performing at such coffeehouses as the Chess Mate. His income at that time was about $300 a week. "Detroit was a good town for exposure" and "the first major American city where you could find yourself," he has recalled, as quoted in the Detroit *News* (October 20, 1974). Although he was still largely unknown, some of his songs had already been turned into hits by other performers. His jet-age hobo song "Early Morning Rain" was recorded by Johnny Cash and by Peter, Paul and Mary, who also made his "For Lovin' Me" internationally popular, and Marty Robbins' rendition of Lightfoot's "Ribbon of Darkness" had reached the top of the country and western charts. When Lightfoot made his New York City debut at Town Hall later that year, Robert Shelton, writing in the New York *Times* (November 29, 1965), commented on his "rich, warm voice" and "dexterous guitar technique" and added: "With a little more attention to stage personality, he should become quite popular."

Having in the meantime placed himself in the hands of Albert Grossman—who also managed the careers of Bob Dylan, Ian and Sylvia, and Janis Joplin—Lightfoot was well on his way to success. Under contract to United Artists, in 1966 he produced his first LP album, *Lightfoot,* a collection of fourteen songs, eleven of which were his own compositions. That same year he was voted Canada's top folksinger, and in 1967 he was designated his country's top male vocalist. Between 1966 and 1969 Lightfoot made four additional albums for United Artists: *The Way I Feel, Did She Mention My Name?, Back Here On Earth,* and *Sunday Concert.*

Although his five United Artists albums had sold over 500,000 copies, Lightfoot felt that he could do better internationally, especially in the United States, where he was now earning over $5,000 a night for his personal appearances. Therefore, on Grossman's advice, in late 1969 he signed a contract with Warner Brothers-Seven Arts to record exclusively under its Reprise label, an arrangement that promised to bring him at least $1,000,000 over a five-year period. His albums for that company include *If You Could Read My Mind* (released earlier as *Sit Down, Young Stranger,* 1970), *Summer Side of Life* (1971), *Don Quixote* (1972), *Old Dan's Records* (1972), *Sundown* (1974), *Cold on the Shoulder* (1975), *Summertime Dream* (1976), and *Endless Wire* (1978). A cross-section of his hits was released by Reprise under the title *Gord's Gold* (1975), and United Artists issued a two-volume compilation of his earlier favorites, *The Very Best of Gordon Lightfoot* (1975). Warner Brothers Publications has brought out several books of Lightfoot's songs, complete with words, music, and guitar chords, including *Old Dan's Records* (1973), *Sundown* (1974), *Cold on the Shoulder* (1975), *Gord's Gold* (1976), and the two-volume *Gordon Lightfoot Anthology* (1971-74).

Admittedly a compulsive composer, in the mid- and late 1960's Lightfoot would at times lock himself in a hotel room for days to force his pace, but in recent years he has relaxed his work schedule. He has produced songs under a wide range of conditions: for example, in 1967, during a one-week railroad trip through England, he wrote sixteen songs, most of which he included in his *Back Here on Earth* album. Lightfoot reportedly wrote "I'm not Sayin' " while watching a hockey game on television; "For Lovin' Me" while in transit following a performance in London, Ontario; and his 1974 hit "Carefree Highway" while driving from Flagstaff to Phoenix, in Arizona.

Of the hundreds of songs that Lightfoot has written over the years, perhaps the most highly praised have been those dealing with Canada's history and natural splendors. "Lightfoot is to me what a real Canadian is. . . . I've seen parts of Canada through his eyes," the painter Robert Markle quotes one of his students as saying in *Maclean's* (December 1971). One of Lightfoot's all-time favorites is his "Canadian Railroad Trilogy," in which he tells of a time "Long before the white man, and long before the wheel,/When the dark green forest was too silent to be real." Although he denies that he is a protest singer, he has on occasion included incisive social commentary in his songs. In "Black Day in July" he recalls the 1967 Detroit riots; his "A Patriot's Dream" is an antiwar ballad; in "Ode to Big Blue" he laments the slaughter of the whale; and his epic twenty-five verse "Doomsday Song" satirizes some ills of our time, including pollution.

Other Lightfoot songs include "Christian Island" and "Too Late for Praying," which touch on religion; "Don Quixote," a tribute to one of his literary heroes; "The Pony Man," a children's song; "Alberta Bound," which contrasts the city with the countryside; "Old Dan's Records," which evokes nostalgia for the "old-time tunes"; and "Wreck of the Edmund Fitzgerald," a ballad about the 1975 sinking of an ore carrier in Lake Superior. In addition to performing his own songs, Lightfoot retains some material written by others in his repertoire, including Ewan MacColl's "The First Time," Hamilton Camp's "The Pride of Man," Bob Dylan's "Girl From the North Country," Kris Kristofferson's "Me and Bobby McGee," and Leroy Van Dyke's tongue-twisting Nashville-type ditty "The Auctioneer," as well as such traditional folksongs as the Appalachian Mountain ballad "Copper Kettle" and the Newfoundland sailor song "Harbour Le Cou."

Lightfoot's popularity was considerably enhanced by his bittersweet love ballad "If You Could Read My Mind," one of a series of songs that he wrote in the summer of 1970. By late 1974 it had sold 700,000 copies as a single and had been recorded by some sixty artists. But it was his "Sundown," a song about a "special girl," that made his name a household word in the United States. It was eventually included in the top forty of both the country and western and the rock music charts, and the *Sundown* album sold some 1,500,000 copies during its first year on the market. According to at least one perceptive critic, Geoffrey Stokes of the *Village Voice* (February 14, 1974), the sensitivity shown in "Sundown" represents a maturing on the part of Lightfoot from the adolescent "love 'em and leave 'em" male chauvinism rampant in many of his earlier songs about relations between the sexes.

During the 1960's Lightfoot frequently performed in such nightclubs and coffeehouses as the Bitter End in New York City, the Cellar Door in Washington, D.C., the Troubadour in Los Angeles, and the Riverboat in Toronto, but in recent years he has virtually eliminated club appearances. By the mid-1970's he had scaled down his earlier schedule of some seventy concert appearances a year to about fifty-five. His annual concerts in Toronto's Massey Hall, which he considers "home," are consistently sold out, as are his frequent performances on the Canadian college circuit, and his concerts in such locations as New York's Carnegie Hall and Avery Fisher Hall, and Washington's Constitution Hall. His annual concert tours take him from coast to coast in Canada and the United States, and to the British Isles, Scandinavia, Australia, and other parts of the world. Lightfoot has taken part in major folk festivals, including those at Newport, Rhode Island, Stratford, Ontario, and Saratoga, New York, and he has occasionally appeared as a guest on television programs, such as the Nashville-based *Johnny Cash Show*. In June 1976 he and other entertainers staged a televised benefit show at Toronto's Maple Leaf Gardens to raise funds for the Canadian Track and Field Association and the Canadian Olympic Association.

Usually appearing onstage in a fringed buckskin jacket, blue jeans, and boots, Lightfoot, who once referred to himself as a "cosmopolitan hick," accompanies himself with equal facility on a six-string or twelve-string guitar and is generally supported by two or more backup musicians. "I try to set up a coffeehouse atmosphere at center stage, a small intimate space where everyone's thoughts are focused on the same thing at the same time," he has explained. He designs most of his album covers and has his own publishing firm, Early Morning Productions. In March 1978 Lightfoot was presented with the Canadian recording industry's Juno award for the fifteenth time, as top folksinger. By 1976 he had eight gold albums, with sales of over 100,000 copies, to his credit, as well as one platinum album—for *Sundown*—representing sales of over 1,000,000. Canada's Medal of Service was awarded to Lightfoot in 1970 in recognition of his general contribution to the good of the country.

Gordon Lightfoot, who makes his home in a large Victorian-style house in an exclusive district of Toronto, has two children from a failed marriage that resulted, according to Jan Hodenfield of the New York *Post* (December 18, 1974), in "the largest alimony settlement ever granted in Canada." A tall, stocky, blue-eyed, blond-bearded man, Lightfoot tries to convey the rough-hewn image of a cowboy or a lumberjack. His reticence and insistence on privacy have been sometimes interpreted as shyness or arrogance. Occasionally temperamental, he stormed off the stage during an Avery Fisher Hall concert in 1974 because of imperfections in the sound system. He refuses to talk to reporters for *Rolling Stone* who once implied that he was alcoholic, although he admits that he can "put it away pretty good." Lightfoot devotes his summers to sailing his yacht, canoeing, and spending time with his children. When asked about his ambitions by Emily Fisher of the Washington *Post* (December 27, 1974), Lightfoot said: "I just want to retain my youthful outlook in everything—not grow old, congeal. Stay curious, questioning."

References: Canadian Composer p4+ S '70 pors; Macleans Mag 84:26+ D '71 por; Toronto Globe and Mail p27 Je 5 '76 por; Washington Post B p1+ D 27 '74 por; Baggelaar, Kristin and Milton, Donald. Folk Music: More Than a Song (1976); Illustrated Encyclopedia of Rock (1977); Okun, Milton. Something to Sing About (1968)

Lopez, Nancy

Jan. 6, 1957- Golfer. Address: b. c/o Mark H. McCormack Agency, 1 Erieview Plaza, Cleveland, Ohio 44114

The successor apparent to Mickey Wright as the greatest female golfer is the personable, popular Nancy Lopez, of whom Miss Wright has said: "Never in my life have I seen such control in someone so young." In the rookie year that began when she joined the Ladies Professional Golf Association in July 1977, Nancy Lopez broke the rookie earnings records for both men and women, and in 1978, her first full season on the women's tour, she clubbed into oblivion the LPGA prize money record of $150,734 set by Judy Rankin in 1976. By August 6, 1978, when she racked up her eighth victory of the season—five of the wins were consecutive, a record—her season's winnings were $153,097, and she was hoping to come close to $200,000 in total 1978 earnings. Her earnings in golf are supplemented by endorsements and commercials that come her way through the Mark H. McCormack Agency, which manages her.

Miss Lopez is a tough competitor, but she stirs no overt jealousy among the women she defeats, partly because of her warm personality and partly because they know that she is good for the tour. "There has never been anyone quite like her," veteran Carol Mann has said. "Her game is characterized by great strength, unbelievable poise, and impeccable putting. . . . Nancy has been a tremendous draw and has focused nationwide attention on the tour, which is something we all wanted. In addition to all this, she happens to be a dear person."

Of Mexican-American descent, Nancy Lopez was born in Torrance, California on January 6, 1957 to Domingo and Marina Lopez. Shortly after her birth the family moved to Roswell, New Mexico, where her father owns the East Second Street Body Shop, an auto repair shop. Her mother died in September 1977, with little warning, following an appendectomy. Miss Lopez has one sibling, an older sister, Delma (Mrs. Bernie Guevara).

Domingo Lopez became interested in golf when he was about forty, as a form of therapeutic exercise for his wife, who had chest pains. At the age of seven, Nancy was following her parents around the Roswell public course, and when she was eight her father gave her a sawed-off four wood. In less than a year she was playing rounds with him, and by the age of eleven she was beating him.

Her father began coaching her seriously, teaching her, above all, to "play happy." "I owe a lot of my mental game to my father because he always had a good attitude toward everything," Miss Lopez told James Gross of *Newsday* (May 28, 1978). "I'm very confident in myself and I love what I'm doing. I'm very relaxed when I'm playing because it's not a job. It's a game." Gross quoted Mr. Lopez: "I tell her, 'Don't be afraid. If you're behind, just give them another good round. Hit the ball and let it fly. If you blow one hole, forget it and go on to another. You can't bring the hole back.' "

Growing up, Nancy Lopez was forbidden to do the dishes or other household chores, because her father knew that "these hands are meant for golf," and for five years she wore dental braces that the family could barely afford. Domingo Lopez explained to his wife, "Mama, she got to. Our Nancy's gonna be a public figure." As Frank Deford observed in a cover story on Miss Lopez in *Sports Illustrated* (July 10, 1978), "Her father brought her up to be a champion, and her mother brought her up to be a lady; together they raised her as royalty."

Miss Lopez won her first "peewee" tournament when she was nine, by 110 strokes, and at twelve she won the first of three state women's tournaments. Playing on the otherwise all-boy golf team at Godard High School in Roswell, she ranked number one and led the team to a state championship. During her senior year she finished second in the Women's Open. To finance her traveling to tournaments, the family skimped, foregoing a new house and even a washing machine.

Outside of golf, Nancy Lopez was, by her own description, "just a normal little person." She was a Girl Scout and an all-round athlete, participating in basketball, swimming, track, gymnastics, and flag football. Her best friend was a Mexican-American, but most of her friends were Anglos and her upbringing in general was anglicized. (She speaks very little Spanish, and she does not have the accent common to many Mexican-Americans in New Mexico.) Nevertheless, she sometimes experienced discrimination, especially when she played at the exclusive country club in Roswell.

While attending the University of Tulsa (Oklahoma) on an athletic scholarship, Miss Lopez won the intercollegiate title. Dropping out at the end of her sophomore year to turn pro, she finished second in her first three professional tournaments. In those early days on the pro tour she would lie awake nights "wondering how [she] would react if ever [she] got the lead," as she recounted in the interview with Frank Deford for *Sports Illustrated*. Too often, she admitted, she played in the safe, prevailing LPGA style, trying to avoid bogeys rather than going for birdies. The turning point was the death of her mother, which, she has said, "somehow made [her] more powerful mentally." "More ready to win," in memorial tribute to her mother, she had her first victory on February 27, 1978, when she took the Bent Tree Classic at Sarasota, Florida by one stroke from Jo Ann Washam. The impetus for the victory was ironical because, according to Miss Lopez's father, she had previously been trying "too hard for Mama." In an interview with Grace Lichtenstein for the New York *Times Magazine* (July 2, 1978), Domingo Lopez explained: "As long as you try too hard in any sport you aren't going to win. As soon as she won the first one, she relaxed."

In the Sunstar tournament on the Rancho Park course in Los Angeles on March 12, 1978 Miss Lopez shot a one-under-par 71 to move ahead of Debbie Austin and score her second straight LPGA victory. The following month, she narrowly missed a third straight victory when, in the Kathryn Crosby/Honda Civic Classic in San Diego, she failed to sink a putt and lost in a sudden-death playoff to Sally Little. At Lutherville, Maryland on May 14 she won the Greater Baltimore Classic by three strokes over Donna Caponi Young, and a week later she came from four strokes behind to force a playoff and beat JoAnne Carner in the first hole of a sudden death in the Coca-Cola Classic at the Forsgate Country Club in Jamesburg, New Jersey. Shooting a women's course record 65 at the Wykagyl Country Club in New Rochelle for an 11-under-par 277, she won over JoAnne Carner in the $100,000 Golden Lights Tournament on May 29. At the King's Island course in Mason, Ohio on June 11, 1978 Miss Lopez set a tournament record in taking the LPGA championship with a 72-hole total of 275. With her 54-hole total of 214 five under par at the Locust Hill Country Club in Rochester, New York the following week she won the Bankers Trust Classic and thereby set a new record for consecutive victories on the LPGA tour, with five.

Miss Lopez's winning streak ended with a thirteenth place finish in the Lady Keystone Open in Hershey, Pennsylvania on June 25, 1978. The following week she finished second, behind Jane Blalock, in Noblesville, Indiana, and at the end of July at Indianapolis she tied for ninth with Sandra Post and Peggy Conley in the United States Women's Open, which Hollis Stacy won for the second year in a row. Resuming her winning stride, she won the European Ladies Professional Golf Association championship at Sunningdale, England by three strokes on August 6, 1978. She carded a one-over-par 73 in the final round at Sunningdale to finish with a 72-hole total of 289. Mary Dwyer finished second, with 292, and JoAnne Carner and Sally Little shared second place, with 292. After the victory, her eighth in 1978, Miss Lopez told a reporter that she was gunning for Mickey Wright's record of thirteen tournament victories in a year. "I'm really excited now," she said. "I guess I'll think about that thirteenth when I hit twelve."

A fierce competitor, Miss Lopez is at her best when she is under pressure or has to come from behind. With, or despite, her unorthodox swing, she averages 240-yard drives. "The unorthodoxy of the Lopez swing has probably been overrated, since many golf writers say nobody has a perfect swing," Grace Lichtenstein observed in her New York *Times Magazine* article. "Nancy brings her driver back nearly in slow motion, her wrists unusually thrust forward. But somewhere on the downswing the club becomes properly aligned and she follows through in a sweeping, comfortable arc that leaves the club hanging behind her back." Her weaknesses are trap shots and soft shots with a wedge. "But," Dale McNamara, her coach at the University of Tulsa, has pointed out, "she doesn't get in traps very often. Anyway, the two most important clubs in the bag are the driver and the putter and she's just magnificent with them."

"Her game can be awe-inspiring," Jeff Williams, the sports news editor of *Newsday* (July 30, 1978) wrote. "She is a marvelous putter, combining skill with aggressiveness. She is long off the tee and solid on the fairway. She is also warm and gracious in the press tent, where her smile catches the flash of the cameras and the glare of the television lights and sends a glow across the room." When Williams asked her why she was such a good putter, Miss Lopez replied: "I practise a lot. I think putting is the most difficult thing. You have to feel it. When I'm over the ball I'm thinking about my stroke, about keeping it low, keeping the backstroke slow and coming through it slow, not with a fast jab."

Except for occasional outings with good friends like Donna Young and Jo Ann Washam, Miss Lopez tends to keep to herself off the course, but on the course she is well liked and considered a good partner. She is the darling of the galleries, which are swelled with her following, known as "Nancy's Navy," in emulation of Arnold Palmer's "Arnie's Army." Her gallery is not only larger than those of other players; it is younger, shriller, and less respectful of links etiquette. The larger and louder it is, the more elated she becomes, and she especially appreciates the handsome young male groupies among her fans. "When I'm playing, I concentrate," she has said, "But when I'm practising I check out the guys. I'm a sucker for men's looks." Miss Lopez recently broke off her engagement to a young man who was in college with her, but she still intends to marry someday. At last report, she was dating Tim Melton, a Pennsylvania sportscaster.

Nancy Lopez has been described as "attractive," "vibrant," "pretty in everything she does," and "big-boned and busty." Once a plump 170, she has dieted down to 135 pounds, and—published reports of five feet seven inches notwithstanding—she is five feet four and a half inches tall. The adjective most often applied to her eyes is "laughing," so that Frank Deford, when he interviewed her for *Sports Illustrated,* found it "odd, given her happy public aspect, that her eyes are naturally mournful." Others have observed that her public poise belies a basically emotional temperament.

Golf's current idol keeps in close touch with her father and her sister. She reportedly still drives a Thunderbird, but her dream car is a Mercedes 450-SL. To relax, she watches television or goes to a movie. Raised a Roman Catholic, Miss Lopez does not attend church regularly, but she prays often and invariably wears a gold cross when she plays. She believes that her success at golf has a divine purpose: the edification of others. She told Grace Lichtenstein in the New York *Times Magazine* interview: "I feel that's why God put me on this earth. I feel like I'm making people believe in a lot of things. I'm not a Jesus person. I don't preach to anybody, but I believe there's a lot of power in the Lord."

References: N Y Daily News p92 Je 25 '78 por; N Y Sunday News mag p8+ Jl 23 '78 pors; N Y Times Mag p7+ Jl 2 '78 pors; Newsday S p10+ My 28 '78 pors; Newsweek 91:77 Je 12 '78 por; Sports Illus 49:24+ Jl 10 '78 pors; Us 2:60 Je 13 '78 por

Lucas, George

May 14, 1944- Motion picture director; writer; producer. Address: c/o Twentieth Century-Fox, 10201 W. Pico Blvd., Los Angeles, Calif. 90035

In the new wave in American cinema pioneered by Francis Ford Coppola, the most successful of the *wunderkinder* is George Lucas, the creator of *Star Wars* (1977), a technically ingenious, visually stunning space fantasy that has broken all box-office records and attracted a large cult following. Lucas who was known as "the kid" to his associates until he began wearing a beard, is typical of the current breed of post-Hollywood, or post-studio, film maker in that he grew up with television as well as movies, was trained academically in film, and works in cooperation rather than competition with other directors. His first feature film, *THX 1138* (1971), was described by him as a "science-fiction documentary." That film, a chilling look at a dehumanized world, seemingly futuristic but actually a grim extension of our own drug-oriented society, was also the first made under the auspices of American Zoetrope, Francis Ford Coppola's company. Out of American Zoetrope too came the surprise hit of 1973, *American Graffiti,* a slice of nostalgia evoking the writer-director's own adolescence.

With *Star Wars,* his third feature, Lucas is being acclaimed a master among screen craftsmen, and his swashbuckling intergalactic adventure story is already being acknowledged as a classic of its genre. That genre is hard to define, falling as it does between science fiction and the fairy tale, between the tradition of *2001: A Space Odyssey* and that of *The Wizard of Oz.* The much talked about market for wholesome family screen fare may be exaggerated, as distributors complain, but certainly *Star Wars* is a strong indication of the trend away from the cynical and the sordid, toward films that excite a sense of wonder. The movie won Oscars for film editing, art direction, costume design, original score, visual effects, and sound and a special Oscar for sound effect editing.

George Lucas was born on May 14, 1944 in Modesto, California. The son of a retail merchant of office equipment who was also a spare-time farmer, he was raised on his father's walnut ranch just outside Modesto. Growing up, he aspired to become a motor racer and spent much of his time tinkering with automobiles. As an adolescent who, as he says, "barely squeaked through high school," he "cruised" McHenry Avenue in Modesto, with his car radio blaring pop tunes full blast, in a Fiat that he had souped up for racing. He changed his mind about a racing career when, a few days before his graduation from high school, a near-fatal accident in the Fiat crushed his lungs and sent him to the hospital for three months.

Lucas' second career choice was art, but he could not persuade his parents to send him to art school. As a social-science major at Modesto Junior College, he became interested in cinematography and began experimenting with an 8-mm. camera owned by a friend. "We did trick animation, ran our movies backwards," he told Paul D. Zimmerman of *Newsweek* (May 3, 1971). "We were so excited, like a pair of aborigines with some new machine."

While racing sports cars, Lucas met cinematographer Haskell Wexler, who encouraged his film making and helped him gain admission to the University of Southern California's film department. At USC he made a *cinéma vérité* science-fiction short based on his realization that "we were already living in the future that everybody was talking and writing about in the 1930's—you know, rockets, television, glass skyscrapers, the world of the comics and 1984." The imaginative documentary, titled *THX-1138:4EB,* won first prize at the Third National Student Film Festival, among other awards.

Regardless of whether or not he was "exploitative," as some have charged, director Roger Corman earned a claim to the title of progenitor of the new wave of American film makers by giving students like Gary Kurtz (who would later produce *American Graffiti* and *Star Wars)* and Francis Ford Coppola the opportunity to work for him for little or no pay and thus gain experience. In his turn, Coppola took an interest in the more promising students at USC. Especially impressed with Lucas, he allowed him to sit in on the shooting of *Finian's Rainbow* (Warner Brothers, 1968) and to shoot a short documentary of Coppola directing *The Rain People* (Warner Brothers, 1969). Lucas did similar documentation of Carl Foreman and J. Lee Thompson making *McKenna's Gold* (Columbia, 1969).

Coppola was instrumental in getting Warner Brothers to sign Lucas to a contract to add a plot to the electronic wizardry of his short *THX 1138:4EB* and develop it into the full-length feature *THX 1138,* set in a grim twenty-fifth century world in which human beings, having desolated the face of the earth, live underground in a robotized society where numbers have replaced names. The expanded script was written by Lucas in collaboration with Walter Murch, who also worked on the sound. Cast in the title role was Robert Duvall, as a defector from the subterranean Orwellian social system, wanted for the crimes of love, sex, and "drug evasion." The film was shot on location in Los Angeles, and the special effects, editing, mixing, and other post-production work was done at American Zoetrope, the super-modern facility Coppola had just set up in a warehouse in San Francisco.

Released tardily and halfheartedly, with little publicity, by Warner Brothers in 1971, *THX 1138* disappointed some critics who, apparently expecting the usual science-fiction formula, dismissed it as "tedious" or "fleshless." But most of them recognized Lucas' sophistication and brilliance, and even the most negative tended to acknowledge his philosophical insight and technical legerdemain. Kenneth Turan of the Washington *Post* (April 17, 1971) found Lucas' strength to reside in "a very personal vision" strong enough to "transform what may sound like a collection of cheap effects into a visually gratifying science-fiction film." Arthur Knight of the *Saturday Review* (April 3, 1971) suspected, correctly, that in surrounding "pitiful zombies" with "stunning visuals and sounds," Lucas was trying to tell us of "the horror that . . . already surrounds us." The reviewer for *Newsweek* (March 29, 1971) classed *THX 1138* as "an extremely professional first film" by "a child of our age, fascinated by the beauty of technology and aware of its dehumanizing potential."

THX 1138 gave Lucas the reputation within the film industry of being, as he says, a "cold, science-fiction, underground, surrealistic, arty, steel-veined guy." Dispelling that image was his second feature film, *American Graffiti,* based on his own coming-of-age in Modesto. "It all happened to me, but I sort of glamorized it . . . ," he told Judy Klemesrud in an interview for an article in the New York *Times* (October 7, 1973). "I went through all that stuff, drove the cars, bought liquor, chased girls. I think a lot of people do, which is the whole idea behind the title—a very American experience. I started out as Terry the Toad, but then I went on to be John Milner, the local drag race champion, and then I became Curt Henderson, the intellectual who goes off to college. They were all composite characters." He said that he intended the movie to be about "the end of a political era, a sociological era, a rock era . . . a warm, secure, uninvolved life."

Specifically, *American Graffiti* focuses on one summer night, in 1962, in the lives of four teenagers who have just graduated from high school. The quartet of adolescents was played by Richard Dreyfuss, Ronny Howard, Paul Le Mat, and Charlie Martin Smith, with support from the then equally unknown Cindy Williams and Suzanne Somers. Written by Lucas in collaboration with Gloria Katz and Willard Huyck, it was produced by Gary Kurtz and Francis Ford Coppola (who lent his name to the production in order to attract major studio backing). As a special favor to his protégé, Haskell Wexler collaborated on the color photography, which was done with lighting described by the writer-director as "jukebox" (and by his wife, facetiously, as "ugly").

Shot on location in Modesto in twenty-eight days on a shoestring budget of $780,000—much of which went to pay for the rights to the period pop songs that fill the soundtrack—*American Graffiti* became a smash hit soon after its release by Universal Pictures in June 1973, and within two years it grossed a total of $50,000,000. Critics greeted it, almost without exception, with raves, and in some instances with heartfelt emotion. Writing in the New York *Times* (December 2, 1973), Aljean Harmetz observed that, despite its "charm and gentle humor," it is a "melancholy" film, "a metaphor for what we once had and lost." Writing in the same newspaper (August 5, 1973), Stephen Farber noted the "sympathy, affection, and thorough understanding" with which Lucas "brings the past alive" and hailed *American Graffiti* as "a work of lasting art." The Academy of Motion Picture Arts and Sciences nominated *American Graffiti* for five awards, including those for best picture, best director, and best screenplay of 1973. The picture also won the Golden Globe Award for best motion picture comedy and the New York Film Critics and National Society of Film Critics awards for best screenplay.

As soon as he saw *American Graffiti,* Alan Ladd Jr., then vice-president in charge of creative affairs at Twentieth Century-Fox, where he is now president, contracted Lucas to go ahead with *Star Wars,* at that time still just an idea in Lucas' head. The contract called for a budget of $8,500,000, a ridiculously low figure in view of the ambitiousness of the project. (As it turned out, the film went only about $1,000,000 over budget.)

Lucas says that he made *American Graffiti* for sixteen-year-olds and *Star Wars* "for kids of all ages." Deploring the fact that "nobody except Disney makes movies for young people anymore," so that "all they've got is Kojak and Dirty Harry," he delved back into "Flash Gordon" and the other comics, books, films, and television shows that fed his own fantasy life as a child, with a view to opening "up the whole realm of space" for a new generation. "Science fiction is okay, but it got so involved with science that it forgot the sense of adventure . . . ," he told Donald Godard in an interview for an article in the New York *Times* (September 12, 1976). "I want to give young people some sort of faraway exotic environment for their imaginations to run around in."

Writing eight hours a day for three years, George Lucas came up with a screenplay set "a long time ago in a galaxy far, far away." The story opens with the capture of Princess Leia Organa by agents of the evil Galactic Empire, which has destroyed her planet, Alderaan, in its campaign to wipe out all vestiges of resistance in the galaxy. By imperial starship she is taken to the Empire's dreaded Death Star, a moon-sized space station where she is imprisoned and interrogated by Grand Moff Tarkin (Peter Cushing) and the sinister space magician Darth Vader, Dark Lord of the Sith (played under black armor by David Prowse), regarding the pirated plans of the Death Star, which, in rebel hands, could make the otherwise impregnable command station vulnerable. Those blueprints have been entrusted by the Princess to the squat, ambulatory computer "droid" R2-D2 (Artoo-Detoo, manned by three-foot-eight-inch-tall Kenny Baker), who, along with his companion "droid," the prissy, fussy robot C3-PO (See-Threepio, played in tin-man fashion by Anthony Daniels), gives the movie much of its campy humor.

As the plot unfolds, the two droids travel to the desert planet of Tatooine, where, by happy chance, the cybernetic pair contact young rustic Luke Skywalker (Mark Hamill), and the man for whom the Princess' message was intended, wise old wizard-warrior

Ben Obi-Wan Kenobi (Alec Guinness), who possesses, or is in touch with, the mysterious, all-pervasive power known as "the Force." After numerous encounters with strange creatures including a bar full of partying and brawling alien freaks, Luke and Ben take off with the droids just in the nick of time in the Millenium Falcon, a Correllian pirate starship, a converted freighter, piloted by soldier-of-fortune Han Solo (Harrison Ford) and his simian-like "Wookie" copilot Chewbacca (Peter Mayhew). In the end the Princess is rescued and in a spectacular climactic space "dogfight" the rebels wipe out the villains, except for Darth Vader, who escapes—presumably to fight again in the first of the planned sequels to *Star Wars*.

Star Wars was shot on location in Panavision and Technicolor in Tunisia and on forty-five sets spread over eleven sound stages in England. Most of the shooting in England was done at the EMI Elstree Studios in Borehamwood, just outside of London, where production designer John Barry, following Lucas' strict instructions, gave the props and sets of other planets, caves, starships, and so on, a "lived in" look, a departure from the shiny, sanitized, and artificial effect traditional in science-fiction films. For the huge rebel hangar scene, with its squadron of X-wing and Y-wing fighter craft, the set had to be filmed on the largest sound stage in Europe, at Shepperton Studios in Middlesex. The stunning, realistic special photographic effects were done by the Industrial Light and Magic Corporation, a complete in-house system set up especially for the purpose by John Dykstra in a warehouse in Van Nuys, California. Original sound effects for the galactic languages, robots, and the like were collected or created by Ben Burtt. The original music was recorded by the London Symphony Orchestra, conducted by John Williams, who wrote the score, and the elaborate stereo soundtrack was mixed at the Samuel Goldwyn Studios in Hollywood in the high-fidelity Dolby System.

Produced by Gary Kurtz and Lucasfilm Ltd., *Star Wars* was released by Twentieth Century-Fox in May 1977. The enthusiastic response of critics and public was immediate and sweeping, cutting across most of the usual barriers of taste, opinion, and age. Newspapers, trade papers, newsweeklies, and intellectual journals of opinion carried notices freighted with adjectives like "magnificent," "grand," "glorious," and "exhilirating" and with phrases like "excellence of construction," "thrilling narration," and "rip-roaring good story." Reviewers described it as a combination of *The Wizard of Oz,* science-fiction comics, the swashbucklers, westerns, and air-battle movies of the 1930's and 1940's, and even *Sir Gawain and the Green Knight*. It is "a remarkable confection," the critic for *Time* (May 30, 1977) wrote, "a subliminal history of the movies wrapped in a riveting tale of suspense and adventure, ornamented with some of the most ingenious special effects ever contrived for film." In the *National Review* David Brudnoy (July 22, 1977) observed that the movie's "visual splendor" and even its "utterly ludicrous dialogue" serve to flesh out the "two-dimensionality" of the lead characters. Brudnoy ended his review: "*Star Wars* is as old-fashioned and uplifting as Faith and Love, as familiar as Superman, and as bright and new as next spring."

Star Wars is expected to gross $300,000,000, and the toys, books, and other spinoffs it is generating are expected to bring in an additional $200,000,000. Lucas Film Ltd., whose long-term share will be an estimated $40,000,000, has set up four subsidiary corporations: the Star Wars Corporation, which will make the film sequels; Medway Productions, under the aegis of which other films will be made or released, including the complete *American Graffiti,* which is five important minutes longer than the version released by Universal in 1973; a special-effects company, Sprocket Systems Inc.; and Black Falcon Ltd., for handling spinoffs. In addition, Lucas has invested in Super-snipe, a Manhattan art gallery specializing in comic book art.

Outside of his own work, Lucas is helping Francis Ford Coppola in the cutting of his sprawling Vietnam war epic "Apocalypse Now." Lucas, Coppola, Steven Spielberg, John Milius, and Martin Scorsese form a mutually supportive group, often trading scripts and percentages of interest in their films with each other. A friend of the five told an interviewer for *Time* (May 30, 1977): "They all seem to have had repressed childhoods of one form or another. Marty Scorsese is asthmatic. Francis Coppola had polio when he was a child, and Steve Spielberg is slight of build, like George. They all work out their fantasies on film." Lucas was quoted as describing himself as "inherently conservative," the "opposite" of Coppola, who is "impulsive, always on the edge of trouble."

An admitted introvert, Lucas found overseeing 900 employees in the making of *Star Wars* "excruciating," and he is turning over the direction of the first of the sequels to Irvin Kershner. He makes movies because he likes to make them, he says, but his intensity as an *auteur* is such that he gets a bad cold and cough whenever he directs. Some describe his demeanor on the set as "dictatorial," "Machiavellian," and "hardheaded," but his anger is usually expressed not by an explosion of words but by brooding silence. "But if he's wrong," John Dykstra reports, "he'll change his mind rather than say, 'I'm the director, I've made a decision, and that's it.' " Dykstra says he admires in Lucas his singlemindedness, his perfectionism, his sensibility, and his "gift for popular narrative."

George Lucas and Marcia (Griffin) Lucas, a film editor whose credits include *Star Wars* and *Taxi Driver*, met when they were working as editors on a documentary film for the United States Information Agency. They were married in 1969. The Lucases live in a Victorian house surrounded by trees on a hill in a suburb of San Francisco. Among the house's furnishings is Lucas' 1941 Wurlitzer jukebox, on which he plays selections from his collection of 78-rpm records. The couple's social life is confined to a relatively small circle, away from the Malibu and Beverly Hills crowd. For recreation Lucas enjoys "flicking out" in movie theatres—as opposed to exhibition rooms—and plays an occasional game of tennis.

George Lucas is a short man with thick, dark, wavy hair, horned-rim glasses, and a wardrobe consisting largely of blue jeans, corduroys, sweaters, sneakers, and the like. His religious belief, developed when he was recuperating from his automobile accident, is a faith roughly the same as the concept of "the Force" articulated in *Star Wars*. Lucas feels that there is "a destiny of sorts" about the commercial success of his work. "I'm trying to set up an alternative film making that allows me to do what I want, within certain parameters. We're trying to make a company that will respect the personality and individuality of film makers."

References: N Y Times II p1+ O 7 '73 por, II p15 S 12 '76; Newsweek 77:50+ My 3 '71 por; People 8:64 Jl 18 '77 por; 8:104+ Ja 2 '78 pors; Sat R/World 1:40+ F 23 '74 por; Time 109:61 My 30 '77 por, 111:82 Mr 6 '78 por

---

Lyle, Sparky

July 22, 1944- Baseball player. Address: b. Texas Rangers, Arlington Stadium, 1500 Copeland Rd., Arlington, Tex. 76011

Among active relief hurlers, baseball's increasingly respected specialists in "firefighting," none has been more consistently successful than Sparky Lyle. With the New York Yankees, Lyle was the first reliever to win the Cy Young Award in the American League, in 1977. (The only previous relief artist to win the award was a National Leaguer, Mike Marshall, in 1974.) After a mediocre start in the minor leagues, Lyle developed a moderate fastball and, more important, a dreaded slider, a pitch that breaks sharply low and away from lefthanded batters and low and in to righthanders. With that simple but overpowering arsenal the insouciant, unflappable southpaw earned a bullpen position with the Boston Red Sox in 1967, and between 1972 and 1978 he used it to protect threatened leads for the Yankees.

Recognition as perhaps the most valuable player on the New York club in the 1970's did not come to Lyle until 1977, when his dramatic rescues of other pitchers' victories, usually in late-inning crises, made possible the winning of the American League pennant and the world championship. As of the end of the 1977 season, Lyle had made a record 621 major-league appearances on the mound without a single start, and his 185 "saves" were the most accumulated by any relief pitcher since the save system was initiated in major-league statistics in 1969. His total eleven-year major-league statistics were a staggering 201 saves, a dazzling 70-54 record, and a fine 2.44 earned-run average. In 1978, Lyle, complaining that he was then being under-employed by the Yankees, was traded to the Texas Rangers.

Albert Walter Lyle was born in Du Bois, Pennsylvania on July 22, 1944, the first of the three children of Albert Lyle, a house remodeling contractor, and Margaret Lyle. Lyle, who was nicknamed "Sparky" by his father, grew up in Reynoldsville, Pennsylvania, where he played high school basketball and football. (The school had no baseball team.) The University of Colorado offered him a football scholarship, but he turned it down, because, as he has said, he "hated school."

Lyle began pitching early in childhood, and his mother often served as his catcher until, when he was eleven, he developed a curve ball. During his school years Lyle played sandlot ball, and after graduating from high school, while working as a manual laborer at the Jackson China Company in Reynoldsville, he pitched for an American Legion team. Although he had no fastball to speak of at that time, he had a reputation as a strikeout king, one who retired as many as thirty-one batters in a single game. (That game went seventeen innings.) Signed by the Baltimore Orioles, he played for Bluefield and Fox Cities in the Baltimore farm system in 1964, winning six games and losing three. Drafted by the Boston Red Sox in 1965, he was assigned successively to Boston clubs in Winston-Salem, Pittsfield, and Toronto, clubs for which he won a total of eleven games, lost a total of nine, and brought his minor-league earned run average to 3.25.

During his years in the minors Lyle taught himself the slider, on the advice of former Boston slugger Ted Williams, who told him that he had found it the most difficult pitch to hit. As quoted by Steve Jacobson in *Newsday* (September 19, 1976), Lyle has recalled the night in Pittsfield when, after long experimentation, the knack for the slider finally came to him, as he was lying in bed with a baseball in his hand: "It was three A.M. and suddenly it came to me. I went outside and threw against the wall of the tavern next door by the street lights. It never broke then like it does now, but I had it."

Called up to Boston in the midst of the 1967 season, Lyle pitched in twenty-three games and posted an ERA of 2.30 to help the Red Sox win the American League pennant. Finishing the season with a strained ligament in his pitching arm, he did not play in the 1967 World Series, which the Red Sox lost to the St. Louis Cardinals. After posting win-loss marks of 6-1 in 1968 and 8-3 in 1969, he had his least impressive major-league season in 1970, when he won one game, lost seven, and allowed an average of 3.90 runs per game. In 1971 he snapped back, racking up six wins, as against four losses, and sixteen saves.

After Eddie Kasko replaced Dick Williams as manager of the Red Sox, the Boston club came to rely on Bill Lee more than Lyle for relief work, and Lyle sought out of the team. Meanwhile, Ralph Houk, then manager of the New York Yankees, had been eyeing Lyle covetously, as Houk later recounted: "He could handle both left and right handed hitters, which is most important for a reliever. And he had that look about him, like he just knew he could get you out. I was crazy about him."

The Yankees succeeded in obtaining Lyle in March 1972, when the Red Sox, desperate for a first baseman, traded him for Danny Cater. Responding to Ralph Houk's confidence in him and dependence on him, and inspired by the opportunity to pitch in Yankee Stadium, regarded by him since childhood as a hallowed site, Lyle came into his own in New York in 1972, winning nine games, losing five, allowing only 1.92 runs per game, and setting a New American League record for saves, with thirty-five. The Yankees won no title that year, but, thanks to Lyle, they were pennant contenders for the first time in eight years.

After a less successful season in 1973 (5-9 in fifty-one games, with twenty-seven saves and a 2.51 ERA), Lyle entered into a protracted contract dispute with the Yankees, who wanted to cut his salary from $75,000 to $65,000. He held out until the end of the 1974 season, in which he strengthened his bargaining position with club records of sixty-six relief appearances, fifty-nine games finished, a 9-3 win-loss tally, and a stunning 1.66 ERA. On October 2, 1974 Yankee owner George Steinbrenner capitulated, and Lyle was signed to a retroactive contract of $87,500 for 1974 and a contract of $93,000 for 1975.

Lyle slumped in 1975, recording only six saves and five victories, as against seven defeats and an ERA of 3.13 in forty-nine appearances. In 1976 he was back in top form, leading the American League with twenty-three saves and bringing his lifetime total to 175, a new record. In sixty-four trips to the mound he had a 7-8 record and a 2.26 ERA. In the 1976 playoffs, in which the Yankees defeated the Kansas City Royals, he allowed no runs in one inning pitched, and in two appearances against the Cincinnati Reds in the World Series, totalling two and two-thirds innings, he struck out three, gave up one hit and no walks, and allowed no runs. The Reds won the series in four straight games.

In 1977 Lyle reached career highs with seventy-two appearances—a new record—130 innings pitched, and thirteen wins, as against five losses, and he racked up twenty-six saves and a league-leading 2.17 ERA. The average would have been 1.79 were it not for one bad day, September 15, when he allowed Boston six runs in one and one-third innings. In the playoffs against Kansas City he pitched in four of the five games and, with the pennant on the line, he won the final two. In the fourth he threw five and one-third innings of two-hit ball, and in the decisive fifth game he pitched a scoreless inning and a third to gain credit for the victory. In the World Series opener against the Los Angeles Dodgers he pitched three and two-thirds innings, giving up a hit that tied the game in the ninth and then getting eleven straight outs, as the Yankees won. They went on to take the series, four games to two.

Before the 1977 season Lyle had signed a three-year contract, originally estimated at $375,000 and later raised to a reported $500,000. At the end of the 1977 season George Steinbrenner gave him a $20,000 bonus, but

Lyle received nothing additional after winning the CY Young Award, on October 26, 1977. "The only thing the Yankees have done for me since I won the award," he complained to a reporter in February 1978, "is sign two new relief pitchers." Although Lyle is chronically late for spring training, his tardiness in arriving at Fort Lauderdale, Florida in February 1978 was interpreted as a protest against Steinbrenner paying him only half the money he was putting out for the new, younger relievers Rich Gossage and Rawly Eastwick. Actually, Lyle was more worried about there being enough work to go around in the Yankee bullpen. He needs to work regularly to stay tuned up, as he has pointed out in numerous interviews, and besides, at thirty-three, he didn't want to waste his "last three or four years of production just sitting out there." He said he would rather be traded than idle.

When Lyle finally arrived in Fort Lauderdale on February 24, 1978, George Steinbrenner had a 100-piece band, along with 28 pom-pom girls, greet him at the airport playing "Pomp and Circumstance," the song the Yankee Stadium organist always plays as Lyle strides to the mound for his relief chores. The reception did little to appease Lyle, and the financial argument between him and the Yankee front office continued into the beginning of the 1978 season. But as for Sparky's concern about possible idleness in the bullpen, Manager Billy Martin's assurances that he would see plenty of action seemed borne out in the early weeks of the season. By the second week in May he had pitched in ten games, the number in which he had worked over a similar span the previous year. But as the season progressed, Martin and his successor, Bob Lemon, let Lyle languish in the bullpen, calling on him mostly for long relief. He ended the season with a 9-3 record, but he had only nine saves and his ERA was 3.47. Lyle was happy to be traded to the Texas Rangers, on November 10, 1978.

Lyle is a simple-spoken, unassuming man who says he never aspired to be a starting pitcher. He loves his work-under-pressure and does not let the tumultuous reception he receives when called to the mound distract him from it. Nor does he allow his concentration or confidence to be undermined by thoughts about yesterday's failures or achievements. His motto is, "Past performance means nothing. Only today's game counts." "When I walk across that white line," he told Joseph Durso in an interview for the New York *Times* (July 14, 1972), "I have no friends, only enemies. I throw a slider, fastball, curve, and letup, and I don't finesse them. I'm cool and I guess I'm calculating. And I don't think I ever lost a night's sleep over a ball game or an unpaid bill." Ralph Houk once said of Lyle, "He's got the ideal disposition for a relief pitcher. Nothing scares him." And Ron Swoboda has observed, "He is the only pitcher I ever saw who never complained that his arm was stiff after he pitched a lot."

On April 29, 1977 Sparky Lyle married Mary Fontaine Massey. By a previous marriage, to Judy Ann Fusco, Lyle has a son, Dane Lyle. The Texas reliever is a sturdy, mustachioed man seldom seen on the field without a large wad of chewing tobacco in his left cheek. Six feet one inch tall, he weighs a little over 200 pounds when he is in condition and up to 225 when he isn't. Among the many fines he has received was one for reporting to spring training overweight.

The Texas lefthander has described himself as "aggressive" on the mound and "gentle" in private life. Lyle's favorite recreations include photography, collecting old canes, driving his 1925 Maxwell, and listening to jazz, and one of his regrets is that he cannot play a musical instrument. Blessed with a sly, irrepressible sense of humor, he never takes himself too seriously, and he is notorious for his locker room pranks, which have included sitting naked on a birthday cake and showing up in a body cast, feigning injury in an accident. Lyle periodically returns to Reynoldsville to see his old buddies there and keep his success in perspective. He is happy that baseball rescued him from "that rut," but, with his live-for-now philosophy, he would probably accept a return to the boondocks with equanimity. Bob Lemon, who succeeded Billy Martin as manager of the Yankees in 1978, has said, "If something happened, Sparky would be the same person. He wouldn't groan and moan. He would have a lot of wonderful memories. He wouldn't second-guess himself. He's smelled the flowers."

References: N Y Daily News p55 O 14 '77; Newsday p12+ S 19 '76 pors; N Y Times p36 Ag 14 '72; Baseball Register, 1976; Who's Who in Baseball, 1978; Who's Who in Professional Baseball

---

McBride, Lloyd

Mar. 9, 1916- Labor union official. Address: b. United Steelworkers of America, Five Gateway Center, Pittsburgh, Pa. 15222

In a referendum that followed one of the most bitter and highly publicized campaigns in recent American labor history, the St. Louis union leader Lloyd McBride was chosen to be installed as international president of the

Lloyd McBride

United Steelworkers of America in June 1977, succeeding the retiring I. W. Abel. Although they reflected the anxious time that the steel industry was undergoing, the strife and publicity attending the campaign sharply contrasted with the career of a man who steadily rose through the ranks of the USW by election to a series of progressively more responsible offices without fanfare and without a challenge. McBride had served the USW, of which he was a pioneering organizer, as a local union president, staff representative, subdistrict director, and finally district director, developing a reputation as an able administrator and a skilled negotiator. With its 1,400,000 members in 5,301 locals in the United States and Canada, the USW is the largest and one of the most powerful of the AFL-CIO's 109 affiliates.

Lloyd McBride was born in Farmington, Missouri on March 9, 1916 and has lived and worked most of his life in St. Louis, to which his family moved when he was four years old. His father was employed as a painter at a steel fabricating plant there, the Foster Brothers Manufacturing Company, but early in the Depression, in 1930, he lost his 75-cents-an-hour job. Fourteen-year-old Lloyd McBride, who had just graduated from Yeatman Junior High, felt obliged to leave school and go to work to contribute to the support of the family. The same plant that had laid off his father hired him, but at 25 cents an hour. "This was the sort of indignity that workingmen had to endure in those days," he has recalled.

Low wages and hard working conditions made McBride eager to be among the first at Foster Brothers to join the Steel Workers Organizing Committee in 1936. Once the plant was organized, he served on the committee that negotiated the first contract for the newly chartered Local 1295. Because, however, the contract was "kind of weak," as McBride remembers it, Local 1295 called a strike in 1937 for an improved contract. During the first week he helped to organize a sitdown among the workers to discourage strikebreakers. Ordered in on the eighth day, the St. Louis police surrounded the building, menacing the strikers with blackjacks. To avoid bloodshed, the strikers vacated the plant, but the strike continued for seven more weeks before an agreement was reached. By that time the office of union president had become vacant.

The members of Local 1295 thereupon turned to McBride, then twenty-two, to head their union, electing him president by acclamation. His acceptance of heavy responsibilities in service to the labor movement prevented him from resuming his formal education, but gave him abundant opportunity to develop his aptitude for leadership. After becoming president of Local 1295, he served as a volunteer organizer of the Steel Workers Organizing Committee until 1940, when its chairman, Philip Murray, appointed him staff representative and organizer. Murray was also president of the Congress of Industrial Organizations, which in 1942 chartered the union that grew out of the Steel Workers Organizing Committee, the United Steelworkers of America. During that year McBride, who had been serving since 1940 as president of the St. Louis Industrial Union Council of the CIO, was elected president of the CIO Industrial Union Council for the state of Missouri.

During World War II, in 1944, McBride resigned from the union council to enter the United States Navy. Released after two years of military duty, he returned to the Steelworkers to be assigned as union staff representative in Granite City, Illinois, just across the Mississippi River from his St. Louis home. In 1958 he moved up to the post of subdistrict director at the same office, providing for a membership that included workers in basic steel, foundries, and fabrication shops. He achieved a major advance in the United Steelworkers hierarchy with his election in 1965 as director of District 34, which has headquarters in St. Louis and covers the southern part of Illinois and all of Missouri, Kansas, Nebraska, and Iowa.

As district director McBride gained the reputation of being an aggressive organizer and recruiter who deserves much of the credit for increasing the district's membership by 33 percent over his twelve-year tenure, to its present total of some 36,000 workers in diverse industries, despite the fact that during the same period several major plants were closed. Union members and steel company officials alike have described McBride as a tough administrator and a determined bargainer. During some of the years that he held the post of district director, he served as secretary and later chairman of basic steel negotiations with Armco Steel Corporation and chairman of the multiplant bargaining unit with the American Steel Foundries.

When I. W. Abel became president of the United Steelworkers in 1965, only a handful of local unionists took part in bargaining and ratification of contracts. Having pledged to reform the bargaining process and give members a voice in important decisions, in 1966 Abel established industry conferences for basic steel, nonferrous metals, containers, and aluminum. Eventually, nineteen conferences were organized to take into account all areas of USW activity. McBride served as chairman of two of the conferences: the Foundry and Forgings Industry Conference and the Lead Workers Conference. He also acquired some experience in international labor relations as a delegate to meetings of the International Metalworkers Federation in Geneva, Switzerland.

Few union elections in recent years have attracted as much national attention as the 1977 campaign for the United Steelworkers presidency. McBride's involvement began three years earlier when several fellow members of the USW executive board urged him to consider running for the post to be vacated upon the mandatory retirement of President Abel. Having never aspired to such a high office, McBride hesitated for some time. He later explained his feelings to Lee Dembart of the New York *Times* (February 11, 1977): "How could a person who went to work at 14 ever dream of becoming president of our union?" A bid for the presidency, moreover, would mean venturing into the limelight after being accustomed for years to remaining largely behind the scenes in his work for the betterment of his district members. He was also aware that he lacked the colorfulness that often makes a candidate popular. "I haven't attempted to make myself a character or to create a picture of being a public figure," Dembart quoted him as saying. "You can't be flamboyant and at the same time deal responsibly with the problems with the union."

McBride's candidacy, formally announced in October 1975, did not have the immediate approval of all other members of the USW's "official family." Some hoped to become candidates themselves, and although united in their desire to thwart the rumored candidacy of Edward Sadlowski, director of District 31 with headquarters in Chicago, they disagreed as to who could best accomplish that end. At the Steelworkers' biennial convention in the summer of 1976, the last significant challenger to McBride's candidacy, USW's international vice-president, John S. Johns, stepped aside, leaving the way open for Abel to back a "unity slate," headed by McBride, for the top USW executive posts. As expected, Sadlowski, the insurgent candidate, opened his campaign shortly afterward.

To many observers, the Steelworkers' race was crucial not only to the future of the steel industry, but also to the character of the American labor movement in the years ahead. A. H. Raskin of the New York *Times* (September 27, 1976) felt the election would serve as a barometer of worker sentiment. He described the contest as a power struggle between younger, more rebellious union members determined to stop the "collaborationist" trend and return labor to the confrontationist tactics of the 1930's and older trade unionists who supported "responsible," "mature" unionism. Partly because of Abel's tacit endorsement, McBride was viewed as the establishment candidate. Sadlowski accused him of practising "tuxedo unionism" and of being unresponsive to the needs and interests of the rank and file. For his part, McBride assailed Sadlowski as an "irresponsible" radical who would upset the stable labor-management relations that had been achieved in the steel industry and a man whose support was based not on his accomplishments but on his appeal to outsiders, to "limousine liberals."

Of more importance to the business community and to government officials than the ideology involved was the potential impact of the election on the conduct of labor-management relations in the steel industry. The basic steel contract, which the USW negotiated with the ten major steel companies on an industry-wide basis, was due to expire in 1977. Bargaining in basic steel is governed by the terms of the Experimental Negotiating Agreement, a no-strike agreement first used in 1974. Considered by Abel to be the crowning achievement of his career, that agreement mandated binding arbitration for the settlement of unresolved contract issues, thereby eliminating the threat of strikes that had contributed to boom-bust cycles in the steel industry in the 1960's. McBride and Sadlowski differed fundamentally on the Experimental Negotiating Agreement, which McBride intended to support as long as he found that it served the best interests of the members, while Sadlowski argued for the strike as labor's most important weapon.

The two candidates were also at odds over extending the democratic process within the union, particularly in regard to the question of rank-and-file ratification of the steel contract. The USW permits membership ratification in many of its industrial jurisdictions, but in basic steel a contract is voted on by the 600-member Steel Industry Conference. Sadlowski vowed to change the procedure, but McBride asserted that membership ratification would destroy the union's ability to negotiate on an industry-wide basis.

From the onset of the contest the brash, articulate, and somewhat fiery Sadlowski attracted more attention than his opponent. But although undramatic in his campaign style, McBride had the advantage of a reputation for militancy. A high-ranking USW staff member told a reporter for *Business Week* (January 24, 1977), "Lloyd may be a terrible candidate, but he might become the gutsiest president we've ever had." His record of accomplishment as a diligent leader proved more persuasive than Sadlowski's assets. Some 500,000 steelworkers of the United States and Canada went to the polls on February 8, 1977 and elected McBride their fourth international president by a 3-2 margin.

One of the first challenges facing the president-elect was the 1977 contract negotiations in basic steel, in which he participated with President Abel. Both had indicated that their highest priority would be the elusive goal of job security in the steel industry, and as the talks opened on February 14, 1977, Abel defined the union's goal as "a job for life with a decent, respectable income for life." The new agreement, concluded in April, fell somewhat short of the lifetime security plan, but provided substantial improvements in income security by offering increased protection against layoffs and plant close downs for workers with twenty years or more of service.

Although McBride planned no radical departures from Abel's policies, as soon as he was installed as president, on June 1, 1977, he made it apparent that he would bring an invigorating style of his own to the direction of USW's new and expanded top echelon. One USW official, quoted in *Business Week* (June 6, 1977), described him as a "tight-fisted administrator who is obsessive about keeping spending under control and demands performance and accountability of staff members." Discussing his insistence upon the accountability of others, McBride criticized, in particular, politicians who seek union support during an election year, yet fail to keep their promises to labor once they are in office. He spoke of his interest of creating a new post in the USW—that of chief political spokesman for the union—and hinted at greater political activism for the USW in the years ahead.

Among McBride's other proposals were measures to step up his union's organizing efforts in the fabricating industries. He also indicated that better working conditions and improved health and safety regulations would be high on his list of priorities. During the campaign, much of Sadlowski's support had come from his appeal to the younger, alienated worker who was dissatisfied with his job and with the way in which his union represented him, although steelworkers are among the nation's highest paid industrial workers. Before his election, McBride had pledged to establish a new union department to develop programs to deal with problems "arising from a changing workplace," and he reaffirmed his pledge shortly after his inaugural.

So troubled had the country's steel industry become by the fall of 1977 that A. H. Raskin opened his labor news analysis of October 18 by asserting, "The United Steelworkers of America is a union under siege." With foreign steel imports accounting for 20 percent or more of the American market, steelmakers signaled their intention to close down older, less profitable plants, laying off thousands of workers. Many labor specialists, therefore, saw as McBride's most serious challenge the task of helping to maintain the cooperative spirit in labor-management relations that had been fostered by the Experimental Negotiating Agreement, so that both union and industry officials could seek new ways to increase productivity in steel plants.

Lloyd McBride was elected a vice-president and member of the executive council of the AFL-CIO in September 1977. He was recently appointed by President Jimmy Carter to be a member of the Advisory Council for Trade Negotiations. He is a member of the executive board of the AFL-CIO Industrial Union Department, the board of directors of the American Arbitration Association, the labor policy advisory committee of the United States Department of Labor, and the Committee for National Health Insurance, and is a vice-president of the American Immigration and Citizenship Conference.

Since 1937 Lloyd McBride has been married to the former Dolores Neihaus; they have two children, Larry, a teaching brother in the Society of Mary, and Sharon, a wife and the mother of two children. McBride has been described in the press as a "trim and compact" man with a "grandfatherly" air. Playing golf is his favorite recreation, but he has remarked, "If I break 100 I feel very good." McBride has served on the advisory board of the Salvation Army and is a member of the Harry S. Truman Library Institute, among other organizations. In May 1977 he received an award of appreciation for his work as a trustee of the Coro Foundation of St. Louis, a nonprofit educational foundation that trains young people for careers in public life.

References: Bsns W p77+ Je 6 '77 por; N Y Times p11 F 11 '77 por; Steel Labor p10+ Je '77; U S News 82:70+ Ja 17 '77 por; Wall St J p5 Ag 30 '76

MacLaine, Shirley

Apr. 24, 1934- Actress; entertainer. Address: b. c/o Pickwick Public Relations, 545 Madison Ave., New York City, N.Y. 10022; W. Norton & Co., 500 Fifth Ave., New York City, N.Y. 10036

NOTE: This biography supersedes the article that appeared in *Current Biography* in 1959.

Hoofer, singer, dramatic actress, comedienne, political activist, feminist, author, and world traveler—Shirley MacLaine is a Renaissance woman whose gamine personality and outspokenness are legendary. Once known as "movietown's clown princess," she came to Hollywood by way of the Broadway musical stage, rose to stardom playing goodhearted tarts and sad-sack heroines and, among other distinctions, received Academy Award nominations for her performances in *Some Came Running* (1958), *The Apartment* (1960), and *Irma La Douce* (1963).

During the 1960's she traveled extensively and became involved in liberal and humanitarian causes. In the 1970's she gained renown as a brilliant and indefatigable star of the international revue stage and of Emmy-award-winning television specials; played an important role in the Presidential campaign of George S. McGovern; led a group of women on a tour of the People's Republic of China, where she made a documentary film; and published two best-selling volumes of autobiography. She returned to the screen in 1977 after an absence of several years in the ballet film *The Turning Point*, for which she received her fourth Oscar nomination.

Of Scotch-Irish descent, Shirley MacLaine was born Shirley MacLean Beaty in Richmond, Virginia, on April 24, 1934. Her father, Ira O. Beaty, who was in the real estate business, had been a band leader and teacher in his youth, and her mother, Kathlyn (MacLean) Beaty, had acted in little theatre productions and taught dramatics. Her brother, actor Warren Beatty, whom she has called her "companion in adjustment and rebellion," is three years younger than she. "I was born into a cliché-loving, middle-class . . . family," she has recalled. "We were all Baptists. . . . We were taught to respect all material possessions. . . . We lived according to what our neighbors thought."

Before Shirley was three, her mother enrolled her in a ballet class, and within a year she was performing in the famous Mosque recitals in Richmond. Later, when the family moved to Arlington, Virginia, she attended the Washington School of Ballet five afternoons a week, and by the time she was twelve she was performing with the school ensemble in ballets presented by the National Symphony Orchestra at Washington's Constitution Hall. Eventually she grew too tall for the ballet, and she had difficulty keeping a straight face while dancing. Her teachers, Mary Day and Lisa Gardiner, encouraged her to try Broadway musicals, and when she was sixteen she spent a summer in New York, dancing in the chorus of a City Center revival of *Oklahoma!*

After graduating from Washington and Lee High School in Arlington in 1952, Miss MacLaine headed once more for New York. She obtained a summer job in the chorus of *Kiss Me Kate* at the Music Circus in Lambertsville, New Jersey and then worked for a time as a dancer with a traveling industrial show that promoted Servel refrigerators. In May 1953 she joined the chorus of Rodgers and Hammerstein's Broadway musical *Me and Juliet*.

Next, Miss MacLaine obtained a chorus spot in the successful Richard Bissell-George Abbott musical *The Pajama Game*, which opened at Broadway's St. James Theatre on May 13, 1954. In addition, she acted as understudy in the role of Gladys for the show's leading dancer, Carol Haney. When Miss Haney injured her ankle at a matinee a few days after the show's opening, Miss MacLaine took her place and earned enthusiastic applause. Her performance was seen by Hollywood producer Hal B. Wallis, who signed her to a long-term film contract. Soon thereafter, Wallis loaned her out to Alfred Hitchcock, under whose direction she made her movie debut in the black comedy *The Trouble with Harry* (Paramount, 1955). Critics reviewing the film noted Miss MacLaine's flair for comedy, as well as her "elfin" beauty and "wanton charm." She gained further attention in Hal Wallis' *Artists and Models* (Paramount, 1955), a Jerry Lewis-Dean Martin farce. In a complete change of pace, she then portrayed the

Indian princess Aouda in Michael Todd's epic *Around the World in 80 Days* (United Artists, 1956).

Miss MacLaine returned briefly to the stage in the winter of 1956-57 as costar in the West Coast touring production of Terence Rattigan's comedy *The Sleeping Prince*. Her next three films—the low-key Western *The Sheepman* (MGM, 1958), the Thornton Wilder comedy *The Matchmaker* (Paramount, 1958), and the family melodrama *Hot Spell* (Paramount, 1958)—did little to advance her career. But her portrayal of Ginny, the tragicomic floozy enamored of returning soldier Frank Sinatra in *Some Came Running* (MGM, 1958), based on James Jones' novel, placed her in the front ranks of serious actresses. Sinatra remembers how he and director Vincente Minnelli, watching Miss MacLaine on Dinah Shore's television show, saw in her "the cuteness, the strength, the humor—everything we wanted in Ginny" and signed her for the role the following day. Commenting on the character in an interview in *Life* (February 17, 1959), Miss MacLaine asserted: "I loved this girl so much, I could have played her scenes any way . . . Minnelli wanted—even standing on my head."

Critics generally found her interpretation of the role to be fine, zestful, and poignant. "She isn't conventionally pretty," the reviewer for *Variety* (December 24, 1958) wrote, "Her hair looks like it was combed with an eggbeater. But . . . she elicits such empathy and humor." Presented with a Foreign Press Award, Miss MacLaine also received an Academy Award nomination but lost out to Susan Hayward.

Costarred with David Niven, Miss MacLaine portrayed a naïve country girl who comes to New York to seek a career in the farce *Ask Any Girl* (MGM, 1959). Her performance won for her the Silver Bear of the International Berlin Film Festival as best actress of the year. She next appeared as a dipsomaniac in *Career* (Paramount, 1959), a McCarthy-era soap opera, and had a brief role in the crime-caper *Ocean's 11* (Warner, 1960). At Frank Sinatra's request she costarred with him as the owner of an 1890's Paris bistro in *Can-Can* (Twentieth Century-Fox, 1960), based on the 1953 Cole Porter-Abe Burrows Broadway musical. Critical response to the film was mixed, and some reviewers responded favorably to her efforts. "Her music hall madam has the raucous self-assertion and the defenseless sentimentality necessary to give the film the animal vitality it has," Paul V. Beckley wrote in the New York *Herald Tribune* (March 20, 1960). During the filming in 1959 Miss MacLaine had engaged in a much publicized exchange of views with visiting Soviet Premier Nikita S. Khrushchev, who had expressed shock at the sexuality of the can-can as performed by her ensemble.

In Billy Wilder's comedy *The Apartment* (United Artists, 1960), about an amiable young insurance clerk—played by Jack Lemmon—who lends his apartment to his bosses for their extramarital affairs, Miss MacLaine turned in a much acclaimed performance as a vulnerable elevator girl who is jilted by Fred MacMurray and ultimately won by Lemmon. A critic for *Variety* (May 18, 1960) observed that "her ability to play it broad where it should be broad, subtle where it must be subtle, enables the actress to effect reality and yet do much more." And in the view of Paul V. Beckley of the New York *Herald Tribune* (June 16, 1960), her portrayal was "as subtle a piece of work as she has turned in so far." Awarded the best actress prize at the 1960 Venice Film Festival, Miss MacLaine also received her second Academy Award nomination but was edged out by Elizabeth Taylor.

Miss MacLaine's films in the early 1960's included the farce *All in a Night's Work* (Paramount, 1961), the melodrama *Two Loves* (MGM, 1961), and the comedy *My Geisha* (Paramount, 1962), produced by her husband, Steve Parker, in Japan. She portrayed Gittel Mosca, a brash Bronx girl in love with a Midwestern lawyer played by Robert Mitchum in the film version of William Gibson's play *Two for the Seesaw* (United Artists, 1962); and she was seen as the tragic schoolteacher Martha Dobie in William Wyler's adaptation of Lillian Hellman's drama *The Children's Hour* (United Artists, 1962).

In an effort to gain more independence and greater financial rewards, Miss MacLaine freed herself from her contract with Hal Wallis in 1963, paying the producer $150,000 in an out-of-court settlement. By 1964 she was earning $800,000 per film and ranked sixth at the box-office. She made frequent guest appearances on television, and she became known as a member of the "Clan," or "rat pack," which included Frank Sinatra, Dean Martin, Sammy Davis Jr., and members of the Kennedy family. She sounded off to interviewers on topics ranging from fashion to politics and received a publicity buildup as the "ring-a-ding girl," the "queen of kooks," and a "new-style star" who had maintained her own identity. "She reached the summit of Big Rock Candy Mountain," C. Robert Jennings wrote in the Washington *Post* (March 23, 1969), "without benefit of cheesecake, good clothes, great looks, Ultra Brite smiles, romantic scandal, studio manipulations—even without a swimming pool."

Meanwhile Miss MacLaine had scored another hit in the role of a brash Parisian prostitute, opposite Jack Lemmon, as a policeman who becomes her pimp, in *Irma La Douce* (United Artists, 1963), adapted from the Broadway musical. After researching the role in the brothels and alleyways of the Les Halles district of Paris, she turned in a performance that Bosley Crowther of the New York *Times* called "cheerful, impudent, and droll." Her portrayal earned her a Golden Globe award from the Foreign Press Association as well as the designation as the year's best actress in a poll by *Film Daily*. Nominated for her third Academy Award, she lost again, this time to Patricia Neal.

Her next two films, the satire *What a Way to Go!* (1964) and Steve Parker's production *John Goldfarb, Please Come Home* (1965)—both released by Twentieth Century-Fox—failed to evoke enthusiasm from critics. Although she received plaudits for her portrayal of the brassy girl friend of American gangster George C. Scott in one of the episodes of *The Yellow Rolls-Royce* (MGM, 1965), she acknowledged to interviewers that she wasn't happy with herself as an actress and was tired of playing "hookers and doormats." Easing up on her filming schedule in the mid-1960's, she devoted herself to social activism, self-education, and travel.

No stranger to political and social causes, Shirley MacLaine had campaigned for Adlai E. Stevenson and John F. Kennedy and had taken part in the unsuccessful effort in 1960 to save convict-author Caryl Chessman from death in the San Quentin gas chamber. In the mid-1960's she became active in civil rights struggles and traveled to the South to help register voters. She was also a vocal participant in protests against United States involvement in Vietnam. Chosen as a delegate to the 1968 Democratic National Convention, she supported Senator Robert F. Kennedy for the Presidency and, after his assassination, turned to another antiwar candidate, Senator George S. McGovern. In her spare time she read voraciously, prompting the late Ernie Kovacs to remark: "If you've got Shirley MacLaine for a friend, who needs an encyclopedia?"

Miss MacLaine traveled extensively, not as a tourist but as a world citizen eager to know at first-hand the remote areas of the earth. Carrying only one small suitcase, she journeyed to Western and Eastern Europe, the Soviet Union, Africa, Southeast Asia, and India. She lived among members of the Masai tribe in East Africa, was detained by border guards during a government crisis in the Himalayan kingdom of Bhutan, and studied Yoga during a six-week stay in India in 1967. There, she became involved in humanitarian causes, supporting, among other projects, an orphanage for 150 boys—"dustbin and gutter babies"—near Calcutta. Miss MacLaine recounted her early life and career, as well as her travel experiences, in her widely acclaimed, best-selling book *Don't Fall Off the Mountain* (Norton, 1970). "What makes her story so engaging," a critic for *Newsweek* (January 11, 1971) wrote, "is her balance and sanity and her willingness to reject or assimilate experience with her eyes, mind, and heart wide open."

Between trips, Shirley MacLaine appeared in such films as the crime thriller *Gambit* (Universal, 1966), with Michael Caine; Vittorio De Sica's *Woman Times Seven* (Embassy, 1967), a showcase for her multifaceted talents that turned out to be a critical and financial failure; and the comedy *The Bliss of Mrs. Blossom* (Paramount, 1968). In the lavish production of the musical *Sweet Charity* (Universal, 1969), directed by Bob Fosse, Miss MacLaine, as the good-hearted, simple-minded dance-hall hostess, tried mightily to duplicate the success that Gwen Verdon had achieved in that role on Broadway two years earlier, but the film failed at the box office. She did little better in the role of a prostitute disguised as a nun in the off-beat Western *Two Mules for Sister Sara* (Universal, 1970), with Clint Eastwood.

Sponsored by the British television tycoon Sir Lew Grade, Miss MacLaine made an ABC-TV series, *Shirley's World*, produced by Sheldon Leonard, in which she played a globe-trotting photojournalist trying to make her way in a male-dominated world. But the program, which made its debut on September 15, 1972, was generally panned by the critics and folded in less than four months. Under her arrangement with Grade she also made two low-budget films that were well received in art houses: *Desperate Characters* (Paramount, 1971), about a harassed middle-class couple in contemporary New York, which earned her a Silver Bear award at the Berlin Film Festival; and *The Possession of Joel Delaney* (Paramount, 1972), a psychological suspense thriller in which she played a well-to-do divorcee involved in spiritualism.

Such issues as the Vietnam conflict, the Kent State massacre, the growing conservatism of the Supreme Court, government attacks on the press, crime, and the continuing civil rights struggle—especially as it concerned women—impelled Miss MacLaine to work once more for the Presidential candidacy of McGovern. As a delegate to the 1972 Democratic National Convention in Miami she served on the platform committee and fought successfully to keep the abortion issue off the party platform, fearing that otherwise Richard Nixon and his supporters might use it against the Democratic candidate. At McGovern's request she assembled a women's council for the campaign with Congresswoman Bella Abzug of New York. "But her main value to the candidate [was] still as a cross-country, Jill-of-all-skills," a reporter for *Newsweek* (September 25, 1972) wrote. "[She] has pounded pavements, rapped with college students, raised $50,000 in one evening in her own living room, and substituted for McGovern in a speech to a steelworkers' convention." With Shirley Chisholm, Bella Abzug, Gloria Steinem, and others, Miss MacLaine appeared in the partly documentary, partly satirical feminist film *Year of the Woman* (1973) that was made at the Miami convention.

In the spring of 1973 Miss MacLaine accepted an invitation to make a six-week tour of the People's Republic of China at the head of a delegation of twelve American women from various walks of life. While there, she produced and codirected a documentary film, *The Other Half of the Sky: A China Memoir.* Shown on public television in the United States, and internationally acclaimed, it was nominated for an Academy Award. Defending the film against charges that it was propagandistic, she wrote in the New York *Times* (April 6, 1975) that she merely recorded what she had observed on the trip, and added: "There is something going on in China that is certainly worth seeing and . . . understanding, I mean, one of the largest experiments in social organization in modern history." She discussed the China trip, the McGovern campaign, and other topics, in her best-selling second volume of memoirs, *You Can Get There From Here* (Norton, 1975).

The China experience motivated Miss MacLaine to nurture her own talent. "I was not a soldier or a philosopher or a politician," she wrote. "But—I could dance. I could sing. I could make people laugh. I could make people cry." She headed for a dance studio and gym, lost weight, stopped smoking, and put together a nightclub act that in July 1974 opened to rave reviews at the MGM Grand Hotel in Las Vegas. Sharing the stage with a chorus line of five and a band, she took her act on a tour of the United States. For CBS-TV she starred in two Emmy-winning specials—*If They Could See Me Now,* in November 1974, and *Gypsy in My Soul,* with Lucille Ball, in January 1976—and she also appeared as a guest in early 1976 in the ABC-TV bicentennial special *The American Spirit.* In February 1976 she launched a successful tour of twelve European and Latin American cities with a triumphant appearance at the London Palladium, and in April of that year she had a two-week engagement at the Palace Theatre in New York, where she set an all-time box-office record. The Columbia LP album *Shirley MacLaine—Live at the Palace* was released shortly thereafter. She was designated female musical star of the year in the 1976 Las Vegas Entertainment Awards. Her third television special, *Where Do We Go From Here?* was presented on CBS-TV in March 1977.

Miss MacLaine returned to the screen for the first time since 1972 in *The Turning Point* (Twentieth Century-Fox, 1977), directed by Herbert Ross and costarring Anne Bancroft and Mikhail Baryshnikov. Although some critics panned the "soap opera" quality of that film about the love-hate relationship between two aging ballerinas, others found it to be an important women's film and felt that the team of MacLaine and Bancroft was quite effective. "Together they are dynamite," wrote a reviewer for *Variety* (October 19, 1977), who asserted that *The Turning Point* would rank as one of Miss MacLaine's career highlights. Among her current projects is a film about Amelia Earhart, in which she will star as the ill-fated woman aviator, and she has been working on her third book, a novel. In 1977 Miss MacLaine performed at President Jimmy Carter's inaugural, took part in Bella Abzug's unsuccessful New York City mayoral campaign, and visited Cuban Premier Fidel Castro.

Shirley MacLaine has for some years been separated from, but is still friendly with, her husband, Steve Parker, whom she married on September 17, 1954, and who lives in Tokyo. Their daughter, Stephanie Sachiko, born in 1956, makes her home in Honolulu. Miss MacLaine has reportedly parted from her long-time friend, journalist and author Pete Hamill. Her abundant energy, exuberance, and resilience have been noted by a number of interviewers. Blue-eyed and freckle-faced, with light auburn hair, Miss MacLaine is five feet six inches tall, weighs 118 pounds, and has what Lee Langley in the *Guardian* (October 16, 1970) called a "funny, croaky, up and down voice." She maintains her trim figure through exercise, yoga, and diet. Commenting on her varied life, she once told Sheilah Graham: "I want to be hungry sometimes. I want to be thirsty. I want the struggle, I want the pain, I want the rain so I can enjoy the sunshine."

References: International Motion Picture Almanac, 1977; MacLaine, Shirley. Don't Fall Off the Mountain (1970), You Can Get There From Here (1975); Parish, J. R. The Paramount Pretties (1972); Thomson, David. A Biographical Dictionary of Film (1976); Who's Who in America, 1976-77

Malamud, Bernard (mäl'ä-mud)

Apr. 26, 1914- Writer. Address: b. c/o Bennington College, Bennington, Vt. 05201

NOTE: This biography supersedes the article that appeared in *Current Biography* in 1958.

Among urban American Jewish writers who came into prominence in the post-World War II years, Bernard Malamud stands out as a compassionate observer of commonplace lives, a novelist and short story writer for whom the Jew serves as a universal symbol of the afflicted who somehow manage to survive adversity. In the singular world of his fiction, the natural and the supernatural inter-

Bernard Malamud

mingle with sometimes startling results, and a sense of unreality enshrouds a landscape of tenements, shops, and city streets that often seem more like states of mind than actual places. Typically, Malamud is concerned with what critic Ihab Hassan has described as "the drama of personality fulfilling itself." His short stories, often drawn from Yiddish oral tradition, fill several volumes, including the National Book Award-winning *The Magic Barrel* (1958). His novels belong to no single literary convention, but blend realism and symbolism in ways that create an impact comparable, in the opinion of some critics, to that of the great nineteenth-century Russian novels. Chief among these are *The Assistant* (1957), which established Malamud as a leading figure among postwar American Jewish writers; *The Fixer* (1966), which captured both a Pulitzer Prize and a National Book Award; and *The Tenants* (1971), which with its insights into contemporary race relations affirmed Malamud's continuing importance on the literary scene.

Bernard Malamud was born on April 26, 1914 in Brooklyn, New York, the older of the two sons of Max and Bertha (Fidelman) Malamud. His parents, who had emigrated from Russia early in the century, earned a marginal living as proprietors of a grocery store. Malamud, whose boyhood, according to his account, was "comparatively happy," grew up in a household where both Yiddish and English were spoken and the emphasis was on the cultural rather than the religious aspects of Judaism. He has fond memories of the Yiddish theatre on Manhattan's Second Avenue, where two members of his mother's family were performers, and of listening to his father's tales of Jewish life in Czarist Russia. His boyhood interests included the films of Charlie Chaplin and the novels of Horatio Alger and Frank Merriwell.

Encouraged to develop his budding talents as a narrator and writer by his teachers and by his father, who bought him the twenty-volume *Book of Knowledge* to celebrate his recovery from a bout with pneumônia when he was nine, Malamud made up stories for his friends and spent evenings in the back room of the family store, trying to put his stories down on paper. Later, at Erasmus Hall High School in Brooklyn, he was one of the editors of the literary magazine and acted in student plays. After his mother's death, when he was fifteen, he nings in the back room of the family store

In 1932 Malamud enrolled in the College of the City of New York and, after graduating with a B.A. degree in 1936, he worked in a factory, in various stores, and as a clerk in the Census Bureau in Washington, D.C., writing fiction in his spare time. "I had written a few stories in college, [and] after graduation I began to write again," he has recalled. "The rise of totalitarianism, the Second World War, and the situation of the Jews in Europe helped me to come to what I wanted to say as a writer." As a graduate student at Columbia University, Malamud began, in 1940, to teach classes in English at Erasmus Hall Evening High School while devoting his days to writing, and he continued that routine for several years after he obtained his M.A. degree in 1942. In 1949, after a year as a teacher at Harlem Evening High School, Malamud moved with his family from New York to Corvallis, Oregon to join the faculty of Oregon State College as an instructor of English. He remained there until 1961, eventually becoming an associate professor. Meanwhile, with the appearance of his work in such magazines as *Harper's Bazaar*, *Commentary*, and *Partisan Review*, he had begun to establish a reputation as a short story writer.

Combining realism and fantasy, Malamud's first novel, *The Natural* (Harcourt, 1952), chronicled the rise and downfall of a talented baseball player. Roy Hobbes—the "natural" of the title—is the victim of his own uncontrollable passions, both in his professional endeavors and his sexual relationships. Often humorous, *The Natural* is contemporary in subject matter but has been compared in form to medieval legends of the Holy Grail. Viewed alongside his later works, it is an uncharacteristic book, notably in the absence of Jewish characters. A number of reviewers found the novel unduly self-conscious and baffling in its use of symbolism. It earned high praise, however, from several prominent critics, including Leslie Fiedler, who liked its "simple joy," its "zest and rewarding nuttiness," and its balanced use of myth and reality.

Having obtained a Partisan Review Fiction Fellowship, Malamud took a leave of absence from the college in 1956-57 and spent a year in Europe, most of it in Italy. With the publication of his next novel, *The Assistant* (Farrar, Straus, 1957), he emerged as a major American Jewish writer. Set in Brooklyn during the Depression, *The Assistant* is about a young Italian-American tough named Frankie Alpine who robs a sick, luckless, eternally suffering Jewish grocer, Morris Bober, then goes to work for him out of a mixture of pity and guilt. Alpine assumes Bober's own sorrows until, transformed by love, and influenced by boyhood memories of stories about St. Francis of Assisi, he takes on the identity of a Jew after the grocer's death. Here, as in subsequent works, Malamud uses Jewishness as a metaphor for the life of the spirit, and for a strict code of personal morality and salvation. In his view, Alpine's conversion represents hope and redemption, although in a limited and somewhat ambiguous sense.

William Goyen summed up the acclaim the book received when he wrote in the New York *Times* (April 28, 1957): "*The Assistant* will reaffirm . . . [Malamud's] talent as a writer about simple people struggling to make their lives better in a world of bad luck. The clarity and concreteness of his style, the warm humanity of his people, the tender wit that keeps them firm and compassionable, will delight many." Theodore Solotaroff, analyzing Malamud's work in his *The Red Hot Vacuum* (Atheneum, 1970), viewed *The Assistant* as "a revelation," because "it restored a sense of the dynamics of character and of the older intention of fiction to show the ways men change." In the opinion of Sidney Richman, who saw in it a successful effort to join lyrical symbolism with the resources of the naturalist-realist tradition, *The Assistant* seemed to "belong to no convention, unless it be to Dostoyevsky's fiercely visionary 'extra-realism.'" *The Assistant* brought Malamud the Daroff Memorial Award and the Rosenthal Award of the National Institute of Arts and Letters in 1958.

Thirteen of Malamud's short stories that had previously appeared in magazines were collected in 1958 under the title *The Magic Barrel* (Farrar, Straus). Spare and sharply focused, the stories are marked by a straightforwardness of language that derives from the Jewish tradition of storytelling. While three of the stories have an Italian setting, the others are situated in the New York Jewish ghetto—which is, in effect, the Eastern European *shtetl* transplanted to the New World. Frequently the stories concern the possibility of an individual's spiritual growth or renewal through extremes of personal experience. For example, in the title story, an admittedly "Godless" rabbinical student named Leo Finkle, marries a matchmaker's daughter —"half-whore, half-goddess"—in whom he envisions his own salvation. In "The Last Mohican," Arthur Fidelman, "a self-confessed failure as a painter," goes to Italy to study Giotto and experiences a kind of rebirth through his encounters with a Jewish refugee con man named Shimon Susskind. And in "The Angel Levine," the Jewish tailor Manischevitz must believe the extraordinary—that his black visitor is a messenger sent by God—if he is to overcome his Job-like misfortunes. Adapted from Malamud's story, the film *The Angel Levine*, starring Zero Mostel and Harry Belafonte, was released by United Artists in 1970.

Although *The Magic Barrel* received a few unfavorable comments, most critics praised the book. Richard Sullivan, writing in the Chicago *Sunday Tribune* (May 18, 1958), found it to be a "gentle work with a curious, almost magical charm" and observed that each story was "a small, highly individualized work of art." Alfred Kazin, in a review included in his book *Contemporaries* (Little, 1962), felt that Malamud had captured both "the guttural toughness of big city speech and the classic bitterness of Jewish dialogue . . . with an intimacy of understanding that is utterly remarkable." Malamud received a National Book Award for *The Magic Barrel* in 1959. From 1959 to 1961 he held a fellowship in the Ford Foundation's humanities and arts program.

Although Malamud's third novel, *A New Life* (Farrar, Straus, 1961), is broader in scope and freer in form than either *The Natural* or *The Assistant*, it is considered one of his less successful works. In an effort to explore new territory, Malamud set the book in the Pacific Northwest. His protagonist, S. Levin, a thirty-year-old romantic and ex-alcoholic, tries to start a new life but is frustrated by his past. By his love for the wife of a literature professor at the "cow college" where he goes to teach, Malamud's suffering hero finally achieves a kind of redemption. Despite some superb satire of academia, evocative descriptions of the Northwest and, in the words of Jessamyn West, "one of the most attractive heroines in recent novels," several critics complained that the book was structurally deficient and unconvincing and that the characterization of S. Levin lacked coherence. Malamud left Oregon in 1961 and settled with his family in Vermont, where he began teaching in the division of language and literature at Bennington College.

Idiots First, a collection of eleven of Malamud's short stories, was published by Farrar, Straus in 1963. As David Boroff observed in the *Saturday Review* (October 12, 1963), "the central figure in many of the stories is the *schlemihl* . . . but Malamud, through the transfiguring power of his warmth and compassion, has invested that figure with dignity as well as pathos." Malamud's stories are "sometimes crazy, often vulgar, but always drawn with vigor," M. H. Wagner wrote in *America* (October 26, 1963). "The local color . . . is put on so thick that the reader can almost smell the garlic." The title story of *Idiots First* describes a dying man's efforts to provide for his feeble-minded son. Others include "Black Is My Favorite Color," a sensitive story of race relations; "The Jewbird," concerning an assimilated Jewish family visited by a bird that embodies everything the father wants to forget; and two more stories about the artist Fidelman in Italy—"Still Life" and "Naked Nude."

Malamud's most ambitious novel to date, *The Fixer* (Farrar, Straus, 1966), relates the ordeal of an impoverished Jewish handyman in Czarist Russia who is accused by anti-Semitic officials of "ritual murder." In his development from an ignorant peasant to a humane philosopher, a disciple of Spinoza who learns that "there's no such thing as an unpolitical man, especially a Jew," Yakov Bok—the "fixer" of the title—represents the triumph of individual will and virtue over the destructive forces of history. In conceiving *The Fixer*, Malamud was originally inspired by his father's account of the case of Mendel Beiliss, a Jew tried and acquitted in Kiev in 1913, and he was also influenced by the Dreyfus case, the Sacco-Vanzetti case, the civil rights struggle in the South, and "what had happened in Nazi Germany." He considers *The Fixer* "a myth, an endless story," rather than an individual case study. The final draft of the book, which took him nearly three years, was preceded by a trip to Russia and six months of intensive study.

While some readers found the book dull, and the reviewer for *Time* (September 9, 1966) considered it "an abdication" for Malamud to "retreat into someone else's history," most critics considered it a work of great political and psychological relevance and some found in it influences of Tolstoy, Dostoyevsky, and Kafka. "*The Fixer* is realistic in the most precise sense of the term," Granville Hicks wrote in the *Saturday Review* (September 10, 1966). "But the story is told so purely and with such power that it has . . . the universal meanings of legend." In Hicks's view, Yakov Bok is "one of the most fully rendered characters in modern literature." Malcolm Bradbury, writing in the *Guardian* (April 7, 1967), thought Malamud's Russia of 1910-1913 "superbly created and finely detailed." A best seller, *The Fixer* earned Malamud his second National Book Award as well as a Pulitzer Prize in 1967. A screen adaptation of *The Fixer*, directed by John Frankenheimer, was released by MGM in 1968.

From 1966 to 1968 Malamud was on leave from Bennington as a visiting lecturer at Harvard University. His next book, *Pictures of Fidelman: An Exhibition* (Farrar, Straus, 1969), opens with the three previously published stories and continues Arthur Fidelman's futile search for artistic fulfillment in Italy with three new pieces, "A Pimp's Revenge," "Pictures of the Artist," and "Glass Blower of Venice." Perhaps the most unrestrainedly humorous of Malamud's works, the book is marred, in the opinion of some critics, by its occasional reversion to crude burlesque and a general lack of artistic control. Among those who praised its brilliant wit and incisive satire was William Kennedy. In his review for the *National Observer* (May 12, 1969), he singled out the surrealistic collage "Pictures of the Artist," in which Fidelman, attempting to sculpt the perfect hole, disappears into hell. "In this episode," Kennedy wrote, "Malamud soars out of sight of all his previous stylistic achievements."

From Fidelman's conflict over whether to perfect his life or his art, Malamud turned next to the conflict between two writers—one Jewish, the other black—in *The Tenants* (Farrar, Straus, 1971). The confrontation in a condemned tenement between Harry Lesser, a moderately successful novelist struggling to complete his magnum opus, and Willie Spearmint, a novice, divided in his loyalties between art and revolution, becomes a microcosm of the relationship between white and black in contemporary America. The book offers two possible conclusions: a happy one, culminating in a double wedding, and a disastrous one, ending in mutual destruction. In the postscript, the word "mercy" is repeated 113 times by Levenspiel, the landlord, who seems to act as a sort of one-man Greek chorus.

Explaining his motivation, Malamud told Israel Shenker in an interview for the New York *Times Book Review* (October 3, 1971) that he considered *The Tenants* a warning against fanaticism. Although critics were not unanimously enthusiastic about *The Tenants*, most agreed that it was a work of considerable importance. "Malamud has rushed in where angelic liberals fear to tread." Anatole Broyard wrote in the New York *Times* (September 20, 1971). "He has seized contemporary history by the horns. . . . He has taken a subject that could . . . degenerate into propaganda and shaped it into art."

Malamud's short story collection *Rembrandt's Hat* (Farrar, Straus, 1973) includes "Talking Horse," a fantasy about the strange relationship between a man-horse and his deaf-mute trainer, and "The Man in the Drawer," a grimly realistic account of a Jewish American visitor to Soviet Russia who agrees to smuggle out a manuscript by a Jewish writer. Helen Rogan, writing in *Newsday* (June 17, 1973), found the stories stylistically irritating and the characters' "wretched passivity" exasperating. But Robert Keily, in his review in the New York *Times* (June 3, 1973), was moved by the book's "wistful and ironic humor." He concluded that Malamud was "a writer that one learns to trust," one who "gently reminds us of what we already knew or should have known."

A new novel by Malamud, *Dubin's Lives*, is scheduled to be published by Farrar, Straus & Giroux in early 1979. Malamud has continued to contribute to magazines, and his work is represented in a number of anthologies. Some of his writings were compiled into *A Malamud Reader* (Farrar, Straus, 1967). Malamud was elected to the National Institute of Arts and Letters in 1964 and to the American Academy of Arts and Sciences in 1967.

Bernard Malamud was married on November 6, 1945 to Ann de Chiara, who is of Italian background. The couple live in Bennington, Vermont. They have two children, Paul and Janna. In recent years Malamud has been teaching on a quarter schedule at Bennington College and spending several months each year in New York City. A scholarly looking man with brown eyes, a fringe of graying brown hair, and a mustache, Malamud is five feet eight inches tall and of medium build. He tries to do some writing each day and likes to spend his leisure time reading, listening to music, visiting art galleries, playing poker, going on walks, and playing lawn bowls with his children or resident guests. Commenting on his method of writing, Malamud told Israel Shenker: "The idea is to get the pencil moving quickly. . . . I go over and over a page. Either it bleeds and shows its beginnings to be human, or the form emits shadows of itself and I'm off. I have a terrible will that way." A novel or story is finished when he "can no longer stand working on it." In his first-person entry in *World Authors*, Malamud said that he was motivated to write by a desire to explain life to himself and stay in touch with his fellow men. The purpose of a writer, he feels, is "to keep civilization from destroying itself."

References: Guardian p8 Mr 6 '72 por; N Y Times Bk R p20+ O 3 '71; Sat R 39:37+ S 10 '66 por; Contemporary Authors vol 5-8 (1969); Richman, Sidney. Bernard Malamud (1966); World Authors: 1950-1970 (1975); Who's Who in America, 1976-1977

Mamet, David (Alan)

Nov. 30, 1947- Playwright. Address: b. c/o Howard Rosenstone & Co., Inc., 850 7th Ave., New York City, N.Y. 10019

Until recently, few theatregoers outside of Chicago had ever heard of a young playwright named David Mamet. Although his work was praised by local critics, Mamet, like many other regional playwrights, was virtually unknown to the New York theatre until the Broadway openings of *American Buffalo* (1977), which was named best play of the year by the New York Drama Critics Circle, and *The Water Engine* (1978). The prolific Mamet has had nine plays produced in the last three years, most of them spare one-act dramas with only two or three characters and a single set. Critics occasionally fault him for his reliance on verbal acrobatics at the expense of plot and character development. They nonetheless concede that he has an eavesdropper's ear for everyday speech and manages to turn the most mundane conversations into a kind of contemporary poetry that has been called "one of the relative wonders of our present theatre." Mamet was recently named playwright-in-residence and associate director of the Goodman Theater in Chicago.

David Alan Mamet was born on November 30, 1947 in Chicago, Illinois and grew up in a Jewish neighborhood on the city's South Side. He attended local elementary schools but, following his parents' divorce in the late 1950's, divided his secondary education between Rich Central High School in suburban Olympia Fields and the Francis W. Parker School in Chicago. Mamet traces his acute awareness of the "music of language" to the influence of his father, Bernie Mamet, an attorney and "amateur semanticist," and his understanding of the rhythms of action and speech to his years of piano lessons and to a stint as a busboy at Second City, Chicago's famous improvisational comedy cabaret. While still in high school he got his first taste of the theatre by working as a backstage volunteer at a neighborhood playhouse.

Following his graduation from high school, Mamet resisted his father's wish that he obtain a law degree, choosing instead a more liberal education at the experimental Goddard College in Plainfield, Vermont. There he studied literature and theatre and wrote his first play, a semi-satirical revue called *Camel*, to fulfill his advanced degree thesis requirement in English literature. In the midst of his graduate study he took eighteen months off to study acting at the Neighborhood Playhouse in New York City. During that period he worked evenings as the lighting man and, later, as the house manager for the long-running Off-Broadway musical, *The Fantasticks*. After taking his degree, Mamet worked as a supporting actor on the New England strawhat circuit, but within a few months he reluctantly gave up his dream of becoming a professional actor because, as he candidly admitted to one interviewer, he was "terrible."

Finding himself out of work, Mamet applied for a short-term teaching job at Marlboro College in Marlboro, Vermont, falsely listing his "new play" as one of his qualifications for the position. The ruse worked, for Mamet was hired not only to teach acting but also to stage his non-existent drama. He quickly wrote *Lakeboat*, a one-act play drawn from his brief experience in the Merchant Marine, and produced it as an exercise for his students. Returning to Chicago a few months later, he worked as a cabdriver, short order cook, factory worker, and high-pressure telephone salesman for a fly-by-night real estate firm that sold "worthless" land in Arizona and Florida. But he missed teaching and in 1971 returned to his alma mater as a drama instructor and artist-in-residence.

While teaching at Goddard, Mamet wrote several short plays because he found it was easier just to write something for his acting classes than to waste hours in a fruitless search for appropriate material. Recruiting his best students, he formed the St. Nicholas Company, an acting ensemble named after the patron saint of troubadours, to stage some of his works as well as such classics as Eugene O'Neill's *Anna Christie*. Confident of his developing skills as a playwright, Mamet returned to Chicago in 1972 and made the rounds of the local theatres. The Body Politic, an experimental theatre, staged his one-act comedy, *Duck Variations*, the Center Youth Theater of the Bernard Horwich Jewish Community Center presented *Mackinac*, a children's play set on Mackinac Island, and *Marranos*, a story about life in Lisbon during the Inquisition, and the avant-garde Organic Theater produced *Sexual Perversity in Chicago*. Mamet's career received an unexpected boost in 1974 when his *Sexual Perversity in Chicago* won the Joseph Jefferson Award, which is given annually to the best new Chicago play. During those months he supplemented his income by teaching theatre classes at the University of Chicago and at Pontiac State Prison in Pontiac, Illinois.

In August 1974 Mamet and three young associates—Steven Schachter, William H. Macy, and Patricia Cox—resurrected the St. Nicholas theater company as the St. Nicholas Players. Their first production was Mamet's *Squirrels*, the story of an older writer who, stymied by the phrasing of a prose passage about squirrels, turns to younger writers for stimulation. "We had a wonderful time," Mamet recalled in a recent interview, "but nobody came to see it. I'm sure in the course of the run, we didn't have 100 people." Then Mamet turned director for an ambitious production of O'Neill's *Beyond the Horizon* that was roundly panned by the critics. The group's next presentation, Mamet's *The Poet and the Rent*, which was described by its author as a comedy for "kids of all ages," prompted one Chicago critic to ponder in verse: "I wonder will I ever watch/a play by David Mamet/That he'll manage not to botch/And spare my thinking, Dammit!?" Despite their early hardships, David Mamet and the St. Nicholas Players profited from the mutually beneficial relationship. The company provided Mamet with a sorely needed outlet to the public, giving him the opportunity to see almost all his plays performed before live audiences. And Mamet's growing local reputation brought prestige to the fledgling troupe.

Although Mamet's career flourished in Chicago, he remained a virtual unknown in the rest of the country, and the manuscripts he regularly submitted to New York producers were just as regularly rejected. Finally, in 1975, the St. Clements Theater, an Off Off Broadway house that often showcases young talent, introduced David Mamet to New York audiences with a double bill consisting of *Duck Variations* and *Sexual Perversity in Chicago*. The stagings were, in Mamet's words, "a cross between a vanity presentation and a good basement production," but the response was sufficiently enthusiastic to lead to a formal run at the Off Broadway Cherry Lane Theater in Greenwich Village. Opening on June 16, 1976, the two plays were an immediate hit with critics and audiences alike, and *Time* magazine placed them on its list of the ten best plays of 1976.

In *Duck Variations*, two garrulous elderly Jewish men while away an afternoon sitting on a park bench swapping hilarious bits of misinformation about the habits of ducks and other assorted subjects. "What emerges," according to T. E. Kalem, a theater critic for *Time* magazine (July 12, 1976), "is a vivid sense of their friendship, the fear of solitude, the inexorable toll of expiring lives." Edith Oliver, who reviewed the play for the *New Yorker* (November 10, 1975) during its Off Off Broadway run, was also touched by the beautifully developed relationship between the two characters. "There is more here than just geriatric humor; there is also imagination and understanding," she wrote. In her view, Mamet "cherishes characters even more" than he "cherishes words."

Its companion piece, *Sexual Perversity in Chicago,* is the story of two erstwhile swinging singles whose tentative, fragile relationship is sabotaged and eventually destroyed by the meddling of well-meaning friends and by their own misconceptions about love. Staged in a series of quick blackouts, the play relies heavily on humor to make its point about the perverse sexual attitudes that many modern men and women "carry around like concealed weapons," in the words of critic Allan Wallach. "My sex life was ruined by the popular media," Mamet admitted to C. Gerald Fraser of the New York *Times* (July 5, 1976). "There are a lot of people in my situation. The myths around us, destroying our lives. . . . Voltaire said words were invented to hide feelings. That's what the play is about, how what we say influences what we think." And, as more than one critic noted, behind the "uncannily credible" dialogue, the macho "pickup chatter," and the occasionally "brutal, dirty, monosyllabic observations," was an aftertaste of "underlying sadness" and "loneliness."

The quality that most impressed critics about Mamet's two short plays, however, was the young writer's mastery of language. Voicing the consensus of his colleagues, Allen Wallach in the June 17, 1976 edition of *Newsday* wrote: "Mamet has captured some of the wonderful ludicrousness of ordinary conversation, as though he had spent his days wandering through Chicago with a tape recorder. He is brilliant at showing how little is communicated when people exchange half-digested scraps of information and receive opinions they never bother to examine." Others praised Mamet's "flair for natural dialogue," his "exactness of expression," his "compelling" silences, and his terse, crosscut exchanges. Mamet readily agrees that he has, as he once put it, "a certain flair for dialogue," but he is more concerned with "language as poetry." "It has to be poetry," he told Mark Zweigler of *After Dark* (August 1976). "If it's not poetic on the stage, forget it. If it's solely serving the interest of the plot, I'm not interested. As a consequence, I go overboard the other way."

While *Duck Variations* and *Sexual Perversity in Chicago* continued their run at the Cherry Lane, David Mamet made the move to Broadway with a revised version of *American Buffalo,* which opened at the Ethel Barrymore Theater on February 16, 1977. Earlier productions of the play had broken box office records at the Goodman Theater's Stage 2 in Chicago in late 1975 and, a few months later, had won for Mamet an Obie Award as the best new playwright of the year. Set in a filthy, cluttered junk shop, *American Buffalo* is a penetrating character study of three small-time crooks who are planning to burglarize the home of a coin collector who has just purchased a valuable American Buffalo nickel. During the course of their wrangling, the men gradually reveal their idiosyncrasies, inadequacies, misconceptions, and failures in gutter dialogue that, according to most critics, contained an unusually high percentage of profanity and obscenity, even for the contemporary stage. In the end, unable to agree upon a plan of action, the three call the whole thing off.

Mamet conceived his play as an attack on the American business ethic and created his foul-mouthed hoodlums as stand-ins for members of the corporate classes who perform imaginary jobs. "We excuse all sorts of great and small betrayals and ethical compromises called business," he explained to Richard Gottlieb, who interviewed him at length for a New York *Times* profile (January 15, 1978). "There's really no difference between the *lumpenproletariat* and stockbrokers or corporate lawyers who are the lackeys of business. Part of the American myth is that a difference exists, that at a certain point vicious behavior becomes laudable." The majority of critics found Mamet's implied suggestion that *American Buffalo* was the American capitalistic system in microcosm interesting but felt that the play itself was too insubstantial to "support the weight of such ideas."

Not even the superb performances of Robert Duvall, Kenneth McMillan, and John Savage as the ludicrously inept thieves redeemed the evening for Brendan Gill of the *New Yorker,* John Beaufort of the *Christian Science Monitor,* and Richard L. Coe of the Washington *Post.* However, several of their colleagues—Clive Barnes of the New York *Times,* Martin Gottfried of the New York *Post,* and Christopher Porterfield of *Time*—were quite taken with Mamet's "exciting," "gripping," "compelling," and "very funny" play. The main criticism leveled at *American Buffalo* was its "inaction" and "static plot." But virtually every critic, even those who, like the New York *Times*'s Walter Kerr, believe that "language alone isn't drama," was fascinated by Mamet's keen ear for "everyday language" and the "cadence of loneliness" and his uncommon ability to find in rough street language "a crude kind of poetry." In spite of its flaws, *American Buffalo* ran for 150 performances and was voted the best play of 1977 by the New York Drama Critics Circle.

During his formative years in Chicago, Mamet often spent his idle afternoons at his father's downtown law office, where he would, as he remembered in a recent interview, "sit in the back room, type letters, make phone calls, play with rubber stamps, and just knock out ideas—type up thirty pages of notes about something." Over several months he accumulated some twenty scenes about actors—"those individuals whom we elect to live out our dramas for us upon a stage"—which he eventually worked into a full-length play entitled *A Life in the Theater.*

Centered around a young method actor touring in a stock company with a disenchanted theater veteran, *A Life in the Theater* examines the different ways in which the two men prepare offstage and perform onstage in a variety of roles. Beneath its comic exterior it paints a wry, affectionate, and often ironic picture of the illusionary nature of the theatre and the universal relationship between student and teacher. After a promising premiere run at the Goodman Theater Stage 2 in February 1977, the play opened at the De Lys Theater Off Broadway on October 20, 1977 to some of the most enthusiastic reviews Mamet had yet received. Typical of the favorable comments was that of Edith Oliver, who wrote in her *New Yorker* review of October 31. 1977, "Mr. Mamet has written—in gentle ridicule; in jokes, broad and tiny; and in comedy, high and low—a love letter to the theater. It is quite a feat, and he has pulled it off." But there were a handful of dissenters, including a critic for *Harper's* magazine (May 1978) who complained that the play was largely "surface flamboyance, sight gags and gimmickry, lush language and posturing" and, worst of all, a "tedious, offensively banal caricature of what daily life in the theatre is actually like."

Originally written in 1976 for National Public Radio's *Earplay* series and rewritten "in bunches" for the stage, *The Water Engine* is a Depression-era fable about a naïve inventor who designs an automobile engine that runs on water, only to have it stolen away from him by corrupt industrialists. Performed as a radio drama with the actors speaking into old-fashioned microphones and with a sound effects man supplying the aural punctuation, *The Water Engine* is, for a Mamet work, "crazy with action." Although the innovative play received only lukewarm reviews from the Chicago critics when it premiered there in May 1977, it generated such excitement during its short stay at the New York Shakespeare Festival's Public Theatre that it was quickly moved to Broadway. New York critics, although more receptive to Mamet's experiment than their Midwestern counterparts, greeted the production with mixed reviews, some calling it "disappointing," others hailing it as "brilliant" and "extraordinary." The New York *Times* reviewer Richard Eder, one of Mamet's most enthusiastic supporters, saw in *The Water Engine* a "growing sense of emotion and magic" as well as the expected "pointillistic verbal brilliance."

Eder was similarly impressed by *The Woods*, an intense, emotional two-character play that examines some of the same issues as *Sexual Perversity in Chicago*, but from a less detached perspective. Directed by Mamet himself, the play had its world premiere at the St. Nicholas Theater in Chicago on November 16, 1977. That same month the St. Nicholas Players staged *The Revenge of the Space Pandas, or Binky Rudich and the Two-Speed Clock*, a children's play Mamet describes as being "about kids from Waukegan who accidentally end up in the fourth planetary gulag," and the Yale Repertory Theater in New Haven, Connecticut produced one of his earlier plays, *Reunion*, the touching account of a young woman who seeks out the alcoholic father she has not seen in twenty years, and as a companion piece, *Dark Pony*, a ten-minute depiction of an idyllic father-daughter relationship.

A slightly built man of medium height with short dark hair and dark eyes, David Mamet has been described by *Cue* reporter Marilyn Stasio as "precisely the type of young man that corporate executives and university faculty love to write references for. He is young, bright and personable. Neat, sober and responsible. Honest, alert and probably dozens of other virtuous things as well." Witty, articulate, and highly literate, Mamet interlards his conversations with literary quotations. He keeps his tendency toward moroseness and depression at bay by running four miles daily. For relaxation, he goes to B-movies to "eat popcorn and talk back to the screen." Although he still considers himself to be a Chicagoan and admits to feeling claustrophobic in New York, Mamet recently moved into a Manhattan apartment, which he shares with his wife, Lindsay Crouse, the actress, whom he married on December 21, 1977.

Passionately devoted to his craft, Mamet tries to write every day, usually in the morning. His filing cabinet is crammed with scores of unfinished plays, snatches of conversations overheard in pool halls, restaurants, or on the street, and character sketches. Despite his aversion to television, he recently agreed to write a children's play for public television and a drama for one of the commercial networks. He also completed the screenplay for a movie version of *Sexual Perversity in Chicago*. Mamet still enjoys teaching and, in 1977, gave a playwriting course at Yale University. His long-range plans include a novel, a book on the aesthetics of theatre and, in five or ten years, the formation of another acting company. But, most of all, he would "like to write a really great play someday."

References: After Dark 9:42+ Ag '76 pors; N Y Sunday News III p3 F 13 '77 por; N Y Times p7 Jl 5 '76 por, II p1+ Ja 15 '78 por; Newsday II p4+ Ag 22 '76 por; Newsweek 89:79 F 28 '77 por; Time 109:54+ F 28 '77 por

---

Manilow, Barry

June 17, 1946- Musician; recording artist. Address: b. c/o Arista Records, 6 W. 57th St., New York City, N.Y. 10019

In the four years since the release of his first single recording, the chart-topping

Barry Manilow

"Mandy," Barry Manilow, the country's leading exponent of romantic pop, has had an uninterrupted string of ten Top Ten singles and six hit albums. All of his releases have been awarded Gold Records and the last four LP's passed the Double Platinum mark, signifying more than two million copies sold. At one point, Manilow had five albums on the charts simultaneously, a feat equalled only by Frank Sinatra and Johnny Mathis.

A talented composer and arranger of simple, melodic, very commercial tunes, Manilow first captured national attention in the early 1970's, singing the infectious jingles for McDonald's, Kentucky Fried Chicken, Pepsi-Cola, and other products. Then, after four years as the musical director of Bette Midler's sensational stage shows, he took the spotlight himself with his special brand of soft, contemporary pop-rock that some music critics have labeled bland, middle-of-the-road schmaltz, probably because of its undeniably widespread appeal. Manilow disagrees with his detractors: "My work is not MOR [middle of the road]. I'm not Led Zeppelin, but I'm not saccharine either. My music is well thought-out, adult, professional tunes. . . . All I'm really trying to do is to bring back intelligent music."

The only child of Harold Pincus and Edna Manilow, Barry Manilow was born on June 17, 1946, in Brooklyn, New York. After his father deserted the family two years later, the child was raised by his mother and grandfather in the poor, tough Williamsburg section of Brooklyn, where he was, as he once put it, "the kid [other children] always beat up." Introduced to music by his mother, Barry Manilow began taking accordion lessons when he was seven, piano lessons when he was thirteen. In a short time, he was an accomplished pianist, playing classical pieces and Broadway show tunes with equal facility. His performance of Manuel de Falla's lightning-fast "Ritual Fire Dance" won for him the "best musician" award from his fellow students at Brooklyn's Eastern High School.

In the late 1950's Edna Manilow married Willie Murphy, a trucker with a passionate interest in modern jazz. When Murphy took his stepson to hear Gerry Mulligan, the jazz saxophonist, Manilow immediately "turned on to cool, West Coast jazz." "It really got to me," he said years later, as quoted in *Newsweek* (March 31, 1975). "That's when I decided there was more to music than squeezing out 'Lady of Spain' and 'Tico Tico.' " He began adding to his record collection jazz LP's and Broadway cast albums, but unlike the majority of his peers, he had no interest in rock 'n' roll. As he told Gerrit Henry, who interviewed him for *After Dark* magazine (June 1976), "I really did not *like* 'Rock Around the Clock.' I think the Beatles finally convinced me there was something going on in rock. . . . After that rock got better—better than the same old four chords, which never really turned me on."

After graduating from high school, Manilow considered a career in music, but in the interests of practicality, he enrolled at City College in New York City as an advertising major. Bored by marketing and merchandising courses, he transferred to the New York College of Music a year later and remained there until his money ran out several semesters short of graduation. Supporting himself with a job in the CBS mailroom, he attended evening classes at Juilliard for about a year. Meanwhile, at CBS, he worked his way up to film editing for the network's local affiliate station. At first assigned to insert commercials in the daytime reruns of such series as *Leave it to Beaver* and *My Little Margie,* he was eventually named film editor of *The Late Show,* the nightly feature movie spot, for which he arranged a new theme to replace Leroy Anderson's "Syncopated Clock." In his off hours, Manilow coached aspiring singers, supplied "instant arrangements" to vocalists at Broadway auditions, and played piano in local night spots. "I was *the* piano player in New York, very cheap, playing for anybody who wanted me," he told one reporter. In the late 1960's he left CBS to hit the road with singer Jeannie Lucas. The two toured the country for six months, playing "the entire Holiday Inn circuit," as Manilow put it.

On his return to New York, Manilow accepted a job as music director of the WCBS-TV series *Callback,* a weekly afternoon showcase for young talent. The program offered him an extraordinarily rich opportunity to write arrangements. "I did sixteen of them a week," he told Gerrit Henry, "from honky-tonk to opera to rock 'n' roll to legit Broadway stuff, sitting down, writing out parts for this little band I had. I learned more about arranging there than ever before—and about editing songs for time and commercial breaks and being tight. . . . I came out with quite a lot of knowledge." On the air for two seasons, *Callback* won Manilow his first Emmy citation. On the strength of his performance Manilow was named music director for a series of pilots for Ed Sullivan Productions.

In early 1970 *Callback*'s executive producer, Linda Allen, introduced Manilow to Bro Herrod, the director and producer who was putting together a musical adaptation of *The Drunkard,* a mid-nineteenth-century melodrama by W. H. S. Smith. Hired as Herrod's musical director, Manilow wrote new arrangements for such familiar tunes as "Strolling Through the Park," and "Whispering Hope" and composed a handful of new songs to enliven the play. Although most critics found the short-lived, Off Broadway production to be only mildly amusing, several of them singled out Manilow's "delightful," "appropriate," and "eminently singable" score for special praise.

Throughout the early 1970's Manilow played occasional club dates in New York City, but he derived most of his income from writing, singing, and arranging musical commercials. Among his most successful commercial credits were Kentucky Fried Chicken ("Get a bucket of chicken/Have a barrel of fun"), Maxwell House Coffee, Dodge Charger, Pepsi-Cola ("Join the Pepsi people/Feelin' free, feelin' free"), Dr. Pepper, Stridex, Band-Aids, McDonald's ("You deserve a break today"), and State Farm Insurance. A medley of those catchy, familiar jingles elicited enthusiastic applause from audiences on Manilow's subsequent national tours. As Jack Kroll noted in *Newsweek* (March 31, 1975), "Ironically, [Manilow's] greatest composition may well be not one of his smooth pop tunes . . . but the misty, haunting pastoral cry of the insurance agent, 'Just like a good neighbor, State Farm is there.' "

In the spring of 1972, while subbing for the house pianist at the Continental Baths, a Turkish bath-cum-nightclub on Manhattan's Upper West Side, Manilow accompanied the flamboyant Bette Midler, who was back at the Baths for a return engagement after a successful swing through the midwest. "It was hate at first sight," Manilow told Steven Gaines in an interview for the New York *Daily News* (December 17, 1976), "but we rehearsed anyway, and Saturday night came, and there I was at the Continental Baths in a roomful of naked men and towels and Bette came onstage looking like my mother with a fox around her neck and a turban on her head. I was rolling under the piano. I cried during the ballads and she totally knocked me for a loop."

Despite their initial aversion to each other, the pair worked so well together that Miss Midler asked the pianist to be her musical director. Manilow immediately accepted her offer and, working closely with her, selected and arranged the old songs from the 1940's, 1950's, and 1960's—novelty numbers, blues, and rock—that were to make Bette Midler a star. Her high-voltage performances of his arrangements of Glenn Miller's "In the Mood," the Andrews Sisters' "Boogie Woogie Bugle Boy," the Dixie Cups' "Chapel of Love," and other hits invariably brought down the house. Some of those restylings are included on her Grammy Award-winning LP, *The Divine Miss M,* and on *Bette Midler,* both of which were coproduced by Manilow. Rock critic Gerrit Henry attributes much of the "wonderful, kicky, style-happy beauty" of those two LP's to Manilow's "having 'painted a picture' orchestrally for each particular number."

At about that time, Manilow, following up a suggestion from his friend Ron Dante, a record producer, scraped together enough money to record three of his own tunes: "Sweet Life," "I Am Your Child," and "Sweetwater Jones." His demos in hand, he made the rounds of the recording companies. Taken by his haunting original music and by his pleasantly boyish baritone, Bell Records executives signed him for a solo album. Just before the LP, *Barry Manilow,* was scheduled for release, Manilow embarked on a national tour with Bette Midler. Taking advantage of the opportunity, Bell arranged for him to push his record by opening the second act of Miss Midler's stage show. "I was totally convinced that Bette's audience was going to kill me," he admitted to Don Kowet in an interview for *TV Guide* (February 18, 1978). "But they never did kill me. They would react after songs. They would laugh at my terrible jokes. Nobody was more surprised than I was." Audiences were particularly enthusiastic about "Could It Be Magic?" a melancholy love song based on a Chopin prelude that crescendoes to a climax of almost overpowering emotional impact. That song earned him his first standing ovation, at a performance at the outdoor Red Rock Amphitheatre in Colorado, and attracted the attention of dozens of FM disc jockeys, who might otherwise have ignored his debut album.

After Miss Midler's tour wound up in New York City, Manilow struck out on his own. With a small backup group he played Paul's Mall and the Bijou in Philadelphia, Pennsylvania, the Great American Music Hall in Atlanta, Georgia, and other rock 'n' roll clubs, using the royalties from his commercials to pay the bills. Back in New York, Clive Davis, the new president of Bell (later, Arista) Records, was cleaning house. One of the few performers he kept under contract was Barry Manilow. As soon as the singer returned to the city, Davis set up recording dates for a second album and a single. For the single, Davis selected "Mandy," a revision of a song called "Brandy," written by Scott English and Richard Kerr, that had been a smash hit in Great Britain.

Described by one critic as "an all-stops-out tearjerker," "Mandy" was perfectly suited to Manilow's affecting voice and heart-catching phrasing. Nine weeks after its release "Mandy" was the number one record in the country and its inclusion on *Barry Manilow II* (1974) helped boost the sales of that LP past the $1,000,000 mark. Manilow was stunned by his sudden success. "I was scared stiff," he told Don Kowet. "How was I supposed to follow that? What I finally realized was, what people were connecting with was not just a nice record. They were getting out of this particular song a personality. There was a person singing this song. He was moving them."

Manilow followed up "Mandy" with a succession of Top Ten singles, including "It's A Miracle," "Could It Be Magic?" "I Write the Songs," "Tryin' to Get the Feeling," "This One's For You," "Weekend in New England," "Looks Like We Made It," "Daybreak," and "Can't Smile Without You," and the best-selling albums *Tryin' To Get the Feeling* (1975), *This One's For You* (1976), and *Even Now* (1978). With the exception of the uptempo "It's A Miracle" and the toe-tapping, cheerfully optimistic "Daybreak" and "Can't Smile Without You," his singles are decidedly romantic. His albums, however, are eclectic collections of sentimental ballads, soft rock numbers, nostalgic tunes reminiscent of the 1940's, and a dozen other styles from samba to bebop to rhythm and blues. Some pop music critics have dismissed his songs as "bubblegum"; others contend that he is one of the few contemporary musicians to master the sophisticated "pop art song." However, virtually all of them recognize Manilow's superb musicianship and the craftsmanlike arrangements that give each piece "the same surface sheen, and the same underplayed but noticeable rhythmic vitality," as *New York Times* reviewer Robert Palmer once noted.

Although a sizeable proportion of his material is written by other composers (Bruce Johnston, for instance, wrote the smash hit "I Write the Songs"), Manilow composes more than half of the songs he records. His most recent LP, *Even Now,* features eight Manilow compositions, with lyrics by his most frequent collaborators, Marty Panzer, Adrienne Anderson, and Enoch Anderson. "The words I sing best to a melody are words about love," he conceded to Robert Windeler, who interviewed him for *People* magazine (August 8, 1977). "Listening only to my singles, you'd think that's all I sing about. On albums I do take it a step or two further. I'm possibly breaking through into slightly new ground with more intelligent lyrics than 'Baby, oh, baby' and more sophisticated rhythm and arrangements that go beyond a guitar and drum. Arranging is my strongest suit," he continued. "It's what separates me from everyone else. . . . I'm only a fair singer, I write nice songs, but I'm a great arranger."

To promote his recordings, Manilow took to the road for crosscountry tours in 1975 and again in 1976. Accompanied by an accomplished group of musicians and by his backup trio, Lady Flash, he played to packed houses in a seven-month, ninety-eight-city swing that included a two-week, sold-out stand at the Uris Theatre on Broadway in December 1976. His performances there won him a special Tony award and provided the material for his first double album, *Barry Manilow Live.* Within weeks of its release in the spring of 1977, that album claimed the top spot on the pop music charts.

Reviewers of Manilow's live performances have occasionally complained about his "stilted" and "awkward" gestures, his apparent addiction to the "golly-gee whiz school of patter," and his "breathless strainings and barely reached notes." Yet it is just those qualities—the awkwardness, the appealing catch in his voice—that so endear him to his thousands of fans. Manilow himself attributes at least part of his success to "the big emotional element in [his] personality." "I try to be human and natural on records," he explained to Dennis Hunt in an interview for the *Los Angeles Times* (December 4, 1976). "You can hear me spitting, you can hear me making mistakes. . . . There's a more human element in a song if my voice cracks or if you can hear me sighing. It's emotional, it's realistic, it's the real me." Reflecting the sentiments of the record-buying public, the American Guild of Variety Artists named Manilow Top Vocalist of the Year in 1976. He also won *After Dark* magazine's 1976 Ruby Award for Performer of the Year, *Photoplay*'s nationwide "Favorite Pop Music Star" poll in 1977, and the 1977 Top Male Pop Vocalist trophy at the American Music Awards.

Working hand-in-hand with his producer and director, Manilow created a kind of musical autobiography for his first network television special. "I wanted a show that would be truly special, not just linoleum floors and shiny light bulbs," he told one interviewer. "No parade of guest stars. No filler like having me sing 'Bye Bye Blackbird' with Lee Majors." Broadcast on ABC-TV on March 2, 1977, *The Barry Manilow Special* lured an estimated 38,000,000 viewers, making it one of the highest rated shows of that season. The program later won an Emmy as the outstanding variety special of 1976-77. *The Second Barry Manilow Special,* which was telecast by ABC on February 24, 1978, was equally successful in the ratings.

Tall and lean, Barry Manilow has shaggy, reddish-blond hair and large, blue, "puppy-dog" eyes. Reporters have found him to be an easygoing and talkative man with a self-deprecating sense of humor. He is a hard worker, and when he is not recording or on tour he spends hours at the piano composing new songs. For relaxation, he plays backgammon or word games, watches television, and goes to "scary" movies. Married in the late 1960's to his high school sweetheart, he was divorced about a year later. Manilow lives with his beagle, Bagel, in a plush cooperative apartment, which was decorated by his longtime "lady," Linda Allen, on Manhattan's Upper West Side. According to some reporters, he has become something of a recluse in the past year or two. "It's not that I'm so private," he told Chip Orton of *Us* magazine (March 7, 1978), "I'm just not sensational. I'm consumed with my work. I'm dedicated to it, I live for it. I don't have star friends. I don't go to crazy parties just to be seen. I don't rip hotel rooms apart when I'm on tour. Sure, I'll throw a tantrum once in a while. But nobody pays any attention to me anyway! . . . If I'm boring, then I'm boring. I don't care. If the press and the critics want to dump on me, let 'em. It's going to get worse, as far as that's concerned, so I'm totally prepared for it. . . . It may make for good reading that I'm unhappy, you know, but I'm *not* unhappy! I'm having a fabulous time."

References: After Dark 9:43+ Je '76 pors; N Y Post p23 D 18 '76 por; Newsweek 85:69 Mr 31 '75 por; People 8:44+ Ag 8 '77 pors; TV Guide 26:18+ F 18 '78 por; Who's Who in America, 1976-77

Mansfield, Michael J(oseph)

Mar. 16, 1903- United States Ambassador to Japan. Address: b. United States Embassy, Tokyo, Japan

NOTE: This biography supersedes the article that appeared in *Current Biography* in 1952.

When Michael J. ("Mike") Mansfield was asked several years ago to have his portrait painted for posterity, he declined with the comment: "When I'm gone, I want to be forgotten." It is unlikely, however, that the self-effacing veteran Montana Democrat, who held the post of majority leader in the United States Senate from 1961 until his retirement in 1976—longer than any other person—will have his wish granted. In 1977 President Jimmy Carter called upon him to serve as United States Ambassador Extraordinary and Plenipotentiary to Japan, one of the most sensitive diplomatic assignments in the world.

A former professor of Far Eastern history at the University of Montana, Mansfield was known as a leading authority on Asian affairs during his thirty-four years in the House of Representatives and the Senate. His expert assessment of conditions in Southeast Asia made him an early critic of American involvement in the Vietnam war. Over the years he has taken a liberal position on such issues as civil rights, protection of the interests of labor and the consumer, and limiting executive powers. Reflecting a consensus of opinion, Helen Dudar described Mansfield in the New York *Post* (June 26, 1971) as "the kind of man who cannot be discussed without mention of 'decency' and 'honor' and 'integrity.' "

Michael Joseph Mansfield is the oldest of the three children, and only son, of Patrick and Josephine (O'Brien) Mansfield, who were immigrants from Ireland. He was born on March 16, 1903 in New York City's Greenwich Village, where his father was a porter at the Van Rensselaer Hotel. Mike, whose mother succumbed to illness when he was a small boy, grew up in the home of an aunt and uncle in Great Falls, Montana. There he helped out in the family grocery store and attended public and parochial schools but dropped out before completing the eighth grade. By the time he reached his teens, he was anxious to see the world. "I hopped freight cars and got caught and sent home twice," he has recalled. "Once I spent the night in jail in Great Falls."

Shortly before his fifteenth birthday Mansfield enlisted in the United States Navy. The youngest Montanan to serve in World War I, he crossed the Atlantic seven times in military transport service on the USS *Minneapolis* before the Navy found out that he was under age and discharged him. He then spent one year in California with the Army and two years, beginning in November 1920, in the Philippines, China, and Siberia with the Marine Corps, but he never rose above the rank of private first class.

Back in Montana in 1922, Mansfield took a job working half a mile below ground as a "mucker" or shoveler in the copper mines of Butte. At the age of twenty-four he enrolled as a special student in the Montana School of Mines. During his year there, he met his future wife, Maureen Hayes, a teacher in Butte, who persuaded him to complete his high school education by taking correspondence courses. "[She] put some sense into me, told me I ought to go to school and make something of myself," Mansfield has recalled. "It was my wife who really got me started, who pushed me, and thank the Lord she did." In 1930 Mansfield finally left the mines—where he had in the meantime become a mining engineer—and enrolled in the University of Montana at Missoula, again as a special student. Three years later he obtained both his high school diploma and his B.A. degree.

After two Montana towns refused to hire Mansfield as a high school teacher because of his Roman Catholic faith, he returned to the university. Aided by a $25-a-month stipend as a graduate assistant and by his wife's earnings and the money she received from cashing in her life insurance, he obtained his M.A. degree in 1934 and joined the university faculty as an instructor. Although not considered an especially brilliant lecturer, he was popular among his students and eventually became a full professor of Far Eastern and Latin American history and political science. During the summers of 1936 and 1937 he did additional graduate work at the University of California in Berkeley.

"There's a little bit of political blood in all the Irish," Mansfield has observed, in explaining how he became interested in winning the seat in the United States House of Representatives for Montana's First Congressional District, which comprises the mining region in the western half of the state. Although he ran last in a three-man race in the 1940 Democratic primary, he was determined to try again. In 1942 he won a close race in the same district to fill the seat vacated by the retirement of Republican Congresswoman Jeannette Rankin.

Soon after Mansfield entered the Seventy-eighth Congress in January 1943, the House leadership, recognizing his forte, placed him on the Foreign Affairs Committee. The Montana freshman also impressed President Franklin D. Roosevelt, who sent him to China on a confidential mission in late 1944. When Mansfield returned in January 1945 he reported that he had found the Chinese demoralized and divided. Although he advised Roosevelt that the Nationalist leader Chiang Kai-shek was "the one man who can make Chinese unity and independence a reality," he indicated that he was impressed with the strength of the Communists, whom he regarded as "more agrarian reformers than revolutionaries." Mansfield later observed that the breakdown of American-Chinese relations following the Communist victory on the mainland in 1949 was one of the great failures of United States foreign policy. He is also credited with having helped to convince President Harry S. Truman that Hirohito should be retained as Emperor of Japan. In November 1949 Truman offered Mansfield the post of Assistant Secretary of State for Public Affairs, but the Montanan preferred to remain in Congress. He agreed, however, to serve as a delegate to the ninth Inter-American Conference at Bogotá in 1948 and to the sixth session of the United Nations General Assembly, which opened in Paris in November 1951.

Representative Mansfield maintained a liberal voting record during his five terms in the House. Among other measures, he supported the extension of price controls, immigration of displaced persons to the United States, increases in the minimum wage rate, economic aid to Greece and Turkey, the Marshall Plan, and a bill to establish an economic recovery program for Asia. He opposed the peacetime draft, the Taft-Hartley bill, poll taxes, funds for the House Un-American Activities Committee, and the Twenty-second Amendment to the Constitution. In addition to serving on the House Foreign Affairs Committee, Mansfield also was a member of a select committee on problems of small business, and in 1950 he headed a special committee to investigate campaign expenditures.

In 1952 Mansfield challenged the Republican incumbent Zales N. Ecton for his United States Senate seat in what turned out to be a heated campaign. When Wisconsin Republican Senator Joseph R. McCarthy visited Montana to campaign for Ecton, he accused Mansfield of "Communist-coddling practices" and of being "either stupid or a dupe," but Mansfield survived McCarthy's calumnies. Despite Republican candidate Dwight D. Eisenhower's landslide victory in the Presidential race in November, Mansfield defeated Ecton by a 5,800-vote margin out of 260,400 ballots cast and took his place in the Senate at the opening session of the Eighty-third Congress in January 1953.

Members of the inner circle of Senate Democrats, notably elder statesman Richard

B. Russell of Georgia and Majority Leader Lyndon B. Johnson of Texas, soon counted Mansfield as one of their own. He was assigned to the Foreign Relations Committee, and he also served on the Senate Appropriations, Policy, and Steering committees. In 1954 he was the Senate's Democratic representative at the Manila Conference, which established the South East Asia Treaty Organization (SEATO), and in 1958 he attended the thirteenth United Nations General Assembly.

In 1957 Mansfield became assistant Senate majority leader, or "majority whip." When Johnson took office as Vice-President in 1961, the Montana senator succeeded him as Senate majority leader at the request of President John F. Kennedy. Unlike his predecessor, Mansfield never browbeat his fellow senators. Some criticized his style as an abdication of strong leadership, but he refused to act tough. "In the first place, I could not do it," he has confessed. "In the second, if I were to do it and I got away with it, the result would be temporary. Sooner or later they'd just tell you to go to hell and do what they wanted to anyway." Mansfield delegated much of his power as legislative head of his party, preferring to work through the Democratic Policy Committee, which he headed. He also gave the Senate Democratic Conference the authority to approve his selection of committee chairmen and distribution of committee assignments.

Aware that a successful majority leader must deal responsibly with the minority party, Mansfield never hesitated to praise Republicans when they helped to win passage of important legislation such as the Civil Rights Act of 1964. He became an especially good friend of George D. Aiken of Vermont, the senior Republican in the Senate, with whom he had breakfast regularly, and who once said: "there isn't a Republican who would raise a finger to hurt Mike." Considered virtually unbeatable, Mansfield was reelected to his Senate seat with 76.2 percent of the vote in the 1958 race against Republican Lou R. Welch and obtained 64.5 percent of the vote in the 1964 contest with Alex Blewett. While his margin of victory was slightly reduced in 1970, when sporting goods dealer Harold E. "Bud" Wallace of Missoula attacked his unpopular stand in favor of gun control, Mansfield's 61 percent of the vote was still considered a landslide.

Although Mansfield supported Lyndon B. Johnson in his unsuccessful bid for the 1960 Presidential nomination—considering him "the greatest majority leader the Senate ever had" —he maintained a strong bond of affection with John F. Kennedy. "We had a very, very close, very warm relationship," he has recalled. After Kennedy's assassination in November 1963, Mansfield delivered an emotional eulogy that his taciturn nature made all the more powerful. During the 1964 Presidential campaign he declined President Johnson's offer of the second spot on the Democratic national ticket, preferring to remain in the Senate.

Mansfield's early concern over Vietnam—an issue that eventually brought him into conflict with President Johnson—prompted him to warn the Eisenhower and Kennedy administrations that the Saigon government would have to be popular with the people and based on social justice if it were to survive. Although he agreed with the Johnson Administration's original plans for a negotiated settlement in Indochina, he increasingly criticized the escalating American military involvement there. On several occasions he took the initiative in sponsoring measures aimed at ending the hostilities. His end-the-war amendment to a Selective Service bill, calling for a ceasefire and a phased withdrawal of United States troops from Vietnam coupled with the release of American prisoners of war was passed by the Senate in 1971 but rejected by the House. In addition, he cosponsored the war powers bill, introduced in the Senate in 1973, to limit the President's authority to involve the nation in undeclared international conflicts.

Despite his opposition to American military involvement in Indochina, Mansfield considers the United States a Pacific power and rejects isolationism. "There's hardly a place in the world where you don't know within an hour any event that's happened there," he has observed. "We *have* to live with one another." During his visits to the Orient he made friends with several Asian leaders, and his close ties with Prince Norodom Sihonouk, the exiled Cambodian neutralist leader, reportedly helped to pave the way for President Richard Nixon's visit to Communist China in early 1972.

The Vietnam experience convinced Mansfield that "Congress had handed its power over to the President on a silver platter." Furthermore, President Nixon's impoundment of funds appropriated by Congress and his broad interpretation of executive privilege indicated to him that the balance of power was "dangerously tilted in the direction of the executive." Mansfield became one of Nixon's most persistent critics, especially after the Watergate revelations shook the Administration's credibility. "To excise Watergate and what it implies before it becomes fatal to liberty is a fundamental responsibility of this Government," Mansfield said in February 1974. "The people of this nation, in their overwhelming number, do not want government by the whim or the will of the most powerful and influential."

Mansfield's voting record in the Senate generally received ratings of 80 percent or better from liberal groups such as the Americans for Democratic Action, the Committee on Political Education of the AFL-CIO, the Consumer Federation of America, and the National Farmers Union. By contrast, the conservative American Security Council and the Americans for Constitutional Action gave him ratings of 0 and 6 percent respectively for 1974. The Senator takes pride in his legislative initiatives to lower the voting age to eighteen, to establish the Senate Watergate Committee, to investigate the nation's intelligence agencies, and to save Montana's Flathead Lake from the Army Corps of Engineers. His key votes in the Senate in recent years include those in favor of equal enforcement of integration laws in the North as well as the South, tax reform, reductions in American troop strength in Europe, the Equal Rights Amendment, the use of federal funds for abortions, creation of a consumer protection agency, reduction of federal penalties for using marijuana, federal subsidization of Presidential elections, and protection of the rights of American Indians.

Mansfield also tried to ensure that Montana received its fair share of federal revenue and that its interests were protected. Preferring to keep in personal touch with his constituents—who look upon him as something of a folk hero—Mansfield once said: "I never intend to forget the people who put me here. If a man takes the time to write me, I think he deserves a real answer."

Announcing his intention to retire from the Senate, Mansfield told his colleagues on March 4, 1976: "There is a time to stay and a time to go. Thirty-four years [in the House and Senate] is not a long time, but it is time enough." On September 17, 1976 he made his last appearance in the Senate, and on the following day he embarked on a tour of China and the Philippines with Senator John H. Glenn Jr. of Ohio. His final act as a Senator was his participation in a meeting of Congressional leaders in Georgia with President-elect Jimmy Carter in November 1976. Mansfield's plans to devote his time to "loafing and fishing" in Montana were cut short, however, when President Carter named him in March 1977 to a five-member commission to visit Vietnam and Laos to seek information about missing United States servicemen.

On March 30, 1977 the Carter Administration announced that Mansfield would succeed James D. Hodgson as American Ambassador to Japan. Officially nominated on April 7, Mansfield was confirmed in the post by his former Senate colleagues two weeks later. After presenting his credentials to Emperor Hirohito in June, he took over as head of the United States Embassy in Tokyo, which —with some 700 employees—is the largest American legation in the world. Although the Japanese gave an enthusiastic welcome to the man who some five years earlier had championed the return of Okinawa to their control, the new Ambassador faced a number of problems. One of major concern to the Carter Administration was the decision on the part of the energy-starved Japanese to reprocess nuclear wastes into plutonium, which is not only a fuel for generating electricity but also a key ingredient for the manufacture of nuclear bombs. Mansfield was also charged with the task of reconciling the Tokyo government to President Carter's plans for large-scale American troop withdrawals from South Korea and inducing the Japanese to limit the volume of exports to the United States. According to *U.S. News & World Report* (October 31, 1977), Mansfield has been criticized by some Americans in Tokyo for "taking the Japanese side" in trade disputes. On the other hand, he is said to have been "unambassadorially blunt" in warning the Japanese of growing protectionist sentiment in the United States.

Mike Mansfield's wife and mentor, the former Maureen Hayes, whom he married on September 13, 1932, is the daughter of a Butte coal dealer. Their daughter, Anne, lives in England with her husband, Robin Morris, a professor of economics at Oxford. The pipe-smoking, Lincolnesque Montanan is six feet tall, weighs 170 pounds, and has thinning black hair that is turning gray. His recreations include listening to jazz, watching movies, and reading history and detective stories. His laconic manner has become something of a legend. According to Senator Edward M. Kennedy of Massachusetts, his favorite answers are "yep," "nope," "maybe," "could be," and "don't know." When, shortly after he assumed his ambassadorial post, a Tokyo newspaper featured an editorial about him with the headline: "A Giant Walks Among Us," Mansfield responded: "I'm no giant. I'm just a fellow embarking on a new career."

Skeptical about the wisdom of recent American foreign policy, Mansfield told a graduating class at Montana State University in 1972: "The pursuit of ideological struggle has not led us to any victories. Rather, it has projected us into a hodgepodge of foreign aid, military alliances, and into overseas operations. The warm human concern of Americans for other people has been distorted by ideological warfare; and we have plunged without warrant into the internal political and social affairs of other nations everywhere in the world. . . . In the end we came to the disaster of Vietnam. It is part of the price which has been exacted for the obstinate pursuit of the obsolete in foreign policy." Nevertheless, he is optimistic about the American future. "The country is still young, got lots of room," he told Louise Sweeney of the *Christian Science Monitor* (June 10, 1976). "Hopefully the purgatory which we've gone through in Watergate and . . . Southeast Asia will make us a better people, a better nation."

References: Christian Sci Mon p14 Je 10 '76 por; N Y Post p22 Ag 16 '64 por, p22 Je 26 '71 por; N Y Times p12 Mr 5 '76, p31 N 2 '76 por; Sat Eve Post 246:10+ O '74 por; Washington Post A p1+ S 25 '66 por, A p13 O 5 '77; Congressional Directory, 1976; Leaders in Profile: The United States Senate (1975); Ralph Nader Congress Project, 1972; Who's Who in America, 1976-77

Mansfield, Mike *See* Mansfield, M. J.

Marriner, Neville

Apr. 15, 1924- British conductor. Address: b. c/o Harold Holt Ltd., 134 Wigmore St., London W. 1, England; c/o Columbia Artists Management, 165 W. 57th St., New York City, N.Y. 10019; h. 67 Cornwall Gardens, London S.W. 7 4BA, England

In his two decades as conductor and artistic director of the Academy of St. Martin-in-the-Fields, the London-based chamber music ensemble renowned for its interpretation of baroque music, Neville Marriner has secured an enviable reputation for musicianship and spirited communication. Neville Marriner began his career as a violinist and headed the second violin section of the London Symphony Orchestra before he developed his ad hoc group of freelancers into one of the world's leading chamber orchestras. The Academy's more than 200 recordings, each of which currently sells thousands of copies, are treasured by collectors for their impeccable intonation, crisp tempos, and distinctive élan. Marriner has in recent years branched out into symphonic orchestra conducting, and on May 15, 1978 it was announced that he has been appointed to succeed Stanislaw Skrowaczewski of the Minnesota Orchestra in Minneapolis, beginning with its 1979-1980 season.

Neville Marriner was born in Lincoln, England on April 15, 1924 to Herbert Henry Marriner, a carpenter, and Ethel May (Roberts) Marriner. His father introduced him to music at an early age by instructing him in violin and piano. When interviewed by Alan Blyth for an article in *Music and Musicians* (December 1968), Neville Marriner recalled: "You could say that family music was for us what television is for most people today." Intensive violin lessons with a well-known teacher, Frederick Mountney, helped to contribute to Marriner's success in talent competitions, which he once described to Dorle Soria in an interview for *High Fidelity/Musical America* (June 1970) as "rather brutal regional talent scouting." Although Marriner was recommended at thirteen for study at London's Royal College of Music, he was allowed to enter as a scholarship student only after graduating from the Lincoln School in 1939, at fifteen. "I remember getting off the train at King's Cross with no money for a taxi and not knowing my way," he told Dorle Soria.

Marriner's musical training was interrupted by his service with Army reconnaissance from 1941 until 1943, when he was invalided out for a five-month stay in the hospital. He afterwards returned to the Royal College of Music, where he received his A.R.C.M. degree in 1944 and captured the Tagore gold medal, among other prizes. During the next five years he studied violin under René Benedetti at the Paris Conservatory, served briefly as the director of string studies at Eton College, Windsor, and became a professor at the Royal College of Music, an appointment, he told Dorle Soria, that made him "feel very old."

Having realized early in his career that he did not aspire to become a concert violinist, Marriner directed his attention to ensemble playing. During the late 1940's and early 1950's, "the formative and informative years" of his musical education, he joined the David Martin Quartet and the Virtuoso String Trio. He and Thurston Dart, a young mathematician turned musicologist and harpsichordist whom Marriner had first met when they were both "slightly shopspoiled by the war, and were convalescing in and around London," teamed up to perform and record duos. They also formed the Jacobean Ensemble, a small instrumental group that presented rare seventeenth and eighteenth-century music in the vigorous and infectious manner that Dart propounded. "Stylistically," Marriner explained to Alan Blyth in an interview for *Gramophone* (October 1974), "I feel I owe a great deal to Thurston Dart. When you played with him, whatever you did felt right, authentic. There was nothing awkward about his playing and it rubbed off on me. If you've spent the first part of your life on one instrument, you need someone like that around to guide you."

Beginning in 1952 Marriner gained his first orchestral experience as a violinist with the London Philharmonia under such eminent conductors as Arturo Toscanini, Wilhelm Furtwängler, Herbert von Karajan, and Guido Cantelli. Four years later he joined the London Symphony Orchestra, where he headed the second violin section for over a decade. Encouraged and tutored by Pierre Monteux, with whom he studied one summer at his home in Hancock, Maine, Marriner developed a marked taste for conducting. "The actual mechanics of conducting are not difficult," he has explained. It's getting the confidence. It's like taking a driving test."

The Academy of St. Martin-in-the-Fields, a chamber music group that Marriner founded in the late 1950's at the Church of St. Martin at London's Trafalgar Square, derives its name from the so-called "academies" of renaissance and eighteenth-century dilettanti. "The name was chosen without much thinking," he told Dorle Soria, "because, when we started, we never thought we would even get off the ground. And then we were stuck with it." The gusto and expertise of its small group of players—several of whom held first desks with leading London orchestras—won the approval of music lovers and critics from the very beginning. After attending one of its inaugural (1958-1959) season's concerts on January 29, 1959, for example, Harold Rutland registered in *Musical Times* (March 1959) his unqualified approval of the Academy's "spirited, clean-textured and stylish" performance of string works by Handel, Corelli, Bach, Gluck, and Geminiani.

Increasingly well-known through its broadcasts over BBC's Third Programme to listeners whom Marriner has described as "a general radio audience, a sort of wallpaper audience," the Academy grew rapidly from its origins as an "after-evensong" chamber music group into one of the most innovative and highly paid ensembles in the world. It secured its reputation with a series of highly praised recordings, beginning with discs released in the early 1960's by the recording company known as L'Oiseau-Lyre. In reviewing a L'Oiseau-Lyre issue of Italian concertos performed by the Academy, Richard Franko Goldman spoke for other critics when he referred to Marriner in *Musical Quarterly* (April 1966) as "a musician of refinement, intelligence, and taste," and called the playing "exquisite, a model for the modern baroque ensemble or chamber orchestra."

With more than 200 records in his discography, Marriner is justifiably proud of his Academy's success on such labels as Decca's Argo, EMI, CBS, and Philips. He recently signed a ten-year exclusive contract with Philips, under the terms of which he agreed to 100 discs: 90 with the Academy, 10 with other orchestras. In his account of an Academy recording session for *High Fidelity/Musical America* (February 1968), Edward Greenfield called Marriner "a recording manager's dream, because he understands technical problems as well as most technicians, and accepts the necessity of retakes." Marriner is convinced that chamber music recordings can generate as much physical excitement as a symphony orchestra.

Notwithstanding his loyalty to the Academy, in the late 1960's and the 1970's Marriner increasingly relinquished its directorship except for its annual tours and recording sessions. Instead he conducted to unanimous acclaim such far-flung chamber orchestras as Lisbon's Gulbenkian Orchestra, Tel Aviv's Israel Chamber Orchestra, and Sydney's Australian Chamber Orchestra. His debut with the New York Chamber Orchestra at Lincoln Center's Philharmonic Hall on August 23, 1971 during one of the annual Mostly Mozart festivals left no doubt in the mind of critic Harris Goldsmith in *High Fidelity/Musical America* (December 1971)—"of his first-rate musicianship and of his ability to lead." A similar occasion five years later, on August 25, 1976, this time at Alice Tully Hall, fired the enthusiasm of Speight Jenkins who the next day in the New York *Post* commended Marriner for a "definitive all-Mozart evening which culminated in the best 'Haffner' Symphony (No. 35 in D Major, K. 385) that this listener can remember hearing."

The growing critical acclaim of Neville Marriner led in 1969 to his directorship of the Los Angeles Chamber Orchestra, a fledgling group of about forty players founded at the Los Angeles Music Center's Mark Taper Forum. In preparing its annual fall and spring concert seasons Marriner coped patiently with a host of problems from funding to firing; he gradually molded the ensemble into what he has called "one of the best in the business," with a repertory that includes both the staples of chamber music and the challenging new music. When asked by Edward Greenfield in an interview for the *Guardian* (June 22, 1974) to compare the Los Angeles Chamber Orchestra with the Academy, Marriner diplomatically explained: "Man for man, [the Americans] play their instruments so much better," but "they are much less well equipped to play in a large ensemble, where British players quickly form themselves into an orchestral section."

It was in London during its first European tour in the summer of 1974 that the Los Angeles Chamber Orchestra made its first recordings: an all-Stravinsky program for EMI and a Josef Suk, Leos Janacek, and Richard Strauss offering for Decca. At that time Marriner, in the same *Guardian* interview, deftly parried the question of possible conflict of interest with the Academy, remarking to Edward Greenfield: "I like both to have style, but I want them to have different styles." He further observed that the Los Angeles Chamber Orchestra plays "nineteenth-century music marvellously, twentieth-century too. Mozart they play well, but they are slightly abrasive in Italian music, Vivaldi—Corelli and so on." When he was about to succeed André Previn as artistic director of London's South Bank Summer Music Festival for a three-year stint starting in 1975, he assured the press that the programming would reflect his personal tastes and steer clear of avant-garde music. He replaced the previously predominant trios, quartets, and small chamber music ensembles with the Academy as resident orchestra and expanded the repertory to include works by such divergent composers as Brahms, Mendelssohn, Schumann, Stravinsky, and Tippett.

When, in the fall of 1977, Marriner resigned as director of the Los Angeles Chamber Orchestra, he explained: "The idea of growing old as violinist never appealed to me, and the idea of growing old as part of a string quartet never appealed to me. But I would like to grow old as music director of a symphony orchestra, and that requires long-term views, of course." Critical response to his occasional symphonic guest conducting appearances, primarily in the United States, indicated that Marriner's aspirations were not unfounded. In reviewing in the New York *Times* (April 23, 1977) Marriner's debut in an all-Mozart program with the New York Philharmonic Orchestra at Avery Fisher Hall on April 21, 1977, Donal Henahan pronounced him an "assured and unequivocal leader" with "few peers as an 18th-century specialist." "His beat was precise and carefully subdivided to help out sections or individual players who may need special consideration, and it never lapsed into the meaningless arm-pumping that so often passes for conducting even among well-known maestros." Few critics who attended Marriner's return engagements with the New York Philharmonic during its Music in May series in the spring of 1978 would take issue with that assessment.

Continuing to expand his image, Marriner recently conducted his first opera, Puccini's *La Boheme*, for Sadler's Wells in London, and he is scheduled to conduct opera at the Aix-en-Provence Festival, in France. His other future commitments include an agreement to be principal guest conductor with the Südwestfunk Orchestra in Stuttgart, Germany beginning in 1980. Most importantly, Marriner has been named to succeed the Polish-born conductor Stanislaw Skrowaczewski as music director of the Minnesota Orchestra (formerly the Minneapolis Symphony Orchestra), starting with the season of 1979-80. Beginning with 1979, he will be music director of the Meadow Brook Festival, featuring summer concerts of the Detroit Symphony.

Neville Marriner, who has been described by one interviewer as "jaunty" and "showmanlike" and by another as "gentle, smiling, and warm," has brown eyes and thick brown hair and carries a trim 160 pounds on his five-foot eight-and-a-half-inch frame. In nervous moments he chain-smokes one of his favorite self-indulgences, Henri Winterman cigars. In his mid-fifties he is driven by the conviction that "10-year plans are too long and five-year plans are too short." He is an honorary fellow of the Royal Academy of Music and has received some of Europe's top recording awards, including the Grand Prix du Disque, the Edison award, and the Mozart Gemeinde prize.

Marriner's marriage to Diana Margaret Carbutt on May 10, 1949 ended in divorce eight years later. On December 20, 1957 he married Elizabeth Mary Sims. They live in a Regency-style apartment in South Kensington, London, but also spend some time in their seventeenth-century country home in Devon and their "very Jane Austen" house in Lyme Regis. The conductor has two grown children: Susan Frances and Andrew Stephen, a promising clarinetist whom his father would rather see lead "a quiet life as a cricketer" than become a musician.

References: Gramophone 45:478 Mr '68 por, 52:661+ O '74 por; Guardian p10 Je 22 '74 por; Hi Fi/Mus Am 20:4+ Je '70 por; Mus & Mus 17:34 D '68 por; Washington Post L p3 N 13 '77 pors; International Who's Who, 1977-78; International Who's Who in Music and Musicians' Directory, 1976; Who's Who, 1977-78

Martin, Steve

1945(?)- Comedian. Address: b. c/o Warner Brothers Records, Inc., 3300 Warner Blvd., Burbank, Calif. 91510

After struggling for years as a television comedy writer for such acts as the Smothers Brothers, and as a virtually unknown entertainer, Steve Martin, a former philosophy student, attained fame almost overnight as a stand-up comic. Martin started in show business as a teen-ager at Disneyland, traveled the arduous route of opening for rock groups, performed in second-rate nightclubs, and ap-

Steve Martin

peared on television talk shows before reaching the stratosphere of the entertainment world. By 1977 he had become a fixture on such television programs as the *Tonight Show Starring Johnny Carson* and *Saturday Night Live,* on both of which he occasionally still serves as guest host, and his performances in nightclubs and concert halls are consistently sold out. His hilarious LP album *Let's Get Small* brought him a Grammy award in 1978.

Self-described as "a ramblin' kind of guy . . . a crazy kind of guy . . . a yew-neek kind of guy," Steve Martin is an uninhibited clown, usually attired in a decorous, tailored white suit. Wearing such familiar props as his fantastic balloon hat, bunny ears, fake nose and glasses, or an arrow through his head, he often succumbs to manic attacks of "happy feet." His jumble of material includes weird tales, funny songs, one-liners, slapstick, and parodies of himself and of show business. Martin's brand of comedy, with its "barely controlled lunacy," may be surrealistic, frivolous, racy, or sometimes downright gross, but it is generally apolitical. His characteristic expressions, such as "Well, excuuuuuse *me!*" and "We're havin' some fun now, eh folks?" are widely mimicked by his exuberant devotees.

While sources are vague about the date and place of his birth, Steve Martin, the son of Glenn and Mary (Lee) Martin, was probably born in Waco, Texas about 1945. At the age of five he moved with his parents and older sister from Waco to Inglewood, California. His father, a real estate agent, occasionally acted in local theatrical productions. Steve Martin remembers that he became irretrievably stagestruck at three, after seeing a Jerry Lewis movie, and at five he began to entertain. "I'd watch the skits on the Red Skelton show, memorize 'em and then go to school and perform during 'Show and Tell,' " he told Tony Schwartz for a *Newsweek* cover story (April 3, 1978).

In 1955 the Martin family moved to Garden Grove in Southern California's Orange County, two miles from Anaheim, where Disneyland had just opened. There, ten-year old Steve soon landed his first after-school job. Rigged out in 1890's style, with a straw hat, vest, and bow tie, he sold twenty-five-cent guidebooks to the amusement park. During his eight fun-filled years at the Magic Kingdom he also sold trick ropes in Frontierland and novelty devices at the joke shop, performed magic tricks at Merlin's on Main Street, and was taught by a friend, John McEuen, to play the banjo. He was especially fascinated by vaudeville comedian Wally Boag who had an act at Disneyland's Golden Horseshow Revue that included "good, clean" comedy routines, songs, and balloons twisted into outlandish animals. After memorizing the entire act, Steve Martin, at sixteen, was featured as "Mouth and Magic" in a Wally Boag production called "It's Vaudeville Again." At the same time he moonlighted at local coffeehouses, appearing as the straight man in a two-man comedy act with his friend Morris Walker. At eighteen Martin left Disneyland and went to work at nearby Knott's Berry Farm, where he appeared in a melodrama at the Birdcage Theatre four or five times daily. After each show, he presented a ten-minute mélange of comedy, magic, and banjo-playing.

Although Martin considered school of secondary importance and was admittedly "mostly a goof-off," he nevertheless graduated from Garden Grove High School and enrolled in a junior college. Inspired by a girlfriend and fellow performer named Stormy, who introduced him to W. Somerset Maugham's *The Razor's Edge* and assured him that "knowledge is the most important thing there is," he then entered Long Beach State College to major in philosophy. But when after three years of studying "like crazy" and earning straight A's he read Ludwig Wittgenstein's view that all philosophical problems are merely problems of semantics, he became disillusioned and dropped out of college to return to the performing arts. "It was the only thing that had real meaning because it had no meaning," he observed in the *Newsweek* interview. "In art, truth comes and goes according to fashion. It can't be measured. You don't have to explain why, or justify anything. If it works, it works. As a performer, non sequiturs make sense, nonsense is real." In 1967 Martin enrolled in a television writing course at UCLA and began performing his comedy routines to mixed reviews at such local nightclubs as Mr. Ledbetter's in Westwood. "Sometimes I'd kill, but a lot of times there'd be no reaction at all," he told the *Newsweek* interviewer. "I developed the theory that anyone can be great sometimes; the hardest thing is to be consistent."

Martin received his first major break when he submitted material to Mason Williams, the head writer for *The Smothers Brothers Comedy Hour*, who had once seen his act. Hired for the controversial CBS-TV show at $500 a week, Martin became one of its ten writers to share an Emmy award—for telecasts presented in March 1968. Now in demand as a writer, he went on to prepare material for such performers as Glen Campbell, Ray Stevens, Pat Paulsen, and John Denver, and after writing routines for Sonny and Cher he was invited to appear on their show as one of the background characters. Martin also helped to write an episode for Dick Van Dyke's NBC-TV special *Van Dyke and Company*, telecast on October 30, 1975, that was nominated for an Emmy award.

Although he was now earning $1,500 a week, writing for others did not satisfy Steve Martin. "Comedy comes down to a split second and by the time it leaves the typewriter to the director to the star, it was gone," he told Dave Hirshey of the New York *Sunday News* (October 23, 1977). "That's why I left." On his slow route to stardom through performing his own material, Steve Martin now endured a depressing period opening for "stoned-out" rock groups in small California clubs. "It was horrible," he recalled in the interview with Hirshey. "I was a total drug casualty. I had a beard and long hair. I wore a turquoise squash blossom necklace and a conch shell belt and those old band uniform frock coats right out of Sergeant Pepper's Lonely Hearts Club." Unable to function as a comedian in such a chaotic atmosphere, Martin left the rock scene after about two years. "There's got to be order for my comedy to work," he has explained, "because chaos in the midst of chaos is *not* funny, but chaos in the midst of order *is* funny."

In what Dave Hirshey has termed his "Straight Arrow Period," Steve Martin trimmed his hair, shaved off his beard, donned a neat three-piece white suit, and hit the Las Vegas circuit, opening for such headliners as Sonny and Cher, Helen Reddy, and Ann-Margret. But although on one occasion Elvis Presley visited him backstage to praise his "oblique sense of humor," Martin's act failed to ignite the enthusiasm of Las Vegas audiences. Later, after touring the Playboy Club circuit, Martin commented: "It's blow-your-brains-out time. Absolutely the worst audiences in the world. You learn technique, though, you sharpen your ad lib." In 1973 he made the first of many guest appearances on Johnny Carson's *Tonight Show*. "It's rumored that Carson moved to the West Coast to be closer to me," he later observed.

Disillusioned by his failure to make a real hit with nightclub audiences, by 1975 Martin was seriously considering leaving show business. Then he decided to change his routine, turning to a more bizarre, outrageous kind of humor, and his prospects immediately improved. His popularity soared, and people began to imitate him. A turning point in his career occurred in August 1975, when he headlined a two-week sold-out engagement at San Francisco's Boarding House, a club where he had failed to make much of an impression when he appeared there the first time in 1972. Reviewing a subsequent performance by Martin at the Cellar Door in the nation's capital, Alex Ward wrote in the Washington *Post* (October 8, 1975) of the "upcoming star" who "defies classification," and added: "This man is strange. And funny. See him at your own risk." Soon Martin was appearing with increasing frequency on such programs as *Dinah!*, the *Merv Griffin Show*, the *Dick Cavett Show*, the *Tonight Show*, the *Hollywood Squares*, and the *Gong Show*. He was both a writer and guest performer with ABC-TV's *John Denver Rocky Mountain Christmas Show*, presented in December 1975, and he appeared as a regular for four weeks in the summer of 1976 on CBS-TV's *Johnny Cash Show*.

Martin's popularity was further enhanced in the fall of 1976, when he was showcased for the first time on NBC-TV's irreverent *Saturday Night Live*. About the same time he was seen on a *Home Box Office* television special that had been taped earlier that year at the Troubadour in Los Angeles. In January 1977 he substituted for the first time for Johnny Carson as host of the *Tonight Show*. (All in all, by the spring of 1978 he had been seen on that program over forty times, including five times as host.) In April 1977 he performed before a capacity crowd at the 3,200-seat Dorothy Chandler Pavilion in Los Angeles, and later that year he appeared with Bette Midler and others in a CBS-TV special honoring *Rolling Stone* magazine on its tenth anniversary.

In October 1977 Martin embarked on a sixty-day tour that grossed over $1,000,000, performing for an estimated 500,000 fans at college campuses and auditoriums in fifty cities from coast to coast. Analyzing the comedian's appeal in a review of the final performance of his national tour, at the 9,000-seat Anaheim Convention Center, Dan Sullivan wrote in the Los Angeles *Times* (December 12, 1977): "Mr. Martin is an original. Most comics have a single face. He is a spinner, a Jekyll and Hyde—which is why we laugh at him, and identify with him too." He alternates "between frenzy and sobriety" in what seems to be "the healthiest (and certainly funniest) kind of therapy . . . that probably accounts for the temptation to imitate it when one comes home." Sullivan also noted that Martin played country music on the banjo "seriously and well."

To Mary Beth Crain, also writing in the Los Angeles *Times* (December 4, 1977), the character Steve Martin assumes is "selfish, amoral, pompous, inept, garish, crude, rude," thereby allowing the audience "to delight in their superiority over the fool before them." A critic for *Variety* (October 26, 1977), reviewing Martin's performance in a show at Harrah's Club in Reno, commented that "there is no middle ground when it comes to this off-the-wall, nonsensical, visual, often childish, and rapid style of comedy; one likes it or one does not." According to Kathy Lowry of *New Times* (September 2, 1977), Steve Martin's comedy is "more accessible, blander —Velveeta as compared to Limburger," than that of such peers as George Carlin, Robert Klein, Lily Tomlin, and Richard Pryor.

Deploring what he viewed as the "anti-intellectual" quality of his humor, Marvin Kitman of *Newsday* (April 20, 1978) expressed concern that Martin presages the decline of American comedy and suggested that he was literally "giving American humor an arrow in the head." Don Shirley complained in the Washington *Post* (September 16, 1977) that Martin's comedy "tickles the mind without really piercing it." In his article in *Rolling Stone* (December 1, 1977), David Felton suggested that Martin "basically has one joke and he's it," but added: "He breaks down barriers. He allows us to see the comedian in all of us." As Robert Hilburn observed in the Los Angeles *Times* (February 23, 1978), Martin conveys the attitude that "it's O.K. to be yourself, as silly as you want to be in this overly cool, protective, conservative world: *Let it all hang out.*" And Tom Shales of the Washington *Post* (September 15, 1977) concluded: "Steve Martin is a cranked-down prophet for a new age of self."

In a serious self-analysis given to David Felton in the *Rolling Stone* interview, Martin said: "I think ultimately, when I'm at my best, it's a total . . . presentation . . . of a human being, onstage, being vulnerable, being afraid, being confident, fooling myself, you know, lying to myself. . . . The different little jokes and things are held together by an attitude of that personality." Martin has cited Jack Benny, Red Skelton, Jerry Lewis, Pat Paulsen, and Lenny Bruce, among those who have inspired him, but since his material is unique, influences are difficult to detect. A self-styled nihilist and existentialist, Martin considers politics a "depressing subject" and tries to keep his act purposely apolitical and atopical. As he has explained, he tries in his routines to present "little personal private observations of the world in general" and to show "how you have to become completely crazy in order to survive."

In his comedy routines, likeable Steve Martin, "who has made a joke out of telling a joke," also becomes the "odious creature" who is aghast when his 102-year-old mother asks to borrow $10 for food, and who shot his girlfriend because he did not want to drive her home. He teaches his audiences to sing-along his granny's free-verse credo: "Be courteous, kind, and forgiving . . . be oblong and have your knees removed. Be tasteless, rude, and offensive"; and he comes out with such nonsensical phrases as: "Is it O.K. to yell movie in a crowded fire house?" Martin boasts about buying a $300 pair of socks, a fur sink, an electric dog polisher, and a gasoline-powered turtleneck sweater. His repertoire of gags includes such subjects as taking hostages and "demanding $100,000 cash, a getaway car, and that the letter "M" be stricken from the English language"; giving his cat a bath but having the fur stick to his tongue; and dating Jacqueline Onassis after meeting her in a laundromat. He often punctuates his comedy routines with such phrases as: "Let's go with *Professional Show Business!!!*" or, "Okay—that's enough *funny comedy gags!*"

Martin's routine about a drug that makes one small instead of high became the title number of his LP comedy album *Let's Get Small,* which was released by Warner Brothers Reprise Records in 1977 and captured a Grammy award in February 1978. That same month he was nominated for an Academy Award for his eight-minute comedy film *The Absent-Minded Waiter* (Paramount, 1977), in which he played the title role, and he was presented by the UCLA student body with its second annual Jack Benny Award for entertainment excellence. Martin has contracted with NBC to star in two television specials. He appears as the villainous Dr. Maxwell in the recently completed film *Sergeant Pepper's Lonely Hearts Club Band,* and he intends to write and star in "Easy Money," a "rags-to-riches-to-rags comedy," as well as "White Man's Vacation," a mock travelogue, for Universal Pictures. He has accepted the lead in George Lucas' forthcoming comedy thriller, "Radioland Murders." Among his other projects is a book of short stories, "Cruel Shoes," which is to be privately printed. His most recent album, *A Wild and Crazy Guy,* was released in late 1978.

Although Steve Martin's "rubberized lips and gangly limbs" are among his most noticeable characteristics on stage, he has what Kathy Lowry of *New Times* describes as "a beach boy handsome face betrayed only by a thick shock of prematurely gray hair and piercing eyes." According to Tom Shales of the Washington *Post,* he now lives "a vegetarian life without drugs or booze," which, he says, completes his "refreshingly reactionary image." Something of a recluse offstage, he is unmarried, but he has on occasion dated such eligible young women of the entertainment world as singer Linda Ronstadt and, more recently, actress Bernadette Peters.

Martin makes his home in Aspen, Colorado, in a house that is heated by solar energy, with his two cats, Betty and Dr. Forbes. He is an avid collector of late nineteenth-century American art and, as his manager, Bill McEuen, has revealed, "he often sits with the doors shut, totally silent, and looks at oil paintings." In his interviews with Louise Farr in *New West* (April 11, 1977) Martin observed: "With paintings, you can be, sort of like, safe. You get them and they stay exactly the same. They don't bother you. . . . They take the place of people, sometimes, too." He enjoys reading old magic books, art books, museum catalogs, and the *New Yorker;* listening to Irish folk music; playing an occasional game of horseshoes with his neighbor John Denver; and skiing. But for real relaxation from the rigors of touring, Steve Martin resorts to more outlandish pastimes. "Every time I've been to New York I've tried to lift the Metropolitan Museum of Art off the ground," he told Wayne Robins of *Newsday* (September 27, 1977). "This time, I've gotten it up two or three inches."

References: N Y Sunday News mag p17+ O 23, '77 pors; New Times 9:55+ S 2 '77 pors; New West 2:67 Ap 11 '77 por; Newsweek 91:60+ Ap 3 '78 pors; People 9:86+ My 1 '78 pors; Rolling Stone p58+ D 1 '77 pors

---

Martins, Peter

Oct. 27, 1946- Dancer. Address: b. c/o New York City Ballet, New York State Theatre, Lincoln Center for the Performing Arts, New York City, N.Y. 10023

As the citation accompanying his 1977 *Dance* magazine award noted, Peter Martins is "the personification of the premier danseur noble," with his masculine elegance, prodigious technique, and indefinable stage presence. Those qualities have brought him to his present eminence as one of the top box office attractions of the ostensibly "starless" New York City Ballet. Schooled in the rigidly classical Bournonville tradition of the Royal Danish Ballet, Martins was for several years a principal dancer with that company before joining George Balanchine's iconoclastic City Ballet in 1969. Under Balanchine's guidance, Martins came into his own as a versatile dancer of astounding physical capabilities, equally at home in the restrained classical purity of *The Nutcracker*, the lighthearted hoofing of *Union Jack*, or the flashy double *tours en l'air* and multiple pirouettes of *Tchaikovsky Pas de Deux*. "To me, dancing is a total expression of myself," he said in a recent interview. "In these last few seasons, I have become aware that I'm not just a ballet dancer. That's become a superficial term to me. I look at dancing differently now. I just see myself as a *dancer*."

Peter Martins was born in Copenhagen, Denmark on October 27, 1946. His father, a structural engineer, and his mother, a concert pianist, divorced shortly after their son's birth, and the boy was, as he once put it, "brought up by women." Despite the influences of his mother and of his aunt and uncle, both principals with the Royal Danish Ballet, the boy had no interest in the dance. Nevertheless, Mrs. Martins took the stubborn seven-year-old along when she shepherded her two older daughters to the open auditions for the Royal Danish Ballet School. "The school didn't take my sisters," Peter Martins told John Gruen in an interview for Gruen's book, *The Private World of Ballet* (1975). "They took me. They already had too many girls. When they saw this little white-haired boy in the waiting room, they just grabbed me, gave me an audition, and, the next thing I knew, I was a member of the Royal Danish Ballet School."

For the first six years, Martins, admittedly the "most undisciplined, belligerent kid around," openly hated the school's strict daily routine. After a full day of traditional ballet classes followed by academic lessons, the children performed nightly with the resident opera and ballet companies. "Three thousand people [watched] while we ran around the stage foraging in the singers' pockets for cookies," he informed Tobi Tobias, who interviewed him for a *Dance* magazine (June 1977) profile. "Too much for a child of eight, nine, ten. Never saw your friends, never had time to play. Never." Martins rebelled twice—once when he was about twelve, and again when he was sixteen, but under the demanding yet sympathetic tutelage of Stanley Williams, he settled down and passed the company's rigorous examinations and was named an "aspirant," a position somewhat comparable to that of an apprentice.

While still an aspirant, Martins danced his first solo in Hans Brenaa's short ballet, *Moods*. Fired by the occasional appearances of the legendary Erik Bruhn, whom he copied "like mad," Martins was an eager pupil in Vera Volkova's character and mime classes and willingly put in extra hours to develop the speed and technical precision required for the ballets of August Bournonville, which dominated the Royal Danish Ballet's repertory. To increase his stamina and strengthen his muscles, he took up soccer and tennis and worked out with body-building equipment.

When he was eighteen, Peter Martins was accepted into the company's corps de ballet, probably because, in his words, "they needed boys on the back row." At first he danced corps parts in traditional ballets, but when the company directors realized that he could dance better alone they assigned him leading roles in such contemporary ballets as Frank Schaufuss' *Garden Party* and Birgit Cullberg's *Moon Reindeer*. Within two years, he was named a principal dancer. The youngest male principal in the company, he appeared in such Bournonville ballets as *Napoli*, *La Sylphide*, and *Konservatoriet* and in the contemporary ballets of John Cranko, Frederick Ashton, George Balanchine, and Kenneth MacMillan. He was also featured in several new ballets by Flemming Flindt, the director of the Royal Danish Ballet, among them, the full-length *The Three Musketeers; The Miraculous Mandarin*, a gruesome melodrama; *The Young Man Who Must Marry;* and *Gala Variations*, a classical pas de deux choreographed especially for Martins and Kirsten Simone. Strangely enough, he was never entrusted with leading roles in *Giselle* or *Swan Lake*.

Visiting choreographers were so taken with Martins' astonishing technique and elegant line that they often asked him to perform with their home companies. After months of refusals, the Royal Danish Ballet reluctantly granted him a leave of absence in mid-1967. In August of that year, he rushed to Edinburgh, Scotland to replace the injured Jacques D'Amboise in the New York City Ballet's touring production of George Balanchine's *Apollo*. Dancing with ballerinas whom he had met for the first time only the day before, Martins turned in a confident and authoritative performance as the boyish god.

Impressed by Martins' eloquent interpretation of that difficult role, Balanchine invited him to appear as a guest artist with the company during its 1967-68 New York season. New York audiences first saw Martins as the courtly cavalier to Suzanne Farrell's Sugar Plum Fairy in Balanchine's popular production of *The Nutcracker*, City Ballet's traditional Christmas offering. In January 1968 he once again filled in for the ailing D'Amboise, taking his place in *Symphony in C*, Balanchine's physically demanding abstract ballet, in the Petipa-influenced "Diamonds" movement of *Jewels*, and in *Apollo*. Although Walter Terry found Martins ineffective as the mature god, he was impressed by his portrayal of the youthful Apollo. "He explores this area fearlessly, but with the awkward, probing, impulsive steps of a child," Terry wrote in the *Saturday Review* (February 3, 1968). "Martins handles the remarkable *gaucheries* which Balanchine has devised better than any other Apollo I have ever seen."

Throughout 1968 Martins jetted back and forth between performances with the Royal Danish Ballet in Europe and guest appearances with the New York City Ballet in the United States. "The situation became absurd," he told Gruen. "I wanted to be a free man. I wanted to be free of the Royal Danish Ballet and its strict policies." Finally, in 1969, he "decided to take [his] chances" with the New York City Ballet. By his own account, he spent most of his first year with the company in the Ginger Man, a restaurant across the street from the Lincoln Center for the Performing Arts complex, the City Ballet's home base. Unused to Balanchine's unconventional and experimental classes, Martins injured himself repeatedly. Frustrated by the consequent inactivity—he danced, on the average, once a week—and by Balanchine's abrasive personality, he considered leaving the company and, at one point, began contract negotiations with American Ballet Theatre, a more classically oriented company. "I was only capable of doing one thing—classical ballet," Martins told Maria Hodgson in an interview for the New York *Times* (May 11, 1975). "Balanchine wanted to change me. He was bored with my technique and wanted something different. . . . He used to tell me I was stupid, stubborn, that I thought the world of myself, that I would never grow. Then I began to listen, and I realized that he was right." Returning to the fold, Martins took extra sessions with his old mentor, Stanley Williams, and put in an hour's warmup at the *barre* before attending Balanchine's morning workout. By the mid-1970's he was so accustomed to Balanchine's methods that he regularly taught company classes in the maestro's absence.

Over the next few years Martins took on principal roles in such standard City Ballet offerings as *Chopiniana*, Michel Fokine's abstract romantic ballet; Balanchine's one-act version of *Swan Lake; A Midsummer Night's*

Dream; Firebird; Serenade, an archetypical example of Balanchine's neoclassicism; *Allegro Brillante,* a plotless choreographic exercise; Jerome Robbins' *Dances at a Gathering; Liebeslieder Walzer;* the abstract classical ballets *Divertimento No. 15* and *Ballet Imperial;* and *Tchaikovsky Pas de Deux,* a showpiece of classical pyrotechnics comparable in virtuosity to the *Grand Pas Classique.* He also danced in the world premieres of Balanchine's *Duo Concertante,* an extended pas de deux, and *Violin Concerto,* and in Robbins' *The Goldberg Variations, The Afternoon of a Faun,* and *In the Night,* a companion piece to *Dances At a Gathering.*

Because he likes to "slip into" the classical repertory now and again, Martins occasionally took time off from the City Ballet to dance Prince Siegfried in *Swan Lake,* Count Albrecht in *Giselle,* Prince Florimund in *The Sleeping Beauty,* or James in *La Sylphide* with a number of major international companies, including the London Festival Ballet, the National Ballet of Canada, and the Royal Danish Ballet. His interpretation of James, the quintessential romantic hero, in the Royal Danish Ballet's faithful staging of Bournonville's *La Sylphide* at the Metropolitan Opera House in New York City in May 1976 was unanimously applauded. "Martins was breathtaking in every respect," Nancy Goldner noted in the New York *Times* (June 13, 1976). "His mime was crystal clear and melodious, his acting full-bodied and yet subtle, and his dancing impeccable."

Although both technically and physically Martins is the ideal premier danseur noble, on more than one occasion he has admitted that he is easily bored by the classics. "There you are, most of the time, standing off to the side, your hand to your brow, or—aaah—held over your heart," he explained to Tobi Tobias. "There's not enough movement, and the acting becomes self-indulgent. You wait and you wait and you wait, and after a while, you do your one little variation. . . . I don't want to be a cavalier, a prince; I want to be a dancer." Because there is "so much dancing" in the Balanchine ballets that dominate the repertory of the City Ballet, Martins has refused to be enticed by lucrative offers from American Ballet Theatre. "I don't think there's a single person [at ABT] to teach me anything," he has said. Nevertheless, he has acknowledged that the incredible physical feats, superb control, and "recklessness" of Mikhail Baryshnikov, the electrifying former ABT principal dancer now with City Ballet, have had a "tremendous influence" on his dancing. He cheerfully confessed to one interviewer that he steals "every big trick in [Baryshnikov's] repertory."

Martins has been similarly challenged by the impeccable performances of Suzanne Farrell, his most frequent partner. Ideally matched, the two have dazzled critics in innumerable ballets, including John Taras' *Daphnis and Chlöe;* Balanchine's *Chaconne,* the first pas de deux created especially for them; and in Jerome Robbins' *In G Major* and *Other Dances,* a series of lyrical duets and tour-de-force solos originally commissioned for Baryshnikov and Natalia Makarova. Unlike many male dancers of comparable technical skill, Martins enjoys partnering because, as he once put it, he likes being "responsible for making [the ballerina] look good." In addition to Miss Farrell, he has partnered Melissa Hayden, Patricia McBride, Gelsey Kirkland, Kay Mazzo, Allegra Kent, and Karin von Aroldingen.

Martins has always considered the directorship of a major ballet company his ultimate career goal, but he was taken by surprise when, in 1976, the Royal Danish Ballet asked him if he would be interested in assuming the company directorship upon the resignation of Flemming Flindt in 1978. Because he felt that he was too young and too inexperienced, Martins declined. He enclosed with his letter of refusal a twenty-five-page list of suggestions. Among other things, he recommended that the company, which had taken a decidedly radical turn under Flindt, immediately restore its traditional Bournonville repertory, "not because they are venerable fossils, but because they are so damn good," and, for variety, revive its Balanchine, Ashton, and Robbins ballets.

Just a few months later, on January 8, 1977, Martins directed a small company of friends—Suzanne Farrell, Heather Watts, Daniel Duell, and a few other City Ballet dancers temporarily unemployed due to the company musicians' strike—in a full evening of dance at Brooklyn College's Whitman Hall. The varied bill of fare included the second movement of Robbins' *In G Major,* the premieres of Robert Weiss's *Reflection,* Richard Tanner's *Songs of Innocence/Songs of Experience,* and *Calcium Light Night,* Martins' first effort as a choreographer, and as a main course, four Balanchine staples: *Allegro Brillante, Tarantella,* the *Agon* pas de deux, and an excerpt from *Who Cares?* Despite Martins' insistence that it was "just a petit four on the program," *Calcium Light Night,* then in an unfinished state, evoked the most enthusiastic response of the evening.

Critics were equally enchanted when *Calcium Light Night,* brilliantly executed by Daniel Duell and Heather Watts, received its official premiere at the New York State Theatre in Lincoln Center on January 19, 1978. The ballet, which takes its name from one of the several Charles Ives's compositions that served as its inspiration, is a tongue-in-cheek exercise in pure movement, consisting of seven showy solos—four for the male dancer, three for the female—and two duets, one of which amounts to "a near tug-o-war," according to one critic. To Walter Terry, who reviewed the performance for the New York *Trib* (January 23, 1978), *Calcium Light Night* was "Martinized Balanchine," blending, like many of Balanchine's works, "ballet and modern (or at least 'free') dance techniques." But although Terry recognized Balanchine's unmistakable imprint in the "flexed feet," the "sudden angularities," and the "swift shifts in directions," he reported that Martins was only "influenced, not enslaved, by his august mentor." Buoyed by his success, Martins is eager to do a second ballet. "Choreography is all I can think about now," he told Jennifer Dunning in an interview for a New York *Times* (January 29, 1978) profile. "Ideas about music keep coming, my legs keep dancing in my living room. . . . I'd do two ballets a season if it were up to me but I think they'd prefer my services as a dancer."

Peter Martins is a strikingly handsome man, with strong, Nordic features, large, melancholy gray eyes, and fashionably styled, light-blond hair. At six feet one and one-half inches, he is unusually tall for a dancer. Like all professional dancers, he puts in a long day of classes, rehearsals, and performances, rarely getting to bed before 2:00 A.M. When he has a few free hours, his favorite recreation is reading, especially the novels of Ernest Hemingway and John Steinbeck. Although he dislikes the stress and nervous tension of New York City, he seldom takes vacations. "My body can't take it," he explained to one interviewer. "When your body is that trained, that refined, you must make your muscles go in certain directions every day."

Martins lives rather modestly in a renovated brownstone on Manhattan's Upper West Side, within easy walking distance of Lincoln Center. His mid-1960's marriage to Lise La Cour, a principal dancer with the Royal Danish Ballet, ended in divorce in 1973. His son Nilas, whom he affectionately describes as "a little ballet kid who stands at the *barre* every day and points his feet," is a student at the Royal Danish Ballet School. A year ago father and son appeared together in Copenhagen in the Royal Danish Ballet's production of *The Nutcracker*. Although he realizes that dancers have a brief professional career, Martins is unconcerned about the future. "My prime time as a human being will be when I'm in my forties, when I am the most clever, most handsome, the best human being," he told Jennifer Dunning. "Not the nicest, but the most disciplined. Then I will have something to say."

References: Dance Mag 42:73+ Ja 20 '68 pors, 51:30+ Je '77 pors; N Y Post p13 N 8 '75 pors; Sat R 51:36+ Ja 20 '68 por; Gruen, John. The Private World of Ballet (1975); Scavullo, Francesco. Scavullo on Men (1977)

Means, Russell (Charles)

Nov. 10, 1939- Organization leader
Address: b. Wanblee, South Dakota 57577

On December 29, 1890, in the final massacre of the American Indian Wars, a United States Cavalry unit slaughtered Chief Big Foot and 350 of his tribe, mostly women and children, at Wounded Knee, South Dakota, and left their grotesquely frozen bodies lying in the snow. Eighty-three years later, Russell Means, in the most dramatic incident of his career as a leader of the American Indian Movement—a militant civil rights organization founded in 1967—and several hundred followers took control of the hamlet of Wounded Knee and held it, under federal siege, for seventy-one days. Means, an Oglala Sioux, contended that their occupation of the village was a "liberation" justified by the federal government's breach of the 1868 Fort Laramie Treaty, which gave the Black Hills to the Sioux, and of more than 300 subsequent treaties. "If the federal government once again turns a deaf ear and closes its eyes to the Indians," Means warned, "the Indian Wars will start all over again. There will be death. I don't consider that a threat. That's reality."

Russell Charles Means was born on the Pine Ridge Reservation in South Dakota on November 10, 1939, the oldest son of Harold ("Hank") Means, a mixed-blood Oglala Sioux, and Theodora (Feather) Means, a full-blooded Yankton Sioux. He owes his Anglo-Saxon surname to his great-grandfather, Gus Means, a minor functionary for the Bureau of Indian Affairs. After World War II broke out, Hank Means, a welder and auto mechanic, moved his family to California, where he found work at the Mare Island Navy Yard near San

Francisco, but Mrs. Means returned to the reservation for the births of her other sons, Ted, in 1941, and the twins, Bill and Dale, in 1946. Russell Means has fond memories of those visits to the reservation, remembering with special pleasure the buckboard rides on dirt roads, the picnics around the family graves—a modern adaptation of a traditional Indian burial rite—and the mock battles the Sioux staged for tourists.

Means attended the Bureau of Indian Affairs school on the reservation and later the public schools in Vallejo, California. He was a good student, earning better-than-average grades in English and history, an excellent athlete, and an enthusiastic Boy Scout. Despite his occasional emotional problems, common to most adolescents, Means was comparatively happy until, at sixteen, he transferred from a racially mixed high school in Vallejo to San Leandro High School, which was almost entirely white. Faced with a daily barrage of ethnic insults from taunting classmates, Means grew resentful and surly. "I guess I was sort of what you'd call a boy named Sioux," he said, as quoted in *The Road To Wounded Knee* (Bantam, 1974). "Every time some wise guy would mouth off I'd figger I had to defend myself for bein' Indian. I got to know what it was like to hate to see it rain."

Virtually ostracized by his fellow students, Means drifted into delinquency and began to experiment with drugs. As a result, his grades plummeted, and he barely graduated from high school. Trying to make a new start, Means moved to Los Angeles, but after a harrowing drug experience, he kicked that habit only to become addicted to alcohol.

Returning to San Francisco, Means worked briefly as a ballroom dance instructor, and, with his father and uncle, took part in an abortive attempt, in 1964, to take over Alcatraz Island. (Means was not involved in the more famous Indian seizure of the island in 1969.) Between 1964 and 1968 he wandered around the West, working as a cowboy, day laborer, circus roustabout, and even as an executive with an employment agency. During those ramblings he attended five colleges, among them, the University of California at Los Angeles and Arizona State University, at Tempe, but never earned a degree.

In the late 1960's Means accepted a job with the Rosebud Sioux tribal council on the Rosebud Reservation in South Dakota, but a few months later, applied for relocation to Cleveland, Ohio. There he directed the government-funded Cleveland American Indian Center. At one seminar sponsored by the Center, he met Dennis J. Banks, a cofounder of the newly formed American Indian Movement (AIM). Excited by its militancy, he founded the second AIM chapter, in Cleveland, and later gave the group its first national media exposure when he and a handful of other Indians seized control of the *Mayflower II* in Plymouth, Massachusetts on Thanksgiving Day, 1970. The noisy confrontation between the Indians and costumed "Pilgrims" attracted network television coverage and made Means a national hero to dissident Indians and to sympathetic white radicals.

Over the next two years Means stage-managed a prayer vigil atop Mount Rushmore, directed an unsuccessful attempt to take over the Bureau of Indian Affairs' central information office, and filed a $9,000,000 damage suit against the Cleveland Indians baseball club, charging that the team's cartoon mascot, Chief Wahoo, demeaned Indians. As he explained to John Koster in an interview for the Bergen County (New Jersey) *Record*'s Sunday supplement, *At Ease* (October 31, 1971), Means hoped that those guerrilla theatre tactics would focus public attention on the Indians' plight. "We don't want civil rights in the white man's society—we want our own sovereign rights. . . . In all our demonstrations we have yet to hurt anybody or destroy any property," he emphasized. "However, because the white man is such a violent dude, and because he digs violence so much, we have found that the only way the white man will listen is by us creating a disturbance in his world."

In February 1972 an angry Russell Means led a contingent of 1,300 Indians into Gordon, Nebraska to protest the public humiliation and suspicious death of Raymond Yellow Thunder. The town's white authorities acceded to the Indians' demands and ordered a second autopsy. Two white townsmen were eventually indicted for manslaughter. The city council also suspended a police officer accused of molesting jailed Indian women and organized a multiracial human rights council. The elated Indians hailed the Gordon protest as their greatest victory to date, but as he left town, Means warned, "We came here to put Gordon on the map. If things don't get better for Indian people, we're coming back to take Gordon *off* the map."

Hounded out of Cleveland by irate baseball fans, who ridiculed his indictment of Chief Wahoo, Means resigned his job as director of the Indian Center and returned to South Dakota in mid-1972. At the annual Rosebud Sun Dance celebration later that summer, Means helped to plan the Trail of Broken Treaties, a series of cross-country caravans scheduled to converge on Washington, D.C. during national election week in November 1972. The mass demonstration was designed to dramatize the Indians' claim that the federal government had for more than 100 years consistently broken its promises to the Indians regarding land and social services.

Having been assured adequate housing by the Department of the Interior, the Indians arrived in the capital on November 2, ready to present their list of twenty demands—most of them involving the restoration of a treaty-making relationship between the United States and the "Indian tribes and Nations"—to government officials. But the promised quarters turned out to be cramped and rodent-infested, and the low-level government representatives sent to confer with the Indians were officious and patronizing. Infuriated by what he saw as one more example of the government's duplicity, Means led a protest march to the Bureau of Indian Affairs. After a brief scuffle its officials surrendered the building to the Indians, who immediately renamed it the Native American Embassy.

When talks with the government collapsed, Means ordered his followers to secure the building against the expected assault by riot police. "Those of us who have painted our faces have taken a vow to die for what we believe in," Means told reporters. "We Indians have never been afraid to die, because we know where we're going." Although the occupiers were disowned by conservative Indian leaders as "Maoists" and "renegades," they won support from such unlikely bedfellows as Stokely Carmichael, the black militant, Dr. Benjamin Spock, the antiwar spokesman, and Reverend Carl McIntyre, the right-wing, pro-Vietnam war activist.

On November 6—election eve—a United States District Court Judge ordered the forcible eviction of the Indians. Outraged, they smashed furniture and office equipment, ransacked files, and carried off valuable Indian paintings and artifacts. The following day they agreed to evacuate the building after the White House promised to look into the quality and effectiveness of federal programs and to consider Indian self-government. On leaving the building, Means told reporters he had removed files that documented the "scandalous if not criminal" exploitation of Indians by the government, and he assured them that finding that proof was a major accomplishment of the AIM occupation.

A few days later, Means returned to Pine Ridge to attend a meeting of the Oglala Sioux Landowners Association, of which he was a member, but Dick Wilson, the president of the Oglala tribal council, had obtained a court injunction prohibiting Means or any other AIM member from speaking at or attending a public meeting on the reservation. After being twice arrested for challenging the court order, Means began to organize demonstrations to protest the alleged harassment of Indians by white police. On February 6, 1973 AIM declared a day of mourning for Wesley Bad Heart Bull, stabbed to death by a white man who was later charged with second-degree manslaughter. When court officers in Custer, South Dakota refused to change the charge to murder, the Indians, led by Means, rampaged through the tourist town. Seventy-eight Indians, including Means, were arrested for rioting and arson.

A few weeks later, the traditional chiefs of the tribe and the Oglala Civil Rights Organization asked for Means's help in impeaching Dick Wilson for misusing tribal funds and repeatedly violating the tribal constitution. Following a short meeting with Wilson, Means was severely beaten by the president's "goon squad." The next day, February 27, 1973, Means and an estimated 200 armed supporters seized Wounded Knee and announced that they were setting up a traditional tribal government, independent from the "puppet" government at Pine Ridge. The Indians demanded a Senate investigation of the Bureau of Indian Affairs and of the 371 broken treaties, recognition of Indian sovereignty, and the removal of Wilson as tribal council president. "The government has two choices," Means announced, as quoted in *Newsweek* (March 12, 1973). "Either they attack and wipe us out like they did in 1890, or they negotiate our reasonable demands." When heavily armed federal marshals and FBI agents surrounded the hamlet, Means told reporters that he fully expected to be killed. "I hope by my death, and the deaths of all these Indian men and women, there will be an investigation into corruption on the reservations and there's no better place to start than Pine Ridge."

As the armed stand-off, punctuated by sporadic gunfire, continued into the spring, support for AIM poured in. Sympathetic Indians slipped through the lines to join the occupation forces, and church and civil rights groups airlifted supplies to the besieged town. But the more conservative Indians, goaded by Dick Wilson, stepped up their attacks on AIM, charging that Means was a Communist tool and that his followers were "clowns and idiots . . . [who] should be prosecuted to the full extent of the law." Wilson even set up his own roadblock to keep medicine, food, and other essentials out of Wounded Knee.

After several weeks of fruitless talks, on April 4 Means negotiated a stand-down, in which he would surrender himself to federal custody and be flown to the White House to work out an agreement ending the siege. But when Means arrived in Washington two days later, the government flatly refused to negotiate until the Wounded Knee activists laid down their weapons. Refusing to order an unconditional surrender, Means stalked out of the meeting. "The Indians' last treaty with the government lasted all of seventy-two hours," he told waiting newsmen. "The government broke it before the ink was dry." Shadowed by FBI agents, Means crisscrossed the country to drum up financial support for his cause. He was eventually arrested and incarcerated for the duration of the occupation when he announced his intention to return to Wounded Knee in defiance of a court order. The confrontation ended on May 8, 1973, when the remaining 120 Indians surrendered according to the terms of an accord signed three days earlier in which the government agreed to meet with Sioux elders to discuss the Indians' charges and to begin an investigation of the tribal government.

While under federal indictment on ten felony charges for taking part in the Wounded Knee occupation, Russell Means challenged Dick Wilson for the presidency of the tribal council. Promising to destroy what he called "the white man's tribal government at Pine Ridge" and to reinstitute "a type of government where all Indians would have a voice in making decisions," he easily won the twelve-man primary in January 1974, defeating Wilson by more than 150 votes. But two weeks later, he lost in the run-off election to Wilson, garnering 1,530 votes to the incumbent's 1,709. Although two independent federal probes sustained AIM's charges that the election was marred by threats, ballot-stuffing, and open bribery, the BIA failed to order a new election. Nevertheless claiming victory, Means said: "The press has continually claimed that we were a band of 200 outsiders at Wounded Knee. . . . The 1,500 votes, according to this illegal election, have verified and vindicated and exonerated the American Indian Movement on the Pine Ridge Reservation."

Resplendent in Indian regalia, Russell Means opened the AIM trial on February 12, 1974 with an attention-getting speech. He told the jury: "We have had no way to express our manhood on the reservation except for five ways. Those five ways are athletics, joining the service, grabbing the bottle, beating our women, or cutting our hair, putting on a tie and becoming a facsimile of white people." Although the judge, in a pretrial ruling, had refused to let Means and his codefendants base their case on an 1868 treaty, the defense team clearly intended to put the government on trial by dramatizing the Indians' grievances. The trial dragged on for months as the six defense lawyers, led by Mark Lane and William M. Kunstler, kept government witnesses on the stand for days, cross-examining them exhaustively. Their persistence was rewarded with evidence of illegal wiretaps, phony exhibits, perjured testimony, and other government misconduct. On September 16, 1974 United States District Court Judge Fred Nichol dismissed the charges against Means and castigated the prosecution for its handling of the case.

Since the trial Means has survived several attempts on his life—at least one, he claims, by paid political assassins—and he has been arrested repeatedly. After he was acquitted of a murder charge in 1975, his brother Ted remarked, "This is the seventh time that Russell has been charged with a violent crime and has been found innocent. Russ is a very committed person, and that's why all these charges are brought against him—because they recognize him as a true leader." Means was eventually convicted of riot charges stemming from the 1973 Custer demonstration and faced a possible twenty-year sentence, but his attorneys worked out a compromise, and he served only one month in jail. In November 1977 he began serving a term for rioting in a South Dakota state penitentiary.

Russell Means is an imposing figure, standing well over six feet in height, with a roughly handsome, scarred face, piercing dark eyes, and long black hair, usually worn in braids. He favors casual Western attire and often wears traditional Indian jewelry. A few years ago he voluntarily underwent the ritual self-torture of the Sioux Sun Dance, in which votaries pierce the flesh of their chests and dangle from skewers attached to long rawhide thongs as a flesh sacrifice to Wakan Tanka, the Great Spirit. As photographed by an NBC News crew, the incident was spliced into a documentary called *The Great American West*, which was telecast as part of the nation's Bicentennial Celebration on July 4, 1976.

In the late 1950's Means married an Indian woman in Los Angeles. The two were divorced shortly after the birth of their second child. A later marriage to a Hopi woman, by whom he had two children, also ended in divorce. When he is not traveling on the lecture circuit, Means lives on the Pine Ridge Reservation. "This is my home," he told one reporter. "I don't run."

References: Biog N 923+ Ag '74 por; Harpers 248:30+ Je '74; Burnette, Robert, and Koster, John. The Road To Wounded Knee (1974); Mencarelli, James. Protest (1975)

Meriwether, W(ilhelm) Delano

Apr. 23, 1943- United States government official; physician; athlete. Address: b. Room 729-H, Department of Health, Education and Welfare, 200 Independence Ave., S.W., Washington, D.C. 20201; h. 4010 Rickover Rd., Silver Spring, Md. 20902

One of America's most appealing sports heroes is Dr. W. Delano Meriwether, the award-winning sprinter whom the magazine *Sports Illustrated* once called the "champion of the armchair athletes." A clinical and research hematologist whose studies have centered on leukemia and sickle cell anemia, Meriwether first took up competitive running as a diversion from the depressing as-

W. Delano Meriwether

pects of his work in 1970, at twenty-seven. Without any previous training in track or any other organized sport, he captured two National Amateur Athletic Union sprinting championships in 1971 and 1972 and quickly became legendary for his unorthodox yet speedy running form, his eccentric track costume, and his low-key manner. Although he missed out on 1972 and 1976 Olympic competition because of injuries, Meriwether has continued to please American track crowds and to compete abroad for United States teams in South America and the People's Republic of China. Since 1973 his professional career has taken him to Washington, where he has served as a special assistant in the Department of Health, Education and Welfare. Dr. Meriwether was most recently in the news in 1976, as the director of the federal government's ambitious swine flu immunization program.

The only son of Wilhelm Roscoe Meriwether, a high school principal and former science teacher, Wilhelm Delano Meriwether was born on April 23, 1943 in Nashville, Tennessee. He has one younger sister, Sue, who is also a teacher. Raised in Charleston, South Carolina from the age of two, Meriwether attended Charleston public schools, including Burke High School. Although interested in high school athletics, the future sprinter took no part in them, for his school had no track team, and he was considered too light for football. "There wasn't much use for a guy who was six feet tall and weighed 135 pounds," he told Sandy Treadwell of *Sports Illustrated* (January 18, 1971). ". . . I liked basketball but the football players were outstanding in basketball." Instead, he confined his extracurricular activities to playing saxophone in the school band. An excellent all-round student, Meriwether especially enjoyed biology and after school worked in a veterinary hospital as a caretaker. There he became interested in dog parasites and prepared exhibits on them that twice took him to the National Science Fair, where he won an American Veterinary Medical Association prize and a National Science Fair award.

Although the Supreme Court decision outlawing segregation was handed down in 1954, Meriwether attended all-black public schools through his 1960 graduation from high school. "I was not an activist," he told John Dorsey of the Baltimore *Sunday Sun* (September 12, 1976). ". . . I admired the people who did the sitting in, and it was necessary. But I thought the thing for me to do was a little different." After high school, Meriwether went to Michigan State University on an academic scholarship. Enrolled in a preveterinary course there, he was accepted into veterinary school after two years, but he decided that medicine would offer him more of a challenge. After his third year at Michigan State he left without completing his undergraduate degree to become the first black student at Duke University School of Medicine in Durham, North Carolina, where he studied on a National Medical Fellowship from the Sloan Foundation. Influenced by his instructor Dr. Charles Mengel, Meriwether developed a strong interest in medical research at Duke and decided to become a hematologist. After receiving his M.D. degree from Duke in 1967, he interned for a year at the University of Pennsylvania School of Medicine in Philadelphia and spent a year of residency at the Ohio State University Medical Center in Columbus.

In 1969 Meriwether joined the Baltimore Cancer Research Center, affiliated with the National Institutes of Health, as a clinical associate. For a year he worked with young leukemia patients and then concentrated on researching the effects of experimental drugs on leukemic mice. In an effort to take his mind off the tragic plight of the leukemia victims he treated, he took up running in the evenings on a high school track. Then, during the 1970 summer season he entered several local meets and sprinted the 100-yard dash in impressive times.

Despite his good showing in local meets, the newly developed runner was hardly a candidate for stardom in the fiercely competitive world of American track and field. At twenty-seven he was already old for a sprinter and had behind him none of the years of meticulously coached preparation that sprinters customarily receive before competing nationally. Meriwether never even had a coach. Nonetheless, while watching the greatest American sprinters on television one Sunday afternoon in July 1970, he suddenly said to his wife, "Hey, I think I can beat those guys," a remark that proved prophetic.

On the basis of his performance in the 1970 races, Meriwether wangled invitations to several major meets of the indoor track season, during the winter of 1971. At the first one, the National Invitational Meet in College Park, Maryland, in January, he stunned the sports world by beating record-holding sprinters Charlie Greene and Ivory Crockett in the 60-yard dash with a time of 6.0 seconds, just .1 second off the world indoor record.

Meriwether's upset victory made him a favorite with reporters and track fans. Sportswriters competed with each other in describing his unorthodox outfit (snug gold swimming trunks, a white hospital shirt, and gold and white suspenders) and his even more unorthodox running style (poor starts out of the block compensated for by incredible bursts of speed as the race progresses). His improbable victory and his image as the talented amateur who wins despite all the odds against him appealed to armchair athletes everywhere.

A few weeks after his College Park win, Meriwether won the 50-yard dash at the Boston AA meet and was chosen its outstanding athlete. Despite a number of injuries, the hematologist finished his first indoor season with an impressive two wins, three seconds, and one third. In the summer of 1971 Meriwether thrilled his fans at the 83d Annual National Amateur Athletic Union outdoor championships in Eugene, Oregon, when he captured the AAU 100-yard dash championship with a stunning time of 9 seconds, a feat that would have broken the world record if the wind had been a little lighter. That summer he was a member of the United States team that competed at the Pan-American Games in Cali, Colombia. During the 1972 indoor track season Meriwether won a second AAU championship, at Madison Square Garden, in February, when he ran the 60-yard dash in 6.2 seconds. At the end of that season he was honored with the Tangueray Sports Award, the Benrus Sports Award, and the Outstanding Athlete Award of the Southern Atlantic AAU.

Despite the rigorous demands of his newfound athletic career, Dr. Meriwether continued his commitment to medicine. In 1971 he left Baltimore for Boston, to become a research and clinical fellow in medicine at Harvard Medical School and a research fellow in medicine at Boston City Hospital's Thorndike Memorial Laboratory, where the principal subject of his research was sickle cell anemia. Two years later, he moved to Washington, D.C. to take up a one-year White House Fellowship. Assigned to the Department of Health, Education and Welfare as a special assistant, he traveled on fact-finding missions to the Sahel drought area of the sub-Sahara, to South Africa, and to the Soviet Union. Asked to stay on at the end of his year's assignment, in 1974 he became special assistant to Assistant Secretary for Health, Dr. Theodore Cooper. In that position he spent most of his time working on federal nutrition programs until Dr. Cooper appointed him, in April 1976, to serve as director of the national swine flu immunization program.

The federal immunization program had been proposed by President Gerald Ford in March 1976, in the face of mounting alarm that a potentially lethal new strain of influenza might be about to strike the United States. The new strain of influenza virus, popularly called "swine flu" because it is a mutation of a virus that brings on a flu-like disease in pigs, had caused the illness of several hundred persons and the death of one young man in an isolated outbreak at the Fort Dix, New Jersey Army post. New strains of influenza always cause concern because severe epidemics occur when populations are exposed to new flu viruses to which they have not had the chance to develop immunity. The "swine flu" virus seemed especially dangerous because it was believed to be similar to the viral agent that caused the influenza pandemic of 1918-19, which killed 500,000 Americans and 20,000,000 persons worldwide.

Unprecedented in scope, the $135,000,000 national influenza immunization program marked the federal government's first attempt to provide free inoculation to every adult American who wanted it. As its director, Meriwether was in charge of coordinating the efforts of the National Institutes of Health in Bethesda, Maryland, the Center for Disease Control in Atlanta, and state health departments across the country. He was responsible for purchasing the vaccine from the manufacturers, having each batch tested for strength, purity, and other factors, and distributing it to state health departments, which would then make it available to the public through free clinics.

In retrospect, Meriwether's odds against successfully implementing the swine flu program would seem to have been even more formidable than those he faced in becoming a track champion. In the first place, public support for the program was limited, with grumblings heard in many quarters that it was merely a political strategm designed to make Ford look good in an election year. Even within the medical community there was considerable debate on the need for widespread swine flu inoculation, for many epidemologists suspected that the Fort Dix outbreak was a freak occurrence not likely to be repeated. Furthermore, Meriwether was working against an extremely tight deadline, since to be effective the vaccine would have to be administered to a substantial proportion of the American population before the start of the flu season in November.

After many delays, swine flu vaccine finally became available to Americans on October 1, 1976, but Meriwether's troubles were only beginning. Within two weeks the program was suspended in several states following the deaths of thirty-five persons who had recently been inoculated. Although the program was resumed within a few days after the Center for Disease Control assured an uneasy public that the vaccine was not connected to the deaths, Meriwether was never able after that to drum up much public enthusiasm for obtaining the inoculation. By December 4, 1976 only 34,900,000 persons had been immunized, not nearly enough to hold down the ravages of an epidemic if it had been going to occur. Fortunately, it did not. Then, on December 16, the program was permanently halted when the vaccine was found to be statistically related to the incidence of a mysterious paralyzing disease called the Guillan-Barre syndrome, which is usually temporary but can, and in the case of one recently inoculated person did, cause death.

Professional recognition of Meriwether's accomplishments have included the Columbus Society of Internal Medicine Award for Excellence in Research (1969), the Public Health Service's J.D. Lane Award for Research (1971), and the Distinguished Medical Alumnus Award from Duke University (1974). In 1971, 1972, and 1975 Meriwether was named one of the Outstanding Young Men of America. His scientific papers on cancer research and other subjects have been published in such journals as *Biochemistry, Nature, Blood, Oncology, Cancer Research,* and the *Journal of the American Medical Association.* He is a member of Phi Kappa Phi and the American Federation for Clinical Research and a fellow of the American College of Physicians.

In his spare time Meriwether manages to keep in training and he continues to run competitively. In May 1975 he traveled to the People's Republic of China as a member of a United States national track team. Prevented from trying out for the United States Olympic team in 1972 by an injury, Meriwether got to the semifinals of the trials for the 1976 team before being knocked out of competition by a pulled hamstring muscle.

Married to the former Myrtle Lillian Capehart, whom he met while attending Duke Medical School, W. Delano Meriwether has two daughters, Myrtle, who is nicknamed Mitzi, and Margo. Mrs. Meriwether, a former public school teacher, is currently assistant director of the Welfare Rights Organization child care center in Washington, D.C. The Meriwethers live in a modest suburban home in Maryland, from which the doctor sometimes commutes the fourteen miles to his HEW office by bicycle. Six feet two inches tall with long legs, powerful thighs, and broad muscular shoulders, Meriwether, whose weight is now 165 pounds, is said to have the perfect physique for sprinting. "My original reason for running was not to compete," he told Dennis McBride of *Runner's World* (December 1976). "One knows there are biological and physiological benefits that any human being can accrue from running. That, coupled with the enjoyment I receive from running, makes it worthwhile. . . . The competitive element is really a bonus. It gives you something to look forward to and makes life interesting."

References: Baltimore Sun S 12 '76 por; Ebony 27:59+ F '72 pors, 32:55+ D '76 pors; N Y Post p25 Ag 16 '76 por; N Y Times p42 Je 28 '71 pors; Sports Illus 34:14+ Je 18 '71 por, 34:20+ F 22 '71 pors; Outstanding Young Men of America, 1972

Miller, G(eorge) William

Mar. 9, 1925- United States government official. Address: b. Board of Governors, Federal Reserve System, Washington, D.C. 20551

When President Jimmy Carter nominated G. William Miller as chairman of the seven-member Board of Governors of the Federal Reserve System in December 1977, he ended months of speculation over whether Dr. Arthur F. Burns would be reappointed to a third consecutive term in that post. Burns, who had tried to control inflation by tightening the money supply, frequently clashed with the President's economic advisers. Miller, the chairman and chief executive officer of Textron, Inc., a multinational conglomerate that manufactures a wide variety of products, ranging from zippers to air-cushion vehicles, holds views more in line with those of Carter Administration officials. A tough, pragmatic manager, Miller, who is a lawyer by profession, joined Textron in 1956 as an assistant secretary; four years later he was president of the corporation. Since assuming the chairmanship of the Fed in March 1978, he has, while maintaining the Fed's traditional independence, worked closely with the White House in planning a joint assault on inflation by the government, private industry, and labor groups.

George William Miller, the son of James Dick and Hazle Deane (Orrick) Miller, was born in Sapulpa, Oklahoma on March 9, 1925. The following year, the Millers, hoping to cash in on the discovery of oil in the Texas Panhandle, moved to Borger, Texas, where James Miller opened a furniture store. When his business failed during the Depression, he found a job in a carbon-black plant. Bill Miller worked at odd jobs after school and on weekends to supplement the family's income.

After graduating from Borger High School in 1941, Miller attended Amarillo Junior College for a year, then entered the United States Coast Guard Academy in New London, Connecticut. Immediately after receiving his B.S. degree in marine engineering in 1945, he was shipped to the Pacific, where he served four years as a line officer, mainly in Okinawa and Shanghai. He left the Coast Guard in 1949 to attend graduate school at the University of California at Berkeley. A superior student, he edited the *California Law Review* and, in 1952, took his J.D. degree at the top of his class.

Declining more lucrative offers from West Coast law firms, Miller joined Cravath, Swaine & Moore, a prestigious Wall Street firm, at an annual salary of $4,000. While working for the firm Miller helped Textron, Inc., then a relatively small textile manufacturing concern in Providence, Rhode Island, win a proxy battle for control of the American Woolen Company in 1955. The victory gave Textron the additional $100,000,000 in assets that helped Royal Little, its chairman and chief executive officer, diversify the company's range of manufactured goods by acquiring businesses outside of the textile field. Impressed by Miller's business acumen, Little hired the young lawyer in 1956 as an assistant secretary in charge of checking out acquisition prospects. Miller was so successful in his new post that, within a year, he was promoted to vice-president and treasurer.

When Rupert C. Thompson Jr. succeeded Little upon his retirement in June 1960, Miller became Textron's president and chief operating officer. Under Thompson's direction Textron continued to purchase diversified manufacturing companies, but he shifted the corporation's priority from acquisitions to stabilization and internal growth. To increase the efficiency of Textron's component enterprises, Miller supervised the introduction of hundreds of administrative reforms.

Miller's interests went far beyond the confines of Textron's boardroom. In his capacity as chairman of the advisory council to President John F. Kennedy's Committee on Equal Employment Opportunities in the early 1960's and, later, as an outspoken charter member of the National Alliance of Businessmen, he tried to convince his corporate peers that providing jobs for blacks and other minorities would not only "contribute to the full development of our human resources," but also "stimulate our national economy."

Long concerned about the broad social consequences of economic and technological progress, Miller frequently spoke about the businessman's responsibility to control the possible negative effects of scientific advances. "I don't believe [that] it's inconsistent for business to be concerned with wise management of a country's resources," he told the National Council on the Humanities in November 1967. "Nor is it inconsistent for business to be concerned with human and spiritual values, because it is in our long-term interests." Miller also found time for politics. In 1966 he served as campaign committee chairman for the reelection of United States Senator Claiborne Pell. Two years later, he was a Rhode Island delegate to the Democratic National Convention and, subsequently, the national chairman of Businessmen for Humphrey-Muskie.

In January 1968 Thompson stepped down as Textron's chief executive officer and was succeeded by Miller. Although Thompson retained the corporate chairmanship, Miller became the effective head of the company, one of the biggest conglomerates in the country. With operations in four major manufacturing areas—aerospace, consumer goods, industrial equipment, and metal products—Textron turned out a diversified line of products, including Gorham silverware, Shaeffer pens, Speidel watchbands, Homelite chain saws, and Bell UH-1 ("Huey") helicopters, the workhorses of the Vietnam war. In his first year as chief executive officer, Miller continued his predecessors' policy of aggressive acquisition, purchasing Bridgeport Machines, a maker of small milling machines; True-Trace, a producer of tracing controls for machine tools; Talon, a zipper manufacturer; and Polaris, a manufacturer of snowmobiles. By the end of that year, Textron achieved record sales of $1.7 billion.

During the next three years of Miller's leadership, Textron stood up well before the recession that severely crippled other conglomerates. While the earnings of Litton, Transamerica, and other highly diversified companies declined sharply, Textron's profits went down by only 10 percent. Miller attributed his company's superior performance to its development of "cost-effective" facilities, its conservative management of assets, and its economically sound, "operationally oriented" acquisition policy. Unlike other conglomerates, Miller explained, Textron never assumed during the boom years of the mid-1960's that profitable acquisition prospects could be found simply "by throwing darts at a board."

Looking toward the future, Miller developed an ambitious foreign expansion program designed to make Textron "a planetary corporation" within the decade of the 1970's. Because Textron, a collection of manufacturing concerns, had diminishing opportunities for further growth in an increasingly service-oriented American economy, Miller turned his attention to international expansion. "We decided that it was easier to extrapolate our conglomerate management skills to manufacturing overseas than to service industries in the United States," he explained, as quoted in *Business Week* (October 7, 1972). "I understand how to control manufacturing costs, but I'd be at a loss to control some of these services outfits that have 347 locations and no 'things.' "

The first of what Miller calls "Little Textrons," Textron Atlantic, Inc., was established in 1970 in Brussels, Belgium. In addition to overseeing European production operations for some Textron companies, it serves as a vehicle for acquisitions in Western Europe. Soon afterward, Textron Pacific, Inc. was set up to facilitate expansion into Asia. Equally interested in the economic opportunities opening up in Eastern Europe and the Soviet Union in the mid-1970's, Miller okayed pilot projects in Poland and Yugoslavia, visited Moscow to promote the export of Textron products to the Soviet Union, and, in 1974, welcomed a Soviet trade delegation to Textron's corporate headquarters in Providence.

To generate growth through internal expansion, Miller routinely spent more than 2 percent of Textron's sales on the research and development of new products, an unusually high percentage for a company that was not a major defense contractor. Much of the money went into product innovation at Bell Aerospace and Bell Helicopter, whose sales had declined with the winding down of the Vietnam war. The initial payoff from this investment came as early as 1973, when Iran ordered dozens of the new helicopters. "As a multimarket company, we're not wedded to a classic textbook sort of organization designed for a single product or market," Miller explained to a reporter for *Business Week* (October 7, 1972). Unlike independent companies, a conglomerate can, as Miller put it, "provide an umbrella for a period of product development and market introduction that's just too costly for an independent company to tackle alone."

In an effort to diversify the corporation's operations still further, Miller revised Textron's acquisition policy, which had previously centered on the purchase of small manufacturing concerns. For example, during Miller's tenure, Textron bought the Security Corporation, an insurance company, and the American Research and Development Corporation, a data processing and pollution control organization. One of Miller's major disappointments at Textron was his aborted attempt to buy into the financially ailing Lockheed Aircraft Corporation in 1974. Under the terms of the proposed agreement, Textron would have invested in Lockheed in exchange for control of 45 percent of its common stock. But because many security analysts believed that the assumption of Lockheed's staggering financial liabilities was too great a risk for Textron, the corporation's stock prices dropped sharply and Miller, to prevent additional losses, pulled out of the deal.

Named chairman of the board of Textron in 1974, Bill Miller presided over a period of phenomenal growth that exceeded the ambitious ten-year goals of an annual 10 percent compound increase in net income and an 8 percent annual increase in sales volume that he had set two years earlier. Only in 1975—a recession year—did Textron fail to meet Miller's goals. Net income for the first three quarters of 1977 was up an astonishing 17 percent over the same period in 1976 and total sales volume for that year topped $2.8 billion. With Textron's sales mushrooming, Miller took time off to serve as chairman of the United States Industrial Payroll Savings Plan. To drum up sales of the savings bonds, he toured the country, speaking to business groups and labor organizations. At President Jimmy Carter's urging, he agreed to head the Labor Department's new H.I.R.E. (Help Through Industry Retraining and Employment) program, which was set up to find jobs in the private sector for at least 100,000 veterans.

On December 28, 1977 President Carter named G. William Miller to succeed Arthur F. Burns as chairman of the Board of Governors of the Federal Reserve System upon the expiration of Burns's second four-year term on January 31, 1978. Since only one corporate executive had ever held the post, the President's selection of Miller, whose sole experience in the financial field was his membership on the board of the Federal Reserve Bank of Boston, came as a complete surprise.

Citing Miller's record as a skillful manager of the complex Textron enterprise, the business community applauded the President's "imaginative" and "inspired" choice. Because of his longstanding commitment to jobs programs, liberals, too, were pleased by Miller's appointment.

Unlike Dr. Burns, who had pursued a policy of limiting economic expansion because he believed that inflation was a greater danger to the economy than unemployment, Miller argued that unemployment and inflation could be "tackled simultaneously." Moreover, at a news conference following the announcement of his appointment, he maintained that the Federal Reserve Board's monetary policies "should be in harmony with the [fiscal] policies of the President." (Burns had vigorously defended the Fed's independence from White House influence.) Cautiously avoiding specific policy statements, he came across as a fiscal moderate in testimony before the Senate Banking Committee. Among other things, he told the Senators that his predecessor's monetary policies had been "generally correct," that he supported measures to insure "full employment with price stability" and a "sound and stable dollar," and that he intended to maintain the Fed's traditional independence.

Still smarting from widespread public criticism about its cursory examination of the financial affairs of Bert Lance, the former director of the Office of Management and Budget, the Senate demanded a full-scale investigation of Miller's involvement in Bell Helicopter's payment of a $2,900,000 commission to Air Taxi Company, an Iranian outfit that acted as the sales agent in Bell's successful 1973 bid for an Iranian government contract. Air Taxi was allegedly partly controlled by General Mohammed Khatemi, the head of the Iranian air force and the brother-in-law of Mohammed Riza Shah Pahlevi. The Security and Exchange commission was also looking into the payment.

Under the direction of Senator William Proxmire, the chairman of the Banking Committee and a determined opponent of Miller's appointment, the confirmation hearings dragged on for five weeks. At one point, Proxmire asked Miller to withdraw his name because of the ongoing SEC probe. Maintaining that he had run a "super-clean" company, Miller refused. He insisted that he had not known about Khatemi's alleged connection with Air Taxi and repeatedly defended Bell's payment as a legitimate sales commission. When no evidence was uncovered to dispute Miller's claim, the Banking Committee closed its hearings on March 2, 1978 with a fourteen-to-one vote in favor of the nominee. The lone dissenter was Proxmire.

Immediately after assuming office on March 8, 1978, Miller took steps to shore up foreign confidence in the dollar, which had been taking a beating in the European money markets. Among other things, he called for a national energy policy to reduce consumption of foreign oil and a tough anti-inflation program. Because monetary policy can go only so far in controlling inflation, he recommended a joint effort by government and the business community to keep spending and taxing down. To reduce the spiraling rate of inflation, which he conceded was "creeping up faster than expected," Miller warned Americans that they "must be willing to sacrifice." As examples of necessary inflation-fighting sacrifices, he listed reductions in federal pay increases (a "demonstrable sacrifice for the private sector to follow"), a voluntary freeze on the salaries of top corporate executives, a moderation of the pass-through cost increases caused by higher labor costs and increased Social Security taxes, and a temporary deferment of such expensive social programs as national health insurance. "If inflation is not curbed, there will be slower growth," he explained, as quoted in *Business Week* (April 10, 1978). "If it is not curbed, it is only a question of whether the slowdown will come sooner or later and whether it will come through a decline in the growth rate or as outright recession."

In April 1978 the Federal Reserve Board decreased the growth in the currency supply and tightened credit in expectation of even greater inflation. Miller also asked President Carter to postpone the proposed tax cut for three months, thus cutting the next year's federal deficit by $8 billion. "If we send out a signal loud and clear that we are reducing the deficit, everything else will fall into place," he told reporters. Nevertheless, on April 25, he reassured worried members of the Senate Banking Committee that the economy was "rebounding" and that he expected further improvements in employment and in both consumer and business spending.

G. William Miller has been described as "a feisty little guy, with a boyish grin and a broken nose, and that spontaneous, optimistic American attitude that trouble is inevitable but everything is possible." He is an enthusiastic amateur photographer and enjoys playing golf and squash and sailing off the coast of Massachusetts, where he has a summer home. A lifelong music lover, he regularly attends performances of the Metropolitan Opera in New York City. Miller and his wife, the former Ariadna Rogojarsky, a Russian emigrée he met in Shanghai, were married on December 22, 1946.

References: N Y Times III p3 My 12 '68 por, D p3 D 29 '77; Newsweek 91:50+ Ja 9 '78 por; Time 111:30 Ja 9 '78 por; U S News 85:90+ O 2 '78 pors; Wall St J p1+ Ja 6 '78; International Who's Who, 1978-79; Who's Who in America, 1976-77; Who's Who in the World, 1976-77

Mondale, Walter F(rederick)

Jan. 5, 1928- Vice-President of the United States. Address: b. The White House, 1600 Pennsylvania Ave. NW, Washington D.C. 20500

NOTE: This biography supersedes the article that appeared in *Current Biography* in January 1969.

When Jimmy Carter assumed the Presidency in January 1977, the one experienced Washington hand in the White House was his Vice-President, Walter F. Mondale. During his twelve years in the United States Senate, Mondale compiled a left-of-center voting record, particularly in the area of social legislation, comparable to that of his mentor and fellow Minnesotan, Hubert H. Humphrey. Not content to be a "ceremonial Vice-President," he transformed the office into a post of considerable power and responsibility. More than any of his predecessors, Mondale is an "assistant President," a "full-scale partner," as President Carter once put it, with real surrogacy.

The middle son of his father's second family, Walter Frederick ["Fritz"] Mondale was born in the village of Ceylon, Minnesota on January 5, 1928 to Theodore Sigvaard Mondale, an impoverished farmer turned Methodist minister, and Claribel Hope (Cowan) Mondale, a part-time music teacher. The original Norwegian surname of Mundal was Americanized to Mondale by his great-grandfather. The Mondales moved from one tiny pastorate to another in the farm belt of southwestern Minnesota until 1937, when they settled in Elmore. Theodore Mondale, whom his son once described as a "purist populist," who believed in the social gospel, regularly discussed politics with his wife and children at mealtimes.

During his somewhat mischievous youth Walter Mondale fought the stereotype of a preacher's son. At Elmore High School he devoted more time to his extracurricular activities than to his studies. He was a star athlete in football, basketball, and track, a founder of the Republicrats, a student political organization, and a talented enough singer to win an "A" rating in the state music contest and earn pocket money by singing "in a screeching baritone," as he puts it, at weddings and funerals.

After graduating from high school in 1946, Mondale enrolled at Macalester College, a small liberal arts institution in St. Paul. To pay his tuition, he took odd jobs and spent his summers toiling in the fields beside migrant farm workers. He dropped out for a year upon the death of his father in 1949, but returned to school—this time, at the University of Minnesota—as soon as he had saved up enough money. In 1951 he was awarded a B.A. degree *cum laude*.

At Macalester, Mondale had become active in state and local politics. In 1947 he organized the student volunteers, popularly known as "the Diaper Brigade," who helped Hubert H. Humphrey, Orville L. Freeman, Karl F. Rolvaag, and others in their struggle to exclude ultra-leftist elements from the newly merged Democratic-Farmer-Labor party. The following year Mondale helped Humphrey, then mayor of Minneapolis, to win election to the United States Senate by successfully managing his campaign in the Second Congressional District, a traditional Republican stronghold. In 1949 he went to Washington with Humphrey to serve as executive secretary of Students for Democratic Action, the campus affiliate of the liberal Americans for Democratic Action. Returning to Minnesota in 1950, Mondale managed Orville Freeman's unsuccessful bid for state attorney general.

In 1951 Mondale enlisted in the United States Army. He spent the next two years at Fort Knox, Kentucky, serving first in the crew of an armored reconnaissance vehicle, then as a specialist in education programs. Discharged with the rank of corporal in September 1953, Mondale entered the University of Minnesota Law School on the G.I. bill. He graduated in the top quarter of his class with an LL.B. degree in 1956. Admitted to the Minnesota bar later that same year, Mondale practised law privately until 1960.

In recognition of Mondale's efficient management of his successful campaign for a third term as governor, in 1958 Orville Freeman appointed him special assistant to the attorney general of Minnesota. Two years later, when the attorney general resigned, Freeman named Mondale to fill out the remaining eight months of the unexpired term. He was elected to that office in November 1960 and reelected in 1962 by one of the largest margins in Minnesota history.

As a diligent and aggressive prosecutor, Mondale focused his attention on civil rights, antitrust litigation, and consumer protection legislation. His highly publicized investigation of alleged financial irregularities in the Sister Elizabeth Kenny Foundation led to indictments and convictions for fraud, the foundation's liquidation, and the passage of a law regulating fund solicitation by charities. In 1963 Mondale attracted national attention when he championed the cause of Clarence Earl Gideon, a Florida convict who had asked the United States Supreme Court to establish the right to free counsel for indigents charged with major crimes in state courts. He filed a brief in support of Gideon's position and persuaded colleagues from twenty-three states to sign it, helping Gideon to win his case.

When Humphrey was elected to the Vice-Presidency in 1964, Governor Rolvaag appointed Mondale to complete Humphrey's term in the United States Senate. In 1966 the voters affirmed the Governor's choice when they returned Mondale to the Senate by a comfortable margin. In 1972 he obtained 56.7 percent of the vote to win a second full term in Congress. Sworn in on January 4, 1965, Mondale began a legislative career that was to rival those of the most liberal members of Congress, among them, Humphrey and the Kennedy brothers. Always troubled by the "powerlessness" of the poor, he defended the rights of "people who don't have the power to insist on being heard." He enthusiastically supported the "Great Society" programs of President Lyndon B. Johnson and spoke up in favor of legislation designed to improve the quality of life, especially for the poor, the elderly, and the very young.

An outspoken advocate of civil rights legislation, Mondale took to the Senate floor in the midst of the inner-city riots following the assassination of Dr. Martin Luther King Jr. in April 1968 to argue in favor of the open housing provisions of the Civil Rights Act of 1968. After a compromise that Mondale later called "a miracle," the Senate passed the bill, the first of its kind in nearly 100 years. As chairman of the Select Committee on Equal Educational Opportunity, he was credited by some political analysts with almost singlehandedly holding back a stream of antibusing bills. Occasionally accused of hedging on the issue, Mondale supported busing as one constitutional tool to end racial segregation in the public schools. In his arguments he stressed the benefits of quality integrated education rather than the inflammatory and misleading issues of racial balance and busing.

Appalled by staggering cost-overruns in the development of new weapons, Mondale denied additional appropriations for the production of antiballistic missiles, multiple intercontinental reentry vehicles, and supersonic transport airplanes. He even opposed continued funding for NASA's proposed reusable space shuttle and for the Skylab program, believing that the money could be better spent on urgent social problems. In his opening statement at the July 1969 hearings on the plight of migrant workers, he said: "Three minutes after we launched our men to the moon from Cape Kennedy, I banged the gavel here in Washington to open hearings on the miserable conditions of the blueberry pickers in eastern North Carolina. . . . Perhaps we belong on the moon, but we surely belong there, in North Carolina . . . with all the resources the nation could mobilize, if it only wanted to do so." To obtain firsthand knowledge of the problem, Mondale marched to the Mexican border with Cesar Chavez's United Farm Workers and visited Indians and Eskimos living in squalor on reservations in the West and in Alaska. Largely because of Mondale, migrant workers won the right to unemployment benefits and legal services.

Mondale probably expended more of his energies on the problems of children than on any other issue. His ambitious child-care program, written into the Economic Opportunity Act of 1971 and providing funds for health care, educational assistance, nutritional aid, day care centers, and developmental services, was vetoed by President Richard M. Nixon. Similar bills languished without action in 1975 and 1976, but his measures for the prevention and treatment of child abuse and for research into the sudden infant death syndrome proved more successful. He also managed to push through the Senate increased appropriations for education, child nutrition, and existing day-care programs.

On other domestic issues Mondale generally voted with the liberal contingent of the Senate. (His rating from the Americans for Democratic Action has consistently been 90 percent or better.) Among other things, the Senator approved a variety of consumer protection legislation, welfare and tax reform bills, governmental reorganization proposals, and measures to safeguard the environment, including a controversial attempt to delay the construction of the trans-Alaska oil pipeline. During the energy crisis of the mid-1970's he advocated breaking up the vertically integrated giants of the oil industry to encourage competition among the smaller independent companies.

In foreign affairs Mondale supported American involvement in the Indochina war until 1968, but he later called his hawkish stance the biggest mistake of his public career. Since then he has supported all efforts to limit American military activity in Southeast Asia and elsewhere. He offered two successful arms-control amendments and repeatedly criticized America's role as an arms supplier to foreign governments. A proponent of détente with the Soviet Union, he endorsed increased trade between Communist and Western countries and a sharing of responsibility for the development of Third and Fourth World nations.

Having turned down the opportunity to become Senator George S. McGovern's running mate on the Democratic national ticket two years before, Mondale embarked on a cross-country tour in 1974 to test his chances for the 1976 Presidential nomination. After six months of almost daily campaigning, he found himself growing more and more impatient with his image makers and with the hullabaloo of the pre-nomination process. Unable to reconcile the "wrenching internal tug of war," in his words, between his Presidential ambitions and his Senatorial responsibilities, he pulled out of the race on November 21, 1974. "I do not have the overwhelming desire to be President, which is essential for the kind of campaign that is required," he told reporters. "I admire those with the determination to do what is required to seek the Presidency, but I have found that I am not among them."

Mondale analyzed the requirements of the office in his book *The Accountability of Power: Toward a Responsible Presidency* (McKay, 1975). Disturbed by what he called Nixon's "imperial" Presidency, he proposed a "less isolating and less monarchial" Presidential lifestyle. He argued for a redefinition of the office that, while acknowledging "the importance of Presidential power," gave greater importance to "accountable Presidential power" under the checks of the Cabinet, the Congress, the media, and the public.

One of the seven finalists in Jimmy Carter's three-month Vice-Presidential talent hunt, Walter Mondale was tapped for the position on July 15, 1976. In announcing his selection to the press, Carter cited Mondale's long list of qualifications: competence to be President, personal and ideological compatibility, sound judgment in times of difficulty, experience in Washington, acceptance by a wide range of Democrats, and an understanding compassion for people who need the services of government most.

Campaigning energetically for the "Grits and Fritz" ticket, Mondale won over audiences with his earnestness, poise, and self-deprecating sense of humor. His low-key and homespun approach to politicking especially appealed to traditional Democratic constituencies. In his standard stump speech he denounced President Gerald R. Ford's controversial pardon of President Nixon and attacked the Ford Administration's "roller coaster" economic policies. In the precedent-breaking debate with Senator Robert J. Dole, his Republican counterpart, on October 15, 1976, Mondale recovered from initial nervousness to score an impressive victory over his more aggressive opponent. An NBC News poll taken shortly after the debate showed that 51 percent of the viewers preferred Mondale and 33 percent favored Dole. According to most political analysts, Mondale's presence on the ticket proved crucial to Carter's victory in the key Northern states.

Believing that the assignments previous Chief Executives had given their Vice-Presidents had trivialized the office, Mondale outlined in a memorandum to Carter his plans for revitalizing it. His most important role, as he envisioned it, would be that of an impartial adviser and troubleshooter, giving the President a candid and disinterested view on issues, strategies, and political problems. During the hectic two-month transition period Mondale worked closely with Carter in helping to formulate policy priorities and select Cabinet members. Since taking office on January 20, 1977, he has been, in his words, "privy to all the facts and options being considered" by the President. Unlike his predecessors, Mondale has an office in the White House, only a few steps away from Carter's. He attends and, in the President's absence, presides over high-level council meetings, confers with Carter at a regularly scheduled Monday lunch, and often meets with him during the day.

Unencumbered by any Constitutional functions other than his responsibility as presiding officer of the Senate, Mondale is able to "roam through the government . . . across department lines," as he once put it. Although he has admitted to reporters that his position as Vice-President is more speculative and risky and less independent than that of a United States Senator, he told Hedrick Smith, in an interview for the New York *Times* (February 16, 1977), that the job gave him a much better opportunity to influence the course of government.

Just three days after the inauguration, President Carter underscored Mondale's central role in the new administration by sending him as a personal emissary to five Western European countries and to Japan for summit-level talks on common economic and political concerns. Heralding a change from the personal diplomacy practised by former Secretary of State Henry A. Kissinger, the Vice-President emphasized Carter's insistence on close cooperation and consultation among allies. During the course of a second European tour in May, Mondale met privately with South African Prime Minister John Vorster to outline the Carter Administration's human rights policy and its opposition to South Africa's racial discrimination. Despite profound disagreement over apartheid, Mondale persuaded Vorster to support the American-British initiative for black majority rule in neighboring Rhodesia. The following month, in a speech to the World Affairs Council of Northern California in San Francisco, he presented the Administration's official Middle East policy. In his remarks, he reiterated the country's traditional strong support of Israel, but suggested that the Israelis be prepared to accept a return to the pre-1967-war boundaries as well as the establishment of a homeland or "entity" for the Palestinians as conditions for a peace settlement.

On the domestic front Mondale carried to completion several projects begun during his days in the Senate. The Administration's election reform bill, with its provisions for instant voter registration, abolition of the Electoral College, and public financing of Congressional elections, was, in large part, Mondale's handiwork. He also supervised the White House task force working on a reorganization plan for national intelligence operations and toughened its proposals for curbing domestic abuses by the CIA and FBI. As president of the Senate, he cast the tie-breaking vote on an Administration-backed bill increasing payroll taxes for Social Security and, when a filibuster stalled the passage of a key measure in Carter's comprehensive energy package, he used a prearranged parliamentary maneuver to end the delaying tactics.

In an end-of-the-year interview the Vice-President conceded that the Carter Administration had tried to accomplish too much too quickly. As chairman of a newly established executive unit charged with setting priorities among issues and drawing up a timetable for their consideration, Mondale promised a "strong salvo, wisely scheduled" during Carter's second year in office. The new plan, Mondale explained, would "keep the President's time freed-up enough so that he can stay on the fundamental strategic problems facing the country."

Trim and youthful-looking, Walter F. Mondale stands five feet eleven inches tall and weighs 165 pounds. He has brown hair streaked with blond and deep-set pale blue eyes. To unwind, he reads magazines of general interest and books on government and politics or watches vintage movies on television, especially those of W. C. Fields or the Marx Brothers. Bored by spectator sports, he enjoys skiing and tennis and, whenever possible, goes hunting or fishing in Canada. "It's my alternative to psychiatry," he told one interviewer. Mondale and his wife, the former Joan Adams, a clergyman's daughter whom he married on December 27, 1955, are the first residents of Admiral's House, the turreted Victorian mansion on the grounds of the United States Naval Observatory that has been the official home of the Vice-President since 1975. Mrs. Mondale, an art enthusiast, is a skilled potter and the author of *Politics in Art*. The Mondale household also includes three teen-age children, Theodore Adams, William Hall, and Eleanor Jane, two cats, and Bonnie, a blind collie.

References: N Y Post p2 Jl 17 '76 por; N Y Times A p1+ Jl 16 '76, p30 Jl 25 '76, p24 N 4 '76 por, p20 Jl 26 '76; N Y Times Mag p38+ Je 5 '77 pors; Newsweek 88:26+ Jl 26 '76 pors; Time 108:20+ Jl 26 '76 pors; Douth, George. Leaders in Profile (1975); Who's Who in America, 1976-77; Who's Who in American Politics, 1975-76

Monroe, Earl

Nov. 21, 1944- Basketball player; businessman. Address: b. New York Knickerbockers, Madison Square Garden Center, 4 Pennsylvania Plaza, New York City, N.Y. 10001; Tiffany Entertainment Corp., 237 W. 54th St., New York City, N.Y. 10019

In the consensus of fans and sportswriters, the most exciting player in the National Basketball Association is Earl Monroe, guard and captain of the New York Knickerbockers. The aggressive Monroe, who is nicknamed Earl the Pearl, began his professional career as a member of the Baltimore Bullets in 1967. During his four seasons in Baltimore, despite the arthritis that still wracks his knees, he kept audiences electrified with his deft, daring ball-handling, trick body movements, whirlwind penetrations of the enemy line, and quicker-than-the-eye scoring. After joining the star-studded Knicks, he was forced to temper his flair as a solo superstar with close teamwork, and the result has been greater versatility and efficiency without loss of flash or control. As the comedian Woody Allen, a New York fan, has observed, several other players have comparable grace and can fake, spin, pump and double pump, stutter-step, shoot from the hip, and dip, twist, and toss themselves in one direction while the arms move in another and the whole body hangs in space, but what makes Monroe different is "the indescribable heat of genius that burns deep inside him . . . some kind of diabolical intensity."

Going into the 1977-78 season, Monroe's professional career totals were 735 games played, 12,724 field goals attempted and 5,860 made, for a percentage of .461; 4,004 free throws attempted and 3,215 made, for a percentage of .803; 2,977 assists; and 14,935 points, or an average of 20.3 per game. Outside of basketball, Monroe owns Pretty Pearl Records, under the aegis of the Tiffany Entertainment Corporation, which he formed in partnership with Dick Scott.

Monroe was born Vernon Earl Monroe in Philadelphia, Pennsylvania on November 21, 1944 to parents who divorced each other when he was five. His father is Vernon Monroe, a night watchman; his mother, Rose, who became Mrs. John Smith through her second marriage, ran a grocery store until her death several years ago. Monroe has an older sister, Anna (Monroe) James, and a younger sister, Theresa Smith.

Although Monroe grew up in a slum neighborhood in south Philadelphia, surrounded by inducements to delinquency, his family was, he recounts, "pretty well off" and helped to keep him on the straight and narrow. "My mother was a great help," he told Bob Rubin for *Sport* (June 1968), "[and] I learned a lesson from my first cousins [when] they got into trouble."

Also helpful was Monroe's interest in athletics, which at first focused on soccer. After breaking a leg, he turned to basketball, practising long hours daily. At mid-season in his junior year at John Bartram High School in Philadelphia, having sprouted to six feet two inches, he moved up to the pivot-man position on the varsity team, and as a senior he averaged 21.7 points per game and made all-city—without the advantage of a jump shot. "I didn't need one as a center," he explained to Bob Rubin. "Even then, though, the other centers were a lot bigger than me, so I had to develop trick shots. I didn't learn the jump shot until the following year."

Although Temple University in Philadelphia showed some interest in Monroe as an athlete, it would not accept him academically. To make up for his poor high school scholastic record, he took classes at Temple Prep, but after a few weeks he dropped out and took a job as a shipping clerk in a factory. During his year on that job he learned "an awful lot," he says: "I learned what possibilities faced me without college. I learned I hate work. . . . I didn't like to do anything where I have to get up in the morning and punch a time clock."

Recruited by Winston-Salem State College, Monroe majored in elementary education at the predominantly black North Carolina school. As a guard on the Winston-Salem basketball team, he averaged seven points a game in his freshman year, twenty-three in his sophomore year, and thirty in his junior year. In 1966-67, his senior year, he tallied an average of 44.5 points, for a total of 1,329, a small-college national record. The Winston-Salem Rams won the National Collegiate Athletic Association college division title, and Monroe was named NCAA college division Player of the Year.

"A lot of people try to class him as a showman," Clarence Gaines, the Winston-Salem coach, later said of Monroe. "There have been some references, which I resent, that he would be better off playing Globetrotter basketball. . . . This youngster puts so much into the game that some people think he's showing off. It's just part of him, and he makes the complete, successful play with it."

Chosen by Baltimore in the first round of the National Basketball Association's 1967 college draft, Monroe joined the Bullets for the 1967-68 season, in which he scored 1,991 points, fourth highest in the NBA and second highest for a rookie guard, and he was voted Rookie of the Year. The Bullets, who were trying to rise from last place in the NBA's Eastern Division, oriented their offense around Monroe. "We had no set offense," one of his teammates later recounted. "We gave the ball to Earl. He *was* our offense." Sometimes he would pass behind his back to Wes Unseld or Gus Johnson, and the Monroe-Unseld-Johnson fast break became one of the most spectacular in the history of the NBA and one that took the Bullets into the playoffs for four consecutive years. In four seasons with the Bullets, Monroe averaged 23.7 points per game.

Monroe, who found Baltimore a "dull" place, was traded by the Bullets at his own request. He went to New York in November 1971 in exchange for Dave Stallworth, Mike Riordan, and cash. The details of the financial arrangement were not revealed, but the common guess around the National Basketball Association was that Monroe was signed to a multiyear contract for approximately $150,000 a year.

When he arrived in New York City Monroe was suffering from bone spurs on his left heel in addition to the arthritis in his knees that had plagued him from the beginning of his professional career and for which he still undergoes regular treatments. More serious than the physical problems was that of psychological and stylistic adjustment. In Baltimore, Monroe had been the Bullet's cynosure, the stellar attack man, little concerned with defense. In New York, he had not only to become accustomed at first to sitting on the bench, waiting his turn to spell Willis Reed, Walt Frazier, or Dick Barnett, but also to adapt his virtuoso playing style to the team concept employed by the Knicks, whose number included Bill Bradley, Dave DeBusschere, Dean Meminger, and Jerry Lucas. Almost to a man, they were exceptionally good open shooters, working for the free shot with their passing and their ceaseless movement, whereas Reed was at his best under close guard, using his opponent as a pivot around which to whip and score or drawing fouls with his twisting and turning. "I've got to get myself together mentally," he told a reporter. "I'm just not a good open shooter. I'm better when I have to shoot with someone on me."

At mid-season in 1971-72 Red Holzman, the New York coach, made a progress report on Monroe: "I think he's adapted well. He's a good basketball player and capable of playing any style. At times we have tried to exploit his ability to go one-on-one. As we go along I think he'll be a good open shooter. It won't be a problem." Nor was it. Monroe learned open shooting as well as defense, and, contenting himself with fewer points—11.9 per game in 1971-72, 15.5 in 1972-73, and 14 in 1973-74—he contributed significantly to New York's successful NBA championship campaign in 1973. Over the years he played in a total of seventy-six playoff games, averaging 18.6 points per game. In four All-Star games between 1969 and 1977, he scored a total of forty points.

His season tallies increased—to 20.9 in 1974-75, 20.7 in 1975-76, and 19.9 in 1976—after Reed and DeBusschere retired and he and Frazier carried the offense. In an article in *Sport* (November 1977), Woody Allen compared the two guards: "Frazier was the steadier of the two. He did everything perfectly. Monroe was, as always, the more dramatic and explosive one. Consequently, when Frazier dribbled up the middle you could count on your two points because of his smooth-as-satin style. When Monroe drove, his lust for danger took him in directions where he might get the ball slapped away or might miss a shot because of spectacular gyrations, but he would thrill you no end. . . . Monroe takes risks, and while some fail, enough come off to make him an artist."

Monroe became captain of the Knicks in the middle of 1976-77, a season in which the Knicks finished in third place in the Atlantic Division of the NBA's Eastern Conference. New York's 1977-78 season opened with a game against the Kansas City Kings at Madison Square Garden on October 18, 1977. In the New York *Sunday News Magazine* (December 4, 1977) Dave Hirshey described Earl the Pearl in action on that occasion: "Monroe dipped into the past and pulled out the Pearl of yore, rocking, rolling, bobbing, spinning, double, triple, quadruple pumping, *swish!* Jumper right side . . . jumper left side . . . driving left side scoop . . . spinning foul line jumper . . . twisting layup . . . ten straight points, twenty-seven points in twenty-six minutes."

After the game against Kansas City, Monroe facetiously explained one particularly spectacular basket that he had sunk, a twelve-foot jump shot with which he outwitted three towering opponents: "Oh, that was just an old la-la move where you float in the air as long as possible." His teammate Phil Jackson commented, "Forget trying to analyze it. Earl is moving to a different drummer all the time. He's got this tune playing inside his head. If you could hear it, it would be progressive jazz." In a similar vein, Talib Aleem, a member of the Prana People, a group that records for Monroe's Pretty Pearl Records, has said, "Earl's a master musician and he doesn't even know it. His body is his instrument. He's a master at getting the right tempo."

A transformation takes place when Monroe has the ball, as Allen observed. "One is suddenly transported to a more primitive place. It's "Roots" time. The eyes are big and white, the teeth flash, the nostrils flare. He dribbles the ball too high, but with a controlled violence. The audience gets high with anticipation of some new type of thrill about to occur. Seconds later he is moving in aggressively, one on one, against a defender and you sense the man is in trouble. Monroe is double-teamed and now there are two men hanging all over him. Then it happens. A quick twist, a sudden move and he's by both men." Sometimes the twist and move forward are replaced by a series of deceptive flashing arm movements ending with a lightning pass, often behind the back, to a teammate. All of this is done without his eyes betraying in advance where he intends the ball to go.

The Tiffany Entertainment Corporation and Pretty Pearl Records are housed in a cavernous studio on West Fifty-fourth Street in Manhattan. In the *Daily News* interview with Dave Hirshey, Monroe explained how he happened to enter the recording business: "The entertainment field was a natural for me to get into. I've always had a flair for acting and at one time in my life I thought I wanted to be a comedian. I used to perform all the old Pigmeat Markham skits in college, I have every album Richard Pryor ever recorded . . . and I bow to nobody in my admiration for Woody Allen. But the record business afforded me more opportunities. It can run simultaneously with my basketball, plus which I'm a night person." Also, aware that his "time is near," he is anticipating his retirement from basketball, preparing for the time when he will have "to concentrate on just Earl and leave off being the Pearl."

Earl Monroe is six feet three and a half inches tall and weighs 190 pounds. Off the court he tends to be a private person, sometimes a brooding one. He acknowledges that he has a "quick temper," a fact evident in the altercation with a referee in Madison Square Garden for which he was suspended from play in March 1978. Monroe owns a home in Oakland, New Jersey, but he spends most of his time in his town house, a four-storey building on West Eighty-eighth Street in Manhattan. He rents out the first floor of the townhouse and shares the other three with his "lady," Tina DeVone, a fashion model. The Knickerbocker superstar drives a Rolls Royce, plays tennis, enjoys cooking (fish is his favorite food), is interested in astrology, and contributes quietly to social service organizations, especially those concerned with the problems of young people.

References: Ebony 24:45+ F '69 pors; N Y Sunday News Mag p7+ D 4 '77; N Y Post p104 N 1 '76 por; p20 Mr 2 '77; Newsday p96 D 3 '74 por; Sport 45:52+ Je '68 pors, 65:20+ N '77 pors; Sports Ill 29:30+ N 4 '68 pors; National Basketball Association Guide, 1977-78

Moore, Henry (Spencer)

July 30, 1898- British sculptor; painter. Address: "Hoglands," Perry Green, Much Hadham, Hertfordshire, England

NOTE: This biography supersedes the article that appeared in *Current Biography* in 1954.

When, in the England of the 1920's and 1930's, Henry Moore achieved in his early sculpture an audacious fusion of abstraction, distortion, and other radical elements of modern art with ancient and traditional aesthetic concepts, his shocked countrymen blasted his work with ridicule and vituperation. Not until he won the 1948 Venice Biennale international prize for sculpture did he begin to gain the acknowledgement as a central influence in contemporary art that has grown over the years to his recognition as the world's greatest living sculptor. Art historians have devoted scores of studies to his life and work, and tributes paid to him are as uncountable as exhibitions accorded his sculptures, drawings, and watercolors.

The presence of Moore's sculptures in architectural, museum, and open-air settings in cities, parks, and estates throughout the world testifies to a universal appeal that derives principally from his generous feeling for life and from his sensitivity to images of archetypal significance, particularly eternal feminine procreativity and protectiveness. His sculptures of the human figure, moreover, are metaphors of the earth's mountains, valleys, and caverns. As they interact with their environment, they repeat in their undulating shapes both the power and lyricism of nature, infused, if Moore has succeeded, with a vitality of their own, as though they were created by an energy from within. Again, if they fulfill the sculptor's intention, they yield their many meanings and their mysteries only gradually, as they are viewed from every angle, preferably against the sky.

A coal miner's son, Henry Spencer Moore was born in Castleford, a small mining town in Yorkshire, England, on July 30, 1898 to Raymond Spencer and Mary (Baker) Moore. He was the seventh of their eight children, and after the early death of his younger sister, the family indulged him as the youngest child. His devotion to his mother—an intense attachment that he placidly regards as a probable mother complex—accounts in large measure for the primacy of the female figure in his sculpture and for his preoccupation with the mother and child theme. He has also acknowledged the effect on his lifework of his ambitious, strong-minded father, who was determined to give his children cultural and educational advantages that would enable them to escape labor in the dismal mine pits.

Aside from his parents, the most important early influence on Moore's development as a sculptor was probably the rugged landscape of Yorkshire itself, its slag heaps, moors, and outcroppings of rock. He made up his mind at the age of eleven to become a sculptor after hearing his Sunday school teacher tell how Michelangelo, whom he called "the greatest sculptor in the world," created his *Head of a Faun*. Drawing in school and carving pieces of wood and stone had already given him much pleasure. But yielding to his father's insistence that he prepare for a secure profession, in 1910 he enrolled in Castleford Grammar School to train as a teacher.

By the time, however, that Moore began his teaching apprenticeship at the local elementary school in 1916, he had become even more eager to be a sculptor because of the encouragement of two of his teachers. Through the headmaster of the grammar school, T. R. Dawes, whose special interest was English church architecture, he became acquainted with the eleventh-century carvings at the Methley Church in Yorkshire, to which he has ascribed his own early fascination with direct carving. His art instructor, Miss Alice Gostick, gave him a glimpse of the realm of art beyond Yorkshire and later helped him to obtain an educational grant for advanced art study.

During World War I Moore fought in France as a private in the Civil Service Rifles, which he joined in 1917. Gassed in the Battle of Cambrai in the autumn of that year, he was invalided home and in early 1919 was discharged from the army. He briefly resumed his former teaching job in Castleford before entering Leeds School of Art in September 1919 on an ex-serviceman's grant. Although the academic training he acquired there had slight relevance to the revolutionary changes then taking place in aesthetic theory and practice, he had access in Leeds to Sir Michael Sadler's collection of post-Impressionist paintings. At the Leeds Reference Library, moreover, he read Roger Fry's *Vision and Design*, which first brought to his attention the characteristics of primitive art, especially of the African Negro, and the principles of three dimensionality and fidelity to material that Moore soon adopted as his own.

In 1921 Moore entered the Royal College of Art on a scholarship. While living in London he had the opportunity to examine primitive art—both pre-Classical and pre-Columbian, as well as African—in the ethnological section of the British Museum, which he has always regarded as his best school. Although he longed to carve directly in stone, as his ancient mentors had done, academic tradition at the college required him to model in clay or plaster.

Visiting Italy in 1925 on a Royal College of Art traveling scholarship, Moore spent most of his time in Florence, where he delighted in his discovery of Giotto, Masaccio, and Michelangelo, whom he has called "the real sculptural artists of the Renaissance" because of their involvement with three-dimensional forms. Also important to his own development was the monumentality he deeply admired in Michelangelo.

Later in 1925 Moore joined the faculty of the Royal College of Art as a part-time instructor in sculpture, a position that he held until 1932, when he began a seven-year term at the Chelsea School of Art. The receptive young artist found that during the first few years he learned much about sculpture from teaching, and he continued to assimilate into his own work themes and shapes from a wide diversity of sources. At the Museum of Natural History and Geological Museum he studied the rhythms, patterns, and structure of bones, stones, minerals, shells, and cells to learn nature's way of shaping objects.

In his own work, meanwhile, Moore explored a variety of materials—wood, stone, metal, and terra cotta and concrete—as was evident in his first one-man show, in 1928 at the Warren Gallery in London, which also included a selection of his drawings. In 1928, moreover, he undertook his first commissioned work, the relief carving *North Wind* for the Underground Building in St. James's Park, London. Inasmuch as relief carving represented to him a subservience of the sculptor to the architect, he accepted the commission reluctantly. His personification of the north wind is not among his notable works.

The following year is a much more significant date in Moore's career because of his creation of the Leeds's *Reclining Figure* of 1929. That work, which H. H. Arnason in *History of Modern Art* considers "one of his first masterpieces in sculpture," was inspired by the hauntingly powerful sculpture of the Toltec-Mayan rain spirit, *Chacmool*, a limestone reclining figure of which Moore had seen an illustration in a German art book some years earlier. Donald Hall suggested in his 1966 biography of the sculptor that the importance for Moore of the 1929 work lay in the formal variety he achieved in his treatment of the human figure. And Arnason pointed out, "In this and other reclining figures, torsos, and mother-and-child groups of the late 1920's, Moore established the basic themes on which he was to play variations for the rest of his life."

Several of Moore's sculptural pieces of the decade of the 1930's are significant as resolutions to formal problems. His Cumberland alabaster *Mother and Child* of 1931 is an early example of his effort to attain monumentality by making the head of his figure small in proportion to the torso. Because the head is the most important part of the figure, he has explained, it determines the scale of the rest of the piece. Moore's modest studio at that time, in Hampstead, could not accommodate very large blocks of stone, nor could he afford the time or money to execute massive works in metal, but he believed that conveying a sense of monumentality was essential in sculpture.

Early in the decade, also, Moore began to make extensive use of voids to disrupt the solid volume of his wood, stone, and metal pieces. Because of his increasing dependence on that device for realizing three-dimensionality, he was often ridiculed as "the sculptor of the Hole." He has said that "a hole can itself have as much shape-meaning as a solid mass." In some of his work after the 1930's his greater use of bronze and other metals gave him the means of more fully discovering the potentialities of "opened-out sculpture." Apart from its formal purpose, the hole held for Moore the fascination of a mysteriousness much like that of a cave in a cliff or hillside. His penchant for the hole may be an aspect of the surrealism that became apparent in his work in the 1930's in the expression of subconscious drives and feelings, a searching out of the mystery within himself.

As another way of studying spatial relationships between voids and solids, Moore experimented with compositions of two or more separated abstract forms. Apparently unfulfilled, however, by a purely abstract idiom, he translated his discoveries into the human figure. His most abstract designs occur in a series of stringed figures of lead and wire or wood and string executed during the late 1930's, but even those pieces, he has maintained, were based on living creatures, organic forms. Accordingly, Moore wrote in a 1934 essay, "Abstract qualities of design are essential to the value of a work, but to me of equal importance is the psychological, human element. If both abstract and human elements are welded together in a work, it must have a fuller, deeper meaning."

That essay, entitled "The Sculptor's Aim," appeared in a collection of essays edited by Herbert Read, *Unit One,* which took its name from that of a group of avant-garde artists that included Ben Nicholson and Barbara Hepworth, Moore's neighbors at Hampstead. In his essay Moore also discussed vitality and power of expression, asserting, "For me a work must first have a vitality of its own, . . . an intense life of its own, independent of the object it may represent. When a work has this powerful vitality we do not connect the word Beauty with it." He went on to explain, "Between beauty of expression and power of expression there is a difference of function. The first aims at pleasing the senses, the second has a spiritual vitality which for me is more moving and goes deeper than the senses."

Throughout the early years of his career Moore relied on drawing to generate ideas for his sculpture, filling notebooks with sketches as a means of sorting out images he had been carrying in his head. During World War II, however, drawing became for him an end in itself when one evening in London he went down by chance into an underground (tube or subway) station where people had taken refuge from Nazi air raids. "I saw hundreds of Henry Moore Reclining Figures stretched along the platforms," he recalled in an interview for the *Atlantic Monthly* (January 1962). "I was fascinated, visually. I went back again and again." After each visit to various underground stations, he produced from memory in watercolor the scenes that became his celebrated Shelter Drawings of 1940-41. The War Artists' Advisory Committee, which commissioned some of those pictures, also commissioned a smaller series of drawings of coal miners. Moore returned to Castleford in 1942 and ventured into the mines for the first time to make his sketches, which, like his Shelter Drawings and his sculpture, are part of his overall statement of man and his environment.

Besides more fully humanizing his work, Moore's experience with the shelter watercolors pointed the way in his sculpture to groups of two or more figures and to draped figures. The influence of the drawings is evident in his seated figures *Madonna and Child* (1943-44) for the Church of St. Matthew in Northampton, one of his few directly commissioned works, and in his tender family groups and other groups of the late 1940's. His interest in the formal problems of drapery, sharpened by the sculpture he saw during a visit to Greece in 1951, led to his bronze *Draped Reclining Figure* of 1952-53 for the Time-Life Building in London, for which he also executed a large, stone sculptural screen. Another sculpture dating from 1952-53 is one of his most famous and popular pieces, the enigmatic bronze *King and Queen,* the first cast of which was bought for Antwerp's outdoor sculptural museum. Having conceived his *King and Queen,* like most of his sculptural pieces, with an open-air setting in mind and the sky as background, Moore is particularly pleased with the location of another cast of that work, at Glenkiln, Sir William Keswick's estate in Dumfries, Scotland, which is also the home of three other Moore sculptures, among them the *Glenkiln Cross (Upright Motive No. 1,* 1955-56), which links pagan, primitive, and Christian symbols.

Within considerable variety Moore's work maintained a remarkable continuity and consistency as one sculptural figure grew out of another. His elm wood *Internal and External Forms* of 1953-54 echos the protective motif of earlier helmet pieces and is essentially a variation on the mother and child theme. After executing a series of upright, or columnar, figures, he returned in 1957-58 to the reclining figure for a sculpture commissioned for the UNESCO building in Paris. Deliberately avoiding any allegorical interpretation of the meaning of UNESCO, the piece uses free relationships of forms that mingle the human figure and landscape. Although the UNESCO request was for a bronze figure, Moore decided upon stone, believing it would weather more suitably, and went to the Henraux stone quarry at Querceta, Italy to carve his sculpture out of sixty-ton blocks of Roman travertine.

Over sixteen feet long, the UNESCO figure was the largest that Moore had executed before 1963-64, when he completed a massive bronze reclining figure, sixteen feet high and thirty feet across, for New York City's Lincoln Center for the Performing Arts. That two-piece figure, which rises out of the water of a reflecting pool near the Vivian Beaumont Theatre, is the culmination of a series of two-and-three-part sculptures that Moore began in the late 1950's in resumption of the multiple-part experimental compositions he had undertaken in the 1930's.

Even before the installation of the Lincoln Center sculpture, Moore had started work on a series of "locking pieces," including the Brussels *Lambert Locking Piece* of 1963-64, to bring together the divided parts. Having overcome with the UNESCO and Lincoln Center pieces many problems relating to scale and size, he began contemplating sculpture into or through which one could walk. In that direction in 1964 he created for the University of Chicago the monumental, richly symbolic bronze *Nuclear Energy*, which has a clearly architectural quality. His gigantic walk-through *Square Form with Cut*, 1969-70, which stands on a large lawn in the outskirts of Prato, Italy, is a magnificent achievement in white marble, rising eighteen feet high and weighing 170 tons. Moore made the model for *Square Form* in polystyrene, a material that permits easy alteration and stands up well in shipment. But for smaller pieces he prefers models of plaster over internal armature and stretch canvas.

Because of his need to study his figures from all sides, some time after World War II Moore had exchanged drawings for maquettes of wax or plaster as the medium for developing concepts and shapes for his sculpture. He continued, however, his practice of sketching memoranda on problems that he encountered in his sculpture, as is apparent in *Henry Moore: Unpublished Drawings* (Abrams, 1972), a selection from the notebooks he kept from 1921 to 1970. The gift of an elephant skull from Julian Huxley inspired a series of forty etchings that Moore made between 1968 and 1970, excited by complexities of structure that suggested many topographical and architectural forms. One of the subjects that most appealed to him when he turned back to drawing in his seventies was Stonehenge, of which he made a series of lithographs that captured the sense of awesome power and monumentality he had felt on seeing Stonehenge for the first time in 1922.

Like his sculpture, Moore's drawings are wholly free of sentimentality and prettiness, but they often convey warmth and affection, such as his 1972 drawings of sheep, some of which are among the more than 300 drawings included in *Henry Moore Drawings* (Harper, 1974). The engaging sheep of Moore's drawings are those that graze on the grounds of his home in Much Hadham. In 1972 he made a sculpture for them to walk through and rub against, the fourteen-and-a-half-feet high *Sheep Piece*. That is one of the original sculptures, along with casts of others, that Moore has kept for himself on the rolling lands around his house and studios. A former trustee of the Tate Gallery in London, he offered the Tate a large part of his private collection, but when space for public display could not be provided there, he made a gift, valued at some $15,000,000 (or priceless), to the Art Gallery of Ontario in Toronto. In celebration of his eightieth birthday, in 1978, thirty-six sculptures donated by Moore were shown at the Tate, and 200 sculptures, drawings, and prints were displayed in his first major exhibition in his native county of Yorkshire, at Bradford.

Henry Moore moved from London to his Hertfordshire home, a fifteenth-century farm cottage, in 1940 with his Russian-born wife, the former Irina Radetzky, whom he had married on July 27, 1929. Their daughter, Mary Spencer, born on March 7, 1946, is a book illustrator. Since the mid-1960's the family has spent summers at another home, a red-tiled bungalow that Moore built in the suburbs of Forte dei Marmi in Italy, not far from the Carrara quarries. Tending in his stature to invite contrast with the figures of his sculpture, Moore stands five feet four inches tall. He is of solid build with large hands and strong shoulders, and he has blue eyes, bushy brown eyebrows, and white hair. Meditative, mild-mannered, and unpretentious, he is so much his own man that although he accepted an O.M. (Order of Merit) and a C.H. (Companion of Honour), he has refused repeated offers of a knighthood, explaining that "titles change one's name and one's opinion of oneself."

References: Finn, David. Henry Moore: Sculpture and Environment (1976); Hall, Donald. Henry Moore, the Life and Work of a Great Sculptor (1966); International Who's Who, 1978-79; James, Philip, ed. Henry Moore on Sculpture (1971); Russell, John. Henry Moore (1968); Who's Who, 1978-79

Morton, Craig

Feb. 5, 1943- Football player. Address: b. Denver Broncos, 5700 Logan Street, Denver, Colo. 80216

The careers of passing ace Craig Morton and of coach Red Miller have tardily peaked at the same time and in the same place—the Denver franchise of the National Football League. Following seventeen years as an assistant coach, Miller became head mentor of the Denver Broncos after the 1976 season. Then the Broncos, already a defensively strong team, acquired offensive experience in Morton, who had "wasted" (as his fans see it) his first nine and a half years in the NFL as an alternate, under-used quarterback with the Dallas Cowboys and the last two and a half as the hapless, last-place New York Giants' outstanding player and therefore their scapegoat. With Miller as strategist and Morton as offensive field leader, the Broncos won the NFL's 1977 American Conference championship. After the team lost in Super Bowl XII to the National Conference champions, the Dallas Cowboys, largely because of concentrated, calculated pressure put on Morton by his old teammates, there was speculation that Denver would be looking for a new quarterback, but Red Miller insisted, "There will be nothing different next year. Craig is our quarterback."

In a post-season testimonial to the mellow, stabilizing leadership displayed by Morton in his first year with the rambunctious Denver club, Pete Axthelm wrote, in his sports column in *Newsweek* (January 16, 1978): "In a year of confusion, injustice, and blunders by officials that have cast a pall over the entire National Football League, the thirty-four-year-old Morton has emerged as the game's most striking symbol of courage, skill, and dignity. Those of us who maligned him through the first dozen years of his career owe him, at the least, the kind of apology that commissioner Pete Rozelle issues after one of his stripe-shirted 'zebras' blows an obvious call that costs some team its shot at the title." Going into the 1977 season, Morton's career totals were 136 games; 2,192 passes attempted and 1,146 completed, for an average of .523; 16,013 yards gained; 109 touchdowns; and 122 interceptions.

A glassblower's son, Larry Craig Morton was born in Flint, Michigan, on February 5, 1943, and grew up in Campbell, California. In high school Morton was all-state in basketball, baseball, and football. As a second baseman, he received attractive offers from a number of major-league baseball teams, but college had priority in his plans. At the University of California at Berkeley he majored in education and made the 1964 All-America team as the pass-throwing star of the football team. He also continued to attract major-league attention, now as an outfielder, but he preferred football and opted for a career in that sport. The first-round draft choice of Dallas, he joined the Cowboys with a $200,000 contract after taking his college degree in 1965.

During his first two years in Dallas, Morton spent most of his time on the bench, as understudy to Don Meredith. He relieved Meredith in ten games in 1967 and thirteen games in 1968 and succeeded him in the starting quarterback slot in 1969. In an exhibition game just before the 1969 season he dislocated his right index finger, and the injury caused him to miss the season's first game, in which rookie Roger Staubach led the Cowboys to victory over St. Louis. Five games later the injury jinx struck again, as Morton later recounted: "I tore up my shoulder . . . and I tried to keep on playing. For two Sundays it wasn't too bad. I couldn't throw in practice, but at home I'd throw into a pillow to loosen up and then try to throw on Sunday. It got so I was throwing sidearm and not well." The Cowboys finished the season with a 11-2-1 record but lost in the playoffs to Cleveland, 38-14.

Morton underwent surgery on his shoulder after the 1969 season and did not return to the lineup until the fourth game of the following season. Pushing himself too hard, he fell repeatedly on his right elbow, damaging the nerves. Off the field he was having problems too, connected with his nightlife, his business ventures, and the Internal Revenue Service. The distractions affected his game-calling, and Coach Tom Landry began dictating the offensive plays.

On his own, confidentially, Morton submitted to hypnosis, and with the help of post-hypnotic suggestion he rallied dramatically. His passing average, 40 percent in the first nine games of the 1970 season, rose to nearly 60 percent in the final five, in which the Cowboys were undefeated. In one game, against Houston, he passed for five touchdowns, and his total of touchdown passes was fifteen. The victory streak led to the Super Bowl—and there it ended, in a humiliating defeat at the hands of the Baltimore Colts. Contributing to the defeat were two intercepted passes thrown by Morton, and blame was focused on him by fans, especially after word about his experiment with hypnosis leaked out.

Trying to explain the legitimate value of hypnosis to Morton's benighted critics, Edward J. Pullman, director of the Southwest Hypnosis Research Center, said: "The object was to relieve Craig of game pressures, boost his confidence, free him from further injury by conditioning him to relax on the instant of body contact, to keep his elbow from being a conscious hindrance, and just generally to open up the full potential of his abilities."

Apparently, Pullman wasted his breath; booing Morton became routine crowd behavior in Texas Stadium in 1971, and Morton's response to it only made matters worse. Like an orchestra leader calling in the brasses, he would lift both arms in a gesture that appeased his pride but irritated Coach Landry. Although the booing belied a real improvement in Morton—or at least in his passing arm, the right arm, following an operation on the elbow—Landry stopped alternating the two quarterbacks toward the end of the 1971 season, picking Staubach as the regular starter. His chief reason for the choice, he said, was Staubach's "greater mobility." Also probably having some weight in the decision was the fact that Staubach, like Landry, was a "born again" Christian, whereas Morton had not yet come to that state—as he since has—and had a playboy's reputation.

Just when Morton had resigned himself to playing backup, Staubach was sidelined with a shoulder injury, at the beginning of the 1972 season. Suddenly thrust again into the number-one spot, Morton responded with his finest season ever. Dallas linebacker D. D. Lewis later observed, "It was in the back of everyone's mind Craig would fold. But he took the challenge. Instead of folding, he got tougher." Despite his spectacular completion of 185 passes, including fifteen touchdown throws, out of 339 attempted, for 2,396 yards, Morton remained the chief target of the crowd's boos in the team's low moments, but he professed not to care. "Let 'em boo," he said. "When I'm throwing touchdowns and the Dallas Cowboys are winning, I can live without the cheers."

The glory of the 1972 season began to fizzle in the opening playoff game, against San Francisco. With Dallas trailing 28-13, Landry replaced Morton with the recuperated Staubach, who turned the score around with two touchdown passes in the final two minutes, and Morton remained on the bench throughout the NFC championship game against the Washington Redskins, a 26-3 disaster for the Cowboys. Bitterly disappointed, he asked to be traded, but his request was ignored and he spent nearly the entire 1973 season on the Dallas bench. Forcing the Dallas front office's hand by signing to play in the stillborn World Football League, he was sent to the New York Giants in the midst of the 1974 season in exchange for a first-round draft choice (who turned out to be linebacker Randy White).

Given the sole field leadership of the team, including the freedom to call his own plays, Morton threw himself enthusiastically into the task of reviving the Giants, who had not reached the playoffs in over a decade. But by the time the 1975 season began, it was clear that no Giant renaissance was imminent. The team was, as sportswriters observed, a "lazy," spiritless, blundering "mess," giving Morton virtually no support as he tried to do too much by himself. "We didn't get any turnovers, no turnovers at all," he later said. "We were always starting on eighty-yard marches. I would try to force a lot of plays I shouldn't have, but I didn't know any other way to get it going."

Contributing to Morton's problems in New York was an offense devised by Bill Arnsparger, a defensively-oriented coach. "It was very frustrating for Craig," a Giant insider later commented. "He was the victim of a front office that didn't bring in any experienced wide receivers and the victim of a coach who had no offensive philosophy . . . no real offensive system. . . . The more Craig was unable to produce big plays, the more frustrated he became."

John McVay replaced Arnsparger as coach of the Giants midway through the 1976 season, when the team's record stood at a dismal seven losses in as many starts. With the offense-oriented McVay planning the offensive strategy, New York picked up three victories in the remaining seven starts. But as the most conspicuous member of the team, Morton continued to be the most vulnerable to the anger of the crowd when the Giants were losing, and at those times his name could not even come up in the pre-game introductions without drawing verbal fire from the bleachers. By the end of the 1976 season, he had had enough and wanted out.

Meanwhile, in Denver, the Broncos were having problems of their own, falling just short of the championship performance of which the members of the team felt they were capable. Following a player mutiny, the Denver front office fired Coach John Ralston and brought in Red Miller as coach and, in a trade for Steve Ramsey and future considerations, Morton as quarterback. Surrounded by better runners, better receivers, a better defensive unit, (the "Orange Crush"), and a better field goal kicker, Morton suddenly clicked, as did the Broncos. In 1977 Denver racked up twelve victories as against two defeats, the best record in the American Football Conference, and Morton earned a number two ranking among quarterbacks in the conference with 1,929 yards, fourteen touchdowns, a .516 completion average, and, in spite of a painful hip condition that hospitalized him at one point, a 4.0 average rushing. Morton was *The Sporting News* choice for AFC Player of the Year.

The dream of a league championship was shattered in Super Bowl XII by Morton's old team, the Dallas Cowboys, who forced and recovered four Denver fumbles and intercepted three Morton passes to take the NFL title, 27-10. "Our number one plan was to pressure Craig Morton," Landry, the Dallas coach, said after the game. "We did not want to give him time to throw. . . . We just rushed the heck out of him." Harvey Martin, one of Dallas' "front four," said: "We didn't go out to hurt Craig. We went out to put pressure on him because we felt when you pressure Craig, he either throws it up [for interceptions] or throws it away."

The Denver Broncos have the reputation of being one of the more "emotional" teams in the NFL. But Coach Red Miller—who, like Landry in Dallas, calls the plays—is having a tranquilizing effect on the team, fostering a conservative approach. Under his direction and influence, Morton is a more patient quarterback, playing percentages, waiting for the "Orange Crush" to force a turnover, and generally "eating" the ball rather than chancing its falling into the hands of the opposition.

Craig Morton is six feet four inches tall, weighs 210 pounds, and has blue eyes and curly, blondish hair. His calm, quiet self-confidence was reinforced when he, the former worldly hedonist, experienced a religious rebirth in the summer of 1977. "I accepted the Lord into my life," he says, "and I married just a great Christian girl." He and Susie Sirmen, a model he met in Dallas when he was with the Cowboys, were married on November 7, 1977. With his conversion and marriage have come a greater serenity on the field and in the face of his life's problems, including the financial one. He is slowly paying up his enormous past debts, now consolidated in a $38,000 bank loan and a $34,000 federal income-tax lien. Two of the businesses that ran him into trouble were campus bookstores in California—an investment choice reflecting his personal interest in reading. His other recreations include art collecting, playing golf and tennis, and sailing. Unlike less articulate "born-again" athletes, who sometimes make their faith sound ludicrous to other "jocks," Morton is lucid in explaining that his reward is "inner peace" and not success as a quarterback, or, as Molly Ivins wrote in the New York *Times* (January 9, 1978), "a Kingdom yes; a ninety-nine yard pass, no."

References: N Y Times D p 12 Ja 12 '78; Sport 55:64+ My '73 por; Sporting News p3+ N 12 '77 por, 185:5+ Ja 7 '78 por; Sports Illus 48:24+ Ja 6 '78; Football Register, 1977

Muldoon, Robert D(avid)

Sept. 25, 1921- Prime Minister of New Zealand. Address: Parliament House, Wellington, New Zealand

When New Zealand's conservative National party leader Robert D. Muldoon unset incumbent Labour Prime Minister Wallace Rowling in the general election of November 1975, many political pundits saw in Muldoon's landslide the ascendancy of a new era of right-wing populism in the small British dominion "down under," 1,200 miles southeast of Australia in the southwest Pacific. Actually, Muldoon's victory probably had less to do with politics than with style and economics: in a time of worldwide recession, the pugnacious Muldoon was the most experienced finance minister in the British Commonwealth. Holding his own finance portfolio as Prime Minister, he has been hewing to a narrow line between too much and too little stimulation of the economy so as to avoid increasing inflation and the foreign deficit on the one hand or unemployment on the other. Despite his best efforts, New Zealand's annual rate of inflation and its balance of payments deficit are still high—approximately 13.5 percent and $1 billion, respectively, as of the beginning of 1978—but the unemployment figure, 16,500 in a population of 3,200,000, is proportionately one of the world's lowest.

A descendant of late nineteenth-century Liverpool Irish and English immigrants—including a Methodist missionary—Robert David Muldoon was born on September 25, 1921 in Auckland, New Zealand's largest city. After his father suffered a severe stroke, when Muldoon was eight, his mother supported the family on her meager earnings as an upholsterer. "As a schoolboy during the Depression," he writes in his autobiography, *The Rise and Fall of a Young Turk* (Reed, 1974), "I saw hardship beyond anything seen today. . . . Hardship is relative." At the age of five, he tore a muscle in his left cheek in a fall and acquired the facial defect, most evident when he smiles, which, as he says, his friends call a dimple and his enemies "a scar or a smirk."

On completing his secondary education at Mt. Albert Grammar School in Auckland in 1940, Muldoon joined the army, where he took advantage of the accounting classes offered. During World War II he served first in New Caledonia and the Solomon Islands and then in Italy, where he saw combat as an infantryman.

Ending the war with corporal's stripes, Muldoon took the examination of the New Zealand Institute of Cost Accountants in Italy, in the tent of his commanding officer, Major John Marshall, whom he would later succeed as leader of the National party. After the war he studied cost accountancy in London on the New Zealand equivalent of the G.I. Bill, and in 1946 he became the first person from outside Great Britain to win the Leverhulme Prize of the London Institute of Cost and Management Accountants.

In 1947 Muldoon returned to New Zealand and joined the Auckland firm of cost accountants which today bears the name Kendon, Mills, Muldoon, & Browne. Despite familial ties to the Labour Party—his grandmother had been an ardent supporter of the party during the Depression—Muldoon chose in 1947 to join the right-of-center National party, and while pursuing his career in accountancy he began to make a name for himself as an enthusiastic party worker. He held a number of National party district offices before making his first bid for the House of Representatives that constitutes New Zealand's unicameral Parliament, in 1954. Running on a staunchly anti-Communist platform, he lost the 1954 election and a second Parliamentary bid, for the Waitemata seat, three years later. He was finally elected, to the Tamaki seat, in the 1960 election that inaugurated the twelve-year reign of the National party government headed by Keith J. Holyoake.

With his taste for political infighting, Muldoon stood out among his party's so-called young Turks, backbenchers with a tendency to quarrel with their own Parliamentary leaders as well as with the Labour opposition. Muldoon relished his growing national reputation as an independent-minded politician with a stinging wit in Parliamentary repartee and press conferences, and he acknowledged that he was "essentially a counter-puncher in verbal battles," with a retort "usually a little harder than the original blow." On one occasion he was officially censured for allegedly offensive comments he had directed to the Speaker of the House.

Muldoon's rise in the hierarchy of the National party government was rapid. As Parliamentary Under-Secretary to the Minister of Finance for four years beginning in 1964, he guided the changeover of New Zealand's currency to the decimal system. In 1967 he served as Minister of Tourism and Publicity until, toward the end of the year, he was given the finance portfolio on the death of Harry R. Lake.

As Minister of Finance, Muldoon immediately earned credit for his deft handling of a temporary balance-of-payments crisis and a subsequent devaluation of the New Zealand dollar; and over the years, as the architect of frequent mini-budgets, he acquired a reputation for hard-nosed fiscal conservatism. The emerging unemployment problem in a country accustomed to near-zero joblessness, coupled with an already rising inflationary rate occupied much of his attention and presented him with a dilemma: the tighter his fiscal policies, the more he would ultimately be blamed for contributing to unemployment. Internationally, as New Zealand governor of the International Monetary Fund, he became a spokesman for small countries dependent on the export of raw materials and farm products from the great Western industrialized nations. A strong advocate of free international trade, Muldoon argued that the industrialized powers must reverse their protectionist trade policies if small nations producing primary products are to avoid chronic trade deficits.

The National party won a narrow but workable majority in the 1969 elections, in which Muldoon retained his Tamaki seat with a comfortable majority. The stringent 1970 national budget that he worked out for the Holyoake government included an unprecedented payroll tax designed to stiffen employer resistance to wage demands, but New Zealand's powerful trade unions continued to push for wage hikes in keeping with an inflation rate then exceeding 10 percent. By 1972 Muldoon had instituted a series of measures bringing the inflation rate down to 4.5 percent per year.

Muldoon was Deputy Prime Minister from February 1972 to December 1972, when Labour returned to power under Norman E. Kirk and Muldoon became deputy leader of the Opposition under his former army superior, Sir John Marshall. Two years later, on the death of Kirk, Wallace E. Rowling was designated Prime Minister, and almost simultaneously low-keyed "Gentleman Jack" Marshall was replaced in the leadership of the National party by the aggressive, unabashedly abrasive Muldoon, who had emerged as the best hope that the party had for an early return to power.

Muldoon was relentless and unstinting in his attacks on the Labour government's economic policies, especially its increasing imposition of state control, its cautious approach to such problems as falling wool and beef prices, and its depletion of exchange reserves. Committed to coping with unemployment, the government had tried to do so first by spending the foreign reserves built up by Muldoon when he was Finance Minister and subsequently by borrowing internationally to keep domestic industry going.

In his 1975 campaign Muldoon accused Rowling of mortgaging New Zealand's future by borrowing more than $2 billion abroad and declared that drastic belt-tightening was necessary to cut imports and reduce a $970,000,000 balance-of-trade deficit. Because he coupled his platform of economic austerity with the populist-chauvinist slogan, "New Zealand the way you want it," urban liberals denounced him as a rabble-rousing demagogue, but the large crowds on the hustings cheered his stands against "creeping socialism" and for tougher immigration laws. He proposed reducing the number of immigrants annually from 30,000 to 5,000 not only by toughening restrictions on non-British immigrants but also by limiting British migrants (except those from Australia) to those with special skills or family ties. He also proposed the deportation of South Pacific immigrants convicted of crimes. What he tried to stress was not racism but immigration's drain on jobs, housing, and money. On other fronts, he called for government intervention against strikes; suggested that he would soft-pedal the proposal, made by Labour to the United Nations, for a nuclear-free zone in the South Pacific; and promised to work for resumption of athletic contacts with South Africa.

Even the most sanguine of Muldoon's supporters were surprised at the magnitude of his victory at the polls on November 29, 1975, which gave the National party a two-thirds majority in the eighty-seven-seat House of Representatives. In keeping with the practice common in British dominions, where the technical ruler is Queen Elizabeth II, Governor General Sir Edward Denis Blundell formally ratified the choice of the electorate by officially designating Muldoon chief executive of New Zealand.

Assuming the position of Minister of Finance as well as Prime Minister, Muldoon addressed himself first and foremost to New Zealand's economic problems. In January 1976 he eliminated the government's expensive dairy, postal, electrical, and gasoline subsidies and initiated a "user pays" policy for rail service, energy, and the like. One effect was an aggravation of inflation, but another was a more realistic view of the true cost of goods and services on the part of New Zealanders of average income. The inflation rate, which had dropped a little when curbs were put on installment buying of cars, television sets, and luxury items, fell appreciably further under temporary limits on wages, prices, and rents but rose again when the controls were removed.

The annual budget submitted by Muldoon in July 1977 included support for livestock and agricultural production but otherwise was designed to cut the inflation rate through such devices as severe restrictions on overseas travel and the importing of liquor, tobacco, and other luxury items. By September the economy had slowed to such a point that the Prime Minister found it necessary to introduce a $180,000,000 mini-budget to boost exports, employment, and consumer spending. He scheduled a 5 percent across-the-board cut in income tax for February 1978 and a $25 supplementary allowance for couples with dependent children for November 1978.

The business community has generally approved of Muldoon's pragmatic, *ad hoc* "fine tuning" (the Prime Minister's phrase) of the New Zealand economy, but labor has been less than happy, especially with his support of voluntary unionism, and his testy relationship with the press has developed into a chronic feud during his premiership. He has stirred controversy with his stated intention to consolidate the nation's two television news services and his decisions to revive sports competition with South African teams and to permit port visits by American nuclear-powered submarines.

The loudest public uproar was over proposed legislation that would authorize the Security Intelligence Service—directed by Muldoon himself—to intercept private mail and to wiretap telephone conversations. In October 1977 an estimated 10,000 people demonstrated against the bill in the streets of Wellington, and some of the demonstrators carried their protest into the House of Representatives, where they verbally assaulted members of Parliament, especially Prime Minister Muldoon. For the first time in New Zealand's history, police had to be summoned forcibly to remove disorderly persons from Parliament's public galleries.

In his foreign policy Muldoon has reemphasized New Zealand's ties to ANZUS, the Australian-New Zealand-United States defense pact. He has traveled widely as Prime Minister, largely in an effort to find new markets for New Zealand's farm exports. With such trade considerations in mind, he has made official visits to the People's Republic of China, Great Britain, France, Egypt, South Korea, Japan, and the United States. In Washington on November 9, 1977 he met with President Carter and reportedly pressed for an easing of American tariffs on imports from New Zealand.

Robert D. Muldoon and Thea Dale Flyger were married in 1951 and have two daughters, Barbara and Jennifer, and one son, Gavin. Muldoon is a stocky man with what has been called a bulldog scowl that reminds some of Winston Churchill. His favorite activity outside of politics is horticulture, especially the growing of lilies. Though raised in the Methodist and Anglican churches, he is now a Baptist. In an interview with Terry Coleman of the *Guardian* (March 26, 1977), the Prime Minister said that what is regarded as his "extreme-right Tory" position is really that of a patriotic "pragmatist." He explained: "I want to preserve the New Zealand that I see. I want to preserve an egalitarian society which is living in one of the loveliest countries in the world, and I want to see that no one disturbs or destroys our way of life."

References: Christian Sci Mon p8 D 1 '75; Economist p49 D 6 '75 por; Guardian p13 Mr 26 '77 por; N Y Times p1+ N 30 '75 por, p12 D 4 '75 por; International Who's Who, 1976-77; Muldoon, Robert D. The Rise and Fall of a Young Turk (1974); Who's Who, 1976-77

Musgrave, Thea

May 27, 1928- Composer; conductor. Address: b. c/o Novello Publications, Inc., 145 Palisade St., Dobbs Ferry, N.Y. 10522

Music in many forms—vocal and choral pieces, chamber and orchestral works, ballets, and operas—carry the individual and recognizable signature of the Scottish composer Thea Musgrave, who in recent years has herself conducted the premieres of her major compositions. "Moving from its generalized neo-classic background into rich unclassifiable territory," as Harold Blumenfeld wrote in the Los Angeles *Times Calendar* (October 25, 1977), her fresh, lucid, and intuitive musical idiom is also marked by its dramatic structure. Miss Musgrave uses the term "dramatic-abstract" in discussing many of her orchestral and chamber music compositions: "dramatic in presentation" and abstract because they have no program. In her so-called "space music" the instrumentalists sometimes move around the orchestra or the concert hall. Another inventive technique is her dramatic use of electronic tape in conjunction with the live performance, as in her opera *The Voice of Ariadne*. Her warmth, humor, and theatrical quality help make her music accessible to ever increasing audiences in the United Kingdom, Europe, and the United States. Now a resident of the United States, Miss Musgrave teaches at the University of California in Santa Barbara.

The only child of James P. and Joan (Hacking) Musgrave, Thea Musgrave was born in Edinburgh, Scotland on May 27, 1928. From about the age of five she was attracted to music and habitually made up snatches of tunes; but her idealistic desire to help people led her to decide upon medicine as a career. After she had completed her public school education at Moreton Hall in Oswestry, England, in 1947 she entered Edinburgh University. Although enrolled in premedical courses, she became tempted by the resources for musical study available at the university. She realized, as she explained in an interview for *High Fidelity/Musical America* (February 1976), "that music, too, had a very important mission, to help humanity on the *next* level." She went on to say, "I also felt that, in this commercial and technological age, I wanted to make an artistic statement."

At the University of Edinburgh, Miss Musgrave acquired a solid, fairly orthodox grounding in music, studying harmony and analysis with Mary Grierson, the aide and biographer of the celebrated Scottish musicologist Donald Francis Tovey, and counterpoint and the history of music with the Viennese composer Hans Gál. She was awarded the Tovey prize and in 1950 the Bachelor of Music degree. On a postgraduate scholarship she began four years of study, from 1950 to 1954, in Paris, where she became familiar with the music of Bartók and Stravinsky and then Dallapiccola, which led her to Webern and to Schönberg and eventually to Stockhausen and Boulez.

Along with investigating experimental work in the serial idiom, Thea Musgrave experienced what Leslie East in *British Music Now* (1975) called the "sobering influence" provided by Nadia Boulanger. Recalling that legendary teacher, Thea Musgrave told Hans Heinsheimer, who quoted her in *Opera News* (September 1977), "I was her student at the Conservatoire, where she was not permitted to teach composition. So she gave a class called 'piano accompaniment.' But we never did any accompanying on the piano—we did score reading, figured bass. . . . It was a general musicianship class, unbelievably stimulating. . . . In addition, I had private lessons with her every week. Yes, and there were her incredible dinner parties where one could meet her students from way back, composers, all kinds of visitors from all over." One of the lessons she learned was "the importance of every bar"; ideally, in composing, she believes, "there is no arbitrary right or wrong way. . . . One just has to be guided by one's own human and musical experience and then be prepared to answer for every note." Miss Musgrave was the first British composer to win the Lili Boulanger prize.

While still an apprentice, Thea Musgrave wrote her first dramatic work, *A Tale for Thieves* (1953), a ballet with a scenario based on Chaucer's *The Pardoner's Tale.* Because she found in Scotland many early opportunities for her to be heard, almost all her compositions have been performed soon after the writing. The first of her many commissions was "A Suite O' Bairnsangs" for voice and piano (1953). Her first major success was the large-scale diatonic and tonal *Cantata for a Summer's Day* (1954), sung by the Saltire Singers, with whom she later performed on several tours as a pianist. By the time the *Cantata* had its premiere at the Edinburgh International Festival, Miss Musgrave was working on her first opera, *The Abbot of Drimock* (1955), for which Maurice Lindsay wrote a libretto based on a Scots Border tale that is a variant of the story Puccini used for *Gianni Schicchi.* One critic noted the "Brittenesque idiom" of the music, and Norman Kay, in his full-length evaluation of Thea Musgrave (*Music and Musicians,* December 1969), pointed in *The Abbot* to "the shadow of Stravinsky of the Piano Concerto" and the importance of "the pull towards free chromaticism.'" That one-act chamber opera was revived in March 1977.

The chromaticism and serial elements that infiltrated Miss Musgrave's "Five Love Songs" for soprano and guitar (1955) were developed further in *Obliques,* both for orchestra and the string quartet, in 1958. A strict application of the serial technique became evident for the first time in the 1958 aria "A Song for Christmas." Although Miss Musgrave's next piece, *Scottish Dance Suite* (1959) for orchestra, was entirely tonal, in the lyrical *Triptych* (1959) she demonstrated her "personal adaptation of serialism,'" and her next two important works, *Colloquy* for violin and piano and *Trio* for flute, oboe, and piano (both 1960), in their "fluid" serial application, as Leslie East wrote, set the "cornerstone of the distinctive style that emerged later." Serialism served for Miss Musgrave as a lasting discipline, even though she broke out of its confines after about two years.

During the early 1960's Thea Musgrave's work was distinguished by the well-made *Serenade* for flute, clarinet, harp, viola, and cello (1961); *Sir Patrick Spens* for tenor and guitar (1961), "a little gem," as Kay termed it, written at the request of Peter Pears; Chamber Concerto No. 1 (1962); two substantial choral works, *The Phoenix and the Turtle* (1962) and *The Five Ages of Man* (1963); and *Marko the Miser* (1962), a tale for children to mime, sing, and play. Concurrently, from 1959 to 1965, Miss Musgrave was busy as an extramural lecturer for London University. Turning down as many as eight commissions for concert or incidental music works, for television and films, she became wholeheartedly involved with the writing of her three-act opera, *The Decision* (1964-65). With a libretto by Lindsay based on a true incident, that drama of the ordeal of an entrapped miner, John Brown, was "an emphatic success" when first performed at Sadler's Wells on November 30, 1967, Stanley Sadie reported in *Musical Times.*

Neither tonal nor serial, Thea Musgrave's first full-length opera "provided the turning point," as Leslie East perceived, in her search for "a truly individual voice, . . . a voice of uncommon richness and strength." According to East, "The wrestling with concrete dramatic problems in *The Decision* obviously contributed to the compelling desire to explore dramatic qualities in abstract instrumental terms." In the following period of marked development Miss Musgrave wrote Chamber Concerto No. 2—in homage to Charles Ives (1966), the first of her "dramatic-abstract" works, which display an awareness of the possibilities of free interplay between various soloists and the rest of the players. Impersonating Rollo, an invention of Ives that symbolizes the typical Victorian conservative, the viola becomes a disruptive and thereby comedic element in the work. The Chamber Concerto No. 3 (1966), with thematic material derived from the names of Viennese composers, was also a "'drama for instruments,' but in a much less specific way," Miss Musgrave explained. "It explores the virtuosic possibilities of the eight players who dominate the texture in turn (the players concerned standing up to play)." In her Concerto for Orchestra (1967), she has the clarinet "instigate a sort of cadenza-revolt among a group of concertante soloists," as Desmond Shawe-Taylor described the lively conflict in the *Sunday Times*. Concerto for Clarinet and Orchestra (1968) employs in essence two directors—the conductor on the podium and a peripatetic soloist-catalyst, pitted against different sections in turn. In its complex melodic texture, the players are freed from bar lines and controlled by the composer with a system of notational cueing.

The "space music" device in Thea Musgrave's "concert-platform dramas" reappears in *Night Music* for Chamber Orchestra (1969) with especially prominent parts for two horn players, who explore contrasting musical ideas dependent on their changing positions in the orchestra. The timpanist in *Memento Vitae* (Concerto in Homage to Beethoven, 1969-70) has an unusual soloistic role. In Concerto for Horn and Orchestra (1971), written for Barry Tuckwell, the soloist is stationary, while the other horn players eventually take up positions behind sections of the audience, simulating the effect of stereophonic sound in the hall. The viola section of the lyrical and witty Viola Concerto (1973), composed for Miss Musgrave's husband, Peter Mark, a violist, usurps the normal place of honor from the first violins and at one point seems to be taking a master class from the soloist. Adding to a spate of critical superlatives, Shawe-Taylor judged it in the London *Times* "the most original and stimulating new music [he had] heard for some while." He continued, "The whole score is written, so to speak, *con amore* and breathes a spirit of happiness that is rare and refreshing in the world of modern music."

Space Play (1974), another dramatic composition, is a concerto Thea Musgrave wrote on commission from the Serge Koussevitsky Music Foundation. As described by Martin Bernheimer of the Los Angeles *Times*, it is "an elegantly orchestrated squabble for nine strategically placed instruments" that "engage in a vital, multi-layered 'conversation' that spans polite discourse, inane chatter, witty interruptions, imitative competition and climactic hyperbole." Bernheimer also admired *Orfeo II* (1975) as "a lovely work, full of ethereal shimmer and clever pathos." A Guggenheim fellowship for 1974-75 gave Miss Musgrave the time to write that brief opera, which features a solo flutist as Orpheus.

In 1973, in a self-educating exploration, Thea Musgrave made a series of eight broadcasts, entitled *End or Beginning*, on Great Britain's Radio 3, dealing with the possibilities of electronic music. Her own initial use of prerecorded electronic tape had served to enhance the supernatural effects in the two-act ballet, *Beauty and the Beast* (1968-69). Referring to her *Soliloquy* for guitar and tape (1969) and *From One to Another* for viola and tape (1970), Leslie East wrote, "Musgrave creates a dramatic dialogue between past (the tape) and present (live soloist) ranging from blatant confrontation to gentle interweaving and vitalized by the tensions of coordination with the tape by the soloist." Taped sound is even more forcefully exploited as a dramatic intensification of the protagonist's anguish in *The Voice of Ariadne*, a three-act chamber opera composed between 1971 and 1973 and given its world premiere in the latter year at the Aldeburgh Festival.

Thea Musgrave had found her story for *The Voice of Ariadne* one day in 1969 while browsing in a London bookstall where by chance she came upon Henry James's *The Last of the Valerii* and realized that the voice of the statue in that novella would call for electronic tape. "I recorded the voice so that the words can always be clearly understood," Miss Musgrave explained, as quoted in the New York *Times* (September 25, 1977), "and what I've done at certain times is to superimpose several voices, with an echo effect, and add electronic sounds suggesting the sea and distance." After attending the United States premiere of the opera in New York in the fall of 1977, William Bender wrote in *Time* (October 10, 1977), "*Ariadne*'s music has the blush of innocent freshness to it. It floats from atonality to tonality and back with dramatic precision, bringing to life the libretto's strange world and humanizing its perplexed cast of characters." Although the romantic libretto, written by Amalia Elguera, pleased many critics, some thought its psychological symbolism puzzling.

From Amalia Elguera's unfinished historical play, "Moray," Thea Musgrave took the story line for her fourth opera, *Mary, Queen of Scots* (1975-77), of which she herself was the librettist. Writing her own libretto proved to be a rewarding experience for the composer because she enjoyed being free to change the words when reworking a musical theme. In his critique in the London *Times* (September 8, 1977), William Mann applauded "a fine text, fluent and unmannered in diction" and a score in which "orchestra and vocal interest are cunningly balanced."

When *Mary, Queen of Scots* had its premiere in September 1977 as part of the Edinburgh International Festival, Thea Musgrave added to her credits of composer and librettist that of conductor. She had made her first important appearance as a conductor several years earlier when she filled in for the regular conductor at a special Christmas performance in Edinburgh of *Beauty and the Beast*. Her only instruction in conducting had been two three-hour lessons with the French musician Jacques-Louis Monod, but her thorough knowledge of the score helped her to overcome the disadvantage of inexperience. Since then she has conducted only her own work and has been especially eager to take charge of her music in its first performance so that the players will be able to heed her intentions as the composer. She conducted the Scottish National Orchestra in the first performances of Concerto for Horn and Orchestra in 1971 and Viola Concerto in 1973, the Philadelphia Orchestra in the first American performance of Concerto for Orchestra in 1976, and the Los Angeles Chamber Orchestra in the first performance of *Orfeo II* in 1976. Other notable premieres that she has conducted are those of *The Voice of Ariadne* in England in 1973 and in New York in 1977. The American premiere of *Mary, Queen of Scots*, by the Virginia Opera Association in Norfolk in late March 1978, was directed by David Farrar and conducted by Miss Musgrave's husband.

Hans Heinsheimer described Thea Musgrave in *Opera News* (September 1977) as "a tall, slim, casually but well-dressed woman with an exuberant personality, a quick-on-the-trigger mind, good looks, and a persuasive smile." When she began teaching at the University of California at Santa Barbara, she met Peter Mark, a Columbia and Juilliard graduate who was teaching viola. They were married in London on October 2, 1971 and now divide their time between Santa Barbara, where they have a house overlooking the Pacific, and Norfolk, Virginia, where they are involved with building up the regional opera company, of which Mark is artistic director. She has contributed to London musical life through her work on such committees as central music advisory panel for the BBC, music panel for the Arts Council of Great Britain, and executive committee of the Composers' Guild of Great Britain. She has also served on the committee of award for Commonwealth Fund of New York, the selection committee for the Harkness fellowships. In 1973 she became an honorary fellow of New Hall, Cambridge and in 1976 she received an honorary doctorate from the Council for National Academic Awards, presented by Prince Charles.

On November 10, 1975 Sarah Caldwell conducted the New York Philharmonic in a performance of Thea Musgrave's Concerto for Clarinet and Orchestra, which was included in a concert, "A Celebration of Women Composers," cosponsored by *Ms.* magazine. Disclaiming any relevance of the women's issue to her work, Miss Musgrave was quoted in *Time* (November 10, 1975) as saying, "Music is a human art, not a sexual one. Sex is no more important than eye color." For men as well as women, composing is hard, and, she has insisted elsewhere, for her, the struggle has been "to be a *good* composer." On another occasion she told a reporter for *Time* (October 10, 1977), "The fight is not so much for women composers, but for composers—and artists. Period."

References: Hi Fi 26:MA-7+ F '76, 27:MA-6+ S '77 por; Keynote 118:23+ O '77 pors; Music and Musicians 18:34+ D '69 por; Musical Times 104:866+ D '63 por, 114:790+ Ag '73; N Y Times II p19+ S 25 '77; Opera N 42:45+ 9/77 por; Time 110:72 O 10 '77 por; British Music Now (1975); Dictionary of Contemporary Music (1974); New College Encyclopedia of Music (1976); Who's Who, 1977-78

Neier, Aryeh (nī′ər är′ē-ā)

Apr. 22, 1937- Organization official; university professor. Address: b. c/o American Civil Liberties Union, 22 E. 40th St., New York City, N.Y. 10016; New York University School of Law, 40 Washington Square, S., New York City, N.Y. 10003

Known since its founding in 1920 as the "watchdog" of the Constitution and the Bill of Rights, the American Civil Liberties Union moved into a much more activist position under the leadership of Aryeh Neier, its executive director from 1970 to 1978. The A.C.L.U. has continued to uphold such traditional principles as freedom of expression, due process of law, and separation of church and state, but it has in recent years expanded into the more controversial areas of legal equality for women, prisoners' rights, antiwar dissent, school busing, impeachment of public officials, sexual privacy, and the defense of First Amendment rights of such extremist groups as the Ku Klux Klan and the Nazis. A staff member of the A.C.L.U. since 1963, Neier served with distinction as executive director of its New York State affiliate from 1965 to 1970. Although not a lawyer, he has over the years demonstrated a solid understanding of legal problems involved in the organization's work. Rejecting the description of the A.C.L.U. as a "watchdog" organization, Neier told Rita Delfiner of the New York *Post* (October 29, 1970): "Being a watch-

Aryeh Neier

dog is sitting back and waiting for some intruder to violate someone's civil liberties. We have to be a good deal of a hounddog." In the fall of 1978 he left his A.C.L.U. post to join the law faculty of New York University as a visiting professor.

Aryeh Neier—whose first name means "lion" in Hebrew—was born in Berlin, Germany on April 22, 1937, the younger of the two children of Wolf Neier, a teacher, and Gitla (Bendzinska) Neier. His parents had come to Germany some years earlier as Jewish refugees from Eastern Europe. He remembers his mother telling him that she deliberately prolonged her pregnancy so that he would not be born on April 20, which was Adolf Hitler's birthday. In 1939, shortly before the outbreak of World War II, the parents brought Aryeh and his sister Esther to England, where he lived through the London blitz and obtained his first schooling. Three of his grandparents and several other relatives became victims of the Nazi Holocaust.

After coming to New York City from England in 1947, the family lived first in the Bronx and then in the Flatbush section of Brooklyn, where the father became a high school language teacher. Aryeh Neier attended New York public schools and graduated in 1954 from Stuyvesant High School, where he had been active in debating. In 1955 he became a United States citizen. From high school Neier went to Cornell University, where he majored in labor relations. There he organized a speakers' group that on one occasion invited an editor of the Communist *Daily Worker* to lecture after he had been denied permission to speak at the City College of New York. While still a student, Neier worked for a time as a mediation and arbitration intern and union organizer with the United Mine Workers. "Over the years, I have accumulated my share of derogatory records," Neier recalled in his book *Dossier* (Stein & Day, 1975). "I have been arrested. My Selective Service file contains a notice from the ROTC at Cornell that I am not suitable officer material because of my negative attitude toward military training."

On graduating from Cornell with a B.S. degree in 1958, Neier obtained a job as labor secretary with the League for Industrial Democracy, an educational and lobbying organization that advocated a social order based on production for use rather than profit; in that post he worked closely with Norman Thomas, who had formerly headed the organization. When, later that year, the league's executive director resigned, Neier was appointed to succeed him, and he remained with the League for Industrial Democracy until 1960. His next position was with *Current* magazine, a monthly review of public affairs, where he was associate editor from 1960 to 1963.

Neier joined the staff of the American Civil Liberties Union as a field development officer in 1963, helping to organize legal support for civil rights activists in the South. "When I started to work for the A.C.L.U. in 1963, . . . the civil rights movement was in full flower," Neier recalled in an article in the Los Angeles *Times* (June 11, 1978). "We knew the battle would be harsh . . . , but we all had hope. . . . Much progress has been made since then. . . . We got demonstrators out of jail. We got blacks on juries. We overturned discriminatory election laws. We obtained decisions that struck down laws against interracial marriage. We won court rulings against school and housing segregation. We made employers pay damages to a few of the many victims of job discrimination."

In the spring of 1965 Neier was named executive director of the New York Civil Liberties Union, a statewide A.C.L.U. affiliate. Shortly after taking office, in an interview with Timothy Lee of the New York *Post* (May 13, 1965), he expressed concern about police abuses, especially against minority groups, and the "hysteria" on the part of some citizens about "coddling criminals" as a result of recent court decisions safeguarding the rights of criminal suspects. "We're going to shift the emphasis . . . from fire fighting to fire prevention," Neier told Lee. "We're going to try to eliminate the basis for civil liberties complaints. We are looking forward to procedural safeguards like a civilian review board, but we're proposing legislative steps too." In response to the demands of the N.Y.C.L.U. and other groups, in May 1966 Mayor John V. Lindsay of New York City announced the creation of an advisory civilian-controlled review board to investigate complaints against police officers. When, a few months later, the Patrolmen's Benevolent Association and the Conservative party called for a referendum aimed at abolishing the review board, N.Y.C.L.U. representatives appeared in court to oppose such a move.

As executive director of the N.Y.C.L.U., Neier also worked to safeguard church-state separation by opposing state aid to parochial schools and prayers in public schools; he condemned official harassment of demonstrators against the Vietnam war; and he fought against Governor Nelson Rockefeller's proposals for compulsory commitment of narcotics addicts. "Although the word is commitment," he told Natalie Jaffe of the New York *Times* (February 27, 1966), "the fact that it's compulsory and there's a maximum sentence makes it sound more like imprisonment." Apart from such traditionally liberal positions, Neier defended the privilege of policemen to join right-wing organizations like the John Birch Society, and on one occasion he personally accompanied American Nazi party leader George Lincoln Rockwell to a legislative hearing to ensure that his rights were safeguarded.

The N.Y.C.L.U. under Neier became involved in a major local controversy in 1968, when it supported the school decentralization efforts of the community control board in the predominantly black and Puerto Rican Ocean Hill-Brownsville section of Brooklyn. The United Federation of Teachers called a strike that fall, protesting that due process rights were violated in transferring noncooperative teachers out of the district. In response, the N.Y.C.L.U. issued a report charging the teachers' union and the city board of education with trying to undermine the district's experiment in community control of schools and contending that the union was using "due process" as a smokescreen to divert attention from its real goal—that of sabotaging decentralization efforts. About 300 members of the N.Y.C.L.U. resigned in protest; some of them charged that the organization had taken sides in a political issue in disregard of the interest of civil liberties. But Neier affirmed in early 1969 that the great majority of the organization's statewide membership of some 27,000 supported its stand on that issue. The N.Y.C.L.U. also drew some criticism from its members when in April 1969 it rejected the stand of four of its staff lawyers who had dissented from a national A.C.L.U. report which condemned student violence.

In the spring of 1970 Neier launched a special litigation project to protect the rights of prisoners while in prison, as the first of a series of planned projects to deal with specific groups. "We're not in a position to confer rights on elements within society which feel deprived," he told Rita Delfiner of the New York *Post*, "but we make it possible for them to try and win their own rights by enabling them to communicate with each other, to organize, to demonstrate, to tell others their opinions."

On September 27, 1970 the A.C.L.U. board of directors announced that Neier had been elected to succeed John de J. Pemberton as executive director. When Neier took office, the national A.C.L.U. had already begun to take a more militant position, notably in its defense in the late 1960's, of such antiwar activists as Dr. Benjamin Spock and the adoption, in July 1970, of a resolution by its national board demanding immediate termination of the Indochina war, an activist trend that was taken even farther by Neier. In the early 1960's 90 percent of the A.C.L.U.'s work had consisted of filing amicus curiae (friend of the court) briefs in civil liberty cases and only 10 percent was actual litigation. By 1972 those percentages were reversed. During the Watergate crisis, the A.C.L.U. helped to initiate the effort to impeach Richard Nixon for abuse of his powers, and the President's resignation in August 1974 was seen by Neier as substantially shifting the balance in favor of civil liberties.

By early 1975 Neier was able to say, as quoted in *Time* (February 17, 1975) that "the best single moment in civil liberties in the past dozen years" had arrived. At that time the A.C.L.U. had just won a $12,000,000 settlement in behalf of 1,200 antiwar demonstrators arrested near the Capitol in Washington, D.C. in May 1971. Furthermore, the organization had recently met with success in lobbying for reinforcement of the Freedom of Information Act and had helped to secure legislation enabling citizens to challenge personal data in government computers. Meanwhile, the membership of the A.C.L.U. had increased over a five-year period from 140,000 to 275,000.

During Neier's tenure the A.C.L.U. also mounted major efforts to extend the protection of civil liberties to persons confined in prisons, mental hospitals, training schools for children, nursing homes for the elderly, and other institutions; it fought for abolition of capital punishment and for making abortions available on the basis of need; and it promoted affirmative action for racial minorities, a goal partly validated by the Supreme Court's compromise Allan Bakke decision of 1978. Neier's tenure as executive director also was marked by some friction in the upper echelons of the A.C.L.U., leading to the resignation of Charles Morgan Jr., head of its Washington office, in the spring of 1976, and that of legal director Melvin L. Wulf in January 1977.

In early 1977 the A.C.L.U. filed a suit in behalf of fifteen Marines belonging to the Ku Klux Klan, challenging the Pentagon's authority to transfer the men from Camp Pendleton, California to ease racial tensions following a clash with black Marines. That action stirred considerable opposition within the ranks of the organization, even though A.C.L.U. lawyers also defended the blacks involved in the case. Discord became even greater when the organization, in the spring of 1978, defended the rights of members of the National Socialist party to stage a march in Skokie, Illinois, a town that included a high proportion of Jewish Holocaust survivors among its inhabitants. The controversy ended for at least the time being when the Nazis, after winning court permission for the parade, decided instead to hold a rally in a Chicago park. Some observers found it ironic that the A.C.L.U. was eager to defend the extreme right, since in the 1950's it refused to defend Communists, and some of its leaders even cooperated with the Federal Bureau of Investigation by supplying it with information about suspected Communist members. "We were wrong in the '50's," Neier told his critics, "but our failures then shouldn't be invoked as an excuse for comparable failures today."

At a day-long convocation on free speech held by the A.C.L.U. at New York's Hilton Hotel on June 13, 1978, Neier asserted: "When we defend the rights of Nazis or the Ku Klux Klan to speak we do so not only in their interests but in our interests. The freedom denied them today could be denied to us tomorrow." The controversy over the Nazis and the Klan was said to be largely responsible for the dwindling of the A.C.L.U. membership to 185,000 by mid-1978.

On April 17, 1978 Neier sent a letter to the A.C.L.U. board of directors, announcing his resignation, to be effective that fall. He denied that he was resigning because of criticism of his policies concerning the Nazis or the Klan but later revealed that he needed "a year or two to reflect on, discuss, and write about" certain questions concerning the A.C.L.U. He expressed the desire to continue to work for the A.C.L.U. on a volunteer basis. In September 1978 Neier joined the faculty of New York University as a visiting professor of law.

Neier has published over 100 articles in newspapers and in such periodicals as the *Nation*, *Crisis*, the *Criminal Law Bulletin*, the *Civil Liberties Review*, and *Crime and Delinquency*, and he has contributed chapters to more than a dozen books. With A.C.L.U. board chairman Norman Dorsen he coedited a series of fifteen handbooks published by Avon Books from 1972 to 1978, dealing with the rights of such groups as mental patients, servicemen, teachers, students, homosexuals, criminal suspects, and the poor.

In his book *Dossier: The Secret Files They Keep on You* (Stein & Day, 1975), which grew out of a 1975 New York *Times Magazine* article, Neier shows how civil liberties are flagrantly violated as a result of the misuse of records kept on individuals by schools, hospitals, courts, credit bureaus, the military, and other institutions. He argues that incriminating dossiers be destroyed and that the denial of employment to individuals because of past records be outlawed. *Dossier* was generally well received by reviewers, as was Neier's second book, *Crime and Punishment: A Radical Solution* (Stein & Day, 1976), in which he presents his views on crime, law enforcement, and correction. Assuming that crime and punishment will always be with us, Neier recommends among other things the decriminalization of such "victimless" crimes as public drunkenness, illicit sexual relations, and narcotics possession, to free police to deal with more serious offenses, and he argues that prison terms for nonviolent criminals can be effectively reduced. As Professor Alan Dershowitz noted, in *Crime and Punishment*, "Neier demonstrates convincingly that there are ways of reducing crime without significantly infringing on civil liberties." Two forthcoming books by Neier, *Defending My Enemy* (Dutton) and *Confinement: The American Way* (Random House), are scheduled for publication in 1979.

In addition to serving as executive director of the A.C.L.U., Neier was executive vice-president of its tax-deductible arm, the American Civil Liberties Foundation. He also served as a lecturer at the School for Continuing Education in New York City in 1968-69 and at the New York police academy in 1969-70, and he has addressed audiences at over 250 colleges and law schools from coast to coast. He has been a member of various boards and commissions, including the American Bar Association's Juvenile Justice Standards Project, the Mental Health Law Project, the Mexican-American Legal Defense and Educational Fund, the National Organization for Reform of Marijuana Laws, and the Committee for Public Justice. His honors include the 1967 humanist award of the Knights of Pythias, the 1974 Gavel Award of the American Bar Association, and a 1975 honorary LL.D. degree from Hofstra University school of law. In 1978 he became a fellow of the New York Institute for the Humanities.

Aryeh Neier was married on June 22, 1958 to Yvette Celton, a marketing director and, according to Neier, very much a liberated woman. With their teenage son, David, they make their home in Hillsdale, New York. Neier, who is six feet one inch tall and weighs 205 pounds, has brown hair and gray eyes and, in the words of J. Anthony Lukas, writing in the New York *Times Magazine* (July 9, 1978), a "moon face and chubby torso" that "disguise a rapier intelligence and formidable debating skill." Although usually mild-mannered, he is occasionally moved to anger by violations of civil liberties. Norman Dorsen has referred to his "iron integrity," and the veteran civil libertarian Roger Baldwin has called Neier "much the best" executive director in the organization's history. For recreation, Neier enjoys vegetable gardening, attending the theatre and the ballet, listening to the music of Bach, playing an occasional game of chess, and reading the history of the seventeenth and eighteenth centuries, "when the human scale was the dominant scale."

References: N Y Post p31 My 13 '65 por, p39 O 29 '70 por; N Y Times p27 Ag 10 '66 por, p29 S 28 '70 por; N Y Times Mag p9+ Jl 9 '78 por; Newsday p5 Jl 23 '78; Time 105: 79 F 17 '75 por; Contemporary Authors vols 57-60 (1976); Who's Who in America, 1978-79

Newton-John, Olivia

Sept. 26, 1948- British singer. Address: c/o MCA Records, Inc., 100 Universal City Plaza, Universal City, Calif. 91608

One of the most successful of the current crop of country pop singers is dulcet-voiced Olivia Newton-John, who hails, ironically, not from Nashville but from England by way of Australia. Miss Newton-John first became well known during the early 1970's in her native England, where she had returned after growing up in Melbourne, and by 1974 her records were topping the charts in the United States. Although music critics are seldom overwhelmed by the blandness of her vocal talents—"if white bread could sing it would sound like Olivia," one of them has quipped—Miss Newton-John's fans flock to her concerts and nightclub appearances and quickly turn her records to gold or platinum. Among her biggest hits are "Let Me Be There," "Have You Never Been Mellow," and "I Honestly Love You." Olivia Newton-John made her film debut opposite John Travolta as a girl-next-door type turned temptress in the musical *Grease*, which was released in the summer of 1978.

Born on September 26, 1948 in Cambridge, England, Olivia Newton-John is the daughter of Bryn and Irene (Born) Newton-John. (The hyphenated name has been in her father's family for two or three generations.) Miss Newton-John's mother is the daughter of the late Nobel Prize-winning German physicist Max Born. Her father, of Welsh descent, taught German at King's College, Cambridge University. Miss Newton-John has an older brother who is a doctor and an older sister who is an actress.

At the age of five Olivia Newton-John moved with her family to Melbourne, Australia, where her father had been appointed head master of University College, an affiliate of the University of Melbourne. (Other sources give Ormond College.) Before he established himself in the academic world, Bryn Newton-John had considered a career as an opera singer, and his large collection of classical music records became an important resource for Olivia. She has also listed among her musical influences the singers Tennessee Ernie Ford, Ray Charles, Joan Baez, and Nina Simone. When she was only ten or eleven, her parents became divorced, an experience that so scarred her emotionally that she is reluctant to experiment with marriage. Although she wanted to be with both her parents, she was given into the exclusive custody of her mother.

By the age of fourteen Olivia had formed a singing group with three girl friends, and not long after that she began harmonizing with a folksinger at a coffeehouse owned by her sister's husband. Miss Newton-John began appearing on local television shows and at fifteen won a talent contest, which had as its prize a free trip to England. After agonizing over the problem of whether she should finish school or go to England, she decided to make the trip, determined to embark on a musical career there, instead of following her mother's wishes by entering the Royal Academy of Dramatic Arts.

Despite her initial reluctance to pull up roots, once the sixteen-year-old singer arrived in England she made it her home. There she ran into a series of misadventures with several groups, including one science-fiction-oriented rock combo that called itself Toomorrow, which, it was hoped fervently by its sponsors, would become the next big British musical sensation. With those ill-starred rock musicians she made a disastrous "space musical" called *Toomorrow,* which she has been trying to forget ever since, and which (mercifully in her opinion), has never been released in the United States. Eventually she formed a successful partnership with another Australian girl singer, Pat Carroll, and the duo began appearing in nightclubs and on television. In 1971, after her partner returned to Australia, Miss Newton-John struck out on her own with her first record, an interpretation of Bob Dylan's "If Not For You." It became a big hit in Great Britain and was followed by two or three more, including "Take Me Home Country Roads," a song first popularized by the homespun performer John Denver. In 1973 the young singer received a further boost to her career when she toured Britain, Japan, and Australia as part of a show headlined by the popular British singer, Cliff Richard.

Until "Country Roads," Miss Newton-John had leaned toward folk music in her singing style, but with that tune she discovered her affinity with country music. She went on to record another country-styled song, "Let Me Be There," which although ignored in Britain, sped up the charts in the United States late in 1973. By the time the singer came to America to tour early in 1974 she was recognized as a promising new singing star. "Let Me Be There" won Miss Newton-John her first Grammy, the 1973 award for best country female vocal performance.

Touring in the United States in 1974 for several months, Olivia Newton-John charmed audiences in Las Vegas at the Hilton, where she played the opening act with Charlie Rich, at Harrah's Club in Lake Tahoe, and at concerts and state fairs around the country. Her subsequent country-flavored singles "If You Love Me Let Me Know" and "I Honestly Love You" ascended to the top of the charts, and when the year was over her recordings had outsold those of every female vocalist with the exception of her fellow Australian Helen Reddy. She was awarded two 1974 Grammies for "I Honestly Love You," one as the record of the year and the other as the best pop vocal performance.

In 1975 Miss Newton-John continued to tour the United States. When she made her debut as a Las Vegas headliner at the Riviera Hotel, the British singer proved to be one of the season's most popular new entertainers. "Her gentle, whispery vocal tone and sweet, delicate appearance/manner are, for the most part, more important in establishing her appeal on stage than range, dynamics, phrasing and the other technical measures of a singer's talent," wrote Los Angeles *Times* (October 7, 1975) critic Robert Hilburn after catching her act. He added that "the key to her appeal in a showroom" is that she "has woven together a pleasant, extremely unpretentious, warmly human show." Miss Newton-John has continued to return to sell-out crowds at the Riviera each year.

By 1975 Olivia Newton-John had three gold singles to her credit in the United States, and her hit song "Have You Never Been Mellow" was well on its way to becoming the fourth. She had also released several chart-scaling albums on the MCA label, including *Let Me Be There* (1973), *If You Love Me, Let Me Know* (1974), *Have You Never Been Mellow* (1975), and *Clearly Love* (1975). In spite of the apathy of many music critics, her albums carried the Midas touch in record stores. Peter Reilly of *Stereo Review* (March 1976) summed up the singer's appeal when he reviewed *Clearly Love,* which sold over 1,000,000 copies in its first ten weeks in the stores: "Olivia Newton-John sounds like a nice girl singing nice songs. . . . As to how well she sings, I really don't think I could tell you, for she seems to come gift-wrapped in such an attractive package of winning ways that I can't help but like her."

After Miss Newton-John's first special was televised on ABC on November 17, 1976, a *Variety* reviewer (November 24, 1976) complained that she lacked "the presence to carry a show." Nonetheless, the program scored high in the ratings, edging out the other networks for the highest percentage of the audience, and a similar reception greeted her ABC special on May 17, 1978, which, simply called *Olivia,* featured Andy Gibb and ABBA, the Swedish musical group, as guest stars.

Nor did the singer's record albums bring about a change of heart in the critics. The *Playboy* critic (July 1976) grumbled that listening to *Come On Over* (MCA, 1976) made one "feel as if you've been wrapped in cotton candy and set out in the sun," while even the loyal Peter Reilly of *Stereo Review* (February 1977) conceded, after hearing *Don't Stop Believin'* (MCA, 1976), that "she's such a complete pro at dishing out the glop that it's relatively painless and pleasant in a sugary sort of way."

"An artist with my image is up for knocking from the so called heavy critics," Miss Newton-John mused during an interview with Steven Gaines of the New York *Daily News* (May 1, 1977). "Basically, I know that I please other people and you can't always please everybody all the time. . . . I read my reviews and if they're constructive, I take note." Although she professed such nonchalance about reviewers, she nonetheless put off her debut in New York City until May 1977, when she appeared at the Metropolitan Opera House in Lincoln Center. She need not have worried. Appearing in the 4,000-seat auditorium, she completely charmed her standing-room-only audience and won some grudging admiration from the critics in attendance. "Miss Newton-John's soprano isn't as negligible as some think," John Rockwell acknowledged in the New York *Times* (May 10, 1977). "There's a nice husky quiver to it, and only at full volume does it become shrill." Most of the critics were especially taken with her rendition of the Webber-Rice song "Don't Cry for Me, Argentina," from the score of the musical *Evita*.

Shortly after making her New York City debut, Olivia Newton-John toured Great Britain, where her appearances included a televised spectacular, in which she performed before the Queen and the Duke of Edinburgh. Back in the United States later in the year, she fulfilled a long-held ambition by costarring in an important film, Robert Stigwood's and Allan Carr's screen version of *Grease*, the long-running Broadway evocation of the 1950's. In *Grease*, which was released in June of 1978, Miss Newton-John appeared opposite John Travolta in the spun-sugar ingenue part of Sandy, singing several new songs and some revivals, as well as originals from the score of the Broadway show.

Like Miss Newton-John's record albums, the movie version of *Grease* fared much better commercially than it did critically. Reviewers found it an overproduced mediocrity, in itself an atavistic throwback to the cretinous musicals of the 1950's, with a cast so overaged it appeared that the students of Rydell High School must have flunked their classes indefinitely without hope of promotion. Its prevailing lifelessness and anemia were not redeemed by the bland presence of Olivia Newton-John, whose cotton-candy image (except for the final sequence, when she is transformed into a sexpot), suffered from the supercharged competition of John Travolta.

Olivia Newton-John has been honored by the Academy of Country Music (1973), the British Country Music Association (1974; 1975), the American Guild of Variety Artists (1974), Billboard (1974), Cashbox (1974; 1975), Record World (1974; 1975; 1976), and by many other organizations, including ASCAP. But the prize that caused the most furor was her award as top female vocalist of 1974 by the Country Music Association of Nashville. Many old guard Nashville musicians were outraged that a pop singer lacking authentic American country "roots" had been so honored, and several, including Miss Newton-John's idol Tammy Wynette, broke away from the CMA to form the Association of Country Entertainers as a result of the incident. Later the British singer mended fences with Nashville by moving her recording operations there from London. Her first Nashville record was *Don't Stop Believin'*. "I really didn't hear about all the talk for a time after it started," she told Gaines of the New York *Daily News*. ". . . I really think now they'll have to admit it's been beneficial to them. Now they're getting a pop audience they never had before. New people are listening to country music because of me."

Miss Newton-John's recent albums for MCA include *Other Side of the Mountain*, *Making a Good Thing Better* (1977), and *Greatest Hits* (1977). Although they have not sold quite so well as her earlier collections, she is still a best seller. All eight of her American-released albums have either turned gold ($1,000,000 in sales) or platinum (1,000,000 units sold). Estimates of the number of records she has sold worldwide, as of 1977, have ranged from ten to twenty-five million.

"Olivia Newton-John has the aphrodisiac qualities of one of my fantasy airline stewardesses (the one on Air Gomorrah)," critic Peter Reilly once confessed, and she seems to affect millions of men similarly. Petite, blonde, blue-eyed, soft-voiced, and pert, the singer, who is known as "Livvy" to her friends, projects an image that was once described by John Rockwell of the New York *Times* (May 10, 1977) as blending "the crinolined, antebellum South with the buoyancy of a modern-day Texas cheerleader." Others prefer to describe her as wholesome, or as a June Allyson type. Unmarried, Miss Newton-John was engaged to British guitarist Bruce Welsh several years ago, and in recent years she has had an on-again, off-again romance with Lee Kramer, an American businessman who has also acted as her manager. She described marriage as "a thing which frightens me" in an interview with Robert Windeler of

People (February 24, 1975). "My parents, my older sister and so many of my friends have been divorced," she explained. "And I'm not ready for children yet." In one of the few songs that she has written for herself, "Changes," she describes the traumatic impact of divorce on a child. An animal lover who once wanted to become a veterinarian, or a mounted policewoman, the singer now resides on a small ranch in Malibu, California where she keeps a number of horses, cats, and dogs, and likes to garden. In the spring of 1978 she cancelled a highly profitable concert tour of Japan scheduled for October as a protest against the recent slaughter of dolphins by the fishermen of Iki Island. Unlike many of her contemporaries in show business, she is reportedly devoid of envy or malice.

References: Biog N 1:1179 O '74 por; N Y Daily News III p1+ My 1 '77 por; N Y Post p33 My 7 '77 por; People 3:38+ F 24 '75 pors; Who's Who in America, 1976-77

Price, Leontyne

Feb. 10, 1927- Soprano. Address: b. c/o Hubert Dilworth, 1133 Broadway, New York City, N.Y. 10010; CAMI, 165 W. 57th St., New York City, N.Y. 10019

NOTE: This biography supersedes the article that appeared in Current Biography in 1961.

Since the early 1950's, when she first came to public attention as Bess in a revival of *Porgy and Bess*, Leontyne Price has become enshrined as something of an American institution, the first black American to achieve the international operatic superstardom denied to her great predecessors, Marian Anderson and Paul Robeson. Miss Price came in for her share of honors after her triumphant debuts at the San Francisco Opera in 1957, the Vienna State Opera in 1958, La Scala in 1960, and the Metropolitan Opera in 1961. Perhaps the ultimate accolade occurred on September 16, 1966, when she appeared as the tragic Egyptian queen in Samuel Barber's *Antony and Cleopatra*, the spectacular work commissioned to open the new Metropolitan Opera House at Lincoln Center. Endowed with a voice of unique color, richness, and wide range, Miss Price seems to have been born to sing such Verdi heroines as Aïda and the Leonora of *Il Trovatore*, interpretations that she has immortalized on recordings. On a much more intimate scale, she has become equally well known, especially in recent years, as a sensitive interpreter of German lieder and French art songs, before such discriminating audiences as those to be found at the Salzburg Festival in Austria.

Mary Violet Leontyne (originally Leontine) Price was born in Laurel, Mississippi on February 10, 1927 to James Anthony and Kate (Baker) Price. Her father worked in a sawmill; her mother—whom she has described as "an incredible woman" and as her "strongest source of inspiration"—worked as a midwife to supplement the family income. Her brother George, whom she calls "the real star of the family," became the first black division chief of staff in the history of the United States Army.

Leontyne Price's parents, who sang in the choir and played in the band of St. Paul's Methodist Church in Laurel, encouraged her early interest in music, especially through listening to recordings. As a young girl she played the piano and sang at church, school, and community functions. A Marian Anderson concert that she attended in Jackson, Mississippi at the age of nine made a lasting impression. "It was just a vision of elegance and nobility," she later reminisced. "It was one of the most enthralling, marvelous experiences I've ever had. I can't tell you how inspired I was to do something even similar to what she was doing. That was what you might call the original kickoff."

After graduating from Oak Park High School in 1944, Leontyne Price studied music pedagogy at the College of Education and Industrial Arts (now Central State College) in Wilberforce, Ohio—just in case, as she told

Edward Greenfield in an interview for the *Guardian* (October 8, 1971), her "frou-frou idea of becoming an opera singer" did not materialize. She began her vocal studies in earnest, however, only shortly before receiving her B.A. degree in June 1948.

Although the Juilliard School of Music awarded her a four-year full-tuition scholarship, Leontyne Price found herself unable to cover her living expenses after arriving in New York City. For a while she feared that she might have to do what some of her friends did—go to work and sing in nightclubs. But Mrs. Elizabeth Chisholm, a long-time family friend from Laurel, came to her rescue with financial assistance. Florence Page Kimball, Leontyne Price's teacher and vocal coach at the time, thought she seemed intelligent and had an attractive voice, but had no intimations of the greatness of her future career.

On the other hand, as Mistress Ford in a Juilliard student production of Verdi's *Falstaff*, Leontyne Price had already so impressed composer and critic Virgil Thomson that he immediately engaged her to sing Saint Cecilia in a revival of his *Four Saints in Three Acts* that was presented in New York and Paris in the spring of 1952. From June 1952 to June 1954, as Bess in a revival of Gershwin's *Porgy and Bess* she appeared before packed houses, both in the United States and under State Department auspices in Europe. Covering the opening in Dallas, John Rosenfield wrote in *Saturday Review* (June 28, 1952): "The voice, a bright and focused soprano, has great impact, but even this is only half of it. She brought a lively theatrical imagination to the role . . . and . . . such vivid detail that the first night audience lost its composure when she took her final curtain call." "Price will no doubt spend a long time in the role of Bess," Paul Hume of the Washington *Post* (August 10, 1952) predicted. "But when she is available for other music she will have a dramatic career."

While singing Bess, Leontyne Price also won recognition as a superlative interpreter of modern compositions, performing works by Igor Stravinsky, Lou Harrison, Henri Sauguet, and John La Montaine at, among other places, the Museum of Modern Art and the Metropolitan Museum of Art in New York and Constitution Hall in Washington, D.C. By the time Samuel Barber asked her to sing his *Hermit Songs* at their premiere at the Library of Congress in Washington, D.C., in October 1953, Leontyne Price was beginning to think of herself as "the contemporary composer's Girl Friday." Her first Town Hall recital in New York City, on November 14, 1954, elicited such mixed reviews as that in the New York *Herald Tribune* (November 15, 1954) of Jay Harrison, who noted her "consistent tremolo" and unevenness of tone but singled out her "personality that literally spills charm over the footlights."

In the role of Floria Tosca in the pioneering NBC-TV production of Puccini's *Tosca* in February 1955 Leontyne Price became a pacesetter as the first black to appear in opera on television. Her Tosca, which brought her to the attention of millions of viewers, won her leading roles in subsequent NBC-TV productions of Mozart's *Magic Flute* in 1956, Poulenc's *Dialogues of the Carmelites* in 1957, and Mozart's *Don Giovanni* in 1960.

On September 20, 1957 Leontyne Price made her debut as Madame Lidoine in the American premiere of Poulenc's *Dialogues of the Carmelites* at the San Francisco Opera. In succeeding seasons she starred in such diverse works as Verdi's *Aïda*, Massenet's *Thaïs*, and Orff's *The Wise Maidens*, not only with the San Francisco Opera but also with the Chicago Lyric Opera and the American Opera Theater. Herbert von Karajan, to whom she gives credit for her European career, featured her in *Aïda* at the Vienna State Opera in 1958, after which she rapidly forged a European reputation with a string of performances at the Verona Arena, the Salzburg Festival, and London's Covent Garden. After her debut as Aïda at Milan's La Scala in May 1960, one Italian critic rhapsodized: "Our great Verdi would have found her the ideal Aïda."

Preceded by her La Scala triumph of a few months before, which gave her more of the self-assurance she needed, Leontyne Price fulfilled a long-cherished dream on January 27, 1961, when she made her debut as Leonora in Verdi's *Il Trovatore* at New York's Metropolitan Opera. She thereby became the fifth black artist to sing a major role at that house since Marian Anderson made the big breakthrough in 1955. "Miss Price overcame . . . technical hurdles with the utmost ease," Winthrop Sargeant wrote in the *New Yorker* (February 4, 1961), "seeming to have sonority and brilliance to spare, and giving the part a special dramatic eloquence, which arose partly from the rich, vibrant quality of her voice and partly from the authoritative artistry with which she used it. Her interpretation was virtually without flaws." She scored in four other roles at the Metropolitan that same season: Aïda, Donna Anna in Mozart's *Don Giovanni*, Cio-Cio-San in Puccini's *Madame Butterfly*, and as the slave girl Liù in his *Turandot*. "Sustaining all of the performances," the reviewer for *Time* (March 10, 1961) observed towards the end of the season, "was the voice, unfurling like a bright banner from the stage and through the opera house."

Despite a few uncongenial roles—most notably that of Tatiana in Tchaikovsky's *Eugene Onegin* and of Fiordiligi in Mozart's *Così fan tutte*—Leontyne Price steadily broadened her repertory in the 1960's to include, for example, Amelia in Verdi's *Un Ballo in Maschera* and Donna Elvira in his *Ernani*. She attracted worldwide publicity as Rudolf Bing's choice to open the new Metropolitan Opera House at Lincoln Center in the world premiere of Samuel Barber's *Antony and Cleopatra* on September 16, 1966. Her year of spartan preparation included the study of works about Cleopatra, whom she considered to be the strongest character she had played to date, as well as the most provocative. Years later, she described the occasion to Irving Kolodin in an interview in *Saturday Review* (September 8, 1972) as the "most grueling" experience of her life, one that left her "almost traumatized for two-and-a-half years." "So much was hanging on it," she explained, ". . . So much to do, so much to think about, so much to cope with in so short a time. It got to the point where it wasn't a matter of how well one performed, but just being able to perform." But at the premiere, in spite of her misgivings, New York *Times* music critic Harold C. Schonberg (September 17, 1966) found Miss Price "in superb voice." Like many reviewers who generally classed the opera itself as at best a minor disaster and at worst a fiasco, Schonberg regretted the empty pomp and panoply of the production, which emphasized "her weaknesses rather than strengths."

Beyond any exceptions were the critical "bravas" Leontyne Price received after her first Metropolitan appearance in Verdi's *La Forza del Destino* on September 29, 1967. Judging her Leonora to be "in the line of such memorable older ones as Rethberg, Milanov, and Tebaldi," Irving Kolodin hailed her maturity as an artist, revealed in her "clear, well-shaped conception of its dramatic as well as musical requirements." Raymond Ericson, writing in the New York *Times* (October 1, 1967) called her "one of the most musical of singers," whose voice possesses "a warm, exciting vibrato at its strongest, and hauntingly pure tone in soft passages."

Although the veteran of 118 Metropolitan performances between 1961 and 1969, Leontyne Price drastically reduced her appearances there in the 1970's. According to Stephen Rubin, who interviewed her for the New York *Times* (September 16, 1973), she regarded herself as "the undernourished darling of the Met," especially in view of the paucity of new productions given her. "I am not a very big temper loser," she told him, "but I *have* a temper, and it's the worst kind. I never throw things, but cerebrally I will get you off my back."

While performing at other leading opera houses and with major orchestras throughout the world, Miss Price concentrated on her "first love"—recitals. The "challenge of bringing to life nineteen or twenty characters in one recital is greater than only one over several hours," she explained to Speight Jenkins of the New York *Post* (January 18, 1973). "Recitals make me sing on my interest, not my capital, which is not always the case in opera, and overall the work has made my voice more elastic." Writing in the same newspaper (March 20, 1971), Harriett Johnson praised her interpretation of Strauss' *Four Last Songs* with the Minnesota Orchestra at Carnegie Hall: "Any artist is always in a dynamic state, expanding, settling in for the long winter of past-prime, or obviously contracting. But she, who had seemed . . . fulfilled beyond further fulfilling, took us further in her art and personality. She was mellow in richness but astringently youthful in promise of more to come. She was a mystery, a prophetess exploring new depths." Somewhat more temperate was Washington *Post*'s Paul Hume who, in his review of February 4, 1974, judged her Kennedy Center recital program of the night before to have been "of vast popular appeal, holding its memorable moments and a notable high level in music of real quality." He added: "No singer after nearly a quarter of a century . . . keeps the voice as it was in the early decades. Miss Price has let unmannerly swoops, improper crescendos, and uneven sounds throughout her lower voice make inroads into the quality of the voice."

Bored with what she called "handkerchief-holding roles—girls who have led sheltered lives and are protected by duennas," Leontyne Price annexed several new operatic roles to her repertory in the 1970's. A phalanx of disappointed critics regretted as "disserving her own interest" her choice of Puccini's Manon Lescaut, which she sang at the Metropolitan Opera House for the first time on February 7, 1975. Among them was Raymond Ericson who deplored in the New York *Times* (February 9, 1975) the "lean, edgy side" of her voice and the absence of the "full, plushy tone one had learned to expect from her." In contrast, her resounding debut as Ariadne in Strauss's *Ariadne auf Naxos* at the San Francisco Opera on October 19, 1977 was, in Arthur Bloomfield's opinion (San Francisco *Examiner*, October 20, 1977), "one of her greatest achievements." A colleague, Robert Commanday of the San Francisco *Chronicle* (October 21, 1977), thought she sang the excrutiatingly difficult arias "as though Strauss had created the role for her."

Leontyne Price has described herself as "a lyric soprano—a juicy lyric, yes, but I've never said I was a dramatic soprano." Her uniqueness, most experts agree, lies in the range and color of her voice which has, as Irving Kolodin has put it, "the same dusky, glowing richness from bottom to top" and spans "a good two octaves, from C to shining C." "I never try an F in public," Miss Price has said. "I sometimes do it in the shower, but there I may just be intoxicated by the soap." During her twenty-year exclusive contract with RCA Victor, Leontyne Price has recorded Negro spirituals, pop tunes, Christmas carols, hymns, American, French, and German art songs, and complete operas by Bizet, Mozart, Puccini, and Verdi. Her latest album, the fourth in a series known as *The Prima Donna*, was released in the summer of 1978. The National Academy of Recording Arts and Sciences has honored her with fifteen Grammy awards. On October 8, 1978 Miss Price performed at the White House.

When interviewing Leontyne Price for the New York *Post* (January 18, 1973), Fern Marja Eckman saw her as "a complex, tense, articulate woman with a wonderfully theatrical face that can summon beauty, majestic proportions and a dramatic Afro that adds impressively to her 5-feet-6." Her speech, according to Speight Jenkins, combines "the Southern drawl of her native Mississippi, a touch of England and a dollop of the Continental-international inflection, all blended into an incredibly musical sound." Her regal manners, which some critics have misconstrued as arrogant, actually stem from her shyness. "I feel terribly self-conscious being in the right place at the right time in the right dress," she explained to Stephen Rubin. To *Newsday*'s Ponchitta Pierce she confided: "I don't like making entrances unless I'm in costume, at 8 o'clock, on stage." As befits the daughter of God-fearing parents and the granddaughter of two Methodist ministers, Leontyne Price is strongly religious. She talks about the Omnipotent, a *Time* interviewer once reported, "as naturally as if he were her neighbor."

Leontyne Price lives alone in a three-story twelve-room Federal Era townhouse in New York's Greenwich Village. On August 31, 1952 she married William C. Warfield, the concert baritone who constarred with her in *Porgy and Bess*, but after years of separation, they were divorced in 1973. Among Miss Price's recreations are collecting records, cooking, dancing, and visiting friends. She is a fellow of the American Academy of Arts and Sciences and a member of Actors Equity Association, the American Guild of Musical Artists, and the American Federation of Television and Radio Artists. The soprano has received honorary degrees from Howard University, Dartmouth College, Central State University, Rust College, and Fordham University. Her other awards include the Presidential Freedom Medal (1964), the Italian Award of Merit (1965), and the NAACP Spingarn Medal (1965).

As one of a handful of "token blacks" who achieved international fame in the 1950's and 1960's, Leontyne Price is acutely aware of her social responsibility. "I am no self-designated Joan of Arc," she told one interviewer at the time of her debut as Cleopatra, "but I feel that I was given this privilege for a reason. . . . I feel that if God sees fit to make this possible, in the various turmoils and misunderstandings that exist, that being given this opportunity as one of my people may be the beginning of a certain dimension, that anyone who wants to aspire to be so completely free artistically as I have been, to be chosen to have what is so important to others on one's artistic merit alone, is truly an American act, and it makes me proud to be an American."

References: Ebony 16:96+ Ap '61 pors, 22:184+ D '66 pors; Holiday 35:103+ Mr '64 por; Mus Am 82:12+ Ja '62 pors; Mus J 28:38+ Mr '70 pors; N Y Times II p21 S 11 '66; N Y Times Mag p37+ O 15 '61 pors; Opera N 25:14+ F 4 '61 pors, 36:14+ F 12 '72 por, 40:16+ Mr 6 '76 pors; Sat R 55:31+ S 9 '72 pors; Stereo R 36:62+ Ja '62 por; Time 77:58+ Mr 10 '61 pors; Encyclopedia of Opera, 1976; International Who's Who, 1977-78; Lyon, H. L. Leontyne Price: Highlights of a Prima Donna (1973); Rollins, C. Famous Negro Entertainers of Stage, Screen and T.V. (1967); Rubin, S. E. New Met in Profile (1974); Sargeant, W. Divas (1973); Smith, F. and Warren, A. Mississippians All (1968); Who's Who, 1977-78; Who's Who in America, 1976-77; Who's Who in Opera, 1976; Who's Who of American Women, 1977-78

Proxmire, (Edward) William

Nov. 11, 1915- United States Senator from Wisconsin. Address: b. Room 5241, Dirksen Senate Office Bldg., Washington, D.C. 20510; h. 4613 Buckeye Rd., Madison, Wis. 53716

NOTE: This biography supersedes the article that appeared in *Current Biography* in 1958.

An idiosyncratic gadfly who models himself after the legendary Senate mavericks Robert M. LaFollette and Wayne Morse, Senator William Proxmire has for two decades practised a kind of pick-and-choose politics that defies pigeonholing. In recent years the Wisconsin Democrat has used his powers as chairman of the Senate Banking Committee and as alternating chairman of the Joint Economic Committee of Congress to fight excessive government spending and to encourage a re-ordering of national priorities. "Housing, hospitals, schools and employment," he argues, "should have priority over military waste, space shuttles, or sending arms and ammunition to warring countries." Although some political commentators have faulted him for his failure to make useful alliances with other Congressmen, members of both parties attest to his knowledge of the issues, painstaking background research, and straightforward, no-nonsense approach to his job. Explaining his singleminded devotion to the United States Senate, Proxmire once remarked, "Politics is my hobby. I eat, breathe, and sleep politics."

William Proxmire

Of German and Irish ancestry, Edward William Proxmire was born in Lake Forest, Illinois, a wealthy North Shore Chicago suburb, on November 11, 1915, the second of the three children of Theodore Stanley Proxmire, a surgeon, and Adele (Flanigan) Proxmire. Dr. Proxmire, a staunch Republican whose window to the world, according to his son, was the editorial page of the then reactionary Chicago *Tribune,* was the chief of staff at Lake Forest Hospital and the founder of the Lake County Tuberculosis Sanitarium in nearby Waukegan.

William Proxmire (he dropped his first name at the age of six after seeing cowboy star William S. Hart in a silent film), was exceptionally hard-working, even as a youngster. He achieved the best academic record of his class at the Hill Preparatory School in Pottstown, Pennsylvania, where he was voted the "most energetic" and the "biggest grind" by his classmates. From there he went on to Yale University, graduating in 1938 with a B.A. degree in English. While at Yale he won boxing titles in several weight divisions and earned a letter in football.

Proxmire continued his education at Harvard University's Graduate School of Business Administration. After taking his M.B.A. degree *cum laude* there in 1940, he joined J. P. Morgan & Company, the New York investment firm, as a student clerk. Six months later he enlisted in the United States Army. Assigned to the counterintelligence corps and the military intelligence service, he spent his entire tour of duty in the United States, much of it in the Chicago area. When he was mustered out of service in January 1946, in the rank of first lieutenant, he resumed his studies at the Harvard Graduate School of Public Administration, where he earned a second master's degree in 1948, taught political theory and comparative government, and completed all the requirements for a Ph.D. degree, except for his dissertation. In the liberal environment of Harvard, Proxmire, much to his father's chagrin, became a Democrat because of his conviction that "on all the critical problems the Republicans found reason not to act."

After leaving Harvard, Proxmire worked for a time as a junior executive for J. P. Morgan & Company, but he was eager to try a career in politics. He characteristically weighed his options and narrowed his list of choices to New Mexico, California, and Wisconsin, finally settling on Wisconsin because he believed the state's traditionally weak Democratic Party offered the best prospects for an ambitious newcomer and outsider. Moving to Madison, Wisconsin, Proxmire took a job as a political and labor reporter on the liberal *Capital Times.* An early practitioner of investigative and advocacy journalism, he clashed repeatedly with his editor over the issue of newspaper objectivity. On one occasion Proxmire published financial information from state officials' tax returns, and, on another, he suppressed a story that implied that a female official of the American Federation of Labor was having an extramarital affair. When a rival newspaper ran the scandalous tale, Proxmire was relegated to writing obituaries, the lowest job on the reporting staff. His journalistic independence notwithstanding, some commentators claim that Proxmire's union organizing activities on behalf of the American Newspaper Guild were the real source of his difficulties with the paper's management.

Proxmire left the *Capital Times* after less than a year to write and broadcast "Labor Sounds Off," a weekly radio news program sponsored by the American Federation of Labor in Madison, and to manage that organization's publication, *Union Labor News.* In February 1950 he announced his candidacy for the state assembly from a Madison district. Proxmire's campaign strategy, then as now, was to make personal contact with as many voters as possible. Concentrating on the predominantly Democratic precincts, he conducted a grueling, seven-month, sixteen-hour-a-day, door-to-door campaign. His diligence paid off in the November general election when he scored an upset victory over his Republican opponent.

As a freshman assemblyman, Proxmire unsuccessfully sponsored measures to establish restraints on lobbyists, limit campaign spending, close tax loopholes, and provide a public advocate for consumers at utility rate hearings. In 1952, rather than run for a second term in the assembly, he decided to try his luck in the gubernatorial contest. No other Democrat dared to challenge the popular Republican incumbent, Walter J. Kohler, and even Proxmire expected to lose. According to Jay G. Sykes, the author of *Proxmire* (McKay, 1972), the candidate predicted, "I'm going to run and lose in 1952, and run and lose in 1954, then I'll win in 1956." As Proxmire had foretold, Kohler beat him soundly in 1952 and narrowly in 1954, but, contrary to his expectations, he also lost his third gubernatorial bid, in 1956, to Republican Vernon Thomson, by 59,000 votes.

With his political career at its nadir, it seemed that Proxmire would have to settle for the presidency of the Artcraft Press Company, a Waterloo, Wisconsin firm in which he had purchased a half-interest in 1953. But when Wisconsin's Republican Senator, Joseph R. McCarthy, died on May 2, 1957, he immediately announced his desire to complete the remainder of the Senator's term. After a whirlwind campaign, he easily defeated Clement J. Zablocki, a Milwaukee Congressman, in the July primary for the Democratic nomination only to come up against his old nemesis, Walter Kohler, in the general election. Cheerfully accepting the role of the underdog in the race, Proxmire told the voters "My opponent doesn't know what it is to lose. I do. And I'll welcome the support of voters who do, too. I'll take the losers. I'll take the debtors. I'll take those who've lost in love, or baseball, or in business. I'll take the Milwaukee Braves." Proxmire defeated Kohler by a decisive 123,000 votes in the special election on August 27, and the following year he easily turned back a challenge from Republican Roland J. Steinle to win election to his first full term in the United States Senate.

In Washington Proxmire quickly emerged as a determined, fiercely independent legislator. Angered by Senate Majority Leader Lyndon B. Johnson's refusal to appoint him to the Finance Committee, he attacked the autocratic control Johnson and his fellow Texan, Speaker of the House Sam Rayburn, exerted over Congress. "When you get these two men together with the power to make committee assignments," he charged in a February 1959 floor speech, "you see the obsequious bowing, scraping Senators and Congressmen around them." Proxmire also criticized Johnson's penchant for compromising with conservatives on civil rights legislation and for supporting the oil depletion allowance. He took on President John F. Kennedy, too, arguing against the President's nomination of Texan John B. Connally as Secretary of the Navy, a post with jurisdiction over oil reserves, and filibustering for nineteen hours in an attempt to prevent the appointment of another Texas oilman, Lawrence J. O'Connor Jr., to the Federal Power Commission. In 1961 and 1962 Proxmire opposed Kennedy on five major issues that were decided by five or less votes in the Senate. Such intransigence marked Proxmire as a troublemaker, and in a poll conducted by *Pageant* magazine shortly before the 1964 election he was ranked fourth lowest among Senators. He managed to ride President Johnson's coattails to a 112,000-vote victory over Wilbur Renk, but he believes that the poll cost him at least 200,000 votes.

Chastened by the 1964 campaign, Proxmire decided to be "more pragmatic." The emergence of Senator Michael J. Mansfield of Montana as an open, democratic Majority Leader, moreover, removed the basic cause of his disaffection. As he gained seniority on the Appropriations Committee and on the Banking, Housing, and Urban Affairs Committee, the Senator's influence grew. He found an outlet for his skills when, in 1967, he became one of the two alternating chairmen of the Joint Economic Committee, a body composed of ten Senators and ten Representatives, and took over its subcommittee on economy in government.

Generally speaking, Proxmire is a liberal on issues of social policy, and he normally receives ratings of 80 percent or higher from such liberal organizations as the Americans for Democratic Action and the AFL-CIO's Committee on Political Education. He has supported limitations on foreign aid to authoritarian regimes, a volunteer army, a relaxed monetary policy to spur the economy, and wide-ranging civil rights legislation. The Senator is especially proud of his role in the defeat in 1964 of Republican efforts to undo the Supreme Court's one man-one vote ruling. During his second term Proxmire became increasingly conservative on fiscal policy, a development that surprised critics who once called him "Billion Dollar Bill" because of his support for expensive government programs that required deficit spending. Proxmire, however, describes himself as a "pragmatic electric" who picks the best from available policies and programs, and Wisconsin voters apparently approve his choices. In 1970 they awarded him 71 percent of their votes and in 1976, 73 percent.

Senator Proxmire's major legislative accomplishments have been in the area of consumer protection. He sponsored the far-reaching Consumer Credit Protection Act, signed into law by President Johnson in 1968. Popularly known as the Truth-in-Lending Act, that measure requires lenders to inform prospective borrowers of their finance charges in writing. The Senator describes the law as "perhaps more valuable to the consumer borrower than any credit card in his wallet." His tireless efforts in behalf of the bill's passage prompted *Sales Management* magazine to give Proxmire first place on its list of "Consumerism's Twelve Shakers and Doers" in Congress. Continuing to work toward improved consumer protection legislation, he offered in 1970 an amendment to restrict the mailing of unsolicited credit cards and limit the liability of persons whose cards are illegally used. Proxmire's Fair Credit Reporting Act of 1970 broke new ground by guaranteeing people the right to review and correct the personal files maintained by credit reporting agencies.

Although he is known as an outspoken critic of the defense budget, Proxmire insists that he is not antimilitary. He was a hawk on Vietnam long after Wisconsin's other Democratic Senator, Gaylord Nelson, became a dove, and he maintained a rather ambiguous position on the war until 1970, when he voted in favor of the Hatfield-McGovern end-the-war amendment. To refute his detractors, he even mounted in his office—which is otherwise bare of decoration—a framed poster proclaiming, "National defense is a life insurance policy. We must be No. 1." Proxmire worries, however, that the United States has become a "national security state" that spends too much on defense frills at the expense of essential domestic programs. He organized and led the floor fight for legislation to prevent generals and admirals from using enlisted men as personal servants, and he repeatedly chastised the military for spending exorbitant sums on elaborate defense systems and strategic weapons, like the B-1 bomber, that promise to be of little value.

Proxmire's subcommittee on priorities and economy in government created a stir in 1969 when it learned about a staggering $2 billion "cost overrun" in the production of the C-5A jumbo cargo plane. As the Senator pointedly remarked, that cost overrun amounted to "more than we were spending on aid to elementary and secondary education in the entire country." His subcommittee report, *The Economics of Military Procurement,* and his own book on the subject, *Report from Wasteland: America's Military-Industrial Complex* (Praeger, 1970), led to the adoption of new uniform accounting practices that allow the federal government to estimate the costs of its defense programs with greater accuracy.

As his book *Uncle Sam: The Last of the Bigtime Spenders* (Simon & Schuster, 1972) attests, Proxmire has uncovered waste in almost all government departments. He is particularly appalled by the enormous sums allotted to popular pork-barrel projects, arguing that the practice diverts money from more productive use in the private sector. Although he has supported the goals of the space program from its inception, he has often come out in favor of cheaper and safer unmanned exploration. "If we put far greater emphasis than we have up until now on the unmanned exploration, we could have an extremely active space program for $2 to $3 billion a year," he explained to one interviewer. For that reason he opposed the costly space shuttle project.

Appealing to fellow fiscal conservatives and to environmentalists, the Senator waged a long uphill battle against the production of the "perfectly trivial" and ecologically hazardous supersonic transport plane (SST). "This is an issue of priorities," he said in a floor debate on the subject in December 1970. "This year we are spending about $150,000,000 to combat air pollution. On this SST project we are asked to spend $290,000,000 to increase air pollution." When the SST appropriations bill was finally turned down by Congress in March 1971, Proxmire received much of the credit for the defeat. Later that same year he failed by only one vote in his effort to prevent the government from bailing out the Lockheed Aircraft Corporation, which was on the verge of bankruptcy. Proxmire, who is the author of *Can Small Business Survive?* (Regnery, 1964), maintained that the "Lockheed story is a classic example of economic malpractice" and suggested that the mammoth aerospace company take "its lumps because that is how the American business system works." He was just as adamantly opposed to the establishment of a special federal agency to assist other ailing corporate giants, including the Penn Central Railroad. "It's very hard to justify," he explained to one reporter. "It's a matter of keeping these old dinosaurs alive when they shouldn't be. If they can't cut it, they ought to go through bankruptcy. Let the forces of the market work."

Early in 1975 Proxmire began issuing a monthly "Golden Fleece" award for the "biggest or most ridiculous or most ironic example of government waste." As chairman of the appropriations subcommittee that reviews the budget of the National Science Foundation, he singled out for special attention six of its projects, including an $84,000 study of romantic love proposed by Dr. Ellen Berscheid of the University of Minnesota. Subsequent Golden Fleece Awards went to the National Institute of Alcohol Abuse for its $102,000 attempt to discover if drunken fish were more aggressive than sober fish and to the Law Enforcement Assistance Administration, which had earmarked $27,000 for research to determine why inmates want to escape from prison. Some political commentators, among them Vic Gold, have belittled Proxmire's "awards" as a publicity gimmick. "No demagogue ever lost a headline by underestimating the Capitol Hill news media's taste for 'exposé' items with a Yahoo zinger," Gold wrote in a piece for *Harper's* magazine (October 1976).

Proxmire's accession in 1975 to the chairmanships of the Banking, Housing, and Urban Affairs Committee and of its housing subcommittee failed to cause the "reign of terror on Wall Street" predicted by some worried businessmen despite the Senator's promise to use those posts to keep a close watch on the banking, housing, and consumer credit industries. Among other things, he suggested centralizing bank regulatory functions, now shared by the Comptroller, the Federal Deposit Insurance Corporation, and the Federal Reserve Board, in a new Federal Banking Commission and tightening the loan policies of the nation's financial institutions. Because of the "easy money" practices of most banks, he argues "there are millions of genuine tragedies, and many of them are people who perhaps shouldn't be borrowing in the first place." He has also given some attention to an overdue review of federal housing policies, which are, in his view, "a great and tragic failure" and "in large part responsible for crime and our other urban problems."

Proxmire's position on the Banking Committee has put him in the midst of New York City's fiscal woes. Fearful that the city's imminent financial collapse in 1975 would end up costing Washington even more money and time, he was an early advocate of aid for the beleaguered city. But because he was worried that the extension of such aid set a dangerous precedent, he demanded as the price of his support a commitment from the city to balance its budget, cut back on the number of municipal employees, curb wages, reduce crippling pension and welfare benefits, end rent control, and begin charging tuition at the City University.

At the time of the original agreement Proxmire assured his skeptical colleagues that it was a one-time-only contingency loan and when he convened hearings, in December 1977, on the city's continuing financial crisis he took a hard-line approach, even going so far as to suggest that bankruptcy was "a more viable option . . . if the city can't make it on its own." Although he conceded that New York City had made progress in some areas of fiscal reform, he criticized its efforts as inadequate and suggested that, with new austerity measures and increased state aid, the city could function without additional federal assistance. Despite Proxmire's opposition to the $2.3 billion in long-term loan guarantees proposed by President Jimmy Carter, the majority of political observers agree that the Senator will eventually support a continuation of the present seasonal-loan program.

A trim six-footer with blue eyes and graying brown hair, William Proxmire looks younger than his years. Meticulous about his appearance, he has had a well publicized hair transplant and, reportedly, a less publicized facelift. A physical fitness enthusiast and the author of *You Can Do It: Senator Proxmire's Exercise, Diet, and Relaxation Plan* (Simon & Schuster, 1973), he follows a rigorous daily schedule. After rising at 6:00 A.M., he does 250 pushups and other calisthenics, then runs the almost five miles from his house to the Capitol. He eats a high-protein breakfast and a light lunch in his office, where he usually works standing at an elevated desk. After putting in a ten- or eleven-hour day (he has not missed a roll call vote since April 1966), he walks home. Shunning the frantic Washington social whirl, he is invariably in bed by 10:00 P.M. On weekends he usually returns to Wisconsin to confer with local political leaders and with his constituents. In 1972 he combined his exercise and campaign regimens in a running tour of the 1,200-mile perimeter of the state. Questioned about the feat, Proxmire said, "Well, I may be crazy, but I love it."

Senator Proxmire's devotion to politics has taken its toll on his personal life. His first marriage, to Elsie Borden Rockefeller, a great grand-niece of John D. Rockefeller, ended in divorce in 1955. Politics was again the villain when in June 1971 Proxmire separated from Ellen Hodges Sawall Proxmire, the former executive secretary of the Wisconsin Democratic party, whom he had married on December 1, 1956. In February 1975, however, the Senator announced that he and his wife "had resumed their life together." Ellen Proxmire is the author of *One Foot in Washington: The Perilous Life of a Senator's Wife* (R. B. Luce, 1964) and the owner-operator of Washington Whirl-Around, a sightseeing business. The Proxmires have a son and a daughter, Theodore and Elsie ("Cici") from his first marriage, two daughters from her first marriage, and a son, who is named Douglas Clark, in honor of Senators Paul H. Douglas of Illinois and Joseph Clark of Pennsylvania, the Democratic veterans who were Proxmire's mentors when he was a neophyte in the Upper House.

References: Atlan 226:6+ D '70; N Y Daily News p112+ Mr 11 '73 pors; N Y Times p37+ S 19 '77 por; N Y Times Mag p28+ Ap 4 '71 pors, p8+ My 28 '78 pors; Nat Observer p22 Ja 20 '73; Douth, George. Leaders in Profile (1975); Sykes, Jay. Proxmire (1972); Who's Who in America, 1976-77

Qabus bin Said (kä-bo͞os′ bin sä-ēd′)

Nov. 18, 1940- Sultan of Oman.
Address: Sultan's Palace, Muscat, Oman

As ruler of the strategically located, oil-rich Sultanate of Oman, at the mouth of the Persian Gulf, Qabus bin Said has attracted wide attention with his efforts to modernize his realm, which was once a self-isolated backwater of the Arab world, afflicted with poverty, disease, and illiteracy. Since he ascended the throne in July 1970 after deposing his father, Said bin Taimur, he has gone a long way toward bring-

Qabus bin Said

ing Oman into the twentieth century by instituting far-reaching reforms and development projects, by removing the rigidly puritanical laws to which his people had been subjected, and by ending the country's isolation.

The Al Bu Saidi dynasty, of which Sultan Qabus bin Said is the fourteenth reigning monarch, has been in control of Oman since 1741, when its founder, Ahmed bin Said Al Bu Saidi, expelled the Persians from the country. Under Ahmed's rule, and in the century that followed, Oman was a significant maritime power, engaged in general commerce and the slave trade, and for a number of years it controlled territory extending to Baluchistan and East Africa. Although the Sultanate of Muscat and Oman—as the country had been known until 1970—remained formally independent over the years, during the nineteenth century it came increasingly under the hegemony of Great Britain, which considered it an important link in its sea route to India. More recently, in view of their dependence on Persian Gulf oil, the British have continued to exercise considerable influence on Oman, but in a more indirect and circumspect manner.

Born in Oman on November 18, 1940, Qabus bin Said Al Bu Saidi is the only son of Sultan Said bin Taimur Al Bu Saidi and his second wife, who came from a Bedouin family. (In some sources his given name is transliterated from the Arabic as Qaboos, and the standard patronymic form "ibn" is used instead of the regional variant "bin.") Qabus bin Said's parents also had two daughters; his father's other marriages were childless. Because of Sultan Said's puritanism and tyrannical nature, Qabus led a lonely and restricted childhood. Denied servants or companions, he was raised in seclusion in the royal palace at Salalah, the principal town of Dhofar province, which his father preferred as a residence to Muscat, Oman's capital. At the Sultan's command, Qabus was forbidden to visit the beaches, to indulge in games, or to talk to his tutors about anything unrelated to his studies. As Wendell Phillips, the American archaeologist and sometime adviser to Said bin Taimur, recalled in his book *Unknown Oman* (McKay, 1966), the father downgraded the youth's self-image and repeatedly warned him that he would have to work or starve.

Nevertheless, Said bin Taimur was acutely aware of his son's intelligence. When Qabus turned sixteen he was sent by his father to England and enrolled in a private tutorial academy for Arab princes run by Philip C. Romans in Bury St. Edmunds, Suffolk. There, over the next five years, he became a serious student, determined to make up for the deficiencies of the education he had received at home. He also qualified as an expert horseman, learned to drive an automobile, and developed a lifelong taste for classical music.

On completing the course of study, Qabus entered Sandhurst, the British military academy. He graduated in September 1962 and then, as a lieutenant in the Cameronians (Scottish Rifles) Regiment, served for six months—or, according to some accounts, a year—with the Army of the Rhine in West Germany. Following his discharge he went on a round-the-world trip under the chaperonage of Major Frederick C. L. Chauncey, a retired British officer who served as his father's vizier. He then returned to Bury St. Edmunds, where he devoted himself to the study of government and economics. He familiarized himself with the affairs of Shell Petroleum Ltd., the British subsidiary of Royal Dutch Shell and the leading shareholder in Petroleum Development (Oman) Ltd., a key factor in his country's developing economy. According to some accounts, Qabus also attended Oxford University for a time.

In 1965 Sultan Said ordered Qabus to return to Oman to commit the Koran to memory in the Bedouin tradition and to study the history of the Oman tribes. In Salalah, Qabus was placed under house arrest in a four-room residence adjoining the royal palace. For the next six years, according to Paul Maubec of the Washington *Post* (December 27, 1970), "Qabus lived the life of a prisoner, except that he could have all the books and records he wanted," and he was "desperately lonely." Forbidden to marry, or to receive guests without royal permission, Qabus saw his father only about once a year during that period.

Sultan Said's despotism affected not merely his son but the whole of Oman's population of some 700,000, whose way of life had remained virtually unchanged for centuries. Described in *Time* (August 10, 1970) as "one of the most stagnant societies on earth," Oman, during Said's reign, had only two elementary schools and one hospital, no newspapers or radio service, and no paved roads. Slavery still existed, and all political activity was banned. Since the sultan did not trust his own subjects, the army and government were largely staffed by foreigners, mostly Britishers, Indians, and Pakistanis.

Obsessed by concern for his personal safety, and haunted by the memory of how he had deposed his own father in 1932, Said bin Taimur lived the life of a recluse in his palace in Salalah, companioned by a small entourage of slaves, concubines, and bodyguards. Ruling with an iron hand despite his isolation, he tried to exercise total control over his subjects. It was forbidden, for example, to build or repair a house, buy an automobile or bicycle, or travel beyond one's home district, without his permission. The repressiveness and aridity of Omani life were heightened by Said's strict enforcement of the puritanical rules of the Ibadi sect of Islam which included absolute bans on motion pictures, music, dancing, smoking, and wearing European-style clothes.

As Robert Geran Landen pointed out in his book *Oman Since 1865* (Princeton Univ. Press, 1967), such conditions could not long endure. The country desperately needed "an accommodation with modern realities," and Landen predicted that unless a new generation of Westernized leaders—personified, in his view, by Qabus bin Said—came to power, Oman would be taken over by "a revolutionary modernizing regime." That threat seemed likely to become a reality since, as a result of Said's ineptitude and popular discontent with his policies, a minor tribal uprising that had begun in Dhofar province a few years earlier, had expanded into a full-scale guerrilla war against the Omani army by the late 1960's. Said's inability to suppress the guerrillas, who were backed by the People's Republic of China, Communist South Yemen, and Palestinian radicals, became a matter of grave concern to the region's two conservative powers, Saudi Arabia and Iran, as well as to Great Britain and the United States. Much discontent was also generated by the fact that Said was pocketing Oman's oil income—which had risen from $3,100,000 in 1967, when exports began, to some $70,000,000 a year by 1970—and that he apparently had no intention to spend any of it on projects aimed at dealing with the nation's urgent needs.

The hopes of Said's diverse opponents naturally focused on Qabus bin Said, who shared their concerns. In due course a coup was organized, but Qabus' own role in it remains obscure, since he was at that time still kept in confinement. The plot involved the coordinated efforts of several groups in Omani society and was known to have been planned and carried out with the complicity of the British, although Foreign Office spokesmen have denied any involvement.

On July 23, 1970, while British-officered Omani troops stood outside to prevent interference, a party of Askari tribesmen led by Sheik Buraik bin Hamoud, the son of the governor of Salalah, stormed the royal palace. There was little resistance, although Sultan Said suffered minor wounds, having, according to some accounts, shot himself in the foot while attempting to draw his pistol. Escorted by a British officer, the deposed Sultan was quickly taken to the RAF base at nearby Masirah and from there was flown in a British plane to Bahrain and then to England. Until his death in 1972 he lived on a pension in London's Dorchester Hotel.

Officially, Said was reported to have retired for reasons of poor health and old age. But a few days after the coup, Qabus announced: "I have watched with growing dismay and increasing anger the inability of my father to use the new-found wealth of this country for the needs of his people. That is why I have taken control." Discussing the coup with Dana Adams Schmidt of the New York *Times* (September 5, 1970), Qabus said: "I would have liked to have had a normal relationship with my father, but he was a man who ruled by fear. And in the end what I had to do transcended personal relationships." Meanwhile, the Omani people joyously acclaimed their new ruler with singing and dancing in the streets. Virtually all influential elements of Omani society—government officials, wealthy merchants, and tribal chiefs—immediately pledged their fealty to Qabus.

One of Qabus' first acts on taking power was his abrogation of the moralistic laws imposed by his father. Then, trying to end the guerrilla warfare that plagued the country, he offered a blanket amnesty to the Dhofar insurgents, but it was accepted by only a few. He also invited Oman's approximately 2,000 expatriates—many of whom had acquired technical training abroad and were working in other Arab countries—to return home without penalty. Among those invited to return from exile was Tariq bin Taimur, his father's half-brother, whom he appointed Prime Minister. In his newly established Council of Ministers, Qabus retained the defense and foreign affairs portfolios for himself. The other ministerial posts were given to Omanis, many of them his relatives, but for the time being most key administrative and technical jobs continued to be held by foreigners. In sharp contrast with his reclusive father, Qabus solidified his base of popular support by going on a series of tours of his realm, visiting towns and tribes that had never, in living memory, experienced a royal visit. He also instituted regional councils to deal with local affairs, and he regularly granted audiences to enable citizens to present their problems to him.

During his years under house arrest Qabus had formulated in his mind a long list of Oman's requirements. Now, inexperienced but filled with enthusiasm, he tried to implement all of his ideas simultaneously. The projects he began in the early 1970's included the construction of a road network, a transportation system, a modern deep-water harbor at Muscat, a new $15,000,000 royal palace, and a hotel for foreign businessmen, as well as schools, hospitals, and other public buildings. He initiated a telecommunications system, two radio stations, a weekly newspaper, water desalinization plants, and such industrial facilities as cement and fertilizer factories, a petrochemical complex, and an oil refinery.

In addition, he took steps to modernize agriculture and the fishing industry; to establish a public school system for both boys and girls as well as a national health service; and to reorganize and expand the 12,000-man armed forces and the police. To brighten the lives of his subjects he indulged in such colorful extravagances as having the air force drop bonbons to children in inland areas and setting up public color television sets in every town and village.

At first Qabus seemed to be fairly successful in getting his various projects under way. Although Oman, with about 2 percent of the Middle Eastern petroleum reserves, is far from being the wealthiest of the Arab oil states, its resources are substantial in proportion to its population. Nevertheless, various problems soon arose. A number of projects were hindered or made more expensive by official corruption. In 1971 strikes, riots, and other labor difficulties erupted at the oilfields and in several towns, where the persistent need for Indian and Pakistani technicians and skilled workers caused dissatisfaction among Omanis, who felt that they were entitled to the best jobs. Furthermore, Qabus bin Said's foreign financial advisers repeatedly warned him that he was trying to do too much too fast and as a result was overspending at a dangerous rate.

On the international scene, Qabus made considerable headway in his efforts to end Oman's isolation. As David E. Long noted in *The Persian Gulf* (Westview Press, 1976), he had two major aims in the sphere of foreign affairs: to garner support in the struggle against the Dhofar rebels, and to gain recognition for his regime, especially among Arab nations. The latter goal was especially important, since in the past Oman's neighbors had come to resent Said's close relationship with the British and, led by Saudi Arabia, had supported rival claimants to the throne. The last such instance had occurred in 1955, when a Saudi-backed contender, the Imam Ghalib, had been thwarted with the aid of British troops.

Soon after Qabus came to power, Oman for the first time established diplomatic relations with the Arab states. In 1971, the year Oman joined both the Arab League and the United Nations, Qabus went on a state visit to Riyadh, the capital of Saudi Arabia. In recent years, the Omani army has been aided by combat troops and air units from Iran and Jordan in its continuing struggle against Dhofar rebel forces, known since 1972 as the Popular Front for the Liberation of Oman and the Arab Gulf. Within the spectrum of Middle Eastern politics, Qabus has aligned his country with the moderate powers. For example, in November 1977 Oman was one of the few Arab countries—along with Morocco, Tunisia, and the Sudan—that supported Egyptian President Anwar Sadat in his peace overtures to Israel.

By 1975 Qabus was encountering serious financial difficulties, despite the fact that Oman's oil income for that year had risen to $1.8 billion. Having accumulated a number of foreign debts, the Sultan found it difficult to obtain credit from banks in Great Britain and Western Europe, and a number of projects had to be halted abruptly. Chastened by that experience, and by the realization that Oman's oil resources might be depleted within a decade and a half, Qabus—who was now serving as his own finance minister—began to rely more on his advisers. In his 1976 New Year's message he declared: "We all have to plan realistically, to proceed in accordance with our resources." Granted a sizeable loan by Saudi Arabia to meet immediate obligations, Qabus ended some of his more extravagant projects, implemented a series of institutional and staff changes recommended by his bankers, and adopted an austere new development program that showed promise of success. Meanwhile, Omani armed forces had begun to make major inroads against the Dhofar insurgents, although government claims of total victory in early 1976 were apparently premature.

Sultan Qabus bin Said was married in 1976 to his cousin Kamilar, the daughter of Tariq bin Taimur. (Some sources suggest that he may have previously been married, about 1970, to the daughter of a tribal chief.) A handsome, brown-eyed man with a flowing black beard, Qabus has been described as introspective and gentle in manner. He usually wears the traditional Omani turban and long robe with a *kunjar*, or curved dagger in his belt, and on rare occasions he appears in his uniform as commander of the Omani army. His favorite recreations include reading, horseback riding, and shooting, and he has a passion for collecting classical recordings. The British government has conferred the honorary title of Knight Commander of the Order of St. Michael and St. George (K.C.M.G.) on him.

As quoted by Paul Maubec in the Washington *Post* (December 27, 1970), Qabus has said of himself: "I am a man with one foot in my country—backward as it is, with its tribal customs, its life dominated by Islam—and the other in the twentieth century. I must be very careful to keep my balance." Although he has been schooled in the progressive political philosophy of the West, he has thus far refrained from instituting a democracy in Oman. "You cannot run before you walk," Qabus has explained. "Most of the people do not even know what a vote is. . . . In these conditions to draft a constitution, to set up a parliament would be like building a huge dome without either walls or foundations. It might perhaps give a nice impression to the outside world, but it would be nothing but a big show."

References: N Y Post p33 Ja 18 '74; N Y Times p2 S 5 '70; Time 97:34+ F 15 '71 por; Washington Post D p1+ D 27 '70 por; International Who's Who, 1977-78; Peterson, J. E. Oman in the Twentieth Century (1978); Who's Who in the Arab World, 1974-75

Ram, Jagjivan

Apr. 5, 1908- Minister of Defense of India. Address: h. 6 Krishna Menon Marg, New Delhi, India 110011

Known popularly as "Babuji," or "Respected Father," India's Defense Minister, Jagjivan Ram, is the unofficial leader of that country's 85,000,000 "Untouchables"—also known as Harijans (children of God), the name applied to them by the late Mohandas K. Gandhi. A member of almost every Indian Cabinet since the nation became independent in 1947, Ram has attained a level of political success that is extraordinary, because traditionally, upper-caste Hindus have shunned and despised their Untouchable coreligionists, who were believed to be suffering divine punishment for unworthiness in previous incarnations. Normally, Harijans hold the most menial jobs, and very few reach positions of eminence. Nevertheless, Ram has carved such a solid niche of power for himself in Indian politics that by defecting from the ruling Indian National Congress to the opposition during the election campaign of March 1977, he was able to play a major role in bringing down Prime Minister Indira Gandhi's authoritarian government. Although Ram claims to stand for "scientific socialism adapted for Indian culture," he is regarded by many as a pragmatist rather than an ideologue.

Jagjivan Ram was born on April 5, 1908 in the village of Chandwa, near the town of Arrah, in British India's eastern Bihar province, to Shobi Ram and his wife, Vasanti Devi. Jagjivan was one of eight children and the youngest of three sons. He entered the village primary school in 1914, the Agrawal Middle School in 1920 and the Arrah Town High School in 1922. Because his father, a farmer, owned about fifty acres of land in a relatively tolerant area of Bihar, Jagjivan in his early years escaped the worst of the insults normally visited upon the Untouchables. But on leaving his native village to enter high school at Arrah, he began to suffer the humiliations associated with his status, even though he had earned a scholarship on his own merit, turning down a grant that had been set aside for Untouchables. It was during his high school years that Ram first became interested in Mohandas K. Gandhi's independence movement and began to subscribe to its periodical *Young India*.

On invitation from a visiting orthodox Hindu educator who was impressed by his facility for language, Ram entered Benares Hindu University in 1926 to study science. At that center of conservative Hinduism, Ram continued to suffer harassment because of his status. On one occasion, for example, a barber, upon learning what caste he belonged to, left him half-shaved. Another time, his landlord threatened to lock him out of his rooms. "I told him that if he broke my lock, I would break his head," Ram has recalled, as quoted in *Time* (February 16, 1970). After two years of preparatory studies at Benares, he entered Vidyasagar College of Calcutta University in 1928 and earned his B.Sc. degree there in 1931.

On completing his formal education, Ram decided to devote all of his time to social reform. In 1931 he joined Gandhi's Congress party. Four years later he was one of the founders of the All India Depressed Classes League, a political organization formed to gain equality for Untouchables, and he was elected its general secretary as well as president of its Bihar branch. Elected a member of the Bihar legislative council in 1936, Ram served as parliamentary secretary with the Bihar government from 1937 to 1939. He also pioneered in organizing a rural labor movement, and in 1937 he formed the Bihar provincial Khet Mazdoor (Agricultural Labor)

Sabha. His influence over the Untouchables in Bihar brought them over to the Congress party. From 1940 to 1946 he was secretary of the Bihar Provincial Congress Committee, and during those same years he served as vice-president of the Bihar branch of the All-India Trade Union Congress.

Meanwhile, in 1940 Gandhi had launched his movement of symbolic nonviolent civil resistance, or Satyagraha, against Indian participation in World War II. In December 1940, after speaking at a number of meetings in support of Gandhi's movement, Ram was arrested by British authorities, and he remained incarcerated until September 1941. Shortly after the All India Congress Committee had called for independence in August 1942, Ram was jailed again, but he was released in October 1943 because of ill health.

Ram emerged as the undisputed leader of the nationalist-oriented Untouchables in 1946, when his Depressed Classes League swamped the rival Scheduled Castes Federation in provincial elections. On September 2, 1946 he was sworn in as Labor Minister in the provisional government headed by Jawaharlal Nehru, established to ease India's transition to independence, and he was, at thirty-eight, its youngest member. After India became independent in 1947, Ram continued to hold the Labor portfolio under Prime Minister Nehru until 1952.

In 1947 Ram asserted that industrial enterprises "which do not provide a decent standard of living for their workers have no social claim to survival." During his tenure as Labor Minister he secured the passage of important social and economic legislation, including the Minimum Wages Act for agricultural laborers; the Employees' State Insurance Act, which provided maternity and sickness benefits for employees in nonseasonal factories; and amendments to the Trade Unions Act compelling employers to negotiate with labor unions. A delegate to meetings of the International Labor Organization since 1947, Ram was elected president of its 1950 conference in Geneva.

Continuing to express concern over the plight of the Untouchables, Ram asserted in 1952 that neither the provision in India's constitution abolishing untouchability nor the state laws guaranteeing equality were enforced. He warned that "if communism ever spreads in the country, it will be due to the misery and suffering of the poor and downtrodden classes" and noted that the Harijans, who constituted nearly one-sixth of India's population, were becoming increasingly conscious of their rights.

Meanwhile, after the general elections that ended in February 1952, Ram became Minister for Communications, a post that he held until 1956, and in that office he planned the reorganization of airlines that resulted in the nationalization of Air-India. His tenure as Minister of Railways and Transport in 1956-57 and Railways Minister from 1957 to 1962 was reportedly marred by some scandals and fatal accidents, but he was responsible for the construction of new railroad lines and the introduction of sleeper coach facilities. In 1961 Ram was backed for the post of deputy party chief by V. K. Krishna Menon, the leader of the Congress party's left wing, and by Mrs. Indira Gandhi, Nehru's daughter, who saw him as a counterweight to the right-wing Congress party leader, Morarji Desai. But Nehru forestalled an intraparty conflict over the deputy post by reducing it in importance and cancelling elections for it. Ram served as Minister of Transport and Communications from April 1962 until August 1963, when Nehru asked him and five other Cabinet ministers to resign following state election defeats for the Congress party. Under what was known as the Kamaraj Plan, they were assigned to full-time party work to revitalize the organization at the grass roots.

Following Nehru's death in May 1964, Ram at first supported Morarji Desai against centrist Lal Bahadur Shastri for succession to the Prime Ministership. When Desai's effort faltered, Ram unsuccessfully tried to secure a consensus for Indira Gandhi and then offered himself as a candidate. But although Ram had great influence with the approximately fifty Harijan members of the Congress party's parliamentary delegation, he failed to block Shastri and was excluded from the new Prime Minister's Cabinet.

After Shastri's death in January 1966, Ram helped Mrs. Gandhi win the Prime Ministership over the conservative Desai and was appointed Minister for Labor, Employment, and Rehabilitation. In 1967 he received the Food and Agriculture portfolio, which he held until 1970. In the summer of 1969 Ram was mentioned by Mrs. Gandhi as a possible candidate to succeed the late Zakir Husain in the largely ceremonial but highly prestigious Presidency of India but the post went to V. V. Giri. When in the fall of 1969 the Congress party's old guard, led by Desai, broke with Mrs. Gandhi in protest against her nationalization of fourteen major banks and other policies, Ram backed the Prime Minister. He was under attack from members of the Congress party's old guard for allegedly having neglected to pay $2,718 in income taxes on earnings from investments over a ten-year period. Nevertheless, a convention in Bombay in December 1969 elected him president of Mrs. Gandhi's ruling faction of the Indian National Congress, which proclaimed its commitment to further nationalization to speed the transformation of India from capitalism to socialism.

In June 1970 Ram was named Defense Minister, becoming one of the four members of Mrs. Gandhi's "inner Cabinet." Although he relinquished his post as party chief in the reorganization that followed the elections of early March 1971 he retained the Defense portfolio. In the crisis that erupted in late March as a result of Pakistani suppression of the Bengali autonomy movement in what was then known as East Pakistan, Ram emerged as a key spokesman for the Indian government, which supported the rebels. Tensions mounted on the India-East Pakistan border as thousands of Bengali refugees crossed the frontier into India, and a series of clashes occurred. When the skirmishes intensified in October, Ram warned of the consequences of a Pakistani attack. "We will not be satisfied merely by defending our borders," he declared. "We will push the enemy back into his territory and see that fighting takes place in enemy country and not on our soil." His warning was implemented in December 1971, as Indian troops swept into East Pakistan and helped establish the independent nation of Bangladesh.

Defense Minister Ram announced in May 1972 that India was developing the technology for carrying out underground nuclear explosions. The blasts, he said, would be used for the extraction of copper and nickel ores and for the exploitation of the country's oil resources. Two years later Ram defended India's first such explosion against criticism from the United States, Western Europe, Pakistan, and China, asserting that India would use nuclear technology only for peaceful purposes. He noted that his country was the only one to date that had conducted its initial tests underground to avoid the danger of nuclear fallout.

When Ram was shifted from the Defense Ministry to that of Agriculture and Irrigation in October 1974, he reportedly complained bitterly and accepted the new post only after repeated pleas from Mrs. Gandhi, who cited the critical food shortages, inflation, and unrest plaguing India at the time. Although Ram's power to dispense patronage within the Congress Party declined during that period, he remained an active member of the government. In November 1974 he attended the World Food Conference in Rome, where he called for the establishment of an international food security council to develop a strategy for eliminating hunger and malnutrition. Ram chided the industrial and oil-producing countries in January 1975 for not doing enough to help the poor nations.

In the wake of mounting opposition to her authoritarian rule and efforts to remove her from office, Prime Minister Gandhi's administration declared a state of emergency on June 26, 1975 and arrested thousands of its opponents. Ram backed that action, and on July 21 he introduced a resolution in Parliament approving the emergency declaration. It was passed two days later, and for the next eighteen months all fundamental civil liberties were suppressed while opposition leaders were jailed without trial. Meanwhile, Mrs. Gandhi and her son, Sanjay, in an effort to subject the government to "housecleaning" and to rejuvenate the administration, weakened the traditional system of political patronage. As a result, Ram's influence within the Congress party, already in decline before the emergency, was eroded further.

On February 2, 1977, two weeks after Prime Minister Gandhi had relaxed the state of emergency and announced parliamentary elections for March, Ram and five others resigned from the Cabinet and the Congress party. Explaining his action, Ram declared in his letter of resignation that Indians were being "deprived of all their freedoms" and that "a fear psychosis" had engulfed the nation. Rather than join the hastily established Janata (People's) party coalition of opposition groups, he and his five colleagues created the Congress for Democracy, which called for the end of all restraints imposed under the emergency. He said, however, that his group would try to avoid running candidates for seats being contested by the Janata organization. Calling for Mrs. Gandhi's defeat, he declared that the main goal of the coming elections was to correct "the illegitimacy that predominates in several aspects of our national life."

Prime Minister Gandhi denounced Ram's defection, asserting that he had been involved in the making of decisions under the emergency rule and had never objected to the actions of her government. Explaining his initial support of the state of emergency, Ram told Martin Woollacott, as quoted in the *Guardian Weekly* (February 13, 1977): "I never thought Mrs. Gandhi would go on contracting the basis of democracy within the organization and the Government." Ram also claimed that if he had resigned before elections were called, there might never have been any new elections. Congress party leaders loyal to Mrs. Gandhi responded to Ram's resignation with a resolution condemning it as an "act of bad faith not expected from a person of his seniority."

Although Ram's Congress for Democracy ran candidates for fewer than fifty of the 542 seats up for election in Parliament's lower house (Lok Sabha), his defection gave the opposition a crucial boost. With wide support among Untouchables as well as a strong political base in Bihar, India's second most populous state, Ram was one of the country's few politicians with a nationwide following. In addition, when he split with Mrs. Gandhi, Ram brought with him five other Congress party leaders, including H. N. Bahuguna, the recently deposed chief minister of Uttar Pradesh, India's most heavily populated state.

Therefore, although the Janata party won a lower house majority in the elections of

March 16-20, 1977, Ram, whose organization won twenty-eight seats, hoped to be chosen Prime Minister. He was disappointed when the Janata party instead chose Morarji Desai, who had broken with Mrs. Gandhi in the 1969 Congress party split. At first Ram refused to serve in the new Cabinet, reportedly because he felt that he was not consulted enough on the formation of the Cabinet and that his party was inadequately represented. But on March 27 he relented and accepted the post of Minister of Defense. On May 1, 1977 Ram announced that the Congress for Democracy would formally merge with the Janata party.

Over the years Ram has served in a variety of organizational posts, including the chairmanship, in 1974-75, of the Indian Institute of Public Administration. He is a past president of several trade unions and has sat on the governing bodies of a number of educational institutions. Some of his speeches have been compiled in the book *Jagjivan Ram on Labour Problems* (Delhi, 1951), edited by Shachi Rani Gurtu; and a lengthy biographical sketch of him is included in the volume *The Working Man* (Patna, 1954), published by the Jagjivan Ram Abhinandan Granth Committee. Ram holds an honorary D.Sc. degree from Vikram University in Ujjain.

Raised in a culture in which parentally arranged childhood marriages were customary. Jagjivan Ram took a bride at the age of eight. In 1935, two years after his first wife's death, he married Indrani Devi. They have a son, Suresh, and a daughter, Mira. Ram is a burly man, five feet five inches tall, with thick features. A teetotaler who lives a simple life, he enjoys tending his carnations and roses, reading, and playing bridge or tennis. He is well versed in economics and mathematics and takes an interest in India's performing arts.

References: Guardian (Manchester) Weekly p6 F 13 '77 por; N Y Times p4 F 3 '77; Time 95:20 F 16 '70 por; International Who's Who, 1977-78; Times of India Directory and Yearbook, 1977; Who's Who, 1978-79

Raskin, A(braham) H(enry)

Apr. 26, 1911- Journalist. Address: b. National News Council, 1 Lincoln Plaza, New York City, N.Y. 10023; h. 136 E. 64th St., New York City, N.Y. 10021

During a journalistic career that spanned more than four decades, A. H. Raskin came to be regarded as the dean of American labor reporters — "the best in the business," in the words of fellow newsman Murray Kempton. As the chief labor correspondent for the New York *Times* and, later, as the assistant editor of its op-ed page, Raskin won acclaim for his good judgment and independence as well as for his thorough knowledge of his subject. The most recent of his many awards are the Columbia University Journalism Award for 1976 and the 1978 Distinguished Service Award of the Institute of Collective Bargaining and Group Relations. Raskin retired from the New York *Times* in 1977 and the following year, in March, became the associate director of the National News Council.

Abraham Henry Raskin was born on April 26, 1911 in Edmonton, a middle-sized industrial city in the province of Alberta, Canada, one of the two sons of Henry Raskin, a fur trader, and Mary (Slatkin) Raskin. His brother Bernard, also a journalist, edited the *Pilot*, the monthly publication of the National Maritime Union of America. In about 1913 the Raskins moved from Canada to Seattle, Washington, where they lived for the next eleven years. In 1920 they became citizens of the United States. Taking advantage of the reopening of trade relations with the Soviet Union after the hiatus caused by the Russian Revolution, Henry Raskin went to Russia in 1924 to buy Siberian furs. His wife and sons intended to join him in Moscow, but when they reached Berlin, they learned that their promised Soviet visas had been denied. Mrs. Raskin and the two young boys had to remain in Germany until Henry Raskin finished his work in the Russian capital.

As A. H. Raskin explained in a letter to the editor of *Current Biography* on December 4, 1977, Germany was at that time in economic turmoil. Spurred by Allied insistence on reparations for World War I, the rate of inflation was calamitous, and when the Raskins arrived in Berlin, the German mark stood at the disastrously high rate of 1,000 to the American dollar. Before the year was out, however, the rate had soared to an all-time peak of 4.2 trillion to the dollar. "Although I was only twelve years old and obviously Americans with dollars were in an advantaged position," Raskin wrote, "the impact on the Germans of this degree of inflation left an indelible impression. Never in my later career as a labor writer and analyst could I accept with equanimity the notion that 'a little inflation can be a good thing.' "

Reunited in 1924, the Raskins returned to the United States and settled in New York City. There A. H. Raskin attended Townsend Harris Hall, a secondary school, where his extracurricular activities included playing soccer and working on the student paper. On his graduation in 1927 he entered CCNY, now City College of the City University of New York. He majored in education and government and, in his free time, edited the triweekly student newspaper, the yearbook, the literary magazine, and the student handbook and served as president of the senior class. In recognition of his achievements he was awarded the Student Council Major Insignia, and was admitted to Phi Beta Kappa. In 1931 he obtained his B.A. degree.

Raskin's abiding interest in journalism, amply reflected in his extracurricular activities, made his career preference a foregone conclusion but, during the Depression, the problem was, as he once put it, "to translate choice into a job." Because of nationwide hiring freezes in almost all fields, Raskin stayed on at CCNY as a graduate student, supporting himself by working as the local college correspondent for the New York *Times*. When economic conditions began to improve, he left school in March 1934 to join the regular reporting staff of the New York *Times*. Assigned at first to cover unemployment and the work-relief agencies, he took on the daily labor beat when substantial numbers of people returned to work toward the end of the decade.

Warned by a City College administrator that Raskin, who had been an aggressive and occasionally abrasive campus correspondent, constituted a potential political risk to the New York *Times*, that newspaper's management asked Neil MacNeil, its senior copy editor, to monitor the young journalist's work. Although Raskin's unfailingly accurate reportage never justified the allegation, wary New York *Times* editors balked at giving him a byline. Despite the lack of nominal recognition, Raskin quickly gained a reputation among his colleagues as a top reporter. A feisty, hard-digging journalist in the Ben Hecht tradition, he was invariably at the center of the action in an era noted for its stormy labor relations.

His diligence paid off in countless exclusives and page-one stories. On one day alone, in 1936, the front page of the New York *Times* carried five articles by Raskin, all of them without a byline. Three years later, bullpen copy editor Raymond McCaw, who was taken with one of Raskin's unsigned pieces, ordered the composing room to add the byline "A. H. Raskin" to the article. According to Gay Talese, in his book *The Kingdom and the Power* (World, 1969), journalistic gossip had it that the *Times* management felt that Raskin's given name was "too Jewish" and not in keeping with the newspaper's Establishment image. Whatever the reason behind McCaw's decision, the byline with initials remained.

Raskin's uncanny ability to be in the right place at the right time is perhaps best illustrated by his coverage of the often turbulent convention of the American Federation of Labor in New Orleans, Louisiana in November 1940. At that convention David Dubinsky, the president of the International Ladies' Garment Workers' Union, introduced a resolution calling on the AFL to break up labor racketeering in its member unions. He was vehemently opposed by Joseph S. Fay, the head of the Union of Operating Engineers. While Raskin was interviewing him, Dubinsky was physically assaulted by Fay and the reporter was inadvertently drawn into the fray. At the height of the melee Raskin suddenly thought: "Hey, I should be covering this thing." He released Fay, raced to the Western Union office in the hotel lobby, and filed his account of the fistfight. The story appeared on the front page of the New York *Times* the next day.

Shortly after the United States entered World War II, Raskin was called up by the United States Army. He spent the next four years at the Pentagon as chief of the labor branch of the Army's industrial services division. Awarded the Distinguished Service Medal for his wartime contribution, Raskin was discharged from military service in 1946 with the rank of lieutenant colonel, but he continued to serve the federal government as a civilian. In 1947 he was named to President Harry S. Truman's Committee on Universal Training, and he later served as a consultant to Truman's Secretary of Defense, George C. Marshall, and several government agencies.

Returning to the New York *Times* in 1946, Raskin became its national labor correspondent. During the next fifteen years he reported on every aspect of the American labor scene, from the complaints of the plant assembly line worker to the concerns of manufacturers and corporate executives. As Talese has pointed out in *The Kingdom and the Power,* Raskin's singleminded pursuit of the news sometimes brought him into conflict with Arthur Krock and James B. ("Scotty") Reston, who successively headed the tightly-knit Washington bureau. Considering themselves the elite corps of *Times*men, the Washington correspondents resented Raskin's persistent attempts to track down leads in the nation's capital. In some instances where Raskin's reports differed from their own, they even went so far as to try to discredit him. For example, in 1949, a year of general economic decline and high unemployment, Raskin learned from one of his sources that President Harry S. Truman intended to ask Congress for funds to help local and state governments run their emergency work-relief programs. Ignoring Krock's uncooperative bureau, Raskin did his own research and filed a front-page story outlining Truman's plans. Outraged by Raskin's scoop, Krock's assistant, Luther Huston, ordered bureau reporters to prove that the story was untrue and fired off an angry letter to the *Times* management in New York. According to Talese's account of the incident, Huston's letter arrived in New York on the same day Truman sent his work-relief message to the Capitol, thus vindicating Raskin.

Many of Raskin's analytical articles from the 1950's and the early 1960's attracted national attention. One of his most widely praised pieces was a four-part series on the status of blacks in the North, which the New York *Times* published in April 1956. In that series he wrote that despite the headway made during the war and the postwar economic boom, "Negroes keep bumping against 'invisible' promotion ceilings in most fields and against walls of almost total exclusion in some." Nevertheless, Raskin concluded that there were "solid reasons for believing that a durable change [was] under way," among them, fair employment laws, federally financed job training programs, and unification in the labor movement.

Raskin's four-part series on the chronically unemployed, published in the New York *Times* in April 1961 and similarly acclaimed by his peers, gauged the impact of technological advancements on the American worker. The problem, as Raskin saw it, was that of striking a balance between economic rejuvenation and full employment so that men did not become "permanent sacrifices on the altar of industrial efficiency." He perceptively scrutinized the problems bedeviling the White House, industrialists, and union leaders, but it was his sensitive presentation of the plight of the long-term jobless that really distinguished the series.

Unlike many economic analysts, Raskin has an unerring feel for the graphic narrative details that lend human interest to a news story. For instance, his article of April 8, 1961 contains the following evocative description: "Outside a weather-battered tenement on the edge of the mill district, a mangy dog had jumped into an overflowing garbage pail and was gorging himself on refuse. In a first-floor kitchen, woolen socks were drying on the open door of a gas stove. . . . Farther back were the squeals of six children of stepladder ages and the mewling of two kittens being mauled." Some of Raskin's best pieces have been anthologized in *Labor in a Changing America* (Basic Books, 1966) and *American Labor Since the New Deal* (Quadrangle, 1971).

As he doggedly tracked down leads in corporate boardrooms and union local backrooms, Raskin attracted a number of powerful enemies, including James R. ("Jimmy") Hoffa, the president of the International Brotherhood of Teamsters, and Michael J. ("Mike") Quill, the international president of the Transport Workers Union (TWU), who had been verbally tangling with the journalist ever since 1953, when the New York *Times* had prematurely, but correctly reported the TWU's willingness to settle a transit strike on the city's terms. In December 1957 Quill strongly objected to Raskin's analysis of his "crisis atmosphere" bargaining tactics during the New York City transit workers' contract dispute. At one union meeting he tore up one of Raskin's articles and recommended that a Congressional committee investigate the reporter to "find out how many checks [he] gets under the table as well as over the table." Unruffled by the accusation, which was, in his words, "utterly without foundation," Raskin issued a public statement saying he would "cooperate fully" in any inquiry into his "sources of income."

In 1961 Raskin was elevated to the editorial board of the New York *Times*. Although technically separated from the news staff, he continued to cover the labor beat and in 1963 tackled what was perhaps the most difficult assignment of his career: an analysis of the printers' strike that shut down all the daily newspapers in the New York metropolitan area for 114 days. Published on April 1, 1963, the 15,000-word article was a brilliant piece of informed, objective reportage. Displaying a firm grasp of the complex issues and personalities involved in the strike, Raskin gave a step-by-step account of the behind-the-scenes negotiations and unhesitatingly condemned the obstinacy and shortsightedness of the participants on both sides of the dispute.

Although some of Raskin's superiors, among them Amory H. Bradford, the New York *Times*'s general manager and chief spokesman during the bargaining, found the article disturbing, fellow newspapermen, almost to a man, praised Raskin's piece as an example of journalism at its best. To James A. Wechsler of the New York *Post* it seemed easily "the most unconventional and distinguished journalistic endeavor of recent (or ancient) years," one notable for its objectivity, perceptiveness, and "extraordinary honesty." In his column of May 7, 1964 he took the New York *Times* to task for not including Raskin's name in its annual list of submissions for the Pulitzer Prize. The wrap-up article eventually won for Raskin a George Polk Memorial Award, a Page One Award from the New York Newspaper Guild, a Silurian Society Award, and a Heywood Broun Memorial Award.

Appointed assistant editor of the New York *Times* editorial page in October 1964, Raskin, in addition to his routine editorial work, occasionally filled in for John Oakes, the editorial page editor. On one of those occasions, in November 1966, he okayed an emotional lead editorial commenting on the absurdity of a Christmas truce in Vietnam that halted the killing for just a few hours. When Arthur Ochs ("Punch") Sulzberger, the publisher of the New York *Times*, read the editorial in an early edition, he ordered it killed. Instead, Oakes rewrote the editorial, and a toned-down version ran in subsequent editions.

Over the years Raskin contributed a number of articles to the New York *Times Magazine*, *Commentary*, the *Saturday Review*, the *Atlantic*, the *Reporter*, the *Harvard Business Review*, and other periodicals. Among his subjects were the growth of organized labor as big business, the implications of civil service strikes, and the "mixed and mixed-up" American economy. In addition, he profiled such prominent labor figures as John L. Lewis, George Meany, Walter Reuther, James R. Hoffa, and W. Willard Wirz. His only book to date, *David Dubinsky: A Life With Labor*, was published by Simon & Schuster in 1977.

When Raskin reached the mandatory retirement age for New York *Times* executives in April 1976, he resumed his career as a full-time correspondent, and, for the next year, reported on the interrelationships among labor, economics, and government on a daily basis. A former lecturer in labor history and labor law at Columbia University's School of Social Work, he returned to Columbia as an adjunct professor at the Graduate School of Business. In December 1977 Raskin left the New York *Times* to accept the editorship of the *Journal of International Labor Affairs*, a new quarterly of the United States Department of Labor, but budget difficulties blocked publication of the magazine after copy had been assembled for the first issue. He had earlier told *Current Biography:* "I leave daily journalism convinced that there is no more satisfying field nor any more useful, but I would be remiss if I did not note that there is also none in which it is more essential that responsibility be an obsessive concern in exercise of the special protections accorded by the First Amendment." In March 1978 he became associate director of the National News Council, an independent, nonprofit agency that examines complaints of inaccuracy or unfairness in the media and also works to uphold the First Amendment by protecting the press from unjust attack.

A gray-haired man with brown eyes, A. H. Raskin weighs 165 pounds and stands five feet eleven inches tall. His favorite recreation is bicycle riding. Raskin and his wife, the former Rose Samrock, an artist, have lived in New York City ever since their marriage on September 27, 1933, with the exception of their four years in Washington during World War II. They have two children, Jane and Donald. Raskin is a member of the Society of the Silurians, the New York Newspaper Guild, the International Press Institute, and the American Academy of Political and Social Science. He is a trustee of the Lowell Mellet Fund for a Free and Responsible Press, a director of the James Gordon Bennett Foundation, and a board member of the Jewish Family Services of New York, the Legal Aid Society of New York, and the Industrial Relations Research Association.

References: Newsweek 51:76+ Ja 13 '58 por; N Y Times p34 D 1 '77 por; Who's Who in America, 1976-77

Rockefeller, John D(avison) 4th

June 18, 1937- Governor of West Virginia. Address: b. Office of the Governor, State Capital, Charleston, W. Va. 25305

A scion of one of America's most powerful families, John D. Rockefeller 4th, better known as Jay, went to West Virginia as an anti-poverty social worker in 1964 and was elected Governor of the "Mountain State" twelve years later, after having served in the state legislature and as Secretary of State. Rockefeller, a Democrat in a family prominent for its Republicanism, is expected by many to go on to bid for national office. But whatever his future, he is in the meantime devoting his energy—and the magnetism of his name in the investment world—to improving the economic condition of his adopted state, the only state that lies entirely within Appalachia. "The psychology in West Virginia today is not that we are poor but that we have unlimited opportunities . . . ," he has said. "We are blessed with 17,000 square miles of coal and a growing coal industry at a time

John D. Rockefeller 4th

when suddenly coal is again critical to the energy of the nation." An environmental protectionist, he cautions West Virginians at the same time to "be certain not to sacrifice the rugged beauty which surrounds us, this gift from God."

John Davison Rockefeller 4th is the great-grandson of John D. Rockefeller Sr., the oil tycoon who founded the Standard Oil Company and became the wealthiest man of his time. John D. Sr. was joined in his business and philanthropic work by John D. Jr., among whose children were Nelson A., the former Governor of New York and Vice-President of the United States, Winthrop, the late Governor of Arkansas, David, the chairman of the Chase Manhattan Bank, and John D. 3d, the former chairman of the board of trustees of the Rockefeller Foundation and director of Rockefeller Center Inc. The Governor of West Virginia was born in New York City on June 18, 1937, the only son among the four children of John D. Rockefeller 3d and Blanchette (Hooker) Rockefeller. His sisters are Sandra, Hope, and Alida.

At birth Jay Rockefeller was given the name John, without the middle initial. "As a boy," he has recounted, "I was told I should make up my own mind whether I wanted to carry on the full name, which I think stands for public service, a sense of responsibility, and a high standard of demand on oneself. When I was twenty-one I wrote a letter to my father saying I wanted the name and the responsibility."

Among Rockefeller's favorite recreations as a schoolboy were baseball, basketball, and watching Abbott and Costello movies. He was a shy, private child, according to boyhood friends, and he himself says that he was never without a sense that his "was not a typical youth." To teach him the value of money, his father gave him a weekly allowance of fifteen cents, out of which he was to allocate a nickel each for spending, saving, and charity.

In 1954 Rockefeller graduated from Phillips Exeter Academy in Exeter, New Hampshire and entered Harvard University. "Uninspired" at Harvard, in 1957 he went to Japan, which he felt offered him "the chance to have an extraordinary experience, regardless of who I was." During three years as a student of Japanese language and culture at International Christian University in the Tokyo suburb of Osawa, he restricted his budget to fifty dollars a month in order to share as fully as possible in the austere life of his Japanese fellow students.

Back in the United States, Rockefeller in 1961 took his B.A. degree at Harvard and enrolled in the Yale University Institute of Far Eastern Languages, where he specialized in Chinese studies because he "wanted to be our first Ambassador to China." Soon after he arrived at Yale he was appointed to the National Advisory Council of the Peace Corps, whose director, Sargent Shriver, had been impressed with reports Rockefeller had written from Japan for *Life* magazine and the New York *Times*. In 1962 he joined the Peace Corps as a special assistant to Shriver and soon afterward moved to the Department of State to become an assistant to the Assistant Secretary for Far Eastern Affairs.

Rockefeller left the Department of State, he later explained, because he "wasn't given much to do" and he realized he "knew nothing about the American people" and "had never made an input into this country." He might have added a more important reason —his views on China and the Vietnam war were dovish in the extreme and therefore anathema to Secretary of State Dean Rusk. Meanwhile, as the godfather of the child of a friend from the Peace Corps who had married a West Virginian, he had become well enough acquainted with West Virginia to think of it as the place he might want to make his "input." Accordingly, he joined Action for Appalachian Youth, a federally financed program under the aegis of VISTA (Volunteers in the Service of America), and went to Emmons, West Virginia in 1964.

The West Virginia in which Rockefeller took up residence was a state of natural beauty marred by pockets of grinding poverty. In Emmons, a backwoods town fifteen miles south of Charleston in the foothills of the Appalachians, almost all of the sixty families were on welfare. The land was too hilly for farming, and the few coal mines in the area had either shut down or reduced their crews

Many of the people were illiterate. "Even worse than the physical conditions was the attitude of the people," Rockefeller later observed. "They had adopted the philosophy of failure."

Wearing clothes bought in a surplus store, and driving a battered Land Rover, Rockefeller jolted over Emmons' unpaved roads, meeting the mountain folk. "The people thoght I was either a Republican organizer, a federal agent looking for moonshine stills, or a state official checking on welfare recipients," he later recalled. The hill people had been so exploited and were so suspicious of carpetbagging do-gooders, that it took him six months just to win their trust. His efforts to inspire united self-help in Emmons brought only modest results—a community association, a temporary meeting hall, the beginnings of a library, and school bus service to Charleston for the first time—but the impact of the experience on Rockefeller himself was "tremendous," as his friend Charles Peters, the editor of *Washington Monthly*, has observed: "It took this raw material [Rockefeller] and made it committed." Rockefeller's wife Sharon, the daughter of Senator Charles Percy, Republican of Illinois, told Louise Sweeney of the *Christian Science Monitor* (July 27, 1977) that her husband had come to see that "you can't meet everyone's needs by focusing on individual services, that government can do it better."

Rockefeller was a registered Republican until 1966, when he switched his party allegiance, declaring, "Through association, experience, inclination, philosophy, and now by choice, I'm a Democrat." He filed to run for the House of Delegates, the lower house of the West Virginia state legislature, explaining, "I now realize that the job of helping the poor to help themselves cannot be done in just one community. . . . You have got to make changes at the top."

With his campaign receiving unusual national press coverage (some of which unduly stressed the memory of John F. Kennedy, with his money, taking the 1960 West Virginia Democratic Presidential primary from Hubert H. Humphrey), Rockefeller breezed to victory in the Democratic primary, receiving a record 23,000 votes, 7,000 more than his closest rival, and in the general election of November 1966 he won election from Kanawha County by a comfortable margin. In the legislature he fought for tax and election reform and supported a successful strip-mining control bill.

Running for the nomination for West Virginia Secretary of State on a "clean elections" platform in 1968, Rockefeller defeated two other candidates in the Democratic primary by a combined margin of 3-1. During the general election campaign, his appearances on the stump often drew larger crowds than those of the candidates for governor, and his growing national prominence was such that he was invited to make the primary nominating speech for Hubert H. Humphrey at the Democratic National Convention. He declined.

A scandal involving former Governor W. W. Barron and five other Democrats contributed to a sweep of the Republican ticket headed by gubernatorial candidate Arch Moore Jr., but Rockefeller came through untouched, winning over John Calebs, 332,835 votes to 214,559, to become Secretary of State. The position of Secretary of State in West Virginia is largely ceremonial, with the only real power being the supervision of elections, but for Rockefeller it served as the springboard for becoming the leader of the Democratic party in West Virginia. As such, in 1970 he successfully backed candidates who opposed what he called "reactionary, unresponsive elements" in the State Senate—meaning those Senators who had opposed Rockefeller's election-reform efforts. He also used his influence as state Democratic leader to fight what he described as the "spreading cancer" of strip mining, surface mining that scars the landscape and causes erosion. Rockefeller contended that such mining, about 18 percent of that done in the state, was not only ecologically but economically bad, because it competed with the deep mines. In 1971 the legislature voted a two-year prohibition on strip mining in counties where it was not already in practice.

Along with the "carpetbag" charge, strip mining became a crucial issue in the 1972 gubernatorial election in which Rockefeller challenged incumbent Arch Moore, whom the mining interests backed. Rockefeller tried to focus on other issues, such as roads and jobs, but the mining issue remained dominant with the public, which had been led to believe that a vote against strip mining meant a vote against mining in general and therefore against jobs. Moore took the election by 73,000 votes.

"West Virginians just felt like they had to kick me once before they would accept me. They had to see if, rejected, I would stay," Rockefeller commented after his defeat. After vowing to try for the governorship again in four years, he accepted the position of president of West Virginia Wesleyan College in Buckhannon, West Virginia when it was offered to him in 1973. During his two-year presidency of Wesleyan he donated $250,000 to the college for the building of a physical education center, which bears his name.

In 1976, in his second gubernatorial bid, Rockefeller swamped his opponents in the primary, winning almost 50 percent of the vote in a field of eight candidates, and went on to challenge former Governor Cecil Underwood in a campaign that contained little of the acrimony of four years before. (Arch Moore was prohibited by law from running for a third term.) Apparently persuaded that advances in technology made possible the reclamation of strip-mined land, Rockefeller no longer opposed strip mining, and the mining lobby supported him. He also backed off from his advocacy of gun control laws, abortion on demand, and the right of public employees to bargain collectively, and he stressed road and highway improvement, jobs, and West Virginia's need for a sound financial manager in the State House. The carpetbagger charge was put to rest when he revealed that he had rejected an offer from his uncle Nelson, then Governor of New York, to fill out the term of New York Senator Robert Kennedy following Kennedy's death in 1968. At the polls in November 1976 Rockefeller easily defeated Underwood, 489,949 votes to 251,754.

In his inaugural address on January 17, 1977 Governor Rockefeller said: "Today we leave behind the defeatism of the past. . . . Reach out, West Virginia, for your fair share of the American dream. I ask you to take some risks with me. . . . There is no magic wand to instantly transform long-neglected roads into superhighways or West Virginia into Camelot. My name is Rockefeller, but that will not pay your bills." The Governor's popularity with the electorate remained high in the months following his inauguration, and his handling of the emergency created by devastating floods in southern West Virginia in April 1977 reinforced that popularity. A poll by the Charleston (West Virginia) *Gazette* released a week after the floods showed a 68 percent approval of his job performance.

Governor Rockefeller's first year in office coincided with President Jimmy Carter's promotion of his federal energy program, with its emphasis on coal as an alternative fuel to oil. The hoped-for passage of the federal energy legislation buoyed up the spirits of West Virginians, so that the Governor could conclude, on the basis of polls taken for him, that "West Virginians feel more confident about the state's future than they do about the nation's—and it's usually just the opposite." In May 1978 Carter appointed Rockefeller chairman of his special commission to study the problems of the coal industry.

Governor Rockefeller is a lanky man, six feet six and a half inches tall, with brown hair, blue-gray eyes, an aquiline nose and a voice that has been described as ranging from "drawl-soft West Virginian" to "Eastern establishment." He dresses conservatively, in pin-stripe suits and the like, and his manner has been characterized as "easy," "loose," and "charming." In her *Christian Science Monitor* article Louise Sweeney described him among reporters at a press breakfast as "bantering but enormously informed and quotable." He told Miss Sweeney that he did not share the disdain toward the family wealth expressed by some of his cousins: "I think it's primarily a blessing. Obviously it's a responsibility. . . . But it's been a great advantage to me. . . . I'm very happy about it." His net worth has been estimated at $19,700,000.

John D. Rockefeller 4th and Sharon Lee Percy were married on April 1, 1967. They have three children, Jamie, Valerie, and Charles. Mrs. Rockefeller says of her husband: "He's intelligent, extremely fair, and balanced, never angry. And he's wise, and always has been; he has an ageless quality." The Governor's recreations and hobbies include listening to baroque music, collecting oriental art, playing racketball, tennis, and basketball, and going on hikes. A friend has observed, "He has a terrific sense of humor about the business of being a Rockefeller. It's something he can joke about."

References: Christian Sci Mon p6 Jl 27 '77 por; Life 60:41+ Ap 1 '66 pors; New Repub 159:16+ D 7 '68; N Y Times Mag p30+ O 4 '70 por; Parade p8+ Jl 19 '70 pors; Penthouse 8:83+ N '76; Sat Rev 55:27+ Ag 26 '72 pors; Collier, Peter, and Horowitz, David. The Rockefellers: An American Dynasty (1977); Who's Who in America, 1977-78

Rohatyn, Felix G(eorge) (rō'ə-tən)

May 29, 1928- Financier. Address: b. Lazard Frères & Co., 1 Rockefeller Plaza, New York City, N.Y. 10020; h. 1125 Park Ave., New York City, N.Y. 10021

The man whose name has been most closely associated with the rescue of New York City from bankruptcy during the fiscally troubled period that began in the mid-1970's is Felix G. Rohatyn, the so-called "wizard" of Lazard Frères & Company, one of New York's most venerable and prosperous investment banking firms. Serving by the appointment of Governor Hugh L. Carey as the unsalaried chairman of the Municipal Assistance Corporation and a member of the Emergency Assistance Control Board, he has struggled through a crisis intensified by shifting monetary figures and uncertainties of federal government cooperation to fulfill a three-year plan for paying off the city's debts and imposing on it a balanced budget. Rohatyn had acquired his reputation as a public-spirited financier and a persistent, cool-headed negotiator when he headed the New York Stock Exchange's Crisis Committee during Wall Street's ordeals of 1970-71.

Felix G. Rohatyn

Felix George Rohatyn was born in Vienna, Austria on May 29, 1928, the only son of Alexander Rohatyn, a Polish Jew, and Edith (Knoll) Rohatyn, a native of Austria. The name Rohatyn, which also belongs to a small Polish town, is of Tartar origin. A prosperous investor and speculator, his grandfather was a member of the Vienna Stock Exchange and head of the bank Rohatyn & Company. He also had business interests in breweries in Austria, Romania, and Yugoslavia, which Alexander Rohatyn managed until 1934, when the growing menace of Nazism made him decide to take his family to France. In Orlèans he also worked as managing director of a brewery. For about six months his son had the job of cleaning and filling barrels with beer.

Rohatyn's parents were divorced in the late 1930's, and his mother remarried. In 1942, during the German occupation of France, Felix fled with his mother and stepfather, Henry Plessner, to the United States by way of Spain, Casablanca, and Rio de Janeiro. In an interview with Peter Hellman for an article in the New York *Times Magazine* (March 21, 1976), Rohatyn recalled his sudden departure from France: "I spent our last night in a hotel room stuffing gold coins into toothpaste tubes. We had been well off, but that was all we got out. Ever since, I've had the feeling that the only permanent wealth is what you carry around in your head."

In high school in Manhattan, the McBurney School, Rohatyn improved his English to such a degree that he eventually lost all trace of a foreign accent. When he graduated in 1944, he enrolled in Middlebury College, which he had chosen partly because its Vermont location would give him opportunities to ski. He was accepted, along with a black student, into a non-Jewish fraternity, Alpha Sigma Psi, which was promptly expelled by the national society, but kept its membership intact in a local organization. As a student majoring in physics, he became greatly influenced in his way of thinking by Professor Benjamin Wissler, head of the physics department, who had, as Rohatyn once put it, "a coldly brutally logical mind." Reflecting on his college experiences, he mentioned two factors that helped him most in his work in investment banking, as quoted in *Business Week* (March 10, 1973): "First, I never took a course in economics. Second, there was an extremely rigorous intellectual process demanded of you."

Equipped with those two advantages, as well as his B.S. degree, Rohatyn took a summer job in New York in 1948 as a trainee in Lazard Frères & Company. Lazard's senior partner, André Meyer, a friend of Rohatyn's stepfather, offered the young man a full-time position with the firm in Europe. He worked in England, France, and Switzerland for a year or so before serving with the United States Army from 1951 to 1953, during the war in Korea. Later, in Lazard's Paris office, he specialized in foreign exchange, an area to which he continued to be assigned after he returned to New York in 1955. The following year at his request he was transferred to a service of Lazard that appealed to him much more, corporate finance and restructuring. As the protégé of Meyer himself, he became so accomplished in the skills and techniques of arranging deals and mergers that Meyer once said, as reported in *Fortune* (November 1977), "He is better than the teacher." Rohatyn was made a general partner in Lazard Frères in 1961.

Another executive who has been immensely important in Rohatyn's career is Harold S. Geneen, head of International Telephone and Telegraph, which he developed into a diversified multinational conglomerate. Rohatyn sold Avis Corporation, then owned by Lazard, to ITT in 1965 and became a director of ITT in late 1967. He also serves on the boards of Engelhard Minerals and Chemical Corporation, Pfizer, Howmet Corporation, Owens-Illinois, and other corporations. His ability to make use of the knowledge gained through his directorships, together with his adroitness as a negotiator, accounts for much of his success in the mergers and acquisitions he has engineered for Lazard.

Among the major ITT acquisitions that Rohatyn masterminded was the 1970-71 takeover of the Hartford Fire Insurance Company, a massive and extraordinarily complex deal that involved the sale of a block of Hartford stock to Mediobanca, a Milan bank. The acquisition was compared to a Chinese puzzle in *Fortune* magazine, which also reported that the Securities and Exchange Commission "spent years .assembling the pieces," in its investigation of its legitimacy. During the early 1970's, moreover, Rohatyn helped ITT over a series of antitrust suits brought by the federal government, with the result that ITT obtained a favorable out-of-court settlement. Other mergers that he brought off included Kinney and Warner Brothers, and Loews Theatres and Lorillard Corporation. He was unsuccessful in realizing his highly complicated 1973 proposals for merging the faltering Lockheed Aircraft Corporation with Textron. Although he worked out a refinancing plan for Lockheed that he is said to consider his best and that he found very satisfying intellectually, Textron was apparently unconvinced.

Because of his spectacular record of solving intricate financial problems, Rohatyn was called to the rescue of Wall Street during the grim twelve-month period of 1970-71 when the financial community was close to disaster. As chairman of the Surveillance Committee of the New York Stock Exchange, which was also known as the Crisis Committee, he led a small, pivotal group of financiers in skirting a collapse by finding sources of capital, arranging mergers, and taking other emergency measures. "Everybody seemed to come to a decision that we just couldn't let a major firm go bankrupt," he said, as quoted in the New York *Times* (January 24, 1971). "We just had to make the decision that if we let one go under there would be a panic." Bernard J. Lasker, then chairman of the board of governors of the New York Stock Exchange, later recalled that over weekends he and Rohatyn together would sometimes make as many as 150 phone calls a day to keep companies from folding and to try to restore others.

Rohatyn's belief that the bankruptcy of a major company could not be risked because it might precipitate an irremediable collapse seems to have foreshadowed his conviction some five years later during the New York City financial crisis that a default by the city would have far-reaching disastrous consequences. Assailing the indifference of the Ford Administration to New York's plea for financial help, he challenged Secretary of the Treasury William E. Simon's contention that a city default would have "a tolerable and temporary" effect on the financial markets. As reported in the Washington *Post* (September 25, 1975), he warned that if federal officials were wrong in their estimate of the impact, they would "regret their decision a half hour after they let the city default." He asserted that a default could "mortally wound" New York State as well as the city and that repercussions from that double adversity could be felt both nationally and internationally.

On another occasion Rohatyn likened a default by New York City to "someone stepping into a tepid bath and slashing his wrists—you might not feel yourself dying, but that's what would happen." Beginning in May 1975 he worked doggedly as a member of an advisory panel appointed by New York Governor Hugh L. Carey to find a way for government and private financing sources to help the city stave off bankruptcy. The plan that the committee developed, not entirely without opposition from Mayor Abraham D. Beame and some other city officials, called in part for the creation of a new state agency, the Municipal Assistance Corporation, which would have the responsibility of borrowing money for the city to cover its "cash-flow" interruption so that it could pay its enormous debts.

When the New York State Legislature, on June 10, 1975, approved "Big Mac," as the agency was quickly dubbed, Rohatyn became one of the original nine voting members of the corporation, five of whom were appointed by the governor and four by the mayor. On September 11, 1975 Governor Carey chose him chairman of MAC, succeeding William M. Ellinghaus, president of the New York Telephone Company, whom Carey named to the powerful Emergency Financial Control Board, which was mandated by the state to exercise ultimate control over the city's budget. Rohatyn, who had attended many of its meetings as an observer for MAC, was himself appointed in July 1976 as one of the three businessmen on the control board, which is also made up of the governor, the mayor, and the city and state controllers.

As both chairman of MAC and a member of EFCB, therefore, Rohatyn was perhaps the principal figure in carrying through an overall three-year plan of financing a reformed budget. The attempt to raise several billion dollars to finance New York City's debt through June 1978, when the budget would be balanced, encountered considerable hindrance because of MAC's difficulty in selling its bonds, which the federal government refused to guarantee. Rohatyn handled one crucial situation after the other by appealing to the city's banks and unions, devising plans to exchange city notes for MAC bonds, and seeking out other resources.

From time to time when the financial outlook brightened, rumors circulated of Rohatyn's intention to leave MAC now that his job was completed, but he continued to stay on to face new emergencies. New York City, for example, ended a four-month threat of insolvency in March 1977 by producing a moratorium-financing plan to pay off a short-term debt of $983,000,000. The approval of the plan by the Emergency Financial Control Board led Secretary of the Treasury W. Michael Blumenthal to indicate that the federal government would extend its seasonal loan program to help the city avert bankruptcy. At that time Rohatyn was quoted as saying, "This is the last of the great financial crises" (New York *Times*, March 11, 1977), and he spoke of his possible retirement in the near future.

In January 1978, however, Rohatyn warned MAC's board of directors that a "genuine crisis" was again building up and that the city was "about to enter a storm fully as dangerous and unpredictable as any we weathered in 1975." He repeatedly expressed disappointment at the failure of the Carter Administration to understand the urgency of New York's fiscal troubles and its need for long-term federal help rather than seasonal loans. He also criticized the Democratic Administration for delay in carrying out its pledge of a takeover of welfare costs, pointing out that New York City's staggering welfare and Medicare burden necessitates cuts in municipal services that threaten to cripple the city. A federal assumption of welfare, he insisted, tied to tax reductions by state and local governments and economic development programs would be a key to urban recovery. In August 1978 President Carter signed a $1.65 billion long-term federal loan guarantee bill. Three months later an agreement was finally reached on a $2.55 billion financing plan for New York City.

Although Rohatyn has long worked and prospered within the country's conservative financial circles, he considers himself a liberal Democrat. One of his favorite proposals is for the creation of a regional financing agency for the Northeast similar to the Reconstruction Finance Corporation of the New Deal era. Discussing his idea in an address in May 1976 before the Brooklyn Chamber of Commerce and the Brooklyn Downtown Development Association, he argued that "New York City by itself is no longer a viable economic unit" and that cooperation among neighboring states is essential to the economic survival of the Northeast. Again, at a meeting in November 1976 in Saratoga Springs, New York, he outlined to the governors of seven Northeastern states his plan for an energy and economic development corporation projected to finance its undertakings through federally guaranteed taxable bonds.

During the years that Rohatyn has served as chairman of MAC, he saved a good part of his time and energy for Lazard Frères, but refused André Meyer's request that he give up his work for the city. According to Wyndham Robertson in *Fortune* (November 1977), "Rohatyn's talents have made him the most important producer in Lazard, and also the best paid. He receives 11 percent of the firm's profits"—more than Meyer and more than Michel David-Weill, who had recently been designated to succeed Meyer as head of the firm. Robertson went on to report, "Both Meyer and David-Weill say they asked Rohatyn to take over and run the New York firm, but Rohatyn has consistently disavowed any interest in the job. He explains: "A lot of it is just grind—dealing with personnel, administration, and accounting—or stroking or soothing egos, or knocking heads."

Remarking that everyone has an indulgence of his own, Rohatyn once admitted, again according to *Fortune*, "MAC is my indulgence —my *péché mignon*," which is literally translated as "cute sin." He has also explained his dedication to New York finance as a form of repaying a debt to the city. "I am rather sentimental about New York because it took me in," he told a group of students at the New School for Social Research in March 1976. ". . . It's been good to me. It's an intellectually exciting place to be." He has been a director of the New York City Heart Association, the Alvin Ailey Dance Company, and Independence House, a rehabilitation center for young people from seventeen to twenty-one who have been released from jail and need help in finding jobs. In 1976 he received the Thomas Jefferson Award of the American Institute for Public Service.

Hellman described Felix Rohatyn in the New York *Times Magazine* as "a compact man with dark wiry hair, fierce black eyebrows and light blue eyes." Public service seems so congenial to him that he was at one time mentioned as a possible mayoral candidate. Although he has never sought elective office, he supported the bid for the Democratic Presidential nomination of Senator Edmund S. Muskie in 1972 and Senator Henry M. Jackson in 1976. He also served as cochairman of the Friends of Governor Carey, formed to raise money to pay off Carey's 1974 campaign debt. On June 9, 1956 Rohatyn married Jeannette Streit, whose father was a founder of the English Speaking Union. They have three teen-aged sons, Pierre, Michael, and Nicolas, who live with their mother, from whom Rohatyn is separated. He shares most of his recreational time with his sons—skiing, playing tennis, cheering for the Rangers at hockey games, and going to the movies.

References: Bsns W p132+ Mr 10 '73 por; Fortune 96:117+ N '77 por; N Y Post p20 S '75 por; N Y Times III p1+ Ja 24 '71 por, p21 Mr 8 '72 por, III p5 Je 23 '74 por, p18 Jl 22 '75, p39 Mr 11 '76 por; N Y Times Mag p19+ Mr 21 '76 por; Village Voice p17+ Ag 2 '76 por

---

Ronstadt, Linda

July 30, 1946- Singer; recording artist.
Address: b. Elektra/Asylum/Nonesuch Records, 665 5th Ave., New York City, N.Y. 10017

The reigning torch singer of country rock music is Linda Ronstadt, a so-called "Los

Ronstadt, Linda

Angeles eclectic" who prefers to think of herself not as a country singer ("because I don't consider myself that pure") but rather as "a pop singer with country roots and rock 'n' roll roots." The waifishly photogenic Miss Ronstadt began her career as lead singer of the soft folk rock group the Stone Poneys, which surfaced with the modest hit "Different Drum" in 1967. As a solo singer—backed early on by the "laid-back" California cowboy sound of the group that later grew into the Eagles—she was sustained by a strong cult following for several years, until she entered the mainstream of pop stardom with "You're No Good" and "When Will I Be Loved?," hit singles drawn from *Heart Like a Wheel,* the first of her five consecutive platinum (million-selling) albums. In 1977 Miss Ronstadt received the Grammy Award, her second, for "best pop vocal performer, female," for her recording of "Hasten Down the Wind."

Miss Ronstadt, whose powerful and vibrant soprano voice, though untrained, has acquired ever greater finesse, pliability, and richness over the years, does little writing of her own material but has a rare talent for bringing to life the lyrics of others, especially heartache ballads and smoky blues. Her repertoire ranges from driving oldies like "Heat Wave" and "That'll Be the Day" to J. D. Souther's mellow "Faithless Love," Karla Bonoff's introspective "Lose Again," the Celtic-Southern ballads of Anna McGarrigle, and Lowell George's "Willin.' "

Linda Ronstadt, who is of upper-class Mexican and German descent, was born on July 30, 1946 in Tucson, Arizona, where her father Gilbert Ronstadt, runs a large hardware store. Her maternal grandfather was Lloyd Copeman, the inventor of an electric stove and of a prototype of the microwave oven. She was raised in a musical household, where the mother, known as "La" Ronstadt, played the ukelele and the father sang Mexican songs, accompanying himself on the guitar. (Mr. Ronstadt is the coauthor, with Linda and her friend bass player Kenny Edwards, of "Lo Siento, Mi Vida" on the album *Hasten Down the Wind.*)

From early childhood Linda Ronstadt was exposed to her father's collection of recordings by the Mexican *rancheros* singer Lola Beltrán, her older sister Suzie's Hank Williams collection, and the country and western, top 40, blues, and gospel music broadcast by KFRF, a Mexican radio station just across the border from Del Rio, Texas. Her first experience performing in public was with a local folk group formed by Suzie (who is now a housewife) and Linda's other older sibling, Pete (a policeman). Linda's younger brother, Mike, now in his early twenties, also aspires to a singing career.

Linda recalls how she rebelled against the discipline at St. Peter and Paul Parochial School in Tucson: "The nuns hated me. They hated the way I talked about boys. I was too giggly and wore too much makeup and dressed too sexy." Her rebelliousness continued through Catalina High School and into a few months at the University of Arizona. In 1964, at eighteen, she dropped out of school and moved to Los Angeles at the urging of Bob Kimmel, a guitar player whom she had met in Tucson and who was already living in Los Angeles.

In Los Angeles, according to Ben Fong-Torres in *Rolling Stone* (March 27, 1975), Linda "sought a career in music and became the object of attention—the kind that led to too many wrong relationships, too many years of hating her own records and concerts, too many sad songs to sing." Kimmel (rhythm guitar) and Ronstadt hooked up with Kenny Edwards (lead guitar) to form Linda and the Stone Poneys, a group that underwent many additions and subtractions of personnel during its short history. In her *Rock Encyclopedia* (1969) Lillian Roxon described the Stone Poneys as "playing the kind of melodic folk pop that only started getting underway . . . when the early Beatles hard rock (and its imitators) had given way to the folky sound of the *[Lovin']* Spoonful and the Mamas and the Papas and, as a matter of fact, the folky sound of [the] middle and late Beatles."

The earliest recording by Linda and the Stone Poneys was the Capitol single "Some of Shelley's Blues"/"Hobo (Morning Glory)" released in January 1965, and their first album was *We Five Sounds,* issued by Capitol in January 1967. Mike Nesmith's "Different Drum," one of the cuts on their second album, *Ever-*

green (Capitol, 1967), became their first single to reach the charts. Before it hit, Capitol Records sent the group on a promotional tour. "We did things like open for Butterfield at the Cafe au Go Go *[in New York]*—which was worse than *[when we had opened for]* Oscar Brown *[at the Troubadour in Los Angeles]*," Miss Ronstadt recalled in the interview with Ben Fong-Torres for *Rolling Stone*. "Here we were rejected by the hippest element in New York as lame. We broke up right after that. We couldn't bear to look at each other."

Edwards left immediately, but Kimmel and Ronstadt stayed together long enough to hire some help and go on tour as a second act with the Doors. In the last Capitol album under the Stone Poney name, *Linda Ronstadt, Stone Poneys, and Friends, Volume 3* (1968), session musicians made up the entire backup for Miss Ronstadt. Later backup musicians included Glen Frey and Don Henley, who went on to form the Eagles, and Andrew Gold, who is now a solo star.

"Her recordings with the Stone Poneys attest to both an abundance of ability and an utter lack of finesse," Janet Maslin wrote in *New Times* (February 7, 1975). "Though Ronstadt, as an early synthesizer of country rock, weighed in as an important footnote in rock history, she had yet to purge her voice of nasality or her style of perfunctoriness. Her material, like her arrangements, seemed selected at random."

In Janet Maslin's opinion, similar problems afflicted Miss Ronstadt's subsequent solo albums on the Capitol label: "Though *Hand Sown . . . Home Grown* featured Linda at her liveliest (on 'The Only Mama That'll Walk the Line' she displayed a guttural growl that has since vanished from her repertoire), its arrangements of country style tunes tended toward trendy but inappropriate psychedelia. (Ronstadt so disliked the album's jangly, electronic versions of 'Silver Threads and Golden Needles' that she later recorded a far more sedate version). Then came *Silk Purse* (with Linda posed in a pigpen—and *still* managing to look like cheesecake—for the cover shot), an album that overcompensated for the ebullient raggedness of its predecessor." Miss Ronstadt herself has said of *Silk Purse:* "I hate that album. . . . I was working with Nashville musicians and . . . I couldn't communicate it *[the California style]* to them." The one song she liked on the album was Gary White's "Long, Long Time," which became a moderate hit as a single.

Linda Ronstadt, the singer's third solo album, sustained the pensive mood of "Long, Long Time" but not always with perfect credibility. Except in her gentle rendition of Eric Anderson's "Faithful," as several critics pointed out, she often seemed "outside" the sensibility of the tender songs she was singing. "Blessed with all the subtlety of a whizzing cannonball," Janet Maslin observed, "Ronstadt could only sugar-coat highly verbal, relatively abstract songs like Jackson Browne's 'Rock Me on the Water' or Liv Taylor's 'In My Reply.' "

Miss Ronstadt's early years as a soloist, the late 1960's and early 1970's, were her "bleak years," as she calls them. "Once they *[the record company executives]* finally got me solo they had me on the road forever. I opened for people like Alice Cooper and the Mothers of Invention. I made a lot of bad records, did bad shows, and got scared really badly. My confidence was shredded, everything went wrong, but I stayed on the road. I was in a coma for about eight years." During one particularly hectic year, 1972, when she toured with Neil Young and had to sing engagement after engagement before Young fanatics impatient for their idol to appear, she says she resorted to cocaine and amphetamines to keep herself going. She now prefers to keep herself toned up by regular jogging.

Exacerbating Miss Ronstadt's personal identity crises and professional insecurity during her "bleak years" was her reliance on boyfriends as her producers and managers, including J.D. Souther, whom she continues to admire as a musician and as a songwriter. It was not until she moved from Capitol to Asylum Records and acquired Peter Asher as her producer and manager that she really found herself. The move to Asylum and the beginning of her full association with Asher did not occur at the same time. Asher began to work with her as a collaborator in the production of her first LP for Asylum, the album *Don't Cry Now*—which included her rendition of the Eagles' "Desperado," perhaps one of her finest recordings up to that time—released in 1973. He became her sole producer and manager with *Heart Like a Wheel* (1974), her last commitment under her Capitol contract.

Heart Like a Wheel was the first of Miss Ronstadt's albums to sell more than a million copies, or, in the jargon of the trade, to "go platinum," and two of its cuts, "You're No Good" and "When Will I Be Loved?," became top singles. Contributing to the success of *Heart Like a Wheel* were backup vocals by Miss Ronstadt's friend Maria Muldaur and arrangements and guitar playing by Andrew Gold. "Ronstadt's singing remains top-notch on the album," Janet Maslin observed, "but she no longer carries the full burden of holding the listener's attention; Asher uses strings, singers, and the usual backup artillery more to provide a setting for her voice than to amplify it. . . . She is working as part of an ensemble now, for the first time in her career. . . . Though the success of *Heart Like a Wheel* is not entirely hers, it is a jubilant success . . . and . . . promises a bright and expansive future."

Prisoner of Disguise (Asylum, 1975) also sold more than a million units—as did *Linda Ronstadt's Greatest Hits* (Asylum, 1976)—but it was widely criticized as a "remake" of *Heart Like a Wheel.* Reviewing her fourth straight platinum LP, *Hasten Down the Wind* (Asylum, 1976), in the Washington *Post,* (September 1, 1976), Larry Rohter wrote: "In view of the response to . . . *Prisoner in Disguise,* it's a move that comes in the nick of time. When Ronstadt repeated the formula that worked so well for her on *Heart Like a Wheel,* mixing ballads by J. D. Souther and James Taylor with revamped versions of old rockabilly and country tunes, a lot of people thought they had her pegged. This time out, she has added new ingredients to the mix." Among the cuts were the bittersweet title song by Warren Zevon; an updated version of Buddy Holly's rollicking rock classic "That'll be the Day," which was already out as a hit single; two reggae, or Jamaican folk rock, songs; and several songs by Karla Bonoff, including "Someone to Lay Down Beside Me," with harmony by Miss Bonoff and Wendy Waldman. Besides "Lo Siento, Mi Vida," Miss Ronstadt herself wrote the mournful ballad "Try Me Again," in collaboration with guitarist Albert Gold.

Simple Dreams, Miss Ronstadt's twelfth LP and fifth platinum album, was released by Asylum in October 1977. Besides the haunting title song by J. D. Souther, it included Linda's version of the old Roy Orbison tune "Blue Bayou," Eric Kaz's complex, morose "Sorrow Lives Here," the Rolling Stones' salty rocker "Tumbling Dice," Warren Zevon's "Poor, Poor, Pitiful Me," and "I Never Will Marry," sung in duet with Dolly Parton, a singer long admired by Miss Ronstadt because "she uses her sexuality in a non-threatening way." Noting Miss Ronstadt's frequent substitution of a female presence in lyrics originally intended for males, Peter Herbst in *Rolling Stone* (October 20, 1977) called the "sub-theme" of the album "a joyous 'anything you can do' statement. . . . What she's telling us, I think, is that she can live on the edge with the best of them." Reviewing the album in the Toronto *Globe and Mail* (October 12, 1977), Paul McGrath observed: "It's difficult to hear in her new recordings the same primitive yelper I used to know when she played with the Stone Poneys. . . . Her angelic voice. . . , even with the hillbilly filtered out, is as charming as could be." Her most recent album is *Living in the U.S.A.,* released in the fall of 1978.

Miss Ronstadt still tours for a good portion of each year, but the tours, under Peter Asher's management, are better organized and less hectic than they once were. The band that she led on her tour in the autumn of 1977 included her old Stone Poney sidekick Kenny Edwards on bass, Waddy Wachtel on lead guitar, Dan Dugmore on steel-pedal guitar, and Don Grolnick on piano. Reviewing a performance by Miss Ronstadt in the Universal Amphitheatre in Los Angeles in September 1977, Mikal Gilmore wrote in *Rolling Stone* (November 17, 1977): "Linda Ronstadt onstage in a Cub Scout outfit . . . has got to be the epitome of coyness. But that coyness was underscored . . . by a stark vulnerability. . . . Her persona [is] the central prop: a wary, repeatedly shattered heart, but ultimately a heart that survives."

After witnessing a performance by Miss Ronstadt at Radio City Music Hall in New York City the following month, Robert Palmer of the New York *Times* (October 31, 1977) observed that "of all the singers who have been classified against their will as Los Angeles eclectics, she has the surest grasp of her diverse materials and the strongest, most affecting voice." In his review in the same day's New York *Post* Carl Arrington wrote: "It has taken effort for her to learn how to make the most of her good looks, great voice, and natural charm. Now, as she presumably goes into her prime . . . for all her pin-up girl looks, it is her music that has made her successful. She has expanded her range of interpretive styles to include everything from . . . Neil Young's 'Love is a Rose' to her cover of the Elvis hit 'Love Me Tender'. . . . Ronstadt is still a nightingale whose songs of romance seem to tumble out of the pages of *True Confession* magazine. Broken dreams and anguished love are still her bread and butter, but it is nice to hear her singing them with less hurt and more heart. She sounds happier."

Linda Ronstadt's "status as the biggest single female superstar of rock" at first "puzzled and disappointed" Susan Lydon of the *Village Voice* (November 7, 1977), who found "embarrassing" the singer's "public persona as the apotheosis of the eternally heartbroken, lonely, and rejected single woman." "But in truth . . . every single woman I knew, even the most hard-core feminist, experienced those same emotional needs, and with precisely the same passionate intensity that Linda's soaring, searing soprano expressed so acutely."

Miss Ronstadt had the honor of singing at President Jimmy Carter's inaugural concert in January 1977. On the occasion of receiving her second Grammy Award, in February 1977 she said, quoting George Bernard Shaw: "Competition is for race horses, not artists. I'm not going to give it back, though." Then she added: "I think Emmylou Harris is the best." The year before she had not even bothered to attend Don Kirshner's rock music awards television show for an award as best female vocalist.

Linda Ronstadt is five feet two inches tall and tries to keep her weight around 110 pounds by attention to diet and exercise. Her big, wide eyes are brown and her hair, which usually hangs in bangs, is raven. Uncomfortable in what she calls "clothes," she usually wears jeans, track shoes, peasant blouses, and other informal attire on stage as in her private life. According to those who have interviewed her, she has a bright, winsome manner, a face that lights up easily into a grin, and, in general, the appearance of a "seventeen-year-old who has spent three days on a bus."

The singer lives in a $200,000 house she owns on the beach at Malibu, California, where she often entertains "straight" friends as well as show business colleagues. Over the years her name has been linked by gossip columnists to numerous men, including comedians Albert Brooks and Steve Martin, rock musicians Mick Jagger and Lowell George, and songwriter Tom Campbell. Governor Jerry Brown of California has been her escort on several social occasions, and she has what she describes as a "platonic" friendship with songwriter Adam Mitchell, who has recently been living in her house at Malibu. Outside of her own repertoire, Miss Ronstadt's tastes in music range widely: from old jazz standards and Nelson Riddle's masterful arrangements for Frank Sinatra to Ireland's great contemporary folk band the Chieftains. According to recent reports, Miss Ronstadt is planning a permanent move to New York City.

References: People p88+ O 24 '77 pors; Rolling Stone p34+ Mr 27 '77 pors; p14+ D 2 '76 pors; New Times 9:69+ O 14 '77; Time 109:58+ F 28 '77 pors; Washington Post mag p21+ O 9 '77 pors; Stambler, Irwin. Encyclopedia of Pop, Rock, and Soul (1974)

Saura (Atarés), Carlos (sou're)

Jan. 4, 1932- Spanish film director; writer. Address: b. c/o Elías Querejeta Producciones Cinematográficas, Maestro Lassalle 21, Madrid 16 h. María de Molina 12, Madrid 6, Spain.

Among the gifted and innovative film directors taking artistic advantage of the permissive atmosphere of post-Franco Spain is Carlos Saura, who is usually considered that country's leading filmmaker of his generation. Although internationally known to *cinéastes* because of the prizes bestowed on his films at such prestigious festivals as Berlin and Cannes, Saura remained relatively unknown in the United States until 1977, when *Cousin Angelica* and *Cria!* were commercially released to the accompaniment of critical acclaim. Before that, his films *The Hunt* and *Garden of Delights* had earned him the respect of some influential American reviewers who agreed with Roger Mortimore of *International Film Guide* (1978) that "Carlos Saura is the only Spanish director since 1939 (except Berlanga) who has remained true to himself."

As an *auteur*, Saura has been responsible for the scripts of all his films to date, and since *The Hunt* (1966), his third full-length motion picture, his producer has been Elías Querejeta. Another long and significant collaboration in Saura's career has been that with his real-life companion Geraldine Chaplin, who has performed in half of his films, the last of which, *Los ojos vendados (Blindfolded)*, represented Spain at the 1978 Cannes Film Festival.

Only a child when the forces of General Francisco Franco won the Spanish Civil War in 1939, Carlos Saura was born in Huesca, a province of the Aragón region extending to the Pyrenees, on January 4, 1932 to Antonio Saura Pacheco and Fermina Atarés Torrente, the second of their four children. The others are Pilar, Angeles, and Antonio, who is a well-known abstract expressionist painter. A native of the Murcia region on the Mediterranean, Carlos Saura's father is an attorney formerly in the civil service;

his mother is a pianist whose playing of works by the contemporary Catalonian composer Federico Mompou would surface in the film director's memory years later as the musical background for one of his films.

The Saura family moved to Madrid in 1935, the year before the outbreak of Spain's Civil War. In Enrique Brasó's *Carlos Saura* (1974), the definitive book about the director and his work, Saura is quoted as saying: "I recall my childhood very well, and in a sense I think the war must have left a greater mark on me than I realize. It is possibly the period of my life that I remember most accurately." From the very first day of the Franco uprising, Saura told Brasó, he clearly remembers an endless succession of things: wartime songs, the games children played, the bombings and blackouts, the hunger and the dead. One ineradicable memory is that of a bomb that fell on his school, and the bleeding face of a little girl struck by flying glass, an episode he later incorporated in a film.

Another Civil War recollection of Saura is of having been taught to read by a priest related to his family, who took shelter with them in order to escape from anticlerical republican extremists. He began his *bachillerato* (high school) studies with his brother at a preparatory school run by the Augustinian Friars in Getafe, south of Madrid. There he and some of his fellow students came upon wartime corpses in a basement hiding place, surrounded by weapons and ammunition—an incident that he later used in his film *The Hunt*. Saura finished his secondary education at a secular school in Madrid. Often playing hookey, he attended neighborhood movie houses and sat through one screening after another of such films as *The Prisoner of Zenda* or those starring Loretta Young and Lana Turner, and other movie queens of the period.

Because of his aptitude for mathematics, Saura began to study industrial engineering after finishing secondary school, but he soon realized that he had made a mistake in his choice of that career. Falling back on a talent that he had cultivated since he was a small boy, he earned a bohemian livelihood from 1950 to 1953 as a roving photographer at the Santander and Granada music festivals and elsewhere in Spain. In November of 1951 he held a one-man exhibition of his pictures in the Royal Photography Society of Madrid, and in March of 1953 took part with members of a group known as "Tendencias" in a collective show. He also contributed to the first Exposition of Fantastic Art at Madrid's Clan Gallery, and to the International Exposition of Abstract Art in Santander during the summer of 1953. During those years he prepared an enormous collection of photos of the various regions of the country for a book on Spain that never saw publication.

Acting on the suggestion of his brother Antonio, Saura signed up for the 1952-53 course at the Instituto de Investigaciones y Experiencias Cinematográficas in Madrid. Everyone in the school at that time was strongly influenced by the German Expressionist filmmakers and by Sergei Eisenstein and Vsevolod I. Pudovkin, which led to an overemphasis of the epic concept. The arrival in Spain of the great neo-realistic films from Italy during the 1950's proved to be exhilarating, and it fathered a new generation of filmmakers in Spain as it did in the rest of Europe. In the same year that he entered the Instituto Saura enrolled in Madrid's school of journalism, but he soon dropped out.

Carlos Saura was the only student approved for graduation in the 1956-57 class of the Instituto, on the basis of his exercise entitled *La tarde del domingo* (Sunday Afternoon), a 35mm sound film shot on location with a hand-held camera at a dance hall frequented by off-duty maids. Although Saura now considers it merely a sentimental rehearsal in the neo-realist vein, it contained the seeds of ideas and techniques that he would further develop in his first full-length feature, *Los golfos* (The Urchins). Before making *La tarde del domingo*, Saura had taken part in an uncompleted documentary by Eduardo Ducay entitled *Carta de Sanabria* that he considers an attempt at "cinéma verité" long before that approach was employed by others abroad, as well as several other experimental films. From the academic year of 1957-58 through 1963-64, Saura was a professor, first at the Instituto and then at the Official Cinema School.

The year after he graduated from the Instituto, Saura both wrote and directed a 45-minute documentary in color on the photogenic Spanish province of Cuenca. He now feels that its chief defect was its long commentary, in which most of the text was superfluous, an observation in keeping with his conviction that he is more at home with images than with scripts. Notwithstanding Saura's reservations, *Cuenca* (1958) won several awards at Spanish film competitions.

Those who attended the Cannes Film Festival of 1960 saw Carlos Saura's social exposé *Los Golfos* as in some ways similar to Luis Buñuel's *Los Olvidados* and Jean-Luc Godard's *A Bout de Souffle*, neither of which Saura had seen at that time. About youngsters from the Madrid slums trying to make their way in bullfighting, *Los Golfos* was played largely by nonprofessional actors speaking lines from a script by Mario Camus, Daniel Sueiro, and Carlos Saura himself. It not only marked a break with the escapist pap of the Francoist film but made a serious commitment to the Spanish film as a work of art. Sent to Cannes with ten minutes sliced off, *Los Golfos* failed to make much of an impression there and finally had an unsuccessful release on the commercial circuit in 1962. Whatever its inadequacies, *Los Golfos* enjoys the distinction of being the first Spanish film made entirely on location. It was also at the Cannes Film Festival of 1960 that Saura first met Luis Buñuel, whose *Viridiana* (1961) was coproduced by the producer of *Los Golfos;* the hurly-burly in Spain over the audacities of the Buñuel film may explain why Saura did not receive another opportunity to direct a movie until 1963, when his script *Llanto por un bandido* (Lament for a Bandit) was accepted by a three-nation production group involving Spain, Italy, and France.

With Lino Ventura, Lea Massari, and Philippe Leroy, and with Francisco Rabal in the title role of "El Tempranillo," a celebrated nineteenth century Spanish bandit, *Llanto por un bandido* had grandiose ambitions that were thwarted by inadequate financial resources. Saura's attempt to keep the script on an intimate level was frustrated by the producers, who wanted an action picture, and who saw to it that the cutting and editing were done in Italy without his supervision. To make matters worse, the opening sequence in which seven bandits were executed by garroting (a scene featuring such Spanish intellectuals as Buñuel and Antonio Buero Vallejo in cameo roles) was deleted by the censor, much to Saura's dismay. Despite those flaws, *Llanto por un bandido* was an entry at the 1964 Berlin Film Festival and was later shown at the Museum of Modern Art in New York.

It was at the Berlin Film Festival, in 1966, that Carlos Saura won his first important international award, a Silver Bear, for his *La Caza (The Hunt)*, a film that also marked the beginning of his long and mutually satisfactory association with producer Elías Querejeta. After his unhappy experience with the ruthless scissoring of *Lament for a Bandit,* Saura had vowed he would never again make a film over which he did not exercise full control. Filmed in 1965, *La Caza* was a multileveled study of the mounting violence unleashed among four hunters on a rabbit shoot, with the deepest level of meaning, which apparently escaped the censors, related to the hunters' Spanish Civil War background. *La Caza* was presented at three other foreign film festivals that year—New York, London, and Acapulco—and marked Spain's first entry at the New York Film Festival. Bosley Crowther of the New York *Times* (September 20, 1966) considered *The Hunt* "a strong, surprising entry . . . which should give the New York cinema intelligentsia a new regard for film-making in Spain." Crowther's encomium for the power and penetration of *The Hunt* ended with a recommendation for its wider exposure in the United States.

When *The Hunt* was released commercially in New York City the following spring, it was hailed by Crowther in a *Times* review of April 30, 1967 as a film "so good, so substantial and powerful that it would be a credit to any director in the world." Amazed that anyone just getting started in movie directing could turn out such an incisive and meaningful finished product, Crowther found the explanation in Saura's "passion to get something said." Thanks to that passion and his "disciplined directorial skill, which is manifested by his command of a mobile camera and a hard-nosed cast," concluded the critic, "Mr. Saura has made a picture that clearly ranks alongside H. G. Clouzot's . . . *The Wages of Fear.*"

Peppermint Frappé, which Carlos Saura scripted with Rafael Azcona and Angelino Fons and directed in 1967, was his first film starring Geraldine Chaplin and José Luis López Vázquez, and won him another Silver Bear at the 1968 Berlin Film Festival. Miss Chaplin handled the intricate dual roles of Ana and Elena in a work dominated by a climate of sexual repression and eroticism. Enrique Brasó has characterized *Peppermint Frappé* as an exploration of Eros and Thanatos (love and death), and considers it as both a bold new course and perhaps the director's most formally perfect venture so far.

Saura has described his next film, *Stress es tres, tres* (1968), as possibly the one he exercised the greatest freedom in directing. *Stress es tres, tres (Stress is Three, Three)* starred Geraldine Chaplin, Juan Luis Galiardo, and Fernando Cebrián as protagonists of a marital triangle that begins in playfulness and winds up as deadly serious. "What I am trying to do in *Stress,*" Saura told Jean Bratton for the New York *Times* (November 26, 1967), "is somewhat in the vein of *The Hunt.* It is the study of a seemingly developed society, the crisis of the modern Spaniard." Although it was entered at the Venice Festival of 1968, it is not generally considered one of his better efforts.

The deadly games that people play was also the concern of Saura's *La Madriguera* (variously translated as *The Den* or *The Honeycomb).* Filmed in 1969 and saturated with fantasy, it featured Miss Chaplin and Per Oscarsson as a married couple that manages to draw closer through a series of childish skits and charades until death becomes inevitable when one partner refuses to continue playing. Saura has been quoted as having remarked at the time he directed *La Madriguera:* "Each time, I'm less interested in producing a reflection of an objective reality." That film signaled Saura's return to the Berlin Film Festival, in 1969.

Fantasy also pervaded the script on which Saura collaborated with Rafael Azcona and directed in 1970 under the title of *El jardín de las delicias (The Garden of Delights)* with a cast headed by José Luis López Vázquez. Not without black humor, the film depicted a reenactment of the past by the family of a wealthy Spaniard who lost his memory in an accident and is thus unable to recall the number of his Swiss bank account. The criticism of the Franco régime only implicit in *The Hunt* and several of Saura's subsequent pictures became bolder in *The Garden of Delights*, which was shown at the 1970 New York Film Festival and at the Vienna Festival in 1972. In her review for the *New Yorker* (March 13, 1971), Pauline Kael found it visually elegant though too tightly controlled. She was unable to retain her interest in the central figure because of Saura's "sedate, measured style" that, while lending "an air of authority and intelligence" to the movie, grew "rather stilted."

Reportedly, Carlos Saura has admitted that he wrote and directed *Ana y los lobos (Ana and the Wolves)* in 1971 to annoy the censor for having tampered with and delayed approval for *The Garden of Delights*. Whatever his motivation, *Ana* was not released until 1972. A frontal attack on ecclesiastical, military, and sexual taboos, *Ana and the Wolves* is about a young governess (played by Geraldine Chaplin) employed in a decaying mansion by three brothers, who symbolize for Saura "the three monsters of Spain: perversions of religiosity, repressed sexuality, and the authoritarian spirit." Nevertheless, he views the three as appealing monsters rather than frightful, whose impotence eventually makes them dangerous and homicidal. Roger Mortimore found in *Ana* "the same richness familiar from *Peppermint Frappé* onwards, fantasy presented as fact and fact as fiction. One of the joyous messages of Saura's films is that what matters is what one thinks has happened rather than what actually has happened." *Ana and the Wolves* was exhibited at the Cannes Film Festival.

The first film made in Spain from the viewpoint of those who lost the Civil War, *La prima Angélica (Cousin Angelica)* was the object of paint and stink-bomb attacks when it had its premiere in Madrid in 1973. It starred José Luis López Vázquez in the demanding alternate role of a middle-aged man with Republican sympathies and that same man as a boy visiting his Falangist relatives during flashbacks to the 1930's. When it opened in the United States in 1977, *Cousin Angelica* gave Saura his broadest American exposure to date and provided critics with much to admire. The *New York Times* reviewer Vincent Canby (May 13, 1977) called it a "fine, sorrowful and poignant Spanish film, . . . a voyage into the past quite unlike any other I've ever seen in a movie." He found *Cousin Angelica* "extraordinarily compelling" even for those not familiar with the subtleties of Spanish life, and the *New Yorker* critic Penelope Gilliatt (May 23, 1977) agreed that it was a "wonderful Spanish picture." *Cousin Angelica* earned a Jury Prize at the 1974 Cannes Film Festival.

"Breed ravens and they'll pick your eyes out" is the Spanish proverb that served Saura for the title of his 1975 film *Cría Cuervos*, which was released in the United States in 1977 under the awkward and misleading title of *Cría!* An intricate and somewhat convoluted film about the vulnerabilities of an orphaned childhood, *Cría!* not only shuttles back and forth between past and present but also occasionally leaps forward into the future. Like much of Saura's work, it is an elaborate and introspective exercise in both memory and anticipation. Although some American reviewers entertained reservations about the film's paucity of event and lack of movement, they were unanimous in acclaiming the virtuoso performances of Geraldine Chaplin and young Ana Torrent. Deservedly, *Cría Cuervos* received the Special Jury Award at the 1976 Cannes Festival.

Geraldine Chaplin was again featured in Saura's *Elisa, vida mía* (1976), which costarred Fernando Rey as her father, a novelist secluded in an isolated house in Castile whose conversations with Elisa after a twenty-year separation are incorporated into his writing, so that real life and fiction become intertwined. After his death, Elisa continues to work on his unfinished book. In an interview regarding *Elisa, vida mía*, Carlos Saura declared that after making eleven films he felt he now spoke for himself with a simplicity and concreteness that enabled him to make more personal films without sticking slavishly to a script. In looking back over his years of filmmaking, Saura saw them as an unconscious progress from the general to the particular, during which his scope had gradually narrowed to concentrate on "two or three characters intimately seen and somehow representative" of him. Thus, going along with the popular belief that everything one does is autobiographical, he admitted that *Elisa, vida mía* was, among all his films, the one closest to his own thoughts. It was an entry at the 1977 Cannes Film Festival.

In 1978 Carlos Saura completed *Los ojos vendados (Blindfolded)*, which had its premiere in May of that year in Madrid during the same week that it was exhibited at the Cannes Film Festival. Dealing with political torture in Latin America and starring Miss Chaplin and José Luis Gómez, *Los ojos vendados* was seen by the Madrid movie critic César Santos Fontenla in *Informaciones* (May 20, 1978) as both a summing up of Saura's previous work and the opening up of a new path in his career.

Probably the most political and accessible of all of Saura's films, *Los ojos vendados* is by no means cryptic or confusing despite its multiple levels of meaning. It is the first genuine sample of what Saura can achieve now that he has been liberated from the heavy hand of censorship under the Franco dictatorship. "While Franco was alive I felt obliged to make films that were a criticism of the repressive mechanism of Francoism," Saura has said. "Franco was like a wall, a barrier, beyond which it was impossible to advance. Now Franco is dead and we can forget about him."

A lanky, craggy-faced man with an intense and piercing gaze, Carlos Saura somewhat resembles the American playwright Arthur Miller. He shares a penthouse apartment in Madrid with Geraldine Chaplin, their young son, Shane, and his two grown sons, Carlos and Antonio, from his marriage to Adele Medrano. Roger Mortimore has pointed out that Miss Chaplin's relationship with Saura and his art is not unlike that of Anna Karina with Jean-Luc Godard, while Elías Querejeta has been as vital to him as Harriet Weaver was to James Joyce. Although listening to music and reading compete for his leisure-time attention, photography remains his major hobby. In recent years there have been retrospective "hommages" to Saura in both France and Czechoslovakia, and the Luis Buñuel Cinema Prize jury in his own country selected him as the film figure of 1977.

References: Brasó, Enrique. Carlos Saura (1978); International Film Guide (1978)

Schlafly, Phyllis (Stewart) (shläf'lē)

Aug. 15, 1924- Author; social activist; politician. Address: 68 Fairmount, Alton, Ill. 62002

The nation's leading foe of the Equal Rights Amendment is Phyllis Schlafly, an ultraconservative author, lecturer, and politician whose unremitting opposition to feminist goals has made her, according to one reporter, "the anathema of the women's movement." The Equal Rights Amendment, a far-reaching guarantee of equal rights for women, is widely supported by women's groups, both major political parties, and many labor unions. After it was passed by Congress in 1972, ERA seemed destined to gain quick ratification in the thirty-eight states needed for it to become the Twenty-seventh Amendment to the Constitution. Yet by 1977 the amendment appeared hopelessly stalled three states short of ratification. Congress, however, voted to extend the seven-year deadline for approval of ERA in late 1978.

If ERA is not ratified, many believe that it will be primarily owing to the efforts of Mrs. Schlafly, who claims that equality would be a step down for most women who are, in her words, "extremely well treated." Mrs. Schlafly has campaigned tirelessly against the amendment, making speeches and establishing chapters of her Stop ERA and Eagle Forum women's organizations nationwide. Long active in conservative Republican politics and a three-time unsuccessful candidate for Congress, Mrs. Schlafly publishes a monthly newsletter called the *Phyllis Schlafly Report* and has written eight books, the best-known of which is *A Choice Not an Echo,* which championed the ill-starred 1964 Presidential candidacy of Barry M. Goldwater. In the mid-1970's she was a commentator on the CBS Radio editorial series, *Spectrum.*

The elder daughter of John Bruce and Odile (Dodge) Stewart, Mrs. Schlafly was born Phyllis Stewart in St. Louis, Missouri on August 15, 1924. Her father, an engineer and inventor, has been characterized by family friends as "so conservative they teased him about being a monarchist." Because the Stewart family suffered some financial reverses during the Depression, Mrs. Stewart clerked for a time in a department store, taught school, and then obtained a job as a librarian for the St. Louis Art Museum.

Both Phyllis and her sister, Odile, were educated at the Academy of the Sacred Heart, a Roman Catholic parochial school in St. Louis. After Phyllis graduated from the academy as valedictorian of her class in 1941, she attended a Catholic college, Maryville College of the Sacred Heart. Two years later she transferred to Washington University in St. Louis. As a college student she worked the night shift at a federal small arms factory that was supplying guns and ammunition for World War II. At first she fired rifles and machine guns to test ammunition; later she worked in a laboratory on photographs of weapon misfirings.

In 1944 Phyllis Stewart graduated Phi Beta Kappa from Washington University and was awarded a $500 scholarship, a substantial grant at that time, to do graduate work at Radcliffe in Cambridge, Massachusetts. After obtaining her M.A. degree in political science from Radcliffe in 1945, she obtained her first job, which consisted of doing research for several Congressmen in Washington. The following year she returned to St. Louis to work as an aide in the successful Congressional campaign of Republican Claude I. Bakewell. From 1946 to 1949 she worked for the First National Bank of St. Louis Union Trust Company as a librarian and researcher.

While working for the bank, Miss Stewart met John Fred Schlafly Jr., a lawyer from a wealthy Alton, Illinois family who was interested in conservative political causes. They were married on October 20, 1949. Quitting her job, Mrs. Schlafly devoted much of her time to community volunteer work. She helped on fund drives and served as president of the Radcliffe Club of St. Louis, as a director of the Alton YWCA, and as a director of the local chapter of the National Conference of Christians and Jews. Eventually she became the commentator on a weekly radio broadcast sponsored by that conference.

Phyllis Schlafly also remained active in Republican politics. In 1952 she made her first bid for political office, when she sought the Republican nomination for Congress from the Twenty-fourth District of Illinois. She won the primary but was defeated in the general election by the incumbent Democrat, Melvin Price. In 1956 she was a delegate to the Republican National Convention, in 1960 she was an alternate, and then again a delegate in 1964 and 1968. In 1960 she again ran unsuccessfully for Congress, that time as a write-in candidate.

Meanwhile, Mrs. Schlafly was mother to a growing brood. Her first child, John F., was born about a year after her marriage, and in the years that followed she gave birth to five more children, Bruce S., Roger S., Phyllis D., Andrew L., and Ann V. Apparently adept at reconciling the demands of motherhood with an active political career, she has recalled: "As a nursing mother I took each of my six children to political meetings across the state."

An ardent anticommunist, Mrs. Schlafly did research for Senator Joseph R. McCarthy during the early 1950's; founded, with her husband, the Cardinal Mindszenty Foundation in 1958 to alert the world to the dangers of communism; and published two bibliographical pamphlets, *Reading List for Americans* (1954) and *Inside the Communist Conspiracy* (1959), both of them compendia of right-wing titles. Eighty-six out of the 116 titles in the second list were also included in the approved reading list of the John Birch Society. Among them were *A World Gone Crazy* by Robert H. Welch Jr., the founder and president of the John Birch Society, *America's Retreat from Victory* by Senator Joseph R. McCarthy, and several books by Dean Manion. In 1962 Mrs. Schlafly gained an opportunity to share her conservative views with a wider public when she began broadcasting a weekly radio program that was carried on eighteen stations as a public service presentation. The program was sponsored by "America Wake Up," a right-wing organization that her husband had helped to found.

Mrs. Schlafly was an enthusiastic supporter of conservative Arizona Senator Barry M. Goldwater's Presidential aspirations in 1964. To boost his campaign, she wrote her first book, *A Choice Not an Echo* (1964), which was printed in paperback under the imprint of Père Marquette Press, a company that she herself established as a mail-order operation in Alton, Illinois. The book became such a best seller that over 3,000,000 copies were distributed before election day.

The success of *A Choice Not an Echo* launched a series of Père Marquette books on the subject of national defense that were written by Mrs. Schlafly in partnership with a retired United States Navy Rear Admiral named Chester Ward. The first of those books was *The Gravediggers* (1964) in which the authors contend that such "gravediggers" as Secretary of Defense Robert S. McNamara and Presidential advisers McGeorge Bundy and Walt W. Rostow were deliberately weakening the United States' military position so that the Russians could bury America. In *Strike from Space* (1965), Mrs. Schlafly and Admiral Ward "revealed" plans for a surprise nuclear attack by the Soviet Union and a counterplot by "defeatists" in the American government who wanted "to disarm unilaterally so the Soviets could feel they did not need to attack." In *The Betrayers* (1968) they castigated "today's Alger Hisses" who were betraying the country to the communists with a "no-win" policy in Vietnam. Without her collaborator, Mrs. Schlafly also wrote *Safe—Not Sorry* (Père Marquette, 1967), in which she contends that the communists instigated the urban ghetto riots in 1967.

Meanwhile, Mrs. Schlafly had ridden the wave of conservatism within the Republican party to election, in the spring of 1964, as first vice-president of the National Federation of Republican Women. That office put her in direct line to succeed to the presidency in 1967. The disastrous defeat of Goldwater by President Lyndon B. Johnson in 1964, however, brought about a resurgence of liberal power in the Republican party. After a bitter floor fight at the 1967 convention of the National Federation of Republican Women, Mrs. Schlafly was passed by for the presidency in favor of a more liberal candidate.

Although she did not formally break with the National Federation of Republican Women after losing the 1967 election, Phyllis Schlafly did establish, for her supporters within that group, a separate women's organization called "The Eagles Are Flying." She also founded the Eagles Trust Fund to support conservative political candidates and began publication of the *Phyllis Schlafly Report* to educate the members of her women's group on the issues and inform them of which political candidates they should support. In 1970 she made her third try for Congress, losing to Democratic incumbent George Shipley. One of the largest contributors to her campaign that year was reportedly the ultraconservative insurance multimillionaire W. Clement Stone.

It was in the February 1972 issue of the *Phyllis Schlafly Report* that Mrs. Schlafly first attacked the Equal Rights Amendment, then pending before Congress, as a threat to family life and the American woman. The amendment, which has been repeatedly put forward by feminists since 1923, states simply that first, "equality of rights under the law shall not be denied or abridged by the United States or by any State on account of sex," and secondly, "Congress shall have the power to enforce, by appropriate legislation, the provisions of this article." In the spring of 1972 ERA seemed like an idea whose time had finally come, and after its approval by Congress, in March, it was quickly ratified in twenty-two states, by the end of the year.

Meanwhile, Mrs. Schlafly was setting up a Stop-ERA organization with chapters around the country. Later she established a second group, the Eagle Forum, which she calls her answer to "women's lib," and it too joined the fight against ERA. Other allies in the fight to halt ERA have included conservative churchwomen's lay groups, some labor unions, and a number of pro-family, antifeminist organizations, some of which are ad hoc committees established by the John Birch Society.

Mrs. Schlafly has concentrated her opposition to ERA primarily around the issues of military service and financial support laws. She contends that under ERA "mothers will have to be drafted" and "women will be sent into combat and onto warships with men." ERA supporters concede that women would be eligible for military conscription, if it is ever reinstated, but they argue that mothers could be exempted as fathers have been in the past, and that only those women physically qualified would be eligible for combat duty. On the subject of financial support, Mrs. Schlafly has asserted that ERA "will make a wife equally responsible to provide a home for her family and to provide 50 percent of the financial support of her family." Legal specialists, however, have agreed that ERA would establish the principle that whoever is able would be required to provide the support, and laws to that effect are already on the books in several states. Mrs. Schlafly has also argued that ERA would legalize homosexual marriages and require unisex toilets in public places. Neither argument has been seriously supported by legal opinion.

At first many observers tended to discount Mrs. Schlafly and her Stop-ERA forces. Nick Thimmesch in the *New York Times Magazine*, however, wrote on June 24, 1973, "Sophisticates are advised not to laugh at Mrs. Schlafly, or her views." His advice proved sound, for in 1973 the ERA bandwagon slowed, with only eight more states voting to ratify. In 1974 three states approved ratification. Since then only North Dakota has ratified, in 1975, and Indiana, in 1977.

Since 1973 Mrs. Schlafly has nationally aired her viewpoint on a variety of subjects as one of the commentators on the CBS Radio network program *Spectrum*. She has continued to publish books, including *Mindszenty the Man* (Cardinal Mindszenty Foundation, 1972), of which she is coauthor with Josef Vecsey, and *Kissinger on the Couch* (Arlington House, 1975), a lengthy indictment of the former Secretary of State and his policy of détente with Russia that she wrote with Admiral Ward. Mrs. Schlafly's latest book is *The Power of the Positive Woman* (Arlington House, 1977), in which she summarizes her opposition to the issues championed by what she calls the "femlib fanatics." It was a selection of the Conservative Book Club. In November 1977 Mrs. Schlafly and her Stop ERA and Eagle Forum organizations sponsored a rally at the Houston Astro-Arena in opposition to the four-day, government-sponsored National Women's Conference in Houston. For a time it appeared that Mrs. Schlafly would challenge Senator Charles H. Percy of Illinois in the March 1978 Republican primary for the Senate nomination, but in December 1977 she announced she would not enter the race.

Mrs. Schlafly served as president of the Illinois Federation of Republican Women from 1960 to 1964. Since 1973 she has been a commentator on the Chicago radio station WBBM program, *Matters of Opinion*. Her awards have included the Woman of Achievement in Public Affairs award of the St. Louis *Globe-Democrat* (1963), the Woman of the Year designation from the Illinois Federation of Republican Women (1969), seven George Washington Honor Medals from the Freedoms Foundation at Valley Forge, and the Brotherhood Award of the National Conference of Christians and Jews (1975). She is a member of the Junior League of St. Louis, Pi Sigma Alpha, and the Daughters of the American Revolution, for whom she served as national chairman of the bicentennial committee (1967-70). Mrs. Schlafly has denied persistent reports that she used to belong to the John Birch Society, even though Robert Welch once described her, in the March 1960 issue of the society's *Bulletin*, as "a very loyal member of the John Birch Society."

Phyllis Schlafly, who has been called "the Gloria Steinem of the Right," is, like Miss Steinem, a glamorous and articulate advocate of her cause. An immaculately groomed woman, Mrs. Schlafly is five feet seven inches tall, weighs a trim 135 pounds, and wears her streaked blond hair in upswept curls. In fashion, she favors conservative dresses, often baby blue, set off with white pearls. Although she sometimes likes to pass herself off as a housewife who operates her activities out of the kitchen of her six-bedroom Tudor house overlooking the Mississippi River in Alton, her feminist opponents have pointed out that she is a professional politician who employs full-time domestic and secretarial help. Sally Quinn of the Washington *Post* (July 11, 1974) characterized the ERA foe as "a walking contradiction." "Her outward demeanor and dress is one of a feminine, bridge-playing, affluent housewife. She smiles a lot, giggles, worries about her appearance and makes polite conversation," Miss Quinn observed. "Yet, on the podium she comes on like a female George Wallace. She is tough and aggressive, totally unlike the role she espouses for most women." Mrs. Schlafly began law school at Washington University in St. Louis in 1974 and is scheduled to graduate in 1978.

References: Ms. 2:55+ Mr '74 por; N Y Daily News p39 N 22 '77 por; N Y Times p44 D 15 '75 pors; National NOW Times p8+ D '77 por; Newsweek 90:35 Jl 25 '77 por; Contemporary Authors 1st rev. vols 25-28 (1977); Who's Who in America, 1976-77

Schorr, Daniel (Louis)

Aug. 31, 1916- Journalist; author. Address: h. 3113 Woodley Rd., NW, Washington, D.C. 20008

NOTE: This biography supersedes the article that appeared in *Current Biography* in 1959.

During his controversial twenty-three-year career with CBS News, Daniel Schorr was one of the few broadcast correspondents who practised old-fashioned print journalism within the narrow confines of television newscasting. His experience, legwork, and bold initiatives made him the most effective and attention-getting reporter in American broadcasting, although his brash aggressiveness occasionally brought him into head-on conflict with the network's corporate executives. In February 1976 Schorr was suspended by CBS after he gave a copy of the suppressed report of the House Committee on Intelligence to the *Village Voice*, and seven months later he resigned following a highly publicized Congressional investigation. "In this country there is always a pendulum swinging between the need for disclosure and the need for national security," he said in a recent interview. "I was there and I stood there as the pendulum swung back from disclosure, and I got knocked down by the pendulum." Since his resignation, Schorr has devoted himself to lecturing and writing a regular column for the Des Moines *Register* and *Tribune* newspaper syndicate.

A second-generation member of a Russian-Jewish immigrant family, Daniel Louis Schorr was born on August 31, 1916 in New York

City to Louis and Tillie (Godiner) Schorr. He has one younger brother, Alvin Louis, who is a social scientist and author. After his father died in the early 1920's, Daniel Schorr began working at odd jobs to supplement his mother's income as a seamstress. "I grew up with a sense that you had to make your own way without help," he told Philip Hilts in an interview for the Washington *Post's Potomac Magazine* (March 28, 1976). "*Nothing* is on a platter."

Always interested in journalism, Schorr edited the student newspaper and the yearbook at DeWitt Clinton High School and, in his free time, worked as a stringer for the Bronx (New York) *Home News* and the *Jewish Daily Bulletin*. Following his graduation from high school in 1933, Schorr enrolled at the College of the City of New York, where he majored in sociology and worked on the undergraduate newspaper, *The Campus*. During his college years he worked part time for several metropolitan dailies and for the Jewish Telegraphic Agency. After taking his B.S. degree in 1939, Schorr signed on as a full-time assistant editor of the Jewish Telegraphic Agency. He then moved on to the New York *Journal-American* and, in 1941, to ANETA, the Netherlands news agency, as its New York news editor. Drafted into the United States Army in 1943, he was stationed at Camp Polk, Louisiana, where he worked in the public relations office of division headquarters, and in headquarters of the Fourth Army at Fort Sam Houston, Texas, where he worked in intelligence until he was discharged, with the rank of sergeant, in 1945.

Rejoining ANETA after the war, Schorr moved to The Hague to reorganize that agency's news operations on the Continent. He resigned in 1948 to free-lance and over the next few years contributed pieces on the Low Countries to the New York *Times*, the *Christian Science Monitor*, the London *Daily Mail*, *Time*, and *Newsweek*. His on-the-scene reports from flood-ravaged Holland attracted the attention of Edward R. Murrow, who recruited Schorr for CBS News in 1953. As a member of the staff of the network's Washington bureau, he covered the Capitol Hill and State Department beats for eighteen months and made occasional side trips to Latin America and Europe. In September 1955 he opened the first CBS News bureau in Moscow. Indifferent to the "guidelines" issued by the Kremlin, he ignored any attempt at censorship and repeatedly read on the air passages that had been deleted by the Russian government. His forthright reports won him the 1956 Overseas Press Club award for best television interpretation of foreign news. Schorr, who was denounced by *Komsomolskaya Pravda* as a "provocateur" and "adventurer," was not allowed to return to Moscow after his annual year-end visit to the United States in 1957.

For the next few years Schorr was a roving diplomatic correspondent, reporting from United Nations headquarters in New York City and from the major European capitals. His assignments included a tour of Austria, France, Poland and the United States with Soviet Premier Nikita S. Khrushchev and a trip to Asia and South America with President Dwight D. Eisenhower. It was during Eisenhower's second term that Schorr first incurred Presidential wrath. In April 1959 he reported from a NATO conference in Paris that John Foster Dulles, Eisenhower's trusted Secretary of State, intended to resign within days. Denying what he called the "utterly irresponsible" story, the President's press secretary publicly excoriated Schorr, but one week later, Dulles resigned. Eisenhower's successor, President John F. Kennedy, so objected to Schorr's inclusion of German criticism of American foreign policy in his reports from Bonn that he asked CBS to transfer the reporter. "Any story I'm interested in is usually one that somebody is interested in keeping people from finding out about," Schorr told Frank Getlein in an interview for the Washington *Star* (February 29, 1976). "I take an unholy delight in puncturing pretense."

In the midst of the 1964 Presidential campaigns, Schorr reported from Munich that Senator Barry M. Goldwater, the frontrunning Republican candidate, planned to take a post-convention trip to Germany to "link up" with German conservatives, adding that the Senator intended to stay at Berchtesgaden, "Hitler's onetime stomping ground." In response to the demands of an outraged Goldwater, who accused CBS of waging a campaign of falsification, Fred W. Friendly, the president of CBS News, ordered Schorr to make a complete retraction. A few days later, Schorr explained that he had not meant to imply that Goldwater intended to join forces with German rightists. What he had meant to say was that "a process of gravitation" was apparent in Germany. For the duration of the campaign Friendly personally cleared every Schorr tape alluding to American politics. It was, as Schorr wrote years later, the "first big black mark" on his record.

In 1966 Daniel Schorr returned to the United States and, on his own initiative, set out to cover the "Great Society" and whatever fit into that broad concept, even if it meant trespassing on another reporter's beat. With the encouragement of Richard Salant, the new president of CBS News, he submitted well-researched pieces on poverty, pollution, education, and health care to the network's regularly scheduled radio and television news broadcasts and prepared cogent analyses of the same subjects for *CBS Reports*, the award-winning documentary series. Perhaps his most controversial contribution to *CBS Reports* was "Don't Get Sick in America," a chilling examination, first broadcast in April 1970, of President Richard M. Nixon's feeble response to the nation's rising health care needs. Aurora Publishers released the report in book form under the same title in 1970.

Unlike many of his younger colleagues, Schorr has the print journalist's built-in antagonism to what he calls the "stage-craft, image-making and slogan-selling" of television. "[I'm] kind of a stray newspaperman in a strange land," he told Barry Furlong in an interview for *New York* magazine (June 16, 1975). "My typical way of operating is not to go stick a camera and a microphone in somebody's face and let him say whatever self-serving thing he wants to say, but to spend a certain amount of time getting the basic information, as though I was going to write a newspaper story. . . . [I] may end up putting a mike in somebody's face, but it is usually for the final and hopefully embarrassing question," he added. "By the time I have a story, his 'no comment' is all I need." Over the years of his almost daily network reporting, Schorr mastered the art of shaping his two-minute pieces for maximum impact in order to snare a place in the tight evening news line-up. "There were several years when my livelihood depended on not only getting the story but selling it," he once explained. "I'm trying to sell an editor who has a short front page."

The siege mentality of the Nixon White House offered Schorr an unparalleled opportunity for investigative reporting. A "real media enemy," in the words of one Administration aide, Schorr earned a spot on Nixon's "enemies list" for repeatedly pointing out the shortcomings of Nixon's programs. Furious, the President ordered an FBI investigation of Schorr on the pretext that he was in line for a top federal job. When he was assigned to cover the byzantine Watergate scandals in August 1972, Schorr accepted the assignment with some reluctance because Watergate was, in his view, "a classic example of a story in search of pictures." Nevertheless, he attacked the assignment with his usual singlemindedness, contributing pieces on the break-in and campaign financing to the network's unprecedented, twenty-three-minute, two-part Watergate "enterpriser" as well as almost daily updated reports. His Watergate coverage won him three Emmys for outstanding achievement within a regularly scheduled news program in 1972, 1973, and 1974.

Schorr often clashed with top officials of CBS over what he saw as capitulation to the Nixon Administration. He was appalled by the network's decision in June 1973 to abandon its "instant analysis" of Presidential addresses and by the conciliatory treatment accorded President Nixon on his resignation. Convinced that it was wrong for the media "to take on the role of nation-healers," he told Duke University students on January 17, 1975 that CBS executives had been so relieved when Nixon failed to blame the press for his resignation that they reciprocated by "soft-pedaling Nixon's wrongs and establishing a general atmosphere of sweetness and light." To restrain its outspoken employee, CBS for a time required Schorr to submit the texts of his speeches for advance permission.

After working for a few weeks on general assignment, which he found highly uncongenial, Schorr was transferred to the intelligence beat in October 1974 to investigate the CIA's questionable activities at home and abroad. At first, he followed the leads of newspapermen and concentrated on the CIA's clandestine operations in Chile and its illegal surveillance of American dissenters. But in February 1975 he struck out on his own, parlaying a tip about President Gerald R. Ford's off-the-record remark to New York *Times* editors into a CBS exclusive. Having confirmed his story, Schorr reported that Ford was concerned about possible CIA involvement in foreign assassinations. His report broadened the scope of the Rockefeller Commission's investigation into CIA activities and prompted the usually staid Richard Helms, a former director of the CIA, to berate "Killer Schorr" on national television.

As the network's chief intelligence reporter, Schorr compiled an impressive list of scoops, although in his haste to outmaneuver his rivals from NBC and ABC, he occasionally overstepped the boundaries of journalistic prudence. For example, he included in one report an interview in which Air Force Colonel Fletcher Prouty falsely accused Alexander Butterfield of being the CIA's contact officer in the White House. When Butterfield denied the charge, Schorr admitted that he had not verified Prouty's statement with a second source. "You can't check on the validity of everything during a live interview," he said as quoted in *Time* (July 28, 1975). "I can't be in a position of suppressing Prouty. What if he's right? I can't play God."

In the course of his work, Schorr covered both the Senate and House intelligence investigations. While the House Intelligence Committee, headed by Representative Otis G. Pike, was meeting in secret session in late January 1976 to review its findings on illegal CIA and FBI operations, several Washington correspondents, among them, Daniel Schorr, learned the substance of the report from various sources. On Friday, January 23, the Pike Committee voted nine to four to publish the report. Over that weekend Schorr began broadcasting news items based on his Xeroxed copy of the report, and on Monday, January 26, the New York *Times* published its detailed analysis. Three days later the full House voted, 246 to 124, against publication. When Schorr realized he possessed the sole copy of the document outside the government, he made what he has since called "an inescapable decision of journalistic conscience" and moved to publish the suppressed report.

Having in mind a paperback edition with his own introduction, Schorr asked Richard Salant to sound out CBS's publishing subsidiaries, and when they showed no interest, he contacted the Reporters Committee for Freedom of the Press, a Washington-based group that aids journalists embroiled in First Amendment disputes. The Committee put him in touch with Peter Tufo, a New York lawyer and literary agent, who eventually made the report available to Clay Felker, the publisher of the *Village Voice,* a liberal weekly newspaper, and the trendy *New York* magazine, in exchange for a promised donation to the Reporters Committee. (The Committee eventually refused the donation to avoid charges of profiteering.) Schorr was a little disappointed by the arrangement, but as he told Nora Ephron in an interview for *Esquire* (June 1976), "Once you start down a certain line, the steps by which one thing leads to another come very swiftly. You find yourself saying, 'By God, I don't care if this appears in *Pravda* as long as it appears.' In the end you're amazed at how far you've come from what you originally wanted to do."

The day after the *Village Voice* hit the newsstands, the Washington *Post* identified Schorr as the anonymous source of the Pike report. Schorr immediately issued a statement explaining that rather than cooperate in what might be the total suppression of the report, he had arranged for its publication. Much to his surprise, the press reaction turned out to be almost entirely negative, with most columnists and editors, liberal as well as conservative, agreeing with Peter Lisagor, the chief of the Chicago *Daily News*'s Washington bureau, that "selling any document is intolerable for a newsman whether it's for personal profit or for charity."

Anticipating trouble from their conservative affiliate stations, nervous CBS network news bosses shifted Schorr to general assignment. Then, after the House of Representatives voted to investigate their reporter, they relieved Schorr "of all reporting duties for an indefinite period." According to Les Brown, the New York *Times*'s media correspondent, Schorr was actually suspended because of his "ambiguous behavior," his "evasiveness," and his alleged unmanageability. In his *Clearing the Air* (Houghton Mifflin, 1977), Schorr himself admitted that he let his superiors suspect Leslie Stahl, a CBS colleague, while he worked out a general plan "for shedding [his] ill-conceived anonymity." At the time, however, he thought his silence would "provide an additional layer of protection for [his] source."

Subpoenaed to testify before the House Committee on Standards and Ethics in September 1976, Schorr appeared under protest. He contended that the investigation was irrelevant because he had obtained the report after the Pike Committee had approved its publication. In any case, he pointed out, most of the findings had been public knowledge before the *Village Voice* published its special supplements. Fully supported by the journalistic community, Schorr eloquently defended a reporter's rights under the First Amendment: "For a journalist, the most crucial kind of confidence is the identity of a source of information. . . . To betray a source would be to betray myself, my career, and my life. I cannot do it. To say I refuse to do it is not saying it right. I cannot do it." The House dropped its case and CBS's top executives wired Schorr commending his immense service to his fellow journalists, to the Constitution and the public's right to know, prompting rumors that he would be reinstated. But on September 28, 1976 he resigned because he felt that his reinstatement would cause tension within the organization.

Since leaving daily broadcast journalism, Schorr has drawn on his four decades of experience to write and lecture about television. Like many communications specialists, he worries that television's unique blend of fact and fantasy has desensitized viewers to such an extent that they are unable to distinguish between the real and the unreal. In Schorr's opinion, however, television newsmen—"the guardians of reality"—have fought "a valiant rear-guard action," minimizing rumor and panic, particularly in times of national crisis by "a steady stream of information and actuality." He remains confident that Americans will become saturated with escapist fantasy and return "from dreamland seeking an old-fashioned answer from an old-fashioned reporter to an old-fashioned question, 'What's the news?' "

Daniel Schorr stands five feet eleven inches tall and weighs about 185 pounds. He has gray hair, brown eyes shielded by thick eyeglasses, a perpetually furrowed brow, and, according to one interviewer, "a voice from a gravel pit." For a man of his years, he has boundless energy and plays an aggressive game of tennis. For relaxation, he likes to read and to listen to music. Schorr and his wife, Lisbeth (Bamberger) Schorr, whom he married in 1967, have two children, Jonathan and Lisa. Mrs. Schorr is a member of the council of the Institute of Medicine of the National Academy of Sciences and also of H.E.W. Secretary Joseph A. Califano's Advisory Committee on National Health Insurance Issues and a consultant on health to the Children's Defense Fund. The Schorrs make their home in Washington, D.C. and often vacation in Aspen, Colorado.

References: N Y Times p13 F 27 '76 por; New York 8:41+ Je 16 '75 por; Newsweek 87:49 F 23 '76 por; Time 106:42+ Jl 28 '75 por; Washington Post Potomac p11+ Mr 28 '76 por; Who's Who in America, 1976-77

Schroeder, Patricia (Scott)

July 30, 1940- United States Representative from Colorado. Address: b. 1507 Dirksen Office Building, Washington, D.C. 20510; h. 836 Dexter St., Denver, Col. 80220

In 1972 Patricia Schroeder was elected to the House of Representatives from Colorado's First Congressional District. It was the first time the state had ever sent a woman to the United States Congress. Relatively unknown at the time of her election, she has since become increasingly popular nationally as well as in her home district because of her outspokenness and activism. Representative Schroeder, the self-appointed gadfly of the House Armed Services Committee, is a well-informed and articulate opponent of the increasingly spendthrift defense budget, who helped to formulate the first comprehensive alternative defense posture and suggested that the surplus money might be better spent on social welfare programs. Her decidedly liberal legislative record has been praised by consumer activists, environmentalists, feminists, and other politically progressive groups.

Patricia Schroeder was born Patricia Scott on July 30, 1940 in Portland, Oregon, the daughter of Lee Combs and Bernice (Scott) Scott. After receiving her primary and secondary education in the public schools in Portland, she attended the University of Minnesota in Minneapolis, Minnesota. A brilliant student, she completed her studies there in three years and graduated, *magna cum laude* and Phi Betta Kappa, with a B.A. degree in 1961. Miss Scott continued her education at Harvard Law School, receiving a J.D. degree in 1964. In one of her law classes at Harvard, she met James White Schroeder. They were married on August 18, 1962. As fellow law students, the two shared professors and books and became accustomed to working together as a team. Both planned careers in law, although Jim Schroeder was equally interested in politics.

After leaving Harvard, the Schroeders moved to Denver, Colorado, where Pat Schroeder, as she prefers to be called, was hired as a field attorney for the National Labor Relations Board, responsible for the Colorado, Wyoming, and Utah area. She held that position until she temporarily stopped working following the birth of her first child, Scott William, in June 1966. She worked as a Democratic precinct committeewoman in 1968 and, in 1969, resumed private practice as an attorney. In addition, she was a lecturer and law instructor at the Community College of Denver in 1969 and 1970, at the University of Denver in 1969 and at Regis College from 1970 to 1972. With the birth of her second child, Jamie Christine, in 1970, Mrs. Schroeder once again cut back on her working hours, but within a year, she was back on the job full time, working as a hearing officer for the Colorado Department of Personnel and as legal counsel for Planned Parenthood of Colorado.

In the meantime, James Schroeder was pursuing his political ambitions. Defeated in his race for the Colorado state legislature in 1970, he decided to turn his talents to campaign management for the 1972 Congressional contest. Because the Republican incumbent, James D. ("Mike") McKevitt, was expected to win reelection easily, Schroeder was hard-pressed to find a liberal Democratic challenger willing to run the risk of an almost certain defeat. As Pat Schroeder explained a few years later, "I never saw myself as a candidate. But . . . I was the only person [Jim] could talk into it!" Although Pat Schroeder filed her candidacy for the House of Representatives in May, she was so certain she would lose that she kept her jobs through the election, so that she would have "something to go back to."

Relying heavily on grass-roots volunteers, the Schroeder campaign, headed by Jim Schroeder, was often favorably compared to Senator George S. McGovern's superbly organized Presidential primary campaign. Like Gary Hart, McGovern's campaign manager, Jim Schroeder favored novel guerrilla tactics, including the "mini-poster," an especially effective new technique. One poster featured a dejected elderly woman with a cane walking haltingly down a deserted street. Its slogan—"Cheer up. The Olympics are coming"—referred to the boiling public controversy over the efforts to make Colorado the site of the 1976 Winter Olympics, a costly proposal that Pat Schroeder strongly opposed. A mini-poster of a tombstone noted that some American troops had been withdrawn from Vietnam and another featuring a Mexican-American child read: "This little radical troublemaker is out to get something from you—hope." Even some of Pat Schroeder's aides thought the posters were "too strong," but they succeeded in drawing attention to the virtually unknown candidate.

As the mother of two young children, Pat Schroeder raised some eyebrows among those voters who believed women should stay home with their children, but, characteristically, she decided to laugh off some objections by occasionally opening her stump speeches with a cheery "Hi! I'm that nut you've been hearing about, the one who doesn't shave under her arms, the one who leaps over barricades uttering obscenities, the one who keeps her kids in the freezer." Rejecting her political elders' advice to take a safe, middle-of-the-road stance, particularly on more controversial issues, Mrs. Schroeder came out against the Vietnam war and called for a reordering of national priorities to emphasize education, child care, health services, and protection of the environment.

Virtually ignored at first, Pat Schroeder eventually won the support of local Democratic groups and of organized labor. With those endorsements, she wrested the September Democratic primary from Clarence Decker by some 4,000 votes and, on November 8, 1972, upset Congressman McKevitt, capturing 51.6 percent of the vote, despite President Richard Nixon's sizable plurality in the district.

On her first day on Capitol Hill, Pat Schroeder ran up against the entrenched male chauvinism that would bedevil her throughout her freshman term. According to an account in *People* (May 15, 1978), when a male colleague, on meeting her for the first time, asked her how she could be "the mother of two small children and a member of Congress at the same time," she replied coolly, "I have a brain and a uterus and I use them both." Even after several years in office, Mrs. Schroeder conceded that being one of a handful of women among some 400 men in the clubby atmosphere of the Capitol was not an easy lot. As she told Lawrence Van Gelder, who interviewed her for the New York *Times* (December 23, 1976), "I think no one in the world would ever say that it is simple. I would also say that most of the women who are qualified have dealt with this issue all their life."

Because of her background and interests, Pat Schroeder might easily have chosen membership on a House committee concerned with quality-of-life issues. Instead she lobbied her way on to the powerful Armed Services Committee against the stubborn opposition of F. Edward Hébert, its autocratic chairman. She explained her reasoning to Judith Viorst in an interview for a *Redbook* (November 1973) profile: "Everyone is always talking about our defense effort in terms of defending women and children, but no one ever asks the women and children what they think. As a woman with children I want to be able to say there are other things we can do to protect us than build bases." Since the Armed Services Committee controlled about 40 percent of the national budget, she was eager to expose what she saw as the waste and folly of defense policies and divert the excess dollars to expanded social welfare programs. She was also deeply interested in military labor-management policies and in military criminal justice.

A few months after taking office, Mrs. Schroeder threatened the long-standing cordial relationship between the Committee and the Pentagon when she denounced the billion-dollar 1974 military procurement authorization bill as "frivolous," a "boondoggle," and "a colossal waste of money." Annoyed by the Committee's "fixation with technology" and its apparent belief that "killing an enemy fifteen times over makes us more secure than if we can kill him only five times over," she tried for weeks to persuade her colleagues to modify the bill, then filed a minority report outlining possible additional Pentagon cuts.

In the seven pages of her "additional views" that became part of the public record, Representative Schroeder condemned the Armed Services Committee, the "Pentagon's lobby on the Hill," for being "frightened of vigorous and open debate" and ridiculed its penchant for holding closed hearings and for calling only those witnesses who agreed with the Pentagon's proposals. She continued her criticism of the Armed Services Committee in "A Freshman in the Weapons Club," a scathing article that appeared in the November 5, 1973 issue of the *Nation*. Belittling the endless questions—"Is it bigger? Is it faster? Is it more maneuverable? Does it give closer, more comfortable shaves?"—about a new weapon that are routinely asked of Pentagon spokesmen, she took her fellow committeemen to task for failing to ask "the whys and what-fors." "What comes into play is the military equivalent of the Peter Principle: the capacity of American technology to produce a particular system governs the nature of the Pentagon's request," she wrote.

After taking part in dozens of weapons procurement hearings, Pat Schroeder concluded that "mere logic" was an "inadequate tool" in dealing with Department of Defense brass. "However useless a defense concept, however premature its implementation, however extravagant its cost, an argument to proceed is deemed conclusive [by the Pentagon] on one of two grounds," she wrote. "Either the Russians are doing it and so must we do it to avoid falling behind, or the Russians are not doing it and therefore we must in order to stay ahead." In a thinly veiled reference to her frequent battles with Committee Chairman Hébert, she pointed out the value of debate and dissent. "Muting dissonant voices is a mark of insecurity rather than strength," she said. "We need the confidence to discuss military issues without bitterness. The wisdom allegedly acquired by mere political longevity can, moreover, easily be overestimated. I doubt that experience will persuade me that it is wiser to spend $350,300,000 on a Safeguard ABM system that is useless in the first instance and severely limited by the SALT agreement in the second."

The septuagenarian Hébert, who had achieved the chairmanship through seniority in 1970 after spending thirty years in the House, did not tolerate dissenting opinions and rewarded or punished committee members according to whether they agreed or disagreed with his views. Stinging from Pat Schroeder's relentless attacks, Hébert was openly contemptuous of her. He even refused to okay her appointment to the United States delegation to a SALT disarmament conference on chemical warfare in Geneva, Switzerland, telling her, "I wouldn't send you to represent this committee at a dogfight." The State Department eventually waived the rule requiring the chairman's approval of all nominations and Mrs. Schroeder made the trip. On her return, she renewed her challenge of Hébert. To bolster her arguments with hard facts, she hired her own experts on budgets and weaponry and carefully prepared for each confrontation. Although she was, more often than not, on the losing end of the debate, Mrs. Schroeder believes that her fight against the Pentagon's "outrageous" requests helped to create "a political climate conducive to meaningful reform."

On the House floor, Congresswoman Schroeder concentrated on consumer, environmental, and social welfare issues. Among other things, she introduced and sponsored the far-reaching child abuse bill that authorized federal assistance for treatment centers and educational programs, cosponsored a measure expanding the Head Start program, and supported proposals for increased school lunch subsidies and year-round recreational facilities for underprivileged children. To help the elderly, she approved cost-of-living Social Security increases, improved emergency medical services and nutritional programs, rollbacks in prices, rents, and interest rates, and property tax reform at the local level.

By reelection time in 1974, Mrs. Schroeder had impressed many political pressure groups with her effectiveness. Not surprisingly, she received 100 percent ratings from the National Education Association, the National Council on Senior Citizens, and the Consumer Federation of America. For her efforts in behalf of governmental reform, the League of Women Voters also awarded her a 100 percent rating. Considered to be too popular to lose, she was unopposed in the primary election, but came up against a scrappy Republican challenger in Frank K. Southworth in the November general election. Southworth set "a nasty tone," in Mrs. Schroeder's words, by ignoring "the really important issues," such as continued increases in defense spending and the faltering economy, to concentrate on the more explosive topics of busing and abortion. Undaunted, she deftly turned the situation to her advantage and trounced Southworth, taking 58.5 percent of the vote to his 40.8 percent. In 1976 Republican state representative Don Friedman cut into her majority by capitalizing on the voters' growing disenchantment with the state's young Democrats, but she still garnered 54 percent of the votes to win reelection to a third term.

When Mrs. Schroeder returned to the Armed Services Committee in January 1975, F. Edward Hébert was deposed, the victim of a change in the House rules governing committee chairmanships that she helped instigate. But the new chairman, Melvin Price, while more evenhanded than his predecessor, was just as pro-military. To register their opposition to the rubber-stamp approval of the annual increases in the defense budget, Pat Schroeder and a few other doves, including Otis G. Pike, Les Aspin, and Ronald V. Dellums, submitted an alternative defense posture statement, which eliminated hundreds of millions of dollars from the Pentagon's 1976 defense request. As in past years, she continued to vote down appropriation bills for sophisticated weapons systems, including the B-1 bomber and nuclear powered aircraft carriers, saying that she did not oppose "reasonable strength," but "unreasonable redundancy."

On the domestic front, Representative Schroeder remained an outspoken advocate of revised national priorities, governmental reform, children's rights, and women's rights. "Women's issues are 'people issues,'" she told one reporter. "It's a matter of not wasting human potential—making sure there are no roadblocks in anyone's way." The chairman of the National Task Force on Equal Rights for Women, she approved federal payment of abortions and called the Supreme Court's ruling that companies may deny sick pay for pregnancy "gender-based discrimination." To demonstrate her support of improved child-care facilities under federal guidelines, she brought her own children to the House floor on "Working Mother's Day."

In addition, Mrs. Schroeder favored increased federal funding of education at all levels and supported busing to achieve racial integration in the schools. Long interested in governmental reforms, she approved easier voter registration, public financing of elections, Congressional control of the national budget, and cosponsored the so-called "sunshine bill" requiring open committee and agency meetings. Despite her considerable achievements, Mrs. Schroeder has complained that her job can be slow and exasperating. "You just wish the institution were more effective," she said, as quoted in the *Saturday Evening Post* (November 1974). "You want to bring it into the twentieth century so when people call, you can respond. . . . If I can stay and can continue to take strong stands, it's worth it. If I have to backpedal to do it, then it's not."

Tall, slender, and girlish, Pat Schroeder has blue eyes, shoulder-length brown hair, and a wide, easy smile. As a fellow Congressman once remarked, "she looks like a mommy on her way to a PTA meeting." She used to enjoy skiing and flying (she has a pilot's license), but since moving to Washington, she has had little time for recreation. Although she attends two or three official functions a week, she shies away from cocktail and dinner parties, preferring to spend her evenings with her children and husband. Now an attorney with a Washington-based international law firm that allows flexible hours, Jim Schroeder has willingly subordinated his career ambitions to his wife's because he believes she is "doing a good job at something important." The Schroeders live in a red-brick, split-level house in Fairfax County, Virginia and, for their frequent trips to Colorado, maintain a condominium in Denver.

References: Christian Sci Mon p12 Mr 21 '73 pors; Family Circle 87:26+ Jl '75 pors; Ms 4:62+ Je '76 pors; Newsweek 86:77 N 24 '75 por; Redbook 142:97+ N '73 por; Sat Eve Post 246:9 N '74 por; Who's Who in America, 1978-79

Scotto, Renata

Feb. 1936?- Opera singer. Address: b. c/o Robert J. Lombardo, 30 W. 60th St., New York City, N.Y. 10023

Not without reason, American music critics have referred to the 1976-1977 Metropolitan Opera season as "the season of Renata Scotto." After opening the house in October 1976 as Leonora in Verdi's *Il Trovatore*, she went on to triumph in two of its new productions and to enter its archives as the star of its first live telecast. Like the tempestuous Maria Callas, Scotto bends the conventions of opera to her own needs and talents. She first won international fame for her bel canto heroines in 1957, when she substituted on short notice for Maria Callas in La Scala's Edinburgh Festival production of Bellini's *La Somnambula;* she then ventured into Verdi and such verismo composers as Puccini, with whom she is particularly identified. Equally at home in the Italian repertory from 1830 to 1870, Scotto is noted for her intensely individual interpretations that combine vocal agility with passion, scrupulous attention to detail, and insight into characterization. If the opinion of the Italian conductor Carlo Faria is to be trusted, she is neither a lyric coloratura, dramatic, or spinto soprano but that extreme rarity, a *soprano sfogato,* a *soprano d'agilità.*

Renata Scotto, the younger of two daughters of a policeman, was born in late February, in the mid-1930's, in Savona, Italy, a town on the Ligurian coast north of Genoa. She started singing as a young child. "I'm born to sing," she told New York *Post* interviewer Joyce Wadler (October 9, 1976). "I was singing when I was 4 years old, but I don't know why. I sing for everybody, but never for nothing, they always have to give me something, like a piece of candy." For Stephen

Rubin of the New York *Times* (November 19, 1972) she recalled: "I used to put on my mother's clothes and go to the mirror and perform. I was a difficult child—nice but difficult. Every moment I wanted to be a star, a prima donna, and I'd go to my mother and say, 'Mama, you like this? Mama, LOOK at me!' I would sing and perform and my mother said, 'Enough already. *Basta!*' This happened all the time."

Although Renata Scotto sang extensively in church choirs, she dreamed of an operatic career only after she had seen Verdi's *Rigoletto* starring the great baritone Tito Gobbi at Savona's opera house. "I got his autograph and gazed at it for a month," she has told interviewers. At fourteen she began studying voice, piano, and violin in her hometown; at fifteen she auditioned for baritone Emilio Ghirardini in Milan. "He thought it was a joke," the soprano has recalled. "A baby with her whole family coming along for protection! But when I sang 'Stride la Vampa' for him he said my voice was 'beautiful' and to come back in a year and a half."

At sixteen Renata Scotto moved to Milan for vocal study, taking lessons first with Ghirardini, then with Merlini, and finally with Mercedes Llopart who, impressed by the possibilities of her upper register, transformed her from a mezzo-soprano to soprano. Her first operatic appearance as the courtesan Violetta in Verdi's *La Traviata* in Savona led to her entry in a national competition for young artists, in 1953. Her prize-winning aria, Violetta's "Sempre libera," brought her a formal debut as Violetta at Milan's Teatro Nuovo, but cost her her lodgings. "I had been living in a convent with some very strict nuns," she explained to an *Opera News* interviewer (January 1, 1966). "They didn't approve of my debut role, so I moved."

That December, Renata Scotto triumphed in the demanding secondary role of Walter, a strolling minstrel, in Catalani's *La Wally*, which opened La Scala's 1954-1955 season. Although the famed Milanese opera house quickly proffered her other supporting roles she sensibly accepted leads in provincial Italian opera centers instead. "I wanted to move fast. I studied hard. I was very ambitious," she has explained. From 1954 to 1957 she gained valuable experience in such parts as Adina in Donizetti's *L'Elisir d'Amore* and Lisa in Tchaikovsky's *Pique Dame*.

Her acclaimed performances as Violetta, Adina, Mimi, and Donna Elvira during a spring 1957 engagement with an Italian touring company at London's Stoll Theatre led London reviewers to call her "a delicious little soprano" and "the darling of the season." Writing in *Opera* (July 1957), Andrew Porter predicted: "There seems to be no doubt that Renata Scotto is destined to go to the first rank of operatic singers." Her big breakthrough came during the Edinburgh Festival of 1957, when, having joined La Scala there as an emergency standby, she unexpectedly was called upon to replace Maria Callas, who had refused to sing a fourth unscheduled performance of Bellini's *La Sonnambula*. Mastering the role of Amina in three days, Renata Scotto scored an unqualified success on an evening that she remembers as the most beautiful in her career. In comparing her with Callas, the critic for *Opera* (October 1957) concluded: "The beauty and freshness of her voice and her unaffected stage personality made her a more credible Amina than her predecessor."

A few months later Renata Scotto repeated her Amina at La Scala to critical acclaim. In demand throughout Italy, she expanded her horizons in the 1960's, recruiting fans in European opera capitals as well as in such far-flung places as Buenos Aires, Moscow, and Tokyo. Although her Covent Garden debut as Cio-Cio-San in Puccini's *Madama Butterfly* on September 10, 1962 met with only a mixed reaction from the critics, her vocal pyrotechnics as Mimi in his *La Bohème* eight days later were unanimously applauded. On October 13, 1965, five years after her appearances as Mimi and Micaela with the Chicago Lyric Opera in the fall of 1960, Renata Scotto made her debut at the old Metropolitan Opera House in *Madama Butterfly*. Many critics found her edgy high notes, inaudible soft phrases, and exaggerated gestures only minor flaws in view of her inborn musicality and overwhelming dramatic involvement. John Ardoin, writing in *Opera* (January 1966) called her performance "one of the handful of supreme characterizations to be seen at the Metropolitan today." In his review for the New York *Times* (October 14, 1965) Raymond Ericson praised her "combination of Japanese grace and Italian volatility, emotions flying through her body and across her face with seeming spontaneity."

The love affair between Renata Scotto and the New York public intensified with her first Metropolitan Lucia in Donizetti's *Lucia di Lammermoor* on December 13, 1965. After hearing her enchanting Adina in a Christmas Eve performance of *L'Elisir d'Amore*, a New York *Times* critic, Howard Klein (December 25, 1965), reported: "She can float a pianissimo high note square on pitch, crescendo, diminuendo . . . toss off scales, ride gossamer-like portamentos from high to low notes, and spit out words like a vixen."

After a whirlwind European schedule that included her Gilda in a new production of *Rigoletto* that opened the Teatro dell'Opera season in Florence on November 19, 1966 shortly after the disastrous Arno flood, Renata Scotto returned to the United States in the winter of 1966-1967. Of greater significance perhaps than her Metropolitan Opera Lucias, Butterflys, and Violettas were her recital debuts at Washington's Constitution Hall and New York's Philharmonic Hall in January 1967. On each occasion she presented a program of Italian arias, rounded off with selections by Beethoven and Gluck. William Bender typified the generally favorable reception when he wrote in the New York *World Journal Tribune* (January 30, 1967): "As a recitalist, she is every bit as theatrical as she is in the opera house. Even the merest whisper of a phrase is charged with emotion. Her emotionality, though, is not of the temperamental sort. Hers is a warm, effusive appeal." Among the few dissenters was the New York *Post's* Harriett Johnson (January 30, 1967), who objected to the soprano's shrill tones, especially in Beethoven's "Ah! Perfido!": "Miss Scotto must learn that a flute is not a trumpet, no matter how much the woodwind yearns to be brass."

Plagued by vocal difficulties in the late 1960's, Renata Scotto was—in the judgement of New York *Times* critic Harold C. Schonberg (October 9, 1967)—"a puzzling singer, capable of great sensitivity and also of tones that can make one wince." She also adopted a number of affectations, notably inaudible pianissimi and distorted rhythms, which Andrew Porter, writing in the *New Yorker* (May 26, 1973), described as a "set of absurdly regal gestures" grafted on "the dear little Miss Muffet appearance." Overcoming those deficiencies—"I mature in the head and in my studying," she once observed—the controversial Renata Scotto sprinted to even greater fame in the 1970's.

Her scintillating Elena in Verdi's *I Vespri Siciliani* opened the 1970-1971 season at La Scala. After making a spectacular Covent Garden appearance in *La Sonnambula* in February 1971 she exacted critical homage as Amina at the Metropolitan Opera in October 1972, despite the obvious drawbacks of appearing in a production that had originally been created for Joan Sutherland in 1963. Taste, expressiveness, and technical precision also marked her Alaide in Palermo's Teatro Massimo production of Bellini's *La Straniera* at the 1972 Edinburgh Festival, leading *American Record Guide* (December 1972) critic George L. Mayer to declare unequivocally in his review: "She is a *major* Bellini singer."

Renata Scotto's increasing popularity among American operagoers not only in New York but also in such centers as San Francisco, Dallas, and Philadelphia contrasted sharply with her stale Metropolitan Opera repertory of Lucias and Butterflys in inadequately rehearsed and tired old productions. Wistfully citing the two opening nights and ten new productions accorded her at La Scala, she told Stephen Rubin in her interview with him: "I know the public. They like me and want me in something different, something new."

The short-lived Renata Scotto vs. the Metropolitan dispute was settled, according to her manager Robert Lombardo, when the post-Rudolf Bing management "made it very evident that this was a new ball game and they were interested in Renata Scotto." In the fall of 1974 the soprano showcased her undeniable assets in a few electrifying performances of a new production of *I Vespri Siciliani*. On New Year's Eve of that year she made Cio-Cio-San "a living, breathing, mature, sentimentally tragic figure," Speight Jenkins testified in the New York *Post* (January 2, 1975), showing herself "in first-class state—clear-voiced, with the edge in her voice working for her and under perfect control and with warmth and inner fire to burn." In June 1975 the Metropolitan Opera's concert performance of *Madama Butterfly* in Central Park, in which she starred, attracted an estimated 100,000 persons, the largest in the history of the parks series. On January 23, 1976, in a tour de force, Renata Scotto became the first soprano in Metropolitan Opera history to sing all three heroines in Puccini's trilogy, *Il Trittico*. Critics were as enthusiastic about her portrayal of the disparate leads—passionate Giorgetta, despairing Sister Angelica, and girlish Lauretta—as they were about her vocal acrobatics.

Her real home runs in the Metropolitan Opera's "new ball game," however, came with the 1976-1977 season. Renata Scotto opened it on October 11, 1976 as Leonora in Verdi's *Il Trovatore* and also graced it with a grand total of forty-two performances, starring in two new productions: Meyerbeer's *Le Prophète* and Puccini's *La Bohème*. In *La Bohème* she sang not only Mimi—which she views as the "most pathetic and human of all Puccini's roles for women"—but also Musetta, because she loves the part. On March 15, 1977 she became known to millions of television viewers in an historic PBS telecast of *La Bohème* live from Lincoln Center. High on her list for future Metropolitan Opera roles are Luisa Miller, Manon Lescaut, and Norma. She sang the last-named role with fine technique and rich intonation but with, some critics felt, as yet limited vocal depth, both at Turin, Italy in April 1974 and at Cincinnati, Ohio in the summer of 1977. Her Adriana Lecouvreur, which she sang at the San Francisco Opera in September 1977 and at the Metropolitan in March 1978, transformed Cilea's cloying opera of the same name into a compelling dramatic experience, transcending its usual candy-box sweetness.

Her unusually flexible voice enables Renata Scotto to disregard voice categories. Calling herself simply a soprano, she continually expands a repertory that already encompasses some fifty roles. One Metropolitan Opera administrator has said: "The marvelous thing is that she's so incredibly versatile." Although she undertakes music of such early composers as Monteverdi and Purcell, she has staked most of her reputation on combining the bel canto repertory of Bellini and Donizetti with the verismo repertory of Puccini and Mascagni. Alluding to her *forte* of the past few seasons—singing verismo roles with bel canto technique and drama—she told New York *Times* interviewer William Livingstone (October 17, 1976): "My technique is secure enough that I think I can do this without damaging the voice."

For two decades Renata Scotto has amply fulfilled the promise noted in September 1960 by an *American Record Guide* critic who acclaimed the then relatively unknown soprano's third recording, a full-length *Lucia di Lammermoor* with Giuseppe di Stefano, on the Mercury label. Her extensive recordings for such companies as EMI, Harmonia, Cetra, Deutsche Grammophone, RCA, and Columbia feature Italian arias and complete operas, including a 1967 *Madama Butterfly* under Sir John Barbirolli that some critics regard as the definitive *Butterfly* recording. "Records I do not only for commercial reasons but because they are important as documents of the art," Renata Scotto told Robert Jacobson in an *After Dark* (October 1977) interview.

The music critic Louis Biancolli once described the dark-haired short-statured Renata Scotto as "a small plump woman with a large plump voice," while to Alan Rich she seemed "a living doll somewhat in the shape of a Christmas pudding." Having lost forty pounds recently through diet and exercise, she now belies those descriptions. Mild-mannered and aware of the proprieties, she is not a highly temperamental artist, although she can be "a little bit difficult," as her wrathful attack on the Callas cultists for detracting from her 1970 La Scala *I Vespri Siciliani* attests. "She expects the world at her feet," as one interviewer put it, "but is in no way haughty about the request." Her unpretentious mannerisms and dress prompted another's comment that she may appear for an afternoon recital "looking like a suburban matron who dressed early for an evening dinner dance," communicating with her audience as directly as "a woman talking over the back fence to a neighbor." Offstage, however, she jealously guards her personal life: "Then I am Renata Scotto, woman, private," she assured Stephen Rubin.

In 1960 Renata Scotto married Lorenzo Anselmi, a violinist and concertmaster with the La Scala orchestra who, she jokes, "fell in love with her voice before he could see her face" during a recording session. Their first meeting, she insists, was "like, uh, un *tempesto* . . . a thunderstorm." To prevent long separations, Anselmi resigned his position to become his wife's teacher and coach. She vocalizes daily, convinced that the way to sustain a career is always to give the public a little more with each new appearance.

The soprano's New York-based career led the Anselmis, who have two children, Laura and Filippo, to purchase a nine-room Park Avenue cooperative in 1976. At Gorganza near Mantua the family still maintains a summer country house "like a poem" along the Po River, where Renata Scotto enjoys swimming, fishing, cooking, and gardening. Among her other recreations are painting, crocheting, and taking home movies. She rarely attends operas. "I know what it is to sing," she told Joyce Wadler, "and I cannot relax; I don't get nervous when I sing, but when others sing, for them I get nervous."

References: After Dark 10:54+ O '77 pors; Newsday II p10+ O 10 '76 pors; N Y Post p37 Mr 21 '67 por, II p19 O 9 '76 por; N Y Times II p15 N 19 '72 por, II p19+ O 17 '76 por; Opera News 30:26 Ja 1 '66 por, 37:12+ Ap 21 '73 por; Opern Welt 1: 46+ Ja '70 pors, 5:38+ My '73 pors; Stereo Review 25:70 Ag '70 por; Washington Post B p1+ Je 24 '75 pors; Encyclopedia of Opera, 1976; Rubin, Stephen E. The New Met in Profile (1974); Who's Who in Opera, 1976

Sedaka, Neil

Mar. 13, 1939- Composer; recording artist. Address: b. Neil Sedaka Music, 1370 Ave. of the Americas, New York City, N.Y. 10019

In a career that spans two decades the singer and songwriter Neil Sedaka has gone from fame to obscurity, then back to fame again. An idol of teenagers in the late 1950's and early 1960's, Sedaka was engulfed by the wave of British rock groups that inundated the pop music charts in the mid-1960's. But his continued success as a songwriter paved the way for his comeback as a performer in Great Britain in 1970. A handful of Gold Record-winning hits and six Broadcast Music Incorporated awards, signifying a minimum of 400,000 radio plays, marked his phenomenal resurgence in the United States in 1975. Sustained by concert, nightclub, and television appearances, Sedaka's second career has turned out to be even more successful than the first. "It was the impossible dream," he said in a recent interview. "The Impossible Dream! To come back fifteen years later, to a new audience, with a new approach."

Neil Sedaka was born on March 13, 1939 in Brooklyn, New York, one of the two children of Mac Sedaka, a taxi driver, and Elea-

Neil Sedaka

nor (Appel) Sedaka, Sephardic Jews who had emigrated from Istanbul, Turkey. Following in the footsteps of his grandmother, a concert pianist who had studied with Walter Damrosch, the composer and conductor, Neil Sedaka showed such musical promise that his fourth-grade teacher at P.S. 253 in Brooklyn's Brighton Beach section urged his parents to give him private piano lessons. At the age of nine he was accepted as a scholarship student in the preparatory division of the Juilliard School of Music, which he attended for the next eight years, while continuing his education in the local public schools.

In the early 1950's Howard Greenfield, an older boy who lived in the same apartment building, asked Sedaka to compose music for a poem he had written. "We had to wait until my mother left for shopping because it would have blown her mind; I was so into my classical music," Sedaka told Tom Nolan in an interview for a *Rolling Stone* (December 4, 1975) profile. "We sat down and wrote a song called 'My Life's Devotion.' I was over the moon! It was not a bad song for a thirteen- and a sixteen-year-old." Because of his small size, eyeglasses, braces, and high-pitched voice, Sedaka had been ridiculed and ostracized by his peers, but his music gave him an entree to local teenage social functions. "I started to write and play popular music . . . because I was tossed aside and that was a way to be accepted by other thirteen-year-olds," he admitted to Norma McLain Stoop, who interviewed him for *After Dark* (September 1976). "It worked in my favor. Not only was I invited to parties, but I was suddenly the life of every party I attended."

By Sedaka's own reckoning, he and Howard Greenfield wrote "a song a day for three years," most of them ballads in the style of such singers as Patti Page and Johnny Ray, but they switched to rock 'n' roll after Sedaka heard the Penguins' version of "Earth Angel," a hit of 1954. Eager to cash in on the rock market, the two made the rounds of New York's music publishing houses and recording companies. Jerry Wexler of the fledgling Atlantic Records organization bought a few of their songs, which were eventually recorded by such rhythm-and-blues artists as LaVern Baker, the Cardinals, Clyde McPhatter, and the Clovers.

Meanwhile, Sedaka continued his classical music training and in 1956 he was selected by Artur Rubinstein, Jascha Heifetz, and other distinguished judges to perform over radio station WQXR as one of fifteen winners in the annual citywide New York *Times*-sponsored Musical Talent in Our Schools competition. After graduating from Brooklyn's Abraham Lincoln High School, he enrolled in Juilliard's college division on a piano scholarship. There he studied under Adele Marcus, the teacher of jazz pianist Cy Coleman, for two years, but he abandoned his embryonic career as a concert pianist in favor of a more lucrative vocation as a pop songwriter when Connie Francis' recording of his song "Stupid Cupid" hit the "Top Forty" charts in the summer of 1958.

Sedaka signed on with Aldon Music, a small publishing firm owned by Don Kirschner and Al Nevins, a member of the vocal group the Three Suns. Kirschner, who eventually launched "bubble gum" rock and fabricated such pop groups as the Monkees and the Archies, employed a number of apprentice rock 'n' roll songwriters, including Gerry Goffin, Carole King, Barry Mann, Cynthia Weil, and Howard Greenfield. In their cramped quarters in the Brill Building on Broadway, Sedaka and Greenfield churned out one tune after another for Bobby Darin, Roy Hamilton, Dinah Washington, the Ames Brothers, and other singers. Encouraged by Kirschner and Nevins, Sedaka decided to cut a demonstration record of his own. "I had been writing songs for other people who would interpret the songs quite differently from the way I saw it," he explained to Milton Esterow of the New York *Times* (June 16, 1962). "I had sung in the choral group at high school, so I decided to give it a try."

On the strength of that demo record, Steven Sholes, an RCA executive, signed Sedaka to a contract. For his first single Sedaka wrote "The Diary," a rhythm-and-blues number, backed by "No Vacancy." "The

Diary" first appeared on *Billboard* magazine's "Hot 100" list on December 14, 1958, remained on the chart for nearly four months, and at one point reached fourteenth place. He followed that up with "I Go Ape," a mildly successful rocker, and "Oh! Carol," a Top Ten hit he has since described as "a simple, ordinary, layman thing" that, although written for Carole King, appealed "to all the Carols."

Other Sedaka hits—"Stairway to Heaven," "Calendar Girl," "Little Devil," "Happy Birthday, Sweet Sixteen," "Next Door To An Angel"—followed quickly, and "Breaking Up Is Hard To Do" topped the charts in the summer of 1962. His albums, including *Little Devil and Others* (1961) and *Neil Sedaka* (1963), were equally successful. Between 1959 and 1963 Sedaka sold more than 25,000,000 records and earned several hundred thousand dollars annually. He played to wildly enthusiastic fans in concert halls and auditoriums throughout the United States and in several foreign countries. For his appearances on stage and on such television shows as Dick Clark's *American Bandstand* and the *Ed Sullivan Show*, Sedaka formed a backup quartet called the Tokens, who later had a number one hit of their own with "The Lion Sleeps Tonight." "I had to keep pinching myself to believe it," he told Tom Nolan. "I used to drive down Kings Highway, in Brooklyn, with the top down in my first car, a white convertible Chevy Impala. . . . I can't describe to you the feeling of pushing the buttons in the car and . . . there were my songs blaring on the radio!"

Then came the British rock invasion of 1964, and sales of Neil Sedaka's records plummeted. Locked into a repetitious pattern of "formula" singles by his recording company, he was unable to crack charts dominated by the Beatles, the Rolling Stones, the Dave Clark Five, Manfred Mann, and other British groups. "The most I could do was change the tempo a bit," he told Tom Nolan. "'Little Devil' sounded like 'Stairway To Heaven,' 'Next Door To An Angel' was very similar to 'Breaking Up Is Hard To Do.' So . . . I blew a good thing." For a few years Sedaka continued to tour abroad, singing standards, "golden oldies," and even a medley of Eddie Cantor's songs, performed in blackface, but he spent most of his time composing new tunes. A shrewd analyst of musical trends, he wrote a number of chart-making hits for Tom Jones ("Puppet Man"), the Fifth Dimension ("Working On A Groovy Thing"), Andy Williams ("One Day Of Your Life"), Davy Jones ("Rainy Jane"), and other singers.

Believing it would be easier to break back into performing in Great Britain, where he still had a core of faithful fans, Sedaka moved to London in 1970. There a re-release of "Oh! Carol" and a new single, "Beautiful You," received the widespread radio play needed to nudge them both on to the pop charts. Backed by a group that went on to international success as 10cc, he toured constantly, playing everything from small pop clubs to the august Royal Albert Hall. Because the members of his audience wanted to hear what he calls his "old stuff," he obliged them with a medley of his past hits in his stage act, but he concentrated on his newer material and eventually record-buyers stopped looking on him as, in his words, "a ghost from the past." Over the next few years Sedaka's singles, including "That's When The Music Takes Me" and the chart-topping "Laughter In The Rain," and albums—*Emergence, Solitaire,* and *The Tra-La Days Are Over*—appeared on the Top Forty with increasing regularity. One British critic commented: "If the old dog has been learning new tricks, he has learned them a great deal faster, and better, than most of the young ones."

In 1974 Neil Sedaka asked his friend Elton John, the flamboyant British rock superstar, to arrange for the American release of his British hits on John's Rocket Records label. "I had been put in a box. There was no breaking out of it unless I had an endorsement like that," Sedaka explained to Tom Nolan. Convinced that Sedaka had handed him "gold bricks," Elton John agreed to release and promote "Laughter in the Rain," a soft rock number with a tricky but haunting melody. Released in early 1975, "Laughter" sold more than a million copies in less than two months. In preparing for his first American recording in several years, Sedaka and Elton John culled material from his three best-selling British LP's. Sedaka agreed in advance to forfeit his royalties from the album, preferring to plow back his share of the profits into the promotion of his comeback. *Sedaka's Back* (Rocket, 1975), featuring "Laughter" and another Sedaka-Greenfield winner, "Love Will Keep Us Together," went gold within weeks of its release. A version of "Love Will Keep Us Together" by the Captain and Tennille became the runaway hit of the summer of 1975 and won the National Academy of Arts and Sciences Grammy award as Record of the Year in February 1976.

The fastest-breaking single of his career, "Bad Blood," a raucous rocker with a reggae beat and somewhat raunchy lyrics, zoomed to the top of the charts in September 1975 and won for Sedaka his second Gold Record in as many attempts. Although a few critics complained about the record's "macho misogyny" and some radio stations refused to play it, Sedaka defended "Bad Blood" as "just a fun rock 'n' roller." "I just like to keep changing," he told Larry Sloman (November 6, 1975). "I'm real happy with 'Bad Blood' because the lyric line is a little controversial, with words like 'bitch' and such. I was concerned at first because my image was so wholesome," he admitted, "but I like it because it's not such a goody-goody two-shoes thing. That's the mistake I made in my first career. The songs were too predictable."

Taking advantage of his resurgent popularity, Sedaka prepared a second LP, *The Hungry Years* (Rocket), for release in the fall of 1975. Among the eleven songs—all but one collaborations by Sedaka and lyricists Howard Greenfield or Phil Cody—were "Bad Blood"; "Tit For Tat," a rocker with an early 1960's flavor; ballads such as "New York City Blues" and "The Hungry Years"; "Stephen," a plaintive hymn to Stephen Foster; and a torchy version of "Breaking Up Is Hard To Do." Sedaka wrote both the words and the music for the eleventh number, "Lonely Night (Angel Face)," which became a Gold-Record-winning single for the Captain and Tennille. Discussing the thematically unrelated material of *The Hungry Years* in a review for *Rolling Stone* (November 20, 1975), Stephen Holden commented: "Sedaka is far more concerned that a pop album work as entertainment than as 'art'. . . . [His] singing is perfectly consistent with his material —dry, energetic, and detached, allowing just the right amount of pathos."

Sedaka's appearance as an opening act for the Carpenters at the Riviera Hotel in Las Vegas in August 1975 gave him his most important public exposure in the United States in a decade. When, three months later, he returned to the Riviera as a headline act, the opening-night audience tendered him six standing ovations. Suddenly in demand from the casino-hotels of Las Vegas and Lake Tahoe to the nightclubs of New York City, Neil Sedaka spent about nine months out of the year on tour. He capped a successful concert season in 1976 with two sold-out appearances in the Great Performers Series at Lincoln Center's Avery Fisher Hall in March and on September 17 starred in his first television special, *Neil Sedaka: Steppin' Out*, for NBC.

In composing a tune, Sedaka, who writes an average of fifty songs a year, tries to please himself as an artist and, at the same time, please the masses. "I'd like to think that I'm a craftsman," he explained to Nik Cohn of *New York* (August 4, 1975). "I sit at the piano and, more often than not, something comes to me. I try to make a song that's commercial . . . but I don't believe in making big gestures." Two of his most recent albums, *Steppin' Out* (Rocket, 1976) and *A Song* (Elektra Asylum, 1977), give further proof of Sedaka's ability to assimilate various styles, from funky rock to country. Most critics agree, however, that he is most at home with soft rock songs, such as "Sing Me" and "You Gotta Make Your Own Sunshine" and fast numbers like "Steppin' Out" and "Good Times, Good Music, Good Friends." When, on the rare occasions that reviewers find fault with a Sedaka LP, their most frequent complaint is the "high choirboy" pitch and timbre of his voice that sometimes give his slower songs a "spun-sugar quality." In 1977 Sedaka bought back all his songs—more than 110 in all—from Kirschner Entertainment Corporation for a reported $2,000,000 and founded Neil Sedaka Music. His most recent album is *All You Need Is the Music* (Elektra Asylum, 1978).

A short, dark, energetic man who was once described as looking more like "a friendly uncle" than a pop star, Neil Sedaka is, according to his friends, gentle, civilized, modest, and "altogether decent." Although open with reporters about his career, he tends to be reticent about his private life. Married since September 11, 1962, Sedaka and his wife, the former Leba Margaret Strassberg, have two children, Dara Felice and Marc Charles. They enjoy tennis and skiing, dinner parties with close friends, and quiet evenings at home. Sedaka, a resident of Westport, Connecticut, also has a home in upstate New York and an apartment in Manhattan.

Sedaka still plays classical music, usually Beethoven, Bach, or Ravel, for his own diversion, and he intends to return to the concert stage in about five years. "It will take me about a year to get back into that kind of music and, hopefully, take my audience with me into the concert halls. . . . I *do* miss that feeling of involvement in the great music," he added. "I'm not putting down *my* music. I feel, I hope, that I'm a contribution to American music, but a critical person must please himself artistically first. I have always been concerned with developing, growing, topping my last work as an artist."

References: After Dark 9:44+ S '76; N Y Daily News p86 S 1 '76 por; N Y Post p31 F 7 '76 por; Rolling Stone p34 D 4 '75 pors; Seventeen 35:76+ S '76 por; Stambler, Irwin. Encyclopedia of Pop, Rock and Soul (1974); Who's Who in America, 1978-79

Serban, Andrei (chər-bän')

1943(?)- Theatrical director. Address: b. Yale Repertory Theatre, 1120 Chapel St., New Haven, Conn. 06520

Among the young directors in the forefront of experimental theatre is Romanian-born Andrei Serban, who began working in the United States in 1969 under the sponsorship of Ellen Stewart, founder of La Mama Experimental Theatre Club in New York. His

Andrei Serban

imaginative productions of the Greek classics and the plays of Shakespeare, Chekhov, and others have been staged at the La Mama Annex in Manhattan's East Village, the Vivian Beaumont Theatre at Lincoln Center, and the Yale Repertory Theatre in New Haven, of which he became assistant director in the summer of 1977. He has also toured Europe and the Middle East with his Great Jones Repertory Project, creating his unique form of theatre in caves, forests, and ruins and on mountaintops and beaches. A onetime disciple of the English director Peter Brook, Serban experiments resourcefully with sound, gesture, movement, and space to achieve powerful and surprisingly novel effects from well-known and conventional plays.

Andrei Serban was born in Bucharest, Romania about 1943. His father was a photographer and sculptor, and his mother, a schoolteacher. Even as a child he displayed a sense of theatre, entertaining his parents and their guests with puppet shows and plays that he enjoyed making up. In Bucharest's Park of the Icons, he organized his playmates in stick-and-fist fights to enact ferocious, dramatic battles. On completing his secondary school courses, he became one of the few chosen from hundreds of applicants for admission to the state's Institute of Theatrical and Cinematographic Arts in Bucharest. During his apprenticeship there in directing plays he worked on proscenium stages with conventional settings.

Although experimental theatre was not encouraged in the socialist state of Romania, Serban staged a production of *Julius Caesar* as a Kabuki play, the traditional Japanese popular drama with stylized singing and dancing. Describing the official reaction to his oriental rendering of Shakespeare, Serban told Jan Hodenfield, who interviewed him for the New York *Post* (January 31, 1976), "The whole question of social realism, which was the hard line of the arts, was entirely contradicted by the production. Of course, it was a scandal." With similar defiance Serban blended grim realism and abstract dance in his version of another Elizabethan drama, the blood-drenched *Arden of Feversham.* Despite his controversial beginning, by 1966, when he took his student theatre to Zagreb, he was becoming recognized as one of Romania's most promising young directors.

Serban's work at the Yugoslav theatre festival that year particularly impressed the American visitor Ellen Stewart, who in 1962 had originated New York's avant-garde Cafe La Mama (now the La Mama Experimental Theatre Club). After three years of persuading she succeeded in bringing him to New York, with the help of a grant from the Ford Foundation. As an acknowledged force in the Romanian theatre, Serban occupied a privileged position, so that he had no difficulty in obtaining a passport to visit the United States. Once here, however, he was not pleased with the type of theatre he found. As he explained to Richard Eder of the New York *Times* (February 13, 1977), "Coming here in the 60's and seeing the whole looseness of the avant-garde, where the idea was to be free in this very sentimental way, in this loose way, smoke drugs, let the hair grow—it seemed so cheap to me. There's something in me more connected to discipline and intensity than to this freedom and looseness." Serban was also frustrated by the fact that he spoke almost no English and had to communicate through gestures and French.

While Serban deplored the laxity that he saw in much of the avant-garde theatre, he admired the explorative abstract dance of Merce Cunningham and the productions of Joseph Chaikin's Open Theatre, which resulted from experimental collaboration between director and actors in creating drama. As he told Julius Novick during an interview for the New York *Times* (February 2, 1976), "It was really discovering a geographical territory and an emotional and a psychological territory which I was of course very influenced by, and something in me had to change."

In 1970 Serban decided to make his directorial debut at La Mama with *Arden of Feversham,* repeating the three-hour version he had staged in Romania. But after struggling in vain to remember his blocking and movements, he felt compelled to start all over again. He explained to Richard Eder, "I realized that what was necessary was nothing. To start from zero. To start from that energy that provokes theater action. We tried to discover this impulse usually called shameful, animal, that had to be revealed either not at all or all the way." To uncover the core of the melodrama, Serban cut the play to fifty minutes, keeping only the key words and phrases, stripping it down to a series of violent physical actions that verged at times on mime. Recalling the play in the *Soho Weekly News* (January 6, 1977), Robb Baker described it as "a whole world of mind and feelings telescoped, encapsulated into the physical bodies of a handful of actors—a triumph." Along with *Arden*, on a double bill that the New York *Times* critic Clive Barnes called "remarkably sophisticated and explosive," Serban offered *Ubu*, an adaptation of Alfred Jarry's nineteenth-century French comedy *Ubu Roi*.

When Peter Brook, the highly inventive and versatile British theatrical director, saw La Mama's production of *Arden*, he invited Serban, along with two members of the cast, to his International Center of Theatre Research in Paris in 1970. Though he held the title of assistant director, Serban had little to do other than observe Brook's techniques. Brook believed that words were often ineffective in drama, either because of debasement of their meaning or because actors felt restrained by them. At his Center of Theatre Research he devised exercises to find new sounds and patterns of movement. Serban supposed that the aim of the exercises was to develop an actor's skills, until he saw that Brook discontinued them as soon as they began to accomplish that purpose. "What I slowly realized," Eder quoted Serban as saying, "was that something in the perception of one's own elements, one's tools, started to take place. Acting is looking with one's own resources. To have a different sense of one's resources is to have a different perception, and that affects the quality of one's acting."

Working with Brook through 1971, Serban accompanied him to Iran to take part in a production of *Orghast*, a theatrical experiment performed in the ruins of the ancient Persian capital of Persepolis. For Serban, *Orghast*, which employed an invented language, was too cold and intellectual to be satisfying, but he acknowledged to Eder, "It fed me for the next five years." He retained, moreover, his deep respect for Brook, under whose guidance he had begun to develop the distinctive ideas that mark his form of theatre: the emphasis on raw sound and physical movement through which his actors attempt not merely to represent emotions, but to create them and transmit them to an audience. Brook's influence more likely confirmed Serban's own concepts of theatre rather than implanted new ones, inasmuch as Serban's staging of *Arden* and *Ubu* had earlier subordinated text to patterns of sound and movement.

Soon after he returned to New York, Serban assembled his own company and started to build on what he had learned in Paris. In La Mama's basement theatre he staged a version of *Medea* using both the original Greek dialogue of Euripides and the Latin of Seneca. His bold experiment sacrificed a literal understanding of the tragedy for an entirely emotional one. Language no longer functioned as a medium for expressing ideas; words were used instead for their qualities of sound and resonance, for the fundamental emotion they evoked. In early rehearsals for the play Serban had actors give speeches in Elizabethan English as a means of informing the audience of developments in the plot, but he found those intrusions destroyed the mood of the play and discarded them. Essential to the sensuous effects that the director sought was the musical score of *Medea*, composed by Elizabeth Swados, who also collaborated with Serban on later productions.

Quite a number of influential drama critics attended the Off-Off-Broadway performances of *Medea*. Henry Hewes of the *Saturday Review* (March 11, 1972) judged it "the most dedicated and pure piece of theater we have seen in some time." Clive Barnes in the New York *Times* (January 26, 1972) wrote of the "authority and integrity" of the production and called it a "potent theatrical event" that "offers deep insights into the nature of the dramatic experience." *Medea* won the Drama Desk Award for 1971.

In 1972 Serban directed a student production of *Romeo and Juliet* at Long Island's Nassau Community College, where in 1970 his visiting production of *Arden* had created an uproar because of nudity in the play. Serban told Alan Wallach, who interviewed him for *Newsday* (February 16, 1972), that his approach to Shakespeare was to treat him as a contemporary genius, not a "classical big statue." Believing that audiences had grown insensitive to Shakespeare's lines through an overfamiliarity with the play, he directed the actors to sing much of the dialogue. The play was staged in "fragments," Serban's manner of getting at the essence.

Serban resumed his interpretation of Greek tragedy in 1973 with a production of Euripides' *Electra*, created for the Festival Octobre à Bordeaux under the auspices of Jean-Louis Barrault. Back at La Mama the following year, he added *The Trojan Women* to his repertory of Greek plays, all three of which he presented at the new La Mama Annex in 1974 (at the rate of two plays a night) under the collective title *Fragments of a Trilogy*. As in his first production of *Medea*, audiences heard ancient Greek in each play, as well as a variety of archaic languages and music from a mixture of primitive cultures. The inclusion of non-Greek material depended upon the individual themes of the plays. In *The Trojan Women*, for example, a play about the imprisonment of civilization, Serban, working closely again with Elizabeth Swados, introduced cries and laments from American Indians, along with songs from Africa and tunes from the Balkans and Romania.

The productions that comprised *Trilogy* were also unusual for the use Serban made of space in presenting them in a huge room with a proscenium stage at one end and galleries along the sides. As the plays began in darkness, members of the audience had no place to sit and no clear idea which way to direct their attention, because spotlighted action occurred sporadically throughout the room. Richard Eder, describing the experience in the New York *Times* (January 24, 1976), compared the condition of the audience to the emotional state of a street crowd witnessing an historical event too vast to be immediately understood. In the second part of *Trilogy* actors ushered the spectators to their seats and the action grew distant, tableaux-like. In Serban's productions there was none of the hostility toward the audience that marked much avant-garde theatre in the 1960's. "Serban's drive throughout these plays," Stanley Kauffmann pointed out in the *New Republic* (September 23, 1974), "has been toward their mythic essences, to distill and crystallize the subconscious, even preconscious elements that made them part of our communal heritage centuries before the plays were written down, the elements that have kept them vital through the centuries since."

As a change from classical tragedy to what he called "something simple and light," in 1975 Serban presented Bertolt Brecht's *The Good Woman of Setzuan* as a work in progress at the La Mama Annex, to which he returned with a full production of the fable the following year. Also in 1975 he staged Brecht's *The Three-Penny Opera* for the American Conservatory Theatre in San Francisco. During Serban's tour of Europe that year *Trilogy* won the Bitef Festival Grand Prize in Belgrade. In late summer he closed the ninth Iran Festival of the Arts with a four-hour mobile production of *Trilogy,* which began at the gates of Persepolis and proceeded through the ruins of the city.

Grants awarded to Serban by the Rockefeller Foundation in March 1976 and the Guggenheim Foundation in April relieved him of some of his financial difficulty in developing his company. His earlier acceptance, however, of an offer of assistance from the French government committed him to another tour abroad. In the spring of 1976 Serban and his company settled in La Rochelle, on the west coast of France, to rehearse a production of *As You Like It,* with Renaissance-like music composed by Elizabeth Swados and much of the dialogue metamorphosed into mime. The Shakespearean comedy had its premiere about two months later in a forest at Perigny. Other productions, both of Shakespeare and the Greek classics, that Serban presented on his European tour that summer used caves, abbeys, amphitheatres, and churches as settings.

At the invitation of the producer Joseph Papp, Serban left his company to stage Chekhov's *The Cherry Orchard* at Lincoln Center's Vivian Beaumont Theatre in early 1977. Irene Worth's portrayal of Madame Ranevskaya and Santo Loquasto's beautiful set won the general applause of critics. But many of them blasted Serban for a stress on farcical elements that not only broke with the traditional presentation of the play, but also, some charged, violated the playwright's intention. Describing Serban's staging as "anti-Chekhovian," Brendan Gill protested in the *New Yorker* (February 28, 1977), "If Mr. Serban is wanton in removing so much that Chekhov has cunningly inserted, he is also, on occasion, gratuitously vulgar." In the *New Republic* (March 26, 1977) Stanley Kauffmann took Serban to task for abandoning Chekhov's realism in favor of an abstract presentation that he contradicted by the inclusion of both literal and symbolic devices. Jack Kroll of *Newsweek* (February 28, 1977), however, was delighted: "Serban's *Cherry Orchard* is the most beautiful production of a classic play in years, a clear-eyed act of love and homage that won't be easily forgotten." Serban defended his interpretation in a letter to the New York *Times* (March 13, 1977), justifying, for instance, his use of symbolism by pointing to places in Chekhov's text that contained "elements of another nature."

Later in 1977 Serban directed a second play at the Beaumont, Aeschylus' *Agamemnon,* combining the original Greek with Edith Hamilton's English translation in a text that was then "sound structured" by Miss Swados. With a few changes the same production moved outdoors during the summer to the Delacorte Theatre in Central Park. Like *Fragments of a Trilogy, Agamemnon* gave Serban abundant opportunity to indulge his penchant for mythic import, archetypal characterization, ritualized movement, ceremony, spectacle, and mime. The play gratified some reviewers and dismayed and confused others. Walter Kerr of the New York *Times* (June 12, 1977), who found the production "visually provocative, systematically dehumanized, dramatically sterile," devoted his review to a string of questions about Serban's staging. In reply Robert Brustein, director of the Yale Repertory Theatre, defended Serban's version of *Agamemnon* in a letter to the New York *Times* (June 13, 1977).

A month later Brustein, who is also dean of the Yale School of Drama, announced that Serban had been appointed associate director of the Yale Repertory Theatre. Serban was also assigned to conduct workshops for advanced students in acting and directing at the School of Drama. The first play that he directed for the Yale company was August Strindberg's *The Ghost Sonata*, which opened the repertory theatre's twelfth season in New Haven, Connecticut on September 30, 1977.

For some years after moving to the United States, Andrei Serban lived modestly in a room at La Mama, with his dog Io (in Greek, "the wanderer"). He was pictured in the *Village Voice* (January 26, 1976) as "a striking figure—tall, thin, and blonde . . . a cross between Sherlock Holmes and Andy Warhol." Although Serban is often named among the new theatrical directors who promote their own concepts at the expense of the playwright, he has insisted, as quoted in *Newsweek* (February 28, 1977), "I'm not an innovator. I'm trying to make a synthesis of many things and from them create an ambience which is my own."

References: After Dark 10:26+ Je '77 por; Keynote p4+ Jl '77 por; N Y Post p8 Ja 31 '76; N Y Times II p5 Ja 18 '76, C p1+ D 31 '76, II p1+ My 8 '77 por; N Y Times Mag p42+ F 13 '77 pors; Newsweek 89:78+ F 28 '77 por; Soho Weekly N p13+ Ja 6 '77; Village Voice p107+ Ja 26 '76

Shange, Ntozake (shang'gā en-to-zä'kē)

Oct. 18, 1948- Poet; playwright. Address: c/o New York Shakespeare Festival Public Theatre, 425 Lafayette St., New York City, N.Y. 10003

The surprise hit of the 1976-77 Broadway season was Ntozake Shange's Golden Apple and Outer Critics Circle award-winning *For Colored Girls Who Have Considered Suicide/ When the Rainbow Is Enuf*, a personal and poignant evocation of the wounded sensibility of black womankind. Miss Shange, whose background is upper middle-class Afro-American, began her career as a poet and performer in San Francisco, where she originally recited in poetry bars much of the material distilled in *For Colored Girls*. After seeing the "choreopoem" about "abused visions" and "misused love" Off Off Broadway, producer Joseph Papp moved the show, with Miss Shange in the cast, first into his Off-Broadway New York Shakespeare Festival Public Theatre and then uptown, where it ran for almost two years at the Booth Theatre. In her passionate and lyrical stage creation Miss Shange examined, through seven personae, the various facets of the inner space of a person whose experience encompasses not only the common "things that happen to people: illness, anxiety, shattered love affairs, being misunderstood, an inability to actualize visions," but those same things compounded by blackness and womanhood in today's American society. Among Miss Shange's other works for the stage is *A Photograph*, presented at the Public Theatre in the 1977-78 season. "I write about pain," the poet-playwright has said. "Apathy stops me up. I think I write choppy prose, but the very choppiness of the prose releases my poetry."

Ntozake Shange was born Paulette Williams on October 18, 1948 in Trenton, New Jersey, the oldest child of Paul T. Williams, a surgeon, and Eloise Williams, a psychiatric social worker. She was named after her father, who, she says, "wanted a boy." Miss Shange has two brothers and a sister, all of whom, following her example, have replaced their "slave names" with African ones: Siwi, Bisa, and Ifa Iyaun. With her younger siblings she grew up in Trenton, at Sampson Air Force Base in upstate New York, and in St. Louis, Missouri.

Miss Shange's childhood was an extraordinarily privileged one, filled with a range of activities extending from dancing and violin lessons to family musicales and reading sessions. Through her father, who played percussion and painted in addition to working as a ringside physician, she met such musicians as Dizzy Gillespie and Miles Davis and such prizefighters as Muhammed Ali. Artists and authors, including W. E. B. Du Bois, were frequent visitors in the Williams home.

But Miss Shange feels that she was "living a lie" for the first sixteen years of her life, as she explained to Allan Wallach of *Newsday* (August 22, 1976): "[I was] living in a world that defied reality as most black people, or most white people, understood it—in other words, feeling that there was something that I could do, and then realizing that nobody was expecting me to do anything because I was colored and I was also female, which was not very easy to deal with. You work very hard and then they say, 'Well, we couldn't possibly use that.'" Another interviewer quotes her explanation of how "all this rage" came to "the most correct" of children: "It was there all the time, but I was just trying to be nice."

In an interview for the *New Yorker* (August 2, 1976) Shange referred to her childhood as "a double life." "Reading was the real life. I read all the Russians in English (my goal in life was to free Raskolnikov from his guilts) and the French in French and the Spaniards with the aid of dictionaries." In English, her earliest favorite authors were Mark Twain, Herman Melville, Carson McCullers, and Edna St. Vincent Millay. Later, Simone de Beauvoir and Susan B. Anthony contributed to the raising of her consciousness. "Faulkner has always been a trial—I have to pretend to be white to understand what he's saying about blacks."

Her most traumatic childhood memory is of the time when, because she was "gifted," she was bused fifteen miles to integrate a previously all-white school in St. Louis: "I was not prepared for it. I was rich and somewhat protected. Now I was being harassed and chased around by these white kids. My parents were busy being proud." As she told Edmund Newton of the New York *Post* (June 12, 1976), "You can't raise somebody like they're regular and then have everybody acting like they're not and expect no problems."

At Barnard College, the sister school to Columbia College at Columbia University in New York City, Miss Shange elected the course in American studies, with a major in Afro-American music and poetry. "I was a good all-American girl [at] a good all-American school, studied hard, kept my virginity, and married a lawyer," she later said. "When he left me, I didn't know what to do, so I stuck my head in the oven. My aunt came in and pulled me out." There were several subsequent abortive attempts at suicide, including one by an overdose of pills.

While at Barnard, Miss Shange became active in the student protest, civil rights, and black liberation movements in which, she found "they didn't treat women right." "I didn't speak up," she has recounted, "because those same men I was shuffling for I was interested in. . . . I became a promiscuous person."

After she obtained her bachelor's degree with honors at Barnard in 1970, Miss Shange went on to the University of Southern California, in Los Angeles, where she worked part time and held a teaching fellowship while earning her master's degree in American studies. It was there in 1971 that she decided to change her name. As she later explained, "I had a violent resentment of carrying a slave name; poems and music come from the pit of myself, and the pit of myself isn't a slave." She consulted friends from the Xhosa tribe in South Africa, who took her down to the Pacific Ocean and baptized her Ntozake Shange. The first name means "she who comes with her own things." The second, the name of the man with whom she was then living, means "who walks like a lion."

After taking her master's degree, Miss Shange taught in the Women's Studies Program at Sonoma State College in Rohnert Park, California. When she was driving home to Oakland after class one day, in a depressed mood, the sight of a rainbow inspired her with the thought that women, especially black women, could survive on the realization that they "have as much right and as much purpose for being here as air and mountains do [or as] sunlight does." She has recalled herself thinking: "We can minimize those scars or those sores that we don't want in us. We can modulate them to the extent that they become at least not malignant. And we forget that. So that's what the rainbow is: just the possibility to start all over again with the power and the beauty of ourselves. . . . Rainbows come after storms; they don't come before the storm."

Meanwhile, Shange had been writing a constant stream of poetry as a release for her frustrations and as an expression of the feminism and third-world attitudes developing in her in the heady ambiance of San Francisco. She began reading her poetry in women's bars, improvising with dancer and musician friends of hers, especially choreographer-dancer Paula Moss, who has recalled the genesis of what would become *For Colored Girls Who Have Considered Suicide/When the Rainbow Is Enuf*: "She [Miss Shange] had this poetry and I had this dance and so we just started to put it out there and see if it would work. At first we had no idea that we would ever be paid or that anyone would ever really look at this as a piece of theatre; we just did this so we would have an outlet. We would go to small bars or schools or something and give a workshop and Ntozake would read and then we would combine the two together. And I guess that's why she calls it a "choreopoem"; she likes movement to her work because her work is something of a song. I used to use her voice as music; I would just dance to her reading, her poetry, and that would be my music."

Moving to New York City, Miss Shange and Miss Moss first performed the choreopoem there on July 7, 1975 at the Studio Rivbea, a jazz loft in Soho. Director Oz Scott, who saw the show there, offered to help with the staging and recruited actresses to fill out the cast of seven women. The developing production moved to the Old Reliable bar, a Lower East Side poets' hangout, and then to Demonte's, a bar down the street from the Old Reliable, where it was seen by Woodie King Jr., the busiest black producer in New York. Produced by King and directed by Scott, the choreopoem was staged at the Henry Street Settlement's New Federal Theatre from November 1975 to June 1976, when Joseph Papp began producing the show at his New York Shakespeare Festival's Anspacher Public Theatre.

In his review of the Off-Broadway production in *Newsweek* (June 14, 1976) Jack Kroll wrote: "Shange's poems aren't war cries—they are outcries filled with controlled passion against the brutality that blasts the lives of 'colored girls'—a phrase that in her hands vibrates with social irony and poetic beauty." Marilyn Stasio wrote in *Cue* (June 26, 1976): "In this theatre piece of staged and danced readings [Miss Shange's] poetry touches some very tender nerve endings. Although roughly structured and stylistically unrefined, this fierce and passionate poetry has the power to move a body to tears, to rage, and to an ultimate rush of love. It helps if this body is black and female, because that is the experience Shange writes about. Seven vital dancer-actresses, including the author, enact [a story of] 'movin' from Mama to whatever was out there.' Through their encounters with rapists, abortionists, and an assortment of evil lovers, they grow in the beauty and strength of their womanness."

After its highly successful Off-Broadway run, *For Colored Girls* opened uptown at the Booth Theatre on September 15, 1976 with Janet League, Aku Kadago, Trazana Beverley, Paula Moss, Rise Collins, Laurie Carlos, and Ntozake Shange (who left the cast after one month) playing, respectively, the Lady in Brown, the Lady in Yellow, the Lady in Red, the Lady in Green, the Lady in Purple, the Lady in Blue, and the Lady in Orange. "The final production at the Booth," Miss Shange wrote in the introduction to the published text of the play (Macmillan, 1976), "is as close to distilled as any of us in all our art forms can make it. . . . The cast is enveloping almost 6,000 people a week in the words of a young black girl's growing up, her triumphs and errors, [her] struggle to be all that is forbidden by our environment, all that is forfeited by our gender, all that we have forgotten."

Critics called the Broadway production a "compelling" cry of "pain, anger, defiance, scorn, and finally anguish," a "howling protest" that "fills a vacuum until now undescribed in literature," and "a gripping celebration of the pain, the dignity, and the triumph of black women in their quest for identity." In the Booth Theatre *Playbill* Colette Dowling wrote: "The women in *For Colored Girls* come from very different backgrounds than [Miss Shange's]. This may account, then, for the occasional false note. . . . Still, the sense of confusion and the struggle to find her own way in the world is vivid and authentic." After the Broadway production closed, on July 16, 1978, national companies continued to tour the United States, Canada, and the Caribbean with *For Colored Girls*.

The second major work by Miss Shange to be staged in New York was *A Photograph: A Study of Cruelty*, produced by Joseph Papp at the Public Theatre in the 1977-78 season. That "poemplay" was about a black woman dancer named Michael (Michele Shay), a free spirit who lives with a gifted but unsuccessful young black photographer, Sean David (Avery Brooks), and bears the brunt of his bitterness. *A Photograph* received mixed notices, with most critics comparing it unfavorably with *For Colored Girls*. Richard Eder of the New York *Times* (December 16, 1977), for example, said: "In *For Colored Girls* Ntozake Shange arranged her acid and lyrical perceptions into a fine, loose-jointed set of meditations and sketches [that did not need] a formal dramatic structure. [She] is something besides a poet, but she is not—at least not at this stage—a dramatist. More than anything else she is a troubadour. She declares her fertile vision of the love and pain between black women and black men in outbursts full of old malice and young cheerfulness. They are short outbursts, song-length; her characters are perceived in flashes, in illuminating vignettes. Some of these things are found in *A Photograph* [but] the perceptions are made to do the donkey-work of holding up what attempts to be a whole dramatic structure, and they fail."

John Simon, one of the few critics who had panned *For Colored Girls* ("just a bunch of self-indulgent monologues and paltry dancing thrown together pell mell"), felt vindicated by the negative reviews his colleagues gave *A Photograph*. In *New York* (January 16, 1978) Simon called *A Photograph* "exactly the same drivel" as *For Colored Girls*, full of "moonings, gripings, and self-aggrandizings" that are "pure paste, . . . glue posturing as nectar." Attributing the success of *For Colored Girls* to "the knee-jerk liberalism of white producers, critics, and audiences," Simon wished that those who "gushed" over *For Colored Girls* and "loathed" *A Photograph* would resee the former: "They might now find in it all the obtuseness and obnoxiousness of the latter minus the spell of novelty, which helped take them in. The rest was done by Miss Shange's being both black and a woman—two wronged minorities."

While *A Photograph* was playing in the Public Theatre's Lu Esther Hall, Miss Shange was performing Sundays in another part of Joseph Papp's theatrical complex, the Public Theatre Cabaret, as the leader of a trio of poets, the Satin Sisters. In *Where the Mississippi Meets the Amazon,* directed by Oz Scott, Miss Shange and back-up poets Thulani Nkabinda and Jessica Hagedorn recited, in partial collaboration, to the music of a five-piece jazz band, dramatic poems that each had written for herself. Mel Gussow of the New York *Times* (December 20, 1977) singled out Miss Shange as "the truest poet and most dramatic performer" of the three. "Her images burgeon with sensuality, as in the hyperbole of the title poem. She invests her work with urgency, and her sister performers take the lead from her. The tone of the show is set by the trio's initial murmuring 'feel good, feel good,' exhorting themselves and the audience to relax and be joyful."

According to recent reports, Miss Shange has been writing another play, with the working title "In the Middle of a Flower," and has been making a film under a grant from the American Film Institute. The movie is based on her novella *Sassafras, Cypress, and Indigo,* the title of which derives from natural dyes used by slaves in the old South. That novella, about three sisters trying to define the life of women in the contemporary world, was published by Shameless Hussy Press, the small publishing house in San Lorenzo, California that first published the poems that make up *For Colored Girls.* In 1977 another small press, Heirs Inc., published Miss Shange's collection of prose and poems *Natural Disasters and Other Festive Occasions.* Among the periodicals to which she has contributed are *Black Scholar, Yardbird Reader, Third World Women, Margins,* and *West End Magazine.* Miss Shange lectured at Douglass College at Rutgers University in the spring semester of 1978, and she was planning to travel to Cuba, Angola, and Mozambique in the fall of 1978. In that same year St. Martin's Press published her latest book of poetry, *Nappy Edges.*

Dumbfounded at one critic's interpretation of *For Colored Girls* as racist, Miss Shange has said, "I love too many people in the world for that." She has also denied being "revengeful" toward black men, saying that she was only trying to be "honest" about her "own experience" of frustrated tenderness: "I wanted to be wonderful and loving, to hold the hand, make the cake, fix the necktie. It's a kindness no one wants if he's never had bread and butter. People can't afford to be open with you if every moment of their lives they're being abused. . . . It would mean I was stronger than them." In an interview for *Time* (July 19, 1976), Miss Shange told Jean Vallely that on occasion she still felt such emotional "pain and despair" as to make her wish to leave her body: "Like in my poem, which says I want to jump right out of my bones and be done with myself. I meant that literally. Death could not be worse." But in her interview with Allan Wallach for *Newsday* she said that she had learned how to cope with those moments: "I call my therapist, or I go to bed, or I leave town [because] whatever that stress is, it'll pass—which I didn't know before."

Ntozake Shange and David Murray, the jazz musician who led the combo in *Where the Mississippi Meets the Amazon,* were married in an informal, unofficial ceremony, with friends as witnesses, in San Francisco in July 1977. Although she still regards San Francisco as her "spiritual, emotional, and creative home," Miss Shange continues to live in New York City, where her successive residences have been in Harlem, Chelsea, and Greenwich Village. The poet-playwright has been described by interviewers as a "sensitive," "hardy," "handsome," and "tough-talking" woman with big brown eyes that are "alternately pleading and laughing." Prominent in her wardrobe are colorful head scarves and African jewelry, including pendant earrings and nose ornaments. Her favorite drink is dry wine, and she is a heavy cigarette smoker. As she wrote in *For Colored Girls,* "Ever since I realized there waz someone callt/ a colored girl an evil woman a bitch or a nag/ i been tryin not to be that & leave bitterness/ in somebody else's cup."

References: Christian Sci Mon p23 S 9 '76 por; Ebony 32:136 Ag '77 por; N Y Amsterdam News D p10+ O 9 '76 pors; N Y Daily News p59 Je 15 '76 por; N Y Post p15 Je 12 '76 por; N Y Times p27 Je 16 '76; C p6 D 16 '77; New Yorker 52:17+ Ag 2 '76; Newsday II p4+ Ag 22 '76 por; Washington Post B p1+ Je 29 '76

Silverman, Fred

Sept. 13, 1937- Broadcasting executive.
Address: b. NBC, 30 Rockefeller Plaza, New York City, N. Y. 10020

When ABC, CBS, and NBC unveiled their program lineups for the 1978-79 television season in September 1978, it was possible, for the first time in broadcasting history, to watch programs selected by one man—Fred Silverman—on all three networks. Aggressive, unorthodox, and fiercely competitive, Silverman oversaw

Fred Silverman

network programming at CBS for five years before moving to ABC in 1975. In less than two years he took that network from third to first place in the annual ratings race. His strategic scheduling, attention-getting promotion, and intuitive grasp of public taste have made hits of such series as *All in the Family, M*A*S*H, Kojak, Charlie's Angels, Happy Days,* and *Battlestar Galactica.* In early June 1978 Fred Silverman took over as president and chief executive officer of NBC, succeeding Herbert S. Schlosser. Since he is responsible for all network broadcasting operations, Silverman is second in power only to Edgar H. Griffiths, the chairman of RCA.

The son of a television repairman, Fred Silverman was born on September 13, 1937 in New York City, New York. He attended public schools in Rego Park, in the borough of Queens, and continued his education at Syracuse University's School of Speech and Dramatic Arts. After taking his B.A. degree in 1958, he went on to Ohio State University for graduate study in broadcasting. For his master's thesis, he analyzed the programming practices of ABC, the youngest of the three television networks, from 1953 to 1959. Among other things, he chastised ABC's "pasteboard programmers" for failing to realize that network television was "basically a business."

Shortly after he received his M.A. degree in 1959, Silverman signed on as a staff producer at WGN-TV, an independent outlet in Chicago, Illinois. Faced with stiff competition from the more moneyed network-affiliated stations, he came up with several imaginative and inexpensive counter-programming schemes that snared first place for WGN in local Friday evening ratings. Eventually promoted to director of program development, Silverman remained with WGN for three years, then moved on to WPIX-TV, an independent station in New York City, early in 1963.

Six weeks later, Michael H. Dann, CBS's program director, hired Silverman to oversee the network's highly profitable daytime schedule. Impressed by his "unbelievable" instincts, Dann gave Silverman virtual autonomy over the game shows, soap operas, and children's programs that constituted the bulk of the daytime lineup. Silverman replaced weary situation comedy reruns with first-run animated cartoon series, thereby almost singlehandedly changing the concept of Saturday morning children's programming, and his highly acclaimed *Children's Film Festival,* an unconventional addition to the juvenile schedule, won for the network a coveted George Foster Peabody Award. By adding imaginative new soap operas to the afternoon lineup, he managed to retain an average 40 percent share of the audience. In recognition of his contributions to CBS's continuing dominance of the ratings, he was named vice-president of daytime programs in July 1966 and, in February 1970, was advanced to vice-president of program planning and development.

When Mike Dann left CBS in June 1970 to join the Children's Television Workshop, Fred Silverman succeeded him as vice-president in charge of programs. The new fall season was already set, but in the spring of 1971 Silverman carried on the "deruralization" of the network roster begun by Robert D. Wood, the president of the CBS television network. He axed thirteen shows, including the cornfed comedies *Green Acres* and the long-running *Beverly Hillbillies,* and ordered an extensive revision of the remaining series. To replace the canceled shows, Silverman selected eight new series, including the provocative and irreverent *All in the Family,* expressly designed to attract the eighteen-to-forty-nine-year-old viewers who are the prime marketing targets of television advertisers.

Having weathered initial objections to its adult themes and uninhibited dialogue, *All in the Family* went on to become the most-watched television show in the United States by May 1971. Buoyed by the success of *All in the Family* and its equally popular spinoffs, *Maude, Good Times,* and *The Jeffersons,* Silverman endorsed plot outlines that broached such controversial topics as menopause, breast cancer, premarital sex, impotence, alcoholism. and abortion. Other CBS comedy entries—*The Mary Tyler Moore Show, The Bob Newhart Show, Rhoda, M*A*S*H*—offered a brand of sophisticated humor especially attractive to younger, better-educated, and more affluent urban viewers. To satisfy the need for adult drama,

Silverman introduced *Cannon, Kojak,* and *Barnaby Jones,* crime series built around strong central characters; *The Waltons,* a gentle, old-fashioned tale of a backwoods family during the Depression; dozens of strategically scheduled dramatic specials; and such award-winning made-for-television movies as *Catholics* and *The Autobiography of Miss Jane Pittman.*

Silverman's consummate skill as a programmer is perhaps most evident in the annual Nielsen ratings averages. At the close of the 1973-74 television season, for example, CBS had nine of the ten top-rated shows; of those nine programs, seven were Silverman entries. Their quality is reflected in the number of Emmy Award nominations they won for the network. For one typical season, that of 1974-75, CBS garnered 117 nominations and thirty-five Emmy Awards. Notwithstanding his uncanny talent for reading the public's mind, Silverman had his share of flops, among them *Me and the Chimp, Big Eddie, Planet of the Apes, Khan!, Dirty Sally,* and the highly touted *Beacon Hill,* a saga about Irish-Americans in Boston circa 1920. Other ambitious projects, including a suggestion to replace Merv Griffin's late-night talk show with original ninety-minute dramas and a weekly prime time "family movie" package, were vetoed by CBS's top brass as being too risky.

Increasingly frustrated in his role as the "custodian of [CBS's] dominance," Silverman accepted when Franklin S. Pierce, the president of the ABC television network, offered him a job as president of the ABC entertainment division in June 1975. Such was Silverman's reputation as a money-making programmer that the announcement of his defection to ABC caused that network's stock to jump two full points on the New York stock exchange, even though ABC was still reeling from its worst season in years. Rather than watch such trivia as *Nakia, Kodiak, Kung Fu,* and *Kolchak,* viewers had deserted the network in droves. (ABC averaged 2,000,000 fewer viewers per night than second-place NBC). To recapture that audience, Pierce and Martin Starger, Silverman's predecessor, bought such action-oriented shows as *S.W.A.T., Baretta,* and *Starsky and Hutch,* appealing situation comedies like *Welcome Back, Kotter* and *Barney Miller,* and dramatizations of the bestsellers *Roots* and *Rich Man, Poor Man.* The fundamentals for a hit season were on the drawing board when Silverman assumed his post on June 16, 1975, but it took his talent for scheduling to turn a promising program roster into a ratings winner.

Recognizing that ABC's future rested with younger viewers, Silverman gambled on using fast-paced, unsophisticated situation comedies in the so-called "family viewing hour" from 8:00 to 9:00 P.M. (E.S.T.) and shifted *The Six Million Dollar Man,* which had shown signs of fading, to an earlier time slot on Sunday evenings. Both moves paid off almost immediately in higher ratings. In a radical departure from routine network scheduling practices, he broadcast *Rich Man, Poor Man* not as a made-for-television movie or as a one-shot drama special, but as a limited series in eight weekly installments. The so-called "mini-series," pioneered in the United States by PBS, proved so successful that it was quickly copied by CBS and NBC.

Because he believes that an enduring series depends on "well-delineated, attractive, appealing" characters, Silverman directed the producers of *Happy Days* to shift the emphasis from the rather colorless Richie Cunningham to Fonzie, the swaggering, street-wise biker, thus converting that piece of 1950's nostalgia into a smash hit. Contending that familiarity is the key to successful programming, Silverman has always favored spinoffs. (Between them, *The Mary Tyler Moore Show* and *All in the Family* spawned five top-ranked series for CBS.) He resurrected Jaime Sommers, who had supposedly been killed in an episode of *The Six Million Dollar Man,* supplied her with bionic limbs, and surrounded her with familiar faces from the parent show for *The Bionic Woman.* Shirley Feeney and Laverne DeFazio were plucked from *Happy Days* for *Laverne & Shirley,* a kitschy blue-collar comedy about two working girls in Milwaukee in the late 1950's.

To give those and other new shows an added boost, Silverman "hammocked" them between proven hits or slotted them opposite weak older programs or untested new ones. Almost all the new series—*Laverne & Shirley, The Bionic Woman, Family, Donny & Marie*—introduced during the "second season," which began in January 1976, were hits and ABC finished off the year in second place, just six-tenths of a point behind first-place CBS in the annual Nielsen ratings. It was the network's first profit-making season since its formation in 1953.

Over the next two seasons Silverman strengthened ABC's position, quickly replacing weak or fading series with sure-fire audience pleasers like *The Love Boat, Fantasy Island,* and *Eight Is Enough.* To cut down on the competition, he lured Nancy Walker away from CBS's *Rhoda* and NBC's *MacMillan,* Redd Foxx from NBC's *Sanford and Son,* and Harvey Korman from CBS's *The Carol Burnett Show* and raided MTM Productions, a regular CBS supplier, for top writers, producers, and directors. As always, he kept a close watch on all aspects of program production, from the development of the plot outline to the editing of promotional spots.

The most popular of Silverman's entries were the sexually titillating *Charlie's Angels, Three's Company,* and *Soap. Charlie's Angels,* a voyeuristic crime drama with sadomasochistic overtones, featuring three shapely young female private investigators, broke into the Nielsen top ten in its first week and regularly received a phenomenal 55 to 60 percent audience share. *Soap*, a farcical exploration of sexual hangups, relationships, and aberrations, drew the fire of outraged religious and secular groups even before it was first broadcast. Caving in under the pressure, several ABC affiliates refused to carry the program, and some sponsors threatened to withdraw their commercials. In closed-circuit messages to affiliates and in public speeches, Silverman defended *Soap's* "socially redeeming" aspects, such as its "very positive" role models and its belief in "the sanctity of the family unit" and he urged delegates to the annual convention of the American Association of Advertisers in Chicago in November 1977 not to become "the pawns of pressure groups."

With *Roots*, a mini-series broadcast on eight successive nights in January 1977, ABC achieved the highest-rated week in the history of network broadcasting. Silverman used the same ploy the following September when, in a surprise move that stunned his competitors, he opened ABC's 1977-78 season two weeks early with *Washington: Behind Closed Doors*, a riveting mini-series based on John Ehrlichman's *roman à clef*, *The Company*. ABC immediately placed first in the ratings and remained there with fifteen of the top twenty series and such critically acclaimed television movies as *Eleanor and Franklin* and *The Trial of Lee Harvey Oswald*. The midseason Nielsens gave ABC a 20.7 rating, followed by CBS with 18.6 and NBC with 17.9.

To retain first place, Silverman ruthlessly scrapped failing and marginal shows, including *Mr. T. and Tina*, *Holmes and Yoyo*, *Blansky's Beauties*, and *The San Pedro Beach Bums*. Disregarding the popular success of most of his shows, a few influential television critics came down hard on what they saw as Silverman's predilection for sex, violence, and "greasy kid-stuff." In an interview for the Washington *Post* (January 18, 1978], Silverman conceded that, in some cases, the charges were justified, but he questioned the validity of the "very, very elitist point of view" that dismissed popular entertainment as junk and trash. He elaborated on that theme in his speech to the Hollywood Radio and Television Society in November 1977: "Implicit in much of their criticism is the notion that television's primary role is to lift the public to some higher level of aesthetic appreciation. We're certainly not going to apologize for what we're presenting to the American public. I believe television is providing quality across the board. From *Eight Is Enough* to *The Love Boat*, there's something for everyone."

In the summer of 1977, after working for almost fifteen years as a programming director, Silverman complained publicly that the life of a television executive was "boring, with a capital B." "It isn't fun anymore," he said, as quoted in *Time* (September 5, 1977). "When I joined CBS, it was terrific. You made a couple of changes in mid-season and put on a couple of summer shows, and that was all there was to it. Now . . . there are fifteen seasons and 180 specials and it is a totally different business." Dissatisfied and restless, Silverman considered several career options before negotiating with Edgar H. Griffiths, the head of RCA, NBC's parent organization, to become the new president and chief executive officer of NBC, a position presenting a challenge that went far beyond the scope of his duties at ABC. According to the terms of his three-year contract, signed in January 1978, Silverman is to receive a six-figure annual salary, variously reported to be $500,000, $800,000, and $1,000,000, plus bonuses and stock options.

Following a four-month "enforced retirement" to honor his expiring ABC contract, Silverman took over the helm of NBC on June 9, 1978. In a closed-circuit address to affiliates three days later, he pledged to make NBC both "the audience leader" and "the most respected network." "We will have a genuine commitment to quality and responsibility because we recognize the importance of broadcasting in this country, the reliance that people place on it, and the obligation that places on us," he said. Redefining leadership to mean "more than competitive success," he downplayed "short-term, artificial rating advantages" and stressed the importance of "helping society understand its problems and meet its challenges." To that end, he promised more news and information programming and innovative, stylish entertainment programs that refreshed the medium without violating "general standards of taste."

Forced to compete with the powerhouse 1978-79 lineup he himself had drawn up for ABC, Silverman moved quickly to improve NBC's opening position. Working closely with his programming executives, he canceled a handful of questionable series and substantially rearranged the announced schedule. One last-minute entry was *Lifeline*, a weekly documentary series about doctors and their patients that Silverman believes could be "the single show that changes the face of prime time television." To get NBC off to a fast start, he studded the opening weeks of the season with special previews, films, and such stunts as a silver anniversary salute to *The Wonderful World of Disney* and the first full-length telecast of *Dumbo*. Although he planned to continue the long-form, mini-series, and "events" programming that has so prominently figured in NBC's schedule for the past few years, Silverman ordered his deputies to concentrate on building the successful series that are, in his view, the "most important element in an effective schedule." Moreover, with only one program—*Little House on the Prairie*—solidly entrenched in the top twenty, he gave the go-ahead for some thirty pilots to be used as possible midseason replacements.

The opposite of the stereotypical dapper, smooth-talking broadcast executive, Fred Silverman has, according to one reporter, "the build of a football guard and the manner of a comedian." He is a short, stocky man with blue eyes and graying brown hair. By his own admission, he is a "very private" person and rarely grants interviews. His colleagues and competitors describe him as a chronic workaholic and a compulsive winner. "I think there is a philosophy that is good no matter what you are doing, that is to always act as if you're in last place," he explained, as quoted in *Time* (September 5, 1977). "You just shouldn't take success for granted, because you can turn around one day and say, 'My Lord, it is all gone.' " In his rare hours of relaxation he watches television (he is especially fond of *60 Minutes*) and reads bestsellers. Silverman and his wife, Catherine Ann Kihn Silverman, his former secretary, and their two children, Melissa Anne and William Laurence, live in an apartment on Central Park West in Manhattan.

References: Life 71:46+ S 10 '71 pors; N Y Times p38 Ja 21 '78 por; N Y Times Mag p19+ Mr 7 '76 por; New Times 7:55+ O 1 '77 por; TV Guide 25:2+ My 7 '77 por, 25:25+ My 14 '77 por

---

Smith, Virginia B(eatrice)

1924- College president. Address: b. Vassar College, Poughkeepsie, N.Y. 12601

Among the signals that Ivy League elitism is diminishing in the Seven College Conference—consisting of the "Seven Sisters," Vassar, Barnard, Radcliffe, Bryn Mawr, Smith, Mount Holyoke, and Wellesley, the major Eastern schools founded as upper-class colleges for women—was the election of Virginia B. Smith to the presidency of Vassar College in 1977. Miss Smith, whose breeding was blue-collar and public school, is a champion of the liberal arts who brings to her post in Poughkeepsie an awareness of the shortcomings of higher education, experience in federal funding of colleges, universities, and individual students, and a commitment to affirmative action. At the time of her present appointment, she was director of the Fund for the Improvement of Postsecondary Education in the United States Department of Health, Education, and Welfare, an agency set up largely in response to recommendations by the Carnegie Commission on Higher Education, of which she had been a member. Miss Smith, a protégée of Clark Kerr, former president of the University of California, began her career as a lawyer, economist, and teacher on the West Coast.

Vassar College, founded in 1861, is the oldest of the so-called Seven Sisters. Coeducational since 1968, it now has a male student enrollment rapidly approaching 50 percent of a total student body of approximately 2,300. "If quality liberal arts education is to flourish rather than just survive, it must be nourished, . . . and the potentially disastrous and probably unnecessary struggle between vocational and liberal arts education must finally and fully be put to rest," Miss Smith has said. "And all of this must be accomplished in a nondiscriminatory and nonsexist context. Because of its unique qualities, Vassar could well be in the forefront of such an effort."

One of six children of a tool and die operator, Virginia Beatrice Smith was born in 1924 in Seattle, Washington. After attending Seattle public schools and taking B.A., M.A., and J.D. degrees at the University of Washington, in Seattle, she did further work at Columbia University, in New York City. Her major academic focus, outside of law, was on labor economics.

Miss Smith's first professional position was that of an economist in the Seattle district Office of Price Administration, which she held from 1944 to 1946. She was a research fellow at the Institute of Labor Economics at the University of Washington in 1946, and she taught economics and business at the College of Puget Sound in Tacoma, Washington from 1947 to 1949, when she moved to Seattle Pacific College. While teaching at the College of Puget Sound and at Seattle Pacific College, she practised law part time.

During her last two years at Seattle Pacific College, Miss Smith chaired the small school's department of economics and business administration. In 1952 she joined the faculty of the University of California's Berkeley Extension, as an instructor and coordinator of public programs in the Institute of Industrial Relations. On a leave of absence, in 1956-57, she studied adult and trade union education in England.

After her return to Berkeley, Miss Smith became administrative analyst on the staff of the president of the university, Clark Kerr, under whom she had studied labor economics at the University of Washington. Moving up the executive ladder, she ultimately, beginning in 1965, served as assistant vice-president in charge of policy development. Concurrently, she was associated with the law office of Sam Kagel in San Francisco, chiefly as a labor-management arbitrator, and she chaired the California State Wage Board and served on the women's advisory council of the California Fair Employment Practices Commission.

Clark Kerr, dismissed as president of the University of California when Ronald Reagan took office as Governor in 1967, asked Virginia Smith to move with him to the Carnegie Commission on Higher Education, a newly created "think tank" of which Kerr became chairman and Miss Smith assistant director and associate director, successively. In addition to her administrative duties, she had the major staff responsibility for the commission's reports.

The first of the commission's reports, *Quality and Equality: New Levels of Federal Responsibility* (McGraw-Hill, 1968), proposed a $200,000,000 federal foundation to expand educational opportunities "for all able young people both for their own benefit and for the benefit of the nation" through grants to schools for innovative projects and scholarships to individuals who might not otherwise have an equal opportunity for higher education. When Thea Gutman, in an interview for *Vassar Quarterly* (Summer 1977), asked her if she had any second thoughts about the report's recommendations, she replied that she and her colleagues had not been "realistic about how centralization follows money." She explained: "I'd be more inclined now to say let's find every way we can to get even more emphasis on diversity of funding sources, on self-reliance, in order not to have a situation where outside forces can dictate so much of what must be done. I'd like to see small amounts of money used for leverage to make rigid forces less rigid, but I would hate to see coordination become centralization. Often people think you can streamline organizations by coordinating everything into large units. But unless great care is taken, the large, streamlined units are often less responsive and function less well than several smaller units."

Another commission report, *The Campus and the City: Maximizing Assets and Reducing Liabilities* (McGraw-Hill, 1972), explored the "unfocused" relationship of higher education with the city, "by far the most difficult [relationship] to deal with and [one which] indeed seemed to elude any reasonable analysis," as Miss Smith later wrote in "The City and the Campus," a chapter based on the commission report that she wrote for *Education and the State* (American Council on Education, 1975). Among other reports were *Institutional Aid: Federal Support to Colleges and Universities* (McGraw-Hill, 1972) and *Less Time, More Options: Education Beyond the High School* (McGraw-Hill, 1971).

In 1973 Virginia Smith left the Carnegie Commission on Education—which has its headquarters in Berkeley—to serve in Washington, D.C. as the first director of the Fund for the Improvement of Postsecondary Education, established largely as a result of the commission's recommendations. Authorized by Congress in 1972, the fund was set up within the education division of the United States Department of Health, Education, and Welfare for the purpose of "improving postsecondary educational opportunities by providing assistance to educational institutions and agencies to encourage a broad range of improvements and innovations." In the four years of her tenure, Miss Smith, in consultation with a board of advisors appointed by the Secretary of Health, Education, and Welfare, was responsible for dispensing over $43,000,000 in grants. In accordance with the expressed guidelines of the fund, the grants were "comprehensive" in range, "responsive" to stated needs and proposed solutions, "action-oriented" (the fund does not underwrite basic research), and "risk-taking" (it does consider unproven ideas).

Descriptions of 340 diverse projects that received support from the fund while Miss Smith was administering it are contained in two issues of *Resources for Change* (United States Government Printing Office, 1976 and 1977). The aggregation of award recipients represents, as Miss Smith wrote in the foreword to the 1977 volume, "not capital resources, but those non-capital resources essential to improvement—people, institutions, and ideas." Hopeful that the volumes would build awareness of "new avenue[s] of action," she called them "a small step toward a dissemination of strategy in which the 'field' talks to the 'field'." The problems addressed by the academic institutions receiving grants included the extension of educational opportunities to "under-served" groups, "meeting individual needs in a mass system," developing more meaningful standards for awarding academic credentials, and "preserving institutional vitality in the face of growing rigidity and regulation." Miss Smith explained to Thea Gutman: "We were not determining in advance what to provide money for; we were interested in their [the applicants'] solutions to problems in the guidelines. . . . We always had to determine if there was a commitment within the institution or if it was just a plea for money."

Virginia Smith's style of leadership at the fund was, typically, participatory, as her deputy director, Chuck Bunting, told Thea Gutman: "Decisions are not hers so much as ours." Miss Smith herself said, in an interview with Liva Baker for *Change* magazine (September 1977): "I've always been a firm believer in joint decisions. Changes don't come about by a laying-on approach. I've never had any sort of marginal idea that hasn't been improved by discussing it with the people it affected." The fund's program officer, David Justice, observed that she "built the fund from a gleam in the eye of some legislators to what it is now." Almost, if not equally, as important as her building of the fund was her successful fight to keep it from being absorbed by the National Institute of Education.

Abroad, Miss Smith headed the United States delegation to the UNESCO Conference on Higher Education in Bucharest, Romania in 1974 and served on the faculty of an international seminar on adult educational needs in Salzburg, Austria two years later. In a poll of 4,000 leaders in the field of higher education conducted by *Change* in 1975, Miss Smith was ranked among the forty-four most influential leaders in the field.

In May 1976, in anticipation of the retirement of Alan Simpson as president of Vassar College, a presidential search committee, composed of seven college trustees, five faculty members, and two students, was formed. On April 7, 1977, after an eleven-month search in which 450 candidates were considered, Elizabeth Runkle Purcell, the chairman of the committee, announced the unanimous choice of Virginia B. Smith. One of the other members of the committee, Mary Bunting, a Vassar alumnus and former president of Radcliffe College, observed that Virginia Smith alone, of all the candidates, had a clear, acute awareness of the innovative role that a president of Vassar could play in American education in this time of transition. "So many candidates failed to see this position as a place to do something for American education," Mrs. Bunting said. "Not only Vassar but all undergraduate liberal arts colleges need a new sense of what their mission is."

In accepting the invitation to become the eighth president—the second woman president—of Vassar College, Miss Smith observed that association with Vassar would be "accepted eagerly" at any time but that she found it "particularly challenging" at this critical stage in American higher education. In an editorial in the campus newspaper, *Miscellany News*, she was seen as bringing to Vassar "a unique perspective on national educational trends and a knowledge of government funding for private colleges," and she was encouraged in her intention to "bring a renewed commitment to women, liberal education, and affirmative action to the presidency."

Before she took office, Miss Smith spoke at Vassar's spring 1977 commencement. On that occasion she reiterated her defense of liberal education, a defense she considers especially important at a time when a recessive job market within an inflationary economy gives an advantage to those arguing for education "for the job." She said: "It is strange that a nation so practical in so many ways could apply such shortsighted practicality to the questions of liberal arts and vocationalism. I've heard estimates that today's graduates will change their jobs four times over during their careers and that 80 percent of all of today's jobs have skills that can be learned within six weeks. Why, then, would we be so shortsighted and so impractical as to waste four years on preparation for initial entry to that kind of 'job market?' "

Thus, when Miss Smith took office at Vassar on July 1, 1977, her first priority was to define and establish the validity and life-enrichment potential of a liberal arts education, "so that policy makers and others would understand its real potency" over and beyond mere "job readiness." High among her other priorities was adaptation to the changing composition of the student body (the freshman class entering Vassar in September 1977 was 42 percent male, 41 percent public-school-trained, and 6 percent black). Rejecting the two extremes of forcing students into the mold of rigid standards on the one hand or accommodating students to the detriment of standards on the other, she took a "more reasonable approach," that of looking at "these students' needs—extreme special needs, perhaps." As she had earlier explained, "The problems that this new block of students bring are probably problems that the students who are already there have; they may be less acute and so they have not been recognized. As you vary the entrance standard—to the extent that your student body becomes less homogeneous—you may have to give more attention to what goes on between entrance and exit. . . . We don't fully understand our exit standards because we've always worked on admission standards."

To overcome the fragmentation of knowledge caused by specialization, Vassar, like many other colleges and universities, had developed interdisciplinary programs in the late 1960's. At the time Miss Smith became president, the trend was back to "the basics"—a movement regarding which she had a word of warning: "We could lose much in going back to the basics if the basics look exactly as they did before. Going back to the basics should mean using the discipline to serve the development of integrating abilities. It is not so important in undergraduate education that a person control a whole body of knowledge as that the person be able to think analytically, to use judgment, to understand the relations between what he has learned and what he may not know. I don't think we've given enough attention to the integrating forces, either in education or society. We tend to think that the way to integrate is just to combine everything, rather than having the integration develop within the individual." Miss Smith's burden at Vassar was lightened financially, at the time she took over, by a $15,000,000 bequest to the college, the largest in its history.

Virginia B. Smith is a soft-spoken, gray-haired woman with a casual, informal manner. Those who know her describe her as "self-effacing to a fault," "intellectually tenacious," "thoughtful," and "succinct." As a former colleague of hers once observed, "Virginia Smith says more of importance about higher education, in fewer words, than anyone else." Miss Smith's sources of recreation include poker and the humor of columnist Art Buchwald, cartoonist Garry Trudeau, and comedian Woody Allen. She also enjoys rowing and canoeing during vacations, most of which she spends at her home in Walnut Creek, California.

References: Change 9:34+ S '77; N Y Times A p24 Ap 8 '77 por; Vassar Quarterly 73:7+ Summer '77 por

---

Snyder, Gary

May 8, 1930- Poet. Address: c/o New Directions, 333 6th Ave., New York City, N.Y. 10003

Gary Snyder's vigorous poetry celebrates the sights and sounds of the American forests and waters and the joys of a simple, organic lifestyle at the same time that it mourns the destruction of those values by modern society. Grounded in a rigorous study of anthropology, American Indian lore, Oriental languages and cultures, and Zen Buddhism, Snyder's poetry is as much acclaimed for its moral vision as for its beauty. "As a poet I hold the most archaic values on earth," Snyder once declared. "They go back to the Neolithic: the fertility of the soil, the magic of animals, the power-vision in solitude, the terrifying initiation and rebirth, the love and ecstasy of the dance, the common work of the tribe. . . . I try to hold both history and wilderness in mind, that my poems may approach the true measure of things and stand against the unbalance and ignorance of our times." Snyder first rose to prominence during the mid-1950's in association with the Beats. In 1956 he left for Japan, where he spent the greater part of the next decade studying Buddhism in a monastery. Since settling permanently in the United States in 1968, he has become something of a hero of the counterculture, who has used his position to speak out on his ecological and environmental concerns. His volumes of poetry include *Myths and Texts* (1960), *The Back Country* (1968), and *Regarding Wave* (1970), and he has published a book of essays entitled *Earth House Hold: Technical Notes and Queries to Fellow Dharma Revolutionaries* (1969). His 1974 volume of poetry and essays, *Turtle Island,* won the 1975 Pulitzer Prize for Poetry. Since 1971 Snyder has made his home in a remote area of the Sierra foothills in Northern California, where he is at work on his partly published *magnum opus, Mountains and Rivers Without End.*

Born on May 8, 1930 in San Francisco, California, Gary Snyder is the son of Harold and Lois (Wilkie) Snyder. He has one younger sister. Snyder's paternal grandfather was an I.W.W. labor organizer and a homesteader in the state of Washington. His mother's family came from Colorado. When he was less than two years old, his family moved to Washington, where they eked out a living as subsistence farmers. When he was not doing farm chores, Snyder spent much of his time in the woods, hiking, camping, and learning the names of trees and plants. He also borrowed books from the public library to learn about woodcraft and American Indian lore.

In 1942 the Snyders moved to Portland, Oregon, where Gary graduated from the eighth grade. In Oregon he continued to spend much of his time outdoors, camping and hiking in the woods around the Columbia River or south of Portland. Beginning in 1943 he spent three summers working at a camp at Spirit Lake, Washington, where he first became acquainted with alpine wilderness and had his first experiences with backpacking and mountain climbing. During the summers of 1946 and 1947 he worked in Portland for a radio station music library, as a copyboy for the United Press and the Portland *Oregonian*, and as a free-lance radio actor. At the age of fifteen he became a member of the adult club, the Mazamas Mountain Climbers, which required the scaling of a snow-covered peak for membership. It was also around that time that his parents became divorced.

Snyder became acquainted with poetry early, before he was able to read, when his mother read verse to him at bedtime. By the age of seven or eight he was writing his own poems and by fifteen or sixteen was writing seriously and consistently. After graduating from Lincoln High School in 1947, he was admitted to Reed College, in Portland, mostly on the strength of some of his poems that he had shown to a Reed professor. There Snyder majored in anthropology and literature and became friends with poets Philip Whalen and Lew Welch. During his summers in college, Snyder worked as a seaman, as an excavator for the Park Service at the archaeological site of Fort Vancouver, and as a timber scaler on the Warm Springs Indian Reservation in Oregon.

After graduating from Reed with a B.A. degree in 1951, Snyder began graduate studies in linguistics at the University of Indiana. But by that time, he had become involved with meditation and after one semester decided that his interests lay, not in pursuing an academic career, but in studying Zen Buddhism and developing his poetry. He therefore returned in the spring of 1952 to San Francisco and soon after began several years of graduate study in Oriental languages at the Berkeley campus of the University of California.

While writing and studying, Snyder supported himself with a variety of odd jobs, including one as a burglar alarm installer. During the summers he headed north to jobs in the woods. In 1952 he worked as a fire lookout for the United States Forest Service on Crater Mountain in the Baker National Forest and the following summer on Sourdough Mountain in Baker. In 1954 he began the season as a lookout in the Gifford Pinchot forest in Washington, but he was abruptly fired, without explanation, as a security risk. Later that summer he found work as a choker setter for the Warm Springs Lumber Company, and the following summer he worked on a trail crew at Yosemite National Park. Out of those rugged outdoor work experiences, as well as out of his experiences as a seaman, Snyder wrote many of the poems that were later to be published in his first volume of poetry, *Riprap* (Origin Press, 1959). The title poem refers to the process, as the poet explained in *New American Poetry*, "of picking up and placing granite stones in tight cobble patterns on hard slab."

Snyder met Kenneth Rexroth, the patriarch of the San Francisco poets, in the autumn of 1953. Two years later he met Allen Ginsberg and Jack Kerouac. Soon after, Ginsberg, Kerouac, and Snyder, along with Philip Whalen, Michael McClure, and Philip Lamantia gave the celebrated poetry reading at the Six Gallery in San Francisco that launched the Beat movement. Rexroth served as master of ceremonies at the event, which marked the first public reading of Ginsberg's poem, *Howl*. In the fall of 1955 Kerouac and Snyder began sharing a small house in Mill Valley, outside San Francisco, and they remained roommates until Snyder left for Japan the following May. Kerouac later created an exuberant portrait of Snyder during that period in the character of "Japhy Ryder," the hero of his autobiographical novel, *The Dharma Bums*.

When Snyder left for Japan, it was with a scholarship from the First Zen Institute of America to study Zen Buddhism in Kyoto. He was to live in Kyoto, except for a few interruptions, until 1967. During part of that period he lived in the monastery of Daitoku-ji, where Oda Sesso, his Rinzai Zen master, was head abbot. Snyder's first departure from Japan occurred in August 1957, when he signed on as a wiper in the engine room of the tanker *Sappa Creek* in Yokohama and traveled around the world with it for the next eight months, disembarking in April 1958 in Los Angeles. He then spent nine months in San Francisco before returning to Japan. In 1961-62 he again left Kyoto, spending four months traveling through India with Allen Ginsberg, Peter Orlovsky, and his wife, the poet Joanne Kyger. On that trip he met the Dalai Lama. Snyder's next departure from

Japan was in 1964-65, when he spent the academic year teaching English at Berkeley, taping a National Educational Television program with Philip Whalen, and giving poetry readings at colleges around the country. After suspending his Zen studies. Snyder spent over a year longer in Japan, experimenting with communal living as part of a group called the Banyam Ashram, which lived on an isolated island off the coast of Kyushu.

During the period that Snyder was living in Japan, his poetry began to be widely published in journals, as well as in several volumes. Soon after the publication of *Riprap* in 1959, a second volume, *Myths & Texts* (1960) was published by LeRoi Jones's Totem Press in association with Corinth Books. Although it represents some of Snyder's earliest adult poetry—written in the years following his graduation from college—*Myths & Texts* is the poet's most complete work and one of his most highly regarded volumes. Steeped in the mythology of American Indians and Far Eastern cultures and permeated with the theories of such anthropologists as Joseph Campbell, *Myths & Texts* clearly shows the influence of Snyder's college studies and his collegiate field work with Indians. Yet it also exhibits a well-developed exposition of the poet's attitudes toward the relationship between nature and man. The first section of *Myths & Texts* is entitled "Logging," which for Snyder is a metaphor for man's rapacious destruction of his environment: "San Francisco 2x4s/were the woods around Seattle:/Someone killed and someone built, a house,/a forest, wrecked or raised/All America hung on a hook/& burned by men, in their own praise." The second series of poems are called "Hunting," which for Snyder is a sacramental activity in harmony with nature, provided that it is pursued for food and not for sport. In the concluding section, Snyder organizes the poems around the theme of "Burning," which he sees as a cleansing and renewing process: "Sweet rain, the fire's out/The black snag glistens in the rain/& the last wisp of smoke floats up/Into the absolute cold/Into the spiral whorls of fire/The storms of the Milky Way." The many esoteric allusions of *Myths & Texts* indicate the young poet's indebtedness to Pound, and some critics, including James Dickey, have likened the book to Pound's *Cantos*.

"Travel, the sense of journey in space that modern people have lost . . . and rise and fall of rock and water. The naked burning rocks of Oman after thirty days at sea. History and its vengeful ghosts," wrote Snyder in *New American Poetry* (1960) to describe his major work, *Mountains and Rivers Without End*. Begun in 1956 and published in sections since 1961, the long poem is to consist of approximately forty parts when it is finished. Snyder has said that he patterned the dramatic structure of the poem after a certain kind of Japanese *No* play and named it after a Chinese sidewise scroll painting. Especially notable among the early sections of the poem, published in *Six Sections from Mountains and Rivers Without End* (Four Seasons Foundation, 1965) and *Six Sections . . . Plus One* (Four Seasons, 1970) are "Bubbs Creek Haircut" and "The Market." In the latter poem Snyder creates a haunting picture of Far Eastern poverty: "they eat feces/ in the dark/ on stone floors./ one-legged animals, hopping cows/ limping dogs blind cats." The plight of the American Indian is treated in several of the more recent sections of the poem, including "The Hump-Backed Flute Player" and especially "Ma," which is written in the form of a letter by an Indian woman to her son.

In 1968 Snyder published a collection of poems written about his experiences in the Far West, Japan, and India from the mid-1950's to mid-1960's in *The Back Country* (New Directions, 1968). The title refers both to the wilderness and the far reaches of the unconscious mind, which Snyder sees as analogous. The collection is notable for such earthy wilderness poems as "A Berry Feast," and for haiku-like verses such as those in "The Public Bath" ("the baby boy/ on his back, dashed with scalding water/ silent, moving eyes/ inscrutably/ pees.").

Later that year, after the publication of *The Back Country* and the birth of his first son, Snyder returned to settle permanently in the United States. The poems of his next collection, *Regarding Wave* (New Directions, 1970; an earlier, limited edition was published by Windover in 1969), reflect Snyder's new domesticity and his love of family life. At the same time, Snyder became an increasingly public figure, using the prestige generated by his personality and lifestyle, as well as his work, in order to speak out on ecological and environmental issues. During the late 1960's, for example, Snyder took part with Alan Watts, Allen Ginsberg, and Timothy Leary in a symposium called "Changes" that was sponsored by the *City of San Francisco Oracle*. Soon he was regarded as one of the leading spokesmen of the counterculture, or what he calls "the Great Subculture," a tradition which, he contends in his popular collection of journal entries and essays *Earth House Hold* (New Directions, 1969), "runs without break from Paleo-Siberian Shamanism and Magdalenian cave-painting; through megaliths and Mysteries, astronomers, ritualists, alchemists and Albigensians; gnostics and vagantes, right down to Golden State Park."

In recent years Snyder has described his poet's vocation as that of "shaman/healer," a mission especially evident in the latter sections of *Mountains and Rivers without End* as well as in his Pulitzer-Prize winning volume, *Turtle Island* (New Directions, 1974), whose title, the poet explains in an introduction, is an Indian name for the North American continent. The poems of *Turtle Island* protest the ravages of the bulldozer, the strip-miner, and the nuclear reactor, while pointing the way to a simpler and more loving lifestyle. As Bob Steuding wrote in *Gary Snyder* (1976), "In one sense, *Turtle Island* is the work of a veteran teacher; Snyder, acting in the role of *roshi,* offers his help, his instructions, his magic."

Although his poetry has been faulted for its emphasis on the poet's everyday life and experiences, a tendency that some critics have found boring or even egotistical, the prevailing critical opinion of Snyder was probably best summed up by Alan Williamson, who described him in the *New Republic* (November 1, 1975) as "one of the two or three best craftsmen among poets under fifty, and the most impressive moral thinker." Snyder's poems have appeared in *Janus, Evergreen Review, Black Mountain Review, Big Table, Kulchur, City Lights Journal, Poetry,* and other journals, as well as in many anthologies. *Cold Mountain Poems,* Snyder's respected translations of the seventh-century Chinese Zen hermit poet, Han-shan, were published in a 1965 edition of *Riprap* (Four Seasons) and in *A Range of Poems* (Fulcrum, 1966), a British collection of his poems. Snyder has also translated some of the poems of the twentieth-century Japanese poet, Miyazawa Kenji. Those translations are included in *A Range of Poems* and in *The Back Country*. In 1977 City Lights Books published a collection of essays by Snyder entitled *The Old Ways.* In addition to his Pulitzer, Snyder's awards have included a Bollingen fellowship (1966-67), the poetry award of the National Institute of Arts and Letters, and a Guggenheim fellowship (1968-69). Snyder is a member of the California Arts Council.

"He is like a wiry Chinese sage with high cheekbones, twinkling eyes, and a thin beard," the late Orientalist Alan Watts once wrote of his friend, Gary Snyder, "and the recipe for his character requires a mixture of Oregon woodsman, seaman, Amerindian shaman, Oriental scholar, San Francisco hippie, and swinging monk, who takes tough discipline with a light heart." A powerfully built man of medium height, Snyder has long, sandy hair usually worn in a pony tail, a reddish beard, and blue-gray eyes. From 1950 to 1952 he was married to Alison Gass. In 1960 he married Joanne Kyger; they were divorced in 1965. Since August 6, 1967 he has been married to a Japanese, Masa Uehara. Their wedding ceremony took place on the rim of an active volcano on Suwa-No-Se Island, while both were living in the Banyan Ashram. Snyder and his wife have two sons, Kai and Gen. Their home is on an isolated ridge near Nevada City, California, about 150 miles from San Francisco in the foothills of the Sierras. They have no electricity in the house, which Snyder himself built. Although he tours the country reading his poetry and lecturing, Snyder told Peter Barry Chowka of *East West Journal* (July 1977) that North American society is "too large and too populous to have any reasonable hope of keeping your fingers on it. . . . What I realistically aspire to do is to know what's happening and to stimulate what I think is really strong and creative in my own viable region, my actual nation: northern California/southern Oregon, which we call Kuksu country, subdivision of Turtle Island continent."

References: East West Journal 7:24+ Je '77 pors, 7:34+ Jl '77 pors, 7:19+ Ag '77 pors; Contemporary Authors vol 9-10 (1967); Kheridian, David. Six San Francisco Poets (1969); Steuding, Bob. Gary Snyder (1976); Who's Who in America, 1976-77; World Authors, 1950-1970 (1975)

Somoza (Debayle), Anastasio

Dec. 5, 1925- President of Nicaragua. Address: c/o Residencia de El Retiro, Managua, Nicaragua

Cast in the classic mold of the Latin American strongman, Anastasio Somoza Debayle, the President of Nicaragua, has leaned heavily for his support on the United States government and his tight control of his country's armed forces. A West Point graduate who advanced to the top of Nicaragua's military establishment during the administrations of his father and older brother, Somoza served as President from 1967 to 1972 and was reelected for a six-year term in 1974. Although his regime witnessed some economic growth, its gains were overshadowed by well-documented charges of official corruption, the brutal repression of political opponents, and the continued poverty of many of Nicaragua's 2,300,000 citizens. Dismissing charges that his political power is geared to perpetuating his family's dynasty and preserving its wealth, Somoza has said, as quoted in the Miami *Herald* (July 31, 1977): "Dynasty, hell. We're a family that likes politics and knows [its] job."

A native of León, Nicaragua, Anastasio Somoza Debayle was born on December 5, 1925 to Anastasio Somoza García, a moderately prosperous coffee planter, and Salvadora Debayle de Somoza. His family also included an older brother, Luis, a sister, Lilian, and an illegitimate half-brother, José Rodríguez Somoza. On his mother's side, Somoza is a great-grandson of former Nicaraguan President Roberto Sacasa and a grand-nephew of ex-President Juan Bautista Sacasa. He is also a great-grandnephew of former President Víctor Román y Reyes. In 1932, the year before United States Marines removed their almost continuous presence of over two decades from Nicaragua, Anastasio Somoza García was chosen to head the new American-sponsored Guardia Nacional de Nicaragua. Although it had been ostensibly established to safeguard a new democratic system, Somoza García soon made the Guardia Nacional his personal political instrument, and after organizing a coup to overthrow President Juan Bautista Sacasa he was elected President of Nicaragua without opposition in late 1936. Over the next twenty years, as *Jefe Director* of the Guardia Nacional, and as President from 1937 to 1947 and again from 1950 until his assassination in 1956, Somoza García dominated Nicaragua, becoming in the process the nation's wealthiest citizen.

Anastasio Somoza Debayle, known since childhood as "Tachito," obtained his elementary education at the Instituto Pedagógico de Managua. Among his schoolmates was Pedro Joaquín Chamorro Cardenal, who eventually became the prize-winning publisher of the opposition newspaper *La Prensa* and who continued to be Somoza's principal adversary until he was gunned down by unidentified assassins in downtown Managua on January 10, 1978. From 1936 to 1942 Somoza studied at the La Salle Military Academy in Oakdale, Long Island, New York. Meanwhile, in July 1941, he became a sublieutenant in the Guardia Nacional, and soon, in preparation for his entry into the United States Military Academy at West Point, he was promoted to first lieutenant. After his promotion to captain in July 1942 he served briefly as a military instructor with the first presidential battalion.

Returning to Nicaragua in June 1946 after completing four years at West Point, Somoza was promoted the following month to major and appointed inspector general of the army. His dizzying rise through the ranks prompted some cynics to observe, as quoted in Richard Millett's book *Guardians of the Dynasty* (Orbis, 1977), that he was "the only cadet in the Academy's history to receive an army as a graduation present." In 1947 Somoza became commander of the first Presidential battalion and then of the fifth battalion, as well as chief of operations of the army. Promoted to colonel in 1948, he was appointed by his father as the first Nicaraguan director of the Academia Militar, previously under United States control. He became chief of the military staff and commander of general headquarters in 1950, assistant director of the army's official review in 1952, and commander of the national air force as well as de facto *Jefe Director* of the Guardia Nacional in July 1956.

When Anastasio Somoza García was assassinated in September 1956, his older son, Luis, was appointed by the national congress to finish his unexpired term, while Anastasio Somoza was formally named *Jefe Director* of the Guardia Nacional. Elected to the Presidency in February 1957, Luis Somoza liberalized some aspects of Nicaraguan life and restored a constitutional ban on consecutive Presidential terms as well as a prohibition on immediate succession to the Presidency by relatives. Meanwhile, Anastasio Somoza Debayle—who was promoted to brigadier general in 1957, to major general in 1960, and to division general in 1964—molded the Guardia Nacional into the strongest military force in Central America and foiled a number of anti-government plots. Continuing its close ties with the United States, the Guardia Nacional helped to prepare the ill-fated American-sponsored Bay of Pigs invasion of Cuba in 1961 and took part in the United States intervention in the Dominican Republic in 1965.

Consolidating his position under René Schick Gutierrez, a "Somoza man" who succeeded Luis Somoza as President in 1963, Anastasio Somoza Debayle began to campaign for the Presidency in 1965. Despite the misgivings of his brother, whose moderate, civilian-oriented administration contrasted with his own hard-line military approach, Anastasio Somoza Debayle won the Presidential nomination of Nicaragua's dominant Partido Liberal Nacionalista (PLN) on August 1, 1966. His chief opponent in the 1967 elections was the Conservative leader Dr. Fernando Agüero Rocha, the candidate of the National Opposition Union (UNO), a coalition of Conservatives, Christian Democrats, and Independent Liberals. To comply with the constitutional ban on military officers campaigning for political office, Somoza resigned his post as *Jefe Director* of the Guardia Nacional.

Somoza surprised observers with an American-style campaign described by Marshall Smith in *Life* (April 28, 1967) as a "whistle-stopping, baby-kissing tour of the countryside." At an opposition rally on January 22, 1967 Agüero Rocha, in an admitted coup attempt, tried in vain to persuade the Guardia Nacional to turn against Somoza, and in the violence that followed, scores of his supporters were killed or wounded. Somoza's victory, tainted by the opposition's charges of fraud, was lopsided, since he garnered 480,162 of the 652,244 votes cast February 5, 1967.

Succeeding Lorenzo Guerrero Gutiérrez, who became interim President after Schick's death in August 1966, Anastasio Somoza Debayle was inaugurated as Nicaragua's thirty-fifth President for a five-year term on May 1, 1967. After the ceremony, Somoza again took over the post of *Jefe Director* of the Guardia Nacional and also acquired the resounding title of *Jefe Supremo*—or commander-in-chief—of Nicaragua's armed forces.

As President, Somoza diverted funds to education and health programs by imposing unpopular austerity measures and emphasized the modernization and diversification of agriculture. Although cotton, Nicaragua's main export crop, had suffered from several years of bad harvests, the per capita income of Nicaraguans grew by over 8 percent between 1968 and 1971, and manufacturing increased by almost 10 percent. Nevertheless, many continued to live in poverty, and opposition to Somoza's regime mounted. The abrogation, in 1970, of the fifty-six-year-old Chamorro-Bryan Treaty, which had given the United States the exclusive right to build an interoceanic canal across Nicaragua, removed one of the few sources of friction between the two countries.

In March 1971 Somoza arrived at an agreement with Agüero Rocha and other Conservative leaders providing for dissolution of the national Congress in September 1971 and the election, five months later, of a constitutional assembly. When he resigned the Presidency in May 1972, he turned power over to a three-man junta—two Liberals and one Conservative—that was to rule until the drafting of a new constitution in 1974. Actually, he never relinquished power, since he continued to serve as head of the armed forces and leader of the PLN.

Meanwhile, on December 23, 1972 Nicaragua was assaulted by a series of earthquakes that virtually destroyed the capital city of Managua and left some 10,000 persons dead and about 300,000 homeless. As head of the armed forces and president of a national emergency committee, Somoza took charge of relief efforts and the distribution of millions of dollars worth of emergency supplies from abroad. but his reassumption of chief executive powers under martial law prompted renewed attacks on him and weakened the Liberal-Conservative coalition. His insistence that Managua be rebuilt on its original site—which had been struck by major earthquakes in 1885 and 1931—aroused suspicion. After all, the Somoza family owned much of its real estate and held monopolies in industries essential to the city's reconstruction.

A new constitution, adopted on April 24, 1974, enabled Somoza to run for a second presidential term. It allocated 60 percent of the seats in the Chamber of Deputies to the PLN and 40 percent to the Conservatives, while in effect barring other parties from electoral politics. With Conservative candidate Dr. Edmundo Paguaga Irías as his only opponent, he was reelected to the Presidency, for a six-year term, on September 1, 1974, receiving 748,985 of the 815,758 votes cast. Shortly after the elections, Pedro Joaquín Chamorro and others, calling the election a sham, organized a broad-based opposition, the Union Democrática de Liberación (UDEL), which included Conservatives and Christian Democrats as well as members of the two illegal Communist parties.

A more immediate threat to Somoza—who began his second presidential term on December 1, 1974—was that posed by the Frente Sandinista de Liberación Nacional (FSLN). It was named after General César Augusto Sandino, who fought United States Marines and the Guardia Nacional in the early 1930's and was killed in 1934 on orders of the elder Somoza. Founded in 1961 and reportedly financed and trained by the Cuban government of Fidel Castro, the FSLN was crushed in the late 1960's by Guardia Nacional operations against guerrillas. By the early 1970's, however, the Sandinistas had renewed their guerrilla activities, especially in the northeastern agricultural provinces of Matagalpa and Zelaya.

On the evening of December 27, 1974 a band of FSLN guerrillas staged a dramatic raid on the home of former Agriculture Minister José María Castillo, who was giving a party in honor of United States Ambassador Turner B. Shelton, a close friend and confidant of Somoza. Since the hostages included Somoza's friends and relatives, the President reluctantly yielded to the guerillas' demands. A ransom of $1,000,000—scaled down from the original demand for $5,000,000—was paid to the raiders; fourteen FSLN political prisoners were freed and flown to Cuba on a Somoza-owned plane; and the government was forced into allowing the broadcasting and publication of a 12,000-word communiqué that denounced the Somoza regime as "the most despicable dictatorship in Latin America" and called for its overthrow. Immediately after meeting the demands, Somoza proclaimed martial law, imposed strict censorship, and launched a campaign against the FSLN.

Meanwhile, Somoza again stressed agrarian reform. Among other projects, he instituted in 1976 a peasant welfare program known as INVIERNO, partly financed by the United States Agency for International Development but considered by critics as a blind for anti-guerrilla activities. Soaring international coffee and cotton prices brought Nicaragua a trade surplus in 1976 for the first time in four years, but little was done to alleviate the maldistribution of income among Nicaraguans.

Somoza's cozy relationship with the United States was enhanced by his cameraderie with fellow West Point graduates in the American military establishment and by his shrewd ability to cash in on American concern over the spread of Communism in the Western Hemisphere. United States aid to Nicaragua since the mid-1940's reportedly has exceeded $250,000,000, and the United States Army School of the Americas in the Panama Canal Zone has trained more than 4,000 Nicaraguans. Under Somoza Nicaragua has maintained more or less cordial relations with other Central American countries. It supported Panama's demand for a renegotiated Canal Zone treaty with the United States, joined in efforts of neighboring countries to raise taxes levied on banana-exporting companies, and endorsed Guatemala's claim to Belize, but the use of Costa Rican territory as a base of operations by Nicaraguan rebels has remained a source of friction between those two countries.

The Somoza family's business property, excluding investments abroad, has been estimated to be worth about $500,000,000 and includes 20 to 30 percent of Nicaragua's arable land, much of it dedicated to producing such leading exports as cotton, coffee, bananas, sugar, and beef. Other Somoza properties include LANICA, the Nicaraguan airline, in which the late Howard Hughes was a partner; MAMENIC, the national shipping line; financial institutions and communications media; and such diverse enterprises as hotels, laundromats, and parking meters; and various manufacturing industries. According to Jack Anderson (New York *Post*, August 18, 1975), who called Somoza "the world's greediest ruler," over 50 percent of Nicaragua's private property is controlled by the Somoza family. "If I gave away my title and . . . my political connections, I'd still be the strongest man in the country," Somoza once boasted, as quoted in the *Wall Street Journal* (October 22, 1973).

Furthermore, Somoza staffed most of the strategic government and military posts with his relatives and cronies. Officers of the Guardia Nacional reputedly augmented their salaries through control of gambling and prostitution and were said to have operated a lucrative black market dealing in looted goods and foreign aid supplies following the 1972 earthquake. Five years after the earthquake, most of Managua remained devastated, while thousands of persons continue to huddle in temporary ramshackle shelters.

Those conditions fueled the resentment of the opposition and led to renewed guerrilla activity by the FSLN in the mid-1970's. The intensity of the Somoza regime's anti-guerrilla campaigns led Nicaragua's Roman Catholic hierarchy, headed by Archbishop Miguel Obando Bravo to issue a pastoral letter in January 1977 that was banned from publication but read from pulpits throughout Nicaragua, charging that Guardia Nacional troops engaged in widespread torture, rape, and summary executions. The damning case against the Somoza regime was further documented by Amnesty International, which issued a blistering report in August 1977, charging that "the populations of entire peasant villages have been exterminated or taken away as prisoners of National Guard troops."

In keeping with President Jimmy Carter's avowed concern for human rights, the United States government withheld economic and military aid from Nicaragua during much of 1977, and responding to United States pressure, the Somoza regime, on September 19, 1977, lifted the martial law that had been in effect for thirty-three months. About two weeks later the Carter Administration announced that "conditional approval" would be given to a previously suspended arms sale to Nicaragua, amounting to $2,500,000.

After suffering a heart attack on July 25, 1977, Somoza was treated for coronary artery disease at the Miami Heart Institute for thirty-nine days before returning to recuperate at his Pacific shore home, Hacienda Montelimar. During his absence, his half-brother, Major General José Rodríguez Somoza, the inspector general of the Guardia Nacional, served as interim head of the armed forces. In view of Somoza's weakened condition, the opposition UDEL issued a manifesto in October, calling for his resignation. Hoping to take advantage of the unsettled political situation, the FSLN launched an offensive in several sectors of Nicaragua on October 13, 1977, and its leaders vowed to continue the struggle until the Somoza government was overthrown.

On August 22, 1978 FSLN guerrillas seized the National Palace and held about 2,000 hostages captive for two days until allowed to fly to Panama with fifty-nine released political prisoners and $500,000 in ransom money. Calling for Somoza's resignation, business, political, and civilian groups began a general strike three days later. Instead of yielding to their demands, Somoza imposed martial law and a curfew in September. After four weeks of bloody fighting in some of Nicaragua's largest cities, in early October Somoza agreed to hold talks with leaders of the Broad Opposition Front and with a panel of mediators from the United States and Latin America. But because the guerrillas still clamored for Somoza's immediate resignation, observers held out little hope for a peaceful resolution of the crisis.

In 1950 Anastasio Somoza Debayle married his first cousin, Hope Portocarrero, a native of Tampa, Florida, whom he met while attending West Point. Their oldest son, Anastasio Somoza Portocarrero, a Harvard Business School graduate and a major in the Guardia Nacional, is reportedly being groomed to succeed his father. The other Somoza children are Julio Nestor, Hope Carolina, Carla Ana, and Roberto Eduardo. The tall and corpulent Nicaraguan strongman, who speaks fluent English peppered with American slang, is as extroverted as his late father and older brother. A former close friend, now admittedly hostile, was quoted in Richard Millett's *Guardians of the Dynasty* as referring to Somoza's "psychic imbalance" and his "megalomania and self-deification." Somoza, who serves as board chairman of a number of companies, has traveled extensively, since 1948, on diplomatic missions and state visits, and holds a number of foreign decorations and honors. An aviation enthusiast, he has a United States pilot's license.

References: N Y Times p14+ F 7 '67 por; New Repub 176:14+ Ap 9 '77; Newsweek 69:56 F 13 '67 por; Sat R 5:19+ N 12 '77; Campos Meléndez, Silvio. Somoza ante la historia (1972); International Who's Who, 1977-78; Millet, Richard. Guardians of the Dynasty (1977)

Spacek, Sissy (spā'sek)

Dec. 25, 1949- Actress. Address: b. c/o Bill Treusch Associates, 853 7th Ave., New York City, N.Y. 10019

Although no longer in her teens, the freckle-faced, Texas-born actress Sissy Spacek achieved stardom in the title role of *Carrie* (1976), which—along with *The Exorcist* and *The Omen*—is one of a new genre of phenomenally successful motion pictures about children or adolescents who use supernatural powers to wreak havoc on their surroundings. Miss Spacek's talent, combined with her fragile, innocent appearance, gave her enough credibility as a maladjusted teen-ager who resorts to telekinesis to avenge herself on her tormentors to earn her an Oscar nomination and an award from the National Society of Film Critics. Earlier, Miss Spacek had won acclaim for her portrayal of the teen-age companion of a young mass murderer in *Badlands* (1973). She again dazzled critics, in 1977, with her performance in Robert Altman's *Three Women* (1977), prompting the writers of a *Newsweek* cover story (February 14, 1977) to single her out as the "most promising" new actress in motion pictures.

Sissy Spacek was born on Christmas Day, 1949, in the small Texas town of Quitman, ninety miles northeast of Dallas. Her parents, Virginia and Edwin Spacek, named their daughter Mary Elizabeth, but her two older brothers began calling her Sissy when she was a child, and she has been known by that name ever since. Her father, who is of Czech ancestry, was the county agent for the United States Department of Agriculture before his retirement. Miss Spacek remembers her childhood as a kind of "fairy-tale existence" in which days were spent on "squirrel safaris" and "frog-giggin'" excursions with her brothers in the piney woods near Quitman, or riding her horse, Buck, in local rodeos and practising barrel races and square dances on horseback. A popular student at Quitman High School, she made her mark there as a cheerleader, drum majorette, fire marshal, contributor to the school newspaper, officer in the Spanish Club, singer in the choral group, member of the local 4-H Club, and homecoming queen. Ironically, in view of her future career, she was turned down for a role in the senior play.

At thirteen Miss Spacek began her musical training on a $14.95 guitar she ordered from a Sears Roebuck catalog. With the aid of an instruction booklet and a recording she taught herself to play "Little Brown Jug" and then took advanced lessons from a Church of Christ preacher. Eventually she developed enough skill to sing and play at school assemblies and to give guitar lessons at fifty cents an hour.

The "fairy tale existence" of Miss Spacek's early years came to a tragic end about 1966, when her brother Robbie, an outstanding athlete, was stricken with terminal leukemia. To spare her the ordeal of witnessing her brother's deteriorating health, her parents sent her to New York City to spend the summer with a cousin, actor Rip Torn, and his wife, actress Geraldine Page. Through them she came into contact with the world of professional show business.

Determined to establish herself as a rock singer, Sissy Spacek made the rounds auditioning for New York talent agents. But although she succeeded in obtaining booking for three appearances on the *Tonight Show Starring Johnny Carson*, stage fright caused her to feign illness on each of those occasions. Once an agent offered her a long-term management contract, but her father, whose permission she had to have because she was under age, saw that it could tie her up for too long a period and refused to sign. When, shortly after her return to Quitman, her brother died, the shock changed her outlook on life and made her aware, as she explained to Michael Wolff in *New Times* (February 4, 1977), "that there isn't all the time you thought there was supposed to be." After two days at the University of Texas, she dropped out and returned to New York to pursue a career in music. Her parents agreed that if that was what she really wanted to do, they would place no obstacle in her way.

For about three years Sissy Spacek was a familiar sight around the stage doors and music studios in the Times Square area, "the funny kid" with the big twelve-string guitar, singing country rock tunes of her own composition. She performed in Washington Square Park and took part in hootenannies at the Bitter End, a Greenwich Village bistro, while supporting herself by singing background vocals for airline and bubblegum commercials and for the soundtrack of Andy Warhol's film *Lonesome Cowboys* (1969), or working as a salesclerk at a Madison Avenue boutique. She also appeared as an extra in the aptly named Warhol movie *Trash* (1971).

After a photographer friend prepared a professional portfolio for her, Miss Spacek briefly tried her hand at modeling, but aside from appearing in a perfume ad in the *New Yorker* she met with little success. In 1971 a record promoter talked her into changing her name to Rainbo and recording a song entitled *John, You Went Too Far This Time*, about a nude album cover that John Lennon and Yoko Ono had recently made. But when the song failed to make a hit, Sissy Spacek began to entertain second thoughts about her future in rock music.

At the suggestion of a young agent named Bill Treusch, Miss Spacek directed her energies into acting. She attended the Lee Strasberg Theatrical Institute for six months and discovered to her amazement, that she already knew the things being taught there. Unlike her classmates, she had few inhibitions and emotional blocks to overcome. Therefore, instead of wasting her time studying, she began to frequent motion picture casting offices. On the advice of a friend she auditioned, successfully, for a role in the big-budget film *Prime Cut*, an underworld melodrama starring Lee Marvin and Gene Hackman that was filmed on location in Calgary, Alberta, Canada and released by National General Pictures in 1972.

In her film debut Sissy Spacek played a drugged teenage orphan rescued from the clutches of a white slaver. Although *Prime Cut* was blasted by the critics for its violence and sadism and failed at the box office, some of its actors, including Sissy Spacek, got good notices. Judith Crist wrote in *New York* magazine (July 3, 1972): "The film's sole virtue is Sissy Spacek, a lovely twenty-year-old with an exquisitely appealing face, who, alas, makes her debut herein as the nymphet. Presumably, a beginner can't be a chooser."

Convinced that her future lay in motion pictures, Miss Spacek left New York and moved to California. She was tested and turned down for roles in several major Hollywood movies before landing her next assignment, in a low-budget, independent art film called *Badlands* (Warner, 1973). Written, produced, and directed by Terrence Malick, *Badlands* tells the story of an alienated young mass murderer, played by Martin Sheen. As his fifteen-year-old girlfriend, Sissy Spacek portrayed an emotionless and vacuous creature whose life revolves around Hollywood gossip magazines and romantic fantasies. Loosely based on the real-life 1950's murder spree of Charles Starkweather and Caril Ann Fugate, *Badlands* created a sensation at the eleventh annual New York Film Festival, where it won praise for its director and stars. Vincent Canby noted in the New York *Times* (October 21, 1973) that "Miss Spacek manages the rather grand feat of being simultaneously transparent and mysterious, sweet and heedlessly cruel." In his *New Times* article, Michael Wolff observed that "Sissy, because she can dismiss her own presence in a way Faye Dunaway never could . . . , shows in the simplest terms of ennui and American girlhood how a fifteen-year-old . . . could tag along on a murderous ride." Despite all its accolades, however, *Badlands* was a box-office failure.

Two years passed before audiences again had the opportunity to see Sissy Spacek on the big screen. In the meantime she appeared on television in two episodes of *The Waltons* and in such made-for-television movies as the independently produced *Ginger in the Morning,* in which she played the title role, and, in 1973, *The Girls of Huntington House,* a melodrama about a home for unwed mothers. In 1974 she portrayed the pregnant teen-age daughter of Cloris Leachman in Tennessee Williams' "The Migrants," a *Playhouse 90* drama about the poverty and hardships of itinerant fruit pickers, filmed on location in New Jersey. During the filming Miss Spacek spent some time among real migrant families, an experience that she described as "heartbreaking." In *Katherine,* an *ABC Sunday Night Movie* presented in October 1975, she played a young heiress, apparently inspired by Patricia Hearst, who rejects her parents and joins a terrorist group. According to John J. O'Connor of the New York *Times* (October 19, 1975), "Miss Spacek's Katherine was thoroughly convincing from chic college girl to revolutionary in jeans and granny glasses."

Shortly after her marriage to art director Jack Fisk, Sissy Spacek worked with her husband as a set decorator on *Phantom of the Paradise* (Twentieth Century-Fox, 1974) a horror film directed by Brian De Palma. Two years later, De Palma and Fisk were preparing another horror film, *Carrie,* when De Palma remembered the art director's talented actress wife. He invited her to try out for a supporting part but in the end decided to cast her in the title role. Based on a novel by Stephen King, *Carrie* (United Artists, 1976) concerns a teen-age high school misfit who uses her telekinetic powers to liquidate the people who had made her life miserable—her fanatically religious mother (played by Piper Laurie), her teachers, and her schoolmates. To prepare for the role, Miss Spacek tried to live the part of a persecuted outcast. "In . . . my dressing room I had religious pictures all round the walls," she told Andrew Veitch of the *Guardian* (January 14, 1977). "I tried to create a little world. I never lost the character, even when I went home with Jack."

Although the film itself received mixed reviews, Miss Spacek's performance catapulted her into stardom. Her achievement was perhaps best summed up by Gary Arnold, who wrote in the Washington *Post* (November 3, 1976): "She responds splendidly to every mood and transformation the role requires: panicky, hysterical schoolgirl; wretched but sensitive daughter . . . ; the momentarily happy, glowing young woman at the prom; a maddened, bulging-eyed vessel of wrath; a contrite, concerned, tragic child. It's been several years since a young American actress has been encouraged to make such an impact, and it's exhilarating to watch Spacek take advantage of this opportunity." *Carrie* became one of the top moneymakers of 1976, and the National Society of Film Critics honored Sissy Spacek with its Best Actress of the Year award. She was also nominated for an Oscar at the Academy of Motion Picture Arts and Sciences awards ceremony in March 1977 but lost to Faye Dunaway.

In her next venture, *Welcome to L.A.* (United Artists, 1977), filmed before *Carrie* but released later, Sissy Spacek received sixth billing as a housemaid who likes to work topless and who picks up extra cash as a hooker. Produced by Robert Altman and directed by Alan Rudolph, *Welcome to L.A.* haphazardly examines the interrelationships of a cross-section of decadent Californians. The film was generally panned by critics, who found it a dull and depressing imitation of Altman's *Nashville.*

Impressed by Sissy Spacek's performance in *Welcome to L.A.* despite the film's shortcomings, Robert Altman cast her in *Three Women* (Twentieth Century-Fox, 1977), which he wrote, produced, and directed. *Three Women* is a dream-like tale of Pinky, an ingenuous Texas girl who attaches herself to a more sophisticated woman, played by Shelley Duvall. After a severe trauma and attempted suicide, the young girl awakes from a coma and assumes the name and personality of her companion. The third woman, played by Janice Rule, remains more or less in the background. Saturated with Freudian imagery and symbolism, *Three Women* was seen by some critics as a masterpiece, enhanced by the performances of its stars. "Sissy Spacek has already demonstrated her ability to shuttle between utter innocence and troubled quirkiness with the utmost ease, or to grow from ugly duckling into radiant maturity," John Simon wrote in *New York* magazine (April 25, 1977). "As Pinky, she reconfirms it stunningly." Robert Altman was quoted in *Newsday* (April 24, 1977) as saying of Miss Spacek: "She is as good an actress as I've even seen work," one who "is able to become whatever you ask her to transmit." For her performance in *Three Women* she received the New York Film Critics' best supporting actress award.

On March 12, 1977 Miss Spacek broke away from her string of offbeat, dramatic roles to act as hostess of NBC-TV's pseudo-counterculture variety show *Saturday Night,* on which she performed comedy sketches, demonstrated her baton twirling skills, and sang her own songs. During the summer of 1977 she was scheduled to begin work on a film to be titled "Illusion" and to be directed by Nicholas Roeg in Vienna that she has described as "a bit of a mystery and a bit of a love story." On January 25, 1978 in the PBS-TV film *Verna—USO Girl* she played a starlet entertaining frontline troops. Gary Arnold wrote in the Washington *Post* (January 22, 1978) that the film "doesn't begin to exploit the emotional resources and variety of moods Spacek has revealed in theatrical movies like *Carrie* and *Three Women.*" Brian De Palma has said that he would like to cast Miss Spacek as Janis Joplin in a film about the ill-fated rock singer.

Sissy Spacek and Jack Fisk, who met while working on *Badlands,* were married on April 12, 1974 in a small chapel in Santa Monica, California, with a Hungarian sheepdog as their only witness. Miss Spacek is five feet two inches tall, weighs ninety-two pounds, and has green eyes and strawberry blonde hair that reaches almost to her waist. She retains her pleasing Texas drawl because she feels that an accent adds color to an actress's personality. She recently bought a cabin near her hometown of Quitman and visits there often. "Texas is the place that keeps me most grounded," she told Larry Gordon of *Circus* magazine (July 21, 1977). "When I get real nuts, I can go back there and walk in the woods and swim and water ski and go riding. It's a little cocoon. It's great." In California, she and her husband live in Topanga Canyon, in "a little tract house" that they have completely remodeled with skylights and French doors and windows. Outside is a giant hot tub that they share with their friends, mostly artists and sculptors. A well-organized person, Miss Spacek keeps their modest dwelling spotless. "If I get hit by a car, I want to go out knowing I returned my neighbor's cake pan," she told an interviewer for *Time* (December 6, 1976).

Discussing her views on personal success with Larry Gordon, Sissy Spacek observed: "You have to know your own talent and keep plugging along. . . . Of course a lot has to do with luck and timing and you have to be able to deal with it emotionally. . . . I'm lucky. I have a real strong family and lots of security and love. And if it all ended tomorrow, I'd just do something else." Among the activities that she might like to engage in at some future date, Miss Spacek has mentioned writing and directing films, resuming her efforts to establish her career as a singer, writing a children's book, and publishing some of her own poems.

References: Chicago Tribune VI/VII p6+ Jl 17 '77 por; N Y Times II p13+ D 12 '76 por; New Times 8:55+ F 4 '77 por; Newsday II p4+ Ap 24 '77 por; Newsweek 89:56+ F 14 '77 por; People 8:35+ Ag 22 '77 pors; Seventeen 33:200+ Ap '74 pors

Spielberg, Steven

Dec. 18, 1947- Motion picture director, writer, producer. Address: b. c/o Columbia Pictures, Colgems Square, Burbank, Calif. 91505

"Making movies is an illusion, a technical illusion that people fall for," Steven Spielberg, the extraordinarily gifted, visually inventive young film maker, remarked recently. "My job is to take that technique and hide it so well that never once are you taken out of your chair and reminded of where you are." Having learned his craft behind a television camera, Spielberg became, at age twenty-seven, the hottest director in Hollywood with the release of his second film, the blockbuster *Jaws,* which has, to date, grossed more than $400,000,000 worldwide, easily shattering all previous box office records.

A technical virtuoso with uncanny cinematic instincts, Spielberg is an expert at audience manipulation, skillfully taking his viewers from heart-stopping terror in *Jaws* to wide-eyed amazement in *Close Encounters of the Third Kind.* His three films have netted him twelve Academy Award nominations, six Oscars, and legions of fans, among them several influential reviewers who rank him with the top Hollywood directors. According to critic Frank Rich, Spielberg is one of the few American directors who "actually knows how to tell a story on screen."

Steven Spielberg was born on December 18, 1947 in Cincinnati, Ohio, the eldest of the four children of Arnold Spielberg, an electrical engineer and computer expert, and

Leah (Posner) Spielberg, a former concert pianist. As Arnold Spielberg accepted executive level positions with a succession of major electronics firms, the family moved from Ohio to Haddonfield, New Jersey to the suburbs of Phoenix, Arizona. There Steven Spielberg was active in scouting and in Little League baseball, but his major interest was film making. The official 'family photographer,' he used his father's 8mm motion picture camera to record outings and camping trips. Soon, he was setting up shots, staging the action, experimenting with different camera angles and technical tricks, and dreaming up story lines for short horror films starring his three younger sisters. "I killed them all several times," he told one reporter.

Despite his interest in and developing talent for the medium, Spielberg's parents sheltered him from all but the most innocuous films, mostly Walt Disney features, and even "kept a blanket over the television set." As he recalled to Jerry Tallmer in an interview for a New York *Post* (June 28, 1975) profile, the first picture he saw—at the age of five or six—was Cecil B. De Mille's circus extravaganza *The Greatest Show on Earth:* "My father said: 'It's going to be bigger than you, but that's all right. The people in it are going to be up on a screen and they can't get out at you.' But there they were up on that screen *and they were getting out at me.* I guess ever since then I've wanted to try to involve the audience as much as I can, so they no longer think they're sitting in an audience."

By the time he was in high school, film making had become Spielberg's "escape"—"something fun to do to keep [him] away from studying algebra and French." He made dozens of 8mm and 16mm shorts, financing his expensive hobby with his well-paying tree-painting business. He also shared his father's passion for science fiction and astronomy and spent hours stargazing through his homemade reflecting telescope. That interest led to his first feature-length film: *Firelight,* a two-and-one-half-hour 8mm epic about a team of scientists investigating mysterious lights in the night sky. It was "all very hard-edged and sci-fi," he said in a recent interview. "Things with jaws came out of the ships to gobble up everything in sight."

When he was in his late teens, Spielberg moved with his family to San Francisco, California. He would have liked to study film, but his high school grades were so poor he could not get into any of the major film schools. Instead, he attended California State College at Long Beach, graduating in 1970 with a B.A. degree in English. During his college years he went to the movies constantly, even though the majority of the films produced in the late 1960's were, he thought, "plastic dreck." To learn more about film making, he regularly bluffed his way on to movie studio lots and observed such directors as Alfred Hitchcock and Franklin Schaffner until he was bodily ejected from the set.

Throughout that period, Spielberg made "very esoteric," "personal" films until, in an "attack of crass commercialism," he made *Amblin',* a slick, lyrical twenty-two-minute short about a boy and girl who hitchhike from the Mojave Desert to the Pacific Ocean. Although Spielberg himself later dismissed the short as "a Pepsi commercial," it nevertheless impressed enough people to win awards at the Venice and Atlanta film festivals. More importantly, it attracted the attention of Universal Pictures' executives, who paired it with *Love Story* (1970) for national distribution. On the strength of *Amblin',* Sidney Sheinberg, then head of Universal's television division, signed the young director to a seven-year contract.

Spielberg's first assignment for Universal was directing Joan Crawford in the pilot of *Night Gallery.* Subsequently, he directed episodes of *The Psychiatrists, Marcus Welby, M.D., The Name of the Game, Owen Marshall,* and *Columbo,* treating each project seriously, as if it would be his "diploma to feature films," although most of the scripts were, in his words, "1950's sub-B" material. He got his first chance at a feature film in 1971 when he was handed the script for *Duel,* a thriller that was scheduled to be telecast as a movie-of-the-week. In *Duel,* a mild-mannered traveling salesman, played by Dennis Weaver, is relentlessly pursued along a remote highway by an unseen, homicidal driver in a huge semi-trailer truck. Through skillful cross-cutting, Spielberg maintained the nail-biting suspense for nearly ninety minutes until Weaver finally outwitted the anonymous trucker.

Shot in just sixteen days for about $350,000, *Duel* grossed more than $5,000,000 in theatrical release in Europe and Japan and won several major foreign awards. Despite the fact that it has never been shown in theatres in the United States, *Duel* has attracted a large cult following and many film critics consider it to be the finest television movie ever made. Spielberg's subsequent made-for-television movies, *Savage* and *Something Evil,* although less successful than *Duel,* were generally well received. Television reviewers were especially taken by the camera tricks and frightening visual effects he used in *Something Evil,* an occult tale starring Sandy Dennis and Darren McGavin.

Inundated with feature film offers after the first broadcast of *Duel,* Spielberg, finding none of them to his liking, took a year off to develop his own screenplays. The first of these was *The Sugarland Express* (Universal, 1974), a comedy-drama drawn from a newspaper account of a desperate young couple's fruitless attempt to rescue their baby from a foster home in Sugarland, Texas. Working from his own story, polished into a taut script by Hal Barwood and Matthew Robbins, Spielberg coaxed exceptional performances from his leading actors, particularly from Goldie Hawn, as Lou Jean Poplin, the distraught, determined, and dangerously impulsive mother who bullies her husband, portrayed by William Atherton, into breaking jail, hijacking a highway patrol car, and speeding toward Sugarland with the police in pursuit. Moreover, displaying a surprising command of action sequences, he choreographed the spectacular multi-car chase with the assurance of a seasoned veteran. In his hands, as one critic noted, "the cars are as eloquent as the characters."

Paul D. Zimmerman of *Newsweek*, Judith Crist of *New York*, Pauline Kael of the *New Yorker*, and Gary Arnold of the Washington *Post* all commended Spielberg for a sense of composition and movement that, in the words of Miss Kael, "almost any director might envy." Those reviewers and others were also taken by his dramatic flair and by his "satiric but strangely beautiful" vision of Middle America. As Miss Crist observed in her highly favorable review for *New York* magazine (April 1, 1974), "The triumph of *The Sugarland Express* . . . goes beyond its technical accomplishments and substance to Spielberg's own viewpoint. . . . He has held up a mirror and showed us our baser selves clearly and truly, to powerful effect."

Despite the positive critical reaction, *Sugarland* fared badly at the box office. Nevertheless, its producers, Richard Zanuck and David Brown, were sufficiently impressed with Spielberg's work to entrust him with the filming of *Jaws*, Peter Benchley's best-selling novel about a killer shark that terrorizes a beach community. Spielberg approached the project with characteristic energy and enthusiasm. "My feeling about sharks is that they've had 80,000,000 years to get their act together," he told Joseph Gelmis in an interview for *Newsday* (July 6, 1975). "Parts of the book terrorized me. I tried to translate my fear into visual language. It became a picture book of fears, phobias, and anxieties."

At times the anxieties were as intense behind the scenes as they were before the cameras. Slowed down by frequent inclement weather, labor strikes, irritated local residents, technical problems with the mechanical sharks, and endless script revisions, the location shooting on Martha's Vineyard, originally scheduled for ten weeks in early summer in 1974, dragged on into September. At one point, Spielberg was almost fired because of mounting production costs. When the picture was finally completed, it was more than 100 percent over its original $3,500,000 budget. *Jaws* (Universal, 1975) more than made up the deficit in short order, grossing a staggering $60,000,000 in its first month of domestic release.

Critical response to *Jaws* was as overwhelmingly enthusiastic as its public reception. Although the principal actors—Richard Dreyfuss as Hooper, the bookish, broadly comic marine biologist; Robert Shaw as Quint, the grizzled, macho shark hunter; Roy Scheider as Brody, the beleaguered local chief of police—came in for their share of good notices, the superlatives were reserved for Spielberg. In the eyes of many critics the young director was as much a master of foreboding atmosphere as Hitchcock and, like him, used the "tension-relaxation rhythm" of alternating terror and humor to great effect. The fast-paced suspense was heightened by brilliantly realized special effects, by the superb underwater photography, and by the expert editing of Spielberg and Verna Fields. Gary Arnold, writing in the Washington *Post* (June 15, 1975), favorably compared the montage "panic on the beach" sequence to the famous Odessa Steps sequence in Sergei Eisenstein's silent masterpiece, *Potemkin*. Spielberg's "dynamic sense of movement [creates] a compelling sense of flight, confusion, and anxiety," Arnold wrote. "There has never been an adventure-thriller quite as terrifying yet enjoyable as *Jaws*, and it should set the standard in its field for many years to come."

In his next film, *Close Encounters of the Third Kind*, Spielberg brought together the social comment of *The Sugarland Express* and the nerve-jangling suspense of *Jaws*. Believing in the existence of intelligent life elsewhere in the universe, he had written a screenplay about a friendly encounter between humans and extraterrestrials while he was editing *Sugarland*. Spielberg objects to the adversary relationship between men and alien beings introduced by the extraterrestrial invasion films of the 1950's and carried on by such popular television series as *Star Trek* and *Space: 1999*. "In thirty years of UFO reportings, the encounters have been very benevolent," he told an Associated Press correspondent in a December 1976 interview. "No sci-fi death rays, no radiation poisoning. . . . That's the attitude I take in the picture. I have tried to take interspace relationships out of the science fiction closet and give them an aura of respectability."

To assist him in his monumental undertaking, Spielberg assembled a top-flight technical crew, including Joe Alves, the talented art director who had worked with him on his first two features; Douglas Trumbull, the special effects wizard of Stanley Kubrick's science fiction classic *2001: A Space Odyssey*; composer John Williams, who had scored

Sugarland and *Jaws* and, incidentally, *Star Wars;* Vilmos Szigmond, his director of photography on *Sugarland,* and four other first-rank cinematographers; and more than forty model makers, animators, optical effects specialists, matte artists, and electrical engineers. He selected his cast with equal care, choosing Richard Dreyfuss as Roy Neary, Spielberg's "Mr. Everyday Regular Fella," who is transformed by his encounter with UFO's; François Truffaut, the internationally acclaimed French director, as Claude Lacombe, the enigmatic scientist leading the team of UFO investigators; Melinda Dillon, Teri Garr, and Bob Balaban, all with impressive stage credentials, for the important secondary parts; and Cary Guffey, a winsome four-year-old, for the pivotal role of Barry Guiler, the trusting child who is briefly kidnapped by the aliens.

Principal photography for the film, which was shot on location in Wyoming and India and in a huge, converted World War II dirigible hangar outside Mobile, Alabama, was completed in five months, but the editing and the intricate matching of visual and aural special effects took more than a year. Throughout this period, the project was shrouded in secrecy to protect the film, particularly its 350 special effects, from fast-buck, made-for-television imitations. Spielberg was making last-minute changes right up to the film's release date in November 1977. Meanwhile, the stock of Columbia Pictures, which had invested $18,000,000 in the venture, fluctuated wildly with the advance reports, particularly when William Flanagan, a financial analyst, predicted in *New York* magazine's November 7, 1977 issue that *Close Encounters* would be "a colossal flop."

A few reviewers—Molly Haskell, Judith Crist, William Wolf—agreed with Flanagan's assessment, calling the film "preposterous," "trivial," "simple-minded," "shallow," and "steeped in pretension." But because the overwhelming majority of the critics agreed with the thousands of viewers whose enthusiasm for the picture was reflected in the box office receipts—as of May 1, 1978 the gross was in excess of $154,000,000—the words most often used to describe *Close Encounters* were "breathtaking," "stunning," "dazzling," "moving," and "brilliant." Even Stanley Kauffmann, who had detested the director's earlier efforts, was so "happily engulfed" by Spielberg's "dazzling epiphany" that he "just didn't want to *leave* this picture."

Like most viewers, Kauffmann was especially enchanted by the awesome thirty-minute climax in which dozens of brightly colored UFO's skitter across the sky, heralding the approach and landing of a gargantuan mothership of staggering beauty. That enormous starship carries on a delightful musical conversation in a kind of "intergalactic Esperanto," as one reviewer put it, with Lacombe's computer-controlled ARP synthesizer before disgorging a score of captivating childlike aliens. "[It was] one of the most overpowering, sheerly cinematic experiences I can remember," Kauffmann wrote in the *New Republic* (December 10, 1977). Other critics were charmed by the magical Disney-like touches in some sequences. "What lifts this film into orbit," Frank Rich observed in his critique for *Time* (November 7, 1977), "is the breathless sense of wonder [Spielberg] brings to every frame. . . . *Close Encounters* is a celebration not only of children's dreams but also of the movies that help fuel those dreams."

Inevitably, *Close Encounters* was compared to George Lucas' *Star Wars.* Spielberg contends that the two films are "quite dissimilar." "*Close Encounters* is an earthbound movie," he explained in a recent interview for *Penthouse* (February, 1978). "Its roots are in the familiar routine of suburban life. *Star Wars* is a beautiful, enchanting space opera—a fantasy. . . . I want people to walk out of [*Close Encounters*] with more questions than they had when they walked in," he continued. "I want them to consider the possibility that we are not alone in the universe, that the stars are not simply a kind of nocturnal wallpaper to be viewed indifferently. People should enjoy looking up at night, exercising their imagination a little more."

To those who fault him for his alleged over-reliance on mechanical devices and optical tricks, Spielberg counters that his films, to date, "have required a great deal of sleight of hand to be effective." "I've been involved in erector sets for five years, and I'd like to do people stories very much," he told Judy Klemesrud of the New York *Times* (May 15, 1977). "I think I can deal with actors as comfortably as I can with a model airplane kit. . . . I'm very frustrated when I see movies like [Bernardo Bertolucci's] *The Conformist* and [Truffaut's] *Small Change* and I haven't taken a position personally on how I feel about the world. I think my films will eventually get around to that, but I never want to stop entertaining."

Spielberg draws much of his inspiration from his friends, writer-directors George Lucas, John Milius, Martin Scorsese, Paul Schraeder, Francis Ford Coppola, and a handful of other inventive young film artists who make up a kind of loosely knit cinematic cooperative. They exchange scripts, ideas, suggestions, rough cuts, and even percentages of profits "like kids trading baseball cards," as Spielberg put it, and also protect each other's films from unwarranted actions by the studios. Committed to helping talented young people break into the business, Spielberg often uses American Film Institute apprentices as assistants on his films and recently acted as executive producer for *I*

Wanna Hold Your Hand (Universal, 1978), a comedy directed by Robert Zameckis, a twenty-five-year-old newcomer. Future projects include producing and directing "Growing Up," a low-budget comedy, from a script by Zameckis and Robert Gale; producing "The Continental Divide," a love story, for Columbia; and directing "1941," a comedy written by protégés Zameckis and Gale, and a "much less fantastic" sequel to *Close Encounters*. He is also collaborating with George Lucas on a science fiction film.

A slim, boyish man, Steven Spielberg stands about five feet ten inches tall and has thick, tousled dark brown hair and "dreamy, far-away" eyes, usually shielded by aviator glasses. He dresses casually, often in sweaters, jeans, and running shoes, and is never without an 8mm synchronized sound motion picture camera. He does not smoke, drink, or take drugs, and rarely attends Hollywood parties, preferring to spend his leisure hours at his Laurel Canyon, California home, which he shares with Amy Irving, the actress. Those who know him say he is friendly, unassuming, disarmingly straightforward, and good-humored. Spielberg, however, describes himself as "a very enclosed person who makes open, impersonal movies." He has boundless energy and often puts in a twenty-hour day when he is working on a film. "I do my best work when I'm in the pits emotionally," he told one interviewer. "Sometimes I'm in the pits for six months straight, but it's okay because my creative juices don't flow as well when I'm happy. . . . The only time I feel totally happy is when I'm watching films or making them."

References: N Y Post p15 Je '75 por; N Y Times II p 13+ My 15 '77 por; Newsday II p1+ Jl 6 '75 por; Newsweek 83:82+ Ap 8 '74 por, 90:98+ N 21 '77 pors; Penthouse 9:100+ F '78 por; Washington Post C p1+ My 31 '75 pors

---

Springsteen, Bruce

Sept. 23, 1949- Rock musician; songwriter. Address: b. c/o Columbia Records, 51 W. 52nd St., New York City, N.Y. 10019

Viewed as the rock messiah destined to revitalize the pop music of the 1970's, Bruce Springsteen "burst just like a supernova"—to borrow a phrase from one of his hit songs—on the rock scene in 1975, with the release of his *Born to Run*. Although Springsteen's tightly knit song-stories about alienated adolescents, sung in his raspy voice to hard-edged rock accompaniment, had made him a cult hero with a fanatical following in the Northeast by 1973, his first two albums failed to attract national attention. But *Born to Run* perfectly reproduced the street punk confidence and driving energy of his electrifying live performances with the E Street Band. "He can do everything," one rock critic wrote in 1975, "and do it until you are moved to dance, or to cry. And sometimes, he can move you to tears and boogaloo in the very same song. . . . He is a pure original."

Of Dutch and Neapolitan Italian descent, Bruce Springsteen was born in Freehold, a working-class town in central New Jersey, on September 23, 1949. His father, Douglas Springsteen, drifted from job to job; his mother, Adele Springsteen, was a secretary. He and his two younger sisters attended a neighborhood parochial school, where he was an indifferent student. "I lived half of my first thirteen years in a trance or something," he told James Willwerth in an interview for a *Time* (October 27, 1975) magazine cover story. "People thought I was weird because I always went around with this *look* on my face. I was thinking of things, but I was always on the outside looking in. . . . From the beginning my guitar was something I could go to. If I hadn't found music, I don't know what I would have done."

Entranced by Elvis Presley's performance on a television special, Springsteen scraped together $18 to buy a battered, second-hand guitar. He quickly taught himself to play the instrument, then moved on to the harmonica and piano. By the time he was fourteen, he was adept enough at all three to play in local pick-up bands. When his family moved to California in 1965, Springsteen remained behind to finish his schooling. Following his graduation from the local public high school, he enrolled at a neighborhood community college, but he dropped out a few months later after having a run-in with a guidance counselor.

Throughout that period, Bruce Springsteen spent virtually all his free time playing and writing music. "Music was my way of keeping people from looking through and around me," he said in a recent interview. "I wanted the heavies to know I was around." As the leader of a succession of hard rock bands, among them, the Rogues, the Castiles, the Steel Mill, and Dr. Zoom and the Sonic Boom, Springsteen gradually acquired a following along the New Jersey coast. His bands, which changed personnel almost as often as they changed names, played local clubs, private parties, firemen's balls, trailer parks, prisons, state mental hospitals, a rollerdrome, even a shopping center parking lot. In the late 1960's Springsteen joined the hippie migration flocking to San Francisco. There he played the legendary Fillmore West with the rock group known as Child, but when he failed to land a record contract, he returned to the New Jersey club circuit, with occasional side gigs in such Greenwich Village night spots as the Cafe Wha? and Max's Kansas City.

Springsteen got his first big break in 1972 when a friend introduced him to Mike Appel, an aggressive young rock producer and manager, who immediately signed him and arranged an audition with John Hammond, the vice-president of talent acquisition at Columbia Records. After hearing Springsteen sing his own "It's Hard To Be a Saint in the City," Hammond immediately put him under contract to Columbia. "The kid absolutely knocked me out," Hammond said later, as quoted in *Newsweek* (October 27, 1975). "I only hear somebody really good once every ten years, and not only was Bruce the best, he was a lot better than Dylan when I first heard him." Clive Davis, then president of Columbia Records, was so taken by Springsteen's first single, "Blinded By the Light," that he read the lyrics aloud at a company meeting. (Although Springsteen's record never hit the charts, a subsequent version by the British group Manfred Mann went all the way to number one in 1977.)

Promoting Springsteen as a singer-songwriter in the Bob Dylan mold, Columbia released his first album, *Greetings From Asbury Park*, in January 1973. The LP effectively showcased Springsteen as a songwriter of dazzling potential, but the smooth, soft, folk rock sound–he sang solo, accompanied by a single acoustic guitar—contradicted his local reputation as a hard-driving rock 'n' roller. Although a few reviewers thought the album was "inconsistent," "uneven," "unlistenable," and "a touch too Dylanesque for comfort," most praised it extravagantly. Unfortunately, because many disc jockeys were irritated by Columbia's hard-sell promotional comparisons to Dylan, *Greetings* was virtually ignored by the major FM rock stations, and its album sales were slow.

Meanwhile, Springsteen's kinetic performances with the E Street Band continued to galvanize rock aficionados. Alternately menacing and enticing, Springsteen struts, swaggers, and dances around the stage with relentless energy. He sings, growls, sobs, and whispers his lyrics "with all the fist-clutching and arm-flailing of a method actor psyching himself out," as one critic reported. Intoxicated by his high-voltage performances, Springsteen's audiences spend most of their time on their feet, clapping and stomping to the infectious beat, and singing along when the band breaks into exuberant renditions of such rock classics as Elvis Presley's "Wear My Ring Around Your Neck," Manfred Mann's "Sha La La," Mitch Ryder's "Jenny Take a Ride" and "Devil With a Blue Dress On," Sam Cooke's "Cupid," or Gary ("U.S.") Bonds's "Quarter to Three."

Backed by his E Street Band, Springsteen assembled for Columbia a second album that was much more representative of his live performances than *Greetings* had been. *The Wild, the Innocent and the E Street Shuffle*, which one critic described as a "free association autobiography," was released to generally favorable reviews in November 1973. Some critics, among them, Bruce Pollock, were captivated by Springsteen's impressionistic, evocative descriptions of abandoned beach houses, sleazy bars, and steamy city streets crowded with punks, pimps, and prostitutes. "Springsteen is a word virtuoso," Pollock wrote in the New York *Times* (December 16, 1973). "His lyrics are intuitive, emotional, a mass of flung images that spin toward you from all directions and somehow hang on a canvas—great swatches of local color that blend into a landscape of remembered adolescent scenes and dreams." But despite the almost unanimous enthusiasm of the trade press, the LP, although it sold somewhat better than *Greetings*, failed to make the charts.

Disappointed by his back-to-back failures, Springsteen concentrated on live performances. For a time, he dutifully toured the country as the opening act for such established rock groups as the phenomenally popular Chicago, but he felt so out of place in the mammoth 15,000- and 20,000-seat halls commanded by the top-selling artists that he finally restricted his performances to clubs and small auditoriums. By doing so, he limited his exposure. "They [large audiences] just won't listen to you," he explained to one reporter. "Some groups just go out and plow through it, but I can't do it that way. And it showed. We played thirteen or fourteen gigs in them big halls and we sold no records. We didn't start selling records until we started playin' smaller places."

By playing to packed houses at the Bottom Line and at Avery Fisher Hall in New York City and in similar settings throughout the East and Midwest, Springsteen eventually attracted the attention of influential rock critics, most of whom wrote wildly enthusiastic reviews. One review in particular changed the course of his career. After seeing Springsteen perform at the Harvard Square Theater in Cambridge, Massachusetts in April 1974, Jon Landau told readers of Boston's *The Real Paper:* "I saw rock and roll future and its name is Bruce Springsteen. . . . He made me feel I was hearing music for the very first time." "Landau's quote helped reaffirm a belief in myself," Springsteen said later, as quoted in *Newsweek* (October 27, 1975). "It helped me go on. I realized I was getting through to somebody." Cashing in on Landau's confident prediction, Columbia immediately launched a promotional campaign touting Springsteen as "the future of rock 'n' roll."

Spurred by Columbia's renewed interest in his career and by his increasing popularity, Springsteen holed up in a New York studio to work on a third album. It took him more than three months to complete the first cut and title track, "Born to Run," a four-and-one-half-minute "mini-opera" built around the guitar line from "Telstar," a mid-1960's hit. In that song, as in several others, Springsteen captured the boredom and desperation of urban adolescence: "By day we sweat it out in the streets of a runaway American dream/At night we ride through mansions of glory in suicide machines/Baby, this town rips bones from your back/It's a death trap, a suicide rap/We gotta get out while we're young/'Cause tramps like us, baby, we were born to run." Released as a single to fuel the growing Springsteen craze, "Born to Run" zoomed straight to the top of the charts.

While his fans waited impatiently, Springsteen made little progress on his album, despite his weeks of work. To get a fresh point of view, he persuaded Jon Landau to coproduce the album. "Things had fallen down internally," Springsteen said, as quoted in *Rolling Stone* (October 9, 1975). "[Landau] was able to point out reasons why we weren't progressing. Nobody knew why; we were completely in the dark. Jon was a super-important figure. He came up with the idea, 'Let's make a rock 'n' roll record.' His whole thing was to help me do things my way, but to make it easier." In June 1975, more than a year after he had begun working on the album, Springsteen sent a rough cut to Columbia executives, who hurriedly embarked on a $40,000 promotional campaign in twelve major markets to push Springsteen's first two albums and, at the same time, generate interest in the unreleased LP. Within weeks, sales of *Greetings* and *E Street Shuffle* doubled and both albums finally made the best-selling charts.

More unified than his first two efforts, Springsteen's *Born to Run* traces a single day in the life of a typical Jersey shore kid during one "soft infested summer," from the slam of a screen door as he leaves the house in the morning, through the endless hours he spends cruising the "highways jammed with broken heroes on a last chance power drive," to a terrifying midnight ride through "Jungleland," where "the hungry and the hunted . . . face off against each other out in the street." The meticulously crafted lyrics and the brilliant orchestrations reminiscent of the layered "wall of sound" popularized in the mid-1960's by Phil Spector, appealed to young record buyers who, in just six weeks, purchased more than 1,000,000 copies of the LP, boosting it into the top spot on the album charts.

Those critics already in Springsteen's camp greeted *Born to Run* with predictable enthusiasm. To John Rockwell of the New York *Times* and Dave Marsh of the New York *Post,* it was "a classic"—"one of the best records of recent years." Greil Marcus, writing in *Rolling Stone* (October 9, 1975) saw it as "a magnificent album . . . , a '57 Chevy running on melted-down Crystals records . . . [that] should crack his future wide open." Even Springsteen's detractors were forced to temper their complaints about "torrential" musical accompaniment, "absurdly inflated" lyrics and "second-hand," "undistinguished" melodies with reluctant praise for the unquestionable brilliance of such songs as "Backstreets" and "Thunder Road."

Often criticized for his derivative melodies, Springsteen readily admitted to interviewers that he had tried to blend "the incredible basicness of the do-ron-rons" of the late 1950's and "the more intellectual approach," typified by Bob Dylan's "Like a Rolling Stone," of the early 1960's. In composing the songs for *Born To Run,* however, he consciously moved away from the flamboyant, alliterative lyrics that marked such early compositions as "Blinded By the Light" ("Madman Bummers and Indians in the summer with a teenage diplomat/In the dumps with the mumps as the adolescent pumps his way into his hat"). "[My] lyrics aren't as flashy now as on the first album," he conceded to John Rockwell in an interview for *Rolling Stone* (October 9, 1975). "Then it was all a lot of images. . . . Lately, I've been trying to deal more with the ideas—with concepts, with themes," he continued. "It gets harder as it gets along. . . . You have to go a little farther than you went the last time. Go a little deeper down into yourself. That's hard to do, because you gotta face emotions and stuff."

As *Born to Run* entered the charts, Columbia poured upwards of $250,000 into an unprecedented promotional campaign that included radio spots, teaser ads in the trade papers, buttons, T-shirts, posters and, in what one columnist saw as "a staggering triumph for the public relations men," simultaneous cover stories in *Time* and *Newsweek*. Columbia's high-powered media blitz, coupled with the effusive praise of rock critics, inevitably provoked a negative backlash. After *Time* and *Newsweek* hit the stands in late October 1975, the number of articles devoted to Springsteen tapered off and *Born to Run*'s ranking in the pop charts dropped sharply. By the end of the year, the album was getting "heavy action" from fewer and fewer FM stations. Springsteen himself strongly objected to the excessive publicity. "The hype just gets in the way," he said, as quoted in *Newsweek* (October 27, 1975). "People have gone nuts. It's weird. All the stuff you dream is there, but it gets diluted by all the other stuff that jumped on you by surprise."

To coincide with the release of *Born to Run*, Springsteen set out on his first national tour. He followed three months of sold-out concerts in the United States with a moderately successful four-city European stint and a series of concerts and club dates in the Northeast. After a well-received two-month swing through the South and Midwest in mid-1976, Springsteen was eager to begin recording his fourth album, but Mike Appel refused to allow Jon Landau to collaborate on the project. To break his contract with Appel, Springsteen filed suit against his manager, charging fraud, breach of trust, misappropriation of funds, and false representation. Appel immediately countersued and obtained an injunction forbidding his client to record.

The long, drawn-out management dispute was finally settled out of court in late May 1977. Although Springsteen immediately set to work on a new LP, the hiatus had damaged his career, perhaps irreparably. "I have started countless numbers of songs which I have been unable to develop to their potential for a lack of a proper recording opportunity," he told an interviewer for *Rolling Stone* (August 11, 1977). "Many of these songs will never be finished." Despite his grim forebodings, he eventually managed to record the album *Darkness on the Edge of Town*, which Columbia released in 1978.

A slight, tightly muscled young man invariably described as "elfin," Bruce Springsteen has curly brown hair, brown eyes, and an impish grin. For several years, he deliberately cultivated the image of a scroungy "Sha-Na-Na reject," as John Rockwell once put it, but he recently shaved his scraggly beard and cut his hair. Totally indifferent to clothing, he wears the same casual attire onstage and off. He does not smoke, seldom drinks, and has never experimented with drugs. Springsteen lives simply in a sparsely furnished beach cottage near Long Branch, New Jersey, where his most prized possessions are his record collection, ranging from Gregorian chants to rock classics, and a customized 1957 Chevrolet convertible. For relaxation, he lounges on the beach, plays pinball machines in boardwalk arcades, and jams with local musicians in neighboring bars. "I want to do everything," he told John Rockwell. "I want to see everything. I want to go everywhere. I know what kind of situation it is. Inside, I got everything straight."

References: Newsweek 86:57+ O 27 '75 pors; Rolling Stone p9+ O 9 '75 pors, p15 My 20 '76 por; Seventeen 34:100+ D '75 pors; Time 106:48 O 27 '75 pors

---

Steel, David (Martin Scott)

Mar. 31, 1938- British political leader. Address: b. House of Commons, London SW 1A OAA, England; h. Cherry Dene, Ettrick Bridge, Selkirkshire, Scotland

Great Britain's traditional two-party system underwent modification in the spring of 1977, when the leader of the small but once formidable Liberal party, a pragmatic young Scotsman named David Steel, concluded an unprecedented temporary agreement for parliamentary cooperation with Prime Minister James Callaghan. The pact, popularly known as the "Lib-Lab" alliance, foiled a move by the Conservative opposition to topple Callaghan's Labor government, thereby enabling the Prime Minister to carry on his plans for national economic recovery, and it placed the Liberals, Britain's third party, into a position of real political influence for the first time in many years.

Steel, who became the youngest Member of Parliament when he was elected to the House of Commons in 1965, is no stranger to controversy. He was dubbed "Herod" for his sponsorship of the 1967 bill to liberalize abortion laws, and more recently he was given the epithet "Judas" by old-guard Liberals, who felt that the 1977 pact with the government compromised their party's independence and ideological purity. Steel's future plans for the Liberal party were described as "wildly, exhilaratingly ambitious" by Simon Hoggart of the *Guardian* (January 21, 1978), who observed: "He might destroy the party altogether, or he might make it the new main force in British politics. . . . The responsi-

David Steel

bility will be his, because he is running it exactly as he wants in exactly his way."

David Martin Scott Steel was born on March 31, 1938 in Kirkcaldy, Scotland, the oldest of the five children (three boys and two girls) of the Very Reverend David Steel, a Presbyterian minister. Steel spent his early years in the Scottish coal mining area of Fife, in Clydeside, and Edinburgh. From the age of eleven until he was fifteen he attended the Prince of Wales School in Nairobi, Kenya, where his father was minister of the parish of East Africa. He remembers spending Christmas of 1952—during the height of the Mau Mau revolt against white rule—at a farm, with loaded revolvers beside the dinner plates. Family debates over African politics and his father's opposition to British methods of flushing out Mau Mau suspects helped to shape his liberal outlook and deep passion for human rights. "I was instinctively anti-Tory as a result of that experience," Steel told Laurence Marks of the London *Observer* (June 20, 1976).

After the family's return to the United Kingdom, Steel attended George Watson's College in Edinburgh, where he edited the weekly newspaper, presided over the debating society, and won prizes for public speaking and composition, as well as the school's merit and service award. At the University of Edinburgh, he studied mathematics, moral philosophy, and law and became an active Liberal under the influence of university rector and Liberal party leader Jo Grimond. In 1959 he was elected president of the Edinburgh University Liberals, which he built into that institution's largest political group, and the following year he became president of the students' representative council. Steel visited the Soviet Union in 1960 as a member of the first Scottish student delegation to that country, and in 1961 he traveled to Poland, Czechoslovakia, Yugoslavia, and Berlin. A college friend, quoted by Laurence Marks in the *Observer,* remembers Steel as a shy, austere man who succeeded with "a mixture of caution, astuteness, modesty and stealth." Steel obtained his M.A. degree from Edinburgh University in 1960 and earned his LL.B. degree there in 1962.

After two years as full-time assistant secretary of the Scottish Liberal party at a salary of £850 a year, Steel was hired in 1964 by the British Broadcasting Corporation as a reporter and interviewer for the weekly Scottish television program *Checkpoint.* By keeping him in the public eye, the media work helped to advance Steel's political career. Having served as the Liberal candidate's campaign manager in a 1963 by-election in Kinross, he had impressed Scottish party leaders as a potential winner. Originally slated to be the House of Commons candidate for the Pentlands district of Edinburgh, which the Liberals had little hope of winning, he was instead offered the candidacy for the more promising Roxburgh, Selkirk, and Peebles district—known as the Borders—for the October 1964 national elections.

Borders party officials were startled when Steel, instead of displaying the humility they expected from a young newcomer, put forth a number of conditions for accepting the candidacy, among them the demand that party functionaries whom he considered incompetent be dismissed. Although he lost the 1964 election, he managed to reduce the Conservative majority from 10,000 to 1,700. In March 1965, following the death of the Tory incumbent, Steel was once more the Liberal candidate for the Borders seat in the House of Commons. Conducting what was described in the London *Daily Telegraph* as a "model campaign," Steel evoked great enthusiasm from his supporters, who hailed him as "the Boy David," and he defeated the Tory candidate, Robin McEwen, by 4,600 votes.

Some eighteen months after taking his seat in Parliament, Steel came into the limelight as the sponsor of a measure to liberalize abortion laws that became the most bitterly contested private member's bill since the end of World War II. Before making his decision, Steel carefully weighed the issues involved and personally saw an abortion performed. In taking over the sponsorship of the bill, he was motivated not only by his belief in its principles but also by his awareness that its public impact would help to further his career. He had important support from the Labor government's Home Secretary, Roy Jenkins, and from a number of newly elected young Labor radicals eager to achieve social change. After some heated debates, the Abortion Act, passed in the House of Commons on July 4, 1967 by a vote of 167 to eighty-three.

In 1967 Steel became a member of the British parliamentary delegation to the United Nations General Assembly, and since 1968 he has been a member of the Foreign Secretary's U.N. Advisory Committee. In keeping with his interests in race relations and African affairs, he served from 1966 to 1969 as president of the Anti-Apartheid Movement of Great Britain. Facing what he has called his "most difficult political decision," Steel opposed the 1969-70 Springboks' rugby tour to Great Britain, and when that all-white South African team played at the Galashiels rugby field in his district, where the sport is almost a religion, he led a protest march of some 200 persons and urged his constituents to boycott the event. In the 1970 parliamentary elections, Steel assumed that he had lost until a second recount showed a 550-vote Liberal majority. Four years later he won the general election by 7,400 votes.

During his five-year tenure, beginning in 1970, as Liberal Chief Whip in the House of Commons, Steel was criticized by some of his party colleagues because he did not consult with them as much as they would have wished and failed to establish close relations with Liberal party organizations in outlying areas. During 1971 Steel was charged with the task of investigating allegations that the highly respected Liberal party leader, Jeremy Thorpe, had once had a homosexual liaison with Norman Scott, a former male model and self-styled author. When Thorpe flatly denied the charges, Steel dropped the investigation, and the case remained dormant for several years. Steel resigned as Chief Whip in 1975, ostensibly to travel and broaden his experience, but his real motive, according to some observers, was to sidestep the smoldering Thorpe affair. From January to July 1976 he was the Liberal party spokesman on foreign and Commonwealth affairs.

From the beginning of his political career, Steel had held the view that the Liberals should be ready to make local arrangements with liberal-minded candidates of other parties, a prospect that was emphatically rejected by his more orthodox party colleagues. After the Conservatives suffered a setback in the February 1974 elections, Prime Minister Edward Heath invited the Liberals to enter a coalition, but Thorpe refused to consider it. Shortly thereafter the Heath government fell and was replaced by a minority Labor government headed by Harold Wilson. In an official party broadcast in mid-1974 Steel suggested that forming a coalition with either Labor or the Conservatives was the key to a Liberal comeback.

In early 1976 renewed allegations about Thorpe's sexual proclivities, although never proven, dominated the headlines. Liberal M.P.'s gave Thorpe a vote of confidence in March, but because they considered his public response to the sexual allegations to be unsatisfactory, they also made plans for a new party leadership election. Thorpe resigned on May 10, 1976 "in the interest of the party," charging that he had been a victim of a "sustained witchhunt" in the press. In the interim, Jo Grimond resumed temporary leadership of the party. Throughout the period Steel remained characteristically uncommitted and refrained from voicing any opinions about the Thorpe case in public.

The campaign for the Liberal party leadership between Steel and the more conservative economist John Pardoe was occasionally marked by mudslinging, but the two men differed more in their political approaches than on issues. Pardoe believed that the party leader should mobilize Liberals to fight for specific objectives, while Steel maintained that Liberalism was primarily a collection of attitudes rather than policies and that the party's success lay in proclaiming those attitudes to the uncommitted voter. Asked about his view toward coalition, Pardoe rejected it without a government guarantee that the next national elections be fought on the basis of proportional representation—long a cherished Liberal goal, since under the existing election system the party received only a small percentage of the parliamentary seats that their popular vote would justify. Although he strongly supported proportional representation, Steel asked voters to "prepare psychologically" for coalition as a "halfway stage towards gaining power."

The Liberal party election of July 7, 1976 has been described as the first grass-roots democratic election ever to be staged by a British political party. In contrast to standard practice, under which a party's leader had been chosen by its members in Parliament, the Liberals instituted a system whereby votes were allocated to local party branches. After defeating Pardoe by a vote of 12,541 to 7,032, Steel called in his acceptance speech for "reawakened individual commitment" and the replacement of the "politics of despair with the politics of hope."

Soon after the 1976 leadership election Steel began planning his coalition strategy in earnest. Public opinion polls since the late 1960's indicated that as many as half of the British voters might support the Liberal party if they thought it could muster enough seats to establish a government. Sharing governmental power, Steel believed, was the key to earning future votes, and he decided to test Liberal reception to his strategy with a speech at the party conference in the fall of 1976. Several prominent Liberals asked him, in the interest of party unity, to tone down his brief allusion to temporarily sharing power. Although aware that the idea of coalition was still heresy to many Liberals, Steel nevertheless went ahead with his speech as planned, and his words were greeted with unexpected enthusiasm.

Steel's chance to implement his ideas came sooner than expected. In February 1977 James Callaghan, who had succeeded Harold Wilson as the Labor government's Prime Minister, lost an important vote on a motion to curtail debate on a bill to grant limited home rule to Scotland and Wales. The opposition Conservatives, led by Margaret Thatcher, then called for a confidence vote, which the Labor government almost certainly would have lost. But Steel, seeing an opportunity to enhance his party's stature and seeking to avoid the new elections that would occur if the Labor government fell, entered negotiations with Callaghan. On March 22, 1977, after five days of consultations, the Prime Minister announced that he had reached an agreement with the Liberals for parliamentary cooperation, and on the following day the Labor government, bolstered by the thirteen Liberal votes in the House of Commons, survived the no-confidence motion by a vote of 322 to 298. The unprecedented accord constituted a severe setback for the Conservatives and for the Labor party's left wing.

The "Lib-Lab" agreement, which gave Callaghan enough support to enable him to continue his economic recovery program, was not actually a coalition pact, since Liberals were not included in the Cabinet. It did not commit the Liberals to support specific legislation but merely pledged them to back the government on confidence votes. In return, the Labor government promised to consult the Liberal leadership on major policy decisions and agreed to consider measures important to them, including benefits for new home buyers, lower income taxes, corporate profit-sharing plans, limited autonomy for Scotland and Wales and, most importantly, the development of a proportional representation system for the forthcoming elections to the European Parliament. The Liberal leaders were convinced that approval of such a system for the European legislative body would help to pave the way for its acceptance in Great Britain.

Despite the fears of its old guard, the Liberals had little to lose by accepting the agreement, since the party's popular support had dropped sharply since 1974. The pact put the Liberals in the national limelight, and it committed the government to taking their wishes into consideration, thus changing the party, in Steel's words, from "a nice little debating society" into a significant political force.

At the Liberal party's annual assembly at Brighton in September 1977 Steel told the 1,500 delegates that by giving the government a clear majority the agreement was "a major political contribution to national stability and recovery." Rejecting the argument of the pact's chief Liberal opponent, Cyril Smith, that the party had sacrificed its independence, Steel pointed out that the Liberals had been able to remain apart from the government while exercising substantial influence over its policies, and that Callaghan had kept his end of the bargain. At the same time, he noted, the Labor party's powerful left wing had been forced to yield much of its previous authority. The delegates voted, 716 to 385, to continue the agreement but added an amendment declaring approval of proportional representation to be "a crucial indicator" of the government's support of the pact.

On December 13, 1977, the House of Commons voted 319 to 222 to reject a proportional representation system for selecting British delegates to the European Parliament. Enraged Liberal M.P.'s immediately convened a party caucus, virtually promising to end the pact. After allowing them to blow off steam, Steel reminded his party colleagues that a general election could be disastrous for the party if it were held before the public became fully aware of the economic benefits brought about by the Liberal-influenced Labor government. He was able to muster support for continuance of the "Lib-Lab" pact by the narrow margin of six to four, only because Jo Grimond, who had opposed it, voted with him out of loyalty.

At a special Liberal party conference held at Blackpool in January 1978, Steel was faced by an angry rebel group that denounced the alliance as "a millstone around our neck" and held it responsible for recent setbacks suffered by the party in by-elections. In a vigorous defense of the pact he pointed out that Callaghan had "delivered precisely what he undertook to deliver." He conceded, however, that it was unlikely that the Liberals would renew the pact when it was due to expire in July 1978, since the forthcoming parliamentary session was scheduled to include debates on topics over which Labor and the Liberals were fundamentally divided. The conference gave its approval to the pact's continuation by a vote of 1,727 to 520. Nevertheless, the "Lib-Lab" pact expired in July 1978.

In addition to his parliamentary and party functions, Steel has continued to appear regularly on radio and television as a political and religious commentator, and he has written articles for leading British newspapers and political weeklies. His publications include the book *No Entry: The Background and Implications of the Commonwealth Immigrants Act, 1968* (Hurst, 1969) and the pamphlets *Boost for the Borders* (1964), *Out of*

Control: A Critical Examination of the Government of Scotland (1968), *The Liberal Way Forward* (1975), and *A New Political Agenda* (1976). Steel was chairman, from 1969 to 1973, of the Scottish advisory council of Shelter, the national campaign for the homeless, and since 1971 he has served on the advisory council of the European Discussion Centre and the council of management of the Centre for Studies in Social Policy. He is a non-executive director of an Edinburgh advertising agency. In December 1976 he was created a Privy Councillor.

David Steel was married in 1962 to Judith Mary MacGregor, a fellow law student who had been introduced to him by Jo Grimond and who is now a nonpractising solicitor. The Steels have two sons and a daughter of their own, and they adopted a fourteen-year-old boy in 1977. They make their home in a rambling house at Selkirkshire in the Borders countryside, near the Ettrick river. A lean and vigorous man, Steel enjoys good food, gardening, angling, driving his Triumph Stag, and riding his horse Hamlet. According to Simon Hoggart, he dresses fashionably, seldom displays emotion, "works extremely fast and extremely hard," and "rarely reads books because he hasn't time."

References: Guardian p9 Ja 21 '78 por; New Statesm p39+ Jl 9 '76 por; International Year Book and Statesmen's Who's Who, 1977; Who's Who, 1977-78

Te Kanawa, Kiri (tu-kä′nä-wä kē′rē)

1946 (?)- Opera singer. Address: b. c/o Artists International Management, Ltd., 5 Regents Park Rd., London NW1 7TL, England

Not since the heyday of Lisa della Casa and Elisabeth Schwarzkopf has a soprano graced the world's operatic stages with both the physical and vocal beauty of Kiri Te Kanawa, who has prompted the critics to overwork the adjective "gorgeous" in her praise. The statuesque singer, who was born in New Zealand of part-Maori ancestry, began her career as a precocious mezzo-soprano, like her colleague from "down under," Joan Sutherland. She continued her musical education in London, where she made a sensational Covent Garden debut as the Countess Almaviva in Mozart's *The Marriage of Figaro* in 1971. Her debut, on three hours' notice, as Desdemona in Verdi's *Otello* at the Metropolitan Opera House in 1974, led the critics to indulge in prophecy more than usual, with one predicting that hers "may prove one of the great voices of our time." Within the last few years her opulent, evenly projected, and dark-hued soprano has gone far to validate some of the extravagant claims of the early 1970's, in a repertory that has expanded to include roles as divergent as Rosalinda in *Die Fledermaus* and the title role in *Arabella*. Meanwhile, Kiri Te Kanawa, who has always been aware that operatic reputations can fade almost as rapidly as floral bouquets in prima donna's dressingrooms, takes all of the uproar with her customary calm and common sense. She hates the word "career." "It's ostentatious," she once explained in an interview. "I may use it when I'm fifty. Right now it's a job."

Proud of her mixed ancestry, Kiri Te Kanawa has said: "I am from New Zealand and ordinary people." She was born to Maori building contractor Thomas Te Kanawa and his Anglo-Irish wife Nell in the North Island port town of Gisborne on New Zealand's Poverty Bay in or about the year 1946. She prefers to keep her precise birthdate private. "I'm not telling exactly," she confided to Anthony Lewis in London for the New York *Times* (December 14, 1971), "so no one will know when I turn fifty." She was the couple's only child but has one stepbrother and a stepsister.

The name "Kiri" means "bell" in some Maori dialects and "skin of the tree" in others. On her father's side of the family she descends from a great chief of the Manupoto tribe of the Maoris, the Polynesian natives who inhabited New Zealand for centuries before the arrival of Europeans. Her mother, who is no longer alive, was a descendant of Sir Arthur Sullivan, the collaborator of W. S. Gilbert. "She was what we call 'Euro pean'," Miss Te Kanawa told Allen Hughes in a New York *Times* interview (February 28, 1974), "and please don't confuse Maori with aborigine. It is, perhaps, the equivalent of your American Indian." Stephen E. Rubin quoted her in another *Times* story (March 3, 1974) as saying: "But I'm not a typical Maori because I was brought up by a white mother who was very domineering."

"She made up her mind when I was three that I would be a singer," Kiri Te Kanawa has recalled. She told Anthony Lewis that she sang "little songs like *Daisy, Daisy, Give Me Your Answer True*" while still a tot. "I had only five or six notes then, but they were loud and dark colored," she said. "My mother played the piano for pleasure, and she must have wanted to be a performer. She was a rather domineering lady, but a lovely lady." Kiri Te Kanawa's mother started her on the piano when she was seven, but the girl loathed every minute of school, because all she wanted to do was sing.

When Kiri Te Kanawa was eleven her family moved to Auckland so that she could have proper singing lessons; since the age of twelve she has trained to be an opera singer to the exclusion of everything else. In Auckland she attended St. Mary's College, a convent school whose singing teacher, Sister Mary Leo, loved music and sensed her pupil's potential. "She had no method or anything, just some sort of gift, a way of bringing the voice out," Miss Te Kanawa has said. By the time she reached her teens, she was singing on New Zealand radio and television, and on a trip to Australia in 1966 she won the important Melbourne *Sun* aria competition, over hundreds of contestants. When she reached eighteen her parents forced her to decide whether to take opera seriously, and she quickly replied "Yes, anything!" "I did *not* want to be a shorthand typist," she has explained in interviews.

With the prize money, the funds she and her parents had saved up, and a $10,000 grant from the New Zealand Arts Council, Kiri Te Kanawa decided to end her schooling and move to London with her mother to complete her voice training. "I didn't actually graduate from school. I fell out. All I wanted to do was sing," Miss Te Kanawa told Anthony Lewis. James Robertson, the director of the London Opera Centre, who had heard her sing in New Zealand, invited her to study at that adjunct to Covent Garden. During her four years there, Miss Te Kanawa's mezzo began to ascend into the soprano range; it is said that conductor Richard Bonynge, the husband of Joan Sutherland, told her she was really a soprano after hearing her voice at a master class at the London Opera Centre.

The repeated interruptions of Dame Eva Turner, the dramatic soprano once famed for her roles in Verdi and Wagner, who conducted a master class with Giovanni Martinelli at the London Opera Centre, irritated not only the small audience at one session but also Miss Te Kanawa herself. Nonetheless, as she observed to Anthony Lewis: "I kept my Maori cool. I thought to myself, we used to eat people like you." She thereupon went to Madame Vera Rozsa, whom she has described as a marvelous teacher who has given her a whole new way of singing. "Without her," Miss Te Kanawa said in one New York interview, "I don't think I would be here now. She would dispute that, but she changed me." Her curriculum at the London Opera Centre included acting and fencing as well as singing, at none of which she claims to have been any good. "I was the worst one there, I think, and I was homesick, but I went through it," she told Robert Jacobson, who interviewed her for *Opera News* (May 1974).

While studying at the London Opera Centre, Kiri Te Kanawa hired an agent and made several auditions for Colin Davis and Peter Hall at the Royal Opera, Covent Garden. On each occasion, Davis and Hall asked her to learn some new role or other. In the meantime, she sang in such Opera Centre productions as *The Magic Flute, Dialogue of the Carmelites, Dido and Aeneas,* and the title role in *Anna Bolena*. She also appeared in smaller parts at Covent Garden (beginning with a walk-on as a flower maiden in *Parsifal*), as well as with the Northern Opera, with the New Zealand Opera, and in concert with the London Philharmonic in Handel's *Alcina* with Joan Sutherland. In mid-1969 Miss Te Kanawa returned to her homeland to perform in *Carmen* with the New Zealand Opera Company, and to make a concert and recital tour. After representing New Zealand at Expo 70 in Japan, she sang the role of Xenia in *Boris Godounov* at Covent Garden during its 1970-71 season.

It was towards the end of 1971 that Miss Te Kanawa, now signed to a five-year contract with the Royal Opera, got her first important international break when it cast her as Countess Almaviva in a new production of Mozart's opera *The Marriage of Figaro* at Covent Garden under the direction of Colin Davis. Earlier that year she had quietly tried out the Countess' role in New Mexico with the Santa Fe Opera, making, in effect, her American debut. Kiri Te Kanawa has since dryly remarked of that unheralded event: "The press didn't want to know me, agents didn't want to know me." Quite the opposite was true when she appeared at Covent Garden on December 1, 1971 as the Countess Almaviva.

Reviewing that auspicious Royal Opera debut in the December 3, 1971 issue of the

Financial Times, Andrew Porter called Miss Te Kanawa's characterization "such a Countess as I have never heard before, not at Covent Garden nor in Salzburg or Vienna" and pronounced it "beautiful, dignified, warmhearted and affecting." He was also impressed by her acting, "warm, beautiful, confident tone" and her "rare sense of legato" summing her up as "a singer of great accomplishment and a vivid character." Reporting on that same performance for the *Observer,* Peter Heyworth wrote: "As soon as her voice, full, warm, radiant and admirably supported, sailed not only with ease but with understanding into the treacherous opening bars of 'Porgi amor', it was evident that we were in the presence of a singer of quite exceptional promise. Miss Te Kanawa has not only the emotional antennae of an artist but the vocal resources and technique to give them flesh. The radiant tenderness with which this Rosina finally forgave her erring spouse was evidence enough that Covent Garden here has a pearl of great price."

That Covent Garden success was followed in the spring of 1972 by another challenge, the role of Desdemona in Verdi's *Otello,* by a tour of New Zealand that summer, and, in the autumn, by her first appearance with the San Francisco Opera as Countess Almaviva. On that occasion the San Francisco *Examiner* critic greatly admired "the grand, creamy, almost spinto sounds of that tall, gorgeous New Zealander Kiri Te Kanawa. . . . Miss Te Kanawa commands a flawless vocal technique, not to speak of a dazzling figure, and it's scarcely surprising she brought the house down." Other roles that she annexed in the early 1970's included those of Mimi in *La Bohème,* Marguerite in *Faust,* and Donna Elvira in *Don Giovanni* as well as Micaela in a new Covent Garden production of *Carmen.* Upon the occasion of her first appearance, as Countess Almaviva, at the Glyndebourne Festival in the summer of 1973, the *Financial Times* critic wrote: "Kiri Te Kanawa scales her voice down with such ease and acts with such lovely, sad dignity and shy sense of fun that one prays Glyndebourne will capture her for many years to come." His prayers were answered, for during the 1973-74 season Kiri Te Kanawa not only scored as Amelia in Verdi's *Simon Boccanegra* but returned to the rustic elegance of Glyndebourne.

Her long-awaited debut at the Metropolitan Opera had been scheduled for March 7, 1974, but when Teresa Stratas reported on the morning of February 9 that she was not feeling well enough to undertake the matinee performance of *Otello* that afternoon, Kiri Te Kanawa was asked on three hours' notice to replace her opposite Jon Vickers. Although she had been grooming herself for the part since late January, she had only watched rehearsals and had never been on stage with the complicated, multilevel sets designed by Franco Zeffirelli. "There was nobody here [when the urgent Met call came], no coach, no accompanist, no one," Miss Te Kanawa later told Joseph C. Koenenn in an interview for *Newsday* (March 15, 1974). "I felt like the loneliest person in the world. I warmed up an hour here [at home] alone and then I caught a taxi. I *literally* spent five minutes on the set before I had to go on."

In spite of her justified nervousness, unfamiliarity with the intricacies of the set, and the threat to her voice posed by a dusty stage, Kiri Te Kanawa's Metropolitan debut was greeted with a salvo of favorable notices. Allen Hughes of the New York *Times* (February 11, 1974), who welcomed her to the Metropolitan roster, wrote: "Miss Te Kanawa won the audience from the very beginning, and did not lose it. Her voice had a lovely fresh sound, her vocal production was smooth, her singing was eloquent, and her acting was touching and invariably believable. She is slim and attractive, and the impression she made as Desdemona was satisfying in every way." He went on to note that Jon Vickers had accurately interpreted the audience's mood by leaving her alone on stage for individual applause at one of their curtain calls.

In her New York *Post* review that same day, Harriett Johnson admired Miss Te Kanawa's amazing poise and voice, which she described as "a large, full, easily produced soprano, that opens up on the top like a luscious role." When Kiri Te Kanawa returned to the Met in *Otello* a month later with a wholly different cast, the New York *Times* reviewer John Rockwell informed his readers (March 10, 1974) that she confirmed the initial impression of excellence, even though she had not yet fully taken "the measure of the part, the house, or her own voice." He detected a slight middle register weakness and a tendency to force herself somewhat at moments of climax. "But these became mere quibbles," he noted, "in the face of such sheer beauty of tone and appearance, musicality of phrasing, and conviction of acting."

After contributing another characterization to the Met, this time as Donna Elvira in Mozart's *Don Giovanni,* a role that she also undertook for the Paris Opéra, as well as making appearances as Marguerite in *Faust* and Fiordiligi in a new Covent Garden production of *Così Fan Tutte* during the 1974-75 season, Kiri Te Kanawa returned in triumph to New York City in February of 1976 to portray the Countess in *The Marriage of Figaro.* So far as Speight Jenkins of the New York *Post* (February 7, 1976) was concerned, nothing went amiss with her performance as "a Countess . . . who defies negative comparison." He went on to document his claim: "She has a radiant voice of large size, which in its sound suggested the sight of a perfect opalescent pearl. Her projection of the text and her musicianship, both in arias and recitatives, created a flowing, natural Mozart style." Casting about for comparisons, he compared her Countess Almaviva to the one created by Victoria de los Angeles, and her beauty reminded him of Lisa della Casa and Jarmila Novotna.

All in all, 1976 turned out to be an eventful year for Kiri Te Kanawa. She tackled the new role of Tatiana in Tchaikovsky's *Eugene Onegin*, returned to the Paris Opéra as Fiordiligi in *Così fan Tutte*, and appeared in the film version of Jean-Louis Ponelle's staging of *The Marriage of Figaro* with an all-star international cast including Mirella Freni, Hermann Prey, Maria Ewing, and Dietrich Fischer-Dieskau. That autumn she visited Australia as Mimi in *La Bohème* and as Amelia in *Simon Boccanegra*, then returned to Europe for engagements at Covent Garden and the Paris Opéra. In October she performed at a benefit concert for New Zealand scholarships and United World Colleges at the Royal Opera House.

When the Paris Opéra concluded its presentation of the five major operas of Mozart in May 1977 with a new production of *The Magic Flute*, which in the opinion of some critics failed to fulfill its promise, Kiri Te Kanawa was singled out as one of its main assets. Correspondent David Stevens reported in *Opera News* (August 1977) that in her aria "Ach, ich fühl's"—taken by conductor Karl Böhm at a tempo more largo than andante—"Kiri Te Kanawa sustained the line splendidly, and not just here but all evening long with a Pamina of such ravishingly vibrant tone, eloquent phrasing, and appealing presence that she earned a complete personal triumph with the Paris public."

Of all the soprano roles in the operatic repertory, few seem more suitable for the special combination of physical and vocal beauty of Kiri Te Kanawa than the title role of Richard Strauss's *Arabella*. When, on November 15, 1977, she sang Arabella with the Houston Grand Opera under the baton of Charles Mackerras, Peter G. Davis of the New York *Times* (November 20, 1977) studded his review with such phrases as "mysterious beauty," "breathtaking presence," and "gleaming soprano." Thanks to the miracle of transmission by satellite, Kiri Te Kanawa was seen by millions throughout the United States as Rosalinde when Covent Garden's new production of *Die Fledermaus* was televised by Metromedia stations on New Year's Eve. In spite of heavyweight competition from such international singers as Hermann Prey, she was, in the opinion of Harold C. Schonberg of the New York *Times* (January 4, 1978), the undisputed star of the production, with her large and sensuous voice, charming acting, and resplendent high C.

Determined to avoid overbooking that might impair her voice, Kiri Te Kanawa tries to devote two months each year to vacationing with her husband, an Australian mining engineer named Desmond Park. They were married on August 30, 1967, only about six weeks after they met in London on a blind date, and make their home in Surrey, one of the Home Counties around London. Among the entries on Miss Te Kanawa's burgeoning discography are complete operatic recordings for the Philips and Decca (London) labels, including *Don Giovanni*, *Carmen*, *Parsifal*, and *Fedora*, as well as a Mozart Mass and the Maurice Durufle Requiem. The soprano, whom interviewers unanimously describe as unpretentious, warm, and levelheaded, has enormous brown eyes and brown hair, weighs about 160 pounds, and is five feet seven inches tall. Her recreations include swimming, golfing, and sewing. She has declared her goal in life to be that of being a singing actress and looks upon Janet Baker as her "idol of the world." In 1973 Kiri Te Kanawa became a member of the Order of the British Empire.

References: N Y Daily News p40 F 19 '74 por; N Y Times p54 D 14 '71 por, p32 F 28 '74 por, II p15+ Mr 3 '74 por; Newsday A p12+ Mr 15 '74 pors; Opera N 38:26 My '74 por; Who's Who, 1977-78

Theroux, Paul (Edward) (the-rōō')

Apr. 10, 1941- Writer. Address: b. c/o Houghton Mifflin Company, 1 Beacon St., Boston, Mass. 02107; h. 35 Elsynge Rd., London, SW18 2HR, England

"I have never believed that characters in fiction vanish after the last page is turned," Paul Theroux has said, in the person of the anonymous American diplomat who spins the tales in *The Consul's File*, his dazzling collection of loosely related stories reminiscent of W. Somerset Maugham. "They have other lives, not explicit or remarkable enough for fiction, and yet it would be sad to think they were irrevocable." During his sojourns in East Africa and Southeast Asia in the late 1960's and early 1970's, Theroux, admittedly an "unrepentant eavesdropper," observed the hard-drinking soldiers of fortune, the aging expatriates, the bored diplomats and their discontented wives, the "jungle bashers," the jaded foreign correspondents, the Anglicized Orientals, and the idealistic young Americans who populate his extraordinary novels about life in the post-colonial Third World.

Paul Theroux

An unusually prolific writer, Theroux has published eleven books, nine of them novels, with Houghton Mifflin since 1966. Although each of the novels was well reviewed, sales of his books were slim until the publication in 1975 of *The Great Railway Bazaar: By Train Through Asia,* one of the few travel books ever to become a bestseller. *The Family Arsenal* (1976), *The Consul's File* (1977), and, to a lesser extent, *Picture Palace* (1978), met with similar critical and commercial success. Theroux recently completed a train trip from the northeastern United States through Mexico and Central America to the tip of Argentina, gathering material for his second travel book. Tentatively titled *The Old Patagonian Express,* it is scheduled for publication during 1979.

Of French-Canadian and Italian ancestry, Paul Edward Theroux was born on April 10, 1941 in Medford, Massachusetts, the third of the seven children of Albert Eugene Theroux, a salesman for the American Oak Leather Company, and Anne (Dittami) Theroux. He has two younger sisters, Ann Marie and Mary, and four brothers—Eugene, an attorney and expert in Sino-American trade; Alexander, a novelist; Joseph, a Peace Corps volunteer; and Peter, a student—all of whom write. Encouraged by their father, who read aloud to them daily from the works of such authors as Charles Dickens and Herman Melville, the three oldest boys competed with each other in publishing family newspapers about the day-to-day happenings in the lives of the large Theroux clan.

Following "a very conventional education" in the local public schools, Paul Theroux attended the University of Maine for a year, then transferred to the University of Massachusetts, where his developing passion for writing prompted him to switch his major from premed to English. After taking his B.A. degree in 1963, Theroux volunteered for the Peace Corps, which he has since described as "a sort of Howard Johnson's on the main drag to maturity," to avoid the draft. Assigned to East Africa, he lectured in English at Soche Hill College in Limbe, Malawi until he was expelled in 1965 for his unwitting involvement in an alleged conspiracy to assassinate the president of the country.

With the help of a highly placed African friend, Theroux soon got a job teaching English and what he has called "their version" of current events at Makerere University in Kampala, Uganda. Among his students were several of Idi Amin's officers, who usually came to class very drunk and "very heavily armed, in their three-piece Savile Row suits." He also produced "a kind of university of the air" until the government, then led by Milton Obote, suppressed it. In his spare time, Theroux wrote free-lance pieces for American magazines and newspapers and worked intermittently on a novel.

One of Theroux's faculty colleagues at Makerere was V. S. Naipaul, the West Indian author. Recognizing the young American's talent, Naipaul went over everything he had written, word by word. "They say you can't really teach writing, which is true, but a person met at the right time can set you alight," Theroux observed to Hugh Hebert in an interview for the *Guardian* (April 17, 1973). "I have to write very slowly, or it comes out all wrong. I only write a page or two a day now. But then I was trying to sit at the typewriter and bang out maybe 2,000 words a day. Naipaul said, 'Style is not very important, style's nothing really. But a book needs a reason for being written.' "

Theroux's first novel, *Waldo,* a picaresque account of a juvenile delinquent who becomes a literary success, was published in 1966. Although Theroux himself now dismisses the work as "a beginner's book," a few critics found it to be "a good, funny novel" with "interesting moments." In his next novel, *Fong and the Indians* (1968), Theroux examined the rapidly changing social environment in the developing East African nations that had been his home since 1963. His nonhero, Sam Fong, an apolitical Chinese Catholic grocer, is representative of thousands of Asian immigrant shopkeepers unable to cope with the realities of independence in their adopted countries. Fong's bumbling attempts at economic survival take him through a series of embarrassing and occasionally dangerous predicaments with double-crossing black marketeers, condescending American government officials, and dishonest Indian merchants. The book was not widely reviewed and sold only modestly, but critics discerned a sensitivity at work behind its caricatures and comedy. In her review of what she considered to be a "small masterpiece" for the *Saturday Review* (September 28, 1968), Constance Wagner commented that it "cuts so close to the bone of truth that anyone familiar with the 'developing nations' must regard it as selective and hilarious reportage."

After being trapped in a street riot in Kampala in 1968, Theroux searched the classified advertisements in the local English-language newspapers for a job in a similarly exotic, but safer location. For the next three years he taught seventeenth-century English literature at the University of Singapore and, in his off-hours, wrote innumerable short stories, an interpretative study of Naipaul, *V. S. Naipaul; an Introduction to His Work* (Africana Publishing Corporation, 1972), and two more novels with African settings. In *Girls at Play* (1969), he analyzed with somewhat icy detachment the effects of the psychological and social pressures of an alien environment on a group of English and American schoolteachers at an isolated girls' school in the Kenyan bush. In *Jungle Lovers* (1971) he tested the physical and moral reserves of two men—Calvin Mullett, an ineffectual salesman who peddles life insurance policies to gullible natives, and Marais, the messianic French-Canadian leader of a ragtag band of black revolutionaries—each of whom holds distinctly different misconceptions about Africa.

Impressed by his powerful command of narrative, his Shakespeare-like hints of impending tragedy, and his perceptive awareness of the devastating effects of Africa on romantic Americans and Europeans, reviewers gave Theroux high marks for both *Girls at Play* and *Jungle Lovers*. A similar favorable reaction greeted the publication in 1973 of *Saint Jack*, a product of Theroux's several years in Singapore. The title character of that novel is Jack Flowers, an aging expatriate philosopher-pimp who entices foreign clients to Paradise Gardens, his brothel-cum-resort, by offering them the chance to "participate in a cultural secret" and take away from Singapore "the ultimate souvenir."

Taken as a whole, Theroux's first four novels present a rather dispiriting view of emergent nations. But Hugh Hebert, in his retrospective review of Theroux's work for the *Guardian* (April 17, 1973), perceived "a kind of compassion at work . . . even when he seems to crucify the tattered remnants of the colonial English or the button-bright missionary Americans." Nevertheless, he concluded, "the whole post-colonial mish-mash is for him and his books less a political than a social and personal thing." Theroux readily admitted to Mel Gussow, who interviewed him for a New York *Times* (July 28, 1976) profile, that leaving the United States was "the best thing that ever happened" to him. "My advice to any young writer is to get away from his country, to experience a different culture," he went on. "It wasn't until I developed a kind of skepticism about what people said that it was possible to write about them. You can't write about a society with a complete acceptance of that society."

In 1971 Theroux decided not to renew his contract with the University of Singapore and moved to England to devote himself to writing. In short order, he published his first collection of remarkably diverse short stories, *Sinning With Annie, and Other Stories* (1972), and completed *Saint Jack*. Then, having just returned to Western civilization after nearly a decade's absence himself, he addressed the problem of reverse cultural shock in *The Black House*, a curious hybrid of social satire, intentional eroticism, and gothic horror, in which Alfred Munday, a bored anthropologist sent home to Britain after ten years in the African bush, finds in his cold, eccentric neighbors remnants of primitive tribal savagery. British reviewers raved about the book; their American counterparts were, on the whole, less enthusiastic. Although most of them admired the richly textured descriptive passages, the witty dialogue, and the "wonderfully prickly" main character, some were inclined to agree with Michael Mewshaw, who felt that *The Black House* did "a serious disservice to [Theroux's] talent."

On the day he delivered the manuscript of *The Black House* to his publisher, Theroux left on a four-month railway odyssey through Asia. Writing daily, "bending over [his] rocking notebook like Trollope scribbling between postal assignments, remembering to put it all in the past tense," as he put it, he carefully recorded his impressions of the passing landscape, from the dingy train station in London's Clapham Junction, across the hot, dusty plains of the Middle East, through the steamy Malaysian villages of Bidor, Trolak, Topah, and Klang, with their "names like science fiction planets," to the Tolstoyan villages of the frozen Siberian steppes. In the anonymity of the railway compartment, Theroux's fellow passengers confided in him, telling him "the most personal things." By his journey's end, he had filled the four thick notebooks that, pared down and rewritten, would become *The Great Railway Bazaar: By Train Through Asia* (1975).

"Rarely have subject and sensibility been so splendidly conjoined," Arthur Cooper wrote in his enthusiastic review of *Railway Bazaar* for *Newsweek* (September 8, 1975). "[Theroux] embarks on every project with all senses fully engaged. His eyes scan for the telling—and unusually grotesque—gesture, his ear is cocked for the absurd, his nose can distinguish character from mere affection. It's as if Graham Greene and Joseph Conrad decided to rewrite Baedeker's guides to Asia." Other reviewers, equally effusive in their praise, saw the book as an intensely personal narrative as well as an entertaining and unconventional guidebook to the Orient. Theroux himself views travel writing as a form of autobiography because "travel brings you back to yourself." "The grand tour is just the inspired man's way of heading home," he remarked on the concluding page of *Railway Bazaar*. "And I learned what I had always secretly believed, that the difference between travel writing and fiction is the difference between recording what the eye sees and discovering what the imagination knows. Fiction is pure joy—how sad that I could not re-invent the trip as fiction."

But he had seen fictional possibilities in the glimpse of a lanky, bearded American, apparently one of "an odd community of practically nameless fugitives" from the Vietnam war, loping along the track of the Saigon-Bien Hoa railroad. Theroux developed that shadowy figure into Valentine Hood, the protagonist of *The Family Arsenal* (1976). A disenchanted, idealistic young American dismissed from his minor diplomatic post for assaulting an offensive South Vietnamese government official, Hood sets up housekeeping in a seedy dockside district of London with an odd trio of social misfits: Mayo, a spoiled rich girl turned terrorist, a "barbarian with taste," who steals for ransom a priceless fifteenth-century painting, and Murf and Brodie, bombers for the Provisional Irish Republican Army. Engulfed by violence, Hood murders a drunken bully who has humiliated a street sweeper, setting in motion a chain of events over which he has no control.

Hailed as one of the "most evocative," "intelligently crafted," and "precisely structured" thrillers of recent years, *The Family Arsenal* was an instant critical success. Moreover, reviewers found in it traces of Joseph Conrad's atmosphere, Evelyn Waugh's wit, Graham Greene's craftsmanship and pessimism, Henry James's large-scaled cultural commentary, and Charles Dickens' eye for curious detail. Theroux found those flattering comparisons impertinent and "a bit presumptuous." "They're on Parnassus," he told Mel Gussow. "I'm on a lower slope with my crayola."

Like *The Family Arsenal, Picture Palace*, Theroux's twelfth book in as many years, was inspired by an incident in his life—in this case, a picture-taking session with Jill Krementz, a portrait photographer whose camera is a passport to the world and whose pictures constitute a visual record of her life. Believing in Jack Flowers' dictum that "fiction gives us a second chance that life denies us," Theroux created one of his most remarkable central characters: Maude Coffin Pratt, a crusty, cantankerous, and defiantly independent photographer. At seventy the world-famous Maude gets her second chance when a curator from a major New York City gallery proposes mounting a Pratt retrospective. As she combs through her photographs, selecting representative samples for the exhibit, she re-experiences in the "picture palace" of her mind the two passions—photography and her unrequited incestuous love for her younger brother Orlando—that dominated and shaped her life. It is only as she examines the photographs that she realizes her past is in "all the pictures [she] never took."

Of all Theroux's novels, *Picture Palace* provoked the most divergent critical opinions. Most reviewers commended his reflections on the relationship between an artist's personal life and his work as well as his boldly executed first-person design, but several felt that the incestuous fixation was overemphasized and contrived. Virtually every reviewer, however, complimented the inventiveness at work in Theroux's memorable portraits of celebrities, among them Graham Greene, Evelyn Waugh, Gertrude Stein, Jean Cocteau, Robert Frost, and D. H. Lawrence.

Paul Theroux is a tall, lean, handsome man with thick dark brown hair, worn modishly long, and dark eyes. Disarmingly candid, he readily discusses his work and his life with reporters. He and his wife, Anne (Castle) Theroux, a producer for the BBC whom he married on December 4, 1967, and their two sons, Marcel Raymond and Louis Sebastian, live in Clapham Junction, a rather unfashionable district of South London, in a house crammed with furnishings collected on his travels. "I live [in England] as a foreigner," he told one interviewer, "as if I were living in Costa Rica."

To escape temporarily from the "clammy frugality" of England, Theroux regularly summers on Cape Cod. "I spend the first few weeks eating junk food and reading, then settle down to a routine of cooking, swimming, amusing children, and reading," he said, as quoted in the New York *Times Book Review* (June 4, 1978). "And I try to suppress my envy of golfers, lifeguards, and accomplished tennis players. I write on weekday mornings, but between the playing of 'God Save the Queen' on the first day of Wimbledon and sundown on Labor Day in East Sandwich, I have no deadlines to meet and no lively hope of finishing anything I write."

References: Guardian p12 Ap 17 '73 por; N Y Post p33 Ag 28 '76 por; N Y Times p14 Jl 28 '76 por; N Y Times Mag p22+ Ap 30 '78 pors; Pub W 210:10+ Jl 26 '76 por; Contemporary Authors vols 33-36 (1973); Who's Who, 1978-79

Thomson, Meldrim, Jr.

Mar. 8, 1912- Governor of New Hampshire. Address: b. State Capitol, Concord, N.H. 03301; h. Mt. Cube Farm, Orford, N.H. 03777

A latecomer to politics, the lawyer and businessman Meldrim Thomson Jr., who became the ninety-first governor of the state of New Hampshire in January 1973, has emerged as a champion of the Republican right wing. He has fought against sales and income taxes in the state that ranks lowest in the United States in per-pupil aid to education; he has proclaimed "Truth About United Nations Week" to discredit the world organization; and he has frequently enraged civil libertarians and environmentalists with his policies. Hostile commentators describe Thomson as the "blockhead who runs the Granite State," but the voters had chosen him for three consecutive two-year terms as their governor, and in the primary of September 1978 he was nominated for an unprecedented fourth term. On election day in November, however, the voters of New Hampshire elected Hugh Gallen, the Democratic candidate, as their governor. Observers attributed Thomson's defeat to his veto of legislation designed to prevent consumers from paying part of the costs of building the Seabrook nuclear power plant.

Born in Pittsburgh, Pennsylvania on March 8, 1912, Meldrin Thomson Jr. has roots in New England and in the Deep South. His mother was from Boston, and his father's family had been based in Georgia for several generations. Thomson spent much of his boyhood in Georgia—where the family had moved about 1917—and also lived for a time in Alabama and Florida. Although his father was a civil engineer, the family was, in Thomson's words, "poor as church mice." Influenced by members of his family and by a biography of Abraham Lincoln, Thomson became a Republican early in life, and he remembers his boyish elation when Calvin Coolidge was elected President in 1924. Because of frequent moves he attended thirteen schools in twelve years and barely passed in the fourth, fifth, and sixth grades. "But at twelve I joined the Boy Scouts, and it changed my life," he has recalled. "I made the honor roll that year." Thomson attended the University of Miami and Mercer University in Macon, Georgia. Later he worked his way through the University of Georgia at Athens, where he was the "lone Republican" and served for a time on the faculty as a political science instructor. He ranked third in his class when he graduated from the University of Georgia Law School with an LL.B. degree and eventually became authorized to practise in several states and before the United States Supreme Court.

After practising law in Florida, Thomson joined a law book publishing firm in Brooklyn, New York and became its editor-in-chief. Then he set up his own company on Long Island, New York, where he was elected a member and chairman of the Stony Brook school board. In 1954 he moved to Orford, New Hampshire, a village in the upper Connecticut River valley, and established the Equity Publishing Company. Now run by two of his sons, the firm produces legal textbooks for three states, the Navajo Indian community, the District of Columbia, Puerto Rico, the Virgin Islands, American Samoa, and Costa Rica.

In addition, Thomson served as chairman of the Orford school board, helped to found a statewide organization known as Taxfighters, and was a delegate to the New Hampshire constitutional convention of 1964. He gained political notoriety in 1966, when his community and nine other New Hampshire towns turned down funds offered by the federal government to support a remedial reading program. In a pamphlet, entitled "Federal Control of Schools, Myth or Fact," Thomson warned at the time that "few voters in New Hampshire realize the speed with which federal controls are invading their schools." The episode helped to bring Thomson to the attention of William Loeb, the militantly right-wing publisher of New Hampshire's dominant newspaper, the Manchester *Union Leader*.

With Loeb's support, Thomson sought the Republican gubernatorial nomination in 1968 but lost by a slim margin to Walter R. Peterson Jr., who was elected governor in November. He was again narrowly defeated by

Peterson in the September 1970 primary and then came in third in the general election, running as the candidate of George Wallace's American Independent party, even though he disassociated himself from the racism of the Wallace clique. Finally, in 1972, Thomson edged out Peterson in the September primary by 2,400 votes and then vanquished Democrat Roger J. Crowley Jr. and Independent Malcolm McLane with 42 percent of the vote after campaigning on the slogan "Axe the Tax." In 1974 he defeated state senate president David Nixon in the Republican primary and Democrat Richard Leonard in the November election. After defeating former state health commissioner Gerard J. Zeiller in the 1976 primary by a substantial majority, Thomson beat the Democratic former state senator Harry V. Spanos in the main contest, surviving a regional Democratic landslide.

Soon after taking office in January 1973, Thomson became the center of political controversy. His administrative aide Frederick D. Goode obtained confidential business tax returns from the state tax commission on twelve businesses, most of them operated by allies of the governor's political rivals, and on Dartmouth College, a favorite target of conservatives. Criticized in the press for having failed to seek the legally required prior approval of the Executive Council, Thomson obtained its belated consent. When the New Hampshire Supreme Court ruled that *ex post facto* permission invalid, Thomson promised to continue to interpret the Constitution as he understood it "and not as it is understood by others." The governor received further censure when that same month he asked, without success, to examine whatever files the federally sponsored New England Organized Crime Intelligence System in Wellesley, Massachusetts might have on New Hampshire politicians. Thomson later claimed that he was only making sure that the agency was not keeping improper data and that he was testing its security.

During the first legislative session of his tenure, Thomson established a record by vetoing twenty-seven bills. His freeze on hiring, except on his approval, even for positions already funded in the budget, obstructed much needed improvements in such facilities as the state mental hospital, which had lost its national accreditation in 1972 because of substandard conditions. Republican State Senator Rob Trowbridge commented in 1974: "The guy's a disaster. Everything he touches turns to bitterness. . . . He creates a negative atmosphere." When Democrats learned that Thomson made 256 telephone calls to the Manchester *Union Leader* over an eighteen-month period in 1973-74, a spokesman called him "a toy tiger whose string is pulled by William Loeb."

Thomson threatened to revoke the charter of Franconia College after it hosted a conference on prison reform in 1973, and he charged that Judge Hugh N. Bownes had "endorsed sexual perversion" when his court, in January 1974, refused to ban organizations of homosexual students at the University of New Hampshire. Later that year Thomson cancelled a $750 grant made by the National Endowment on the Arts through the New Hampshire Commission on the Arts to the literary magazine *Granite*, maintaining that the poem "Castrating the Cat," printed in the periodical, was an "item of filth."

Outspoken on national as well as local issues, Thomson has come out against gun control, prison reform, amnesty for Vietnam war resisters, and the Equal Rights Amendment. "Women are already equal," he has said. "I always put women on a pedestal and thought they were better than men." In 1974 he issued an edict forbidding female state employees to use the title "Ms." in official communications. Thomson challenged the United States Supreme Court in June 1975 when he signed a bill to allow voluntary recitation of the "Lord's Prayer" in public schools, and more recently he provoked criticism from proponents of church-state separation by ordering flags on state buildings to be lowered in observance of Good Friday.

To thwart a federal Equal Opportunity Commission survey on the ethnic backgrounds of New Hampshire's public employees in late 1973, Thomson ordered department heads to identify all workers as "Americans." When Roman Catholic priests in 1975 came out in support of a boycott of Gallo wine in sympathy with striking farm workers, Thomson made a show of buying a bottle of it in the presence of reporters. The governor also tried in 1973 to block a $350,000 federal grant to New Hampshire Legal Assistance, which provides legal help for the poor, and he has demanded the right to review the political backgrounds of volunteers for VISTA, the domestic Peace Corps. After signing a bill in September 1977 restoring the death penalty in New Hampshire, Thomson asserted: "I feel like John Hancock when he finished putting his signature on the Declaration of Independence."

Thomson, who believes that "the states should function like fifty laboratories for experimenting in the democratic process, contributing to the whole, but in different ways," has on occasion clashed with authorities in other states. For example, he has advised New Hampshire citizens to ignore New York City's efforts to collect overdue parking fines owed by the state's residents unless there was "solid evidentiary documentation" of their guilt. When the city threatened to seize the cars or New York property of New Hampshire scofflaws, Thomson replied that the Granite State might take a "lien on the Statue of Liberty and relocate it at the entrance to Portsmouth harbor, where people are free from economic deficits and government harassment."

A much publicized dispute between Thomson's administration and that of neighboring Maine began in January 1973, after Maine officials arrested a New Hampshire man for trapping lobsters in Atlantic waters claimed by both states. At issue were control of 2,400 acres of ocean and Maine's right to establish stringent limits on the size of lobsters that fishermen could take. Several confrontations occurred between patrol boats manned by New Hampshire fish and game officers and Maine coastal wardens before Thomson and Governor Kenneth Curtis of Maine agreed in June 1974 to a compromise boundary that ended the "Lobster War." Thomson's real concern in the dispute with Maine was, however, not so much with lobster fishing as with the ownership of the oil and natural gas deposits below the ocean's surface. Convinced that the United States must issue a "declaration of energy independence," Thomson was the only Atlantic coast governor to give unqualified support to a federal plan in 1975 to lease oil drilling sites along the Continental shelf to private companies.

In November 1973 Thomson announced that Olympic Refineries, a company established by the Greek shipping tycoon Aristotle Onassis, would spend $600,000,000 to build a petroleum refinery in the Durham area that would process 400,000 barrels of oil daily. But residents of Durham and environmentalists, concerned by the damage that oil spills might do to the offshore lobster grounds, objected to the plan. Despite a large-scale publicity campaign, a Durham town meeting in March 1974 refused to rezone 3,000 acres to create a site for the refinery. Soon after that the state legislature defeated Thomson's proposal to empower a state commission to overturn a locality's rejection of a refinery. The governor, who has denounced the "environmental mystique," was bitter about his defeat on that issue. "His idea," explained State Senator Trowbridge, "is still that what is good for business on very narrow grounds is good for all Americans, and nothing else matters. . . . He doesn't realize that irreversible mistakes may be made."

Thomson's hopes for developing New Hampshire's energy and industry sparked another confrontation when members of the Clamshell Alliance, an environmentalist group, occupied the construction site for a nuclear power plant in Seabrook on April 30, 1977. The protesters argued that, among other perils, the plant's cooling system would endanger marine life. Thomson, who in his January 1975 inaugural speech had proposed a crash program to build nuclear plants, described the demonstrators as terrorists and called out state police. Of the 1,414 persons arrested most were held in National Guard armories before being convicted of criminal trespass charges in mass trials in a county district court. Confining the prisoners cost New Hampshire approximately $50,000 a day, but Thomson called on "corporations, labor unions and rank-and-file citizens throughout America" to help pay the bill. When a year later members of the Clamshell Alliance planned a "first anniversary ball" at the National Guard armory in Portsmouth, Thomson, as National Guard commander in chief, tried to ban the festivities but was overruled by state courts.

True to his campaign promises, Thomson has steadfastly resisted introduction of an income tax and a general sales tax in New Hampshire, which ranks lowest in the United States in per capita state taxes. For its revenues, the state had in the past relied largely on "sin taxes" levied on liquor, beer, cigarettes, horse racing, and dog racing. But since in recent years those taxes were no longer sufficient to provide for the needs of a growing population, the state has had to depend increasingly on a 7 percent business profits tax. To the dismay of environmentalists and those wanting to preserve New Hampshire's rustic atmosphere, Thomson has mounted a major effort to bring industry into the state, and the result has been an economic boom. Hundreds of companies have moved into New Hampshire, which is exceeded in population growth only by Florida among the states east of the Rockies. Its unemployment rate—3.4 percent in mid-1978—has remained well below the national average, and as a result of Thomson's frugal policies New Hampshire's welfare budget ranks fourth-lowest in the nation, behind those of Alaska, Nevada, and Wyoming. New Hampshire leads the Northeastern states in capital investment, growth of individual real income, and the creation of new employment opportunities, and it has a consistently high bond rating and low public indebtedness.

Although Thomson called Richard Nixon's overtures to China in the early 1970's a "disgrace in the diplomacy of America," he loyally defended the former President during the Watergate crisis. During the 1976 Presidential campaign he sharply criticized Gerald R. Ford and Henry Kissinger and gave his support to Ronald Reagan, indicating that he himself might be a candidate in the event that Reagan did not run. He withdrew his endorsement from Reagan when the Californian asked Senator Richard S. Schweiker of Pennsylvania, a liberal Republican, to become his running mate. In 1975 he and Howard Phillips, a former Nixon aide, set up the Virginia-based Conservative Caucus Inc., to create grassroots political organizations in every Congressional district. Thomson became chairman of the caucus and "Secretary of State" in a "shadow government" monitoring the administration of President Jimmy Carter.

One of Thomson's favorite targets has been Andrew Young, United States Ambassador to the United Nations, whom he has called a "one-world co-conspirator." Following a visit to South Africa in early 1978, he praised its Prime Minister, John Vorster, as "one of the world's great statesmen." When President Jimmy Carter signed the Panama Canal treaties in the spring of 1978, Thomson ordered the flag on the State House in Concord to be flown at half-mast and said: "I find it abhorrent to witness an American President rushing to surrender our sovereign territory."

Governor Meldrim Thomson Jr., who is a Baptist, has been married since 1938 to the former Gale Kelly of Brooklyn, who had been his secretary. He describes her as essential to his political success and admits that "she has a nicer personality than I and probably got votes I couldn't have." They are the parents of six grown children: Peter (who serves as the governor's chief of staff), David, Thomas, Marion Gale, Janet, and Robb; and they have thirteen grandchildren. The Thomsons live in Orford at the 1,300-acre Mt. Cube Farm, which is the base of operations for the governor's Mt. Cube Maple Sugar Company. Thomson rises at 5:30 each morning and runs a mile every day. He often hikes in New Hampshire's rugged mountains and enjoys working in the garden at the State House in Concord.

According to Howard Phillips, quoted in *Newsweek* (June 26, 1978), Thomson exhibits a "bizarre mixture of authoritarianism, paranoia, and simple aggression," while a New Hampshire Democratic spokeswoman quoted in the New York *Times* (March 30, 1978), described him as "very bright, very shrewd, very tough and, when he needs to be, very vicious or very charming." The governor, who has a courtly manner and speaks with a Southern drawl, has a knack of remembering faces and names and enjoys the handshaking duties of a politician. He campaigns tirelessly, spreading a message of economy and decentralization that he believes is the basis of the American concept of government. "My opponents say I'm back in the nineteenth century," Thomson has said. "They are wrong. My beliefs are rooted in the values of the seventeenth century and I'm proud of it."

References: Boston Mag 66:61+ My '74 pors; N Y Times p16 My 11 '77 por, A p1+ Mr 30 '78 por; Newsweek 91:26+ Je 26 '78 por; People 8:41+ N 28 '77 pors; Wall St J p1 O 30 '74; Washington Post A p2 Ag 25 '74 por; Who's Who in American Politics, 1977-78

Tindemans, Leo(nard)

Apr. 16, 1922- Former Prime Minister of Belgium. Address: h. Jan Verbertlei 24, B-2520 Edegem, Belgium

A European statesman in the tradition of his illustrious compatriot Paul-Henri Spaak, Leo Tindemans, the former Prime Minister of Belgium, had devoted much of his time to drafting a blueprint for the political unification of Western Europe. Ironically, he had at the same time found it difficult to cope with the problems of his own strife-torn country. For several decades there has been growing tension between its Dutch-speaking Flemish and French-speaking Walloon populations, and in recent years, partly because of the international oil crisis, once prosperous Belgium has suffered from economic recession, especially in its French-speaking south. Tindemans had been looking for constitutional solutions to the problem of Flemish and Walloon demands for greater autonomy, while trying to maintain a central government strong enough to deal with unemployment, inflation, and industrial decline. After failing to get from his own party full support for a regionalization program designed to ease ethnic tensions and linguistic conflicts, Tindemans tendered the resignation of his government to King Baudouin on October 11, 1978.

A member of a Flemish Roman Catholic family, Leonard Tindemans, the son of Frans and Margaretha (Vercruyssen) Tindemans, was born on April 16, 1922 in Zwijndrecht, Belgium, a suburb of Antwerp. He studied at the State University of Ghent, which granted him the degree of bachelor of commercial, economic, and consular sciences. Later he attended the Catholic University of Louvain, where he obtained a degree in social and political science in 1967, after completing a thesis on the political thought of the noted Flemish statesman Frans van Cauwelaert. He attended an international seminar at Harvard University during a visit to the United States in 1962.

Early in his career, Leo Tindemans worked briefly as a journalist in Antwerp. He then became a civil servant in the economic department of Belgium's Ministry of Agriculture. Tindemans entered national politics as a member, and later as leader of the Flemish wing, of the middle-of-the-road Social Christian party, representing Roman Catholic middle-class and working-class interests. From 1958 to 1966 he was the party's national secretary general. Long interested in the movement for European unity, he eventually became vice-chairman of the European Union of Christian Democrats. In 1961 Tindemans was elected to the Chamber of Representatives—the lower house of Belgium's national Parliament—from Antwerp, to occupy the seat vacated by the death of Frans van Cauwelaert. Concurrently with his national and international activities, he served from 1965 to 1976 as mayor of Edegem, a residential suburb of Antwerp with a population of about 8,000. In addition, he was for a time a visiting professor in the faculty of social sciences at the Catholic University of Louvain.

On June 18, 1968 Tindemans took over his first Cabinet post, as Dutch-speaking Minister for Community Relations in Prime Minister Gaston Eyskens' coalition government of Social Christians and Socialists. The Eyskens government, which took office after a four-month government crisis engendered by a language dispute at the University of Louvain, was formed on the basis of a compromise agreement providing for equal apportionment of Cabinet posts between Flemings and Walloons and establishing dual ministries for education, culture, and community relations between the two language groups. As the Dutch-speaking Minister for Community Relations, Tindemans worked closely with his French-speaking counterpart, Freddy Terwagne, in helping to formulate a plan for the linguistic, economic, and administrative decentralization of Belgium. That plan provided the basis for constitutional reforms adopted by Parliament in 1970 and 1971.

Although those reforms established a framework for resolving the conflicting demands of Flemings and Walloons, their implementation —which required a two-thirds majority in Parliament—was hampered because of squabbles over details. Tensions within the Eyskens coalition, especially over the provision establishing Brussels as a special bilingual area, led to the dissolution of Parliament in September 1971 and the premature holding of new elections two months later. A reorganized Cabinet, headed by Eyskens and again composed of Social Christians and Socialists, entered the troubled political scene on January 20, 1972, with Tindemans as Minister for Agriculture and Middle-Class Affairs. The government collapsed, however, on November 22 of that same year, after linguistic and territorial issues brought about a split in the Social Christian party.

On January 23, 1973 Edmond Leburton, a Walloon Socialist, took office at the head of a grand coalition of Belgium's three leading parties—the Social Christians, the Socialists, and the moderately right-wing Party of Freedom and Progress, or Liberals. Together they controlled 76 percent of the seats in Parliament. The new enlarged Cabinet included Tindemans as Deputy Prime Minister as well as Minister of the Budget and Institutional Problems. But the Leburton government fell within a year, largely because of the failure of plans for the construction of a Belgian-Iranian oil refinery near Liège. The withdrawal of the Socialists, who blamed their coalition partners for the project's failure, was followed by Leburton's resignation on January 19, 1974. A week later, Tindemans was named Prime Minister-designate by King Baudouin and charged with the task of forming a new government. Unable to muster a viable coalition, he recommended the dissolution of Parliament and the calling of new elections.

In the elections of March 10, 1974, from which Tindemans emerged as indisputably the national leader, the Social Christians increased their representation in the 212-member Chamber of Representatives to seventy-two seats—a net gain of five. Determined that a strong government must be established as quickly as possible, Tindemans tried to reconstitute Leburton's grand coalition but was unable to persuade the Socialists to work with the Liberals. He then tried to form a coalition with the Socialists, who decided, however, to enter the opposition in order to increase their support among leftist voters. After making an unsuccessful attempt to persuade the small federalist parties to join the government, Tindemans had to settle for a minority Cabinet with the Liberals, whose thirty seats brought the government's strength only up to 102.

Tindemans' Cabinet of nineteen ministers and six secretaries of state was sworn in on April 25, 1974. After presenting his policy declaration, Tindemans won his first vote of confidence in the Chamber of Representatives on May 4 by 100 to sixty-three, with the federalist parties abstaining. The government gained a slight majority on June 10, when the Walloon Union (Rassemblement Walloon), with twelve seats, agreed to join the coalition, becoming the first federalist party to take part in a national government. To conciliate the federalists, Tindemans immediately took steps to implement the constitutional provisions for greater cultural autonomy. On July 20 the Chamber of Representatives approved legislation setting up nonelective regional councils for the French and Dutch-speaking communities and for Brussels that were to advise the national Parliament. Although the two-thirds majority needed to invest the councils with legislative power was lacking, Tindemans expressed hope that the new institutions might eventually form the basis for more far-reaching legislation.

The Flemish-Walloon conflict was temporarily overshadowed during 1975 by the worsening economic situation. In 1974 the inflation rate had reached a peak of 15.7 percent, and unemployment, closely tied to a decline in exports, was approaching 7 percent of the insured labor force. In March 1975 the government announced a massive allocation of funds to create new jobs in public services, and in May Tindemans issued a decree freezing prices of key commodities, rents, and public utility rates for a two-month period that was later extended to the end of the year. Other measures included government aid for investments, reduced corporate taxes, and the easing of credit restrictions. Pointing out that Belgian production costs were at that time even higher than those of the United States, Tindemans declared: "The terrifying problem facing us is how to make our prices competitive again." In October the government announced an additional twenty-five point economic program to curb inflation, ease unemployment, and encourage exports.

The Tindemans government's belated decision, announced in June 1975, to join its NATO allies Denmark, Norway, and the Netherlands in replacing the obsolete F-106 aircraft with American-made F-16 fighter planes rather than with the more costly French Mirage F-1 nearly triggered a government crisis. The purchase of the Amercian planes was opposed by the Belgian aircraft industry and by Walloons who retained strong ties with France. Tindemans had originally favored the French contract, which he felt might provide the foundation for a flourishing all-European aircraft industry, but he had to go along with the allied countries to ensure standardization within NATO. As a concession to European sentiment, the Belgian government scaled down its purchase order from 116 to 102 planes and announced plans to use the amount saved to establish a European aerospace research fund. After the Walloon Union decided at the last moment to support the government, the purchase was approved by a 112 to ninety-one vote of confidence in the Chamber of Representatives.

During 1975 Tindemans regularly took part in top-level meetings of European statesmen, including the thirty-five-nation Conference on Security and Cooperation in Europe held in July at Helsinki. In May of that year he made a ten-day visit to the People's Republic of China, and in June he accompanied King Baudouin on a trip to the Soviet Union. During a two-day visit to Zaire—the former Belgian Congo—in September Tindemans began to work towards the improvement of ties with that nation, which had become somewhat strained the year before.

In a radio interview on December 7, 1974 Tindemans proposed that the Common Market establish a top-level committee to study the feasibility of the creation of a Western European political union by 1980. A few days later, while attending the Paris summit meeting of the European Economic Community, Tindemans was invited to draft a report on the overall concept of a European union. To prepare for that project, he studied earlier recommendations for European unity and traveled throughout the nine EEC member countries. His forty-one-page report, entitled *European Union: Report to the European Council*, was published in Brussels in January 1976.

Stressing "realistic and realizable" goals, the Tindemans report called on member states to accept an obligation to work toward common objectives on major issues involving economic, defense, and foreign policies, as well as development of energy sources, scientific research, and aid to underdeveloped countries. It proposed the virtual abolition of the right of veto within the European Council. The report suggested a "two-tier approach," in which countries with strong economies would be allowed to proceed more rapidly with joint economic and monetary plans, while giving economically weaker countries, such as Great Britain, Ireland, and Italy, the opportunity to catch up. Citizens of member nations would have certain fundamental rights, including the right to appeal to the European Court of Justice. The European Parliament, to be elected by direct suffrage in all member countries in 1978, would have the authority to initiate programs of common concern.

Although he conceded that his report was not the last word on European integration, Tindemans expressed the hope that it would result in major discussions. His "two-tier approach" to economic issues drew a barrage of criticism from French Socialists and representatives of the British Labor government, but his report was generally well received. To lay the groundwork for elections to the European Parliament, scheduled for mid-1978, a meeting was held in Brussels on April 29, 1976 by delegates of thirteen Christian Democratic and centrist parties from seven of the nine EEC member states. There a new European People's Party—Federation of Christian Democratic Parties of the European Community was founded, and Tindemans was unanimously elected its president.

Tindemans' plan to streamline local administration by merging Belgium's 2,359 towns and villages into 589 larger units was approved by Parliament in November 1975 and endorsed by the voters in the October 1976 local elections. Meanwhile the government's 1975 economic reforms brought little improvement. The inflation rate for 1976 remained above 10 percent, while unemployment rose to more than 8 percent. An austerity program instituted in February 1977 that included wage curbs and increases in indirect taxes set off a series of one-day protest strikes by the trade unions.

A new government crisis erupted on March 4, 1977, when the two Walloon Union members of the Cabinet refused to support the government on a budget vote, as a protest against the administration's failure to rescue the ailing Walloon-controlled steel industry. By dismissing the two ministers, Tindemans reduced the support of the government in the Chamber of Representatives to 106—slightly short of a majority. After vainly trying to persuade the Socialists to join the coalition, Tindemans recommended the dissolution of Parliament and the calling of new elections, a year ahead of schedule. The elections of April 17, 1977 constituted a resounding vote of confidence for Tindemans, who received 134,163 preferential votes, more than any other candidate in Belgium's parlimentary history, and for the Social Christians, who increased their representation to eighty.

Unable to bring the Socialists and Liberals together into a grand coalition with his own party, Tindemans organized a four-party coalition of Social Christians, Socialists, and two federalist parties—the Dutch-speaking People's Union (Volksunie) and the Brussels-based Democratic French-speaking Front (Front Démocratique des Francophones)—that controlled 173 of the 212 lower-house seats. The federalist parties agreed to join the government after Tindemans had assured them of immediate action on a new federalization plan that would include the creation of directly elected regional councils for Flanders, Wallonia, and Brussels. To ensure the cooperation of the Socialists, Tindemans promised to put into effect a new economic program to combat unemployment and inflation and strengthen the nation's industries.

The inauguration of the new government was delayed when four French-speaking members of Tindemans' own Social Christian party refused to be sworn in, complaining that not enough important posts had been allocated to the French-speaking community. They changed their minds, however, after Tindemans assured them that their linguistic group would be adequately represented under the new constitutional provisions. On June 3, 1977 his Cabinet of twenty-three ministers and seven secretaries of state was finally sworn in. Six days later, the government won its first vote of confidence, when the Chamber of Representatives, by a vote of 165 to thirty-three, approved the federalization program. It was described by Prime Minister Tindemans as "a charter of reconciliation" that was "nothing more or less than the redefinition of a country." When, more than a year later, the Flemish wing of Tindemans' party refused to back the Egmont Pact, a plan to divide the country into three linguistic regions, Tindemans resigned.

Leo Tindemans and his wife, the former Rosa Naesens, whom he married in 1960, have two sons and two daughters. Candid and straightforward, the Belgian Prime Minister was once quoted as saying, "I'd rather be foreign minister." He lists his favorite recreations as walking, reading, and writing and is the author of several political studies, including *Ontwikkeling van de Benelux* (Development of Benelux, 1958), *L'Autonomie Culturelle* (Cultural Autonomy, 1971), *Regionalized Belgium: Transition from the Nation State to the Multinational State* (1972), *Een Handvest voor woelig Belgie* (A Charter for Agitated Belgium, 1972), *Dagboek van de Werkgroep Eyskens* (Agenda of the Eyskens Task Force, 1973), and *Europe, Ideal of our Generation* (1976). In 1976 Tindemans received an honorary D. Litt. degree from the City University of London and was awarded the Charlemagne Prize.

References: International Who's Who, 1977-78; Who's Who in Belgium (1962); Winkler Prins Encyclopedie van Vlaanderen (1974)

Toon, Malcolm

July 4, 1916- United States Ambassador to the Soviet Union. Address: b. American Embassy, Ul. Chaikovskogo 19/23, Moscow, U.S.S.R.

Recognizing that the struggle for American-Soviet détente, nuclear disarmament, and Middle East peace requires the skills of a thoroughly trained professional envoy at the American embassy in Moscow, Presidents Gerald R. Ford and Jimmy Carter both chose Malcolm Toon as United States Ambassador to the Soviet Union. During his three decades in the Foreign Service, Toon, who speaks Russian fluently, had become one of the State Department's foremost experts on Soviet affairs and had acquired a reputation for firmness and forthrightness in his conduct as a diplomat. Before being appointed in 1976 to succeed Walter J. Stoessel in the U.S.S.R., he had served as Ambassador to Czechoslovakia, Yugoslavia, and Israel.

Malcolm Toon was born on July 4, 1916 in Troy, New York to George and Margaret Harcomb (Broadfoot) Toon. His parents were natives of Scotland, and in the early 1920's, when his father, a stonecutter, became discouraged in his efforts to earn a living in the United States, they went back to Scotland with their son. After about a year, finding conditions just as difficult in the old country,

Malcolm Toon

they returned to America and settled in the Boston area. Their economic situation improved somewhat in the 1930's, after the elder Toon began working in the street construction business.

During the family's brief stay in Scotland, Toon had begun his primary education. He attended public schools in Medford and Bedford, Massachusetts, and in 1937 graduated from Tufts College (now University) with his B.A. degree. Enrolling in the Fletcher School of Law and Diplomacy, which is on the Tufts campus, he was awarded his M.A. degree from Harvard University upon completing his study there in 1938. The following year he became a research assistant with the National Resources Planning Board in Washington, D.C.

While serving with that newly established federal agency, Toon prepared for and passed the Foreign Service examinations. But with the United States' entry into World War II, he felt that he would have greater involvement in world affairs in the military service than in a low-level post in the diplomatic corps. In 1942 he entered the Naval Reserve as an ensign. During the next few years he served in combat in five campaigns in the South Pacific as a PT-boat commander. Before his discharge in 1946, he had earned a Bronze Star decoration and attained the rank of lieutenant commander.

By the time that Toon was free to take up his deferred Foreign Service appointment, in February 1946, he had recognized that "the major problem of the postwar period would be the Soviet Union," as he recalled in an interview with Michael J. Berlin for the New York *Post* (July 19, 1976). He asked to be sent to Moscow, but he explained, "In those days officers in the very bottom grade were not sent there." Instead, his first posting was what he described as "the next best thing"—Warsaw, where he was sent as an administrative officer in July 1946. The bitter street fighting between the forces of the left and of the right in Poland reminded him of the combat he had recently survived, and he thrived on the excitement during his service there.

On his return to Washington from Poland in November 1949, Toon was assigned to Haiti, in those days regarded as a soft posting where, he told Berlin, "you could spend most of your time lying on the beach and cruising around the social circuit." The prospect of so bland a tour, which would probably have delighted some of his colleagues, led him to request the chief of personnel to assign him to Eastern Europe, where he felt he would have a chance to see some action. Soon afterward he was transferred to Budapest, to serve as political officer from August 1949 to March 1950. With the intensification of the cold war, he was recalled to the United States for training in the Russian language and area study at Middlebury College and Harvard University.

"Then my career logically fell into the so-called Soviet expert path," Berlin quoted Toon as saying. The State Department assigned him for the first time to the United States Embassy in Moscow in June 1951, with the dual designation of consular and political officer. As a political officer specializing in Soviet affairs, he was transferred to Rome in February 1952 and to Berlin in October 1953. In the latter assignment he served also as chief of consular affairs and as liaison officer to the United States section of the Office of Allied Commanders in the four-power administration of the divided city.

When Toon was reassigned to the State Department in Washington in July 1956, he held the titles of foreign affairs officer and supervising foreign affairs officer before taking on the responsibilities in February 1958 of special assistant to the director of the office of East European affairs. From 1956 to 1960 he also served as deputy director of the East-West exchanges staff. The first United States-Soviet cultural exchange negotiation was among the several international conferences in which he participated as a delegate. The others included the 1958 Nuclear Test Ban Conference in Geneva, the 1959 Foreign Ministers' Conference on Berlin in Geneva, and the 1960 Ten Nation Committee on Disarmament in Geneva.

Toon's next appointment in the field was to London in August 1960 as first secretary of the American Embassy. He returned to Moscow in 1963 as counselor for political affairs and in May 1965 attained the rank of consul general, becoming the third-ranking staffer at the American Embassy in the Soviet Union. Soon afterward he was involved in an extraordinary incident that was apparently precipitated by a Stewart Alsop column in the *Saturday Evening Post* describing the KGB (Soviet intelligence) setup in Washington and naming the number-three man in the Soviet Embassy as the head of station.

In a full-page article in the May 29, 1965 issue of *Nedelya*, the weekend supplement of *Izvestia*, the Soviet government newspaper, Toon was termed the head of the American "spy kitchen" and was accused, with Alan Logan, the second secretary of the American Embassy, of heading a network of espionage agents working among American students in Russia. According to Toon, as quoted by Berlin in the New York *Post* (July 17, 1976), the charge was totally groundless. Denying that he ever had anything to do with the CIA, he maintained that the Soviets were simply retaliating by attacking the American counterpart of the man Alsop had accused. They selected him as a target, Toon said, because "they feel uncomfortable with anybody that has some expertise in the [Soviet affairs] field" and wanted to destroy him as an effective Foreign Service officer.

The Russians did not follow up their allegations with any official action against Toon, but about a month later he was transferred back to Washington, where he was appointed director of the State Department's office of Soviet affairs. In 1968 he became acting deputy assistant secretary for East European affairs. As those advancements indicate, his expertise as a Soviet specialist was gaining increasing recognition, and not merely from the State Department, for during that period the Russians accused him both of having masterminded the defection of Svetlana Alliluyeva, Stalin's daughter, in 1967 and of heading a secret interdepartmental committee organized to sabotage the commemoration of the fiftieth anniversary of the Russian Revolution.

During the summer of 1969, about a year after a Soviet invasion of Czechoslovakia put down that country's attempt at liberalization, Malcolm Toon presented his credentials as United States Ambassador in Prague. Richard Nixon's selection of an outspoken diplomat like Toon for that sensitive post, according to Chalmers M. Roberts of the Washington *Post* (April 20, 1969), was meant to serve as "evidence that the President does not intend to let the heavy Soviet hand in Eastern Europe interrupt diplomatic relations with the Communist world." Also by the appointment of Nixon, in October 1971 Toon became United States Ambassador in Belgrade, Yugoslavia. There he played an important role in negotiating an agreement, in January 1973, whereby the Overseas Private Investment Corporation, a United States government agency, would underwrite investments of American capital in joint ventures with the Yugoslavs. He was also on hand to smooth over the difficulties that arose in April 1974, when United States-Italian naval maneuvers in the Adriatic were denounced by the Yugoslavs as reflecting a secret American involvement on Italy's side in the long-standing Italo-Yugoslav dispute over the city of Trieste. While serving in Yugoslavia, in 1973, he attained the rank of career minister.

President Nixon, furthermore, reportedly intended for a time in 1973 to appoint Toon his Ambassador in Moscow, but, instead, at the last moment named Walter J. Stoessel, the State Department's other top Russian expert. On Toon's return to Washington in 1975, after he had completed his tour in Belgrade, he was slated to replace Ellsworth Bunker as the chief American representative at the then forthcoming Middle East Peace Conference in Geneva. When the United States Ambassador to Israel, Kenneth B. Keating, unexpectedly died, however, in May 1975 President Ford chose Toon to replace him at the embassy in Tel Aviv.

Since Toon's expertise and experience were entirely in Eastern European, rather than Middle Eastern, affairs, Ford's choice came as a surprise. Observers, however, explained the decision as stemming from Secretary of State Henry Kissinger's feeling that the Tel Aviv post, in an era of delicate United States-Israeli relations, required a professional diplomat of the highest stature. It was also said that Toon's selection was motivated by his well-known immunity to "localitis"—explained by Berlin in the New York *Post* as a "diplomatic disease that causes ambassadors to break out in cables to the State Department advocating the interests of the countries in which they are stationed." Supposedly that "disease" is endemic among American diplomats in the Arab countries, but Toon wryly commented to Berlin, the immunity "was easy to come by in Eastern Europe."

Ambassador Toon immediately set to work familiarizing himself with the main issues in United States-Israeli relations and with the history and problems of the Middle Eastern region. During his brief tenure in Tel Aviv he set a new style for American diplomats in Israel. Whereas Keating, for instance, as reported in the Washington *Post* (May 9, 1975), had often complained that Secretary of State Kissinger constantly bypassed the embassy to deal directly with Israeli officials, often using Simcha Dinitz, the Israeli Ambassador in Washington, as his conduit, Toon insisted on having a stronger role and more personal participation in communications between Washington and Tel Aviv.

According to Terence Smith, writing in the New York *Times* (November 1, 1975), in his first four months in the Jewish state, Toon "gathered more headlines, generated more controversy, and aroused more arguments about his performance than all his predecessors together." In the fall of 1975 a State Department official told Toon that he had spoken out of turn in commenting on the possibility of American intervention in strife-torn Lebanon and in criticizing Egyptian President Anwar Sadat for making anti-Jewish remarks while on a visit to the United States. Although the views Toon otherwise expressed in Israel usually reflected the instructions he received from Washington, his blunt manner often offended the Israelis.

Heated reaction greeted Toon's criticism of the establishment of Jewish settlements in the occupied West Bank territories and his call for reform of the tortuous Israeli electoral system. The most intense responses were generated by his comments on the Israeli economy and Israeli dependence on aid from the United States. In a radio broadcast in October 1975 Toon advised Israelis "to tighten your belts and temper your appetites" before asking for large amounts of American aid, suggesting that the country attempt to solve its economic problems through an austerity program. Later, in April 1976, at a news briefing for reporters, he criticized the Israelis for trying to pressure the United States Congress into authorizing more aid than President Ford had requested.

Israeli resentment of Toon's style did not, however, preclude acknowledgement of the validity of many of his observations. Critics condemned him for appearing to interfere in Israel's domestic affairs, but they were forced to admit that his advice, though sometimes formulated tactlessly, was nonetheless sound. In fact, many of his proposals, especially in the economic sphere, have been vindicated by the Menahem Begin government's recent initiation of an austerity program, and the need for domestic political reform was a major issue in Israel's 1977 national election.

In September 1976 President Ford indicated that Toon was his choice to replace Stoessel as American Ambassador to the Soviet Union. Instead of routinely giving their *agrément,* or acceptance, as is customary, the Russians delayed for nearly two months, apparently because they hoped to force the President into selecting someone of a more pliable stance on American-Soviet relations. Under pressure from Kissinger, however, they approved Toon's nomination, which was then officially announced on November 24. He presented his credentials at the Kremlin on January 18, 1977.

While the Toon appointment was awaiting Senate confirmation, however, in February 1977 Ford's successor, President Jimmy Carter, withdrew the nomination, reportedly because he intended to give the Moscow post to someone who was not a career diplomat but had great personal influence and political stature. Carter changed his mind after he was persuaded that the United States' relations with the Soviet Union demanded the attention of a professional negotiator of the highest qualifications. The President was also said to have become aware that the replacement of a known hardliner might well be interpreted as a sign of weakness or as a signal that he favored a soft policy. Toon was renominated on April 25 and received Senate confirmation on June 7, 1977.

Customarily, the American Ambassador in Russia delivers a brief Fourth of July address on Soviet radio and television. The text of Toon's remarks on July 4, 1977 included a reference to "fundamental and inalienable rights which cannot be arbitrarily infringed or removed by governmental authorities," and went on to assert that "Americans will continue to state publicly their belief in human rights and their hope that violations of these rights wherever they may occur will end." Soviet authorities demanded that those passages be deleted, and when Toon refused, the traditional broadcast was canceled. Another event that captured headlines in the American press occurred in late August 1977, when a fire raged through the upper floors of the United States embassy building in Moscow, causing considerable damage. Toon denied that Soviet intelligence operatives, intermingling with the firemen, had exploited the emergency to compromise top-secret files and apparatus in the fire-ravaged areas of the building.

In an interview with Fred Coleman of *Newsweek* (July 25, 1977), Toon noted that the achievements of the SALT talks have been rather limited to date and that the Soviets have not been pursuing "helpful" policies in Africa and the Middle East. He pointed out, "The major part of the job [of attaining détente] lies ahead of us. I think we would just be kidding ourselves if we did not recognize that the differences between us on . . . gut issues are very wide indeed." He added, however, that "Soviet policy for the most part is dictated by what the Marxists themselves call objective conditions. And objective conditions at the present call for some measure of détente, some measure of relaxation of tensions." It is also necessary, he said, to counter the Soviet "suspicion, which is hard to dislodge, that the President's [human rights] campaign is aimed at undermining Soviet power inside the Soviet Union and in Eastern Europe as well."

Malcolm Toon received the State Department's Superior Honor Award in 1965. He is said to "run a very tight ship," and Berlin quoted one of his colleagues in the Foreign Service, who described him as being "a very direct, thoughtful man, . . . clear, precise, . . . an accurate reporter and incisive analyst." On August 28, 1943 he married Elizabeth Jane Tayler, a secretary whom he met in Washington during World War II. They have three children—Barbara, Alan, and Nancy. Toon enjoys golf, tennis, hunting, and fishing and belongs to several clubs, including the Pinehurst (North Carolina) Country Club and the Kenwood Golf & Country Club in Washington.

References: N Y Post p22 Jl 19 '76 por; Department of State Biographical Register, 1974; International Who's Who, 1977-78; International Yearbook and Statesmen's Who's Who, 1977; Who's Who in America, 1976-77

Travolta, John

Feb. 18, 1954- Actor. Address: c/o American Broadcasting Company, Television Division, ABC Television Center, 4151 Prospect Ave., Los Angeles, Calif. 90027

"At once mean-looking and pretty, he conveys the kind of threatening sexuality that floors an audience," wrote Frank Rich in *Time* magazine after watching John Travolta, Hollywood's newest erotic symbol, in *Saturday Night Fever*, a slick, frenetic film that exploits the current discomania. Although it was only Travolta's first starring vehicle, he received virtually unanimous critical accolades and an Academy Award nomination as best actor of 1977 for his performance as a troubled Brooklyn youth, macho but vulnerable, who finds his only escape from a dead-end job and a suffocating family on Saturday night at the local disco, where he reigns as undisputed king. Previously, John Travolta had been best-known to members of the subteen set, who idolized him for his charming portrayal of a cocky, somewhat dim-witted high school student in the ABC-TV situation comedy series, *Welcome Back, Kotter*. In 1978 Travolta recruited even more admirers by costarring with Olivia Newton-John in the film version of the long-running Broadway hit musical *Grease*, which casts a backward look at high school students in the rock 'n' roll era of the 1950's.

John Travolta was born on February 18, 1954 in Englewood, New Jersey, the youngest of the six children of Salvatore and Helen (Burke) Travolta. His mother, a former actress who once headed a group called the Sunshine Sisters, worked as a drama teacher and director during John's childhood. In 1931 she established a long-distance record for swimming the Hudson River. Travolta's father, who at one time played semiprofessional football as a quarterback, operated the Travolta Tire Exchange in Hillsdale, near Englewood, until his retirement. Show business obsessed Travolta's close-knit Irish-Italian Roman Catholic family, and his two brothers and three sisters are all involved in the performing arts. Two of his sisters, Ellen and Margaret, appear on television; his other sister, Anne, and his mother have small roles in *Saturday Night Fever;* his brother Joey has launched a singing career; and his brother Sam has been trying to organize a band.

As a child, John Travolta received tap-dancing lessons from Gene Kelly's brother Fred and mimicked James Cagney's song-and-dance routines after watching *Yankee Doodle Dandy* on television. When he was twelve he joined an Actors Studio workshop in Englewood and was given a role in its production of Frank Gilroy's *Who'll Save the Plowboy?* His decision to become an entertainer was his own. "Man, nobody pushed me into show business," he told Tom Burke of *Rolling Stone* (June 15, 1978). "I was aching for it!" Within a few years Travolta was appearing in summer stock and supper club productions of musicals like *Gypsy* and *Bye, Bye Birdie*. In the meantime, he was a reluctant student at Dwight Morrow High School in Englewood. "I was a bit of a clown in school, only an average student. I went out with one girl," he told Edwin Miller of *Seventeen* (October 1976). "I was always involved outside and never did anything like plays in school. I was inhibited by a lot of the people there. My reality was different from theirs. I was interested in show business, and they weren't." Travolta picked up dance steps and rhythms from black students. "Whatever new dance came to school, I learned it," he told an interviewer for a cover story in *Time* (April 3, 1978). "I think the blacks accepted me because I cared about them accepting me. They seemed to have a better sense of humor, a looser style. I wanted to be like that."

At sixteen Travolta obtained his father's permission to drop out of school so that he could concentrate on acting, and about that time his talents were discovered by agents Bob LeMond and Lois Zetter. Within a few months the teenager was obtaining jobs acting in television commercials. At seventeen he moved to New York City, where he at first stayed with his sister Anne and then rented his own Lower West Side cold-water flat. Soon after turning eighteen Travolta made his Off-Broadway debut, playing the part of Private Griggs in a revival of *Rain* that opened on March 23, 1972 at the Astor Place Theatre but closed five days later.

By that time Travolta was occasionally commuting to the West Coast to do guest spots on such television series as *Owen Marshall, Emergency, The Rookies,* and *Medical Center.* Then he landed the minor role of Doody with the first national touring company of *Grease,* the Jim Jacobs-Warren Casey Broadway musical about teenagers in the 1950's. He remained with *Grease* for nine months, beginning with its opening performance in Boston on December 23, 1972. Travolta made his Broadway debut in *Over Here!,* a World War II musical starring the two surviving Andrews Sisters, in which he had the small singing and dancing role of Misfit, one of a group of GI's on their way to the war. It opened at the Shubert Theatre on March 6, 1974 and ran for 348 performances. Meanwhile, he continued to make occasional commercials. Remembering a television spot he did for Mutual of New York in 1974, an executive for that insurance firm said in retrospect, as quoted in the New York *Times* (June 7, 1978): "He was excellent. . . . We knew that the kid was going to be a star."

Travolta made his film debut inconspicuously in a horror film called *The Devil's Rain* (Bryanston, 1975), in which he wore a mask and delivered the lines: "Blasphemer! Get him, he is a blasphemer!" Although he was unsuccessful in his audition for the plum role of Meadows in the Jack Nicholson vehicle *The Last Detail,* the casting director was so impressed by him that he called him when he was lining up actors for the new television comedy series *Welcome Back, Kotter.* After turning down an offer for a Broadway role in *The Ritz,* Travolta auditioned for the *Kotter* series and easily won the role of Vinnie Barbarino, the leader of a street gang called the Sweathogs, whose members make life difficult for Brooklyn high school teacher Gabe Kotter, played by Gabriel Kaplan.

When the show premiered on ABC-TV in September 1975, Travolta was only one of its several featured actors, but within a few months he had emerged as a star. Although critics were relatively unimpressed by the *Kotter* series, it soon became a hit, especially among teens and preteens, who could identify with Barbarino and his peers. "Originally Vinnie was very slick and very tough," *Kotter's* executive producer James Komack told Burt Prelutsky of *TV Guide* (January 1, 1977). "He was a bully and a con artist. But Johnny has a very likable, sweet and even soulful personality. He has a very spiritual attitude, so we made Barbarino a devout Catholic. Because Johnny can play against Barbarino's conceits, he makes him an extremely vulnerable character." As of the spring of 1978, *Welcome Back, Kotter* was continuing to capture high audience ratings.

By early 1976 Travolta had become the heartthrob of the teenybopper set, and his grin adorned posters in adolescents' bedrooms across the country. As a result of his singing in one of the *Kotter* episodes he was persuaded to record for the RCA-subsidiary Midland International Records. His single, "Let Her In," sold over 800,000 copies and reached the number five spot on the *Cashbox* best-seller charts. It was included on his LP album *Can't Let You Go,* which a writer for *Time* (July 26, 1976) characterized as "a bland rock album tailored to subteens." Among his other recordings are the album *John Travolta,* also for Midland, and the singles "Moonlight Lady" and "Slow Dancing." Although Travolta's singing failed to enrapture critics, it continues to thrill the prepubescent set. While promoting his recordings he was mobbed at suburban shopping malls, and on one occasion he had to disguise himself in a policeman's uniform to escape the crowds. In September 1976 he appeared among the guest performers at the second annual Rock Music Awards, broadcast live from the Hollywood Palladium by CBS-TV.

During the summer of 1976 Travolta returned to the East to tour New England with a summer stock production of William Inge's *Bus Stop,* in the starring role of Bo Decker. Then he turned in a brief but effective performance as Billy Nolan, a sadistic high school student who joins Sissy Spacek's tormentors in Brian de Palma's telekinetic horror film *Carrie* (United Artists, 1976). His portrayal of a teenager forced to live shielded from the world by plastic because of his congenital lack of immunity from disease, in the TV film *The Boy in the Plastic Bubble,* presented on ABC in November 1976, brought him critical praise. Pauline Kael commented later in the *New Yorker* (December 26, 1977) that Travolta "gave the character an abject, humiliated sensitivity that made the boy seem emotionally naked."

In late 1976 Travolta signed a $1,000,000 three-film contract with producer Robert Stigwood. The first to be made under that contract was *Saturday Night Fever* (Paramount, 1977), based on a 1976 *New York* magazine article by Nik Cohn entitled "Tribal Rites of the New Saturday Night." Cohn wrote about young blue-collar men and women in Brooklyn whose otherwise empty lives revolve around their weekend binges at discotheques. For his starring role as Tony Manero, the nineteen-year-old king of the 2001 Odyssey disco in the Bay Ridge section of Brooklyn, Travolta underwent a rigorous training that included two hours daily of running and three of dancing. To help him he hired Jimmy Gambino, the trainer whom Sylvester Stallone had used to prepare for the fight scenes in *Rocky*. At the end of five months Travolta was twenty pounds lighter and had, as he told one reporter, "a whole new body." Also in preparation for his part he frequented discos in Brooklyn and even entered a few disco dance contests.

Filmed under John Badham's direction on a $3,000,000 budget in the spring of 1977, mostly on location in Brooklyn, *Saturday Night Fever* was released with a publicity blitz in December of that year. Most critics agreed that the film's impact was equal to the promotion, and although some faulted it as derivative in story line or excessively exploitative, they were in unusual accord in applauding its star's performance. "For Travolta, it's a triumphant starring debut," wrote David Ansen of *Newsweek* (December 19, 1977) in a typical panegyric. "In a less engaging actor's hands, Tony could have been insufferably arrogant and dense. But Travolta's big slab of a face is surprisingly expressive, revealing a little boy's embarrassment and hurt as well as a stud's posturing. Travolta understands Tony with his whole body—needless to say, he can dance up a storm—and you can't keep your eyes off him. It's a fresh, funny, downright friendly performance."

If the critics held any reservations at all about Travolta's performance, it was that he was perhaps too good. Some wondered if he were not typecast, especially since Tony was a character not unlike Vinnie Barbarino. Pauline Kael observed in the *New Yorker* (December 26, 1977): "Travolta gets so far inside the role he seems incapable of a false note; even the Brooklyn accent sounds unerring." But she went on to dismiss the idea of typecasting. "At twenty-three, he's done enough to make it apparent that there's a broad distance between him and Tony, and that it's an actor's imagination that closes the gap," she pointed out. "There's dedication in his approach to Tony's character; he isn't just a good actor, he's a generous-hearted actor." In February 1978 Travolta was nominated for an Academy Award for his performance. He has also received the best actor of the year award from the National Board of Review.

By the time *Saturday Night Fever* was released, Travolta had completed work on the film adaptation of *Grease* (Paramount, 1978), which in its original version was still running on Broadway. Produced by Robert Stigwood and Allan Carr and directed by Randal Kleiser, the film featured Travolta in the starring role of Danny Zuko and costarred country-pop singer Olivia Newton-John. When it was released in June 1978 the critical verdict was negative, although most reviewers conceded that Travolta did as well as he could with the poverty of his material. "His animal magnetism is such that every time he appears on the screen as . . . the punk with a heart of gold, it is impossible to watch anybody else," Robert Martin wrote in the Toronto *Globe and Mail* (June 17, 1978). "The best moments in the film aren't dialogue but shots of Travolta reacting, suddenly becoming macho when he realizes the gang is watching him talk to his girlfriend or smothering a giggle after accidentally elbowing Olivia Newton-John in the breast. These moments alone make *Grease* worthwhile." And Stanley Kauffmann commented in the *New Republic* (July 1, 1978): "John Travolta . . . sings pleasantly, and he does more vivid phallocratic dancing as in *Saturday Night Fever*. He's not really *good*, but that's not his fault—there's no part, just a lot of twaddle. . . . His appeal doesn't yet work head-on, it works sideways, obliquely, through tensions, like Cagney's and Bogart's. . . . But his power is truly powerful, and he should thrive."

Travolta's third film under contract with Stigwood, to be called *Moment by Moment* and to be released by Universal Pictures, is a love story involving a delivery boy and a bored California housewife, played by Lily Tomlin. In March 1978 he formed his own production company and signed a two-picture agreement with Orion Pictures that would net him $1,000,000 per film. Among his future projects is a Paramount picture to be called "American Gigolo" and a new sequel to *The Godfather*, also to be made by Paramount, in which he would star as the son of Michael Corleone. Meanwhile, his contract with *Welcome Back, Kotter* is scheduled to run until 1980. By the time he is thirty, Travolta told Maureen Orth of *Newsweek* magazine (December 19, 1977), he hopes to be directing as well as continuing to star in dramas and musicals.

Just as youngsters tried to ape the style of Elvis Presley in the 1950's and that of the Beatles in the 1960's, the soulful "Travolta look" and the strutting "Travolta walk" have become the rage among contemporary teenagers. Menswear shops have been doing a landslide business selling three-piece white suits and other accessories of the type worn by Travolta in *Saturday Night Fever*, and a fashionable tonsorial parlor is featuring a $25 Travolta haircut. And dance studios report that the "Hustle," as performed by Travolta on screen, is booming in popularity.

John Travolta's main hobby is flying, and his West Hollywood penthouse apartment is filled with model airplanes. A licensed pilot, he owns a single-engine AirCoupe, but he has been grounded for the time being, under the terms of his contract with Stigwood. Travolta also owns a reconditioned commercial DC-3. On the ground he drives a 1955 Thunderbird and a new Mercedes, but his Honda 350 motorcycle has also been declared off-limits by Stigwood.

A well-built six-footer, Travolta has blue eyes, dark hair, a wide mouth, and a dimpled chin. While filming *The Boy in the Plastic Bubble* he met Diana Hyland, who played his mother in the film. They were lovers until her sudden death from cancer, at the age of forty-one, on March 27, 1977. The actor was with her at the time she died in Los Angeles, but returned a few days later to the set of *Saturday Night Fever* in New York. "The pain was on every inch of his body," the film's director, John Badham, recalled to Maureen Orth of *Newsweek*. "Some of the best scenes in the picture were done in that advanced stage of grief." Observers have pointed out that Travolta has been astute in seeking opportunities for artistic and commercial success without being trapped in the role of bubblegum hero that his television series foisted upon him. Still, as a reporter for *Time* (December 19, 1977) commented, "His early start left him without a true adolescence, and emotionally Travolta is an odd combination, half boy, half man—a middleaged man at that. The man plans his career. The boy buys a DC-3 and collects model airplanes." Travolta has undergone seven months of psychoanalysis and now practises Scientology.

References: Ladies Home J p137+ Mr '78 por; N Y Sunday News mag p19+ Mr 13 '77 pors; N Y Times II p15+ D 11 '77 por; Newsweek 90:63+ D 19 '77 pors; People 7:41+ Je 13 '77 pors; Rolling Stone p72+ Je 15 '78 pors; Seventeen 35:137+ O '76 por; TV Guide 25:21+ Ja 1 '77 por; Time 110:69+ D 19 '77 pors, 111:82+ Ap 3 '78 pors; Reeves, Michael. Travolta: A Photo Bio (1978)

Turner, Stansfield

Dec. 1, 1923- Director of Central Intelligence. Address: b. Central Intelligence Agency, Washington, D.C. 20505

Nine directors have preceded Admiral Stansfield Turner in the Central Intelligence Agency since its establishment in 1947. But Turner is the first Director of Central Intelligence to have budget control over the several agencies that form the United States intelligence community and the explicit authority to assign and coordinate intelligence collection tasks. Increased power was accorded him in an executive order signed by President Jimmy Carter in January 1978 as part of a reorganization plan that had as one of its purposes the rehabilitation of the CIA, which in recent years has been beleagured by revelations of abuses of its mandate and by security leaks. Turner, who became the CIA director in February 1977, is an urbane Navy man of strong intellectual bent, a former Rhodes scholar, destroyer commander, systems analyst, writer on naval strategy, president of the Naval War College, and fleet and area commander of the North Atlantic Treaty Organization.

Stansfield Turner was born on December 1, 1923 in Chicago, Illinois, one of two children of Oliver Stansfield Turner and Wilhelmina Josephine (Wagner) Turner. The other child was named Twain. His father was born at Ramsbottom, Lancashire, England, came to the United States in 1909 at the age of ten, entered the real estate business six years later, and by 1929 had risen to the vice-presidency of a Chicago real estate firm. The family's home was in the well-to-do suburb of Highland Park, where Stansfield attended high school.

At Amherst College, in which he enrolled in 1941, Turner took part in student politics, served as president of his class, played football, and became a member of the Naval Reserve. One of his friends and classmates, William H. Webster, is now director of the FBI. After two years at Amherst, Turner transferred to the United States Naval Academy, where he made his mark as an outstanding student, brigade commander, and left guard on the football squad. He and Jimmy Carter were in the same class at Annapolis, but, according to the President, they did not know each other. "He was so far ahead of us," Carter told his Cabinet in a comment on his nomination of Turner, "that we never considered him competition, or even a peer." Although they were members of the class of 1947, they graduated in 1946 under an accelerated program adopted during World War II, with Turner finishing 25th in the class of 820, while Carter ranked 59th.

After a year aboard a cruiser, Turner went to Oxford University as a Rhodes scholar, studying philosophy, politics, and economics, and obtained his M.A. degree in 1950. Returning to sea, he served on destroyers in both the Atlantic and Pacific and earned a Bronze Star and other service decorations in the Korean war. His assignments at sea, including his commands of the USS *Conquest* from 1956 to 1958 and the USS *Rowan* in 1962, alternated with tours of duty in the politico-military division of the Office of the Chief of Naval Operations and in the Office of the Assistant Secretary of Defense for Systems Analysis. The Navy also assigned him to a period of study in the advanced management program at Harvard Business School.

As Turner gradually advanced through the naval grades, acquiring a reputation as an effective and open-minded officer and administrator, his assignments grew more sensitive and important. In 1967, with the rank of commander, he directed the USS *Horne,* a guided missile frigate, off the coast of Vietnam. Moving up to captain, he served for the next two years as executive assistant and military aide to Secretary of the Navy Paul Ignatius, advising on budget, manpower, and other matters. He was awarded his two stars as rear admiral, assisted Admiral Elmo R. Zumwalt Jr., Chief of Naval Operations, on a Navy modernization project, and assumed command of a carrier task group of the Sixth Fleet in the Mediterranean in 1970.

During the early 1970's Turner's assignments continued to increase in responsibility, and he was mentioned from time to time as a possible future chief of naval operations. In 1971 he was named to head the systems analysis division in the office of the chief of naval operations and the following year, shortly after receiving the third star of a vice-admiral, was appointed president of the Naval War College in Newport, Rhode Island. With typical independent-mindedness, Turner dispensed with uniforms at the college, ordered extensive revisions in the curriculum to increase, for example, the reading requirements, beginning with Thucydides' *History of the Peloponnesian War,* and called for examinations in strategy and tactics, analysis and management. The students' year at the college was decidedly not to be a year on the beach. He cautioned in a college address that if the military did not shape up, "the think tanks will be doing our thinking for us." He invited a variety of provocative speakers to seminars and lectures that he organized. One guest was his friend, Herman Wouk, author of *The Caine Mutiny;* another was Jimmy Carter, then Governor of Georgia, who spoke on government reorganization and with whom he thereafter remained in correspondence.

Soon after Turner began his two-year tenure at the War College, his paper "The United States at a Strategic Crossroads" appeared in the *Naval Institute Proceedings* (October 1972). In that paper he noted three significant changes in America's strategic environment—a movement away from a bipolar world, waning domestic support for traditional policies, and changing Soviet capabilities and strategy. He urged a greater emphasis on the "maritime option," naval strategy, arguing that "under the new strategic considerations which we must take into account . . . sea-based forces have increased applicability across the spectrum of our requirements." In December 1974 he contributed "Missions of the U.S. Navy" to *Naval Institute Proceedings,* a paper in which he pointed out that a quartet of missions had evolved—strategic deterrence, sea control, projection of power ashore, and naval presence—and concluded that naval officers "must understand the Navy's missions, continually question their rationale, and provide the intellectual basis for keeping them relevant and pertinent to the nation's needs."

By that time Turner was serving as commander of the United States Second Fleet and NATO Striking Fleet Atlantic, a post to which he had been appointed in August 1974. As Second Fleet commander, on May 12, 1975 in Boston harbor he participated in ceremonies welcoming the first Soviet warships—two guided missile destroyers, the *Boiki* and the *Zhguchi*—to visit an American port since the end of World War II. Four months later he became commander in chief, Allied Forces Southern Europe (AFSOUTH), with headquarters in Naples, Italy, and was promoted to four-star, or full, admiral.

Turner's new responsibilities were reflected in a larger concern with strategic questions. When interviewed by John K. Cooley of the *Christian Science Monitor* (June 24, 1976), he asserted that NATO was more important to the West now than in the past because of the growth of Warsaw Pact power, particularly Soviet strength. For *Foreign Affairs* (January 1977) he wrote an article, "The Naval Balance: Not Just a Numbers Game," which appeared as Congress was taking up the fiscal 1977 Pentagon budget and the nation was debating the lineup of United States-Soviet forces. Turner maintained that opposing navies could not be usefully compared in quantitative or absolute terms and that an analysis of trends was a more sensible approach to the issue of naval capabilities. The question to ask was not, "Who's ahead?" but, "Can we still undertake the old missions or perhaps take on new missions that were impossible yesterday?" He warned that the drawing of "doomsday" pictures might have a negative affect on other countries' perceptions of United States naval effectiveness: "A few extra ships in the budget or at sea may not be enough to overcome an inaccurate perception of weakness." The article was referred to repeatedly the following month when Turner was nominated as director of Central Intelligence under the new Democratic Administration.

Departing from Italy on an hour's notice on February 2, 1977, Turner flew to Washington to meet with President Jimmy Carter, who named him on February 7 to the dual post of primary adviser on foreign intelligence and head of the CIA. Carter's first choice as intelligence chief, Theodore Sorensen, had been opposed by foreign policy hardliners and by conservative Senators, with the result that he withdrew his name from consideration in January. Before announcing the Turner nomination, Carter had consulted with Senator Daniel K. Inouye, chairman of the Senate Select Committee on Intelligence, and other members of that panel.

The nomination of Turner came near the close of a period during which the CIA had been rather extensively criticized in the press and investigated by Congress for illegal activities. Since 1973 the agency had undergone two major reorganizations and had had three directors—James R. Schlesinger, William E. Colby, and George Bush—who, in the words of David Binder in the New York *Times* (November 25, 1976), had become as "interchangeable as Cabinet officers." The general reaction to Turner's nomination was favorable, when, on February 22, he testified before the Senate intelligence committee. He assured the committee that he would conduct intelligence operations "strictly in accordance with the law and American values" and that he would keep the members informed about covert operations. His aims as intelligence chief, he said, would be to provide unbiased intelligence estimates and to restore the reputation of the United States intelligence community. The committee recommended his confirmation 17-0 on February 23, and a day later the Senate unanimously confirmed his appointment. Turner was permitted to retain his Navy commission and remain on the active duty list. As Senator Inouye disclosed, he had agreed not to seek the position of chief of naval operations or chairman of the Joint Chiefs of Staff during his tenure at the CIA, but that agreement would not prevent the President from naming him to either post.

Some reservations about how Turner might handle the intelligence assignment and whether he could control the CIA appeared in the press after his confirmation. According to an editorial in the *Nation* (March 12, 1977) on the Senate hearing, "The signs that Turner will be frank with the responsible committees of Congress about future CIA huggermugger were faint, if they appeared at all; he merely promised to 'study' the matter of protecting the civil liberties of American citizens as the CIA goes about its normal business of spying." On the subject of control, "Suetonius" of the *New Republic* (March 12, 1977), after discussing Turner's career, commented, "The troubling question—wholly unanswered in his flabby, shambling confirmation hearings—is whether even this impressive making of an admiral will enable him to run 'the Company' rather than vice-versa. . . . Bright, sophisticated, polished, apparently at ease with himself and his country's limited place on the planet, he is no Curtis LeMay railing against the sun. But he is not Billy Mitchell either. . . . For his many strengths, he remains very much a man of the system."

Representative of more positive considerations of prospects for change or reform at the CIA under Turner was Frank Getlein's observation in *Commonweal* (March 4, 1977): "I've seen him at work . . . and emerged from the experience in frank admiration of the openness of the mind to unusual suggestions, the willingness to entertain unorthodox assumptions. . . . If Turner brings the same openness to reevaluation to the CIA, it could be the most important thing to happen to the Agency since its inception and an event of great value to the country."

Among the problems pressing Turner almost as soon as he took office was that of trimming the staff over a period of six to eight years by several hundred operatives who were deemed no longer needed because of advances in the United States's technological capability for gathering intelligence. To save money and to reduce speculation among the CIA employees as to who would be dismissed, he decided to cut the time span to two years. In the fall of 1977 he began the paring by having termination notices sent to 212 agents in the directorate of operations, the agency's clandestine branch. Criticized by the expendable agents and many observers as unnecessarily brusque, that action was reported in the press to have further damaged the morale at an agency that only recently, in August, had added to its string of scandals new disclosures about its program, now defunct, of funding secret experiments on human beings in a search for methods of manipulating behavior.

With a view toward a reorganization of the overall United States intelligence operation and toward a restoration of the prestige that the CIA had once enjoyed, among other objectives, on January 24, 1978 President Carter signed an executive order to give Stansfield Turner, as Director of Central Intelligence, "full and exclusive authority" over the budgets (estimated at $7 billion) of all of the country's intelligence agencies, direct control over the CIA, and the responsibility of working through the new National Intelligence Tasking Center in assigning projects to the agencies and coordinating their activities. The various agencies besides the CIA are the FBI, the National Security Agency, State Department Intelligence, Defense Intelligence Agency, Military Intelligence, Treasury Department Intelligence, Energy Department Intelligence, and Drug Enforcement Administration.

The President's order also curbed certain kinds of covert operations that had discredited the CIA, occasionally because of misrepresentation. Assassinations and medical experimentation on unwitting human subjects were prohibited. A special coordinating committee under the chairmanship of the National Security Council director, Zbigniew Brzezinski, was given the responsibility, shared with the President, of supervising all sensitive clandestine intelligence activities. Moreover, Secretary of Defense Harold Brown retained operational control over the electronic signal interception and the satellite surveillance programs. Therefore, although Turner's power increased substantially, he could not be regarded as an intelligence czar. Shortly after the Presidential directive became known, Turner denied in an interview for *Newsweek* (February 6, 1978) that there was any problem in morale at the CIA at the present time. "This place is producing," he asserted. "The President of the United States is pleased with it. And the product is high." He went on to point out, "When you're in a period of transition to new objectives, new methods, new management systems, new styles of openness, of course there are people who are complaining, because it wasn't done the way it was yesterday."

Admiral Stansfield Turner works an average of twelve hours a day; has offices at the CIA headquarters in Langley, Virginia, as well as in the old Executive Office Building next to the White House; confers with Carter for half an hour or longer once or twice a week; and sometimes sits in on Cabinet meetings. He holds honorary degrees from Amherst, Roger Williams, Bryant, and Salve Regina colleges. His decorations include the Legion of Merit. His religion is Christian Science.

On December 23, 1953 Turner married Patricia Busby Whitney of Chicago, and they have two married children. Their daughter, Laurel, is Mrs. Frank G. Echevarria of San Diego, California, where she and her husband work in the community college system. Their son, Lieutenant Geoffrey W. Turner, is in Naval Intelligence. Of distinct military bearing, the admiral stands five feet nine and a half inches tall and weighs 185 pounds; he has blue eyes and gray hair. He is a nonsmoker and a teetotaler. To keep trim he swims, plays tennis and squash, and jogs with his dog, Hornblower, a golden retriever.

References: Cong Q p259+ F 12 '77 por; N Y Post p27 F 8 '77 por; N Y Times p20 F 8 '77; New Repub 176:10+ Mr 12 '77 por; Newsweek 91:19+ F 6 '78 pors; International Who's Who, 1977-1978; Who's Who in America, 1976-77

Vereen, Ben

Oct. 10, 1946- Actor; singer; dancer. Address: c/o Bert Padell, Padell, Kaden & Nadell Co., 405 Park Ave., New York City, N.Y. 10022

After playing minor roles for six years in theatrical productions throughout the United States, the lithe and limber Ben Vereen arrived in his first leading role on the Broadway stage in 1971 as Judas Iscariot in the rock opera *Jesus Christ Superstar*. One year later he opened as the Leading Player in Stephen Schwartz's *Pippin* and was acclaimed as one of the most gifted, energetic, and multifaceted entertainers since the advent of Sammy Davis Jr., one of his childhood idols. The choreographer Bob Fosse, who directed him in *Pippin*, has said: "There's no man like him on the musical comedy stage."

Ben Vereen was born in Miami, Florida on October 10, 1946. He grew up in the Bedford-Stuyvesant section of Brooklyn, along with his four brothers and four sisters, two of whom were adopted. Both of his parents worked to support the family: his father, James Vereen, in a paint factory and his mother, Pauline, as a theatre matron. Vereen attributes his theatrical aspirations to the encouragement of his mother, who as a girl left work in the Louisiana fields to join a troupe of vaudeville entertainers as a wardrobe mistress. "One day, when I was about ten," Vereen told Guy Flatley for a New York *Times* interview (November 5, 1972), "a short white fellow with a bald head came to our door and told me to make my head reach my feet. When I stooped over, the man said to my mother, 'The boy's a born dancer!' " Convinced by the enthusiastic con artist from the Star Time Dance School, his mother enrolled him in that neighborhood institution, which Vereen later referred to as a "rip-off joint." Although he later attended other talent schools, he was more interested in singing gospel songs in the Pentecostal churches that he visited with his godmother and her husband, an itinerant preacher. He sang solos as a child, and during his teens, performed with a group poetically known as the Sensational Twilights of Brooklyn.

Although he had never heard of New York's High School for the Performing Arts, Vereen acted on the advice of his principal at Junior High School 178 and tried out for its entrance audition. "I was a real hick," Vereen admitted to Peter Bailey for an *Ebony* magazine interview (May 1973). "All the other guys had on tights and ballet shoes and there I stood in bermuda shorts and sneakers. They really didn't know what to do with me, but I got in." Despite his own preference for ballet, Vereen eventually proved more suited to modern dance. During his senior year he came to the attention of one of his teachers, Helen Tamiris, the well-known choreographer and dancer, who bestowed her special award for achievement in dance on him at graduation.

Vereen obtained his first professional role through Vinnette Carroll, a teacher in the school's drama department, who had seen him perform in a dance concert during his senior year. In 1965 she was staging an Off-Broadway production of Langston Hughes's gospel song-play *The Prodigal Son* at the Greenwich Mews Theater and signed Vereen to play a small role and understudy the lead. "Vinnette planted the seed, you know," Vereen told Raoul Abdul for his collection of interviews, *Famous Black Entertainers of Today*. "She used to spend a lot of time saying things to me that I really didn't understand at that time, but today I do—about performing and projection. At that time I was going through the transition of tearing from the church and going into theater."

The Prodigal Son opened on May 20, 1965 but closed shortly thereafter. After conducting an unsuccessful search for other work in the theatre, Vereen decided to prepare for a career in the ministry at a Pentecostal seminary in Manhattan. Disillusioned by what he felt was a hypocritical atmosphere, he left the school, and, with the encouragement of former teacher Lester Wilson, began looking for theatre work. In 1966 he joined a summer-stock company in Tannersville, Pennsylvania, where he played Chico in *West Side Story* and choreographed the troupe's version of *Annie Get Your Gun*. He also performed for a while with the Ron Davis Dancers and the Arthur Mitchell Dance Company, in between his bouts of unemployment.

Vereen's luck changed for the better in the fall of 1966, when he auditioned for a choreographer and director of whom he had never heard, for a one-line part in the chorus of the forthcoming Las Vegas production of *Sweet Charity*. When Bob Fosse saw Vereen perform during the cattle-call audition, he yelled, "That's the guy!" He then asked Vereen to notify him when he started cutting records so that he could go out and buy every one of them. Vereen later told Janis Kaye in a Fort Lauderdale, Florida *News & Sun-Sentinel* interview (March 2, 1975) that it was Fosse who taught him to subdue his performances. "Cool it, Ben," Fosse would say to Vereen, "it's a little too much. You're all over the place. Use your hands and your eyes—control it."

Sweet Charity's Las Vegas company opened at Caesar's Palace in December 1966, with Vereen playing Brother Ben. He took over the role of Big Daddy Johann Sebastian Brubeck in the performances given at Boston's Shubert Theater in September 1967 and then moved with the play to the O'Keefe Theatre in Toronto, Canada in January 1968. During the filming of *Sweet Charity*, which was released by Universal Pictures in 1969, Vereen met his childhood hero, Sammy Davis Jr., who was cast in the role of Big Daddy.

Davis invited Vereen to join him in the Chicago and London productions of *Golden Boy*, a musical adaptation of Clifford Odets' 1937 play about a violinist turned boxer. The play opened at the Auditorium Theatre in Chicago in April 1968 with Vereen in the role of the Fight Announcer and as the understudy for one of the leading players. In the middle of one performance in Chicago, Davis fell ill and had the actor who played Eddie Johnson take over his role as Joe Wellington. That complicated cast shuffle meant that

Vereen then had to go on as Johnson. During his performance, he spotted Davis watching him from the wings. As Vereen came offstage after having received the first ovation of his career, Davis quipped, "I'm not going to say anything, because I knew it all the time!" Vereen has often praised Davis in return. As he explained to Janis Kaye, "I'm giving the man flowers while he's alive. I learned a lot from him."

In 1968 Tom O'Horgan first brought Vereen to Broadway, when he hired him to take over the role of Claude in the rock musical *Hair*. Vereen then moved to the Los Angeles company of *Hair* at the Aquarius Theatre in November 1968, first in the role of Hud and then as Berger. The local critics signaled their delight with Vereen by presenting him with a citation as "best all-around performer in a musical." In 1969 he moved back to the Broadway company of *Hair* as Berger. In the following year O'Horgan invited Vereen to join his repertory company, the New Troupe, in performances of his and Sam Shepard's experimental works in the United States and in Europe. Vereen has called his association with O'Horgan "an experience in mental and spiritual awareness; he gave me so much," as reported in the *Ebony* article.

While playing Berger in the San Francisco company of *Hair* after his return from Europe Vereen met Charles Gordone, the playwright who wrote the 1970 Pulitzer-prize winning drama *No Place to Be Somebody*. Gordone cast him as the bar owner and pimp Johnny Williams in the San Francisco production of his play that was presented by the National Shakespeare Company in September 1970. To prepare for his role, Vereen spent four weeks with a number of pimps to familiarize himself with the subterranean world of prostitution. "Maaan, it was a trip," Vereen told Peter Bailey. "Here I was coming from the hearts and flowers scene in *Hair* to a drama and to Gordone. I had to make a quick transition. Gordone had to murder the sensitivity I had developed in *Hair* and used to shout at me, 'That ain't the way to read this play. Get that *Hair* stuff outta your head. This is a nigger play. Read it like a nigger.' He drove us hard, but it was valuable time spent, since he opened up something else in me."

On October 12, 1971 Vereen returned to Broadway as Judas Iscariot, the betrayer of Christ, in *Jesus Christ Superstar* at the Mark Hellinger Theatre. Directed by his old friend Tom O'Horgan, the rock opera dealt with the seven last days in the life of Jesus of Nazareth. During the rehearsals at the Ukranian National Home in lower Manhattan, Vereen told Bob Micklin in a *Newsday* interview (September 28, 1971) that the play represented a "spiritual thing" for him. "All my life I've been bogged down in all that Christian crap," he said, "but in this play I feel I'm getting closer and closer to what Jesus was really talking about."

Vereen's unorthodox and sympathetic portrayal of one of the most abhorred traitors in the history of mankind met with considerable skepticism on the part of many clergymen and critics. A year after *Jesus Christ Superstar* opened, he explained to Guy Flatley why he believed that Judas had been a revolutionist: "What he did he did out of love for the people of Israel. When he placed Jesus in the hands of the establishment, he counted on the people saying, 'You can't do this to our Christ, the man who healed our lame.' He thought they would overthrow the Romans, but they chickened out, man. . . . We pray to a man who was mutilated on a cross. He didn't *have* to die; *we* let him die. And we said, 'Judas, you're the dude, you take the blame.' Yet Judas was noble enough to take his own life—a heavy thing to do, but he did it out of love for Christ. Get behind *that* love. They are two men totally misunderstood."

Although certain that the show would succeed with Broadway audiences, most critics were unimpressed themselves. The reviews ranged from Clive Barnes's temperate criticism in the New York *Times* on October 13, 1971, in which he compared *Jesus Christ Superstar* to one's first view of the Empire State Building—"not at all uninteresting, but somewhat unsurprising and of minimal artistic value"—to the harsher strictures of such critics as Michael McNay of the *Guardian* (October 14, 1971), who felt that the show staggered "from vulgarity to schmaltz and back." With few exceptions, however, critics warmed to Vereen's performance, so that few would disagree with Richard Watts (New York *Post*, October 13, 1971), who considered him "the best and most attractive actor in the cast." Vereen was later nominated for a Tony Award as best supporting actor in a musical for his performance.

Unhappy with the producers of *Jesus Christ Superstar* for not providing adequate publicity for the play and for acting as a divisive force among the members of the cast, Vereen was not too upset when he was fired in June 1972 for refusing to do eight performances a week after recovering from throat surgery. His grief was assuaged by the fact that he had already auditioned successfully for Bob Fosse's forthcoming musical *Pippin*, the show about the coming of age of Pepin, the son of the eighth-century Frankish Emperor of the West, Charlemagne.

After its out-of-town tryouts at the Kennedy Center Opera House in Washington, D.C., *Pippin* moved to New York City's Imperial Theatre on October 23, 1972. According to director Bob Fosse (*Ebony*, May 1973), Vereen's role as the Leading Player "began as a small part, but it kept growing with Ben's ability to take anything and make it into something wonderful." Vereen's performance as master of ceremonies, confidant to Pippin, and prestidigitator who at one point in the play brings Charlemagne back to life, captivated the critics. Richard L. Coe in the Washington *Post* (September 22, 1972) saw a resemblance in his style to Cab Calloway's—"a slinky stride, toothy leer, and a mental hi-de-ho." But Coe hastened to add: "Still, Vereen above all is himself, guiding and mocking poor little Pippin through his human education."

In his interview for *Newsday* (November 12, 1972), Jerry Parker reported on Vereen's reaction to his overnight stardom. "I expected a lot from 'Superstar,' and the critics were good to me," Vereen said. "But with the reviews for this! I was floored. That's a lot to live up to, I don't want to let anybody down. I just stopped reading them. The whole idea of the game for me is work. Not just work, but excellent work." On March 25, 1973 he won a Tony Award as best actor in a musical for his outstanding contribution to *Pippin*.

Vereen's success on the Broadway stage prompted executives at NBC-TV to offer him his own four-segment, summer variety show entitled *Ben Vereen . . . Comin at Ya*, the first installment of which was telecast on August 7, 1975. The following January he appeared as the great jazz musician Louis Armstrong in a made-for-TV ABC *Movie of the Week* presentation. Although a few critics were disappointed with the flaccid script for *Louis Armstrong—Chicago Style*, Arthur Unger expressed a generally held view in the *Christian Science Monitor* (January 23, 1976) that Vereen turned in a "virtuoso performance."

Vereen's most endearing, and certainly most widely viewed, television performance, however, was that of "Chicken" George in the David Wolper production of *Roots*, the eight-part miniseries based on Alex Haley's best-selling book of the same name that traced his family history from its African origins through late nineteenth-century America. Vereen appeared in a number of the eight episodes, which were shown between January 23 and 30, 1977 over ABC-TV. Playing the role of the son of a black slave and her white owner, Vereen impressed millions as a talented trainer of fighting cocks whose success in the white man's world enabled him to return to the farm to obtain his family's freedom from his father. On April 11, 1977 he received one of the Television Critics Circle Awards for best actor for his performance as Chicken George in *Roots*.

Besides the small role he had in the film version of *Sweet Charity*, Vereen played Carlos in Roger Corman's *Gas* (American International Pictures, 1972) and Bert Robbins in *Funny Lady* (Columbia Pictures, 1975), the continuation of the Fanny Brice saga begun by the film's star, Barbra Streisand, in *Funny Girl* in 1968. The character Vereen created for *Funny Lady* was a meld of black entertainers Bert Williams, the Ziegfeld Follies comic, and Bill ("Bojangles") Robinson. The respect Vereen feels for the black, burnt-cork minstrel and vaudeville entertainers, whom he credits with establishing the "first economic stronghold for blacks in this country," led him to base his own nightclub act of the early 1970's on their performing style.

A man of boundless energy, Vereen found time between his performances in *No Place to Be Somebody* and *Jesus Christ Superstar* to tour American military bases with Jane Fonda's antiwar Free the Army show, and, before joining the cast of *Pippin*, worked in a troupe known as the Slam Players that performed for prison inmates. In November 1972 he played at Lincoln Center in *The Gershwin Years*, and, in 1976 entertained at the White House for President Gerald R. Ford and the Prime Minister of Ireland. His first record album, *Ben Vereen—Off-Stage*, appeared on the Buddah label, and he formed and recorded for his own record company during the early 1970's.

The American Guild of Variety Artists presented their Rising Star, Entertainer of the Year, and Song-and-Dance awards to Vereen, making him the first male performer to receive all three at one time. He has also received a Theater World award for his performance in *Jesus Christ Superstar*, a Drama Desk award for best actor in a musical, and a Cleo Award for his work in *Pippin*.

Ben Vereen lives with his second wife, Nancy Brunner, a former ballet dancer, and their four daughters Malaita, Naja, Kabara, and Karon, in a home in Encino, California. He has a son, Ben Vereen Jr., by a previous marriage. Janis Kaye described him as a man who is constantly in motion: "Whether he's shaking hands, posing for pictures, or stepping out of someone's way, every movement has the lithe, graceful quality of a dance step." Still a deeply religious man, he has explored many forms of worship, including Buddhism. "If God has given you a gift, you've got to use it—by giving," he once told a writer for the New York *Post* (August 23, 1972). "If I can't do that, I'll perish. . . . I mean that —I'll blow my brains out."

References: After Dark 5:18+ D '72 pors; Biog N p678 My-Je '75; Christian Sci Mon p26 Ag 20 '75 por; Ebony 28:74+ My '73 pors; N Y Times II p 1+ N 5 '72 por; Nat Observer p24 D 2 '72 pors; Newsday II p3 N 12 '72 por; Time p57+ N 27 '72 por; Washington Post D p1+ Je 1 '77 por; Abdul, Raoul. Famous Black Entertainers of Today (1974); Who's Who in America, 1978-79; Who's Who in the Theatre (1977)

Videla, Jorge Rafaél

Aug. 2, 1925- President of Argentina, Address: Oficina del Presidente, Casa Rosada, Buenos Aires, Argentina

Lieutenant-General Jorge Rafaél Videla, former Army Commander-in-Chief, was sworn in as Argentina's thirty-ninth President on March 29, 1976, five days after a long-expected "clockwork" coup by military forces overthrew the crisis-ridden government of Isabel Martínez de Perón. Seizing the office bloodlessly with at least the tacit majority support of his countrymen, President Videla was a reluctant leader who had earlier resisted strong military pressures to interfere with the elected constitutional government. A lifelong professional soldier of unquestioned integrity, a strict moralist of the old school, and a devout Roman Catholic, he is considered politically moderate in everything but his dedicated anti-Communism.

Videla's move against President Perón, who inherited her post twenty-one months before, on the death of her husband, Juan Perón, came only after widespread certainty of her inability to deal with such crippling national problems as economic deterioration, rampant political terrorism, and government corruption. Once in office, Videla announced a "national reorganization to restore morality and efficiency" by staffing key civilian and government positions, including his Cabinet, with army, air force, and navy chiefs from his tripartite military junta. He has weathered criticism from abroad about Argentine violations of human rights, threats from the military Right, and the depredations of Leftist terrorists whom he has sworn to eradicate. Despite the junta's instability, Videla has made considerable progress in rehabilitating Argentina's "political and economic wasteland," and he has promised a gradual return to civilian rule. His resignation from his military command on August 1, 1978 had no effect on his presidency. Three months earlier, leaders of the junta had publicly announced their decision to continue it into early 1981.

Unlike the colorful Peróns, Jorge Rafaél Videla has almost no publicized personal life, so deep are his roots in the austere Argentine military establishment. His is the kind of figure, wrote Joanne Omang in the Washington *Post* (March 26, 1976), "around whom few anecdotes grow." He was born into an army family on August 2, 1925, in the large provincial city of Mercedes, seventy-five miles from Buenos Aires. His father, Colonel Rafaél Videla, was Commander of the Sixth Infantry Regiment, and his mother, María Redondo de Videla, came from an old Mercedes family. He has a sister, María. At sixteen Videla entered the National Military College, the Argentine equivalent of West Point, where he received his commission in 1944 as an Infantry Second Lieutenant. His advanced education came at the Higher School of War.

In the three decades before he became the potential successor to Mrs. Perón, Videla was a career officer who was best known to those whom he taught and commanded during his long and distinguished service at the National Military College. After being commissioned, he took his first post with the Fourteenth Infantry Regiment in the central province of Córdoba. In 1946 he was a lieutenant in the Vigilance Company in the Ministry of War, and for the next two years he served with the Motorized Army Regiment. Joining the Military College in 1948 as an instructor, he gained a reputation as an excellent teacher and a stern, self-denying taskmaster. He also acquired his military nicknames of *El Hueso* (the Bone), *El Flaco* (Skinny), and, in reference to his stealthy gait, the Pink Panther. Rising to the rank of captain, he attended the Higher School of War during 1951-1954, and then returned to the Military College as a staff officer.

Promoted to Major, Videla was posted to the United States from 1956-1958 as adviser to the Office of the Military Attaché in the Argentine embassy, and he returned to Washington on later assignments, once as a member of the Inter-American Defense Board. Videla also took part in some South American diplomatic missions, for which he was decorated by Bolivia and Venezuela. During 1962-1965, and again during 1966-1968, he was staff officer in the Army General Command. He was promoted to Colonel in 1965 and then studied advanced military strategy for two years at the Army Center of Higher Studies. Appointed chief of the infantry batallion at the Military College in 1958, Videla rose to be chief of the cadet corps in 1968, and, as Brigadier General, served the college's commandant from 1971-1973.

"The army, the strong arm of the nation," Videla said while commandant, "ought to resemble a lion, ready to fight but confined in a golden cage of discipline, whose bars are laws and regulations." But as his military position became more prominent and conditions in Argentina worsened, his stand for political neutrality on the part of the military became increasingly untenable, for in fact, between 1967 and 1973, Argentina was under military rule.

The country reverted to civilian control with the resignation of President General Alejandro Lanusse and the subsequent election in March 1973 of President Hector Cámpora, the handpicked candidate of Juan Perón, who had fled to exile in Spain after exercising virtual dictatorial rule from 1946 to 1955. With the way paved for Perón's return to head the Peronists, still the nation's dominant political force, President Cámpora resigned, and in September 1973 President Perón and Vice-President Isabel Perón were elected in a landslide victory. For a time it seemed that Perón would solve Argentina's two most persistent problems, a declining economy and widespread social unrest, but by the time he died on July 1, 1974, the country was beset with soaring inflation, unemployment, strikes, mounting foreign debts, disunity within Peronist ranks, and terrorism from both Left and Right.

Although she took office with the pledged support of both the Peronists and the military, President Isabel Perón was ill-equipped by experience or temperament for effective leadership. Each of her fumbling moves exacerbated her difficulties, as she reshuffled her Cabinet with disturbing frequency, nationalized foreign-owned industries, paid national debts with new printings of money, and tried unsuccessfully to deal with labor and squabbling groups within her Judicalist Party. In November 1974, finding herself faced with near anarchy, she declared a national state of siege to counteract political violence. She was further hampered by ill health, which twice forced her to absent herself from office, and by the Rasputin-like machinations of José López Rega, her private secretary and Minister of Welfare.

Meanwhile, in 1973, Brigadier General Videla had become Chief of the Army General Staff. His rise to public prominence came two years later, with still another misstep by Isabel Perón. On August 11, 1975, in an effort to indicate military support for her tottering government, she appointed Colonel Vincente Damasco, an active Army officer, Minister of the Interior. General Alberto Numa Laplane, then Commander-in-Chief of the armed forces, supported both Peronism and military involvement in politics. At first he approved the Damasco appointment, but when leading Army generals demanded that both Damasco and Laplane resign their commissions, they were forced to acquiesce, although Damasco remained as Interior Minister. On August 27, after a two-day confrontation with Army officers who denied Mrs. Perón's desire to appoint a younger Peronist officer to Laplane's post (which by Argentine practice would have forced resignations of senior generals), she reluctantly appointed Videla, the Army's choice, as Commander-in-Chief. By doing so, she gained time in her struggle for survival, but her act spotlighted the strength concentrated in the military.

President Perón's respite was short-lived, and Videla emerged thereafter as the new strong man to lead the nation. On August 30, 1975 he began a systematic purge of Army officers sympathetic to Peronism. That same month, when Peronist labor leaders demanded the removal of Victorio Calabro, the governor of Buenos Aires province who repeatedly called for Mrs. Perón's resignation, Videla blocked the ouster attempt. In December 1975, in the course of directing a military investigation of the Anti-Communist Alliance of Argentina (A.A.A.), a right-wing Peronist terrorist group whose "death squads" operated with impunity, Videla uncovered connections between the terrorists and José López Rega's Ministry of Welfare. Those disclosures, in addition to other evidence of financial corruption, eventually compelled the Minister to flee to Spain. Videla also directed an Army campaign of extermination in Tucumán province against the People's Revolutionary Army (E.R.P.), a Marxist guerrilla force considered by the Army as the greatest threat to national security. Videla's forces pursued a "no prisoners" policy, and Videla spent Christmas 1975 in the field with troops who took the lives of hundreds of terrorists.

On December 18, 1975 Mrs. Perón faced an attempted military coup when rightist Air Force officers under the leadership of General Jesús Orlando Capellini seized two air bases near Buenos Aires, flew mock strafing runs over the Presidential palace, and, acting on their own, demanded that the President relinquish her powers to a government headed by General Videla. Moving in consort with the chiefs of the Air Force and Navy, General Orlando Ramón Agosti and Admiral Emilio Massera, Videla met with Mrs. Perón and her Cabinet, and announced to all military commands that he rejected the dissident Air Force officers' demand for a takeover. The coup attempt collapsed. Supported by Peronists in the Congress, the General Confederation of Labor, and her Judicalist Party, President Perón had survived what Juan de Onis in the New York *Times* (December 20, 1975) called "the most serious military crisis that the Peronist movement had faced since it was returned to power." Still viewed as a moderate proponent of a democratic changeover, Videla nevertheless warned the Cabinet that Mrs. Perón had either to give way to a constitutional successor or submit to a military coup.

In the next ninety days President Perón sank deeper into her morass of economic and political problems. Stubbornly insisting at first that she would complete her elected term until March 1977, she ultimately promised a December 12, 1976 general election. But her time had run out, and only fears of full-scale civil war, plus the military's determination to eradicate all terrorists first, delayed a coup.

With the death toll from terrorism estimated at 2,200 during Mrs. Perón's months in office, inflation pegged between 335 percent and 600 percent, and an economy plagued by strikes, unemployment, bankruptcies, and unmeetable foreign debts, the General Confederation of Labor posed the only possible block to military intervention. But by March 22, 1976, when the Videla junta boldly publicized its government plans, a bloodless overthrow was certain. It came on March 24 when Mrs. Perón, headed by helicopter to her residence in Olivos, was instead taken into custody by her Air Force pilots and placed under arrest in the Andean country of Neuquén province. As the country calmly pursued its normal activities, military forces occupied the principal civilian and government offices and declared a state of martial law. On March 25 General Videla, General Agosti, and Admiral Massera announced that Videla would serve as President for three years, with final executive powers entrusted to the three leaders. In an unusually swift reaction, the United States formally recognized the Videla government on March 26.

As if to set the tone of his leadership, Videla was sworn into office on March 29, 1976, in a brief, unadorned ceremony, along with eight Cabinet members, six of whom were from the military. Addressing the nation in a televised inaugural message on March 30, he declared that the coup was "not directed against any social group or political party. . . . We did not act out of an ambition for power, but from responsibility to protect national security." Warning of the need for "sacrifice, effort, and austerity," he also pledged respect for human rights "based not on legal or international declarations, but . . . the result of our profound Christian conviction of the preeminent dignity of man as a fundamental value." A Videla proclamation on March 24 outlined the junta's goals to "restore the essential values" of the nation, put a stop to left-wing subversion, restore the economy, and "assure subsequently a republican, representative, and federal democracy."

To achieve those ends, Videla suspended all traditional functions of Congress, provincial governments, the Supreme Court and other judicial tribunals, organized political parties, and labor unions. As a substitute for Congressional law-making, he created a nine-man military Legislative Advisory Commission, headed by Army General Carlos Dalla Tea. Although the nation was functioning normally within hours after the takeover, with military personnel filling all key positions, arrests of those suspected of subversion or corruption mounted as high as 4,000 in the last week of March. Among those detained or sought were ex-President Cámpora, five provincial governors, Peronist cabinet members, and labor leaders, all accused of harming "the higher interests of the nation." In June 1976 the Videla junta formally charged Mrs. Perón with administrative irresponsibility and embezzlement of public funds. That same month forty-eight political, labor, and student organizations were dissolved, with prison terms set for illegal political activities.

Faced with severe economic problems, on April 2, 1976 President Videla promised to reverse the Populism of Peronism and establish a free market economy. His Minister of the Economy, José Martínez de Hoz, president of Acindar, Argentina's largest steel company, immediately set about to encourage domestic and foreign private investment, increase Argentine production and exports, decontrol the monetary exchange, and return government-held industries to the private sector. Loans of $1.3 billions from Western banks and the International Monetary Fund helped Videla to meet payments on over $8 billion of inherited foreign debts. To check inflation, de Hoz removed price controls, put severe limits on wage increases, and reduced government spending. Helped by bumper wheat crops, by March 1977 Argentina inched towards economic stability, with a billion dollar surplus in foreign trade, government reserves of $2.3 billions, and annual growth rate of 4.5 percent, and an unemployment drop to 4 or 5 percent. But popular dissatisfaction with Videla's economic measures, particularly from labor spokesmen, persisted, in view of inflation still at over 300 percent in March 1977, and with a drop in workers' real wages of 40 percent.

Although Videla announced in December 1976 that his government was close to final victory over the People's Revolutionary Army and the left-wing Peronist Montoneros, Argentina's two major guerrilla groups, political killings, abductions, and arrests remained his most pressing problems. Within a year the death toll rose to 1,500, and the number of those arrested or abducted was estimated at between five and ten thousand. Videla himself escaped three near-miss attempts upon his life by terrorists. As the scope of terrorism spread to include refugees, priests, political figures, Jews, and journalists, often by rightist "death squads" seemingly operating with government sanction, condemnation of Videla's methods swelled. Internally the criticism came from such groups as the Argentine Permanent Assembly for Human Rights and the Roman Catholic Church, and abroad from the Vatican, the United Nations High Commission, Amnesty International, and the governments of Israel, West Germany, and the United States. In February 1977, when the Carter administration reduced foreign aid to Argentina because of its abrogations of human rights, Videla refused all aid entirely. Viewing the targets of his war against subversion as Marxist class divisiveness and the spread of international communism, Videla expressed his pique with foreign critics unfamiliar with Argentina's situation. His goal, he told the nation, was to halt unauthorized terror and secure a government "monopoly of violence" against subversion.

When the national euphoria after the takeover dissipated by the end of 1976, Videla was increasingly faced with opposition to his moderate approach, principally from labor and from rightist military hard-liners wanting an extreme authoritarian regime. Instability within the three-man junta surfaced on December 1, 1976, when Admiral Massera openly disapproved of dialogues conducted with labor and political groups by Major General Roberto Viola, Army Chief of Staff and one of Videla's closest advisers. To consolidate his control of military power, Videla retired a number of hard-line generals, one of whom, General Acdel Vilas, on May 27, 1977, openly suggested the need for a rightist coup. That same month the rightists gained strength with revelations of scandal. One, linking financial corruption to ex-President Lanusse, who is viewed as a potential moderate candidate in any future election, led to his arrest. The other scandal, involving complicated investment ties between the Montoneros guerrilla group and the late David Gaivier, a Jewish Argentine financier, opened doors to rightist charges of Jewish links with leftist subversion, and resulted in the arrest of Jacob Timmerman, publisher of the prestigious liberal newspaper *La Opinión*.

By August 1977 Videla's struggle with rightist military commanders seemed temporarily to have been won, but he had widened his government's definition of dissidents to include journalists, educators, and intellectuals, "the authors," he said, "of political subversion . . . who do not use bombs, but who create far more damage because they destroy the mind." Videla steadily repudiated an "elitist corporativist regime," and, in doing so, maintained support from the populace and civilian political figures. With his tenure never completely certain, Videla remained firm in his promise for the military to give way eventually to a constitutional democracy. Still to be solved were the three main issues splitting the moderate and rightists: protection of individual rights, the role of labor organizations in the nation's economy, and the eventual place of civilians in the Argentine political process.

A tall, gaunt, hard-muscled figure in a plain uniform, ramrod-straight, his arms pressed against his sides, Videla almost always appears in photographs as a model of military severity, his tightclosed mouth, large black mustache, and prominent nose reinforcing the impression. His hatred of corruption and his religious devotion are legendary in Argentina, where the President by law must be a Roman Catholic. Reporters describe him as shy, diffident, and nervous, with his no-nonsense approach often softened by ready smiles and gracious conversation. Unlike some of the five previous military leaders who have ruled Argentina's 25,000,000 people since 1930, Videla seems content with both his colorless image and his popular nickname, "The Reluctant Dragon," a man who although a Latin American leader, has no real appetite for totalitarianism. He is married to the former Alícia Raquel Hartridge, by whom he has had six children.

References: N Y Times p10 D 20 '75 por; Washington Post A p21 Mr 25 '76 por; Britannica Book of the Year, 1976; International Who's Who, 1976-77

Vilas, Guillermo (vē′ läs gē-zher′ mō)

Aug. 17, 1952- Tennis player. Address: h. Buenos Aires, Argentina

After several disappointing years in which he repeatedly lost the big matches, Guillermo Vilas of Argentina finally shook off his runner-up image in 1977 to become a major contender for the top worldwide ranking in men's tennis. A left-handed power player with a formidable artillery of strong ground strokes, hard, accurate serves, and blinding topspin backhands, Vilas collected twenty-one championships in thirty-four tournaments that year, losing just fourteen of the 154 matches he played. His impressive string of victories included Grand Slam triumphs in the French Open and in the United States Open at Forest Hills, where he decisively defeated Jimmy Connors, the reigning champion, 2-6, 6-3, 7-6, 6-0. Despite his phenomenal record, 1977 singles rankings from the Association of Tennis Professionals and the United States Tennis Association placed him, respectively, second, behind Connors, and fourth,

Guillermo Vilas

behind Connors, Björn Borg (the only player who consistently dominates him), and Brian Gottfried. But in March 1978, when the influential *World Tennis* magazine released its rankings for 1977, Vilas topped the list.

Guillermo Vilas was born in Mar del Plata, Argentina, a seaside resort some 250 miles south of Buenos Aires, on August 17, 1952, the only son of José Roque and Mexula Vilas. A solitary youngster whose friends were, in his words, "trees, birds, [and] bicycles," he first took up tennis to meet other children. His father, a well-to-do lawyer and the president of the Club Náutico Mar del Plata, encouraged the boy to play regularly on the club's clay courts. Embarrassed by his frequent mistakes, he practised daily in his family's two-car garage, hitting balls against the doors.

When he was ten years old, Vilas began taking private lessons from Felipe Locicero, a retired tennis pro. Within one year, he was good enough to enter local junior tournaments; within two years, he was playing—and invariably winning—in Buenos Aires. During his first few months on the international junior tournament circuit, Vilas' devastating topspin backhand dazzled such promising players as Jimmy Connors, whom he defeated in the Orange Bowl junior tourney. By the late 1960's he was a regular on Argentina's Davis Cup squad. Uncertain about his future as a professional tennis player, Vilas attended law school in Buenos Aires for a year before turning professional.

His first few years on the international pro circuit, with time out for a short hitch in the Argentine army, were rather uneventful, but as he gained experience in world-class competition, Vilas steadily improved. In 1972 he was the runner-up in the Rothman Sutton Hard Courts tournament and in the Western Pro Championships in Cincinnati. The following year he reached the semifinals of the First National Louisville Classic and, in his first major victory, took the South American title, defeating the up-and-coming Swedish teenager, Björn Borg.

Vilas' career took a quantum leap forward in 1974, when in one three-month stretch, he racked up fifty-four victories in sixty matches. His phenomenal post-Wimbledon surge began in July in Gstaad, Switzerland, where he trounced Manuel Orantes in straight sets to win the Swiss Open. Later that month he took the Dutch Open, beating Barry Phillips-Moore, 6-4, 6-2, 1-6, 6-3. After losing the Washington Star International title to the relentless Harold Solomon in a strenuous match marked by sustained rallies of 100-plus strokes, he bounced back to take the top prize in the Louisville Classic from Jaime Fillol. Mixing solid ground strokes from the baseline, hard overhead smashes, and his patented backhand topspin passing shot, he downed Patricio Cornejo, Don McCormick, Jeff Borowiak, Björn Borg, and Tom Okker, all in straight sets, to reach the finals of the Canadian Open in August. One hour after he overpowered Manuel Orantes, 6-4, 6-3, 6-2, in the men's singles final, Vilas returned to the court as Orantes' partner in the doubles championship. The two erstwhile adversaries subdued a determined German duo to win for Vilas his second title of the day.

Going into the United States Open at Forest Hills, New York in September, Vilas and Borg were in a dead heat for first place in the Commercial Union Grand Prix standings. When some sportswriters suggested that he no longer lost big matches to inferior players because he had finally developed the killer instinct of a champion, Vilas replied, as quoted in *Newsday* (September 4, 1974), "I learned to finish a match. . . . You can call it killer instinct. You learn from experience. [Once] when I was beating an old man [in Argentina], I thought about him being old and not having any money and I was getting sad. Not any more. I learned that he is out there trying to do the same as me and we are equals."

A superlative clay-court player, Vilas, who was seeded ninth, was not expected to survive the third or fourth round on the fast grass courts at Forest Hills. After a nervous, five-set, first-round victory over Ferdi Taygan, Vilas settled down to defeat his next two opponents easily, but he was no match for Arthur Ashe's practised serve-and-volley game. He fell to the older pro in the fourth round, 7-6, 4-6, 4-6, 5-7. The top man in the 1974

Grand Prix points standings, Vilas competed with the seven other finishers in the Grand Prix Masters tournament in Melbourne, Australia in December. Relying on his lethal topspin backhand, he upset John Newcombe, Borg, Onny Parun, Raúl Ramirez and, in the championship, Ilie Nastase. His first-place prize money and the $100,000 bonus for the highest point total boosted his 1974 earnings for the year to $271,110, an amount exceeded only by Jimmy Connors.

Vilas spent the first five months of 1975 in Argentina, perfecting his game and relaxing, but returned to the circuit in time for the major international tournaments. After sustaining some disappointing losses in the semifinals of the Italian Open, the final of the French Open, and the quarterfinals at Wimbledon, he finally hit his stride in the Washington Star International tournament in midsummer. Playing superb defense, he lost only nineteen games in five matches on his way to the title, and in the final match he avenged his 1974 loss by soundly beating Harold Solomon. Seeded first, Vilas carried his winning streak into the United States Pro tournament, where he defeated such players as José Higueras, Arthur Ashe, and five-time U.S. Pro champion Rod Laver, his boyhood idol, before succumbing to Björn Borg in the final.

At home on the new clay-type composition courts at Forest Hills, Vilas breezed through his early-round matches to earn a berth in the semifinals. Up two sets to one and leading five games to none in the fourth set of his semifinal match, Vilas failed to cash in on five set points because his mobility was restricted by a severe groin pull, and he lost that set and the match to Manuel Orantes. Completely recovered by November, he kept Adriano Panatta away from the net with long baseline shots to win the Argentine Open title in straight sets. Once again the Grand Prix points leader, he was eliminated in the semifinals of the Masters tourney.

Because he was bothered by recurrent pain and stiffness in his left wrist, Vilas played steady but unspectacular tennis throughout 1976. Early in the year he won three World Championship Tennis tournaments before losing two successive WCT titles to his close friend and regular practice partner, Björn Borg. The two are remarkably similar players and their matches are often distinguished by incredible rallies. For example, in a final of a WCT tourney in Dallas, Texas in May 1976, which Vilas lost, 6-1, 1-6, 5-7, 1-6, they traded topspin drives, lobs, sliced backhands, and perfectly placed drop shots until Vilas angled a forehand down the line but wide on the eighty-fifth stroke. That victory was Borg's seventh over Vilas in eight matches.

Off to a slow start, Vilas failed to pick up his first 1976 Grand Prix victory until August, when he won the Canadian Open rather easily. He then advanced to the semifinals at Forest Hills by outlasting Eddie Dibbs only to be humiliated by Jimmy Connors, 4-6, 2-6, 1-6. A couple of year-end championships in South America boosted his Grand Prix points total slightly, but he failed to place higher than sixth, his lowest ranking in three years. Discouraged by his performance, Vilas asked Ion Tiriac, a one-time Romanian Davis Cup player and former coach of Ilie Nastase, Adriano Panatta, Björn Borg, and the Boston Lobsters tennis team, for help. "I was all the time Number Three, Number Four, Number Five, but I wanted to be Number One," Vilas explained to Barry Lorge in an interview for the Washington *Post* (January 6, 1976). "So in order to do that, you have to change some things and you have to pick the right guy to do it. . . . For me [Tiriac] is the right one." Tiriac, a glowering, rather sinister-looking man who claims kinship with the historical Count Dracula, signed on as Vilas' full-time coach in January 1977 for an undisclosed percentage of the player's earnings.

Under Tiriac's watchful eye, Vilas polished his clay-court game of deft drop shots, beautifully timed passing shots, topspin ground strokes from the baseline, crosscourt backhands, and well-disguised topspin lobs. For shot-making flexibility, Tiriac advised Vilas to take some topspin off his ground strokes, giving them more pace and depth, and helped him to perfect a flatter, faster first serve. Turning to tactics, Tiriac urged his pupil to adopt a more aggressive game by following his attacking shots into the forecourt. To increase Vilas' speed and stamina, he set up a training regimen of diet and exercise, so that within a few months Vilas was easily the fittest player on the circuit. Tiriac also took over the management of Vilas' business affairs, which the player had heretofore handled with casual neglect.

Before embarking on a five-month round of international tournaments, Vilas helped his country's Davis Cup team to defeat the United States in the 1977 Cup quarterfinals in Buenos Aires. He trounced Brian Gottfried, who had won decisively in their last two meetings, 6-4, 6-0, 6-2 and, while almost hysterical fans rhythmically chanted his name, handily defeated Dick Stockton, 5-7, 6-2, 6-2, 6-2. His victory over Stockton gave the Argentine squad an insurmountable three to one lead in the best-of-five series. Although admittedly "tight," Vilas played with supreme confidence in the French Open, dropping only one set in the first seven matches. Never losing service in the final, he blitzed Gottfried, 6-0, 6-3, 6-0, to win the first Grand Slam title of his career.

Perhaps because he was exhausted by his efforts in France, Vilas fell into a temporary slump. He lost a first-round match in the John Player grass tournament in Nottingham, England to Tim Gullikson, 2-6, 2-6, and a third-round meeting at Wimbledon to Billy Martin. Returning to his French Open form in July, Vilas took first-place honors in the Washington Star International tournament and, coming from behind to defeat Eddie Dibbs, 1-6, 6-0, 6-1, won his third Louisville Classic title in four years. After five consecutive Grand Prix championships, he sat out the Canadian Open.

As a warm-up to the 1977 Forest Hills contest, Vilas entered the Lionel Tennis Week round-robin in Harrison, New York. In the final of that contest he demolished the mercurial Ilie Nastase, 6-2, 6-0, in just fifty-five minutes. It was his thirty-eighth win in a row. Despite his remarkable clay-court streak, the longest by a male player in the history of the game, Vilas was seeded fourth at Forest Hills, behind Connors, Borg, who eventually defaulted due to an injury, and Gottfried. Relying on looping crosscourts off the forehand and blistering down-the-line backhands, he defeated Manuel Santana, Gene Mayer, Victor Amaya, José Higueras, Ray Moore, and Harold Solomon, all in straight sets, to earn the right to oppose Connors in the final. He had dropped only twenty-six of 100 games in the tournament for a phenomenal .808 average and was openly hungry for the title. "It's the same as a guy who never eats," he said, as quoted in the New York *Times* (September 8, 1977). "One day, he eats bread. The next day, he wants a sandwich. The next day, he wants a steak. And the next day, he wants to go to the palace."

After losing the first set of the final to Connors, 2-6, Vilas deftly changed the pace of his backhands, mixing slices with topspin drives, switched to a hard, flat first serve, and began to attack the net. The gamble paid off as he won the second set rather easily, 6-3. Troubled by the swirling winds, and trailing 1-4 in the third set, he shifted to a lower-bouncing undercut backhand and forced a tiebreaker, which he won, seven points to four. As the pro-Vilas crowd cheered wildly, he relentlessly attacked Connors' most vulnerable spot by repeatedly hitting low balls to his forehand, causing the American to commit one error after another. Down 0-5, 0-40 in the fourth set, Connors gamely saved three match points before losing on a late call of a wide forehand. At a press conference after his victory, an elated Vilas told sportswriters, "This tournament doesn't count if you only reach the semifinals or the finals. You have to win for it to count. I came up here to win it and I won it. . . . I was Number three or Number Four, but I wanted to be Number One and now I think I am."

In the last six months of 1977 a newly confident Vilas won eighty-three out of eighty-four matches and twelve out of thirteen tournaments. His only loss came on an injury default to Ilie Nastase in a French tournament in the late fall. The leader in the annual Grand Prix bonus pool for the third time and winner of the $300,000 top prize, Vilas easily qualified for the Colgate Grand Masters round-robin tournament at Madison Square Garden in New York City in January 1978. After winning a surprisingly easy victory over Orantes, 6-4, 6-1, Vilas drew Jimmy Connors in the second round. Their sensational shot-making, with Connors attacking Vilas' backhand and Vilas hammering at Connors' erratic forehand, dazzled a record tennis crowd for more than three hours. The pair split the first two sets. In the third and deciding set, Vilas won eleven of thirteen points for a 4-1 lead, but Connors rallied to play off a match point at 3-5. At 5-5, 0-30, Vilas took charge again with a spectacular backhand passing shot. Visibly tiring and suffering from a pulled tendon in his left ankle, he hung on to win, 7-5.

Assured a slot in the semifinals, Vilas defaulted his third round-robin match to rest his injured ankle. His opponent in the semifinals was Björn Borg, who had beaten him eleven times in fifteen meetings. Favoring his left foot, Vilas played more tentatively than usual and rarely attacked the net. Down two service breaks and 0-3, he admittedly "lost a little concentration" as Borg, showing few signs of the pharyngitis that had sidelined him earlier in the week, took point after point. Vilas never led in the second set and lost the match, 3-6, 3-6. He defaulted his third-place match to Brian Gottfried. A few days later, after an orthopedic specialist diagnosed a severe inflammation of the ligament in his left ankle, Vilas withdrew from a $250,000 tournament in Boca West, Florida, in which he was to have played Connors, Borg, and Vitas Gerulaitas. He rejoined the circuit in March.

Invariably described as "bull-like," Guillermo Vilas, who stands five feet eleven inches tall and weights 165 pounds, has the square, muscular body of a halfback. His handsome, strong-featured face, arresting green eyes, and shoulder-length, curly brown hair, held back by a headband on the court, have attracted a sizeable contingent of tennis groupies. An unworldly young man, he takes little interest in the trappings of the jet-setting tennis superstar. For tax purposes he maintains an official residence in Monte Carlo, but he prefers his four-bedroom flat in Buenos Aires, where he relaxes between tournaments by swimming, playing soccer, dancing, and listening to rock and jazz. To keep fit on vacations, he does 500 pushups daily and sticks to a simple diet of fruits and vegetables.

The sensitive and introspective Vilas reads ravenously, choosing nonfiction over fiction.

"My life is like fiction," he told Barry Lorge. "I am all the time traveling, staying a few days and leaving, meeting different people. Sometimes I eat breakfast in America, fly and have dinner on a different continent. To most people, this is not real. When I read, I like things that people really observe and feel." Although he is shy and dislikes giving personal interviews, he eagerly discusses religion, politics, literature, and philosophy with reporters. In addition to his native tongue, he speaks fluent English and several Romance languages. (He and Tiriac communicate in Italian.) Vilas is currently completing work on a "heavy" psychological screenplay, tentatively titled "The Deciding Years," and on a second volume of poetry. His first book of verse, *Ciento Veinticinco (125)*, a collection of spare, haiku-like poems, sold out its first two printings of 20,000 copies shortly after its publication in 1975. He has also written a book about tennis. "There is so much more to life than hitting a tennis ball," he said in a recent interview. "But right now I am doing the right thing at the right time."

References: Esquire 89:39+ My 9 '78 pors; N Y Times p46 S 12 '77 por; Newsweek 84: 46 D 30 '74 por; People 9:72+ Ja 30 '78 pors; Seventeen 34:28+ D '75 por; Sport 69:98+ S '76 por; Sports Illus 41:93+ S 9 '74 por, 48:116+ My 29 '78 por; Washington Post D p1 Ag 26 '75 pors

---

Vreeland, Diana (Dalziel)

1903?- Fashion journalist; museum consultant.
Address: b. Metropolitan Museum of Art, 1000 Fifth Ave., New York City, N.Y. 10028
h. 550 Park Ave., New York City, N.Y. 10021

One of the "very few great original women" in America, according to Truman Capote, Diana Vreeland has reigned as the undisputed doyenne and high priestess of American fashion since the 1940's, when she was fashion editor of *Harper's Bazaar*. Later, during the 1960's, she moved to *Vogue* as editor in chief and turned that bastion of *haute couture* into a lively chronicle of the decade's culture, society, and chic. Mrs. Vreeland's influence over fashion has extended far beyond that of a reporter. With her own extraordinary sense of style and penchant for fashion dicta, she has exercised a considerable influence on the development of the fashion industry, especially in the United States. In the moneyed and creative world in which she has lived and worked—that of the so-called "Beautiful People," one of the many terms she herself coined—Diana Vreeland has become something of a living legend. Her startling appearance, dramatic manner, outrageous statements, and love of the exaggerated and idiosyncratic have been envied, admired, despised, and imitated, but seldom duplicated. Now in her seventies, Mrs. Vreeland has, since leaving *Vogue* in 1971, begun a new and highly successful career as special consultant to the Costume Institute of the Metropolitan Museum of Art in New York, where she has mounted seven retrospective fashion shows.

The first daughter of Frederick Young Dalziel, a personable Scotsman who worked as a stockbroker, and his beautiful American wife Emily Key (Hoffman) Dalziel, Diana Dalziel was born in Paris around the turn of the century, probably in 1903. Mrs. Vreeland has always declined to pinpoint her birthdate because, as she says, "age is terribly boring and . . . so American I can't get on with it." Mrs. Vreeland had one younger sister, Alexandra. "We were never wealthy, but of course life then was so different," Mrs. Vreeland recalled for Felicia Warburg Roosevelt in *Doers and Dowagers* (1975). "Mother and Father always had a car and chauffeur, and we went to Venice or Deauville in the summer or wherever everybody else went. Our parents spent their days having a good time. They never contributed a bloody thing, and they and all their friends lived the life of Riley." In the glittering Paris of the privileged during the early years of the century, the Dalziels conducted an artistic salon to which came Diaghilev, Nijinsky, Ida Rubinstein, Chaliapin, Isadora Duncan, and Irene and Vernon Castle, who performed their famous Castle Walk while Diana and her sister looked on in delight from the sidelines.

But the most impressive sight of her childhood, Diana Vreeland told Lally Weymouth of *Rolling Stone* (August 11, 1977), was the coronation of George V. "Now please visualize: there was the czar of all the Russias —including *all* the Russias," Mrs. Vreeland told the *Rolling Stone* writer in a speech typical of her italicized way of expressing things. "All the different sorts of horses. The *équipage* of the German states. The kaiser and all his *équipage.* Don't forget the liveries. The animals. Then, don't forget that King George was also emperor of India. You see —the elephants, the rajah, the maharajahs . . . the jewels. The servants. The *elephants.* They came for days through the streets of London. There was a king of the Belgians. There was a king of all those little German states. . . . The whole bit. . . . Then there were the Turks. There were the Japanese. There were the Chinese. My dear, say it. *We saw it.* Until the night was black. Then we were put to bed—get up the next morning. Early, early, early."

In 1914 the Dalziels came to the United States to escape World War I, and they settled in New York City on 79th Street off Park Avenue. Despite the ample opportunities that they gave their children to absorb the culture and society of their special world, the Dalziels seemed little concerned for the formal education of their daughters. In Europe, Diana apparently received no schooling; in the United States she received a few months here and there at such prestigious private schools as Brearley in Manhattan. She did, however, attend ballet class three times a week with the Russian ballet choreographer Michel Fokine, and during several summers in Wyoming she learned to ride horses from no less an authority than Colonel William ("Buffalo Bill") Cody.

Diana Dalziel made her formal debut at a party in 1922, and at that period in her life spent much of her time attending parties and dancing, often at such famed Harlem nightspots as the Cotton Club. While vacationing in Saratoga she met a handsome young Yale graduate named Thomas Reed Vreeland, and on March 1, 1924 they were married. During the first years of their marriage, until the end of 1928, they lived in Albany, New York, where Vreeland was undergoing training in a bank. Then, in January 1929 they moved to London, where he took a job with Guaranty Trust.

Living in London as a young society matron, Diana Vreeland found herself in much the same milieu that she had enjoyed as a child in Paris, except that now she was old enough to take an active part in the fashionable life that she had once only observed. It was for her a period of self-education in which she read, visited museums, traveled, and conversed with members of the smart set, including Evelyn Waugh, Christian Bérard, the artist and set designer, and Cole Porter. She continued her interest in dancing by becoming a member of the Tiller Girls, a chorus line used by Ziegfeld. And, of course, each season she traveled to Paris to shop at the great houses of couture.

In 1936 Mrs. Vreeland's husband obtained a position in New York City, and the couple, with their two children, moved back to the United States. Soon realizing that the higher cost of living on that side of the Atlantic would preclude living in the luxurious manner to which she had become accustomed in Europe, Mrs. Vreeland decided that she must supplement her husband's income. At first she worked on a free-lance basis for *Harper's Bazaar,* writing her famous "Why don't you. . . ?" column, which first appeared in the magazine in July 1936. An offbeat advice column combining snob appeal and luxurious fantasy, it asked its readers why they did not do such things as "turn your old ermine coat into a bathrobe," "remember that nothing is smarter with your shooting tweeds than linen gaiters," and "wash your blond child's hair in dead champagne, as they do in France." Despite, or more probably because of, the grim deprivation of the Depression, the column scored a great hit with readers, and it also inspired a great deal of clever satire from humorist S. J. Perelman, playwrights George S. Kaufman and Moss Hart, and others. Mrs. Vreeland continued writing the column for about two years, until the start of World War II made her sense that the time for frivolity had passed. Around that time she went to work for *Harper's Bazaar* on a full-time basis, and in July 1939 her name went on the masthead as fashion editor.

Although at *Harper's Bazaar* Diana Vreeland had to learn the craft of journalism and the art of putting a magazine together, she was already well schooled in fashion and high society. As she told Felicia Warburg Roosevelt, "Suddenly I found that my *whole background was my future.*" Soon she became part of a triumvirate—the other members were editor in chief Carmel Snow and art director Alexey Brodovitch—who ran *Harper's Bazaar.*

Because of her uncanny ability to spot new style trends as well as her way of creating fashion through her own definite tastes and dictates, Mrs. Vreeland became, over the years, the most respected fashion editor in the business. In March 1962 she made news when she left *Harper's Bazaar* to join the staff of its archrival *Vogue,* where she served a brief stint as associate editor and then, on the retirement of editor in chief Jessica Davis, took over the top post on January 1, 1963.

At *Vogue* Mrs. Vreeland soon began recording, and at the same time shaping, the look of what she called the 1960's "youthquake." She featured pop culture figures like Mick Jagger and Jacqueline Kennedy, discovered or promoted such youthful and often unconventionally beautiful models as Marisa Berenson, Penelope Tree, "Baby Jane" Holzer, Verushka, and Twiggy, and invented a whole galaxy of stylish, often young pacesetters whom she called the Beautiful People. Those Beautiful People, or BP's, included such disparate figures as the Carter Burdens of New York City, Princess Paola of Belgium, and Principessa Luciana Pignatelli of Italy. Among the important fashions that she touted were boots, costume jewelry, pants for women, see-through tops, tights, wigs, the "Swinging London" fashion, and the "ethnic," or peasant, look.

Perhaps the most striking change that Mrs. Vreeland brought to *Vogue* was the way in which she transformed it into a mirror image of what Felicia Warburg Roosevelt called the "Vreeland Mystique." "Her flair, her artistry for the bizarre, follows her like the scent of perfume," Mrs. Roosevelt wrote. "Her offbeat tastes are watched, copied and chronicled by everyone in the fashion world." With breathtaking authority Mrs. Vreeland decreed what was fashionable in the pages of her magazine, often presenting her readers with grotesquely exaggerated looks and outfits totally unwearable outside the pages of *Vogue,* and leaving it up to the reader to translate the look into a livable version. Like her own conversation, the pages of *Vogue* became peppered with her made-up words like "youthquake" as well as surrealistic aphorisms like "pink is the navy blue of India" or "the bikini is only the most important invention since the atom bomb."

The heady days of the Vreeland *Vogue* drew to a close, however, with the recession of the early 1970's, when a decline in advertising revenues led the Condé Nast Corporation, its publisher, to decide that the time had come for a new editor. Consequently Mrs. Vreeland was fired in May 1971 and replaced by her longtime assistant, Grace Mirabella. After a four-month vacation in Europe, Diana Vreeland returned to New York, where she confounded her friends, who expected her to slip unobtrusively into retirement, by soon accepting an assignment as special consultant to the Costume Institute of the Metropolitan Museum of Art. While working for the museum, she has remained on the *Vogue* masthead as consulting editor.

Soon after the death of the Spanish-born Paris couturier Balenciaga in 1972, Mrs. Vreeland began scouring Europe and later the United States for costumes by the designer who dominated *haute couture* through the 1950's and on into the 1960's. The result was her first Metropolitan show, "The World of Balenciaga" which drew some 200,000 viewers during its two-month run in the spring of 1973. For her next show, "The Tens, the Twenties, the Thirties" Mrs. Vreeland assembled luxurious Paris originals designed between 1909 and 1939. That show, which ran from December 1973 through September 1974, drew an even bigger crowd, numbering almost 400,000 persons.

For her third Metropolitan show, "Romantic and Glamorous Hollywood Design," Diana Vreeland collected over a hundred costumes from private collections, individual collectors, film studios, and designers. Although ensembles were shown from all motion picture eras, the emphasis was on the 1930's, 1940's, and, 1950's, when Hollywood films displayed the most glamour, romance, and flamboyance. Unprecedented in its success, the Hollywood costume show was twice extended so that it ran for about a year, beginning in November 1974, and drew some 800,000 visitors.

Diana Vreeland's contribution to the 1976 Bicentennial year was "American Women of Style," for which she chose costumes worn by Consuelo Vanderbilt, Isadora Duncan, Mrs. Charles Dana Gibson, Josephine Baker, Rita de Acosta Lydig, and Irene Castle, among others. A few months later, in December 1976, Mrs. Vreeland opened perhaps her most spectacular show to date, "The Glory of Russian Costume." Part of a cultural exchange program with the Soviet Union, the Russian show featured over a hundred costumes seen for the first time outside the Soviet Union. To many observers the most sumptuous outfits in the show were the brightly colored and richly embroidered peasant costumes. Mrs. Vreeland's sixth show, titled "Vanity Fair: Treasure Trove of the Costume Institute", opened in December 1977 and featured costumes drawn from the 19,000 items that make the Metropolitan Costume Institute the world's largest and most impressive collection of its kind. Costumes for dancers and musicians were exhibited in her seventh show, entitled "Diaghilev: Costumes and Designs of the Ballets Russes," which opened at the Metropolitan Museum of Art in November 1978.

A striking, original-looking woman, Diana Vreeland has never been called a beauty, although she has inspired any number of fanciful descriptions. Cecil Beaton called her "an authoritative crane" and Truman Capote "some extraordinary parrot—a wild thing that's flung itself out of the jungle." Her walk has been compared to a "camel's gait," and her face has been likened to "a cigar store Indian" or "a cross between a silent-screen vamp and Lillian Hellman." Although it is now over a decade old, the description by Eleanor Perenyi in *Show* (March 1964) perhaps still fits Mrs. Vreeland best: "With her black hair, as smooth as if it were polished, her bony, expressive countenance in which the lower lip, often curled voluptuously around a cigarette holder, seems the central point and a body so thin it might be a finely articulated rack on which to hang what . . . are the characteristic 'little nothing' clothes of the mid-century, she might be a rare variety of ruminant. Her hands are beautiful, real instruments of touch that show her respect for fine things. Her voice is another kind of instrument: Anglo-American in accent, it can range from a susurrant murmur suitable to aphorisms . . . to an articulate roar of disapprobation."

Widowed since 1966, Mrs. Vreeland has two married sons, Thomas Reed Vreeland Jr., an architect, and Frederick D. Vreeland, who is in the diplomatic service, and tour grandchildren. Since 1956 she has made her home in a two-bedroom Park Avenue apartment that is decorated in her characteristically flamboyant style. The living room is a mass of brilliant reds, with red rug, red doors, and red paisley-covered couch, chair, and walls. Everywhere are artfully arranged memorabilia and vases of fresh flowers. Her offices at *Harper's Bazaar*, *Vogue*, and the Metropolitan have also been decorated in red. Like everything else about her, Mrs. Vreeland's working habits are legendary. Indisputedly a hard worker, she nevertheless has always insisted on her own idiosyncratic schedule, which includes working at her apartment, often in the bathroom, in the mornings and not showing up at the office until noon. As in former periods of her life, Mrs. Vreeland's social circle includes a number of creative and trend-setting people, including Andy Warhol, Warren Beatty, and Jack Nicholson. The former fashion editor's awards have included the French Légion d'Honneur and the 1963 New York Fashion Designers award. Diana Vreeland became a naturalized citizen of the United States in 1925.

References: N Y Times p30 Mr 28 '62 por; Rolling Stone p38+ Ag 11 '77 pors; Show 3:68+ Mr '64; Roosevelt, Felicia Warburg. Doers and Dowagers (1975); Who's Who in America, 1976-77

Webster, William H(edgcock)

Mar. 6, 1924- United States government official. Address: b. Federal Bureau of Investigation, 9th St. and Pennsylvania Ave., Washington, D.C. 20535; h. 49 Godwin Lane, St. Louis, Mo. 63124

Judge William H. Webster, who took office as director of the Federal Bureau of Investigation on February 23, 1978, is the bureau's third permanent chief—after J. Edgar Hoover and Clarence M. Kelley. A Missouri Republican and a distinguished veteran of the federal bench, Webster had been recommended to President Jimmy Carter by Attorney General Griffin B. Bell after the previous nominee, Judge Frank M. Johnson Jr., withdrew from consideration because of ill health. Webster took office at a time when the Attorney General was contemplating the prosecution of several former high-ranking FBI officials for violating the rights of citizens, and he was charged with the task of restoring public confidence in the Justice Department's main investigative body. Former Republican Congressman Thomas B. Curtis of Missouri has compared Webster's appointment as FBI chief with that of Judge Kenesaw Mountain Landis as baseball commissioner in 1920. "What they are trying to do reminds me of what baseball did after the 'Black Sox' scandal," he observed. "They are bringing in a judge to try and give the institution back its prestige."

William Hedgcock Webster, the son of Thomas M. and Katherine (Hedgcock) Webster, was born in St. Louis, Missouri on

March 6, 1924 and spent his boyhood in Webster Groves, a St. Louis suburb. His father owned farmland, including a cattle ranch, and operated several small businesses. After graduating from Webster Groves High School, Webster went to Amherst College on a scholarship. He interrupted his undergraduate studies to enroll at the midshipman school at Columbia University and spent the years from 1943 to 1946 in the United States Naval Reserve. Released from active duty with the rank of lieutenant, junior grade, he returned to Amherst and graduated with a B.A. degree in 1947.

Having decided on a career in the legal profession, Webster then studied at Washington University Law School in St. Louis, where he obtained his law degree in 1949. That same year he was admitted to the Missouri bar and joined a St. Louis law firm, now known as Armstrong, Teasdale, Kramer, and Vaughan. But he hardly had time to become established before the outbreak of the Korean war in 1950 led to his recall to active duty in the Naval Reserve. As a member of the legal staff he was assigned to defend a seaman accused of theft. Learning that his client had not been advised of his right to counsel before interrogation, Webster instructed the man to keep silent. Although his immediate superiors complained that his interference stymied their efforts to obtain a confession, he received a commendation from fleet headquarters, and his procedure became part of the Uniform Code of Military Justice. Webster has recalled that as a result of that experience he "really became interested in the criminal justice process."

After his discharge as a lieutenant, senior grade, in 1952, Webster returned to the St. Louis law firm, in which he became a partner four years later. Meanwhile he had become active in politics, and in 1958 he served as president of the Missouri Association of Republicans. In 1960 he was appointed United States Attorney for the Eastern District of Missouri by President Dwight D. Eisenhower but resigned after the inauguration of President John F. Kennedy in early 1961. Resuming his law partnership, Webster handled a number of important cases in the 1960's, including the defense of the Mobil Oil Corporation against federal charges that it had fixed prices and the legal preparations for the establishment of MasterCharge as a nationwide credit system. From 1964 to 1969 he served on the Missouri board of law examiners.

In 1971 President Richard M. Nixon appointed Webster judge of the United States District Court for Eastern Missouri. Student demonstrations at Washington University helped him to decide to accept the post, although its $40,000-a-year salary was less than half of what he had been earning in private practice. "A lot of people were saying then that the system didn't work," he has recalled. "I believe it does work, and I saw service on the bench as a way of helping to keep it working." During his tenure as district court judge, Webster compiled a middle-of-the-road record that has been described as better than average by both liberals and conservatives. According to a survey published in the St. Louis *Post-Dispatch* (January 19, 1978), none of the forty-four decisions handed down by him from that bench was reversed by a court of appeals. Among the landmark actions that Webster took as district judge was the issuance of an injunction in 1973, ordering drastic reforms of conditions at the St. Louis city jail.

Named by President Nixon to the United States Court of Appeals for the Eighth Circuit (which serves Arkansas, Iowa, Minnesota, Missouri, North Dakota, and South Dakota), Webster was confirmed in that post by the United States Senate in July 1973. During his four and one-half years on the appeals court, he acquired a reputation as a legal craftsman whose written opinions tended to be dispassionate recitations of the facts and the law. He appeared reluctant to overturn lower-court rulings and jury verdicts, and he rarely disagreed with his colleagues on the three-judge panels, filing dissents in only sixteen out of the more than six hundred cases that he heard.

In criminal cases, Webster was fairly consistent in his support of the prosecution. He affirmed more than 80 percent of the criminal convictions brought before him and generally refused to reverse decisions on the basis of procedural violations that he deemed of minor importance. In one dissenting opinion he argued that a man convicted on "overwhelming" evidence of kidnaping, raping, and murdering a ten-year-old girl did not merit a new trial despite the failure of the authorities to inform him of his rights.

Webster's record on cases involving civil rights escapes easy classification. In one case, for example, he ruled that a black woman was entitled to a trial in her class action suit charging the Pillsbury Company with race and sex discrimination, while in another he agreed with an employer's contention that a black truckdriver with an accident record had been discharged as a result of incompetence rather than prejudice. In 1974 he refused to grant members of the militant American Indian Movement, prosecuted for their occupation of Wounded Knee, South Dakota, a preliminary injunction against the FBI for allegedly violating their rights, and later he dissented from the reversal of conspiracy convictions of four of the Indian demonstrators.

Webster established an important precedent by allowing prosecutors to use mail fraud laws against politicians who deprived the public of such intangible rights as an honest count of votes. On another occasion he reversed a district court ruling that upheld the University of Missouri's refusal to recognize a campus organization for homosexual students. "I have no doubt that the ancient halls of higher learning . . . will survive even the most offensive verbal assaults upon traditional moral values," he said. "Solutions to tough problems are not found in the repression of ideas."

Frank Ruppert, a lawyer for the American Civil Liberties Union, once described Judge Webster as "a man who calls them as he sees them" and who "acts impartially and in regard to the law." But another civil rights lawyer concluded after appearing before him that Webster "doesn't take any chances in favor of the underdog." Disdainful of political labels, the judge has said with some satisfaction: "The liberals who like me think I'm liberal; the conservatives who like me say I'm conservative." In an interview quoted in the St. Louis *Post-Dispatch* (January 19, 1978), Webster remarked: "I think of myself as operating from a position of restraint but being ready to take any judicial actions necessary to achieve the ends of justice. I want to try to avoid overkill." Webster's reputation for evenhanded justice and judicial restraint persuaded a panel of the American Bar Association in 1975 to include him on its list of eleven preferred choices for the vacancy on the United States Supreme Court created by the retirement of Associate Justice William O. Douglas. Webster was one of six finalists considered by the White House, but President Gerald R. Ford eventually selected John Paul Stevens of Chicago.

When Attorney General Griffin B. Bell—relying on his "Bell system" of recruiting, which depends on the advice of trusted friends rather than on a formal search committee—first sounded him out as a possible candidate for the post of FBI director at a conference in London during the summer of 1977, Webster, secure in his lifetime tenure on the Court of Appeals, expressed little interest. But when Bell approached him again following the withdrawal of Judge Frank M. Johnson as a candidate in November 1977, Webster was more receptive. At a forty-minute meeting with President Carter in mid-January 1978, he received assurances that, if selected as FBI director, he would have independence in making appointments in the bureau and in conducting professional investigations, and that he would be guaranteed direct access to the Attorney General.

After the choice had narrowed down to William H. Webster and Federal District Judge Frank J. McGarr of Chicago, Attorney General Bell announced Webster's nomination as FBI chief on January 19, 1978. Enumerating his qualifications, Bell observed: "He reasons well. He's oriented to facts . . . and I'm satisfied that he is a person who's lived a judicial life of such rectitude that the Senate will not find anything in his opinions which will disqualify him." Accepting the nomination, Webster promised "to maintain the high standards and traditions of the FBI" and asserted that he looked on the assignment as a "great adventure." Asked why he was willing to forfeit the security of the bench, Webster responded: "I am an old Navy man. . . . I heard a bosun's pipe and somebody saying 'Now hear this.' And I'm glad to do it."

Among the critics of the nomination was Kenneth E. Tilsen, the defense attorney in the Wounded Knee cases, who charged that Webster had been "unwilling to curb FBI abuses," that he had "a restricted view of the Federal Civil Rights Acts," and that he failed "to recognize basic First Amendment freedoms." The St. Louis civil rights organization ACTION accused Webster of "racism, sexism, and elitism" because of his memberships in the Noonday luncheon club, the Mysterious Order of the Veiled Prophet, the University Club, and the St. Louis Country Club, none of which included members of racial minorities in their ranks.

Webster's supporters outnumbered his critics. "I have a high regard for his intellectual qualities," said the United States Solicitor General Wade McCree, who originally recommended him to Bell. "He's a real straight arrow when it comes to integrity." Republican Senator John C. Danforth of Missouri called him "decent and fair, . . . an excellent lawyer and a first-rate human being." Margaret Bush Wilson, chairman of the board of directors of the National Association for the Advancement of Colored People, commended Webster for his "very real sense of human rights, which includes civil rights," and Theodore McMillian, the first black judge on Missouri's Court of Appeals, thought that he would be "sympathetic and sensitive to black concerns."

Webster persuasively stated his case at the confirmation hearings on his nomination, conducted by the Senate Judiciary Committee on January 29 and 30. He assured the Senators that he adhered 100 percent to the dictum that the FBI "is not above the law" and affirmed his belief that the bureau had no right "to wage war on private citizens to discredit them." In the event that the President or Attorney General asked him to do something that he considered illegal, he would try to persuade them to change their minds, seek help from the Congressional committee that oversees the bureau, or resign. "The use of the FBI for political purposes is to be abhorred," he said. "I don't know to what extent it has been used that way in the past, but it won't be in the future." Questioned by Senator Edward M. Kennedy of Massachusetts about his club affiliations, Webster responded: "I honestly believe that I am as color-blind as any man in this room." He declared that he would quit any club that actively practised discrimination or impeded him in executing his duties. During the hearings he revealed that he had assets of $898,296 and liabilities of $17,489 and promised to have his securities placed in a blind trust. Webster's appointment for a ten-year term as FBI director was confirmed on February 9, 1978 by a voice vote of the Senate.

On February 23, 1978 Webster took his oath of office as director of the Federal Bureau of Investigation and received his FBI badge from the Attorney General in a ceremony at the J. Edgar Hoover FBI Building in Washington, D.C. After paying tribute to his predecessor, Clarence M. Kelley, who retired on the same date, Webster promised to fulfill his duties "with due regard for the rights of all our citizens" and to maintain "the highest standards of professional law enforcement." In his $57,500-a-year post as director of the Justice Department's principal investigative arm, Webster heads a staff of some 19,000 employees, including 8,400 special agents, operating on an annual budget of about $500,000,000. During recent years the image of the FBI had become tarnished by the late J. Edgar Hoover's personal vendettas against black civil rights leaders, by the use of illegal surveillance procedures against political dissenters, and by the efforts of acting director L. Patrick Gray 3d, in 1973, to impede the Watergate investigations under pressure from the Nixon administration.

While continuing Kelley's reform efforts, aimed at modernizing the FBI's investigative facilities, enhancing its public image, and improving staff morale, Webster also devoted himself to reassessing the bureau's priorities. In response to the kidnapping of former Italian Prime Minister Aldo Moro by guerrillas in Rome, he ordered the FBI Academy in Quantico, Virginia to intensify its anti-terrorist program. "When we have epidemics of this kind around the world," he warned, "they are likely to spread to the United States." Late in March 1978 Webster, in compliance with a new law, became the first FBI director to appear before the House Judiciary Committee to explain his agency's appropriations request. He told the Congressmen that the bureau, partly as a result of budget cuts, would no longer trace military deserters, but that it would step up its efforts against "organized and white collar crime, including public corruption." Webster also assured them that the FBI would try to hire more women and members of the black and Hispanic minorities as special agents.

Considerable discontent was generated within FBI ranks by the Justice Department's indictments, in April 1978, of Gray and two other former top FBI officials for allegedly having used illegal methods in tracking down members of the radical Weather Underground, and by the bureau's announced plans to discipline sixty-eight agents accused of various infractions involving citizens' rights. A number of veteran agents were also critical of Webster's appointment, to the second-ranking FBI post, of James B. Adams, whom they considered, according to *Time* (May 1, 1978), "a headquarters hatchet man for the late J. Edgar Hoover." Another problem facing Webster has been public criticism of the FBI practice of using informers, which he considers "the most effective tool in law enforcement today." In a speech before the American Newspaper Publishers Association in Atlanta in May 1978, Webster revealed for the first time the number of informers currently working for the FBI. He assured his audience that the bureau had abandoned its practice of spying on "First Amendment organizations" engaged in dissent and was now primarily concerned with combating crime and terrorism, and he expressed the hope that no restrictions would be placed on the informer system in the new FBI charter currently drafted by Congress.

Webster served as a director of the Visiting Nurse Association from 1961 to 1968 and of the Big Brothers of America in 1966. Active in the Big Brother Organization of St. Louis since 1958, he was its president in 1965-66 and is now its honorary life president. A past chairman of the American Bar Association's corporation, banking, and business law section, Webster also belongs to the Federal, Missouri, and St. Louis bar associations and is a fellow of the American Bar Federation. While on the federal bench he was chairman of the judicial conference advisory committee on criminal rules and served on the ad hoc committee on habeas corpus and the committee on court administration. He is a member of the American Law Institute, Phi Delta Phi, the Order of the Coif, and the Washington University board of trustees, and he has served as president of the Washington University alumni and law alumni associations. In 1972 he was awarded a Washington University alumni citation, and in 1977 he received the Distinguished Alumnus Award of Washington University Law School. Amherst College conferred an honorary LL.D. degree on him in 1975.

William H. Webster was married to Drusilla Lane on May 5, 1950. Their children are Drusilla Lane (Mrs. William K. Busch), William Hedgcock, and Katherine Hagee. The family has a nine-room colonial style home in the St. Louis suburb of Ladue, as well as a 265-acre cattle farm in Callaway County, Missouri that once belonged to Webster's parents. Trim and youthful, Webster is five feet ten and one half inches tall, has brown hair flecked with gray, and dresses conservatively. A Christian Scientist, he neither smokes nor drinks. Acquaintances describe him as a polite, disciplined, and soft-spoken man who is devoted to his family. One long-time friend has said of him: "His ambition is to do something great for his country. Yet he has a sense of humility and is very modest about his achievements." Webster's favorite leisure activities include tennis, amateur photography, horseback riding, and relaxing on the family ranch.

References: N Y Times B p6 F 6 '78 por; St. Louis Post-Dispatch A p1+ Ja 19 '78 por; Time 111:22 Ja 30 '78 por; Who's Who in America, 1978-79

Weissenberg, Alexis (Sigismund) (vīs′ən-berg)

July 26, 1929- Pianist. Address: c/o Columbia Artists Management, 165 W. 57th St., New York City, N.Y. 10019

The brilliant Bulgarian-born French pianist Alexis Weissenberg has been as liberated in his life and career as in his dynamic, idiosyntratic performances. Weissenberg, who began his career as a child prodigy, retreated into a decade-long sabbatical in 1957 because he felt that "facility" had become his "enemy" and he did not want "to end up at the age of fifty still a 'promising' pianist." His absence from the concert and recital stage enabled him to rethink his style, his repertoire, and his goals and to return to public performance strengthened in his openness to change in his own interpretations of works and in his anti-traditionalism in general. "I am against tradition," he has said. "I am of this century and when I play works from the last century I play for audiences conditioned by today's noise, today's flying machines, and today's pollution."

The virtuoso, who has played with most of the great orchestras of the world and whose eclectic repertoire ranges from Bach to Bartók and from Brahms to Stravinsky, is perhaps best known for his solo performances with the Berlin Philharmonic under Herbert von Karajan and for his more than thirty LP's, including works by Rachmaninoff, Beethoven, and Chopin, on the Angel, RCA Victor, and Connoisseur labels. Generally described by critics as a virile romanticist, he has been credited with taking Chopin "out of the salon" and making him "not old-maidish but masculine."

Alexis Sigismund Weissenberg was born on July 26, 1929, in Sophia, Bulgaria, the only child of upper-class Jewish parents, Paul and Lillian Piha Weissenberg, who were later divorced. His mother, herself a pianist, often entertained Russian musicians and other visiting artists from abroad in the Weissenberg home, took her son to concerts regularly, and enrolled him in piano lessons when he was three. Sound obsessed him from his earliest years, Weissenberg told Robert Jacobson in an interview for an article published in a Lincoln Center Philharmonic Hall program (February 1972). "I sang a lot as a child, referring to melodic comparisons in my own mind. Everything was sound, and it had all sorts of effects on me: it made me sad or happy or nervous or impatient or comfortable. And today, . . . sound is part of my inner thinking."

From the beginning, Weissenberg told Jacobson, he was drawn to the Russian pianists. "This kind of pianism became a goal, but it also sounded logical to me, not because it is an effective kind of playing but because I was emotionally much closer to it. There is nothing you can do about temperament. If you are a Slav, you remain a Slav. And you are much more logically connected (in the best sense of the word) with Chopin, Rachmaninoff, Tchaikovsky, and Prokofiev because of your inner system of rhythm, melody, and harmonies."

At five, Sigi, as Weissenberg was nicknamed, began studying composition as well as piano under Pantcho Vladigeroff, and three years later he gave his first public concert. When the Germans occupied Bulgaria, during World War II, he and his mother were captured trying to flee the country and spent nine months in a Nazi concentration camp outside Sofia. In the confusion following an English bombing raid on Sofia they escaped to Turkey, and thence they made their way to Palestine.

In Tel Aviv, Weissenberg studied with Leo Kestenberg and made many appearances with the Palestine Symphony Orchestra, and during the same period he concertized extensively elsewhere in the Middle East and in South Africa. Jan Holcman, who heard him play at that time, later reported in the *Saturday Review* (September 24, 1960) that even then he played "à la Weissenberg, with a certain elegance, his wizardly technique never reducing the artistic conception to the merely metronomic."

To complete Alexis' development "as a real man and real artist," his mother sent him alone in 1946 to New York City, where he studied under Artur Schnabel, Olga Samaroff, and Wanda Landowska. Weissenberg says that he owes a "gigantic" debt to Samaroff because of her great knowledge of pianism generally, and that Landowska helped him to understand how to "go about the ornamentation of Bach" so as to "create the same emotional intensity and structure in a work of Bach as one would in any Romantic piece." The "potent" example that Vladimir Horowitz set for him with the piano was comparable, he explains, to "what Landowska did with the harpsichhord, which she made into something else."

As winner of the Philadelphia Orchestra Youth Contest in 1947, Weissenberg performed Rachmaninoff's Piano Concerto No. 3 in D minor, Op. 30 with the Philadelphia Orchestra under Eugene Ormandy, and the following year his winning of the Edgar M. Leventritt International Award brought him the privilege of playing Chopin's Piano Concerto No. 1 in E minor, Op. 11 with the New York Philharmonic under George Szell. Later in 1948 he toured Mexico, Central America, and South America. Some critics thought that what they considered liberties in interpretation taken by him came close to "distortion," but Howard Taubman, reviewing a Carnegie Hall recital for the New York *Times* in October 1949, reported that Weissenberg, while "imaginative and personal," played "in all speeds and dynamic ranges without abusing the best interests of the piano."

In the 1950's, Alexis Weissenberg saw his career fading rather than flourishing and his talent in danger of stagnation in a deadly cycle of provincial bookings. As he has explained, he was experiencing a problem common to many a performer who begins his career at a very early age and then finds himself experimenting in public with what he should be developing in private and thus "playing a lot of things badly." The major orchestras tend not to re-engage him and he finds himself repeating the same recital again and again on the backcountry circuit —"and how many times a year can you honestly and decently play 'Liebestraum' without going nuts?"

Preferring "no career to a stupid one," and feeling the need of retreating from the concert and recital stage in order to think over what he "had done well," what he "could do much better," and what he "should never do again," he took the "desperate step" of a prolonged sabbatical, beginning in 1957. After spending several years in Madrid, he moved to Paris, where he still makes his home. Artistically as well as musically talented, he supported himself partly with income earned by designing Christmas cards and posters. He also had an inheritance to draw on.

During what he calls his "second formative period" he balanced his private musical activity—including work on his repertoire, studying new scores, and reading about music and musicians—with reading in other fields, taking literature and philosophy courses, and engaging in intellectual discussions with people of diverse interests. In an interview with Roy Hemming for *Stereo Review* (April 1974), he remarked, "I knew that if I took several years off, most people would think I had committed suicide or decided never to play the piano again, or gone off to Tahiti with some exotic girl to live the rest of my life. I might have *loved* to do that, but the climate on Tahiti is very bad for pianos."

Weissenberg resumed his career in 1966, playing Stravinsky's *Petrouchka* in a Swedish television film and giving a concert in Paris. In 1967 he made a television film with the Berlin Philharmonic under Herbert von Karajan, playing Tchaikovsky's Piano Concerto No. 1 in B flat minor, Op. 23, and the following year he opened the Berlin Philharmonic's season in a performance of the same work.

The pianist marked his return to the United States with a performance with the New York Philharmonic of Rachmaninoff's Piano Concerto No. 3 in D minor in February 1967. When he gave a recital that included the five Chopin nocturnes at Lincoln Center's Philharmonic Hall later in the same year, Raymond Ericson of the New York *Times* (November 2, 1967) reported that he still played the piano "as if he had been born for that alone." "Decorative phrases were flicked off lightly;" Ericson wrote, "soft, quick repeated chords were transparently clear; melodic lines were delicately inflected or perfectly even—the tonal weight always absolutely under control." Irving Kolodin, writing in *Saturday Review* (November 18, 1967) voiced the opinion that Weissenberg "may be that rarity among contemporary pianists: a performer who is as good a recitalist as he is with orchestra."

As of 1968, the LP's recorded by Weissenberg on the Angel label included Bach's Chromatic Fantasia and Fugue in D minor, Liszt's Sonata in B minor, and, with the Paris Conservatory Orchestra, the Six Chopin

Works for Piano and Orchestra. On the RCA Victor label he recorded Rachmaninoff's Concerto No. 3, with the Chicago Symphony Orchestra, among other works. Regarding his RCA Victor album comprising Chopin's Sonata No. 3 in B minor, Op. 58, Scherzo No. 1 in B flat minor, Op. 20, and Scherzo No. 2 in B flat minor, Op. 31, a reviewer in *American Record Guide* (September 1968) observed, "Good pianists often come to grief with them. But Weissenberg is not a good pianist —he is a sensational one. To have chosen such a program took nerve; to have carried it off as he does takes genius."

In 1969 Weissenberg made the first of eight visits to Japan, to perform at the Osaka Festival. Three years later he returned for the first time in twenty-eight years to Bulgaria, where he was honored with the title "Artist of the People." In 1974-75, during his annual five-month tour in the United States, he played the Bartók Second Piano Concerto with the Cleveland Orchestra and performed in the anniversary series of the Ninety-second Street YMHA in New York City.

Beginning in 1974 Weissenberg recorded all five of the Beethoven piano concertos with the Berlin Philharmonic under Herbert von Karajan. Discussing the project with Speight Jenkins for *Record World* (November 2, 1974), he spoke of his "responsibility as the pianist to look at the pieces newly, with profound seriousness." Jenkins observed that "a desire to make his audience, all of his audiences, feel moved about music comes through all of what he says."

After hearing Weissenberg play the Third Rachmaninoff Concerto at the Kennedy Center in Washington, D.C., Paul Hume of the Washington *Post* (March 11, 1976) ventured the opinion that no one else, outside of Vladimir Horowitz and the composer himself, has "taken the whole work, with its pianistic fireworks, and made it his own." Reviewing a Carnegie Hall concert featuring Schumann's *Davidsbündlertänze*, Op. 6, and Stravinsky's "Three Movements from *Petrouchka*," Hubert Saal observed that Weissenberg is "a little bearish on lyricism" and "bullish on earthiness" and that "in order to realize his fresh rhythms and vivid color he takes plenty of liberties with accents and tempos." He quoted the pianist as saying, "I don't think there's anything duller than careful playing. You've got to take risks to be original."

Weissenberg, who currently plays about eighty to eighty-five concerts a year internationally, feels that the joy of sharing his music with audiences compensates for the routine, the travel, and loneliness involved. He also feels that the audience should allow the performer "to jump into the music and let himself go." He has said that he has one desideratum: "I do wish that people would stop talking about how I played 20 years ago." On the other hand, he also enjoys listening to Vladimir Horowitz, Glenn Gould, Arturo Benedetti Michelangeli, and other pianists who startle him with their styles and make him forget his own ideas about music.

Alexis Weissenberg, a trim, wiry man who looks younger than his years, is five feet six inches tall. Those who know him report that he is frank, friendly, and disarmingly charming, with a relaxed, unassuming manner. Outside of performances, he tends to dress modishly but casually. A lively conversationalist in seven or eight languages and a gifted mimic and impersonator, he enjoys talking with and entertaining a small circle of friends, but he usually avoids large parties, and he abhors after-concert receptions. He meditates regularly.

Weissenberg is divorced from his wife Carmen, the daughter of a Spanish diplomat whom he married during his sabbatical and by whom he has two daughters. A naturalized French citizen, he lives in Paris in an apartment overlooking the Seine, and he vacations on the Spanish and French seacoasts, sometimes with his children. Occasionally he also vacations in the Swiss mountain resort town of Zermatt, but only for short periods. "I need the quickness of the city, the nervousness," he says. "It recharges me."

References: Cue 44:8 F 10 '75 por; Hi Fi 19:MA7+ Ap '69; N Y Times II p11+ Ag 15 '71 por; Sat R 43:47+ S 24 '60 por; Sr Schol 94:21+ Mr 7 '69; Time 92:59+ D 20 '68 por; Thompson, O., ed. International Cyclopedia of Music and Musicians, 1975; International Who's Who in Music, 1976; Jacobson, Robert. Reverberations (1974); Saleski, Gdal. Famous Musicians of Jewish Origin (1949); Who's Who in America, 1976-77

Wilder, Gene

June 11, 1935(?)- Actor; scriptwriter; director. Address: b. c/o Twentieth Century-Fox, 10201 W. Pico Blvd., Los Angeles, Calif. 90035; c/o Kaplan and Veidt, 667 Madison Ave., New York City, N.Y. 10021

In his pursuit of the risible, Gene Wilder takes a path well trodden by Mel Brooks and others, structuring his films to parody another film or a film genre, with an obsession for screen trivia. But in employing his ingenious comic imagination in the many functions of *auteur*—actor, scriptwriter, director, and producer—he is developing an identifiable style of his own—one that is quieter and more subtle than that of his mentors, slapstick touched with poignancy and romance mingled with the bizarre. When

Gene Wilder

Wilder went to Hollywood in the late 1960's to perform first in *Bonnie and Clyde* and then in *The Producers,* he was an actor with a solid background in the theatre who applied to comedy the same professional skills that he did to serious drama. His other technical proficiencies in cinematic art came to the aid of his career later in *Young Frankenstein,* for which he helped to write a script to suit his goals as an actor, and more recently in *The World's Greatest Lover,* of which he was star, writer, director, and producer.

Born Jerome Silberman in Milwaukee, Wisconsin on June 11, 1935, Gene Wilder is the son of William J. and Jeanne (Baer) Silberman. (Some sources give 1934 as the year of his birth.) His father, who had emigrated from Russia at the age of eleven, was an importer and manufacturer of novelties and souvenirs. His Chicago-born mother was of Polish descent. A heart attack that she suffered when her son was six years old left her a semi-invalid. To cheer her up, the child improvised comedy skits, so that from an early age he was aware of the coexistence of laughter and pain. His older sister, who was taking dramatic lessons, also provided an impetus toward his becoming an actor when he observed with envy the attention and approval that she drew from an audience during a student performance. In press interviews he has given various explanations of why, at about the age of twenty-six, he chose Gene Wilder for his professional name. He told Leo Seligsohn of *Newsday* (December 17, 1977), "I had always liked Gene because of Thomas Wolfe's character Eugene Gant in *Look Homeward, Angel* and *Of Time and the River.* And I was always a great admirer of Thornton Wilder."

After attending the Black-Foxe Military Institute in Los Angeles for a rather brief and dissatisfying period, Wilder completed his secondary school education in Milwaukee at the Washington High School, from which he graduated in 1951. At about the age of twelve, he had begun studying acting with Herman Gottlieb in Milwaukee and in 1948 had made his debut at the Milwaukee Playhouse as Balthazar in *Romeo and Juliet.* His early preference was for comedy, but seeing Lee J. Cobb in the original Broadway production of *Death of a Salesman* (1949-50) turned him toward what he then considered to be a more serious and important form of acting. He attended the University of Iowa, took part in student dramatic productions, played in summer stock during vacations, and obtained his B.A. degree in 1955.

Apparently with the intention of acquiring a classical training in the theatre, in 1955 Wilder enrolled in the Old Vic Theatre School in Bristol, England, where he studied judo, fencing, gymnastics, and voice, but left when he reached the course in techniques of acting. On his return to the United States, he was inducted into the Army and assigned to the Valley Forge Hospital in Pennsylvania. Seeing some connection with acting, he opted for duty in the neuropsychiatric ward. On weekends he studied drama at the Herbert Berghof Studio in New York City. In 1961, when he became a member of the Actors Studio, he began studying with Lee Strasberg. One of the jobs that Wilder took to finance his acting apprenticeship was that of fencing instructor, having acquired at Bristol a skill that also enabled him to work as fencing choreographer for *Twelfth Night* and *Macbeth* at the Cambridge (Massachusetts) Drama Festival in 1959.

On March 6, 1961 at the Off-Broadway Mayfair Theatre, Gene Wilder made his New York debut in the role of Frankie Bryant, the young bumpkin in Arnold Wesker's *Roots.* In his first Broadway appearance, in November of that year, he played the bewildered hotel valet in Graham Greene's comedy *The Complaisant Lover,* giving a performance for which he won the Clarence Derwent Award, presented to a promising newcomer in a supporting role. It was reportedly the gratifying audience response to his inspired portrayal that persuaded him to consider following the comic route. After touring in *The Complaisant Lover,* he returned to Broadway in the spring of 1963 as the Chaplain in Bertolt Brecht's *Mother Courage and Her Children.* That production proved to be significant in his career because of his meeting with Mel Brooks, who every evening used to call backstage for its star, Anne Bancroft, whom he later married. Brooks promised Wilder a part in a movie he intended to write.

Before that promise was kept, however, Wilder continued on Broadway in *One Flew Over the Cuckoo's Nest* (1963), *Dynamite Tonight* (1964), and *The White House* (1964) and also toured in one or two plays. He was a standby for Alan Arkin in the role of Harry Berlin in Murray Schisgal's *Luv*, which had its premiere in November 1964. During the long run of that smash hit the role was taken over by Gabriel Dell and then by Wilder, who was therefore a star of the three-character comedy when it closed in January 1967.

Only a few of the critics, concentrating on Warren Beatty's performance in *Bonnie and Clyde* (Warner Brothers), mentioned the brief appearance of Gene Wilder as Eugene Grizzard, the neurotic undertaker kidnapped by the Barrow gang. But in some later appraisals of the actor, he was remembered as a peerless hysteric in his screen debut of 1967. The following year in *The Producers* (Embassy), the first film that Mel Brooks wrote and directed, he created for Wilder the role of Leo Bloom, a neurotic accountant who carries around a handkerchief-size security blanket. His acting won him an Oscar nomination for best supporting actor. Several reviewers thought the movie hilarious, even though they agreed with the verdicts of Renata Adler of the New York *Times* (March 19, 1968): a "fantastically uneven movie," and Paul D. Zimmerman of *Newsweek* (February 5, 1968): "a hybrid—half miracle and half mess."

Similar reservations, some of them judging the script unworthy of the acting, were often echoed in reviews of Wilder's later pictures. The critic for *Variety* (February 4, 1970), for instance, found that Wilder and Donald Sutherland seemed "superior to their material" in *Start the Revolution Without Me* (Warner Brothers, 1970), playing dual roles in a period farce about two sets of twins switched at birth. In the lead of *Quackser Fortune Has a Cousin in the Bronx* (UM Film, 1970) he portrayed a Dublin peddler of manure who arouses the romantic interest of an American coed at Trinity College. To Judith Crist of *New York* magazine (July 20, 1970), the film was "a pleasant piece of fluffery that does little but showcase further the charming talents of Gene Wilder." Penelope Gilliatt wrote in the *New Yorker* (July 25, 1970), "Gene Wilder, one of the best American actors, plays the dreadful Quackser as best as man could." But through his characterization of Quackser, whom he considered to be innocent and likeable, Wilder achieved what he wanted—a departure from the neurasthenic stereotype in the direction of the comic-romantic hero.

Again, it was chiefly Wilder's graceful performance in the title role of an eccentric candymaker that carried the musical fantasy for children *Willy Wonka and the Chocolate Factory* (Paramount, 1971), which Roald Dahl adapted from his book *Charlie and the Chocolate Factory*. A later musical mainly for children, Stanley Donen's *The Little Prince* (Paramount, 1974), based on Antoine de Saint Exupéry's semiclassic, featured Wilder as the Fox. Some critics deplored the waste of his talent on what they called a disappointment and a disaster, but others thought the film a joy.

The satirical *Everything You Always Wanted to Know About Sex But Were Afraid to Ask* (United Artists, 1972) gave Wilder the opportunity to work with Woody Allen, who, like Mel Brooks, ranks among the foremost American directors, writers, and actors of comedy. One of the funniest of the film's seven skits that reduce to absurdity Dr. David Reuben's popular manual is entitled "What is Sodomy?" and presents Wilder as a general practitioner who, called in to treat a shepherd stricken with love for a sheep named Daisy, becomes himself enamored of the sheep. Discussing the difference between the directing styles of Allen and Brooks with Mel Gussow of the New York *Times* (January 5, 1976), Wilder called Allen more "cerebral." He compared Allen's brand of humor to setting off "1,000 safety matches [that] flare up, make you laugh and die down." Brooks, on the other hand, according to Wilder, "wants to set off atom blasts of humor. . . . He wants gigantic explosions."

Brooks gave full play to his raucous humor in *Blazing Saddles* (Warner Brothers, 1974), a parody of Hollywood westerns in which Wilder portrays an alcoholic gunslinger, Waco Kid, who with his black sidekick, Bart, saves the town from an unscrupulous land grabber. Considerably more cinematically disciplined than that uproarious comedy, Wilder's next picture under Brooks's direction, *Young Frankenstein* (Twentieth Century-Fox, 1974), is another genre spoof, one that carefully re-creates parts of the 1931 Frankenstein film in its parody of Mary Shelley's classic and the old horror movies. Besides conceiving the idea for the production, Wilder collaborated with Brooks on the screenplay and starred as Dr. Frankenstein, a California brain surgeon and teacher who is trying to live down the scandal of his ancestor, Baron Frankenstein, and visits Transylvania when he inherits the family castle. Zimmerman appraised Wilder's portrayal in *Newsweek* (December 23, 1974) as "his finest performance to date." In another 1974 film, the ill-fated screen version of Ionesco's *Rhinoceros* (American Film Theatre), Wilder had the leading role of Stanley (Berenger in the play), the only character who remains a human being.

When asked in interviews why he had become a screenwriter, Wilder explained that no one else was writing the roles that appealed to him, sad men who are funny. The commercial success of *Young Frankenstein* no doubt encouraged him in creating another screen hero for himself, this one the insanely jealous Sigerson Holmes, the title character of *The Adventure of Sherlock Holmes' Smarter Brother* (Twentieth Century-Fox, 1975). That "romantic comedy," as Wilder classified it, spoofs not the revered Sherlock Holmes, but the period detective drama. The writer and star also directed *Adventure,* which was filmed in London and included in its cast such brilliant regulars of the Brooks-Wilder comedies as Madeline Kahn, Marty Feldman, and Dom DeLuise.

Among the critics who welcomed Gene Wilder's directorial debut was Gary Arnold, whose review of *Adventure* in the Washington *Post* (December 19, 1975) called attention to "a lyric streak of the madcap in Wilder" and to his "relatively subtle, ironic touch, which recalls the eccentric style of British film comedy." Arnold summed up, "*Adventure* isn't overwhelming, but it shows wit and flair." Somewhat similarly, comparing Wilder with Brooks, Derek Malcolm of the *Guardian* (December 18, 1975) found Wilder's touch to be "less frenetic . . . not so likely to bruise us half to death in the name of laughter. But it also lacks Brooks's bludgeoning energy, which can transform a comic set piece into a tour de force."

With *The World's Greatest Lover* (Paramount, 1977), his next comedy in the manner of *Young Frankenstein* and *Adventure,* Wilder went a step further, adding the function of producer to that of actor, scriptwriter, and director. He also wrote a song for the movie. As he had done in the earlier films, he approached the drafting of his story line and characters "with the magic 'if.' " In this instance, he related to *Newsday*'s Seligsohn, he asked himself, "What would happen *if* a neurotic baker followed his compulsive dream of fame and romance to Hollywood. . . ?" Claiming the title role for himself, Wilder played the Milwaukee baker, Rudy Valentine, who goes to Hollywood in the mid-1920's to try to compete with Valentino.

"Many of the nutty sequences are clever modern spin-offs on the art of the silent comedy masters whom Wilder clearly reveres," William Wolf wrote in *Cue* (January 6, 1978). "His reverence also extends to Fellini, whose *White Sheik* obviously provided further inspiration." One of the early scenes in *The World's Greatest Lover,* in which the baker gets trapped on the cake conveyor belt, is intended as a tribute to Charlie Chaplin, whom Wilder regards as his patron saint or spiritual father. Wilder has often said that his screenplays are "emotionally autobiographical." In re-creating the golden age of silent movies, he was less interested in authenticity than in his own childhood fantasies of the period.

Besides providing scripts tailored to his own style of acting, Wilder turned to writing in fulfillment of what he called "a maturing process." "I'm more concerned with what I'm expressing than with the act of expression itself," he was quoted as saying in the *Guardian* (December 15, 1975). But he also said that he hoped not to outgrow the desire to act. While continuing to star in his own films, he recently accepted the lead in *Silver Streak* (Twentieth Century-Fox, 1976), which he neither wrote nor directed. In that parody of *North by Northwest* and other train mysteries, Wilder is a romantic publisher who happens to witness a murder as a passenger on a crack Los Angeles-to-Chicago train. Joseph Gelmis' conclusion in *Newsday* (December 10, 1976), "Overwrought script and direction squander a talented cast," summed up critical opinion fairly well, but some reviewers felt that lively scenes of Wilder with Richard Pryor made the film worthwhile.

Gene Wilder's television roles include three on NBC's *Dupont Show of the Week* presentations during 1962: Muller in "The Sound of Hunting," Wilson in "The Interrogators," and the Reporter in "Windfall." He appeared as the Head Waiter in "Reunion with Death" on *The Defenders* (CBS, 1962), Yonkel in "Home for Passover" on *Eternal Light* (NBC, 1966), and Bernard in *Death of a Salesman* (CBS, 1966). More recently he was seen in the TV movie *Thursday's Game* (ABC, 1974) as Harry Evers and in the comedy-variety show *Annie and the Hoods* (ABC, 1974).

One of the members of the cast of *Roots,* along with Gene Wilder, was Mary Mercier, a playwright as well as an actress, whom he had married on July 22, 1960. The marriage broke up, and on October 27, 1967 he married Mary Joan Schutz (some sources give Jo Ayers as the name of his second wife). Before that marriage ended, also in divorce, he adopted his wife's daughter by her earlier marriage, Katharine Anastasia. The blue-eyed, curly blond-haired actor plays bridge and tennis in his spare time and has a serious, winsome manner offscreen that contrasts with the frantic carryings-on so enjoyable to his fans. "My quiet exterior used to be a mask for hysteria," he once said, as quoted in *Time* (July 20, 1970). "After seven years of analysis, it just became a habit."

References: Christian Sci Mon p9 Ja 29 '75 por; Cue 44::27+ N 8 '75 por; Guardian p8 D 15 '75 por; N Y Post p15 D 28 '74 por; N Y Sunday News mag p23+ Ja 18 '76 pors; N Y Times II p15 N 16 '69 por; Notable Names in the American Theatre (1976)

Yalow, Rosalyn S(ussman)

July 19, 1921- Medical physicist. Address: b. Veterans Administration Hospital, 130 W. Kingsbridge Rd., New York City, N.Y. 10468; h. 3242 Tibbett Ave., New York City, N.Y. 10463

In 1977 Rosalyn S. Yalow became the second woman ever to win the Nobel Prize in medicine. She was honored for her development of radioimmunoassay (RIA), an ingenious application of nuclear physics in clinical medicine that makes it possible for scientists to use radioisotopic tracers to measure the concentration of hundreds of pharmacologic and biologic substances in the blood and other fluids of the human body, and in animals and plants. Dr. Yalow invented the technique in 1959 to measure the amount of insulin in the blood of adult diabetics. Since then she and others have applied RIA to scores of medical problems. Used in over 4,000 laboratories in the United States, as well as in thousands of laboratories abroad, RIA is generally acknowledged to be one of the most important postwar applications of basic research to clinical medicine. Dr. Yalow, who trained as a nuclear physicist, performed her pioneering experiments at the Bronx Veterans Administration Hospital in New York, where she is now the senior medical investigator. Her discovery and development of RIA was made in collaboration with the late Dr. Solomon A. Berson, her associate from 1950 until his death in 1972.

The younger child of lower-middle-class Jewish parents, Rosalyn Sussman was born in the Bronx, New York on July 19, 1921. Her father, Simon Sussman, now deceased, ran a small business. He is survived by his wife Clara (Zipper) Sussman, who is now a spirited woman in her nineties. The Sussmans had one son, Alexander. As a child Rosalyn was always encouraged to get the good education that had been denied to her immigrant parents, and she credits her father with having instilled in her the idea that girls could do anything boys could do.

After attending public elementary schools in her neighborhood, Rosalyn Sussman went to Walton High School, where her chemistry teacher urged her to study science. Later, at Hunter College, she was encouraged to pursue a career in physics, although a number of her advisers cautioned that she would probably have to settle for a secretarial job to underwrite her graduate training. With that possibility in mind, she took courses in shorthand and typing during her senior year. By the time she graduated, Phi Beta Kappa and *magna cum laude*, from Hunter with a B.A. degree in physics and chemistry in 1941, however, Rosalyn Sussman was able to put aside her steno pad, for she had been accepted as a teaching fellow in physics at the University of Illinois at Urbana. The only woman among 400 men in the faculty of the College of Engineering, she became, in 1945, the second women to receive a Ph.D. degree in physics from Illinois.

While in graduate school, Miss Sussman met a fellow physics student named A. Aaron Yalow, the son of a rabbi from upstate New York. They were married on June 6, 1943. After obtaining their Ph.D. degrees in 1945, the Yalows returned to New York City where Rosalyn Yalow worked for a year as an electrical engineer for the Federal Telecommunications Laboratory. In 1946 she was hired by her alma mater, Hunter, as a physics lecturer, a post she held until 1950.

After World War II, the Veterans Administration initiated a research program to explore the use of radioactive substances in the diagnosis and treatment of diseases. One of the hospitals chosen for the nuclear medicine project was the VA hospital in the Bronx, which hired Dr. Yalow as a consultant in nuclear physics in 1947. In 1950 she was appointed physicist and assistant chief of the hospital's radioisotope service. That same year, Dr. Solomon A. Berson, a young internist, joined the radioisotope unit. His training and talents so complemented Dr. Yalow's, that, according to Barbara Yuncker of the New York *Post* (November 19, 1976), "they developed a collaboration so symbiotic that they came to believe in mental telepathy." Initially, the two researchers explored the use of radioactive iodine in the diagnosis and treatment of thyroid disease. Later, they measured blood volume by tagging red blood cells or plasma proteins with radioisotopes of phosphorus and potassium. They subsequently found ways in which radioactive iodine could be used to tag insulin and other hormones and proteins in order to study the body's normal methods of making and destroying such substances. While conducting those studies, Dr. Yalow and Dr. Berson developed their revolutionary method of radioimmunoassay.

Radioimmunoassay is a laboratory procedure that employs radioisotopes and immunologic methods to measure with a high degree of precision substances in the blood or other body fluids. In the past those substances had often been impossible to measure, either because they were present in too minute quantities or dilute concentrations, or because their chemical properties were too similar to those of other substances. The first step in RIA is to inject the substance to be measured into a suitable laboratory animal, usually a guinea pig or rabbit, in sufficient quantities so that the animal's immunologic defenses produce antibodies in reaction to the substance. Virtually any substance can be thus rendered antigenic, or antibody-producing, although some substances must be treated chemically in order to trigger an immunologic reaction. There is no need to purify the antiserum.

The antigenic substance that is to be measured is then "labeled" with radioactive iodine or another suitable radioactive isotope, and precisely measured amounts of labeled antigen are placed in test tubes containing measured amounts of antibody. Blood or other fluid from the test animal (or patient) is added to some of the prepared test tubes. That fluid, of course, will contain an unknown amount of unlabeled antigen. In the other test tubes are placed standard solutions containing known amounts of unlabeled antigen. After an appropriate reaction time during which antigen—labeled and unlabeled—will bind with antibody, the labeled antigen is separated by special techniques. By comparing the ratio of bound to unbound labeled antigen in tubes containing the laboratory animal's (or patient's) blood with that of the standard solutions, the precise concentration of unlabeled antigen can be determined because the unlabeled antigen exerts an inhibitory effect on the binding of the labeled antigen.

When Dr. Yalow and her associates first used RIA in 1959 to measure the insulin levels in the blood of diabetics, they made the surprising discovery that adult diabetics actually have higher than normal levels of the peptide hormone insulin. Until then, it had been believed that adult diabetics, like children afflicted with the disease, had an insulin deficiency. RIA demonstrated that the elevated blood sugar level in adult diabetics results from some as yet unknown factor that interferes with the action of insulin.

Following their groundbreaking work on insulin retention in adult diabetics, Dr. Yalow and Dr. Berson applied RIA to the study of other hormones. They used RIA to measure the amount of growth hormone (GH) in the bodies of certain unusually small children in order to discover if a deficiency existed that could be treated with GH; to determine whether excessive steroid production of the adrenal gland was resulting from a gland tumor or from stimulation by an overactive pituitary gland; to find out if sterility stemmed from a lack of sufficient sex hormones; to determine whether a patient with an ulcer should be treated medically or surgically; and to discover whether or not a high level of calcium in the blood—a condition often leading to kidney stones—was caused by too much secretion of the calcium-regulating hormone parathyroid.

Dr. Yalow and her colleagues at the Bronx VA Hospital have concentrated mostly on the application of RIA to hormone measurement, but along with other researchers they also have extended the use of RIA into virtually all medical specialties. For example, it has become the preferred method for screening blood in blood banks for contamination by the virus responsible for producing hepatitis in patients receiving transfusions. Physicians use it to measure the degree of protection an anti-rabies injection can give the victim of a bite and to discover if prescribed drugs or antibiotics are present in a patient's circulatory system at levels adequate for effectiveness. RIA has also been used to determine whether a person has recently taken heroin, methadone, LSD, or other abusive drugs, and it can detect the surreptitious administration of such potentially lethal drugs as curare. Indeed the use of radioimmunoassay has become so widespread that Dr. Yalow worries about its overuse. "It's being sold for diagnostic testing where in fact it isn't very useful," she explained to Elizabeth Stone during an interview for a New York *Times Magazine* (April 9, 1978) profile. "I have been to international meetings where the pharmaceuticals are selling kits, and they'll have big displays saying you cannot diagnose diabetes without an insulin assay. Well, I think you get more understanding of the nature of the diabetes with an insulin assay, but it's not *necessary*."

In 1968 Dr. Yalow was named acting chief of the radioisotope service at the Bronx VA Hospital and, in 1969, she became chief of the radioimmunoassay reference laboratory, a post she still holds. The following year the hospital added chief of the nuclear medicine service to her administrative duties. In 1972 Dr. Yalow became a VA senior medical investigator, and in 1973 she became director of the newly established Solomon A. Berson Research Laboratory. During the 1950's Dr. Yalow served as a consultant at Lenox Hill Hospital. She was research professor in the department of medicine at Mt. Sinai School of Medicine from 1968 to 1974 and, in 1974 she was appointed a Distinguished Service Professor at Mt. Sinai.

In 1976 Dr. Yalow became the first woman ever to win the Albert Lasker Prize for Basic Medical Research and the following year, in 1977, she reached the summit of scientific honor when she was awarded the Nobel Prize in medicine. She received half of the $145,000 prize money, with the other half split between Dr. Andrew V. Schally of the New Orleans VA and Dr. Roger Guillemin of the Salk Institute in California, who used RIA to make important discoveries about hormones in the brain. Dr. Yalow immediately banked her share of the cash award. As she explained to an interviewer for *People* magazine (January 2, 1978), "I can't think of anything I want. I wasn't handed college or graduate school or anything else on a silver platter. I had to work very hard, but I did it because I wanted to. That's the real key to happiness."

As only the second woman to win a Nobel in medicine (the first was Gerty T. Cori who shared the prize in 1947 with her husband), Dr. Yalow, in accepting her award at the Nobel Festival in Stockholm, Sweden, in December 1977, took advantage of the occasion to give the cause of feminism a boost. "We still live in a world in which a significant fraction of people, including women, believe that a woman belongs and wants to belong exclusively in the home; that a woman should not aspire to achieve more than her male counterparts and particularly not more than her husband," she told her fellow Nobel laureates. "We cannot expect in the immediate future that all women who will seek it will achieve 'equality of opportunity.' But if women are to start moving toward that goal, we must believe in ourselves or no one else will believe in us, we must match our aspirations with the competence, courage and determination to succeed, and we must feel a personal responsibility to ease the path for those who come after us. The world cannot afford the loss of the talents of half its people if we are to solve the many problems that beset us."

Among the many other awards that have been bestowed upon Dr. Yalow are the American Academy of Achievement Golden Plate Award for Salute to Excellence (1977), "La Madonnina" International Prize of Milan (1977), Modern Medicine's Distinguished Achievement Award (1976), the A. Cressy Morrison Award in Natural Sciences of the New York Academy of Sciences (1975), the Scientific Achievement Award of the American Medical Association (1975), and the Gairdner Foundation International Award (1971). She is a member of several professional fraternities.

Dr. Yalow, who has delivered distinguished lectures before numerous societies and at medical centers around the country, has been awarded honorary doctorate degrees by several universities, including the University of Illinois (1974), the New York Medical College (1976), Yeshiva University (1977), and Hunter College (1978). She is a fellow of the New York Academy of Sciences, a member of the Radiation Research Society, the American Association of Physicists in Medicine, and the Endocrine Society, and an associate fellow in physics of the American College of Radiology. A former secretary of the United States National Committee on Medical Physics (1953-57), Dr. Yalow is a member of Subcommittee 13 of the National Committee on Radiation Protection and the President's Study Group on Careers for Women, and a consultant to the New York City Department of Health's subcommittee on the human applications of radioactive materials. The medical physicist, whose professional list of publications runs to nearly 300 items, is coeditor of the professional journal *Hormone and Metabolic Research* and a member of the editorial boards of the *Mount Sinai Journal of Medicine and Diabetes*. Dr. Yalow found time in her busy professional schedule to host a five-part dramatic series on the life of Marie Curie for the Public Broadcasting Service in the fall of 1978.

Rosalyn S. Yalow and her husband, a physics professor at Cooper Union for the Advancement of Science and Art, live in the Riverdale section of the Bronx, about a mile from the Bronx VA Hospital, where she frequently puts in an eighty-hour week. The Yalows have two children, Benjamin, a computer systems analyst for the City University of New York, and Elanna, a doctoral candidate in educational psychology at Stanford University. The black-haired, brown-eyed physicist is five feet, six inches tall and weighs 150 pounds. Dr. Yalow claims no hobbies and travels only to attend scientific conferences and deliver lectures. "It's true that women are different from men," she told a reporter for the New York *Post* (December 7, 1977). "If you want to be a good wife, you have to work a little harder." Despite the burdens of her professional career, Dr. Yalow leaves her office early enough each evening to cook dinner in her kosher kitchen for her husband, gardens, and cares for her house with cleaning help only one day a week. "I can't think of anything in the world that I would want that I haven't had," she told Barbara Yuncker in the interview for the New York *Post*. "I have my marriage, two wonderful children. I have a laboratory that is an absolute joy. I have energy. I have health. As long as there is anything to be done I am never tired."

References: Hunter News 4:6 Je '77 por; N Y Mirror pBW4 Mr 12 '61 por; N Y Post p39 N 19 '76 por; N Y Times Mag p29+ Ap 9 '78 pors; People 8:95 Ja 2 '78 por; American Men and Women of Science 13th ed (1976)

Zukerman, Pinchas

July 16, 1948- Musician; conductor.
Address: b. c/o ICM Artists Ltd., 40 W. 57th St., New York City, N.Y. 10019

The Israeli-born virtuoso violinist Pinchas Zukerman, a protégé of Isaac Stern who came to the United States as a child prodigy in 1962, is now, at thirty, recognized as one of the finest instrumentalists of his generation, especially when he plays the works of the German late Romantics or of the second Viennese school. Besides playing the violin and the viola, Zukerman is fast developing into a skilled conductor. His greatest love is for chamber music, which he has performed in company with such friends as pianist Daniel Barenboim and cellist Jacqueline du Pré or with such ensembles as the Chamber Music Society of Lincoln Center or the Los Angeles Chamber Orchestra. In whatever capacity he appears before an audience, the dynamic Zukerman is an uninhibited, demonstrative performer, transmitting his passionate conviction in what he is playing or conducting. "As a conductor, he's very musical, very intent, very serious," Isaac Stern has observed. "Time will have to tell whether his conducting career will flower. My hope is that he will keep on enlarging his incredible ability on the violin and viola. He plays with extraordinary clarity and articulation, producing an urgency of sound that demands the ears of the listener."

Pinchas Zukerman, the only child of Jehuda and Miriam (Lieberman-Skotchilas) Zukerman, was born on July 16, 1948 in Tel Aviv, Israel, where his parents, concentration camp survivors from Poland, had settled the year before. The father, now deceased, was a professional violinist, a former member of the Warsaw Philharmonic who taught during the day and played with his own band in nightclubs. Pinchas grew up in Tel Aviv and in a small village outside the city.

At five, Pinchas Zukerman learned to play a recorder given him by his father. Next he tried, but disliked, the clarinet. When he was seven his father bought him a half-sized violin and began teaching him to play that instrument, and soon father and son were playing Mazas' duets together. Later, Pinchas studied at the Israel Conservatory and the Academy of Music in Tel Aviv, under Ilona Feher. "But I had a nice all-around childhood," he assured Sidney Fields of the New York *Daily News* (July 15, 1975). "A lot of friends, a lot of play. Soccer was my game. No one beat me over the head with music.'

"Since my father was a musician," Zukerman recounted when Joseph Roddy interviewed him for the New York *Times* (January 24, 1971), "he knew the struggle it is to get up on the stage and play. So he had me playing in every possible corner of Israel, the opening of a house, bar mitzvahs, everything. I played my little Wieniawski and people loved it [and] I used to play chamber music twice a week with a teacher [Miss Feher]. I had played all the Beethoven quartets by the time I came to America." He could also play the difficult Paganini Caprices.

Zukerman confesses that he was an "arrogant" child prodigy. "But I had reason to be, I guess," he told Stephen E. Rubin, another interviewer for the New York *Times* (November 7, 1971). "It was put in my head that I was good and, of course, after a while you start believing it. I didn't have the emotional support to know there was so much I had to learn." The American violinist Isaac Stern recalls that when he and Pablo Casals heard Zukerman during a visit to Israel in 1961, the child violinist "played, and looked at you, and dared you to dislike him." Stern arranged for him to study with Ivan Galamian at the Juilliard School in New York City with the help of a scholarship from the American-Israel Cultural Foundation.

In 1962 Vladeck Grodecki, an Israeli businessman, paid Zukerman's air fare to the United States. His parents followed six months later, but Jehuda Zukerman was unable to find suitable work in New York and moved with his wife to Montreal, Canada. While studying at Juilliard and at the Professional Children's School and the High School of Performing Arts, Pinchas Zukerman lived with the parents of pianist Eugene Istomin.

Spoiled by early adulation, Zukerman found it difficult to adjust at Juilliard, where he was, for the first time, a prodigy among prodigies, and he rebelled against Ivan Gamalian's insistence that he go back to the basics and practise long hours. His arrogance was not his only problem, as he explained to Sidney Fields: "It was a lonely time, a very lonely time. I didn't know a word of English. In junior high school where I went to learn it the only subject I passed was geometry, only because the teacher spoke some Yiddish. I hated Professional Children's School and the High School of Performing Arts. I played a lot of hookey. I haunted the pool halls, and almost got into trouble. When Isaac Stern found out he pinned me against the wall. He did everything but punch me. He got me to see that music isn't a profession; it's a way of life. I was sixteen. There was still time, thank God."

Zukerman made his New York debut playing two movements from Lalo's *Symphonie Espagnole* in a concert given at Town Hall by the New York Orchestral Society on October 27, 1963 for the benefit of the United Nations Children's Fund. On that occasion the reviewer for the New York *Times* (October 28, 1963) was impressed with his "personality capable of projecting with incredible force the most vivid emotional qualities," with "his vigorous rhythmic sense," and, above all, with "the high degree of spontaneity present throughout."

On May 16, 1967 Zukerman was co-winner, with Kyung Wha Chung of Korea, of the Leventritt International Competition. That honor led to a recording contract and a contract with Sol Hurok, who booked him on a tour of the United States and Canada. Filling in for Isaac Stern, who was ill, at the Westbury (Long Island) Music Fair on April 8, 1968, Zukerman, assisted by pianist Charles Wadsworth, played Ernest Bloch's *Nigun*, Schumann's Sonata in A Minor, and Stravinsky's Divertimento from *The Fairy's Kiss* in addition to works by Bach and Vivaldi. Ron Eyer of *Newsday* (April 9, 1968) found his playing on that occasion "intensely, voluptuously romantic" but "tasteful" and "executed with consummate artistry."

Early in 1969 Zukerman made his first appearance with the New York Philharmonic, playing Mendelssohn's Concerto in E Minor under the direction of Leonard Bernstein. In May 1969 he and his friend Daniel Barenboim, the young Israeli pianist, offered a program of sonatas by Beethoven, Mozart, and Schumann at the Brighton (England) Festival, and the following February, Zukerman and Isaac Stern performed together music for two violins by Leclair, Prokofiev, and Spohr in a program presented by the Chamber Music Society of Lincoln Center. Reviewing the latter event for the New York *Times* (February 7, 1970), Harold Schonberg noted "the impeccable teamwork" of the two musicians and Zukerman's "tone, rhythm, security of bow and finger, authority, [and] personality."

In his second visit to England, in 1970, Zukerman recorded the complete Beethoven trios with Daniel Barenboim and Barenboim's wife, the cellist Jacqueline du Pré. Edward Greenfield of the *Guardian* (March 17, 1970), who was present in the EMI studios during some of the recording sessions, noted "the technical finesse, the warmth of feeling between these three players, their spontaneous response to each other as well as the detailed care of their preparation." Greenfield wrote: "The beauty of these relationships as we see them from the outside lies in the lightness of personal contact; when necessary, a mutual criticism set in humor, which allows a sublime image of the relationship to emerge in the music-making. Like kids at play, they perform as angels. Zukerman has joined the husband-and-wife team as a brilliant catalyst to their complementary qualities." Greenfield noted that the "serious-faced verbal teasing of Barenboim" and "the tongue-in-cheek fun of du Pré" was matched by the "ebullient clowning of Zukerman."

The intimate circle of musician friends also included Itzhak Perlman, Vladimir Ashkenazy, and Zubin Mehta. When performing with the Los Angeles Philharmonic Orchestra under Mehta, Zukerman developed the habit of joining the string section before and after his solo and, while fiddling with the others, observing Mehta's use of the baton, in order to compare it with that of Barenboim, who was doing more and more conducting in addition to playing the piano. Later he would tease both friends about their podium technique. In one of his frequent appearances away from Los Angeles, Mehta conducted Barenboim, Miss du Pré, and Zukerman in Beethoven's Triple Concerto at Carnegie Hall in November 1970.

For his first solo recital in New York City, Zukerman offered a varied program of works by Mozart, Schubert, Schumann, Brahms, Wieniawski, Bloch, and Schönberg. In his review in the New York *Times* (April 5, 1971), Allen Hughes wrote: "With Lawrence Smith as a splendid assistant at the piano, Mr. Zukerman played with absolute interpretive authority and complete mastery of the violin. . . . Each work came out with just the right stylistic emphasis, and it is a particular pleasure to report that Mr. Zukerman played Schönberg with just as much conviction as he did the Wieniawski, for example. There was nothing dutiful or condescending in his approach to any of the pieces and in each of them beauty of tone and rightness of phrasing were ever present." The recital was filmed in its entirety by Christopher Newpen as a BBC television documentary.

During the 1972-73 season Zukerman's performances included appearances with the New York Philharmonic, the National Symphony Orchestra, and the Cleveland Orchestra. As a conductor, Zukerman made his debut with the English Chamber Orchestra in a program of baroque music, including Haydn's Symphony No. 46 and an orchestral version of Verdi's String Quartet, at Lincoln Center in April 1974. In his review of that performance Raymond Ericson of the New York *Times* (April 28, 1974) wrote: "He obviously has music in his fingers, elbows, and shoulders, and he used them to get an honest and delightful performance of the Verdi from his fine players."

"When I started conducting," Zukerman has recalled, "I felt very uncomfortable on the podium, and very naked without the violin. I didn't know what to do with myself." Using some of the basic movements of violin playing helped," he said. "But that was only part of the problem, because the baton, unlike the violin, produces no sound. . . . The difficult thing is to make music from gestures." In his review in the New York *Times* (January 23, 1975) of a performance by Zukerman as conductor-violinist with the Israel Chamber Orchestra, Harold C. Schonberg advised Zukerman to "give a downbeat, and everything else will take care of itself."

Later in the same year, in July, when Zukerman conducted and played at the opening of the Mostly Mozart Festival at Lincoln Center, Schonberg commented in the New York *Times* (July 22, 1975) that "his instincts as conductor" in the "Jupiter" Symphony were "all in the right direction." He also observed that, as his own soloist in the Violin Concerto, Zukerman was "a modern performer in the best sense of the word . . . avoiding a throbbing vibrato, etching each phrase clearly, keeping a steady rhythm, approaching the notes literally though without pedanticism." Schonberg added that Zukerman "produces a large tone that is capable of infinite modulation" and "is not even afraid to produce a hard steely sound when it suits his purpose."

In addition to the violin, Zukerman played the viola in performances of, respectively, three movements of Mozart's Serenade in D K.203 and Telemann's Viola Concerto in G with the Musica Aeterna Orchestra under the direction of Frederick Waldman at the Metropolitan Museum of Art in November 1976. In New York in 1977 Zukerman gave a recital at Lincoln Center, in February, played with the New York Philharmonic, in April, conducted the Philharmonic, in June, and performed with the Chamber Music Society of Lincoln Center, in September.

Away from New York, Zukerman gave master classes in Aspen, Colorado during the Aspen Music Festival in the summer of 1977; during the 1977-78 season conducted the Toronto Symphony and was soloist with the Berlin Philharmonic; and in July 1978 performed at the Caramoor and Tanglewood festivals. Back in New York later in July, he conducted at the Mostly Mozart Festival. On his 1978-79 schedule were engagements with the New York Philharmonic and the Chamber Music Society of Lincoln Center.

On the Angel, Columbia, and Deutsche Grammophon labels, Pinchas Zukerman has recorded a repertoire ranging from Bach to Kabalevsky. As a writer for Cue (April 15-April 28, 1978) noted, "The album of Brahms violin and viola sonatas (with Daniel Barenboim as pianist), and the Elgar Violin Concerto (Barenboim conducting) "capture the sure musicality and glowing tone that led the London *Times* to declare him 'absolutely without peer among violinists.' "

Pinchas Zukerman is a muscular, bearded man, six feet tall and weighing 185 pounds, with brown eyes and brown hair. He likes spicy foods, drinks very little alcohol, smokes cigars, plays tennis, goes horseback riding, and enjoys spectator sports. Zukerman and the flutist Eugenia Rich were married in a Jewish religious ceremony on May 26, 1968. With their two children, Arianna and Natalia, they live in a nine-room apartment overlooking the Hudson River in Manhattan. Pointing to a Picasso lithograph in his apartment when being interviewed by Bridget Paolucci for *High Fidelity/Musical America* (August 1978), Zukerman said: "I love the simplicity, the flowing line. People tell me I play such long lines. There's no stoppage in music; even rests are coming from somewhere and going somewhere."

Pinky, as he is known to his friends, described his feeling for music to Eleanor Blau in an interview for the New York *Times* (February 18, 1977) in these words: "It's like walking in a desert and all of a sudden you need water. If you can transmit this to the audience, this wonderful need for music, well, that is what you are always trying to do." He said that his practising is done now "mostly in the head" and that except for ironing out a few "tricky" passages he just studies the scores. "I think about it. I'm constantly inside of music."

References: N Y Post p39 Jl 18 '75 por; N Y Times II p 15+ N 7 '71 por; II p17+ Jl 16 '78; N Y Times Mag p56+ Ap 18 '76 pors; Who's Who in America, 1978-79

OBITUARIES

ALVAREZ, WALTER C(LEMENT) July 22, 1884-June 18, 1978 Physician; physiologist; author; authority on the digestive tract and its diseases; was consultant in internal medicine at Mayo Clinic from 1934 to 1950; simultaneously, was professor at Mayo Foundation at University of Minnesota; edited several periodicals, including *Modern Medicine* and *Geriatrics;* wrote prolifically for popular as well as professional publications; in addition to some thousand articles and a syndicated newspaper column, produced numerous books, including *Little Strokes* (1966) and his autobiography, *Incurable Physician* (1966); died in his native San Francisco. See *Current Biography* (September) 1953.

Obituary

N Y Times B p12 Je 20 '78

ASCOLI, MAX June 25, 1898-Jan. 1, 1978 Former publisher; writer; political scientist; in 1949 helped to found the *Reporter,* a biweekly liberal magazine of news interpretation, of which he was publisher and editor until its demise in 1968; author of several books on government and politics, including *The Power of Freedom* (1949); member of the graduate faculty of the New School for Social Research (1933-50); died in New York City. See *Current Biography* (February) 1954.

Obituary

N Y Times p24 Ja 2 '78

BERGEN, EDGAR Feb. 16, 1903-Sept. 30, 1978 Comedian; most popular ventriloquist in history of show business; played low-keyed straight man for his "star," the tophatted, monocled, wise-cracking wooden dummy, Charlie McCarthy, supported by the buck-toothed hayseed Mortimer Snerd and the old maid Effie Klinker; appeared in vaudeville and on Chautauqua circuit before making radio debut with Rudy Vallee (1936); had own, consistently successful radio program (1937-57); received special Academy Award for motion picture appearances (1937); also appeared on television and on nightclub circuit; died in Las Vegas, Nevada ten days after announcing retirement. See *Current Biography* (May) 1945.

Obituary

Washington Post B p8 O 1 '78

BEST, CHARLES H(ERBERT) Feb. 27, 1899-Mar. 31, 1978 American-born Canadian physician; physiologist; biochemist; co-discoverer of insulin for use in treatment of diabetes; was youngest member of team, working at University of Toronto in 1921, which isolated the hormone—a pancreatic excretion that turns sugar into energy—that now saves or lengthens lives of tens of millions of diabetics around the world; later headed department of physiology at the University of Toronto and the Banting-Best Institute, where he and his associates developed histamine, an antiallergic enzyme, and heparin, an anticoagulant used to slow blood clotting in heart surgery; died in Toronto. See *Current Biography* (June) 1957.

Obituary

N Y Times p24 Ap 1 '78

BIRDWELL, RUSSELL (JUAREZ) Oct. 17, 1903-Dec. 15, 1977 Public relations counsel; publicized hundreds of Hollywood stars, including Carole Lombard and Ronald Colman, and such major films as *The Outlaw* and *Gone With the Wind,* as well as such business organizations as the Celotex Corporation; author of the semiautobiographical *I Ring Door-Bells* (1939) and *Women in Battle Dress* (1942), a report on British women in World War II; died in Oxnard, California. See *Current Biography* (July) 1946.

Obituary

Variety 289:62 D 28 '77

BOBST, ELMER H(OLMES) Dec. 16, 1884-Aug. 2, 1978 Corporation executive; pharmacologist; philanthropist; president of American branch of F. Hoffmann-La Roche (1928-44), which he developed into a leading producer of vitamins; president (1945-54), board chairman (1954-67), and then honorary chairman of firm now known as Warner-Lambert Pharmaceutical Company; White House adviser on nation's health in administration of his close friend Richard M. Nixon; among other philanthropies, donated $11,000,000 to New York University toward construction of Elmer Holmes Bobst General Library and Study Center, dedicated in 1972; died in New York City. See *Current Biography* (December) 1973).

Obituary

N Y Times p32 Ag 4 '78

BOYER, CHARLES Aug. 28, 1899-Aug. 26, 1978 Actor; appeared in over seventy motion pictures, often as a romantic lover, and more recently in character roles; acted on stage and in films in his native France before settling in Hollywood in early 1930's; was perhaps best known for portrayal of Pepe Le Moko in *Algiers* (1938), which brought him an Academy Award nomination as best actor; also received three other Oscar nominations; appeared on Broadway stage in such plays as *Don Juan in Hell* (1951) and *Lord Pengo* (1962); cofounder (1951) and star of Four Star Playhouse television series; died in Phoenix, Arizona, of an overdose of sleeping pills, two days after his wife's death. See *Current Biography* (February) 1943.

Obituary

Variety 292:4+ Ag 30 '78

BRACE, GERALD WARNER Sept. 23, 1901-July 20, 1978 Author; professor of English at Boston University (1939-71); explored various aspects of New England life and extolled such virtues as self-control and moderation; wrote eleven novels, including *The Wayward Pilgrims* (1938), *The Garretson Chronicle* (1947), *Bell's Landing* (1955), *Winter Solstice* (1960), *The Wind's Will* (1964), and *The Department* (1968); also published literary criticism and reviews; died in Blue Hill, Maine. See *Current Biography* (Yearbook) 1947.

Obituary

N Y Times p22 Jl 22 '78

BRADEN, SPRUILLE Mar. 13, 1894-Jan. 10, 1978 Former United States government official; diplomat; known as a crusader for democracy in his service as Ambassador to Colombia (1939-42), to Cuba (1942-45), and to Argentina (1945); Assistant Secretary of State for Latin American Affairs (1946-47); in later years consultant to United States companies dealing with South American countries; died in Los Angeles while on a visit. See *Current Biography* (September) 1945.

Obituary

N Y Times B p2 Ja 11 '78

BREECH, ERNEST R(OBERT) Feb. 24, 1897-July 3, 1978 Former corporation executive; began career as cost accountant, in 1920; became, successively, comptroller of the Yellow Cab Manufacturing Company, president of North American Aviation, vice-president of General Motors, and president of Bendix Aviation Corporation; after World War II, in the position of president, helped rebuild Ford Motor Company; later, was chairman of Trans World Airlines; died in Royal Oak, Michigan. See *Current Biography* (September) 1955.

Obituary

N Y Times B p2 Jl 5 '78

BREL, JACQUES Apr. 8, 1929-Oct. 9, 1978 Belgian-born French composer, lyricist, and singer; performed in Paris bistros and cabarets (1953-67), becoming leading "troubadour pop" artist in France; wrote over 500 songs, many of them in bitter-sweet or cynical, anti-establishment mood, of which some were presented in English translation in Off-Broadway revue *Jacques Brel Is Alive and Well and Living in Paris* (1968-72); produced and starred in French version of musical *Man of La Mancha*, presented in Brussels and Paris (1968); died at Bobigny near Paris. See *Current Biography* (March) 1971.

Obituary

News World p47 O 10 '78

BRUCE, DAVID K(IRKPATRICK) E(STE) Feb. 12, 1898-Dec. 5, 1977 Statesman and diplomat; helped to administer the Marshall Plan after World War II; first member of the Foreign Service to hold the three top diplomatic posts in Europe, as Ambassador to France (1949-52), to West Germany (1957-59), and to Great Britain (1961-69); filled highly sensitive assignments as representative to Vietnam Peace Talks in Paris (1970-71) and liaison officer to Peoples Republic of China (1973-74); Ambassador to NATO (1974-76). Died in Washington, D.C. See *Current Biography* (September) 1961.

Obituary

N Y Times p1+ D 6 '77

BURGESS, W(ARREN) RANDOLPH May 7, 1889-Sept. 16, 1978 Banker; economist; vice-president (1936-38) of Federal Reserve Bank; vice-chairman (1938-48) and executive committee chairman (1948-52) of National City Bank of New York; board chairman of City Bank Farmers Trust Company (1948-52); as deputy secretary (1953-54) and undersecretary (1955-57) of United States Treasury, played key role in formulating Eisenhower administration's economic policies; United States Ambassador to NATO (1957-61); died in Washington, D.C. See *Current Biography* (June) 1949.

Obituary

Washington Post C p4 S 18 '78

BUTLER, JOHN M(ARSHALL) July 21, 1897-Mar. 16, 1978 Former Republican Senator from Maryland; lawyer; elected to six-year Senate term in 1950 and reelected in 1956; a staunch conservative, supported Senator Joseph R. McCarthy in his anti-Communist crusade, the controversial "witch-hunt," as liberals viewed it, that agitated the American national soul in the 1950's; sponsored legislation to outlaw Communist party; died in North Carolina, enroute from vacation in Georgia. See *Current Biography* (May) 1954.

Obituary

N Y Times B p2 Mr 17 '78

CAIN, JAMES M(ALLAHAN) July 1, 1892-Oct. 27, 1977 Author; known for lean, uncluttered crime novels that race terrifyingly to dénouement in the inexorable undoing of culprit or culprits; with the now classic *The Postman Always Rings Twice* (1934), introduced recurrent theme of perfidious wife conspiring with lover in murder of husband for profit; for sixteen years was screenwriter in Hollywood, where eight of his works, including masterpieces *Mildred Pierce* and *Double Indemnity*, were filmed; began career as journalist and, to the end, described himself as "newspaperman"; died at home in University Park, Maryland. See *Current Biography* (December) 1947.

Obituary

N Y Times p26 O 29 '77

CATTON, BRUCE Oct. 9, 1899-Aug. 28, 1978 Historian; former journalist and United States government official; author of over a dozen volumes vividly recreating American Civil War from "enlisted man's eye-view"; won

1954 Pulitzer Prize in history and National Book Award for *Stillness at Appomattox* (1953), the concluding volume of a trilogy that includes *Mr. Lincoln's Army* (1951) and *Glory Road* (1952); senior editor of *American Heritage* magazine since 1959; was awarded Presidential Medal of Freedom (1977); died at Frankfort, Michigan. See *Current Biography* (Yearbook) 1954.

Obituary

Time 112:76 S 11 '78

CHAPLIN, SIR CHARLES (SPENCER) Apr. 16, 1889-Dec. 25, 1977 British-born actor, writer, producer, and director; one of great film personalities of all time; starred in scores of silent two-reel comedies, usually in role of tragicomic "little tramp," before founding own Hollywood studio in 1918; wrote, produced, directed, and acted in such full-length classics as *The Kid* (1921), *The Gold Rush* (1925), *City Lights* (1931), *Modern Times* (1936), *The Great Dictator* (1940), and *Monsieur Verdoux* (1947); received special honorary Academy Award in 1972; was knighted by Queen Elizabeth II in 1975; died at Corsier-sur-Vevey, Switzerland, where he had lived in voluntary exile from United States since 1952. See *Current Biography* (March) 1961.

Obituary

N Y Times p1+ D 26 '77

CHAPMAN, OSCAR L(ITTLETON) Oct. 22, 1896-Feb. 8, 1978 Former United States government official; lawyer; strategist and troubleshooter for the Democratic party during the Administrations of Franklin D. Roosevelt and Harry S. Truman; Assistant Secretary (1933-46), Under Secretary (1946-49), and Secretary of the Interior (1949-53); member of the Washington, D.C. law firm of Chapman, Duff & Lenzini; died in Washington, D.C. See *Current Biography* (February) 1949.

Obituary

N Y Times B p2 F 9 '78

CHASE, ILKA Apr. 8, 1905-Feb. 15, 1978 Actress; author; appeared in a score of Broadway plays, including *The Women* (1936-38), in which she played Sylvia Fowler, and in about the same number of films, including *Fast and Loose* (1930) and *The Animal Kingdom* (1942); as a writer was noted for her acidulous wit in her autobiographical *Past Imperfect* (1942), the novel *In Bed We Cry* (1943), which she adapted into a play in which she starred, and a variety of other literary works; was also a popular radio and TV personality; died in Mexico City. See *Current Biography* (May) 1942.

Obituary

N Y Times B p11 F 16 '78

CHAVEZ, CARLOS (ANTONIO DE PADUA) June 13, 1899-Aug. 2, 1978 Mexican composer; conductor; in early works adapted Mexican Indian rhythms and harmonies to contemporary idiom, but later turned to traditional romantic style; founder and director of Orquesta Sinfónica de México (1928-48); founder and director of National Institute of Fine Arts (1947-52); director of National Conservatory (1928-29, 1934); guest conductor of many of world's leading orchestras, including New York Philharmonic, Boston Symphony, and Philadelphia Orchestra; died in Mexico City. See *Current Biography* (May) 1949.

Obituary

N Y Times B p2 Ag 4 '78

CHURCHILL, CLEMENTINE OGILVY HOZIER, BARONESS *See* Spencer-Churchill, C. O. H., Baroness of Chartwell

CLAY, LUCIUS D(UBIGNON) Apr. 23, 1897-Apr. 17, 1978 Retired general of the Army; business executive; in 1947 became military governor of Germany and commander in chief of the United States armed forces in Europe; supervised the rehabilitation of postwar Germany and resisted the threat of Soviet domination by organizing the Berlin airlift of 1948-49; accepted a variety of political and government assignments while serving as chairman and chief executive officer of the Continental Can Company (1950-62) and senior partner in the investment banking house Lehman Brothers (1963-73); died in Cape Cod, Massachusetts. See *Current Biography* (June) 1963.

Obituary

N Y Times p42 Ap 18 '78

COLE, DAVID L(AWRENCE) May 1, 1902-Jan. 25, 1978 Labor relations specialist; lawyer; helped to develop the system of arbitration in the settlement of labor disputes; during the labor-troubled 1930's, 1940's, and 1950's was an impartial participant in mediating and arbitrating major conflicts in steel, transportation, public utilities, and other fields; served on federal and state committees concerned with labor-management relations; died in Paterson, New Jersey. See *Current Biography* (January) 1949.

Obituary

N Y Times B p2 Ja 26 '78

CONANT, JAMES BRYANT Mar. 26, 1893-Feb. 11, 1978 Chemist; educator; diplomat; researcher and teacher in organic chemistry, mainly at Harvard University (1919-33); president of Harvard (1933-53); United States High Commissioner to West Germany (1953-55) and Ambassador to West Germany (1955-57); during late 1950's and early 1960's made a series of controversial studies on American public school education, recommending wide-ranging reform; died in Hanover, New Hampshire. See *Current Biography* (February) 1951.

Obituary

N Y Times D p9 F 13 '78

COZZENS, JAMES GOULD Aug. 19, 1903-Aug. 9, 1978 Author; noted for his meticulous craftsmanship and sharp delineation of character; wrote some sixteen books, including Pulitzer Prize-winning novel *Guard of Honor* (1948), set against a military background, and best-selling *By Love Possessed* (1957), which won the Howells Medal of the American Academy of Arts and Sciences and was made into a motion picture; also wrote many short stories, for *Saturday Evening Post, Collier's*, and other magazines; died in Stuart (Florida) Memorial Hospital. See *Current Biography* (June) 1949.

Obituary
Washington Post B p6 Ag 19 '78

CRAIG, CLEO F(RANK) Apr. 6, 1893-Apr. 21, 1978 Former utilities executive; spent entire career with American Telephone and Telegraph Company, beginning with a job as plant attendant in 1913; was promoted to positions in several divisions and elected to the board of various subsidiaries before serving as A.T.&.T.'s president (1951-56) and chairman (1956-57); died in Ridgewood, New Jersey. See *Current Biography* (September) 1951.

Obituary
N Y Times p22 Ap 22 '78

CROSBY, BING May 2, 1904-Oct. 14, 1977 (*Variety* places birth date three years earlier) Singer; actor; one of best-loved entertainers in history of American show business; noted for mellow, effortless renditions of such hits as "White Christmas" and "Blue Skies"; vocalist with dance bands, including Paul Whiteman's, in 1920's; was featured regularly on radio, beginning in 1931, and, later, irregularly on television; sold over 300,000,000 records; appeared in scores of films, including popular "Road" comedies with Dorothy Lamour and Bob Hope; won Academy Award as Father O'Malley in *Going My Way* (1944); engaged in various business, sports, and philanthropic enterprises; died of heart attack while playing on La Moraleja Golf Course near Madrid, Spain. See *Current Biography* (June) 1953.

Obituary
N Y Times p1+ O 15 '77

DALY, JAMES (FIRMAN) Oct. 23, 1918-July 3, 1978 Actor; accumulated over 600 television credits, including role of Dr. Paul Lochner in *Medical Center* series and Emmy award-winning performance in Hallmark Hall of Fame production *Eagle in a Cage* (1965); on stage, appeared in such Broadway productions as a revival of *Major Barbara* (1950) and *J.B.* (1959), in which he replaced Pat Hingle in starring role; also appeared in films *The Court Martial of Billy Mitchell* (1955), *Planet of the Apes* (1968) and others; died in Nyack, New York. See *Current Biography* (October) 1959.

Obituary
N Y Times B p2 Jl 7 '78

DIX, WILLIAM S(HEPHERD) Nov. 19, 1910-Feb. 22, 1978 Librarian of Princeton University (1953-75); chairman of the United States Commission for UNESCO (1955-61); president of the American Library Association (1969-70); as chairman of the shared cataloging committee of the Association of Research Libraries (1964-68) worked for Congressional acceptance of an amendment providing for the Library of Congress' international program of centralized cataloging; died in Princeton, New Jersey. See *Current Biography* (June) 1969.

Obituary
N Y Times B p2 F 23 '78

EAMES, CHARLES June 17, 1907-Aug. 21, 1978 Designer; architect; popularized modern furniture in post-World War II years with his mass-produced form-fitting Eames chairs, made of molded plywood and other materials; pioneered in use of multimedia techniques in the production of educational documentary films; noted for his designs of buildings, fabrics, machinery, and toys, and his techniques for planning exhibits; design consultant for Westinghouse Electric, IBM, and other corporations; won many honors, including Kaufmann International Design Award (1960), which he shared with his wife and collaborator, Ray Kaiser Eames; died in his native St. Louis, Missouri. See *Current Biography* (January) 1965.

Obituary
Washington Post C p8 Ag 24 '78

ECCLES, MARRINER S(TODDARD) Sept. 9, 1890-Dec. 18, 1977 United States government official; business executive; a principal architect of the government-spending policy of Roosevelt's New Deal legislation; member (1936-51) and chairman (1936-48) of the Federal Reserve Board; directed several major financial and industrial companies in Utah and the West; died in Salt Lake City. See *Current Biography* (April) 1941.

Obituary
N Y Times p38 D 20 '77

EGHBAL, MANOUCHEHR Oct. 13, 1909-Nov. 25, 1977 Iranian physician and politician; was professor of infectious diseases at University of Teheran (1940-53); appointed to succession of increasingly important government administrative posts (1943-50); served as permanent Iranian representative to UNESCO (1961-77); headed National Iranian Oil Company (1963-77); died in Teheran. See *Current Biography* (May) 1959.

Obituary
N Y Times p24 N 26 '77

EGLEVSKY, ANDRÉ Dec. 21, 1917-Dec. 4, 1977 Ballet dancer; a classicist acclaimed for his technical virtuosity; performed with many European and American companies, including the New York City Ballet (1951-58); in latter part of career opened a ballet school in Massapequa, New York and formed his own company, Eglevsky Ballet; died in Elmira, New York, where his company was scheduled to perform. See *Current Biography* (February) 1953.

Obituary

N Y Times p40 D 5 '77

ELIOT, MARTHA MAY Apr. 7, 1891-Feb. 1978 Pediatrician; official of the United States Children's Bureau (1924-56); made contributions to social welfare as well as child care through work with the World Health Organization, UNICEF, and other organizations; was affiliated with Yale University (1921-46) and Harvard University (1956-60); the first woman president of the American Public Health Association (1947-48); died in Cambridge, Massachusetts. See *Current Biography* (October) 1948.

Obituary

N Y Times B p2 F 23 '78

EVANS, BERGEN Sept. 19, 1904-Feb. 4, 1978 Writer; professor of English at Northwestern University (1932-75); author of *The Natural History of Nonsense* (1946), a witty debunking of fallacies; as an authority on usage wrote *A Dictionary of Contemporary American Usage* (1957) and was host of two television programs concerned with language, *The Last Word* and *Down You Go;* died in Highland Park, Illinois. See *Current Biography* (Yearbook) 1955.

Obituary

N Y Times p28 F 5 '78

FABIAN, ROBERT (HONEY) Jan. 31, 1901-June 14, 1978 Former British police official; author; joined London police department in 1921; moved to Criminal Investigation Department at Scotland Yard two years later; was chief of Yard's "Flying Squad" from 1943 to 1945; after his retirement, in 1949, wrote crime feature stories for Kemsley newspaper chain; recounted thirty of the cases he solved as a detective in *Fabian of the Yard* (1950), which became basis of a television series; also wrote *London After Dark* (1954); died in Epsom, Surrey. See *Current Biography* (April) 1954.

Obituary

N Y Times B p18 Je 15 '78

FINE, JOHN S(YDNEY) Apr. 10, 1893-May 21, 1978 Former Governor of Pennsylvania; state Republican party leader; lawyer; before election to four-year term as Governor, in 1950, served as judge on, successively, Court of Common Pleas of Luzerne County and State Superior Court; died in Wilkes-Barre, Pennsylvania. See *Current Biography* (September) 1951.

Obituary

N Y Times D p10 My 22 '78

FISCHER, JOHN Apr. 27, 1910-Aug. 18, 1978 Journalist; worked for United Press and Associated Press in Europe and Washington, D.C. before World War II and in government posts during war; joined staff of *Harper's Magazine* in 1944; served as its editor in chief (1953-67) and then as contributing editor, and wrote its column "The Easy Chair"; author of *Why They Behave Like Russians* (1947), *Master Plan, U.S.A.* (1951), and other books; died at Yale-New Haven Hospital in Connecticut. See *Current Biography* (May) 1953.

Obituary

Washington Post C p3 Ag 21 '78

FITCH, AUBREY (WRAY) June 11, 1883-May 22, 1978 United States naval officer; aviator; commander of one of American task forces in battle of Coral Sea (1942) that helped to thwart Japanese assault on Australia; superintendent of United States Naval Academy (1945-47); served briefly as special assistant to Under Secretary of the Navy before retiring in 1947 with rank of admiral; died at New Castle, Maine. See *Current Biography* (October) 1945.

Obituary

N Y Times B p2 My 24 '78

FORD, BENSON July 20, 1919-July 27, 1978 Automobile manufacturer; grandson of automobile pioneer Henry Ford and brother of Ford Motor Company chairman Henry Ford II; joined Ford Motor Company in 1940; served on its board of directors (1941-78) and as a vice-president (1948-78); former chief executive (from 1948) of Lincoln-Mercury Division; chairman of Ford Dealer Policy Board (1956-78); died aboard his yacht on Cheboygan River in Michigan. See *Current Biography* (February) 1952.

Obituary

N Y Times B p2 Jl 28 '78

FRANÇOIS-PONCET, ANDRÉ June 13, 1887-Jan. 8, 1978 French diplomat; writer; president of the standing committee of the International Red Cross; as Ambassador in Berlin (1931-38) during the rise of Nazism warned repeatedly of Hitler's war preparations; High Commissioner in West Germany (1949-58); Ambassador in Bonn (1955); author of books on German literature and politics, including *The Fateful Years* (1949); died in Paris. See *Current Biography* (October) 1949.

Obituary

N Y Times p36 Ja 10 '78

FRICK, FORD C(HRISTOPHER) Dec. 19, 1894-Apr. 8, 1978 Baseball executive; former newspaperman and radio commentator; president of National League of Professional Baseball Clubs (1934-51); national commissioner of baseball (1951-65); helped to promote racial integration in major league baseball and presided over its expansion from coast to coast; was elected in 1970 to baseball Hall of Fame, which he had helped to found in 1938; author of *Memoirs of a Lucky Fan* (1973); died in Bronxville, New York. See *Current Biography* (May) 1945.

Obituary

N Y Times B p2 Ap 10 '78

GAINZA PAZ, ALBERTO Mar. 16, 1899-Dec. 26, 1977 Argentine newspaper publisher and editor; in 1943 succeeded to the control of family-owned *La Prensa,* an objective and editorially independent daily paper; was forced into exile in 1951 by the dictatorial President Juan Perón, who also seized the paper; resumed management of *La Prensa* in 1956, after the overthrow of Perón; was widely honored for journalistic integrity; died in Buenos Aires. See *Current Biography* (April) 1951.

Obituary

N Y Times p38 D 27 '77

GANNON, ROBERT I(GNATIUS), REV. Apr. 20, 1893-Mar. 12, 1978 Jesuit priest; was president of Fordham University in New York City from 1936 to 1949; earlier, had been dean of St. Peter's College in Jersey City, New Jersey and teacher of English and philosophy and director of dramatics at Fordham; later was retreat master at St. Ignatius Retreat House in Manhasset, Long Island; as educator, was a traditionalist, against permissiveness and loose curricula in undergraduate studies; wrote autobiographical *The Poor Old Liberal Arts* (1962), among other books, and published two collections of his witty speeches. See *Current Biography* (March) 1945.

Obituary

N Y Times A p19 Mr 13 '78

GARST, ROSWELL 1898(?)-Nov. 5, 1977 Agriculturalist; businessman; a leading authority on production of hybrid corn; proprietor of model farm at Coon Rapids, Iowa and a partner in Garst & Thomas Hybrid Corn Company, which he founded there in 1930; advised Eastern European Communist governments on improved methods of agricultural production during 1950's and 1960's; acted as host to Nikita S. Khrushchev during Soviet Premier's United States tour in 1959; author of book *No Need for Hunger* (1964); died at Carroll, Iowa. See *Current Biography* (April) 1964.

Obituary

N Y Times p38 N 7 '77

GAUD, WILLIAM S(TEEN, JR.) Aug. 9, 1907-Dec. 5, 1977 Former United States government official; financial consultant; assistant New York City corporation counsel (1935-41); law partner in Carter, Ledyard & Milburn (1946-61); assistant administrator (1961-64), deputy administrator (1964-66), and administrator (1966-69) of Agency for International Development; vice-president of International Finance Corporation (1969-74); consultant to World Bank Group (1974-76); national chairman of Population Crisis Center (1976); died in Washington, D.C. See *Current Biography* (January) 1969.

Obituary

N Y Times B p13 D 7 '77

GOLDMARK, PETER C(ARL) Dec. 2, 1906-Dec. 7, 1977 Engineer; corporation executive; revolutionized recording industry by developing long-playing phonograph record for Columbia Broadcasting System (1948); also contributed substantially to development of color television and other aspects of communications technology; chief television engineer (1936-44), director of engineering research and development (1944-50), and vice-president (1950-54) of CBS; president of CBS Laboratories (1954-71); founded Goldmark Communications Corporation (1971); died in automobile accident in Westchester County, New York. See *Current Biography* (December) 1950.

Obituary

N Y Times A p1 D 8 '77

GROSS, MASON W(ELCH) June 3, 1911-Oct. 11, 1977 University president; foundation executive; as sixtieth president of Rutgers, the State University of New Jersey (1959-71), was noted for fostering expansion of its facilities, doubling its student enrollment, reforming its curriculum, defending academic freedom, and maintaining a peaceful campus atmosphere during period of student unrest in 1960's; president of Harry Frank Guggenheim Foundation (1971-77); died at Red Bank, New Jersey. See *Current Biography* (June) 1969.

Obituary

N Y Times D p20 O 12 '77

HARRIMAN, E(DWARD) ROLAND (NOEL) Dec. 24, 1895-Feb. 16, 1978 Financier; began banking career in the firm of his brother, W. Averell Harriman; partner of Brown Brothers Harriman & Company (since 1931); director (since 1924) and chairman (1946-49) of the Union Pacific Railroad; president and chairman of the American National Red Cross (1950-53); founder in 1938 of the United States Trotting Association; died in Arden, New York. See *Current Biography* (March) 1951).

Obituary

N Y Times D p12 F 17 '78

HARRIS, BUCKY Nov. 8, 1896-Nov. 8, 1977 Baseball manager; member of baseball's Hall of Fame; joined Washington Senators as player in 1919; continued to play second base for seven years after becoming Washington's manager, in 1924, the year he led the Senators to their first pennant and first world championship; later managed four other teams, including the championship New York Yankees of 1947; returned to Washington to manage Senators twice; died in Bethesda, Maryland. See *Current Biography* (June) 1948.

Obituary

N Y Times D p23 N 10 '77

HIGHET, GILBERT (ARTHUR) June 22, 1906-Jan. 20, 1978 Classicist; university professor; literary critic; was Anthon Professor of Latin Language and Literature from 1950 to 1972 at Columbia University, where he had taught Latin and Greek since 1937; inspired enthusiasm for learning as a stimulating teacher, as the author of books on the Greek and Roman influence on Western literature, among other subjects, and as the broadcaster of a weekly radio program during the 1950's; died in New York City. See *Current Biography* (September) 1964.

Obituary

N Y Times p24 Ja 21 '78

HOBBS, LEONARD S(INCLAIR) Dec. 20, 1896-Nov. 1, 1977 Aircraft engineer; business executive; headed team that developed prototypical J-57 split compressor turbojet engine, which powered first American jet airliners and military aircraft; joined Pratt & Whitney, a subsidiary of United Aircraft Corporation (now United Technologies Corporation) as research engineer in 1927; vice-president for engineering (1944-56) and then (until retirement in 1958) vice-chairman of United Aircraft; received Collier Trophy for pioneering work on J-57 engine (1953); died in Hartford, Connecticut. See *Current Biography* (October) 1954.

Obituary

N Y Times B p11 N 3 '77

HOLLAND, (GEORGE) KENNETH May 10, 1907-Dec. 9, 1977 Educational administrator; as State Department official and foundation executive, promoted international understanding through cultural and educational exchanges; while president of Inter-American Educational Foundation (1945-46), implemented own plan for development of new schools in Latin America; served as United States representative to UNESCO (1948-50); president Institute of International Education (1950-73); died in Bronxville, New York. See *Current Biography* (March) 1952.

Obituary

N Y Times p28 D 10 '77

HUMPHREY, HUBERT H(ORATIO, JR.) May 27, 1911-Jan. 13, 1978 Democratic United States Senator from Minnesota (1949-64 and since 1970); was elected Vice-President in 1964 as the running mate of Lyndon B. Johnson; Democratic nominee for President (1968); taught political science at Macalester College and the University of Minnesota (1969-70); an ardent and articulate champion of liberalism whose very few deviations from that cause include his support in the 1960's of American intervention in the Vietnam War, a stand he later modified; one of the most influential and beloved leaders in federal government; died at his home in Waverly, Minnesota. See *Current Biography* (April) 1966.

Obituary

N Y Times p1+ Ja 14 '78

JAMES, DANIEL, JR. Feb. 11, 1920-Feb. 25, 1978 Retired United States Air Force officer; championed racial equality in the armed forces; in 1975 became the first black to achieve rank of four-star general; commander in chief, North American Air Defense Command, with headquarters in Colorado Springs, Colorado (1975-78); retired shortly before he suffered a fatal heart attack; died in Colorado Springs. See *Current Biography* (March) 1976.

Obituary

N Y Times p32 F 26 '78

KELDYSH, MSTISLAV (VSEVOLODOVICH) Feb. 10, 1911-June 24, 1978 Soviet mathematician, physicist; government official; a leading authority on vibration theory, especially as applied in aerodynamics; played fundamental roles in development of his country's nuclear, computer, and aerospace technologies; as president of Soviet Academy of Sciences, from 1961 to 1975, was chief spokesman for and overseer of U.S.S.R.'s scientific establishment; was also professor at University of Moscow, member of Communist party's Central Committee, and deputy in Supreme Soviet. See *Current Biography* (February) 1962.

Obituary

N Y Times B p6 Je 27 '78

KENYATTA, JOMO Oct. 20, 1891(?)-Aug. 22, 1978 President of Republic of Kenya (1963-78); respected elder statesman among leaders of newly independent African nations; entered politics full-time as general secretary of Kikuyu Central Association (1928); worked and studied intermittently in England (1929-46); became president of Kenya African Union in 1947 and of Kenya African National Union in 1961; was imprisoned by British (1953-61) as suspected leader of Mau Mau terrorist organization; as President, guided his people into moderately prosperous "African Socialism" and nonalignment in cold war. See *Current Biography* (April) 1974.

Obituary

Toronto Globe and Mail p10 Ag 23 '78

KHACHATURIAN, ARAM (ILICH) June 6, 1903-May 1, 1978 Soviet composer; noted for folk-oriented style inspired by music of his native Caucasus; composed chamber music, symphonies, concertos, motion picture scores, incidental music, and such ballets as *Gayne*, which includes the internationally popular "Saber Dance"; denounced by Soviet authorities, along with Shostakovich, Prokofiev, and other composers for "formalism" (1948), but was later rehabilitated; former deputy to U.S.S.R. Supreme Soviet and chairman of Union of Soviet Composers; was named People's Artist of the U.S.S.R., among many other honors; died in U.S.S.R. See *Current Biography* (March) 1948.

Obituary

N Y Times B p2 My 3 '78

KIMPTON, LAWRENCE A(LPHEUS) Oct. 7, 1910-Nov. 1, 1977 Educator; former chancellor of University of Chicago (1951-60); began career as teacher of philosophy and dean at, successively, Deep Springs College in California and University of Kansas City; during World War II administered University of Chicago's Metallurgical Laboratory, which was then engaged in construction of first atomic bomb; later was dean of students and professor of philosophy at Chicago and at Stanford University; after resigning Chicago chancellorship, was a vice-president of Standard Oil Company; died at home in Melbourne, Florida. See *Current Biography* (June) 1951.

Obituary

N Y Times B p4 N 2 '77

KIPNIS, ALEXANDER Feb. 1, 1891-May 14, 1978 Ukrainian-born singer; one of foremost bassos of his time, noted for richness and dramatic power of his voice; was best known for interpretations of Wagner and Russian operas; also won distinction for song recitals; member of Chicago Civic Opera (1923-30) and Metropolitan Opera (1940-45); appeared as guest at leading European and Latin American opera houses; after retirement from Met, taught at Juilliard School, at New York College of Music, and privately; died at Westport, Connecticut. See *Current Biography* (December) 1945.

Obituary

N Y Times p38 My 16 '78

KOCH, JOHN Aug. 18, 1909-Apr. 19, 1978 Artist; representational painter of the more fashionable people, lifestyles, and interiors of Manhattan whose technical facility and graceful manner assured his success even during the flourishing postwar years of abstract expressionism; won considerable critical respect with the renewed interest in realism in the 1960's; died in New York City. See *Current Biography* (May) 1965.

Obituary

N Y Times D p14 Ap 20 '78

KRAG, JENS OTTO Sept. 15, 1914-June 22, 1978 Social Democratic Prime Minister of Denmark (1962-68; 1971-72); expert in political economy; in Foreign Ministry and various other Cabinet posts, beginning in late 1940's, strove to reconcile Europe's rival trade organizations; as Prime Minister, led Denmark into European Economic Community, in 1972; later became Common Market's chief representative in United States; died at his summer home near Fredrikshavn, Denmark. See *Current Biography* (October) 1962.

Obituary

N Y Times D p13 Je 23 '78

LANGER, WILLIAM L(EONARD) Mar. 16, 1896-Dec. 26, 1977 Historian; one of foremost authorities on diplomatic history; faculty member (from 1927), Coolidge Professor of History (1936-64), and then professor emeritus, at Harvard University; chief of research and analysis branch of Office of Strategic Services during World War II; author of *The Franco-Russian Alliance 1890-1894* (1929), *European Alliances and Alignments 1871-1890* (1931), and *Diplomacy of Imperialism 1890-1902* (1935), among other books; editor of *Encyclopedia of World History* (1940) and multivolume *Rise of Modern Europe* series; died in Boston, Massachusetts. See *Current Biography* (December) 1968.

Obituary

N Y Times p31 D 27 '77

LEAKE, CHAUNCEY D(EPEW) Sept. 5, 1896-Jan. 11, 1978 Pharmacologist; educator; a pioneer researcher in the development of modern drugs; administrator and/or professor of pharmacology in several universities, including Ohio State University (1955-62) and the University of California Medical School at San Francisco (since 1962), also lectured and wrote on the history and philosophy of medicine; served as president of the American Association for the Advancement of Science (1960) and other organizations; died in San Francisco. See *Current Biography* (April) 1960.

Obituary

N Y Times B p6 Ja 13 '78

LEAR, WILLIAM P(OWELL) June 26, 1902-May 14, 1978 Industrialist; electrical engineer; inventor; founder and president (1939), and later board chairman, of Lear, Inc.; chairman of Lear Jet Corporation (1963-67) and Lear Motors Corporation (1967-69); held some 150 patents in such areas as radio, electronics, automotive engineering, and aviation technology; developed, among other innovations, first practical car radio, automatic pilot for aircraft, eight-track stereo cartridge, and Learstar jet airplane; died in Reno, Nevada. See *Current Biography* (July) 1966.

Obituary

N Y Times D p12 My 15 '78

LEIBOWITZ, SAMUEL S(IMON) Aug. 14 1893-Jan. 11, 1978 Former judge; began career as a criminal defense lawyer in New York City; while defending nine black Alabama youths in the Scottsboro case in the 1930's brought about a Supreme Court ruling banning exclusion of blacks from juries; judge of Kings County Court in Brooklyn (1940-61); justice of Supreme Court of New York (1961-69); died in Brooklyn. See *Current Biography* (January) 1953.

Obituary

N Y Times B p2 Ja 12 '78

LLOYD, (JOHN) SELWYN (BROOKE) *See* Selwyn-Lloyd, Baron

LOMBARDO, GUY (ALBERT) June 19, 1902-Nov. 5, 1977 Canadian-born bandleader; introduced "sweetest music this side of heaven," a velvety sound with slow tempo and simplified arrangements, to popular dance music in 1920's; with his Royal Canadians, remained a national institution even after his vogue passed, into the swing, bop, and rock eras; known for nearly half a century for New Year's Eve broadcasts from the Roosevelt and Waldorf-Astoria hotels in New York City; died in Houston, Texas. See *Current Biography* (February) 1975.

Obituary

N Y Times p38 N 7 '77

LUBIN, ISADOR June 9, 1896-July 6, 1978 Economist; member of President Franklin D. Roosevelt's "brain trust"; served as United States Commissioner of Labor Statistics (1933-46) and in other key government posts; was appointed special assistant to the President in 1941; after World War II, served on Allied Reparations Commission in Moscow and represented United States on U.N. Economic and Social Council; New York State Industrial Commissioner (1955-59); died at Annapolis, Maryland. See *Current Biography* (January) 1953.

Obituary

N Y Times p22 Jl 8 '78

McCARTHY, JOE Apr. 21, 1887-Jan. 13, 1978 Former baseball manager; managed the Chicago Cubs (1926-30), the New York Yankees (1931-46), and the Boston Red Sox (1948-50); while managing the Yankees won eight American League pennants and seven World Series titles; first manager to win pennants in both the American and National leagues; was elected to baseball's Hall of Fame in 1957; died in Buffalo, New York. See *Current Biography* (May) 1948.

Obituary

N Y Times p24 Ja 14 '78

McCARTHY, JOSEPH VINCENT *See* McCarthy, Joe

McCLELLAN, JOHN L(ITTLE) Feb. 25, 1896-Nov. 27, 1977 United States Senator from Arkansas; first elected in 1942, served seven consecutive terms in Senate; was chairman of Permanent Investigations Subcommittee (1955-72) and Appropriations Committee (1973-77); best known for heading Senate investigations into organized labor in 1950's and organized crime and campus antiwar demonstrations in 1960's; in recent years, worked on revision of United States Criminal Code; died at his home in Little Rock. See *Current Biography* (April) 1950.

Obituary

N Y Times p40 N 29 '77

McCLOSKEY, MARK A(LEXANDER) Oct. 21, 1891-Nov. 13, 1977 Social worker; public official; specialist in youth education, recreation, and rehabilitation; former chairman of New York State Youth Commission (1955-60); early in career was, for sixteen years, associate head worker with Hudson Guild Settlement House in Manhattan; directed National Youth Administration for New York City from 1936 to 1938; during World War II served as director of recreation in the Federal Security Agency and of Office of War Community Services; died in Northfield, Vermont. See *Current Biography* (November) 1955.

Obituary

N Y Times p44 N 15 '77

McGINLEY, PHYLLIS Mar. 21, 1905-Feb. 22, 1978 Writer of well-crafted light verse that celebrated life in the suburbs; winner of the 1961 Pulitzer Prize in poetry for *Times Three: Selected Verse from Three Decades* (1960), becoming the first writer of light verse so honored; also wrote essays and several books for children; died in New York City. See *Current Biography* (November) 1961.

Obituary

N Y Times B p2 F 23 '78

McKEEN, JOHN E(LMER) June 4, 1903-Feb. 23, 1978 Former drug company executive; chemical engineer; president (1949-65) and chairman (1950-68) of Chas. Pfizer & Company; developed that minor Brooklyn chemical plant into one of America's largest pharmaceutical companies, the manufacturer of penicillin and Terramycin, among other products, with sizable foreign and domestic markets; died in Palm Beach, Florida. See *Current Biography* (June) 1961.

Obituary

N Y Times p32 F 26 '78

MARKEL, LESTER Jan. 9, 1894-Oct. 23, 1977 Journalist; as innovative Sunday editor of the New York *Times* (1923-64), set the pattern for multisection Sunday papers nationwide; was proudest of his establishment of Sunday *Times*'s interpretative "Week in Review" section; beginning in 1963, moderated *News in Perspective* program on national public television; after retirement as associate editor of *Times*, in 1968, was consultant to National Educational Television network, died at home in Manhattan. See *Current Biography* (December) 1952.

Obituary

N Y Times p1+ O 24 '77

MARSHALL, S(AMUEL) L(YMAN) A(TWOOD) July 18, 1900-Dec. 17, 1977 Military historian; journalist; United States Army officer; chief of orientation for Army, founder of Army News Service, and chief historian in Central Pacific and European theatres, during World War II; author of some thirty books, including *Bastogne* (1946), Korean war saga *Pork Chop Hill* (1956), and *Vietnam Primer* (1967); after retirement from active duty (1960) with rank of brigadier general, served as Vietnam war consultant to Pentagon; died at Fort Bliss, Texas. See *Current Biography* (November) 1953.

Obituary

N Y Times p44 D 18 '77

MENZIES, SIR ROBERT G(ORDON) Dec. 20, 1894-May 14, 1978 Prime Minister of Australia (1939-41; 1949-66); dominant Australian political figure during World War II and postwar years; as head of conservative coalition of Liberal and Country parties, removed wartime economic controls, encouraged private enterprise, and led Australia into anti-Communist foreign policy that included participation in Korean war and support of Pacific Defense Pact and SEATO; author of autobiography *Afternoon Light* (1967) and other books; was knighted by Queen Elizabeth II in 1963; died at his home in Melbourne. See *Current Biography* (January) 1950.

Obituary

N Y Times p38 My 16 '78

MESSERSCHMITT, WILLY June 26, 1898-Sept 15, 1978 German aircraft pioneer; director and chief designer of Bayerische Flugzeugwerke, later known as Messerschmitt A. G. Augsburg (1927-45); developed Me-109 fighter plane, which ruled skies in early stages of World War II; also designed Me-262 twin-engine jet fighter; was found to be a "reluctant beneficiary" of Hitler regime by de-Nazification court (1948); resumed production of planes in late 1950's; later became honorary board chairman of Messerschmitt-Bölkow-Blohm G.m.b.H. and adviser to Hispano Aviación of Spain; died in West Germany after major surgery. See *Current Biography* (April) 1940.

Obituary

Newsday p23 S 16 '78

METCALF, LEE Jan. 28, 1911-Jan. 12, 1978 Democratic United States Senator from Montana (since 1961); as member of the House of Representatives (1953-60) and as Senator advocated bills favoring conservation, aid to education, and consumer protection and other liberal legislation; died in Helena, Montana. See *Current Biography* (February) 1970.

Obituary

N Y Times B p2 Ja 13 '78

MONTOYA, JOSEPH M. Sept. 24, 1915-June 5, 1978 Former United States Democratic Senator from New Mexico (1965-77); member of Senate Select Committee on Presidential Campaign Activities, or Watergate Committee (1973); served in elective state offices in New Mexico for some twenty years before entering United States Congress in 1957; as Senator, supported interests of farmers, organized labor, consumers, and poor and was an early opponent to United States military involvement in Vietnam; was defeated in bid for third Senate term (1976); died in Washington, D.C. See *Current Biography* (March) 1975.

Obituary

N Y Times D p17 Je 6 '78

MOORE, SIR HENRY R(UTHVEN) Aug. 29, 1886-Mar. 12, 1978 British naval officer, retired; was navigator in battle of Jutland in World War I; served as naval assistant at Washington Conference for Limitation of Armaments in 1921 and 1922; directed the climactic sea-air assault on German ships off Norway, thus earning rank of full admiral and command of Home Fleet; after World War II, headed Admiralty's delegation in Washington and represented Britain on Military Staff Committee advising United Nations Security Council; died in Kent, England. See *Current Biography* (September) 1943.

Obituary

N Y Times B p2 Mr 15 '78

MOREELL, BEN Sept. 14, 1892-July 30, 1978 United States naval officer; during World War II organized and commanded 250,000-man Naval Construction Battalions, or Seabees, which built Pacific shore installations to back up naval action against Japanese; federal administrator of strike-bound petroleum and coal industries (1945-46); after retirement from active naval service with rank of admiral (1946), served as president of Turner Construction Company and then (1947-58) as chairman of Jones and Laughlin Steel Corporation; died in Pittsburgh, Pennsylvania. See *Current Biography* (June) 1946.

Obituary

N Y Times D p7 Jl 31 '78

MORO, ALDO Sept. 23, 1916-May 8, 1978 Italian political leader; former law professor; served as Minister of Justice and Foreign Minister, and in other Cabinet posts, during more than thirty years in Italian politics; Prime Minister (1963-68, 1974-76); leader of Christian Democratic party since 1976; was noted for skill in political maneuvering; helped to formulate compromise plan (1976) for parliamentary cooperation between Christian Democrats and Communists; was found dead in Rome, fifty-four days after his abduction by members of terrorist Red Brigades. See *Current Biography* (June) 1964.

Obituary

N Y Times A p1+ My 10 '78

MURPHY, ROBERT D(ANIEL) Oct. 28, 1894-Jan. 9, 1978 Former career diplomat; business executive; a principal planner of the World War II Allied landings in North Africa (1942); many diplomatic posts included political adviser for Germany (1944) and Ambassador to Belgium (1949-52) and to Japan (1952); Under Secretary of State for Political Affairs (1959); in later years served as chairman of Corning Glass International and director of Corning Glass Works; died in New York City. See *Current Biography* (November) 1958.

Obituary

N Y Times B p9 Ja 11 '78

NESTINGEN, IVAN A(RNOLD) Sept. 23, 1921-Apr. 24, 1978 Former government official; lawyer; Democratic mayor of Madison, Wisconsin (1956-61); an early supporter of the Presidential candidacy of John F. Kennedy, who appointed him Under Secretary of Health, Education, and Welfare, in which post he served from 1961 to 1965; died in Washington, D.C. See *Current Biography* (March) 1962.

Obituary

N Y Times B p4 Ap 26 '78

OBOLENSKY, SERGE Oct. 3, 1890-Sept. 29, 1978 Socialite; businessman; member of one of Russia's oldest noble families, distantly related to Romanov czars; emigrated from Russia in 1919; after coming to United States in 1924, held various positions in banking and hotel administration, including that of executive vice-president in charge of international development with Hilton Hotels (1948-49); later headed promotion consultant firm of Serge Obolensky Associates; died at his home in Grosse Pointe, Michigan. See *Current Biography* (October) 1959.

Obituary

Washington Post B p8 O 1 '78

PAPASHVILY, GEORGE 1895(?)-Mar. 29, 1978 Author; emigrated from Soviet Georgia to settle in the United States in 1923; with his American wife, Helen, wrote *Anything Can Happen* (1945), a lighthearted account of his madcap adventures and misadventures in discovering America and adapting to its ways; also with his wife, recounted a visit to his birthplace in *Home and Home Again* (1973) and published books about Soviet Georgian folklore and cuisine; died in Cambria, California. See *Current Biography* (March) 1945.

Obituary

N Y Times B p2 Mr 31 '78

PAUL VI, POPE Sept. 26, 1897-Aug. 6, 1978 262d Supreme Pontiff of Roman Catholic Church (1963-78); served with Vatican Secretariat of State (1923-54) and was close adviser to Pope Pius XII; Archbishop of Milan (1954-63); was created a Cardinal in 1958; after his election as Pope, reconvened Second Vatican Council (1962-65) begun by his predecessor, Pope John XXIII; carried out such reforms as creation of Synod of Bishops and replacement of Latin Mass with vernacular, but resisted demands for modification of Church doctrines concerning Papal infallibility, priestly celibacy, and ban on artificial means of birth control; championed world peace, human rights, social justice, and ecumenism; died at his summer retreat at Castel Gandolfo, Italy. See *Current Biography* (November) 1963.

Obituary

N Y Times A p1+ Ag 7 '78

PAYNE, FREDERICK G. July 24, 1900-June 15, 1978 Former Republican Senator from Maine; was Mayor of Augusta, Maine from 1935 to 1940; served two terms as Governor of Maine, from 1949 to 1953; after one six-year term in United States Senate, was unseated by Democrat Edmund S. Muskie in 1958; died in Waldoboro, Maine. See *Current Biography* (December) 1952.

Obituary

N Y Times B p4 Je 16 '78

PEI, MARIO (ANDREW) Feb. 16, 1901-Mar. 2, 1978 Italian-born American philologist; educator; writer; taught romance philology at Columbia University from 1937 to 1970; made the formidable study of world linguistics and etymology a fascinating pursuit in well over a score of books, including acclaimed companion volumes *The Story of Language* (1949) and *The Story of English* (1952); in addition, wrote several books in other genres or on other subjects, including *The Consumer's Manifesto* (1960) and *The America We Lost: The Concerns of a Conservative* (1968); died in Glen Ridge, New Jersey. See *Current Biography* (October) 1968.

Obituary

N Y Times p36 Mr 5 '78

PERVUKHIN, MIKHAIL G(EORGIEVICH) Oct. 14, 1904-July 1978 Former Deputy Prime Minister of the U.S.S.R.; electrical engineer; industrial manager; directed Soviet fuel, energy, and chemistry programs during World War II; later supervised nuclear weapons research and foreign aid; was member of the Communist party's ruling Presidium, from 1952 until 1957, when he was ousted by Nikita S. Khrushchev; served as Ambassador to East Germany from 1958 until 1962; was reported dead in *Pravda* on July 25, 1978. See *Current Biography* (March) 1956.

Obituary

N Y Times B p2 Jl 26 '78

PETERSON, F(RANK) RAYMOND Nov. 13, 1895-Nov. 26, 1977 Banker; was national bank examiner for federal government (1922-35); rose through ranks to become chairman and chief executive officer of First National Bank of New Jersey (1946-75); president of American Bankers Association (1949); died at his home in Hackensack, New Jersey. See *Current Biography* (February) 1950.

Obituary

N Y Times p34 N 28 '77

PURTELL, WILLIAM A(RTHUR) May 6, 1897-May 31, 1978 United States Republican Senator from Connecticut (1952-59); staunch supporter of President Dwight D. Eisenhower; helped to sponsor legislative proposals for restricting rights of labor unions; headed several manufacturing companies in Connecticut before entering politics in 1950; died at Hartford, Connecticut. See *Current Biography* (June) 1956.

Obituary

N Y Times D p21 Je 1 '78

RATTIGAN, SIR TERENCE (MERVYN) June 10, 1911-Nov. 30, 1977 One of most successful British dramatists; master of the "well-made" play that "unashamedly says nothing—except possibly that human beings are strange creatures"; wrote many hits for London stage—some of which also became successful on Broadway or in film adaptation—including *The Winslow Boy* (1946), *The Browning Version* (1948), *The Sleeping Prince* (1956) and *Separate Tables* (1956); also wrote motion picture scripts; died in Hamilton, Bermuda. See *Current Biography* (December) 1956.

Obituary

N Y Times B p23 D 1 '77

RATTNER, ABRAHAM July 8, 1895-Feb. 14, 1978 American-born Jewish painter who lived in France between the two World Wars and became identified with the Franco-American art world; was noted for intense, vividly colored designs with religious themes and moral concerns, executed on canvas and in tapestries and stained-glass windows; was also a printmaker; died in New York City. See *Current Biography* (March) 1948.

Obituary

N Y Times D p16 F 15 '78

RENNERT, GUNTHER Apr. 1, 1911-July 31, 1978 German opera director and producer; noted for imaginative stagings of operas ranging from preclassical to contemporary; as general manager of Hamburg Staatsoper (1946-56), restored it after wartime devastation into one of Europe's leading opera companies; headed Bavarian Staatsoper in Munich (1967-76); as free-lance director, staged operas in world's leading houses, including the Metropolitan; also directed plays on German and Austrian stage; died in Salzburg, Austria. See *Current Biography* (June) 1976.

Obituary

N Y Times B p2 Ag 2 '78

RITCHARD, CYRIL Dec 1, 1898-Dec 18, 1977 Australian-born actor; singer; director; was best known for Tony Award-winning portrayal, on Broadway, of the rascally Captain Hook in musical version of *Peter Pan* (1954) and for New York stage performances in *Visit to a Small Planet* (1957) and *The Roar of the Greasepaint, the Smell of the Crowd* (1965); also appeared on television and in motion pictures and directed operas and plays; died in Chicago, Illinois. See *Current Biography* (January) 1957.

Obituary

N Y Times p34 D 19 '77

ROCKEFELLER, JOHN D(AVISON), 3d Mar. 21, 1906-July 10, 1978 Philanthropist; financier; arts patron; grandson of oil industrialist John D. Rockefeller; among many other institutional posts, served as director of Rockefeller Center (1932-62); as president of Rockefeller Brothers Fund (1940-56); and as chairman of Rockefeller Foundation (1952-71), General Education Board (1932-71), Colonial Williamsburg (1934-54), Lincoln Center for the Performing Arts (1961-70), and Asia Society (1964-74); collected Asian and American art; delegate to Japanese peace treaty conference in San Francisco (1951); died in automobile collision in Westchester County, New York. See *Current Biography* (June) 1953.

Obituary

N Y Times A p1+ Jl 11 '78

ROSS, NELLIE TAYLOE Nov. 29, 1876-Dec. 19, 1977 First woman Governor in United States; served as Democratic Governor of Wyoming (1925-27), completing unexpired term of her late husband, William Bradford Ross; director of United States Mint (1933-53); died in Washington, D.C. See *Current Biography* (May) 1940.

Obituary

N Y Times B p11 D 21 '77

ROSTAND, JEAN Oct. 30, 1894-Sept. 3, 1977 French biologist; author; son of famed dramatist Edmond Rostand; as an independent researcher and scholar, became a leading authority on genetics, evolution theory, embryology, and crustaceans; author of over fifty books, including *A Biologist's View* (1956), *Can Man Be Modified?* (1959), and *Evolution* (1962), as well as works of fiction, philosophical essays, and sociological treatises; was honorary president of French peace movement and free thought movement; elected to French Academy (1959); was awarded UNESCO's Kalinga Prize for popularization of science (1959) and grand literary prize of city of Paris (1962). See *Current Biography* (December) 1954.

Obituary

France (French Embassy Press and Information Office) p2+ O '77 por

ROTHERMERE, ESMOND CECIL HARMSWORTH, VISCOUNT May 29, 1898-July 12, 1978 British newspaper publisher; Conservative Member of Parliament (1919-29); chairman (1932-71) and then president of Associated Newspapers Ltd., a chain that includes the conservative London *Daily Mail* and the *Evening News;* chairman of Newspaper Proprietors Association (1934-61); died in London, England. See *Current Biography* (December) 1948.

Obituary

N Y Times D p16 Jl 13 '78

RUBICAM, RAYMOND June 16, 1892-May 8, 1978 Advertising executive; writer; in 1923 cofounded Young & Rubicam, largest advertising agency in United States and second only to J. Walter Thompson Co. internationally; was president of ad agency until 1944, when he became chairman; introduced to advertising the use of Sunday comic strips and direct involvement of agency in development of ideas, talent, and programs for such radio series as *Henry Aldrich*; died at home in Scottsdale, Arizona. See *Current Biography* (December) 1943.

Obituary

N Y Times p42 My 9 '78

RUEFF, JACQUES (LEON) Aug. 23, 1896-Apr. 23, 1978 French economist; a leading advocate of return to gold standard in international monetary system; as financial counselor to President Charles de Gaulle's government, drafted reform program (1958) that helped to restore French economic stability; author of *The Age of Inflation* (1964) and other books; first economist to be elected to French Academy (1964); died in Paris. See *Current Biography* (February) 1969.

Obituary

N Y Times p40 Ap 25 '78

SAID BIN TAIMUR Aug. 13, 1910-Oct. 19, 1972 Sultan of Muscat and Oman (1932-70); subjected people of his oil-rich Persian Gulf realm to repression and poverty; maintained close relations with Great Britain; after being deposed by his son Qabus bin Said (who became Sultan of Oman) in 1970, lived in exile at Dorchester Hotel in London, England until his death. See *Current Biography* (October) 1957.

Obituary

International Who's Who, 1973-74

SCHIPPERS, THOMAS Mar. 9, 1930-Dec. 16, 1977 Conductor; noted for a musical style of freshness, authority, and seeming spontaneity; principal interpreter of the music of Gian-Carlo Menotti, with whom he founded the Spoleto Festival of Two Worlds in 1958; as a regular conductor of the Metropolitan Opera, beginning in 1955, conducted a record number of opening-night performances; became musical director of the Cincinnati Symphony Orchestra in 1970; conducted the New York Philharmonic and La Scala Opera, among other world-renowed orchestras; died in New York City. See *Current Biography* (April) 1970.

Obituary

N Y Times p28 D 17 '77

SELWYN-LLOYD, BARON July 28, 1904-May 17, 1978 British statesman; Conservative party politician; as Foreign Secretary, from 1955 to 1960, was regarded as a principal architect of controversial Suez invasion, in 1956; earlier served as Minister of Defense and, later, as Chancellor of the Exchequer; was member of House of Commons for thirty-one years until he accepted life peerage in 1976; died at home in Oxfordshire. See *Current Biography* (April) 1952.

Obituary

N Y Times B p14 My 18 '78

SHAW, ROBERT Aug. 9, 1927-Aug. 28, 1978 Actor; author; wrote five novels, thrillers with depth, including *The Hiding Place* (1959) and Hawthornden Prize-winning *The Sun Doctor* (1961); began acting career as member of Shakespeare Memorial Theatre at Stratford-on-Avon, in 1948; later accrued stage credits with the Old Vic, in the West End, and on Broadway, where he made debut as actor in *The Caretaker* (1961-62) and as author with the hit *The Man in the Glass Booth* (1968-69), his dramatization of his novel of the same name; on screen, was perhaps best known for roles as villains in *From Russia With Love* (1964) and *The Sting* (1973), as Henry VIII in *A Man for All Seasons* (1966), and as fanatical shark hunter Quint in *Jaws* (1975); played title role in network special *Luther* (ABC, 1968), among numerous other television assignments; died in Tourmakeady, Ireland. See *Current Biography* (May) 1968.

Obituary

Washington Post B p4 Ag 29 '78

SIDES, JOHN H(AROLD) Apr. 22, 1904-Apr. 3, 1978 Retired Navy officer; an authority on missile warfare and the first commander of robot-weapons warships; in 1960 was promoted to the rank of admiral and made commander in chief of the Pacific Fleet guarding the Far East and the United States West Coast, a post in which he served until 1963; died in Coronado, California. See *Current Biography* (January) 1961.

Obituary

N Y Times B p10 Ap 6 '78

SPENCER-CHURCHILL, CLEMENTINE OGILVY HOZIER, BARONESS OF CHARTWELL Apr. 1, 1885-Dec. 12, 1977 Wife of Sir Winston Churchill; married Churchill on September 12, 1908; was widely respected for her graciousness and resoluteness in supporting her husband's career in politics and government, especially during his years as Prime Minister; led a busy public life of her own in her service to the Red Cross, YWCA, and various community welfare causes; died in London. See *Current Biography* (July) 1953.

Obituary

N Y Times p1+ D 13 '77

SPROUL, ALLAN Mar. 9, 1896-Apr. 9, 1978 Former bank official; worked for thirty-seven years in the Federal Reserve System, for the first ten years in San Francisco and later in New York, serving as president and chief executive officer of the Federal Reserve Bank of New York from 1941 to 1956; was an authority on the world monetary system as well as national economy and finance; died in California. See *Current Biography* (December) 1950.

Obituary

N Y Times p40 Ap 11 '78

STEINBERG, WILLIAM Aug. 1, 1899-May 16, 1978 German-born conductor; was noted for serious, restrained, and precise baton technique; came to United States in 1938 as protégé of Arturo Toscanini; conducted San Francisco Opera (1944-52) and Buffalo Philharmonic (1945-52); as musical director of Pittsburgh Symphony Orchestra (1952-76), made it into one of most highly rated ensembles in United States; also served as musical director of London Philharmonic (1958-59) and Boston Symphony (1969-72); frequent guest conductor with New York Philharmonic, Metropolitan Opera, and other leading orchestras; made many recordings; died in New York City. See *Current Biography* (March) 1958.

Obituary

N Y Times B p2 My 17 '78

STONE, EDWARD D(URELL) Mar. 9, 1902-Aug. 6, 1978 One of foremost American architects; combined traditional and innovative elements in his style; founded own firm in 1935; taught at New York University (1935-40) and Yale (1946-52); chief of planning and design section of United States Army (1942-45); worked on design of Radio City Music Hall, Museum of Modern Art, American pavilion for 1958 Brussels World's Fair, United States Embassy in New Delhi, Kennedy Center for the Performing Arts in Washington, D.C., General Motors Building in New York City, among many others; died in New York City. See *Current Biography* (June) 1958.

Obituary

N Y Times C p10 Ag 8 '78

TREFFLICH, HENRY (HERBERT FREDERICK) Jan. 9, 1908-July 7, 1978 Animal dealer; known as "Monkey King of America"; for over fortv years, until his retirement in 1973, headed New York City animal importing firm that brought in more than 1,500,000 monkeys and thousands of other animals, birds, and reptiles and sold them to zoos, circuses, medical laboratories, and private buyers; supplied such animal celebrities as chimpanzee Cheetah, featured in Tarzan films; died in his home in Bound Brook, New Jersey. See *Current Biography* (January) 1953.

Obituary

N Y Times B p2 Jl 10 '78

UNTERMEYER, LOUIS Oct. 1, 1885-Dec. 18, 1977 Author; editor; lecturer; an influential anthologist and early champion of modern poetry whose collections of other writers' poems influenced the taste of American readers, especially students, for half a century; produced more than ninety books, mainly anthologies, but also several volumes of his own prose and poetry; died at his home in Newtown, Connecticut. See *Current Biography* (January) 1967.

Obituary

N Y Times p63 D 20 '77

UTLEY, FREDA Jan. 23, 1898-Jan. 21, 1978 Journalist; author; lecturer; correspondent for British newspapers in Japan and China in 1920's and late 1930's; author of books on the Far East, including *China at War* (1939); while working in Moscow at the Institute of World Economy and Politics (1930-36) became disillusioned with Communism, which she indicted in *The Dream We Lost* (1940) and other writings; died in Washington, D.C. See *Current Biography* (December) 1958.

Obituary

N Y Times D p7 Ja 23 '78

VASILEVSKY, ALEXANDER M(IKHAILOVICH) Sept. 30, 1895-Dec. 5, 1977 Soviet military officer; after twenty-five years of military service, named deputy chief (1941-42) and chief of staff (1942-49) of Russian Army; helped plan pivotal battle of Stalingrad during World War II; was Josef Stalin's minister of defense

(1949-53), but downgraded to deputy minister (1953-57), then inspector-general (1959-77) after confrontation with Premier Nikita S. Khrushchev; died in Moscow. See *Current Biography* (October) 1943.

Obituary

N Y Times B p4 D 7 '77

VELASCO ALVARADO, JUAN June 16, 1910-Dec. 24, 1977 President of Peru (1968-75); general in Peruvian army; headed leftist military junta that deposed civilian President Fernando Belaúnde Terry and carried out important economic and social reforms while nationalizing major industries; was overthrown in August 1975 in middle-class-supported coup headed by General Francisco Morales Bermúdes; died in Lima, Peru. See *Current Biography* (June) 1970.

Obituary

N Y Times p26 D 25 '77

WARNER, JACK L(EONARD) Aug. 2, 1892-Sept. 9, 1978 Motion picture producer; with three older brothers, pioneered in production, distribution, and exhibition of films; cofounder (1923), chief of production, president, and then board chairman of Warner Brothers Pictures; helped to produce first successful sound motion picture, *The Jazz Singer* (1927), and many other films, including such classics as *The Life of Emile Zola* (1937), *Casablanca* (1943), and *Treasure of the Sierra Madre* (1948); produced Academy Award-winning *My Fair Lady* (1964); died in Los Angeles. See *Current Biography* (January) 1945.

Obituary

Washington Post C p4 S 11 '78

WHITEHEAD, (WALTER) EDWARD May 20, 1908-Apr. 16, 1978 British business executive; after joining Schweppes Ltd. in 1950, promoted its tonic water abroad and became well known to Americans as debonair, bearded Englishman in advertisements extolling virtues of "Schweppervescence"; president (1953-67) and then chairman of Schweppes (USA) Ltd.; held rank of commander in British Royal Navy; was created Commander of the Order of the British Empire (1967); lived in Bahamas after retirement from Schweppes in 1971; died in Petersfield, England. See *Current Biography* (January) 1967.

Obituary

N Y Times p77 Ap 18 '78

WHITEHILL, WALTER MUIR Sept. 28, 1905-Mar. 5, 1978 Librarian; man of letters; director of the Peabody Museum of Salem (Massachusetts) from 1936 to 1942 and of the Boston Athenaeum since 1946; wrote *Spanish Romanesque Architecture of the Eleventh Century* (1941), several books on Boston, including *The Boston Public Library* (1956) and *Boston: A Topographical History* (1959), and several more on American maritime history; crusaded successfully for the restoration of Boston's Quincy Marketplace and the salvaging of other historic sites in the Hub city; died in Boston. See *Current Biography* (June) 1960.

Obituary

Time p73 Mr 20 '78

WILLIAMS, JAY May 31, 1914-July 12, 1978 Author; best known for his historical, science fiction, and adventure novels for children and young people, such as *The Counterfeit African* (1944), *The Sword and the Scythe* (1946), and *Eagle Jake and Indian Pete* (1947); also wrote adult historical novels, including *The Good Yeoman* (1948), about the Robin Hood legend, the nonfiction book *The Fall of the Sparrow* (1951), about extinct animal species, and mystery stories published under the name Michael Delving; died during visit to Great Britain. See *Current Biography* (Yearbook) 1955.

Obituary

N Y Times p28 Jl 16 '78

WILSON, I(RVING) W(HITE) Sept. 26, 1890-October 16, 1977 Industrialist; guided growth of Aluminum Company of America into billion-dollar business; joined Alcoa as electrochemical research technician in 1911; rose through the company's executive ranks to president (1951) and chairman of the board (1957); retired in 1960; died in Pittsburgh. See *Current Biography* (July) 1952.

Obituary

N Y Times p34 O 17 '77

WOOD, PEGGY Feb. 9, 1892-Mar. 18, 1978 Actress; author; began her fifty-seven-year acting career starring in musical comedies, including *Maytime* (1917); later went into such dramatic roles as female lead in *Blithe Spirit* (1941), accumulating more than seventy Broadway credits in all; on television, played title character in CBS television series *Mama*, beginning in 1949; won Academy Award nomination for best supporting actress as Mother Superior in *The Sound of Music* (1965), one of her few, scattered film credits; served in high offices in ANTA and other actors groups; outside of acting, wrote a number of books, including two volumes of memoirs and several novels; died in Stamford, Connecticut. See *Current Biography* (December) 1953.

Obituary

N Y Times p38 Mr 19 '78

WRISTON, HENRY M(ERRITT) July 4, 1889-Mar. 8, 1978 Educator; as president of Brown University, from 1937 to 1955, reorganized curriculum in accordance with his dictum that the essence of education is "the individual search for something significant"; had earlier been teacher of history at Wesleyan University and president of Lawrence University, later headed American Assembly, a public-issues "think tank" at Columbia University; during Eisenhower Administration, headed advisory committees on reorganization of United States diplomatic corps and White House formulation of national goals; died in New York City. See *Current Biography* (May) 1952.

Obituary

N Y Times D p19 Mr 9 '78

YOUNGDAHL, LUTHER W(ALLACE) May 29, 1896-June 21, 1978 Federal judge; as three-term Republican Governor of Minnesota, beginning in 1947, campaigned against gambling liquor, and vice, broke up rackets, and reformed mental institutions; in 1951 resigned governorship to accept appointment as judge of United States District Court for District of Columbia; was proudest of his defense of First Amendment rights in dismissing 1952 and 1955 indictments against Owen J. Lattimore, a principal target of Communist-hunting Senator Joseph R. McCarthy; died in Washington, D.C. See *Current Biography* (March) 1948.

Obituary

N Y Times D p13 Je 23 '78

BIOGRAPHICAL REFERENCES

Almanac of American Politics, 1978
American Architects Directory, 1970
American Bar, 1965
American Catholic Who's Who, 1976-77
American Medical Directory, 1972
American Men and Women of Science 13th ed (1976)
Asia Who's Who (1960)

Baseball Register, 1976
Biographical Directory of Librarians in the United States and Canada (1970)
Biographical Directory of the American Congress, 1774-1971 (1971)
Biographical Encyclopaedia & Who's Who of the American Theatre (1966)
Biographical Encyclopedia of Pakistan, 1971-72
Biographic Directory of the USSR (1958)
Burke's Peerage, Baronetage. and Knightage, 1970

Canadian Who's Who, 1973-75
Celebrity Register (1973)
Chi è? (1961)
China Yearbook, 1971-72
Chujoy, A., and Manchester, P. W., eds. Dance Encyclopedia (1967)
Concise Biographical Dictionary of Singers (1969)
Congressional Directory, 1978
Congressional Quarterly Almanac, 1978
Contemporary Authors (1962-78)
Contemporary Dramatists (1973)
Contemporary Novelists (1976)
Contemporary Poets (1975)
Contemporary Poets of the English Language (1970)

Debrett's Peerage, 1974
Department of State Biographic Register, 1972
Dictionary of Contemporary American Artists (1977)
Dictionary of International Biography, 1975
Dictionary of Latin American and Caribbean Biography (1971)
Dictionnaire de biographie française (1964)
Directory of American Judges (1955)
Directory of American Scholars (1974)
Director of British Scientists, 1966-67
Directory of Medical Specialists, 1972-73

Encyclopedia of Pop, Rock and Soul (1974)
Episcopal Clergy Directory, 1972
Ewen, D., ed. Composers of Today (1936); Living Musicians (1940); First Supplement (1957); Men and Women Who Make Music (1949); American Composers Today (1949); European Composers Today (1954); The New Book of Modern Composers (1961); Popular American Composers (1962; First Supplement, 1972); Composers Since 1900 (1969)

Feather, Leonard. Encyclopedio of Jazz (1960); Encyclopedia of Jazz in the Sixties (1966)
Filmgoer's Companion (1977)
Foremost Women in Communications (1970)

Grove's Dictionary of Music and Musicians (1955)

Hindustan Year Book and Who's Who, 1963
Hoehn, M.A., ed. Catholic Authors (1957)
Hvem er Hvem? 1973

International Authors and Writers Who's Who, 1978
International Motion Picture Almanac, 1977
International Television Almanac, 1977
International Who's Who, 1978-79
International Who's Who in Art and Antiques, 1976
International Who's Who in Music, 1975
International Who's Who in Poetry (1974-75)
International Year Book and Statesmen's Who's Who, 1978

Japan Biographical Encyclopedia & Who's Who, 1964-65
Jews in the World of Science (1956)
Junior Book of Authors (1951)

Kelly's Handbook to the Titled, Landed and Official Classes, 1964
Kleine Slavische Biographie (1958)
Kras Bla Bog, 1964
Kürschners Deutscher Gelehrten-Kalender, 1970

Leaders in Education (1974)
Leaders in Profile (1975)

McGraw-Hill Modern Men of Science (1966-68)
Martindale-Hubbell Law Directory, 1977
Middle East and North Africa, 1977-78
More Junior Authors (1963)

Nalanda Year-Book and Who's Who in India and Pakistan, 1958
National Cyclopaedia of American Biography current vols A-L (1926-72)
New Century Cyclopedia of Names (1954)
Nordness, Lee, ed. Art USA Now (1963)
Notable Names in the American Theatre (1976)
Nouveau Dictionnaire National des Contemporains (1968)

Official Catholic Directory, 1976

Panorama Biografico degli Italiani d'Oggi (1956)
Political Profiles (1976-77)
Poor's Register of Directors and Executives, 1974
Prominent Personalities in the USSR (1968)

Quién es Quién en la Argentina, 1968-69
Quién es Quién en Venezuela, Panama, Ecuador, Colombia, 1956

Robinson, Donald. 100 Most Important People in the World Today (1972)

Slonimsky, Nicholas. Baker's Biographical Dictionary of Musicians (1958)
Something About the Author (1971-77)

Third Book of Junior Authors (1972)
Thomas, S. Men of Space (1960-68)
Thompson, K. A. Dictionary of Twentieth-Century Composers (1973)
Thompson, O., ed. International Cyclopedia of Music and Musicians, 1964
Turkin, H., and Thompson, S. C. Official Encyclopedia of Baseball (1959)
Twentieth Century Authors (1942; First Supplement, 1955)
Two Hundred Contemporary Authors (1969)

Vem är Det, 1973

Webster's Biographical Dictionary (1971)
Wer ist Wer? (1975)
Who is Who in Music (1951)
Who's Who, 1978-79
Who's Who in Advertising (1963)
Who's Who in Africa, 1973
Who's Who in America, 1978-79
Who's Who in American Art (1978)
Who's Who in American Education, 1967-68
Who's Who in American Politics, 1977-78
Who's Who in Art (1974)
Who's Who in Australia, 1971
Who's Who in Austria, 1971-72
Who's Who in Baseball, 1971
Who's Who in Belgium (1962)
Who's Who in California, 1965
Who's Who in Canada, 1969-70
Who's Who in Chicago and Illinois (1950)
Who's Who in Colored America, 1950
Who's Who in Communist China (1969)
Who's Who in Engineering, 1964
Who's Who in Finance and Industry (1977-78)
Who's Who in France, 1976
Who's Who in France (Paris), 1953-54
Who's Who in Germany (1972)
Who's Who in Insurance, 1978
Who's Who in Israel, 1978
Who's Who in Italy, 1957-58
Who's Who in Labor, 1976
Who's Who in Latin America Pts 1-7 (1945-51)
Who's Who in Library Service (1970)
Who's Who in Malaysia, 1967
Who's Who in Music, 1969
Who's Who in New York, 1960
Who's Who in New Zealand (1968)
Who's Who in Opera, 1976
Who's Who in Philosophy (1969)
Who's Who in Professional Baseball (1973)
Who's Who in Publishing (1971)
Who's Who in Railroading in North America (1959)
Who's Who in Space, 1966-67
Who's Who in Spain, 1965
Who's Who in Switzerland, 1970-71
Who's Who in the Arab World, 1974-75
Who's Who in the East, 1977-78
Who's Who in the Midwest, 1978-79
Who's Who in the Netherlands, 1962-63
Who's Who in the South and Southwest, 1976-77
Who's Who in the Theatre (1977)
Who's Who in the USSR, 1972
Who's Who in the West, 1978 79
Who's Who in World Aviation and Astronautics (1958)
Who's Who in World Jewry (1972)
Who's Who of American Women, 1977-78
Who's Who of British Engineers, 1970-71
Who's Who of British Scientists, 1971-72
Who's Who of Jazz (1972)
Who's Who of Rhodesia, Mauritius, Central and East Africa, 1965
Who's Who of Southern Africa, 1970
Wie is Dat? (1956)
Women Lawyers in the United States (1957)
World Authors: 1950-1970 (1975)
World Biography (1954)
World Who's Who in Science (1968)
World's Who's Who of Women (1974-75)

PERIODICALS AND NEWSPAPERS CONSULTED

ALA Bul–American Library Association Bulletin
After Dark
Am Artist–American Artist
Am Libs–American Libraries
Am Scholar–American Scholar
Am Sociol R–American Sociological Review
America
Américas
Arch Forum–Architectural forum (disc.)
Arch Rec–Architectural Record
Archaeology
Art N–Art News
Arts
Arts & Arch–Arts & Architecture
Atlan–Atlantic Monthly
Aviation W–Aviation Week and Space Technology

Barron's
Bet Hom & Gard–Better Homes and Gardens
Biog N–Biography News
Book-of-the-Month Club N–Book-of-the-Month Club News
Book W–Book Week (disc.)
Broadcasting
Bsns W–Business Week

Cath World–Catholic World
Christian Sci Mon–Christian Science Monitor
Columbia J R–Columbia Journalism Review
Commonweal
Cong Digest–Congressional Digest
Cong Q–Congressional Quarterly Weekly Report
Coronet (disc.)
Cosmop–Cosmopolitan
Cue
Cur Hist–Current History
Cur World Leaders–Current World Leaders

Dance Mag–Dance Magazine

Ebony
Ed & Pub–Editor & Publisher
Encounter
Esquire

Facts on File
Family Circle
For Affairs–Foreign Affairs
For Policy Bul–Foreign Policy Bulletin
Forbes
Fortune

Good H–Good Housekeeping
Guardian

Harper's
Hi Fi–High Fidelity
Hi Fi/Stereo R–Hi/Fi Stereo Review
Holiday
House & Gard–House & Garden

Illus Lond N–Illustrated London News
Intellectual Digest (disc.)

Ladies Home J–Ladies' Home Journal
Lib J–Library Journal
Life
London Observer
Look (disc.)

McCall's
Mag Wall St–Magazine of Wall Street
Mlle–Mademoiselle
Modern Maturity
More (disc.)
Ms
Mus Am–Musical America
Mus Courier–Musical Courier (disc.)
Mus Mod Art–Museum of Modern Art Bulletin

N Y Daily News
N Y Tribune (disc.)
N Y Herald Tribune Bk R–New York Herald Tribune Book Review (disc.)
N Y Post
N Y Rev of Books–New York Review of Books
N Y Sunday News
N Y Times
N Y Times Bk R–New York Times Book Review
N Y Times Mag–New York Times Magazine
N Y World-Telegram–New York World-Telegram and Sun (disc.)
N Y World Journal Tribune (disc.)
Nat Geog Mag–National Geographic Magazine
Nat Observer–National Observer
Nation
Nations Bsns–Nation's Business
Nature
New Leader
New Repub–New Republic
New Statesm–New Statesman
New Times
New York–New York Magazine
New Yorker
Newsday
Newsweek

Opera N–Opera News

Penthouse
People
Philadelphia Inquirer
Playboy
Pop Sci–Popular Science Monthly
Psych Today–Psychology Today
Pub W–Publishers Weekly

Read Digest–Reader's Digest
Redbook
Reporter–The Reporter (disc.)
Rolling Stone

Sat Eve Post–Saturday Evening Post
Sat Night–Saturday Night
Sat R–Saturday Review
Sci Am–Scientific American
Sci Mo–Scientific Monthly
Sci N L–Science News Letter
Science
Show Bus Illus–Show Business Illustrated (disc.)
Spec–Spectator
Sport
Sports Illus–Sports Illustrated
Sr Schol–Senior Scholastic

Theatre Arts (disc.)
This Week–This Week Magazine (disc.)
Time–Time
Times Lit Sup–London Times Literary Supplement
Toronto Globe and Mail
Travel
TV Guide

U N Rev–United Nations Review
U S News–U.S. News & World Report

Variety
Village Voice
Viva
Vogue

Wall St J–Wall Street Journal
Washington M–Washington Monthly
Washington Post
White Plains Reporter Dispatch
Wilson Lib Bul–Wilson Library Bulletin

Yale R–Yale Review

CLASSIFICATION BY PROFESSION—1978

BUSINESS AND FINANCE
- Backe, John D.
- Ball, Lucille
- Bunker, Ellsworth
- Elliott, Osborn
- Ford, Henry, II
- Fox, Carol
- Haldeman, H. R.
- Klein, Calvin
- Laker, Frederick A.
- Miller, G. William
- Muldoon, Robert D.
- Rockefeller, John D., 4th
- Rohatyn, Felix G.
- Thomson, Meldrim, Jr.

COMMUNICATIONS
- Bond, Edward
- Brownmiller, Susan
- Elliott, Osborn
- Haldeman, H. R.
- Hooks, Benjamin L.
- Howe, Irving
- Jay, Peter
- Raskin, A. H.
- Schorr, Daniel
- Vreeland, Diana

DIPLOMACY
- Bunker, Ellsworth
- Jay, Peter
- Mansfield, Michael J.
- Toon, Malcolm

EDUCATION
- Gardner, John
- Giamatti, A. Bartlett
- Howe, Irving
- Koch, Kenneth
- Lamm, Norman
- Malamud, Bernard
- Smith, Virginia B.

FASHION
- Beene, Geoffrey
- Fawcett-Majors, Farrah
- Hemingway, Margaux
- Klein, Calvin
- Vreeland, Diana

FILM AND TELEVISION
- Andersson, Bibi
- Ashley, Elizabeth
- Asner, Edward
- Backe, John D.
- Ball, Lucille
- Clark, Roy
- Davis, Sammy, Jr.
- Deneuve, Catherine
- Dern, Bruce
- Fawcett-Majors, Farrah
- Gish, Lillian
- Goodson, Mark
- Hayden, Sterling
- Hemingway, Margaux
- Herzog, Werner
- Keaton, Diane
- Lucas, George
- MacLaine, Shirley
- Martin, Steve
- Newton-John, Olivia
- Saura, Carlos
- Schorr, Daniel
- Silverman, Fred
- Spacek, Sissy
- Spielberg, Steven
- Travolta, John
- Vereen, Ben
- Wilder, Gene

GOVERNMENT AND POLITICS
- Bokassa I, Emperor
- Brezhnev, Leonid I.
- Byrd, Robert C.
- Church, Frank
- Cleland, Max
- Costanza, Margaret
- Desai, Morarji
- Dukakis, Michael S.
- Elliott, Osborn
- Fälldin, Thorbjörn
- Flood, Daniel J.
- Geldzahler, Henry
- Goldwater, Barry M.
- González, Felipe
- Haldeman, H. R.
- Hooks, Benjamin L.
- Jay, Peter
- Johnson, Frank M., Jr.
- Jorgensen, Anker
- Kennedy, Edward M.
- Koch, Edward I.
- Mansfield, Michael J.
- Miller, G. William
- Mondale, Walter F.
- Muldoon, Robert D.
- Proxmire, William
- Qabus bin Said
- Ram, Jagjivan
- Rockefeller, John D., 4th
- Rohatyn, Felix G.
- Schroeder, Patricia
- Somoza, Anastasio
- Steel, David
- Thomson, Meldrim, Jr.
- Tindemans, Leo
- Toon, Malcolm
- Turner, Stansfield
- Videla, Jorge Raphaél
- Webster, William H.

INDUSTRY AND LABOR
- Ford, Henry, II
- Jorgensen, Anker
- McBride, Lloyd
- Ram, Jagjivan

INTERNATIONAL RELATIONS
- Bukovsky, Vladimir
- Muldoon, Robert D.
- Tindemans, Leo
- Toon, Malcolm

LAW
- Byrd, Robert C.
- Church, Frank
- Dukakis, Michael S.
- González, Felipe
- Johnson, Frank M., Jr.
- Neier, Aryeh
- Schroeder, Patricia
- Smith, Virginia B.
- Webster, William H.

LITERATURE
- Adams, Richard
- Aleixandre, Vicente
- Auchincloss, Louis
- Bond, Edward
- Clark, Eleanor
- Didion, Joan
- Donoso, José
- Gardner, John
- Giamatti, A. Bartlett
- Graves, Robert
- Hayden, Sterling
- Howe, Irving
- Koch, Kenneth
- Malamud, Bernard
- Shange, Ntozake
- Snyder, Gary
- Theroux, Paul

MILITARY
- Cleland, Max
- Somoza, Anastasio
- Turner, Stansfield
- Videla, Jorge Raphaél

MUSICAL COMPOSITION
- Frampton, Peter
- Giulini, Carlo Maria
- Lightfoot, Gordon
- Manilow, Barry
- Musgrave, Thea
- Sedaka, Neil
- Springsteen, Bruce

ORGANIZATIONS
- Hooks, Benjamin L.
- Kuhn, Maggie
- McBride, Lloyd
- Means, Russell
- Neier, Aryeh
- Schlafly, Phyllis

PERFORMING ARTS
- Andersson, Bibi
- Ashley, Elizabeth
- Asner, Edward
- Bond, Edward
- Clark, Roy
- Davis, Sammy, Jr.
- Dern, Bruce
- Fox, Carol
- Frampton, Peter
- Gish, Lillian
- Giulini, Carlo Maria
- Keaton, Diane
- Lightfoot, Gordon
- MacLaine, Shirley
- Mamet, David
- Manilow, Barry
- Marriner, Neville
- Martin, Steve
- Martins, Peter
- Musgrave, Thea
- Newton-John, Olivia
- Price, Leontyne
- Ronstadt, Linda
- Scotto, Renata
- Sedaka, Neil
- Serban, Andrei
- Shange, Ntozake
- Springsteen, Bruce
- Te Kanawa, Kiri
- Travolta, John
- Vereen, Ben
- Weissenberg, Alexis
- Wilder, Gene
- Zukerman, Pinchas

PHILOSOPHY AND RELIGION
- Hooks, Benjamin L.
- John Paul I, Pope
- Lamm, Norman
- Lefebvre, Marcel

SCIENCE AND MEDICINE
- Gould, Laurence M.
- Meriwether, W. Delano
- Yalow, Rosalyn S.

SOCIAL ACTIVISM
- Brownmiller, Susan
- Bukovsky, Vladimir
- Corrigan, Mairead
- Hooks, Benjamin L.
- Kuhn, Maggie
- MacLaine, Shirley
- Means, Russell
- Schlafly, Phyllis

SOCIAL SCIENCE
- Gould, Laurence M.
- Howe, Irving
- Mansfield, Michael J.
- Smith, Virginia B.

SPORTS
- Ali, Muhammad
- Carew, Rod
- Fidrych, Mark
- Guthrie, Janet
- Karpov, Anatoly
- Lyle, Sparky
- Meriwether, W. Delano
- Monroe, Earl
- Morton, Craig
- Vilas, Guillermo

VISUAL ARTS
- Anuskiewicz, Richard
- Chryssa
- Geldzahler, Henry
- Moore, Henry

OTHER CLASSIFICATIONS
- Carter, Lillian
- Carter, Rosalynn

CUMULATED INDEX—1971-1978

For the index to 1940-1970 biographies, see Current Biography Cumulative Index 1940-1970